Emperor of Japan

Emperor of Japan

MEIJI AND HIS WORLD, 1852 – 1912

Donald Keene

COLUMBIA UNIVERSITY PRESS

NEW YORK

Columbia University Press wishes to express its appreciation
for assistance given by the Japan Foundation
toward the cost of publishing this book.

Columbia University Press
Publishers Since 1893
New York   Chichester, West Sussex

Library of Congress Cataloging-in-Publication Data

Keene, Donald.

Emperor of Japan : Meiji and His world, 1852–1912 / Donald Keene.

p. cm.

ISBN 0-231-12340-X (cloth : alk. paper)

1. Meiji, Emperor of Japan 1852–1912. 2. Japan—History—Meiji period,
1868–1912. 3. Emperors—Japan—Biography. I. Title.

DS882.7.K44 2002

952.03′1′092—dc21   2001028826

Columbia University Press books
are printed on permanent and durable acid-free paper.
Printed in the United States of America

c 10 9 8 7 6 5 4 3 2 1

To the Memory of Nagai Michio (1923–2000)
Friend and Teacher

CONTENTS

PREFACE

At the northern end of the Gosho, the grounds surrounding the old imperial palace in Kyōto, just inside the wall marking the perimeter, there stands a small house. In the early years of the Meiji era, when American missionaries were first allowed to reside in the old capital, they used the house for a time to store their furniture and other belongings while they searched for a domicile. Today it attracts little attention, even though it is one of the few houses belonging to the nobility to have survived not only the conflagration that swept through the Gosho in the middle of the nineteenth century but also the dilapidation and destruction following the move of the capital to Tōkyō in 1868.

Outside the fence that protects the house and garden from intruders is a small wooden marker inscribed Sachi no i, the Well of Good Fortune, and inside, barely visible over the top of the fence, is a more considerable stone monument. These two reminders of the past are all that alert the visitor to the fact that the building possesses greater significance than as an example—a very unimpressive example—of nineteenth-century traditional Japanese architecture. In fact, Emperor Meiji[1] was born in this house in 1852, and (according to unreliable tradition) he was first washed in water from the Well of Good Fortune.[2]

Meiji was born in this inconspicuous building rather than in the imperial palace itself because his mother, Nakayama Yoshiko, had been obliged by custom to leave her quarters in the palace when it became evident that she would soon give birth. It was traditionally believed that a birth polluted the building where it occurred, and for this reason children of the emperor were normally born near their mother's house, often in a separate building that was likely to be destroyed when no longer needed. Ironically, this little house has lasted longer than the elaborate residences of the nobility that once surrounded it, vying proud roof against roof.

In preparation for the imperial birth, Yoshiko's father, the acting major counselor Nakayama Tadayasu, had erected this "parturition hut" next to his own, more substantial dwelling. He at first attempted to persuade his neighbors to let him use land they were not actually occupying, but even though the child who was to be born might well become the emperor, he was refused by all and, in the end, had to build on his already crowded property. Like many other nobles at the time, Tadayasu was too poor to pay the costs of even so modest a structure—two small rooms with a bath and toilet attached—and had to borrow most of the money needed for the construction.[3]

Although the house is itself unimpressive, it is strange all the same that the birthplace of a deified emperor, whose shrine in Tōkyō, the Meiji jingū, attracts millions each New Year and many thousands of worshipers even on quite ordinary days, should be the object of so little interest and treated so casually. Only recently has the little house, badly neglected over the years, been given new tiles for its roof. This unmitigatedly utilitarian dwelling, with bare boards on the floor and not a trace of ornamentation anywhere, hardly suggests that this is where a prince was born who became Japan's most celebrated emperor.

The indifference displayed toward Meiji's birthplace characterizes also, in a curious way, general knowledge of the man: even Japanese who believe that Meiji was the greatest Japanese ruler of all time may have trouble recalling a single accomplishment that might account for so glorious a reputation. Meiji is associated, of course, with the "Meiji Restoration" of 1868, the beginning of Japan's modern history, but he was only fifteen when it occurred and, at that age, was obviously incapable of making a significant contribution to the Restoration or to the momentous changes that immediately ensued. His name is associated also with victories in wars with China and Russia and with the securing of an alliance with England, although his role in these events was surely that of a benign presence, not that of a formulator of policy or military strategy. Yet it is also true that throughout his reign and even much later, he inspired men to perform extraordinary deeds of valor. There was no question in the minds of the men who effected the changes of the new regime that he was the guiding spirit.

The general lack of knowledge of the man is not the result of any large-scale suppression of evidence. There is ample documentation for almost every occurrence of Meiji's life from his birth to his death. The official chronicle, *Meiji tennō ki* (Record of the Emperor Meiji), lists, on a virtually day-to-day basis, not only events in which he directly participated but relevant occurrences in the world around him. Many books and articles recalling Meiji's daily life and personality were published after his death by people who knew him, but these books somehow fail to leave much impression. As the first emperor ever to meet a European, he figures also in the journals of foreign dignitaries who visited Japan. Their accounts, less inhibited than those by the comparatively few Japanese who were admitted to his presence, are of particular interest for their candid descriptions of his appearance from the time he first appeared before the public; but even they tell us little about the man.

In addition to the host of facts in the twelve closely printed, stout volumes of the official record, there are innumerable legends and anecdotes about Meiji, notably the gossip concerning such subjects as his amours and the amount of liquor he consumed. There are even people who proudly claim to be illegitimate descendants, usually with only the flimsiest of evidence. Indeed, so much material is available that it might seem that the only requirement for a scholar who intended to write a well-rounded biography was patience; but Meiji's biographers have rarely succeeded in the most essential task, creating a believable portrait of the man whose reign of forty-five years was characterized by the greatest changes in Japanese history.

It may be that the biographers, whether or not they are willing to admit it even to themselves, have reached the frustrating conclusion that the personality of Emperor Meiji had no greater depth or complexity than the pieces of paper printed with his portrait, the conventionalized image of a monarch before which his subjects bowed in reverence without ever wondering what might lie beneath the surface. In order to illustrate their contention that Meiji had a "human" side, biographers often relate anecdotes suggesting that underneath his impassivity he felt great affection for his consort or that he thought constantly of his people or that he possessed a wonderful sense of humor; but such anecdotes are seldom memorable or even believable. Debunking critics of more recent times tend to portray Meiji either as a cipher who was incapable of performing the acts attributed to him or, conversely, as a ruthless tyrant whose actions betrayed his indifference to the welfare of his subjects. They are probably equally mistaken, and their efforts only deepen the mystery of Meiji's abiding fame and the immense number of his worshipers.

Unlike Queen Victoria, his near contemporary, Meiji kept no diary and wrote virtually no letters. Meiji's father, Emperor Kōmei, left many letters, most of them filled with the passionate anger that developments in the world had aroused in him; but the rare surviving letters of Meiji are without interest. Apart from his signatures on state documents, hardly anything in his handwriting survives.[4] There are very few photographs, perhaps no more than three or four altogether, although many less exalted Japanese of his day were frequently photographed. The portrait paintings made both while he was alive and after his death, whether showing him inspecting a silver mine or presiding over a conference on drafting a constitution, were effigies not meant to be literally accurate, the work of artists who had probably never had so much as a glimpse of Meiji's face.[5]

One way of knowing Meiji, apart from the official records and the unofficial, sometimes untrustworthy, reminiscences of his chamberlains, is by reading the poetry he composed. It is estimated that in his lifetime Meiji wrote more than 100,000 poems. Despite the conventional language and imagery that marks them all, they contain bits of autobiographical interest and suggest his feelings on various occasions; but the documents for which he is best known—the rescripts on the army and on education—were composed by other men, and it is difficult to find in their wording anything of Meiji's personal beliefs.

The testimonies written after his death by people of the court who knew him are unsatisfying and sometimes mutually contradictory. One man recalls that Meiji was an unusually healthy and active boy, somewhat of a bully perhaps, a champion sumo wrestler in his youth. Another man, who knew him equally well, contends that as a child Meiji was delicate and prone to illness, testimony that makes one question accounts of his prowess at sumo. The story that Meiji fainted the first time he heard gunfire has been repeated by many biographers but denied by others. When faced with such contradictions, a modern reader tends to suspect the worst—that although Meiji as a boy was in fact sickly and timid, his biographers invented anecdotes that made him appear to have been a sturdy little son of Yamato. But can the man who many years earlier served as Meiji's playmate have been lying when he recalled how regularly Meiji used to thrash him?[6]

These contradictions are not confined to his boyhood: his intelligence, judiciousness, concern for his people, and other qualities befitting a sovereign have been questioned by recent scholars. To cite a minor example of such contradictions: Is it true that (as one chamberlain stated in his memoirs) Meiji not only received a dozen or more Japanese and foreign newspapers every day but examined them assiduously?[7] Or is it true (as another chamberlain claimed) that during the early part of his reign, Meiji read the headlines but later on did not even glance at a newspaper?[8] There also are contradictions in his reported daily behavior that make it extremely difficult to decide what he was really like. If, as often mentioned, he was simple in his tastes and so reluctant to spend money on himself that his uniform was patched,[9] how does this square with his reported penchant for diamonds and French perfume?[10]

It is difficult to feel that one knows Meiji even after plowing through the twelve volumes that record every day of his life. We know precisely when he set foot outside the Gosho for the first time, but what we really want to know is not the hour but the impression produced on him when he emerged from the walled enclosure that had been his entire world and (like Shakyamuni Buddha before him) saw, for the first time, poverty, illness, and death.

Those who knew him personally praised his fortitude, his evenhandedness, and other admirable qualities. Even if we accept their praise as literal truth, we would like to know how it happened that a prince, raised mainly by ignorant women and devoted to the traditional, elegant pastimes of the nobility rather than to the use of weapons, a descendant of many generations of monarchs who had never participated in warfare, is remembered above all as a soldier, a man rarely seen out of uniform?

When writing about Meiji, it is often difficult to keep one's attention focused on the man himself because he was surrounded by officers of extraordinary ability and vividly contrasting personalities. Historians tend to discuss Meiji's reign in terms of these men, leaving only a ceremonial role for the emperor in whose name their glorious achievements were performed. Yet surely it would be unfair to attribute Meiji's extraordinary reputation solely to his having been, quite by chance, the emperor at a time of cataclysmic changes. In a more negative view, his youth and inexperience unquestionably helped the architects of the Restoration; one can easily imagine how their work would have been impeded at every stage if Meiji's father, Emperor Kōmei (whose hatred of foreigners was implacable), had not providentially died at the early age of thirty-six. But Meiji was also capable of making important decisions even while he was young; for example, his intervention prevented the invasion of Korea advocated by Saigō Takamori and a majority of the other ministers. On many later occasions, Meiji's actions—notably his repeated tours of the country—helped create in his subjects an awareness of Japan as a unified, modern country. To label Meiji a mere cipher is as inappropriate as to dismiss Queen Victoria in the same terms.[11]

Meiji's first name, Sachinomiya, or Prince Sachi, was given to him by his father a week after the infant's birth. He was later known as Mutsuhito, the name that appears on documents he signed throughout his reign. Meiji, the name by which he is now normally known, was his posthumous designation; it was also the *nengō*, or reign-name, used in Japan instead of Western chronology. Until the adoption of "Meiji" as the name for Mutsuhito's entire reign, the *nengō* was traditionally changed several times during the reign of a single emperor—at two fixed points in the cycle of sixty years, or when a series of natural disasters were attributed to an inauspicious *nengō* or when some prodigy of nature required recognition in the calendar. The name Meiji, meaning "enlightened rule," was the *nengō* used for his reign from his first full year as a sovereign, 1868, until his death in 1912. It is now used also to characterize the whole of Japanese culture during a period of rapid and sometimes violent change.

I shall attempt in these pages to find Emperor Meiji, a man who was born in a country that for centuries had refused almost all contact with the West but who in his lifetime saw Japan transformed into not only a world power but also a member of the community of nations.

Emperor of Japan

Chapter 1

There are two portraits of Emperor Komei (1831–1867). The first, often reproduced, shows him sitting on a raised tatami (the *gyokuza*, or jeweled seat),
dressed in court costume and wearing the distinctive headgear of an emperor,
a hat with a tall, projecting plume-like band. His oval face, turned somewhat
to the right, is composed and utterly without expression, in the typical manner
of formal court portraits. Nothing (except perhaps the angle of the plume)
indicates that this portrait was painted in the nineteenth, rather than, say, the
thirteenth century, and no attempt was made to suggest in the depiction of
Kōmei's features his long suffering during an unusually turbulent reign. Judging
by this portrait, Kōmei differed little from his ancestors, the emperors of the
previous 200 years, most of them figureheads who contributed little to the nation. During their lifetimes, their existence was unknown to most Japanese;
today even their names have been forgotten. Kōmei, however, despite the bland-
ness of his features in this portrait, is distinctly remembered.[1]

The second portrait creates quite a different impression. The face reveals a
strong personality of which wrath seems to be the principal component. Kōmei
was indeed angry throughout much of his life. His surviving letters and other
documents make it plain that almost every development during his reign infuriated him, and his response to each was not merely anger but frustration
over his inability to prevent the impending changes in the government and
society.

Kōmei was born on July 23, 1831. His father was Emperor Ninkō, the 120th emperor according to the official chronology. His mother was not the emperor's consort but a *gon no tenji*, or lady of the bedchamber, the daughter of the nobleman Ōgimachi Sanemitsu. Officially, however, Kōmei was considered to be the empress's own child. As the fourth son of Ninkō, he normally would not have succeeded to the throne, but all his elder brothers had died by the time he was born. The mortality rate among children of the imperial family at this time and even much later was astonishingly high. Of Ninkō's fifteen children, only three lived past their third year; of Kōmei's six children, only one (Meiji) survived him; and of Meiji's fifteen children, only five lived to be adults.[2] It is not clear why the mortality rate should have been so much higher at the imperial court than among contemporary Japanese peasant families;[3] but it has been ascribed to various causes, such as excessively early marriage (the heir to the throne normally married by his sixteenth year), the backward state of medicine as practiced by the court physicians, and the unhealthy, gloomy atmosphere prevailing in the palace. Perhaps also—though this is rarely suggested—the extremely limited choice of women of the nobility as mothers of imperial children tended to promote inbreeding.

Especially after the beginning of the eighteenth century, emperors did not live long, although there were a few exceptions. Sakuramachi died at thirty; his successor, Momozono, at twenty-one; Go-Momozono, at twenty-one; Ninkō (Kōmei's father), at forty-six; and Kōmei himself, at thirty-six. Accession to the throne was accordingly early: Kōmei's grandfather, Emperor Kōkaku, ascended the throne at nine; his son, Ninkō, at seventeen; Kōmei, at fifteen; and his son, Meiji, also at fifteen. Under other circumstances, the accession of an inexperienced boy emperor might have created severe problems in the country's administration, but in fact it hardly mattered to the Japanese state whether the emperor was a venerable exemplar of monarchical wisdom or a mere child; he took no part in the government, and his only public activities were the performance of prescribed rituals and ceremonies.[4] The shogun did not have to ask the emperor's advice when planning a course of action, and once he had made a decision, he did not seek the emperor's consent. This situation would change with Kōmei.

Kōmei grew up in the Gosho, the area in the center of the city of Kyōto (about 220 acres) where the buildings of the palace were situated and where most of the *kuge* (nobles) lived; this was the imperial family's entire world. According to Higashikuze Michitomi (1833–1912), it was the policy of the shogunate to cloister the emperor as if he were some sort of living god removed from the world of mortals, and it was strictly forbidden to inform him of new or unusual happenings.[5] Higashikuze, who was selected to be Kōmei's playmate when he was ten years old, related in his old age everything he could remember about Kōmei's boyhood, fearing that unless he set down his remembrances, the old traditions might be lost forever. His memory was extraordinary, extending to minute details of the many ceremonies he witnessed—exactly who was present, how they were dressed, what gifts were offered, and so on. Here is his account of a typical ceremony:

> On the seventh day of the sixth month, his ninth birthday,[6] there was the ceremony of "first reading." It was not that the prince had never read anything before he was nine. He had in fact already read the *Classic of Filial Piety* and the *Great Learning*—Takatsukasa, the general of the left, was his tutor—and the ceremony was purely a formality. The prince sat at the middle level wearing an ordinary court costume, his sleeves held back by threefold purple cords and laced trousers with violet hexagonal patterns. The middle counselor Koga Takemichi brought forward a desk and placed it before the prince. Then Kiyohara Arikata of the third rank came forward and seated himself before the desk. He read the preface to the old text of the *Classic of Filial Piety* three times. The prince immediately afterward read through this text in the same way. Kiyohara of the third rank withdrew, and Koga, coming forward, removed the desk. The prince then withdrew to the inner quarters.[7]

The education of a prince consisted largely of reading aloud, with the aid of a tutor, Confucian texts such as the *Classic of Filial Piety*. At first he would read the words without understanding their meaning, but eventually he would be able not only to read texts in classical Chinese but to compose poetry in that language. Calligraphy was an equally indispensable attainment of a prince, and the selection of the proper calligraphy tutor was a matter of crucial importance. Finally, a prince was expected to be able to compose Japanese poetry in the classic verse form, the *tanka*.

Apart from these elements of a traditional education, a prince seems to have learned little else from books—perhaps no more than the essentials of Japanese and Chinese history and geography. Some emperors were fond of reading Japanese fiction, and others enjoyed such entertainments as the *bugaku* dances performed at the court as they had been for a thousand years; there are records also of nō being performed in the imperial palace. But these avocations were considered to be merely diversions, distinct from the serious study that the shogunate had enjoined on the imperial household as its principal occupation.

In 1615 a code of approved behavior for the nobility was drawn up by the former shogun Tokugawa Ieyasu, his son Hidetada (the titular shogun), and the nobleman Nijō Akizane, who had served as *kampaku*, or chancellor. This code, known as *Kinchū narabi ni kuge shohatto* (Regulations for the Imperial Palace and Nobility), consisted of seventeen articles, presumably in imitation of the Seventeen Article Constitution drawn up by Prince Shōtoku in 604. The first and most important article enjoined the emperor and his courtiers to devote themselves to scholarship and the arts. The emperors of the Tokugawa period seem to have taken this to heart: scholarship (the study of a limited number of

Confucian classics) and the arts (chiefly *tanka* and calligraphy) were the central elements of their education. The Confucian classics were studied not in the hopes that a prince might one day rival scholars of the Tokugawa period in reinterpreting the texts; it was enough for members of the court to be familiar in general with the teachings of Confucius and to be able to quote his words at appropriate times. The remainder of the seventeen articles dealt with specific matters, such as appointments to court offices, inheritance of property by nobles, precedence among the various noble houses, and the treatment of members of the nobility who had entered priestly orders.

Even if they resented the supremacy of the shogunate and recalled nostalgically the distant past when the emperor reigned supreme, most emperors and members of the aristocracy did not chafe under the regulations to which they were subjected. The world they lived in was tiny, but they seemed unaware of its limitations, and matters of the most minute concern could occupy their minds for decades. Even those who resented the interference of the shogunate in their lives and the presence in Kyōto of officials sent from Edo who monitored their every action were well aware that they could not survive without the annual stipends the shogunate paid them.

In the case of the lower ranks of the aristocracy, the stipends they received were often insufficient to maintain their households even at a modest level, and many resorted to working on the side, preferably at pursuits that were not considered to be demeaning, such as making copies of the calligraphy of old masters or painting cards for the New Year's game of *karuta* (cards); they counted on the appeal of their illustrious names to sell their handiwork. The family of Iwakura Tomomi (1825–1883), who emerged as the most prominent noble of the late Tokugawa and early Meiji periods, was so poor that they had to rent their house as a gambling den, taking advantage of their immunity as nobles from police regulations. But even the poorest of the nobles were proud of their lineage and their social status, and they were respected by society as a whole, although some of them, as we know from the testimony of the nobles themselves, behaved outrageously, stopping at nothing in their desperate eagerness to make money.[8]

The poverty of the emperor and the court has often been exaggerated, especially by popular historians who have fabricated tales of the drastic expedients to which even emperors resorted merely to stay alive. In fact, they lived reasonably well, even by the standards of the daimyos of the time, whose wealth similarly tends to be exaggerated.

The life of an emperor during the Tokugawa period must have been extremely boring, however. Apart from the consolation of nocturnal pleasures (Gomizunoo had thirty-seven children and Gosai, twenty-seven), each day seems to have been occupied mainly with ceremonies, repeated identically from year to year. But perhaps the aspect of an emperor's life that we would find most oppressive was the narrow confines of the area in which he could move. This had not always been true. Although the emperors never traveled very far from the Gosho, they made occasional imperial progresses to different parts of the city. For example, in 1626 Gomizunoo was entertained for four days at Nijō Castle, the official residence of the shogun in the capital. But from 1632, the year when the shogun Tokugawa Iemitsu (1604–1651) began to rule in his own right after the death of his father, Tokugawa Hidetada, the shogunate did not permit the emperors to leave the Gosho. On a few occasions, it is true, fires in the Gosho might compel an emperor to take refuge at a temple else-where in Kyōto, but it is not much of an exaggeration to say that the successive emperors were prisoners of the state.

Abdicated emperors were freer to travel outside the Gosho. The Shugaku-in, in the hills northeast of the city, was originally built about 1650 as a pleasure resort for the retired emperor Gomizunoo. It was visited from time to time in later years by other abdicated emperors, but it had not been used for many years, and when the retired emperor Kōkaku requested permission in 1823 from the shogunate to visit the Shugaku-in, hasty repairs had to be made before the visit could take place. The occasion passed splendidly:

> The cloistered emperor Gomizunoo was the first to visit the tea pavilion of the Shugaku-in, at the foot of Mount Hiyoshi. The cloistered emperor Reigen had also frequently stopped here. After the death of the cloistered emperor Reigen in 1732, for a period of about a hundred years, the place fell into rack and ruin, and the imperial visits ceased. In the autumn of 1824, the military were commanded to make fresh repairs, and reverting to their old practice, they performed this service. Accordingly, on the twenty-first day of the ninth month of 1825 the retired emperor [Kōkaku] paid his first visit. The route he took was as follows: he left the Gosho by the Seiwa-in Gate, proceeded to Masugata, crossed the Kamo River, and then rested a while at Nitta Yamabana. Great crowds of people cheered him, shouting "Banzai!" They filled the streets, gazing at him reverently. Truly this was proof of an auspicious reign.[9]

Although emperors who had abdicated and entered priestly orders were al-lowed this degree of freedom by the shogunate, this was not true of reigning emperors; from 1632 until 1863, when Kōmei went to worship at the Kamo and Iwashimizu Shrines, the successive emperors hardly ever left the Gosho, and then only because of some disaster. None of them had seen the sea or Mount Fuji or the city of Edo, where the shoguns reigned. During his entire lifetime, an emperor would never have seen more than a few hundred of his subjects, and virtually none of the Japanese would ever have had even the barest glimpse of him. The people of Kyōto were, of course, aware that the emperor lived behind the walls of the Gosho, but except for such rare occasions as when the retired emperor Kōkaku visited the Shugaku-in, they never saw even the palanquin in which he was borne, let alone the man. He was invisible to all but a handful of high-ranking courtiers, a presence behind curtains who excited awe and reverence but who was remote from the world of human beings.

Higashikuze Michitomi was one of the very few at the court for whom the future emperor Kōmei was both a human being and a friend. He recalled Kōmei's proficiency in his studies: "He was able to read the Four Books and the Five Classics[10] without difficulty and learned enough even to lecture on them. He did not study Japanese books very much, but he received instruction in composing *tanka* from his father and composed them every day. His poems were extremely good. In *gagaku* [music] he received instruction from Hamuro, the major counselor, and he was a skillful player of the flute."[11]

Kōmei was officially named the crown prince in 1840, when he was in his tenth year. Higashikuze recalled that before the ceremony, imperial commands had been issued to seven Shintō shrines and seven Buddhist temples to pray that the ceremony would not be interrupted by wind or rain.[12] The actual ceremony took place in the Shishinden (Hall for State Ceremonies). At the conclusion, the emperor presented the prince with the *tsubogiri no goken*, the sword indicating that the recipient was next in the succession.

Higashikuze did not actually become the prince's companion until 1842, but he knew from reports how Kōmei looked on that occasion two years earlier: "His hair was arranged in the *agemaki* style, divided on top to left and right in loops over his ears, in the manner of the hair of the two boys in attendance on Prince Shōtoku in the famous portrait. This was because he had not yet had his *gembuku*."[13]

Probably Higashikuze knew of this ceremony only from other people, but he was present for Kōmei's *gembuku*, or initiation into manhood, the second most important rite of the prince's life, which began on May 11, 1844, with the ceremony of blackening the prince's teeth. Kōmei disliked this so much that he had to be forced. (It is not hard to imagine the thirteen-year-old boy squirming and perhaps shrieking as the nasty black liquid was rubbed against his teeth.) The next two days were spent rehearsing the ceremony. As Higashikuze explained, "This was something that happened only once in an emperor's lifetime, and there were so few people who could remember what had happened the previous time that everybody had to consult books during the rehearsals."[14]

Before dawn on the day of the ceremony the prince was dressed in his costume for the occasion. All the nobles wore formal robes with trailing skirts and carried broadswords inlaid with mother-of-pearl. The emperor appeared, followed by a woman attendant bearing the crown prince's crown. Inside the Hall for State Ceremonies, the officers of the Imperial Palace Keeper's Bureau (*tonomoryō*) opened the curtains. The crown prince's tutor led him to the platform, whereupon the chancellor, Takatsukasa Masamichi, came up beside the prince. Kujō, the minister of the right, supported the prince's train. At this solemn moment all the nobles prostrated themselves. Those of lesser rank did the same outside the building. The minister of the center, Konoe Tadahiro, placed the crown on the prince's head, and Koga Takemichi, the acting middle counselor, bound his hair. Konoe again came forward, removed the crown, and left. Koga came forward and rearranged the prince's hair. When this was done, the prince withdrew to the inner quarters and changed his costume.[15] The ceremony was over.

Emperor Ninkō, Kōmei's father, died at dawn on February 23, 1846. Nobody expected him to die: he was in the prime of life (only forty-six years old) and was endowed with an exceptionally strong constitution. He had been suffering from nothing worse than a cold, but one day when he got up to go to the toilet, he discovered that he could not stand. He was supported by court ladies, but they were not able to hold up the heavy man, and he had to crawl to the toilet. On the way he had a fatal attack. His death was not immediately announced; instead, it was stated that he was so severely incapacitated he wished to abdicate. But an emperor could not abdicate without the permission of the shogunate. A fast messenger was therefore sent to Edo by the Kyōto deputy *shoshidai*,[16] but Ninkō had died long before the reply was received.

The emperor's death was formally announced on March 13. One week later, there was a simple ceremony to mark Kōmei's succession to the throne, and on the following day Ninkō was placed in his coffin. Then, on March 30, it was announced that the lady-in-waiting (*miyasudokoro*) Kujō Asako (1834–1897) had been named *nyōgo*, the highest rank of court lady below the empress, signifying that Kōmei now possessed the equivalent of a wife.[17]

Most of the events described in the official record of the early years of Kōmei's reign have little historical importance. There were memorial services for the late emperor Ninkō, purification and other Shintō rites, an eclipse of the moon, a cockfight—all reported with equal thoroughness and a wealth of citations. Perhaps the most important event was the opening of instruction at the Gakushū-in (a school for children of the nobility). The entry for October 19, 1846, by contrast, leaps from the page: "Word of the coming of foreign ships having reached the capital, the emperor sent a message to the shogunate on sea defenses."[18]

This was the first expression in centuries of an emperor's views on foreign policy and could only have been the result of extreme consternation on the part of the fifteen-year-old Kōmei (or his advisers) on learning of the threat of foreign intrusion. The entry for June 9, 1847, is in the same vein: "The counselor Nonomiya Sadanaga was appointed as the imperial envoy to the special festival of the Iwashimizu Shrine. He was asked especially to pray for peace and tranquillity within the four seas, at a time when foreign warships have intruded into Japanese waters."[19]

This was the first of many prayers that Kōmei would offer to the gods, asking their assistance in ridding Japan of foreign intruders. Never in his lifetime, however, did Kōmei see any foreigners. Indeed, he probably knew next to nothing about them at the time his prayers were offered at the Iwashimizu Shrine, and he learned little more during the rest of his reign; but he was absolutely sure that the presence of foreigners (or, more specifically, Western foreigners) was an intolerable affront to the Land of the Gods.

The reference to foreign warships in Kōmei's prayers was probably to the two American warships that entered Edo Bay in the summer of the previous year under the command of Commodore James Biddle, who attempted unsuccessfully to draw up a treaty of commerce with the magistrate of Uraga. A French warship also visited Japan in 1846. Kōmei referred to both in his *semmyō* (message from the throne) offered to the Iwashimizu Hachiman Shrine, and he prayed that if the foreigners ever came to Japan again, the god of the shrine would raise a wind that would blow them away and leave the country in peace.[20]

Kōmei never swerved in his antiforeign sentiments, even though at times, powerless to do otherwise, he reluctantly agreed to allow the foreigners to remain in Japan temporarily until the moment had arrived to drive them all into the sea. His xenophobia was formed early in his life and remained with him to the end; surely it was one of the elements that contributed to the fierceness of the expression in his portrait.

On October 31, 1847, the coronation of Kōmei took place in the Hall for State Ceremonies when he was in his seventeenth year. He delivered a *semmyō*, praying for peace and asking for the assistance of all his subjects. Judging from the surviving accounts, the ceremony was carried out with magnificence, and on the following day persons who were not normally allowed to approach the imperial palace were able to get a glimpse of the splendor of the occasion.[21]

Kōmei's life after his coronation differed little from the routine that had been established in previous reigns. There were religious observances, poetry gatherings, and the resignations and promotions of palace officials. When necessary, Kōmei would compose a *tanka*, usually phrased in unclouded language:

ume yanagi	As plums and willows
iromeku haru no	Take on the colors of spring
niwa no omo ni	Within the garden,
asahi majiete	Mingling with the morning sun
uguisu no naku	The song thrushes are singing.[22]

The only disturbing events during the next few years were eclipses of the sun and moon, which regularly caused a suspension of all court events. Kōmei attended performances of *bugaku* and nō in the palace, gazed at the moon at appropriate times, and attended various rites and gatherings. Almost every one of his acts occurred on the prescribed day, the same day each year. Scarcely a personal matter except for a rare illness appears in the pages of the official chronicle. Outside the Gosho, fires and floods destroyed houses and bridges, and the emperor responded to each calamity by ordering prayers for the welfare of his people to be offered at the major shrines.

The increasingly frequent appearance of foreign ships in Japanese waters caused consternation, but the most that Kōmei could do in response to the threat was to send messengers to the usual seven shrines and seven temples with instructions to pray for peace.

Moments of happiness also appear in the official chronicle, as when Kōmei's consort put on a maternity belt, followed two months later by the birth of his first child, a daughter. Thirteen days later a son was born to a concubine, but mother and infant died the same day, the first example of what became a familiar pattern of births and deaths in the imperial family during Kōmei's reign. The fact that this son's mother was not the emperor's consort did not diminish the importance of his birth, nor did it lessen the emperor's disappointment over his death, but he lived for so short a time that the usual command to show respect for the dead by abstaining from making noise within the capital was not issued.[23]

The record of the events of the early years of Kōmei's reign is hardly engrossing, but every so often the reader's knowledge of later events lends interest to a seemingly matter-of-fact statement. For example, the entry for August 8, 1851, states that the emperor sent a messenger to Prince Arisugawa Taruhito (1835–1895) informing him of his consent to the marriage of his sister, Princess Kazunomiya (1846–1877), to the prince.[24] She was only five at the time, and the marriage arrangement was based solely on dynastic considerations; but ten years later, when the shogun asked for her hand, this engagement would present a serious obstacle.

Again, the official record for October 15, 1851, states laconically that a prince was born.[25] Without prior knowledge of who was born on this day, it would take considerable reading in the pages that follow the bare announcement to realize that the newly born prince was the future emperor Meiji.

Chapter 2

The *Record of the Emperor Kōmei* supplies minimal information on the birth of the future emperor Meiji, but the *Record of the Emperor Meiji* is extraordinarily detailed from the moment when the *gon no tenji*, Nakayama Yoshiko (1835–1907), felt labor pains, beginning about eight in the morning.

At once Yoshiko's father, the acting major counselor Nakayama Tadayasu (1809–1888), sprang into action. In the hour of the serpent (9 to 11 A.M.) he sent for three court physicians and a midwife, who appeared promptly. He also informed in writing Chancellor Takatsukasa Masamichi (1789–1868), the court spokesmen (*gisō*),[1] and the military liaison officers (*buke densō*)[2] of the impending birth of an imperial child. Messages were relayed at once to other affected men and women officials in the palace. The baby was born about noon, halfway through the hour of the horse. Messages were again sent out. Emperor Kōmei received word while he was sitting in the north garden of his residential palace, admiring the chrysanthemums in the flower beds and drinking saké before lunch. It is reported that when he heard the news of the birth of a son, he looked exceptionally pleased and drank a considerable quantity of saké.[3]

No sooner was the prince born than he and the placenta were wrapped in a *ukeginu*, a square piece of white lined silk. After the birth of the prince had been announced, all fires in the Nakayama house were extinguished. They were relit with fire taken from the house of Kawabata Dōki (1835–1902), a merchant whose family had for many years been the official purveyors of rice cakes to the palace. The extinguishing of household fires was probably in keeping with the belief that even fire was polluted by being in the same house where a birth had occurred. It is curious that the new fire came from a merchant's house rather than from a shrine or the monastic retreat of some member of the imperial family, but the Kawabata family had enjoyed special status ever since the late Muromachi period, and fire from their house, known for its purity, was used in the palace kitchens.

Before the birth, Nakayama Tadayasu had borrowed safe-delivery charms from various auspicious temples and individuals. He was now able to return them with thanks and presents. A court lady sent by the emperor to inspect the prince left with him a protective dagger and a sleeved coverlet (*kaimaki*). The baby would receive many other presents that though traditional, may appear bizarre to contemporary readers. First, however, was the ceremony of cutting, binding, and cauterizing the umbilical cord.[4] The placenta was washed and placed in an earthenware vessel which, in turn, was placed in a bucket of unpainted wood, wrapped in white silk, and displayed on a stand in the next room along with a pair of knives, two blue stones, and two dried sardines.[5] In front of them a lamp was kept burning day and night, and a screen was placed around them. The wooden bucket was decorated with designs in white paste showing pines, bamboos, cranes, and tortoises but not plum blossoms (usually associated with pines and bamboos in artistic compositions) because plum blossoms fall, an inauspicious association.

After the umbilical cord had been cut, the baby was given his first bath. In keeping with the old custom, the water had been drawn from the Kamo River and was mixed with well water. For the next few days, until the baby was given swaddling clothes, he was dressed in an undershirt and a sleeveless coat. His bedding was laid on a *katataka* (a thick tatami that has been sliced in half on the bias, leaving one end much higher than the other) in the main room of the little house where he was born. A pillow was placed at the high end of the tatami to the east or to the south, and it was guarded by two papier-mâché dogs facing each other. Between the two dogs were placed sixteen articles of cosmetics. Behind them was a stand on which the "protective dagger" the prince had received was placed along with an *amagatsu* doll[6] also wrapped in white silk but with red silk pasted to the ends of its arms and its feet. In the *tokonoma* (alcove for hanging paintings) was another stand on which were placed two buckets of unpainted wood with designs in white. In one was a packet of rice and two silken cords looped into rosettes, and in the other were three blue stones and two hardheads.[7] The grains of rice were wrapped in paper flecked with silver foil, and every time the prince was moved from one spot to another, these ornamental grains of rice were scattered to dispel evil spirits. The white silken cords were each about twelve feet long. Each time the prince sneezed, from the moment of his birth until his seventh night, a knot was made in a cord; it was believed that the more he sneezed, the longer he would live. To the east of his bedding stood two clothes racks, both draped with sashes of red and black silk flecked with gold leaf. At first, these were the only touches of color in the room. In accordance with custom, the baby's clothes were white, decorated also in white with the usual felicitous designs of pines, bamboo, cranes, and tortoises. On the 101st day after the birth, the white would be replaced with colors.

In the meantime, word was sent to Tsuchimikado Hareo (1827–1869), the chief of the Department of Yin-Yang, requesting him to appear as soon as possible. Before any major decision was made or after any important occurrence, an expert in yin-yang divination was summoned to interpret its meaning or prescribe the course of action to be taken. Tsuchimikado's family were hereditary diviners for the imperial family, and their recommendations were always given great weight. When Nakayama Yoshiko's delivery was approaching, Hareo had given elaborate instructions as to the direction in which the accouchement should take place, depending on the day of the month it actually occurred.

There had been a scare when Yoshiko had run a high fever in her fifth month of pregnancy, but she had survived the danger to give birth safely. All the same, no chances could be taken at this stage, and Hareo's advice was urgently needed. Unfortunately, he lived at some distance from the palace, and by the time he arrived the baby was already being fed. Hareo nevertheless gave the customary instructions exactly as if he had arrived on time: he announced how the umbilical cord should be cut, the bath prepared, and the baby washed. He gave supplemental instructions for removing the fetal hair, putting the baby in swaddling clothes, burying the placenta, and so on. The instructions were mainly for form's sake, since most of his prescriptions had already been implemented. One matter remained to be decided, the site for burying the placenta. For reasons of direction, Tsuchimikado chose the Yoshida Shrine, east of the city. The approval of the palace was needed, and a messenger was sent. By the time approval was received, it was already dark.

Meanwhile, Nakayama Tadayasu and his son Tadanaru (1832–1882) had reported to the military liaison officers that they had been polluted by the birth. Tadayasu reported this also to his colleagues at the palace offices where he worked. This, too, was for form's sake. Far from being distressed by the pollution he had suffered, Tadayasu was ecstatic, as we can gather from his poem:

ama terasu	How marvelous that
kami no mi-mago wo	Today I rejoice, thinking,
ware ya to no	The holy grandson
mono to yorokobu	Of the gods that shine in heaven
kyō no ayashiki	Is none other than my own!

The poem, though devoid of literary merit, perfectly expressed Tadayasu's sentiments.

Every conscious act performed during the following days followed the pre-scriptions of a yin-yang diviner, but these were not the sole considerations. On the seventh day after the infant's birth, Tadayasu had a yin-yang diviner purify the chamber in which the birth had taken place. The official seventh-night service was about to be conducted when someone realized that it was exactly 100 nights since Princess Yoriko, the infant's elder sister, had died, so the ceremony was postponed to the following night.

The burial of the placenta was the next major consideration. This ritual generally took place within a day or two after the birth. Even before the baby was born, Nakayama Tadayasu had dug two holes in his property, but Tsuchimikado decided that neither was auspicious. His interpretation of geomantic signs led him to prefer the Yoshida Shrine, but in any case, the burial could not be carried out immediately. The three days after the birth belonged to the *doyō* period when digging in the earth was avoided for fear of a curse. The day after *doyō* ended, there was a change of season, also an unpropitious time for digging. *Muikadare*, the sixth day after the birth, when the infant's downy hair was shaved and a name was bestowed, was also avoided, and the following day was the anniversary of Princess Yoriko's death. Each of these events precluded the possibility of digging a hole in the ground, even though a team of men had already scouted the precincts of the shrine and decided on the proper spot. The burial of the placenta finally took place ten days after Meiji was born.

As yet Kōmei had not laid eyes on his newly born son. We can imagine how eagerly he was awaiting the moment, but tradition was more important than the claims of paternal affection. Not until thirty days after the prince's birth was he taken to the palace to see his father. Before he set out, a white line was drawn across the hairline of his forehead, then dotted with mascara. Under it was written in rouge the character for *dog*, an example of protective magic. Nakayama Yoshiko, the infant's mother, carrying him in her arms, made the journey (a few hundred yards) in a palanquin. She took with her the special gifts she had received when first she put on a maternity belt and, later, when she had given birth.

The palanquin set out for the palace about eleven in the morning. Two men cleared the way, and another ten attendants also preceded the palanquin which was borne by eight men. Four officers in formal attire walked beside the palanquin. Two court physicians and a majordomo, dressed in court costumes, followed. Other men, all wearing linen jackets, drew up the rear, and various dignitaries walked separately from the procession. If these people had been in the least desirous of arriving promptly at the palace, the journey from Nakayama's house should not have taken more than ten minutes, but the procession followed the incredibly roundabout route prescribed by a yin-yang diviner. When they finally arrived, the emperor was waiting in his private apartments with his consort. They both gave dolls to the baby. The baby responded by presenting 100 pieces of gold and a box of fresh fish for the palace sanctuary (*naishidokoro*) and gifts of ten quires of fine paper, seaweed, dried bream, and a barrel of saké for the emperor. Other gifts followed. Then the infant declared that he wished to take up residence in his mother's apartments. His great-grandmother, Tadayasu's mother, moved there to serve him day and night.[8]

At the end of the year, Tadayasu followed the Kyōto custom of a baby's maternal grandfather giving him as his first New Year presents a *buriburi* and a *gitchō*. A *buriburi*, made of wood and shaped like a melon, was covered with auspicious drawings of cranes and tortoises and the like. Those with wheels were pulled with a string. The *gitchō*, also of wood, was about two feet long and shaped like a mallet. Two wooden balls went with the *gitchō*. These two items invariably were presented together as typical New Year gifts. Although they were originally toys, children were no longer allowed to play with them, perhaps because they had become too costly.

The presents given to the baby prince, who by this time had acquired the name Sachinomiya (Prince Sachi), and those given in return were more or less the same kind of gifts that were exchanged in moderately affluent households in Kyōto at that time. Money was also given, but compared with the presents with which contemporary royal families in Europe feted the birth of their off-spring, the celebration was austere.

Sachinomiya also received dolls and toys, gifts more appropriate for a baby. From this time on, every milestone in Sachinomiya's development was carefully recorded—his first use of chopsticks, his first sitting with crossed legs, his first experience of mosquito netting. The peaceful atmosphere in the palace did not last long, however. Six months later, in July 1853, an American fleet commanded by Commodore Matthew Calbraith Perry arrived in Japanese waters with the demand that documents brought from Washington be delivered to the Japanese government, the initial step in the process of opening the country after the long era of seclusion.

Perry's fleet first appeared in Japanese waters at dusk on May 26, 1853, when his ships entered the port of Naha in the Ryūkyū Islands. The political status of the Ryūkyūs was difficult for the Americans to understand. The islands were tributary to both the Japanese (more specifically, to the Satsuma domain) and the Chinese but had a king of their own. British, French, and American ships had been calling at the islands since the early years of the century, although they were forbidden to enter ports in the main islands of Japan. Up to now the foreign ships had generally appeared one at a time, but Perry's fleet boasted five. Perry went ashore and proceeded to the Okinawan capital, Shuri, where he rented a house. Satisfied with his negotiations, he presented the islanders with agricultural tools and vegetable seeds and, in return, was given firewood, water, and food. The island had been all but opened to foreign ships.

Perry's fleet also visited the Ogasawara (or Bonin) Islands, whose only inhabitants were some thirty people of mixed ancestry—English, American, Portuguese, and Hawaiian. Perry purchased a tract of land on the main island from the American settlers, intending to build an office, a pier, and a coaling station. This accomplished, he returned to Naha preparatory to sailing to his main objective, Japan.

None of these events was known in Kyōto, where life in the palace continued unruffled. On the fifth day of the fifth month, the little prince celebrated his first Boys' Day. The traditional streamers were flown in his honor, and he was presented with martial toys—a helmet and a spear. He was now living in his grandfather's house, and Kōmei, not having seen the prince in some time, was eager for another visit. The doctors he consulted were cautious, estimating that the best time for a visit would not be until after the boy's birthday in the ninth month. However, if the emperor desired to see his son sooner, this was also permissible, providing he avoided the extreme heat of the sixth and seventh months.[9] When Nakayama Tadayasu's opinion was asked, he replied that Sachi-nomiya was exceptionally healthy. He was seen regularly by doctors, and they rarely found anything wrong with him. There was no reason why a meeting could not take place immediately. Accordingly, the boy was sent to the palace that day and was given playthings by the emperor and his consort.

Three days later, on July 8, 1853, Perry's fleet of four vessels entered the fortified harbor of Uraga, not far from Edo. An officer of the Uraga magistracy, Nakajima Saburōsuke, and the interpreter Hori Tatsunosuke[10] proceeded to the *Susquehanna*, Perry's flagship. At first the Americans would not let the Japanese aboard, but after Hori had negotiated (in English) with the officers, they were permitted to board the ship, where they displayed the order that all foreign ships calling at Japanese ports must be expelled. Perry (who did not meet the Japanese) sent word through his second in command that he had brought a letter from the president of the United States requesting a trade treaty but that he could show this document only to a high-ranking Japanese official.

The following day Kayama Eizaemon, another officer of the magistracy pretending to be the magistrate himself, visited the American ship. He did not see Perry but instead the captain of the ship, Buchanan, and two other officers and informed them that Uraga was not a place where foreigners could be received, that state documents could not be accepted, and that the ships should proceed to Nagasaki. Buchanan replied that unless the Japanese government appointed a suitable official to receive the document, Perry would land, by force if necessary, and present the document to the shogun himself. Kayama promised to report this to the shogunate and to give a reply in three days.

The real magistrate of Uraga, Ido Hiromichi (d. 1855), reported to the shogun on the presence of the American fleet at Uraga and warned that the defenses were inadequate. In the meantime, boats were sent from the American fleet to sound Edo Bay, to the annoyance of the shogunate officials who were powerless to prevent it. When word reached Edo that the American fleet was in internal Japanese waters, there was great consternation. The receipt of documents from foreign countries was prohibited by law, but if the Americans were refused, this would surely bring on some disaster. The best thing, the officials decided, was to put up with the affront for the time being, accept the letter, and, after the American fleet had left, to consult fully before determining the national policy.

On July 9 two high-ranking Japanese officials went to Kurihama, southwest of Uraga, where they met Perry and accepted the letter from President Millard Fillmore. They informed him that the shogun was gravely ill and could not make any immediate decision on major policies[11] but promised that an answer would be forthcoming the next year. Perry accepted this and said he would return.

As yet, no word of these developments had reached Kyōto. The Gion Festival was celebrated as usual, and a week later Kōmei's birthday was the occasion for eating red rice and exchanging auspicious gifts such as dried cuttlefish.

The letter from President Fillmore did not reach the shogunate until July 14. It caused great worry and was the source of rumors that shook the whole society. The elder statesman (rōjū) Abe Masahiro (1819–1857) summoned a meeting of his colleagues, but opinions were so divided that no decision could be made. Two senior figures, Tsutsui Masanori (1778–1859) and Kawaji Toshiakira (1801–1868), argued that the American request to open the country should be accepted; they contended that after more than 200 years of peace, military preparations had become lax, and people no longer possessed their old resoluteness. Abe Masahiro sent for Tokugawa Nariaki (1800–1860), the daimyo of Mito and the political figure most respected by the shogunate officials because of his seniority and his special interest in national defense. Nariaki knew in his heart what difficulties would be involved if the American request were rejected and fighting ensued, but he did not wish to accept the foreigners' demands. When asked his opinion, he advocated taking a firm stand against the Americans. Many others agreed with him, but the shogunate was divided between those who advocated opening the country and those who insisted that it be kept closed.

On July 15 the shogunate directed the Kyōto shoshidai, Wakisaka Yasuori (1809–1874), to inform the court of the visit of the American ships. The court had long worried about the possibility of such a calamity and so was greatly alarmed when it received the report. The perturbed emperor directed the seven shrines and seven temples to pray for seventeen days for peace within the four seas, for the longevity of the imperial throne, and for the tranquillity of the people.

On August 5 the shogunate sent to the various daimyos copies of the translation of the American president's letter. The shogunate had previously made all decisions by itself, but now that the order established more than 200 years ago seemed to be crumbling, it had no choice but to give the daimyos a voice in national policy.

Perhaps the most outspoken was Kuroda Nagahiro (1811–1887), the daimyo of Fukuoka, who contended that in view of world circumstances, it was not feasible for Japan alone to remain permanently secluded from all other countries. He was in favor of granting the American request for trade but restricting it to Nagasaki and limiting the agreement to five or six years. He also was willing to allow the Americans to use some deserted island as a coaling station but argued against Japan's providing the coal on the grounds that any privilege given to the Americans would then be demanded by the Russians, the British, and the French.

In any case, trading privileges, he continued, should be restricted to the Americans and the Russians, the latter because as far back as 1804 they had requested it. Other countries should be firmly refused. If the other countries objected, what harm could there be in using the might of the Americans and Russians to hold them off? If it was considered inadvisable to allow trading privileges to two countries, the Americans would be preferable. Good relations with them would earn their gratitude, and they could be used against the countries of Europe. This would be an instance of the strategy of using barbarians to control barbarians. But if the Americans were flatly refused, war would certainly be unavoidable, and once that happened, Japanese ships would be attacked everywhere, and the sea-lanes would be closed. Not only would Edo be unable to survive a single day, but the conflict would leave permanent damage. In view of the lack of defense preparations and the improbability of Japan's winning a war, peace must be made the main objective lest the Russians attack and capture Japan's northern territory.

The most urgent need, Kuroda declared, was sea defense. The law against building big ships should be contravened. Models should be adapted from the West. Instructors and workmen skilled in shipbuilding and the manufacture of arms should be invited to Japan, and the Japanese should be allowed the freedom to travel abroad. As the result of the long years of peace, he concluded, people high and low alike had come to crave comfort. Their spirits had fallen into a decline. The time had come for a revival of military preparedness.

Kuroda's recommendations did not go all the way to advocate opening the country, but it is astonishing that so soon after the American fleet first appeared off Uraga, an influential daimyo was proposing—with no other provocation than a letter from an American president asking for coaling rights—the dismantling of a system that had successfully lasted for more than 200 years. Naturally he did not propose abolishing the rule of the shogun, nor did he mention (as some men would before long) the importance of the emperor in a new Japan; but he was clearly in favor of ending the country's seclusion, a basic condition of the Tokugawa state.

Kuroda was surprisingly frank in his appraisal of Japan's military capacity. The regime was founded on rule by the military class, and martial training had never been neglected, but Kuroda could see little chance of Japan's winning a war with a foreign power. His appraisal of his country's military strength may have been excessively pessimistic: the intense warfare that immediately preceded the establishment of the Meiji government belied his warning of a decline in the fighting spirit of the samurai class.

Not all the daimyos shared Kuroda's fear of defeat in a war with a foreign power. Shimazu Nariakira (1809–1858), the daimyo of Satsuma, sent a letter to the shogunate declaring that accepting the Americans' demands would harm the prestige of the shogunate and invite contempt abroad. He admitted that if war were to break out immediately between the Japanese and the Americans, it would be "difficult to count on certain victory." He therefore proposed that if the Americans came again, the Japanese should enter into protracted diplomatic negotiations aimed at delaying a firm answer for three years. During this time military preparations should be completed, national strength restored, and then, with one blow, the foreign barbarians could be exterminated.[12] His opinion was shared by most of the other daimyos, and from this time on, the word jōi—expulsion of the barbarians—became the battle cry of the advocates of national defense.

The court in Kyōto did not receive a translation of the American letter until August 16, and it was nine days later before the members of the court met to discuss the contents. The tempo of life at the court was still ponderously slow. On this occasion the chancellor (Takatsukasa Masamichi) the two court spokesmen (Hirohata Mototoyo and Karasumaru Mitsumasa), and the two military liaison officers (Sanjō Sanetsumu and Bōjō Toshiakira) met in the emperor's study. Previously, foreign affairs had always been left to the disposition of the shogunate, but now it was also necessary to win the consent of the Court Council.

The courtiers might have been expected to reject unanimously any action that might result in opening the country to foreign barbarians, but Takatsukasa, surprisingly, was in favor of granting the Americans' request. He pointed out that although in principle the country was closed to all foreigners, in fact the Japanese had traded with China and Holland for many years. Thus agreeing to trade with the Americans would merely increase the number of trading partners from two to three. He stipulated, however, that they must confine their commercial activities to Nagasaki and that if they violated this rule, they must be driven off by force. The unfortunate fact, he said, was that the Japanese military had lost its old fortitude and vigor and had become cowardly, lazy, and effeminate. It had no conception of how to fight foreigners. The best solution, therefore, was to permit trade and accept the profits.

Most of the others disagreed with Takatsukasa, but on the following day he sent a message to the shogunate asking it to inform the court in advance of whatever measures it proposed taking in the event the Americans returned. This unprecedented request was honored by the shogunate, and for the first time in at least 250 years, it solicited the court's opinion before making any decisions.

President Fillmore's request that provisions be supplied to ships operating in that part of the Pacific undoubtedly seemed quite reasonable to the Americans in terms of practices prevailing throughout the rest of the world. War was not openly threatened, but the implications were clear, and the Japanese were aware that they had to respond or face reprisals. At such a time—especially when the shogun was debilitated—the shogun's government needed the support of the daimyos, not only those who were in league with the Tokugawa family (the *fudai* daimyos), but also those who pursued a more independent course (the *tozama* daimyos). Even that array of force might not be enough in this new emergency. Help was needed also from the emperor, even though he did not have a single soldier or gun at his command.

Once a precedent of consulting with the emperor had been established, it proved difficult for the shoguns in future years to ignore his wishes.

Chapter 3

The court had not yet recovered from the shock of Perry's unexpected visit when it was informed by the shogunate on September 19 that a Russian fleet of four ships, under the command of Vice Admiral E. V. Putiatin (1803–1884), had entered Nagasaki Harbor.[1] On his arrival, Putiatin announced to the officials in Nagasaki that he had brought from his government a letter concerning trade between the two countries. His orders had initially called for him to proceed to Edo and conduct negotiations there, but the Russian government later decided it would be better to show respect for Japanese law by proceeding to Nagasaki, the port designated for intercourse with foreign countries, in this way establishing a contrast with the Americans, who had brazenly sailed into Edo Bay.[2]

Soon after the arrival of the Russian ships, various Japanese dignitaries came aboard along with a Dutch interpreter. They were informed by the captain of the *Pallada* that Vice Admiral Putiatin had brought a letter from his government to the Japanese government. There was also a note for the Nagasaki magistrate that, it was said, should be delivered immediately. After some hesitation, the officials accepted the note. It contained a declaration in extremely polite language of the profound respect for Japanese law that had impelled the Russian fleet to call at Nagasaki rather than Edo. This was a mark of the czar's ardent desire for harmonious relations between the two countries.

The officials at once sent word to Edo reporting the arrival of the Russians and asking whether or not to accept the letter from the Russian government. After waiting some time for an reply, Putiatin sailed to Shanghai to pick up supplies and perhaps to find additional orders from his government.³ When there was still no answer even after he got back from Shanghai, he announced that he had no choice under the circumstances but to go to Edo. The alarmed Nagasaki officials sent word by fast messenger to Edo, mentioning how much more accommodating the Russians were than the Americans and suggesting that the Russians might be used to blunt the edge of American demands. They added that if the Russian overtures were met with the usual suspiciousness, Japan risked incurring the enmity of a country that was twice as big as the United States.

Shortly before the messages from Nagasaki reached Edo, the shogun Tokugawa Ieyoshi died, and the senior officers of the shogunate, in mourning and faced with organizing a new regime, did not get around immediately to responding to the problem of how to answer the Russians. After considerable debate, they decided to accept the letter from the Russian court, falling back on the precedent established by accepting the American president's letter.

The letter (in Russian but with translations into Chinese and Dutch) from Count Karl Robert Nesselrode, the minister of foreign affairs, expressed his hopes for establishing peace and good relations between the two countries, for settling the disputed border between Japan and Russia on the island of Sakhalin, and for opening ports to trade.⁴ Most senior members of the shogunate favored accepting the Russian requests, but Tokugawa Nariaki, the shogunate's adviser on maritime affairs, was strongly opposed, and the discussions dragged on. The shogunate finally agreed that the best course was to delay.

Putiatin grew increasingly impatient over the failure of the shogunate officials to return with an answer from Edo, as promised by the Nagasaki officials, and threatened again to sail to Edo if they did not appear within five days. Four days later, the tardy officials, headed by Tsutsui Masanori and Kawaji Toshiakira, arrived with the shogunate's reply to Nesselrode's letter. First, it said, the establishment of the border was a difficult matter that would require considerable time to determine. Maps would have to be drawn, consultations made with affected parties, and so on. Second, the laws of their ancestors strictly prohibited opening the ports. However, in view of world developments, the government did recognize the necessity of opening the country, but a new shogun had just taken office and the situation was still too confused to give an immediate answer. Reports would have to be submitted to Kyōto and to the various daimyos. After due consideration of the issues, they expected to be able to come up with a proposal in three to five years.⁵

It is apparent from the message's wording how desperately the shogunate wanted to stall off a decision; but even more important was the admission that despite the long tradition of isolation, the Japanese now had no choice but to open the country. This awareness of the change in world conditions was not communicated to the court, however, because of the anticipated outraged resistance by Emperor Kōmei.

Putiatin was disappointed by the reply. He moved now to the offensive, informing the shogunate's representatives that with the exception of the southern part of the island of Sakhalin, all the islands north of Etorofu (Iturup) were Russian territory. Tsutsui replied that Japan had possessed Kamchatka as well as (it went without saying) the Kuriles and Sakhalin. He proposed that shogunate officials be dispatched to Sakhalin the following spring to ascertain the situation. In the meantime, the Russians would be free to obtain firewood and water at any place on the Japanese coast except for the vicinity of Edo. He promised also that if Japan made trade concessions to another country, they would apply to Russia as well.

Putiatin was still not satisfied, but he left Nagasaki early in the first month of 1854, saying he would return in the spring. The most influential men in the country were by now aware that the policy of isolation could not last much longer. As early as the seventh month of 1853, as we have seen, Kuroda Nagahiro, the daimyo of Fukuoka, had formally proposed lifting the ban on constructing large ships. In the eighth month, Shimazu Nariakira, the daimyo of Kagoshima, sent a letter urging the shogunate to purchase ships and weapons from Holland. Abe Masahiro (1819–1857), the chief senior councillor (*rōjū shuseki*) of the shogunate, who had long advocated building ships that (unlike the small fishing boats that operated off the Japanese coast) were capable of making ocean voyages, decided on October 21 to lift a prohibition that had been in effect for more than 220 years. The shogunate ordered several steam warships from the Dutch, and soon several domains started building large ships, intended for the shogunate. In August 1854 the shogunate decided on the flag to be flown on the new ships: a red sun on a white ground.[6]

The reactions of the court in Kyōto to the Russian intrusion and later developments are not recorded in the official chronicle. It is not clear whether or not the emperor and his advisers, even after being informed of the arrival of the Americans and the Russians, were aware of how greatly the situation had already changed with respect to opening the country. In any case, other matters that were closer at hand seem to have monopolized the attention of those in the old capital. A terrible heat wave in the eighth month had dried up most of the wells, including the one on Nakayama Tadayasu's property, and he feared that this might have a bad effect on the infant prince. He decided to drill a new well at the spot recommended by a yin-yang master. When the water from the new well was tasted, it was found to be exceptionally pure, and the delighted Tadayasu declared that henceforth this water would be used to meet the prince's needs. Word of this reached the emperor, who was highly pleased and gave the well the name Sachi no i (Sachi's Well) because of its special connection with Sachinomiya and because *sachi* meant good fortune.

In November the prince celebrated his first birthday. We might have expected that he would receive elaborate gifts from members of the court, delighted that an imperial offspring had attained this milestone in his life, but most of the presents were in fact bestowed by the prince—on the emperor, the imperial princesses, the consort, the ladies of the court, and members of Tadayasu's household. He also invited to his birthday party the various doctors, wet nurses, and others who had served him. The little prince obviously had no part in choosing the ritual gifts, such as boxes of fresh bream, buns filled with bean paste, and saké; but he was probably glad to receive the dolls and toys presented to him by the emperor and members of the court, including his mother, Nakayama Yoshiko.

During the following week, however, the prince was afflicted with a severe illness marked by vomiting and fever. Doctors of every sort were summoned, and they prescribed traditional Chinese medicines with such exotic names as *shisetsu* (purple snow). When these failed to have any effect, messengers were sent by members of the court to various shrines to pray for the prince's recovery. At times he seemed better, only for a relapse to set in. The court was plunged in gloom, as people remembered how many children of the imperial family had died in infancy. Numerous gifts—most of them totally unsuited to an infant—were offered in the hopes of comforting the prince, and his mother maintained a constant vigil over his sickbed. Ryōjo, the former chief abbot of the Kakushō-in, was summoned to perform incantations. The prince's great-grandmother, Nakayama Tsunako, distraught at the possibility that they might lose him, composed this poem:

kono kimi no	How must all the gods
ima wa to miyuru	And the buddhas look upon
kanashisa wo	Our grief-stricken hearts
kami mo hotoke mo	When it seems this little prince
ika ni miruran	Has reached his final hour?[7]

That night Nakayama Yoshiko collapsed with a mysterious illness that rendered her insensible to her surroundings. In addition to Buddhist incantations and readings of the sutras, yin-yang diviners were now called in to pray and twang their bows. These rites were apparently efficacious: by the end of the month, both the prince and his mother seemed to have recovered. But it was not long before the prince was stricken again, and another set of priests was summoned to pray for him. He was not completely cured until the end of the year. Although knowledge of medical science was steadily progressing in Japan—largely as the result of the increased study of European medicine—it was clear that it had yet to make headway in the palace. Indeed, apart from the number of prayers said on his behalf, a member of the imperial family was unlikely to receive medical treatment as effective as that given to persons of far humbler status.

On November 23 Tokugawa Iesada (1824–1858), the fourth son of the previous shogun, was officially appointed by the emperor as the thirteenth shogun. The emperor also named Iesada *seii taishōgun*, or "great general and subduer of barbarians." This title, always of major importance as a sign of the shogun's legitimacy,[8] had possessed little military significance because the country was not threatened by barbarians; but at a time when the appearance of foreign ships was causing great consternation, it suddenly acquired immediacy. Emperor Kōmei sent the two *buke densō* to Edo with an imperial message: the shogun was informed that his most important task as the "great general and subduer of barbarians" was to reassure the people of the country by driving off the foreign ships, in this way avoiding national disgrace and future troubles. Chancellor Takatsukasa Masamichi sent a message of his own to Abe Masahiro, the senior adviser of the shogunate, asking what steps the shogunate was planning to calm the emperor's uneasiness with respect to the American ships. Abe replied that no decision had as yet been made but vowed he would do nothing without considering the emperor's peace of mind. He also urged that in the future the emperor communicate his wishes without constraint, promising to do whatever he was asked.[9]

The court had left the disposition of all state business to the shogunate, but ever since 1846, when Kōmei sent a message to the shogunate asking about sea defenses, he had repeatedly expressed dissatisfaction with the shogunate's apparent reluctance to dispose of the barbarians. On March 31, 1854, without consulting the emperor, the shogunate signed the Treaty of Kanagawa with the United States. It provided that the ports of Shimoda and Hakodate would be opened to American ships, that an American consul might reside in Shimoda, and that firewood, water, and food would be supplied to ships in need of them. There was no mention of trade in this treaty of peace and amity, but the foundations for trade had been laid. The choice of Shimoda and Hakodate, both extremely inconvenient places, no doubt reflected the shogunate's desire to keep the foreigners at arm's length.[10]

It is not clear when the court first learned of the treaty. In any case, its attention was diverted from the foreign menace by another disaster. On May 5 a fire broke out in the palace and, fanned by a strong wind, quickly consumed the main buildings. The emperor was hastily evacuated to the Shimogamo Shrine along with other members of the imperial family. The fire spread so rapidly that the six or seven of the emperor's personal attendants who managed to arrive in time to escort him to safety went barefoot. Another officer hurried to the Nakayama house and evacuated Sachinomiya to the same shrine. The devastation caused by the fire was not restricted to the palace: more than 5,400 houses belonging to inhabitants of Kyōto were reduced to ashes before the fire was extinguished.

The Shimogamo Shrine had been designated as the place of refuge in the event of a conflagration in the palace, but it was much too small to hold the members of the imperial family and their attendants. The empress returned temporarily to her original family, and others took refuge in one temple or another. The Nakayama house was one of the few inside the Gosho to escape destruction, and the prince returned there on May 15.[11]

The imperial family's troubles were by no means at an end. At the end of June, Sachinomiya's temperature suddenly shot up, and at first he did not respond to treatment. He eventually recovered, to the relief of everyone, only for a great earthquake to shake Kyōto, the most violent ever recorded for the region. It caused many deaths and destroyed innumerable houses. Even though the Nakayama house again escaped destruction, it was so small and crowded as to seem especially vulnerable to earthquakes. As long as the tremors continued, Sachinomiya was kept in the garden, where, according to the official record, he tranquilly suckled at his nurse's breast.

Even during the various calamities, the emperor continued his study of poetry and was inducted into the secret traditions. To express his congratulations on the emperor's achievement, the prince, it is recorded, sent an official with a box of dried cuttlefish. Presents were offered at the court on every conceivable occasion, but they were rarely of the kind favored by European royalty. The most frequently offered item was fresh fish. No doubt fresh fish, especially from the sea, was a rarity in Kyōto, situated miles inland, but it was hardly in the same class with caviar, let alone a Fabergé Easter egg. The court in Kyōto indeed lived frugally by the standards of royalty elsewhere, the austerity of their lives probably occasioned not so much by economic stringency as by long-standing traditions and perhaps also by preference.

Even more upsetting to the emperor than the fire and the earthquake was the sudden appearance of the Russian warship *Diana* in Ōsaka Bay on November 7, 1854.[12] Putiatin, whose flagship in the previous year had been the old tub *Pallada*, had now returned aboard a modern warship. The *Diana* remained in Ōsaka for about two weeks, creating immense consternation in the capital. One can easily imagine how Kōmei, who bitterly opposed the slightest concession to the foreigners, reacted to the intrusion of a foreign warship almost on his doorstep. He not only ordered prayers for the nation's safety to be offered at the usual seven Shintō shrines and seven Buddhist temples but also reduced his daily meals to a minimum and observed austerities. The citizens of the capital were alarmed, and the shogunate, seeking to reassure them, commanded various domains to defend Kyōto and environs. Some officials even favored moving the emperor to Ōsaka Castle, more easily defended than the Gosho, but before further steps could be taken, the Russian ships had weighed anchor and left for Shimoda.

Negotiations between the Japanese—Tsutsui and Kawaji—and the Russians—headed by Putiatin—began in Shimoda on December 22. Putiatin, eager to obtain a treaty, expressed his government's willingness to cede to the Japanese the island of Etorofu, even though the Russians had positive proof it belonged to them, providing the Japanese would permit trade between the two countries. Some progress was made, but the negotiations were adjourned for two days. The following day, a great earthquake struck Honshū, accompanied by a powerful tsunami that was particularly severe at Shimoda. Countless people on the shore were swept out to sea by the roaring waves, and the badly battered Russian ships narrowly escaped being dashed against the rocks. The Russians earned the gratitude of the Japanese by rescuing some Japanese from the sea.[13]

Shimoda was almost completely destroyed by the tsunami, and talks between the Japanese and Russians could not be resumed for ten days. The negotiations were protracted.[14] In the meantime, the court in Kyōto decided that an unlucky *nengō* (reign-name) had been responsible for the recent disasters, and Confucian scholars were commanded to prepare a list of suitable new *nengō*. The shogun chose from among the names presented to him Ansei, or Peaceful Government, a term derived from a passage in the early Confucian text *Hsün Tzu*, which states that if the common people are at peace with the government, the ruler will enjoy peace in his office.[15] Despite its auspicious name, the Ansei era (1854–1860) would not be characterized by peaceful government.

One of the first events of the Ansei era was peaceful enough—the baby prince first put on colored clothes in place of the white clothes he had hitherto worn. Naturally, yin-yang diviners were consulted before so momentous a step was undertaken. Tsuchimikado Hareo, the head diviner, decided that ten o'clock in the morning on the sixteenth day of the twelfth month (February 3, 1855) was the appropriate time. There was snow that day, and the baby prince, no doubt suitably bundled up for the cold, set out that morning for the temporary palace where his father resided, accompanied in his palanquin by his great-grandmother. Other members of his mother's family, including Nakayama Tadayasu and his wife, walked behind the palanquin, reaching the palace at the prescribed hour. Not until noon, however, was Sachinomiya dressed in his first colored costume, a cloak of deep crimson worn over a white glossed-silk robe, both presents from the emperor. A ritual meal was served at which the prince was attended by his mother, Nakayama Yoshiko. After the ceremony, he was taken by his grandfather, Nakayama Tadayasu, to the temporary palace where the emperor granted him an audience and offered him two cups of saké. After having his clothes changed once again, the prince appeared before the emperor, who congratulated him and offered another cup of saké. Fruit and other delicacies were served, followed by gifts of dolls and toys, and the prince's clothes were changed for the third time, this time to bright red. The ceremonies lasted until about four in the afternoon. On this occasion, the emperor gave the prince twelve sets of clothes, and other members of the court added to this wardrobe. Sachinomiya also gave presents to the emperor and others, mainly fish, which was followed by a general exchange of gifts among those who had participated in the ceremony.[16]

Five days later, unbeknownst to the emperor and his court, a treaty of friendship was signed with the Russians in Shimoda. The Japanese were more generous in their concessions to the Russians than they had been with the Americans, perhaps influenced by their favorable impression, perhaps also out of sympathy for Putiatin, who had visited Japan four times in order to obtain the treaty and who had suffered the loss of his ships in the tsunami and later storms.[17] After being stranded in Japan, the Russians eventually returned to their country, some in an American transport hired for the purpose, others in a German merchant ship, and still others in a ship built by Japanese ship's carpenters under Russian supervision. By the summer of 1855, the last Russians had left Japan.[18]

Although the court was unaware of these developments and the official chronicle of Meiji's life, insofar as it mentions events in Kyōto, is devoted mainly to such milestones in his life as a bout of chicken pox that left pockmarks on his face and his first steps as a baby, the court must have sensed impending danger. Regardless of whether members of the court favored keeping the country closed or opening it, they were agreed on the necessity of strengthening the national defenses. A court order was issued to collect temple bells and recast them as guns and cannons. The shogunate prohibited the use of copper, iron, lead, and other metals for Buddhist statues or ritual implements.[19]

Natural disasters also continued to afflict the country. In September 1855 heavy rains and winds caused the rivers in the capital to rise dangerously, and all but two bridges over the Kamo River were swept away in the flood. On November 11 a great earthquake struck Edo, destroying half the city and causing numerous deaths and injuries.

The one bright spot of 1855 for the court was the completion of a new palace, replacing the one destroyed by fire in the previous year. It had taken a year and seven months, as opposed to two years and ten months for the previous palace, completed in 1788. Although the country was faced with urgent problems of defense, Abe Masahiro ordered that rebuilding the palace take precedence, a sign of the importance he placed on "relieving the imperial mind." When asked his wishes for the new palace, the emperor replied that although he could think of various improvements that might be made, he would be satisfied, in view of the national emergency, if the palace were rebuilt without changes. That the shogunate should have asked the emperor's wishes, and that the emperor declined to be extravagant because of the national emergency, shows how great a change had occurred not only in their relations but in the emperor's awareness of political developments.

The cost of the new palace was met with contributions from the shogunate and the various daimyos, notably Maeda Nariyasu of Kaga (1811–1884), the richest of the daimyos. The emperor, his consort, the prince, and the others of the court moved in procession to the new palace on January 1, 1856. The prince was attended by his great-grandmother. She had shaven her head when she entered Buddhist orders but, for this joyous occasion, wore a wig.

Chapter 4

As 1856—the third year of Ansei—opened, Emperor Kōmei, installed in his new palace, was able to enjoy what for his turbulent spirit were rare moments of tranquillity. But even at this relatively peaceful time, there were occasions for alarm. Foreign ships were observed with increasing frequency in the waters off Ōsaka, and the shogunate, fearing that this must cause the emperor grave concern, reinforced Kyōto with guards from the Hikone, Kōriyama, and other domains; but perhaps reassured by the splendor of his new palace, the emperor felt no special need of extra guards and sent a message to the chancellor asking that their numbers be gradually reduced.[1]

The emperor, however, was never entirely free from worry. At this time, he seems to have been bothered less by the presence of foreigners in Japan (his usual source of unhappiness) than by Sachinomiya's health. At the end of the previous year, the prince had run a fever. The area around his mouth was swollen, and he had trouble eating. The chief abbot of the Kakushō-in rushed to the palace and spent the night in prayers. Jinkai, the abbot of the Gojō-in, performed spells, apparently to good effect: on the same day the prince seemed better, although the respite was only temporary. On February 15 the prince's temperature suddenly shot up. He was racked with coughing and could not fall asleep until midnight. The only nourishment he could take was sugar-water. On the seventeenth he was able to swallow a little rice gruel but slept very little. The emperor prayed for his recovery at the sanctuary and offered rice to the gods. The empress had prayers said at the Gion Shrine, and Jinkai once again performed spells.

The prince did not recover fully for another ten days. Of course, every child has illnesses, and parents worry each time their child has a cold; but in the case of children of the imperial family, each illness, however slight, may have seemed like a presage of death. When the physicians' remedies seemed ineffectual, the only hope lay in prayers. Probably, too, as time went by and no other son was born to the emperor, each fluctuation in the prince's health was a matter of grave concern to the entire court.

On April 29 of that year, Sachinomiya visited his father in the imperial palace. Although he was not yet three years old, he already displayed characteristic stubbornness: he refused to get into the palanquin that had been provided, and his nurse had to carry him in her arms. The prince also so disliked having people stare at him that a curtain was stretched along the path from Nakayama Tadayasu's house (where the prince lived) all the way to the palace gate. Although the curtain shielded him from the eyes of the curious, it forced people to make a detour around his path. But despite the inconvenience, the curtain was used whenever he went to the palace. He generally walked the short distance accompanied by members of his mother's family and a chamberlain or two.[2]

The emperor grew increasingly fond of his son and sometimes kept him in the palace overnight or even for a month at a time. Nakayama Tadayasu missed having his grandson in the house, but judging that it was best for the child to become accustomed to the palace, he contrived to stay out of his sight when on duty there. Sometimes the prince played in the empress's garden. His great-grandmother, Nakayama Tsunako, who often accompanied him, composed this poem as she watched him cross the little stone bridge in the empress's garden:

noboru beki	The child of the sun
kagiri shirarenu	Destined to rise to
hi no miko no	Incalculable heights
watarisometsuru	Has crossed for the first time
ama no iwahashi	The stone bridge of heaven.[3]

On August 21, 1856, two months after this peaceful scene was celebrated in Tsunako's poem, the American consul, Townsend Harris, arrived in Shimoda aboard the warship *San Jacinto*. Four days later, he called on the magistrate of Shimoda, Okada Tadayasu, and informed him that henceforth he would be residing permanently in Shimoda. Okada, apparently acting on orders from the shogunate, did not recognize Harris's right to remain in Shimoda and enumerated the existing regulations prohibiting foreigners from staying in Japan. Harris, refusing to be swayed, insisted that his residence in Japan was in accordance with the Treaty of Kanagawa, and if the officials failed to accord him the treatment appropriate to a consul, he would go directly to Edo and complain in person. After keeping Harris waiting a full month, the shogunate finally agreed to let him reside in Shimoda. In the meantime, Harris had raised the American flag at the Buddhist temple Gyokusen-ji, which he called the consulate. The shogunate commanded its representative in Kyōto, the *shoshidai*, to report this development to the chancellor.[4]

Two days after Harris's arrival in Shimoda, Jan Hendrik Donker Curtius (1813–1879), formerly the chief merchant of the Dutch trading station on Deshima but now the Netherlands government commissioner, sent (by way of the Nagasaki magistrate) a letter to the shogunate in which he urged that the policy of the closed country be abandoned. He predicted that if Japan persisted in this policy, it would lead to war with the major countries of the world. He also called for the old regulations against Christianity to be lifted, deploring in particular, as contrary to good relations with other countries, the use of *fumie* (images, generally of the Virgin Mary) that the Japanese were obliged to tread on to demonstrate that they were not Christians. He pointed out the advantages to Japan of trade with foreign countries and advised the Japanese to set up a schedule of import duties and encourage the production of wares suitable for export. He suggested also that men from countries with relations with Japan be permitted to bring their wives and children to live with them in the open ports. Finally, Curtius asked that the restrictions on foreign ships be lifted and the laws revised with respect to permission to leave the ports and to travel to Edo.[5]

Twelve years earlier (in 1844) Willem II, the king of Holland, had sent a letter to the shogunate asking that the country be opened to trade. The haughty officials did not deign to respond, but since then the situation had changed dramatically, and the shogunate now felt that it had to give serious consideration to Donker Curtius's suggestions. At the council meeting, virtually all those present spoke in favor of opening the country speedily. Only Abe Masahiro, worried about the reactions of the various domains and fanatical patriots, said that the time was not yet ripe for such action. No one defended the longstanding tradition of the closed country.[6] The shift in policy had occurred with startling swiftness.

These developments seem not to have been transmitted yet to the court in Kyōto. The prince's third birthday (fourth by Japanese count) was celebrated with gifts—mainly fish—from the emperor and other members of the court. A week later, by command of the emperor, the prince went to live in the palace. The departure from the house of his grandfather, Nakayama Tadayasu, was accompanied by religious incantations and other ceremonies, but because of the prince's dislike of riding in a palanquin, the palanquin sent for him was loaded instead with protective amulets and the like, and it was only pretended that the prince was aboard. His mother, Nakayama Yoshiko, rode beside the amulets, ostensibly to watch over the (invisible) prince. Various physicians, secretaries, and other dignitaries accompanied the palanquin the short distance to the palace gate.

As soon as the prince entered the palace, he was taken to the emperor, who gave him a cup of saké along with a box of dainties. The empress gave him mixed sweets and toys. The prince offered similar gifts in return. Although he was only three years old, he was expected to participate in the stylized ritual of gift giving and receiving. It is hard to imagine the little boy's reactions to the role he was obliged to play. Perhaps he thought of the ritual behavior as a game, but gradually he must have become aware that bowing and exchanging presents was not a game but his life. Many years later, the German court doctor Erwin Baelz overheard Itō Hirobumi remark to Prince Arisugawa, "'It is really very hard luck to be born a crown prince. Directly he comes into the world he is swaddled in etiquette, and when he gets a little bigger he has to dance to the fiddling of his tutors and advisers.' Thereupon Itō made a movement with his fingers as if he were pulling the strings of a marionette."[7]

For all the privileges that a prince received, it was a painfully constricted life with almost no freedom. But human feelings were not completely suppressed. Probably the prince felt closest to his great-grandmother, Nakayama Tsunako, who had (in the words of the official chronicle) "devoted herself solely to his upbringing for four years, forgetting sleep and food."[8] We can easily imagine how upset she must have been when she realized that now that he was to live in the palace, she would no longer be able to see the prince when she chose.

The prince was to stay in the apartment of his real mother, Nakayama Yoshiko, three rooms in the western part of the Hana goten (Palace of Flowers).[9] Soon after his birth, Yoshiko relinquished to Kōmei's consort all rights over her child. The boy addressed the consort as his mother and showed her the expected reverence. Although Yoshiko was a court lady of some importance, the most she could hope for was the privilege of waiting on her son. She was not to suggest to him (though eventually he would know) that she was his real mother. After examining Yoshiko, then known as Nii no tsubone, Dr. Baelz wrote in 1893,

> She is the Emperor's real mother, whereas the Empress Mother ordinarily so called, Kodai Kogo, is the widow of the late Emperor. It is to the latter that the Emperor has to pay the duties of a son. He visits her ceremoniously several times a year. On the other hand he never sets foot across the threshold of his real mother's house, for she is only a subject. She may visit him if she has asked permission and he has granted it. Strange flowers of etiquette![10]

Perhaps it was because of Kōmei's compassion for a woman who had been deprived of her child that the prince was left in her care. As late as the beginning of the twentieth century, even empresses who gave birth to princes were not normally so fortunate, as their children were taken from them and left with strangers, in accordance with palace custom. Dr. Baelz reported about the eldest son of Emperor Taishō (the future Hirohito),

> At five went to call on Count Kawamura. The crown prince's son has been put under the care of this elderly admiral, who must be nearly seventy. What a strange idea! I hoped that the unnatural and cruel custom of taking little princes away from their parents and handing them over to strangers had fallen into desuetude. It is not so, however. The poor crown princess was compelled to hand over her baby, which cost her many tears. Now the parents can see their child only for a brief period once or twice a month.[11]

Even though he was now living with his mother, the prince was not able to sleep soundly in the palace. The rooms of Yoshiko's apartment may have seemed cold and bleak in comparison with the Nakayama house, where he had spent most of his life up to this time. He probably missed his grandparents and especially his great-grandmother. But the only remedy for his sleeplessness that occurred to the palace staff was to summon eminent Buddhist prelates who burned holy fire and pronounced spells in order to drive away the demons responsible for the prince's insomnia.[12]

Life inside the palace fell increasingly behind life elsewhere in Japan. Traditional rites were performed exactly as in the past, and they, rather than modern medicine, were used to cure illness. Although the efficacy of vaccination against smallpox had become fairly well known elsewhere in Japan, and Meiji as a small boy was secretly vaccinated,[13] Kōmei refused to be vaccinated, which may have led to his untimely death.

The pleasures of life in the Gosho belonged to the past. In the spring of 1857, for example, a pavilion was built in the palace garden following plans sketched by the emperor himself. He gave the completed building the name Chōsetsu—Listening to the Snow—and had the minister of the left, a noted calligrapher, inscribe a plaque to hang over the door.[14] It is agreeable to think of Kōmei in his pavilion composing poetry or listening not only to the snow but to *gagaku* music. Nothing seemed to have changed from the past; but from outside the palace there came increasingly loud and jarring noises.

On February 28, 1857, Donker Curtius addressed another warning to the magistrate of Nagasaki, presumably intended for the shogun. He reported (what the Japanese already knew) that China had been defeated in the Opium War with England and had been required by the peace treaty to open the ports of Amoy, Canton, Shanghai, Ningpo, and Fuchow. Although the Chinese had done this unwillingly, the ports that were opened had prospered as the result of foreign trade, and the people had greatly benefited. However, at Canton, in contravention of the treaty, the port was not opened, and mobs tore down the British flag. The city was bombarded by the British fleet and reduced to ashes. The Europeans and Americans blamed this reaction on the Chinese officials' failure to behave in a responsible manner, and the contemptuous laughter they directed at the Chinese had still not stopped.

Donker Curtius revealed at this point why he had taken the trouble to inform the Japanese of these developments. Although what had happened in Canton did not directly concern the Japanese, it should serve as a warning to them that once they had signed a treaty, they had to live up to its provisions and not alter them willfully. He continued, "From what I have recently heard from the American official who has been dealing with the magistrate at Shimoda, your country has repeatedly procrastinated in making replies to negotiations. It has happened frequently, too, that there has been haggling over trifles or disavowals of promises. This is not the way to create ties of trust with foreign countries. Again, in correspondence with other countries your country's attitude is often arrogant, and when addressing them the language used is that of giving commands to a vassal state. This is something that all foreigners find disagreeable. At present the major countries in the world are England, America, Russia, and France. Your country is about to open commercial relations with these great Powers. You should change your old ways as soon as possible, realize the fruits of friendly relations, move with the times, and in this way respond to general trends in the world."[15]

Donker Curtius's words were reasonable, and the threat to Japan from the foreign powers of which he warned was real. But the basic premise of his argument, that Japan, too, would be reduced to ashes if it failed to accept the universal morality of trade, did not make sense to persons reared according to Confucian principles. Trade might be mutually beneficial to the countries involved, as Donker Curtius stated; but if a country chose to refuse such benefits, why must it be annihilated? The shogunate officials were indeed haughty, and the tactics of delay they practiced may well have been exasperating, but if the foreign visitors would only realize that they were unwanted and go away, they would avoid humiliation.

Such thoughts are likely to have passed through the minds of members of the shogunate even if they realized that Japan's isolation could not be prolonged much longer. Improved means of transportation, including the steamship, had reduced the effectiveness of the barrier of distance that had protected Japan and made opening the country all but inevitable. But this was not necessarily an unmitigated disaster. There were probably benefits to be derived from foreign trade quite apart from the commercial profits mentioned by Donker Curtius. The *rangakusha* (scholars of Dutch learning) had been studying European science for a century, and they were convinced that it was essential for the Japanese to be aware of developments abroad in medicine, navigation, geography, and other branches of learning that could benefit Japan. It was clear, too, that if Japan had been able to import foodstuffs from abroad, many lives could have been saved during the recent famines.

Even the emperors in Kyōto, normally isolated from their people, had on one occasion at least been made aware of the suffering caused by a famine: in 1787 some 70,000 persons massed around the Gosho praying to the emperor— as to a god—for relief from hunger.[16] Emperor Kōkaku and the retired empress Gosakuramachi were moved to compassion and gave what they could to feed the hungry.[17] Kōkaku was so shocked by the people's misery that he broke precedent by asking the shogunate to relieve the people's distress, the first time during the Tokugawa period that an emperor intervened in a matter of state policy.

It is unlikely that Kōmei, relaxing in his Pavilion of Listening to the Snow in the early summer of 1857, had an occasion to recall his grandfather's gesture. The life that he led at this time was agreeable, thanks to the generous allowance he received from the shogunate, and there was no immediate reason to worry about the welfare of his people. Instead, the chief threat to his happiness was the foreign barbarians. His prayers to the gods conveyed his fervent hope that the foreigners would leave as soon as possible, and this wish remained paramount in his mind.

Before long, the cry of sonnō jōi—Respect the emperor and drive out the barbarians!—would be on the lips of countless patriots, but Kōmei himself wished only to drive out the barbarians. Far from seeking to profit by this new respect for the emperor and to deprive the shogun of political power, Kōmei was fiercely outspoken in his opposition to those whose "respect for the emperor" involved the overthrow of the shogunate. Not only was he conservative in his politics, but he was also well aware how indebted he was to the shogun for his comfortable life. His repeated bursts of anger seem to have been occasioned by frustration that he was being kept from enjoying the peace of his Pavilion of Listening to the Snow. But Kōmei's tranquillity lasted only as long as he remained unacquainted with developments elsewhere in Japan.

On the fifth day of the fifth month, the day when families with sons set up pennants shaped like carp, Kōmei gave the prince an audience and with his own hands hung from the prince's shoulder an ornamental scent bag. Later that day, he visited the prince's room, an exceptional honor, and inspected the pennants like any other father. This may have been the last unclouded day of his life: a week later, he received the first report concerning the fortifications along the coast around Ōsaka that had been constructed by the shogunate in response to the increasingly frequent appearances of foreign ships in a region that was dangerously close to the capital. Two gun emplacements each had been built at the mouths of the Kizu and Aji Rivers; forty heavy guns had been cast; and the construction of Western-style ships was being planned. These were major undertakings, and quick results could not be expected.[18]

Kōmei's apprehension on learning of the closeness of foreign ships was doubtless tempered somewhat by relief over these energetic preparations to defend the region around the capital, but the world seemed to be moving in a direction that was hateful to him. A few weeks later, on June 17, 1857, the magistrates of Shimoda joined with Townsend Harris in signing the Treaty of Shimoda, a further step in opening Japan to the barbarians.

Not satisfied with the provisions of the Treaty of Kanagawa, Harris had secured by negotiation and compromise an arrangement far more favorable to the United States. The "convention," as Harris called it, opened the port of Nagasaki to American ships and gave Americans the right of permanent residence at Shimoda and Hakodate. It also provided the basis for extraterritoriality: "Americans committing offenses in Japan shall be tried by the American Consul General or Consul, and shall be punished according to American laws."[19] In later years, the Japanese made immense efforts to persuade foreign governments to relinquish this privilege, an infringement on their sovereignty, but probably the magistrates in Shimoda did not foresee the magnitude of their concession.

Harris's next triumph occurred when as the result of his repeated requests, the shogunate decided to permit him to proceed to Edo for an audience with the shogun. A number of influential clans opposed this decision, but the shogunate, disregarding them, informed the court of its action. Harris left Shimoda on November 23, 1857, accompanied by his Dutch interpreter, Henry Heusken,[20] and escorted by a great many soldiers provided by the shogunate, anxious to ensure that no mishap occur on the way. In the number of soldiers, the heralds, and in many other respects, it was much like a daimyo's procession. Harris wrote in his diary, "The whole train numbered some three hundred and fifty persons."[21]

On December 7, 1857, the shogun Tokugawa Iesada granted Harris an audience in the Hall of State Ceremonies.[22] Officials of the shogunate were arrayed in tiers; the shogun was seated on the highest level, leaning on an armrest. Harris, after bowing three times, advanced toward the shogun and described his mission. He presented the letter from President Franklin Pierce to the emperor of Japan—it was still believed that the shogun, usually known as the tycoon, was the sovereign of the country—investing Harris with power and authority to "agree, treat, consult, and negotiate" concerning a treaty of commerce between the two countries. Harris's journal continues, "Here I stopped and bowed. After a short silence the Tykoon began to jerk his head backward over his left shoulder, at the same time stamping with his right foot. This was repeated three or four times."

It is hard to imagine what these gestures were intended to convey, but the intent was friendly. The shogun's brief reply to Harris ended, "Intercourse shall be continued forever."[23]

Five days later, Harris visited the *rōjū* (senior councillor) Hotta Masayoshi. He enumerated the reasons why at a time when the invention of the steamship and telegraph had made communications vastly easier among nations and the whole world had become like one family, each country must maintain friendly relations with all other countries. There were two requirements: the stationing of diplomatic personnel in the capitals of other countries and the opening of free trade.

Harris warned the Japanese of the danger of the British waging a war with Japan if they failed to obtain a commercial treaty. The British navy might well occupy Sakhalin and Ezo, and if the British and French forces that were at the moment pressing on Peking were successful, France was likely to demand Korea, and England might demand Taiwan from the Chinese. America, though, desired only peaceful relations; moreover, if the Japanese relied on the Americans, they would repel the excessive demands of the British and French. Harris warned that if war broke out with England, Japan would lose. Finally, he promised that if Japan signed a treaty with the United States, the latter would include a guarantee to prohibit the sale of opium, in this way distinguishing America from England.[24]

The threat of British ships seems to have been effective. Although some powerful daimyos opposed a treaty (like Tokugawa Nariaki, who loudly insisted on *jōi*), on January 16 Hotta Masayoshi invited Harris to his residence and informed him of his willingness to inaugurate trade relations, to permit a minister to be stationed in Japan, and to open some other port in place of Shimoda.[25]

Hotta informed the Kyōto *shoshidai* of these developments and directed him to report them to the emperor. The court quickly countered with the command not to open any port in the region of Kyōto. Later that month, by order of the shogunate, two officials delivered a detailed report on recent dealings with foreign countries. The precedent of keeping the court abreast of current developments had been firmly established.

Hotta sent word that he would be going to Kyōto in order to obtain imperial consent to the treaty with America. This does not seem to have reassured Kōmei, who decided to ascertain the opinions of senior court officials before Hotta arrived in Kyōto. He sent a letter to the chancellor commanding him to ask the prime minister, the minister of the left, and the minister of the right their frank opinions on foreign affairs. On hearing the rumor that Hotta was bringing with him a large sum of money, the emperor wrote to Chancellor Kujō Hisatada: "Do they suppose I can be bought? If, as long as I am the ruler of this country, I allow myself to become a mere dummy and permit trading with foreign barbarians, I shall lose the confidence of the people and will leave a shameful reputation for generations to come. I would have nowhere to hide myself from the gods or from my ancestors. I urge all of you to take these considerations to heart and not let yourselves be led astray by money."[26]

Even during these hectic days there were occasional agreeable interludes. In the eleventh month of 1857, Sachinomiya, in his sixth year, composed a poem,[27] the first of his 100,000 *tanka*.

Chapter 5

The senior councillor Hotta Masayoshi (1810–1864), accompanied by two senior officials, Kawaji Toshiakira and Iwase Tadanari, left Edo for Kyōto on March 6, 1858, bringing with him lavish gifts for the emperor from the shogun Tokugawa Iesada. On the same day, Hotta sent a letter to the military liaison officers (*buke densō*) stating that the purpose of his visit to Kyōto was to report on the circumstances of the signing of the treaty with America. Two days later, Hotta invited to his lodgings the two military liaison officers and the three court spokesmen (*gisō*) and described to them in detail the situation prevailing in the world. Arguing that it was no longer possible for Japan to maintain its isolation, he showed the officials the draft of the commercial treaty and asked for the court's approval.[1]

A few members of the court, notably the former chancellor Takatsukasa Masamichi and his son Sukehiro (1807–1878), favored granting the shogunate's request, but Kōmei sent letters to the minister of the left, Konoe Tadahiro (1808–1898) and the chancellor, Kujō Hisatada (1798–1871), urging them to respect his wishes. His letter to Kujō reiterated his unyielding opposition to making any concessions to the foreigners. If the Americans were allowed what they sought, how could he face his ancestor, the deity of the Great Shrine of Ise? If the Western barbarians insisted on opening the ports to trade, Japan should not renounce the use of arms.[2]

Hotta's mission to the court proved to be fruitless. At the audience with Hotta on April 5, the emperor repeated his conviction that signing a treaty with America imperiled the Divine Land. Hotta was given a letter in which Kōmei expressed his deep concern.[3] He emphasized that if the treaty signed several years earlier opening the port of Shimoda to foreign ships, an event of grave significance to Japan, were modified in the manner the Americans asked, this would constitute a blemish on the national honor. Kōmei's initial draft of the letter had left ultimate disposal of the matter to the shogunate, but a group of eighty-eight nobles protested so strongly against the shogunate's policy of accommodating the foreigners that the language of the letter was made even more outspoken. Hotta left Kyōto on May 15 greatly disappointed.

Perhaps the most striking aspect of Hotta's visit was the vociferous opposition expressed by the nobles. It is easy to imagine that the members of the aristocracy at this time were effete courtiers, powdered, painted, and dressed in the mode of the distant past. Such aristocrats probably existed, but from this time on, many of the *kuge* class displayed unwonted resolution and even audacity in their efforts to return power to the emperor. This phenomenon is sometimes attributed to the practice, widespread among nobles of this time, of taking wives from the samurai class, thereby infusing the aristocracy with new vigor. This is hard to prove, but in any case, it becomes increasingly inappropriate to think of the courtiers as exemplars of gentle decadence or as epigones of the Heian court. From this time, aristocrats would be prominent in all activities directed against the shogunate.

In the fourth month of 1858, the shogunate appointed the daimyo of Hikone, Ii Naosuke (1815–1860), as *tairō*.[4] The emperor soon afterward wrote a letter in which he predicted that Ii would make a strong attempt to secure imperial sanction for the treaty. However, he declared, there was absolutely no chance of his changing his mind.[5] Kōmei, whose allegiance to the shogunate was absolute, nevertheless insisted on his privilege of refusing to cooperate with its policies when he thought they were mistaken.

Kōmei became increasingly outspoken in his condemnation of the policy of allowing foreigners into the country. On July 27, 1858, he sent envoys to the Great Shrine of Ise, the Iwashimizu Hachiman Shrine, and the Kamo Shrine to pray for divine protection. In a *semmyō* he asked the gods, if warfare should break out between Japan and the foreign barbarians, to send a divine wind (*kamikaze*) like the one that had destroyed the ships of the Mongol invaders in the thirteenth century. He also asked the gods to punish those who, by their failure to repay the blessings they had received from the country, showed themselves disloyal—meaning those who favored opening the country.[6]

Kōmei's prayers went unanswered. On July 29 the Shimoda magistrate Inoue Kiyonao met with Townsend Harris aboard the warship *Powhattan*, then anchored off Kanagawa, and signed the treaty of amity and commerce between the United States and Japan.[7] The treaty included a schedule of dates during the next five years when ports in addition to Shimoda and Hakodate—Kanagawa (Yokohama), Nagasaki, Hyōgo (Kōbe), and Niigata—were to be opened to foreign ships.

On July 31 the shogunate sent word to the court reporting the conclusion of the treaty with America, explaining that because of the great urgency involved, there had been no time to seek the court's advice. When the court received this letter, Kōmei was predictably furious. He sent for the chancellor and gave him a letter in which he announced his intention of abdicating the throne.

Kōmei was driven to take this extreme step probably because it was the only act of which he was capable that might cause the shogunate to alter its policies. If Kōmei had abdicated—the shogunate would have had to concur in this decision—his successor would have been either his son, only six years old, or a prince of a collateral line. A child-emperor might prove a disaster in these critical times, and the accession of a cousin not in the direct line of succession would probably have aroused resentment if not factionalism.

Kōmei's letter opened with a conventional presentation of the uniqueness of the Japanese imperial institution, especially the unbroken line of descent, contrasting it with the practices in China where in the past even persons of the lower classes had ascended the throne because of their unusual ability. Kōmei lauded the single line of emperors in Japan, but his real emphasis seems to have been on the difficulty for a man to serve adequately as emperor, even though he had not been selected for his ability. Even an unquestioning believer in the profound significance of the unbroken line of emperors would have to admit that not every occupant of the throne was outstandingly suited to the office; indeed, the *Records of Japan* describes emperors who were cruel and perverse. Kōmei was probably more gifted than any emperor of the century prior to his accession, which may account for his dissatisfaction with the role he was obliged to play and, ultimately, with himself. Using conventional language, but in a way that suggests these were probably his real feelings, he described his unworthiness to occupy the throne. He declared that he should have firmly declined to succeed to the throne on the death of his father, but at the time he was so overcome with emotion that he hardly knew what was happening even as he underwent the rites of accession. Despite his ignorance, he had devoted his every energy since then to serving the gods and in particular his first ancestor, always striving to keep from besmirching the sacred line. It had been beyond his meager capacity to rule the country as he wished, and he frequently had had occasion to sigh over his failure. Ever since the disastrous fire of 1854 that destroyed the imperial palace, there had been incidents of unrest in many parts of the country, and the people could not be tranquil. He blamed this entirely on his own lack of virtue, and this had caused him immense grief.

Most recently, foreign ships had been appearing in Japanese waters, and worst of all, an American envoy had come to ask for friendship and trade. He was sure that despite the amicable words pronounced by the foreigners, they entertained in their hearts the ambition of swallowing up Japan at some future time. If the foreigners were refused, it was likely to lead to war. He had been informed that because of the years of peace and good government, the temperament of the people had become indolent, and military preparations were not ready. In sum, the Japanese forces were no match for an enemy. But even recognizing the special circumstance of a long protracted peace, was it not lamentable that those charged with subduing barbarians had lost the qualifications of their office?

The emperor had left political matters to the shogunate and had hesitated to express his opinion for fear of worsening relations between the military and the court, but this had led to a difficult situation. At a loss what to do and having only limited ability, he had decided to relinquish the throne. Because Sachinomiya was too young to be his successor at a time when the nation faced a grave crisis, he therefore proposed one of the three princes of the blood.[8] It was definitely not because he desired to lead a life of ease and pleasure that he was abdicating; it was because he wished someone more capable than himself to deal with the problems of state. He asked the chancellor to forward his request to the shogunate.[9]

The letter plainly indicated Kōmei's dissatisfaction with the shogunate's inability to handle the foreigners. Although he did not mention this in this letter, he had become increasingly convinced that the foreigners had to be expelled, whatever the cost; their presence in Japan was an affront to the gods and to his ancestors. What makes this and his subsequent letters in a similar vein memorable is the impression they convey of a tormented human being. It is true that much of the phraseology is stereotyped, but no other emperor, at least for hundreds of years, had expressed such bitter frustration, such a sense of powerlessness, despite the grandeur of his title. Kōmei had become a tragic figure, and from this point until the terrible conclusion of his life, he had only brief periods of respite from anger and despair. To find parallels in Japanese history we would have to go back to the exiled emperors Gotoba and Godaigo. Perhaps Richard II, at least as Shakespeare portrayed him, resembled Kōmei even more closely in his awareness of how little control he possessed over his destiny. The barrage of letters Kōmei directed to the officers of his court, lamenting each new development, is without parallel in the correspondence of Japanese sovereigns. The letters are signed with pseudonyms, most often *kono hana*, or "these flowers," a reference to the ancient Naniwazu poem:

naniwazu ni	At Naniwa Bay
saku ya kono hana	How these flowers are blooming!
fuyugomori	Prisoned by winter,
ima wa harube to	How these flowers have blossomed
saku ya kono hana	For now it is the spring.

Did Kōmei use this pseudonym in the hopes that he, too, would, after a long winter, know the spring?

Toward the end of the letter, he denied that he was giving up the cares of office in order to lead a life of pleasure, but paradoxically, that is the kind of life that the shogunate and many members of his court thought was most appropriate for him. Only toward the end of his reign when his feelings turned from frustration to desperation did he indulge heavily in saké and women.[10] Kōmei emerges in this letter as a moving figure, a man of intelligence schooled in traditions that were rapidly becoming untenable in an age of change enforced from without.

Kōmei's request that he be allowed to abdicate apparently never reached the shogunate. By dint of firm persuasion, Kujō Hisatada managed to mollify Kōmei, promising that a senior shogunate official would come to Kyōto to explain the situation. But in the seventh month of 1858, the shogunate signed treaties (similar to the one concluded with America) with Holland, Russia, and England.[11] On September 11 Kōmei, enraged by this new development, responded with an imperial edict declaring his intention of abdicating and demanding an explanation from the shogunate for its disregard of the imperial will.

After receiving the letter, Kujō Hisatada replied that although it was evident that the emperor had reason on his side, the matter was of such grave importance that he would have to give it his mature consideration before offering an opinion. He met with the Court Council. Most of the members agreed that the imperial message should be forwarded to the shogunate but felt that intemperate language should be avoided. When Kujō showed Kōmei's letter to senior court officials, Konoe Tadahiro, the minister of the left, advocated sending a copy of the letter to Tokugawa Nariaki, the former daimyo of Mito, urging him to persuade the shogunate to reform the government and take steps to protect the country from foreign insult. If Nariaki could induce two or three of the major domains to join him, the emperor's wishes could be carried out completely.[12]

This was a dangerous plan. It proposed violating the shogunate's order, which had expressly prohibited the court from communicating directly with the domains; worse, if it were successful, it would surely foment dissension, the one thing the shogunate most feared and hated. There was a sharp division of opinion among members of the Court Council, some afraid that sending the letter would ultimately harm the court and others insisting that unless the letter was sent immediately, the emperor would certainly abdicate. In the end, one copy of the letter was given to the representative of the Mito clan living in the capital, and another to a shogunate official stationed in the palace for transmission to the shogunate.

In his letter, Kōmei recognized that signing a treaty with America had, under the circumstances, been inevitable, but he reproved the shogunate for not having followed his suggestion that the major domains be consulted before taking further diplomatic steps. He also expressed concern over unrest within the country and urged a policy of *kōbu gattai*, the union of aristocracy and military. This phrase summed up Kōmei's ideal of cooperation by the court and shogunate in driving out the foreigners, as opposed to the more familiar *sonnō jōi*, and it would figure prominently in the discourse of the late Tokugawa period.

Once again, Kōmei was dissuaded from abdicating. On September 23 word of the death of the shogun Tokugawa Iesada reached the capital. He had died more than a month earlier, but the shogunate had kept this a secret, and only at this time was the court informed. The shogun's death may have inhibited Kōmei from following up on his plan to abdicate. In any case, at the beginning of the ninth month he managed to get Kujō Hisatada, the chancellor and a supporter of the shogunate's policies, replaced by Konoe Tadahiro, a man whose attitudes he found more congenial.

On October 13, 1858, Manabe Akikatsu (1804–1884), a senior councillor (*rōjū*), arrived in Kyōto. This seemed to be in keeping with the promise that the shogunate had made to send a senior official, but Manabe had no intention of apologizing to the emperor for having signed a treaty with the Americans without obtaining imperial consent. Rather, he had come by command of Ii Naosuke to restore Kujō Hisatada to his former position as chancellor. That was not all. He intended to rid the capital of all those who opposed the shogunate's policies. This marked the beginning of what was known as the Great Purge of the Ansei era. Eight samurai leaders of the *sonnō jōi* faction were executed, including such admired men as Yoshida Shōin, Hashimoto Sanai, and Rai Mikisaburō. Yoshida Shōin's crime had been to join the plot to assassinate Manabe on his way from Edo to Kyōto, but the "crimes" of the others were by no means so clear. Members of the aristocracy (even those of the most exalted families) who were suspected of *sonnō jōi* leanings were also questioned and forced to resign their offices. Others, judged to be more deeply involved, were confined to their quarters or ordered to shave their heads and become Buddhist priests.

Manabe, perhaps by way of consolation, brought for the emperor lavish gifts from the new shogun, Tokugawa Iemochi. Kōmei, however, declined to give Manabe an audience.[13] His feelings toward the shogunate official who had removed Konoe Tadahiro, his choice as chancellor, and replaced him with Kujō Hisatada, a man he did not trust, can easily be imagined. Manabe had a meeting instead with Kujō, reinstalled as chancellor, and told him why, in view of world conditions, Japan had to sign treaties of friendship and commerce with various foreign powers. He also presented to Kujō the memorials sent by various daimyos and a copy of the provisional treaty with America. These documents were afterward submitted to the emperor.

That same day, November 29, the emperor promoted the new shogun to the senior second court rank and on the following day named him "great general subduing barbarians." It may have seemed to Kōmei as if he were bestowing the highest honor in his power on a likely enemy. During the next months, Kōmei continued to write letters expressing his rage over the prevailing situation. At the end of the year, he finally gave an audience to Manabe Akikatsu, who was about to return to Edo. He gave him a letter that opened, "Friendship and commerce with the foreign barbarians constitutes a fatal flaw in the Imperial Land, a pollution of the Divine Land." The emperor urged a return to "the good system of the closed country [*sakoku*]."[14] He was willing to pardon the signing of the treaties, although he himself did not approve of them, in view of conditions both inside and outside Japan. Nonetheless, the breathing space obtained by signing the treaties should be used to implement the policy of *kōbu gattai*. Although this concession was the first of many that Kōmei would have to make, his ultimate objective, freeing Japan of the barbarians, never wavered.

The sixth year of Ansei (1859) opened with the traditional New Year festivities at the palace. There were exchanges of presents, performances of *bugaku*, and the consumption of ritual food and drinks. Sachinomiya, now in his seventh year, was presented by the court with a cask of saké and appetizers; he had reached an age when he could participate in some court activities. On February 21 he witnessed *bugaku* for the first time in the company of the emperor and received, also for the first time, a cup of saké from the emperor's hand.

On May 24 four nobles who had been arrested by Manabe Akikatsu in the previous year—Takatsukasa Masamichi, Konoe Tadahiro, Takatsukasa Sukehiro, and Sanjō Sanetsumu (1802–1859)—were granted their "request" that they be allowed to shave their heads and enter Buddhist orders. This was the shogunate's punishment for the courtiers' audacity in communicating directly with Tokugawa Nariaki. Takatsukasa Masamichi and his son Sukehiro had been among the few nobles to support opening the country to foreign trade, but they had been persuaded by "men of high purpose" (*shishi*), mainly lower-ranking samurai of nationalistic beliefs, to shift to favoring the closure of the country, thereby angering the shogunate.

Before the shogunate could pass sentence on these men, the Kyōto *shoshidai* Sakai Tadaaki (1813–1873) informed them that he wished them to commit suicide, but they refused to comply. Kōmei, taking pity on the men, sent a letter to the chancellor Kujō Hisatada asking him to intercede with Sakai and obtain a pardon for them, but Manabe proved to be adamant. He had firm proof that secret communications had been exchanged between these men and Nariaki. Court secrets had been passed to Mito samurai, and samurai of Mito and Fukui had been incited to subversive activity. It was possible that these men had been deluded by the wild ideas of vagabonds, but regardless of the reasons, they had acted in contravention of *kōbu gattai*.[15]

On April 9 Kōmei had secretly sent a letter to Sanjō Sanetsumu relating his special respect and affection for the accused men. During the reign of Emperor Ninkō, Takatsukasa Masamichi had served for a long period as chancellor, and when that emperor had suddenly died, bringing the inexperienced Kōmei to the throne, he had helped him in every conceivable way, acting almost as the regent. Kōmei could not bear to think of this man, who was now aged, being found guilty of a serious crime. Again, Konoe Tadahiro had been Kōmei's tutor, his teacher of calligraphy, and the one who had placed the cap on his head when Kōmei had his *gembuku* ceremony. The other two men had also served diligently and well during the previous reign. When the foreigners came to Japan, all four men had done everything humanly possible to accord with his wishes. They may have made mistakes at times, but they could not possibly have entertained seditious plans regarding the shogun.[16]

Kōmei's letter concluded with the hope that he might be able to persuade the shogunate to show leniency. Sanjō Sanetsumu received this letter at the village outside the capital where he was living in retreat. Although he was suffering from illness, he rose from bed, changed to a court costume and cap, and, after first purifying himself, read the letter. He wept at the graciousness of the emperor's compassion. He felt sure that the praise for his services to the court would demonstrate that he had not been unfilial to the spirits of his ancestors and would save him from leaving a shameful name to his descendants. Nonetheless, Sakai sternly refused Kōmei's plea for leniency, and even for a stay in implementing the punishment of the four men. Kōmei, still reluctant to order the men to shave their heads, asked them once again if this was really their wish. They answered that it was, no doubt resigned to their fate, and Kōmei finally had no choice but to issue the command.

Sakai Tadaaki appears as the villain in accounts describing how the Ansei purge affected the court, but he was only the agent of shogunate power in Kyōto. Behind his unfeeling rejections of every attempt by Kōmei to obtain leniency for men who had served him and his father was the decision by Ii Naosuke, the most powerful man in the shogunate, to erase all opposition. Ii began the purge almost as soon as he took office as *tairō* in 1858 and continued it until he was assassinated two years later. The purge was occasioned mainly by the need Ii felt to remove opposition to shogunate policies with respect to treaties with foreign powers, but it also had a domestic aspect, the naming of a successor to the office of shogun. The purge proved to be a total failure and ultimately contributed to the shogunate's collapse, but the two years during which arrests and imprisonments were carried out would be remembered as a reign of terror.

For Kōmei, the purge was a source of personal humiliation. Surely it was not necessary for the security of the shogunate that old men who had faithfully served Kōmei and his father before him should be made to enter Buddhist orders merely because at some stage they had expressed opposition to the trea- ties. But Ii was determined to make an example of each, even if this meant incurring Kōmei's hatred. Rarely has the contradiction between the reality and the actuality of imperial authority been so clear. It must have been galling for the emperor, performing the prescribed rituals in the robes of his office, to recall that there was not a single command he could pronounce that might not be contravened by the shogunate.

The chronicle of the year 1859 mentions also epidemics and other disasters that affected the whole country. A third daughter was born to Kōmei, only for the second daughter to die, perhaps a victim of the epidemic. For Kōmei there seems to have been one comfort, his son, Sachinomiya, and the process of his gradually becoming a worthy heir to the throne provided the only bright spots in a year otherwise marked by calamities.

Chapter 6

Sachinomiya's schooling began in 1859 when Prince Takahito (1812–1886) was appointed as his calligraphy teacher. The fact that Sachinomiya's first teacher was a calligrapher suggests the importance attached to being able to write a distinguished hand. Although calligraphy was of only minor importance to a European prince, in Japan it was an indispensable element in the education of the aristocracy. A member of the imperial family was required to display his skill as a calligrapher on relatively few occasions, but it was essential that whenever he did write, his handwriting would be not merely acceptable but an imposing mirror of his character. It is difficult to say how proficient Emperor Meiji eventually became, however, because so little survives in his handwriting.[1]

Sachinomiya had actually begun calligraphy practice during the previous year, but this instruction was apparently casual; now that he was in his eighth year, he was expected to study calligraphy (and other subjects) systematically under appropriate tutors. Prince Takahito was chosen to teach the prince calligraphy because his family had long been renowned for its penmanship. On May 5 he brought the Naniwazu poem as a model for the writing of *kana*,[2] and Prince Takahito and his pupil exchanged gifts, each presenting a box of fresh *tai* (bream) to the other. The first formal lesson in calligraphy was a most important step in the education of a prince, and that no doubt was why *tai*, a traditional feature of celebrations, were exchanged.[3]

From this time on, Prince Takahito came several times a month on appointed days to offer calligraphy instruction to Sachinomiya. On June 4 the pupil presented for his teacher's approbation some characters of which he had made fair copies, an occasion for a further exchange of gifts. By August 10 the young prince, apparently pleased with his own progress, was presenting to attendants samples of his calligraphy—one or two characters each, most frequently *naka* and *yama*.[4]

In the meantime, he had commenced another kind of study, reading the Confucian classics. On May 29 Fusehara Nobusato (1823–1876) was appointed as his reading tutor. During the first session with his pupil, he read a passage from the *Classic of Filial Piety* three times. Naturally, a boy of seven could not be expected to understand a Chinese philosophical text, even when read in Japanese pronunciation; but before long, Sachinomiya was able to recognize characters and read them aloud, following his teacher. This method of learning, known as *sodoku*, was surprisingly effective, as we know from the generations of Japanese who learned Chinese in this way and were later able to read and write it competently; but it must have been excruciatingly boring for a boy to recite by the hour words that meant nothing to him.

As soon as Sachinomiya completed the *sodoku* reading of the *Classic of Filial Piety*, Emperor Kōmei commanded that he begin reading the *Great Learning*.[5] In a *sodoku* class of boys of the same age, there might at least have been the pleasure of friendly emulation or perhaps fun shared at the expense of the teacher, but Sachinomiya at first had little companionship in his lessons. The nobleman Uramatsu Tarumitsu (1850–1915) became Sachinomiya's sole school playmate in 1861, when he was eleven and the future emperor Meiji was ten (by Japanese count). He recalled in conversation,

> I waited on him every day, morning until evening, never leaving his side whether he was studying or exercising, until it was time for him to go to bed. The prince generally wore a kimono with long sleeves of colored silk crepe and trousers of white silk. He did not wear new clothes each day but dressed very simply. His hair was so arranged that his frontlocks were swept over his sidelocks on both sides and was arranged on top in a boyish style. The only difference between my way of doing my hair and his was that his sidelocks were puffed out.
>
> His studies began with *sodoku* reading of the Four Books and the Five Classics. I was his partner. We were taught by the late Fusehara Nobusato, but occasionally Ano Okumitsu substituted. The textbooks were written in fair copy by Mr. Fusehara. When we finished one book, he would present His Majesty with the next. We read aloud in unison, in the manner of an old-fashioned temple school.[6]

Thus far the instruction had been considered to be informal, meaning that Sachinomiya and his companion studied in private with their tutor, but on June 25, 1862, their formal instruction began. Emperor Kōmei commanded the master of yin-yang divination Tsuchimikado Hareo to determine the proper hour for the initiation. Everything was to follow the precedent set in 1839 when Kōmei underwent the same formalities. The most distinguished members of the court witnessed the ceremony, which had for its climax Fusehara Nobusato's reading three times lines from the preface to the *Book of Filial Piety*.

Sachinomiya was not an especially diligent pupil. Anecdotes about his dislike of study have been preserved, and he himself recalled in later years that his mother, Nakayama Yoshiko, had been quite strict with him, not giving him lunch until he had finished that day's assignment.[7] Still later, in 1905, he composed a poem recollecting those long-ago days:

tenarai wo	How I regret now
monouki koto ni	My childish disposition
omoitsuru	When I decided
osanagokoro wo	That writing practice was
ima kuyuru kana	Such a boring waste of time.

The following poem was composed about the same time:

takeuma ni	I remember now
kokoro no norite	Those days when I neglected
tenarai ni	My writing practice
okotarishi yo wo	Because my only interest
ima omou kana	Was riding a bamboo horse.[8]

Another anecdote relates how Nakayama Tadayasu, then in charge of Sachinomiya's education, lost his temper when in the midst of a lesson, his pupil suddenly stood up and went without explanation to his private quarters. Tadayasu decided that there was no point in continuing his instruction, to which he devoted his every effort, if the prince behaved in so undisciplined a manner. He penned a note resigning his post and saying he did not intend to appear again before the prince. Tadayasu's son, Takamaro, pleaded that the prince was still too young to realize what he was doing, but the enraged Tadayasu would not listen. Just then a messenger came from the palace asking Tadayasu to return immediately, but he obstinately refused. Takamaro, insisting that refusal was in contravention of a subject's duties, finally succeeded in persuading his father to relent. When Sachinomiya saw Tadayasu, he apologized, saying he was at fault, and promised never to behave that way again. He said, "Please don't lose your temper, but look after me as before." Tadayasu was deeply moved. When he saw Takamaro later that day, he said, "His Highness is an enlightened prince. I was too hasty. It was my fault." He wept aloud.[9]

The story has a pleasant ending, but it implies that Sachinomiya was capable of thoughtless and even cruel behavior. We know from the testimony of his childhood playmate, Kimura Teinosuke, that even as a child, Sachinomiya was fully aware of his power over subordinates:

> His Majesty had an extremely impetuous streak that went with his un-yielding disposition. If ever anything occurred that failed in some way to please him, he would usually at once clench his little fists and strike whoever was at fault. I can't tell you how many times I was the recipient of blows from his gracious fists. At any rate, I tended to be insufficiently in awe of him, perhaps because I was a year younger, and I was always venturing to do something contrary to his wishes, and each time he deigned to strike me smartly.
>
> One day a certain daimyo presented him with a goldfish bowl with five or six goldfish swimming in it. I was greatly intrigued and watched the fish by His Majesty's side, but when he went into the next room I immediately put my hands inside the bowl and chased the fish until I actually succeeded in catching one. The goldfish died, much to my con-sternation, and while I was wondering helplessly what to do, His Majesty came back into the room and saw what had happened. He flew into a rage, and with a cry of "Tei-bon!" he clenched his fists and struck my head three times. I ran away, but he came running after me, and favored me with another blow, as I recall. . . .
>
> And although I don't recall the reason, on another occasion I was the recipient of his anger for some mischief I had done, and I was hit in the head nine times in succession. When I think back on it now, I realize that my mischief had caused me to trouble the imperial mind, and even now I feel the cold sweat oozing from my armpits.[10]

Another unappealing anecdote relates how an elderly noble who had been placed in charge of Sachinomiya from the time of his birth began to feel that the boy was too active for him to handle. He was thinking of asking to be replaced by a younger noble when one day he saw Sachinomiya playing by a pond in the Gosho. The boy called out, "Grandpa, come have a look! See all the carp in the pond!" The old man went to the pond but could not see any carp. He asked politely where they might be, to which Sachinomiya replied, "There, over there!" The old man stooped over to get a better look, whereupon the boy gave him a shove from behind, and the old man tumbled into the water. The pond was extremely shallow, but being an old man, he had trouble getting back onto the bank. Thereupon His Majesty called out in a loud voice, "Come, everybody! The old man's turned into a carp!" People rushed up and helped pull the man out of the water. It is related that the mud-stained garment that he wore when he fell into the pond became the greatest treasure of his family.[11]

It may be wondered why such anecdotes are included even in works osten-sibly compiled to enhance Emperor Meiji's glory. Probably the harshness—

even brutality—with which he treated a playmate and a harmless old man was considered to be a necessary quality, enabling a prince, who not only was raised by women but for years was dressed and painted like a girl, to be transformed into the stern ruler of the nation. It is related that after the old man suffered the humiliation of being pushed into a pond, he sent Iwakura Tomomi a letter asking to be replaced. But Iwakura summoned him and said, "You have served His Majesty ever since the day he was born, but you still do not understand his greatness. I am well aware of the efforts his training has cost you now that you are old, but I believe that because you yourself were raised as a noble, your only concern has been to make sure that he was well behaved. But Japan is now in a critical state. Imperial power will unquestionably revive. At that time, it will not suffice for the emperor to be well behaved. I can see in this young prince a manly disposition that is capable of maintaining its equilibrium no matter what kind of crisis it may encounter, and I rejoice in my heart. I am returning your letter asking to be relieved of your position."[12]

The manliness of the little prince, ready to use his fists against anything that displeased him, has been emphasized by anecdotalists who prefer not to portray Sachinomiya as a remote figure, hidden by screens from the eyes even of members of the court, or as a prince whose delicate health was a constant source of worry to those around him. They seem to be saying that even if pushing an old man into a pond was not in itself admirable, it was a demonstration of a virile personality.

In other respects, however, Sachinomiya's education, whether provided by tutors or by observation of life at the court, was traditional. He began to compose *waka* poetry even before he had formal instruction.[13] One poem composed at this time survives:

tsuki mireba / kari ga tonde iru / mizu no naka ni / mō utsuru narikeri

When it sees the moon, the wild goose comes flying; it is already
    reflected in the water.

This poem does not scan, and the imagery is confusing, but it is of interest as the earliest example of his poetry. A *tanka* composed a couple of years later shows greater awareness of the metrics:

akebono ni	In the light of dawn
kari kaerite zo	The wild geese are returning
haru no hi zo	On this day in spring;
koe wo kikite zo	I listen to their voices—
nodoka narikeri	They sound so very peaceful.

The repeated use of the emphatic particle *zo*, mainly to fill out the meter, is likely to amuse a modern reader, but this sign of the prince's awareness of metric requirements demonstrates that he had made some progress. From this time, it became usual whenever Sachinomiya had an audience with his father to receive a list of topics on which to compose *tanka*. He would show the results to Emperor Kōmei, a skilled poet, who would correct them. This is how he modified the prince's poem:

haru no hi ni	On a day in spring
sora akebono ni	When dawn is in the sky
kari kaeru	The wild geese return;
koe zo kikoyuru	Their voices can be heard —
nodoka ni zo naku	How peacefully they cry!

Kōmei's guidance was undoubtedly important in the only part of Meiji's formal education that was specifically Japanese in content, a tradition established in the Heian past when emperors not only composed poetry but were well versed in the poetry of the past. Before long, Sachinomiya had become familiar with the poems in the standard collections. His literary preferences were otherwise confined to Japanese martial tales and accounts of Chinese heroes.[14] His childhood companion Uramatsu Tarumitsu recalled that Sachinomiya often mentioned his admiration for the audacity of Toyotomi Hideyoshi or the loyalty of Kusunoki Masashige. At the time he seems to have been less interested in the deeds of his ancestors, perhaps because they were not martial enough to suit his tastes.

Sachinomiya's education differed little in content from that of his father or, indeed, that of his ancestors of centuries earlier. Although the fear of Western intruders had come to obsess Kōmei, he did not consider it essential for his son to learn about the dangerous barbarians. Sachinomiya did not study the geography of the world or consider the advances in science achieved in the West. Only after the Meiji Restoration would his education become relevant to the world in which he lived.

In April 1860 it was decided that Sachinomiya would have his *fukasogi*. This ceremony, at which a child's hair was trimmed, was usually performed between the ages of three and eight for both boys and girls, but in 1858, when Meiji was about to have his *fukasogi*, it was postponed because of the burning of the Sennyū-ji, a temple closely associated with the imperial family. Another ceremony, traditionally performed when a boy or girl was nine by Japanese count, was known as *himo-naoshi* or *himo-toki*; it marked the first time a child wore an adult's sash in place of the cord that was used for children's clothes. It was decided that Sachinomiya should have both ceremonies this year. The yin-yang diviners were consulted, and they settled on May 9 at ten o'clock in the morning for the *fukasogi* and ten days later for the *himo-naoshi* ceremonies.

The preparations for the *fukasogi* were elaborate. The emperor gave the prince innumerable articles of clothing, some to be worn at the ceremony, which are described in three closely printed pages of the official chronology.[15] The *himo-naoshi* was a much simpler affair. These occasions served as a prelude to the far more important ceremony of August 16 when Sachinomiya was officially proclaimed as the heir to the throne. He would henceforth also be considered to be the "true child" of Kōmei's consort, ranking at court immediately after her, and he would live in the same palace. The formal proclamation of Sachinomiya as prince of the blood and heir to the throne would be made in October.

On October 16 the doctor of letters Karahashi Ariteru (1827–1874), who had been commanded by Kōmei to prepare a suitable name for the prince as an adult, submitted three names—Kumihito, Fumihito, and Mutsuhito. On the following day, the emperor commanded that the names be shown to the chancellor, the minister of the left, and other dignitaries with the request that they choose the most appropriate.[16]

On November 11 Sachinomiya was proclaimed as the crown prince. On this occasion, his new name was revealed to the assembled nobles, inscribed by the emperor himself—Mutsuhito.[17] This ceremony was followed by the drinking of toasts of congratulation, the singing of popular songs and nō, and the offering to the prince of numerous presents by the assemblage. The celebration at the court was followed the next month by congratulatory gifts from the shogun.

Once the excitement had died down, Mutsuhito was sent back to his studies. The empress, dissatisfied with his progress in calligraphy, commanded Nakayama Yoshiko to supervise his writing practice every day.[18]

These events, though they probably provided some moments of agreeable diversion for Emperor Kōmei, were overshadowed by the urgent business with which he was now confronted, the shogunate's request for the hand of his sister, Kazunomiya, as the bride of the shogun Iemochi. Kazunomiya was the daughter of Emperor Ninkō, and she had been born in 1846, five months after his death. She and her half brother Kōmei seem to have been unusually close, which may account for the extreme reluctance displayed by both to accept a marriage proposal that was in some respects highly advantageous. The proposal, received from Edo on June 3, 1860, spoke of the marriage's fostering the union of the nobility and the military (*kōbu gattai*), which was Kōmei's avowed political stance. Relations between the court and the shogunate had been strained by the latter's having signed treaties with five Western powers, and a marriage would do much to heal the rift.

A marriage of this nature had first been discussed in November 1858 during a conversation between Konoe Tadahiro, the minister of the left, and Sakai Tadaaki, the newly appointed *shoshidai*. Konoe believed that the marriage would benefit the nation but that Kazunomiya's engagement to Prince Taruhito, arranged when she was five years old, ruled out the possibility of marriage with the shogun. Sakai, however, was unwilling to give up the plan. In the following year, he discussed the marriage with the chancellor and obtained the shogunate's consent. Eventually, word of these negotiations reached Kōmei, who replied that it would not be possible to break the engagement with Prince Taruhito. He also mentioned Kazunomiya's dread of going to Edo which, she supposed in her girlish innocence, was a den of foreign barbarians. Kōmei, feeling pity for his sister, refused to force her into a marriage that inspired such terror.[19] He was, however, fully aware of the political advantages to be gained, and his refusal was no doubt tinged with regret.

That year Kazunomiya celebrated her sixteenth birthday by Japanese count. On July 15 she took part in the moon-viewing ceremony, which was the feminine counterpart of the *gembuku* boys underwent. There is something so innocently appealing in the description of Kazunomiya viewing the moon that it is not difficult to imagine Kōmei's reluctance to lose his only sister.

For its part, the shogunate refused to give up plans for a marriage between the shogun and Kazunomiya. There were also proponents of the marriage at the court. When the emperor asked his opinion, Iwakura Tomomi, then a chamberlain, replied that it was obvious that the shogunate's strength was waning. However, he continued, attempting to recoup imperial power with military force would surely lead to great disorder within the country and might invite foreign intervention. It would be better to consent to the marriage, demonstrating to the world that indeed the nobles and the military were united. In exchange, the shogunate should be obliged to abrogate gradually the treaties it had signed with foreign powers. If the shogunate could be persuaded to agree that henceforth all important matters of state would be submitted to the court for its approval before being put into effect, the shogunate's authority would come to depend on the court. For this reason, he said, Kazunomiya was more valuable to the state than nine tripods of treasure. Iwakura advised accepting the request, providing the shogunate would swear to abrogate the treaties.[20]

On July 6 Kōmei sent a letter to the chancellor Kujō Hisatada concerning the marriage. The tone suggests that he had been affected by Iwakura's advice. Describing his unhappiness over the shogunate's signing treaties with barbarians, a development for which he had no excuse to offer the gods or his ancestors, he mentioned his reluctance to send Kazunomiya, the daughter of an emperor, to a part of Japan where foreigners roamed. However, if the shogunate would demonstrate its resolve to cast out the foreigners, he would attempt to persuade Kazunomiya to marry the shogun.[21]

The response from the shogunate was reassuring. In all matters it agreed with the emperor's sentiments, and it fully intended to drive out the foreigners; but until the country was united and militarily strong, it was not possible to confront external problems. The first step was to display to the country the union of nobility and warriors. Once this was achieved, the next step would be to prepare the defenses of the country against the foreigners. If the emperor permitted the marriage of the princess to the shogun and the resources of the country were in this way unified and strengthened, was it possible that the policy of the shogunate would differ from that of the emperor in its eagerness to drive out the foreigners?[22] The shogunate promised to get rid of the foreigners in seven to ten years, either by negotiations that would lead to annulment of the treaties or by military force.[23]

These assurances had the effect of making Kōmei favor accepting the marriage proposal from Edo. On September 4 he asked the chancellor to get Kazunomiya's mother and uncle to persuade her to accept the proposal.[24] He also commanded him to arrange with Prince Taruhito for the annulment of the engagement.[25] Kazunomiya, however, remained unmoved by their arguments, reiterating that she was desolate at the thought of leaving her brother. A week later Kōmei sent a letter to the chancellor reporting that Kazunomiya could not bear to go to Edo as a bride. He was unwilling to compel her to accept, but he also felt obliged to live up to his part of the agreement with the shogunate. He therefore suggested that in place of Kazunomiya, his only surviving daughter, Sumanomiya, might make an acceptable substitute, even though she was still only a year and a half old. Although he was fond of this infant, he was willing to part with her as a sign of his desire to secure a union between nobility and military. If the shogunate would not accept, he would have no choice but to abdicate.

A copy of Kōmei's letter was shown to Kazunomiya who, on reading his offer to abdicate, was sure she would be unable to eat or sleep if she became the cause of her brother's abdicating the throne. She therefore decided to accept his advice[26] and go to Edo, providing five conditions were met. The first was that she not be required to leave for Edo until after the seventeenth anniversary of the death of her father, Emperor Ninkō, two years hence. She also wished to be able to return each year to Kyōto on the anniversary of Ninkō's death, to pray at his tomb and to inquire after the emperor's health. But the shogunate was unwilling to wait two years; it was eager to celebrate the marriage as soon as possible. Kazunomiya's second condition was that she be able to live in Edo under exactly the same surroundings as in the Gosho. This was accepted by the shogunate. The remaining conditions concerned her choice of attendants.[27]

Kōmei sent a letter to the shogunate in which he listed six conditions of his own: (1) that Kazunomiya's five conditions be accepted; (2) that even if there were a change in the senior councillors, the promise to break diplomatic relations with foreign countries would be maintained; (3) that it be made known throughout the country that the marriage was not forced on Kazunomiya in order to preserve the Tokugawa family but was arranged in the interests of promoting the union of nobility and military necessary for the country; (4) that means be found to take care of persons who had been impoverished as the result of opening trade with the foreigners; (5) that the treatment accorded to Kazunomiya once her marriage was settled on would be reported privately to the throne before any decision was made; and (6) that consideration be given to amends for Prince Arisugawa.[28]

Even after Kazunomiya had given her consent, some nobles still opposed the marriage. A rumor circulated at the court that the emperor's intimate Koga Takemichi (1815–1903) had accepted bribes from the shogunate to expedite the marriage and that the courtiers Chigusa Aribumi and Iwakura Tomomi were his underlings. Kōmei got wind of this rumor and directed the chancellor to squelch it, for once he had agreed to the marriage, he was in no mood to tolerate any opposition.[29]

Finally Prince Taruhito was persuaded to abandon his suit for Kazunomiya's hand. A rumor was deliberately circulated that he had been unenthusiastic about the marriage because Kazunomiya had been born in *hinoeuma* (the year of the fiery horse), an ill-omened year for women. Then it was discovered that the young shogun had been born in the same year, whereupon it was decided that a marriage between two people born in an otherwise unlucky year was extremely lucky.[30]

At this period the education of Mutsuhito and the matter of Kazunomiya's marriage seem to have fully absorbed the court's attention. but we should not forget that 1860 was also the year of the first Japanese mission sent to America. Even as the shogunate was promising to expel the foreigners in return for the hand of Kazunomiya, it was taking the irrevocable step of sending officials abroad for the first time since the country was closed more than 200 years earlier.

Chapter 7

The year 1861 was one of the two "revolutionary" years in the cycle of sixty when the *nengō* was invariably changed. But even if it had not been a "revolutionary" year, the stormy events of 1860 provided ample reason to change the *nengō*, and the new year had begun inauspiciously. A fox was observed in the palace garden, and Emperor Kōmei commanded Nakayama Tadayasu to have it exorcised; but prayers and offerings had no effect. Night after night the fox yelped directly under the prince's quarters, until finally (at the empress's suggestion) he moved to her pavilion.[1]

The country was in the grip of severe inflation. Word of the hardships that high prices had inflicted on the common people reached the ears of the emperor, who gave the *shoshidai* fifty pieces of gold, instructing him to use the money to alleviate suffering in the province of Yamashiro, the area around the capital. The *shoshidai* refused the money, obeying the order of the shogunate, which had other plans for providing assistance.[2] The shogunate seems to have been reluctant to allow the emperor to become actively involved in relieving the distress of his subjects.

Japan's relations with foreign countries were also strained. On March 13, 1861, the Russian corvette *Posadnik* under Captain Birilev cast anchor at the Tsushima Islands between Japan and Korea. Under pretext of making necessary repairs to the ship, Russian officers and men went ashore and soon erected barracks and other buildings, seemingly as a permanent encampment. The inhabitants of the islands and the Russians clashed, resulting in the deaths of several Japanese. The shogunate sent the magistrate for foreign affairs to Tsushima to demand that the Russians leave, but they refused.[3]

Russia was not the only European power to realize the strategic importance of Tsushima. The British had asked the shogunate to open a port there, and a warship had made soundings in nearby waters. This action gave the Russians the excuse to "protect" Tsushima from the British. They warned the shogunate of the threat of British occupation of the islands and, urging the need for adequate defenses, offered to build gun batteries and lend cannons to the Japanese.[4] The shogunate rejected this proposal; but when the Russians had more or less occupied the islands, it had no choice but to turn for help in evicting them to Sir Rutherford Alcock, the British minister, following the principle of "using barbarians to fight barbarians." Two British warships under Sir James Hope, commander of the East Indian Fleet, were sent to Tsushima. After receiving a severely phrased warning from Hope, the Russians withdrew from the islands.[5]

News of these developments, which in the past would probably have been kept from the emperor, soon reached Kōmei, causing him extreme distress; but it was not until the following year (1862) that he commanded the daimyo of Tsushima to strengthen Japan's sea defenses.[6] The emperor's personal intervention in a matter that in the past would not have been brought to his attention suggests how greatly his authority had increased.

The change in the *nengō* from Mannen to Bunkyū took place on March 29, the day recommended by the yin-yang diviners. The change seemed at first beneficial. For a time, members of the court were again able to enjoy such traditional diversions as garden parties, performances of nō, and other entertainments. There were also sad occasions: the death of Kōmei's infant daughter Sumanomiya was another instance of an imperial child whose life was cut short.

The period of respite at the court was brief: antiforeign sentiments were rising to a frenzied intensity even as the shogunate was seeking to promote better relations with European countries.[7] On June 5 fourteen *rōnin* from Mito attacked the British legation in Edo. The minister, Sir Rutherford Alcock, escaped injury, but members of his staff were wounded. Although the Mito domain remained in the forefront of the *jōi* movement, other domains were readier to reach an accommodation with the foreigners. Mōri Takachika, the daimyo of Hagi, sent Nagai Uta (1819–1863) to Kyōto and directed him to transmit his views on the necessity of opening the country and, in this way, achieving *kōbu gattai*. Nagai met with Ōgimachisanjō Sanenaru (1820–1909) and expressed his master's strong conviction that a revision of the national policy was imperative.

Although Nagai delivered his long, rambling statement to Ōgimachisanjō, it was clearly intended for Emperor Kōmei. It opened with the (by now familiar) description of the sorry state of the Japanese military caused by the centuries of peace. Surely, it continued, the emperor must be enraged when he sees that the shogunate is not only powerless to resist the intrusion of the barbarians but ready to sign treaties of friendship and commerce without even consulting him.

No doubt he is also disturbed when he realizes that he can no longer depend on the military to protect him. The shogunate has no firm policy with respect to the barbarians but contents itself with temporizing expedients. The emperor has not been kept fully informed of developments, but hotheads have gathered around the throne to call for the abrogation of the treaties with the foreign powers. If the treaties are broken, the foreign powers will surely not accept this peaceably but will initiate military action against Japan. Nagai added that he would not oppose fighting the foreigners if there were any chance of success, but he believed that it would be folly to risk national survival in a war that the Japanese could not hope to win.

For 300 years, he continued, the court in Kyōto has entrusted both internal political decisions and foreign policy to the shogunate. For this reason, the foreigners suppose that the shogunate is the government of Japan and, now that they have concluded treaties with the shogunate, imagine that Japan is their ally. If the treaties are abrogated, their wrath will lead immediately to war. The entire country will soon be in peril. For example, it would not take more than four or five foreign warships to blockade Kyūshū, and the rest of the country would suffer the consequences. It is uncertain whether Kyōto can be defended, and if the capital were defiled by the hooves of foreigners' horses, the humiliation would affect all the other provinces, even those not directly under attack.

Nagai believed that this unhappy situation had arisen because of the policy of *sakoku* (closure of the country) adopted by the shogunate after the Shimabara rebellion. Earlier in Japanese history, not only foreigners had visited Japan freely but facilities had even been erected to accommodate them. Indeed, isolation from other countries was by no means true to ancient Japanese traditions. Had not the goddess of the Ise Shrine promised that imperial influence would extend everywhere the sun shone? The empress Jingū's conquest of the Three Han Kingdoms of Korea was in accord with the intentions of her divine ancestor, and if she had known about countries farther away than the Three Han Kingdoms, she probably would have continued her conquests. But now the government, far from extending Japanese territory abroad, passively allows barbarians to enter the country. Even supposing that *sakoku* were desirable, it could be successfully maintained only if the country possessed striking power; isolation that depended entirely on Japan's island situation was bound to fail. At present the most urgent need is the power both to defend and to attack.

Nagai begged the emperor to change his views on *sakoku* and, returning to the policy of his ancestors, extend imperial authority abroad. He should establish a policy of insisting that all five continents offer tribute to the imperial land, in this way transforming a national calamity into a national blessing. There would be peace within the country, thanks to the union of the court and the military, and once Japan possessed an abundance of warships, imperial rule could be imposed throughout the world.[8]

Mōri Takachika (through his emissary Nagai Uta) was attempting to persuade Emperor Kōmeiō to abandon his support for *sakoku*, not by preaching the brotherhood of man, but by reminding him of the Sun Goddess's promise of Japanese domination of the world once the court and the military had united. Several steps remained to be explained between the present, when the debilitated Japanese military are no match for the foreigners, and the future, when countries all over the world will pay tribute to Japan; but it was hoped that profits from trade with foreigners would enable the Japanese to strengthen their armaments.

As Takachika had expected, Ōgimachisanjō passed on the contents of Nagai's memorial to the emperor who was pleased to receive it. Kōmei did not approve of dismantling *sakoku*, but he favored strengthening Japanese military capacity, and he never wavered in his support of *kōbu gattai*. He commanded Takachika to use his influence to promote understanding between the Court Council and the shogunate and bestowed on him this poem:

kuni no kaze	Even if stormy winds
fukiokoshite mo	Should rage through the country,
amatsuhi wo	I shall wait for them
moto no hikari ni	To return the sun in heaven
kaesu wo zo matsu	To its pristine radiance.

As the result of Nagai's exertions, the shogunate ultimately agreed to ask Takachika to serve as its intermediary in negotiations aimed at achieving *kōbu gattai*. Unfortunately for Nagai, however, the wording of the document he submitted to Ōgimachisanjō was deemed to include disrespectful language, leading to a controversy that ended with Nagai's dismissal.[9]

During most of that year, 1861, the main matter occupying the court's attention was Kazunomiya's journey to Edo as the bride of the shogun. The date of her departure, the end of October 1861, was initially set in 1860. The shogunate hastily repaired the roads along which she would travel; but the emperor sought a delay on the grounds that the princess should be in the capital in the spring of the following year for the services on the seventeenth anniversary of the death of her father, Emperor Ninkō. This request was submitted to the *shoshidai*, Sakai Tadaaki, but he was opposed, citing the preparations that had already been completed. Nonetheless, the shogunate yielded to the extent of allowing Kazunomiya to leave as late as the middle of the November.

Even after this arrangement had been reached, a fresh obstacle to the marriage arose. Since the middle of 1860, the shogunate had been privately conducting negotiations with Prussia, Belgium, and Switzerland for opening diplomatic relations, and at the end of the year a treaty with Prussia was signed.[10] When Kōmei received word that the shogunate was concluding three new treaties with foreign countries, he was, predictably, enraged, and he declared that the engagement of Kazunomiya and the shogun should be broken. He said that it was precisely because he had trusted the shogunate's promise to abrogate the treaties that he had consented to the marriage. The chancellor and other court officials, panic stricken at the thought of the effect that Kōmei's decision might have on relations between the court and the shogunate, attempted to mollify him, and in the end succeeded in getting him to agree to postponing for a few years (rather than terminating) the marriage plans. When Kazunomiya was asked her opinion, she answered with startling frankness that she had never wished for the marriage and that she hoped that she would not have to go to Edo until every last foreigner had been expelled and the East was peaceful; if this failed to happen, she hoped that the wedding would be called off.[11]

The marriage was preserved by an adroit maneuver by Sakai Tadaaki, who objected to transmitting to the shogunate the angry reactions of the court. He insisted that the information he had given concerning the new treaties had been privately transmitted to the chancellor and that it would be a violation of confidence if a formal protest were lodged with the shogunate. Kōmei was eventually persuaded to leave everything to the chancellor. On New Year's Day of 1861, the shogunate sent the court a message explaining in detail the circumstances of the three new treaties and promising once again to expel the foreigners in seven to ten years.

Several other crises threatened to destroy the marriage plans, but in September 1861 Emperor Kōmei, his anger abated, agreed that Kazunomiya should leave for Edo in November. Princess Chikako, as Kazunomiya was now officially known,[12] left Kyōto reluctantly.[13] She visited the Shugaku-in, which had been refurbished for her grandfather, Emperor Kōkaku, and on the return journey worshiped at the Kamo and Kitano Shrines. She attended a performance of nō in the palace. When she went to pray at the Gion Shrine for a safe journey, the emperor and the prince watched as her procession left the palace gate. On November 17 she visited the palace to bid farewell to the emperor, empress, and prince and received presents from them. Before her departure, the emperor wrote the princess a letter asking that when she was married, she would use her influence over her husband to effect the expulsion of the barbarians. Finally, the day she dreaded, the day of her departure, arrived. On November 22 her palanquin left the Katsura Palace, accompanied by court officials. A year later, when patriots decided that the princess's departure for Edo had been an unspeakable affront to imperial dignity, the two nobles who accompanied her all the way to Edo (Chigusa Aribumi and Iwakura Tomomi) were punished for their role in the affair.[14]

The marriage procession was on a grand scale—as many as 10,000 armed men,[15] horses, and an enormous amount of food, gifts, and baggage, including a dismantled Kyōto-style house that was to be erected in Edo, in keeping with the second of Kazunomiya's five conditions for agreeing to the marriage. The princess traveled in the utmost luxury, with frequent stops along the way at places of touristic interest, not reaching Edo until December 16, though two weeks was usually ample time for the journey. The huge number of people in her entourage was deemed essential to guarantee her absolute safety. (There had been rumors that the princess might be abducted along the way.) Males over fifteen were forbidden to cross the path of the procession, and in the cities men were ordered to remain in back rooms, leaving the women to bow from their doors. The route taken was devious, in part to avoid places with inauspicious names; for example, in order not to cross Satta Pass, whose name suggests *satta*, or "divorced," the procession left the Tōkaidō, the normal route to Edo, and took a long detour through the mountains along another highway. Unfortunately, there was no way of avoiding the *enkiri enoki*, whose name meant "broken vows nettle-tree," highly inauspicious before a marriage, but every last leaf on the tree was concealed with straw matting so as to protect the princess from any harmful effects from its name.[16]

The marriage between the princess and the youthful shogun did not take place until March 11, 1862, but even before then, opponents of the marriage had resorted to violence. On February 14, 1862, the senior councillor Andō Nobumasa (1819–1871), a leading proponent of both *kōbu gattai* and the marriage, was set upon by six *rōnin* from Mito while on his way to the shogun's castle. One man fired a shot into Andō's palanquin, wounding him. The other five men attacked with drawn swords, but Andō was protected by some fifty retainers (the assassination of Ii Naosuke having alerted shogunate officials to the danger of traveling without sufficient escort), who quickly disposed of the would-be assassins.

The *rōnin* carried with them a manifesto in which they stated why they had been impelled to take this action.[17] They accused Andō of having deceived the court: although he had given *kōbu gattai* as the reason for making the emperor's sister marry the shogun, in reality it was no more than a scheme for obtaining imperial consent to the treaties with the foreigners. The *rōnin* had been aroused in particular by a rumor circulating at the time. Hori Toshihiro (1818–1860), a shogunate official who committed suicide under mysterious circumstances, was said to have left behind an open letter to Andō accusing him of disloyalty.[18] According to the letter, Andō had, at the instigation of Townsend Harris, plotted to depose the emperor. To this end, he had employed two scholars of national learning to produce examples from the distant past of emperors who had been dethroned.[19] The assassins, believing the rumors and angered by Andō's apparent friendliness with foreigners, decided that he had defiled the sacred Way of a true subject. For this reason they had no choice but to impose Heaven's punishment on him. The term *tenchū* (divine punishment), though ancient in origin, first came into vogue at this time as a justification for the political murders of the 1860s.

Having narrowly escaped death at the hands of assailants, Andō might have been the object of sympathy, and his position might have become even stronger than before; but in fact, he lost the considerable political power he had enjoyed as the leader of the shogunate faction favoring economic reform and trade with the West, probably because the anti-shogunate forces had moved into the ascendancy.

One other crisis occurred before the marriage could take place. The shogunate had promised Princess Chikako that she would be allowed to return to Kyōto for the services in memory of her father to be held on the seventeenth anniversary of his death, but her departure for Kyōto was repeatedly delayed. The princess finally sent her senior lady-in-waiting in her stead. Kōmei was angered by the shogunate's failure to keep its promises, but the latter argued that the long journey would fatigue the princess before her wedding.

Chikako was treated with the utmost deference at the wedding. The ceremony went on for about ten hours, sufficient time for the bride to change costume many times. Her feelings on first encountering her husband were not recorded, but the marriage, despite its political background and later problems with her mother-in-law, was as happy as any dynastic marriage could be. The princess's wedded life lasted for only five and a half years, until Iemochi's sudden death, but when she herself was on her deathbed, she asked to be buried in the Tokugawa tomb rather than in Kyōto.

The marriage of the emperor's sister and the shogun achieved the aim of bringing about closer relations between the imperial family and the shogunate, and it ushered in a brief period when the emperor enjoyed greater influence than he had in centuries.[20] Kōmei unswervingly favored *kōbu gattai* and opposed those who advocated overthrowing the shogunate, but tension mounted as the shogunate continued to sign treaties of commerce and amity with foreign countries, even though the court desired nothing more than to have every last foreigner expelled from Japan.

Shifts of policy were frequent and abrupt in all the factions, resulting at times in surprising alliances or hostilities. In the past, Satsuma had often behaved like a separate kingdom, almost independent of the shogunate, but at the end of 1861 the youthful daimyo, Shimazu Tadayoshi (1840–1897), sent envoys to the capital, offering to serve as a conduit in transmitting imperial wishes to the shogunate. The envoys offered Kōmei a sword, for which he expressed gratitude in a poem inscribed in his own hand:

yo wo omou	There can be no doubt
kokoro no tachi to	This sword possesses a heart
shirarekeri	That cares for the world;
saya kumori naki	Brightly and without a cloud
mononofu no tama	Shines the soul of the soldier.[21]

When Shimazu Tadayoshi and his father received the poem, they were moved to tears.

In June 1862 the Satsuma daimyo and his father sent envoys to the capital informing the former minister of the left Konoe Tadahiro and the acting major counselor Konoe Tadafusa of their support for the emperor and their conviction that change in the shogunate was of urgent importance. They also expressed fears that the emperor was insufficiently protected, and for this reason, they had decided to send troops of their own into the capital. Konoe Tadafusa, alarmed, tried to fend off this unwanted assistance, but the Satsuma leaders would not listen. On June 15 some 1,000 Satsuma soldiers entered the capital. Their leader explained that they wanted to see some high-ranking court officials dismissed and the chancellor Kujō Hisatada replaced by Konoe Tadahiro. They also had demands concerning the reorganization of the shogunate. What they sought was the dismissal of officials who opposed *kōbu gattai*. They demanded that the shogun swear fealty to the court. Once the imperial dignity was fully ensured by this action, ways should be considered of how it might be extended overseas.[22] That night, possibly as a test of the genuineness of Satsuma's promises of loyalty, the emperor commanded Shimazu Hisamitsu to quiet the turbulent *rōnin* in the capital.

Five days later, Hisamitsu moved into action. Before he arrived in Kyōto, the samurai and *rōnin* who supported *sonnō jōi* supposed that he would lead them in an attack on the shogunate, but when he made it plain that reform and not destruction of the shogunate was his aim, they were much disappointed. Members of the Hagi and other domains who favored violent action met at the Terada-ya, an inn in Fushimi south of the capital, with malcontent members of the Satsuma domain to plan the assassination of the chancellor and Sakai Tadaaki. The plotters and members of the Satsuma domain who were obedient to Hisamitsu's orders clashed. The rebels were massacred, and the emperor, greatly pleased, bestowed on Hisamitsu a dagger from the imperial collection, praising him for his victory over lawless men. Shimazu Hisamitsu had won a high reputation at the court.

Mutsuhito figures hardly at all in this part of the chronicle of his life. We know that he saw off Kazunomiya when she left for Edo, and perhaps he was aware (even at the age of ten) of her sadness. In June there was a ceremony, patterned on the one Kōmei had undergone at the same age, to commemorate his beginning the study of the Confucian classics, although in fact he had started three years earlier. An epidemic of measles that summer caused alarm in the palace, and prayers were said to preserve the prince. Another baby sister died, less than a year old. On a more pleasant note that same year, Mutsuhito first tried his hand at painting.

These bits of information are scattered among the prosaic events recorded in the official chronology. It is easy to miss the facts of lasting importance. For example, the section describing events of September 1862 records in detail the religious observances at various shrines, the emperor's evening spent admiring the moon, and his presentation of gifts to the crown prince. These and similarly unexciting events are followed by the entry for September 14, which opens with a flat statement: three nobles—Iwakura Tomomi, Chigusa Aribumi, and Tomi-nokōji Hironao—accused of having cooperated with the shogunate in sending Kazunomiya to Edo, were confined to their houses, relieved of their posts, and urged to become Buddhist priests.[23]

Behind this surprising development was the great intensification of pressure from supporters of *sonnō jōi* as their numbers swelled with malcontents and their actions became more reckless. Anyone who opposed them was likely to be threatened if not killed. Just a month earlier, Shimada Sakon, a retainer of Chancellor Kujō Hisatada, was attacked and killed. His head was exposed at Shijō-kawara, and his severed limbs were thrown into the Takase River. This initiated a wave of terror, which the extremists called *tenchū*, or "divine punishment." When the shogunate showed itself powerless to suppress the disorder, the terrorists gained the upper hand. They singled out for special attack "four villains and two ladies,"[24] members of the court whom they charged with responsibility for Kazunomiya's marriage to the shogun. They found support among the nobles, and the *jōi* faction now controlled some of the major domains. Despite his repeated statements of support for the shogunate, Kōmei declared at this critical moment that he had not in any way deviated from his sworn mission of *jōi*,[25] an avowal that probably encouraged the perpetrators of "divine punishment."

It is hard to imagine what effect these developments may have had on Mutsuhito's development. Was he still too young to understand what was happening in the world outside the Gosho? Or was he deliberately sheltered from the raging controversy and news of the murders? Or did even this prince, living deep within the Gosho, become aware, when people he had often seen at the court ceased to appear, that major changes had occurred? Did Kōmei explain to his son why he was always so agitated and fatigued? In any case, the harsh realities of the times were gradually intruding into a world that had been guided for centuries by traditional conceptions of order and decorum. Now change would be the rule.

Chapter 8

The changed relationship between the emperor and the shogun is vividly illustrated by an incident that occurred on January 17, 1863. The imperial envoy Sanjō Sanetomi (1837–1891) and the vice envoy Anegakōji Kintomo (1839–1863) arrived at Edo Castle on this day with a message from Emperor Kōmei to be delivered to the shogun. The brief text reiterated his unswerving desire for every last foreigner to be expelled from the country. He urged the shogunate to decide on a concrete plan for putting *jōi* into effect and to convey this plan without delay to the lords of the various domains. Once the plan had been carefully considered and approved by a majority, the ugly barbarians could be eradicated.[1] What was unusual was not the content of the message, a restatement of views that Kōmei had often expressed, but the manner in which the letter was presented by the imperial envoy to the shogun.

It had been the custom when an imperial envoy had an audience with the shogun for the shogun to receive him while seated on the upper level[2] of the hall of audiences. The imperial envoy would prostrate himself on the lower level, following which a herald would announce his rank and name. Then the envoy, in response to a nod from the shogun, would move up to the upper level on his knees and, bowing low, transmit the message from the emperor. When he had finished, he would withdraw, still on his knees. Sanjō Sanetomi, finding this practice repugnant and denigrating to imperial prestige, communicated to the Kyōto deputy (*shugo*), Matsudaira Katamori, his wish that the shogunate show greater deference toward an envoy from the emperor.[3]

Sanjō's protest was taken to heart, though presumably only after much debate in the shogunate. On this occasion, the envoy went directly to the upper level, and it was the shogun, at first seated on the middle level, who had to wait for a sign from the envoy before moving to the upper level in order to receive the imperial letter. It is hard to imagine a more striking example of the change in the relations between the shogunate and the court, but this was by no means the only instance of the shogunate's new attitude of reverence toward the emperor.

The shogunate was faced with a dilemma. It clearly wished for better relations with the court, which necessitated obeying Kōmei's injunction to expel the barbarians, but the most intelligent men in the shogunate—for example, Tokugawa Yoshinobu (1837–1913) and Matsudaira Yoshinaga (1828–1890)—were aware that opening the country was inevitable. The shogun probably had no alternative in the end but to reply to Kōmei in terms of assurances that he fully intended to carry out the principle of *jōi*.

The change in the relative importance of the emperor and the shogun was quickly noticed by the leaders of the different domains, and many daimyos found it necessary to visit Kyōto. The shogunate had strictly prohibited them from entering the capital, and the normal route taken by daimyos on their way to Edo from the west of Japan skirted the city of Kyōto; but at this juncture the prohibition had lost force, and daimyos now called regularly in Kyōto. Indeed, the center of politics had moved from Edo to Kyōto. Profiting by the sudden increase in its importance, the court used the influence of the visiting daimyos to persuade the shogunate to change features in the system that it found objectionable. This was the first time in at least 500 years that the emperor possessed such political importance. The main thrust of court politics was not, however, aimed at securing greater power for the emperor but at achieving the goal of *jōi*.

The change affected the nobles as well. Until this time they had nothing to do with national politics; instead, their political concerns were restricted to the palace and its ceremonies. Now, however, nobles began to take an active part in the government, a step toward the restoration of imperial authority.

The new importance of the emperor was underlined in 1863 when the shogun visited the capital, the first time there had been such a visit in more than 200 years. Iemochi wished to demonstrate both his reverence for the court and his profound desire to achieve *kōbu gattai*. The shogun was preceded by his most important advisers, including Tokugawa Yoshinobu, who visited the palace on February 27 and was received by the emperor. Three days later, Yoshinobu called at the Gakushū-in, the school for sons of the nobility founded by Kōmei's father. On this occasion he proposed that the old practice of requiring junior members of the imperial family to enter Buddhist orders be discontinued; instead, they should be named *shinnō* (princes of the blood) and allowed to remain in the laity. He also proposed that after many years of confinement in the Gosho, the emperor should tour the country in the spring and autumn in the manner of the monarchs of olden times. Finally, he suggested that Prince Son'yu (who had been condemned to perpetual confinement during the Ansei purge) be allowed to return to the laity. All three proposals were calculated to ingratiate him (and the shogun) with the emperor.

The last proposal was quickly implemented: on March 18 an imperial command was issued to Prince Son'yu enjoining him to let his hair grow out.[4] Before long Prince Nakagawa, as he was now known,[5] became the confidant of the emperor, the member of the court he most trusted. He has attracted curiously little attention from modern scholars, but he was not only a power behind the throne[6] but a man of considerable influence whose career was marked by vicissitudes suggested by his frequent changes of name. His presence at the Shōren-in, especially during the early 1860s, was a magnet drawing patriots from all over the country.

The enhanced political importance of Kyōto at this time, confirmed by the shogun's visit, did not mollify the extremists, who maintained their loathing of anyone suspected of collaborating with the shogunate. Another wave of terrorist activity swept over the capital. Some men were killed, and others were threatened with death. On the night of March 10, 1863, four assailants killed the Confucian physician Ikeuchi Daigaku (1811–1863). The murderers, following the tradition of such assassinations, left behind a note explaining why they had killed Ikeuchi:

> This individual always enjoyed the favor of exalted personages. In the period around 1858 he allied himself with samurai of just principles and exercised himself on their behalf in various ways but in the end betrayed them, entering into communication with corrupt officials and causing the deaths of many loyal samurai from different domains, in this way himself escaping punishment. His crimes are such that heaven and earth cannot hold him. For this reason, divine punishment has been administered, and his head is exposed.[7]

Ikeuchi had been one of four heroes of the *jōi* faction, along with Umeda Umpin, Yanagawa Seigan, and Rai Mikisaburō. At the time of the Ansei purge, the shogunate, considering Ikeuchi to be particularly dangerous, pursued him. In the end he gave himself up, but instead of being put to death, he was released after a relatively brief imprisonment, giving rise to the suspicion that he must have cooperated with the shogunate.

Not content with just killing Ikeuchi, his assailants cut off his ears, delivering one to Nakayama Tadayasu and the other to Ōgimachisanjō Sanenaru, together with notes warning that unless they resigned their positions, they would be dealt with in the same manner. These nobles were accused of being two-faced—in public advocating righteous action but in private favoring compromise and half-hearted measures. The assassins asserted that moreover, the two men had taken bribes in return for services rendered to the cause of *kōbu gattai*; this, they declared, had led to their hatred. Tadayasu was enraged by the false accusations made against him, but in the end both he and Ōgimachisanjō, alarmed by the threat to their lives, resigned their posts, pleading ill health. Tadayasu was replaced by Sanjō Sanetomi as the guardian of Prince Mutsuhito.

Incidents of violence and intimidation multiplied in 1863 as samurai and *rōnin*, intoxicated with the principle of *jōi*, went on a rampage, killing and maiming; and they kept up tension in the city by circulating false rumors. There were more than seventy incidents of murder, arson, and intimidation during the year, each explained by a statement left by the head of the victim or pasted on a wall. The shogunate authorities were powerless to control the disorders, and it was left to the court—in whose name the outrages were committed—to remonstrate with the unruly "patriots." The emperor, never wavering in his support of the shogunate, gave orders for samurai belonging to the sixteen domains stationed in the capital to assemble at the Gakushū-in, where they were instructed not to meddle in politics and especially not to throw unsigned missives into the houses of gentlemen. They were told that if they had complaints, they should send them under their signature to a responsible official. The emperor also summoned the daimyos of the sixteen domains and directed the chancellor to inform them of his views on carrying out *jōi*. He urged them to feel free in the future to visit the Gakushū-in and express their views, especially on matters pertaining to national defense.

Living people were not the only victims of the violence. On March 11 nine men broke into a hall at the Tōji-in containing wooden statues of the Ashikaga shoguns, cut off the heads of the first three, and carried them to the Sanjō Bridge, where they were displayed with signs explaining the crime of each.[8] The gesture was interpreted by persons of the time as a covert attack on the Tokugawa shoguns, and the representatives of the shogunate in Kyōto were quick to respond. The perpetrators of the crime were arrested, and the appropriate punishment was much debated.[9]

On April 21 the shogun Tokugawa Iemochi arrived in the capital with more than 3,000 retainers. He proceeded to Nijō Castle, the official residence of the shogun in Kyōto. The visit was potentially dangerous. The city was filled with partisans of *sonnō jōi*, and any one of them might have staged a suicidal attack on the shogun. On the following day, Iemochi sent Tokugawa Yoshinobu to the palace to express his apologies for the incompetence he had displayed in governing the country ever since becoming shogun. He nevertheless asked that the emperor, following time-honored custom, renew his authorization to rule. His wish was granted.[10]

On April 24 Iemochi himself went to the palace to pay his respects. The emperor granted the shogun an audience, graciously welcoming him and offering a ritual cup of saké. Later the emperor summoned Iemochi to his study, where the two men chatted. The emperor's manner of receiving the shogun was polite but not deferential: the court had decided that the shogun ranked below the minister of the center (*naidaijin*), the fifth highest rank in the court government.

The reverence with which Iemochi begged the emperor to grant the benefit of his divine wisdom if ever any action of the shogunate failed to meet with his approval also contrasted strikingly with the arrogance displayed by Tokugawa Iemitsu in 1634 during the last visit of a shogun to the capital. At that time the Tokugawa family was at the height of its power and the shogun was accorded higher rank than the chancellor.[11] This time the meeting was dominated by the presence of the emperor.

During his audience, Kōmei made his usual request—that Iemochi carry out the announced policy of *jōi*. After the audience ended, Iemochi visited Prince Mutsuhito's residence, where he left rich gifts, including a fine broadsword, 500 pieces of silver, twenty pieces of gold, two hanging scrolls, a flower vase, and bolts of brocaded silk. On the following day, the emperor sent an envoy to Nijō Castle with return gifts from himself and the prince.

Once the formalities of the occasion were over, the emperor was again tormented by anxiety and indignation over the continued presence of foreigners in the country. On April 28 he voluntarily left the Gosho for the first time in his life[12] in order to offer prayers at the two Kamo Shrines for the realization of *jōi*.[13] He was accompanied by the *kampaku*, the minister of the right, and various lesser nobles. The shogun was also in attendance, together with Tokugawa Yoshinobu, various daimyos, as well as experts in protocol. It rained that day, but when the imperial palanquin passed before Iemochi and the others, they all leaped off their horses, discarded their umbrellas, and knelt along the road.[14] Vast numbers of Kyōto's inhabitants turned out for a rare glimpse of the emperor, or at least of his palanquin.[15] It has often been recounted that Takasugi Shinsaku (1839–1867), a extremist *jōi* proponent from Chōshū, called out sarcastically as the shogun passed, "*Seii taishōgun!*" alluding to the shogun's inability to live up to his title of "conqueror of barbarians."

Iemochi's visit proved to be a great success for Emperor Kōmei. Savoring his triumph, he was reluctant to allow his guest to leave. However, on April 7 Iemochi, having spent far longer in the capital than the originally planned ten days, announced that he was returning to Edo. Members of the court were disappointed. At the time the courtiers were divided into two main factions: those who sought to promote *kōbu gattai* and those who believed Iemochi's presence in the capital provided an opportunity to discomfit him and perhaps eventually to overthrow the shogunate. Their reasons differed, but both factions hoped Iemochi's stay would be prolonged, enabling them to realize their goals; but the shogunate was frantically eager for him to return to Edo to deal with the repercussions of an incident that had occurred in the autumn of the previous year.

An Englishman, Charles Richardson, along with three companions, had ridden past the procession of the daimyo of Satsuma, Shimazu Hisamitsu, allegedly without showing proper respect. Richardson was killed at a place called Namamugi, and the British demanded reparations from both the shogunate and the Satsuma clan. The shogunate eventually complied with the British demands, but at the time of Iemochi's visit to Kyōto, the matter had not yet been settled, and he was urgently needed in Edo for the negotiations.

When Iemochi informed Kōmei of his forthcoming departure, the emperor said that he would be unable to control his feelings of desolation if Iemochi returned to Edo. He begged Iemochi to reassure him by remaining a while longer. Iemochi, deeply moved, acceded to the emperor's wishes. The grateful emperor showered Iemochi with gifts, and Prince Mutsuhito, accompanying his father, appeared for the first time before the shogun.

On May 28 Kōmei traveled to the Iwashimizu Hachiman Shrine to pray for deliverance from the foreign menace. Originally the journey had been planned for a week earlier, and the emperor had commanded the shogun to accompany him. These plans were upset when Nakayama Tadamitsu (1845–1864), the seventh son of Nakayama Tadayasu, suddenly resigned his office and, alleging illness, fled the capital.[16] Reports had it that Tadamitsu, along with some *rōnin* from Chōshū, was planning to intercept the procession on its way to Iwashimizu and to kill the shogun. On May 17 the emperor, getting word of the plot, ordered a postponement of the pilgrimage. Tokugawa Yoshinobu advised that the visit be dropped altogether, and the emperor himself manifested increasing reluctance to go, but he was forced by extremists to make the journey as planned.

Kōmei described the circumstances in a letter he sent to Prince Nakagawa on May 29. He had decided on a further postponement because he was suffering from vertigo, his chronic complaint, and was apprehensive about the long journey. The chancellor, Takatsukasa Sukehiro, replied to the emperor that although a postponement was reasonable under the circumstances, it would be difficult to change plans; so he advised the emperor to resign himself to going. Soon afterward, Sanjō Sanetomi requested an audience with the emperor. He said that he had come to see whether the emperor was really ill or only pretending. He refused to hear of a postponement but insisted that the emperor make the journey, regardless of whether he was ill. Afterward, other officials joined the discussion, some saying that the emperor was pretending to be ill because he was unwilling to make the journey and others declaring that if the emperor withdrew to his private quarters, they would drag him out and put him bodily into the imperial palanquin. The emperor, all fear and trembling, had no choice but to yield. The chancellor was deeply upset by what had happened, but he, too, was powerless to alter the situation. Neither the emperor nor the chancellor was a match for the "hot-blooded nobles" (*kekki no dōjō*). Kōmei urged Prince Nakagawa to ask Shimazu Hisamitsu to help persuade the irresponsible nobles to open their eyes, for if they continued to have their own way, it would surely lead to disaster.[17]

Other sources relate that places where the emperor might rest had been provided on the way in case he was stricken with illness on the journey. He certainly was unwell. When he went to pray in the main shrine building at Iwashimizu, he stumbled and had to be lifted to his feet; and persons in his retinue supported him throughout as he made the round of fifteen lesser shrines.

It is ironic that Kōmei's adversaries, members of the *sonnō jōi* faction, were pledged to revere the emperor; yet they blatantly disregarded his wishes and even threatened him with physical violence if he refused to visit Iwashimizu. They were willing to die for him, but on their own terms.

The nobles had arranged for Iemochi to accompany the emperor to Iwashimizu and for the emperor to present him there with a *settō*, an ornamental sword worn as a sign that the wearer was a surrogate of the emperor. Acceptance of the sword would have put the shogun in a difficult position by compelling him to carry out the emperor's policy of expelling the barbarians, a step the shogunate was reluctant to take. Iemochi seems to have learned what was in store for him. He declined, on grounds of illness, to take part in the pilgrimage, sending Tokugawa Yoshinobu in his stead; but when Yoshinobu was summoned to the shrine to receive the sword, he pleaded sudden illness and refused to leave his lodgings.[18] We can imagine how upset Kōmei must have been by this double rebuff. Perhaps his own illness was psychosomatic. It was understandable in terms of natural apprehensions not only over what was for him a distant journey but also over the possibility of abduction or even murder on the way.

The men who threatened the emperor were not assassins or even uncouth samurai but members of the upper ranks of the nobility, men belonging to a class that is usually depicted as corrupt and effete rather than as hot-blooded. Kōmei looked for succor not to members of his court or to the shogun but to someone who might be described as a hothead, Shimazu Hisamitsu, the de facto ruler of Satsuma, who in the previous year had sent troops to Kyōto to suppress radical loyalists in the Terada-ya incident. While at the Iwashimizu Shrine, the emperor prayed for *jōi*, but he may also have prayed for deliverance from those who most vociferously supported him, the *sonjō* faction, as the *sonnō jōi* adherents came to be called.

There is no evidence as to how much Prince Mutsuhito knew of these developments. He was still only eleven years old and probably did not discuss political matters with his father. When Kōmei left for Iwashimizu, the prince (and the empress) saw him off and welcomed him back, but the prince was probably unaware what an ordeal the visit to Iwashimizu had been for his father. It is likely, however, that he knew something of the activities of Nakayama Tadamitsu, his youthful uncle.

Tadamitsu was appointed as a *jijū*, or chamberlain, in 1858, at the age of thirteen. His main function as chamberlain was apparently to serve as the playmate of his nephew, Mutsuhito, seven years younger than himself. In the same year he became a chamberlain, Tadamitsu participated in the protest staged by eighty-eight nobles against the treaty of trade and amity with foreign powers signed by the shogunate. He was guided in his precocious advocacy of *jōi* by the teachings of such patriots as Takechi Zuisan (1829–1865), Kusaka Genzui (1840–1864), and Yoshimura Toratarō (1837–1863), men who would perish in the fighting of the last days of the shogunate.[19]

The dominant figure in Tadamitsu's education as a patriot was Tanaka Kawachinosuke (1815–1862), a retainer of the Nakayama family who had known Tadamitsu from childhood days. Like Tadamitsu's other mentors, Tanaka was involved in the incident at the Terada-ya. He was arrested by Satsuma troops, and on the ship bearing him to captivity, he and his adopted son were stabbed to death and their bodies thrown into the Inland Sea. Perhaps the chief lesson Tanaka taught Tadamitsu was that loyalty, hitherto associated with particular domains, was more properly directed at the *kokutai*, the national essence, as embodied in the person of the emperor.

On September 30, 1862, Tadamitsu visited Takechi Zuisan's lodgings. He informed Takechi that he had decided that Iwakura Tomomi must be killed and that he needed Takechi's help. His reasons for killing Iwakura were not stated, but Takechi's diary mentions Tadamitsu's belief that Iwakura planned to poison the emperor or at least to place a curse on him.[20] Takechi told Tadamitsu to give up his plan, but Tadamitsu replied that once he had made up his mind to do something, he could not stop until he had accomplished it. Takechi, at a loss how to argue with someone in Tadamitsu's overwrought state, agreed to discuss the plan with his associates. One of them, the extremist noble Anegakōji Kintomo, said he had heard that Tadamitsu often behaved in a wild and disorderly manner. He added that he was not sure whether or not Tadamitsu was really an "advocate of justice" who was upset over the times.[20]

Takechi informed Sanjō Sanetomi of the plot, and the latter probably told Nakayama Tadayasu. Late that night Tadamitsu went to Takechi's lodgings to say that he had been obliged to call off the attack. Apparently Tadayasu forbade Tadamitsu to take part in the plot. Tadamitsu threatened to commit suicide, to which Tadayasu replied, "If you are so intent on it, I don't suppose you'll stop, no matter what I say to stop you. But killing him, there's no getting around it, would be a reckless act. You should first denounce his crimes to the appropriate official, and if that official refuses to look into the matter, you may take matters into your own hands. If you are unwilling to listen to reason, kill your father first."[21]

Faced with his father's stern opposition, Tadamitsu had no choice but to give up his plan. But the next day, November 2, he summoned Takechi and told him, in a quick change of decision, that he had decided to kill the rogues that day after all and asked Takechi to get support from the Satsuma, Chōshū, and Tosa domains. Takechi respectfully listened to Tadamitsu and then went to the chancellor to warn him that unless Iwakura and the others were banished to some distant place, Tadamitsu would join with men from three domains to carry out "divine punishment." Two days later, notes were thrown into the houses of three nobles—Iwakura, Chigusa Aribumi, and Koga Takemichi—warning that if they did not leave the city in two days, their heads would be exposed on the riverbed of the Kamo River, and punishment extended to their entire family. The threats, but also the prevailing *jōi* atmosphere in the Court Council, had the desired effect: Iwakura shaved his head and a few weeks later moved to exile in Iwakura Village, north of the capital. This did not end Tadamitsu's obsession with killing Iwakura, whom he repeatedly blamed for every occurrence that displeased him.

Tadamitsu, braving his father's disapproval and seemingly indifferent to the likelihood that he would be disowned, continued his wild and precipitous activities even after he had succeeded in getting rid of Iwakura. Tadayasu naturally worried about his wayward son, whose whereabouts were unknown. In April 1863 he petitioned the court to relieve Tadamitsu of his office, stating his fear that extreme concern over the danger to the nation might have driven Tadamitsu out of his senses. He said he would continue to search for his son and, when he found him, would determine whether he was mad.

For a time Tadamitsu took refuge in Chōshū, making sudden, disconcerting appearances only to vanish just as suddenly, making him less than a welcome visitor, even though his ties with the imperial family were an asset to the *jōi* cause. A letter sent on May 22, 1863, from Chōshū reported that on seeing the foreign ships and weapons that had been bought by the domain, which stood in the forefront of the *jōi* movement, Tadamitsu had been so enraged to think that foreign weapons were being used in the sacred cause that he urged the domain leaders to destroy them. They were unwilling to accept this suggestion, and the indignant Tadamitsu rode off to the port city of Shimonoseki.[22]

In September 1863 the Tenchū-gumi (Divine Punishment Group) was organized by Yoshimura Toratarō and others, with Tadamitsu as the central figure. These loyalist fanatics were based in Yamato Province, where at first they enjoyed some success in burning government buildings and killing officials, but their revolt was crushed. Tadamitsu was assassinated in 1864 by a band of killers sent by the Chōshū domain.[23]

Prince Mutsuhito was too young to be aware of the details of the *jōi* movement, but he probably knew something of Tadamitsu's activities and perhaps also of the tenets that inspired him. Almost nothing is known about Meiji's political views when he ascended the throne at the age of fifteen, but he seems not to have shared his father's reverence for the institution of the shogunate. Perhaps Tadamitsu helped form the young prince's conception of what rulership should mean in Japan. Tadamitsu's behavior was so erratic that one can hardly imagine him systematically imparting to Meiji a political philosophy, but the example of a young noble risking his life in the attempt to overthrow a regime he hated, in the face of his father's opposition and the weight of tradition, may have stirred the boy who would soon be emperor.

Chapter 9

On June 9, 1863, Tokugawa Iemochi reported to the throne that the foreigners would be expelled on June 24.[1] Twice before he had set a date, but both times he had had to postpone action. It was doubtless with extreme reluctance that he settled on still another date. He was well aware how woefully inadequate Japanese military preparations would prove if the foreigners resisted eviction. But he had no choice: he was under constant pressure from the court, and he had promised when he was given the hand of Kazunomiya that he would carry out *jōi*.

After learning of the court's determination to expel the foreigners, the Chō-shū domain had hastily erected fortifications along the coast. On the day set for *jōi* to commence, the domain demonstrated its eagerness to be the first to put *jōi* into practice by shelling some foreign ships. An American merchant ship anchored off the northern Kyūshū coast was the first victim. This action was followed a few weeks later by the shelling of a French and a Dutch warship as they passed through the Shimonoseki Straits. When word of these encounters reached the court, the emperor appointed the nobleman Ōgimachi Kintada as "supervisor of *jōi*" and sent him to Hagi with gifts for the daimyo of Chōshū and his son and a message praising them for their initiative in having led all the other domains in carrying out *jōi*.[2] It was obvious that sooner or later, the foreign powers would retaliate for these attacks, but Kōmei had long since been resigned to the possibility of war.[3]

The emperor's confidence of victory in a war with the foreigners seemed confirmed by Satsuma's successful resistance to the British soon afterward. The British had demanded reparations from both the shogunate and the Satsuma domain for the murder of Charles Richardson at Namamugi. The shogunate paid in May, but Satsuma had failed to respond. The British sent a fleet of seven warships that entered Kagoshima Bay on August 12, 1863, to demand that the daimyo Shimazu Mochihisa execute the men responsible for the Namamugi incident and pay indemnities to the families of those killed and wounded in the incident. The daimyo was given twenty-four hours to reply. The answer from the domain stated that the guilty persons had fled and could not be found. As for the indemnity, the domain could not pay without authorization from the shogunate.

On August 15 at dawn, the British warships suddenly seized three steamships belonging to the domain. At noon the Satsuma batteries opened fire on the British fleet, and it was returned. The firing lasted until late in the afternoon. Many houses and temples in Kagoshima were destroyed by fire, and there were numerous casualties among the Satsuma forces; but the British also suffered considerable damage, and the fleet left without scoring a decisive victory. When Shimazu Mochihisa informed the court of his battle with the British, the emperor sent a message of congratulations.[4]

The court responded enthusiastically to the news, and in anticipation of armed conflict with the foreigners, members of the imperial family and the nobility were commanded to wear swords when entering or leaving the palace precincts. This was a novel experience for them, for it had been centuries since members of the court took themselves seriously as potential combatants. The chancellor, Takatsukasa Sukehiro, asked the daimyos residing in Kyōto their opinions concerning the advisability of a *jōi* campaign personally led by the emperor. The daimyo of Tottori, Ikeda Yoshinori (1837–77), replied, "Yes, personal leadership by His Majesty would be desirable. But if His Majesty and the nobles have not the slightest knowledge of military matters, how can they possibly be successful? The daimyo of Aizu, Matsudaira Katamori, is now in Kyōto serving as the military governor, and there are other daimyos in Kyōto with their troops. They should be asked to drill their troops [in the vicinity of the palace], so that the nobles' eyes will become familiar with the sight of soldiers and their ears with the roar of cannons. Only then will it be fitting to discuss personal command by His Majesty."[5]

Emperor Kōmei accordingly asked Matsudaira Katamori to have his soldiers drill outside the Kenshun Gate. It rained that day, but the emperor nevertheless watched the drill from an observation post at the gate. He was accompanied by the empress and the crown prince, as well as by many ladies of the court, nobles, and daimyos. Katamori personally led more than 3,000 troops in his command. The drill began about four in the afternoon. All the soldiers wore helmets and armor, but some units carried guns, while others brandished spears, bows, and other traditional arms. The soldiers blew conch horns, banged bells and drums, waved swords and spears, fired guns and bows, and occasionally emitted war cries. There was little suggestion of modern warfare.

Another drill was held at the Kenshun Gate on September 17. This time, troops not only from Aizu but also the Tottori, Tokushima, Yonezawa, and Okayama domains participated. Once again Prince Mutsuhito observed. Troops of the Yonezawa domain armed with Western-style guns staged maneuvers. The chronicle of Meiji's reign states,

> The roar of guns echoed to the heavens, and powder smoke obscured the sky. Boys and girls among the spectators turned pale with fright, but the prince tranquilly gazed on throughout with no change of expression. There had been no instance in modern times of an emperor personally watching the maneuvers, and it was absolutely unheard of for a prince of his tender years to accompany the emperor at such a time. Among the courtiers were those who said that it was a violation of time-honored custom for armed men to run about within the nine gates, even granting it was a drill, and that to play with weapons in the vicinity of the imperial sanctuary was a profanation of divine authority. Such were attitudes at the time.[6]

On September 25 Kōmei announced his plan to visit the tomb of Emperor Jimmu and the Kasuga Shrine to pray for *jōi*. He planned also to go on to the Great Shrine of Ise for the same purpose. He revealed that he was considering taking personal command of the *jōi* forces. The *jōi* faction among the nobles, believing this would provide a good opportunity for a campaign against the shogunate, conferred with Chōshū samurai and *shishi*. Guessing this would happen, the *kōbu gattai* faction became highly disturbed and appealed to Prince Nakagawa for help in getting the emperor's proposed journey to Yamato canceled. Prince Nakagawa went to the palace at dawn on the twenty-eighth to ask the emperor why he had decided to take the serious step of assuming personal command. Taken aback by this unexpected question, the emperor answered that he had not yet decided whether to assume personal command. He had long desired to worship at the tomb of Emperor Jimmu, but the rest of his statement had been intended to mollify Sanjō Sanetomi's faction.[7] It was clear to Prince Nakagawa that the emperor was being manipulated by advocates of *jōi*.

That night, by command of the emperor, Prince Nakagawa conferred with the former chancellor Konoe Tadahiro and others of the *kōbu gattai* faction. They decided they would have to expel the nobles who had been plotting to "alter" the court, meaning by "alter" to disrupt the court's traditional relations with the shogunate. Before dawn on the morning of the thirtieth, a meeting of the Court Council was held, attended by nobles and also the Kyōto military governor and the Kyōto deputy (*shoshidai*). The nine gates to the Gosho were bolted shut, and no one was allowed to enter except by personal command of the emperor. Soldiers of various domains were ordered to guard the gates. At four in the morning, blank shots were fired by cannons to signify that martial law had been put into effect. Hearing the noise, nobles of the *jōi* faction came rushing to the palace, but the gates were tightly shut and they were unable to get in.

At this point Prince Nakagawa, in the presence of the emperor, read a message from the throne: "Ever since this spring it has not infrequently happened that the court spokesmen [*gisō*] and other officials have conspired with the Chōshū domain to misrepresent my commands. The matter of my taking personal command is the worst such instance. From now on Sanetomi and the rest are to cease attending court and to remain in seclusion in their homes."[8]

Sanjō Sanetomi and his confederates were relieved of their posts and replaced by such partisans of *kōbu gattai* as Nakayama Tadayasu and Ōgima-chisanjō Sanenaru. A further edict stated that the emperor's journey to Yamato had been called off and that although there had been no change in the policy of *jōi*, this was not an appropriate time for the emperor to assume personal command. The *jōi* faction quickly grasped that their hour of glory had ended; and when the Chōshū samurai left Kyōto to return to their province, seven nobles, including Sanjō Sanetomi, went with them.[9] The *kōbu gattai* faction was now in control of the court.

These momentous events ushered in a period of relative tranquillity at the court. On November 3 a birthday party was held for Prince Mutsuhito, modestly celebrated with an exchange of presents, mainly fish, followed by a smaller gathering at which Nakayama Tadayasu read a congratulatory message to Nakayama Yoshiko, his daughter and the mother of the crown prince. That day, in his own house, Tadayasu drank a toast to the long life and health of the prince. He nostalgically recalled the past when the prince lived in his home. The prince was now twelve years old (by Japanese count). The years that had passed had misted over like a dream, and the changes in the times had occurred in the twinkling of an eye. No doubt Tadayasu was thinking of the kaleidoscopic changes in his own situation at the court as first one faction and then another acquired control. Later that month Tadayasu's wife, Aiko, had an audience with her grandson, the prince. It was the first time in seven years she had seen him, and she was moved to tears, recalling the past.

On December 26 Mutsuhito's companion Uramatsu Tarumitsu, having reached the age of fourteen, asked permission to bid farewell to boyhood days and wear the clothes and hair style appropriate to an adult. Permission was granted, and the occasion was celebrated with gifts from the emperor, the empress, and the prince, who (in addition to more practical gifts) gave his friend illustrated editions of traditional books of warfare and prodigies.[10] The prince had colored in some of the illustrations and scribbled in some of the books, evidence that he had read them, perhaps as an escape from the Confucian texts he was forced to read.[11]

The prince's study of *tanka* continued, at first under the guidance of his father and later (from February 1864) under the court poets, Reizei Tametada (1824–1885) and Yanagihara Mitsunaru (1818–1885). Not knowing that the prince had already received instruction from his father (and occasionally from the court lady Hirohashi Shizuko), Tametada considered it his duty to inform the emperor that it was high time for the prince, now in his thirteenth year, to begin the study of *tanka*. The emperor was too busy at first to respond. On February 19 Tametada composed two poems explaining why he thought the prince's *tanka* lessons should begin. The second was

hajime yori	There is no flower
hana ni nioeru	That has a flower's fragrance
hana wa nashi	From the beginning:
hana wa tsubomi no	A flower starts becoming
hana ni naritsutsu	A flower while in the bud.

In February 1864[12] the shogun Tokugawa Iemochi visited Kyōto by command of the emperor. Six days after he arrived at Nijō Castle (on February 22), the emperor appointed him as minister of the right and general of the right guards. Iemochi went to the palace to express his gratitude.

The emperor's reply was by no means cheerful: "Alas! wherever you look, in the conditions that obtain today, you will see that the dangers threatening us are great and imminent indeed. At home, the scene is virtually one of disintegration and collapse: public order has broken down, high and low are disunited, and the people suffer extremes of distress. Abroad, we are subjected to the insults of five arrogant powers; conquest by them seems certain to be our fate. Thinking of this, I can neither sleep by night nor yet swallow food. And alas! however one regards these facts, the responsibility is not yours. The fault is mine and lies in my own want of virtue."[13]

Although conventional in phraseology, the emperor's words seem to come from the heart. And when later in the letter he declared that he loved the shogun as his own son and asked that the shogun love him as a father, he revealed personal affection for Iemochi. He urged Iemochi to live up to his title of "subduer of barbarians," adding, "The subjugation of the hated foreigner is the greatest of the national tasks facing us. It will finally become possible only if we raise forces with which to chastise them. However, it is not my wish that the expulsion of foreigners be carried out recklessly. I ask you, rather, to evolve a suitable plan with due deliberation and report it to me."[14]

The letter, written in more direct language than most documents of the time, forcefully stated Kōmei's position. He favored cooperation with the shogunate in restoring the country's stability and prosperity by driving out the ugly barbarians, but he did not approve of the rash assaults on foreigners of the kind committed by the Chōshū samurai. He conveyed his concern about the urgency of the situation by using two old locutions, *ruiran* and *shōbi: ruiran* is a pile of eggs that will tumble over at the least provocation, and *shōbi* is danger so close that it singes one's eyebrows.

Iemochi's visit was otherwise pleasant and leisurely, lasting until the fifth month. There were many occasions for giving and receiving presents, and Iemochi was invited to all the feasts and entertainments held in the palace. The *jōi* faction at the court had lost its strength as the result of Sanjō Sanetomi's flight to Chōshū, and there was also something of a lull in antiforeign activities elsewhere in the country.

The first incident to disrupt the calm took place on July 8. The Chōshū domain had sent a petition to the court asking that Sanjō Sanetomi, the daimyo Mōri Yoshichika, and his son Sadahiro be pardoned and allowed to return to the capital. The court refused to intervene, leaving the matter to the shogunate to decide. The *rōnin* of the domain, learning of the refusal, were incensed. Some of them secretly gathered in Kyōto at a restaurant called the Ikeda-ya to plan the next step. But the shogunate got word of this gathering and sent the celebrated Shinsengumi, an elite band of swordsmen organized by the shogunate and led by Kondō Isami (1834–1868), to attack the place. All the *rōnin* were either killed or captured.[15]

When news of the Ikeda-ya incident reached Hagi, the domain, furious, sent a force of more than 1,000 soldiers to Kyōto under Fukuhara Echigo (1815–1864). Their numbers were augmented by *rōnin* of like convictions, and they camped in different areas around the city. They sent a petition to the court and the shogunate, once again asking for pardon. The Court Council decided on July 27 that either Mōri Yoshichika or his son would be permitted to visit the capital; and if he stated that he repented of his actions, the court was prepared to relent. At the request of Tokugawa Yoshinobu, the court also insisted that the Chōshū forces around the capital withdraw from their positions and return to Chōshū. These terms were rejected. Instead, the Chōshū domain drew up its own plan: to set fires in Kyōto on a day of strong winds. In the ensuing confusion, the forces would kill Matsudaira Katamori, the Kyōto military governor, and Prince Nakagawa; persuade the emperor to move to Chōshū; attack the Shinsengumi; replace the Aizu daimyo with the Chōshū daimyo in the office of the Kyōto military governor; and compel the shogun to carry out *jōi*.[16]

The particular enmity displayed toward Prince Nakagawa and Matsudaira Katamori probably originated in rumors circulating at the time that these two men had adopted the proposal of Sakuma Shōzan (1811–1864) that the emperor be moved to Hikone. This was not the first time there had been such a rumor. In July 1863, Ogasawara Nagamichi (1822–1891), a member of the Council of Elders and an advocate of opening the country, had sailed from Edo to Ōsaka with 1,500 shogunate troops. It was rumored that he intended to force the court to open the country and that if it did not, he would set fire to the capital, tie up the nobles, and, in one mighty blow, destroy the city. It was further rumored that the shogunate intended to move the capital to Hikone.[17] Now, a year later, similar rumors reached the ears of the Chōshū patriots.

The Confucian scholar Sakuma Shōzan, as the supposed originator of the plan and as an advocate of opening the country, was especially hated by the *rōnin*, and they assassinated him in Kyōto on August 12.[18] This rash action on the part of Chōshū men aroused other domains to demand a punitive expedition against that domain.

Pro- and anti-Chōshū forces gathered around the capital. The Court Council sent a message on August 19 to the Chōshū domain asking it to withdraw immediately all forces from the area. It promised also that if the domain obeyed the imperial command and then appealed for a pardon, its plea would be seriously considered. But the Chōshū samurai refused to obey; instead, they submitted a memorial to the court listing Matsudaira Katamori's crimes and their determination to wreak divine punishment on him. Messages explaining why the domain had no choice but to open hostilities were tossed into the nobles' houses.

The court was thrown into a panic. The chancellor, Prince Nakagawa, Tokugawa Yoshinobu, and others were received in audience by the emperor, who issued a edict ordering the subjugation of Chōshū. By this time, fighting had begun at Fushimi, and gunfire could be heard even in the palace. Yoshinobu ordered all gates to the palace closed.

By seven the next morning rebel soldiers were pressing close to the palace gates. Fukuhara Echigo's troops were repulsed by soldiers of the Ōgaki domain, but other rebels managed to get as far as the Hamaguri and Nakadachiuri Gates. The noise of the fighting was described as resembling 10 million bolts of thunder, and the palace buildings shook as if in an earthquake.[19] The main rebel effort was concentrated on the Hamaguri Gate, defended by the Aizu domain. A fierce battle ensued, and the rebels had all but broken through the gate when reinforcements from Kuwana and Satsuma arrived and joined the forces to attack and rout the Chōshū forces. Success at the Hamaguri Gate encouraged the loyalists, and by the time the battle was over, five hours after it began, the rebels had been crushed.[20]

Great consternation had been aroused in the palace by the fighting. By order of the emperor, Prince Mutsuhito was moved from his own quarters to the "residential palace" along with the empress and Princess Sumiko. Boarded palanquins (*itagoshi*) were ready to evacuate members of the imperial family in case of an emergency. The emperor, in full court dress, sat impassively, seemingly unruffled by the furious activity around him.[21] Courtiers were dressed for fighting, their sleeves tied back and their feet shod in straw sandals, quite unlike their normal appearance. The palace grounds swarmed with soldiers in armor, and shells smashed the doors of the palace gates, at times staining them with blood. Suddenly flames shot up outside the gates and spread in all directions. The fierce fires burning along Karasuma Avenue threatened to engulf the palace. The confusion inside the palace was indescribable, as members of the court wondered where they should flee. Only the intervention of Matsudaira Katamori, who insisted that they must not attempt to escape, saved them from being caught between the two warring armies.[22]

The next day, taking advantage of their success, the loyalists executed more than thirty men of the *sonnō jōi* faction who were being held in the Rokkaku prison. Bodies of the dead were piled up and exposed for three days outside the palace gates, a place that for more than 250 years had not seen warfare. Some 28,000 buildings in the capital, including temples and shrines, were destroyed by fire during the fighting. The fires were not extinguished for days.

Even after the Chōshū rebels had been defeated and the capital once again took on a semblance of calm and order, there were still disturbing occurrences. One night a group of men broke into the palace and attempted to steal the imperial palanquin. When word of this reached Tokugawa Yoshinobu, the commander of palace defense, he rushed to the palace and found some 300 men in the inner courtyard of the emperor's "residential palace." Yoshinobu ordered them to disperse and sent word to the chancellor and Prince Nakagawa who came rushing to the scene. They asked the emperor to move to a safer place. Later, at Yoshinobu's request, the emperor moved to the Hall of State Ceremonies. Prince Mutsuhito and the empress accompanied him. Some of the court ladies, terrified and not knowing what was going on, were weeping and wailing. The prince was so startled that he fainted and was revived by an attendant.[23]

A corrupted form of this account has become an established part of postwar writings about Prince Mutsuhito. For example, one (unfriendly) biographer wrote, "When the Chōshū clan fired shells at the Hamaguri Gate in the seventh month of 1864, [Meiji], frightened by the roar of the explosions, fainted. From this act, one can surmise that he had a weak-spirited, cowardly nature."[24] Probably what made the prince faint was not the roar of cannon at the Hamaguri Gate (the attack at this gate had taken place a day earlier) but being wakened in the middle of the night and suddenly carried off to the Hall of State Ceremonies amid shrieking women. The shrieks were occasioned by a freak accident: the maidservant of a certain lady, accompanying her mistress from one building to another, accidentally dropped a jar containing liquid used in blackening teeth. The sound of the jar breaking against the board floor was mistaken for gunfire, and the smell of the liquid that spilled out was so strong that it caused panic.[25]

The incident in itself was of no intrinsic importance, but it is startling to find in the sober pages of the chronicle of Meiji's life an anecdote that might more appropriately appear in a medieval romance. Who were the mysterious figures in the courtyard? Why did they want to steal the emperor's palanquin? Why was no trace ever found of even one of the 300? Why was the maid carrying a jar of teeth-blackener at this critical moment? Why should the sound of one jar breaking against the floor have thrown so many people into a state of panic?

On the day after this mysterious incident, the prince sent for his grandfather Nakayama Tadayasu. Taking out some picture books, he asked the old man to explain them. It is reassuring that even in this dangerous period, the worst to have faced the imperial family in centuries, the twelve-year-old prince remained a boy for whom real adventure did not take the place of adventure stories.

Chapter 10

The year 1864 was filled with disasters. Only two weeks after the violence in the Gosho, a fleet of warships from England, France, America, and Holland bombarded Shimonoseki in retaliation for Chōshū's attack on foreign ships. The action by the allied fleet had taken place at the suggestion of the British minister, Sir Rutherford Alcock, who had grown impatient with the shogunate's procrastination and believed that the use of force was necessary.

Earlier that year a Japanese mission had been sent to France under the minister of foreign affairs, Ikeda Nagaoki (1837–1879), to negotiate closing the port of Yokohama to foreign ships. Although the shogunate was not in favor of this, it felt obliged to honor the promise it had made to the court. Ikeda soon learned that the French were totally unwilling to discuss the matter. Instead, they demanded reparations for the attack on French ships and guarantees that in the future they would be able to pass unharmed through the Shimonoseki Straits. Ikeda, convinced that the shogunate must change its fundamental policies, signed a treaty on June 20, 1864,[1] accepting the French demands, even though he had not been authorized by his government to do so.[2] He decided, also in disregard of orders, not to visit England or other countries, feeling sure that they would be equally unwilling to consent to closing Yokohama to foreign ships.

When representatives in Edo of the four nations learned of the treaty after Ikeda's unexpectedly early return, they asked the shogunate to implement its provisions, but it replied that it was not bound by the treaty because Ikeda had violated the terms of his commission. (He and his colleagues were subsequently removed from their posts and punished.) The four nations, exasperated by what seemed to be another example of the shogunate's dilatory tactics, took matters into their own hands. An allied fleet set sail for Shimonoseki despite the shogunate's attempts to forestall this action and Chōshū's desire to negotiate a peaceful settlement. On September 5 the fleet opened fire on the Chōshū batteries, and after three days of fighting, the foreigners landed and demolished the fortifications. Mōri Yoshichika, the daimyo of Chōshū, was forced to sue for peace and to accept the conditions laid down by the allies: that foreign ships passing through the Shimonoseki Straits would be accorded friendly treatment; that the gun batteries would be neither replaced nor repaired; that firewood, water, food, and coal would be supplied; and that an indemnity of 3 million dollars would be paid.

A lull followed until November when Tokugawa Iemochi assumed command of an expeditionary force sent to chastise Chōshū for the unruly behavior of its soldiers in the capital. In an effort to reassert the shogunate's authority, he ordered various domains to provide troops. Some refused, making excuses; they were obviously reluctant to assist the shogunate. Although Chōshū had been branded as traitorous, its courageous stance was widely admired, and when word was received of the bombardment of Shimonoseki by the allied fleet, sympathy for Chōshū spread throughout the country. Aware of these feelings, the shogunate asked Chōshū only to apologize and to issue a statement of submission. Mōri Takachika agreed to these conditions and, as a sign of compliance, offered up the heads of three of his major advisers. He also promised to obey the shogunate's wishes with respect to the disposition of Sanjō Sanetomi and the other nobles who had taken refuge in Chōshū.[3]

This victory by the shogunate was not impressive, but at least it provided a breathing space in its domestic and foreign troubles. Although life at the court had, at least on the surface, resumed its normal calm, vague apprehensions continued. Nakayama Tadayasu felt so upset over a recurrent dream of Prince Mutsuhito that he sent a retainer to the Kitano Shrine to pray for the prince's safety. His wife, sharing his anxiety, sent messages asking about the prince's health.[4]

Even after the new year, 1865, began, the disposition of Sanjō Sanetomi and the other nobles who had taken refuge in Chōshū was still being debated. One of those who advocated exiling the men to Kyūshū was Saigō Takamori (1828–1877), his first appearance in the *Record of the Emperor Meiji*.[5] On February 7 the *nengō* Genji was changed to Keiō, as the previous *nengō* was blamed for the violence that had threatened the sanctity of the palace in the previous autumn.

The new *nengō* did not greatly improve the situation. On July 14 Tokugawa Iemochi arrived in Kyōto. The arrival of the shogun in the capital, an event that a few years earlier would have been of extraordinary importance, had now become almost routine. Iemochi reported to the emperor that despite Mōri

Takachika's professed repentance for his crimes, *jōi* agitators in his domain were again making ominous noises. Moreover, Takachika had sent underlings to foreign countries to purchase large supplies of weapons. Iemochi claimed to have positive proof that Takachika was secretly trading with foreigners, and he had decided to march against him.

Iemochi was stating his intentions to the emperor before he actually moved against Chōshū. This in itself would have been inconceivable even ten years earlier; it would not have occurred to the shogun to inform the emperor of political or military plans. Iemochi probably intended his communication mainly as a report of the situation, but Kōmei interpreted the report as a request for his permission to attack Chōshū. His first reaction was to invite Iemochi to the residential palace where he personally poured saké for the shogun in a gesture of friendship and as a sign of approval of Iemochi's plans. After the emperor had retired to his private apartments, the court spokesmen, the military liaison officers, and other palace officials took Iemochi aside to inform him that the emperor had been so pleased by Iemochi's repair of the imperial tombs, completed earlier that year, that he was considering bestowing "god names" on his ancestors Hidetada and Iemitsu. Iemochi firmly declined this honor, only to be informed that this was a most unusual gesture on His Majesty's part and that the shogun must accept it without hesitation.[6] Iemochi yielded to what in effect was an imperial command, another instance of the change in relations between the emperor and the shogunate.

On November 16, 1865, nine warships of England, France, the United States, and Holland appeared off the coast of Settsu Province. A message was sent ashore demanding in the names of these countries that the shogunate open the port of Hyōgo and that it secure the emperor's approval[7] for the treaties. In return for these favors, the allies were willing to forgo two-thirds of the 3 million–dollar indemnity for the Shimonoseki incident. However, if the shogunate would not grant these two demands immediately, the foreigners would go to Kyōto and make the same demand of the court. And if the court likewise refused to accept the demands, they would meet again amid "gun-smoke and a rain of bullets."[8] The Japanese were given seven days to make a reply.

The members of the Council of Elders stationed in Hyōgo, Abe Masato and Matsumae Takahiro, favored granting the foreigners' demands. They argued that there was no time to consult the court, and if they were to insist on doing so anyway, this would surely lead to warfare in which many lives would be lost and incalculable damage inflicted by the foreign powers. When the emperor learned of their attitude, he was extremely upset. He ordered that the two men be stripped of their official rank and commanded the shogunate to have the men confined to their residences, there to await further orders.[9] The shogunate obeyed, although it was unprecedented for the court to issue such orders concerning shogunate personnel. No explanation for this action was provided in the wording of the imperial command, but we know from other sources the desperate steps that Tokugawa Yoshinobu took to keep the foreigners from opening hostilities.[10]

First of all, Yoshinobu summoned the shogunate officials to Ōsaka Castle to hear their opinions. None of them had any suggestions to make other than to yield to the foreigners' demands, as agreed at the previous meeting. Only Matsudaira Nobutoshi looked dissatisfied. This encouraged Yoshinobu to ask Nobutoshi privately to get Inoue Yoshiaya, the Ōsaka magistrate, to inform the foreigners when next they conferred that although the shogunate had privately decided to open the port of Hyōgo, as requested, "to tell the truth, in our country there is an emperor who is higher than the shogun. There is a rule that in important matters even the shogun must obtain the emperor's permission before putting them into effect. In other words, because the port of Hyōgo is an important matter, he must of course request the consent of the emperor. It will take at least ten days to obtain this consent."[11]

This was a startling admission by the shogunate. Until this time the foreigners had assumed that the "tycoon" was the supreme ruler of Japan and that the mikado was no more than a "spiritual sovereign." The shogunate officials encouraged them in this belief. Townsend Harris recorded in his journal, "They spoke almost contemptuously of the Mikado, and roared with laughter when I quoted some remarks concerning the veneration in which he is held by the Japanese. They say he has neither money, political power, nor anything else that is valued in Japan. He is a mere cipher."[12]

The persistence of the belief that the shogunate was the legitimate government of Japan and that the shogun was therefore the highest power in the country was reflected also in the message sent to the shogun Iemochi on this occasion by the newly arrived British representative, Sir Harry Parkes. He addressed the shogun as "Your Majesty." It is true that one of Parkes's demands was for "the sanction of the Treaties by the Mikado,"[13] but the tone of the letter implies that the shogun had it in his power to obtain this "sanction" from a figurehead.

Now, however, a high-ranking officer of the shogunate had openly admitted that the emperor ranked above the shogun and that the port of Hyōgo could be opened only if the emperor gave his permission. Faced with this new revelation of Japan's power structure, the foreigners had to reconsider their previous assumptions.[14] Before long, the British would openly back the emperor and the French the shogun, extending to Japan their rivalry in Europe; but on this occasion, the four allies agreed with surprisingly little resistance to a delay of ten days while the emperor's authorization was sought. They still did not trust the shogunate officials' assurances and declared that they wanted proof that the emperor's permission would definitely be forthcoming. Inoue Yoshiaya replied that he could not produce any proof. In Japan, he added, it was the custom when promising some important matter to seal it in blood. He declared, "I will therefore, before your eyes, cut my finger and give you my seal in blood." He drew his dirk and was about to cut his finger when the startled foreigners stopped him, saying that they believed his promise.[15]

Yoshinobu's decision, notably supported by Inoue Yoshiaya, gave the shogunate ten days' leeway during which to obtain Emperor Kōmei's consent to the treaties. This in itself would be difficult enough, but a new problem had arisen. Iemochi felt so resentful of what he considered to be the court's usurpation of the shogunate's powers, displayed in dismissing two shogunate officials, that on November 21 he addressed a message to the throne stating that because of his youth and incapability, he was unable either to calm the mind of the emperor or to reassure the people, and he wished therefore to yield his post to Tokugawa Yoshinobu. He also begged the emperor, in view of the perilous international situation, to give his consent to the treaties. On the same day that he presented this memorial, Iemochi left Ōsaka for Edo. When he reached Fushimi, south of Kyōto, he received word from Chancellor Nijō Nariyuki stating that his request to resign could not be granted immediately and that it would be a mark of disrespect toward the court if he returned to Edo without obtaining permission. Iemochi was directed to attend court the following day to present in person his reasons for wishing to resign.[16]

The reprimand issued by the court to Iemochi could hardly have been more blunt. There was now no question as to who was stronger, the emperor or the shogun. Iemochi, changing his plan, went to Nijō Castle in Kyōto. He ordered Tokugawa Yoshinobu, Matsudaira Katamori, and other important shogunate officials in the capital to go to the palace and explain the need for speedy imperial consent.

Yoshinobu was later summoned to the palace, where he discussed with the chancellor and other court officials the advisability of imperial sanction for the treaties. Kōmei listened to the discussion from behind bamboo blinds. The meeting began at six in the evening and went on through the night without the participants' reaching a decision. On the following day, at Yoshinobu's suggestion, some thirty senior officials of the domains stationed in Kyōto were asked to express their opinions. Men from Aizu and Kōchi, the first to speak, strongly urged the opening of the country and denounced its closure. Men from the other domains, almost without exception, favored imperial approval of the treaties, and the court finally decided to give its approval, even though it was a bitter defeat for Kōmei. He was moved especially by the plea to accept the treaties voiced by Prince Nakagawa, who warned that if the foreigners were refused, the whole region stretching from Hyōgo to the capital would go up in flames, the safety of the throne itself would be endangered, and the Great Shrine of Ise would be reduced to ashes. The prince said he could all but see these disasters before his eyes.[17]

Even now, when the emperor enjoyed greater power than in 500 years, he was unable to ignore the wishes of the majority of the domains. It was infuriating to be obliged to give his consent to treaties that he hated, but he had no choice, and he preserved a modicum of independence by refusing to consider opening the port of Hyōgo.[18] Although many men continued to profess their willingness to lay down their lives in the imperial cause, it was clear even to the emperor that badly equipped Japanese soldiers would be no match in a war with the foreigners.

Despite his announced intention of returning to Edo, Iemochi lingered in the Kansai region until December 20. A week earlier, he and other high shogunate officials were received in audience by the emperor. Iemochi apologized profoundly for his inadequacy, especially in the recent controversy; but the emperor assured him that they would work together as in the past and, by strengthening national defenses, prevent humiliation by foreign countries.[19]

The rest of 1865 was uneventful, and Prince Mutsuhito's name seldom appears in the chronicle for 1866. In August he completed the *sodoku* reading of *Mencius*. It had taken a little more than a year, a considerable improvement in speed over his reading of the *Analects*, which had taken more than four years. The emperor praised the prince for his diligence and encouraged him to keep up the good work.

All the same, evidence suggests that the emperor's chief worry at this time may have been the prince's education. He feared that the prince had been overly influenced by the palace ladies responsible for his upbringing, particularly that they might have indoctrinated him with their *sonnō jōi* beliefs. Kōmei wrote to Kayanomiya (the new title of Prince Nakagawa), "As the result of the education he has received at the hands of these women, Sachinomiya has become unpleasant toward me and is more than I can cope with. He believes that people who obey the commands of the emperor are bad and that there are no troublemakers. He's only a child, but one can't be too careful." He accused the court ladies of being at the root of the trouble and threatened once again to abdicate.[20]

About this time Iwakura Tomomi, living in retreat north of the capital, wrote a statement of his views that included an admonition to the emperor urging him to give up his life of "pools of saké and forests of flesh" and to think seriously of politics.[21]

These bits of evidence seem to indicate that the placid life at the court recorded in the chronicles may mask less agreeable realities—the prince mouthing *sonnō jōi* slogans even to his father, the emperor trying to forget his frustration by diverting himself with liquor and women.

We would like to know more also about the activities of Kayanomiya, who is generally described as "crafty."[22] After the successful palace coup in September 1863, largely managed by this prince, the emperor bestowed on him the name of Prince Asahiko and named him *danjō no in*, a high position open only to princes of the blood that carried with it the privilege of remonstrating with the emperor.[23] However, there was a strange rumor that Kayanomiya had placed a curse on the emperor. According to this rumor, in the summer of 1863 the prince sent an arrow and a large sum of money to a priest of the Iwashimizu Hachimangū named Ninkai with whom he was friendly. Ninkai bought a pheasant and then used the arrow to shoot it to death. He offered the pheasant on the altar, at the same time placing a curse on the emperor and praying that Kayanomiya would take the emperor's place on the throne. Ninkai's machinations were detected by a samurai of the Tottori clan who killed Ninkai and removed the pheasant from the altar.

The rumor was brought to the attention of the emperor, but because he had absolute faith in Kayanomiya, he dismissed the matter as mere gossip and declared that he and the prince were a true example of branches from different trees that had grown together.[24] As a sign of his confidence, the emperor increased the prince's stipend and built him a splendid new palace.[25]

The incident seems hardly credible, but some at the court believed it. If nothing else, it suggests that the atmosphere surrounding the court was such that even stories of black magic could be accepted as truth. It also suggests why, toward the end of the year, the deaths of both the emperor and the shogun quickly gave rise to rumors of poison and conspiracy.[26]

For the shogunate, 1866 was a year of unmitigated disasters. This time, the disasters did not originate with the foreigners, who were content with negotiating tariff reductions and other unexplosive issues. Rather, the shogunate had announced in the spring of the previous year that it was preparing for a second expedition against Chōshū, to be commanded personally by the shogun. This announcement prompted Chōshū to acquire modern weapons and to organize its troops on Western lines. More important, it led to an alliance between Chōshū and Satsuma, hitherto bitter enemies. The first phase of this alliance was exemplified by Satsuma's serving as the channel for purchasing armaments for Chōshū from European merchants in Nagasaki. Early in 1866 Saigō Takamori sent Kuroda Kiyotaka (1840–1900) to Shimonoseki to sound out leading men of Chōshū about cooperation between the two domains.[27] In February 1866, Sakamoto Ryōma (1835–1867) and Nakaoka Shintarō (1838–1867) of Tosa, who had already served an important role in bringing the two domains together, met with Saigō to plan active cooperation between Satsuma and Chōshū.[28] No longer would the rallying cry be *jōi*; instead, the overthrow of the shogunate and the restoration of imperial rule would unite the two domains. An agreement between Chōshū and Satsuma was reached by Kido Takayoshi (1833–1877) and Saigō in March with the help of Sakamoto Ryōma.[29]

The shogunate army marched against Chōshū in July 1866. Morale was extremely low. Some domains that had been counted on to strengthen the shogunate forces refused to send soldiers, and others sent only small detachments. The Chōshū forces, however, were well trained and supplied, although their numbers were modest. The opening engagements were forerunners of the many shogunate defeats that characterized the war. The most notable fact about this warfare was that it was fought with guns, not with swords or bows and arrows. It was Japan's first modern war.

During the midst of this losing war, Tokugawa Iemochi, who had been unwell for some time, fell seriously ill in Ōsaka.[30] Almost immediately, the question of the childless Iemochi's successor was raised. His own choice was Kamenosuke, the three-year-old son of Tokugawa Yoshiyori. It is baffling why he should have favored a small child as his successor at a time of national crisis. No one else, not even Iemochi's wife, Princess Chikako,[31] agreed with his choice, and he was finally induced to submit to the emperor a memorial asking that if he should die, Tokugawa Yoshinobu be appointed as shogun and commander of the army sent to conquer Chōshū.[32] Tokugawa Iemochi died in Ōsaka on August 29, 1866, at the age of twenty.

On September 19 the emperor summoned a council of senior nobles to discuss the recommendation he had received from the daimyo of Kagoshima that hostilities with Chōshū be terminated in view of the national emergency and that all efforts be devoted instead to strengthening the country's defenses.[33] The court spokesman Ōgimachisanjō Sanenaru strongly supported this. None of the other nobles uttered a word, but the emperor, speaking from behind blinds, declared that the attack on Chōshū must not yet be aborted. Sanenaru bowed before the emperor's voice but persisted in his arguments with ever greater intensity and in the end could not refrain from "shedding tears of blood and howling in lamentation." It is extraordinary that Sanenaru had the courage to insist on his beliefs, even when he knew that the emperor opposed them. It is also difficult to imagine any other despotic regime, whether in Asia or Europe, where this would have been possible, although perhaps Sanenaru's strong connections with the powerful Satsuma domain gave him courage.[34] On September 12, at another session of the council, Kōmei finally rejected the Satsuma proposal.[35]

Although the shogunate at first kept Iemochi's death a secret, someone had to take command of the expeditionary force. On September 8 Tokugawa Yoshinobu was chosen. Just before he was to set out for the front, Yoshinobu received word that Kokura, a stronghold of the shogunate in northern Kyūshū, had fallen. This news made him decide to suspend hostilities in the war with Chōshū. He sent word of this decision to the chancellor, who relayed it to the emperor. As might be expected, Kōmei was extremely displeased and insisted that Yoshinobu carry out his mission. On September 24 Yoshinobu went before the emperor to explain the futility of the situation. Only then did the emperor accept the decision to cease hostilities.

On September 28, a month after Iemochi died, his death was officially announced, providing an excellent pretext for discontinuing the war with Chōshū on the following day.[36] A war that had brought neither glory nor advantage to anyone had ended not with a bang but a whimper. But it had changed forever the Japanese conception of martial conflict.

Chapter 11

The death of Tokugawa Iemochi came as a blow to Emperor Kōmei. He had enjoyed the young man's company and for a time believed that together they could realize the ideal of *kōbu gattai*. If the emperor had been able to forget this ideal and to accommodate himself to the newer ideal of restoration of imperial rule, he would surely have been more fortunate. He would have had the support of the great majority of not only the nobles but also the samurai class, but he refused to abandon his old convictions. To the exasperated men around him, he seemed maddeningly obstinate, but his extreme reluctance to change was an instance of conservatism in the strict sense; each concession caused him pain and chagrin. After the defeat of the shogunate armies in the war against Chōshū, the emperor was in the ironic position of using every means at his disposal to oppose those who sought to make him the undisputed ruler of Japan.

On October 8, 1866, soon after Tokugawa Yoshinobu announced the cessation of hostilities in the war with Chōshū, a group of twenty-two nobles presented a petition to the court requesting an audience with the emperor. They said it was to communicate to him their heartfelt convictions at a time of national emergency. The nobles were led by Nakamikado Tsuneyuki (1820–1891) and Ōhara Shigetomi (1801–1879), but it was Iwakura Tomomi who, behind the scenes, planned this collective appeal.

Iwakura had been living in enforced retreat outside Kyōto ever since being accused in 1862 of having plotted with the shogunate to send Kazunomiya to

Edo; but he was a born machinator, and it did not take him long to reestablish old contacts. He had frequent visitors, notably those of the *sonjō* faction, who kept him informed of the latest developments.[1] Impressed by the bold stand of Ōgimachisanjō Sanenaru during the discussion before the emperor on the advisability of continuing the Chōshū war, Iwakura conceived the idea of having a group of nobles present their collective views to the emperor, in this way lending weight to their opposition to Kōmei's unwavering allegiance to the shogunate.

Iwakura, who was strongly in favor of the proposal presented by Satsuma for ending the conflict with Chōshū, drew up a program for creating a court government that would be amenable to the proposal. The nobles would open by asking that the court administration exclude Chancellor Nijō Nariyuki and others whose attitudes they found objectionable, such as Prince Asahiko, Tokugawa Yoshinobu, and Matsudaira Katamori. Next they would ask that nobles at present living in enforced seclusion be allowed to return to the court. Finally they would ask that Konoe Tadahiro be reappointed as chancellor. The ultimate purpose of these (and other) remonstrances would be to restore imperial rule, profiting by the confusion that had been created in the shogunate by the shogun's death.[2]

In response to the nobles' petition for an audience, the emperor appeared along with the chancellor Nijō Nariyuki, Prince Asahiko, and other dignitaries. Ōhara Shigetomi, a senior member of the court, stepped forward to present the requests of the assembled nobles to the emperor. He asked, by way of preliminary, that the daimyos of the various domains be summoned in the near future by the court to hear the emperor's commands, in this way bypassing the shogunate. The three requests he made were not exactly the same as Iwakura's: that nobles who had been imprisoned or confined to their quarters because of their involvement in political incidents be set free, that the army formed to punish Chōshū be disbanded, and that the Court Council be reorganized.[3]

Ōhara spoke without circumlocution, both because of his upright character, for which he was known at the court, and because at the age of sixty-five, he may have believed he had little to lose. All the same, this kind of courage had not often been witnessed at the Japanese court.

Kōmei's response was predictable: he demanded in a rage why he was being bothered by such insignificant matters. What, he asked, did the assembled nobles mean by referring to this as a national crisis? The real crisis had occurred in the winter of the previous year when he had been forced to consent to the treaties. If the nobles were now so deeply moved by patriotism as to ask for an audience with him, why did they not offer their advice at that time, when it was genuinely needed? They had remained silent and did not say one word. How dare they burst in on him in this way? This could only be considered a case of lèse-majesté.[4]

The chancellor, a mild-mannered man, intervened, blaming himself for having aroused the emperor's wrath. He explained that the unhappy state of the times had impelled Ōhara to make his plea. Why would a man speak so bluntly unless he were deeply moved by concern for the country? Nijō Nariyuki concluded by saying that he himself could not escape blame because as chancellor, he stood highest among the nobles.[5]

Ōhara answered comfortingly, assuring the chancellor that he was not at fault; but when Prince Asahiko spoke in terms similar to Nijō Nariyuki's, apologizing for his failure to offer good advice, Ōhara turned on him and said, "Yes, you really are to blame. You should resign and apologize to the whole country."

He then addressed the emperor: "Your Majesty, if I might have your reply, I will leave immediately." The emperor answered that he would be willing to speak to Ōhara alone a few days hence. Obviously the prospect of another mass meeting was unwelcome. Prince Asahiko suggested that the emperor detain Ōhara and ask him to speak his mind in full, but the emperor said he needed more time to consider the three proposals. He dismissed the nobles, but after conferring with Prince Asahiko and others, he agreed to summon the daimyos and to meet with Ōhara on October 11. This information was passed on to the twenty-two nobles, who were still waiting for an answer, and they left at two in the morning.

Perhaps we should see behind the events of that day the hand of Iwakura Tomomi, who had decided that imperial rule could not be restored as long as Nijō Nariyuki and Prince Asahiko were still in power. Iwakura had used Ōhara in his attempt to get rid of the two men, but he still had to contend with the emperor. On October 12 Nijō Nariyuki, faced with impeachment at the hands of the nobles, resigned, alleging ill health. The emperor refused to accept his resignation. Prince Asahiko also expressed a wish to be relieved of his post, saying that he was unequal to the heavy responsibilities, but the emperor calmed the prince's anger and persuaded him to remain. These steps halted further action for the time being, for any attempt to push charges against Nijō and Asahiko would be construed as an attack on the emperor himself.

Invitations to the conference were sent out on October 15 to twenty-four daimyos, urging them to take part in a discussion of matters of national importance in the presence of the emperor. Only three daimyos (plus the heirs of two others) had appeared in Kyōto by November, the rest claiming to be too ill to attend. So little enthusiasm was displayed that the conference seems not to have taken place.

On November 25 the emperor issued a decree punishing Nakamikado Tsuneyuki, Ōhara Shigetomi, and the rest of the twenty-two nobles who had petitioned him, declaring they were guilty of lèse-majesté. Nakamikado and Ōhara were confined to their residences, and the others were ordered to refrain from attending court. Ōgimachisanjō Sanenaru, who was suspected of aiding the derelict nobles, was also ordered to remain in his house. The emperor had resorted to these measures in the hopes of stifling the nobles' opposition to his policies.

On January 10, 1867, the emperor conferred on Tokugawa Yoshinobu the title of barbarian-quelling great general, a gesture showing that his loyalty to the concept of *kōbu gattai* had not changed. This proved to be one of the last acts of his reign. A week later, on January 16, he attended a performance of *kagura* dances at the palace sanctuary, even though he had been feeling unwell for some days. The court doctors said his illness was nothing worse than a cold and not sufficient reason to miss the dances, but before the performance was over, he felt so poorly that he left. From this point on, his illness worsened. Two days later, he took to his bed with a high fever. On January 20, the physicians announced that he had smallpox. On investigation it was discovered that a page named Fujimaru had caught smallpox but, after a long illness, had finally been cured. Fujimaru had begun to appear at the court again, and it was suspected that the emperor had caught the sickness from him.[6]

According to the courtier Higashikuze Michitomi, a friend from childhood days, Kōmei was blessed with an exceptionally fine physique. He was very strong and had never been sick before.[7] It probably seemed unlikely to those who knew him that he would fall prey to illness. Even today, scholars are divided between those who believe Kōmei died of smallpox and those who believe he was poisoned. No one disputes the fact that he contracted smallpox, but it is strange that the source of his smallpox should have been a boy who had recovered and was presumably no longer infectious. Again, it is strange that the emperor was the only person at the court to contract the disease, especially because his contacts with Fujimaru were casual. These are a few of the mysteries relating to the death of the emperor at the early age of thirty-six.

We can trace the course of Kōmei's illness from the letters and diaries written by people who attended him, including Nakayama Tadayasu and Nakayama Yoshiko, the grandfather and mother of Prince Mutsuhito. The day after the emperor suffered his first attack of illness while watching *kagura*, he developed a fever, and he began to suffer from delirium and sleeplessness, as well as from a loss of appetite. On January 20, spots appeared on his hands, which on the next day spread to his face. The palace physicians diagnosed the illness as smallpox, and this was reported under the signatures of fifteen doctors.[8] The illness followed its normal course, and after several days during which the emperor could swallow only mouthfuls of hot water, there was a noticeable change for the better, followed by steady improvement each day. On January 24 it was officially reported that the emperor had suffered an extremely light case of smallpox.[9] It seemed that he was well on the road to complete recovery, and the priest Tankai, who had been commanded to recite prayers for seventeen days for the emperor's recovery, was allowed to return to his temple.[10]

A party was even scheduled to celebrate the emperor's recovery; but on

January 30 he suffered a violent bout of vomiting and diarrhea. Different accounts mention the purple spots that appeared on Kōmei's face on that day, and the blood that issued from the "nine apertures." He died in agony a short while later.[11]

Thus far, all the accounts are in agreement, but the unexpected turn for the worse in the emperor's illness, just when he seemed to be out of danger, soon led to rumors that the change was the result of arsenic poisoning. These rumors have persisted and have occasioned painstaking research into the characteristics of death by poison as opposed to smallpox. A curious blank in the official report of his illness, beginning on January 31, has suggested to some scholars that the relevant facts were deliberately erased. Some members of the court expressed doubts, even at the time, about the optimistic prognosis reports issued by the emperor's doctors. The nobleman Yamashina Tokinaru wrote in his diary that he had heard that the emperor had suffered extreme pain on January 24 and that his illness was spreading to other parts of his body, despite the official announcements that his condition was improving.[12]

Smallpox was by no means unusual in Japan at that time, but the particularly virulent, nearly always fatal variety (called hemorrhaging pustular smallpox or black smallpox)[13] was much less common than the milder forms. Furthermore, the symptoms of the most dangerous forms of smallpox closely resemble those of arsenic poisoning, and this fact induced some scholars to trace step by step the parallels between the course of Kōmei's illness (as recorded in contemporary documents) and the symptoms of arsenic poisoning (as given in medical books). Even before 1945, when it first became possible to discuss such matters freely, a few scholars had expressed the belief that Emperor Kōmei was poisoned,[14] and rumors to this effect go back as far as Sir Ernest Satow, who in *A Diplomat in Japan*, written largely between 1885 and 1887, recalled that in February 1867 — not many days after Kōmei's death — at the port of Hyōgo,

I met some native traders, who were greatly interested in the approaching opening of the port, and discussed various suitable sites for a foreign settlement. They also conveyed to me the news of the Mikado's death, which had only just been made public. Rumour attributed his decease to smallpox, but several years afterward I was assured by a Japanese well acquainted with what went on beyond the scenes that he had been poisoned. He was by conviction utterly opposed to any concession to foreigners, and had therefore been removed out of the way by those who foresaw that the coming downfall of the *Baku-fu* would force the court into direct relations with Western Powers. But with a reactionary Mikado nothing but difficulties, resulting probably in war, was to be expected. It is common enough in eastern countries to attribute the deaths of important personages to poison, and in the case of the last preceding Shōgun rumours had been pretty rife that he had been made away with by Shitotsubashi. In connexion with the Mikado I certainly never heard any such suggestion at the time. But it is impossible to deny that his disappearance from the political scene, leaving as his successor a boy of fifteen or sixteen years of age, was most opportune.[15]

Satow's remarks make it clear why scholars over the years have been attracted to the theory that some person or persons, despairing of progress under so reactionary a monarch, decided to get rid of Kōmei by poisoning him. It is obvious, as Satow said, that if Kōmei had continued to block the efforts of those who sought to overthrow the shogunate and create a new form of government in Japan, it certainly would have been far more difficult, perhaps even impossible. His successor, a fifteen-year-old boy, was quite another matter. Some of the leaders of the Restoration referred to him as a *gyoku*, a jewel in their hands that made possible the revolutionary changes they planned. Scholars, reflecting on this fact, have found the sudden death of a still young and energetic emperor too great a piece of luck to accept without skepticism; surely, they argue, it could not have been an accident.

But if Kōmei was poisoned, the question is, who did it and how? Nezu Masashi, the most outspoken of the exponents of the assassination theory, believed that the poisoning was the work of nobles who had accepted bribes from the shogunate to promote the marriage of Kazunomiya; these men included Chancellor Kujō Hisatada, Minister of the Interior Koga Tatemichi, Iwakura Tomomi, and Chigusa Arifumi.[16] He believed that these men suborned a court lady to administer the poison.

The name that most frequently appears in discussions of possible poisoners is Iwakura Tomomi. One story has it that Iwakura, knowing that Kōmei was in the habit of licking his writing brush when pondering his words, put poison on two new brushes that were presented to the emperor the day before his mortal illness began.[17] But this theory conflicts with other evidence concerning the progress of the emperor's illness. If his illness was initially caused by poison that had an immediate and terrible effect, he would not have gradually shown symptoms of smallpox, nor would it have seemed a few days later that he was on the way to recovery. Obviously, this theory is hard to sustain.

More common is the theory that Iwakura's younger sister, Horikawa Motoko, administered the poison; but she entered Buddhist orders in 1863 and never returned to service in the palace, making it improbable that she could have gained access to Kōmei's sickroom. Several other court ladies have been implicated, but it is not clear why only a woman could have fed the emperor the fatal dose.[18]

The conjecture that Iwakura must have been behind the poisoning was doubtless inspired by his reputation as a schemer,[19] but there is otherwise no evidence that he planned the assassination or even that the death of Kōmei was welcome to him. Indeed, it has been argued that Iwakura was confident that he could manipulate the emperor, a man whom he nevertheless respected and believed to be absolutely essential to the court's reform. It is said that on learning of Kōmei's death, his first thought was, "I am finished!" and he considered completely withdrawing from the world.[20]

Haraguchi Kiyoshi, the leading proponent of the "death by illness" theory, has taken great care to establish that it was not in Iwakura's interests for Kōmei to have died at this time.[21] He has also painstakingly examined all the evidence concerning the symptoms of the emperor's illness, as recorded in contemporary documents (including some used by proponents of the assassination theory), and compared these symptoms with those observed during the smallpox epidemic in Nagoya in 1946, when close to 18,000 persons were stricken.[22] His conclusion was that Kōmei died of illness; consequently, no one administered poison and no one planned the deed. It is unlikely we shall know the cause of Kōmei's death unless permission is granted to examine his remains for possible traces of arsenic.

During the early stages of the emperor's illness, Prince Mutsuhito had been in attendance each day at his father's bedside, dressed in brightly colored clothes, perhaps to cheer the sick man. But once the doctors decided that the malady was smallpox, the emperor commanded that for fear of contagion, the prince not visit his sickroom until he had recovered. Mutsuhito, however, had been vaccinated against smallpox. Years before, when he was still living in the house of his grandfather, Nakayama Tadayasu, the latter asked a doctor of Dutch medicine to vaccinate the boy. When the emperor on his deathbed was informed, he expressed relief that there was no fear of contagion. Needless to say, Kōmei himself had refused to be vaccinated.[23]

Emperor Kōmei's death was kept secret for several days, perhaps because his illness had been so sudden that the court was not prepared for the funeral rites. During these days, the grief-stricken Prince Mutsuhito could not go into mourning—or succeed to the throne. Although the accession would have to take place soon, an unexpected problem immediately arose: the prince had not yet had his *gembuku*, and it was therefore unclear what costume he should wear when the accession ceremony was performed. An official commanded to search for precedents discovered that Emperor Kōkaku, who had come to the throne in 1779, had his accession ceremony while costumed as a boy. Accordingly, Mutsuhito's hair was arranged in a suitably youthful style.

The sudden death of his father must have come as a profound shock to the prince, and his daily life immediately changed. His clothes and food and even the place where he slept were unfamiliar, which must have been disquieting as well. On February 4 the emperor's death was at last announced, and a period of mourning began. The following day the body of the late emperor was placed in a coffin, and the prince paid his final respects.

Determined that the funeral conform to ancient precedents, members of the court asked Toda Tadayuki, an expert in such matters, to investigate. He reported that ever since middle antiquity, it had been the practice to cremate deceased emperors and to erect nothing more than a small stone pagoda at the spot where his ashes were buried. However, after the death of Emperor Gokō-myō in 1654, a more impressive funeral service had been held, consisting of a pretended cremation followed by burial. It was decided that Kōmei's body would also be buried, within the precincts of the Sennyū-ji in Kyōto.[24]

The new emperor's accession took place on February 13, 1867. The ceremony was surprisingly simple. The prince appeared at four in the afternoon and seated himself at the prescribed place in the Hall of State Ceremonies. Two court ladies had already placed the regalia to the right of the emperor's seat. The emperor commanded the former chancellor to serve as regent and to perform in his stead the duties of his office. Following this, the emperor withdrew to his private quarters. Announcements were read to the assembled nobles concerning their privileges and prerogatives, which were to remain unchanged from the previous reign. Gifts were offered in honor of the accession by the widow of the shogun Iesada and by the wife of Tokugawa Yoshinobu but not by Princess Chikako, who was still in mourning for her husband, the shogun Iemochi.

Perhaps the happiest person on this occasion was Nakayama Tadayasu. Like Fujiwara no Michinaga some 850 years earlier, he rejoiced that he was now the grandfather of an emperor. No doubt he was saddened by the death of Emperor Kōmei, but grief was probably not his prevailing emotion. He sent this poem to his daughter, Nakayama Yoshiko, describing his feelings:

kanashiku mo	Grief-stricken, and yet
kanashiki uchi ni	Even amid the sadness
ureshiku mo	There is also joy,
ureshiki koto wa	A happiness created
kyō no hitokoto	By what has happened this day.

The young emperor also composed poetry on this occasion. Most of the forty *tanka* evoked his grief over his father's death, but three also mentioned the heavy weight of responsibility he felt on becoming emperor. He showed the poems to Nakayama Tadayasu, who was moved to tears.[25] Unfortunately these poems have been lost, but from this time on until the end of his life, poetry was very nearly the sole outlet for Emperor Meiji's personal feelings.

Chapter 12

The year 1867 did not begin happily for Emperor Meiji. The court was in mourning, and the usual New Year's festivities were canceled. Naturally, the young emperor felt grief over the death of his father, Emperor Kōmei. It is not clear to what degree the son and father had been spiritually compatible, but they saw each other frequently: for years it was the prince's practice to go every afternoon to pay his respects to his father and to ask for criticism of his poetry. He had no reason to anticipate that Kōmei, still only thirty-six, would suddenly die; and his education, in the traditional mode, had not prepared him adequately for the responsibilities of the position of emperor, especially at this difficult time. The strain he experienced may account for the nightmares that troubled his sleep at this time. Letters and diaries by members of the court allude to his insomniac suffering. The courtier Chigusa Aribumi wrote to Iwakura Tomomi, "Night after night, something comes beside the pillow of the new emperor and threatens him, causing him great anxiety. Yesterday, as I told you, he commanded prayers to be said. The rumor seems to be true."[1]

Prince Asahiko also mentioned the nightmares in his diary entry for February 9:

Something strange has been happening of late. I gather that persons close to the late emperor are gossiping to the effect that a figure, looking like Shōki in popular depictions, has been making appearances. He has a sword that he wears at his side. The following morning [the new emperor] has a fever.[2]

On February 15 Prince Asahiko wrote in his diary:

Myōsen'in has returned to the capital and I have heard many stories from him. According to one of his accounts, the new emperor is not well. In the past few days his cold has become worse. Ever since his accession to the throne the former emperor has appeared in the antechamber before the new emperor—and only him—day and night alike.[3]

If, recalling *Hamlet*, we accept the possibility of Kōmei's ghost coming back to this world to inform his only son that he has been murdered and to command the son to avenge him, we can only conclude that this ghost was far less persuasive than the ghost of Hamlet's father. The ghost kept the boy emperor from sleeping, but it did not rouse him to avenge his father's unnatural death, nor (judging from his subsequent actions) did he even become distrustful of persons at the court who might have administered the fatal dose of poison.

The ghost may have been the young emperor's chief cause of distress as the new reign began, but other members of the court were too busy disposing of the previous reign's unfinished business to worry about the ghost. One urgent problem was rectifying the unfortunate situation in the women's quarters of the palace. Nakayama Tadayasu sent a letter at this time to the minister of the interior, Konoe Tadafusa, emphasizing the need to enforce strict discipline in the women's quarters. He deplored the laxness that had come to prevail as the result of inadequate supervision of the palace ladies during the final years of Kōmei's reign.

If we can believe Tadayasu's comments, the atmosphere in the women's part of the palace resembled that of the licensed quarter.[4] Tadayasu believed, however, that the tender years of the emperor, who was not yet interested in a harem, provided a unique opportunity for removing offenders and restoring palace traditions. The senior palace lady (Tadayasu's grandmother, Nakayama Isako) was so extremely debilitated that she had to be replaced immediately. Other ladies who had served the late emperor were to be given generous gifts of money (depending on the length of their service) and asked to retire. Female attendants who were still young—in their early twenties or younger—were to be encouraged to marry into suitable families. Women of twenty-four or twenty-five and older would be permitted either to remain in their present posts or to shave their heads. Tadayasu's daughter, Nakayama Yoshiko, at first expressed the intention of entering Buddhist orders so that she might consecrate her remaining years to prayers for the repose of Emperor Kōmei; but she was persuaded to "remain in this world" because so many court ladies who had served Kōmei entered Buddhist orders after his death that it was feared there would not be enough ladies left at court who were familiar with the ceremonies. Yoshiko reluctantly agreed and subsequently devoted herself mainly to the education of her son, the new emperor.[5]

On February 19 an amnesty was proclaimed as part of the mourning for the late emperor and the celebration of the accession of the new emperor. Seven nobles who had been disgraced for their roles in incidents of 1863 and 1864 were pardoned and permitted to attend court again. Ten days later the amnesty was extended to cover four nobles of the *jōi* faction who were then living under house arrest, including Prince Taruhito.

On February 23 the court issued a directive to the shogunate commanding it to disband the expeditionary army that had been sent to punish Chōshū. The failure of an army composed of troops from many domains to defeat a single domain had plainly revealed the shogunate's weakness. Morale was low, and the death of the shogun Iemochi further contributed to the lack of enthusiasm for the shogunate's cause. The shogunate, at last abandoning all hope of successful prosecution of the war, ordered its troops to return to their original commands, saving face by giving as the reason the death of the late emperor.[6]

Emperor Kōmei was buried on March 5 at the imperial burial ground at the Sennyū-ji in Kyōto. In keeping with the provisions of his will, the traditional funeral rites after the death of an emperor—the proclamation of days of national mourning, the wearing of mourning dress, the employment of professional keeners to bewail the death, and so on—were not observed, but precautions against disturbances in the cities were taken. For a period of one year, festivities and the wearing of expensive clothes were forbidden.[7] The new emperor could not leave the palace to accompany the late emperor's coffin to the grave, but he saw off the funeral cortege from the Gekka Gate.

At the beginning of March, the first changes in the new emperor's daily life were made. He moved on March 7 to the Hall of Mourning (*iroden*), a temporary building of simple construction where, dressed in coarse clothes and surrounded by only the humblest articles, he prayed for the repose of his late father. He remained there for two weeks when, after putting aside his clothes of mourning and undergoing rites of purification, he returned to the main palace building. On the following day, various state officers came to pay their respects to the new emperor and to offer presents. The new reign had begun.

The posthumous name Kōmei, derived from a passage in the *Classic of Filial Piety*, was bestowed on the late emperor on March 21,[8] but the *nengō* was not changed with the new reign. Following the precedent of Kōmei's reign, when the *nengō* Kōka was retained for about a year after Kōmei succeeded to the throne, the *nengō* was not changed until October 23, 1868, almost two years after Kōmei's death. At this time it was decided that in the future each emperor's reign would have only one *nengō*.[9]

The beginning of a new reign was, of course, a matter of the utmost concern to the various foreign powers. The French government consistently supported the shogunate in what it anticipated would be a struggle for power. On March 29 the shogun Tokugawa Yoshinobu gave an audience to the French minister plenipotentiary Léon Roches in Ōsaka Castle and asked his opinion concerning reform of the shogunate. Roches warned that the shogunate must not seek to scrap any of the treaties it had concluded. He noted that various domains, alleging that the shogunate did not really wish to open the country, had entered into independent negotiations with the British to open ports they controlled. The French, with the interests of the shogunate in mind, believed that it was necessary to open the ports of Shimonoseki and Kagoshima in place of Hyōgo and Niigata (which had long been the subject of dispute). Opening these ports would demonstrate the shogunate's sincerity and at the same time would seize the initiative from the Kagoshima and Chōshū domains. Roches also urged the shogun to educate and guide the young emperor and to display firmness in dealing with the many daimyos. He promised that France would stand by the shogunate; this assurance should permit the shogunate to carry out decisively and fearlessly its announced policy of opening the country. Yoshinobu was impressed by Roches's advice and from this time often summoned him for consultation.[10]

On April 11 the shogun asked nine major domains their opinions on the desirability of opening the port of Hyōgo. Urging their support for this action, he said he was well aware that the late emperor had strictly forbidden opening the port; but, he added, it would by no means be easy to alter treaties already signed with the foreigners that promised to open Hyōgo. Even before he received responses from the nine domains, he requested imperial authorization, pointing out the many changes in the situation since Kōmei had refused permission. Not only had there been the war with Chōshū and the death of the shogun Iemochi, but the foreigners had become far more vocal in demanding that Japan carry out the provisions of the treaties. The country had no choice but to comply. Rather than passively acquiescing, the Japanese should look with fresh eyes at the world situation. In the spirit of the old dictum "Within the four seas all men are brothers; all men should be treated with equal benevolence," a renewal of the country should be initiated at the outset of the new reign. In this way the evil practices that had lingered from the past would be purged, and within a few years the nation would prosper. The glory of the imperial country would redound to the four seas, and the imperial mind would be set at ease.[11]

The different domains were divided in their opinions, and it was by no means certain that the shogunate could win over its feudatories to the policy of opening the country. Most important, the court was not persuaded by Yoshinobu's arguments. The reply received from the court stated that in view of the previous emperor's opposition, opening the port of Hyōgo would not be feasible; the new emperor was reluctant to show disrespect for his father's wishes. The shogun was asked to reconsider.[12]

Yoshinobu, however, was unwilling to abandon his plan. On April 29 he sent a memorial once more asking for imperial authorization. He apologized for insisting, even after having received a refusal, and he was fully aware that subjects should bow before the wisdom of the former emperor; but he could not remain silent in view of the urgency of the situation, which affected the destiny of the country. Although he was aware that by advocating the observance of the treaties, he risked incurring the displeasure of the court, he asked, in the interests of national safety and prestige, that the court reconsider its opposition to opening the port of Hyōgo. The court's reply to this letter was a reiteration of its refusal. The shogunate was further directed to inform the court of its obedience to this command.[13]

Even the court could not ignore indefinitely the menace of foreign intervention. On July 24 the regent, Nijō Nariyuki, sent a message to Yoshinobu stating that in view of the opinions expressed by the shogun and other important figures, the court had no choice but to give imperial sanction to opening Hyōgo.[14]

Presumably the young emperor had little or nothing to do with these decisions by the court. Indeed, it is not clear if any attempt was made to acquaint him with policy decisions. One of the rare references to his education at this time is the mention by Nakayama Tadayasu in his diary of delivering lectures to the emperor on *Kimpishō*, a thirteenth-century study of court practices and usages, and *Tzūzoku sangokushi*, a seventeenth-century Japanese translation of a Chinese account of warfare at the end of the Han dynasty.[15] These two works formed part of the traditional education of a ruler but hardly provided the kind of knowledge the emperor needed at this moment. Apparently Tadayasu did not consider that the emperor's increased political importance necessitated a different kind of education. Perhaps he hoped that Meiji, unlike his father, would confine his interests (like the emperors who reigned earlier in the Tokugawa period) to poetry, matters of protocol, and the literature of the distant past.

Although the supporters of *sonnō* had declared their reverence for the emperor, their allegiance to his cause was usually expressed in terms of opposition to the shogun rather than in terms of the benefits they expected to accrue after the overthrow of the shogunate. Little thought was given to the role the emperor would play once the throne had been restored to power. Surely no one assumed that he would become an absolute dictator, imposing his will on the population. Probably Tadayasu and the others around the young emperor hoped that the place of the shogunate in governing the country would be taken by the nobility, under the vaguely defined aegis of the emperor.

Although Roches had recommended that special attention be given to the young emperor's education, his words seem not to have been heeded. Meiji's mother, Nakayama Yoshiko, continued to supervise his calligraphy and his composition of *tanka*, and he also had instruction in these subjects from Prince

Takahito and Prince Taruhito.[16] But not for another year or more, when Kido Takayoshi first concerned himself with the emperor's education, was any thought given to the kind of scholarly preparation appropriate to a modern monarch.

Even after its defeat in the war with Chōshū, the shogunate remained the only effective central government. The most the court could do was to refuse to consent to plans made by the shogunate, especially with regard to foreign relations; it did not initiate plans of its own. The shogunate was, of course, far more experienced than the court in dealing with foreigners, but it was now faced with problems it had not encountered as long as *sakoku* lasted.

A dispute with Russia over the future disposition of the island of Sakhalin made it necessary to send two shogunate officials to St. Petersburg to negotiate with the Russians. At the time both Japanese and Russian colonists were living on the island, giving rise to incessant clashes. The Japanese proposed that the island be divided at the fiftieth parallel; the Russians demanded the whole island but offered in exchange to yield Etorofu and three small islands to the Japanese. The negotiations dragged on, but finally, on March 18, 1867, a provisional treaty was signed that left the island open to people of both countries but urged that friendlier relations based on mutual sincerity prevail, a pious hope that could not have satisfied settlers from either country. The mission nevertheless marked an important step in the history of Japanese diplomacy: it was the first time that Japanese envoys traveled abroad to negotiate a treaty.[17]

Yoshinobu did his best to cultivate foreign diplomats living in Japan. His first contact was with the British minister plenipotentiary, Sir Harry Parkes, to whom he granted an audience at Ōsaka Castle. On this occasion he witnessed a display of horsemanship by British cavalry, followed by the formal dinner he offered by way of indicating friendship. During the following days he gave audiences to French, Dutch, and American representatives. He treated them all with the greatest courtesy, giving them personal assurances that the treaties would be carried out to the letter.[18]

When tension arose in Korea as the result of the slaying of a French missionary and several American sailors, some Japanese advocated forming an alliance with Korea to fight against the foreigners; but the shogunate instead sent envoys to Korea to persuade the Koreans that it would be to their disadvantage to become involved in warfare with the foreigners. The shogunate offered to serve as an intermediary in settling the dispute. Three of its officers sent a message to the American minister, asking the Americans to respond positively if the Koreans agreed to mend their ways and enter into negotiations.[19]

It is astonishing that the Japanese, cut off from contact with most foreign countries for two and a half centuries, felt able to give advice to another country on the conduct to be observed among nations. Probably the Japanese feared that if Korea were invaded by troops sent by Western powers, this would adversely affect Japan, Korea's close neighbor. Japanese intercession was effective: toward the end of 1867, the Americans thanked the Japanese for help in averting a war.[20]

At this time the young emperor's attention was probably preoccupied by quite a different matter, the arrival of his bride. On July 27 Haruko,[21] the younger sister of Acting Major Counselor and General of the Left Guards Ichijō Saneyoshi, visited the palace and was received in audience by the emperor in his study. The purpose of this visit was to acquaint the emperor with her appearance and demeanor. If he disliked her, he was free to reject her as his bride, but he was probably predisposed in her favor because of her family and her accomplishments. Haruko's father was the late Minister of the Left Ichijō Tadaka, and her mother was the daughter of Prince Fushiminomiya Kuniie. Her pedigree was impeccable, and her scholarly and artistic attainments were no less impressive. As a small child (between the ages of three and four) she had been able to read aloud the poetry in the anthology *Kokinshū*, and at five she had composed *tanka* of her own. At seven she had done *sodoku* reading of a text in classical Chinese under the guidance of the Confucian scholar Nukina Masanori, with whom she also studied calligraphy. At twelve she had begun *koto* lessons and later also studied the *shō*. She was fond of nō and enjoyed singing passages from the plays at breaks during her studies.[22] She had studied the tea ceremony and flower arrangement with masters of the day. She had never suffered any major illness, perhaps because she had been vaccinated against smallpox when she was eight.[23]

These qualifications (and others) made her seem to members of the court like an ideal bride for the young emperor. There was one slight problem. She was older than her prospective husband. This in itself was not an insuperable obstacle: the consorts of the emperors Reigen, Sakuramachi, and Ninkō had been older than their husbands. But Haruko was three years older, a difference in age that normally was avoided as inauspicious. The regent solved this problem by changing her birth date from 1849 to 1850.[24] All was now ready for her appearance before the emperor.

On this occasion Haruko wore a white *habutae* silk kimono with embroidered patterns and trousers of a deep purple. She arrived in a wickerwork palanquin about one in the afternoon, accompanied by her ladies. In the emperor's study she and the emperor exchanged greetings and partook of refreshments and saké. Haruko offered the emperor gifts, including a box of fresh fish. She withdrew at about seven and went to the palace of the dowager empress where she was again given refreshments. She changed costume before taking leave of the emperor. He presented her with various gifts, including a tobacco pipe, ornamental hairpins, and an incense box. Later the emperor highly praised her comportment. The acting major counselor Yanagihara Mitsunaru, pleased with this expression of approval, asked the highest-ranking members of the nobility if they had any objection to Haruko's being named as *nyōgo*.[25] Everyone was in favor, so all barriers to her being appointed as the emperor's consort had been cleared.

Two days later, on July 29, the military liaison officer Hino Sukemune went as the emperor's envoy to the house of Ichijō Saneyoshi to inform him that his sister had been chosen as the emperor's bride. Word quickly spread, and there were numerous visitors to the Ichijō household. The shogunate donated 15,000 *ryō* for wedding and other expenses and announced that it would henceforth provide an annual stipend of 500 sacks of rice for her expenses. However, as the result of the political changes that occurred in the following year, the shogunate could not devote much attention to the marriage, and only a small portion of the promised money was ever delivered. Gifts came from other sources, but the total available for the wedding was sufficient for only a simple ceremony.

Even after Meiji's future consort had been definitively chosen, the wedding could not take place immediately. He would be in mourning for his father for a full year after Kōmei's death. Moreover, he had not yet had his *gembuku* (initiation into manhood), which was essential before his marriage, but this ceremony could take place only after the period of mourning was over.

Serious problems of quite another nature arose before the wedding could be celebrated. Unsettled conditions in the city of Kyōto caused concern about Ichijō Haruko's safety. She was assigned a bodyguard of ten samurai in July, and plans were drawn up for evacuating her to one or another temple in the event of a disturbance. In case of a serious emergency, she was to take refuge in the palace of the empress dowager. This in fact happened at the beginning of 1868, when the proclamation of the shogun's return of government to the emperor gave rise to disorder within the city. During the fighting between troops loyal to the emperor and those of the shogun, the sound of gunfire could be heard even within the Gosho. Plans for the marriage were temporarily left in abeyance.

The death of Haruko's brother, Ichijō Saneyoshi, in May of that year posed yet another problem—if special care had not been taken to ensure that Haruko ate separately from the rest of her family, her brother's death would have polluted her and caused still further delay in the wedding. All the same, by the end of 1868 the situation had stabilized sufficiently for the marriage to be celebrated on January 11, 1869.[26]

Early that morning Haruko's chamber was decorated in preparation for the ceremony. A yin-yang diviner was summoned to determine the precise time for her to put on her marriage robes. The diviner recommended eight in the morning, at which time Konoe Tadahiro, in charge of the ceremony, tied the robes. At two in the afternoon a palm-woven carriage was brought to the southern stairs of Haruko's chamber. Two nobles bore the shafts. A waiting woman placed inside the carriage an incense burner and a sword bestowed by the emperor earlier that morning. Haruko boarded the carriage, accompanied by two ladies-in-waiting. Nobles pulled the carriage as far as the Middle Gate, where oxen were attached. Once the escort was ready, the carriage moved out of the Double Gate. When it reached the northernmost gate of the palace, the oxen were unhitched, and the carriage shafts rested on a stand. An official reported the arrival of the carriage to the guards, whereupon court officials pulled the carriage inside the gate. They passed through the Genki Gate (inner northern gate) and reached the northeast gate of the Higyōsha, a palace building. Here, members of the escort surrounded the carriage with curtains and screens to prevent outsiders from observing Haruko as she descended from the carriage. The ladies of her escort followed her, bearing the sword and the incense burner. They moved through various passageways into the prince's palace, where Haruko seated herself, the sword and the incense burner at her side. Nobles who had arrived by a more direct route came forward to offer congratulations.[27]

After a short rest Haruko reappeared wearing five layers of robes and with her hair rearranged. She went to the Higyōsha where she was offered refreshments. Soon afterward she was informed of her appointment as *nyōgo*. Normally the announcement of appointment as *nyōgo* was made the day after a palace lady had entered the emperor's service, but because Haruko was also to be named empress, the appointment as *nyōgo* took place on this day. The title of empress was a signal mark of favor: Kōmei's consort had never received it.[28]

Haruko's appointments as *nyōgo* and empress were proclaimed by officials whose precisely executed movements as they performed the ceremonies probably suggested an elaborate ballet. When these formalities were at last completed, Haruko was ready to go to the Seiryōden (residential palace) where she would enter the presence of her future husband. She was accompanied by Konoe Tadahiro and Nakayama Tadayasu. One court lady held Haruko's train while two others carried the sword and incense burner. Next the Night Palace Ceremony took place. At eight the emperor went to the Chamber of Purification where he put on straw slippers. He entered the curtained enclosure from the western door, and Konoe Tadahiro removed the slippers. Next the empress entered the curtains. Nakayama Tadayasu, as both a relative of the emperor on the maternal side and an aged man whose wife was still living, covered them with the royal quilts. Next he offered rice cakes that would be eaten by the newlyweds on the third night of the marriage. These cakes were customarily prepared and offered by a married couple of advanced years.[29]

When this ceremony had ended, a court lady took the cakes to the Higyōsha where they would be kept for three days in a lucky direction. Next a maid of honor (*myōbu*) took an oil lamp with a cloth wick and lit it with flame from a hanging lantern in the northeastern corner of the Night Pavilion and took it to the Willow Pavilion where she transferred the flame to the lacquered lantern.

At this point Tadahiro and Tadayasu withdrew. For three days the flame would be kept burning in the lantern. That night, palace ladies by turns would hold aloft the imperial sword.

Next the private ritual of drinking saké took place in the Ordinary Residence. The empress sat to the north. At the third cup, she herself poured the saké and offered it to the emperor, and then she received a cup from his hand. Afterward they partook of a simple meal and then withdrew to the empress's palace. At last the newlyweds were alone.

Needless to say, every act performed during this series of ceremonies was prescribed by tradition. This was an event of dynastic significance, and it was believed that the couple's happiness, fertility, and longevity would be reflected in the country's prosperity. The union of Meiji and his bride would not, as it happened, be blessed with children, but Haruko would be a far more prominent public figure than any consort for many hundreds of years.

Chapter 13

The main issues facing the shogunate at the beginning of 1867 were the opening of the port of Hyōgo and the disposition of the rebellious Chōshū domain. For some months the court kept up its bitter opposition to opening Hyōgo to foreign ships, but on June 26 high-ranking nobles were summoned to the palace to hear discussion of the matter. The acting major counselor Daigo Tadaoki expressed the opinion that even though Emperor Kōmei had forbidden opening the port, under present conditions it could not be avoided. He pointed out that Kōmei had in fact authorized the opening of three ports (though not Hyōgo because of its proximity to Kyōto) and that there really was no major change. His eloquence swayed the other nobles, and in the end imperial authorization for opening the port was granted. It was also decided to treat Chōshū leniently.[1]

Now that the long-debated issue of the port of Hyōgo had at last been settled, on July 7 the shogunate further decided to permit foreigners to conduct business in Edo and Ōsaka. With this, full compliance with the provisions of the treaties signed with the foreign nations had been achieved. This did not signify that all the shogunate's problems had been solved: major and minor problems constantly arose, and increasingly the young emperor was obliged to take part in decisions.

One minor problem arose as a direct consequence of the foreign settlements. On July 14 the Nagasaki magistrate arrested and imprisoned sixty-eight Christians. Christianity had been prohibited in Japan for about 250 years, but "hidden Christians" in the region of Nagasaki had preserved the religion without guidance from ordained priests or even from Christian books. Over the years the beliefs of these Christians had steadily drifted from orthodox teachings, and by now the hymns they sang, originally in Latin, had become gibberish, memorized by believers who had no idea of the meanings. Most of the Christians were poor fishermen and peasants. If suppressing such a cult had been a purely religious matter—if, say, it involved a heterodox Buddhist sect—it could have been achieved without difficulty, but the suppression of a Christian sect immediately involved the foreign powers, which were highly sensitive to attacks on their religion.

As far back as 1857, as the result of negotiations between Townsend Harris and the senior councillor Hotta Masayoshi, it had been agreed that foreigners should be able to practice their religions without hindrance, and the Americans obtained permission to erect a Protestant church in the foreign settlement. At the same time French priests were active in promulgating Catholicism, especially in the area of Nagasaki. The hidden Christians, overjoyed by the arrival of coreligionists, openly visited the church erected by the French and appealed to the French minister for support. Some, rejoicing that their hour had at last come, flaunted their new importance, leading to conflicts even within families.[2] Buddhists, angered by the government's slowness in punishing the Christians, even though the religion was still prohibited, threatened to take matters into their own hands and kill the Christians. The latter responded by arming themselves with bamboo spears. After the arrests on July 14 the French and Portuguese consuls in Nagasaki demanded the release of the Christians and, when this was refused, reported the matter to their legations, urging them to negotiate with the shogunate for release of the prisoners.

On August 24 Tokugawa Yoshinobu granted the French minister Léon Roches an audience in Ōsaka Castle. Roches had previously asked the shogunate to free the Christians, only to be informed that they had violated a national law and so their arrest was unavoidable. The meeting between Yoshinobu and Roches was arranged at Roches's request, ostensibly to discuss trade. The shogunate had become increasingly dependent on France as a source of weapons, and the French were in a strong position to make demands with respect to the Christian prisoners. In the hopes of making an even more powerful impression on Yoshinobu, the French invited him aboard a French warship to observe blank firing and the maneuvering of the ship. The next day he began negotiations for the release of the prisoners.

On September 3 the councillor Itakura Katsukiyo (1823–1889) met with Roches to discuss the issue. Two days later Yoshinobu sent a letter to Napoleon III explaining that Christianity had long since been prohibited in Japan and that the arrest of the Christians had been obligatory. He asked that French priests cease proselytizing among Japanese subjects. Finally he agreed to free the imprisoned Christians. They would be placed in the custody of village officials and encouraged to move to other localities.[3]

This action did not end the repressive measures directed against the hidden Christians. In April 1868 when the signboards erected by the shogunate listing five prohibitions imposed on the populace were replaced by injunctions of the new imperial government, the prohibition on Christianity remained unaltered. The third injunction stated: "The Christian heretical sect is strictly prohibited. Anyone arousing suspicion should be reported to the village office. A reward will be bestowed."[4]

Even Emperor Meiji became involved in the discussions of how the Christians were to be brought under control. On May 9 princes of the blood, nobles of high and low ranks, and various daimyos were summoned into the imperial presence and commanded to express their opinions concerning the disposition of the Christian believers in Nagasaki. They were informed that despite the prohibition newly issued in the previous month, the number of Christian believers had continued to grow and that there were now more than 3,000. If no punitive action were taken, this might well have serious consequences. For this reason the chief justice of the Nagasaki courts had been given permission to dispose of the Christians as he saw fit.

Earlier Councillor Inoue Kaoru (1835–1915) had gone to Nagasaki to observe the situation with respect to the Christian believers and had been greatly upset. After his return to Kyōto, he had discussed the situation with Kido Takayoshi, who subsequently conferred with the vice president (*fukusōsai*), Sanjō Sanetomi. They concluded that the best course would be to explain patiently their errors to the leaders of the believers. Those who responded to the command to abandon the forbidden faith would be required to discard their pictures of Jesus and swear an oath before the Japanese gods. Those who refused to yield to persuasion would be put to death. This opinion, reported to the throne, was the occasion for the gathering in the emperor's presence.[5] On the following day those who had attended the meeting submitted their recommendation: the majority favored death for all Christian believers.

The British minister Sir Harry Parkes was enraged when he learned that even on the new signboards, Christianity was prohibited. Parkes was famous for his terrible temper, and it is not difficult to imagine his fulminations when on May 4 he called on Sanjō Sanetomi to protest against the wording of the signboards and the disposition of the Christian believers in Nagasaki. Iwakura Tomomi, Prince Akira, and the councillor Ōkuma Shigenobu were also present; Ōkuma was eventually able to calm Parkes.

On May 27 Meiji summoned Kido and commanded him to go to Nagasaki to dispose of the matter. The signboards were changed: the word "heretical" in the phrase "heretical Christian sect" was deleted, but a separate item was added proscribing heresy.[6] On June 14, 1868, 114 Christian leaders were turned over to the Hagi, Tsuwano, and Fukuyama domains for imprisonment. More than 2,400 believers were eventually imprisoned under extremely harsh conditions in seventeen different places. About 500 of them recanted under pressure from the authorities and were released, but the rest persistently refused to change their faith, displaying great strength in their convictions. Many of those who recanted subsequently reverted to their old beliefs. All prisoners were finally released and allowed to return to their homes in March 1873 after the government decided that further imprisonment would serve no useful purpose.[7]

The suppression of Christianity was not one of the major problems facing the shogunate during the closing months of its existence. It could not have been of great importance to members of the court either, preoccupied as they were with efforts to overthrow the shogunate. Nevertheless, they felt it advisable to have the debate over the disposition of the Christians take place in the presence of the emperor. He also participated in most of the future discussions of state policy, although the official records never indicate his reactions.

The most pressing problem facing the shogunate was, of course, its continued existence. Because the mounting opposition to the shogunate is a subject already treated by many historians, suffice it to say here that the alliance between Chōshū and Satsuma, formerly bitter enemies, was the key factor in galvanizing the opposition to the shogunate. The anti-shogunate domains, mainly in west Honshū, Kyūshū, and Shikoku, had become increasingly dissatisfied with the shogunate's monopoly of the highly lucrative foreign trade. But when discussing their grievances, they normally did not mention this; instead, they spoke of the need to restore imperial rule. A contemporary historian has written, "It needs hardly be said that the internal disturbances at the time of the Restoration were definitely not caused by loyalist convictions. Fundamentally, they resulted from the aspirations of the major domains in the southwest, headed by Satsuma and Chōshū, to be independent of the shogunate."[8]

Even if these were the real aspirations of Satsuma, Chōshū, and the other domains that ultimately overthrew the shogunate, they needed a rallying cry, and "Restore power to the emperor!" served this purpose. The shogunate under Tokugawa Yoshinobu, especially after its humiliating defeat in the war with Chōshū, took desperate measures to stave off collapse. With France's help, it rapidly increased its store of modern weapons, and under Yoshinobu's leadership, many reforms were launched. Senior shogunate statesmen, notably Oguri Tadamasa (1827–1868), attempted to push through plans for making the shogunate into an absolutist regime, believing this was the only way it could ensure its authority over rebellious domains.[9] As early as 1866 Oguri privately discussed the advisability of abolishing the domains and replacing them with prefectures, a measure that eventually was adopted by the Meiji government in 1871, but the shogunate lacked sufficient support to carry out so daring a plan.

The daimyos of the major domains, especially in the west and south, joined forces in alliances. But for all the reverence they professed for the court in Kyōto, their chief concern seems to have been preserving their own power. Initially at least, they seem not to have hoped to substitute the absolute authority of the emperor for the authority of the shogunate,[10] as hardly any of the daimyos or their retainers rose above anxiety over the survival of their particular domains to consider what was desirable for the country as a whole.[11]

The shogunate's authority was weakened also by populist uprisings calling for change, at their height during the summer of 1866 during the war with Chōshū.[12] These uprisings, stemming from anger over the skyrocketing prices of food, especially rice, had the effect of creating opposition to the shogunate at a time when it desperately needed unity in its struggle with Chōshū.[13]

In the meantime, men from the major domains in Kyūshū, Shikoku, and western Honshū were consolidating plans for restoring power to the court. In March 1867 Gotō Shōjirō (1838–1897), a councillor (*sansei*) of the Tosa domain, met Sakamoto Ryōma (1835–1867), a renegade of the same domain, in Nagasaki. Gotō was duty bound to arrest Sakamoto, but instead he listened to the views of a man known for his advanced political ideas. The two men agreed that the only way out of the impasse in which the government found itself was for the shogun voluntarily to relinquish his powers to the court.[14]

Four months later, in July 1867, Gotō, with two other Tosa men, Sakamoto and Nakaoka Shintarō (1838–1867), in attendance, met in Kyōto with three leaders of the Satsuma domain—Saigō Takamori (1828–1877), Ōkubo Toshimichi (1830–1878), and Komatsu Tatewaki (1835–1870)—and drew up a pact between the two domains. The language and political ideas embodied in this pact closely resemble those originally expressed by Sakamoto in his *Senchū hassaku* (Eight Proposals Composed Aboard Ship), written while on his way from Tosa to Kyōto several weeks earlier.[15]

After promising to do everything in their power to restore rule to the emperor, the two domains agreed to eight articles. The first article declared that all powers for deciding the administration of the country resided with the court. Subsequent articles expressed their belief in the necessity to erect (with money provided by the various domains) a parliamentary building in Kyōto from which would emanate the laws governing the entire country. The parliament would consist of two chambers, and the members of the lower house of this parliament, selected for their righteousness and blamelessness, would include persons from all walks of life, ranging from high-ranking nobles to samurai and even commoners. Daimyos would take their places in the upper chamber. But before these changes could occur, the shogun would have to resign his office, resume his status as a daimyo, and return his political powers to the court. New treaties should be concluded with foreign countries that would provide for fair commercial practices.[16]

In October of the same year, Satsuma and Chōshū concluded a pact that was specifically aimed at overthrowing the shogunate. Ōkubo Toshimichi and Ōyama Tsunayoshi (1825–1877), central figures in Satsuma, traveled to Yamaguchi, where they communicated to Mōri Takachika (1819–1871), the daimyo, the frustration of their own daimyo over his failure to persuade the shogunate to mend its ways. They declared that there was no way to solve the nation's problems except by using military force to overthrow the shogunate. They asked that Chōshū send troops to support their own in Kyōto, where they were guarding the imperial palace.[17]

Impressed by Ōkubo's arguments and his straightforward answers to the questions put to him by members of the Chōshū domain, Mōri Takachika agreed without hesitation to support Satsuma and to send troops to Ōsaka. He added, however, that guarding the imperial palace was a heavy responsibility, and if by some mischance, the emperor were captured by the enemy, everything would be lost.

There was contact also between the Kyōto aristocrats and the samurai who were planning the overthrow of the shogunate. Iwakura Tomomi, still living under house arrest at Iwakura Village, had maintained relations with the principal Satsuma leaders, and he was otherwise kept abreast of recent developments by visitors from the various domains. In July, Nakaoka and Sakamoto called on him and urged him to make up his differences with Sanjō Sanetomi, his personal enemy. Iwakura agreed, and Nakaoka was also able to persuade Sanjō to forget old grievances. In this way the loyalist nobles were united both in their opposition to the shogunate and in their support of the major domains.[18]

In November 1867 Yamauchi Yōdō (1827–1872),[19] the former Tosa daimyo, sent a letter to Tokugawa Yoshinobu urging him to return the government to the court. Yōdō was by no means a militant supporter of the restoration of imperial authority, but Gotō Shōjirō adroitly persuaded him that Yoshinobu himself would welcome such a proposal. In this way Yōdō would show his respect for the emperor and his compassion for the shogun. Gotō also stressed that Satsuma and Chōshū were planning military action against the shogunate and that the best way to avoid warfare was for the shogun to resign his office. Yōdō was so determined to avoid such a conflict that he declared he would not send one Tosa soldier to Kyōto. This was a disappointment to Gotō, who had promised Saigō and Ōkubo to return to Kyōto with Tosa troops, but he had obtained the desired letter from Yamauchi Yōdō.[20]

The letter itself, apart from its reiterations of awe and dread over the propriety of addressing such a missive to the shogun, and an account of Yōdō's recent illness, contains a vaguely worded expression of the belief that the time had come to change a system that had lasted for hundreds of years and to restore rule by the emperor. It concludes with Yōdō's confession that worry over the predicament in which the country found itself had caused him to shed tears of blood.[21]

An appended proposal, signed by Gotō Shōjirō and three others of the domain, was more specific. It listed seven points, some derived from Sakamoto's recommendations and others from the Satsuma–Chōshū pact, opening with the proposal to establish a parliament in two chambers in which all classes of society would serve. The second article urges the establishment of schools in the cities where students would be instructed in the arts and sciences. The third article calls for new treaties and the establishment of fair trading practices.[22] The next article stresses the importance of land and sea defenses. Military installations should be built between the capital and Settsu Province, and the court itself must be defended by well-equipped troops under the emperor's personal command. The fifth article calls for basic reforms of old evils and not mere surface changes. Some court practices, sanctioned by centuries of observance, would have to be completely altered before Japan could stand independent among the nations of the globe. Finally, members of the parliament would have to be impartial and fair in their judgments and not get bogged down in arguments over trivialities.[23]

The letters were received by Itakura Katsukiyo of the Council of Elders and delivered to Yoshinobu. Gotō had been instructed to obtain Satsuma's approval for Yōdō's proposal, but at first Saigō refused, saying that plans for attacking the shogunate had been completed and that it was too late to give advice to the shogun. He said that he could not prevent Tosa from carrying out its plans but that Satsuma would act as it thought best. Gotō, not discouraged by the refusal, approached other Satsuma men and found them willing to support the letter. In the end Saigō and Ōkubo agreed to postpone military action.[24]

On November 9, 1867, a secret imperial command was issued to Satsuma and Chōshū ordering them to subjugate Tokugawa Yoshinobu:[25]

> Imperial Edict. Minamoto[26] Yoshinobu, borrowing the authority of successive generations and depending on the strength of his pack of bandits, has wantonly impaired the loyal and the good and has frequently disobeyed imperial commands. In the end, not fearing to distort the edicts of the late emperor and not caring that he has plunged the populace into an abyss, his all-pervasive evil threatens to overturn the Land of the Gods. We are father and mother of the people. If We fail to strike down this traitor, what excuse shall We have to offer to the spirit of the late emperor? How shall We make Our profound amends to the people? This is the cause of Our grief and indignation. It is unavoidable that the period of mourning be disregarded.[27] Implement the wishes of Our heart by slaughtering the traitorous subject Yoshinobu. When you have speedily accomplished this great deed to save the nation, you will enable the people to enjoy the lasting peace of the mountains. This is Our wish. See to it that you are prompt in carrying it out.[28]

The edict is highly unusual in its strong, even violent, language. It is strange that although it is written in the first person (using the imperial pronoun *chin*), it is signed by three noblemen.[29] For this reason the document has been labeled by some as a forgery, and by others as a pseudoedict inspired by Iwakura Tomomi but in fact composed by Tamamatsu Misao (1810–1872), a learned, former Shintō priest who served as Iwakura's "brain."[30] According to Iwakura himself, the edict was shown to the emperor by Nakayama Tadayasu and approved by him before being sent to the two domains.[31] But it is doubtful that Tadayasu would take to the emperor a document that was kept extremely secret (it was not shown even to the regent).[32]

This edict was followed the next day by a much shorter one, ostensibly from the emperor himself, commanding Satsuma and Chōshū to kill Matsudaira Katamori and Matsudaira Sadanori.[33] Although both domains sent replies promising complete obedience to the best of their abilities, neither edict led to the prescribed murders.

On November 8 Tokugawa Yoshinobu addressed a letter to the court requesting permission to return his authority to the court, and this prompted the emperor to call off the edicts issued to Satsuma and Chōshū.[34] Historians have debated why Yoshinobu decided at this point to yield his authority.[35] Within the shogunate itself, many men had recognized that a change was inevitable. On November 8 Yoshinobu assembled at Nijō Castle the senior officials of forty domains with incomes of more than 100,000 *koku* to discuss the return of rule to the emperor (*taisei hōkan*). Itakura Katsukiyo showed them the draft of Yoshinobu's memorial to the throne requesting permission to surrender his office. He asked their opinions. Most of the officials withdrew without committing themselves, but after the meeting, Komatsu Tatewaki from Satsuma, Gotō Shōjirō and Fukuoka Takachika from Tosa, and Tsuji Igaku from Aki lingered behind to thank Yoshinobu for his sacrifice and urge him to take decisive action. They were joined by men from other domains. Yoshinobu at last made up his mind, and that day he gave the memorial to the two military liaison officers.[36]

Yoshinobu's memorial to the throne was couched in familiar language, tracing the long history of his family's service to the throne and the favors it had received and blaming his scant virtue for the present difficult situation in which the country found itself. In yielding his authority, he looked up to the emperor's wisdom for guidance. If all joined to ensure the security of the imperial land, he felt sure that Japan would be able to stand on equal terms with foreign countries. On the following day, November 10, Yoshinobu was summoned to the court and informed that the emperor had granted his request to return his powers to the court.

The official proclamation of the resumption of imperial rule was not made until January 4, 1868, but the decision had been made: in principle, the emperor was now the sole ruler of Japan. His reactions to this event are unknown. Not even a poem survives that might give a clue to his feelings, something similar to what Queen Victoria wrote in her journal the day she became queen: "I am very young, and perhaps in many, though not in all things, inexperienced, but I am sure, that very few have more real good will and more real desire to do what is fit and right than I have."[37] All the same, the emperor was aware that the line of Tokugawa shoguns, begun with Ieyasu in 1603, had ended and that for the first time in more than 500 years, an emperor ruled without a shogun.[38]

On the same day Iwakura Tomomi received a pardon from the emperor and permission to attend court once again. Earlier, someone learning of Iwakura's intention of restoring power to the emperor had compared his plan with that of the Kemmu Restoration—when (in 1333) the emperor Godaigo was empowered to rule without a shogun. Tamamatsu Misao disagreed, holding that the scope of the present restoration was so huge that its only real precedent was the founding of Japan by Emperor Jimmu.[39] It had been more than 670 years since Minamoto Yoritomo first founded his shogunate and more than 260 years since the Tokugawa shogunate was founded.

About a month later foreign envoys in Japan received this communication:

> The emperor of Japan announces to the sovereigns of all foreign countries and to their subjects that permission has been granted to the Shōgun Tokugawa Yoshinobu to return the governing power in accordance with his own request. We shall henceforth exercise supreme authority in all the internal and external affairs of the country. Consequently the title of emperor must be substituted for that of Tycoon, in which the treaties have been made. Officers are being appointed by us to the conduct of foreign affairs. It is desirable that the representatives of the treaty powers recognize this announcement.[40]

The message (as translated) was dated February 8 by the solar calendar and signed Mutsuhito.

Chapter 14

Restoration of imperial rule, the dream of many Japanese ever since cries of *sonnō jōi* were first raised around the country, had at last been achieved. Political power was (at least in principle) in the hands of the court, but the court still had no organs of administration or legislation. On November 27, 1867, senior members of the Court Council met at the house of the regent Nijō Nariyuki to determine basic policies but failed to reach a decision.[1] Proponents of rule by the emperor had not given adequate consideration to the problems they were likely to encounter when they assumed responsibility for running the government.

By imperial decree, major state decisions and policies with respect to foreign countries were to be determined by a council consisting of daimyos with incomes of more than 100,000 *koku*.[2] However, it was clear that it would take time for these men to assemble in Kyōto, and in the meantime decisions were urgently needed in order to dispose of the mountain of accumulated major national and international problems. The court seemed powerless to act; indeed, this period has been characterized as one during which there was no government in Kyōto.[3]

Despite the earnestness of the shogun's words and actions when he returned power to the court, many daimyos, in both Edo and Kyōto, were indignant over Yoshinobu's decision. They held meetings to discuss what the return of power to the emperor signified, and some personally visited Yoshinobu to express their discontent. He patiently explained the inadvisability of divided allegiances within a country and urged them to return to their domains. Above all, he warned them not to do anything rash. But daimyos living in Edo, regardless of whether they were allies or enemies of the Tokugawa family, ignored his plea for caution. They supported the shogunate against the court, some so strongly that they refused to obey commands issued by the court. Many samurai, angered by the change in the government, advocated increasing military preparations in order to seize control by main force. Some urged Prince Asahiko, perpetually lurking behind the scenes, to restore shogunate authority.[4]

Restoration of the emperor had not brought peace and order to the capital. Tension was heightened by incessant rumors. On November 14 Iwakura Tomomi went incognito to the Satsuma residence in Kyōto to inform the samurai of an urgent matter. According to a former official with whom he was in close contact, a samurai of the Ōgaki domain had proposed that the Council of Elders order soldiers to set fire to the Satsuma residence; then, taking advantage of the confusion, they would abduct the emperor and spirit him off to Ōsaka Castle. This rumor, though probably groundless, seemed so serious to Iwakura that he felt obliged to warn the Satsuma retainers to take emergency precautions.[5]

Assassinations—a conspicuous a feature of the period—also contributed to the tension. On December 10, 1867, Sakamoto Ryōma and Nakaoka Shintarō, who had played a major role in arranging the alliance between Satsuma and Chōshū, were assassinated in Kyōto.[6]

Restoration of imperial rule had yet to be formally proclaimed, but the court in Kyōto was already faced with practical problems now that the shogunate was no longer administering the country. When the regent and other members of the court met with Tokugawa Yoshinobu and senior retainers of resident daimyos on December 16, the following were some of the problems brought up for consideration: What arrangements should be made for soldiers from different domains to take turns in guarding the city of Kyōto and the grounds of the imperial palace? How would money to be raised for building the Ōmiya Palace?[7] What would the functions of the *shoshidai* and lesser officials be? How would the issuance of paper currency be regulated?[8]

In principle, such matters were to be decided by an assembly of senior daimyos, but very few of them had yet appeared in the capital, as they were waiting to see the way the wind was blowing before leaving their domains. The court finally decided to leave everything as in the past, at least for the time being. We can all but see the smile of amusement on Yoshinobu's face as he contemplated from a distance the spectacle of the nobles helplessly floundering in their new and unfamiliar tasks.[9]

On December 17 the emperor issued an edict to three nobles who had taken a prominent part in the restoration movement—Nakayama Tadayasu, Ōgimachisanjō Sanenaru, and Nakamikado Tsuneyuki—instructing them to direct Satsuma and Chōshū to discontinue for the time being their attacks on the shogunate.[10] On December 20 Yoshinobu again formally requested permission to resign his post, but the regent Nijō Nariyuki rejected his petition, commanding him to remain in office until the assembled daimyos could decide on his future. Obviously the court still had not made up its mind how to deal with this man, powerful even in defeat.

Some historians have even suggested that Yoshinobu used the return of power to the emperor as a means of strengthening his position. Foreigners in Japan suspected that Yoshinobu had some ulterior motive for giving up his office. Sir Ernest Satow recalled that when the English were informed that Yoshinobu had long been intending "to surrender the government to the Mikado," they were skeptical:

> This of course we did not believe, our view being that he was tired of being badgered by Satsuma, Chōshū, Tosa and Hizen, and that in order to give unity to his own party, he had resolved to call a general council, which possibly might reinstate him by a majority of votes, and thus establish his authority more strongly than ever.[11]

As far back as July 23, 1867, Itakura Katsukiyo and Nagai Naoyuki, two high-ranking officials of the shogunate, had hit on the plan of having the shogun serve as regent during the emperor's minority, in this way preventing any division between the court and the shogunate.[12] Nothing seems to have come of this proposal, but toward the end of that year, Nishi Amane (1829–1897), the "brain" of Yoshinobu, drew up the first bill to be presented to the Assembly of Daimyos dealing with the form of the future government.

The bill called for a division of power into three branches—the government, the court, and the daimyos. By "government" was meant administrative authority. The head of the Tokugawa family, known as the *taikun* (tycoon), would be the chief of this branch. He would establish his government in Ōsaka and rule the whole country through officials appointed unilaterally by himself with the exception of the presiding officer, who would be selected by the tycoon from among three candidates proposed by the daimyos.

The "daimyo" branch of the government was the legislature. It would consist of two houses, the upper house composed of daimyos and the lower house, of samurai, one from each domain. The legislature was authorized to debate important matters such as the laws, the budget, foreign policy, and issues of war and peace. The tycoon would be the presiding officer of the upper house. In cases when the upper and lower houses failed to reach agreement on some item of legislation, the tycoon was entitled to cast three votes, as opposed to one each for the upper and lower houses, thus ensuring him always of the decisive vote. The tycoon also had the right to dissolve the lower house.

The third branch of the government—the court—was of only nominal significance. The emperor was expected to affix his seal of approval to laws passed by the legislature, but he did not possess the power of the veto.[13]

If this bill had been approved by the Assembly of Daimyos, it would have given Yoshinobu far greater power than he had ever possessed. His authority would have been further enhanced by impoverishing the daimyos, for they would be required to give two-thirds of their income for national defense and much of the rest for education, exploitation of mines, a telegraph system, and railway lines. Nishi Amane wrote at the time, "Just as in Turkey people call [the ruler] the sultan, and in Russia they call him the czar, there is no reason why in our country we should not call him the tycoon."[14] Yoshinobu probably expected to be supported by a majority of the daimyos, enabling him to rule as an absolute monarch. Even Fukuzawa Yukichi, the apostle of Japanese enlightenment, wrote favorably of "the tycoon monarchy."[15] It is not clear what Yoshinobu himself desired. Some scholars believe that he was aiming at an absolute dictatorship; others, that he sought to establish a government based on a league of the different domains in which he would have the principal role.[16]

On January 4, 1868, the restoration of imperial rule was formally proclaimed. Early that morning, the chamberlain Chigusa Aritō was sent to inform Iwakura Tomomi that he had been released from house arrest. He was commanded to attend court immediately in full regalia. Iwakura must have presented a rather strange appearance, wearing his court cap perched on a head that had been completely shaven (in the manner prescribed for a person doing penance under house arrest). He arrived at the court bearing a box containing the proclamation of the Restoration and other documents. Ushered into the presence of the emperor, Iwakura offered him the proclamation that, he declared, was based on the emperor's own views. Iwakura then withdrew. Presently the young emperor moved to his study, where princes of the blood and high dignitaries had assembled, and (probably behind a screen that kept the assemblage from seeing him) read aloud the proclamation announcing the restoration of imperial rule, the abolition of the office of chancellor or regent and that of the shogunate, and the establishment of a new form of government consisting of a *sōsai* (Prince Arisugawa Taruhito), ten *gijō*, and twenty *san'yo*.[17]

That night an important meeting was held in the presence of the emperor. Nakayama Tadayasu, the presiding officer, explained that the session was being held to place the imperial government on a firm footing by effecting thoroughgoing reforms. No sooner was it announced that the session was open to discussion than Yamauchi Yōdō got up to propose that Yoshinobu be allowed to participate in the deliberations. Ōhara Shigetomi disagreed, whereupon Yōdō launched into the praises of the peace and prosperity the Tokugawa family had brought to Japan for more than 200 years. He expressed admiration for Yoshinobu's willingness to relinquish powers inherited from the long line of his ancestors solely in order to bring about a better, lasting government; and he criticized the sinister activities of a handful of nobles who, in the name of the emperor, a mere child, were attempting to obliterate Yoshinobu's achievements.[18]

Iwakura was not one to take criticism calmly. He demanded to know how Yōdō had the effrontery, at a meeting held in the presence of the emperor, to make such accusations. He asserted that the glorious success of the Restoration was due to the emperor's extraordinary ability and that every single action of that day originated in the emperor's judgments. He declared that Yōdō had been guilty of grave disrespect in suggesting that persons were taking advantage of the youth of the emperor to steal power.[19]

Taken aback by the accusation, Yōdō apologized profusely for his impropriety of speech,[20] but his slip did not immediately cause others to support Iwakura. Matsudaira Yoshinaga (1828–1880), the daimyo of Echizen (who had just been named a *gijō* of the new government), also spoke on behalf of Yoshinobu, invoking the centuries of Tokugawa achievements. Iwakura interrupted Yoshinaga to declare that if Yoshinobu had any sense of responsibility, he would at once resign his rank[21] and return to the government his land and people; this was how he could assist the great achievement of the Restoration and entitle himself to a place in the assembly. When Yoshinobu returned his powers to the government, Iwakura continued, he surrendered no more than an empty name; but there was no indication he would yield his title and land, his real power. Iwakura concluded by asking rhetorically how a man like Yoshinobu could be forgiven and allowed to participate in the deliberations.[22]

Ōkubo Toshimichi was the first to support Iwakura. He urged the court to order Yoshinobu to return his land and people and that if he did not, he should be subjugated. Ōkubo was known for his gravity and taciturnity, but the outrage he felt on hearing the sympathy displayed toward the Restoration's archenemy seems to have inspired fiery eloquence.[23]

Gotō Shōjirō spoke next. He prudently supported Yōdō and Matsudaira Yoshinaga, calling for a fair and just Restoration, which apparently meant lenient treatment of Yoshinobu. Gotō was followed by other speakers: Tokugawa Yoshikatsu, the daimyo of Owari, and Asano Mochikoto, the heir of the daimyo of Aki, both agreed with Yōdō and Yoshinaga, but Shimazu Tadayoshi, the daimyo of Satsuma, supported Ōkubo. At this point Iwakura, noticing that Nakayama Tadayasu had taken aside several nobles and was conferring with them, demanded how they could be whispering in a corner by themselves when they should be devoting every energy to debating the rights and wrongs of the issue before the emperor. The emperor commanded a recess in the session, as the discussion seemed unlikely to end soon.[24]

During the recess Saigō Takamori, who was outside the room, remarked that it would take only one short sword to settle the discussion. His words reached Iwakura's ears[25] and inspired new resolve. He addressed himself to Asano Mochikoto, who, although he had supported Yōdō, seemed to be wavering. Iwakura said that he was ready to deal with Yōdō, even if this meant shedding blood in the presence of the emperor. After promising to support Iwakura, the startled Asano sent a retainer to inform Gotō of Saigō's remark and Iwakura's determination. Gotō, quick to size up the situation, recommended to Yōdō that he yield lest there really be bloodshed, a suggestion that Yōdō had no choice but to follow. Gotō also persuaded Matsudaira Yoshinaga to reconsider. It may be that Gotō's change of heart was inspired by his hopes of obtaining a post in the new government.[26] In any case, when the emperor returned to the hall and the meeting was resumed, everyone was in agreement with Iwakura. Not a single voice was raised against his proposal that Tokugawa Yoshinobu be asked to surrender his rank and his land. The meeting ended at midnight.

Iwakura's success in winning over even those who had spoken most strongly in favor of Tokugawa Yoshinobu bespeaks remarkable diplomatic skill at playing off one man against another. Perhaps the most effective weapon he used against the opposition was his assertion that the emperor had approved of every step Iwakura had taken, including the demand that Yoshinobu relinquish his rank and land. But had Emperor Meiji in fact approved? Or was the claim an invention of Iwakura's, intended to overcome the supporters of Yoshinobu by citing an authority they could not oppose? Surviving documents do not tell us one way or the other. Meiji was certainly young—fifteen years old by Western count—but not so young that he could not have formed political opinions. Kōmei's exasperation with his son may well have been caused by Mutsuhito's anti-shogunate sentiments, instilled in him by his mother's family or by the ladies of the rear palace (*ōoku*). This is only conjecture. The most important fact is that Meiji was present throughout the discussions, and they could not have failed to produce a strong impression.

On January 5, 1868, the day after the momentous meeting, Tokugawa Yoshi-katsu and Matsudaira Yoshinaga, both *gijō* of the new regime, went to Nijō Castle to inform Yoshinobu that his request to resign as shogun had been granted by the emperor and that a private injunction (*naiyu*) had been issued ordering him to surrender his rank and return his land. When their palanquins entered the castle grounds, soldiers loyal to the shogunate surrounded them and screamed insults, calling them lackeys of "Satsuma bandits" and traitors to the cause of Yoshinobu. The two daimyos, paying no attention to the clamor, proceeded directly to Yoshinobu's room and, pushing aside the abusive guards, delivered the message.

Yoshinobu listened in deferential silence and then gave his response in measured terms. He expressed gratitude for the emperor's kindness in granting his request to return the government to the court. He stated also that he personally had no objection to resigning his rank and giving up his land. But if this were announced without preparation, it would cause great consternation among his direct retainers and might well lead to an unfortunate situation. He asked for a delay in responding to the throne. Yoshikatsu and Yoshinaga agreed.[27]

As Yoshinobu predicted, when the soldiers of the shogunate and allied domains in Nijō Castle learned of the latest imperial command, they were enraged and blamed it entirely on Satsuma. An armed conflict seemed likely at any minute. In the hopes of defusing the situation, Yoshinobu left for Ōsaka Castle, taking with him the daimyos of the three domains that backed him most strongly—Aizu, Kuwana, and Bitchū.

At this juncture, when the battle lines between the supporters of the emperor and those of the shogunate had been tightly drawn, a minor incident provided a kind of comic relief. The first anniversary of the death of Emperor Kōmei was approaching, and suitable observances were necessary. However, the finance magistrate reported, the court had insufficient funds for the purpose. Iwakura thereupon suggested that the best plan was to ask Minister of the Interior (naidaijin) Tokugawa Yoshinobu to supply the money. The magistrate accordingly went to Ōsaka Castle and, explaining the situation to Yoshinobu, requested a gift of a couple of million ryō.

He could not have come at a worse moment. Yoshinobu was reluctant to give money (which he could ill afford) at a time when people inside the castle were seething with fury against the advocates of rule by the emperor; but the magistrate pleaded so eloquently that in the end Yoshinobu directed the finance magistrate to give 1,000 ryō and promised that the local governor in Kyōto would supply additional funds. The memorial ceremonies took place on January 27, 1868, four days before warfare broke out between shogun and court, with money from an enemy of the court.

On January 14, when Yoshinobu granted an audience in Ōsaka Castle to the ministers of England, France, Italy, America, Prussia, and Holland, he informed them of the changes in the government but insisted that he was still in charge of all dealings with foreign countries because the new government was not yet ready to handle such matters.[28] Three days later, Yoshinobu announced that he would not be bound by the proclamation of the Restoration and called for the court to rescind it. In a message sent to the sōsai Prince Taruhito, Yoshinobu stated his objections. He had asked to return the political powers he had received from his ancestors, deferring to public opinion, because he hoped to establish a government in accord with the principles of peace and justice, but to his astonishment, armed men from a few domains had suddenly intruded into the imperial palace and, with the collaboration of nobles who had been disgraced during the previous reign,[29] were attempting to carry out unprecedented changes that threatened to corrupt usages of the court dating back thousands of years. He continued, "Even supposing these changes originate with the emperor, is it not our duty as loyal subjects to remonstrate with him? It must be said, moreover, that the signs of disorder in the country have their origins in the youth of the present emperor. This is especially the case in foreign relations: if they twist the wishes of the emperor and deal with foreign countries on the basis of temporary expedients, they will lose the trust of other countries and do great harm to the imperial land."[30]

Up to this point Tokugawa Yoshinobu had behaved like a dutiful subject, accepting without question edicts from the emperor, but now he seemed to be anticipating the outbreak of warfare between his forces and those professing loyalty to imperial rule. He justified his refusal to comply with the proclamation of the Restoration in terms of the traditional Confucian duty of a subject to remonstrate with his lord when he believed the lord had been led astray by evil or ambitious advisers. This would be his stance during the ensuing Boshin war.[31]

The outbreak of fighting between the forces of the shogunate and those of the emperor was precipitated by a series of incidents of arson and looting in and around Edo, committed by *rōnin* acting under direction from Saigō Takamori.[32] It is assumed that the Satsuma leaders—Saigō and Ōkubo—were deliberately trying to provoke the shogunate into committing some act that would give them an excuse for opening hostilities against the shogunate. But although these incidents aroused anger, the crucial provocation occurred quite by chance: on January 18 the outworks of Edo Castle burned, and the shogunate blamed this on Satsuma *rōnin*.[33] On the same day, Satsuma *rōnin* opened fire on the office of the Shōnai domain, which was entrusted with policing the city. Two days later, shogunate troops surrounded the Satsuma residence in Edo and demanded that the *rōnin* responsible for various unruly incidents be turned over. When this was refused, shogunate troops opened fire, and in the ensuing exchange of gunfire, men on both sides were killed. Finally the shogunate troops set fire to the residence and burned it to the ground.

Word of this action took three days to reach Kyōto. In the meantime, on December 28, 1867, the emperor reviewed a military drill by some 2,000 soldiers of the Satsuma, Chōshū, Aki, and Tosa domains. The purpose of the review may have been to rouse the troops' fighting spirit by the emperor's proximity or, conversely, it may have been to inculcate the young emperor with a martial spirit. (He rode a horse for the first time this year.) Satsuma troops dominated not only in numbers (making up 1,500 of the 2,000 soldiers) but also in their equipment, notably their British uniforms and caps.[34] When the review was over, the emperor offered gifts to the unit commanders and saké to the ordinary soldiers.

Word of the clash in Edo reached Ōsaka Castle on the following day, just after Tokugawa Yoshinobu had finished writing a letter accepting the demands that he return his position and land to the emperor's government.[35] Soldiers in the castle were enraged by the news, and Yoshinobu, carried away by their anger, changed his mind and decided to send shogunate troops against Kyōto on the first day of the lunar new year (January 25).

The shogunate army outnumbered by three times the 5,000 men of the Satsuma, Chōshū, and allied domains. It is true that some of the shogunate troops were mercenaries, but others had been drilled by French instructors and were equipped with modern weapons. When Saigō learned about a clash between the shogunate and the imperial armies at Toba (between Ōsaka and Kyōto), he is reported to have exclaimed, "One burst of gunfire at Toba makes me happier than getting a million allies."[36] He must nevertheless have felt considerable apprehension over the outcome of the battle. Even before the fighting started, he composed a memorandum concerning the safety of the emperor in the event that Kyōto was immediately threatened.[37] The emperor, disguised as a court lady and accompanied in a court lady's palanquin by the dowager empress, was to be escorted by Satsuma and Chōshū soldiers to a safe place in either Aki or Bingo.[38] It is hard to imagine that even a wig and a heavy application of cosmetics would have made the resolutely masculine face of Emperor Meiji resemble a woman's, but escaping in feminine disguise was a tradition.[39]

The fighting began on January 27, 1868. Forces of the Aizu and Kuwana domains advancing on Kyōto by way of Toba and Fushimi were met there by imperial troops, mainly from Satsuma. The leader of the shogunate army's advance party declared that by command of the former shogun, he and his men were on their way to Kyōto. If any attempt were made to stop them, they would respond with force. The Satsuma troops' reply was a burst of cannon and rifle fire. According to some accounts, one Satsuma shell hit a gun carriage near where the shogunate army commander, Takigawa Tomotaka, was mounted on a horse. The startled horse bolted, threw Takigawa, and ran wild along the Toba highway. A column of shogunate troops strung out along the highway was thrown into a state of panic by the sudden burst of fire and the wild horse, a bad beginning for their offensive.[40]

The bolting of the horse was an accident, but the imperial forces were also helped by a secret weapon, the brocade pennant carried by imperial forces when doing battle with traitors. On October 10, 1867, Ōkubo Toshimichi and Shinagawa Yajirō (1843–1900, a Chōshū leader) visited Iwakura Tomomi at his place of exile to discuss the stratagem of restoring imperial rule. Iwakura showed the others the design of a pennant conceived of by his "brain" Tamamatsu Misao, and asked them to have some made. In Kyōto, Ōkubo bought red and white damask, which Shinagawa took to Yamaguchi to be made into pennants. Half the pennants were kept in Yamaguchi; the other half, at the Satsuma residence in Kyōto.[41]

On January 28 the emperor bestowed on Yoshiaki, the prince of the Ninna-ji, a brocade pennant and the settō[42] as a sign that he had been appointed as "great general, conqueror of the east."[43] Those opposing Prince Yoshiaki's forces were condemned not merely as enemies but specifically as "enemies of the court"(chōteki). Although Tokugawa Yoshinobu had been at pains to insist that he was fighting not the court but Satsuma, the brocade pennant gave the Satsuma troops the status of authorized defenders of the emperor. The brocade pennant was a powerful factor in the defeat of the ex-shogun's army, for it not only bolstered the morale of the Satsuma forces but also made the shogunate army hesitate over the propriety of attacking the emperor's forces.[44]

Prince Yoshiaki was a strange choice as the commanding general.[45] Apart from his lineage as a member of the imperial family, he had no qualifications for the post. He entered the Ninna-ji in 1858 as a boy of twelve, and neither while at the temple nor afterward did he receive military training. His position of commanding general was undoubtedly symbolic, real command being left to men like Saigō Takamori, an eager participant in battle.[46] Perhaps it did not make much difference who was in command—warfare in Japan still retained many of the medieval traditions of individual combat.

Regardless of who deserves credit for the victory at Toba, it was decisive. The shogunate army fled the field. They sought to regroup at Yodo Castle, the stronghold of a member of the Council of Elders, only to be refused admission, to their intense surprise and consternation. This betrayal by forces presumed to be loyal to the shogun was only the first. The second came two days later when the Tsu domain, assigned to guard the Yamazaki area, the gateway to Ōsaka, turned its guns on the shogunate forces. On the previous day a messenger from the court (with the help of the brocade pennant) had persuaded the domain to desert the shogun and offer its allegiance to the court.[47]

On the evening after this disaster Yoshinobu gathered advisers and military leaders in Ōsaka Castle to plan strategy. Voices were raised asking Yoshinobu to raise morale by assuming personal command of the shogunate forces. He agreed, much to the delight of all present. That night he slipped out of Ōsaka Castle, planning to board the shogunate warship *Kaiyō maru*. The ship had not arrived, and while waiting, he went aboard the American warship *Iroquois*.[48] He sailed for Edo the next morning on the *Kaiyō maru*, taking with him only a few high officials. When the remnants of the shogunate army learned the next morning that Yoshinobu had escaped, they abandoned Ōsaka Castle and fled. Yoshinobu later said that he had never intended to take arms against the court, that once the brocade pennant appeared, he lost all desire to fight.[49]

The war had not ended, but the victory of the imperial forces at Toba meant that they now controlled all of western and southern Japan. Although they still had to gain control of Edo and the northern regions, the emperor's regime had scored a major success.

Chapter 15

On February 9, 1868, just a week after the capture of Ōsaka Castle, Emperor Meiji finally had his *gembuku* ceremony. In honor of this event, an amnesty was proclaimed, and nineteen nobles who for various offenses had been forbidden to attend court were pardoned. It was on this occasion that the imperial message was delivered to the ministers of six countries, informing them that the emperor would henceforward exercise supreme authority in both the internal and external affairs of the country.

Behind the stiff, formal language and the insistence on the emperor's new authority, the message contained the implication that although his father had bitterly opposed the treaties that the shogun signed with the foreign powers, the present emperor recognized their validity. It was an indirect admission by the court that relations with foreign countries were inevitable and a recognition that it was desirable for them to be friendly.[1]

After the emperor's envoy, Higashikuze Michitomi, had shown to all the ministers the translation of the emperor's message, "a fire of questions was directed against the envoy, who answered them well."[2] The atmosphere was surprisingly like that of a modern press conference. The questions from Léon Roches, the French minister, revealed that he was still committed to supporting the shogun, but the other ministers merely promised to report the message to their governments.

On the same day a public proclamation was issued notifying the people that conditions had changed so greatly that friendly relations with foreign countries, the cause of so much grief to the previous emperor, had now been approved. The people were enjoined to do their best to accord with the emperor's wishes, a warning that incidents of violence against foreigners would not be tolerated. In addition, in order to increase respect for Japan abroad, military preparations would be speeded up, and inequalities in the treaties would be revised in accordance with international law.[3]

During the pause before the war against the shogunate army was resumed, this time east of the barrier of Hakone, Princess Chikako, the former Kazuno-miya, sent a messenger to the commander of the eastern sea circuit, Hashimoto Saneyana (a relative on her mother's side), asking that the Tokugawa family be spared the stigma of being called "enemies of the court" (*chōteki*). She pointed out that the outbreak of war had been completely unforeseen by Yoshinobu and that he had returned to Edo once he had been branded as a *chōteki*. In view of his mistakes, probably nothing could be done for him, but she begged that out of pity for her the Tokugawa family be spared the label of enemies of the court. If the imperial army crushed the Tokugawa family, she doubtless would kill herself. Her life meant nothing to her, but the thought of dying together with *chōteki* was too painful to bear. She implored the court to grant her plea.[4] She now had come to identify herself with the Tokugawa family.

A request from Princess Chikako could not be totally ignored, but it had little effect in Kyōto. Various daimyos asked that Yoshinobu be forgiven, providing he made a formal apology. This course was favored by Iwakura, who sent an envoy to Edo urging Yoshinobu to agree. But the answer, which struck Iwakura as lacking in sincerity, set him on a course of uncompromising opposition to the former shogun. By this time tens of thousands of Satsuma and Chōshū soldiers were pressing on Edo Castle from land and sea.

Yoshinobu himself vacillated between submission to the imperial army and a policy of resistance to the end. On February 9 he sent a letter to Sir Harry Parkes, the British minister, announcing that the Tokugawa regime was still in control of foreign relations. He declared that Parkes would be violating the treaties if he met with a representative of the imperial government. Two days after asserting his authority in this manner, Yoshinobu dismissed Oguri Tada-masa, the most uncompromising advocate of resistance among his advisers, suggesting that he was ready to seek peace. On February 11 Yoshinobu sent a letter to Matsudaira Yoshinaga and Yamauchi Yōdō, the two members of the imperial government most disposed to show him leniency, insisting that the fighting at Toba and Fushimi had occurred without his permission. He expressed bewilderment as to why he was being pursued and asked them to intercede on his behalf.[5]

On February 13 Yoshinobu had the first of three meetings in Edo Castle with Roches. The French minister still supported the Tokugawa government and believed that despite the setback at Toba and Fushimi, it would eventually be victorious. Yoshinobu informed Roches that he would do everything in his power to keep the Tokugawa family's ancestral lands. He asserted that the emperor was now a prisoner, unable to do anything of his own volition, that the so-called imperial government was actually in the hands of Satsuma and Chōshū.

At their second meeting Yoshinobu declared his intention of retiring from active life and of yielding his position to Tokugawa Mochitsugu, the daimyo of Kishū. On February 15 Yoshinobu again wrote to Yoshinaga and Yōdō, this time informing them (as he had informed Roches) that he intended to retire, both because he had been stigmatized as a *chōteki* and because he was in poor health. He asked the two daimyos to clear his name of the charge of being an enemy of the court.

On February 23 Yoshinobu had his final meeting with Roches. He gave Roches a statement of his position, defending his actions since returning power to the emperor. He insisted that he had intended not only to observe the treaties with the various governments but also to "improve" them, suggesting that when revised, the treaties would be even more advantageous to foreign countries. Perhaps he planned to authorize the introduction of Christianity.[6] However, Yoshinobu added, there was a limit to what he could endure, and he appealed to the foreign countries for their understanding. This may have been an indirect way of saying that although he would compromise on many issues, he would not tolerate intrusion into his domains. Yoshinobu's statement could not have surprised Roches, as he had prepared the rough draft.

Roches, alone among the foreign diplomats, clung to the judgment that a stable government under the tycoon offered the best possibility for trade with the West. Parkes, much quicker to realize that the imperial regime in Kyōto would eventually become the government of the whole country, wrote off Yoshinobu as a failure who was now no more than the ruler of a single domain.[7] On March 4 Yoshinobu left Edo Castle to enter a life of seclusion at the Daiji-in, a subtemple of the Kan'ei-ji in Ueno. He stated that he would henceforth give himself exclusively to submission and penance. He took full responsibility for having incurred the emperor's wrath and said he was prepared to accept divine punishment. His only request was that the priest Prince Kōgen come to Edo and pray for his salvation.[8] Kōgen, until this time an obscure priest whose only distinction was that he was a member of the imperial family, would before long emerge as a rival for the throne of Emperor Meiji.

While Yoshinobu was vacillating over the proper course of action, dissension of another kind arose within the government in Kyōto concerning the future site of the capital. Ōkubo Toshimichi proposed that the capital be moved to Ōsaka. Moving the capital would be a sign that the ways of the old regime, associated with the Kyōto nobility, had been rejected in favor of a new and enlightened government. Ōsaka was well suited to commerce with foreign countries, and this would promote a "rich country and strong army" (*fukoku kyōhei*). Most important, moving the emperor from the Gosho would end the isolation from his people. He would, like monarchs abroad, mingle with the common people in the new capital, accompanied by a mere one or two attendants.[9]

When Ōkubo's plan was brought before the Court Council on February 17, it was vociferously attacked by the nobles, including the *gijō* Nakayama Tada-yasu, the grandfather of the emperor, as a plot by the Satsuma and Chōshū domains to reap private benefits. A more important reason for the nobles' opposition was doubtless their attachment to Kyōto, the focal point of their whole lives.[10]

Although Ōkubo's plan for moving the capital was not immediately approved, his earnest plea, made at the same time, that the emperor leave the enclosure of the Gosho and take personal command of the punitive force to be sent to the east did not go unheeded. On February 25 the emperor left the Gosho for the first time since he was a small child. He visited Nijō Castle, formerly the symbol of shogunate power in the capital, traveling in the *sōkaren* (the informal palanquin used by the emperor) and carrying with him the sword and jewel of his office. On his arrival he was met by the president (*sōsai*) Prince Taruhito. He then went to the Hall of Audiences in the keep of the castle where he took his place on the upper level (*dan*) behind bamboo blinds. The *sōsai*, *gijō*, and senior counselors (*san'yo*) sat on the middle level, and the junior counselors and others below. A discussion ensued on the advisability of the emperor's taking personal command of the campaign against the rebels and on the establishment of the position of a supreme commander. When the discussion had ended, the *sōsai* was called behind the blinds, and the emperor spoke this command: "Yoshinobu and his rebel underlings have now fled to Edo Castle, where they are abandoning themselves to greater and greater outrages. His Majesty cannot endure a situation in which the seas to the four directions boil over and the people are about to fall into misery. He has decided in his wisdom to assume personal command of the expedition. You should be aware in this connection that he intends to choose a suitable person to serve as supreme commander. All military forces of the great and small domains in the home provinces and the seven circuits should accordingly make preparations. Within a few days His Majesty will take council on the war and issue his commands. When the various units receive orders, they are to assemble at once. He commands the various units to join forces and strive to achieve victory in loyal battle."[11]

Prince Taruhito was appointed as supreme commander on March 1 and received a brocade pennant, to be guarded by two platoons of soldiers from Tsuwano. He was a relative by marriage of Tokugawa Yoshinobu and, for this reason, had especially asked to be placed in command of the punitive expedition. He took formal leave of the emperor on March 7.

Detailed instructions concerning the conduct of the army were issued by Prince Taruhito. They include such provisions as an insistence that all in the army receive the same treatment, regardless of rank or birth and that damaging shrines and temples, setting fire to civilian houses, stealing property, and selling coercively were strictly prohibited. When foreigners were caught committing acts of disorder or disrespect, they were to be arrested and their guilt established before being turned over to the ministers of their country for examination; they must not be shot or slashed to death, nor should their houses be entered without good reason. The intent of these provisions was obviously to convince the world that the imperial army was operating in accordance with internationally recognized codes of warfare and was by no means a band of ruffians killing and looting as they moved across the country.

The court's desire for improved relations with foreigners is apparent also in its decision to permit foreign ministers to be presented to the emperor. There was strong opposition, particularly by the denizens of the imperial palace. Matsudaira Yoshinaga and Iwakura Tomomi appeared before the emperor to explain that it was a principle observed in all countries that the monarch give audiences to the ministers of foreign countries. On March 9 an announcement was made that the emperor would permit the ministers of foreign countries to come into his presence. It was further explained that the unusually prompt proclamation of the emperor's decision was necessitated by his imminent departure to lead the expeditionary army.[12] Meiji's willingness to meet foreigners indicates that he had not been infected by the hatred of foreigners that had plagued his father.

Following the emperor's proclamation, a memorandum was prepared justifying the decision to grant audiences to foreign ministers by citing instances from ancient Japanese history of emperors who had accorded such audiences. These instances, though of shaky historical authenticity, were cited because of the great importance that the Japanese court always attached to precedents. The memorandum admitted that there was no precedent for the emperor's meeting foreigners from countries other than China and Korea but blamed this on the slow development in Japan of the art of navigation. Now, however, the country was in contact with the whole world, and a failure to observe practices common to all countries would result in a loss of trust in Japan. Compromise was thus necessary in the interests of international relations.[13]

As a first step in improving relations with the foreigners, they were allowed to visit the city of Kyōto. Sir Ernest Satow gave a cheerful account of sightseeing in the old capital and expressed the hope that the foreign ministers could henceforth reside in that city (despite its climate) rather than in Edo, "for it was naturally supposed that the government of the country would in future be conducted from Kiōto."[14]

Just at this juncture a grave incident of antiforeign character occurred in Sakai. Eleven French sailors, members of the crew of the *Dupleix*, were killed by Tosa men. According to Japanese accounts, they (and six companions) were wandering through the streets of Sakai in a disorderly manner when they were attacked by the Tosa samurai, who were fulfilling their duty of maintaining order. Satow's account was quite different: "These Japanese massacred a boat's crew of inoffensive and unarmed men, who were never alleged to have given the slightest provocation." The French minister, Léon Roches, at once sent a message demanding the heads of the Tosa samurai responsible for the incident; 150,000 dollars for the families of the dead sailors; the apology of Prince Yamashina, the foreign minister; the apology of Yamauchi Yōdō, the daimyo of Tosa; and the exclusion of armed Tosa samurai from the treaty ports.[15] The Japanese agreed to all these conditions.

Twenty Tosa men were found guilty of having killed the French sailors and were condemned to kill themselves. After eleven had committed *seppuku*, the French ship's captain witnessing this display of samurai fortitude raised his hand to stop the proceedings, and Roches asked that the lives of the remaining nine men be spared. Satow regretted this action: "One could only regret that Captain du Petit Thouars judged it necessary to stop the execution when eleven had suffered, for the twenty were all equally guilty, and requiring a life for life of the eleven Frenchmen looked more like revenge than justice."[16]

Satow had previously witnessed the *seppuku*[17] of a condemned officer of the Bizen domain[18] and been impressed by the dignity of this form of punishment. He seems not to have found it horrible that eleven men had slit open their abdomens and then had their heads cut off, perhaps because at the time public executions not only were common in Europe but were performed in a carnival-like atmosphere. He wrote,

> As for being ashamed of having been present at a *harakiri* on the ground that it was a disgusting exhibition, I was proud to feel that I had not shrunk from witnessing a punishment which I did my best to bring about. It was no disgusting exhibition, but a most decent and decorous ceremony, and far more respectable than what our own countrymen were in the habit of producing for the entertainment of the public in the front of Newgate prison.[19]

On March 23 the French minister, Roches, and the Dutch political agent, Dirk de Graeff van Polsbroek, were granted an audience by Emperor Meiji.[20] About two in the afternoon, the emperor, dressed in an informal robe and carrying the imperial sword and jewel, appeared in the Hall of State Ceremonies and seated himself behind his screen of state. Assistant President Sanjō Sanetomi and Adviser to the Throne Nakayama Tadayasu stood beside him inside the screen; Foreign Minister Prince Akira[21] and Assistant President Iwakura Tomomi stood outside the screen, with lesser officials to the right and left. The vice minister for foreign affairs, Higashikuze Michitomi, led the French minister into the imperial presence, where he bowed. The voice of the emperor could be heard: "We are pleased to learn that the emperor of your country is well. We hope that the relations between our two countries in the future will be ever more cordial, lasting and unchanging."[22]

Roches's reply was considerably longer, concluding with the prayer which he made on behalf of Napoleon III for the prosperity of Japan and for divine protection of the emperor himself. When this ended, the French minister left and the Dutch minister was led before the emperor, who vouchsafed virtually the same words he had pronounced to Roches. Afterward the two envoys were offered tea and cakes. The English minister was to have had an audience immediately afterward. He had already left the Chion-in, the temple where he and his party were staying, and was proceeding on horseback toward the palace, escorted by both English and Japanese, the latter including Nakai Hiroshi (1838–1894) and Gotō Shōjirō. When the procession reached the corner of Shinmonzen and Nawate, two men

sprang out from opposite sides of the street, drew their swords, and attacked the men and horses, running down the line and hacking wildly. Nakai observing what was passing jumped down from his pony and engaged the fellow on his right, with whom he had a pretty tough fight. In the struggle his feet got entangled in his long loose trousers, and he fell on his back. His enemy tried to cut off his head, but Nakai parried the blow, receiving only a scalp wounds, and pierced the man's breast at the same time. This sickened him, and as he was turning his back on Nakai he received a blow on the shoulder from Gotō's sword, which prostrated him to the ground, and Nakai jumping up hacked off his head.[23]

The other assailant, after slashing many other Englishmen, charged at Satow, wounding his horse. After this narrow escape, Satow moved up to the head of the procession to protect the minister. He saw "Sir Harry Parkes, in his brilliant uniform of an Envoy and minister calmly sitting on his horse in the middle of the cross-roads." The second assailant was soon captured. "Assisted by a retainer of Sanjō's we examined him. He expressed great penitence, and asked that his head might be cut off and exposed publicly to inform the Japanese nation of his crime."[24] He insisted that they had no accomplices (although three men were later exiled as such). Many in the capital sympathized with the attackers, sharing their belief that if foreigners were admitted into the palace, it would fatally weaken the Land of the Gods and that if foreigners were allowed to see the emperor's face, it would be a desecration of the imperial majesty.[25]

When the emperor learned of the attack on Parkes, he expressed profound regret, and members of his government rushed to Parkes's side. He responded to their expressions of sympathy, saying that "a graver outrage had been committed upon the Mikado than upon himself, and he felt assured that the government would know how to vindicate the honour of their sovereign."[26] So many of Parkes's escort had been severely wounded in the attack that it was not possible to appear before the emperor that day. The Chion-in

> was turned into a hospital. Our wounded men, bleeding as if their life must ebb out, lay patiently in the verandah, waiting their turn for the assistance of the surgeons, who, stripped to their shirts, seemed almost to multiply themselves, so swift and skilful were they. Shirts and sheets were being torn up into bandages, buckets of bloody water were being emptied and filled again. Everything one touched was sickening, wet, and red. It was a nightmare. Presently the head of the man whom Nakai had killed was brought in—a terrible sight.[27]

The delayed audience of Parkes and A. B. Mitford, the junior interpreter,[28] with the emperor took place on April 14. Mitford wrote, "Our own retinue was sadly reduced. Our mounted escort could only muster two men, who with drawn swords rode on either side of Sir Harry." When the Englishmen reached the Gosho, they were surprised that it was not even fortified and that it was surrounded by plain whitewashed walls, but Mitford commented, "Still, in spite of its studied plainness, the Gosho was not without a certain grandeur of its own."[29]

When Parkes and Mitford were ushered into the Presence Chamber, they saw Emperor Meiji, probably the first foreigners ever to glimpse a Japanese emperor:

> In the centre was a canopy supported by four slender pillars of black lacquer draped with white silk, into which was woven a pattern in red and black. . . . Under the canopy was the young Mikado, seated in, or rather, leaning against, a high chair. Behind him knelt two Princes of the blood, ready to prompt him. . . .
> As we entered the room the Son of Heaven rose and acknowledged our bows. He was at that time a tall youth with a bright eye and clear complexion; his demeanour was very dignified, well becoming the heir of a dynasty many centuries older than any other sovereignty on the face of the globe. He was dressed in a white coat with long padded trousers of crimson silk trailing like a lady's court-train. His head-dress was the same as that of his courtiers, though as a rule it was surmounted by a long, stiff, flat plume of black gauze. I call it a plume for want of a better word, but there was nothing feathery about it. His eyebrows were shaved off and painted in high up on the forehead; his cheeks were rouged and his lips painted with red and gold. His teeth were blackened. It was no small feat to look dignified under such a travesty of nature; but the *sangre Azul*[30] would not be denied. It was not long, I may add, before the young sov-

ereign cast adrift all these worn-out fashions and trammels of past ages, together with much else that was out of date.[31]

The emperor's greeting to the English was more or less the same as that to the French and Dutch ministers, but he added his regret that an "unfortunate affair" had occurred while they were on their way to the palace three days earlier. Parkes gallantly replied that the emperor's gracious words had caused him to forget the unfortunate incident completely.[32] Mitford later wrote that the emperor, "because of his extreme youth and the novelty of the situation to one who had only recently left the women's apartments," showed symptoms of shyness. "He hardly spoke above a whisper, so the words were repeated aloud by the Prince of the Blood on his right side and translated by Itō Shunsuke."[33]

Three days after Parkes and Mitford were presented to the emperor, the first clash occurred between the imperial forces advancing on Edo and the Shin-sengumi, a band of some 200 men under the command of Kondō Isami (1834–1868). The imperial forces under Itagaki Taisuke were victorious.[34] Perhaps the most memorable thing about the march of the imperial troops to Edo was the song they sang, "Tokoton'yare," composed by Shinagawa Yajirō (1843–1900) during the battles at Toba and Fushimi.[35] This song spread not only throughout Japan but also to England, where the music and part of the Japanese words were incorporated into the operetta *The Mikado*, composed in 1885: *Miyasama, miyasama, ouma no mae no, pira pira suru no wa nan jai na, tokoton'yare ton'yarena. Arya chōteki seibatsu seyo to no nishiki no mihata ja shiranka, tokoton'yare ton'yare na.*[36]

Chapter 16

The young emperor's first act of major historical significance was undoubtedly the promulgation of the Charter Oath in Five Articles on April 7, 1868. The swearing of this oath before the gods of heaven and earth, in the presence of "the hundred officials" including nobles and daimyos, was preceded a day earlier by an edict that announced the renewal of various ceremonies of Shintō worship after the extremely long hiatus imposed by the military regime. The stated purpose of the edict was to revive the union of rites and rule that had existed in ancient times.[1]

A central element in the plan of restoration was the reestablishment of the Jingikan, the Ministry of Shintō. It had originally been established at the beginning of the eighth century, but for centuries had possessed little more than vestigial significance. Now, however, Shintō priests and the performance of Shintō ceremonies at the court and at shrines were to be placed under its supervision, and the priests were to resume functions that had long been left to surrogates. The renewed importance of the Shintō priesthood and the insistence on separating Shintō from Buddhism were made more explicit four days later when Shintō priests who served concomitantly as Buddhist priests were ordered to yield their Buddhist ranks and positions, give up their Buddhist robes, and let their hair grow out.[2]

For more than a thousand years, most Japanese had believed simultaneously in both Shintō and Buddhism despite the inherent contradictions between the two religions. For example, according to Shintō belief, the present world is lovely and a source of joy, but *yomi*, the world after death, is a place of foulness and corruption. According to Buddhist texts, on the contrary, this world (*shaba*) is a place of trial and suffering, but one's actions in this life can enable one to enjoy after death the joys of paradise. These and other fundamental differences were generally minimized by those who discussed religious matters. Instead, the doctrine of *honji suijaku*, which explained the Shintō divinities as avatars in Japan of the eternal Buddhist divinities, was widely accepted.[3] In keeping with the projected return to the system of religion and government that had prevailed in the time of Jimmu, the first emperor, Buddhism, a foreign religion, was now rejected and even persecuted.[4]

Even during the long period when Buddhism played a far more prominent role in the state and emperors regularly entered Buddhist orders and were known posthumously by their "temple names" (*in*), Shintō was never neglected by the imperial family. The most important rites performed by the emperor were those of Shintō, beginning each year with *shihōhai*, the ceremony of worship of the four directions, carried out at four o'clock on the morning of New Year's Day. The emperor prayed to the star under which he was born, to the gods of heaven and earth of the four directions, and to the tombs of his father and mother for abundant crops, a long reign, and peace in the realm— all benefits in this world, in keeping with Shintō's this-worldly outlook. Mention of the star under which the emperor was born was an indication that the Shintō rituals had been greatly influenced by Taoism. The court was dependent on *on'yōji*, priests of yin and yang, for predictions by divination of good or bad fortune. No action of consequence was undertaken in the palace without consulting an *on'yōji*.

Japanese religious life at the commencement of the Meiji era included elements of Shintō, Buddhist, Taoist, and other beliefs as well as what might be called superstitions. The decision to accord special importance to Shintō, and especially to the Jingikan, was, of course, closely connected with the enhanced importance of the emperor, who, according to Shintō belief, stood at the apex of the world.

The ritual accompanying the emperor's pronouncement of the Charter Oath was entirely Shintō. The ceremonies began that day in the Hall of State Ceremonies with the gathering of nobles, daimyos, and lesser officials, all dressed in court robes, making a dazzling sight in their different colors. The ceremonies proper opened with the sprinkling of salt water and scattering of rice, by way of purification. Next the head of the Office of Shintō Worship, Shirakawa Sukenori, sang *kamiuta* (god-songs) for the descending god. After the offering to the gods had been made, the emperor, attired in informal robes and accompanied by the two assistant presidents (Sanjō Sanetomi and Iwakura Tomomi), the two ministers of state (Nakayama Tadayasu and Ōgimachisanjō Sanenaru), and various other dignitaries, entered and took his place on the throne. It faced south,[5] with the *shinza* (seat of the gods) diagonally to the right. Screens depicting the four seasons were placed around the throne.

Sanjō read aloud a Shintō prayer, beginning with an invocation to the gods of heaven and earth.[6] After Sanjō had finished, the emperor advanced to the anise bush before the altar, bowed in prayer, and made an offering of white and red cloth on sprigs of sacred wood. Sanjō then read aloud the emperor's Oath in Five Articles:

> Deliberate assemblies shall be widely established and all matters decided by public discussion.
>
> All classes, high and low, shall unite in vigorously carrying out the administration of affairs of state.
>
> The common people, no less than the civil and military officials, shall each be allowed to pursue his own calling so that there may be no discontent.
>
> Evil customs of the past shall be broken off and everything based on the just laws of nature.
>
> Knowledge shall be sought throughout the world so as to strengthen the foundations of imperial rule.

It is well known that the text of this oath was not composed by Meiji himself, but by two samurai-scholars, Yuri Kimimasa (1829–1909) and Fukuoka Takachika (1835–1919), and then revised by Kido Takayoshi.[7] Its significance has been discounted by some scholars who contend that the seemingly liberal ideals expressed in the articles masked the real intent of the oath, which was to win the country's support before the attack on Edo Castle, scheduled for the following day.[8]

It would be a mistake to suppose that the five articles of the oath signified an intention by the leaders of the government to create a parliamentary democracy in the near future. But whether or not the oath was genuinely progressive, the language was unprecedented in Japan or, indeed, any other country in the orbit of Chinese civilization. Deciding "all matters by public discussion" was definitely not traditional, nor had the administration of affairs of state been considered to be a privilege shared by the lower classes — regardless of how one defines "lower classes." The fourth article — "Evil customs of the past shall be broken off and everything based on the just laws of nature" — is admittedly vague and subject to conflicting interpretation; but the customs of the past were normally praised and contrasted with the degenerate ways of the present, not characterized as "evil." The last article, stating that knowledge should be sought throughout the world, seemed even to contradict the basic concept of "restoration," which looked back to Japan's own past, rather than to the rest of the world, for guidance. In later times the principles enunciated in the five articles were qualified, watered down, and sometimes ignored, but they were never repudiated, and they survived as ideals for those who hoped to make Japan into an enlightened modern state.[9]

After the reading of the oath, the nobles, daimyos, and others present all signed their names to a document expressing profound admiration for the provisions of the Charter Oath. They swore to obey the emperor's wishes even at the cost of their lives and begged the emperor to take comfort from their determination to do their utmost to implement the oath. Nobles and daimyos who were unable to be present on this occasion visited the court afterward to sign their names, a total of 767 persons.[10]

What impression did this ceremony have on the emperor himself? If he expressed his opinions to those around him, they have been lost. It is likely that owing to his youth, he was not consulted in the preparation of the text. Conceivably, he first learned the contents of the five articles when he heard them read aloud by Sanjō Sanetomi; but it is hard to imagine that the ceremony— the most impressive of his reign up to this point—and the reading of the Charter Oath failed to move him. The idealism embodied in the articles may well have affected him precisely because he was young and inexperienced. Certainly during the early part of his reign, he showed himself to be sympathetic to the tenor of the oath he had sworn to observe.

On the same day as the Charter Oath was promulgated, a letter written in the name of the emperor was made public. The letter described the great achievements of his ancestors, contained words of comfort for his people, and promised to exalt the nation's prestige in the eyes of foreign countries:

> Ever since, quite unexpectedly, We succeeded to the throne, young and weak though We are, We have been unable to control Our apprehension, day and night, over how We are to remain faithful to Our ancestors when dealing with foreign countries. It is Our belief that when the authority of the court declined in the middle ages and the military seized power, they maintained on the surface worshipful respect of the court, but in reality their respect intentionally isolated the court, making it impossible for the court, as the father and mother of the entire people, to know the people's feelings. In the end, the emperor became the sovereign of the multitude in name only. That is how it happens that although awe of the court today is greater than ever before, the prestige of the court has diminished correspondingly, and the separation between those above and those below is as great as that between heaven and earth. Under these conditions, how are We to reign over the country? Now, at a time of renovation of rule of the country, if even one of the millions of people in this country is unable to find his place in society, this will be entirely Our fault. Accordingly, We have personally exerted Our physical and spiritual powers to confront the crisis. It is only by stepping into the shoes Our ancestors wore in

ancient times and throwing Ourself into governing the country that We fulfill Our Heaven-sent mission and do not violate Our duty as the ruler of the hundred millions.

In ancient times Our ancestors personally disposed of all state affairs. If anyone behaved in a manner inappropriate in a subject, they themselves would punish the guilty. The administration of the court was simple in every respect, and because the emperor was not held in awe, as he is today, emperor and subjects were close; those above and those below loved each other; the blessings of heaven pervaded the land; and the majesty of the country shone brightly abroad. In recent times the world has become much more civilized. At a time when every other country is progressing in all directions, only our country, being unfamiliar with the situation prevailing in the world, stubbornly maintains old customs and does not seek the fruits of change. It fills Us with dread to think that if We were idly to spend a peaceful existence in the palace, enjoying the tranquillity of each day and forgetful of the hundred years of griefs, Our country would in the end be subject to the contempt of all others, bringing shame to Our ancestors and hardship to the people. For this reason We have sworn, along with many officials and daimyos, to continue the glorious work of Our ancestors. Regardless of the pain and suffering it may entail, We intend personally to rule over the entire country, to comfort you, the numberless people, and in the end to open up the ten thousand leagues of ocean waves, to proclaim the glory of our country to the world and bring to the land the unshakable security of Mount Fuji. You of countless numbers have become accustomed to the evils inherited from the past and to think of the court only as a place to held in awe. Not knowing the acute danger threatening the Land of the Gods, you manifest extreme surprise when We bestir Us, and this has given rise to doubts of every kind. The people are confused, but if a time should come when they prevent Us from carrying out Our plans, this would mean not only that We had wandered from the Way of the ruler but that they had caused Us to lose Our ancestral patrimony. You of countless numbers give due consideration to Our aspirations and join with Us. Cast away private thoughts and choose the general good. Help Us in Our work and ensure the safety of the Land of the Gods. If We can comfort the spirits of my ancestors, this will be the greatest happiness of Our life.[11]

The letter is of special interest because it is so unlike anything Kōmei or any earlier emperor would have written. The main point seems to be the emperor's desire for closer contact between himself and his people. He blames the military for having created an aura of awe about the throne that made it impossible both for the people to know the emperor and for the emperor to be aware of his people's feelings. He intends now, he says, to leave behind the passive role of the emperor and take positive action on behalf of his country. It is a call for cooperation in the great changes that are about to occur, although it would not have occurred to Meiji's predecessors that the cooperation of the people was essential.

On April 8, the day after the swearing of the Charter Oath, signboards listing five prohibitory decrees were erected, replacing those of the shogunate. The first three proscriptions were similar to those long favored by the shogunate, and the remaining two were expedients designed to meet the present crisis.

The first injunction was traditional: "The five moral rules of human conduct are to be properly followed. Widows, widowers, orphans, childless old people, the maimed, and the disabled are to be pitied. There must be no murders, arson, theft, or other evil deeds."

The second injunction perpetuated the shogunate's prohibition on conspiracies, appeals by irregular processes, mass desertions of villages, and various other acts of insubordination. The third signboard strictly forbade Christianity and, promising a reward, urged people to report to the authorities anyone suspected of practicing Christianity.

These first three injunctions can hardly have surprised anyone, but the remaining two were more to the point. The fourth was apparently intended to discourage those who still harbored feelings of *jōi* from attempting by intimidation or bloodshed to rid the country of foreigners:

> The policy of the Imperial Government has been completely changed: that is to say, the court, for good reasons, has opened relations with foreign countries and concluded treaties with them in accordance with international law. Accordingly, foreigners must not be harmed; anyone who violates this is contravening the court's command. Such action will not only create danger for the nation but will be a breach of international faith that impairs the prestige of the empire. It will be punished appropriately.

The fifth injunction was probably intended to discourage those who, dissatisfied with conditions at home, planned to take advantage of the greater ease of travel since the fall of the shogunate to move to more congenial places: "Samurai and commoners are strictly prohibited from absconding from their native provinces. Anyone who has complaints to make about his province or his master is permitted to present them to the cabinet [*dajōkan*]."

These signboards, erected all over the country, were much better known to the mass of the population than the Charter Oath pronounced before nobles and daimyos.[12] The fourth injunction was of particular importance, spelling the end of the *jōi* part of the slogan of *sonnō jōi*.

Just at this time, negotiations were under way in Edo between Saigō Takamori and Katsu Kaishū (1823–1899), a councillor of Yoshinobu, for the surrender of Edo Castle. The opinions of a foreigner, the British minister Sir Harry Parkes, were sought. According to Sir Ernest Satow,

> [Katsu] said he was ready to fight in defense of Keiki's [Yoshinobu's] life, and expressed his confidence in Saigō's ability to prevent a demand being made which might not only be a disgrace to the Mikado, but prolong the civil war. He begged that Sir Harry Parkes would use his influence with the Mikado's government to obviate such a disaster. This the chief did repeatedly, and in particular when Saigō called on him on April 28, he urged on him that severity toward Keiki or his supporters, especially in the way of personal punishment, would injure the reputation of the new government in the opinion of European Powers. Saigō said the life of the ex-Shōgun would not be demanded, and he hoped that similar leniency would be extended to those who had instigated him to march against Kiōto.[13]

The success of the negotiations that resulted in the bloodless surrender of Edo Castle owed much to this advice from a foreigner. On April 26 sixty men, led by Hashimoto Saneyana (a Kyōto noble) and Saigō Takamori, were admitted to Edo Castle. They were met at the front gate by the new lord of the castle, Tokugawa Yoshiyori, who showed them the greatest deference. It was agreed that the castle would be turned over to the imperial army one week later, on May 4. On that day the stronghold of the shogunate was in fact delivered into the hands of the emperor's army.[14]

In the meantime, an event of equally great significance to Emperor Meiji took place. On April 14 he left the Gosho on his way to Ōsaka as commander in chief of the imperial forces. He rode in the informal imperial palanquin and carried with him the sacred mirror. A brocade pennant fluttered above. Twenty-nine nobles headed by Prince Hirotsune, Sanjō Sanetomi, and Nakayama Tadayasu rode beside him. Prince Taruhito led the advance party. The emperor was seen off by the empress dowager and nobles and officials, all dressed in formal robes. As the imperial palanquin passed along Sakai Street and Sanjō Avenue, crowds knelt in reverence along the way. At eight that evening the procession reached the Hachiman Shrine at Iwashimizu, where the emperor spent the night. Traveling in slow stages, the emperor did not reach the Higashi Honganji Betsuin in Ōsaka, which would be his residence, until the afternoon of April 16.[15]

Perhaps the single most exciting moment for the emperor on this momentous journey outside the capital was his first glimpse of the Inland Sea on April 19 when he reviewed the vessels of his fleet off Mount Tempō. He boarded a light skiff on the banks of the Aji River and sailed down the river, protected by guards lining both banks. At noon he reached Tempō. The *Denryū maru*, a ship belonging to the Saga domain, fired a salute, followed by a salute from a

French warship at anchor and then by a response from the *Denryū maru*. After lunch the emperor observed the spectacle of the fleet maneuvering. Surely this was one of the happiest days of the emperor's life. Not only had he left the walled-in world of the Gosho, but he had seen a large body of water and had been acclaimed by the roar of naval guns.

The war had not ended. Fighting continued in the north, and Enomoto Takeaki had sailed the shogun's fleet off to Hokkaidō. Within the city of Edo there was the menace of the Shōgitai, a military unit that continued to support the deposed shogun even after the castle had been surrendered. Subduing these rebellious elements would take time, but (at least in retrospect) it seems clear that the imperial forces were no longer in serious danger.[16]

In the meantime, the young emperor was enjoying his stay in Ōsaka. On May 22 he granted an audience to the English minister plenipotentiary, Sir Harry Parkes, who brought with him his credentials from Queen Victoria. Parkes was accompanied by Admiral A. B. Keppel, Mitford, Satow, and various members of the legation and naval staffs. The audience took place in the Nishi Honganji. In view of the violence that had been directed against Parkes and his escort at the time of his previous audience, this time security was extremely strict. Satow's description of the audience is well known:

On a dais at the extreme end sat the Mikado, under a canopy supported by black-lacquered poles, and with the blinds rolled up as high as was possible. We advanced up the middle of the room in double column, the one on the right headed by the Admiral and composed of naval officers, the other headed by the minister, and consisting of the legation staff. Everyone made three bows, first on advancing into the middle of the room, the second at the foot of the dais, the third on mounting the dais, which was large enough to afford place for us all. The Mikado rose and stood under the canopy from the moment that we began to bow. The principal minister for Foreign Affairs and one other great personage knelt, one on each side of the throne.

In front of the throne, on each side, stood a small wooden image of a lion; these are of great antiquity and are much revered by the Japanese people. Behind the throne a crowd of courtiers were ranged in a double row, wearing little black paper caps and gorgeous brocade robes of various hues. As the Mikado stood up, the upper part of his face, including the eyes, became hidden from view, but I saw the whole of it whenever he moved. His complexion was white, perhaps artificially so rendered, his mouth badly formed, what a doctor would call prognathous, but the general contour was good. His eyebrows were shaved off, and painted in an inch higher up. His costume consisted of a long black loose cape hanging backward, a white upper garment or mantle and voluminous purple trousers. . . .

Sir Harry stepping forward put the Queen's letter into the hand of the Mikado, who evidently felt bashful or timid, and had to be assisted by Yamashina no Miya;[17] his part was to receive it from the Mikado. Then His Majesty forgot his speech, but catching a word from the personage on his left managed to get out the first sentence, whereupon Itō [Hiro-bumi] read out the translation of the whole that had been prepared be-forehand. Sir Harry then introduced each of us in turn, and next the Admiral, who presented his officers. The Mikado expressed the hope that all was well with the squadron under his command, and we retired back-ward out of the presence into the ante-chamber, bowing as we went, and congratulating ourselves that everything had passed off without a hitch.[18]

Japanese descriptions of audiences granted by the emperor at this time are relatively rare, no doubt out of deference. Ōkubo Toshimichi, who was sum-moned by the emperor on May 1 to his temporary residence at the Higashi Honganji, mentioned in his diary the tears of joy and gratitude he shed at the thought that he, a mere samurai, should have been accorded the extraordinary favor of an audience. He was so overcome that he spent the rest of the day drinking.[19] On May 9 Kido Takayoshi and Gotō Shōjirō were also summoned to the Higashi Honganji for an audience with the emperor. Kido wrote in his diary,

> His Majesty inquired of us about the current situation in the country and of the general state of things in the nations overseas. . . .
> For several hundred years there has been no instance of a common subject without a court rank being granted an audience by the emperor. I am moved to tears by his favor. I only regret that the great enterprise of the Restoration has not yet been carried out completely. In the afternoon the emperor viewed the sumo matches from behind his bamboo screen.[20]

There is also an account, contained in a letter written by Yokoi Shōnan (1809–1869) to his family, of his impressions of the emperor during an audience on July 13:

> His face is long, and his coloring is rather dark. His voice is loud. He is of slender build. As for his looks, I suppose one might say they are about average. But he makes a most imposing figure, and I am overjoyed that I should have seen so extraordinary a person.[21]

Meiji's life while in Ōsaka was much less formal than in the Gosho. He probably enjoyed the relative freedom, although even here his studies contin-ued. On May 4 he witnessed from behind bamboo blinds an exhibition of Japanese fencing. This was followed by lectures on the *Great Learning, Sun*

Tzu, and *San Lüeh;*[22] the latter two are studies of the art of warfare. On May 9 the emperor heard a lecture on *Sun Tzu,* and from then on there were daily lectures (which senior nobles might also attend) on Japanese and Chinese classics. The emperor's education remained one of the principal concerns of those closest to him.

The emperor's visit to Ōsaka served the purpose of turning him into a visible presence at least to his advisers and to select foreigners. But once Tokugawa Yoshinobu submitted to punishment, it was felt that the emperor's duties as commander in chief of the army had ended, and plans were made for his return to Kyōto. This did not please Ōkubo Toshimichi, who wanted the capital moved to Ōsaka and who was afraid that back in Kyōto the emperor would be as remote from his people as in the past.[23]

The emperor left Ōsaka on May 28 and, traveling more quickly than on the way out, reached Kyōto the following day. When his palanquin entered the palace gates, *gagaku* musicians and dancers performed *Genjōraku,* a work conveying joy over an emperor's return.

That day the weather was brilliantly clear, and the common people swarmed to get a glimpse of the emperor's return. The brocade pennants that had flown above the palace gates, signifying the emperor's personal command of the army, were removed. The emperor could enjoy his first triumphal return.

Chapter 17

Shortly after the emperor's return to Kyōto from Ōsaka, a proclamation was issued announcing his personal assumption of all state affairs:[1]

> In keeping with his tender years, His Majesty has hitherto lived in the rear palace,[2] but pursuant to his recent oath, and it being also his wish, he will henceforth live in the front part of the palace. He will proceed to his study every morning about eight,[3] preside there over all state affairs, and direct the *hoshō*[4] to submit reports. At times, when it seems appropriate, he may also visit the Hall of Eight Views.[5] In his leisure time he will study the literary and martial arts. He will retire to his private quarters about four in the afternoon. Such is the daily schedule of arrangements he has graciously proclaimed.

Yokoi Shōnan, a councillor (*san'yo*) of the new government, expressed in the letter (already quoted) his profound admiration for the emperor's dedication to duty. He described how Meiji at his levee, seated on a "throne" (*gyokuza*) — two tatami high placed in the middle of an eight-mat room — gave himself completely to state business. A tobacco tray by his side was the only article of furniture.[6] Two or three *kinjū*[7] waited on him, about six feet away, and ministers were seated in attendance on the other side of the threshold. *Gijō* and *san'yo* came forward to make reports, either singly or together. Yokoi commented that nothing so impressive had been seen for more than a thousand years.[8]

A reorganization was announced at this time, establishing three branches of the government—executive, legislative, and judicial. Obviously those who planned this new system of government had been influenced by American or European examples,[9] but the stated goal of the reorganization was not the imitation of foreign practices but the implementation of the Charter Oath in Five Articles. Although surely no one expected (or desired) that in the near future a democracy would be created with equal opportunities for all to rise in the government (only princes of the blood, nobles, and daimyo were eligible to become first-rank officials), the way was opened for samurai and even commoners of ability to rise to positions of the second rank.[10] Officials were to be elected by ballot to serve a term of four years before rotation,[11] and the reelection of officials would be permitted. All persons, regardless of rank—whether daimyos or mere farmers or merchants—would be expected to contribute to the costs of the new government and enable it to maintain an army and internal security; persons of rank were expected to pay one-thirtieth of their income in taxes.

Many other regulations were promulgated at this time, some very specific on minor points, others in the nature of general admonitions, and all conceived in the expressed hope of building a modern state that would not be inferior to the advanced countries of the West.

The fighting had by no means ended, especially in the northeast and north of the country. High-ranking nobles were dispatched as commanding generals to areas of unrest, even if nothing in their training (or future careers) suggested competence in military matters. For example, Saionji Kinmochi (1849–1940), a man known for his liberal thought but not for his knowledge of warfare, was appointed as commanding officer of the northern provinces on June 15 and left for his post in Echigo the next day. Probably (like other generals chosen from the nobility) he was only a figurehead, but the appointment of such men indicated that it was still believed that martial ability went hand in hand with the traditional education in the Confucian classics.[12]

The most enigmatic figure among the nobles who became involved in the fighting at this time was Prince Yoshihisa. He was born in 1847, the ninth son of Fushiminomiya Kuniie. In 1858 at the age of eleven, he was ordained as a priest at the Rinnō-ji, a imperial temple of the Tendai sect at Ueno in Edo, where he was given the Buddhist name of Kōgen.[13] In 1867 he was appointed as the abbot of the temple, an exalted position for someone of his years. Under other circumstances he might have spent the rest of his life in prayer and meditation, but Tokugawa Yoshinobu, who had left Edo Castle to live at the Kan'ei-ji in Ueno after announcing his submission to the wishes of the court, asked Kōgen to go to Kyōto and intercede on his behalf with the emperor.[14]

Rinnōjinomiya, as Kōgen was known, was first approached on March 3, 1868, by an emissary who suggested that he plead with Prince Taruhito on Yoshinobu's behalf, but he refused. He gave his reasons: having become a priest as a mere child, he was unacquainted with worldly matters and was incapable, at a time of national crisis, of interceding for Yoshinobu. Moreover, although he was accustomed to praising the Buddha and reading the sutras, he had no experience in dealing with people and trying to persuade them. He concluded by saying that if it was necessary that someone go, it should not be himself but a substitute.[15]

The next day Yoshinobu visited Rinnōjinomiya and formally requested him to go to Kyōto. Kakuōin Gikan, the intendant of the Rinnō-ji, answering in place of the prince, reminded Yoshinobu that Rinnōjinomiya's father was now very old and if he went to Kyōto, it might prove difficult to leave his father. This would surely cause anxiety among the people of Edo. Gikan also urged Yoshinobu to send someone else.[16] Mention of "anxiety" among the people of Edo if Rinnōjinomiya failed to return to their city suggests that he was popular or at least well known, perhaps because of his close connections with the court.

Yoshinobu acquiesced that day, but on March 5 he summoned Gikan and informed him that Prince Taruhito, the supreme commander of the imperial forces, had left Kyōto and was now on his way to Edo with his army. He repeated the request that Rinnōjinomiya go to the court personally and on the following day sent him a letter to this effect. On March 7 a group of shogunate officials headed by Yamaoka Tesshū (1836–1888) also sent a letter to Gikan. The persistence of Yoshinobu and the others reflected their belief that if Rinnōjinomiya went to Kyōto and asked for an audience with the emperor, his position was such that he could not be refused. This was, they thought, Yoshinobu's best chance of obtaining the emperor's pardon. The prince at last agreed on March 9 to undertake the mission and set the date of his departure for March 13. He would be accompanied by a retinue similar in number to those who normally accompanied him on his processions, some sixty men including not only priests and samurai but a physician, a legal adviser, a secretary, a cook, three tea servers, and various flunkies including palanquin bearers. All the same, this was a very small procession for someone of his status.[17]

About ten in the morning of March 13 the prince's palanquin left Ueno. He was seen off by the families of his retainers, young and old, who grieved over the parting and worried lest he be detained in Kyōto and not return. The people of Edo, seeing the palanquin pass by, bowed with tears in their eyes, moved by the prince's unselfishness in going to the capital to plead for the Tokugawa family.

The procession reached Odawara on March 17, two days behind schedule, but the prince was feeling so unwell that he could not continue the journey. Two days later, an advance party of the imperial army entered Odawara, and men from the Satsuma, Chōshu, and Ōmura domains, as well as an emissary of the commanding general, met with Gikan. He was asked why the prince was traveling to Kyōto and why he was accompanied by so many soldiers. After a few more questions, the emissary commanded Rinnōjinomiya to remain in

Odawara until the general decided what action he would take. He also insisted that the soldiers of the prince's bodyguard return to Edo. The prince, obeying the command, sent back all members of his retinue except for priests.[18]

On March 26 a samurai from Satsuma informed Rinnōjinomiya that the commanding general would arrive the next day in Shizuoka and asked him to proceed there. The prince left Odawara before daybreak in a heavy rain. As he and his party were passing through Hakone Yumoto Village, they encountered a party of Satsuma soldiers on their way to Odawara. The soldiers began to sing boisterously a song mocking the prince: "Why is the prince going to the capital when it's raining cats and dogs? *toko ton yare, ton yare na.*"[19]

The soldiers approached the prince's palanquin and tried poking at the door with their bayonets and the butt end of their lances. When the palanquin reached the house where the prince was to rest, there were so many soldiers swarming around the building that the prince's party took refuge in a temple. They set out once again, but more soldiers were on the road than before, and they were twice as disrespectful as the previous lot. The prince's retinue had expected to eat lunch at a temple in Hakone, and food for this purpose had been packed that morning, but this temple also proved to be full of soldiers, and they moved on, still hungry. By now it was growing dark, and the rain showed no sign of letting up. A man who had been sent ahead to Mishima came back with word that soldiers were in the house where the prince expected to spend the night, and there was nowhere else to stay. The prince finally found a temple where he could pass the night. The chest containing food and table-ware that had been sent to Mishima in anticipation of his staying there had to be sent back. The prince did not eat dinner until cockcrow.[20] His men slept that night in the open, not bothering to remove their traveling clothes.

The prince reached Shizuoka on March 29 after the long, harrowing journey. He was invited to stay at the temple Sōji-in but declined because he had heard that priests of the Shintō shrine near the Sōji-in had formed a band of partisans who were said to have a particular aversion for Rinnōjinomiya. It is puzzling that they should have entertained strong feelings against a man whose life had been spent almost entirely in seclusion, but word may have reached these Shintō priests that the prince was traveling at the behest of the former shogun.

On March 30 Rinnōjinomiya proceeded to Prince Taruhito's headquarters and was received in audience. He presented Yoshinobu's petition, stated that the former shogun was now living in retreat in Ueno, and asked that his punishment be lightened. Prince Taruhito replied that it was because of Yoshinobu's gross acts of treason that an imperial command had been issued to punish him and that there was no way now to alter these plans. Members of his staff asserted that even if it was true that Yoshinobu had professed submission to the court and was living in a monastery, that was not sufficient reason to call off the expedition. They declared that the excuses for past behavior he made in his petition were proof he still had not admitted his guilt.[21]

Rinnōjinomiya answered that he was pleading not only because he wished to save Yoshinobu but also because he feared it would disturb the emperor's peace of mind if he knew that the people of Edo were suffering because the city had been attacked by the imperial army. This line of argument seems to have moved the officers, and despite their doubts, they agreed to consider his plea.

Rinnōjinomiya had a second meeting with Prince Taruhito on April 5. He asked what Yoshinobu must do to prove that he was really sincere in his submission. Taruhito referred him to his staff officers; although he was the commander in chief, they apparently made the decisions on military strategy. The officers' answer was simple: Yoshinobu must surrender his castle and his fleet. This seemed reasonable to the prince, and he informed Prince Taruhito that he would send a messenger to Yoshinobu to report their reply. He would himself continue his journey to Kyōto, as originally planned. Taruhito objected, saying that Rinnōjinomiya's mission had already been accomplished, and he had no need to go to Kyōto.[22] He directed the prince to return to Edo and urged him to inform Yoshinobu personally of the conditions of surrender. Rinnōjinomiya left for Edo two days later.

There is no documentary evidence for Rinnōjinomiya's feelings at this time, but it is likely that as a prince of the blood, he was angered by both the ill treatment he had received at the hands of the Satsuma soldiers and the peremptory tone with which Taruhito had ordered him to return to Edo. Such feelings of bitterness, added to the resentment he already felt over the expedition against Tokugawa Yoshinobu led by Satsuma and Chōshū, may explain his subsequent willingness to associate with those who were still resisting the imperial army.[23]

Soon after the prince's return to Edo, he was approached by leaders of the Shōgitai, a band of supporters of the Tokugawa family formed on March 4 at the Kan'ei-ji in Ueno, the family temple of the Tokugawas. Kakuōin Gikan was an ardent supporter of the Shōgitai, and his influence probably induced the prince to cooperate (at least passively) with the organization. Men from many domains eagerly inscribed their names in blood on the roster of the Shōgitai, vowing to clear Tokugawa Yoshinobu's reputation and to destroy Satsuma, which they denounced as the embodiment of evil.[24]

During the period before the imperial troops occupied the city of Edo, the Shōgitai was authorized by the former shogunate to patrol the streets and may have in fact helped maintain order; but once the government troops arrived, the Shōgitai turned to provoking incidents and sometimes to robbery. Prince Taruhito ordered the Shōgitai to disband, and officers of the former shogunate, including Katsu Kaishū and Yamaoka Tesshū, supported him, saying that the actions of the Shōgitai in fact imperiled Yoshinobu; but their words had no effect. Gikan snarled at Yamaoka that the order was in the name of the court, but it was the doing of Satsuma and Chōshū. He accused Yamaoka of being the dupe of Satsuma and declared that it was entirely natural that Ueno should be defended by men who honored not merely the former shogun but the whole Tokugawa family going back to the time of Ieyasu. He ended by denouncing Yamaoka as an "ingrate of a false retainer."[25]

The presence of Rinnōjinomiya at Ueno made it difficult for the government forces to stage an attack on the stronghold of the Shōgitai, as it would have been extremely awkward if he were hurt or killed in the fighting. They therefore persuaded the prince's father to send him a letter asking him to return to Kyōto to pay his respects to the emperor. The members of the Shōgitai were enraged to learn this, sure that the prince's departure would be the signal for an all-out attack on the Kan'ei-ji. They sent the prince a message informing him that if he tried to leave Ueno, every single member of the organization would commit *seppuku* before the main temple gate, and the prince would have to step over their dead bodies in order to leave.[26]

The citizens of Edo also implored the prince not to go to Kyōto, believing that his presence was the only thing deterring the imperial troops from setting the city on fire. The prince wavered, one day deciding to remain in Ueno, only to change his mind the next. Some of the priests urged him to go to Kyōto where he would be safe, others opposed his going, fearing that once back in Kyōto he would be compelled to return to the laity, a loss to the Tendai sect. The commander in chief ordered the prince to leave Ueno immediately so that the attack on the Shōgitai could commence, but Gikan intercepted the letter.

Finally Prince Taruhito could wait no longer. At dawn on June 6 the government army opened its attack. The fighting was fierce, but the outnumbered Shōgitai was compelled to fall back, and early that afternoon Satsuma troops took the temple's Black Gate. That morning as usual, the prince went to the hall of worship to read the sutras. When the sound of gunfire was heard, the other priests tried to persuade him to leave, but he would not go until he had completed his reading. In the meantime, the priests produced some nondescript clothes they had prepared for an emergency, and the prince put them on in place of his priest's robes.

Where was he to flee? He and the few priests with him wandered that day from place to place, afraid of capture. It seems not to have occurred to the prince to give himself up to the government troops, preferring (it would seem) any hardship to surrender. At one place a merchant who had long benefited from the patronage of the Kan'ei-ji offered to guide them to safety:

> They followed him into a farmhouse. It consisted of one small room, and was not a place where the prince could be asked to stay. When they opened the storeroom they saw agricultural tools, straw, dried grass, all

piled up. In one corner there was a board floor, about nine feet square, and in front of it a dirt floor. They installed the prince on the boards, and the priests sat reverently before him on the dirt floor. When the prince said he was cold, they borrowed two dirty and stained quilts. The prince, noticing the hesitance of the priests, told them not to worry. He took the quilts and threw them over his head. It was three in the morning. There were so many mosquitoes that the prince was unable to sleep the whole night long.[27]

The next morning an attendant priest made breakfast for the prince. The dishes were dirty and cracked, but he made rice balls and some unpleasant-smelling *miso* soup. "The prince said that were it not for such circumstances, he would never have known the taste of the soup of the common people. He forced himself to drink a mouthful, then put it aside with a smile."[28]

The prince was able to accept with a smile the hardships of his flight, but parties of government troops were searching the area for remnants of the Shō-gitai, and the commander in chief ordered that anyone knowing the where-abouts of Rinnōjinomiya report it immediately. Troops were sent to surround and search the residence of the daimyo of Kishū, for it was thought that the prince might take refuge with his sister, the daimyo's wife. These actions con-vinced the priest of the temple where the prince had taken refuge that Prince Taruhito was not to be trusted. He urged the prince to flee by sea to the north and arranged for the prince, in disguise, to be escorted to Shinagawa, where he could board a ship of Enomoto Takeaki's fleet.[29]

Late that night the prince and others in his party were rowed out to the *Chōgei maru*, where they were courteously received. Enomoto came to the ship from his flagship, the *Kaiyō maru*. Speaking privately to the prince, Enomoto asked if he wished to go to Taruhito's headquarters. If so, he would send an escort with the prince, men ready to give up their lives. But if the prince was absolutely determined to go to the north, he would obey his command. The prince replied that his temple in Ueno had been destroyed by flames and he had nowhere to go. Everywhere in Edo was dangerous. Even if he took refuge with Taruhito, he would not be safe. For this reason he would prefer to go to the north, where there were branches of his temple that had not been affected by the warfare. There he would wait for the imperial army to pacify the entire country. Enomoto agreed to do as the prince asked, but he asked him to write a declaration affirming that this was indeed his choice.[30] This suggests that Enomoto foresaw that Rinnōjinomiya might become the head of a faction con-testing rulership of the country with Emperor Meiji.

According to one unverifiable source, the prince's declaration was cast in the form of an imperial edict in which he appointed Enomoto and his staff to important positions in his newly created court.[31] If this actually happened, it indicates that the prince had taken on the attributes of an emperor.[32]

The documentary evidence gives a confusing impression of Rinnōjinomiya. Afraid of becoming involved in the warfare, he escaped to the north to await the victory of the imperial forces. But the north was the center of shogunate activity, and it is hard to reconcile his seeming innocence with his subsequent cooperation with the rebels. Whether or not he chose to recognize it, the presence of a member of the imperial family enabled the rebels to raise the brocade pennant of legitimacy.[33]

A league of antigovernment domains in the north and northeast had been formed in May, and an oath of allegiance was signed on June 22.[34] When Rinnōjinomiya appeared a month later, he was asked to be the "symbol" of the league. The members hoped he would serve as its military leader, but he, as a priest, declined. On August 5 he was chosen to be the "leader." At a meeting of the league that day, a seven-point statement defining the prince's status was drawn up. The first three points were as follows:

1. His Highness will temporarily reside at Shiroishi Castle.
2. His expenses will be met with the income from former shogunate lands in Ōu.
3. The Shōgitai will continue to protect him.

Rinnōjinomiya moved to Shiroishi Castle on August 30. At the gathering of the various domains, he served as the leader of the league in both name and reality.[35] The daimyos of the Sendai and Yonezawa domains were chosen as his viceroys (sōtoku), and lesser appointments were made, in effect setting up a rival court to the one in Kyōto. According to a document written by Kikuchi Yōsai (1788–1878),[36] the nengō was changed that day in the north to the first year of Taisei, and Rinnōjinomiya was enthroned as the emperor Tōbu.[37] It is not clear how much credence should be given to this document, which is not supported by other evidence, but its existence suggests that such a development seemed plausible.

The prince remained in the north until the fighting ended. On October 22, 1868, when the league had lost most of its members and the end was in sight, he wrote an apology declaring that he deeply repented of his actions toward the court.[38] Rumors circulated that partisans of the league were planning to spirit the prince away aboard a ship bound for foreign parts, and orders were given to maintain a strict watch, but in fact he remained in Sendai (and later in Shiroishi) until he left on November 30 for Tōkyō. In the following month, it was decided that Rinnōjinomiya had violated his moral obligations and, for this reason, would be left in the charge of his father. He was to proceed immediately to Kyōto and give himself to penitence."[39] On November 17, 1869, he was released from penitence and restored to his position as an imperial prince. The court showed great leniency toward a prince who, willingly or not, had been a central figure in a revolt against imperial authority. That same year he went abroad, at first to the United States and England and later to Germany, where he studied military science.[40] He was named Kitashirakawanomiya in 1872, and it was by that name he was known during the rest of his career. He died of illness in Taiwan in 1895 while serving as general of the Household Guards Division.

Prince Asahiko, another controversial member of the imperial family, was exiled to Hiroshima on October 1, 1868, because of his involvement in a plot to overthrow the government. He had already been confined to his house because of suspicious activities in the previous year, but in August 1868 an informant disclosed that the prince was plotting to restore the Tokugawa family. He planned to send Enomoto Takeaki with his fleet to various places where soldiers would be landed, raising the standard of revolt.[41] An investigation found him guilty, and he was deprived of his title of prince of the blood, his rank, and his status as an adopted son of Emperor Ninkō. However, his punishment was gradually lightened, and in February 1872, he was pardoned and his status restored.[42]

The best-known revolt against the imperial government during this period was undoubtedly the one staged by Enomoto Takeaki. Five months after Edo Castle was surrendered to the imperial army, Enomoto escaped with eight warships. After calling at Hirakata (where he put Rinnōjinomiya ashore), he went on to Ezo (Hokkaidō), establishing himself at the modern Five Point Fortress near Hakodate, where he overwhelmed the defenders from the Matsumae and Hirosaki domains. On January 14, 1869, Enomoto sent a message to the court through the British and French ministers asking permission to develop the northern region. In a reply sent on January 26 to the two ministers, Iwakura Tomomi declared that Enomoto's words and actions did not match, that he would not be able to escape the name of traitor.[43] This severe response may have occasioned Enomoto's declaration of the "Ezo republic," which won the conditional recognition of the British and French squadrons that happened to be in Hakodate. The attempt to create a country where supporters of the shogunate could live in the traditions of the shogunate ended in failure on June 27, 1869, when Enomoto surrendered to imperial forces led by Kuroda Kiyotaka, but of all the revolts accompanying the Meiji Restoration, his lasted the longest.[44]

This was the last major revolt against the authority of the imperial government during the period immediately following the Meiji Restoration, although there were similar, but smaller, incidents. W. E. Griffis wrote of

one more attempt, in 1871, to set up a rival Mikado and reinstate the old order of things. . . . Everything was planned on the time honored method, which was, first of all, to get possession of some one of the princes of the Imperial blood. With a Son of Heaven in their grip the usurpers could give the color of sanctity and law to their proceedings done in his name.[45]

In April 1871 still another plot was uncovered. Two nobles (Toyama Mitsu-suke and Atagi Michiaki), outraged over the sharp rise in prices that had caused suffering among the people, the deterioration of Kyōto since the capital had been moved to Tōkyō, and (above all) the rampancy of foreigners and foreign influence in the country, plotted to change the government and carry to fruition Emperor Kōmei's ideal of *jōi*.[46] They attracted members of the nobility, includ-ing retainers of Prince Asahiko. According to Griffis, "Part of their plan was to burn Tōkyō, carry back the Emperor to Kyōto, and change the whole system of government."[47] One of the conspirators advocated blowing up the govern-ment buildings of Kyōto Prefecture and massacring the evil officials inside. Another conspirator was more interested in wiping out the foreigners in Kōbe. Fortunately the culprits were arrested before they could carry out their plans. Even after they were arrested, Toyama and Atagi manifested contempt for the laws promulgated by the court and were obviously still plotting to break the laws. For this reason, they were ordered on January 12, 1872, to commit suicide. Their followers were also punished: some reduced to commoners and others sentenced to life imprisonment.[48]

In addition to these high-level conspiracies, there were many incidents of peasant revolt—126 in 1868 alone, many of them in the general area of Kōzuke Province.[49] Such revolts were often fomented by former adherents of the sho-gunate and other malcontents, but they tended to be directed against rich mer-chants or local authorities rather than the central government, and for this reason some revolts actually helped the government.[50]

It is not known how much the young emperor knew about these manifes-tations of discontent with imperial rule. He certainly was familiar with the situation[51] and would have heard about the activities of Rinnōjinomiya and Prince Asahiko, members of the highest aristocracy as adopted sons of Emperor Ninkō. The victories of the government armies in the north were reported to him, along with reassurances that the situation was under control. His attention may, however, have been diverted from military matters by his forthcoming coronation and journey to Edo, events that affected him more directly than fighting in remote parts of the country. But as he undoubtedly was aware, all the various revolts would have to be quashed before the menace of a restoration of the shogunate was forever ended.

Chapter 18

The coronation of Emperor Meiji took place on September 12, 1868. The ceremony had originally been planned for December of the preceding year, but conditions in the country were too unsettled to permit much display. The time to prepare the ceremony properly also was insufficient, so the coronation was put off until the following year.[1] Because of other, more urgent matters at hand, the details of the ceremony were not considered until June when Iwakura Tomomi asked Kamei Koremi (1824–1885), a former daimyo but now an officer of the Ministry of Shintō, to examine old records to determine authentically Japanese rituals that should be observed at the coronation. Iwakura was sure that most of what was considered to be traditional was in fact copied from Chinese models, and he believed that in a time of great changes, it was appropriate that the ceremony be revised so as to constitute a model for future coronations.

A formal order was issued in the eighth month to Kamei and Fukuba Bisei (1831–1907) to compile a new-style set of procedures for the coronation. At this point Fukuba made a suggestion that was hardly in keeping with ancient tradition. Years before, Tokugawa Nariaki (1800–1860) had presented Emperor Kōmei with a globe in the hopes that it would not only familiarize him with the general configuration of the world but also inspire in him an ambition to make Japanese prestige shine in all quarters of the globe. Fukuba suggested that if the globe were made a focal point of the coronation, it would stir lofty thoughts in the officials present and deepen their knowledge and that it would impress the common people with the sublimity of the ceremony of accession to the throne.[2] He also proposed that the Shintō prayers offered at the coronation embody the respect with which the mass of the people offered their congratulations. Iwakura, too, wished to involve the whole people in rites hitherto restricted to the high nobility.

Naturally, a master of yin-yang was consulted as to the best time for the ceremony. He decided the coronation should take place on September 12 at eight in the morning. The officials appointed to preside over different aspects of the ceremony prescribed many changes based on their readings of ancient Japanese texts. Offerings were made to the principal Shintō shrines with prayers that there be no wind or rain on the day of the coronation.[3] Shintō officials were sent to the tombs of Jimmu, Tenchi, and Meiji's immediate three predecessors, to inform them of the coronation.

The ceremonies were elaborate, every movement of the participants planned. Early that morning the emperor put on his coronation robe. It was similar to the robes worn by Shintō priests, a departure from the traditional Chinese-style robes. At ten he crossed the bridge connecting the Residential Palace and the Hall of State Ceremonies where the ceremonies would be performed. Two maids of honor went before him. Next came two ladies of highest court rank, one bearing the sacred sword and the other, the jewel.[4] The emperor was followed by an official who carried the scepter. Another official supported the emperor's train. The emperor entered from the rear curtained enclosure inside the hall and seated himself on the throne, still invisible to the assemblage. The two women officials placed the sword and jewel on a stand to the emperor's left and withdrew. The scepter was offered to the emperor. Next, at the sound of a gong, two court ladies raised the bamboo curtain, and for the first time the emperor became visible. The master at arms called out, and the entire assemblage prostrated themselves in worship. An official offered the nusa[5] to the emperor, and the head of the Ministry of Shintō then approached to receive and remove the nusa. When this ceremony had ended, there was a call for another reverence, and the entire gathering bowed in unison. Then a herald,[6] Reizei Tametada, advanced to the designated place and, lifting the text, read in a loud voice the proclamation of the emperor's succession and prayers for his longevity and the prosperity of the country.

After the reading of the proclamation, a musician sang the ancient poem:

watatsumi no	As I count over
hama no masago wo	The grains of sand on the shore
kazoetsutsu	Of the great ocean,
kimi ga chitose no	I shall know then just how long
ari kazu ni sen	Your reign will endure, my lord.[7]

When the song was over, at a command from Fusehara Nobutaru, the assemblage bowed again. Prince Takahito advanced on his knees to the emperor's seat to inform him that the ceremony had ended. A gong was struck, at which the maids of honor lowered the bamboo curtain, and the emperor, once again hidden from sight, withdrew. The *gijō* and *san'yo* went to the Kogosho to offer their congratulations to the emperor on the successful completion of the ceremony. Others who had been present at the ceremony left at a signal from the drums, and the ceremony was concluded at noon. It had been raining steadily up until this point, but the skies suddenly cleared, to the delight of all, who took this as an auspicious sign. Officials were given a holiday, and the common people rested from their labors so that they might join in the celebration.[8]

As a further step in cementing the ties between the emperor and his people, the emperor's birthday was proclaimed a national holiday, the Feast of Tenchō.[9] Observance of the emperor's birthday as a holiday had begun as far back as 775, but the custom had long since fallen into abeyance. Its revival at this time was thus another instance of the intention to restore ancient practices.

On October 23 it was announced that the *nengō* had been changed from the fourth year of Keiō to the first year of Meiji and that henceforth there would be only one *nengō* for an entire reign.[10] The name Meiji was derived from a passage in the *I Ching*, the ancient Chinese book of divination: "The sage, facing south, listens to the world; facing the *light*, he *governs*." The day before the new *nengō* was announced, the emperor himself had visited the sanctuary (*naishidokoro*) where he drew lots to determine the new *nengō* from among several names submitted by scholars. Although he probably did not realize it at the time, the emperor had also chosen the name by which posterity would know him; earlier emperors were known by a place-name from the site of their residence or (as was true of Meiji's father and grandfather) by a posthumously chosen title. The name Meiji, interpreted as meaning "enlightened rule," came to seem an accurate description of his reign. Names like those of his father and grandfather, auspicious though they were, would have been less appropriate to the era.

Once the coronation was out of the way, the next task ahead of the young sovereign was his visit to Tōkyō. This journey had been announced as far back as September 19 in a proclamation stating that the emperor made no distinction in importance among "all lands within the seas, east and west." For this reason, he had given Edo the new name Tōkyō—"Eastern Capital." The stated reason for the journey was the desire he had long entertained of comforting the people of the east who had suffered from the warfare that had raged since the spring of that year.[11] The visit seemed so important to Iwakura Tomomi that he insisted on having the date of the emperor's departure officially announced on the day after the coronation. He submitted on October 13 a proposal naming who would accompany the emperor to Tōkyō and who would remain in Kyōto to run the government and defend the city during the emperor's absence.

There were protests against overhastiness, as some people felt that Prince Asahiko's plot and the escape of the shogunate's fleet were evidence that the eastern region had not yet been completely pacified. But Etō Shimpei (1834–1874), who is credited with originating the plan of moving the capital to Tōkyō, stressed the urgency of an imperial visit. He argued that the people of the eastern region had long been accustomed to receiving benefits from the shogun and were as yet unfamiliar with the emperor's benevolent influence. With the fall of the Tokugawa family, these people felt as if they had been deprived of their master and did not know where to turn. If, because of fear of the rebel fleet, the emperor's journey to Tōkyō were delayed, the regime would lose credibility both at home and abroad and might, by missing a unique opportunity, do itself irreparable harm. The combination of Etō's eloquence and Iwakura's political acumen carried the day for those who favored a visit in the immediate future.[12]

Opposition nevertheless continued to be heard, not only from those who were worried because the northern provinces had not been completely pacified, but also from those who, remembering the huge expenses incurred by the government ever since the fighting at Toba and Fushimi, feared that the cost of the journey of the emperor and his entourage would represent a serious drain on the country's already straitened finances. The people of Kyōto also were apprehensive lest the journey to Tōkyō be the prelude to a move of the capital to that city. (It was known that the san'yo Ōkubo Toshimichi favored such a move.)[13]

The inhabitants of Tōkyō were eager for an imperial visit, the sooner the better. Now that the shogunate had been dismantled, the city had lost its political importance, and it was feared that it might fall into neglect. This fear was not confined to the people of Tōkyō. Sir Ernest Satow wrote in his diary,

Now that the daimiōs whose wants had been supplied by the merchants and shopkeepers had left for their country homes, the population would naturally decrease. It was a sad thing that Yedo should decline, for it was one of the handsomest cities in the Far East. Though it contained no fine public buildings, its position on the seashore, fringed with the pleasure gardens of the daimiōs, and the remarkable huge moats surrounding the castle, crowned with cyclopean walls and shaded by the picturesque lines of pine-tree, the numerous rural spots in the city itself, all contributed to produce an impression of greatness.[14]

Satow's elegiac tone indicates that he expected the city to lose its greatness and even its physical beauty now that the shogun and the daimyos had left. The samurai quarters seemed lonely or even dead. The only way Tōkyō could recover its importance was by being chosen as the capital of Japan. This was precisely what Ōkubo intended, and when he returned on October 28 to Kyōto from Tōkyō, where he had been serving as an adviser to the commanding general of the Eastern Expeditionary Army, he argued so vehemently in favor of an immediate imperial visit to Tōkyō that the Court Council at last set a date for the emperor's departure, November 6. During the following week, there was good news from the northeast: on November 1 the Sendai domain surrendered to government forces.

The emperor's palanquin left the capital for Tōkyō as scheduled. That morning at eight the emperor went to the Hall of State Ceremonies, where he boarded his palanquin. He carried with him the sacred mirror, one of the three emblems of his authority. He was accompanied by a procession of more than 3,300 people headed by Iwakura Tomomi, Nakayama Tadayasu, and various daimyos. Katō Akizane, the daimyo of Mizuguchi, served as guardian of the sacred mirror. The procession was seen off from the Dōgi Gate of the palace by the dowager empress and Princess Sumiko. Nobles and daimyos living in Kyōto lined up outside the southern gate to watch the emperor depart. Along the streets of the capital, old and young, men and women, bowed in worship as the imperial palanquin passed. No action was taken to clear the roads in the path of the procession, but even without the usual admonitions, the bystanders were reverent and orderly. The sound of hands clapping in worship continued without a break.[15]

The procession moved eastward to Awata-guchi where it stopped briefly at the Shōren-in, an imperial Tendai temple, long enough for the emperor to have lunch. The emperor afterward transferred to a board palanquin, a relatively modest palanquin used by the imperial family on long journeys. The procession went by Keage Slope to Yamashina on the other side of Higashiyama. On the way the emperor worshiped from afar the tomb of Emperor Tenchi. At about two that afternoon the procession reached Ōtsu, where the emperor established his temporary residence at the official inn. The sacred mirror was installed in another building.

At this point Acting Middle Counselor Ōhara Shigetomi came galloping up. He urged that the imperial palanquin return to Kyōto. He reported that on November 2, in the midst of the festival of the Toyouke Great Shrine, the shrine's torii had spontaneously fallen over, and the priests, interpreting this as a warning from the Great Goddess Amaterasu, had sent a swift messenger to Kyōto to inform the court. Ōhara had been opposed from the start to the emperor's journey to the east and resorted to this expedient in the hopes of obstructing the procession. Iwakura, however, was unmoved; he promised to offer special prayers and sent Ōhara back to Kyōto.[16]

That day (and this would be true of every stop on the journey to Tōkyō) the emperor directed an official to see that offerings were made at all Shintō shrines along the way. In addition, money was given to very old people, filial children, chaste wives, loyal servants, and people who had contributed to public enterprises. Persons who were ill, who had met with accidents, or who were in desperate poverty were also comforted with monetary gifts. The money involved in all this largesse came to a large sum, but fortunately most of the journey's expenses were paid by rich merchants of Kyōto and Ōsaka.

The procession moved steadily ahead along the Tōkaidō, the highway link-ing Kyōto and Tōkyō. News arrived of the surrender of the Aizu domain on November 8, of the Shōnai domain on November 9, of the Nagaoka domain on November 19, and of the Morioka domain on November 22. The only re-sistance to the imperial government that remained was by Enomoto Takeaki in Ezo.

What did the young emperor think of this first ambitious journey? He seems not to have recorded his feelings in poems, soon to become his chief means of expression, but there are occasional clues to what had particularly impressed him. On October 12 he stopped his palanquin to watch peasants reaping the rice harvest. Iwakura asked a peasant for some rice ears, which he offered to the emperor for his inspection, and the Owari daimyo presented the emperor with this *tanka*:

karishi ho no	When I see how few
sukunaki mireba	Are the ears of the harvest
aware nari	I am moved to pity.
ōmitakara no	What must be the feelings of
kokoro ya ika ni	His Majesty's loyal subjects?

The emperor, it is recorded, gave cakes to the peasants, by way of comforting them.[17]

On November 14, at Shiomizaka on the Shizuoka coast, the emperor caught his first glimpse of the Pacific Ocean. This was probably the first time in re-corded history an emperor had actually seen the ocean. Although the emperor kept his reactions to himself, Kido Takayoshi exclaimed that from this day forth the imperial glory would shine across the seas.[18] The next day when the emperor crossed Lake Hamana, the surface of the lake was perfectly calm, and the em-peror, it is said, looked exceedingly pleased. Iwakura composed a *tanka* on this occasion that he modestly did not include in his own account of the journey:

nami kaze no	The lake of Arai
arai no umi wa	Known for its waves and wind is
na nomi nite	Rough in name alone:
mi-fune shizuka ni	The royal boat has smoothly
watarimashikeri	Glided across the water.[19]

There were other moments of interest along the way. At the Ōi River, known as the widest and most difficult to cross in Japan, a plank bridge had been constructed to facilitate the emperor's crossing. At the Abe River there was a boat-bridge, an even more novel experience for the emperor. But the most memorable event for him was seeing Mount Fuji on November 20. This was probably the first time an emperor had seen this mountain, so celebrated in Japanese literature. Meiji commanded each of the members of his escort to compose a poem about Fuji by the time his palanquin arrived in Tōkyō.

The emperor arrived in Tōkyō on November 26. He was met at Shinagawa by Commander in Chief Prince Taruhito, Sanjō Sanetomi, and the governor of Tōkyō Prefecture and was escorted into the city by princes of the blood, nobles, and daimyos all attired in formal costume and wearing swords. This impressive display was at the suggestion of Iwakura Tomomi, who believed that the people of the Kantō region, having long lived under a despotic regime, had fallen into savage ways and that the best way to control their fierceness and soften their dispositions was to expose them to the costumes and etiquette of the court.[20]

The emperor's procession stopped briefly at Zōjō-ji where he changed from his traveling palanquin to the phoenix palanquin (*hōsha*). The procession entered Edo Castle by the Wadakura Gate, musicians leading the way. At two that afternoon the emperor entered the castle, which henceforth would be known as Tōkyō Castle and considered to be the royal seat. Tens of thousands of people watched the procession with expressions of awe, weeping to think that this day they had beheld the ruler of their country.[21]

The fighting had not yet ended; indeed, on December 4 government forces in Ezo suffered a setback at the hands of Enomoto Takeaki's forces. But the prevailing opinion seems to have been that the rebels no longer presented a serious threat to the regime.[22] On December 15 Prince Taruhito returned the brocade flag and *settō* to the emperor, signifying that resistance to the government forces had been terminated in the northeast.

On December 17 in commemoration of his visit, the emperor offered to the people of Tōkyō, a vast amount of saké. A total of 2,990 barrels was distributed. In addition, 550 pewter saké containers and 1,700 bundles of dried cuttlefish were given away along with the saké. The total cost was more than 14,038 *ryō*, but the people of Tōkyō enjoyed a two-day binge. The event inspired a very early example of Meiji literature, a quatrain by Ōnuma Chinzan (1818–1891):

> The Son of Heaven has moved the capital and bestowed his largesse;
> The boys and girls of Tōkyō look lovely as flowers.
> Observe how "Duck Waters" have lost out to "Seagull Crossing";
> Quite a few of the nobles have forgotten about home.[23]

Mention of "largesse" refers to the distribution of saké. "Duck Waters" (the Kamo River in Kyōto) now seems so much less attractive to the Kyōto noblemen than "Seagull Crossing" (the Sumida River in Tōkyō) that they have forgotten about their ancestral homes. Indeed, when it was announced on January 10 that the emperor would return to Kyōto early in the following month, Sanjō Sanetomi, a leader of the nobility, opposed the decision to leave Tōkyō. He argued that the rise or fall of the country depended largely on the attitude of the people of the eastern region; that is, if the emperor were to return so soon to Kyōto, he would surely lose their hearts. The prosperity of Tōkyō, he said, affected the prosperity of the entire country; even if Kyōto and the surrounding region were lost, the country would not be lost, provided Tōkyō was not lost.[24]

While in Tōkyō, the emperor met people of special importance to him. He gave an audience to Kazunomiya, now known as Princess Chikako, and probably reminisced about her brother, the late emperor Kōmei. He also gave an audience to Tokugawa Akitake (1853–1910), Yoshinobu's younger brother and now the Mito daimyo, who had spent a year studying in France, and asked him about conditions abroad. Evidently Akitake's reports impressed Meiji, who frequently thereafter summoned Akitake to obtain information about the West. In January, Akitake, who was still only fifteen years old, was ordered to go to Ezo where, as the daimyo of Mito, he was expected to crush the rebel forces in Hakodate.[25] No doubt he was sent less because of martial talents than because of his name: it was probably hoped that the presence of a Tokugawa—the brother of the last shogun—on the side of the government forces would spiritually weaken the supporters of Enomoto Takeaki.

During Meiji's stay in Tōkyō, negotiations were opened with the foreign diplomats living in Yokohama on a number of matters: the end of their policy of neutrality in the conflict between the government and the rebels; the destruction of the rebels in Hakodate; the disposition of the Japanese Christians; and the issuance of paper money. The negotiations did not go smoothly. The foreign representatives, headed by the redoubtable Sir Harry Parkes, refused to consider any request that seemed to threaten the sacred right to trade—in Hakodate and anywhere else.

On January 2 a foreign trade center was opened in Tōkyō at Tsukiji, which was also made available to foreigners for residence. Samurai were forbidden to enter the settlement without written permission. This restriction on the passage of samurai into the concessions was probably intended to allay the foreigners' fear of sworded samurai, but it had the effect of lowering their prestige. Before long, the samurai were given the task of protecting foreign ships, something none of them could have foreseen. Ōnuma Chinzan wrote a poem on their plight:

> A little Yang-chou—that's the new Shimabara;
> Our browbeaten Japanese warriors guard the barbarian ships.
> "Please don't come here wearing your swords—
> Please come instead with a hundred thousand coins."[26]

In the winter of 1868, at the same time that daimyo mansions in Tsukiji were demolished to provide living space for the foreigners, a new licensed quarter, named after the old Shimabara in Kyōto, was opened nearby. The last two lines of the poem indicate that for the prostitutes of the new Shimabara, money counted more than a customer's rank. This surely was no less humiliating for the samurai than the duty of protecting foreigners, despite their *jōi* convictions of a few years earlier.

On January 5 and 6 the emperor received the ministers from foreign countries, evidence of his hope for increased and better relations between Japan and the rest of the world. In Western diplomatic practice, there was nothing remarkable about the emperor's receiving foreign diplomats and providing refreshments for them, but it was unprecedented in Japan. It is all the more astonishing when one recalls that Kōmei, who considered that the presence of foreigners on the sacred soil of Japan was an unspeakable offense to the gods, had died less than two years earlier. The young emperor was willing not only to meet foreigners but was affable to them.

On January 11 the emperor boarded a Japanese warship for the first time and observed the maneuvering of the fleet. He had frequently been urged by Sanjō Sanetomi and Iwakura Tomomi to ride out to the sea off Yokohama, but his grandfather, Nakayama Tadayasu, had been opposed, fearing that the sacred sword and jewel might be lost. In the end the emperor decided to inspect the ships, but when he set out, he left the sword and jewel at the Hama Palace, heavily guarded. While the emperor was aboard the *Fuji*, an American warship fired a twenty-one-gun salute, to which the *Fuji* responded. The court officers accompanying the emperor (including the *gijō* Nakayama Tadayasu and the *san'yo* Ōkubo Toshimichi) were startled by the noise, but the emperor remained absolutely calm, and his expression was even one of special pleasure. On later occasions he revealed the same self-possession when he heard explosions and similar noises in his vicinity, in contrast to the apocryphal story that as a child he fainted on hearing the sound of gunfire.

The emperor's outing to sea was a complete success. The perfect weather and the emperor's evident pleasure in the day were interpreted as a favorable sign for the future of the Japanese navy. On the following day the emperor issued a command for further study of how the navy might be strengthened.

On January 15 the *hoshō* Iwakura Tomomi and the assistant foreign minister, Higashikuze Michitomi, visited the British legation in Yokohama in the hopes of persuading the foreigners to end their policy of neutrality in the warfare between the government and the supporters of the shogunate. The main reason for the urgency of this request was their desire to obtain possession of the American-built ironclad *Stonewall Jackson*. This ship had been ordered by the shogunate, but before it could be delivered, the country was torn by fighting. Because the foreign powers had adopted a position of neutrality, they were unwilling to turn over the ship to either side. The government had several times requested that the foreigners abandon their neutrality, but they had refused, and the *Stonewall Jackson* remained at anchor in Yokohama Bay. Iwakura and

Higashikuze argued that the war was in effect over and that there was therefore no reason to maintain a policy of neutrality. According to Satow, Sir Harry Parkes replied at this time that his colleagues "were willing to make a declaration that the war was over, but were not willing to give up the 'Stonewall Jackson'; and that in order to justify her retention they would not withdraw their notifications of neutrality."[27]

Parkes did everything possible to persuade the other foreign ministers, and thanks to his intercession they finally agreed to abandon their neutrality.[28] It is hard to know what to make of Iwakura's statement that "the mikado's government" was far from desiring to use the *Stonewall Jackson* to attack Enomoto. No sooner was neutrality lifted than the government bought the ship from the Americans and sent it to Hakodate, where it performed valiantly in naval engagements. But the leniency to the rebels promised by Iwakura at this time was no lie. It is true that after Enomoto surrendered on June 27, 1869, he was imprisoned for three years, but he received a special pardon in 1872 and was appointed to the Office for the Development of Hokkaidō.

Other leaders of the rebellion were treated with similar lenience. After the warfare in the northeast had ended, the emperor issued a pronouncement stating that he did not intend to be the sole judge of the former rebels, that in order to ensure absolute fairness, the punishments would be decided by a consensus of opinions. With respect to Matsudaira Katamori, the daimyo of Aizu, the emperor favored reducing by one degree the normal punishment of death in such instances of rebellion. This recommendation was in fact adopted not only in Katamori's case but also for all the other daimyos. Not one of those who fought against the government was executed. Katamori was exiled to Tottori but, before long, was pardoned. Other daimyos were deprived of their domains, but most were soon given new ones. Kido Takayoshi alone held out for the death penalty, saying that although he did not hate the rebels, he hated their crime and could not forget the many loyal soldiers who had died because of their rebellion. He believed that the law must not be twisted in order to be lenient, but his words failed to sway the others in the government, and leniency was the order of the day.[29]

The emperor left for Kyōto on January 20, promising to return to Edo in the spring. He was accompanied by a procession of 2,153 men, considerably fewer than on the outward journey, a sign that less danger from hostile elements was expected. Along the way the emperor again saw Mount Fuji and admired Miho no Matsubara. He had every reason to feel satisfied. During the less than three months since he had left Kyōto, the northeast of the country had been entirely pacified, and although there was still resistance in Hakodate, even the ministers of the various foreign countries were agreed that the war had been won. The city of Edo, long the shogunate's stronghold, was his. Moreover, the unprecedented passage of the emperor's palanquin along the

Tōkaidō had undoubtedly enhanced his prestige among people in places far from the capital.[30]

The imperial palanquin returned to Kyōto on February 5, in time for the funeral services in memory of Emperor Kōmei on the eighth. Three days later Ichijō Haruko, the bride of Meiji, entered the palace, an appropriately felicitous ending to one of the most important years in Japanese history.

Chapter 19

The year 1869 began under far happier circumstances than any other in recent memory.[1] The ceremonies performed at the palace in Kyōto on New Year's Day were traditional, following ancient precedents. In Tōkyō, too, nobles, daimyos, and other officials resident in the city gathered at the castle to offer their congratulations. New Year's messages were received from the British and American ministers.

On the fourth of the month the senior officials—*hoshō, gijō, san'yo,* and the like—were summoned to the palace to hear a rescript from the emperor read by the *hoshō,* Iwakura Tomomi. The emperor's message conveyed his fear that his lack of virtue might result in impairment of the sacred, unbroken dynastic thread he had inherited from his ancestors. It might also prevent him from understanding fully the hardships under which many of his people lived because of the continuing warfare. But he expressed his determination to extend the achievements of his ancestors and his joy that he was served by officials such as those who had gathered this day before him. He asked that they not hesitate to correct and remedy his faults.[2]

The emperor's message was largely conventional in its phrasing, and it is unlikely he had any part in composing the text;[3] but it is clear that he expected to participate in whatever future decisions were made by the government. He would be present not only at meetings of his cabinet but at innumerable official functions, almost to the day of his death. Usually he did not say a word during the discussions at the meetings he attended, but his presence added enormously to their dignity and importance.

It did not take long for the festive New Year atmosphere to be harshly interrupted. On February 15 at about two in the afternoon, the *san'yo* Yokoi Shōnan was returning by palanquin from the court when, just as it passed Teramachi, several men suddenly began to fire pistols at the palanquin. Yokoi pushed open the door and, emerging from the conveyance, attempted to defend himself with his dirk, but he had been weakened by a recent illness and, powerless to resist, was killed on the spot. The assassins got away despite the efforts of Yokoi's retainers and servants.

When word of the assassination reached the emperor's ears, he was extremely perturbed. He immediately sent a court attendant to Yokoi's lodgings to ascertain what had happened. The emperor presented the retainers and servants who had been wounded in the attack with 400 *ryō* for medical treatment. The next day he directed the Kumamoto daimyo Hosokawa Yoshikuni to see to it that Yokoi was buried with suitable honors, and he himself contributed 300 *ryō* for the expenses. These immediate, warmhearted reactions are memorable if only because they contrast sharply with his impassivity in later years when men, even those closer to himself than Yokoi, were assassinated. His youth may account for the spontaneous concern he displayed at this time. Later, as his concept of the appropriate behavior for a monarch developed, such spontaneity tended to be replaced by a detachment that seldom permitted him to display personal feelings.

Yokoi Shōnan's assassins were eventually found on Mount Kōya after a widespread search and such measures as sealing off all entrances into the city of Kyōto. The captured murderers declared that they had killed Yokoi because they despised him as a traitor, a man in contact with the foreigners who planned to propagate Christianity in Japan.[4] They were imprisoned in the Kyōto residence of the Fukuoka domain where they soon became objects of compassion: the daimyo of Fukuoka asked that they be treated with leniency, and many people urged an amnesty. Even the government prosecutor, in the hopes of justifying the assassination, searched for evidence that Yokoi might have acted improperly. Such sympathy suggested that behind the enlightened facade of the new regime, the old xenophobia persisted, and the murder of anyone who favored the foreigners would be condoned. The four assassins were not executed until November 1870.

Needless to say, Yokoi's purpose had not been to convert the Japanese to Christianity. He was a convinced Confucianist (the teacher of Motoda Nagazane, Meiji's conservative tutor) and never abandoned this belief. Yokoi had been a passionate advocate of *jōi* in early years but had shifted to *jitsugaku*,[5] practical learning. This, in turn, led him to favor the importation of foreign learning, including Western economic and political ideas. Christianity was by no means fundamental to his thought, but as one Western authority on the period has stated, "Christianity appeared to Yokoi as the ethic of practicality or rationality. . . . Yokoi, more perceptive than much later Japanese writers, in seeing the intimate relationship between Western technological and economic power and Christianity, perceived the relationship between modernity and an adequate ethic."[6] The assassins declared that they feared that the pristine purity of traditional Japanese beliefs might be defiled by foreign influence, and they refused to recognize that Yokoi's learning was of value to the new Japan.

Yokoi was ahead of his time. Sir George Sansom, tracing the development of Yokoi's political thought, believed that eventually "he even developed ideas of universal peace and the brotherhood of man, propounding a kind of One World doctrine."[7] A traditional Confucian education might well foster a belief in the brotherhood of man, but this was not the aspect of Confucianism most typical of Japan at the end of the Tokugawa period. The men who assassinated Yokoi believed that their violence was authorized by the Confucianism they had absorbed as young samurai; both tolerance and intolerance were justified according to Confucian texts.

The young emperor's studies, typifying what people of the time supposed to be orthodox Confucianism, consisted of reading canonical works of Chinese thought, along with a few works of Japanese history. Six lectures on the *Analects* and six on the *Records of Japan* were delivered in his presence each month. Somewhat later the curriculum was expanded to include (among Japanese works) Kitabatake Chikafusa's *Jinnō shōtōki*,[8] as well as others of the Four Books of Confucianism. As yet no attempt was made by his mentors to acquaint Meiji with the geography or history of the world, let alone science.

The one concession to the modern age made by his tutors at this time was to permit Meiji to ride horseback six times a month. His interest in riding had been awakened two years earlier when he rode a horse for the first time, and in the following year he had many occasions to witness displays of horsemanship. Kido Takayoshi, who became one of the emperor's rare friends, related in his diary how the emperor had rolled up the bamboo screen of his royal box and commanded Kido to ride at the Grand Equestrian Review. Kido rode so brilliantly that the emperor placed a flowering branch on his tray of food and cakes and gave him so much saké that Kido became intoxicated.[9] Before long, horsemanship became an obsession with the emperor—to the distress of some members of the court, who thought he should spend more time reading books and less time on horses.[10] Such activities of the young emperor strikingly contrasted with the sedentary life led by his father, who not only never rode a horse but virtually never left the Gosho; they may also account for Meiji's closeness to the samurai class, the repository of Japanese martial traditions.

On February 25, 1869, the emperor attended a display of riding, and he himself, dressed in white with crimson trousers, mounted a horse. The other riders included not only daimyos (whose education had naturally emphasized martial sports) but members of the aristocracy, including Sanjō Sanetomi and Meiji's grandfather, Nakayama Tadayasu. Originally the emperor had been encouraged to ride in order to free him from the debilitating effects of having been raised mainly by women; now the passion he had developed for riding was communicated to those around him. He esteemed men to the degree that they demonstrated ability in the saddle.

The emperor's education was a matter of great concern to the men serving him. Kido's diary reveals again and again his particular anxieties, especially in the following decade. Iwakura Tomomi was also aware of the necessity of surrounding the young emperor with the proper advisers. On March 5, 1869, he sent a memorandum to Sanjō Sanetomi in which he stressed the importance of cultivating *kuntoku*, the virtue of the ruler. "Now, at the beginning of the renovation of imperial rule, the emperor is not rich with years, and for this reason he should not be without guidance for even a single day."[11] Iwakura recommended that persons be selected from among the nobility, the daimyos, and the senior samurai for their sincerity and strict morals, their ability and lofty purpose, or for their knowledge of Japan, China, and the West. Iwakura stressed that the emperor was intelligent and possessed of outstanding virtue and that once he had grasped the essentials, the government would have the man it needed.

At first there were few concrete proposals. In 1871 the emperor's study schedule was changed to include some materials relating to modern times. A program was drawn up for each ten days of instruction. On four of the ten days the emperor was lectured on "Success Stories from the West," the Japanese translation of Samuel Smiles's *Self-Help*, published only a few months earlier. It must have been startling for a young man—whose knowledge of books had been confined mainly to Confucian texts and accounts of the divine descent of the Japanese emperors—to read descriptions of men like Benjamin Franklin who had been able, thanks to their native intelligence and hard work, to overcome the barriers of poverty and class. The emperor was also expected to study German every day,[12] but before long it was decided that the press of official business was too great to permit him to continue these lessons.

Despite the introduction of the new, imported learning, the old-style culture still prevailed at the court. On February 21 the first concert of the reign was held in the palace, attended by the emperor and empress. All the performers were members of the court: the *shō* was played by eight nobles, including the former minister of the left; the *hichiriki*, by six nobles; the flute, by another six nobles, including the emperor's grandfather, Nakayama Tadayasu; the *biwa*, by three nobles; and the *koto*, by five other nobles. The ability to play one of the musical instruments used in *gagaku* was prized at the court, just as it had been in the Heian period.

Meiji does not seem to have studied any musical instrument, but from early childhood he had composed *tanka* under his father's guidance, and he retained this avocation during the rest of his life. On February 19 Meiji attended the first poetry gathering (*utagokai*) of his reign. The emperor's poem was on the topic "Spring Breezes Cross over the Sea":

chiyo yorozu	An indication
kawaranu haru no	Of spring, unchanging a thousand,
shirushi tote	Ten thousand ages:
umibe wo tsutau	How gentle are the breezes
kaze zo nodokeki	Blowing along the seacoast!

The empress's poem on the same topic was

oki tsu nami	The waves offshore are
kasumi ni komete	Swathed in mist and above the sea
haru kinu to	In all directions
kaze mo nagitaru	The wind has now abated,
yomo no umizura	Telling us that spring has come.[13]

There is little or no individuality in these poems; they express pleasure over the arrival of spring in exactly the same manner as had innumerable court poets of the preceding millennium. No attempt was made to surprise with the language or images, because composing these metrically exact poems was above all a demonstration of familiarity with the court culture.

Another aspect of court tradition can be detected in the laconic announcement on March 20 that Natsuko, the daughter of Acting Major Counselor Hashimoto Saneakira, had been appointed as lady-in-waiting (*tenji*). On the following day the emperor granted her an audience and bestowed on her a cup of saké.[14] The saké was followed by gifts of silken cloth. The girl was only twelve, too young to become a concubine of the emperor, but three and a half years later, on November 12, 1873, she gave birth to a daughter by the emperor and died the same day.

Although the marriage of the emperor and empress was happy, they seem to have recognized early that she was barren. Even if the emperor had been reluctant to share his bed with another woman, he had the duty of providing an heir to the throne; and from about this time, he spent his nights with carefully selected women of the high nobility in the hopes that one or more of them would conceive. The women were mainly girls in their teens (Hashimoto Natsuko was fifteen at the time of her death) and, though of impeccable ancestry, were poorly educated. Indeed, their sole ambition was to give birth to an imperial child. Fierce rivalries developed among these women for the emperor's attentions. However, even if a woman was fortunate enough to bear the emperor's child, she was unlikely to know the joys of motherhood, as the baby would be taken away from her and officially treated as the child of the empress.

All the same, as we know from the example of Nakayama Yoshiko, Meiji's mother, the mother of an imperial child received superior court rank and other marks of favor. Even if her child died, she continued to live in comfort, lonely though her life might be.[15]

Meiji had fifteen children by five women, inconspicuous figures at the court who in surviving photographs look almost identical in their rigid hairdos and formal court robes. It is difficult to say if the emperor had any favorites, although two (Sono Sachiko and Ogura Fumiko) served him much longer than the others. Sono gave birth to eight of Meiji's children, four of whom survived. In Europe the illegitimate children of kings were not eligible to succeed to the throne, but according to Japan's different traditions, no distinction was made between children born to the empress and those who came into the world from the "borrowed" womb of another lady.

There has long been gossip about Meiji's love life, and even today some people proudly insist that they are illegitimate descendants. Extremely little evidence supports such claims.[16] Gossip has it that the emperor was often attracted by pretty geishas and commanded them to share his bed that night. This may actually have happened, but nothing written by the men who knew the young emperor personally confirms this supposition. Meiji was always provided with a half-dozen young ladies of the aristocracy who were his concubines. Those who displeased him were easily replaced; he had no need to look elsewhere.

It is easy to imagine that a young man, still not twenty, who was under pressure to beget children, the sooner the better, might throw himself into physical pleasures to the detriment of his studies. Kido's diary, especially from 1874, frequently mentions that the emperor's education was at a standstill, implying that his mind was on other matters. That year, at the request of the imperial tutors, Kido urged the emperor to demonstrate by devotion to his studies that he was worthy of his divine lineage. Perhaps this was an indirect way of advising him not to spend too much time with his ladies.

Although by this time a fairly comprehensive plan for the emperor's education had been drawn up, including not only the classics of Chinese philosophy and Japanese history but also European history and the German language, the emperor's progress was slow. Kido reported in his diary after a meeting with Fukuba Bisei, who lectured on Japanese history, and Katō Hiroyuki (1836–1916), who lectured on German law,

> They are anxious about the emperor's progress in his studies; so, taking advantage of my service with the imperial household, they asked me to make certain that his study schedule is better organized, and to assist him in directing more serious attention to his books. I gave them my opinions, and all agreed; therefore, I have decided to report our findings directly to the throne.[17]

Kido apparently felt emboldened by the affability the emperor had always shown him to recommend that he exert himself even more than before to "fulfill his divinely appointed task." A year later Kido bluntly told the emperor that "unless he concentrates his efforts on fulfilling his divinely appointed task, we, his humble subjects shall have no end of worry."[18]

A prime source of concern was the emperor's indulgence in drinking. Kido described how, after a performance of *kyōgen* at the house of Nakayama Tadayasu, some of those present feared the emperor might go "too far in his merriment" at the drinking bout that followed.[19] Many of those who served the emperor, including the chamberlain Takashima Tomonosuke (1844–1916), attested to his capacity for liquor. Takashima recalled that no matter how heavily the emperor might have been drinking the night before, the next morning he never showed the slightest sign of a hangover. Not only had the emperor an exceptionally strong constitution, but he seems to have required less sleep than an average man. When he awoke, even after only four or five hours of sleep, he would go promptly to his office, ready for work. Takashima mentioned with admiration,

> His diligence was extraordinary. Every morning he would rise early and go to his office, not retiring to his private quarters until five or six in the afternoon. Sometimes he did not leave even then but would command, "This evening let's have a party in my office." He would talk for hours, until late at night. Then, when it was time for His Majesty to go to bed, people would at once bring bedding from the back palace. It was by no means unusual for us chamberlains to spend the night in the corridors on night duty.[20]

The empress worried about her husband's drinking. That interpretation has been given to her poem:

hana no haru	I hope you will observe
momiji no aki no	Moderation when drinking
sakazuki mo	From your saké cup
hodohodo ni koso	Amidst the springtime flowers
kumamahoshikere	Or the crimson autumn leaves.[21]

The empress seems to have mentioned springtime flowers and colored autumn leaves because these were (and still are) the seasons when the largest quantities of saké are consumed.

During his youthful years, Meiji drank Japanese saké by preference, but in later years he switched to French wine and champagne. His capacity for drink was exceptional, but he was not always able to hold it. Hinonishi Sukehiro, who served the emperor as a chamberlain from 1886, recalled that Meiji drank two bottles of champagne at one sitting. When he drank that heavily, he had trouble walking, so the chamberlains did everything they could to restrict the amount of champagne he imbibed.[22] The emperor never left the dinner table as long as there was anything left to drink. Normally, he would retire to his private quarters by eleven at night, but anecdotes relate how he sometimes drank until very late at night.

Yet as all sources agree, he went early every morning to his office to conduct business of the day. Although he may at times have neglected his studies, to the disappointment of Kido and others of his advisers, his strong sense of duty never permitted him to neglect state business. His profound awareness of what it meant to be the emperor of Japan deeply impressed foreign commentators, who compared him favorably with the reigning monarchs of Europe. Charles Lanman, writing in 1882, was typical in his praise:

> Unlike many of the princes and royal personages of Europe, he is not addicted to self-indulgence, but takes delight in cultivating his mind; sparing no pains nor personal inconvenience to acquire knowledge. Although still young he frequently presides at the meetings of his Privy Councillors, . . . He often visits his executive departments, and attends at all the public services where the Imperial presence is desirable. While prosecuting his literary as well as scientific pursuits, he subjects himself to the strictest rules, having certain hours for special studies, to which he rigidly conforms. In his character he is said to be sagacious, determined, progressive and aspiring; and from the beginning of his reign he has carefully surrounded himself with the wisest statesmen in his Empire, and these have naturally assisted in his own development; so that it is almost certain that the crown of Japan has been worn in this century by one who was worthy of the great honor.[23]

Lanman went on to commend Meiji for "his zealous aspirations, almost free from prejudices, to adopt from other nations all that he deems beneficial for the promotion of the national welfare" and declared that he bore a striking resemblance to Peter the Great. Kido might have found such praise excessive, but anyone acquainted with the foibles of European royalty was likely to admire Meiji's dedication to his office.

Japanese found other aspects of Meiji's character to praise. His simplicity and avoidance of extravagance and display were often mentioned. One chamberlain recalled that the writing brush he used was worn away at the end and that he used sticks of ink to the last morsel, grinding the ink himself. Year after year he wore the same old-fashioned uniform, decorated with "frogs," long after everyone else had shifted to more modern uniforms. The uniform was often mended. When his shoes became old and loose, the chamberlains bought him new ones, but he commanded them to repair the old ones. The emperor was aware that it sometimes cost more to repair old clothes and shoes than to replace them with new ones, but he consistently followed the principle: "If something can be repaired and used again, it should be repaired."[24] Many memorialists commented on the dustiness of the curtains in the palace and on the blackened condition of the *shōji*, the results of Meiji's insistence on thrift (and on the use of candles rather than electricity).

Although none of his tutors described Meiji as scholarly, Takatsuji Osanaga (1840–1921) recalled that he listened to lectures with rapt attention and that whenever he did not understand something, he would ask questions until the meaning was perfectly clear.[25] Katō Hiroyuki delivered lectures on constitutional and international law each week before the emperor, but unfortunately, the emperor's obligation to deal with state business took precedence over his lessons, and he fell behind the schedule Katō had set. Accordingly,

> it was arranged to increase by one hour each day the time of his study, and for him to be in his office every day at seven in the morning in summer and half-past eight in winter. His Majesty's diligence was truly inspiring. He rose every morning at five and was waiting in his office when the tutors arrived.[26]

Katō made extract translations from Western books concerning constitutions; the division of powers into legislative, executive, and judiciary; the system of self-government of cities, towns, and villages; and the history of constitutions in Europe from the end of the eighteenth century to the middle of the nineteenth century. At first he used as his teaching materials his translations of various German authorities, especially Johann Bluntschli, but he feared that if the emperor depended exclusively on translations, he would not acquire a real understanding. Katō therefore decided to switch to reading texts in the original German, but it soon became evident that the emperor had no time (and perhaps no aptitude) for learning a foreign language. But, Katō insisted, he was a diligent pupil:

> His late Majesty was by nature extremely thorough and steady. He seemed unwilling ever to stop halfway; he refused to stop until he had understood to his own satisfaction the basics. If, for example, I stated something one day which he did not understand, he would ask questions the next day until he fully understood. Progress was slow, but once he had grasped something, he never forgot it and would always make full use of it. This ability always made me marvel. As an educator, I have come in contact with many students over the years, but I have never encountered anyone like His Majesty who, though there was never an examination, would apply himself to his studies in this way entirely for the sake of mental training.[27]

The emperor's remarkable memory was mentioned by many who knew him. Vice Admiral Ariji Shinanojō (1843–1919) recalled:

There was not one palace ritual or ceremony or any other historical fact with which he was unfamiliar. He never forgot the name of anyone to whom he had ever granted an audience, however humble the person's station might be. He attended the graduation ceremonies at the army and navy academies and at the university, and he never failed to remember the names of graduates who received a prize for scholarly excellence or who delivered a lecture in his presence. . . . When he invited someone to dine with him, he would describe what had happened when he last met that person and everything that had been discussed on the occasion, all as vividly as if he could see before his eyes long-ago memories.[28]

Even allowing for a certain amount of exaggeration in Ariji's praise as he recalled the recently deceased emperor, it is clear that Meiji had a retentive memory. He was not an intellectual; the accounts of those who knew him recall words of the *Analects*: "The firm, the enduring, the simple and the modest are near to virtue."

The "firm" aspect of Meiji's personality was conspicuously displayed in his active participation in military maneuvers; he even led the troops on horseback with drawn sword. During his first maneuvers, there was violent wind and rain, but the emperor remained completely unperturbed, an inspiration to the troops. This sangfroid would be typical of his behavior throughout the rest of his reign. No matter how uncomfortable or even tragic the circumstances, he was never known to complain or feel sorry for himself.

At this stage of his reign, Meiji was an inexperienced youth who had no choice but to depend on the brilliant men around him. Although these men were deferential and unquestionably revered him as their sovereign, they may also have rather intimidated him by their knowledge of not only politics and warfare but also literature and philosophy. Perhaps the emperor's apparent lack of enthusiasm for his studies, about which Kido complained, was occasioned by feelings that he could never attain their level of accomplishment.

As yet Meiji had few occasions to demonstrate his mettle. If he had died young or had lived no more than the thirty-six years of his father, he might be remembered only vaguely as the emperor who reigned at the time of the Restoration. A combination of longevity and dedication to duty, however, eventually made this youth the most celebrated of the long line of emperors.

Chapter 20

The most important event of 1869, at least as far as Emperor Meiji was concerned, was his second visit to Tōkyō. The earlier visit had been an enormous success, but the people of Kyōto felt rather neglected when they learned that the emperor had bestowed saké and other gifts on the people of Tōkyō. After his return to Kyōto early in the new year, he accordingly bestowed equally vast quantities of saké on the people of Kyōto,[1] perhaps hoping in this way to allay their fear that the old capital might soon be displaced by the new capital in the east.

Despite such gestures, apprehension that the capital would be moved to Tōkyō continued. On March 5 Iwakura Tomomi drew up a statement in which he specifically addressed this fear. Iwakura mentioned how upset many people in Kyōto and Ōsaka were by rumors that the capital was about to be moved to Tōkyō. It was true that in the previous year Edo had been renamed "Eastern Capital" (Tōkyō), but, Iwakura insisted, this was definitely not a sign that the emperor contemplated changing the seat of his authority. Rather, the decision was inspired by his desire to treat east and west alike, on the basis of his conviction that all parts of Japan "within the four seas" were equally dear to him. Kyōto had been the capital for more than a thousand years, ever since the time of Emperor Kammu, and was the site of the tombs of the successive emperors. Iwakura was certain that the capital would not be moved from Kyōto to Tōkyō, not even a thousand years hence, that there was absolutely no danger that Kyōto would be abandoned. The emperor, desiring to spread the light of imperial rule far and wide, even to Ezo and the farthest island of the Kuriles, now felt it necessary to make a second journey to the east in order to extend the benefits of the new government to parts of the country that had yet to be blessed by his benevolent influence. Iwakura conceded that some men in council advocated changing the capital, but he personally was unconditionally opposed. If the emperor should in his wisdom command that that the capital be moved, it would be unavoidable, but in his capacity as a subject, Iwakura would not praise such a decision.[2]

Plans gradually took shape for the second imperial journey to the east, regardless of whether or not it was intended as a harbinger of a forthcoming move of the capital. On March 20 it was announced that the imperial palanquin would make a detour on the way to Edo in order that the emperor might worship at Ise. This decision changed the character of the journey; that is, it would not simply be political, extending imperial influence to distant parts of the country, but religious as well, affirming the close relationship between the emperor and Shintō that would be emphasized in years to come. Another announcement ten days later disclosed the date of the emperor's departure (April 18) and declared that the keynote of the reception along the way was to be simplicity. Overeager officials were not to bother people going about their business along the roads or to interfere with agricultural labor. This insistence on simplicity may have been intended to establish a contrast with the traditional ostentation of a daimyo's procession. The stress on agriculture suggests another important purpose of Meiji's travels—to bring the emperor closer to his people at their place of work.

On April 2 the emperor sent a special message to the people of the northern region where the rebellion against imperial authority continued. He declared that just as every part of the country was the emperor's land (*ōdo*), so every person living on this land was like his child, and he would be deeply upset if he thought that even one person had failed to find a place in society.[3] The phraseology was Confucian, but it also radically differed from what earlier emperors would have said; it is hard to imagine Emperor Kōmei being distressed to learn that one of his subjects had not found a place in society. The young emperor not only felt close to his subjects—every Japanese, regardless of his status or in what part of the country he lived—but worried about their happiness and was loath to do anything that might interfere with their daily employment.

Another way in which the emperor brought himself closer to his people was by opening to the public his private gardens. On April 5 the Fukiage Garden inside Tōkyō Castle was opened for three days, an unprecedented event. The citizens were overjoyed and flocked to the castle in such numbers that eight people died in the press, and many others were injured. The emperor donated 300 *ryō* in gold to the families of the victims.[4]

Meiji left on his journey as planned. He was accompanied by members of the high nobility, including Sanjō Sanetomi, and his grandfather, Nakayama

Tadayasu. He was also accompanied by an unwanted bodyguard of *shinpei*— soldiers who had volunteered to serve as his bodyguard in Kyōto. An English resident, John Black (1827–1880), described them:

> Their idea was that they were especially imbued with the "ancient spirit of Japan"; and their creed—"devotion to the Mikado and death to the foreign barbarians." These men, then, threw themselves in his path, imploring him not to leave the sacred city, nor pollute himself by intercourse with foreigners; and, when His Majesty was deaf to their entreaties they said there was nothing left for them but to accompany him, and protect his person. As they were some 2,000 strong, ready enough with their trenchant blades, they were allowed to have their way; and so they came trooping to the capital.[5]

The early part of the emperor's journey was along the Tōkaidō, as on his previous journey, but after stopping at Seki the procession took the Ise Road to Matsuzaka, where the emperor spent the night. On the following day the procession reached the building of the Outer Shrine at Ise where he spent the night. The next morning the emperor, attired in the golden costume worn on state occasions, left his quarters in the imperial palanquin and proceeded to the shrine itself where an elaborate ceremony of worship was performed. After lunch the emperor set out again, this time to worship at the even more important Inner Shrine. He was accompanied by civil and military officers, all in formal attire. After a brief rest the emperor bathed. At two in the afternoon he worshiped at the shrine.

Because this was the first time in history that an emperor had worshiped at the most important of Shintō shrines, a new set of rituals for the occasion had been drawn up by the Ministry of Shintō at the emperor's command. The priests compared Meiji with two ancient emperors, Jimmu and Keikō,[6] and praised his wisdom and virtue in the most extreme superlatives.[7]

When Meiji was about to leave, Tōdō Takakiyo, the heir of the Tsu domain, paid a visit and offered the emperor a telescope and some cakes.[8] The telescope, like the globe that had occupied a prominent place at his coronation, seems to have been intended to enlarge the horizons of the young emperor, who now was making his acquaintance with the heartland of his country.

After Ise he visited the Atsuta Shrine. The procession rejoined the Tōkaidō at Okazaki and from there went on to Tōkyō. Although the journey itself was unmarred by any unpleasantness, apprehension was felt over reports received of continuing warfare in the north. Three of Enomoto Takeaki's warships had raided government ships anchored in Miyako Bay, and Fukuyama Castle fell to the rebels. It was feared that they might extend their attacks deeper into Honshū. From this time on until June 16, when Enomoto surrendered and the gates of the Five Point Fortress were opened to the imperial forces, the slow progress of the campaign against the rebels was a constant source of worry.[9] Enomoto was urged to surrender, politely and sometimes even with gifts. Some of his men, a few hundred at a time, surrendered, exhausted by the long struggle and by the lack of provisions, but Enomoto held out until the bitter end, refusing to abandon his old allegiance.

Once he was settled in Tōkyō, Meiji's life soon resumed the familiar routine of lessons in the Chinese and Japanese classics, along with riding practice. But although his personal life was unruffled, and there is no indication he took part in the decisions made by the government at this time, many proclamations were issued in his name. For example, on May 14 it was announced that a history office was being established by imperial command to prepare a revised history of Japan. The emperor declared,

> A national history is an everlasting, immortal canon; the compilation was a great enterprise of our ancestors. However, there has been no continuation since the *Sandai jitsuroku*.[10] Is this not a grave deficiency? Now that the abuses of the military regime, which had prevailed since the Kamakura period, have been ended, and government has been revived, I wish to found a history office which will continue the achievement of our ancestors and will promote education and culture throughout the country.[11]

He appointed Sanjō Sanetomi as chief editor.

Many problems faced the government. The subjugation of the rebels in the north was both discouragingly slow and costly. The paper currency issued by the government to help pay the costs of the warfare was not readily accepted by the public. At first the government attempted to redress the perceived inequality between paper money and gold by setting the value of 120 *ryō* in paper as the equivalent of 100 *ryō* in specie. This had the result of encouraging speculators to manipulate the currency. The government then declared that paper and specie had the same value, whereupon (a perfect example of the workings of Gresham's law) bad money drove the good money from circulation.[12] The measures and countermeasures adopted by the government were signs of both its inexperience and the continuing crisis.

Similarly the policy for the punishment of crimes swung from extreme severity to relative liberality. On May 26 the military decreed that for violating the edict against factions, the head of the faction would be put to death and the other members placed under confinement. Soldiers who deserted while in the possession of weapons and uniforms would be executed, but those who returned their weapons and uniforms before deserting would, if a first offense, be imprisoned for fifty days; second offenders would be exiled. Persons who without cause demanded money or coercively touted would, depending on the degree of their crime, be executed or sent to distant banishment.[13] It was later decreed that the leaders of the opposition to the government forces in the recent warfare in the northeast would be beheaded. Those who were already dead would be subject to a mock execution and their family line exterminated. The severity of these measures in no way accorded with the promise of generous treatment extended to Enomoto.

On June 2 the *kōgisho kaigi* voted to abolish the death penalty for believers in Christianity, substituting whipping. But the spirit of the old regime was by no means dead: on June 7 the *kaigi* voted not to prohibit *seppuku*,[14] and a few weeks later the same body unanimously voted not to prohibit the wearing of swords. In August, though, various forms of cruel punishments were abolished, including exposure, public parading of the guilty, and sawing off the head.

The lightening of the sentence against Christians probably was a gesture in the direction of the foreign powers, which continued to protest against the prohibition against Christianity. The Ainu had also attracted the sympathy of the foreigners. The government was aware that local officials in the north had at times cruelly mistreated the Ainu and that some Ainu, responding to the kind treatment of foreigners, had come to prefer them to the Japanese. The government feared that foreigners might, under the name of relieving the distress of the Ainu, incite them to rise against the Japanese. In order to prevent this from happening, Japanese immigration to Hokkaidō was encouraged.

Acts of violence against foreigners continued. The British minister was enraged by these incidents and pressed for apprehension of the culprits. On May 14 the *gijō* Tokudaiji Sanetsune and Hachisuka Mochiaki called on the British minister with apologies, but he failed to understand what they meant. Accordingly, the *hoshō* Sanjō Sanetomi, the *gijō* Ōgimachi Sanenaru, and the *san'yō* Ōkuma Shigenobu called on the minister for further explanation, and on the following day the government issued a strict prohibition on any kind of violence against foreigners. Antiforeign feeling remained strong, however, and the attacks continued, enraging the foreign envoys, who were always ready to create an incident, to the consternation of the Japanese leaders, who had their hands full with domestic issues.[15]

During this period little is recorded concerning the emperor's activities besides his frequent displays of horsemanship. His studies of the Chinese classics had progressed; he was now reading with his tutors the *Book of Poetry* and *Mencius*.[16] On occasion he reviewed troops and observed cannon practice. When the long-sought victory over Enomoto at last came, he gave an audience to senior naval and army officers. It is not clear whether Meiji was kept informed of all developments, but he was definitely involved in the most significant event of this time, the return by the daimyos of their lands and people to the emperor.

On July 25 the emperor issued an edict accepting the request of various domains that they be permitted to return their registers (*hanseki*). Domains that had not made this request were now commanded to return them. Four major domains (including Satsuma and Chōshū) had announced their intention of returning their registers in the first month of the year, and their example had been followed by others. In the end 274 daimyos surrendered their lands and people to the central government and were rewarded by being appointed as governors of their domains.[17] The titles of "nobles" (*kuge*) and "daimyos" (*shokō*) were abolished, both henceforth being known as "peers" (*kazoku*). The administrative unification of Japan had taken an immense step forward.

On August 15 the government was further reorganized with the establishment of additional ministries. Sanjō Sanetomi was appointed as minister of the right, and Iwakura Tomomi and Tokudaiji Sanetsune (1839–1919) as major counselors. The emperor's maternal grandfather, Nakayama Tadayasu, was appointed as head of the Ministry of Shintō. Other men who had figured prominently in the restoration of imperial authority were granted posts of importance in the new government.

Meanwhile the ground was being prepared for another important development in the emperor's activities. In the early summer of 1869, the British minister, Sir Harry Parkes, received word that the duke of Edinburgh, the second son of Queen Victoria, planned to visit Japan in command of the warship *Galatea*. In the previous year the duke had sailed around the world aboard this ship. Although most of his visits to various countries had been largely ceremonial, in Australia he had been wounded and nearly killed by an Irish patriot. His brief visit to Japan would hardly be worth remembering except for the fact that he was the first member of European royalty ever to visit Japan.

When word reached the court of the intended visit, a contemporary account records:

> The "progressivists" desired that His Majesty should once and for all resolve to conform as far as possible to the usages of other sovereigns on such occasions; but a very strong "opposition" denounced, in strong terms, the Mikado's lowering his dignity by making any advance which could be regarded as an admission of equal rank between a foreign Prince of the Blood Royal, and the Imperial and heaven-descended family of Japan.[18]

It took several months before the British minister received a reply from the court. It stated that the emperor was "delighted beyond measure" by the news of the forthcoming arrival of the English prince and added that "His Majesty would be intensely pleased if your Prince would consent to take up his abode in the gardens of O Hama-go-ten, the seaside palace of His Majesty." John Black, whose *Young Japan* gives the most detailed account of the background of the visit, considered it particularly important that after the formal reception of the English prince in the palace, "His Majesty should receive the prince accompanied by the English minister, and a gentleman of the English legation who should act as interpreter, in one of the Garden houses in the Imperial domain and converse with him on equal terms."[19]

The manner of treatment of the visiting English prince was of the highest importance to Parkes, the English minister, who insisted that "the Mikado will be receiving a scion of royalty as his *equal* in point of blood." He also noted that "if at the last moment I see anything derogatory in their [the Japanese] arrangements, I can decline the reception." The Chinese government had already refused to give the duke of Edinburgh "a proper reception," and he was therefore to visit China incognito. Iwakura Tomomi told Parkes that the

> reception of the prince had caused the Government much anxious consideration; for when the subject was first mooted, opinion was by no means uniform as the course to be pursued. An intelligent majority, however, had seen that the occasion was one that should be profited by to mark their friendly feelings toward foreign Powers, and their readiness to promote more intimate relations with them, although at a sacrifice of old ideas and usages. In order, therefore, to receive the prince in a manner that would be acceptable to England, the Mikado would have to adopt a new etiquette.[20]

The duke's reception by Emperor Meiji at the castle in Tōkyō was without precedent. Black commented, "Since that day other princes and distinguished men have been even more familiarly received; but that was after the Court and the country had become so used to these innovations that they ceased to discuss them."[21]

The audience took place on September 4. Every step was carefully planned, beginning with prayers to Kan-jin for his safe arrival.[22] A salute of twenty-one guns would be offered to the duke on his landing in Yokohama. Before his departure from Yokohama, the roads would be cleaned and repaired, and prayers for his safe journey offered to the god of roads. The security arrangements for the duke when he traveled by road from Yokohama to Tōkyō would be similar to those observed when the emperor traveled. According to A. B. Mitford, "The shutters of the upstairs rooms in the houses by the wayside were hermetically sealed with bits of paper stuck across them so that no Peeping Tom should look down upon the august person."[23] Prayers would also be offered at his destination: "On the day on which His Royal Highness may be expected to arrive in Yedo, religious ceremonies will take place at Shinagawa, to exorcise all evil spirits. On His Royal Highness' arrival, a Prince of the Blood will visit him, to inquire after his health."[24]

The eighth of the nine points in the program of the reception that was planned for the duke of Edinburgh was "When His Royal Highness is about to enter the gate of the castle, the ceremony called 'Nusa' will take place." Mitford in his memoirs explained that "nusa is a sweeping away of evil influences with a sort of flapper with a hempen tassel."[25] None of the British objected to this ceremony, but the acting American minister, A. L. C. Portman, prepared a report for the president of the United States entitled "The Purification of the Duke of Edinburgh." According to Fukuzawa Yukichi's autobiography, the report declared:

> Japan is a small secluded country, very self-respecting and very self-important. It is customary, therefore, for its inhabitants to regard foreigners as belonging to the lower order of animals. Actually, when the English prince arrived to be received by the emperor, they held a ceremony of purification over the person of the prince at the entrance to the castle. . . . Such being the ancient rite in the land, they employed this method on the person of the Duke of Edinburgh, because in the eyes of the Japanese, all foreigners, whether of noble lineage or common, are alike impure as animals.[26]

Probably Portman intended these provocative statements as no more than a means of catching the president's eye, but he may have been close to the truth. In the second month of 1868, when the matter of the propriety of the emperor's giving audiences to the ministers of foreign countries was debated, it was finally decided that to allow the foreigners into the palace grounds, but to safeguard the holy precincts, rites of exorcism would be performed at the palace gates in the four directions. The rites performed on the duke of Edinburgh before he was admitted to the palace had the same purpose: the *nusa* ceremony was performed not to shield him from baleful influences but to protect the palace from being polluted by a foreigner.[27] When informed by an interpreter at the American legation of the details, Fukuzawa did not laugh. He wrote instead, "I felt like crying over this revelation of our national shame."

No one in the British party seems to have been disturbed by the implications of the rite, and the meeting of the duke with the emperor took place without incident. On alighting from his carriage within the palace, the duke was received by high-ranking officers who escorted him to a waiting room. After a short interval the duke was conducted to the Audience Chamber, where the emperor stood on a raised dais. After a few words of welcome, to which his guest returned a suitable reply, the emperor invited the duke to meet him more privately in the garden. Mitford recalled,

> After a short delay, during which the princes and dignitaries of the Court came to pay their respects, the Duke was shown to the delicious little Maple Tea-house in the Castle gardens, where tea and all manner of delicacies were served. Then came a summons to the Waterfall Pavilion, where the emperor was waiting; only Sir Harry, the Admiral, and myself went in with the Duke.[28]

Parkes had been apprehensive about the duke's interview with the emperor. He wrote, "I believe the poor young Mikado suffers much from severe shyness and his ministers fear the prince will find him very uninteresting. The Prince himself is rather shy."[29] The reported conversation between Meiji and the English prince, though scarcely sparkling, was normal for such an occasion. The emperor said that it gave him the greatest pleasure to receive a prince who had come from so distant a country, and he begged the prince to remain long enough to repay himself for the fatigue of the journey. In reply the prince expressed his gratitude for the cordial reception he had received and was sure that it would please Her Majesty, the queen. The emperor assured the prince that he was happy to think that this auspicious visit would help cement the friendly relations between the two countries. He begged the duke to express any wish that might occur to him, so that he might have the pleasure of gratifying it. The prince said that so far from being dissatisfied with his reception, it had exceeded his expectations. It had long been his desire to visit a country of which he had heard so much, and he had not been disappointed. And so on. It is not difficult to imagine a similar exchange of remarks today.

From the beginning Alfred, the duke of Edinburgh, had been resigned to the likelihood that the occasion would be a bore, and in his memoirs, not concealing his boredom, Mitford confessed his inability "to become artistically enthusiastic over the presentation of diamond snuff-boxes." The snuff-box in question, presented by the prince to the emperor as a memento of himself just before taking leave, was described by Sir Henry Keppel as "a beautiful gold box, on the lid of which a miniature of himself [the duke] was set in diamonds."[30] The emperor's gifts to his English guests were considerably more artistic.[31] The prince also requested a poem in the emperor's handwriting, which he intended to present to Queen Victoria after his return to England. He received this *tanka*, which has suitably political overtones:

yo wo osame	If one governs the land
hito wo megumaba	And benefits the people
amatsuchi no	Heaven and the earth
tomo ni hisashiku	Will surely last together
arubekarikeri	For all eternity.[32]

Nothing has been recorded concerning the two young men's reactions on meeting. For Alfred, Meiji was probably the ruler of an obscure, though not barbaric, country and, as such, not of much interest; but he probably appreciated the entertainment provided during his stay.[33] Meiji may have been too tense during this first encounter with European royalty to form an opinion of the English prince, but he was aware that he must be ingratiating lest Japan's relations with England, the most powerful foreign country, be impaired. Regardless of the interview's content, the gesture of receiving a foreign prince on terms of equality set a precedent of the highest importance.

A month after the duke of Edinburgh's departure, an Austro-Hungarian mission headed by Baron Antony von Petz arrived in Japan to begin negotiations for a treaty. The baron also brought gifts: a piano for the empress and a life-size statue of the emperor of Austria for the mikado.[34] At the conclusion of the Japanese treaty with the Austro-Hungarian Empire (which was accomplished with unprecedented rapidity), Meiji is said to have written "an autograph letter to his 'brother,' the emperor of Austria."[35] Black, who described these events, commented that "never before until now had any sovereign but the Emperor of China been similarly addressed by the Mikado." In the Europeans' eyes, Meiji had acquired a new set of relatives—all the reigning monarchs of the world.

Chapter 21

When Emperor Meiji left Kyōto in 1869 for his second visit to Tōkyō, the people of Kyōto interpreted this as an omen that the capital would be shifted from their city to the east. They were reassured by Iwakura Tomomi's insistence that the location of the capital would not be changed, but their fears flared up again when it became known that the empress also was planning to go to Tōkyō. Many people in Kyōto were now convinced there was a real danger that the capital would be moved despite official denials, and they gathered at shrines to pray for divine intercession to keep the empress from leaving the city. So great was the consternation aroused by the prospect of the emperor and empress no longer residing in Kyōto that local officials feared conspirators might organize mass protests. If that happened, there was no telling what untoward events might stem from the people's turbulent emotions.[1] Only by exerting all their powers of persuasion were local officials able to calm the residents of the capital.

Whether or not the citizens of Kyōto were justified in interpreting the empress's departure for Tōkyō as a sign that a change of capital was imminent, on November 8, 1869, the empress's palanquin left the Gosho, protected by guards drawn from four domains and headed for Tōkyō. She arrived nineteen days later after a pleasant journey. Apparently quite at home in her new surroundings, she soon afterward gave a party at the Fukiage Garden for senior officers of the government.[2]

Earlier in 1869 when Emperor Meiji was about to leave for his second visit to Tōkyō, the people of Kyōto had been informed that he would return to their city in April or May of the following year and would celebrate his Daijō-e[3] there in the winter of that year. This announcement had quieted their anxiety, only for them to be informed in the spring of 1870 that the emperor's return to Kyōto had been unavoidably delayed because of unsettled conditions in parts of the country and the pressure of state business. A year later, on May 15, 1871, it was announced that the Daijō-e would be performed in Tōkyō instead. On May 24 Major Counselor Tokudaiji Sanetsune was sent as a special envoy to Kyōto to report to the tomb of Emperor Kōmei that conditions in the world and an increased burden of state duties had compelled the emperor to postpone his return to Kyōto. Tokudaiji also visited the empress dowager and informed her that the emperor's return to Kyōto would be delayed for several years.[4]

The emperor did not in fact return to Kyōto (except for brief visits) until 1877. At no point was it officially announced that the capital was now Tōkyō and not Kyōto. All the same, when Meiji at last returned to Kyōto, his journey was characterized as *gyōkō*, a going away from his residence, rather than as *kankō*, a return to his residence, the term used when he returned to Kyōto from Tōkyō in 1868.[5] By 1877 Tōkyō was functionally the capital of Japan, not only because it was the seat of the emperor and all organs of the government, but also because the foreign legations were situated there. However, the government hesitated to make this official, perhaps fearing the reactions of the people of Kyōto. Meiji would be buried in Kyōto, and the coronation of his son, Emperor Taishō, would also take place there in 1915, suggesting the persistence of the belief that in certain respects anyway, Kyōto was still the capital. It might even be argued, in the absence of a proclamation to the contrary, that Kyōto remains to this day the capital of Japan.

The official explanation of why Meiji could not return to Kyōto stressed the urgency of the state business. This was not necessarily untrue, but it is difficult to discover what precisely the emperor's role was in the many changes occurring. The entries in the chronology of his reign that specifically refer to the emperor most often describe the number of times he mounted a horse or the progress of his studies in the Chinese classics.

Riding had become a passion with him. At one time he was spending every other day mainly on a horse. Even those who recognized the desirability of physical fitness felt that the young emperor was devoting too much time to horses. When the *gijō* Nakamikado Tsuneyuki (in Kyōto at the time) learned how frequently the emperor was riding, he sent a letter to Iwakura Tomomi suggesting that he be restricted to six days a month.[6] Although the recommendation seems to have had some effect, the emperor's enthusiasm for riding continued unabated.

Meiji's studies at his time were concentrated on the orthodox books of Confucianism, but he also had instruction in the *Records of Japan* from Hirata Nobutane, the grandson of Hirata Atsutane, the Shintō apologist.[7] His chief tutor, Motoda Nagazane, first appeared before Emperor Meiji on July 17, 1871.

Motoda was born in Kumamoto in 1818. His family was of middle-level samurai status, and he grew up in comfortable circumstances. At the age of fifteen, he determined to study the teachings of the sages and in this way serve his country. Before he reached twenty, he had become friendly with various scholars, including Yokoi Shōnan, and studied Neo-Confucian texts with them. As early as 1847 he expressed to his father his basic philosophical conviction:

> It hardly needs repetition, but the Way of the subject resides in loyalty and filial piety. The way of loyalty and filial piety consists in making clear the principles. The only way to make the principles clear lies in practical learning [jitsugaku]. Everything apart from practical learning is empty language and corrupt Confucianism and, for this reason, is inadequate to make clear the principles. At present I am serving you, my father, with this practical learning. If I should aspire some day to serve his lordship, it would be with practical learning.[8]

The present-day meaning of jitsugaku is "practical learning" (such as engineering or medicine), as opposed to theoretical or philosophical knowledge, but this was not the meaning in Motoda's day. The term goes back as far as Chu Hsi (1130–1200) and originally referred to Confucian studies which, unlike Buddhism or Taoism, stressed the importance of attaining the highest moral virtue not as a goal in itself but because it enabled a man to be of service to the state. In later times the meaning shifted somewhat but, however interpreted, always stressed the unity of thought and action.[9] It can easily be seen that this kind of philosophy, rather than the more abstract considerations of some Confucianists, was well suited to the ruler of a modern state.

Fearing that Motoda's association with a school of Confucianism frowned on by the daimyo of the domain might block his advancement, Motoda's father asked him to give up jitsugaku. Motoda at first refused, but the various illnesses that afflicted him and other members of his family at this time caused him to drift away naturally from his teacher, and this led to a reconciliation with his father.[10] In 1858 Motoda succeeded his late father as adviser to the daimyo of the Kumamoto domain, and when that daimyo died, he accompanied his successor to Edo in 1860. He became actively involved in politics. At first, under the influence of Yokoi Shōnan, he favored a policy of "respect the emperor and open the country," a liberal position for someone who is generally thought of as a hidebound conservative.

At the time of the first Chōshū war, Motoda served with the troops of the Kumamoto domain, in keeping with his profession of kōbu gattai, but he opposed participation in the second Chōshū war. The Kumamoto domain, disregarding his advice, sent troops into combat. They suffered severe losses, which served to enhance Motoda's reputation as a judge of the political situation. He steadily rose in position. In 1871 he was appointed as the tutor (jidoku) to the Kumamoto daimyo, now known as the governor, and joined him in Tōkyō.[11]

Those who heard Motoda's lectures at this time commented on the passion with which he delivered them. Unlike many Confucian scholars, he emphasized not individual phrases but broader themes that truly served to cultivate the mind. A disciple who first heard him lecture in 1871 recalled,

> He would cite many vital examples from ancient and recent times, to such good effect that in the end we not only understood the texts but could not help but being moved to the depths of our hearts. Motoda's every action seemed to be inspired by a desire to follow the Way of the sages. To us young people, everything about him—his speech and actions, his appearance and his attitude—seemed absolutely splendid. We thought of him as a perfect jewel without a flaw. But there was nothing the least unnatural or stiff about him: his imposing air was combined with an indescribable affection and warmth.[12]

About this time, Motoda composed a memorial concerning the court to be presented by the governor as his own views. Though brief, it was highly admired:

> At the time of the Restoration the reason why evil men close to the throne boldly manifested rebellious intent was that the imperial authority had not yet been displayed. The reason why the imperial authority had not yet been displayed was that imperial rule had in fact yet to be carried out. From this time forward, I pray that His Majesty the emperor deign to attend the Hall of Audiences, where ministers will address and debate bills in his presence. If all state affairs are personally decided by the emperor, a just and honorable form of stable government will come into being, and people will for the first time revere it from their hearts. The failure of the provinces to submit to political guidance is to be attributed to the failure to obtain the proper kind of provincial officials. Men of talent should be appointed, and they should spread political education throughout the country. Governors who, like myself, have succeeded to their posts because of lineage should be eliminated. For this reason I respectfully request that I be relieved of my post.[13]

The proposal contained two important points. The first was the desirability of having legislation discussed in the presence of the emperor, who would personally decide whether it should be adopted. It has often been noted that Meiji religiously attended cabinet and similar meetings, even those not of great importance. The emperor's dedication to duty, exemplified by his constant attendance at such gatherings, was probably inspired by Motoda. The second point— the need to end hereditary succession to high offices—was not quickly realized.

Motoda's plan, praised by all who saw it, eventually reached Ōkubo Toshi-michi, who was so impressed that he promised to call it immediately to the emperor's attention. Ōkubo was also looking for a tutor for the emperor and asked the governor of Kumamoto about Motoda's character. The governor replied that he was unable to say whether Motoda was the best man for the position, but he could certainly vouch for his character. Thanks to this recommendation, Motoda was appointed on June 30, 1871, as the emperor's tutor. He delivered his first lecture before the emperor on July 21 on the *Analects*.[14] From then on, he delivered twelve lectures each month on the *Analects* and later on *Nihon gaishi*.[15] Motoda continued to lecture before the emperor until his death in 1891.

When first informed that he had been chosen to be the emperor's tutor, Motoda was astonished and expressed doubts about his qualifications. He believed he was already too old (at fifty-three) to be an effective member of the government, contrasting himself with men in their early forties like Saigō Taka-mori, Ōkubo Toshimichi, Kido Takayoshi, and Itagaki Taisuke, who had already made names for themselves in the new government. He suggested younger men for the post, sure that he would disgrace himself if appointed, and he announced his intention of returning to Kumamoto.[16] But Shimotsu Kyūya (1809–1883), a domain official whom Motoda respected, interrupted, "You can't do that. The combination of Motoda's learning and virtuous behavior with Saigō's valor will make an unbeatable combination."[17] Such praise made it impossible for Motoda to continue his resistance. He wrote in his diary this account of his first audience with the emperor:

Attired in formal wear, I approached the throne on my knees and, bowing my head to the floor, I worshiped the dragon countenance from outside the Mima,[18] then withdrew, still on my knees. This was my first approach to the imperial presence. My mind was filled by turns with awe and joy, and I could not control my profound emotion. When this ceremony was over, I had an interview with the major counselor Tokudaiji Sanetsune and was informed that I had been appointed as the chief tutor [*jidoku senmu*] to the emperor and that I would receive the treatment appropriate to an official appointed with the emperor's approval. At first I declined, saying that I was unworthy of this responsibility, but the imperial command had already been issued, and I did not wish to oppose it. I therefore resolutely accepted the command.[19]

Although some of his contemporaries found Motoda unbendingly conservative,[20] he enjoyed the full confidence of the emperor, as well as the admiration of principal figures in the government, who praised him without qualification. Ōkubo Toshimichi, who rarely had a good word for anyone, said of Motoda, "As long as this man is by His Majesty's side, my mind is at ease." Soejima

Taneomi said, "The man who deserves the greatest credit for the magnitude of His Majesty's moral virtue was Motoda *sensei*. I would have no choice but to give his name as the subject who contributed most to the Meiji era."[21] Although Motoda is virtually forgotten today, he seems to have exerted greater influence on the emperor than any of the celebrated statesmen who surrounded him.

After becoming the emperor's tutor, Motoda resumed his interest in practical learning, which for him meant returning to the basic texts of Confucius and Mencius. He insisted that the Way must be sought in the Six Classics[22] and nowhere else. He admitted the value of Western scientific learning and technology and urged Japanese to study them in the spirit of *kakubutsu*, a term found in the *Great Learning* meaning "an investigation of things." He was convinced, however, that with respect to human relations, the West had nothing to offer, that guidance could be found only in the Six Classics. He added,

> In recent years there have been those who, saying they are fed up with the platitudes of the Chinese classics, delight solely in the novelties of Western books. This in the end is likely to turn into an indiscriminate mania for Western culture, an unspeakable perversion of learning.[23]

The combination of Eastern morality with Western science, first advocated by Sakuma Shōzan during the late Tokugawa era, characterized Meiji's attitude, especially in his later years, which probably can be attributed to the influence of Motoda's teachings as well.

In addition to his lectures in the palace, Motoda wrote essays on subjects such as the national religion,[24] but he is best known for his part in the formulation of the *Rescript on Education* of 1890, which gave great prominence to Confucian ethical ideals and to the principle of *chūkun aikoku* (loyalty to the sovereign and love of country), a two-word crystallization of Motoda's political thought.

The emperor's moral education was traditional, under the guidance of Motoda and others; but his public life was increasingly affected by Western things. His first public appearance before Japanese and foreigners, on April 28, 1870, was during a review of troops,[25] an activity not discussed in the Confucian texts he studied. It was apparently at the insistence of Ōkubo Toshimichi, who wished the emperor to act like a modern European monarch, that Meiji emerged from the shadows of his private quarters into the glare of public attention.

The Austrian Baron Alexander de Hubner, who had an audience with the emperor in 1871, reported that a chamberlain had come for him in "a kind of phaeton built in Hongkong, perhaps the only vehicle that the court possesses, for the use of carriages is unknown at the court. The mikado never leaves his palace." He added in a footnote, "Some months later, on the advice of his reform-minded ministers, the emperor showed himself in a calash before his astonished subjects. This summer (1872), they saw him travel through the streets of Yokohama in a hired carriage. The son of the Gods wore a peculiar European uniform, half sailor and half ambassador!"[26]

Meiji's uniform, with its characteristic gold "frogs" spread across the chest, though European in inspiration, amused the Austrian baron. The emperor continued to wear this uniform long after anything similar was to be seen abroad. Every morning he changed from Japanese nightclothes to Western dress, either his uniform or a frock coat, whenever he left the privacy of the inner quarters. Gradually, too, his diet began to include Western food and drink: we know exactly when he first drank a glass of milk and ate beef.[27]

It was normal for Europeans to deplore the haste with which Japanese discarded their traditional attire and took to wearing Western clothes. Numerous cartoons depict the Japanese wearing ill-fitting Western finery, looking not merely unattractive but comic. However, W. E. Griffis, who had served the daimyo of Echizen through the late Tokugawa period and knew Japan well, disagreed with this view:

> In spite of what artists and lovers of the unique and the strange in the Japanese may say, the natives themselves understand human nature and hold the true philosophy of clothes. Their great ambition is to be treated as men, as gentlemen, and as the equal of Occidentals. In their antiquated garb they knew that they or their country would never be taken seriously.
>
> Very soon we saw a change of dress, not only among soldiers and Samurai but among all the government officers and even in the Mikado himself. . . . It is certain that the laying aside of the Samurai's garb hastened the decay of the old barbarous customs which belonged to feudalism. In fact, this revolution in clothes helped powerfully in the recognition by the whole world of Japan as an equal in the brotherhood of nations.[28]

In December 1871, when Meiji visited Yokosuka, a photograph was secretly taken of the emperor and those accompanying him. Although he was attired in formal robes, of the twenty men in his retinue all but three were in Western clothes.[29]

The customs of the past continued to be given lip service, but one custom after another was rejected as being unsuitable for a modern nation, and some were even prohibited. For example, the blackening of the teeth and shaving of the eyebrows, traditional in the *gembuku* ceremony of high-ranking nobles, was prohibited on March 6, 1870. Two months later, testing the sharpness of one's sword on the corpse of an executed man also was prohibited. Samurai were no longer allowed to reprimand (or even kill) commoners for an alleged trivial offense.[30]

Meiji adapted quickly to both the use of foreign things and the etiquette to be observed when granting an audience to an eminent foreign visitor. He learned that he was expected to shake hands, to smile (although at first he had trouble remembering this), and to ask his visitors polite questions about matters of no interest. Eager palace officials quickly became familiar with foreign behavior and sought to put visitors at ease. They arranged to have European food served at receptions and, discovering that foreign dignitaries disliked removing their shoes at an audience, had the tatami covered with carpets.[31]

As early as 1869, in the hopes of relieving foreigners' nervousness when they saw samurai wearing swords, a proposal to make voluntary the wearing of swords was made. Advocates of change expressed the view that Japanese society had become so peaceful that swords—symbols of the age of unrest and violence from which Japan had happily emerged—were no longer necessary except as ornaments to formal attire. But others sprang to the defense of the sword, which they insisted was the expression of the martial spirit of the imperial country and the seat of the true spirit of the Land of the Gods. They asked rhetorically if anyone who possessed the Yamato spirit would ever discard his swords. These arguments carried weight, and the bill was unanimously defeated.[32]

Nonetheless, on September 23, 1871, a decree was issued permitting samurai to cut their hair and not wear swords. It also made optional the wearing of dress uniform or semi-dress uniform. Several important members of the government, including Kido Takayoshi, had already cut their hair in anticipation of the decree, and resistance to such signs of modernity and enlightenment seemed to be scant. Even the chamberlains and pages cut their hair.

Despite the claims that law and order had been restored to Japan by the enlightened new regime, the assassinations continued. Anyone who voiced untraditional views lived under the constant threat of being killed, and even the bravest man could not help but feel intimidated, knowing that at any moment he might be felled by an assassin's sword. Fukuzawa Yukichi felt particularly vulnerable because he was known for his advocacy of "enlightened" opinions. He wrote in his autobiography, "Nothing can be worse, more unsettling, more generally fearful, than this shadow of assassination. No one without the actual experience can really imagine it." In 1871, when the university he founded, Keiō gijuku, moved to Mita, he had a trapdoor built in his residence to permit him to escape from any would-be assassin.[33]

The most shocking assassination of the early Meiji era was that of Ōmura Masujirō (1824–1869), a samurai of the Chōshū domain.[34] Ōmura learned Dutch at Ogata Kōan's academy in Ōsaka and later studied Western medicine in Nagasaki. In 1853 he was invited to Uwajima by its daimyo, Date Munenari. By this time, foreign pressure on Japan had mounted, and Ōmura was ordered by the domain to return to Nagasaki to study the construction of warships and navigation. In 1856 he accompanied the daimyo to Edo, where he became a teacher at the shogunate's *bansho shirabesho* (Institute for the Investigation of Barbarian Books). He studied English in Yokohama with the American missionary J. C. Hepburn. Gradually he acquired a reputation as an expert in military matters, and after his return to Chōshū in 1861, he set about reforming its army, insisting on the necessity of combat training for both samurai and commoners. During the second Chōshū war (1866), troops Ōmura had trained routed the shogunate forces, and the same troops distinguished themselves during the fighting at Toba and Fushimi that overthrew the shogunate. Later in 1868 he led the forces that demolished the Shōgitai.

After the Meiji Restoration, Ōmura was appointed to the post of *hyōbu dayū* (minister of war) and, in this capacity, directed his energies to creating a modern army. He was so successful in his efforts that he has often been referred to as the "father of the Japanese army." The most notable feature of his plans was his advocacy of the conscription of commoners, a development that enraged samurai who believed it threatened their special, privileged position. Ōmura's attack on the Shōgitai had also earned him many enemies among disgruntled samurai still clinging to the now repudiated ideal of *jōi*. He had every reason to expect some sort of violence.

In the middle of August 1869, Ōmura traveled to the Kansai region, mainly to establish a school for training noncommissioned officers. He himself was aware of the danger of assassination, as was his friend Kido Takayoshi, who arranged for special police protection. Ōmura had word from an informant that he was being followed by suspicious persons as he traveled about the Kansai, and he took precautions to keep his movements secret; but on the night of October 9, when Ōmura and his associates were relaxing at an inn in Kyōto, a band of eight men, most of them from Chōshū, forced their way in, and a terrible battle in the dark ensued.[35] Ōmura was wounded in several places and barely escaped with his life by hiding in a bathtub full of dirty water. His worst wound, on the leg, did not heal, and he was finally taken to a hospital in Ōsaka. He was treated by the celebrated Dutch doctor A. F. Bauduin, who urged immediate amputation. However, an operation could not be performed on a person of Ōmura's rank without the government's permission, and the permission was so slow in coming that Ōmura died of his wounds on December 7.[36]

Ōmura's assailants were captured and sentenced to death, only to be reprieved at the last moment. As in the case of Yokoi Shōnan, there was considerable sympathy for them, especially among samurai in high places, who shared the assassins' view that Ōmura's restructuring of the army was an intolerable affront to their class. The assassins were not executed for a year after the crime.

The next important victim of an assassin was the counselor Hirosawa Saneomi, who was murdered in his house on February 27, 1871. The assailant was never found, and the motive of the crime remained unknown.[37] The emperor, greatly distressed by the crime and the slowness of the police in apprehending the perpetrator, issued this command:

The disaster with which the late Hirosawa Saneomi met is evidence that We have shown Ourself to be incapable of protecting Our ministers, and

We have let the criminals escape. He makes the third minister to be harmed since the Restoration. This is Our misfortune and a failure of court principles, brought about by the laxness of enforcement of law and order. We profoundly regret this. We charge all in the country to search with the greatest care and to expect the certain apprehension of the criminals.[38]

It must have been galling for the young emperor to have to admit that despite the immense efforts the Japanese were making to persuade Western nations that Japan was a civilized country where law and order were respected, three men high in the government had been assassinated within the space of two years. Many other assassinations and attempted assassinations during the next thirty years created so unfavorable impression on the Western nations that it was difficult for the Japanese to persuade them to end extraterritoriality.

The Japanese nevertheless continued to make rapid strides toward modernization. Railway and telegraph lines soon extended to many parts of the country, and almost every day saw the introduction of some new Western thing, whether an article of clothing, something to eat, a machine, or a book of photographs. Despite their popularity, these importations could not keep people from yielding at times to the passions that had swayed them during the turbulent days at the end of the Tokugawa period.

Like many of his contemporaries, the young emperor was attracted by the new without repudiating the old, finding a place for both in different segments of his life. He loved Kyōto more than anywhere else, but he realized that the new Japan must make a fresh start away from the traditions of the old capital. The son of Emperor Kōmei, who had rejected every aspect of Western civilization, he became the symbolic leader of modern Japan, which boldly took from the West whatever might help it become a modern nation. But he did not neglect to listen to Motoda's lectures on the unchanging wisdom of the East.

Chapter 22

The chief political event of 1871 was undoubtedly the proclamation of *haihan chiken* (abolition of the domains and establishment of prefectures) on August 29. On that morning the emperor summoned to the palace leaders of the four domains that had been most actively involved in both the Restoration and the new government—Chōshū, Satsuma, Hizen, and Tosa. He expressed gratitude for their advocating the return of registers in 1869 and asked their support for the forthcoming major undertaking, *haihan chiken*. The minister of the right, Sanjō Sanetomi, read the emperor's rescript in which he declared it was necessary, in order to protect at home the countless millions of people and to achieve abroad equality with all nations, to extend and unify laws throughout the country and to do away with an institution that by now was significant only in name. The institution was feudalism—the division of the country into domains, each ruled by a daimyo.

The transition from a feudal to a centralized state took place with unbelievable smoothness. On the afternoon of August 29, the emperor sent for the governors of four domains who had proposed a system of prefectures and subprefectures to replace the domains and expressed his pleasure in their recommendations.[1] Later that afternoon he summoned fifty-six domain governors (*chiji*) resident in Tōkyō and informed them by a proclamation (read by Sanjō Sanetomi) of the great change. The daimyos prostrated themselves in token of their submission to the emperor's edict. The same message was delivered on the following day to representatives of daimyos living in their provinces. On September 1 the minister of foreign affairs, Iwakura Tomomi, reported to the ministers of the different countries that the domains had been abolished and replaced with prefectures.

On September 5 when Iwakura visited the acting British minister, F. O. Adams, to inform him personally of the changes, the latter expressed his congratulations for the successful completion of a highly dramatic action. He said it would be quite impossible for a government in Europe to achieve a change of similar magnitude in fewer than several years and without the use of military force.[2]

The impetus for returning the registers had come from the domains themselves, but *haihan chiken* was an imperial command imposed on the domains. There might well have been opposition to the destruction of a system that had lasted (with various modifications) since the end of the twelfth century, a system that guaranteed many privileges to the daimyos and their retainers, but not a voice was raised against the imperial command. This was largely the result of careful preparatory planning. Ōkubo Toshimichi, one of the chief proponents of the plan, had traveled to Satsuma to obtain the cooperation of Saigō Takamori. Saigō was revered as both the chief architect of the Restoration and a man of unsullied reputation; his advocacy of *haihan chiken* was indispensable and, once obtained, influenced many daimyos who might otherwise have protested.

The need for abolishing the domains had by this time become clear to men like Ōkubo as an administrator and to Yamagata Aritomo (1838–1922) as a military man. Yamagata had just returned to Japan after a year in Europe where he had studied different military systems. Although the government seemed not to be menaced by any immediate threat of an uprising, it was obvious that like any other government, it needed military forces to deal with whatever unforeseen crises might arise. William Elliot Griffis said of the government of that time: "Without one national soldier, it possessed only moral power, for the revolution had been carried through because of the great reverence which the Mikado's name inspired."[3]

The funds available to the government were also so limited that the need for cash had become desperate. The replacement of the domains, which had been more or less autonomous, by prefectures under the control of the central government seemed to reformers the only solution, but it was by no means easy to effect. Not only was it likely that the samurai class would fight for what it considered to be its rights, but the common people, most of them unaware of any higher authority than the daimyo, would hardly oppose a daimyo if he chose not to obey the emperor. The daimyo's influence was pervasive, touching the daily lives of all who dwelled in his domain.

Griffis was present when the decree abolishing the domains was received in Fukui, the seat of the Echizen daimyo:

I had full opportunity of seeing the immediate effect of this edict, when living at Fukui, in the castle, under the feudal system. Three scenes impressed me powerfully.

The first was that at the local Government Office, on the morning of the receipt of the Mikado's edict, July 18, 1871. Consternation, suppressed wrath, fears and forebodings mingled with emotions of loyalty. In Fukui I heard men talk of killing Yuri, the Imperial representative in the city and the penman of the Charter Oath of 1868.

The second scene was that in the great castle hall, October 1, 1871, when the lord of Echizen, assembling his many hundreds of hereditary retainers, bade them exchange loyalty for patriotism and in a noble address urged the transference of local to national interest.

The third scene was on the morning following, when the whole population, as it seemed to me, of the city of 40,000 people, gathered in the streets to take their last look, as the lord of Echizen left his ancestral castle halls, and departed to travel to Tōkyō, there to live as a private gentleman, without any political power.[4]

Similar scenes were no doubt enacted in many others of the 270 domains, great and small. It is extraordinary that the daimyos, faced with a loss of hereditary privileges and compensated by only titular recognition as governors of the domains where they had reigned, accepted *haihan chiken* so calmly. The Meiji Restoration had shifted the apex of Japanese society without changing its structure. *Haihan chiken* had a far greater impact: close to 2 million people—the samurai class—had lost their income, formerly granted by the daimyos, and were faced with the prospect of permanent unemployment. Several years later they received lump-sum grants of money from the government to compensate for their loss of positions in the hopes they would use the money to start new careers. But most samurai, unaccustomed to trade and other occupations of the new Japan, soon exhausted the money, and many were forced to perform humble, even menial labor. Ōnuma Chinzan's poem in Chinese, *Shafuhen* (The Ricksha Man), describes one such samurai. It is in the form of a dialogue between a ricksha man and his customer. The customer speaks first:

> "Ricksha boy, why up so early?"
> "To wipe the dust from my ricksha.
> My customers still haven't come,
> But I got up at dawn to be ready."
> "What did you do in the old days?"
> "I was a shogunate retainer with 3,000 *koku*.
> When I left home I rode in a chair or on horseback,
> Proud I was a samurai of high rank.
> Today I have forgotten all that;

I gladly carry merchants in my ricksha.
I pull people east, west, south, north,
All day long, for a couple of strings of cash.
My wife and children are waiting for firewood and rice,
And what money's left I gladly drink up in saké."[5]

It is true that many of the samurai class subsequently found employment in government offices, and they continued for fifty years or more to form the backbone of the intelligentsia,[6] but some never managed to accommodate themselves to the changes. The former samurai who is reduced to pulling a ricksha (or performing some equally disagreeable labor) is a familiar figure in literature of the time, and it was rumored that young women of the samurai class had found employment in the Yoshiwara brothels.

The emperor's authority was obviously greatly enhanced by the change. In principle at least, he was now the sole ruler of the entire country, replacing numerous feudal lords, some of whom had governed their domains more or less independently. The change affected him personally, but he probably was even more directly affected by another change that occurred very soon afterward. In the same month as the *haihan chiken*, the Ministry of the Imperial Household and the emperor's private quarters underwent a major shake-up. Until this time only members of the high-ranking nobility (*dōjō kazoku*) could serve at court, and in keeping with their ancient lineage, it was their practice to cling to precedents and conventions. The emperor's living quarters were dominated by female officials of the nobility, most of them held over from the previous reign. They were unyielding in their conservatism and used their influence over the emperor to forestall changes.[7] Members of the government, even noblemen like Sanjō Sanetomi and Iwakura Tomomi, lamented this situation and attempted to reform it, but practices that had built up over the centuries were not to be altered in a single day.[8]

Saigō Takamori, who had traveled to Tōkyō to support *haihan chiken*, decided that the time had come for change. He insisted that it was essential for "delicate and effeminate old aristocrats" to be replaced by "manly and incorruptible samurai" as the emperor's mentors. After consulting with Ōkubo and Kido, he made a formal proposal to Sanjō and Iwakura, asking for a prompt decision. On August 19 the decision was reached: Yoshii Tomozane (1828–1891), a Satsuma samurai, was appointed as chief of the staff, charged with reforming the Ministry of the Imperial Household and the emperor's private quarters. The nobleman Tokudaiji Sanetsune, long an advocate of change, was commanded to serve the emperor personally in the capacity of a member of the Ministry of the Imperial Household.

Recommendations for reform were soon presented. Henceforth, persons would be appointed as chamberlains without respect to whether they belonged to the nobility or the samurai class. It was hoped that even if there were only a few samurai among the chamberlains, they would eliminate abuses of long standing. The chamberlains were also given a new duty, keeping the emperor informed of matters old and new, Eastern and Western. Senior chamberlains would assist in the emperor's intellectual growth. The changes did not affect only the emperor: it was decided that the empress and her ladies also needed to be familiar with both old and new conditions in Japan, China, and the West and that they therefore should be allowed to listen to lectures delivered before the emperor.[9]

Men in the emperor's staff with aristocratic names like Sanjōnishi, Uramatsu, and Ayanokōji were replaced by samurai with names like Murata Shimpachi.[10] On September 15 all the female officials were dismissed and replaced with younger women.[11] Saigō Takamori, in a letter he sent on January 20, 1872 to his uncle, Shiihara Yosanji, wrote with evident satisfaction,

Among the many changes of every kind, those most to be rejoiced over and prized relate to the emperor's person. Up to now, no one who was not a noble was permitted to come into the presence of His Majesty. Even officials of the Ministry of the Imperial Household who happened to be of the samurai class could not enter his presence. But these bad practices have all been changed, and members of the samurai class have been chosen to serve even as chamberlains. Nobles and samurai have been selected without distinction, and the emperor shows particular favor to chamberlains appointed from the samurai class, a truly admirable development.

The emperor intensely dislikes being cooped up in the women's quarters and remains all day, from morning to evening, in his office. He and the chamberlains read and discuss together the learning of Japan, China, and the West. He is so occupied with his studies that he dresses much more simply than was customary with daimyos up until now. His diligence in his studies is exceptional, far greater than the average man's. The emperor today cannot be as emperors were in the past. Even their lordships Sanjō and Iwakura say that he must be far more active. Fortunately, he is of a brave and wise nature, and he has an extremely robust constitution. The nobles say there has not been so healthy an emperor in recent generations. He goes riding every day that the weather permits, and he has said that he intends shortly to drill one platoon each of his personal guards every other day. It is reported that he is determined to lead a battalion and to be his own grand marshal.[12]

Later in the same month, the cabinet was reorganized, and the offices of minister of the left, minister of the right, and major councillor were abolished, along with various lesser offices. The government was divided into three branches: the executive (*shōin*), headed by the emperor; the legislative (*sa-in*); and the judicial (*u-in*).

Once these major domestic changes had been made, greater attention could be paid to international developments. First in importance was the establishment of the northern frontier. The settlement of Ezo (or Hokkaidō, as it came to be called in September 1869) was an urgent concern lest the Russians get there first. Important officials were sent to administer Hokkaidō and Chishima, which were divided into eleven provinces and eighty-six counties.[13] On October 5, 1869, Ōkunitama was established as the principal god to be worshiped by those engaged in the development of Hokkaidō, and a ceremony of enshrinement was carried out. Major temples encouraged parishioners to emigrate to the new territory.

The chief problem in establishing the frontier between Japan and Russia related to Sakhalin. Both Russia and Japan had established settlements on the island, and the boundary between the two was by no means easy to draw. In March 1870 a commission for the development of Sakhalin was appointed, but in the absence of diplomatic relations between Japan and Russia, it was not possible to negotiate. On March 3 Terashima Munenori (1832–1893), Ōkuma Shigenobu, and Itō Hirobumi met with the American minister resident Charles E. De Long to discuss the question of Sakhalin. The officious De Long, stressing the great importance to the rest of the world in settling the boundary, proposed himself as the mediator. He pointed out the close relations between the United States and Russia and promised that if entrusted with this mission, he would spare no pains in reaching a solution.[14] The Japanese accepted the offer with the proviso that the border be established along a degree of latitude: north of 50 degrees would be Russian territory, and south of 50 degrees, Japanese.

Despite De Long's self-confidence, his negotiations failed to produce a settlement. Minor clashes between Japanese and Russians continued, and the Japanese still had not made up their minds what policy to adopt. They had at least three choices: (1) to pay the Russian settlers a sum of money in return for leaving Sakhalin and then rule the whole island; (2) to divide the island and move Russian settlers north of the boundary, giving them some money for their expenses; and (3) to yield the entire island to Russia, receiving compensation in return.[15]

In June 1871 Soejima Taneomi was sent to negotiate with the Russians in the Russian part of Sakahalin. When he was about to leave, the emperor told him:

> Russia is the country closest to our own, and it is therefore highly desirable that we maintain friendly relations. This is particularly true of Sakhalin where our two peoples live together, coming and going in the course of earning their livelihoods. How could we fail to devote our efforts to pre-

serving this situation? In the past, as far back as 1852, the Russian czar sent an ambassador plenipotentiary to discuss how the border might be settled, but because of circumstances on both sides, the discussions did not bear fruit. Later, in 1867, a treaty was provisionally signed in St. Petersburg, providing for mixed occupation by both peoples. When I examine now the situation on Sakhalin, it makes me wonder whether because of the differences in language and intent, suspicion and even hostility are not likely to arise in people's hearts, leading to hostility and finally to a disruption in the friendly relations between the two countries. It is most urgent that the border be determined. This is a deep concern not only of myself but of the czar of Russia who has been gravely concerned. For this reason I command you, Taneomi, to go with the full powers delegated to you, and negotiate to determine the boundary. I hope that you will profit by this opportunity to settle this matter and enable the people of both countries to continue enjoying their blessings and that our friendship [with Russia] will be ever closer and long lasting. See to it, Taneomi, that you take my words to heart.[16]

It is noteworthy that the emperor spoke of the czar as sharing his concern with achieving a peaceful solution to the border problem; he declared that their mutual desire was peace, which would permit their subjects to continue earning their livelihoods undisturbed. This statement suggests that the emperor now was aware of both the duty of a sovereign toward his people and the desirability of sovereigns of different countries acting in concert.

During the next few months Soejima Taneomi met the Russian envoy Evgenii Karlovich Biutsov many times, but their negotiations failed to settle the status of Sakhalin.[17] In February 1873 Kuroda Kiyotaka, the vice president of land development in Hokkaidō, presented a memorandum urging that Japan abandon Sakhalin completely, declaring that funds would be better spent on developing the huge tracts of land available in Hokkaidō than on attempting to develop the wastelands of Sakhalin. He claimed it was unlikely that the income derived from the sale of grain, coal, or fish produced in Sakhalin would ever sustain the population and praised the Russians for their wisdom in having sold Alaska to the Americans in 1868 for similar reasons.[18]

The situation was not resolved until May 1875 when a treaty was concluded between Minister Plenipotentiary Enomoto Takeaki and the Russian Plenipotentiary Alexander Gorchakov providing that His Majesty, the emperor of Japan, would yield all rights over the entire island of Sakhalin to His Majesty, the czar of all the Russias, in return for the latter yielding to the emperor of Japan the eighteen islands of the Kurile chain. The border between the two countries was established between Shumshu Island, the northernmost of the chain, and Lopatka, at the southern tip of Kamchatka.[19]

In the meantime the emperor's attention was diverted to events occurring far from Japan. Soon after the outbreak of the Franco-Prussian War, fought between July 1870 and May 1871, the Japanese government sent four senior samurai as observers. By the time they reached Europe, the Prussians had been victorious in every battle and were besieging Paris. The Japanese observers went to Paris where they compiled minutely detailed reports on the fighting, the strengths and weaknesses of the combatants, the merits and demerits of the weapons used, the causes of victory or defeat, as well as general conditions in Europe. Without exception, they were deeply impressed by the strength and battle tactics of the Prussian military. Until this time the Japanese had followed French models in organizing a modern army, but the French defeat in the war induced the Japanese to change their mentors: henceforth, the German army would provide the model.[20]

The emperor took an exceptional interest in the war. Takashima Tomono-suke, an army officer, recalled years later how the emperor had carefully ex-amined reports reaching him of the Franco-Prussian War and questioned his advisers about the strategies adopted by the two armies. Soon after the war ended, a German warship called at Yokohama, and the captain offered the emperor photographs of the war. The officer asked permission to explain the photographs, which the emperor readily granted. He listened with great interest as the officer described not only what was shown in the photographs but all that had happened up to the conclusion of the war. Takashima reported that "the dragon face looked unusually pleased as he listened."[21]

The date of this incident is not clear, but needless to say, it was unheard of for the emperor to admit a foreigner into his presence for such a purpose.[22] The emperor again broke precedent when he granted an audience to Adams, the acting British minister, who was being transferred to a superior post. The em-peror expressed his pleasure that the value of his services had been recognized by his sovereign but regretted that Adams was leaving. Under the circumstances, he could not detain him but hoped that he would take good care of himself on the voyage home.[23] There was nothing in the least remarkable in the emperor's words, but they indicated with what rapidity the court had accustomed itself to European usages.

As the result of his armies' victories, the king of Prussia, Wilhelm I, was crowned as kaiser of Germany at Versailles in January 1871 and sent notification of his new eminence to Emperor Meiji. The latter responded with a message of congratulations and two albums of Yamato-e, a return gift for the war pictures the kaiser had sent the previous autumn. The distance between Japan and Europe was still enormous, but Japan had assumed a role important enough in the world for the emperor to be kept abreast of the news of his "cousins," the crowned heads of Europe.

The most important development with respect to bringing Japan into closer contact with the rest of the world at this time was undoubtedly the departure of the Iwakura mission for America and Europe on December 23, 1871.[24] The treaty of commerce signed with the United States in July 1858 had stated that its provisions might come up for reconsideration in 171 months, so this was an appropriate time for the mission to visit the countries with which Japan had signed treaties.[25] The treaties had provided for extraterritoriality and fixed import tariffs, both highly unpopular with the Japanese as infringements on their sovereignty. It was hoped that these objectionable provisions might be eliminated by negotiation.

In February 1871 Itō Hirobumi, then in Washington, wrote to various high-ranking officials proposing that a mission of outstanding officials be dispatched in the near future to Europe and America to examine in each country the situation with respect to friendly relations, trade, and customs duties, as advance preparation for fulfilling the conditions necessary for revision of the treaties. Itō hoped that members of the proposed mission would succeed in convincing persons in the countries they visited that Japan had reached maturity as a modern state and therefore should not be treated as a backward country whose laws and finances could not be trusted. The chief purpose of the mission would be to win the confidence of the major Western countries and to communicate to them the government's desire for revision of the treaties.

In May 1871 the government ordered Councillor Ōkuma Shigenobu (1838–1922) and Yoshida Kiyonari (1845–1891), an official of the Finance Ministry, to examine the advisability of sending a mission to the West in the hopes of revising the treaty. They concluded that a mission should be sent, and the cabinet prepared a statement that was submitted to the emperor.

Starting from the assumption that relations between countries should be on a basis of equality, the statement asked why Japan had signed unequal treaties with foreign countries. It blamed this on the laziness and temporizing habits of the officials of the late Tokugawa period. At the time of the Restoration, men had wished to reclaim Japanese rights and escape from the humiliation to which the treaties subjected Japan, but the treaties were in force and could not be changed. The time had now come to discuss with foreign governments revision of the treaties and friendship based on equality. Because revisions would have to be based on international law, anything in the Japanese system or its laws not in consonance with international law would have to be changed. This might take a year or more, but because it was clearly stated in the treaties that a revision might commence on July 1, 1872, a great opportunity now existed. But the diplomats of each nation would undoubtedly seek the advantage of their own country, and if anything in the Japanese system, laws, or religion was contrary to generally accepted morality, they were likely to attack it and insist on Japan's immediate compliance with their ways as the price of treaty revision. This would not be easy for the Japanese, and the result was likely to be confrontation over the conference table.

A mission might be useful in avoiding this kind of disagreement. Its members would pay courtesy calls on foreign countries to express the hope that the changes in the Japanese government would enable closer ties than before. They would also inform each country that treaty revision was the goal of the Japanese government and propose negotiations. Sending a mission to the countries of Europe and America was the best way to discover what Japan would have to do in order to be accepted as a member of the community of nations. Specialists attached to the mission would observe the countries' systems, laws, economy, education, and so on in order to determine how they might be adopted in Japan. The mission would give the Japanese the opportunity to change their own country in ways that would convince foreign countries that Japan should be considered an enlightened nation.[26]

A second memorandum described some of the changes that would have to be made in Japanese laws, in the freedom for foreigners to come and go and live where they pleased, in education for enlightenment, and in removing obstacles to religious freedom.

It is likely that if these proposals had been followed as they stood and the mission had not attempted to obtain immediate treaty revision, it would have been acclaimed as an unqualified success, but the mission's inability to obtain revision has caused many historians to speak of its disastrous failure. This attitude was not, however, shared by foreigners of the time, who eagerly claimed recognition for their part in a glorious page of Japanese history. W. E. Griffis, writing in 1900, stated,

> Perhaps the most remarkable event of the year 1871 was the dispatch of the great embassy to Christendom, that is, to America and Europe, of which it may be said, without any exaggeration, whatever, that Guido F. Verbeck was the originator and organizer, as we shall see.
>
> From Tokio, November 21, 1871, Mr. Verbeck wrote:
>
> "The government is going to send a very superior embassy to America and Europe. . . . It is my hope and prayer that the sending of this mission may do very much to bring about, or at least bring nearer, the long longed-for toleration of Christianity. . . . Eight or nine of the names are of former scholars of mine. We pray that the results may be good, and further, under the Divine blessing, the boon of religious toleration. I have worked in that direction all I could."[27]

Verbeck recalled that on October 25, 1871, Iwakura had requested him to call. His first question was, "Did you not write a paper and hand it to one of your chief officers?"[28] He was referring to a paper Verbeck had sent to Ōkuma several years earlier, recommending the sending of an embassy to Europe and America. Iwakura said he had not heard of the paper until three days before but was now having it translated.

At the end he told me that it was the *very* and the *only* thing for them to do, and that my programme should be carried out to the letter, . . . The embassy is organized according to my paper. . . . It sailed in two months from the date of my paper becoming known to Iwakura and the emperor.[29]

Griffis added,

One prominent object of the embassy was to secure the removal of the extra territoriality clause in the treaties, that Japan might receive full recognition as a sovereign state. For this, however, the envoys were not, as our American minister, Hon. Chas. H. De Long, told me before they started, armed with full powers from the Emperor.[30]

A question that has divided specialists is whether treaty revision was the mission's prime objective. Those who believe it was emphasize the length of the mission's stay abroad and the great cost and describe the dejection of its members after their return to Japan. It is clear, however, that treaty revision, though ardently desired, was not the original objective. It may be that De Long, who accompanied the mission to Washington, mischievously suggested to the Japanese that the moment had come to ask the Americans to revise the treaties, perhaps hoping that success would redound to his credit in Japan. The extraordinarily friendly receptions that the Japanese mission received wherever it went in America confirmed the belief that the time was ripe for negotiations.[31]

However, when the Japanese arrived in Washington, the secretary of state pointed out that their credentials did not include treaty revision. Ōkubo and Itō accordingly took the long journey back to Tōkyō to obtain the credentials, but despite the time, trouble, and money this had cost,[32] Iwakura decided that unilaterally concluding a treaty with the Americans would be disadvantageous to Japan. Under the most-favored-nation clause in the treaties, Japan would have to extend to every other country whatever concessions it made to the United States without necessarily receiving compensation in return. He decided to break off negotiations with America on treaty revision and instead to conduct negotiations at some future time around a conference table with all nations represented. Iwakura, Kido, and Yamaguchi Naoyoshi called on the secretary of state to inform him that it would not be possible for them to reach agreement solely with the United States and that they would therefore return to the mission's original purpose, paying courtesy calls on the various nations. The mission spent six and a half months in America (including the long wait in Washington) before going on to England and other European countries. But the time was by no means totally wasted, as Kume Kunitake's extraordinary *Beiō kairan jikki*, the detailed account of the travels of the mission, makes absolutely clear.

The philosopher and historian Miyake Setsurei averred that once the mission left the United States, its activities degenerated into an aimless wandering. He said that the members were well aware of this but had no choice but to go on. Miyake admitted that they were intrigued by what they saw in advanced countries and took comfort from the thought that this was enabling them to become familiar with world conditions but said this did not mask their failure, even to themselves.[33] There is no trace of dejection, however, in Kume's lengthy work. Whether or not they were always conscious of it, the members of the mission were helping make Japan into a modern nation.

The Western nations were reluctant, for economic reasons, to consider revising the unequal treaties, as it was to their advantage to continue their control of Japanese import tariffs. If pressed by the Japanese, they could have justified their opposition in terms of the continuing instances of murders and attempted murders of Europeans and their inability to trust Japanese justice to punish the guilty.[34] They could have insisted that the restrictions against Christianity be lifted before treaty revision could be considered. But it was beyond the mission's powers to guarantee such changes. Although the failure to obtain treaty revision was a severe disappointment, the mission had in fact carried out brilliantly the original terms of its assignment. If the members had not hoped to achieve more—to obtain treaty revision—they would not have wasted the months waiting for Itō and Ōkubo to return from Tōkyō, and there would have been no reason to question their success.

In any case, they derived from personal experience a kind of knowledge of the West that could not have been obtained in any other way. They had the good fortune to observe the various Western countries at a time of prosperity and optimism, and they would be able to put this knowledge—whether of advanced machinery or politics or merely the etiquette to be observed at a European reception—to good use in Japan. Considered in this light, the Iwakura mission was a stunning success, and the fruits of the long voyages would be shared by the emperor and the entire Japanese people.

Chapter 23

While members of the Iwakura mission were still waiting impatiently in Washington for Ōkubo Toshimichi and Itō Hirobumi to return from Japan, plans for another "mission" were being made in Japan. Its object would be similar to the one with which the Iwakura mission was originally charged: to examine conditions at the various places visited and to impress on the people at each place the prestige of the new Japanese government. The major difference was that this mission, headed by the emperor himself, would travel not to foreign countries but to distant parts of Japan.

On June 16, 1872, it was announced that the emperor planned in the near future to visit by sea the Chūgoku and Saigoku[1] areas of Japan. In preparation for the actual journey, a full-scale rehearsal was held on this day.[2] The emperor, satisfied with the rehearsal, shortly afterward fixed the date of his departure as July 10. He said, moreover, that he expected this to be the first of many journeys that would eventually take him to every part of the country.

An official statement issued at this time explained the special importance of the journey: ever since the medieval period, the military had kept the emperor shut up inside the walls of his palace, so this would mark the inauguration of a new era. The emperor would travel throughout the country observing its geography, general conditions, people, and climate. It had been a serious fault that no program existed for acquainting the emperor with his country, but this fault was now being remedied. Travels by ship would take the emperor to Ōsaka, Hyōgo, Shimonoseki, Nagasaki, Kagoshima, Hakodate, Niigata, and wherever else on the coasts people had built cities and towns. Such travel would help him devise better plans for the welfare of the entire country. Unfortunately in some villages in the hinterland, people still were ignorant of the court's benevolent intentions, which meant that the emperor's influence could not be said to be wholly pervasive. If the present opportunity to correct this situation was not seized, there would be increasing doubts in the country about what the future held, and this would represent a grave obstacle in the path of progress and enlightenment.[3]

The actual situation vis-à-vis the emperor was even more serious than the statement suggested. At the start of the Meiji era, many, perhaps most, commoners showed almost no interest in him.[4] Ōkubo Toshimichi, aware of this, had long urged that the emperor follow the practice of European sovereigns and show himself to his people. He was sure that it was politically essential to transform the emperor from a mysterious being hidden by walls and curtains into a visible presence familiar to his subjects.

Nothing in the emperor's education had prepared him for a role as a public figure. The early descriptions written by Europeans suggest that he was so ill at ease before strangers that even when he spoke his voice was all but inaudible.[5] His peculiar manner of walking, presumably learned from the ladies of the *ōoku*, was commented on,[6] and his dress and painted face suggested a being who was an anomaly in this world. The change in the emperor's appearance and his decision to show himself to his people would occur not because he personally desired change but in response to the suggestions of advisers like Ōkubo.

The early attempts to "humanize" the emperor were only moderately successful: he did not show himself to the public during his journeys to Tōkyō from Kyōto, and the most that spectators could have seen was his palanquin. However, as early as 1868 images of the emperor began to appear in *nishikie*, the woodblock prints created for the common people's enjoyment, suggesting that interest in the emperor had germinated.[7]

This development, though welcome, did not go exactly according to plan. Ōkubo intended to make the young emperor into a monarch along the lines of Louis XIV, with the hope that this would represent an intermediary stage in the creation of a constitutional monarchy. Japanese monarchical tradition, however, did not provide promising soil for the cultivation of baroque grandeur. In the case of Louis XIV, "the political techniques of European absolutism were extremely visual: art and power joined in the processions when the king visited cities, in the masques in the palaces, and in the splendid palace buildings and gardens. The king became a visible presence by means of these arts."[8] The monarchy in Japan was nonvisual; not only was the emperor himself invisible, but the blank walls around the Gosho in no way suggested the magnificent architecture and gardens surrounding the French king's palace at Versailles.

All the same, when reading an account of Louis XIV and his court, we occasionally may be struck by resemblances to Meiji: "The king was viewed by most of his contemporaries as a sacred figure."[9] Even as a child Louis impressed foreign envoys with his gravity and his poise: "The Venetian envoys noted that in 1643, when he was only five, Louis laughed rarely and scarcely moved in public."[10] He seems to have been schooled in the etiquette of the Spanish court, for it was said of Louis's father-in-law, Philip IV of Spain, that at audiences he remained virtually immobile, "like a marble statue," a description strikingly similar to foreign accounts of Meiji at an audience.[11] But even though shyness as much as ritual behavior accounted for Meiji's immobility at audiences, in France or in Spain the king's statuelike appearance was part of a theatrical presentation. One scholar wrote, "The king's immobility and virtual invisibility should therefore be viewed as part of the theatre of the court. The fact that Philip could not be seen for much of the time was a way of making his public appearances all the more dazzling."[12]

When Louis was a young man, about Meiji's age at the time he became emperor, he appeared to be a model ruler: "The image of the young king projected in the 1660s was that of a ruler unusually devoted to affairs of state and the welfare of his subjects."[13] But it was not long before Louis's apparent concern for his people gave way to increasing absorption with himself and his glory. In contrast, Meiji's concern for his people, exhibited from the time he ascended the throne, continued to grow for the rest of his reign.

The resemblances between the two monarchs are intriguing, but they are brief and intermittent. Japan had no equivalent of the many equestrian statues of Louis XIV; the elaborate paintings showing the king defending the Catholic faith or winning victories in battles with foreign countries; or the poetry, plays, and musical compositions commissioned in order to enhance Louis's image both with his contemporaries and with posterity. What has been called a "department of glory" was founded in France to organize the presentation of the king's image. Meiji's glory had no need of such a "department." Instead, his glory stemmed from the length of his reign and the unwavering impression of his deep concern for the Japanese people, not from any beautified image.

Perhaps the closest resemblance between the two monarchs is found in Norbert Elias's appraisal of Louis XIV:

> In his way Louis XIV is undoubtedly one of the "great men" of Western history, whose influence has been exceptionally far-reaching. But his personal resources, his individual gifts were by no means outstanding. They were mediocre rather than great. . . .
>
> The paradox mentioned just now in connection with the "greatness" of Louis XIV points to a curious circumstance: there are situations in which the most important tasks are not those which can be solved by people with qualities we romanticize somewhat as originality or creativity, people distinguished by extraordinary drive and activity, but by people of steady and placid mediocrity. Such was the situation of Louis XIV.[14]

Ōkubo's efforts to make Meiji into a monarch in the style of Louis XIV were misguided and, fortunately, were unsuccessful, but he was correct in his belief that the emperor must become visible, a figure with whom the Japanese people could identify, a stern but loving father.

Meiji's journey of 1872, which lasted from June 28 to August 15, was triumphant from beginning to end. Unlike the progresses of Louis XIV, or even of daimyos during the heyday of the Tokugawa period, it was to be circumspect: traffic was not to be interrupted on its account; the common people were to go about their work as on ordinary days; there was no need to repair the roads or to hide dirty places; and gifts offered to the emperor were to be refused. The aim was for the emperor to see the country as it actually was, not for him to be treated to artfully disguised Potemkin villages.

There was opposition to the journey, mainly from those who remained in Kyōto. Nakayama Tadayasu, the emperor's maternal grandfather, was astonished that the journey—a major undertaking—had been decided on at a time when conditions were still unsettled, and he had grave fears for the consequences. The journey was only the most striking of the many changes in the life of the emperor. Hashimoto Saneakira (1809–1882), a high-ranking Kyōto nobleman, who had an audience at the palace in Tōkyō with the emperor on June 20, was astonished, after making a profound reverence, to look up and see the emperor dressed in Western clothes sitting on a chair. Hashimoto later noticed that carpets had been laid along the corridors in order to spare the palace officials the trouble of removing their shoes. They sat on chairs when performing their assigned duties.[15]

Hashimoto was by no means the only person dismayed by the rapid Westernization of the court, but regardless of such feelings, when the emperor left the palace at four on the morning of June 28 he was dressed for the first time in what would become his most typical costume—a swallow-tail uniform fastened with hooks.[16] His appearance did not escape criticism from conservative subjects. While the emperor was in Nagasaki, a certain person addressed a memorial begging him to cease wearing Western clothes. Imperial Household Minister Tokudaiji Sanetsune conferred with Saigō Takamori about their response. Saigō sent for the man and shouted at him, "Are you still ignorant of the world situation?" The intimidated man went quietly away.[17] Only three or four years earlier, when *jōi* was still on the lips of many samurai, such a protest might have been heeded.

The emperor set out from the palace on horseback. He stopped briefly at the Hama Detached Palace for refreshments, then at five-thirty in the morning boarded a boat that took him to the warship *Ryūjō*, anchored off Shinagawa. He was accompanied by a suite of more than seventy men (including Saigō Takamori and his younger brother Saigō Tsugumichi) and a platoon of Household Guards. As soon as the emperor set foot aboard the ship, he was greeted with music played by a navy band. Twelve years earlier when the first Japanese mission had traveled across the Pacific to America, the members complained incessantly about the cacophonous "barbarian music" to which they were subjected, but now the Japanese navy played similar tunes for the emperor. His arrival on the ship was otherwise celebrated by hoisting a brocade pennant above the center mast, displaying signal flags, sailors manning the yards and cheering, and firing a twenty-one-gun salute.[18] All but the first of these ceremonies had been learned from Western navies only within the last decade but were already firmly part of Japanese naval tradition.

The first visit of the journey was to the Great Shrine of Ise. On the morning of June 30, the *Ryūjō* and the other ships of the convoy dropped anchor in Toba Bay. From there, a procession set off for Yamada, the site of the Ise Shrine. It was headed by local officials and, following them, members of the Ministry of Works, the Naval Ministry, the Army Ministry, and so on. Two chamberlains carried the imperial sword and jewel. The emperor himself, riding a horse, was protected on either side by chamberlains. Half the platoon of Household Guards led the way, and half served as rear guards for the emperor. The officials accompanying him, attired in swallow-tail coats and carrying Western swords, walked. Commoners who lined the roads welcoming the emperor were astonished at the simplicity of the costumes worn, compared with those that brightened the daimyo processions of the old regime. Kneeling by the sides of the roads, these commoners clapped their hands in worship, as if in the presence of a god. The procession and the reception were typical of the visits made during the journey.

The second stop was at Ōsaka. A Russian warship encountered on the way gave a twenty-one-gun salute, honoring the brocade pennant on the *Ryūjō*. The emperor did not reach his temporary lodgings until ten that night. Along the streets, the people of Ōsaka clapped their hands in worship and shouted, "Banzai!"[19] Foreigners in the Matsushima settlement lit bonfires along the roads and, doffing their hats, saluted the emperor.

On July 7 the emperor left Ōsaka and boarded a riverboat bound for Kyōto. This was his first visit to the old capital in more than three years. It was dark by the time he reached the city, but there were lanterns at every door lighting his way to the Gosho. The people of Kyōto clapped their hands in worship, and, we are told, there was no one who did not weep with emotion on seeing the emperor's face for the first time.[20]

During his brief stay in Kyōto, Meiji met members of his family—his grandfather Nakayama Tadayasu and his aunts Princess Chikako and Princess Sumiko.[21] When he went to worship at the tomb of his father, Emperor Kōmei, he changed from Western clothes to formal court robes. Later he visited a display of Kyōto wares that included not only traditional Nishijin silks but a newly invented rice-pounding machine and Western-style umbrellas. He visited a middle school where he observed classes and listened while pupils were questioned about punctuation, arithmetic, and foreign languages. He also visited a school that had been founded to teach boys and girls of the aristocracy foreign languages (English, German, and French) and manual arts, but now also admitted children of the commoner class. He gave audiences to the foreign teachers. Finally the emperor issued a rescript expressing pleasure over the devotion of the foreign teachers and his hope that they would encourage the pupils to work ever harder at their studies.[22]

Wherever the emperor went on this and later journeys, he never failed to inspect local products and to visit schools where he watched experiments in chemistry and other sciences and listened to the pupils deliver speeches in Japanese and foreign languages. He also reviewed troops at places where there were encampments. These actions show the emperor at what would be his most typical—encouraging the local production of goods, manifesting interest in education, inspiring the troops. He seems to have decided that Japan's future as a modern nation would depend on these three factors: industry, education, and the military. The newspaper *Nagasaki Express*, going beyond conventional expressions of awe and gratitude, praised the emperor's visit to that city for having shaken its inhabitants from obstinate ignorance and eradicated their narrow-mindedness and for having weeded out the thorns that lay in the road to civilization and progress.[23]

Needless to say, wherever the emperor went he was gazed at worshipfully by his subjects. He was welcomed also by foreigners, whether teachers in the schools or state employees (known as *yatoi*) who had been hired to instruct Japanese in Western scientific and mechanical knowledge. Perhaps the most unusual incident of the journey occurred in Kumamoto. When the emperor visited the house of Leroy L. Janes, a teacher at the Yōgakkō, or School of Foreign Learning, Mrs. Janes, standing on the second-floor balcony, scattered flower petals over the emperor as he entered, a greeting he never experienced before or afterward.[24]

A favorite anecdote Meiji often related at dinner with his ministers was of stopping with members of his escort at a foreigner's house in Kagoshima. The old woman who lived there produced a splendid Western meal and refreshments, but (the emperor would conclude with a laugh), "She didn't even know who I was!"[25] It is hard to imagine under what circumstances the emperor and his entourage would drop by a foreigner's house or, no matter how hospitably inclined the old lady might have been, how she managed to produce a splendid meal so quickly, but it is a pleasant story with a familiar theme—the exalted visitor who arrives incognito but is treated hospitably by the aged owner of a humble cottage[26]—and lacks only a line at the conclusion relating that the visitor bestowed a rich gift on his unsuspecting benefactor.

After the emperor boarded ship and left Kagoshima, the common people were permitted to examine the place where he had stayed. Crowds that lined up before dawn accepted with reverence bits of the rush matting on which the emperor had knelt in prayer, and cryptomeria needles from the decorations of the platform where he had enjoyed the cool of evening, which they used as talismans to ward off misfortune.[27]

The emperor's ship proceeded from Kagoshima to Marugame in Shikoku, where he arrived on August 7, a day of rain, lightning, and fierce wind. On the following day it cleared, and from a temporarily established place of worship the emperor directed prayers to the tomb of Emperor Sutoku at Shiramine and that of Emperor Junnin on the island of Awaji; both emperors had perished in exile. That day, word came from Tōkyō of dissension among the various elements composing the Household Guards, the majority of whom came from Satsuma. Saigō Takamori and Saigō Tsugumichi returned by fast ship to Tōkyō, for, as Satsuma men, they were thought to be the only officers who could calm the turbulent elements.[28] The emperor continued his journey as scheduled, calling at Kōbe on his way back to Yokohama.

After his return to Tōkyō, Meiji continued to display particular interest in education. On September 3 the first public library was opened in Ueno. On the following day the emperor sent a message stressing the importance of education and revealing the plans that had been drawn up for education at every level. The number of institutions planned ranged from eight universities to 53,760 elementary schools. All children from the age of six would be required to enter one of several kinds of elementary schools intended to meet the different needs of boys and girls, children in the city and the country, and so on. The model for the educational system would be France. These plans were intended to implement the promise made by the emperor in his Five Article Charter Oath to abolish evil customs and to seek learning throughout the world.[29]

The country seemed at last to be peaceful after the years of turbulence. Twenty-one of the fortified outer gates of Tōkyō Castle were removed, leaving only the foundation stones and stone walls. The special guards who had been assigned to protecting foreign diplomats, residents, and yatoi were replaced by ordinary police. But there were still sporadic outbreaks of peasant revolts in the provinces, and international questions assumed particular importance.

On September 26 judgment was pronounced in the case of the Maria Luz, a Peruvian ship that had been damaged on the way from Macao to Peru and had called at Yokohama on July 9 for repairs. One night while the ship was anchored there, a Chinese laborer escaped by jumping overboard. He was rescued by a British warship and turned over to the Kanagawa authorities. The Chinese complained of gross mistreatment of himself and the 231 other Chinese aboard the Peruvian ship and asked the protection of the Japanese authorities. The Peruvian captain was summoned and the Chinese escapee returned to him, but he was warned that he must treat the Chinese aboard the ship more humanely. He was enjoined with particular severity not to punish the man who had escaped. But the captain not only punished him brutally but continued his cruel treatment of the other Chinese crew members. The acting British minister, R. G. Watson, receiving word of this, personally inspected the *Maria Luz* and discovered that what the escaped Chinese had said was true: the Chinese laborers aboard ship were living under conditions close to penal servitude. He asked Foreign Minister Soejima to look into the matter.

Soejima at once issued orders that the Peruvian vessel not leave the harbor. He learned on further examination that the ship's officers had deceived the illiterate Chinese and, after concluding a contract in Macao that committed the men to virtual slavery, had confined them to the hold of the ship where they were subjected to inhumane treatment. A preliminary hearing was held at which the Peruvian shipping company was found guilty of wrongdoing, and all the Chinese were permitted to go ashore. The Court Council approved the decision on August 27. Each of the foreign countries represented in Japan was informed of the decision and asked its opinion. Only the British supported it. The American consul declined to give an opinion because the matter was not related to his own country, but the other countries opposed the decision, citing the regulations signed in October 1867 for the supervision of the Yokohama foreign residence district and expressing doubts about whether the Japanese government was empowered to deal with an incident that had occurred outside its territory. The presiding judge, Ōe Taku (1847–1921), appealed to Soejima, who announced that the court's decision would be respected.

On August 30 Ōe ruled that the Chinese should be set free. He added that the ship's captain, though deserving a hundred strokes of the lash, would be permitted to leave port on his ship. The Peruvians, still not ready to yield, attempted to prove that the contract signed with the Chinese laborers in Macao was legal and binding. The court confirmed on September 26 Ōe's earlier decision, declaring that the actions of the Peruvian captain had violated international law and were not compatible with Japanese law. Some of the Chinese crew of the ship, encouraged by this decision, deserted, and the captain, perhaps fearing for his life, fled to Shanghai, abandoning the ship. The Chinese government subsequently thanked the Japanese for their friendly action.[30] In June 1873 the matter was submitted to the arbitration of Czar Alexander II of Russia, who two years later upheld the Japanese court's decision.[31]

William Elliot Griffis, a worshipful admirer of Emperor Meiji, described his part in the decision:

> Mutsuhito returned to Yokohama about the middle of August. While here he had a long consultation with the governor of Yokohama, Mr. Oyé Taku, concerning the case of the Peruvian ship *Maria Luz*, which had come into the harbor through stress of weather. It was loaded with the human freight of Chinese laborers, who had been decoyed, practically kidnapped, and cruelly treated. Their condition was made known by one of them swimming off to a British man-of-war then in the harbor.
>
> Mutsuhito, not afraid of "the vice called republicanism," nor of Pe-

ruvian ironclads, nor of the frowns of men behind the age, resolved to strike a blow for human freedom. After due trial in court, the Chinese laborers were landed on Japanese soil and held until the Peking government was heard from. This was Japan's first manifesto in behalf not of herself only but of Asian humanity. Some foreigners severely criticized the Imperial action and even imagined a Peruvian man-of-war coming to demand satisfaction; but the matter was settled by arbitration, the Russian emperor deciding that Japan was right.[32]

Griffis's mention of the emperor's personal role in the settlement of the *Maria Luz* case is not confirmed by other contemporary sources. If Griffis was correct, this was a rare instance of the emperor's intercession in a legal matter. Griffis recalled also, "In the trial at court the cogent arguments of the English barrister, F. V. Dickins, and the translator of Japan's classic verse, helped mightily.[33] Young girls, who had been forced to go into service for vile purposes, were practically set free and the old contracts, which bound them involuntarily for a period of years, were annulled."

Dickins, a fluent speaker of Japanese who had been hired by the Peruvian government to present its case in answer to the argument that the contract made with Chinese laborers constituted slave labor, cited the sale of prostitutes in Japan; if this was legal, the Peruvians had committed no crime. The Japanese were taken aback by his argument, and Ōe, the presiding magistrate, hastily adjourned the court. In the end Ōe ruled that even if slavery did exist in Japan, as exemplified by the sale of prostitutes, it was prohibited to send slaves abroad, and therefore the Peruvian captain, because he intended to send Chinese slave laborers abroad from Yokohama, had violated the law. This tortuous reasoning gave Ōe the authority to order the release of the Chinese.[34]

It was highly embarrassing to the Japanese that their practice of selling human beings had been revealed to the foreign consular officials assembled in the courtroom. Ōe urged the government to prohibit this traffic as soon as possible. On November 1 an epoch-making ordinance was issued strictly prohibiting the sale of human beings.[35] All prostitutes were released from their contracts, and the debts of geishas and prostitutes were canceled because they had been incurred under nonhuman conditions. The contracts of apprentices were also modified to provide that they could not be bound for more than one year.

A series of actions taken by the Japanese government at about this time complicated Japanese relations with two countries closer to hand than Peru — Korea and the Ryūkyū kingdom.

For about 400 years the Japanese had had a trading post in Korea — rather like the Dutch "factory" at Deshima in Nagasaki Bay.[36] The Japanese stationed at the Sōryō (Choryang) Wakan in Pusan were restricted to members of the Tsushima domain: because of its geographic situation midway between Japan and Korea, the island of Tsushima had traditionally served as the intermediary between the two countries. Although the Japanese were subjected to strict surveillance and at times discourteous treatment, they remained because trade—largely barter—was profitable.

Japan's relations with Korea had been strained early in the Meiji era. On being informed that the shogunate (with which it had enjoyed good relations) had been overthrown,[37] the Korean government was reluctant to enter into relations with the imperial government.[38] Then the Japanese government, trying to break the impasse, decided in 1869 to relieve Sō Shigemasa, the former daimyo of Tsushima, of his post as negotiator between the two countries and to carry on its own negotiations. Two members of the Ministry of Foreign Affairs were sent to Korea in March 1870 to inform the Koreans of the change, but the Koreans' only response was that the Japanese message could not be received. The offended envoys returned to Japan where they urged an invasion of Korea (*seikan*).

A Japanese mission sent in October of the same year had no more success. The three envoys asked to meet with local officials, but they were refused. The Koreans said that for 300 years Tsushima had served as the intermediary between the two countries. Why should this tradition be broken now? If the Japanese wished to strengthen the ties between the two countries, the only way was to conform to the old usages. The Japanese were once again rebuffed.

The next mission sent from Tōkyō arrived in Pusan in February 1872. The *hundo*, the officer who dealt with the Japanese, declined to meet members of the mission, alleging illness, and not until April did Sagara Masaki, the chief of the mission, succeed in delivering to the acting *hundo* letters with which he had been entrusted as well as his own statement on the purpose of the mission. In June the *hundo* visited the Japanese station and said that Sagara would receive an answer after his statement had been discussed, but he could not promise when this would be. Sagara and the other Japanese, annoyed by the vagueness of the message and the likelihood of wasting time waiting for a reply, broke the rules by leaving the Wakan and going directly to the provincial headquarters. The commandant not only refused to meet the Japanese but severely rebuked them for having left the trading station and entered a forbidden area.[39]

The Japanese had no choice but to withdraw to the Wakan. Members of the mission returned to Japan in order to inform Foreign Minister Soejima Taneomi of the situation. On September 12 Soejima, who had decided that for reasons of both history and prestige, the trading post should be maintained, presented to the *shōin* a series of proposals that were approved by the Court Council and the emperor on September 20. The first article conveyed Soejima's belief that the Wakan should be maintained as Japan's outpost in Korea.[40]

On September 30 the assistant foreign minister, Hanabusa Yoshimoto (1842–1917), sailed for Korea in order to implement Soejima's proposals. His most important task was to replace the officials at the Sōryō Wakan, vassals of the

Tsushima domain, with Foreign Ministry officials, and to place the post under the ministry's direct control. The Wakan would no longer serve as a trading station for the Tsushima domain, and accounts between the domain and the Korean government would have to be cleared. Once again negotiations dragged on, ostensibly because the Koreans were waiting for the former *hundo* to resume office. Finally on December 10 the Koreans announced their refusal to accept either the wares that Hanabusa had brought with him (by way of settling accounts) or his officials.

The irritation of the Japanese was compounded by their impression that the Koreans, unlike themselves, had refused to adopt a policy of *bummei kaika* (culture and enlightenment), that they were hopelessly behind the times. Korea was still closed to the West, and the Koreans appeared to the Japanese very much as the Japanese had appeared to Europeans, giving rise to an attitude of contempt for Korean backwardness that contrasted sharply with the earlier respect for Korea as the transmitter of Chinese culture.[41]

The Ryūkyū kingdom, another neighboring country, also began to feel the threat of Japan's newly emerging authority. The status of this country had long been ambiguous. In 1186 the shogunate had given the founder of the house of Satsuma the title of *jitō* (manor lord) of Okinawa and the other eleven islands of the "south seas." Internal warfare among the three kingdoms of Okinawa, at a time when warfare in Japan prevented the Shimazu family from sending help to Okinawa, led one of the kings to send a mission to the Ming court in 1372, asking Chinese help in unifying the country; he also asked to become a feudatory. The Chinese agreed and gave the country the new name of Ryūkyū. This change in relations with China did not end the long-standing tributary relationship with Japan: in 1441 the shogun Ashikaga Yoshinori confirmed Shimazu Tadakuni in his rule over the Ryūkyū kingdom. During the Tokugawa period, Ryūkyū remained more or less a possession of the Shimazu family, although it maintained relations with China.

In February 1872 the counselor of Kagoshima Prefecture sent two officials to Ryūkyū, acknowledging mistakes made in the past in administering the islands and expressing hopes for improved relations. The Ryūkyū king, Shō Tai (1843–1901), agreed. In the meantime, Treasury Minister Inoue Kaoru decided that the status of the Ryūkyū kingdom should be clarified. Kagoshima officials resident in Okinawa were ordered to convey the Japanese government's disappointment that the king had not visited the court to congratulate the emperor on the resumption of his personal rule. The king was urged to send a mission to Tōkyō immediately.[42]

Shō Tai, bowing to this command, sent three dignitaries who reached Tōkyō on October 5. On October 16 the mission had an audience with the emperor accompanied by his chief ministers. The ambassador read a memorial addressed by the Ryūkyū king to the emperor in which he voiced the joy that the Restoration had given him, though he came from a distant island. The emperor, in reply, expressed satisfaction that Ryūkyū, which for many years had been a tributary of Satsuma, had demonstrated its loyalty to the throne. The emperor thereupon issued a proclamation bestowing on the king the title of Ryūkyū *han-ō* (domain king) and according him a place in the ranks of the Japanese nobility. Gifts (including textiles, three hunting guns, a saddle, and a pair of cloisonné vases) were given to the king and his consort.[43]

It is strange that the king should have received the title of *han-ō*, even though the *han* (domains) had been abolished. This could only have been a temporary expedient intended to place the Ryūkyū kingdom firmly under Japan's authority. The ultimate aim, not achieved until 1879, was to incorporate the kingdom into the Japanese Empire.

One final event of the fifth year of the Meiji era requires notice—the adoption of the solar calendar. On December 10 the ceremony of changing the calendar was performed preparatory to adopting the solar in place of the lunar calendar. At ten that morning, after worshiping the Great Shrine of Ise from afar, the emperor announced that the third day of the twelfth month would be January 1, 1873. The emperor reported this change to the spirits of his ancestors. Later he went to the *shōin* where he handed to Sanjō Sanetomi a rescript explaining why the solar calendar was to be used.

First the emperor mentioned the inconvenience of the lunar calendar, which required the insertion every two or three years of an intercalary month in order to match the solar year. The solar calendar was far more accurate, requiring only one extra day every four years; it would not err by even a single day for 7,000 years. The emperor had decided to adopt the solar calendar because of its superior accuracy.[44]

The emperor did not mention in this rescript what may have been the chief reason for adopting the solar calendar. Ever since the ninth month of the previous year, Japanese governmental offices had followed the practice of paying salaries monthly. If the lunar calendar were followed, it would become necessary to pay salaries thirteen times every time a year had an intercalary month— obviously undesirable to the government.

Some Japanese felt that they had lost a valuable segment of their lives when the day following the third of the twelfth month became January 1, but although the lunar calendar was no longer officially recognized, its use persisted for some years, especially for religious ceremonies. In most respects, however, Japan was now living within the same temporal frame as the advanced nations of the West.

Chapter 24

The New Year celebrations on the first day of the sixth year of Meiji's reign were in some respects unprecedented. First of all, the beginning of the year was according to the solar, rather than the lunar, calendar. This meant that poets greeting the New Year would not be able to follow the tradition of mentioning haze in the mountains, warm breezes, the melting of ice in the rivulets, and the other signs of the new season; January 1 was much too cold to look for harbingers of spring. Emperor Meiji, whose earlier New Year poems had contained such observations as "the wind blowing along the shore is mild" and "the blowing breezes are balmy" and "the spring breezes that soften the landscapes with each passing day," this year composed a poem devoid of natural imagery.

There were other departures from tradition in the festivities. This was the first New Year's Day on which senior foreign employees of the government were permitted to pay their respects to the emperor. On January 10 another precedent was established when wives of foreign diplomats were permitted to accompany their husbands to the palace in order to offer New Year's greetings to the emperor and empress.[1]

On January 7 the emperor and empress attended together the inaugural lectures of the new year, including one delivered by Motoda Nagazane on the opening chapter of the *Great Learning*. A new schedule of studies had been prepared for the emperor. Each month apart from six days of rest, he would attend twelve lectures on Japanese history and another twelve on *Saikoku risshi hen* (Samuel Smiles's *Self-Help*); this year an attempt was made to balance traditional Eastern learning with Western practical guidance. Modern readers may find it strange that Smiles's popular book was chosen to represent the West, rather than a major historical or philosophical work, but at this point the Japanese sought from the West not wisdom but know-how. In addition to the lectures, the emperor would have three sessions of poetry composition each month, and he was expected to study German every day except on his six days of rest. He would also practice calligraphy and study Japanese grammar.[2]

On January 10 military conscription, decided on toward the end of 1872, was officially promulgated. Men who had reached their twentieth year and were in good physical condition would be conscripted into the army and navy. On January 22 it was decreed that Buddhist nuns might let their hair grow out, eat meat, marry, or return to the laity. On February 1 the emperor, dressed in Western attire, rode a horse fitted with Western trappings. On February 8 new postal rates were put into effect that set a fixed rate for the delivery of letters to any part of Japan, regardless of the distance. On February 12 the first industrial company, for the manufacture of Western-style paper, was established. On March 14 it was decided to end Buddhist ceremonies in the palace, replacing them with Shintō observances. The funerary tablets of the successive emperors and the images of Buddha that had been enshrined in the palace would all be moved to the Sennyū-ji in Kyōto.

This series of events typifies the rapidly changing times, each event affecting many people in their worldly and religious activities and each prefiguring larger changes, but it was less because of these and other internal developments than because of the evolving relations with foreign countries that 1873 ranks as one of the memorable years of Japanese history.

The first major event relating to foreign relations was the issuance on February 27 of an imperial edict commanding the foreign minister, Soejima Taneomi, to proceed to China as ambassador extraordinary and plenipotentiary. His mission was to exchange documents relating to the ratification of the treaty of friendship recently concluded between the two countries and to present a message of congratulations from Emperor Meiji to the Chinese emperor on his assumption of personal rule and his marriage.[3]

Soejima had another, more important task, assigned by an imperial order dated March 9, 1873: to discuss with the Chinese the punishment of the Taiwan aborigines who in 1871 had killed fifty-four shipwrecked Okinawans.[4] Behind this expression of the emperor's concern for his subjects was the implicit assertion (which, it was anticipated, the Chinese would be reluctant to accept) that the Okinawans were Japanese subjects. In the preceding year, as we have seen, the king of the Ryūkyū Islands had been granted the title of domain king, and Soejima officially informed foreign representatives in Tōkyō that Japan had assumed full responsibility for the islands; but the Chinese had not yielded their suzerainty. The emperor's message also indirectly challenged the Chinese claim of exercising sovereignty over the entire island of Taiwan, which they could prove only by punishing the guilty aborigines.[5]

The plan for sending an embassy to China had originated in October 1872 during discussions among Soejima, the American minister Charles De Long, and the American general Charles LeGendre, who, as American consul in Amoy (a port facing the Taiwan Strait), was well acquainted with the problem of the aborigines. Fortunately for Soejima, LeGendre happened to visit Yokohama on his way back to the United States. When consulted, he expressed the opinion that Japan could easily occupy Taiwan with 2,000 men and offered maps and photographs of the island. Soejima, delighted by the prospect of expanding Japanese territory, said there would be no problem in raising an army of 10,000 men, but first it would be necessary to sound out the Chinese government. He intended to present the Chinese with a difficult choice. If they insisted that they had sovereignty over the entire island, they would be obliged not only to punish the aborigines but also to compensate the families of the murdered Okinawans. But if they disclaimed responsibility for the aborigines' behavior, this would give the Japanese ample excuse to invade Taiwan.[6]

On March 9, along with his command, the emperor gave his photograph to Soejima, a high mark of favor. On March 12 Soejima, accompanied by LeGendre (who had by this time resigned from the United States diplomatic service and taken a position with the Japanese Foreign Ministry) and by two interpreters,[7] boarded the warship *Ryūjō* (the former *Stonewall Jackson*), which sailed that day from Yokohama, escorted by the *Tsukuba*, a corvette. The decision to send Soejima to China aboard the most powerful warship of the small Japanese navy was clearly intended to impress the Chinese.[8] It was the first time Japanese warships had been sent abroad.[9]

Soejima was particularly well qualified to serve as an ambassador to China. His calligraphy was the finest of any official of the Meiji government, and he was adept at composing poems in Chinese. This artistic ability—combined with an excellent knowledge of Chinese history, philosophy, and customs—would serve him in good stead when dealing with Chinese officials. His mission as an ambassador benefited also from the gratitude expressed by the Chinese government for his action in freeing the 232 Chinese laborers who had been held as slaves aboard the *Maria Luz*.

On the way to China, the *Ryūjō* and the *Tsukuba* called at Kagoshima, where Soejima took advantage of the opportunity to visit Saigō Takamori.[10] A second stop was made at Nagasaki. When the ships reached Shanghai on March 31, Soejima was invited to a banquet by the Russian grand duke Alexis, whom he had entertained in Japan the previous November. On April 8 the ships sailed from Shanghai to Tientsin but, because of navigational problems, did not arrive until April 20. Two days later Soejima visited the office of Li Hung-chang, the viceroy of Chihli Province, who thanked him profusely for rescuing the Chinese aboard the *Maria Luz*. Soejima exchanged with Li the documents of the treaty of friendship and trade ratified in the previous year. However, General Le-Gendre, who was present at this reception, wrote that Li Hung-chang treated Soejima "coldly" and that "with me he was most rude." When LeGendre was introduced to Li, he asked who LeGendre was and, when informed, replied, "We have made treaties before this one, and we did not find the need for foreigners to advise us; what reason is there for it now?"[11] Li also criticized the Western dress of members of Soejima's embassy, to which Soejima replied:

> If, Your Excellency, the dress of foreigners is not beautiful, it is quite useful, especially on board our men-of-war which are also of foreign style. With our ancient costume our men could not have thought of working in the rigging or at the guns. But since we have changed our dress, we get along very well, so well in fact, that in the ironclad and the corvette which we have brought with us to China there is not a single foreigner.[12]

This was Soejima's first taste of the arrogance of Chinese officials, but he turned Li's criticism to Japan's advantage by contrasting its modern ways with the unbending conservatism of the Chinese.[13] On the following day Soejima had a more cordial meeting with Li at which Sino-Japanese relations were discussed at length. Soejima made full use of his command of Chinese classical literature to criticize the contemptuous and condescending attitude displayed by the Chinese toward foreign countries, saying that it did not accord with the teachings of the sages of ancient times. His criticism seems to have struck home: Li subsequently wrote a letter to a subordinate noting that Japan had grown strong ever since adopting the policy of Westernization and that China was now lagging behind.

Soejima left Tientsin on May 5 and arrived in Peking two days later. He discovered on his arrival that "for over a hundred days," the ministers from the various foreign countries had been engaged in a confrontation with the Chinese court on the matter of how they were to present their compliments to the emperor. They insisted that the Chinese court follow the custom elsewhere of the emperor's receiving the foreign dignitaries standing, but the court wished these dignitaries to follow Chinese custom and kneel before the seated emperor. Neither side seemed willing to yield. The Chinese, ever since the time of Emperor K'ang Hsi in the seventeenth century, when Manchu rule was at its height, had demanded that Europeans prostrate themselves before the emperor. Needless to say, Europeans found kneeling distasteful. In response to the complaints of the Russian envoy, K'ang Hsi replied that while the Russians were in China, they must follow Chinese customs. In return, if a Chinese envoy went to Russia, he would obey Russian customs. The Russian finally yielded. On the day he presented himself before the emperor, he was compelled to kneel in the rain while the emperor sat haughtily ensconced on his throne, protected from the rain by a roof. The Russian had no choice but to execute the required three bows followed by nine kneelings.[14]

Soejima was indignant that the Chinese, not recognizing the altered circumstances of the nineteenth century, still acted as if China were the Middle Kingdom—the center of the world—and required foreign diplomats to humiliate themselves in accordance with precedents established at the court of K'ang Hsi. He did not mention in his memoirs that a similar question had arisen at the Japanese court not long before. In April 1872 the British acting minister, R. G. Watson, arrived in Tōkyō and requested an audience with the emperor in order to present his credentials. Expressing the hope that the traditional manner of receiving foreigners at the Japanese court would be changed, he asked that the emperor, following the general custom in the West, receive diplomats standing, as a mark of mutual respect, instead of receiving them while seated on his *gyokuza*. Soejima, then foreign minister, "strongly and emphatically" refused the request, saying that when diplomats visited a foreign country, they should follow the customs of that country—precisely the attitude of the Chinese court that so annoyed Soejima. He informed the British acting minister that as long as he insisted that the emperor stand during the reception, he would not be permitted to appear before the emperor.[15] Watson left without a word.

Some time later the Russian envoy to Japan, Evgenii K. Biutsov, then engaged in negotiations over the fate of Sakhalin, requested an audience with the emperor. He informed Soejima that he left it to the emperor to decide whether to receive him standing or sitting. Soejima, pleased with this conciliatory attitude, arranged an audience. On this occasion Meiji, to everyone's surprise, received the Russian standing. When the British minister learned of this, he felt embarrassed over his earlier inflexibility and requested an audience, saying this time that it did not matter in which manner the emperor received him. He was granted an audience, at which Meiji again stood to receive the foreign envoy. This was his own decision. He apparently wished to demonstrate that he was willing to accept international standards of etiquette, provided that foreign envoys ceased to demand that he conform to their ways. It is said that the incident made Watson a staunch friend of Japan.[16]

Despite the attitude he had displayed in Japan, Soejima was as reluctant as the Europeans to comply with the Chinese custom of requiring those who had an audience with the emperor to kowtow. He was sure that his country was more advanced than China and that it was no longer necessary for the Japanese to approach the Chinese court with awe and trepidation.

When Soejima met with Chinese officials of the Office for Foreign Affairs on May 24, his first question was why a busy man like himself had been kept waiting so long for an audience with the emperor. An official explained that it was because of Prince Kung's illness. (Illness was recognized in China, as elsewhere in East Asia, as an unanswerable excuse for not meeting visitors.) He mentioned also that the Chinese government was studying the plan for the audience ceremony that had been submitted by the European and American envoys. Soejima demanded why the Chinese thought it necessary to consider the opinions of foreigners concerning a Chinese ceremony, contrasting this with the practice in Japan: "We decide how the foreign envoys are to be received and wait for their arrival; the envoys may therefore be received by the emperor as early as the day after their arrival. We do not tolerate any interference or disagreement on their part, and thus we make clear our imperial authority."[17]

Soejima took out a folding fan on which he had written in classical Chinese a brief statement of his views on how the emperor should receive foreign envoys. He used Confucian terms to evoke the relationship between the head of a state and visiting envoys: it should be that of friends, and sincerity and mutual respect should govern audiences. Soejima stated that the ceremony should conform to the standards of etiquette of the envoy's country, rather than those of the receiving court. This contention was precisely the opposite of the attitude he had displayed in Japan.

Throughout his conversation with the Chinese officials, Soejima quoted the Chinese classics to confirm his views. For example, in berating the Chinese for their contemptuous attitude toward foreigners, he quoted the teaching of the duke of Chou: "Even barbarians are people; if you treat them as barbarians they will be just that, but if you treat them as true gentlemen they will indeed become true gentlemen." He poured scorn on the Chinese for not relying (as he did) on their ancient wisdom.[18]

On June 1 Prince Kung, who seems to have recovered, visited Soejima. Seeking to establish a difference between a Japanese who was familiar with the Chinese classics and ignorant Europeans, Prince Kung said he was sure that Soejima would not object to bowing before the emperor in the prescribed manner. Soejima was enraged and replied that it was beneath his dignity as a representative of Emperor Meiji to grovel before the Chinese emperor. The next day the Office of Foreign Affairs announced its approval of the proposal made by the Western envoys to substitute five bows for the traditional kowtow. Soejima composed a letter of reply stating that he had no intention of complying with the new plan. If he had to bow before the emperor, he expected the emperor to bow back. LeGendre urged Soejima not to send the letter, fearing that it would only make the Chinese more obstinate, but Soejima insisted, predicting that the very extremity of his statements would prove effective.[19]

The negotiations continued. Soejima was determined to be received by the Chinese emperor as an equal (in his capacity as Meiji's ambassador); he also expected to be received ahead of any of the Western diplomats whose rank was only that of minister. Although he was initially opposed on these two points by both the Chinese and the Western ministers, in the end he was victorious. He was accorded the honor due to his superior rank and was even congratulated by the Europeans; and he was consequently received before any of the other envoys at a private ceremony by the emperor.

Soejima still had not touched on what was ostensibly the main business that had brought him to China—the punishment of the Taiwan aborigines. On June 21 he sent Yanagihara Sakimitsu (1850–1894), the first secretary of the embassy, and the interpreter Tei Nagayasu to the Office of Foreign Affairs to discuss the aborigines and China's relations with Korea. His attention at this time to Korea suggests that he was already thinking of punishing the Koreans for their discourteous treatment of Japanese envoys.

During the discussion on Taiwan, Yanagihara insisted that the Chinese had shown they were unable to control the aborigines. He pointed out that in the past the island had belonged to Japan, later to the Netherlands, and still later to Coxinga. The Chinese had never occupied more than half, and their rule did not extend to the aborigines in the eastern part of the island who two years earlier had murdered shipwrecked Japanese. The Japanese intended to send a punitive expedition against the aborigines, but because the part of Taiwan where the aborigines lived was adjacent to Chinese territory, the Japanese had thought it advisable to inform the Chinese of their intentions.

The Chinese replied that they had heard of some Ryūkyū subjects being murdered, but not of any Japanese. The survivors of the attack by the aborigines had been rescued by Chinese officials and returned to their country, the Ryūkyū Islands. Yanagihara objected, saying that ever since "middle antiquity" the islands had belonged to Satsuma and that the Okinawans, being Japanese subjects, were entitled to the protection of the Japanese government.[20]

During the ensuing discussion, the Chinese admitted that their political rule did not extend to every part of Taiwan and that the "wild natives" (as opposed to the "mature natives" who had accepted Chinese rule) were not under their control. This statement was used to justify the Japanese attack in April 1874 on the aboriginal areas of Taiwan.

With respect to Korea, Yanagihara was informed that although the king of Korea received investiture from the emperor of China, the internal administration of the country and questions of war and peace remained in the hands of the Koreans. This admission served to assure Soejima that the Chinese would not intervene if the Japanese attacked Korea.

Soejima concluded his mission with an audience with the emperor.[21] He did not kneel but bowed three times. When his audience was completed, the ministers of Russia, Britain, the United States, France, and the Netherlands were received in a group. Although their credentials had been issued nearly twenty years earlier, only now were they able to present them, largely thanks to Soejima.

After the ceremonies had ended, the various foreign envoys were invited to a formal banquet in keeping with the Chinese custom, but it was so hot that day that the Western ministers had privately agreed to decline the invitation. When Soejima was asked if he also intended to decline the meal, he replied (being familiar with Chinese etiquette), "Certainly not. I gladly accept." This produced a favorable impression on the Chinese princes and officials, who contrasted Soejima's courtesy with the insulting behavior of the envoys of the Western countries who had declined the emperor's invitation. This incident did not, however, cause the Europeans to turn against Soejima. Before Soejima left Peking, the British minister, Sir Thomas Wade, called on him to express the thanks of all the foreign diplomats for solving the problem of how the emperor would receive them, a matter that had impeded communication for many years.[22]

The Chinese also expressed their gratitude for his efforts. When Soejima's ship left Taku (the port of Tientsin), he was given a twenty-one-gun salute, the first time the Chinese had ever fired guns from their forts in honor of a foreigner.[23] Moreover, during Soejima's brief stay in Tientsin on the journey back to Japan, Li Hung-chang visited him at his inn, even though this meant breaking his period of mourning for his deceased brother. The two men spent several hours in conversation. Li also favored him with a letter in which he praised Soejima's conduct of the *Maria Luz* affair and urged that their two countries, both situated in the East, join in perpetual friendship.[24]

Soejima returned to Japan in triumph, confident that Japan could now expand its territory to Korea and Taiwan. He was given a hero's welcome at each of the stops made in Japan before reaching Yokohama. His joy in returning to Japan is suggested by a poem in Chinese he wrote at Nagasaki:

> No sooner am I in Japan than the air is fragrant;
> The mountains and rivers are lovely, nature is true.
> It brings back to mind the days I spent in Peking;
> Sand filled the air, swallowing up human beings.[25]

On July 27 he had an audience with the emperor during which he offered him the text of the treaty he had concluded with China and the gifts from the Chinese court.

In the meanwhile, relations between Japan and Korea had steadily deteriorated because of Japanese anger over the high-handed manner with which their attempts to open trade and diplomatic relations with Korea had been rebuffed. The de facto ruler of Korea, the *taewon'gun*,[26] was determined to prevent the opening of his country to the West and was suspicious of the changes that had occurred in Japan. He insisted that relations between the two countries be in accordance with the precedents established during the previous 300 years.

A crisis occurred in July when members of the magistrate's office that dealt with the Wakan discovered that some Japanese merchants who did not belong to the Tsushima domain had been slipping in and out. The Koreans expressed their strong disapproval by erecting a sign[27] at the gates of the Wakan denouncing this violation of the custom of 300 years. They also expressed dismay over the changed appearance of these Japanese—men who cut their hair in Western

style and wore Western clothes—and declared that such men did not deserve
to be called Japanese. They insisted that the traditional manner of trade between
the two countries, with members of the Tsushima domain serving as the intermediaries, was immutable. Persons from the other Japanese islands were not
permitted to engage in this trade, and the arrival at the Wakan of such persons
indicated that Japan had become a country without laws. The Japanese at the
Wakan were directed to communicate this rebuke to their superiors so that
nothing would happen that they would later regret.[28]

Scholars have persuasively argued that the message was not intended to
insult Japanese in general but referred specifically to the illegal activities of
Japanese merchants who had arrived at the Wakan intending to do business
outside the traditional framework of Korean–Japanese trade.[29] However, this
was not how the Japanese of the time interpreted the message. The apparent
insult to Japanese honor, especially the term "a country without laws" (*muhō
no kuni*), created a furor throughout Japan and precipitated calls for punishing
Korea. When informed of this latest development, the emperor was extremely
upset and commanded Sanjō Sanetomi to dispose of the Korean incident.[30]

Sanjō's report to the cabinet recounted all the irritating encounters that had
taken place between Japanese and Koreans. In 1871 when the government sent
an envoy to Pusan with letters informing the Koreans of *haihan chiken* and
asking for meetings with officials to discuss the possible effect of this change
on the relations between the two countries, he had no success in meeting the
hundo, the Korean officer who dealt with the Japanese at the Wakan. On no
fewer than twenty occasions, the *hundo* claimed to be too ill to see the Japanese.
Later, the *hundo* went to the capital and reported when he returned that an
answer to the Japanese request for a meeting would not be forthcoming until
an official decision had been reached. When the Japanese asked how long it
would take to reach such a decision, they were informed it would be six to ten
years.[31] Most recent was the incident of the offensive signs put up at the entrance
to the Wakan.

Sanjō predicted there was no telling to what humiliations Japanese might
be subjected in the future. The Japanese had tried ever since the Restoration
to enjoy friendly, neighborly relations with Korea, only to meet with insults. A
small number of army and navy units—whose numbers could be reinforced if
necessary—should be sent to protect the Japanese living in Korea. Sanjō concluded by asking the council to approve his proposal.

Saigō Takamori was the first to respond. He opposed sending troops, sure
that such action would arouse the fears and suspicions of the Koreans, who
would take it as a sign that Japan intended to swallow up Korea. This was not
Japan's intention, and to prove this, an ambassador plenipotentiary should be
sent to enlighten them. If they refused to listen and insulted the envoy, their
guilt would be apparent to all the world, and they should then be attacked. He
concluded by proposing himself as the emissary.[32]

Saigō's proposal was supported by most of the leading men in the government, although some key figures were abroad or unable to attend the Court Council's sessions.[33] At this point Sanjō Sanetomi, as was his wont, began to waver. He proposed telegraphing Iwakura to return at once to participate in the discussions, but Saigō sent Sanjō a letter on August 3 urging him to be firm in carrying out the Court Council's decision. On August 16, not having received a response, Saigō went to see Sanjō and spoke his mind in stronger language. He said that if Sanjō waited for Iwakura's return, he would miss a valuable opportunity for action. He was absolutely certain that when the Japanese envoy arrived in Korea, he would be killed; only then would it be appropriate to send an army to punish the crime. He added that there were signs of discontent even in Japan that might result in disorder; it would be desirable to turn the point of accumulated wrath outward and, in so doing, display Japanese prestige abroad.[34]

Realizing that it was useless attempting to dissuade Saigō, Sanjō called a session of the Court Council on August 17 at which it was decided to send an envoy to Korea in the manner Saigō had proposed. The only opposition came from Kuroda Kiyotaka, who claimed that settling the dispute with the Russians over Sakhalin was more urgent, and he also offered himself as a substitute for Saigō.[35]

At the beginning of August the emperor and empress left Tōkyō for Miyanoshita in order to escape the oppressive summer heat. In the light of the emperor's future reluctance to leave the capital for any private reason, this was an unusual concession to human frailty. The emperor enjoyed the surroundings and the food, especially the fish caught in the rivers (he did not like saltwater fish) and the freshly dug taros.[36] But this was an inconvenient time for him to be away from the capital. During the negotiations that followed, it was necessary for members of the government who wished to consult the emperor to travel what was then a considerable distance. On August 19 Sanjō went to Miyanoshita and remained until the twenty-third, visiting the emperor each day. Even though the Court Council had voted to send Saigō to Korea, Sanjō still wavered, hoping that Iwakura would return in time to give his opinions. The contents of his discussions with the emperor are not known, but in the end the emperor commanded the council to wait until Iwakura's return before deciding whether to send Saigō to Korea. The decision should be reached only after thoughtful deliberation and should then be reported to him. Sanjō hurried back to Tōkyō and communicated the emperor's wishes to Saigō.

It is impossible to say whether the command to wait for Iwakura's return originated with Meiji himself or if Sanjō persuaded the emperor in the course of his visits. If this was indeed the emperor's decision, it was his most important political action to date. War with Korea, though ardently desired by many Japanese at this time, would have been a disaster for both countries. Quite apart from the moral issues and the terrible suffering that an invasion would have inflicted on the Korean people, it was by no means certain that the Japanese had sufficient military strength to secure a quick victory. A war might have been costly to both sides.[37]

Saigō wrote ten letters to Itagaki between July 29 and August 17. In the first, he opposed the plan, favored by Itagaki, to send troops to Korea without further delay. He argued that troops were needed to protect Japan from Russian incursions in the north, and war with Korea without sufficient provocation would alienate world opinion. He was sure that it would be far preferable to send an envoy first. The first letter concludes, "If it is decided to send an envoy officially, I feel sure that he will be murdered. I therefore beseech you to send me. I cannot claim to make as splendid an envoy as Soejima, but if it is a question of dying, that, I assure you, I am prepared to do."[38]

In his letter of August 14 he wrote,

> If we fail to seize this chance to bring us into war, it will be very difficult to find another. By enticing the Koreans with such a gentle approach we will certainly cause them to furnish us with an opportunity for war. But this plan is doomed to fail if you feel it would be unfortunate for me to die before the war, or if you have any thoughts of temporizing. The only difference is whether [my death comes] before or after the event. I shall be deeply grateful to you, even after death, if you exert yourself now on my behalf with the warm friendship you have always shown me.[39]

The repetition of the words "dying" and "death" in the course of these letters has suggested to historians that Saigō longed not so much for a solution to the troubled relations with Korea as for death. In a letter to his uncle Shiihara Yosanji dated June 29, he described the illness from which he had been suffering since the beginning of May. Traditional Japanese medicine had proved completely ineffective, and he had resigned himself to the likelihood that his disease was incurable. The emperor had sent his personal physician and also a German doctor whose treatment had brought temporary relief from pain.[40] In Saigō's letter of August 23 to Itagaki, he used the phrase *shi wo miru koto wa ki suru gotoku* — "I look on death as a return." He promised in his letter not to rush into death, but he seemed determined all the same to die in Korea, perhaps because this seemed preferable to a meaningless death from illness.[41]

It seems obvious from his letters as well as his remarks delivered at the Court Council that Saigō thought his death in Korea would provide Japan with a plausible cause for war. Some scholars who wish to exonerate Saigō of the charge of warmongering believe, however, that he was really a man of peace who hoped that he would be able to persuade the Koreans to meet the Japanese halfway. His insistence that the Japanese envoy sent to Korea be attired in court robes and not be accompanied by a military guard or warships has been held up as proof of his pacific intentions. But unless his letters to Itagaki deliberately falsified his real beliefs, as one scholar has claimed,[42] he undoubtedly hoped for war. His death in Korea not only would make this possible but would bring him the satisfaction of having died for a cause. War in Korea would also provide members of the samurai class, who resented their loss of status and were ready for rebellion, with an identity as Japanese soldiers, fighting against a foreign country. Saigō warned that unless action were taken immediately, an invaluable opportunity would be lost, but surely most people today are thankful he was frustrated in his plans.[43]

The emperor returned to Tōkyō on August 31 in order to receive the duke of Genoa, the nephew of the king of Italy, who had arrived in Yokohama a week earlier. On September 9 he granted an audience to Shō Tai, the Ryūkyū king, and on September 12 to General LeGendre. On September 13 Iwakura Tomomi returned to Tōkyō after twenty-one months abroad and visits to twelve countries.

Iwakura's return did not put an end to the advocacy of an invasion of Korea. On October 15 the Court Council once again voted to send Saigō to Korea. But opposition to the plan was developing. In his diary entry for September 3, Kido Takayoshi wrote,

> At 4 I went to Prince Sanjō's where the prince told me, among other things, about Imperial Councilor Saigō's proposal to send an expedition to Taiwan and to subdue Korea. The government is prepared to decide in favor of the proposal, so I am deeply disturbed. At present our common people are undergoing hardships: they are bewildered by a myriad of new ordinances; and several times since last year they have risen in revolt. The government apparently regards this as a normal condition. To speak of planning for the present, nothing is more urgent than proper management of domestic affairs; and to mention our obligations in foreign affairs, nothing is of greater moment than protection for the people of Karafuto [Sakhalin]. . . . Why must we harp on speedy punishment of those guilty of "infringing on our national honor"? At this time the proper management of internal administration must have first priority.[44]

The conflict of interest between domestic and foreign affairs that Kido mentioned characterized future debates on national policy. For Kido, as for other members of the Iwakura mission, the weakness of Japan, certainly when compared with the major countries of the West, was all too evident, and they were sure this was not a time for Japan to engage in a war with Korea. Because Kido was too ill to attend sessions of the Court Council, Iwakura assumed leadership of the antiwar faction. He realized that he needed the help of Ōkubo Toshimichi to stop Saigō from being sent to Korea, but Ōkubo repeatedly refused appointment as a councillor (*sangi*), a necessary condition for attending the Court Council. Even Kido, who had had a falling out with Ōkubo during their travels abroad, joined in persuading Ōkubo to accept. Ōkubo finally agreed, on condition that Soejima also be made a councillor.[45] This was puzzling: far from being an ally, Soejima was a convinced advocate of the invasion of Korea, but Ōkubo may have hoped that even if an ambassador was sent to Korea, the council would choose Soejima, who would not seek death, rather than Saigō, who would.

Meiji appointed Ōkubo as a councillor on October 12. On the following day Soejima was similarly appointed. At the Court Council on October 14 Iwakura delivered his views. He contended that of the three problems facing Japan—settling the dispute with Russia over Sakhalin, punishing the Taiwan aborigines, and sending an embassy to Korea—the last was the least urgent. Saigō, disagreeing, argued that the problems of Sakhalin and Taiwan were not urgent but that the Korean question involved the authority of the throne and country and could not be postponed. He concluded by saying that if the Court Council decided Sakhalin was the most urgent problem, he would be willing to go as an envoy to Russia. During the arguments it became clear that four members of the Court Council (Itagaki, Gotō, Soejima, and Etō) sided with Saigō, and three members (Ōkubo, Ōkuma, and Ōki) sided with Iwakura.[46]

On October 15 Sanjō Sanetomi announced his support for Saigō. This seemed to mean Saigō would definitely be sent to Korea, but the same night Sanjō wrote to Iwakura confessing that he had changed his mind once again, prompted by anxiety over what Saigō might do. On October 17 Ōkubo announced his intention of resigning, as did Kido, by way of protesting Saigō's apparent success. Iwakura failed to appear at the Court Council on October 18, alleging illness. The next day, Sanjō had a nervous breakdown, the result of intense strain over deciding the disposition of Saigō's plan.

When the emperor learned of Sanjō's illness, he sent his personal physicians, including two Germans, to treat him. Later that day, he himself visited Sanjō's house. After leaving, the emperor went to Iwakura's residence, where he delivered his command that Iwakura replace Sanjō as prime minister. On October 23 Iwakura sent a memorandum to the emperor stating his reasons for opposing the sending of an ambassador to Korea, and he asked for the emperor's decision. In the memorandum, Iwakura insisted on the necessity of developing Japan's strength to international levels in order to obtain equal treatment. He pointed out that it had been only four or five years since the Restoration and that this was no time to engage in foreign conflict. Predicting that war with Korea would break out on the day an ambassador arrived, he argued that they should wait until Japan was strong before sending an embassy; otherwise, disaster might follow.[47]

On the following day, October 24, the emperor's decision was received. He supported Iwakura's recommendations.[48] With this, the possibility of an invasion of Korea withered away. Saigō and his supporters among the *sangi* (Etō, Gotō, Itagaki, and Soejima) all resigned because of illness.[49] The emperor was greatly distressed. But there would be no war in Korea.[50]

Chapter 25

The turbulent political developments of 1873 tended to overshadow Meiji's personal life, although it, too, was marked by events of exceptional dramatic interest. In May of that year his *gon no tenji* (concubine) Hamuro Mitsuko, the daughter of Hamuro Nagatoshi (a former acting major counselor), in her fifth month of pregnancy, underwent the ceremony of putting on the maternity sash. On July 1 in preparation for the birth, she moved from the palace to a house belonging to the Imperial Household Ministry. On September 18, 1873, Meiji's first child, a son, was born. The child was stillborn, and his mother died four days later.[1]

On November 2 another *gon no tenji*, Hashimoto Natsuko, the daughter of Hashimoto Saneakira, put on the maternity sash. She had earlier moved to the house of her brother Saneyana for the birth. No doubt the greatest precautions were exercised before the forthcoming birth, especially in view of the recent death of Hamuro Mitsuko and her baby, but on November 13 Natsuko was seized with extreme uterine pains and her condition rapidly worsened. Iwakura Tomomi, Tokudaiji Sanenori, and other officials, learning of her grave condition, rushed to the scene. After first informing the emperor, they decided to ask the doctors to use artificial means to induce the birth, but despite the doctors' efforts, the baby, a girl, was stillborn. Hashimoto Natsuko died the next day.

Meiji was undoubtedly distressed by the loss of his first two children and probably shed tears when he learned that two women on whom he had bestowed his favors, both of the high nobility, had died young; but outwardly he disclosed nothing of his private emotions.

A disaster of quite a different kind struck the emperor and his family on the night of May 5, 1873. The carelessness of a palace lady in not making sure that some embers were fully extinguished caused a fire to break out in a palace storehouse. Guards attempted to extinguish the blaze, but fanned by a strong wind, it spread from building to building of the old Edo Castle until it had consumed the whole in flames. The emperor and empress escaped without harm, and the most vital treasures (including the imperial regalia) were saved, but many important documents and other possessions were reduced to ashes. The emperor made his temporary residence at the Akasaka Detached Palace, the former residence of the Kishū domain. He lived there for more than ten years until the new palace was completed in 1889.

Some alterations were essential in order for the temporary palace to serve as both residence and office for the emperor, but he directed that the strictest economy be practiced.[2] Members of the court expected that a new palace would be erected as soon as possible in place of the one destroyed in the conflagration, but on May 18 the emperor sent Prime Minister Sanjō Sanetomi a message stating that at a time when many other demands were being made on the national finances, he did not wish the palace to be rebuilt. He declared, "It must not happen that for the sake of Our dwelling, public finances sustain losses and the people are made to suffer."[3] The emperor's Confucian training had fostered a stoicism that revealed itself in his lifetime dislike of extravagance and ostentation.

Perhaps the emperor's greatest pleasure at this time was in taking part in military drills and maneuvers. On April 29, 1873, he led the Household Guards (Konoe-hei) to Shimōsa Province. On that morning at six he set out from the palace on horseback. Bugles were blown, the soldiers of the four Guards battalions presented arms, and the emperor, raising his sword, gave the signal for the march to begin. The march continued for some twenty miles with only brief stops for rest. At the destination, tents were erected where the emperor, along with the officers and men, were to spend the night.

That night there was a strong wind and rain, and the tents threatened to collapse. The commanding general, Marshal Saigō Takamori, rushed up to the emperor's tent to make sure that he was safe. The emperor quite calmly replied, "The only thing that bothers me is the rain leaking in."[4] This story, widely reported, was interpreted as an indication of the emperor's affection for Saigō, an impression that scholars today are happy to confirm. The emperor decided that despite the bad weather, the site was ideally suited for maneuvers and gave it a name befitting its new importance, Narashinohara, or "Maneuver Fields."

On June 12 the emperor observed a platoon of Guards soldiers give a demonstration with live ammunition inside the grounds of the temporary palace, the first time guns had been fired within its precincts. When it was proposed that a stand be constructed from which the emperor might observe the maneuvers, he said it would not be necessary, and he sat on a chair under a tree.

The closest glimpses we have of the young emperor at this time are provided by the official photographs for which he sat on October 1873. These were not his earliest photographs. As we have seen, he was included in the photograph taken in the Yokosuka Navy Yard in November 1871. Again in May 1872, still beardless and wearing traditional court attire, he posed for the photographer Uchida Kuichi.[5] The photographs taken on this occasion were intended to be distributed to foreign dignitaries in return for the photographs of monarchs received by the Iwakura mission, but it was officially stated that they were not ready in time for Ōkubo Toshimichi (who had returned briefly from America) to take with him when he went back to Washington. More likely Ōkubo was disappointed that in the photographs, the emperor did not look like the ruler of a modern state and so decided not to present them abroad.[6]

The photographs taken on October 8, 1873, are distinctly more modern, showing Meiji in the Western military uniform that would henceforth be his customary attire.[7] He sits rather uncomfortably on a Western-style chair, his embroidered cocked hat on the table beside him. His hair (cut in March of that year)[8] is parted in the middle, and the moustache and beard familiar from later portraits have begun to make an appearance. His hands are folded on the hilt of a sword. He still looks young, but his expression is severe.[9]

The changes in the emperor's appearance, made in order that he might impress the world as looking like a modern monarch, were echoed by similar (though smaller-scale) changes in the appearance of the empress and empress dowager: in March 1873 they stopped painting false eyebrows on their foreheads and blackening their teeth. Even the old buildings underwent changes: the Gosho, long the hallowed residence of the imperial family in Kyōto, was turned over to the city of Kyōto in February 1873 and, in the following month, was "borrowed" as the site of an exposition. Treasures from the imperial collection, hitherto unseen by the general public, were placed on display for ninety days.

Many of the new edicts promulgated at this time by the "caretaker government"[10] seem to have been intended to display to the world how willing and able the Japanese were to adopt international practices. Japanese were officially permitted to marry foreigners, and the nearly 2,000 "hidden Christians" who had refused to give up their faith were released from imprisonment, ending a long cause of contention between Japan and the West.[11]

Such changes aroused bitter opposition and even revolt among the Japanese people, particularly the lower classes, but the first major uprising of 1873 arose from a simple misunderstanding. The proclamation issued in December of the previous year announcing military conscription had used the term *ketsuzei*, literally "blood tax," a circumlocution for military service. This was interpreted by the peasants of Hōjō as meaning that their blood would be squeezed from them by way of serving their country. The misunderstanding was intensified by rumors of sightings of white-garmented medical personnel. Before long, more than 3,000 men were rampaging through the countryside by way of expressing their hatred of the measure. Their first target, however, was an *eta* (outcast) village that they burned to the ground, allegedly because the *eta*, who had been submissive, were now uppish, encouraged by the new regime. Anger was voiced also over paying taxes for schools, cutting hair in the Western style, and slaughtering cattle. It is evident from the specific grievances that although a misunderstanding over military service was the direct cause of the uprising, it was essentially an expression of resentment of the changes decreed by the government in its efforts to achieve modernization.[12]

Another uprising occurred in Hokkaidō, where a reduction in taxes was demanded because of the poor catches of fish. This particular uprising ended with Kuroda Kiyotaka taking personal responsibility and freeing all those who had been arrested. A much larger uprising was staged by the peasants of Fukuoka Prefecture against merchants who were charging exorbitant prices for rice. The drought from which the peasants were suffering was blamed on the merchants' greed, which was said to have defiled the mountain gods. The uprising, started on June 16, spread in a few days throughout the prefecture, the number of participants allegedly reaching 300,000. The insurgents set fires everywhere, destroyed houses, cut telegraph wires, burned official registers, and killed every official they saw. On June 20 the rebels broke into the cities of Fukuoka and Hakata and on the following day attacked the prefectural office and set it afire. The revolt was finally put down with the help of troops from neighboring prefectures. Although the uprising was directly inspired by hatred of rapacious rice merchants, its scale was so large as to suggest that suppressed discontent over the changes brought about by the new regime had exploded into an unreasoning desire to return to the feudal past.[13]

Hundreds of people died in these uprisings, but it is obvious that even larger numbers would have been killed or injured if militants had succeeded in starting a war in Korea. Fortunately the year concluded without any further disturbances. The last entry for 1873 in the chronology, dated December 31, states that the German doctor Theodor Hofmann, employed by the Ministry of Education, had advised the emperor, who had been drinking very heavily this year, to shift from saké to wine and not to drink more than one bottle a night with his meal.[14] We may imagine that Meiji was depressed by the loss of his first two children and their mothers, and the conflict between advocates and opponents of the invasion of Korea had probably exhausted him. Drink was the most readily obtained comfort.

The new year, 1874, opened with an innovation: for the first time, the empress joined the emperor in worship. On January 4 the emperor attended the *shōin* and listened to various reports and proposals. Even when most given to drink, the emperor never neglected what he conceived to be his duties, such as attending these sessions. During 1874 he attended the *shōin* on more than forty occasions. He also continued to hear lectures delivered by his various tutors. The empress attended the lectures with him. It was planned to have Meiji continue his German lessons, but he disliked them so much that they were discontinued. If he had persisted and actually learned German, it (rather than English) might have become the second language of the Japanese court.

On January 13, 1874, when Iwakura Tomomi was returning in his carriage from the palace where he had dined with the emperor, he was attacked and wounded at Akasaka by some eight or nine assailants. He escaped from the carriage only to fall into the moat from which he crawled up to some bushes on the bank where he hid. In the meantime, the sounds of approaching people frightened away the assailants.[15]

The emperor and empress, shocked to learn of the attack, went to the Imperial Household Ministry where Iwakura was being treated for his wounds. The emperor commanded that he be moved to the palace. When he was informed on January 17 that the culprits had not yet been apprehended, the emperor sent for Sanjō Sanetomi, Ōkubo Toshimichi, and Ōki Takatō and, stressing the gravity of the incident, demanded to know why the assailants were still at large.

That night five of the assailants were arrested, followed by the remaining four. They all were samurai from Kōchi Prefecture, followers of Itagaki Taisuke who were enraged with Iwakura for having prevented Itagaki and Saigō Takamori from carrying out their plan of conquering Korea. They had decided to get rid of Iwakura in the hopes of changing court policy. On July 9 sentence was passed on the would-be assassins: they were to be deprived of their status as samurai and beheaded.[16]

The Korean crisis in the narrow sense had ended by October 1873, but the issue continued to agitate many members of the samurai class. Most samurai had yet to find employment under the new regime, and their economic difficulties compounded the anger they felt over the failure to avenge the supposed insult of a foreign country. A war with Korea might have solved their financial problems and even have ended the mutual enmity that divided the major domains, but deprived of this solution, many samurai became rebellious.

As early as February 1874 there were signs of rebellion among the samurai of Saga Prefecture. Some formed a political party that opposed the government's efforts at modernization and advocated a return to the feudal system, including the policy of *jōi*. It insisted on the importance of strengthening the military. The conquest of Korea, they said, should be delayed until this was achieved; but once internal divisions were ended and the country was strong again, Japan should attack not only Korea but also China, Russia, and Germany.[17] Most of those affiliated with this party were men in their forties or fifties who nostalgically recalled the old days of the shogunate.

The other important party in Saga,[18] the Seikan-tō, was composed mainly of men in their twenties and thirties who in general favored the changes effected by the new regime but resented its failure to send an envoy to Korea, as the majority of the councillors had voted. As a first step, the Seikan-tō advocated implementing this decision, but its ultimate aim was the conquest of Korea. The two parties, though diametrically opposed in many points of view, were alike in that their prime concern was the predicament of the samurai class at a time when there seemed to be no alternative solution to their unhappy idleness. Both groups actively recruited new members and, from the beginning of 1874, began stocking weapons and provisions in preparation for war. The Seikan-tō, whose strength in Saga was only some 2,000 men, revealed that it had allies among the samurai of Kagoshima, Kōchi, and elsewhere.

Although he had resigned his post as *sangi*, Etō Shimpei remained in Tōkyō, under orders to continue serving the government. Despite his defeat on the issue of Korea, he continued to work on behalf of programs he had initiated as minister of justice. He had lost none of the energy that had enabled him to rise from the humblest ranks of the samurai class to the eminence of a *sangi*. Etō, who consistently advocated the creation of a parliament and insisted on the need to respect basic human rights, was one of the signers of a petition submitted to the Sa'in on January 17 calling for the popular election of a legislative body.[19] But on January 13, four days before the petition was submitted, he suddenly left Tōkyō for Saga, in defiance of governmental orders. He was responding to the request of members of the Seikan-tō that he become their leader. The decision to accept, made despite the warnings of friends in Tōkyō,[20] led irrevocably to his tragic end. It is difficult to understand why a man of his intelligence and enlightened views associated himself with an ill-conceived movement that could only end in disaster.[21]

Etō told Itagaki Taisuke and Gotō Shōjirō that he was returning to Saga in order to calm the hotheads of the Seikan-tō; but some sources say that he privately informed an acquaintance that he believed the time had come for a second "restoration."[22] Probably he did not envision at first an out-and-out revolt against the government, but the belligerence of the partisans of war with Korea reached feverish intensity with the arrival of Etō, and this may have affected him.

Alarmed by reports of the situation in Saga, coming on the heels of the attempted assassination of Iwakura, Ōkubo decided to replace the governor of Saga with a henchman, Iwamura Takatoshi (1840–1915), commanding him to restore order. Iwamura, an overbearing, incompetent man who knew nothing about the situation in Saga, was the worst possible choice, and he exacerbated the situation by accidentally making a dangerous enemy. By chance he had as his fellow passenger on the ship taking him to Saga, Shima Yoshitake (1822–1874), a Saga samurai who had served as a chamberlain and later as governor of Akita Prefecture. Shima was traveling to Saga at the request of Sanjō Sanetomi, who had urged him to help calm the situation there. In the course of shipboard conversations with Iwamura, however, Shima became so annoyed by

Iwamura's nasty comments about Saga men and his prediction that it would take him only one sweep of his net to catch all the rebels, that he decided to join Etō to protect Saga from the new governor.[23]

Ōkubo received repeated warnings of imminent conflict in Saga. He felt that it was incumbent on him to suppress the disturbance as quickly as possible and decided to go to Kyūshū to see to it personally that effective measures were taken. On February 10, four days before his departure, Ōkubo was invited to dinner by the emperor, and three days later the emperor received him in an audience at which he expressed his concern.

That same day, after conferring with members of the Seikan-tō, Etō issued a statement saying that if Japan did not punish Korea for its reckless behavior and disrespect, it risked losing its national authority. Tolerating such insults would also make Japan the object of other countries' contempt. For the sake of the emperor and countless millions of Japanese, he and his party had sworn to wipe out the disgrace even at the cost of their lives. They had learned that the government was sending troops against them and therefore had no choice but to open hostilities, looking for inspiration to the example of Chōshū, which had successfully fought a war against the shogunate.[24]

On the following day, February 14, Etō finally made up his mind to attack the government forces in Saga Castle and form a new government. He seems to have believed that he would be joined by disaffected samurai from Satsuma and Tosa,[25] but the only help the Seikan-tō would receive came from Shima and his party.

The attack began at dawn on February 16. The rebels' first objective was the prefectural office inside the grounds of the old Saga Castle. The government forces inside, few in numbers and badly equipped, held out until February 18, when they managed to break through the cordon surrounding the castle and escape to Chikugo, leaving many casualties behind.

This was the Saga forces' only victory during the rebellion. Etō soon realized that he had gravely miscalculated in expecting that men from Satsuma and Tosa would join him once the fighting started.[26] On February 17 Sanjō Sanetomi issued a bulletin to commanding officers in which he asserted that despite the Saga rebels' attempts to win adherents in other prefectures for their policy of attacking Korea, they had been completely unsuccessful. Even Kagoshima had remained calm, and although rumors of an uprising in Tosa (another hotbed of antigovernment sentiment) had circulated, they were without foundation.

On February 19 Ōkubo arrived in Hakata, where he made his headquarters, and issued a proclamation calling for the destruction of the Saga rebels. On the twentieth, government forces advanced into Saga Prefecture and, after a battle on the twenty-second near the border between Fukuoka and Saga, broke through the defense lines of the rebel army. On the twenty-third, deciding that further resistance would only increase the number of victims, Etō told his supporters that he had disbanded the army of the Seikan-tō.[27] He said that he was going to Kagoshima to get help. If he failed in Kagoshima, he would go to Tosa, and if he failed there, he had another plan (which he did not reveal). That night he escaped with seven of his supporters in a fishing boat, heading for Kagoshima in order to ask Saigō Takamori's help in staging another revolt.

The morale of the Saga rebels was greatly weakened by Etō's flight, but they continued their resistance. The most violent fighting of the war took place on February 27, when the government forces were again victorious. The following night Shima, who had declared that he intended to die in Saga Castle, fled with some of his staff to Kagoshima. He had refused to make the declaration of surrender demanded by the government army. The government forces entered Saga Castle on March 1 without bloodshed. Although exchanges of gunfire continued sporadically, by the time Prince Higashifushimi, appointed by the emperor as the commander in chief of the expeditionary forces, arrived on the scene, the rebel resistance had ended. On March 3 Ōkubo, who had arrived in Saga two days earlier, sent a telegram to the Shōin announcing the pacification of the rebels.[28]

On March 1 a search warrant for the arrest of Etō and Shima was issued, giving details of their physical appearance.[29] It was ironic that Etō, who had organized the police, was now being hunted by them. Sympathy was expressed for the fugitives even in the highest circles. Sanjō wrote to Ōkubo on behalf of Shima, admitting that he had taken part in a rebellion but calling attention to his achievements as a devoted loyalist and insisting that he was not an evil schemer. On April 5 after Etō had been captured, Kido proposed to Sanjō that as a convinced believer in action against Korea, Etō should be sent to the front in Taiwan.[30]

Etō's party of fugitives landed in Kagoshima on February 27. They called on Saigō the next day but learned that he was at Unagi Hot Springs. Etō went there on March 1. The two men spoke privately for three hours. About nine that evening, Etō left but returned the next day. This time the conversation between the two men continued for about four hours, sometimes rising to such intensity that their voices could be heard outside. The content of the discussion was not disclosed, but it seems likely that Saigō refused to commit himself to supporting Etō either at this time (when the defeat of the Saga rebels was evident) or at any foreseeable time in the future. He may have stated that because he was no longer in the government, Etō should seek help not from himself but from Shimazu Hisamitsu, an adviser to the cabinet. Shimazu, however, had received on February 2 a command from the emperor directing him to make sure that Saigō did not support the Saga rebels.[31]

On March 3 Etō left Kagoshima, once again by fishing boat. The sea was rough, and he and his small party could get only as far as Sakurajima that night. The next day they visited Ogura Shohei (1846–1877) at Obi. Ogura, only recently returned from study abroad, was an advocate of war with Korea and welcomed the fugitives, hiding them nearby. (He was later to serve a sentence of seventy days for this kindness.)[32]

On March 10 the nine men left for Tosa aboard a fishing boat that Ogura had hired for them, eluding the police on their trail. The journey that followed on sea and land was marked by danger and physical strain. When Etō at last reached Kōchi and met Hayashi Yūzō (1813–1899), whose support he had counted on, he was treated coldly, no doubt because Hayashi knew how close the pursuers were. Etō left Kōchi that night, reluctant to involve Hayashi in his guilt, and wandered in the mountains for three nights in the cold and rain. Etō himself said that never since he issued from his mother's womb had he suffered such hardship.[33]

Etō seems to have hoped somehow to make his way to Tōkyō, where he would disclose the true story of the Saga rebellion to his former associates. If they found him guilty, he planned to turn his sword on himself.[34] On March 28 he emerged from the mountains near the border between Tosa and Awa at Kōnoura, a village by the sea. He hoped to find a boat that would take him to Tōkyō, but he was detected by an alert guard, who asked to see his papers. Etō at first pretended to be a merchant from Ōsaka but soon changed his story and claimed to be a secret agent sent from Tōkyō to find the men responsible for the attack on Iwakura Tomomi. He asked his captor to deliver a sealed letter he had written to Iwakura. The letter, dated March 27, stated that he had been prevented by the strictness of security measures in Tosa from going to Tōkyō and asked Iwakura to give orders that would permit him to proceed to Tōkyō.[35]

A police officer opened the letter and discovered inside Etō's real name. He knew for certain now the man he had captured was wanted by the police but did not know what procedures to follow in arresting someone who until lately had been a councillor. Finally he invited Etō to play a game of *go* with him at another house, leaving Etō's two companions behind. Etō took the white stones; the officer, the black. After each put down one stone on the board, the officer, putting down a second black stone, suddenly shouted, "*Etō-dono, Etō-dono,*" the signal for armed men in the next room to burst in with the cry, "Sir Etō, we have the honor to arrest you."[36] The language they used when making the arrest was comically polite, but all the same, they bound Etō with ropes, like a common criminal. He did not resist.

Etō was treated with kindness by his captors, who purposely allowed the journey to Kōchi, which normally took three days, to last five, perhaps foreseeing that his life had not much longer to run. From Kōchi, he and his two companions were taken by warship and then overland to Saga, arriving on April 4. They were thrown into a hastily built prison.

The trial of Etō, Shima,[37] and others who had participated in the Saga rebellion began on April 8 and was over the next day. The incredible haste was dictated by Ōkubo's impatience to have the proceedings terminated as soon as possible. It was obvious from the start that Etō and the others would be found guilty. The presiding judge, Kōno Togama (1844–1895), had been a protégé of Etō, who had appointed him to his office, but during the trial he addressed Etō with such brutality that at one point Etō cried out, "Togama—how dare you appear before me?"[38] Kōno is said to have hung his head in reply, but the sentence he pronounced on April 13 was harsh, especially considering that there were no precedents in either the old penal code or the new one (devised by Etō) for punishing people who staged rebellions; the crime seems not to have been anticipated. Kōno turned to Chinese law when passing sentence. Etō and Shima would be deprived of their status as samurai and beheaded, and their heads exposed afterward. Other leaders were also to be decapitated, but they would be spared the humiliating public exposure of their heads.

When Etō heard the sentence, he attempted to address the judge, but he was dragged from the courtroom before he could finish. He was executed the same day. Decapitation was normally the work of outcasts, but Prince Higashi-fushimi, the commander in chief, considered that it was a breach of decorum to allow an outcast to execute men of Etō's and Shima's caliber, and they were beheaded instead by a samurai. Etō's final poem, composed immediately before his death, was

masurao no	A warrior even
namida wo sode ni	While wringing his tears
shiboritsutsu	Into his sleeves
mayou kokoro wa	Feels his heart waver
tada kimi ga tame	Only with thoughts of his lord.

Etō's head was exposed for three days. He was forty when he died. It had been exactly three months since he had left Tōkyō on his ill-fated journey to Saga.

In his diary entry for April 13 Ōkubo expressed his satisfaction with the outcome of the trial: "Today everything has concluded satisfactorily. I felt great relief." There was no trace of pity for Etō. Ōkubo wrote, "Etō's disgraceful behavior was shocking," referring perhaps to Etō's final outburst before being dragged from the court. Photographs taken of Etō's severed head for a time were on sale in Tōkyō, but on May 27 the Tōkyō prefectural government ordered everyone who had purchased a photograph to return it to the seller. However, Ōkubo is said to have hung such a photograph in the reception room of the Interior Ministry.[39]

There is no evidence concerning the emperor's reactions to the trial and death of Etō. Perhaps he was more concerned at this time with developments in Taiwan than in the crushed Saga rebellion. Ever since June 1873 when Soejima Taneomi had met with Chinese statesmen to discuss the appropriate punishment for the Taiwanese natives who had killed Okinawan subjects of the emperor, the issue had been hanging fire. In January 1874 Ōkubo and Ōkuma prepared a report on the situation. Their conclusion was that in view of the Chinese government's declaration that the territory of the uncivilized natives did not belong to any country, it was incumbent on the Japanese government to retaliate for the outrage done to its subjects.

On February 6 the ministers and councillors accepted this conclusion, but Kido did not attend the meeting, an indication that he was still opposed to any form of foreign intervention.[40] In March, Ōkuma Shigenobu, Councillor and Foreign Minister Terashima Munenori, Minister Plenipotentiary to China Yanagihara Sakimitsu, and Army Minister Saigō Tsugumichi (1843–1902) met at Ōkuma's house to discuss the proposed campaign against the Taiwan savages. Their report called for troops to leave Kumamoto on March 18 for Taiwan. The plan was not put into effect, but on April 3 Meiji summoned Ōkuma and asked for details. By this time the Saga rebellion had been completely suppressed and the government was in a position to take military action against Taiwan.

On April 6 the emperor granted Saigō Tsugumichi full powers to pacify the Taiwan natives. In a rescript the emperor commanded Saigō to punish those responsible for killing Japanese. In separate instructions the emperor stated that if the natives were left to do as they pleased, this would lead to great harm: "Our purpose in carrying out the conquest is to civilize these savages and set at ease the minds of our good people. You should bear this in mind, and carry out your task with both kindness and resolution. Once the natives are subdued, you should educate them and lead them in the direction of enlightenment. They should be encouraged to perform useful activities in cooperation with our government."[41]

Kido, however, again spoke out against the proposed Taiwan expedition. He noted with surprise that even though only a few days had passed since the Saga rebellion was quelled, people were already calling for the invasion of Taiwan. He asked, "Who does not feel delight at the thought of expanding national power abroad and opening our territory into foreign realms? However, it is the duty of the government to discriminate between inner and outer, central and peripheral. There is an order of priorities, slow or fast, early or late. At present thirty millions of our people still do not receive the protection of the government. Ignorant and poverty-stricken people still cannot be said to possess rights. One must admit that our country is not behaving as a country should." Kido argued that in some respects the present regime was inferior to the feudal system. The people's lack of confidence in the new government was not without cause. Since the Restoration, not a year had passed without a revolt. His own recommendations had been ignored, and military officers had already left for a campaign abroad. He could no longer remain in a cabinet whose views were so remote from his own; he would only be deceiving himself and the world. Even if he were not ill, he would be unable to remain in his post, but in view of his illness, how could he remain and still keep his integrity?[42]

Despite Kido's objections, plans for the attack on Taiwan proceeded. Saigō Tsugumichi and Ōkuma were now in Nagasaki preparing to depart for Taiwan. The protests of the British and American governments, which recognized Taiwan as a Chinese possession, were so strong, however, that the ministers and councillors decided to consult the Chinese government before taking further action. Ōkuma was ordered back to Tōkyō, and Saigō Tsugumichi was told to remain in Nagasaki and await further orders. Saigō protested strongly against any delay. He argued that the troops were ready for the departure and that any delay would impair their morale. The harm would be far worse than the Saga rebellion. He had decided that if he were commanded to halt action, he would return the commission given him by the emperor, become a renegade, attack the savages' haunts, and in this way keep the matter from involving the country. Ōkuma tried to dissuade him, but in vain. That night, Saigō Tsugumichi gave orders to the ships to leave the harbor and loaded firewood and water. Ōkuma sent a telegram to the Shōin reporting that fighting spirit was so high he could not control it.[43]

On April 27 Saigō dispatched a consular official to Amoy with a letter for local officials in which, after expressing neighborly friendship for China, he explained that he was about to set sail for Taiwan in order to fulfill the mission imposed on him by the emperor. His ships would pass territory under Chinese control, but since he had no hostile intentions toward them, he asked them not to interfere. He intended to subdue the unruly natives and make sure they would never again commit outrages against Japanese. He requested that if the savages attempted to take refuge in the areas of Taiwan controlled by the Chinese, they would be arrested and the Japanese informed.

Saigō was impatient to start out for Taiwan but felt obliged to wait for permission from Tōkyō. Finally on May 2 he decided he could wait no longer. More than a thousand soldiers boarded four warships that headed for Taiwan. Ōkuma followed on May 17. His departure from Nagasaki had been delayed by negotiations to purchase an American and a British merchant ship to be used in the operation.[44]

The Chinese were naturally highly displeased that the Japanese had invaded an island that they considered to be their own territory and repeatedly demanded that the Japanese troops be withdrawn. The Chinese, announcing that both Taiwan and Ryūkyū were Chinese possessions, sent two warships to Taiwan which arrived on May 22. The captain of one of the ships met Saigō and asked for a reply to this declaration. Saigō answered that all discussions of the matter were in the hands of the Japanese minister to China, Yanagihara Sakimitsu. As far as he was concerned, the operation against the natives had been more or less concluded. His soldiers were suffering from the heat, and he was waiting only for the command to return to Japan for a triumphant welcome.

Although Saigō had claimed that the operation against the savages was more or less over, the Japanese troops did not immediately leave Taiwan. They continued to battle not only the savages but also the tropical heat and disease. Negotiations with China for disposing of the Taiwan problem continued., with the Japanese anticipating that they might be broken off at any time. In that case, should Japan declare war on China? Most army leaders, including Yamagata Aritomo, opposed a war, contending that Japan was not yet ready, but two generals insisted that Japan had nothing to fear. They averred that even while China was resorting to delaying tactics, it was frantically arming for war and that Japan must not let China gain the advantage. The Court Council, meeting on July 9, announced that it intended to strive for a peaceful solution with China, but if this failed, there would be no alternative to war.[45]

The possibility of a war with China, the model for Japanese civilization for more than a thousand years, naturally caused extreme anxiety, even though some men argued that China was no longer the old China and that Japan therefore must perform necessary tasks—such as educating the Taiwanese natives—in place of a weak and inefficient China.[46]

On August 1 the emperor commanded Ōkubo Toshimichi to go to China to negotiate the issue of Taiwan with the Chinese government. Negotiations did not proceed smoothly. On October 2 the Chinese rejected a Japanese request for an audience with the emperor, declaring that it was insulting for the Japanese to request an audience even as they were massing their troops for an attack. On October 10 Ōkubo delivered what was intended as a final ultimatum, but the Chinese stalled again. Both sides continued to repeat the same arguments.

Finally, however, on October 31 China and Japan agreed to a treaty. It provided that the Chinese would recognize that the Japanese move into Taiwan had been justified; that the Chinese would pay an indemnity for the loss of Japanese lives and for the costs the Japanese had incurred in building roads, erecting buildings, and the like; that acrimonious documents exchanged between the two countries would be destroyed; and that the Chinese would ensure the sea-lanes' safety from attacks by the Taiwan savages. The departure of Japanese troops from Taiwan was set for December 20.[47]

Ōkubo returned from China on December 9 and was granted an audience with the emperor along with other officers who had served prominently in the campaign on Taiwan. The emperor thanked all of them and gave them gifts. On the thirteenth, Madenokōji Hirofusa, the acting minister of imperial household affairs, presented Ōkubo with 10,000 yen in gold, but Ōkubo declined the gift, saying that the successful conclusion of a treaty with China was owing not to his own merit but to the guidance of the emperor. He also mentioned the great expense that had been involved in pacifying the Taiwan savages and noted that the imperial palace had yet to be rebuilt.

On December 23 the emperor, at last yielding to many urgent requests, authorized the rebuilding of the imperial palace, not for his own pleasure, but because the temporary palace was so cramped official functions could not be carried out properly.

The year ended cheerfully. The dangerous rebellion in Saga had been put down with minimal government losses, and the invasion of Taiwan had achieved its real purpose, to make the Chinese admit that Okinawa was Japanese territory; but neither success was a full resolution of the issues involved. The Saga rebellion was a prelude to the much more serious Satsuma Rebellion, and in another twenty years, the dispute with China would lead to the Sino-Japanese War.

The last document of the seventh year of Meiji was a memorial presented to the throne on December 31 by Iwakura Tomomi, in which he outlined the many changes that had occurred since the arrival of Commodore Perry's fleet in 1853. The felicitous developments, such as *haihan chiken* and the sending of the Iwakura mission to America and Europe, were attributed to the emperor's ceaseless pondering of the needs of the country; but there were also many unfortunate events. Indeed, it might be said that only now, after twenty years of turmoil, was the country at peace and the surrounding seas calm. Iwakura's memorial concluded with the prayer that the emperor would devote himself even more intensely to nurturing his ministers' talents so that together they might realize the vision he had entertained ever since the beginning of his reign of restoring the grandeur of Japan.[48]

Chapter 26

The eighth year of Meiji's reign, 1875, was one of the quietest. After the customary New Year observances on January 1, he went the next day to visit the Aoyama Palace and pay his respects to the empress dowager. On the fourth he went to the Shōin to be present at the commencement of state business for the year. Prayers were offered that day to the Great Shrine of Ise, the Kamo Shrines, and the Hikawa Shrine, followed by reports from the different ministries on such subjects as the number of policemen stationed throughout the country "for the protection of the people" and the forthcoming inauguration of postal money orders. Many schools had been built during the previous year, and there were now 1,297,112 elementary-school pupils, approximately one-twenty-fourth of Japan's entire population. Finance Minister Ōkuma Shigenobu offered the prime minister a budget for the coming six months that anticipated a surplus of nearly 40 million yen of revenues over expenditures.[1] In short, all seemed to going well in Japan.

As part of his continuing education, the emperor would hear in 1875 lectures delivered each month by Fukuba Bisei, Motoda Nagazane, and the newly appointed Nishimura Shigeki (1828–1902).[2] He also had calligraphy instruction from Motoda and Chō Hikaru.

The emperor's days were otherwise occupied with performing ceremonies (such as the observances on the anniversaries of the deaths of previous emperors), giving audiences to foreign diplomats, rewarding Japanese for meritorious deeds, observing military drills, and composing poetry. The emperor's poem at the first poetry gathering of the year was on the theme "Capital and Country Greet the New Year." The expression is not complicated:

miyako ni mo	In the capital
tōki sato ni mo	And in distant villages
atarashiki	People are busy now
onaji toshi woba	Welcoming the beginning
uchimukaetsutsu	Of the same New Year.[3]

On January 21 his second daughter was born to the *gon no tenji* Yanagihara Naruko.[4] The delivery was in a building specially constructed on the grounds of the Aoyama Palace. After the disappointment of two stillborn babies, the newborn baby seemed to be healthy, to everyone's immense relief. During the next few days a stream of visitors came to the palace to offer congratulations. On the twenty-seventh, the emperor bestowed on the little princess the name Shigeko.[5] She would live in the Ume Goten (Plum-tree Palace) and for this reason would also be known as Umenomiya. The birth and naming were reported to the gods, and a banquet was held in the palace. Toasts were offered to the long life of the princess and to the greater and greater flourishing of the imperial line. The emperor asked the guests to share his joy.

In February there was a smallpox epidemic. The emperor and empress were vaccinated, which served to give Japanese, who might have otherwise feared an injection of foreign medicine, the courage to have themselves inoculated as well. Even little Princess Shigeko was vaccinated. On February 20 she paid her first visit to the palace, accompanied by her mother, Naruko, her grandfather Yanagihara Mitsunaru, and her uncle Yanagihara Sakimitsu. From this time on, she was frequently taken to the palace. No doubt her father was eager to see the princess as often as possible, but keeping her in the palace would have violated precedent. Meiji was obliged to follow the same custom that had required his own parents to leave him as a small child with his grandparents in the Nakayama household. It was understood that Shigeko would remain with her grandparents until the age of five.

The princess's mother, Yanagihara Naruko, was the most notable of Meiji's concubines. Writing in 1912 about the ladies of Meiji's court, Saitō Keishū described "Sawarabi no tsubone" (her "Genji name")[6] as a model for all women officials in the palace.[7] Saitō declared that she was not only beautiful but extremely intelligent; moreover, despite being exceptionally strict in her behavior, she was also gentle. Everyone in the *ōoku* admired her and agreed it was impossible to find fault with her behavior.

Like the other ladies who served as *gon no tenji*, Naruko was a shadowy presence even in the palace. Unlike court ladies of other ranks, who were encouraged to exercise and occasionally accompanied the empress on excursions, a *gon no tenji* rarely left her quarters within the palace and, never being exposed to sunlight, was likely to have a pallid complexion.[8] Their ranks were higher than those of most ladies of the emperor's entourage (a few were later promoted to *tenji* and rose as high as the first rank), but a somewhat clandestine air surrounded them. Yamakawa Michiko, whose position at the court was considerably inferior to that of a *gon no tenji*, wrote, "*Gon no tenji* are what in vulgar parlance are known as mistresses. Their main task was to look after the emperor, and when he went to the *ōoku*, they would take turns at serving by his side."[9]

Gon no tenji took care of the emperor's personal needs, attending him, for example, when he dressed or took a bath. But their most important function, as Yamakawa Michiko implied, was serving in his bed. This special duty was officially recognized: they were the only court ladies to receive an allowance for cosmetics.[10] The choice of just which *gon no tenji* would sleep with the emperor on a particular night was made not by him but by the senior court lady.[11] He seems not to have had strong preferences among his sleeping partners. If the emperor took a dislike to a concubine, she soon left his service, but this happened rarely. The fact that his last eight children (born between 1886 and 1897) were all born of his union with the *gon no tenji* Sono Sachiko suggests that he preferred her to the others, but it may be simply that she was exceptionally fecund. Several *gon no tenji*, including Ogura Fumiko, never bore him any children.[12]

As the mother of Princess Shigeko, Yanagihara Naruko enjoyed preferential treatment, but the birth of her third child, the future Taishō, was so difficult and accompanied by such hysteria and screams of anguish that she was never again permitted to share the emperor's bed.[13] She was nevertheless promoted to *tenji* and elevated to the second rank and, after her death, to the junior first rank, all as the result of having given birth to a prince who became the heir apparent.[14]

Princess Shigeko lived for only about a year and a half before succumbing to brain fever despite the court physicians' determined efforts.[15] Two years elapsed between her birth and that of the next imperial child. One can imagine how impatiently Meiji waited for word that one of his *gon no tenji* had put on a maternity belt.

In the meantime he spent his days as usual, receiving visitors from at home and abroad, riding, and occasionally issuing rescripts on matters of the day. He was also obliged to read and form opinions on the memorials submitted by his officials. At the end of February, for example, he received a long memorial from Iwakura Tomomi that stressed Japan's weakness when compared with the major nations of the West—no doubt the product of Iwakura's reflections after his travels abroad.[16] An awareness of Japan's military and industrial backwardness, had impelled Iwakura to oppose sending Saigō Takamori to Korea, but in this memorial Iwakura warned instead of the Russian menace to China, using a familiar expression from the Chinese classics: if the lips perish, the teeth will feel the cold.[17] He urged closer relations with China as a bulwark against Russian aggression; the two nations should help and depend on each other like the two wheels of a cart or the wings of a bird. His recommendation was unusual, as Japanese officials of the time thought of China as an enemy, a rival for control of the Korean peninsula, or as a self-satisfied but ineffectual country whose claims to possession of Taiwan could be defied with impunity.

Iwakura also described in his memorial how profoundly he had been impressed by the emperor's powers of judgment. He prayed that the emperor would henceforth deign to decide all matters of state, for if he graciously granted the benefit of his wisdom, what plan could fail? Once the nation, basking in his benevolence, was fully united, it would be able to gain equality with foreign countries, and the imperial glory would not falter for 10,000 years to come.[18] This was more than mere flattery. Perhaps because of his experiences abroad, Iwakura seems to have come to believe that the emperor should be (at least in principle) all-powerful, in this differing from such men as Kido, Ōkubo, and Itō who favored gradual progress toward a democratic state. But the despotism Iwakura had in mind would follow not the European style but the ancient Japanese ideal. The emperor, the descendant of the gods, would rule serenely, untroubled by the political antagonisms of those beneath him, imparting his wisdom to his ministers.[19]

Iwakura may have come to believe in the necessity of an all-powerful emperor because of his observation of the hostility that some major figures were then displaying toward the government. Even though he was minister of the left, Shimazu Hisamitsu had long refused to attend court, alleging illness, and had consistently opposed every innovation. He was especially enraged by the Western clothes that most officials now wore as their normal costume. In addition, Saigō Takamori, back in Kagoshima, showed no signs of returning to Tōkyō, maintaining mute opposition to the government.[20]

On April 14 the emperor attended the Shōin and, in the presence of the councillors and other important officials, announced the creation of the Genrō-in and the Taishin-in.[21] Regional legislatures would also be inaugurated. These measures were intended to be preparatory to the establishment of a parliamentary system of government. Meiji declared,

> At the beginning of our reign, We assembled our various ministers and swore an Oath in Five Articles to the gods. With these articles as the policy of Our government, We have sought a way to enable our people to live in security. Fortunately, thanks to the spirits of Our ancestors and the efforts of Our ministers, we have attained the present short respite. It is evident to Us, however, that this prosperity is not deep-seated, and that many things in our domestic policy have yet to be revived and restored. We now, in an extension of Our Oath, have established the Genrō-in, in this way broadening the sources of lawmaking; created the Taishin-in, in

this way strengthening judicial power; and summoned the provincial officials, in this way preparing the people to think of the public good and thereby laying the ground for the gradual creation of a government with a national constitution.[22]

In April, Iwakura submitted another long memorial to the throne that included the statement "Although the customs and languages of those who dwell in the many countries of this world differ, all are equally human beings."[23] This may seem like a truism to modern readers, but it served as a prelude to Iwakura's analysis of the changes in Japanese relations with foreigners. In the past Tokugawa Ieyasu had closed Japan to all but a handful of Chinese and Dutch merchants in Nagasaki, but this was no longer feasible. Japan could not ignore the achievements of the major nations of the West and the many facilities that contributed to their prosperity and strength. They made steam engines run on the ground and floated steamships on the oceans. The telegraph enabled them in a matter of seconds to be in communication with the most distant parts of the world. Places that in the past were thought to be 10,000 leagues away were now as close at hand as one's own backyard; East and West were neighbors. Unlike the fanatical believers in *jōi* of ten years earlier, Iwakura believed that the Japanese would have to recognize the qualities of men in other countries and learn to live with them.

Despite Iwakura's apprehensions over Russian territorial aims, a treaty was signed at this time with Russia that seemed likely to settle the long dispute over possession of Sakhalin. The treaty provided that the emperor of Japan would cede rights to the entire island in return for receiving from the czar of all the Russias the eighteen islands of the Kurile chain.[24] Not long afterward the czar's decision in favor of Japan in the case of the Peruvian ship *Maria Luz* mollified even Japanese who believed that Russia was Japan's greatest enemy.[25] It seemed likely that better relations between the two countries would prevail, and Meiji expressed his gratitude to the czar.

The acquisition of the Kurile Islands caused attention to be focused on the north. In July 1875 Sanjō Sanetomi, Kido Takayoshi, and Ōkubo Toshimichi presented a memorial asking the emperor to visit Hokkaidō in order to learn about its landscapes and people. They were convinced that if he toured Hokkaidō, it would make the entire country aware of the island. Its great size and possibilities for development would silence petty disputes on other matters, enlarge the imperial authority, and bring enlightenment to the ignorant.[26]

The government also began at this time to devote its attention to Okinawa, at the opposite end of the empire, applying pressure on the Ryūkyū kingdom to conform to Japanese usage. In July an envoy was sent to Shuri Castle with orders for King Shō Tai to discontinue vassal relations with China. Henceforth the Ryūkyū government was not to send envoys to China or to congratulate Chinese emperors on their accession to the throne or to accept appointment to their own throne from the Chinese government. They were to use the *nengō* Meiji. The Ryūkyūans, however, were reluctant to break their historical ties with China.

The remnants of *jōi* sentiments in Japan now took the form of protests over the importation of foreign products, which had caused an imbalance in trade and an outflow of specie. The minister of the left, Shimazu Hisamitsu, was the spokesman for a group of antiforeign partisans that included the emperor's grandfather, Nakayama Tadayasu. The emperor listened to their complaints and promised to give them careful consideration, but there was less and less inclination among members of the court to pay attention to Hisamitsu's protests, whether about the trade deficit, the clothes worn at court, or the solar calendar.[27] Besides, any attempt to prohibit the importation of foreign goods would certainly cause difficulties with the Western powers.

Ōkubo Toshimichi also was concerned about the Japanese trade deficit and had started a more positive program to reduce the deficit. Two years earlier he had employed an American to introduce sheep raising and to build a factory for making blankets in the hopes that this would reduce Japan's imports of wool and help develop hitherto unproductive land. Students of sheep raising were recruited throughout Japan, and in September, after visiting some uncultivated property in Shimōsa Province, Ōkubo himself decided to start his sheep ranch there. Unfortunately this scheme did not help correct the trade imbalance.

The most dramatic event of 1875 was an incident at Kanghwa Island in Korea that September. According to the Japanese version of what happened,[28] the Japanese warship *Un'yō*, on a mission to survey the Tsushima Strait, was passing along the west coast of the Korean peninsula on its way to China when it ran out of firewood and water. The ship anchored on September 20 off Kanghwa Island, and the captain went by boat to look for a place where he might land and obtain water, only to be greeted suddenly with rifle fire followed by blasts of artillery. The *Un'yō* responded with naval gunfire, but the captain, realizing that the water was too shallow for the Japanese ship to approach shore and that he had too few men with him to engage in combat, returned to the ship and ordered the firing to stop. The next day at dawn, the Japanese attacked and occupied the island after a brief but intense clash. The Japanese lost only one man to thirty-five by the Koreans. Sixteen Korean prisoners were taken. The Japanese ship returned to Nagasaki on September 28.[29]

The incident was no more than a minor clash involving a few dozen men on each side, but it was deliberately expanded into a crisis by Japanese officials who used it as an excuse for demanding concessions from the Koreans. When word of the action at Kanghwa Island reached the government, a session of the Court Council was held in the presence of the emperor. The council decided to dispatch a warship to Pusan to protect the lives of Japanese residents of Korea. The emperor, extremely disturbed by these developments, sent for Iwakura and asked for a detailed explanation of the Kanghwa incident, treating it as a matter of major national importance.

Kido Takayoshi, who a few years earlier had opposed Saigō's request to be sent as an envoy to Korea because he believed that strengthening the country internally was more important than avenging a supposed affront to Japanese honor, now changed his mind. He decided that although previously the evidence to warrant attacking Korea had been insufficient, firing on Japanese troops constituted an unmistakably hostile act. He proposed himself as an envoy to Korea. In a letter he sent to Sanjō Sanetomi, he blamed the crises Japan had faced during the recent years—the political upheaval of 1873 and the Saga rebellion—on the failure to establish satisfactory relations with Korea. In 1874, members of the Ryūkyū domain had been killed by Taiwanese savages, but the present event was much more serious—not only had the Japanese flag been dishonored, but (unlike Taiwan) Japanese lived in Korea, and their plight could not be ignored. The first step should be to ascertain whether China was willing to take action to chastise Korea, its tributary state; if not, he (Kido) should be delegated to deal with the Korean government. A Korean refusal to accept blame would justify the use of military force, and the responsibility would be clear. Kido was confident that if the Japanese government left the tactics of negotiations with the Koreans to him, he would do nothing to impair the glory of the imperial land.

Public opinion was aroused over the Kanghwa incident,[30] but the government was prevented from acting immediately because of internal problems, notably the attack directed against Prime Minister Sanjō Sanetomi by Minister of the Left Shimazu Hisamitsu in a letter to the emperor. He declared that if his advice—to dismiss Sanjō—was not heeded, Japan would be enslaved by the Western powers. He urged the emperor to assume full control of the government.[31]

Shimazu's accusations were vague and left the emperor perplexed. On October 22 he sent for Shimazu and, rejecting his petition, stated that Sanjō had served the nation devotedly and enjoyed his confidence. Shimazu Hisamitsu replied that if his petition were not accepted, he would have no choice but to resign his post. The emperor responded that in view of the crisis in Korea, he could not accept Hisamitsu's resignation.

In this and other controversies of the time, the emperor showed a firmness indicating that his period of youthful inexperience had come to an end. Naturally, before making decisions he consulted with his ministers, notably Kido, but the decisions were his own.

On November 1 it was decided at a meeting at Sanjō's house, attended by Minister of the Right Iwakura Tomomi and the councillors, to send an envoy to Korea and to station an envoy extraordinary and a minister plenipotentiary in China in order to be better informed about the situation. Mori Arinori was appointed to the latter post on November 10 with orders to ascertain through the intermediary of the Chinese government why the Koreans had attacked Japanese, who were merely looking for fresh water.

On December 9 an envoy was appointed to proceed to Korea. Kido had repeatedly asked to be sent, but just at this time he suffered a cerebral hemorrhage, and Lieutenant General and Councillor Kuroda Kiyotaka was chosen in his place. Sanjō's instructions to Kuroda described the grievous insult to the Japanese flag but said that the Japanese government did not despair of improving relations with Korea, that it was possible that the incident at Kangwha had been the decision of a provincial official and was not by order of the Korean government. It was essential to determine who had made the decision. If the Koreans were willing to open friendly relations with Japan and allow trade, the envoy was authorized to accept this concession in lieu of reparations for the attack on the Un'yō. If, however, the Korean government refused to accept responsibility for the attack at Kangwha and showed no signs of sincerely wishing to resume the traditional friendship between the two countries, the envoy was authorized to take appropriate measures.[32]

Kuroda sailed for Korea on January 6, 1876, with two warships, three transports, and three companies of marines, some 800 men in all,[33] the maximum the Japanese navy could provide by way of escort. The badly equipped little fleet was by no means as impressive as the ships Commodore Perry had brought to Japan on a similar mission twenty-three years earlier. In case negotiations broke down, secret plans were made for army reinforcements. Leaves for army personnel were canceled, and General Yamagata traveled to Shimonoseki to prepare for a possible military expedition.

The Japanese ships anchored off Kanghwa, a distance of some twenty miles from Seoul. On January 16 the Japanese military paraded to the Treaty House on Kanghwa, where they were met by two Korean commissioners. Kuroda at first thought that there was little hope of arriving at an agreement with the Koreans because of the prevailing unsettled conditions. He asked for reinforcements, but the Court Council refused his request, judging that a premature display of military strength might place an obstacle in the path of peaceful negotiations, by making the Koreans dread the Japanese.

The first meeting between representatives of the two countries lasted for four days. The negotiations were conducted with ritual politeness on both sides but consisted mainly of repetitions of familiar arguments. The Japanese wanted to know why their attempts to secure a treaty of peace and friendship had been consistently rebuffed; the Koreans in return wanted to know why the Japanese had used titles for their emperor that put him on an equal footing with the emperor of China, thereby placing Korea in a subordinate position. After denying any intent of asserting suzerainty over Korea, the Japanese asked why their ship had been fired on at Kanghwa. The Koreans answered that because the Japanese marines were dressed in European-style uniforms, they were mistaken for either French or Americans.[34] They failed to apologize, saying merely that the provincial officials had not recognized that the ships were Japanese. The Japanese delegates then demanded why the Korean government had not informed its provincial officials of the flags flown by Japanese ships and insisted that this required an apology. The Korean commandant replied that he was charged only with receiving the Japanese visitors; he was not authorized to make an apology.

The negotiations dragged on, interrupted by periods of consultation between the Korean commissioners and their government in Seoul, but on February 27, 1876, a treaty of friendship was at last signed between Japan and Korea.[35] After the signing ceremony, the Japanese offered presents to the Koreans, not only the traditional bolts of silk, but a cannon, a six-shooter, a pocket watch, a barometer, and a compass. The gifts (with the exception of the silk) were strikingly like those the Americans had given the Japanese when the first treaty between the two nations was signed, and the treaty itself had almost identical significance: Japan was "opening" Korea, the hermit nation, to diplomatic relations and to trade.[36] One Western scholar later commented,

> As the Western Powers had done with herself, so did she now, without one particle of compunction, induce Korea to sign away her sovereign rights of executive and tariff autonomy, and to confer on Japanese residents within her borders all the extraterritorial privileges which were held to violate equity and justice when exercised by Europeans in Japan.[37]

When word of the signing of the treaty reached the diplomatic community in Tōkyō, the ministers of the various countries asked for an audience with the emperor so that they might express their congratulations. The emperor invited them to a banquet at the Shiba Detached Palace, where each minister had the opportunity to convey joy over the signing of the treaty and hopes for greater and greater friendship between Japan and Korea.[38]

In the meanwhile small changes were affecting the lives of most Japanese almost daily, far more than events in Korea. On March 12, for example, Sunday was officially established as the day of rest. The government hesitated to take this step, for it feared that people might suppose it was out of deference to Christianity. But it was essential to bring Japan into line with the enlightened countries of the West, and in the end the government risked being called subservient to the Christians. A month later, Saturday afternoons were also designated as holidays.

On March 29 a decree was issued prohibiting all persons (except members of the armed forces and the police in uniform) from carrying swords. Violators of this order would have their swords confiscated. For years a debate had been waged over whether samurai should be permitted to wear swords in the old tradition or forbidden as an anomaly in modern Japan. It was at last resolved, no doubt bringing comfort to Europeans, who were always made nervous by the sight of a sword.

On April 4 the emperor, empress, and empress dowager visited Iwakura Tomomi's house, where they were entertained with performances of nō. Although nō had been performed at the palace in Kyōto and the empress dowager in particular was devoted to the art, it had long been associated with the shogunate. In keeping with the Confucian tradition that a well-run government honors "rites and music" (reigaku), the shogunate had chosen nō as its "music" and patronized it. With the fall of the shogunate, the future of nō had become doubtful. Some actors followed the Tokugawa family to "exile" in Shizuoka, but not finding audiences for their plays, most turned to other occupations. Only a handful attempted to maintain nō in Tōkyō. Daimyos still resident in the city on occasion requested performances as part of the entertainment offered their guests, but after the daimyos returned to the provinces, the nō actors no longer had patrons. It is true that when the duke of Edinburgh visited Japan, performances of nō (the first since the Restoration) were presented for his pleasure, but the actors could not wait hopefully for another royal visitor from abroad; they needed income to sustain their families, and none was forthcoming.

Hōshō Kurō (1837–1917), probably the most distinguished actor of the day, requested permission in 1870 to retire from the stage and debated whether to become a merchant or a farmer. Nō was performed in only two theaters—in Kyōto, where the Kongō School maintained its theater, and in Tōkyō, where in 1872 Umewaka Minoru (1827–1909) built a theater at his house in Asakusa. Performances at both theaters were rare.

The performances at Iwakura's house were thus of great importance in the revival of nō. During his travels in America and Europe, Iwakura had been invited on various occasions to the opera which, he was informed, was the most notable variety of European drama. (His hosts probably invited him to the opera because they hoped that even if he could not understand the words, he might at least enjoy the music.) Seeing opera abroad made Iwakura recall the nō, and after he returned to Japan, he asked two members of his embassy to plan a revival of the nō as a suitable entertainment to offer to foreign visitors.

The actors who appeared before the emperor on this occasion included Umewaka Minoru and Hōshō Kurō. In addition to members of the imperial family, four former daimyos, Sanjō Sanetomi, Kido Takayoshi, Ōkubo Toshimichi, Ōkuma Shigenobu, Itō Hirobumi, Yamagata Aritomo, and other major figures in the government also attended. After the planned program of Kokaji, Hashi Benkei, and Tsuchigumo had ended, Hōshō Kurō, at the emperor's request, performed Kumasaka. The emperor, it was reported, looked highly pleased. At the dinner of Western food offered afterward by Iwakura, the emperor favored him and the other ministers and councillors with saké poured by his own hand.

This was the first time the emperor had seen nō in Tōkyō. He seems to have been genuinely fond of it. Sometimes, when in a particularly good mood, he used to sing passages from the plays, and he even taught his court ladies how to sing them.[39] His enthusiasm for nō was undoubtedly an important factor in the preservation of this art at a time when its future looked bleak. From then on, whenever the emperor visited the residences of principal officers of the state or members of the nobility, he was generally entertained with performances of nō.

Meiji's next visit to the house of an adviser took place soon afterward, on April 14. On his way back to the palace from Asukayama, where he had gone to admire the cherry blossoms and to inspect a paper factory, he stopped at the villa of Kido Takayoshi in Somei Village.[40] Summoning Kido into his presence, the emperor uttered these words of praise: "You, Takayoshi, ever since the inception of the Restoration, have dedicated yourself to national duties, and now the country is fortunately enjoying peace. This is due to your accomplishments and those of your colleagues. We have personally paid you a visit and are delighted to be able to share pleasures together."[41]

He gave Kido 500 yen in gold, a large Satsuma ware vase, a pair of silver cups, and three cases of imported wine. He granted Mrs. Kido an audience, strolled in Kido's garden, and then joined in eating a box lunch with the other guests. This was the first time an emperor had ever visited the house of someone of the samurai class. Kido naturally was delighted.[42]

The emperor's plan of traveling to all parts of the country, announced years earlier, had been temporarily postponed as the result of various emergencies—the controversy over sending an envoy to Korea, the Saga insurrection, the expedition to Taiwan, and, most recently, the incident at Kanghwa Island—but now that these crises had been surmounted, the desirability of an imperial tour of the north of Japan was again urged.

On the whole the country was at peace, although peasant revolts (such as one in Wakayama early in May) were signs of residual discontent. In May, Kido submitted a lengthy memorial to the throne opening with the bold declaration that governments were established for the sake of the people but that the people were not under obligation to serve the government. He went on to describe the situation that had prevailed before the Restoration. During the 700 and more years since rule was delegated to the military, the people had always been oppressed by the government, but when the emperor, with supreme benevolence of intent, proclaimed the Restoration, he swept away the accumulation of evil practices. Truly, Kido commented, this must be accounted a great blessing for the people.[43]

Having read this far, one might expect that Kido would go on to urge even stronger steps to eliminate practices lingering from the rejected past. Instead, he warned against excessive changes. For example, with the establishment of prefectures in place of domains, officials had been appointed who were not necessarily natives of the locality they administered. They were therefore less solicitous when dealing with local problems than officials who were familiar with the persons involved and who would be anxious not to acquire a bad reputation that would be inherited by their children and grandchildren.

Kido was in effect pleading for the retention of one of the "evil customs" of the past. On May 19 after visiting Sanjō Sanetomi, he wrote in his diary: "We have been dazzled by the daily changes before our eyes, and we have discarded our customs of several hundred years too readily. In the end we have fallen victim to the disease of excessive rigidity in our approach."[44]

He was particularly upset by the announced plan of ending the stipends given to samurai: "If the plan for termination of stipends is not given up, I hope the government will minimize the troubles of those adversely affected, open the path of livelihood to them, and treat them with generosity."

Kido favored change, but without haste and with due consideration of "human" concerns. He probably transmitted these views to the emperor, for Kido was consulted by the emperor more frequently than any other statesman of the day.

Meiji's reactions are not described. His time was largely occupied by events that related directly to the steady progress of modernization. On May 9, for example, he attended the opening ceremonies of Ueno Park, the first public park in Japan. Refreshments, provided for the occasion by the Interior Ministry, typified the new age, as they included white wine, champagne, and ice cream.[45]

On June 2 the emperor finally set forth on his journey to the northeast.[46] He was accompanied by 230 persons, including members of the cabinet, official historians, chamberlains, and physicians. The first stop of the journey was at Sōka, reached by the procession at three that afternoon. As soon as the emperor had settled in his temporary quarters, he was formally welcomed by the governor of Saitama and other officials. The emperor rose the next morning at four, and the procession set out again. On the way to Gamō Village, the emperor commanded that his carriage be halted in order that he might observe rice planting. The peasants were dressed in their best clothes for the occasion, the men in the paddies wearing white cords to hold back their sleeves and the women red, and all wore sedge hats. As the peasants planted the rice seedlings, they sang songs that echoed far and near. The emperor was fascinated and kept his carriage waiting until he had seen his fill.[47]

The procession reached Satte, the next stop, that afternoon. The emperor sent for the governor and asked him about conditions in the prefecture. The governor described local geographic and living conditions and the products of the region. He mentioned that the greatest hardship endured by the people of the prefecture was the rivers' flooding. The emperor asked if there was no discontent among the people over the system of paying land rent with money rather than produce. The governor replied that most people welcomed the new system, but they would like to have the time of payments divided through the year. As in all future meetings between the emperor and local officials, Iwakura Tomomi and Kido Takayoshi were in attendance.

Almost everywhere the procession went, the emperor inspected elementary schools, listened to the pupils' recitations, and gave gifts (generally, dictionaries or atlases) to those pupils with the best marks. Outside the classrooms he watched the children perform calisthenics. These visits could not have been of great interest to the emperor, but he never indicated anything but pleasure over what he saw. Perhaps he enjoyed seeing his young subjects applying themselves to mental and physical culture; even more, he may have considered that such visits to schools and factories were part of his duties as a sovereign.

Only when there was some sight of unusual interest in the vicinity does the journey seem more than a graciously performed duty. When the emperor visited the Tōshōgū in Nikkō, for example, he carefully examined the architecture, the statues, the treasures from Japan and abroad. He paid his respects also at the tomb of Tokugawa Iemitsu and had documents concerning Ieyasu sent to his lodgings so that he might peruse them at leisure. That night he asked members of his escort to compose poems about the Eight Sights of Nikkō. Meiji felt no hesitation about visiting a site intimately associated with the Tokugawa family.

Wherever the emperor's procession went, it was greeted by crowds lining the roads. Many of the spectators composed poems describing their emotions, hoping that somehow they might be seen by the emperor himself. These farmer-poets were well aware that if they attempted to send their poems to the emperor through proper channels, local officials would see to it that they never reached him; so they either begged members of the entourage to show the poems to the emperor or left them in places where they would most likely attract notice. The head chamberlain collected and arranged such poems and offered them for the emperor's scrutiny every night at dinner.

The emperor also inspected local produce wherever he went and made a point of listening to the songs of peasants of the vicinity. Wherever he went, he was also shown antiques from the distant past, whether paintings and calligraphy or ancient farm utensils. He was pleased to see newly opened farmland and equally pleased by factories, a beginning of industrialization. In Sendai he attended a public display of objects owned by the Date family, including an oil painting of Hasekura Rokuemon, who visited Rome in 1615, worshiping a crucifix and a parchment book in Latin that Hasekura had brought back from Europe.[48] The emperor received gifts from both local officials and humble persons, like the cage of fireflies offered by elementary-school pupils in Furukawa. On occasion he bought local wares that intrigued him.

Probably the emperor found the last place he visited, Hakodate, the most intriguing. He happened to arrive at the Hakodate Hospital for a tour of inspection just when an experiment was being conducted on a toad's blood circulation. He examined the toad through a microscope, the first time he had used this instrument. When he reached his lodgings after a tour of the schools, he found that an exhibition of local wares had been arranged for him, including Ainu utensils and clothes. Later that day, more than fifty Ainu came to pay their respects. At night the garden was bright with hundreds of red lanterns. Every house along the streets had a lantern hanging from the eaves, and even the ships in the harbor were illuminated with strings of lights. All along the shore there were lighted stone lanterns, and in nearby villages, torches burned.

On July 17 the emperor visited the Five Point Fortress, the site of the last resistance to his army, and climbed up the ramparts. He asked a local official about the warfare. When he heard of some fifty Ainu, both men and women, who had come to Hakodate to see the procession, he sent for them and watched them dance.

During the voyage back to Yokohama from Hakodate, the sea was rough, and almost everyone was seasick. But the journey was otherwise a triumph. It is true that Kido Takayoshi, worried about the emperor's lack of exercise, had tried without much success to persuade him to walk or ride a horse, but he seems rarely to have left his carriage or palanquin during the journey.[49] A more serious concern was the accounts of dissatisfaction and even unrest among the samurai class, heard from local officials wherever the procession went. This pent-up discontent would, before the year had ended, explode in violence.

Chapter 27

The rapid pace of modernization continued unabated during the remainder of 1876. On September 4 the *Jingei*, a warship intended for the emperor's personal use, was launched at the Yokosuka shipyard. On the following day the last link in the railway line between Kyōto and Kōbe was completed, and train service between the two cities by way of Ōsaka was inaugurated. On September 7 the emperor issued a rescript to the Genrō-in calling for a rough draft of a constitution to be compiled after making a broad study of the laws of different foreign countries. On September 9 the emperor was presented with two newspapers, one published in Tōkyō and the other in Yokohama; he would henceforth receive a number of newspapers every day. Each of these developments in its own way—transportation, political progress, dissemination of information—suggested the shape of things to come in Japan.

The emperor also entered into closer contact with the heads of various foreign countries. On October 1, for example, he sent a message of congratulations to President Ulysses S. Grant on the opening of the Centennial Exposition in Philadelphia, commemorating the hundredth anniversary of American independence. Two days later he received from the czar of Russia the photographs and architectural drawings he had requested of the Winter Palace in St. Petersburg, to be consulted when building his new residence in Tōkyō.

Not all his subjects were pleased with such developments. Many samurai still clung to their old ideal of *sonnō jōi* and resented each step the government took to make Japan into a modern nation. They were outraged that foreigners were now permitted to buy property in the Land of the Gods and to live outside the foreign settlements. They were especially infuriated by the edicts issued earlier that year commanding them to cut their hair in Western style and to cease wearing swords. Their anger over what they considered to be flagrant violations of Japanese traditions (those of their own class in particular) was intensified by the economic hardships that many were then suffering.

The Saga rebellion, the first violent expression of this anger, had been suppressed with the aid of government troops from the Kumamoto garrison. It occurred to the leaders of "patriotic" groups in Kumamoto that now, when the garrison was far below its normal strength, might be the moment to attack their headquarters. At the time there were four "parties" (tō) in Kumamoto. Two—the Keishin-tō (more familiarly known as the Shinpūren)[1] and the Gakkō-tō—were reactionary, hoping to restore the samurai traditions rejected by the Meiji government. The other two "parties"—the Jitsugaku-tō and the Minken-tō—favored modernization.[2] The wrath of the Shinpūren was roused to fever pitch by the false rumor that the emperor was planning to go abroad.[3]

The leader of the Shinpūren, Ōtaguro Tomoo (1835–1876), decided in October, after having on several occasions performed rites of Shintō divination,[4] that he had at last been given divine authorization for staging an uprising. He was in contact with samurai in other prefectures who shared his convictions, and he hoped that success in Kumamoto would encourage them to stage similar revolts. The mutual bond uniting these men was hatred of the changes (especially in the status of the samurai class) that had occurred since the Meiji Restoration. The members of the Shinpūren were the most extreme. They were not satisfied merely with arresting the spread of Western influence; they were determined to eradicate every trace of it, whether the wearing of Western clothes or the use of the Western calendar. Some members displayed their hatred of electricity, for example, by holding white fans over their heads when they had to pass under telegraph wires, in order to protect themselves from baleful foreign influences. Many carried salt to sprinkle (by way of purification) whenever they saw a Buddhist priest,[5] a Japanese in Western clothes, or a funeral. And one man, convinced that paper money was imitated from the West, refused to touch it lest he be polluted and accepted money only with chopsticks.[6] One ideological decision had fatal repercussions during the impending battle with government forces—their refusal to use modern weapons. The members of the Shinpūren fought with swords and spears against soldiers armed with rifles and cannons.

Late at night on October 24 the men of the Shinpūren—fewer than 200—gathered secretly. They quickly divided into squads, each with a specific assignment. One squad attacked the Kumamoto garrison and, taking advantage of surprise, killed many defenders before setting fire to the barracks of infantry and artillery soldiers. Other rebels, bursting into the telegraph office, smashed the hated foreign instruments, although this meant cutting off communications with the outside world, including their allies. Still others attacked the residences of the prefectural governor Yasuoka Ryōsuke, the garrison commandant Major General Taneda Masaaki, and the chief of staff Lieutenant Colonel Takashima Shigenori. They killed Taneda and Takashima, mortally wounded Yasuoka, and burned down his house.

The slaughter was indiscriminate. The attack on the barracks, completely without warning, caught the unarmed soldiers in their nightclothes, but this did not induce the Shinpūren to capture rather than kill. They showed no mercy even toward men who were too badly wounded to defend themselves. More than 300 soldiers of the garrison were killed or wounded in the battle. Unlike the members of the Shinpūren, the garrison soldiers were conscripts, most of them peasants. It seems to have given the Shinpūren samurai special pleasure to kill lowly peasants who had dared to usurp their place as military men.

At first it seemed as if the rebels had won a complete victory, but once the army officers were able to overcome their surprise and shock, they rallied the remaining soldiers and, by force of numbers and modern weapons, routed the attackers. The rebels were decimated by gunfire; Ōtaguro, badly wounded, commanded his followers to cut off his head, and they did. Most of the survivors committed *seppuku*, maintaining Japanese tradition to the end. By dawn, the fires set by the rebels had died down, and sounds of gunfire could no longer be heard. The battle was over, but it had thrown the city into a state of panic, and many people had fled. The emergency was not lifted until November 3.[7]

The revolt of the Shinpūren had achieved nothing except the deaths of some 500 men who might otherwise have been of service to their country and perhaps to the world. The two long lines of gravestones at the Sakurayama Shrine in Kumamoto where 123 of the Shinpūren are buried, each marked with a name and the age at which the man died, whether in action or by his own hand, are likely to inspire reveries on the swiftness of the fall of the cherry blossoms and similar metaphors for the deaths of samurai. Visitors who stand before these tombs today may be so impressed by the dedication displayed on behalf of a doomed cause as to forget that the attack was brutal in the extreme and that the ideals for which the young men (most in their teens or twenties) died were insensate.

All the same, the 180 or so members of the Shinpūren had demonstrated that it was possible for a small body of men, if their attack was unforeseen and they themselves were ready to risk their lives, to defeat much larger forces or at least to reduce them to a state of terror. This lesson of terrorism was communicated to samurai dissidents throughout Japan, some of whom soon demonstrated that they also were prepared to start a rebellion with a mere handful of men.[8]

Word of the Shinpūren uprising reached the court on October 25. Iwakura Tomomi and Kido Takayoshi immediately informed the emperor of what they had heard, but because communications with Kumamoto had been cut, they did not know the details. The next day after telegraphic service with the Kumamoto garrison had been restored, Sanjō Sanetomi and Ōkubo Toshimichi gave the emperor a fuller report. Officers were dispatched to Kyūshū to obtain firsthand information, and Major General Ōyama Iwao was appointed to replace the murdered Taneda as commandant of the Kumamoto garrison.

On October 23, the day before the battle in Kumamoto, the Shinpūren sent a messenger to the former Akizuki domain in Fukuoka prefecture to inform disgruntled samurai of the planned uprising and to ask them to join the revolt. The Akizuki samurai, angered by the government's refusal to take Shimazu Hisamitsu's advice and halt the increasing Westernization of the country, had been in secret communication with both the Shinpūren and dissidents in Hagi. The political thought of the Kanjōtai[9] (as the Akizuki samurai styled themselves) was marked by one unusual feature, an advocacy of overseas expansion, and the government's refusal to attack Korea had infuriated them.

In response to the Shinpūren's request, the Akizuki samurai, led by Miyazaki Kurumanosuke, agreed to send troops to Kumamoto. On October 26 the Akizuki samurai, who numbered fewer than 200 men, prepared to leave for the scene of the fighting.[10] Not all the former Akizuki samurai agreed with this decision. Some urged Miyazaki to disband the troops, but passions had been aroused, and nothing less than military action would satisfy hot-tempered samurai. The Akizuki samurai set off behind a white banner inscribed in big characters *hōkoku*.[11] Before long, government troops caught up with the rebels and inflicted heavy losses. On November 1 most of the leaders of the Kanjōtai, weary and despairing of success, committed suicide.

The third of the revolts occurred in Hagi. Maebara Issei, a brilliant student of Yoshida Shōin at his celebrated school in Hagi, and later at the Chōshū school for Western learning, had seen active service with both Chōshū and Meiji armies. He had distinguished himself especially in the campaign at Aizu Wakamatsu. After rising to be minister of defense, he resigned in 1870, ostensibly because of illness but actually because he was angered by Kido Takayoshi's recommendations to the Court Council on the treatment of former daimyos. He was dissatisfied also with the political views of senior members of the government, especially their advocacy of modernization. Maebara began to think of starting a revolt and joining forces with other dissidents, especially the Shinpūren.[12]

When Maebara learned that the Shinpūren had staged an uprising, he summoned a group of intimates on October 26 and declared to them that the time had come to revive the national polity. He proposed a lightning attack on Yamaguchi. The others agreed, and he issued a manifesto appealing to men of like views. On October 28 Maebara's supporters assembled, ready for combat. They numbered only about 100 men, but they decided to attack that night. The governor of Yamaguchi Prefecture, getting word that trouble was brewing in

Hagi, sent an official to inform Maebara that the Kumamoto rebellion had been quelled and ordered him to disband his men at once.

Maebara realized that his revolt was doomed: a surprise attack had offered the only possibility of success, but now that the governor had learned his plans and was expecting support from government troops, there was no point in trying to attack Yamaguchi. Maebara thereupon changed his plans: he would win over the samurai of the provinces along the coast of the Sea of Japan and advance with them to Tōkyō where, at the feet of the emperor, they would commit suicides of remonstrance.

With this in mind, Maebara and his men made their way to Susa on the northern coast of Yamaguchi Prefecture, looting as they went. In Susa he mustered additional men and formed them into the Junkoku Army.[13] He planned to go by sea from Susa to Hamada in Iwami Province, but strong winds assaulted his flotilla of fishing boats and forced him to return to Hagi. When Maebara discovered that his secret supplies of ammunition in Hagi had been dumped into the sea, he knew he had no chance of success. He decided to go to Tōkyō and offer his reasons for having staged a rebellion. He and a handful of his men slipped out of Hagi but were captured on November 5. The rest of the Junkoku Army was crushed by land and sea forces of the government.

Samurai with similar views in other places who had been sympathetic to the rebels abandoned their plans to revolt, realizing it would be futile. On December 3 leaders of the failed rebellions in Kumamoto, Akizuki and Hagi, were tried and executed. The samurai rebellions were over for the time being, but peasant revolts in Ibaraki and Mie made it clear how much dissatisfaction still lingered in the country.

On December 31 Kido Takayoshi, the most outspoken member of the administration, sent a memorandum to Prime Minister Sanjō Sanetomi and Minister of the Right Iwakura Tomomi in which he blamed inept administration of the laws for recent revolts by samurai and peasants. However, he said, the ultimate blame lay elsewhere: ever since the crisis of 1873, most of the troubles plaguing the country had originated in Satsuma. As examples of this pernicious influence, he mentioned Satsuma's advocacy of the conquest of Korea and of Taiwan. The government was always in the position of having to follow Satsuma's lead. Kido's harsh interpretation of the actions of the Satsuma samurai may be explained in terms of his Chōshū background, but surely that was not all; he sympathized with peasants who, faced with poverty and hunger because of unsettled conditions, had no other way to express their frustration than by arming themselves with bamboo spears.

Kido proposed a six-point program intended to promote the welfare of the peasant class. One point urged an end to using government money for unnecessary construction, thereby freeing funds to help people in economic distress. Another point declared that the people should not be bound, without first consulting them, by rules and regulations that had been promulgated. Kido concluded by expressing impatience with those who favored delay in opening a parliament on the grounds that the people were not ready for it. They said they favored gradual rather than precipitous change, but they themselves did not hesitate to impose decrees without considering whether or not these decrees were enlightened or appropriate; if that was not precipitous, what was it?[14]

The day after Kido sent his memorandum, the New Year ceremonies for 1877 were performed at the palace in exact conformity to tradition. The emperor was now in his twenty-sixth year. On January 4 he announced that land taxes would be reduced from 3 to 2.5 percent in the hopes of bringing relief to the people. Kido Takayoshi commented in his diary, "I have long requested this action, so I am grateful. My only hope now is that the Imperial purpose will be fully realized, and that it will lead to the well-being of the people."[15] This reduction in state revenues would result in a curtailment of some state services, and the emperor urged officials to practice strict economy.

Behind the emperor's decision, we can detect the presence of Ōkubo To-shimichi, who on December 27, 1876, had sent a memorandum to Sanjō Sa-netomi in which he declared that it was absolutely essential to relieve the plight of the peasants. Not only had the new government done nothing to help the peasants, but it had not even spared the time to consider their problems. The peasant revolts that had lately broken out in various parts of the country were evidence of their unhappiness. It was the duty of the government, which had always insisted that agriculture was the foundation of the state, to enable the peasants to make a decent living.[16] Ōkubo proposed lowering the tax to 2 per-cent, predicting that the relief afforded to the farmers would bring about general prosperity. The 2.5 percent announced by the emperor was presumably a compromise.

On January 4 the emperor rode horseback. This normally would need no comment, but from this day on, riding became a mania with him. He rode almost every day from two in the afternoon until sundown. He continued his intense riding practice not only in Tōkyō but after he went to Kyōto later that month.

The emperor left Tōkyō for Kyōto on January 24. The announced reason for the journey was the emperor's desire to worship at the tomb of Emperor Jimmu at Mount Unebi and of Emperor Kōmei at the Sennyū-ji in Kyōto on the tenth anniversary of Kōmei's death. He was also planning to visit tombs of other emperors in the region of Kyōto and Nara,[17] traveling to and from Kōbe by sea. The emperor, no doubt remembering the rough voyage on his return from Hokkaidō, was unenthusiastic about making two sea voyages and attempted to persuade his advisers to allow him at least to return by land. But they informed him that he would be urgently needed back in Tōkyō and begged him to return by sea because it was quicker than land travel.[18] The emperor eventually yielded, but (as we can tell from the poems composed at this time) he was still apprehensive about the rough seas. The first *tanka* was composed on January

21, the day before the scheduled sailing, although stormy winds in fact caused a postponement:

hageshiku mo	I can hear the roar
fukikuru kaze no	Of the wind blowing this way
oto su nari	With violent force;
ao unabara ni	How the waves will be rising
nami ya tatsuran	In the blue expanse of sea.

The second *tanka* seems to have been composed aboard ship:

kinō kyō	In the fierceness of
umi fuku kaze no	The wind blowing over the sea
hageshisa ni	Yesterday and today
kogiiden fune mo	Ships that were being rowed away
shibashi todemetsu	Have had to be stopped a while.[19]

On the morning of January 24, the emperor and his suite traveled by train to Yokohama, where he boarded the *Takao maru*. The ship, escorted by two warships (the *Kasuga* and the *Seiki*), sailed the same morning. That day he composed the following *tanka*:

nami kaze no	Not dismayed even
tatsu mo itowazu	By the rising wind and waves,
unabara ni	How the ship races
keburi wo tatete	Over the plains of the sea
hashiru fune kana	Raising a column of smoke.[20]

The poem confirms the emperor's confidence in the ship, regardless of the weather, but the sea was rougher than he had expected. The waves rose, whipped by a fierce northeasterly wind and by rain, and the ship rocked so badly it was decided to anchor at Toba until the storm abated. The emperor described his feeling in these words:

fuku kaze ni	Having been battered
arasoitateru	By the rough waves mustered up
aranami ni	By the blowing winds.
kokoro narazu mo	We have had to row the ship back
kogikaeshikeri	Quite against our own wishes.[21]

The storm continued for several days. Not until January 27 were the ships able to resume the voyage, reaching Kōbe the next day. The emperor landed and, after a brief rest at the post office, went by horseback through the city to the railway station, acclaimed by crowds that lined the streets. He traveled by train from Kōbe to Kyōto, where he was again greeted by crowds as he proceeded from Higashi Hongan-ji (where he briefly rested) to the Gosho. He was no doubt moved to return to the scenes of his childhood, but the only surviving expression of his pleasure is found in this *tanka*:

suminareshi	How delightful to think
hana no miyako no	That this year I shall see
hatsuyuki wo	The first fall of snow
kotoshi wa min to	In the flowery capital
omou tanoshisa	Where I lived so many years.[22]

Arriving at the palace, he was welcomed by the empress and the empress dowager. Later that day he granted an audience to members of the imperial family. On January 29 the emperor received members of the nobility in his study. He distributed gifts to various princes and princesses as well as to high-ranking nobles. It may have seemed as if Kyōto's old glory had at least temporarily been restored, although the buildings of the Gosho had suffered from neglect during the emperor's absence in Tōkyō.[23]

That night, quite unknown to those who attended these ceremonies at the court, a group of young men (described as "private school students") raided the army ammunition dump at Sōmuda in Kagoshima, the first clash of the Satsuma Rebellion.

The immediate cause of this action by "students"—samurai who had attended the private schools[24] founded by Saigō Takamori—was the report that the national army, disturbed by reports of unrest, had sent a steamship to transfer ammunition stored in Kagoshima to the Ōsaka Artillery Arsenal. Attacks on army ammunition dumps and on the arsenal attached to the naval shipyard continued during the following week. The vice commandant of the shipyard repeatedly asked the governor of Kagoshima for police protection, but he was ignored. On February 3 the vice commandant closed the shipyard, suspecting that the governor's failure to act was occasioned by his sympathy for the attackers. Two days later the "students" occupied the shipyard and began to manufacture weapons and ammunition.

Behind these actions were the frustration and anger felt by Saigō Takamori and other Kagoshima samurai when his request to be sent to Korea as an ambassador was finally rejected. After returning to Kagoshima they decided that the samurai needed special training to make them effective defenders of the prefecture, which—in their view—was an all but independent country. In June 1874 Saigō founded a school outside the city of Kagoshima at the foot of Shiroyama in buildings that had been the stables of the Satsuma clan. A branch school, smaller in size, was founded within the city itself, and other branches were soon established elsewhere in the prefecture. The guiding spirit of these

"private schools" was Saigō Takamori. A set of maxims, penned by Saigō himself, was displayed at each school, including one declaring that reverence for
the monarch and compassion for the people were the foundation of learning.
If thoroughly investigated, this principle would enable the samurai to perform
their Heaven-appointed duties in a righteous manner.[25]

The instruction given at these schools emphasized the reading of the Chinese classics, especially those relating to the art of war, and the study of the
traditions of the samurai class.[26] No guidance was provided in Japanese learning
(such as Shintō or poetry composition) or in Western technology. The purpose
of the schools was to make members of the samurai class aware that although
they were neglected by the government in Tōkyō, they were the repositories of
Japanese tradition. Even though they emphasized the importance of study, the
private schools closely resembled political parties; the students were committed
to a program of action; and their interest in learning was in no sense academic.

Some Kagoshima samurai, particularly those who came from places outside
the city, were reluctant to attend the schools, but social pressure eventually
obliged them to show solidarity with others of their class. The schools enjoyed
the covert support of the governor, who appointed "students" to local political
offices.

In December 1876 the government sent a police officer named Nakahara
Hisao and various other men[27] to Kagoshima to investigate reports of subversive
activities by the private schools. Soon after arriving they were captured by students of these schools and accused of being spies. Later they were accused of
an even graver crime: their mission, it was charged, was to assassinate Saigō.
Nakahara was tortured and forced to sign a confession admitting his guilt.[28] He
later repudiated the confession, but it was widely believed in Kagoshima—even
by Saigō—that the government wished to kill Saigō.[29] This revelation became
for those associated with the private schools a pretext for starting a rebellion in
order to protect him.

Although the emperor was kept informed of developments in Kagoshima,
he showed no signs of wanting to return to Tōkyō or to take command of efforts
to put down a rebellion against his authority. Instead he spent his days in Kyōto
inspecting schools, a brewery, various factories, and even a stock-farming ranch.
He paid his respects at various Shintō shrines and, in the company of the
empress, the empress dowager, and his aunt Princess Sumiko, attended a program of nō at the Katsuranomiya Palace.[30] He continued these peaceful activities (and visits to the tombs of his ancestors) even as conditions in Kagoshima
rapidly worsened.

On February 6 reports reached Tōkyō on the tense situation in Kagoshima,
causing great surprise and consternation because their content diametrically
contradicted the appraisal prepared by Hayashi Tomoyuki (1823–1907), an officer of the Interior Ministry. After he had inspected conditions in Kagoshima
and returned to Tōkyō, he discounted the seriousness of the reported unrest.[31]

Hayashi now asked to be sent back to Kagoshima so that he might get a better grasp of the changed situation. Sanjō Sanetomi, Kido Takayoshi, and Itō Hirobumi acceded to Hayashi's request, and he was ordered to return to Kagoshima along with Admiral Kawamura Sumiyoshi (1836–1904). They expressed particular concern over the possibility that unrest might spread to other parts of Japan that were close to Kagoshima either geographically or spiritually.[32] In view of the gravity of the situation, they suggested that Hayashi, Kawamura, and the others in the party proceed to Kagoshima by the steamship *Takao maru*, the fastest way to get there.

The *Takao maru* sailed from Kōbe on February 7 and arrived in Kagoshima two days later. A messenger was sent to the prefectural office to report the mission's arrival. Soon afterward the governor, Ōyama Tsunayoshi, came aboard. He informed Hayashi and Kawamura that the students of the private schools were upset because of the report that assassins had been sent to kill Saigō. In fact the whole prefecture was seething with indignation. He relayed Saigō's request that Kawamura (Saigō's cousin) go ashore so that they might discuss the matter. Hayashi replied that it was unlikely that any assassins had been sent to Kagoshima. He urged Ōyama to join with Saigō in calming the agitation.[33]

Hardly had Ōyama left the *Takao maru* than seven or eight small boats approached, each bearing a dozen or more armed men. They attempted by force to board the *Takao maru*, but the captain, cutting the moorings, ordered the ship to proceed toward Sakurajima. Ōyama returned later that day with a message repeating Saigō's eagerness to meet with Kawamura. Hayashi replied that he could not permit Kawamura to go ashore until the turbulence had been calmed. He labeled the attack on a ship belonging to the government an act of lèse-majesté and informed Ōyama before dismissing him that in view of prevailing conditions, the ship would be leaving at once.[34]

The *Takao maru* returned to Kōbe on February 12. It was met by Yamagata Aritomo and Itō Hirobumi, who had gone there when word of the incident in Kagoshima reached Kyōto. That night at an inn in Kōbe, preparations for sending troops to Kagoshima were discussed. There seemed to be no doubt that the outbreak of war was imminent.

Chapter 28

February 1877 was one of the memorable months of modern Japanese history. The Satsuma Rebellion, the last civil war to be fought in Japan, broke out this month, pitting heroes of the Restoration against one another. The war represented a great threat not merely to the evolution toward democracy desired by principal members of the government but to the very survival of the regime. At the start it was by no means certain that the Satsuma Rebellion would fail, and if it succeeded, the entire political configuration of Japan would undoubtedly have changed.

Emperor Meiji was kept abreast of developments from the first stirrings of the rebellion, and he was not indifferent to what he heard; but his life in Kyōto at this time seems to have been completely unruffled by the dramatic events taking place in Kagoshima. He visited schools, listened to pupils recite, and rewarded the bright ones with money for textbooks. At first he rode virtually every day. Once in a while he left Kyōto. On February 5, for example, he visited all the stations on the newly opened railway line between Kyōto and Kōbe. Kido Takayoshi's diary evokes the stuffily formal nature of the ceremonies:

> At 9 the emperor boarded the train to go to Ōsaka station. On his arrival there the Army Band formed ranks and played some music, while several government officials welcomed the emperor. A throne had been prepared in the railway station. The ministers of foreign nations were lined up to the left of the throne; and, as the prime minister was ill, I headed the

line of Japanese officials to the right of the throne. The Grand Master of Ceremonies introduced the Governor of Ōsaka, who headed the delegation of governors, secretaries, head district chiefs, and other officials; and the Governor stepped forward in front of the throne to offer a congratulatory address. The emperor honored him with a message in reply.[1]

Two days later, on February 7, Meiji set out for Yamato Province in order to fulfill a long-standing wish to worship at the tomb of Emperor Jimmu, his distant ancestor. On the way he stopped on the bridge over the Uji River and watched fishermen cast their nets from dozens of little fishing boats. He spent that night at Uji where, admiring the moon, he composed this *tanka*:

mononofu no	Morning Sun Mountain—
yaso Uji kawa ni	Visible in the light
sumu tsuki no	Of the moon that dwells
hikari ni miyuru	In the Uji River known
asahiyama kana	To soldiers of many clans.[2]

On the following day the emperor visited the Phoenix Hall and inspected the buildings and treasures of this famous temple. Afterward he and his escorts traveled to Nara where he stayed at the Tōdai-ji from where he enjoyed the splendid view of nearby mountains.

On February 9 Meiji went to worship at the Kasuga Shrine. Shintō rites were performed, and he listened to *kagura*. In the afternoon he visited an exhibition of treasures from the Tōdai-ji and Hōryū-ji and saw a performance of the nō play *Shakkyō* performed by actors of the Komparu school.[3]

Later that day Emperor Meiji was shown the imperial collection of treasures in the Shōsō-in. Although the building was normally sealed shut, it was opened for this occasion. Inside the Shōsō-in the emperor expressed interest in the celebrated *ranjatai*, an ancient log of incense wood. Ashikaga Yoshimasa in the fifteenth century and Oda Nobunaga in the sixteenth century had received slivers of the *ranjatai*, perhaps as a tribute to their place in history. After he had returned to his quarters that night, Meiji asked for a piece of the *ranjatai*. The director of the museum cut off a sliver two inches long and offered it to the emperor, who broke it into two pieces and burned one. "A fragrant smoke filled the temporary palace."[4] The emperor took back to Tōkyō the remaining piece of *ranjatai*.

On February 11, corresponding to the date in the lunar calendar of Jimmu's coronation,[5] Meiji worshiped before his tomb. In 1863 a spot had been designated as Jimmu's tomb, and repairs had been made during Kōmei's reign. Since then it had been neglected, but from now on it would be shown proper respect. On the day he visited the tomb, the emperor watched folk dances that had been preserved since ancient times at Kuzu in Yoshino as well as *bugaku* dances. Afterward he inspected the machines used to make the famous Miwa vermicelli.

On February 12 Meiji visited sites associated with Sugawara no Michizane, who had passed through this region on his way into exile. That morning there were snow flurries, and a holy purity seemed to fill heaven and earth. The emperor could not bear the thought of leaving a place sacred to his first ancestor and so intimately associated with the history of the country. He said he would like to stay for another day, but the imperial household minister replied that it would cause hardship for people if he prolonged his stay. Besides, the news from Kagoshima was so disquieting that the emperor should return to Tōkyō as soon as possible. The emperor at once agreed.

The emperor's seeming imperturbability in face of threatening news from Kagoshima is little short of astonishing. Of course, his travels in the countryside of Yamato were not merely pleasure excursions. Apart from the importance he attached to paying homage before the tombs of Jimmu and other emperors, his travels (like earlier journeys to Kyūshū and to Hokkaidō) served the vital function of bringing him closer to the people. When he decided to keep to his original plan of visiting Nara, despite the threat of war, he may have been following the advice of Kido Takayoshi, who wrote in his diary on February 10, after describing the alarming situation in Kagoshima, "I maintain that a sudden change of the schedule on account of this civil disturbance is improper; and that if a rebellion breaks out before the end of the tour, the emperor should stay where he is."[6]

In any case, while the emperor was pursuing his leisurely journey around Yamato, visiting schools, spinning mills, and imperial tombs, troops of the Household Guards Division and the Tōkyō and Ōsaka garrisons were being dispatched to Kyūshū. On February 12 in response to intelligence received from the Kumamoto garrison, Army Minister Yamagata Aritomo sent a message to Prime Minister Sanjō Sanetomi concerning strategy. He warned that the situation in Kagoshima was extremely tense. It would be difficult to predict what would occur if war broke out or what changes might result afterward, but they would not be insignificant. Moreover, once Kagoshima moved into action, other provinces in different parts of Japan were likely to join.

Yamagata admitted that he did not know what strategy Kagoshima might adopt in the event of a full-scale rebellion, but he listed three possibilities: Saigō's forces might stage a sudden raid, using steamships, on Tōkyō and Ōsaka; his troops might attack Nagasaki and the Kumamoto garrison to gain control of Kyūshū; or they might ensconce themselves in Kagoshima and, keeping an eye on signs of shifting loyalties throughout the country, wait for the right moment to strike. Yamagata correctly inferred that Saigō would choose the second course—an attack on the Kumamoto garrison—and he believed that the best way to counter such a strategy would be a joint army–navy onslaught on Kagoshima Castle, the nerve center of Saigō's forces. He was sure that once this castle was taken, it would not be difficult to destroy rebellious domains elsewhere.[7]

On February 13 at 8 P.M., Sanjō left Kyōto for the emperor's residence in Nara, arriving at midnight. He had gone to ask the emperor's permission to send warships to Kagoshima. Permission was granted, and Sanjō (at 2 A.M.) withdrew from the imperial presence. He sent authorization to Rear Admiral Itō Sukemaro in Kōbe, who immediately raised the *Kasuga*'s anchor and set sail for Nagasaki. The *Ryūjō* was already there.

Earlier, as signs of impending conflict were multiplying, Iwakura Tomomi had suggested to Ōkubo Toshimichi that if there was a disturbance in Kagoshima, an imperial envoy should be sent to admonish Saigō Takamori and Shimazu Hisamitsu. When word was received of the seizure of arms by "students" of Saigō's private schools, Iwakura proposed himself as the envoy and offered to leave at once for Kagoshima. Ōkubo did not agree, contending that at a time when the emperor was in the western part of the country, Iwakura's responsibilities were too heavy to permit him to leave the capital. But as more and more reports on the situation in Kagoshima reached Tōkyō, it became clear that something had to be done to end the "students' violence." Ōkubo decided to leave for Kyōto to be with the emperor. It was as yet unclear what course of action Saigō and Shimazu would take, and Iwakura decided not to reveal publicly that a punitive force would be sent to Kyūshū.

In the meanwhile the emperor continued his visits to places of interest in the Kansai region. On February 14, attired in court robes, he worshiped at the Sumiyoshi Shrine. Later in the morning he changed to informal clothes and visited the tea house where Toyotomi Hideyoshi had once amused himself. The emperor and his party went next to Ōsaka, where soldiers of the garrison, lined up along the way, presented arms. The houses were decorated with flags, lanterns, and brightly colored pennants in honor of the visit. At the garrison he was greeted with an artillery salute and gave an audience to Yamagata Aritomo and Kido Takayoshi. After lunch he went to the Ōsaka English Language School, where he heard the pupils recite in English and observed a science experiment. From the English school Meiji went to the Ōsaka Teachers Training School where there was a repetition of classroom visits, and he gave prizes to the outstanding students. Finally the emperor proceeded to the Ōsaka Mint where he received various dignitaries and ate a Western meal.

Granted that Meiji was still a young man, the day must nevertheless have been exhausting, and the remainder of the journey was equally taxing. On the fifteenth, among other activities, he quizzed gifted children from city elementary schools about Japanese history, asking about the achievements of six emperors—Keikō, Nintoku, Goshirakawa, Gouda, Ōgimachi, and Goyōzei. After resting briefly he asked a similar group of schoolchildren from the countryside about Japanese geography. On the sixteenth, before leaving Ōsaka, the emperor visited an indigo-dyeing factory and watched stages of the process. He returned to Kyōto that day.

This is one of the moments in the life of Meiji when the biographer would give anything for a glimpse into his reactions. How did he feel when he learned that Kagoshima, a highly important province, was on the brink of secession and likely to be joined in rebellion by other provinces? And how did he react to the possibility that his government's troops might soon be fighting against those commanded by Saigō Takamori, who was not only the hero of the Restoration but a man for whom he had special affection? Perhaps the energy with which Meiji threw himself into routine visits may have been his way of putting such thoughts from his mind. The apathy he displayed during the rest of his stay in Kyōto may have stemmed from the same cause.

On February 16 Ōkubo arrived in Kōbe from Tōkyō and met with Itō Hirobumi and Kawamura Sumiyoshi. The three men had a prolonged discussion, after which Ōkubo and Itō left for Kyōto to meet with Sanjō Sanetomi. On the following day they (and Kido) went to the Gosho where they conferred for several hours in the presence of the emperor. Yamagata, who arrived late, also joined the discussion, and they agreed to send an imperial envoy to Kagoshima. The emperor summoned Prince Taruhito and commanded him to serve as his envoy. Taruhito planned to leave on February 18 aboard the steamship *Meiji maru*. The ship was about to sail when a message arrived from the Kumamoto garrison reporting that a spearhead of Kagoshima rebels had entered Kumamoto Prefecture, and it seemed likely fighting would break out at any moment. Taruhito's departure was delayed.

The entrance into Kumamoto of Kagoshima troops commanded by Saigō began on the fourteenth. All accounts agree that Saigō was reluctant to initiate hostilities, but reports of his intended assassination had incensed his men. On the twelfth he, together with his lieutenants Kirino Toshiaki and Shinohara Kunimoto, had sent a letter to Ōyama Tsunayoshi, the governor of Kagoshima, announcing their intention of traveling with their soldiers to Tōkyō, where they intended to ask questions of the government.[8] On the following day Ōyama in turn sent messages to Sanjō Sanetomi and several governors, informing them that Saigō and his escort would be passing through their prefectures on their way to Tōkyō. He also hinted at Saigō's grievance, the alleged plot on his life.[9] The same message was sent to the garrison.

Before an answer could be received, the Kagoshima army had moved into Kumamoto. Saigō's army consisted of seven battalions of infantry plus artillery and support troops, a total of about 15,000 men,[10] most of them provided with modern weapons. Even after word had been received that Saigō's troops had crossed the border into Kumamoto, the emperor's life in Kyōto at first remained undisturbed. On February 18, for example, he went to Tenryū-ji Village, where he visited the villa of the patriot and poet Yamanaka Ken (1822–1885). After lunch he watched fishermen catch carp in the Ōi River and inspected a paper mill.

That night Prime Minister Sanjō Sanetomi, having decided that there could be no mistaking the rebellious intent of the students of the Kagoshima private schools, conferred with Kido, Yamagata, Ōkubo, and Itō. The next morning he informed the emperor of the crisis, and the emperor issued the command to punish the rebels. Prince Taruhito was named general of the punitive expedition. Army Minister Yamagata Aritomo and Navy Minister Kawamura Sumiyoshi would assist him. The emperor announced his intention of remaining in Kyōto until the rebellion had been suppressed.

Six or seven inches of snow fell on the day Saigō's army left Kagoshima, the heaviest snowfall in fifty years in that normally warm region. Although Saigō's troops had been well trained and maintained discipline, the army must have presented a curious appearance. Saigō, Kirino, Shinohara, and the other top-ranking officers who had not resigned their commissions in the government forces wore the same uniforms as did the men they would fight. Others of Saigō's officers wore naval uniforms, police uniforms, or the dress of civil servants. Officers wore a white armband indicating the unit to which they were attached, and a crepe silk or white cotton sash over their coats. A sword dangled from their left hip, and they carried bright red flags in their right hand. The costumes worn by ordinary soldiers were even stranger. Strangest of all was Murata Shimpachi, recently returned from abroad, who rode into battle attired in a swallow-tail coat and a derby.[11]

The objective of the Kagoshima soldiers was the capture of Kumamoto Castle, the center of government military strength in the southern half of Kyūshū. It was defended by conscripted soldiers, like those who had been slaughtered by the Shinpūren in the previous year. Morale was low, mainly because the men were intimidated by what they heard of the great Saigō, whose fame extended throughout the country.

The garrison could not hope for support from the Kumamoto samurai, some of whom were secretly in communication with the Kagoshima forces. The defenders' only hope was to entrench themselves inside the castle and wait for relief from government troops. Then a fire broke out in the castle's storehouse, reducing almost all the reserves of food to ashes. The garrison had no choice but to requisition food from nearby villages in preparation for what was anticipated would be a siege of some weeks in duration. On February 19 messengers sent by the governor of Kagoshima arrived and attempted to show the commandant, Major General Tani Tateki, three documents—Saigō's original letter asking permission to go to Tōkyō, the governor's response, and a transcript of Nakahara Hisao's confession relating to the planned assassination. The documents were rejected, and the messengers were informed that if Saigō's soldiers attempted to go by the castle, the defenders would have no choice but to stop them. The vanguard of Saigō's army was now a bare five miles away.

The first shots of the war were exchanged on February 19. Units of the Kagoshima army attempted to force their way into Kumamoto Castle but were repulsed by cannon fire from the defenders. General Tani sent a telegram to army headquarters (now in Ōsaka) reporting the opening of hostilities, and Yamagata forwarded the message to Sanjō Sanetomi in Kyōto. A message was sent from Kyōto to Tani urging him to hold firm and to destroy the rebels with one bold attack. The arrival of the first and second brigades was promised by February 25.

The main body of the rebel forces began their attack on the castle from two sides on the twenty-second. They stepped up the attack on the twenty-third but were unable to advance. This made them realize that the peasant-soldiers inside the castle were not as ineffectual as they had supposed, and they resigned themselves to a long siege.

On the night of February 22, in moonlight bright as day, the Kokura Fourteenth Regiment, commanded by Acting Major Nogi Maresuke (1849–1912), and rebel troops clashed. The rebels, raising war cries, fought at close quarters with drawn swords. The government troops fell back, unable to withstand the attack. Later that night in the midst of fierce fighting, the standard bearer of the regiment was killed and the regimental flag was lost. Nogi was horrified and tried, disregarding personal danger, to recapture the flag, but he was held back. The commander in chief of the expeditionary force never asked Nogi what had happened to the flag, preferring to overlook the incident, but Nogi did not forget it, and twenty-five years later he committed suicide to atone for the loss.

In the meantime, Kumamoto samurai began to desert in numbers to Saigō's army, citing the government's addiction to Western practices and the neglect of Japanese traditions which, they believed, had prevented Japan from regaining its ancient glory. Desertions by samurai of this persuasion soon swelled the ranks of Saigō's army to some 20,000 men. The prevalence of *sonnō jōi* thought was not surprising in these samurai; they not only resented the changes that Westernization had brought to their lives but had been stirred by the heroic deaths of members of the Shinpūren. Saigō himself was not anti-Western (George Washington was one of his heroes), but the private school students displayed a strong element of *jōi*, as we can infer from the song they sang, which begins:

> Though this is the Land of the Gods
> Today as in the distant past,
> People are dazzled by stupid foreign ways
> And, paying no attention to the confusion in Japan,
> They borrow their laws from abroad. . . .

Not only was foreign influence decried, but the achievement of the Restoration was questioned:

> When they wiped out the daimyos
> They said they were returning to the past,
> But now we know they were lying. . . .

After singling out Ōkubo and Sanjō for special attack, the song makes this accusation:

> What happened then to their traitorous hearts?
> They sold the country to the dirty foreigners
> And ordered us to give up our weapons and swords
> A decree never heard before or since. . . .

The conclusion of the song, expressing the fascination that death exerted over these samurai, contrasts with the triumphant note typical of the war songs of other countries:

> We've reached a point we can take no more
> We warriors can only do our utmost
> To save tens of thousands of people,
> Today our last, on the road to the other world.[12]

Even after the fighting had begun in earnest, Saigō still insisted that his only objective was to proceed to Tōkyō in order to ask the government some questions. He maintained that there was nothing secret about his plans: the prefectures and garrisons he would pass on his way had long since been informed. But the troops of the Kumamoto garrison had tried to block his passage, and he therefore had no choice but to resist.

On February 28 Governor Ōyama of Kagoshima sent a petition to Sanjō and Iwakura explaining why Saigō's troops had opened fire. He expressed astonishment that the government had ordered that Kagoshima be pacified. He insisted that Saigō's purpose in opening the private schools was to inculcate loyalty and filial piety in the young men of his prefecture. When Saga, Kumamoto, and Yamaguchi had been torn by disturbances, absolute calm had reigned in Kagoshima. What suspicions of his motives had induced the government to order his assassination? It is true that his followers were carrying arms on their journey to Tōkyō, but after all, Saigō's execution had been ordered, and so he had to prepare for any untoward event on the way. He asked that imperial instructions be issued immediately to reassure the people of Kagoshima.[13]

By the time this letter reached Iwakura, however, a new ultimatum had been issued. Saigō, enraged, sent a letter to Prince Taruhito, announcing that if his arguments continued to be ignored, he would have no choice but to employ military force in passing Kumamoto.

The siege of Kumamoto Castle dragged on for fifty-four days until it was relieved on April 14. In the meanwhile communications between the defenders and the outside were almost completely severed, although on occasion a courier slipped through enemy lines to report on conditions inside the castle. On March 4 Kido, who had spent several days at headquarters in Ōsaka, returned to Kyōto and gave a detailed report to the emperor on the progress of the war and future objectives. The emperor was relieved to hear that the situation was turning in the government forces' favor. At the same time, imagining Saigō's grief over having been branded as a traitor, the emperor felt sympathy for him. Kido was moved to tears at the depth of the emperor's affection for a subject who had previously served him well.[14]

Judged in terms of how a European monarch would probably have reacted under the circumstances, Meiji's compassion was remarkable. A European monarch, learning that a man whom he had trusted and favored was now leading a rebellion, would probably have fulminated against the man's ingratitude, never once giving a thought to the pain it might have cost the man to rebel. Meiji's affection for Saigō Takamori may have led him to hope that the confrontation between Saigō's forces and the government forces might still be averted. Indeed, Saigō, Kirino, and Shinohara were not stripped of their court ranks and posts until March 9.

Conversely (and contrary to typical European examples of leaders of rebellions), absolutely nothing suggests that Saigō was dissatisfied with Emperor Meiji or that he hoped another form of government might replace the monarchy. Far from it—Saigō seems to have believed that direct rule by the emperor, even authoritarian rule, was the ideal form of government.[15] This belief was shared by the samurai who fought under him. For them, the ultimate objective of the Satsuma Rebellion was to rid the emperor of the corrupt officials surrounding him so that he might rule undisturbed by their evil influence.

For that matter, men close to the emperor, like Kido Takayoshi, did not (as often in wartime) paint the leader of the enemy as a traitor or an ingrate. Kido said of Saigō that he was definitely not an evil man like Ashikaga Takauji, who had raised the standard of rebellion against the emperor Godaigo; rather, he was ill informed on conditions and had unfortunately allowed momentary anger to destroy himself and harm his country. Saigō's action was to be hated, but the government should consider whether it had made mistakes that had inspired his revolt.[16]

The battle for Kumamoto Castle was crucial. If the castle fell to the rebels and they entered Hizen Province, all Kyūshū would fall into their hands.[17] But if they were defeated in Kumamoto, the war would end in the foreseeable future, for the rebel leaders were not likely to prolong the war by withdrawing to Kagoshima.[18] The relief army was, however, slow in reaching the castle. After overcoming their initial surprise at the fierceness of the resistance of the peasant-soldiers, the rebels settled down to a siege, modeling their tactics on those of the Prussians during the siege of Metz during the Franco-Prussian War.[19]

The government army's first victory was won by a unit of 100 handpicked policemen who, with drawn swords, stormed a fortified place that regular soldiers had failed to take in several days.[20] On March 15 government troops launched an offensive on the enemy stronghold at Tabaruzaka. The most intense fighting of the war caused many casualties on both sides. On the twentieth, the government army, scoring a breakthrough, took the fort at the crest. It is recorded that the corpses of rebel dead were so numerous that they blocked the road and the waters of the moat ran red. The enemy fled. The siege of Kumamoto Castle was not lifted for another three weeks, and the war continued until late September, but the victory at Tabaruzaka foreshadowed the end. Sooner or later, the government army's matériel and numerical superiority would defeat the Satsuma samurai, fierce fighters though they were.

From the outbreak of hostilities, the emperor seems to have been unable to think of anything but the war. He rarely went to his study except to give audiences, but he listened every day to Sanjō Sanetomi give the latest news of the war. He spent most of his time surrounded by women in the residential palace. The emperor's chief officers—Sanjō, Iwakura, Kido, and the rest—had exerted every effort to foster the emperor's moral excellence, and they were deeply concerned about his behavior at a time of national crisis. Sanjō and Kido again and again begged him to appear in his study, but without effect. On March 20 after a meeting with Kido to discuss what should be done, Sanjō went to the palace and remonstrated with the emperor, who finally agreed to mend his ways. Beginning on the twenty-first he would appear every other day in the study to hear reports on progress of the war. He summoned his tutor, Motoda Nagazane, from Tōkyō and questioned him (Motoda was a native of Kumamoto) about the geography. He also asked Motoda to deliver lectures on famous battles of Japanese and Chinese history.[21]

On March 25, at Kido's urging, the emperor agreed to leave the Gosho and ride horseback through the city. Kido, much concerned over the emperor's persistent refusal to emerge from the palace's inner recesses, begged him to tour Kyōto, sure it would cheer him, even if there was a little wind and snow. For all his passion for riding, the emperor had exercised his horse inside the Gosho only twice since the war began; but at ten that morning, accompanied by Kido and various chamberlains and palace officials, he rode out the southern gate. The streets were muddy and the emperor's clothes were soiled by the ride. Perhaps Kido hoped that the sight of the emperor on his horse would cheer the people of Kyōto. The fighting in Kumamoto had been going on for only a month, but people were already weary of the war.[22]

The rebels still tenaciously prevented the government army from lifting the siege of Kumamoto Castle. The government feared that the army's apparent weakness might inspire restive elements in other parts of the country to test their strength against the government's and might even precipitate a collapse of the regime. At a meeting on April 4 Sanjō, Kido, Ōkubo, and Itō decided that if there was no improvement in the situation during the next few days, they would ask the emperor to move to Shimonoseki so as to be closer to the fighting.[23]

Three days later a more drastic step was considered: asking the emperor to take personal command of the expeditionary force. Because there was a shortage of soldiers even with conscription, and the public showed a conspicuous lack of enthusiasm for the war, the one way to arouse enthusiasm would be to ask the emperor to take command.

In the meantime conditions inside the castle were becoming desperate. Food and ammunition were running short, with meals for infantry soldiers consisting of rice gruel twice a day and millet once. One thing that kept up morale was tobacco, but the "tobacco" was actually tea leaves. It was estimated that supplies of food would last for only eighteen days.

On April 12 the full strength of the government army under General Kuroda Kiyotaka put to flight the rebel army between it and the castle. The rebel general, Nagayama Yaichirō, unable to withstand the attack, committed suicide. That afternoon, the commandant of the castle, observing the government army approach, ordered his men into the field to catch the rebel army in a pincer movement. At four that afternoon the Second Brigade, commanded by General Yamakawa Hiroshi, broke through the enemy ranks. The soldiers in the castle raised war cries, waved flags, and their joyful shouts filled the castle. The siege had been lifted.

On April 15 Kuroda entered the castle, and on the next day, Yamagata followed him. The campaign up to this point had resulted in 7,500 casualties, and nine-tenths of the city of Kumamoto had been consumed in flames. Even with the victory at Kumamoto Castle, the war lasted another five months, but the rebels' resources steadily dwindled. Saigō's forces were on the run, and only his brilliant generalship preserved them from encirclement and destruction. Even now he was occasionally able to inflict a defeat on superior government forces.[24]

During this period Meiji showed less and less interest in his studies. He sent Motoda back to Tōkyō in May. Before leaving, Motoda delivered a lecture on the proper behavior for a ruler. Although couched in normally polite language, the implications were clear: "he who has virtue should become the ruler of men; he who lacks virtue must not become the ruler of men."[25] Not only had lectures been discontinued, but not even the prime minister or the councillors could easily arrange to visit the emperor. He had agreed to go to his study regularly, but he went only in the morning, and in the afternoon he relaxed in his private quarters.

The death of Kido Takayoshi on May 26 after a long illness came as a blow to the emperor, but it did not shake him out of his apathy. In July, Sanjō Sanetomi, feeling more responsible than ever for the emperor's education now that Kido was dead, thought the best plan was to have Motoda and Fukuba Bisei come to Kyōto to resume lectures, but he could not send for them without imperial permission. This was difficult to obtain, but eventually both tutors arrived in Kyōto, and the emperor was informed that they wished to devote themselves to his guidance. He expressed his pleasure and declared that he would henceforth devote himself to his studies, but in the end lectures were not given.

On July 28 the emperor left Kyōto to return to Tōkyō. His departure had been delayed several times for fear of the adverse effect it might have on the troops in Kyūshū, but the inconvenience of a government divided between two cities had made his return essential. On the ship returning from Kōbe to Yokohama, the emperor, seeing Mount Fuji rising into the clouds, composed three *tanka*, including

azuma ni to	As the ship hurries
isogu funaji no	Along its course to the East
nami no ue ni	How joyous it is
ureshiku miyuru	When appears over the waves
Fuji no shibayama	The wooded slopes of Fuji.[26]

He scribbled three poems in pencil in a notebook, tore out the page, showed it to his chamberlain Takasaki Masakaze (1836–1912), an accomplished poet, and asked him to criticize the poems frankly. Takasaki deferentially examined them and said that the second of the three was particularly good. The emperor asked what was wrong with the other two. Takasaki replied that nothing was wrong with them, but they were not as good as the second. The emperor asked Takasaki to explain what was superior about the second poem. The conversation continued, the emperor manifesting greater and greater interest. He showed Takasaki some *tanka* composed earlier, and Takasaki analyzed each one carefully. The emperor finally showed him more than thirty poems. The experience helped while away the time aboard ship, but more important, this may have been the moment when the emperor, depressed by the war and apathetic, began to take new interest in life and in his duties as emperor.[27]

On July 4 the *gon no tenji* Yanagihara Naruko put on a maternity belt. The emperor's first three children had all died as infants, and the doctors were determined that the next child should be born in the most favorable environment. In the end, it was decided not to send Naruko to Kyōto for the birth because of her delicate health. A son was born on September 23 at the Umegoten in Tōkyō,[28] the day before the final action of the war in Kyūshū.

Saigō's last stand was at Shiroyama, where he had opened the first private school. At the end, he had only forty men left, and he was severely wounded. Kneeling in the direction of the imperial palace, he bowed his head, and his aide Beppu Shinsuke at once decapitated him. The rebellion had ended.

Chapter 29

The remainder of 1887, at least as far as the emperor was concerned, was occupied chiefly with disposing of the aftermath of the Satsuma Rebellion. The
various generals who had participated in the war were acclaimed with triumphal
returns, shared by soldiers of humble ranks, and decorations were awarded to
the principal agents of the victory. Saigō Takamori was not forgiven his part
in the conflict, but sympathy was already expressed. The day after Saigō's death,
the emperor asked the empress to compose a *tanka* on Saigō Takamori. She
wrote:

Satsuma-gata	On Satsuma shores
shizumishi nami no	The waves that have quieted
asakaranu	Were not shallow—
hajime no chigai	Differences at the beginning,
sue no awaresa	But pathos at the end.[1]

The end of Satsuma resistance meant that there would be no further casualties in an unpopular war. The emperor visited the hospitals where men
wounded during the war were convalescing. Some had lost arms or fingers, and
others had been blinded. The emperor, deeply distressed, commanded that five
maimed men be brought into his presence. He asked them kindly where and
when they had been wounded and whether they still felt pain. Then, with an
expression of sorrow, he touched their scars. The wounded men lowered their

heads and wept with gratitude. Yamagata Aritomo, observing the emperor's gesture of compassion, stood erect and saluted, at which everyone wept.[2]

Again and again in accounts of Meiji's contacts with his subjects at this time and later, we encounter the word *kankyū*, or "tears of emotion." People wept more easily a hundred years ago than they do today, and it was not considered to be unmanly, even for samurai, to weep. The emperor who ten years earlier had been a mysterious being hidden behind the walls of the Gosho had been transformed into an awesome but benevolent presence whose every gesture of affection for his people summoned forth tears.

After the emperor returned to Tōkyō, his life reverted to the pattern he had set before lapsing into apathy in Kyōto. He attended a cabinet meeting thirty minutes each day, beginning at ten in the morning.[3] Once again he had parties in the residential palace with whichever advisers happened to be on duty. On October 4, for example, Takasaki Masakaze and Motoda Nagazane attended him. During their conversation he took up a brush and wrote some big characters, followed by this preface and poem:

Tonight, in the company of my men, I took brush in hand and wrote all kinds of things that I showed them.

aki no yo no	Not tired by the length
nagaki ni akazu	Of a nighttime in autumn,
tomoshibi wo	I lift the lantern
kakagete moji wo	And give myself the pleasure
kakisusamitsutsu	Of scribbling down the words.

According to the record of Meiji's life, "the two men [Takasaki and Motoda], struck by the emperor's solicitude, wept with emotion, and without realizing it, bowed profoundly before him." The empress asked Takasaki if he would not compose a reply. He at once complied with this *tanka*:

asakaranu	In appreciation
mi-gokoro kumite	Of the depth of his feeling
mizuguki no	I have wet my sleeve
mi-ato ni sode wo	As I examined the traces
nurashitsuru kana	Left by the imperial brush.

Motoda, deciding that he could not remain silent, composed two quatrains in classical Chinese. The party was so agreeable to the emperor that from then on he frequently exchanged poetry with those attending him. On October 12 the chamberlain Ogi Masayoshi drew a picture of a gourd. Yamaguchi Masasada wrote a poem on the picture:

kono hisago	I will try drinking
Gankai mata wa	From this gourd to distinguish
Hideyoshi no	What Gankai
medeshi kokoro wo	Or perhaps Hideyoshi
nomiwakete miru	So enjoyed about liquor.

Both the emperor and the empress laughed at the poem.[4] This rare description of their life *en famille* is endearing.

On October 23, after a long lapse, the emperor spent an hour in his study reading with Motoda Nagazane.[5] Gradually his program of studies came once again to include lectures as well as readings. Believing that the works they read together provided models for the virtuous behavior of an emperor, Motoda explained the text in detailed but easily understood language, comparing it with recent history and citing examples of virtuous actions by rulers. Motoda always attempted—and generally succeeded—in arousing the emperor's interest, although at first he was unable to understand what in particular might appeal to the emperor. One night, after the emperor had read how King Hsüan of Chou, moved by the remonstration of Queen Chiang, applied himself to matters of state, he asked his own consort to compose a poem on the theme of "moved by remonstrations, to devote oneself to governing"[6] Meiji admired rulers who took remonstrations to heart and mended their ways.

Motoda was moved by the emperor's newly awakened self-examination after the long period during which he had neglected his studies and also by his readiness to respond to his advisers' criticism. A fuller program of studies was initiated on December 13.[7] Not long before, at a chrysanthemum-viewing party at the Aoyama Palace, the emperor had impressed Motoda by the soundness and excellence of his opinions, particularly with respect to foreign countries. Motoda had never before heard the emperor speak so eloquently and wished that foreigners could have heard him.[8]

The emperor also resumed his frenetic horse riding. His renewed interest was at first welcomed by his advisers, but eventually they decided he was overdoing it, and they feared that out of exhaustion he might fall off his horse. Iwakura Tomomi spoke to him, but to no effect. Even though it rained steadily at the beginning of January 1878, the emperor rode every day on the track inside the palace grounds, not seeming to mind that he was muddy to the shins. The drivers and grooms of the imperial stables were exhausted. On January 12 two *jiho*,[9] Hijikata Hisamoto and Takasaki Masakaze, broached the subject with the emperor. He listened with an amiable look on his face, and when the two men finished speaking, he said, "You have spoken well. From now on I will follow the opinions of the drivers." The two *jiho* were so impressed by the speediness of his acquiescence that they shed tears of emotion.[10]

The next day the emperor went riding with Hijikata. While passing through a pine forest, Hijikata's horse bolted and he was almost thrown. The emperor at once rode up and asked if Hijikata was all right. He was upset to think that just the day before he had been warned about his riding and now his companion was almost thrown. All who heard his words were struck with admiration for his generous and magnanimous nobility.

A subtle change occurred about this time in Meiji's relations with other heads of state. His letter to Patrice de Mac-Mahon, the president of France, bore the superscription "Mutsuhito, Emperor of Japan by grace of Heaven, descendant of an unbroken line of ten thousand generations of emperors."[11] He had not previously used this overpowering title in foreign correspondence. Conversely, the letter sent to him by the emperor of China bore a superscription referring to himself as Great Emperor of the Great Ch'ing Country and to Meiji as Great Emperor of Great Japan,[12] placing the two monarchs on terms of equality, an unprecedented concession from the Chinese court.

Meiji seems to have become consciously aware of Japanese history, whether in terms of the shell mounds discovered in September 1877 by the American scientist Edward Morse, or of the Satsuma Rebellion as an important part of the history of his own reign.[13] He showed renewed interest especially in his ancestors.

The usual court formalities, exchanges of visits and presents, and composition of New Year poems opened the new year of 1878. Toward the end of January, the emperor issued a rescript on the importance of agriculture to the state. Now that all the rebellions had been quelled, the fundamental policies of a well-run state were reiterated.

Only occasionally do we get a hint of problems relating to the throne. The emperor's professed respect for remonstrances seems to have encouraged the men around him to express (naturally in the most respectful terms) their disapproval of his actions. For example, on February 3 the *jiho* on duty, Yamaguchi Masasada begged permission to appear before the emperor, even though it was a Sunday. Braving the displeasure on the emperor's countenance, Yamaguchi asked him to observe greater temperance in his drinking, pointing out that the beriberi from which he had suffered during the previous year might well recur.[14] This year, with New Year and other celebrations, the emperor had been overindulging. At a party on January 10 he had kept drinking until 3 A.M., and just three days before he granted an audience to Yamaguchi his drinking had continued until 5 A.M. Yamaguchi implored the emperor not to drink so much, especially late at night.

The emperor took the "remonstration" with good grace, and, it is reported, he was never again seen with a drunken face.[15] There is no indication why Meiji drank so heavily. Various people who knew him testified to his love for drink, even long afterward. General Takashima Tomonosuke, who had served in the Satsuma Rebellion, recalled,

The tone of the palace at the time was one of virility and martial prowess. The emperor drank very heavily. At times he would assemble favorite members of the court and stage drinking parties. I have not much capacity for liquor, and although it embarrasses me to admit it, I always made my escape and hid. But Yamaoka Tesshū and Major Counselor Nakagawa were heavy drinkers, and they would invariably be summoned when the emperor had a drinking party. Nothing gave him greater pleasure than to drink cup after cup of saké, listening to the tales of deeds of bravery that went with the drink. The cup he used at that time was not the usual small size, but one as big as a drinking glass, and he had it filled to the brim.[16]

Viscount Hinonishi, who became a chamberlain in 1886, wrote that even after the emperor had drunk his coffee at the end of a meal, he would not withdraw to his private quarters as long as there was any liquor left on the table.[17]

Remonstration of a quite different nature was made by the emperor's chief Confucian adviser, Motoda Nagazane. It was proposed about this time (February 1878) that following European models, forestland be attached to the Crown. But Motoda opposed this plan, arguing that the imperial household depended for its preservation not on land but on the ties with the hearts of the people created by "divine virtue and great benevolence." He recalled that in ancient times, the government took only a small portion of the products of the land by way of taxes. Then, moving to the rights of the sovereign and the people, Motoda declared that if there was some right that the people, having performed their duties faithfully, deserved to obtain, the sovereign should bestow it. If there was some right that the sovereign, having ruled virtuously, deserved to obtain, the people should offer it. However, in the present instance, the government was trying to take away what should be the property of the people and to make it the private possession of the imperial household. This represented in effect a struggle for advantage between the imperial household and the people on equal terms, and it did harm to imperial authority. A portion of land taxes should be set aside for the maintenance of the imperial household. Then if the government ruled the people with supreme virtue and great benevolence, they would respond with ever greater love for the imperial household. But if the people's hearts were alienated, even if the imperial household possesses all the land in Japan, the people would fight to take it away.[18]

Motoda's words were heeded, and the plan of co-opting lands for the Crown was not carried out. This instance suggests the power that Confucian remonstration still possessed, but sometimes a would-be remonstrator, enlightened by the emperor's superior virtue, would withdrew his criticism. On one occasion the emperor asked a chamberlain to have his shoes repaired. The chamberlain secretly conferred with two *jiho*, Sasaki Takayuki and Takasaki Masakaze, asking why the emperor should have commanded that his shoes be repaired rather than discarding them in favor of new ones. They replied that this might seem a trivial matter, but it had important implications for the ruler's virtue. If the emperor asked to have his shoes repaired because he respected the value of economy, his command was truly to be admired. However, if he were motivated by stinginess, this was most to be regretted. Takasaki asked the emperor his reasons. He replied that he was planning to give the shoes to the acting chamberlain Fujinami Kototada, but noticing that they were a little worn, he had asked to have them repaired so as to spare Fujinami the expense. Takasaki, realizing how much the emperor loved his ministers, wept with emotion.[19]

Another aspect of the emperor's sovereignly virtue was revealed on April 23 when he donated 20,000 yen to Tōkyō Prefecture for building a hospital to treat beriberi. Having suffered himself from this disease the previous year, he sympathized with others who were afflicted. If his own illness were to recur, it was likely that the doctors, as usual, would prescribe a change of air. Iwakura Tomomi, foreseeing this, proposed building a detached palace for the emperor at some elevated spot with a healthful atmosphere. The emperor replied, "Yes, a change of air is a good cure. But I am not the only one to suffer with beriberi. This illness is common to our whole people. It would be easy enough for me to move to another place, but surely one can't expect the whole population to move. For the sake of our entire people, I want to consider other means of preventing this sickness. When I traveled to the north, I noticed that dozens of soldiers in the garrison were suffering from beriberi, even though their post was on high ground. In my opinion, moving to a better place is not enough to escape the disease. I have heard that this sickness does not exist in the West but is found only in our country. If that is true, the cause must be eating rice. I have heard that a physician of Chinese medicine, Tōda Chōan, cures patients by having them eat beans or wheat instead of rice. I am sure there must be something to it. Chinese medicine should not, however, be discarded wholesale as being outdated. Western medicine and Chinese medicine both have their good points. Japanese medicine is not to be discarded either."[20]

Iwakura, struck dumb with admiration, withdrew. Later Ōkubo Toshimichi also recommended that the emperor move to another location and received the same reply. One cannot be sure that these were the emperor's actual words, but it may have been his first recorded pronouncement of this length. The hospital for which he gave money was opened on July 10. He later gave money for the construction of an insane asylum in Tōkyō, the first ever built in the city.

The emperor had an aversion to the doctors who remained with him to the end of his life. He particularly disliked being examined. In the previous year when he was suffering from beriberi, he had not told the doctors serving him that he felt unwell, and by the time the doctors learned this, the illness was already far advanced. His strong physique generally permitted him to pay little attention to his health. For their part the court doctors still relied on traditional, sometimes unenlightened, practices. When, for example, Princess Chikako contracted beriberi in August 1877, the best the doctors could do was to recommend a change of air. She accordingly went to Hakone, where she died three weeks later on September 2, in her thirty-third year.[21] This tragic end to the life of an unhappy woman, the sister of an emperor and the wife of a shogun, seems to have intensified Meiji's distrust of doctors. It was only after two hours of persuasion by Sasaki Takayuki (1830–1910) that he consented to a physical examination.

The various remonstrances of his advisers, and his own willingness to follow (after an initial show of resistance) what they advised, seem to have brought a new maturity to the emperor. Fortunately he was surrounded by men of extraordinary ability who showed the persistence and even courage required to guide the emperor, who had not yet completely thrown off the effects of his early education in the Gosho.

Among these advisers, probably the most gifted, though the least popular, was the interior minister, Ōkubo Toshimichi. He was undoubtedly the most powerful man in the government, responsible only to the emperor. Ever since he returned from America and Europe in 1873, Ōkubo's aim had been to strengthen the country politically and economically in order to compete on terms of equality with the advanced countries of the West. His methods were often high-handed, and he had aroused the hatred of adherents of both the right (who blamed him for the rejection of the invasion of Korea and the defeat of Saigō Takamori) and the left (who believed that his conservatism had blocked the advance of people's rights). He was unjustly accused of leading a life of luxury while the majority of the Japanese (especially the samurai) were in dire financial straits. Disgruntled samurai in all parts of the country, mouthing slogans reminiscent of those used by *sonnō jōi* advocates of the late Tokugawa period, had made Ōkubo the particular target of their resentment.

A group of samurai in Kanazawa began to plan his assassination. Kanazawa was an unexpected place for a plot. First, the Kaga domain had played an extremely inconspicuous role in the Restoration. Furthermore, the Maeda family enjoyed the largest income of any daimyo—1 million *koku*—and the city of Kanazawa had developed as a center of cultural activity. This prosperity may explain the lack of turbulent political activity at a time when other parts of Japan were deeply involved in the changes of the first ten years of Emperor Meiji's reign.

Some samurai in Kanazawa, however, felt frustrated by the conciliatory tactics that had enabled Kaga to thrive at a time when other domains were embroiled in political disputes.[22] They were embittered particularly by the refusal to send Saigō to Korea and sided with him in his unsuccessful war against the government. One architect of the assassination plot, Chō Tsurahide, journeyed twice to Kagoshima to meet Saigō and to study at a private school.[23] The center of antigovernment activity in Kanazawa was a group of samurai known as the

Sankō-ji faction.[24] This faction never possessed the discipline of a political party but advocated the use of militarism and violence to obtain its ends. The leader, Shimada Ichirō (1848–1878), was the central figure in the assassination. At times the Sankō-ji cooperated with a much larger group, the Chūkoku-sha, which favored popular rights. Although the ideals of the two groups were quite dissimilar, they were alike in opposing the oligarchy headed by Ōkubo. After the crime, some of the Chūkoku-sha's populist beliefs were incorporated in the manifesto sent to the newspapers.[25]

During the Satsuma Rebellion the sympathies of these men were with Saigō. They were enraged when they learned of the supposed plot to kill him, rejoiced over his early victories, and were disconsolate as it became evident that his cause was lost. Toward the end of April 1877, Shimada and Chō visited Kuga Yoshinao (1843–1916), a leader of the Chūkoku-sha, and asserted that they could not stand by indifferently now that Saigō had been defeated.[26] They had concluded that the two men most responsible for Saigō's death, Kido Takayoshi and Ōkubo Toshimichi, must be killed. Kuga did not agree with the proposed assassination but said he would think it over and asked the two men to return a few days later. He hoped that the wait would cool their ardor, but their resolve only grew fiercer. But because Kido then died on May 26, the assassination plot would henceforth be focused on one man, Ōkubo Toshimichi.

Shimada went about recruiting co-conspirators. At first he was cautious about revealing his intention, but by November he was discussing plans freely with would-be associates. It is astonishing that no one betrayed him to the police. No doubt he counted on samurai class loyalty, but on occasion in order to throw potential betrayers off the track, he also announced that he had abandoned plans to kill Ōkubo.[27]

On March 25, 1878, Shimada left for Tōkyō. The poems he composed on leaving his family reveal that although he was intent on killing Ōkubo and undoubtedly sincere when he declared he had no regrets over giving up his life, it was painful to think that he would never again see his wife and children. He composed two poems of parting. The second was "I had known from before that this day would come, but how sad parting makes me now."[28] Although Shimada's poems had no literary distinction, they came from the heart. It is hard to imagine an assassin in any other country but Japan composing poetry before he set out on his deadly mission. No doubt for Shimada, who clearly foresaw his death, these were his farewell poems to the world.

The disappearance from Kanazawa of both Shimada and Chō aroused the suspicions of prefectural authorities that the two men, both known to be extremists, might be plotting something. The central government was also on the lookout for both dissident samurai and members of the movement for freedom and popular rights and had sent innumerable plain-clothes men to every region. As interior minister, Ōkubo Toshimichi controlled the network of police dispatched in all parts of the country, but he may have decided not to pay much attention to peaceful Ishikawa Prefecture.

The first task for the leaders after arriving in Tōkyō was to draw up a statement giving their reasons for wanting to kill Ōkubo. They were following the tradition, going back to the late Tokugawa period, of attaching explanatory notes to the heads or bodies of the victims of assassinations.[29] The assassination statement began as follows:

> Shimada Ichirō, a samurai of Ishikawa Prefecture, and his confederates, making profound obeisance and braving death, looking upward offer our words to His Majesty, the emperor, and looking downward to the 30 million and more of his subjects, make this proclamation. A careful examination of the situation prevailing in the realm has convinced us that the administration and laws neither originate with imperial wishes nor do they stem from public discussion by the people. They are determined exclusively by the assumptions and unilateral decisions of a handful of influential officials.

As these words suggest, the conspirators (like many others both earlier and much later) insisted that they were acting in consonance with the emperor's true wishes, that they would rid him of the corrupt officials surrounding him who prevented him from ruling personally. At the same time, somewhat contradictorily, they also wanted the people's wishes to be heard in the form of public discussion, which was probably a concession to the freedom and popular rights philosophy of Kuga Yoshinao, who framed this vindication of the assassination.

The statement went on to accuse officials of greed and corruption, lining their purses while the vast majority of the ordinary citizens were suffering from privation. Five offenses were singled out: (1) autocratic control of the government achieved by halting public discussion and suppressing civil rights; (2) the arbitrary issuance of laws and the widespread use of influence to intimidate; (3) the depletion of public funds for unnecessary building and useless decorations; (4) the creation of internal dissension caused by the neglect of patriotic and loyal samurai and by suspicions directed at persons who grieve for the country and seek to protect the sovereign; and (5) the loss of national prestige caused by their mistaken methods of dealing with foreign countries.[30]

Although the conspirators' immediate objective was the assassination of Ōkubo, the statement also mentioned others who either must be killed or could not be tolerated. The former category included Iwakura Tomomi and the late Kido Takayoshi; the latter, Ōkuma Shigenobu, Itō Hirobumi, Kuroda Kiyotaka, and Kawaji Toshiyoshi. Still others, like Sanjō Sanetomi, were corrupt but could be expected to fall like dead leaves from a branch once the trunk of the tree—

the arch villains—had been cut down.[31] There were hints that Shimada and his fellow assassins expected a second assassination to follow their own.[32]

The first part of the statement concluded with the hope that in accordance with the oath sworn by the emperor at the time of his accession, the evils of the officials would be corrected, and a parliament be speedily established where public discussions would be held, ensuring the prosperity of the imperial household, the permanence of the country, and the tranquillity of the people.[33] Here, too, reverence for the throne and insistence on the people's rights went together. But it is doubtful whether the assassins understood the high-flown language of the manifesto drawn up by Kuga Yoshinao to justify their crime.[34] Their minds were set on only one thing—killing Ōkubo.

Once the six assassins had assembled in Tōkyō, they began to prepare systematically. They determined on which days Ōkubo went to the Akasaka Palace, the route he took, the distinguishing features of his horse carriage, and, of course, his facial features. They chose for the crime a narrow street that Ōkubo's carriage customarily took in order to avoid crowds. They discovered that councillors were expected to attend the Dajōkan on six days of the month—the fourth, fourteenth, twenty-fourth, seventh, seventeenth, and twenty-seventh—and decided to carry out the assassination on May 14. A few days before the fourteenth, Shimada, brushing off the objections of his fellow conspirators, sent Ōkubo a letter warning him that his life was in danger. Apparently he felt that unless Ōkubo was warned, the reason for the assassination would not be known.[35] Probably Ōkubo shrugged off the threat; it could not have been the first such letter he had received.

In their last-minute preparations, Shimada and Chō wrote letters to their wives, telling them of their determination and expressing their hopes for their children's education.[36] Shimada's letter was in the form of a long poem including such accusations against Ōkubo as "These great villains made false charges to His Majesty, whose name we mention with awe, and devoted every effort to murdering every last worthy minister. They plotted together, deceiving those above and attacking those below. They traded Sakhalin for the Kuriles."[37]

Ōkubo was not the monster portrayed in the statement or the letters sent home by the conspirators. Early that morning, before setting out in his carriage for the palace, he had a conversation with the governor of Fukushima Prefecture in which he predicted that it would take three periods of ten years each to achieve the work of the Restoration. Japan was about to enter the second period, which Ōkubo believed to be of critical importance, when the country would be strengthened internally and the productivity of the people enhanced. He considered that whatever his faults might be, he was the best person to guide Japan during this period. The third period would be in the hands of the next generation.[38] One step in his plan for increasing production was opening new lands, and that morning he discussed plans for building a canal in Fukushima Prefecture.

Normally Ōkubo would have had a pistol in the carriage to protect himself from sudden attack, but that night he was to attend a reception given by the Chinese minister, and directing that the carriage be cleaned for the occasion, he had left the pistol with a subordinate. This may have cost him his life.

The assassination was carried out with the smoothness born of intensive preparations. Two men maimed the front legs of the two horses, and the other four killed one of the coachmen before dragging Ōkubo out of the carriage and killing him with singular brutality. The coup de grâce was delivered to Ōkubo's throat with such savagery that the point of the sword penetrated the earth below. After arranging their weapons neatly on the ground beside the corpse, the six men went to the nearby palace to turn themselves in. They presented the police with a copy of their statement. When asked if they had other accomplices, they replied, "Yes, every one of the 30 million Japanese, except for the officials, are our accomplices."[39]

Word reached the palace soon afterward. Motoda Nagazane had just begun to deliver a lecture on the *Analects* to the emperor in his study. A court official rushed up to inform Motoda of the calamity. Motoda at once reported this to the emperor, who sent a chamberlain to Ōkubo's house to find out precisely what had happened. The chamberlain returned presently with word that Ōkubo was dead. The emperor, severely shaken by the news, sent the chief chamberlain, Tokudaiji Sanetsune, to convey his grief. The empress dowager and the empress sent other envoys.

On the following day the emperor posthumously promoted Ōkubo to minister of the right and contributed 5,000 yen for the funeral expenses. Later that day he issued a formal announcement of grief over the loss of a faithful minister on whom he had depended. He appointed Itō Hirobumi to succeed Ōkubo as interior minister, ensuring continuity in this important post.

The assassination of Ōkubo Toshimichi was deplored even in foreign newspapers.[40] His funeral, the first state funeral in Japan, was on an elaborate scale. Flags were at half-mast, and warships gave twenty-one-gun salutes. The religious ceremonies were entirely Shintō; the general disapproval of Buddhism at the time no doubt accounted for this break with tradition.

The appointment of Itō meant that Ōkubo's policies would not be repudiated, but the assassins' statement seems to have been taken to heart. Even before the assassination, early on the morning of May 14, three *jiho* (Sasaki Takayuki, Takasaki Masakaze, and Yoshii Tomozane), who had decided that a new office should be created to assist the emperor, called on Itō Hirobumi intending to recommend Ōkubo as the man best qualified for the post. Itō concurred, but immediately afterward they learned to their horror of the assassination.

On examining the statement left by the assassins, they could not help but agree, however, that at present the laws neither originated with the emperor nor resulted from the deliberations of the people. They decided that the most urgent need was for the emperor to administer state affairs personally, and they decided to inform the emperor of their conclusion.

On May 16 the *jiho* were granted an audience at which each man expressed his views. Sasaki said that although in principle the emperor governed, in fact he delegated his authority to his ministers. This gave rise to the impression that a handful of powerful officials actually ran the country, which in turn stirred resentment among the people, as one could tell from the recent assassination. Unless positive steps were taken, the great enterprise of the Restoration would end in so much foam. It was essential that the emperor's wishes be put into practice if Japan's prestige was to be extended abroad. The emperor thus must be kept fully informed of developments both at home and abroad.

Takasaki Masakaze came forward to relate that Ōkubo had always been profoundly concerned over the cultivation of imperial virtue. On the day before he was assassinated, Ōkubo had visited Takasaki's house and expressed his anxiety. Takasaki seemed overcome even as he spoke, and he sobbed and wept as he voiced his opinion that it was essential for the emperor to assume personal rule. At this, tears could also be seen in the emperor's eyes. Yoneda Torao also expressed the hope that the emperor would devote himself to state affairs with the same energy he daily devoted to riding horseback. The emperor, changing his expression, said that he gladly accepted their loyal counsels and that he would henceforth pay attention to these matters. He asked the men to join in the task of assisting him. Takasaki, weeping tears of emotion, withdrew.[41]

The emperor seems to have taken his counselors' advice to heart. He would no longer seem indifferent to the running of the state. On May 21, for example, he expressed to the two *jiho* on duty his views on abuses of the time. Some officials had built new houses in Western style. For persons of rank whose position made it necessary to associate with foreign diplomats, there was probably a need for such houses, but in the eyes of the common people, these officials were prospering from the people's sweat and blood and seeking only personal interest. He therefore commanded officials to refrain for the time being from building such houses. If they would wait a few years until the new imperial palace was built before building their own houses, the complaints would disappear of themselves.

The emperor also expressed dissatisfaction that ever since the Restoration, posts in the government had been filled mainly by men from three provinces: Satsuma, Chōshū, and Tosa. This would have to end. There were well-qualified men in all parts of the country—even in the remote northeast regions—and they should be employed.[42] The shock of Ōkubo's death and the remonstrations of the *jiho* seem to have aroused a new sense of responsibility and a new sense of his own authority.

Chapter 30

On May 23, 1878, the emperor decided that he would leave in August on his long-planned tour of the Hokuriku and Tōkai regions. He had originally intended to make the journey in 1877, following his tour of the previous year to the north, but complications arising from the Satsuma Rebellion prevented him from carrying out this plan. The stated purpose of the forthcoming journey, as usual, was to learn from personal observation about regions of his country he did not know and about the people living there.[1]

Remembering his experiences during his travels in the north, the emperor made it clear that he did not wish his journey to cause anyone financial hardship. He mentioned in particular that when he visited schools, the pupils should all wear ordinary attire and not have new hats, shoes, or other items of clothing made in honor of the occasion. He also expressed the hope that when he visited prefectural offices, he would be shown maps of the area, vital statistics, and records of the meritorious deeds of virtuous persons. In addition, he asked that reports be submitted on police stations and the number of patrolmen, methods of encouraging industry, pastureland, the number of cattle, and the size of uncultivated lands and currently cultivated lands. He did not expect this to be a pleasure trip, nor was his object primarily to inspire awe or even affection. His journey was, above all, educational, to give him greater knowledge of his people and how they made a living. No doubt his advisers hoped also that a visit from the emperor would make the inhabitants of remote parts of the country more fully aware of the existence of the government in Tōkyō to which they owed allegiance, a tie transcending regional loyalty.

Nothing corresponding to the element of spectacle, so important to European progresses, was planned.[2] His tours of the provinces differed in one other respect from European examples: no attempt was made to make the Japanese familiar with the face of their emperor either during his travels or on coins or banknotes. Meiji generally traveled in a closed palanquin rather than an open carriage from which he could be seen by spectators. In earlier days his face would have been visible only to members of the highest nobility, and even now he was reluctant to show it. Photographs of Meiji, few and not generally available, were not for public display. Ministers of foreign countries sometimes received a photograph of the emperor when they left Japan, but Japanese, no matter how devoted, could not display their sovereign's photograph.

In 1874 a man in Tōkyō began to sell (without authorization) reproductions of the photographs taken by Uchida Kuichi. This inspired Uchida to ask permission to sell his negatives, prompting a lengthy debate in the government as to the propriety of selling the emperor's photograph.[3] In the end, sale of the photographs was prohibited, and people who had already purchased one were commanded to surrender it. The absence of photographs or other tokens of self-aggrandizement typified the restrained nature of the emperor's journey. The crowds lining the streets of towns and villages through which the procession passed might catch a glimpse of Meiji, but he did not court their attention by wearing a splendid uniform or traveling in a luxurious carriage, and his largesse was confined to small gifts to pupils at elementary schools and to very old people.

Just before Meiji was scheduled to leave Tōkyō, an incident occurred that threatened to postpone his journey. On August 23 soldiers of the artillery battalion of the Household Guards mutinied, angered by a reduction in their pay and the worsening of their rations. The mutiny involved only about 100 men, all (except for two noncommissioned officers) privates, and most from either Kagoshima or Kōchi, two regions known for their military traditions. During the brief revolt, the mutineers killed several officers, fired a cannon at the residence of Finance Minister Ōkuma Shigenobu, and set off with two mountain guns for the Akasaka Palace, where they intended to present their demands. Some ninety men reached the palace, where they were met by regular troops who had been warned they were coming. The mutineers were arrested.

By four the next morning, calm had been restored, but the disturbance, coming not long after the assassination of Ōkubo Toshimichi, made Iwakura and other *jiho* propose that the emperor's journey be postponed. The incident was minor, they admitted, but it might be symptomatic of more serious unrest in the army. Their view was opposed by Sanjō Sanetomi and most of the councillors, who felt that it would be harmful to imperial prestige if the progress was

postponed because of an unimportant incident. After consulting with the *jiho*
Sasaki Takayuki, the emperor decided to leave as planned.

The emperor and his entourage[4] set out on August 30. The first night of the
journey was spent at Urawa in Saitama Prefecture. The next morning when he
granted an audience to officials of the prefecture, the emperor was presented
not (as one might expect) with materials attesting to the happy lives of the
inhabitants but with a report on the dismal conditions under which people at
Nakatsugawa lived. The people of this village of twenty-five houses and a population of 129 were so poor and backward that they had never worn even cotton
clothes, and none of them was literate. When they fell ill, there was no doctor
to attend them, and when they died, no temple where they might be buried.
Their staple food was millet, not rice. Most of these villagers were even unaware
that there were such things in the world as schools, pharmacies, saké shops, or
fishmongers. It was a blot on Emperor Meiji's glorious regime that people were
living under such conditions a bare forty or fifty miles from his residence. Local
officials said they planned to repair the road to the village and to guide the
villagers gradually into the ways of civilization.[5]

The emperor's reactions to this account are not given. Later he visited the
offices of each branch of the local administration, a court, and various schools
where he observed classrooms and rewarded prizes to the best pupils. Next he
visited a museum of industry and toured the exhibits of models of machinery,
minerals, and works of art. He was particularly interested in the tea produced
in Sayama and the silk thread from Koma, as tea and silk were the main Japanese exports at this time. Wherever the emperor went on this journey, he
always showed a special interest in local products.

From Urawa the progress went to Maebashi, where the crowds straining to
get a look at the emperor were especially numerous, and from there to Ma-
tsuida. It had rained almost every day since the emperor left Tōkyō, and the
roads were in terrible condition. At places it was impossible for the emperor's
palanquin to pass, and he had to get down and make his way through the mud.
Fortunately his legs were strong, but the others of his suite, less endowed, trailed
behind him, some with great difficulty. The weather was clear the day he
crossed Usui Pass, and from the highest point he enjoyed a splendid view. Later
the royal progress passed through Karuizawa, Oiwake, and Komoro, but low-
hanging clouds blocked the view of Mount Asama, the most prominent feature
of the landscape.

At Nagano the emperor met the resident priest of the celebrated temple
Zenkō-ji. It was unusual for him to associate with Buddhist priests, and he
seldom visited a temple, but he probably considered that the Zenkō-ji, the heart
of Nagano, could not be ignored. At Takano where he stayed at the local school,
he sent a chamberlain to offer prayers at the graves of men killed in the war of
1868. As the progress moved closer to the scenes of fighting in that war, the

prayers became frequent. In Takano, the emperor bought several varieties of sweets, which he sent to the empress and empress dowager, along with cakes and fruit from Nagano. The gesture no doubt pleased people of the town; and the fact that he bought the sweets, rather than accept them gratis, distinguished him from European monarchs.

The journey from Takano to Kakizaki followed the coast of the Japan Sea most of the way, and the emperor seemed delighted by the splendid scenery. But the journey was by no means easy. The road, narrow and through deep sand, was said to have been repaired, but the little horse carriage rocked each time its wheels sank in the sand. Sunlight pouring through the windows made the interior so hot and humid that Sasaki Takayuki, accompanying the emperor, could not stand being inside. He obtained permission to proceed on foot, but the emperor, stoic as always, endured both the tossing of the carriage and the heat. All the same, when he reached Kakizaki he was feeling so poorly that he sent for his physician, overcoming his dislike of medical treatment.

The rewards of this mainly painful journey were confined to the scenery and sights along the way. At Izumozaki, for example, the emperor watched with great interest hundreds of boats fishing at night. The pains far outweighed the pleasures of travel, however: he spent the whole of each day sitting Japanese-style in a cramped palanquin and at night was obliged by custom to sit bolt upright on a chair until ten, his bedtime, when he was at last able to stretch out. The night that the emperor spent at Izumozaki, his quarters were not only cramped but invaded by swarms of mosquitoes. His chamberlains urged the emperor to retire into the protection afforded by a mosquito netting, but he answered, "The whole purpose of this journey is to observe the suffering of the people. If I did not myself experience their pains, how could I understand their condition? I do not in the least mind the mosquitoes."[6] The emperor's words seem too Confucian to be true, but it accords with other recorded episodes of the journey and gives an indication of the compassion felt for his people by a man who thus far had had little personal experience of suffering.

When the emperor reached Niigata, he was shocked by the number of people suffering from trachoma. He recalled that when he had traveled in the north two years earlier, he had noticed people who suffered from the same disease and had asked a doctor if there was no way of treating it. The doctor answered that there was none that poor people could afford. Now, seeing even more trachoma victims in Niigata, the emperor commanded his personal physician to investigate the causes and possible ways of curing and preventing trachoma. Two days later the emperor received a report blaming the climate, the physical features of the region, and the inadequately clean houses for the spread of trachoma; but the main cause was its infectious nature. The emperor donated 1,000 yen for study of a cure and prevention.

There were a few bright spots on the journey. At Nagaoka the emperor was pleased to see that this city, which had been almost totally destroyed during the war of 1868 and had been desperately poor afterward, was gradually recovering. There was much to remind him of the warfare of ten years earlier. At Fukushima Village, the site of a battle, the positions of the government troops were marked by white flags and those of the rebels by red flags to give the emperor an idea of just how the battle had been fought.[7]

For the most part the journey was miserable. It rained day after day, leaving the roads deep in mud, and even when it cleared, the rivers were so swollen that they were extremely difficult to cross. Years later (in 1899) the emperor recalled the journey in this *tanka*:

natsu samuki	It's now long ago
Koshi no yamaji wo	Since I traveled mountain roads
samidare ni	Soaked by the spring rains
nurete koeshi mo	In Koshi, where it is cold
mukashi narikeri	Even in the summertime.[8]

By the time they reached Oyashirazu Koshirazu, the most dangerous place on the Japan Sea coast, cliffs dropping into the sea and the only road washed by the waves, everyone was exhausted. Once safely passed this frightening place, Meiji stopped his carriage to enjoy the scenery. It was magnificent—he could catch glimpses through the ocean spray of Sado Island and the Noto Peninsula.[9]

Danger of another sort was feared in Kanazawa, for this was where Ōkubo's assassins had plotted, and there might still be unruly elements in the population. Nothing untoward happened; instead, the emperor spent his time as usual—visiting schools, the Kenrokuen garden, and a museum where products from home and abroad were displayed. At Komatsu, the emperor received letters and gifts from the empress and empress dowager. No doubt they gave him as much pleasure as letters from home bring any traveler.

From this point on, the journey was relatively easy. From Kanazawa he went to Komatsu, Fukui, Tsuruga, Ōtsu, and on to Kyōto. One night in Kyōto he entertained the members of his suite with stories of the Gosho before the Restoration. Although his recollections were barely ten years old, they may have seemed echoes of the distant past.

Plans for the emperor to worship at the Great Shrine of Ise during his progress through the Tōkai region had to be altered when typhus was reported in Mie Prefecture. The revised route took the procession through Kusatsu, Ōgaki, and Gifu to Nagoya. At each stop, as usual, the emperor visited schools and exhibitions of local products. There is no suggestion that he was bored or impatient to get back to Tōkyō; his strong sense of duty, submerged temporarily during the Satsuma Rebellion, had again manifested itself and characterized his actions for the rest of his life.

Meiji returned to Tōkyō on November 9. He had traveled some 440 *ri* (more than 1,000 miles) over a period of seventy-two days and had passed through eleven prefectures. Despite the fatigue of the journey, he looked well and seemed to be in good spirits. The day was declared a holiday, and everywhere in the capital he was greeted with flags.

The remainder of the year was generally uneventful, but just before it ended—on December 27—an order was suddenly issued by the Court Council abolishing the Ryūkyū domain. The minister of the interior, Itō Hirobumi, had decided to demote the domain to a prefecture; it would no longer be a kingdom but merely one of many prefectures. The background of this decision was the refusal of the Ryūkyū domain to obey the Japanese order to break its contacts with the Chinese court. The Ryūkyū king had been specifically commanded not to send an envoy to express congratulations when a new emperor ascended the throne of China or to receive appointment by the Chinese emperor as king of the domain. The king had disregarded these orders and had secretly sent a member of his family to the Chinese court to appeal for help against Japan. He had also asked the domain representative in Tōkyō to secure help from the Chinese, American, French, and Dutch ministers. No fewer than fourteen petitions were submitted to the Japanese government asking to return to the old form of dual allegiance to both Japan and China, pointing out that "Japan is our father and China our mother."[10]

The Japanese insisted, however, "For a country to serve two emperors is like a wife serving two husbands."[11] The Ryūkyū kingdom had for centuries served two masters, China and Satsuma, paying tribute to both. This was the only way a small country with few resources and no military strength could maintain its existence. Determined to break the ties between the Ryūkyū Islands and China, the Japanese were exasperated by the king's stalling tactics. Finally Itō decided to abolish the domain, using as a pretext the king's intransigence. He ordered Matsuda Michiyuki (1839–1882), the chief secretary of the Interior Ministry, to draw up a plan for terminating the Ryūkyū domain. The plan called for the enforced removal of the king from Okinawa to Tōkyō. It was approved by the prime minister and the Court Council. The king was ordered to comply within a week with the order issued to him. If he refused, the Japanese government would take "positive measures" to dissolve the domain. In the meantime Ryūkyū officials stationed in Tōkyō were ordered to return immediately to Okinawa, a first step in depriving the domain of its semiautonomous status.[12]

Matsuda Michiyuki left Yokohama for Naha on January 8, 1879. He arrived in Naha on January 25 and on the following day went to Shuri, the Ryūkyū capital, where he met with high officials and read aloud this message from Sanjō Sanetomi:

On May 29, 1875, you sent an alternate-year tributary mission to China and a congratulatory envoy on the occasion of the succession to the throne of the Chinese emperor. Moreover, when you were named king of the domain, you accepted the status of a loyal vassal of China. You were forbidden to continue these practices, but you have not yet submitted a statement of compliance. Again, although you were directed in May 1876, in connection with the establishment of a magistrate in your territory, to turn over all the court business of the domain, you have failed to comply with this to the present, terming this a "supplication." This situation cannot be allowed to persist. If you continue to fail to obey directives, appropriate measures will be taken. This demand is urgent.[13]

After reading this statement, Matsuda gave the document to Shō Hitsu, the younger brother of the king. He added verbally a threat of extreme measures in the event that the order was not obeyed and gave the king until 10 A.M. on February 3 to respond. On January 29 Matsuda sent the king another missive ordering him to submit a statement of obedience, together with an oath. Failure to comply would be interpreted as a sign that the king was likely to repeat his former errors and so would not carry out his promise in good faith. The king was ordered to appear at the branch office of the Interior Ministry along with the king's deputy. But the king did not appear on the third. Instead he sent some senior officials with his reply to Matsuda's letter.

The king, using deferential terms, explained the difficulty of his position. If he refused to pay tribute and offer congratulations to the Chinese court (as Matsuda commanded) and refused appointment as a vassal to that court, his domain would certainly be punished by the Chinese. His small country, caught between two strong countries, was helpless. He abjectly begged for Japanese sympathy.

Shō Tai had never been a commanding figure, but there is something inescapably moving in the spectacle of a king cringing before an official whose sense of mission—disposal of the Ryūkyū problem—left no room for pity. Matsuda, charging that the king's letter was evidence that he still refused to obey the order of the Court Council, announced that he was returning to Tōkyō where he would report in detail what had transpired. He told the Ryūkyū officials to await further orders. When the officials begged him to show consideration, he not only refused but added a new cause of complaint: he was angry that although Ryūkyūans had been directed years earlier to use the reign-name Meiji, they still dated their documents according to the Chinese reign-name Kuang-hsü. He declared that this was absolutely forbidden.

Matsuda left the next day for Tōkyō. On March 11 the emperor issued a command abolishing the Ryūkyū domain and directing the king and his heirs to move to Tōkyō.[14] Okinawa would become a prefecture, and members of the royal family would be given titles in the Japanese peerage. Matsuda sailed once again to Okinawa, this time with more than 160 police and 500 infantry troops.

The king, pleading illness, refused to see Matsuda, but on March 11 he left the palace, the seat of Ryūkyū authority for 500 years where he had lived his entire life, and moved to the residence of the crown prince, Shō Ten.

Shō Tai's resistance seems to have had some effect. On April 5 the emperor sent the chamberlain Tominokōji Takanao to inquire about Shō Tai's health. He privately directed Tominokōji to urge Shō Tai to come to Tōkyō as soon as possible and, in order that the king might travel safely, sent the government-owned ship *Meiji maru* for his use.

Tominokōji arrived in Naha on April 13 and, protected by an escort of thirty police officers, went on to Shuri. Shō Tai declined because of illness to see the emperor's envoy but sent word asking that Shō Ten be allowed to receive him instead. Tominokōji, refusing, went with Matsuda to Shō Tai's temporary residence. He was met at the gate by princes of the royal house and high officials, and Shō Ten led the envoy to Shō Tai's sickroom. The king, with his clothes and hat of ceremony placed on the bed, pretended (as a mark of respect to the emperor's envoy) to put them on. Then, supported by two attendants, he rose from bed and, kneeling, bowed profoundly.

The envoy communicated the emperor's message. Shō Tai expressed thanks in extremely humble language. Tominokōji asked whether he would obey the emperor's command. The king replied that he would answer the following day.

Now that the formal part of the visit was over, Matsuda left his chair and, sitting on the floor, expressed sympathy for the king's illness and the mental anxiety he had suffered during the past months. Tominokōji joined in comforting the king. When they had left the sickroom, they agreed that although Shō Tai looked pale, there was no sign of a wasting illness; but it was clear that he was not merely pretending to be ill.[15]

On April 14 Matsuda summoned the chief officials of the former domain and urged them to persuade the king to make a reply. The king was exceedingly reluctant to leave Okinawa and begged for a postponement of his departure because of illness. Matsuda refused, saying that because Shō Tai's illness was chronic, he could not hope to recover completely. On the fifteenth, Shō Tai's brother Shō Hitsu, along with more than twenty senior officials, begged Tominokōji and Matsuda for a stay of four or five months, proposing that one of the royal princes be sent (as a hostage) to Tōkyō. On the sixteenth, 150 members of the Ryūkyū aristocracy, along with the royal princes and senior domain officials, begged for a stay of ninety days. This was refused outright. It was pointed out that the king would enjoy the special protection of the state during the voyage and that there was nothing to worry about.

Behind the intransigence of the Japanese officials was the fear that the king was delaying his departure for Tōkyō in the hopes that in the meantime, the Chinese would come to his support. The sooner Shō Tai was in Tōkyō, they reasoned, the less chance there was of Chinese intervention.

The king was scheduled to leave on April 18, but on the day before Shō

Hitsu and other high officials made a final appeal to Matsuda. They said this time that it was not only because of Shō Tai's health that a delay of ninety days was sought but because the former domain had been unsettled by recent changes and the king himself was needed to admonish the people and persuade them to continue at their normal occupations. This time they proposed that Shō Ten, the crown prince, be sent to Tōkyō. Matsuda at last yielded but insisted that there was no reason to postpone the departure for ninety days. Therefore he would shorten the period of delay and inform them the next day exactly when the king would have to leave.

Matsuda was not worried by the possibility of unrest. He reasoned also that if the king persisted in refusing to go to Tōkyō, he could be taken by main force. But if Shō Ten was left in Okinawa, he might become the focal point for a rebellion that would lead to Chinese intervention. The best plan was to get both Shō Tai and Shō Ten to Tōkyō. He decided therefore to accept the proposal that Shō Ten be sent to Tōkyō and to state that the decision about whether or not Shō Tai's departure might be delayed would be left to the prime minister. Once Shō Ten was safely in Tōkyō, they could say that Shō Tai's request had been refused. In this way responsibility for sending Shō Tai to Tōkyō would rest at the highest level of the government. An imperial envoy would then be sent to Okinawa to escort Shō Tai to the capital.[16]

On April 18 a delegation of Ryūkyū nobles headed by Shō Hitsu called on Matsuda. This time they asked for a postponement of only eighty days and again proposed that Shō Ten be sent to Tōkyō. Matsuda answered that if they requested fewer than forty days, it might be possible to ask Tominokōji, the imperial envoy, to delay his return. In that case Shō Ten's journey to Tōkyō could be viewed as a gesture of gratitude. On the next day Tominokōji approved the plan, and it was decided that Shō Ten would accompany him to Tōkyō. On April 19 Tominokōji Takanao and Shō Ten left Naha aboard the *Meiji maru*.

The ship reached Yokohama on May 1. On the fifth, Meiji received Shō Ten and five members of his entourage, who bowed in respect from the other side of the threshold. That day Shō Ten offered presents to the emperor and empress. He also requested the prime minister to allow his father a delay in going to Tōkyō, but this was refused. Everything went in accordance with Matsuda's scenario.

On the same day Major Sagara Nagaoki and the court physician Takashina Tsunenori left for Okinawa to examine the king's malady. The two men arrived on May 18 and went with Matsuda to the king's temporary residence in Shuri. Takashina diagnosed the king's ailment as a nervous disorder and hypogastric congestion. He said there was no immediate danger from this illness, but it was unlikely it could be completely cured in a matter of months or even years. Having heard this much, Matsuda produced a document announcing that the government had refused Shō Tai's request for a delay. He would have to leave for Tōkyō within a week. The king at last resigned himself to going to Tōkyō but asked for a delay of three weeks. More than sixty nobles from Shuri, Naha, Kume, and Tomari made the same request, but Matsuda sternly refused. The king's departure was set for May 27.[17]

In the meantime the Chinese had at last protested. On May 10 a letter signed by Prince Kung and other ministers was sent to the Japanese minister in Peking declaring that the Ryūkyū kingdom had for hundreds of years accepted the Chinese calendar and paid tribute. China, respecting its integrity as an independent country, had allowed Ryūkyū complete freedom in its politics and laws. China had also joined with Japan in signing a treaty with Ryūkyū, recognizing it as a sovereign state. Now, however, the Japanese government had imposed its administrative system on Ryūkyū. This not only contravened the treaty of friendship and destroyed another country but ended its ancestral sacrifices. It could only be considered an expression of contempt for China and other countries. Only by giving up its plan to end Ryūkyū sovereignty could Japan promote friendly relations between the two countries.[18]

China was in a poor position to protest. According to the convention signed at Peking in October 1874 by the Japanese plenipotentiary and the Chinese minister of foreign affairs, the Chinese recognized the people of Ryūkyū as Japanese subjects. The Chinese government agreed also to pay an indemnity to the families of Ryūkyū fishermen who had been killed by the Taiwan natives, referring to the fishermen as "people of Japan."[19]

When the Japanese foreign minister received the Chinese protest, he replied that the disposal of the Ryūkyū problem was a matter of domestic policy, that other countries might not intervene. The Chinese retained one hope of dissuading the Japanese: the former United States president, Ulysses S. Grant, who visited China in May, would be going on to Japan. He would bear a communication from Prince Kung and might, with his prestige, change the minds of the Japanese.

On June 9 Shō Tai, who had finally left Naha on May 27, arrived in Yokohama. He was accompanied by his second son, Shō In, and more than forty retainers.[20] He went immediately to the house prepared for him by the Imperial Household Ministry. On June 17 Shō Tai, his eldest son Shō Ten, and some ten other former retainers went to the palace. The emperor granted Shō Tai and Shō Ten an audience. Nothing is recorded of Meiji's reactions on seeing the dethroned king. He may have resented Shō Tai's manifest reluctance to comply with Japanese orders, but he doubtless felt that his government had done everything it could to make the loss of the throne—inevitable because of modern Japan's destiny—as painless as possible. The same day, Shō Tai was appointed to the junior third rank and Shō Ten to the junior fifth rank. Matsuda was decorated for his efforts in disposing of the Ryūkyū problem. A precedent for dealing with deposed monarchs, followed after the annexation of Korea, had been established.

Shō Tai was well treated in exile.[21] It is said that he was happier in Tōkyō than he had been during the thirty-one years of his reign. No doubt he was glad to be spared the eternal bickering of the political parties in Okinawa.[22] Some even say that once in Tōkyō he was as happy as a country bumpkin on his first visit to the city.[23] But he seems nevertheless to have yearned for the land he once ruled. In 1884 he received permission to visit Okinawa for 100 days.

Sasamori Gisuke, a former samurai from Hirosuke, recorded in a diary his experiences during a stay in the Ryūkyū Islands in 1893. Although he was not a partisan of the deposed king, he felt obliged to record instances of the worshipful respect still paid to Shō Tai and his family. In June of that year Prince Kitashirakawanomiya paid a state visit to Okinawa. He paid his compliments to Shō Ten, the son of the deposed king, and offered his respects at the royal tombs. But despite these conciliatory gestures, not one member of the Ryūkyū noble families accepted his invitation to a banquet several days later. Sasamori commented, "What discourtesy!"[24]

Later Sasamori noticed with indignation that on the road from Naha to Shuri, "in front of every house they had spread mats, and men and women sat on them formally in rows. I asked the reason, and I was told, 'Today, at the invitation of the governor, Shō Ten and his family are to pass. Everybody has turned out to pay his respects.'"[25]

Sasamori had many occasions to notice that the Japanese, however benevolently disposed, were treated by the Okinawans as intruders. He reported that there was not a single instance of an Okinawan marrying a person from "the other prefectures," nor was there a single person from "the other prefectures" who had taken up permanent residence in Okinawa.[26] He added that even though people from Europe and America belonged to a different race, they often became naturalized in Japan and married Japanese. He concluded that "the natives' feeling is one of strong attachment to the restoration of the old regime, and for this reason their attitude has not been satisfactory to this day."

The annexation of Okinawa hardly figures in histories of Japan, and Shō Tai rates only a brief entry in biographical dictionaries. He was in no sense an important political figure even while a king, and his last thirty years were spent in obscurity. But somehow, even now, there is something affecting about the downfall of a kinglet, deposed by a major country testing its strength at the start of its modern age.

Chapter 31

None of the many foreign visitors to whom Emperor Meiji gave an audience produced as strong an impression on him as did the former American general and president Ulysses S. Grant. General Grant, as he was known even while he served two terms as president, embarked on a round-the-world journey in 1877. The purpose of the trip was largely political. The glory he had won for his military exploits during the Civil War had been tainted by the widespread corruption of his presidency, and his advisers judged it prudent for him to absent himself for a while from the United States in the hopes that this would make voters forget the scandals. He had ambitions of serving a third term as president.

Grant and his wife began their travels with the voyage to England, where a high point was a stay at Windsor Castle as guests of Queen Victoria. During the next two years they visited many countries of Europe, followed by Egypt, India, Siam, China, and, finally, Japan. They were eager sightseers, but they themselves were also on display. As a biographer of Grant has written, "The unpretentious man in the dark suit was his country's greatest warrior-hero, and the world wanted to have a look at him. The general and his lady were ambassadors of both American simplicity and American power."[1]

In foreign countries, where the scandals of his presidential administration were not widely known (or perhaps more readily tolerated than in the United States), Grant's reputation as a great soldier, the savior of the union, had preceded him, and he was welcomed everywhere. An editorial in the *Times* of London concluded that "after Washington, General Grant is the President who will occupy the largest place in the history of the United States."[2] Kings, queens, and members of the highest nobility were pleased to meet him, although they sometimes commented on his lack of manners.

Wherever he went, he preserved his casual, American ways. When, for example, he called on Bismarck, the most powerful man in Europe, he nonchalantly sauntered into the courtyard of the chancellor's palace and, throwing away a half-smoked cigar, returned the salute of the startled palace guards. Perhaps the greatest triumph of Grant's journey was the reception not by royalty but by the working classes of the north of England, who responded with affection to this man who, they sensed, was one of them.[4] Grant certainly enjoyed the unaffected welcome from miners and other workmen more than the endlessly repeated state dinners. Sometimes on such occasions the tedium would induce him to get drunk. The viceroy of India, Lord Lytton, wrote a letter describing Grant's behavior in these sarcastic terms:

On this occasion "our distinguished guest" the double Ex-President of the "Great Western Republic," who got drunk as a fiddle, showed that he could also be as profligate as a lord. He fumbled Mrs A., kissed the shrieking Miss B.—pinched the plump Mrs C. black and blue—and ran at Miss D. with intent to ravish her.[3]

From India, General and Mrs. Grant went to Singapore, Saigon, Bangkok, and Hong Kong before arriving in China. In Tientsin they met the viceroy Li Hung-chang, who greeted his guest with the simple statement, "You and I, General Grant, are the greatest men in the world." Later he explained that was referring to the success of Grant and himself in putting down huge rebellions within their two countries.[4]

While Grant was in Peking he was asked by Prince Kung, the acting head of the government, to use his influence to settle the dispute between China and Japan over the sovereignty of the Ryūkyū Islands. The prince deplored the attempt of the Japanese "to extinguish this kingdom, which has always paid tribute to China, which has always been friendly." General Grant replied that any course short of national humiliation or national destruction was better than war. "'War,' he said, 'was so great a calamity that it should only be invoked when there was no other way of avoiding a greater, and war, especially between two nations like China and Japan, would be a measureless misfortune.'"[5]

Grant's hatred of war and everything connected with war was astonishing in a man who had enjoyed such great success as a general. He even hated paintings that depicted warfare and told John Russell Young, the writer who accompanied the Grants on their trip around the world, "I never saw a war picture that was pleasant. I tried to enjoy some of those in Versailles, but they were disgusting." Grant was unsparing in his criticism of his own participation in the Mexican War in 1845: "I know the struggle with my conscience during the Mexican War.

I have never entirely forgiven myself for going to that. I had very strong opinions on the subject. I do not think there was ever a more wicked war than that waged by the United States on Mexico. I thought so at the time, when I was a young-ster, only I had not moral courage to resign."[6]

Grant had joined the army because he hated his father's work—he was a tanner—and attending the military academy at West Point offered the only possibility of getting a good education. After graduation he left the army, but because he failed at every business in which he engaged, he had no choice but to become an army officer, despite his hatred of war. He related, "I never went into a battle willingly or with enthusiasm. I was always glad when a battle was over. I never want to command another army. I take no interest in armies. When the Duke of Cambridge asked me to review his troops at Aldershott I told his Royal Highness that the one thing I never wanted to see again was a military parade."[7]

It is ironic that Grant, who was thoroughly disillusioned with the military, was on his way to Japan, where Emperor Meiji was manifesting increasing interest in military reviews and maneuvers. Young noted, "The emperor of Japan is fond of his army, and was more anxious to show it to General Grant than any other institution in the Empire."[8] In the end, Grant, despite his ex-treme dislike, felt obliged to comply with the emperor's wish for Grant to review the Japanese troops.[9]

Grant arrived in Nagasaki on June 21, 1879, aboard the warship *Richmond*. The ship was met by Date Munenari (1818–1892), a nobleman, and Yoshida Kiyonari (1845–1891), the Japanese minister plenipotentiary to America. Young recorded,

> Prince Daté said that he had been commanded by the emperor to meet General Grant on his landing, to welcome him in the name of his Maj-esty, and to attend upon him as the emperor's personal representative as long as the General remained in Japan. . . . Mr. Yoshida is well known as the present Japanese minister to the United States, a discreet and accom-plished man, and among the rising statesmen in the empire. Having been accredited to America during the General's administration, and knowing the General, the government called him home so that he might attend General Grant and look after the reception.[10]

Grant delivered soon afterward his first speech in Japan, which included these words:

> America has much to gain in the East—no nation has greater interests; but America has nothing to gain except what comes from the cheerful acquiescence of the Eastern people and insures them as much benefit as it does us. I should be ashamed of my country if its relations with other

countries, and especially with these ancient and most interesting empires in the East, were based upon any other idea.[11]

Grant had originally planned to visit Kyōto, but an epidemic of cholera had broken out in the Kansai region, and the Japanese government did not want Grant to risk becoming infected. The Americans were disposed to take the threat of cholera lightly, but as the guests of Japan, they were under the charge of the emperor's representatives, who insisted that the Americans not land in the Kansai. They accordingly went on to Yokohama, arriving on July 3.

They were met by an impressive array of dignitaries, including Iwakura Tomomi, who shook hands with Grant. The act of shaking hands seems to have been very important to the Americans: they were greatly impressed the next day when the emperor, on meeting Grant, advanced and shook hands with him. Young wrote, "This seems a trivial thing to write down, but such a thing was never before known in the history of Japanese majesty."[12] The emperor's gesture caused Young to muse, "The Mikado has never failed in courtesy to the princes of other royal families who have visited him. But while he treated English, Russian, and German princes as princes, he has treated General Grant as a friend."[13]

At the request of the Japanese, the first meeting between the emperor and General Grant took place on the Fourth of July, the anniversary of American independence; and the emperor's first greeting to Grant expressed his pleasure that their meeting had occurred on this day. Young's description of Emperor Meiji suggests that despite his expressions of friendship, he was still not at ease with foreign visitors:

> The manner of the emperor was constrained, almost awkward, the manner of a man doing a thing for the first time, and trying to do it as well as possible. After he had shaken hands with the General, he returned to his place, and stood with his hand resting on his sword, looking on at the brilliant, embroidered, gilded company as though unconscious of their presence.[14]

The greetings exchanged by the two men were formal. The emperor said: "I have heard of many of the things you have said to my ministers in reference to Japan. You have seen the country and the people. I am eager to speak with you on these subjects, and am sorry I have not had an opportunity much earlier."

General Grant replied that he was entirely at the service of the emperor. He said he was glad indeed to see His Majesty and thank him for all the kindness he had received in Japan. He might say that no one outside Japan had a higher interest in the country or a more sincere friendship for the people. Probably Grant was sincere in these remarks. He was delighted with the scenery, finding Japan "beautiful beyond description," and the lack of adornment in Meiji's palace had produced a most favorable impression. Young wrote, "The home of the emperor was as simple as that of a country gentleman at home. . . . What marked the house was its simplicity and taste." Again, "Japan has taught the world the beauty of clean, fine-grained natural wood, and the fallacy of glass and paint." Grant's own preference for simplicity and naturalness made him respond to Japanese tastes. He was also impressed when he learned that although there was a project to build a new palace for the emperor on the site of the one that had been destroyed by a fire, "the emperor has prevented it, loath to incur the expense and satisfied with his house as it is."[15]

Young's descriptions of the Japanese dignitaries whom Grant met on the occasion of his first audience with the emperor are valuable because the appearances of these men are so rarely mentioned in Japanese works:

> The Prime Minister [Sanjō Sanetomi] is a striking character. He is small, slender, with an almost girl-like figure, delicate, clean-cut, winning features, a face that might be that of a boy of twenty or a man of fifty. . . . Iwakura has a striking face, with lines showing firmness and decision, and you saw the scar which marked the attempt of an assassin to cut him down and slay him, as Okubo, the greatest of Japanese statesmen, was slain not many months ago.
>
> The emperor stood quite motionless, apparently unobservant or unconscious of the homage that was paid him. He is a young man, with a slender figure, taller than the average Japanese, and about the middle height according to our ideas. He has a striking face, with a mouth and lips that remind you something of the traditional mouth of the Hapsburg family. The forehead is full and narrow, the hair and the light mustache and beard intensely black. The color of the hair darkens what might pass for a swarthy countenance at home. The face expressed no feeling whatever, and but for the dark, glowing eye, which was bent full upon the General, you might have taken the imperial group for statues. The empress, at his side, wore the Japanese costume, rich and plain. Her face was very white, and her form slender and almost childlike. Her hair was combed plainly and braided with a golden arrow. The emperor and empress have agreeable faces, the emperor's especially showing firmness and kindness.[16]

According to Young, the emperor conversed a good deal with Grant during this reception at the Shiba Palace. The interpreter was Yoshida Kiyonari. The content of the conversation was not recorded,[17] but the emperor, apparently impressed with Grant, expressed a desire to have a private and friendly meeting. This was arranged for a time after the general returned from his trip to Nikkō.[18]

The emperor's second meeting with Grant took place on July 7. That morning a military review took place in the presence of the emperor and General

Grant. Apart from the pleasure it no doubt gave the emperor to display his trim and well-equipped troops, he may have supposed (not knowing that Grant detested such military reviews) that this would be of particular interest to his guest. After the ceremony Meiji said to Grant, "A review of so few troops probably doesn't interest you. I have heard that your country has only a small standing army. I am truly impressed that a small army suffices for such a big country."[19] The emperor's comment on the fewness of the American troops may reflect the observations of Japanese who had visited Washington and seen how little police protection was needed for the president of the United States.

After the military review the emperor proceeded to the Shiba Detached Palace, where he was joined by General Grant and his wife. The emperor, welcoming them, shook hands with both. Other guests included the governor of Hong Kong and his wife and the American minister and his wife. General Grant ushered the wife of Prince Taruhito into the dining room, and the prime minister, Sanjō Sanetomi, taking Mrs. Grant's hand, brought her to the table.[20] Not so long before, members of Japanese delegations to the West had been astonished (and even dismayed) by the presence of women at dignified state occasions, but now the prime minister did not hesitate to take a foreign lady by the hand and politely lead her to the table.

After dinner General and Mrs. Grant were invited to another pavilion where they were served coffee. Over coffee, the emperor (interpreted by Yoshida Kiyonari) chatted with the former president. He asked questions and made comments about Grant's journey around the world, including:

"I am sure that in the course of your journey to different countries, during the past year and more, you have not only enjoyed the scenery and other sights but have found much that was of use to you."

"You must have suffered from the heat in India."

"Customs in India differ greatly from those in Europe and America. Among the various customs you noticed, which were the most striking?"

"Did you visit the Great Wall and other famous historical places while you were in China?"[21]

The emperor, who previously had difficulty in conversing with foreign visitors, was now able to go beyond routine comments on the weather and stereotyped expressions of gratitude that the visitor had traveled all the way to Japan. At first, the emperor had been reluctant to eat dinner with foreigners, and it took persuasion by the imperial household minister, Tokudaiji Sanetsune, to change his mind,[22] but he now seems to have enjoyed the occasion, even though the temperature rose to 93 degrees Fahrenheit and he was wearing a dress uniform. The emperor talked not only with Grant but also with the governor of Hong Kong. The empress, conversing with Mrs. Grant, vouchsafed words of comfort over the exhausting journey, to which Mrs. Grant responded by declaring that in none of the many countries she and her husband had visited were they treated with such great kindness as in Japan.[23]

Grant and his wife left for Nikkō on July 17, accompanied by Yoshida Kiyonari and Date Munenari. On the following day, the emperor sent Itō Hirobumi to Nikkō[24] to make sure that the Grants were comfortable there. Grant's stay in Nikkō was probably planned to give him relief from the Tōkyō summer. It may also have been intended to console him for not having been able to visit Kyōto. On July 22 while in Nikkō, he met with representatives of the Japanese government who had come to speak officially concerning the difficulty between China and Japan on the Ryūkyū question. As he had promised Prince Kung and Viceroy Li Hung-chang, Grant communicated the Chinese position. Itō Hirobumi replied that "Japanese rights of sovereignty over Loochoo were immemorial." Grant explained that his entire interest arose from his kind feelings toward both Japan and China. He added that "Japan was in point of war materials, army and navy, stronger than China. Against Japan, China, he might say, was defenseless, and it was impossible for China to injure Japan."[25] Grant's accurate estimate of the relative military strength of China and Japan revealed his expertise as a professional soldier, whereas most foreign observers, even as late as the Sino-Japanese War (1894–1895), were sure that China was far stronger than Japan.

Notes continued to be exchanged between the Japanese and Chinese governments concerning the ownership of the Ryūkyū Islands. Terashima Munenori, the minister of foreign affairs, sent a message to the Chinese government pointing out that the writing, language, religion, and customs of the Ryūkyū Islands were the same as those of Japan and that the islanders' custom of paying tribute to Japan went back as far as the Sui and T'ang dynasties, a thousand years earlier. In the twelfth century, Minamoto Tametomo had traveled to the Ryūkyūs, married the younger sister of the chieftain, and had a son who became king. Terashima's letter recounted also the special relationship between the Ryūkyūs and Satsuma and emphasized that now the domain had been abolished, the Ryūkyū Islands were an integral part of the Japanese Empire.

The Chinese responded with proofs that the Ryūkyūs had long acknowledged Chinese sovereignty and denounced the Japanese for having destroyed an independent country. This, they said, represented an act of extreme contempt toward not only China but all other countries. In their response the Japanese once more cited historical evidence for their claim to sovereignty.[26]

This was surely not a propitious moment for an outsider to intercede, but after his return from Nikkō at the end of July, Grant asked the emperor to set a day for a meeting, perhaps hoping to find an occasion when the tense situation between Japan and China could be discussed. The meeting took place at the Hama Detached Palace on August 10. The emperor arrived that afternoon in informal dress accompanied by Sanjō Sanetomi, Tokudaiji Sanetsune, and the chief chamberlain, Yamaguchi Masasada. Grant, accompanied by his son and his secretary, was led into the imperial presence. The emperor rose and shook hands with Grant. During the conversation that ensued, Sanjō and the interpreter, Yoshida Kiyonari, were the only Japanese present besides the emperor.[27]

The conversation between the emperor, who was then twenty-seven years old, and Grant, who was fifty-seven, lasted for more than two hours. It was recorded in English, presumably by Grant's secretary, but the transcript is too short to be the full text of all that was said during the two hours. The Japanese seem not to have made their own transcript; the English text was later translated.[28] It is unfortunate that Meiji's actual words were not preserved. They might have indicated, for example, just how the young monarch addressed a world-famous general and president who was twice his age.

The conversation opened with the emperor's apologies for not having arranged a meeting with Grant earlier and Grant's expressions of gratitude for the warmth of the reception he had received in Japan. The remainder of the conversation consists mainly of Grant's observations and recommendations. He obviously wished to establish himself in the eyes of the emperor as a friend of Japan and, to this end, was blunt in his denunciation of the attitudes of other Europeans and Americans in Asia: "This side of Singapore I have found but few newspapers or periodicals that are capable or willing to reason things upon common footing between the Asiatics, and Europeans and Americans. 'The Tokio Times' and 'The Japan Mail' are the only papers I have seen that treat eastern nations as if they too had rights that ought to be respected. All the western officials, except very few, are the same. Whatever is their interest they advocate it without regard to the right of China or Japan."

"Sometimes my blood boils to see this unfairness and selfishness."[29]

Later in the conversation Grant repeated his condemnation of European powers in Asia: "European powers have no interests in Asia, so far as I can judge from their diplomacy, that do not involve the humiliation and subjugation of the Asiatic peoples. Their diplomacy is always selfish, and a quarrel between China and Japan would be regarded by them as a quarrel that might ensue to their own advantage."[30]

These are strong words, but they sound plausible coming from a man convinced that American society, unlike that of the European nations, was egalitarian in nature. Although Grant did not name particular offenders, it is likely that he referred especially to England, the chief among the European powers. Describing people at the farewell party given to Grant when he was about to leave Japan, John Russell Young contrasted the American minister John Bingham with the celebrated Sir Harry Parkes:

Mr. Bingham, whose keen face grows gentler with the frosty tints of age, is in talk with Sir Harry Parkes, the British minister, a lithe, active, nervous, middle-aged gentleman, with open, clear-cut Saxon features, the merriest, most amusing, most affable gentleman present, knowing everybody, talking to everybody. One would not think as you followed his light banter, and easy rippling ways, that his hand was the hand of iron, and that his policy was the personification of all that was hard and stern in the policy of England.[31]

Grant thought of himself and his countrymen as being unaffected by the haughty ways of Europeans like Parkes, who never ceased his efforts to obtain for England the greatest possible advantages, regardless of what this might cost the nations of Asia. He told the emperor, "None, except His Majesty's own subjects, can feel more warmly interested for Japan's welfare than I do. In this regard, however, I am a fair representative of most of the American people." He was probably sincere in this declaration, though surely it would not have been difficult to find Americans as selfish as the Europeans attacked by Grant, who warned the emperor especially against foreign indebtedness:

There is nothing a nation should avoid as much as owing money abroad. . . . You are doubtless aware that some nations are very desirous to loan money to weaker nations whereby they might establish their supremacy and exercise undue influence over them. They lend money to gain political power. They are ever seeking the opportunity to loan. They would be glad, therefore, to see Japan and China, which are the only nations in Asia that are even partially free from foreign rule or dictation, at war with each other so that they might loan them on their own terms and dictate to them the internal policy which they should pursue.[32]

Grant also urged the Japanese to be more conciliatory in their negotiations with China over the Ryūkyū question: "Japan in a spirit of magnanimity and justice should make concessions to China. The importance of peace between China and Japan is so great that each country should make concessions to the other."[33] One wishes for a concurring reply from the emperor, but all that he said (at least in the transcript) was, "As regarding Loo Chu, Itō etc. are authorized to talk with you and will do so shortly."

Grant also expressed dissatisfaction with the tariff convention that Japan had signed with foreign countries.[34] Import duties were only 5 percent, far too low, and "export duty is the worst possible thing for any country to have." He declared that foreign governments should agree to the proposed revision of the treaties. (The Americans had agreed, providing other countries followed, but none did.)[35] Finally, after praising the Japanese educational system, Grant indirectly suggested that foreign professors, with their greater experience, be retained to oversee the younger, Japanese teachers: "In the United States we never hesitate to employ foreigners if they are useful to keep them. The men who made your Engineering school, which has no superior in the world, are men who should be kept as long as you can keep them."[36]

Grant's recommendations were on the whole admirable, though his caution against haste in establishing a legislative body, made elsewhere in the conversation, may seem strange in view of his evident admiration of the Japanese people and his own democratic beliefs.[37]

It is hard to measure how much influence the conversation exerted on the emperor or on Japanese policies. Grant's warning against foreign loans was probably the part of the conversation that exerted the greatest effect. When Ōkuma Shigenobu, the new finance minister, tried to find a way out of the government's financial difficulties by floating a foreign loan of 50 million yen, his proposal was defeated, and one reason cited was Grant's warning.[38]

Grant's recommendation that Japan proceed slowly before creating a legislative body accorded perfectly with what most Japanese statesmen favored anyway and need not have been learned from the foreign visitor.[39] Again, the Japanese, long dissatisfied with the tariff regulations that had been imposed on them, did not have to be reminded by Grant of the injustice, but they were as yet unable to compel the European powers to agree to more equitable treaties.

Grant urged that Japan be more conciliatory with respect to the sovereignty of the Ryūkyū Islands, but this recommendation was not followed, nor did the letters he later addressed to Iwakura Tomomi and Prince Kung, proposing that China and Japan negotiate directly, have any immediate effect.[40] On December 1, 1879, President Rutherford Hayes informed Congress that the American government had indicated its willingness to promote a peaceful solution of the Ryūkyū dispute,[41] but advantage was not taken of this offer. Direct negotiations between Japan and China of the kind Grant proposed began at last in August 1880, but even after a settlement was agreed on, the Chinese changed their minds, and possession of the Ryūkyū Islands never again became a matter of negotiation. The outbreak of the Sino-Japanese War in 1894 put an end to any possibility of friendly discussion of the issue along the lines Grant had suggested.

Perhaps the most lasting result of the emperor's conversation with Grant was to give him greater self-confidence when in later years he had to deal with foreign statesmen. However, the cultural impact of Grant's visit on Japan went far beyond the conversation with the emperor. He was greeted by enthusiastic crowds wherever he went, and the streets along which he would travel were decorated with lanterns and bamboo.[42]

The climax of the celebrations occurred on August 25 when a public festival was held at Ueno Park, ostensibly to commemorate the twelfth anniversary of the capital's move to Tōkyō. The emperor was to be present and visible to the crowds, but it was decided to take the occasion to honor Grant as well. The emperor's arrival, greeted with music played by military bands, was followed by displays of mounted archery, swordsmanship, and fireworks.[43] General Grant shared the festivities with the emperor, and when they had ended, as Young recorded, the drive back to Grant's hotel was memorable:

For miles the general's carriage slowly moved through a multitude that might have been computed by the hundreds of thousands, the trees and houses dangling with lamps and lanterns, the road spanned with arches of light, the night clear and mild, all forming a scene the like of which I had never witnessed, and which I can never hope to see again.[44]

This celebration recalls the welcome given to the first Japanese embassies by people in the United States and Europe in the 1860s, but it was even more remarkable: surely many in the crowds that cheered Grant had shouted anti-foreign slogans a dozen years earlier, and some may even have planned to kill every foreigner in sight. Hatred had mysteriously turned to love. The plain former soldier had captured the hearts of the Japanese, even the emperor, not by presenting rich gifts but by his unaffected ways and his delight in Japan.

Grant was depicted in numerous woodblock prints that commemorated his visits to the horse races, exhibitions of calisthenics by schoolchildren, the great waterfall at Nikkō, and the theater. In August he presented a curtain to the Shintomi Theater to express his gratitude for the kabuki play he had attended there on July 16.[45] The play (in one act with two scenes) was by the outstanding dramatist of the time, Kawatake Mokuami, and was called A *Military Account of the Later Three-Year War in Ōshū*. Although it ostensibly depicted how the eleventh-century general Minamoto Yoshiie put down a revolt in the Ōshū region, the play was intended to represent the triumphs of General Grant himself.[46] At the first performance, seventy-two geishas danced, wearing kimonos derived from the American flag—red and white stripes for the body and left arm, and stars on a blue background for the right arm.

Grant was otherwise immortalized by a quasi-biography called *Guranto-shi den Yamato bunshō* (Biography of Mr. Grant: Japanese Documents) by the popular novelist Kanagaki Robun. The covers of the little booklets in which the work was printed from woodblocks show the seventy-two geishas as well as Mr. and Mrs. Grant, both holding fans.

Perhaps Grant's most important contribution to the arts came as the result of watching a program of nō plays at the residence of Iwakura Tomomi. Just at a time when Iwakura had decided to support the revival of nō, Grant arrived in Japan and indicated to Iwakura that he would like to see Japan's classical arts. This was hardly typical of Grant. In Europe he had been invited to the opera frequently and thought of it as "a constant threat." When invited to the opera in Madrid by the United States minister, the poet John Russell Lowell, "After five minutes he claimed that the only noise he could distinguish from any other was the bugle call and asked Mrs. Lowell, 'Haven't we had enough of this?'"[47]

Grant's reactions to nō were quite different. He is reported to have been profoundly moved by the program consisting of Hōshō Kurō in *Mochizuki*, Kongō Taiichirō in *Tsuchigumo*, and Miyake Shōichi in the *kyōgen Tsurigitsune*. Afterward he said to Iwakura, "It is easy for a noble and elegant art like this one, being influenced by the times, to lose its dignity and fall into a decline. You should treasure it and preserve it."[48]

These words, coming from a foreign dignitary, were not ignored. Iwakura realized more than ever the necessity of saving nō and, enlisting the support of former daimyos and members of the nobility, took active steps to ensure its survival. On August 14 a special performance at his residence was attended by the emperor, the prime minister, four councillors, and other dignitaries. The revival of nō was definitely under way.

General Grant took leave of the emperor at a ceremony held in the palace on August 30. Grant expressed his gratitude for the kind and joyful reception he had received everywhere. He had noticed that in Japan there were neither extremely rich nor extremely poor people, a praiseworthy situation that he had not observed elsewhere during his journey. The country was blessed with fertile soil; large areas of undeveloped land; many mines that had yet to be exploited; good harbors where huge, almost limitless catches of fish were unloaded; and, above all, an industrious, contented, and thrifty people. Nothing was wanting in Japan's plan to achieve wealth and strength. He urged the Japanese not to let foreigners interfere in their internal government, so as to enable the country to amass wealth and not be forced to depend on other countries. He concluded by saying that his wishes for the complete independence and prosperity of Japan were not his alone but were shared by the entire American people. He ardently hoped that the emperor and the people would enjoy the blessings of Heaven.[49]

The emperor thanked Grant in a brief speech. According to Young, he read it in a clear, pleasant voice, quite a contrast from the inaudible whispers of his first encounters with foreigners. Here is how Young described his last impressions of the emperor: "The emperor is not what you would call a graceful man, and his manners are those of an anxious person not precisely at his ease — wishing to please and make no mistake. But in this farewell audience he seemed more easy and natural than when we had seen him before."[50]

Grant's visit had been an immense success in all respects save one: it did not enable him to get reelected as president. But he would not forget Japan, and the Japanese, from the emperor down, would remember this unaffected man who behaved so little like a hero.

Chapter 32

On August 31, 1879, Meiji's third son was born to the *gon no tenji* Yanagihara Naruko. The emperor and empress at once sent infant clothes and a "protective sword" to the Aoyama Lying-in Chamber, and that night the imperial birth was celebrated at a congratulatory dinner. Nakayama Tadayasu, Meiji's grandfather, was appointed as the prince's guardian, but because of his advanced age, Ōgimachi Sanenori was chosen to assist him. On September 6 the emperor bestowed on the prince the name Yoshihito; he would also be known as Harunomiya.[1]

The birth of the prince, duly reported to the gods, was celebrated with traditional rituals and a banquet attended by members of the imperial family, cabinet ministers, councillors, palace dignitaries, and the parents of Yanagihara Naruko. No doubt the atmosphere was festive, but surely many of those present were aware that the birth had been exceedingly difficult, and everyone knew that Meiji's first two sons had died in infancy. Perhaps that is why, breaking with precedent, the ministers did not offer congratulations.

From the day the prince was born, he suffered from a rash that covered his body. The scabs dissolved by September 23, and he was given a hip-bath, but it had an adverse effect. On the following day, spasms, starting in his abdomen, gradually spread to his chest. A mucous cough aggravated the pain. The spasms at last diminished by three in the morning, but the infant had still not recovered entirely, and there were frequent, though milder, recurrences that caused the emperor and empress great anxiety. The palace doctors tried every remedy, including acupuncture, and the aged Tadayasu spent days and nights watching over his great-grandchild. Not until December did the prince's illness subside, and even then the attacks recurred every nine days. The baby's mother, Yanagihara Naruko, did not recover her health after the birth, and because the quarters in the Lying-in Chamber were crowded, she was sent back to her apartment in the palace.[2]

The emperor did not get his first glimpse of Yoshihito until December 4. That afternoon, after exercising his horse on the riding ground, he went, still on horseback, to the Aoyama Lying-in Chamber. Nakayama Yoshiko (the emperor's mother) carried the prince in her arms to the emperor, who expressed delight with his son. On the following day the empress paid a visit to her nominal son. It had been decided as far back as September 30 that the prince, who would be considered as the empress's son, would be brought up initially (like his father) at the house of Nakayama Tadayasu; but he suffered a fresh outbreak of illness that day, and his departure was delayed. The move did not take place until December 7. On December 28 the prince, having reached his 120th day of life, had his "first chopsticks" ceremony at the Nakayama house, but the prince's health continued to worry the emperor, and for fear of provoking spasms, he treated the prince with greater indulgence than he ever showed his other children.

Other matters than his son's health occupied the emperor's attention at this time. By this time he was recognized as a "cousin" by the royal houses of Europe, and he accordingly received regular and prolonged visits from foreign royalty. Prince Heinrich of Germany brought Meiji a decoration from his government, the first time any Asian monarch had been so honored. This was also the first foreign decoration that Meiji wore. He received from the duke of Genoa, a somewhat later visitor, the Annunciade, Italy's highest military decoration, and responded by bestowing the Grand Order of the Chrysanthemum on the duke and showing him how to wear it. The emperor also received a bust of himself and portraits of himself and the empress made by the Milanese artist Giuseppe Ugolini.[3]

Apart from visits by foreign royalty, the emperor was regularly informed of events in the lives of other monarchs. He responded correctly to his "cousins," sending messages of congratulation to Alfonso XII of Spain on his remarriage and to the czar of Russia on his narrow escape from assassins.[4]

Matters closer to home also demanded the emperor's attention. In October 1879 some members of the government made a concerted attempt to get rid of Soejima Taneomi by sending him abroad on an unspecified mission. Kuroda Kiyotaka, the leader of the anti-Soejima faction, claimed that foreign newspapers had accused Soejima of having expressed in lectures delivered before the emperor opinions contrary to government policy and of having, while he was foreign minister, colluded with a foreigner—the American general Charles LeGendre—when dealing with the Taiwan incident. Kuroda's charges were supported by other high-ranking officials, including Councillor Saigō Tsugu-michi, but Ōkuma Shigenobu declared that if Soejima were dismissed, he would resign. Itō Hirobumi praised Soejima's scholarship but said that Soejima was not trusted by most people because of his extreme conservatism. He favored sending Soejima abroad to examine political conditions so that he might improve his already superior understanding of the West. Itō suggested that Soejima might be permitted at some future date to rejoin the cabinet.

When asked to render a decision, the emperor conferred with his Confucian adviser Motoda Nagazane, who strongly defended Soejima. He said that he had heard the lectures Soejima had delivered in the presence of the emperor and considered that they embodied profound respect for the majesty of the imperial house and contributed to the exaltation of the imperial virtue. He believed that it was entirely beneficial for the emperor to use Soejima and that he, Motoda, had not detected anything harmful in his words. Kuroda had never heard any of Soejima's lectures and therefore lacked firm evidence for his accusations. To believe unfounded reports, and on this basis to seek to get rid of Soejima, was to question the wisdom of His Majesty. If one were to believe everything that appeared in the newspapers, how many of the cabinet would escape being removed? If Kuroda's self-serving proposal to get rid of Soejima were adopted, this action would surely be widely criticized; but if Kuroda, annoyed that his proposal was rejected, asked to be relieved of his post and permission were granted, would anyone question this decision by the emperor?[5]

The emperor, not rushing into a decision, conferred several times with Motoda, whose opinions he highly valued. Motoda answered with increasing bluntness. He attributed to personal rancor Kuroda's urging that Soejima be removed from his position. There was no fault to find with Soejima; even if 10 million people hated him, the emperor should continue to employ him. Soejima had been employed as the emperor's tutor for only seven months and had not even completed his lectures on the *Great Learning*. How could anyone propose that he be sent abroad at this stage? Even if Kuroda resigned as councillor, there would still be nine other councillors, but if Soejima left, not only would it deprive the emperor of one of the rare people who could contribute to his learning, but it would encourage dissident elements to attack the government, resulting in incalculable harm. In the end Motoda's eloquence carried the day: the emperor decided not to allow Soejima to be sent abroad. Kuroda, who had threatened to resign if his advice was not heeded, remained in office.[6]

At this distance from the events, it seems clear that some personal (or domain-based) enmity was behind the insistence of Kuroda and other Satsuma men that Soejima be removed from his post. But the incident is noteworthy for another reason. One sometimes gets the impression that all the Meiji government's decisions were made by consensus, but this is an instance when the emperor, relying on Motoda, a man above political factionalism, made a decision that differed from the opinions of the majority of his ministers.

About the same time the emperor abolished the office of *jiho*, or adviser, which had been created a little more than two years earlier.[7] Although the *jiho* included extremely distinguished men—Tokudaiji Sanetsune, Sasaki Takayuki, and Motoda Nagazane—from the first they were prevented from carrying out their assigned duty of counseling the emperor, by members of the government who accused them of craving power. Itō compared their would-be meddling in the government with the evils of the eunuchs in China and predicted that this would confuse the functions of the palace and the government. In the end the frustrated *jiho*, angered over being compared with the notoriously corrupt eunuchs and equally angered over Kuroda's attempts to get rid of the *jiho* Soejima, requested that their office be abolished, providing that the ministers and councillors would carry out the functions of *jiho* in addition to their prescribed duties. The cabinet eventually decided to abolish the *jiho* and assigned ministers and councillors to palace duties similar to theirs.

The emperor seems not to have welcomed this decision. On October 20, a week after the office of *jiho* was abolished, he summoned Tokudaiji, Sasaki, Motoda, and the others and informed them that even though the *jiho* had been abolished, if ever they had something to tell him, they should do so without reserve. He personally presented them with bolts of silk and invited them to lunch with the prime minister and the minister of the right. This was not the only instance of a decision by the politicians that displeased Meiji, although they always insisted that their actions were intended to carry out the imperial will.

The principal subject of debate during the latter part of 1879 was education. Meiji's Oath in Five Articles had promised that the Japanese would seek learning throughout the world in order for their country to catch up to the advanced countries. The emperor's abiding interest in education was evidenced by the frequency of his visits to schools wherever he traveled. He himself continued to receive instruction from Motoda Nagazane and others in the Confucian classics. He was particularly affected by Motoda's insistence on *chū* (loyalty) and *kō* (filial piety) as the central Confucian virtues, even though these two virtues had not been stressed in the Confucian writings of China or in those of the Japanese Confucianists of the Tokugawa period. During the Meiji era the four Confucian virtues commonly cited in statements on education—*jin* (humaneness), *gi* (righteousness), *chū*, and *kō*—were seen as adjuncts to the policy of "civilization and enlightenment" favored by the bureaucrats.[8] However, *jin* and *gi* tended to receive less attention than *chū* and *kō*, virtues that lent themselves easily to the new state's policies.

The emperor also listened to lectures delivered on works of Japanese tradition and (to a lesser extent) Western history. His preferences in education, regardless of the subject matter, were conservative, as we can infer from this poem:

yorozuyo ni	What never changes
ugokanu mono wa	Throughout ten thousand ages
inishie no	Are the teachings left
hijiri no miyo no	From the ancient past,
okite narikeri	The holy age of the sages.

The emperor also revealed in his poetry his awareness that traditional learning was insufficient in a modern world:

susumiyuku	It will do no good
yo ni okurenaba	If we fall behind a world
kai araji	That is progressing
fumi no hayashi wa	Even if we penetrate
waketsukusu tomo	The depths of literature.[9]

Despite the emperor's belief in the importance of the learning of the past, the new education tended to be Western in orientation. For example, on July 14, 1876, when the emperor visited an elementary school in Aomori, ten pupils of English gave talks in English and wrote compositions. The following were the subjects:

Speech: Hannibal's speech encouraging his soldiers.
Composition: In celebration of His Majesty's visit to Aomori.
Speech: Andrew Jackson's speech in the U.S. Senate.
Composition: A song in praise of enlightenment and progress.
Speech: Cicero's attack on Cataline.
Composition: A song in praise of education.[10]

The emperor had to leave the school before all the planned talks and compositions could be completed. As he departed, the pupils sang for him a song in English. The emperor gave each of them five yen with which to buy a copy of *Webster's Intermediate Dictionary*. But on his return to Tōkyō, he told Motoda that he thought that the pupils' ignorance of Japan was the fault of "American educational methods" in practice, since the school system was established in 1872.[11]

After his return from his journey of 1878 to Hokuriku and Tōkai, the emperor sent for Iwakura Tomomi and informed him that it was essential to cultivate in the schools traditional Japanese morality. He obviously had not been pleased with Japanese children who, though ignorant of Japanese traditions, glibly delivered speeches in English on Hannibal and Cicero.

The emperor was interested not only in academic institutions but also in technical training schools where "practical learning" was taught. On January 24, 1878, he visited the forerunner of the Faculty of Agriculture of Tōkyō University, and in the rescript pronounced on this occasion, he declared, "We believe that agriculture is the foundation of the nation."[12] This insistence on the importance of agriculture to the nation was, of course, nothing new: Confucian philosophers had been saying the same thing for more than a thousand years. What was distinctive was that the students were learning about modern agricultural methods in a school, whereas in the past they would have been expected to learn how to be successful farmers by laboring in the fields. Such a school was not intended to destroy traditional agriculture or crafts that had been passed down from generation to generation; rather, this formal education in scientific techniques would lead to increased agricultural production and to a more prosperous society.

On July 15, 1878, the emperor pronounced a rescript at the ceremonies opening the engineering university. A school where technology would be systematically taught was new to Japan and an important part of the process of "enlightenment." In order to raise Japanese techniques to the standards in the advanced countries, it was necessary to hire foreign experts as teachers. On his visits to schools throughout the country, Meiji always singled out the foreign teachers for special attention. When they were about to leave Japan after completing their contractual duties, he usually granted them audiences, an honor much less frequently bestowed on Japanese. President Grant, as we have seen, urged the Japanese to retain their foreign advisers. Although he expressed the hope that teaching positions of every kind would be one day filled entirely by Japanese, he noted that it would be unwise "to hurry unnecessarily the dismissal of foreign instructors. . . . I believe that you should keep for as long as they can be kept foreigners, like those of world reputation who have founded His Majesty's Engineering University." His advice was heeded.

Meiji also encouraged Japanese (who could afford it) to study abroad, to observe conditions in other countries, acquire practical learning, and keep Japan from falling behind in progress.[13] He stressed even in his poetry the importance of the absorption of Western civilization:

wa ga sono ni	Here in my garden
shigeriaikeri	They have grown in profusion—
totsukuni no	Because I planted
kusaki no nae mo	And cultivated seedlings
ōshitatsureba	Of plants and trees from abroad.

In 1872 an edict on education had been promulgated providing for the standardization of education throughout the country, mainly along the lines of the French educational system.[14] Although the plan proved to be too idealistic to

be realized with Japan's limited resources, it was indicative of the great importance attached to education from the start of the Meiji era.

Soon after the new school system was promulgated, there were complaints
that the authorities were so determined to carry through the ambitious plan,
regardless of the costs, that they were spending huge sums of money. The
administrators were also charged with excessive interference in the schools. As
the result of these and other complaints, Education Minister Tanaka Fujimaro
(1845–1909) was sent to America to observe education there. On his return he
proposed basic departures from the system instituted in 1872: the educational
system should be changed to accord better with the national strength, the conditions of people's life, and the existing culture. The French system would be
replaced by a decentralized educational system in which responsibility would
be shifted to the localities.[15] A draft bill was submitted in May 1878 for examination by Itō Hirobumi, who made some modifications such as giving greater
autonomy to local authorities and minimizing interference from the central
government. After passing the Genrō-in with further modifications, the bill was
presented to the emperor for his approval.

In the meantime Iwakura Tomomi, charged by the emperor with incorporating traditional virtues into the new education, had concluded that Japan's
educational policies had to be changed. Such men as Sasaki Takayuki and
Motoda Nagazane were convinced that loyalty and filial piety must be the
cornerstone. Moral training (shūshin) had always been a basic part of the
elementary-school curriculum,[16] using such Confucian works as the Great
Learning for texts, but these men felt that shūshin tended to be overshadowed
by foreign learning.

On April 16, 1878, Iwakura and Sasaki had an audience with the emperor at
which he stressed the importance of moral education, regardless of whether a
person was a student of Chinese learning, a devotee of the emperor, or even
(like Fukuzawa Yukichi and Katō Hiroyuki) advocates of Western learning. On
May 5 during an audience with the emperor, Iwakura read aloud the proposal
of someone who favored a republican government—presumably as a warning
against too great a tolerance of dissenting opinions. He urged the emperor to
devote himself more than ever to his Heaven-appointed duties so as to ensure
the fairness of the government's policies. The most essential concern was education. Judging from recent conditions, Iwakura observed, the blind adherence
of many people to Western ways deprives them of independent, self-respecting
thought. If a Westerner says the Analects is a good book, they read it at once;
if a Westerner says it is a bad book, they throw it away without hesitation. It
reminds one of ignorant men or women rushing off to worship at whatever Inari
shrine happens to be popular at the moment.[17]

On June 26, the day after the revised bill was submitted to the emperor, he
promised, in view of the importance of the matter and his own personal interest,
to have a written record of his views prepared. This document, composed by

Motoda, was in two parts. Although it purported to present the emperor's views, they were in fact Motoda's. The first part declared:

> The essence of the teachings for high and low alike of our ancestors and our national classics is that the essential function of education is to teach benevolence, righteousness, loyalty, and filial piety. The Way of human beings should be cultivated by the exhaustive study of knowledge and the arts. However, in recent years only knowledge and the arts have been respected, and in their eagerness to run after the trivialities of "civilization and enlightenment," quite a few men have broken rules of conduct and impaired customs. Moreover, taking the astute proclamation that old, unenlightened customs are to be rejected and learning is to be sought throughout the world as the commencement of the Restoration, such people have promised they will adopt the superior practices of the West and demonstrate they are capable of making improvements each day. But what happens is that they dismiss, as long-standing evils, benevolence, righteousness, loyalty, and filiality and recklessly vie to adopt Western ways. This is to be dreaded for the future and may in the end make them unaware of the great principle of loyalty to one's sovereign and filial behavior toward one's parents. Their attitude does not accord with the basic principles of education in our country.
>
> For this reason, from this time forward, basing ourselves on the teachings of our ancestors, we should teach benevolence, righteousness, loyalty, and filial piety, and our moral teachings should be based chiefly on Confucius. People should revere sincerity and good conduct and study the different disciplines in accordance with their particular talents. As they continue their progress, morality and technical skills, both essential and auxiliary, will all be present, and the teachings of the Great Mean and righteousness will fill the land. Then, in its spirit of independence, our country shall not be ashamed before any nation in the universe.[18]

In his second essay, Motoda touched on his experiences while traveling with the emperor:

> Last autumn when I examined schools in the various prefectures and observed the pupils' scholarly attainments, the instruction offered to children of farmers and merchants consisted entirely of high-flown empty theories. In extreme cases the pupils were able to speak Western languages well but were incapable of translating the foreign words into Japanese. When these children graduate some day and return home, it will be difficult for them to apply themselves once more to their basic occupations. The high-flown empty theories they have learned will be of no use to them either if they wish to become officials. In addition, I heard ev-

erywhere that quite a few of them are so pleased with themselves, they make fun of their elders and obstruct the provincial officials.[19]

Motoda urged the establishment of courses in agriculture and business instead of highbrow knowledge, so that graduates would return to their basic occupations and prosper. The emperor summoned Itō Hirobumi and, telling him of his desire to improve education and correct morals, asked Itō for his views.

Itō's memorial to the throne, after an opening paragraph indicting the collapse of morals that marked the times, declared that in order to remedy the situation it must be treated as a disease and that in order to cure a disease it was necessary to find out what had caused it. He traced the origins of the present undesirable situation in education to the changes brought about by the Restoration. The end of the closed country era and the feudal system meant that the samurai class was no longer bound by traditional discipline and constraints. This liberation, though desirable, entailed the loss of the good qualities in the old system. Deprived of their former means of support, samurai had become involved in partisan politics and infected by radical ideas emanating from Europe.

The deterioration of morals could not be attributed solely to the failure of the new education introduced since the Restoration. But even if the effects of education were not immediate, it was the best cure for the prevailing situation. If the government took the lead in promoting education and remedying the inadequacies of the present system, it was reasonable to hope that Japan would achieve a "civilized" state. Itō expressed opposition to any attempt to create a national religion that would combine old and new in consultation with the classics, as this would require the appearance of a sage, and in any case, it was not for the government to control.

Itō favored technical education as the way to wean young samurai from the Confucian partiality for empty political arguments which in turn had led to their susceptibility to radical ideas from the West. Practical learning, rather than political discussions, should be the core of education. He concluded by recommending that only outstanding students be allowed to study law and politics.[20]

The emperor showed Itō's memorial to Motoda, who recognized it was a serious attempt to amplify the emperor's views on education and to make up for oversights. However, he continued, the views expressed in the memorial suggested that Itō did not perfectly understand the emperor's wishes. Motoda asked to be authorized to prepare a reply, and when he did, it was to reject Itō's views completely. He insisted that the Four Books and Five Classics of Confucianism must be the core of education, followed by works of national learning that treated ethics and, only at the end, Western books. Itō had said that one should not expect immediate results from education, but Motoda asked what would happen in the future if the foundations were not laid today. Itō had urged that no national religion be established, at least at this time, but Motoda demanded when a more appropriate time would be. Even European countries had national religions. Since ancient times, Japan's advances had been achieved by revering the heavenly ancestors and adopting Confucianism. "The national religion of today is none other than a return to the past."[21]

Motoda was pleased, however, that a minister of education had been appointed. The position, long vacant, had recently been assigned to the councillor Terashima Munenori in addition to his regular duties. He hoped that the emperor would communicate to Terashima his wishes on education. The emperor sent for Terashima the next day and gave him Motoda's two essays, Itō's memorial, and the draft bill on education passed by the Genrō-in.[22]

The new educational bill was in forty-seven articles. It prescribed opening schools at every level from elementary to university. Government elementary schools were to be established in every village and town except where satisfactory private schools already existed. In those places that lacked the means to establish schools, touring professors would be provided. A child's education would last for eight years, from the sixth to the fourteenth year. Parents or guardians would be responsible for sending the children to school. Although loopholes in the act permitted parents to get around this obligation, it came close to mandating compulsory education for all Japanese children, a sign of the importance attached to education by the government, despite its chronic lack of funds.

The educational system that emerged from the revisions to the 1872 school system was not a success. The new system that had been laboriously constructed during the past seven years was thrown into confusion, and there was a marked decline in educational standards. The liberalization intended to free education of the straitjacket of bureaucratic administration resulted in a laissez-faire policy that did not appeal to members of the government or the emperor. Accordingly, Tanaka Fujimaro was replaced as minister of education, and his successor, Kōno Togama, who had accompanied the emperor on visits to schools in the countryside, was dismayed by what he observed. He therefore decided to reform the education law by strengthening the central and regional officers' authority.[23] In December 1880 the Genrō-in approved a modified educational law providing that morals (*shūshin*) would rank at the top of all subjects taught.[24]

From about this time, Meiji seemed to assume a noticeably more conservative outlook. Motoda's influence is apparent in the emperor's insistence on Confucian values in education. Of course, each generation tends to contrast the feckless youth of its own time with the uncomplicated but sincere young people of the past. But the shift in educational policy suggests that even though the government was dedicated to progress and the propagation of practical learning, it was not content merely with lamenting the loss of old-fashioned morality but was ready to compel the young to submit to tradition. As Asukai Masamichi wrote, "The route to the Rescript on Education of 1890 had been opened."[25]

Portrait of Emperor Meiji. This photograph, the earliest taken of Meiji, shows him in traditional robes and headgear. *Courtesy the Yokohama Archives of History*

Portrait of Emperor Kōmei. This official portrait reveals nothing of Kōmei's personality. *Courtesy the Collection of Sennyū-ji*

Portrait of Emperor Kōmei. The intense expression on Kōmei's face contrasts with his placid appearance in the earlier portrait.

Portrait of Empress Haruko, posthumously known as Shōken. Unlike the emperor, the empress did not object to having her photograph taken. *Courtesy Charles Schwartz, Ltd.*

Official portrait of Emperor Meiji. This photograph was taken specifically in order to exchange it with photographs of foreign monarchs sent to the emperor. Meiji's hair has been cut, and the beginnings of a mustache and beard are evident. Meiji continued to wear this old-fashioned uniform long after it had disappeared from Europe. *Courtesy Charles Schwartz, Ltd.*

The advisability of an invasion of Korea (*seikan*) being disputed by members of the cabinet. Print by Hashimoto Chikanobu (1877). The figure to the upper left is probably Meiji. Others portrayed in this print include Saigō Takamori, Iwakura Tomomi, Sanjō Sanetomi, Itagaki Taisuke, Etō Shimpei, and Ōkubo Toshimitsu. *Courtesy the Kanagawa Museum*

Portrait of Saigō Takamori. Print by Suzuki Toshimoto (1877). Saigō's mustache and beard, not found in most portraits of him, probably represent the artist's guesswork. *Courtesy the Kanagawa Museum*

The opposing army leaders during the Satsuma Rebellion. Print by Takeuchi Eikyū (1877). The government forces (in Western-style uniforms) and the Satsuma officers (in various costumes) flank Shimazu Hisamitsu. *Courtesy the Kanagawa Museum*

The *seppuku* (ritual disembowelment) of Saigō Takamori. Print by Taiso Yoshitoshi (1877). Saigō in fact died at Shiroyama, not on the sea, but the artist had a lively imagination. *Courtesy the Kanagawa Museum*

Rokumeikan, the building that symbolized Japanese
efforts to achieve modernization. *Photograph courtesy
Dallas Finn*

The visit to Japan of General and Mrs. Ulysses S. Grant, depicted in insets to the upper right and left, celebrated by geisha dancing in kimonos that pay tribute to the Stars and Stripes.
Courtesy the Mary and Jackson Burke Collection

Issuance of the constitution in the state chamber of the new palace, March 14, 1889. Print by Adachi Ginkō.
Courtesy The Metropolitan Museum of Art, Gift of Lincoln Kirstein, 1959

Empress Haruko teaching girls at the Peeresses' School to sing the song she composed. Print by Toyohara Kunichika (1887). The empress wore Western from this time on. *Courtesy the Kanagawa Museum*

皇后宮御製唱歌

左ノ唱歌ハ今般華族女
學校ヘ却下相成ル者也

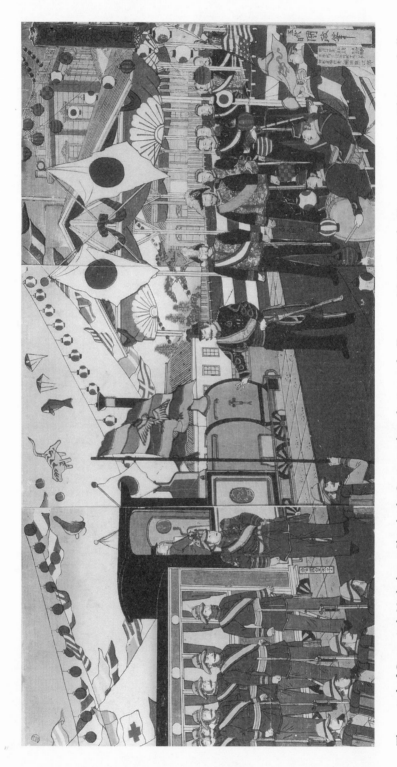

The arrival of Czarevitch Nicholas at Shimbashi Station, where he is met by Emperor Meiji. Print by Kunimasa V (1891). This is a wholly imagined scene, since the future Nicholas II never visited Tokyo. *Courtesy the Kanagawa Museum*

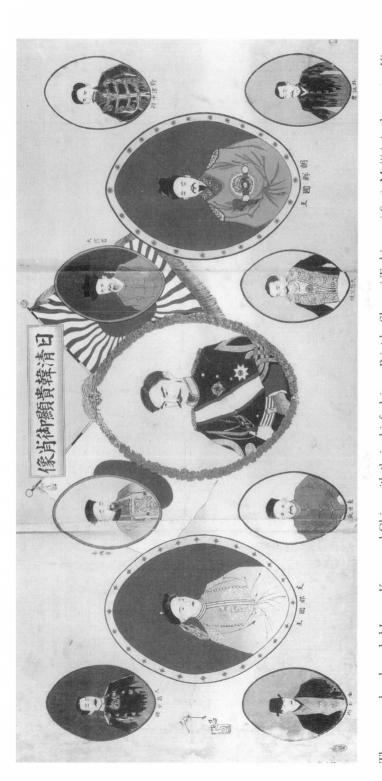

The monarchs who ruled Japan, Korea, and China with their chief advisers. Print by Shunsai Toshimasa (1894). Meiji is in the center; King Kojong, to the right; and Kuang-hsü, "the king of China," to the left. *Courtesy the Kanagawa Museum*

The visit of Empress Haruko to the hospital in Hiroshima where men wounded in the Sino-Japanese War are being treated. Print by Kobayashi Kiyochika (1895). The bandaged patient at the left crouches in awe, and a nurse nearby kneels. *Courtesy the Kanagawa Museum*

Negotiations in Shimonoseki to end the Sino-Japanese War. Print by Kobayashi Kiyochika (1895). To the right, the Japanese delegation is headed by Itō Hirobumi. To the left, the Chinese delegation is led by Li Hung-chang. Two foreign advisers of the Chinese are also present. *Courtesy the Kanagawa Museum*

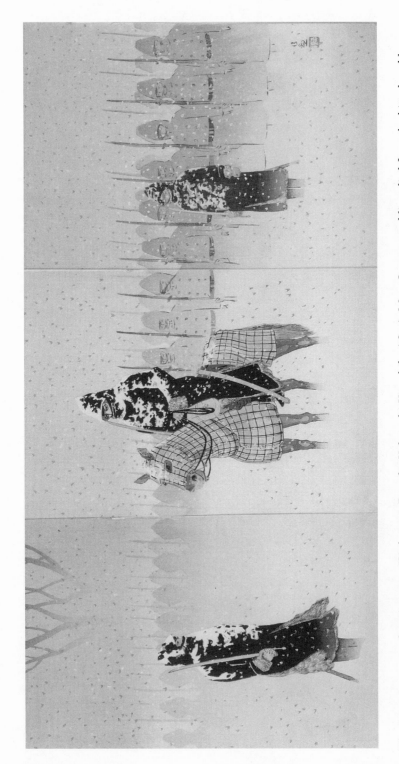

The Japanese army advancing near Weihaiwei. Print by Kobayashi Kiyochika (1895). More Japanese soldiers died from the bitterly cold winter than from Chinese bullets. *Courtesy the Kanagawa Museum*

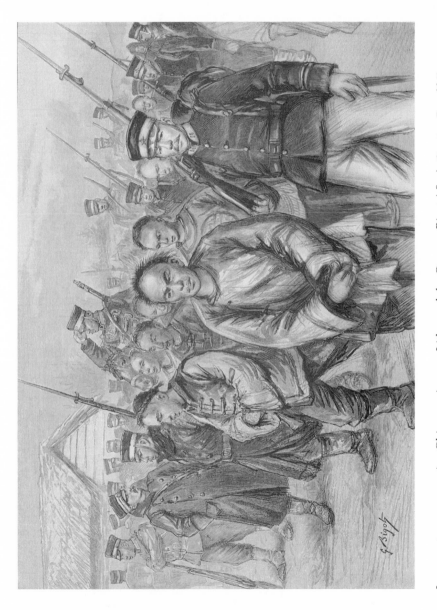

Japanese troops convoying Chinese prisoners. Lithograph by Georges Bigot (1895). *Courtesy Donald Keene*

Russian and Japanese military at the outset of the Russo-Japanese War. Print by Watanabe Nobukazu (1904). The soldiers and sailors of the two nations are facially almost indistinguishable. *Courtesy Print Collection, Miriam and Ira D. Wallach Division of Art, Prints and Photographs, The New York Public Library, Astor, Lenox and Tilden Foundations*

Chapter 33

The customary New Year ceremonies for 1880 were performed by the emperor, now in his twenty-ninth year. The emperor and empress received the duke of Genoa, and Prince Heinrich, the grandson of the German kaiser, telegraphed greetings from his ship in Nagasaki harbor. On the second day of the new year Emperor Meiji sent a telegram of congratulations to Alfonso XII, the king of Spain, not on the New Year, but on his having escaped assassination.[1] More than ever, Meiji was in communication with the crowned heads of Europe, but he may have felt, even as he expressed joy over the narrow escapes of various kings, how remote their world was from his own; surely he had no fears that anyone would attempt to assassinate him.

This was the first year in which Meiji might be said to have routinely exercised his powers as emperor. His councillors' proposals were brought to him for a final decision, not (as in previous years) as a mere formality, but because his opinion was needed, often to break a deadlock within the cabinet. This new responsibility may account for the reduction in his other activities. There was a marked decrease, for example, in the emperor's visits to the empress dowager and in the number of times he went horseback riding. His formal education also suffered: he listened to lectures delivered by Motoda Nagazane and other scholars only twenty-three times between April and December, despite being scheduled to hear them four or five times each week. Instead, Meiji attended meetings of the cabinet almost every day,[2] and he had frequent lunch meetings with high-ranking officers of the government to discuss state business. Itō Hirobumi was particularly eager at this time to establish direct links between the emperor and the cabinet and for the emperor to assume a major role in decision making.[3]

Financial problems were a principal concern of the government during 1880. Government revenues were far from covering expenditures. Although in the previous March the emperor had commanded the ministers, councillors, and others to practice strict economy and had given orders to the imperial household minister for the palace to serve as a model to the nation in its avoidance of wasteful expenses, his orders had little effect. The different ministries insisted that they were unable to cut expenses any further, and the palace's expenses reportedly had actually increased. This was partly due to inflation, but the news prompted another call for economy: the staff was ordered to refrain from having repairs made to the palace that were not absolutely urgent and not to buy anything new.

Believing that a more positive policy than thriftiness was needed to overcome the financial problems, Ōkuma Shigenobu submitted in June 1879 a four-point proposal for remedying the situation. The first point was to redeem a considerable part of the paper money that had been printed to pay the expenses of the 1877 Satsuma Rebellion. The flood of banknotes had resulted in a loss of confidence in their value, and now a silver 1-yen coin was worth 1 yen, 43 sen in paper money. Inflation was rampant, and the only way to restore confidence in the banknotes was to replace nonconvertible notes with notes convertible into specie. The money for redeeming the notes could be raised in part by selling government-owned factories, but Ōkuma's main proposal was to float a foreign loan of 50 million yen to be repaid over twenty-five years. He estimated that these measures would permit the government to redeem 78 million yen in nonconvertible notes.[4] Another 27 million yen in paper money would be redeemed in exchange for convertible bills.

The cabinet was evenly divided on the issue of whether to float a foreign loan. Ōkuma had won over the Satsuma faction, but the Chōshū and allied councillors, headed by Itō Hirobumi, opposed the loan, though not all for the same reasons. Among the strongest opponents was Minister of the Right Iwakura Tomomi, who (as a member of the nobility) was in constant communication with the palace. His allies among the former jiho, especially Sasaki Takayuki and Motoda Nagazane, also continued to have access to the emperor's ear. Motoda spoke strongly against any foreign loan, conjuring up the peril to the nation that this might involve and recalling General Grant's warning against accepting foreign money. The question he (and Iwakura) posed was, what if Japan were unable to repay the loan? Would Japan have to yield part of its territory—say, Shikoku or Kyūshū—in order to satisfy its creditors?[5] The only way to overcome the financial crisis, these men argued, was to practice strict economy.

The emperor was aware of Ōkuma's plan and did not like it, but he was also anxious not to risk a permanent split in the cabinet, such as had occurred at the time of the dispute over Korea. He sought the opinions of the heads of the different ministries, but they also were divided. Unable to get a clear recommendation either way, the emperor finally decided against borrowing money from foreign countries. On June 3, 1880, he issued this rescript:

> Ever since the early years of the Meiji era, there have been many demands on the state that have brought about the present financial difficulties. Today, in the thirteenth year of the era, there is an outward flow of specie, resulting in a loss of confidence in paper money. This was the reason for Councillor Ōkuma's proposal. I have examined this proposal. I have also been informed that there is no unanimity of opinion in the cabinet or in the various ministries. Although I am well aware that it is not easy to dispose of the financial problem, I am convinced that borrowing money from abroad is today an inadmissible solution. Last year Grant spoke at length concerning the advantages and disadvantages of foreign loans. His words are still in my ears. The financial crisis looms before us today, and we must choose a goal for the future. Now is the time for putting thrift into practice. I call on you, my lords, to implement my wishes and, making strict economy your watchword, establish a course for economic recovery. Discuss this fully with the cabinet and ministries, then report back to me.[6]

There was naturally no opposition to the emperor's command, although there was discussion about how to implement it. The emperor's decision in effect had established the palace as the ultimate authority when divisions existed in the cabinet and ministries. Before long, a similar decision would be required of the emperor with respect to the proposal that in order to control the mounting price of rice, the farmers should be required to pay taxes in rice rather than in cash, reverting to the system that had existed under the shoguns. But before this problem came to a head, the emperor set out on another progress, this one to Yamanashi, Mie, and Kyōto Prefectures.[7]

The announcement of the forthcoming journey, made on March 30, set the date for his departure on June 16. In May the people of the Shimo-ina district of Nagano sent a petition to the emperor imploring him to travel through their backward part of the country rather than through Kiso, which already had a fine road and might soon expect the railway. Such a visit would serve to stimulate the production of silk, the local industry, and would give women and children, who could not hope to visit the capital even once in their lifetimes, an unforgettable experience.[8] Although the emperor did not accept the petition, it suggests the people's eagerness for the emperor to visit their region.

In preparation for the emperor's travels, the roads were improved. For example, the road beyond Sasago, formerly a perilous trail into the mountains, had been widened and railings erected at places where there was a sharp drop below.[9] The cost of mending the roads over which the procession would pass soon became the subject of conflicting statements by the newspapers and the authorities. According to one newspaper, each household in the district was required to pay part of the cost of improving the road and of providing flags, roadside lighting, and the like. It was reported that many people, though delighted at the prospect of worshiping the emperor as he passed, had complained that even if they sold all their possessions, they would not be able to raise the 3 yen, 53 sen, 3 rin that was their share of the expenses.[10] The headman of the town of Kita Fukashi, however, denied that vast sums of money were being spent in preparation for the emperor's visit. He insisted that no levy had been imposed on the population, that the expenses would be paid by public-spirited persons.[11]

Perhaps the most striking editorial on the emperor's proposed journey appeared in the *Tōkyō Yokohama mainichi shimbun* on April 4. The writer drew a distinction between necessary and unnecessary travels by the emperor. At the beginning of his reign when people in such places as the northeast or in Kyūshū were unaware there was an emperor who ranked even higher than their feudal lords, it was necessary for him to journey to these places to make people aware of his existence. However, the editorial continued,

> the people of the entire country now know there is an emperor, and they realize there is no one else to whom they should offer their respect and awe. It is a time when he can remain in his palace and govern calmly and without strain. Why, when the country is so well governed, should he be obliged to travel about in his palanquin, braving the burning heat?
> ... In such a time as this, the thirteenth year of Meiji, one can say that an imperial progress is unnecessary.[12]

This view seems to have found receptive ears among the emperor's advisers, and he made only two more progresses during the remainder of his reign.[13]

The same editorial writer also refuted the argument that the emperor's travels were necessary because they enabled him to learn about conditions in the country. He declared that one could learn quite enough about conditions by reading the newspapers. Other people had suggested that it was important for the emperor to see with his own eyes the conditions of misery under which some of his subjects lived, but because the route taken by the emperor's palanquin never passed through such places, he saw only the most prosperous areas. It was insulting to the emperor to say that travel to remote parts of the country was his only way of discovering the hardships suffered by his people.

Another editorial (in the *Chōya shimbun*) was addressed to people who lived along the route that the emperor would travel, urging them to take advantage of this rare opportunity to let him know how they really lived. It was to obtain such information, the editorial said, that the emperor traveled to distant parts of the country. Of course, people would be delighted to have the opportunity of seeing the splendor of the imperial palanquin, but they should not, in their joy over welcoming the emperor, attempt to conceal the true state of conditions. Not only would this defeat the purpose of the progress, but their servility would be an affront to the imperial virtue.[14]

It is hard to imagine what the common people specifically could have done to enlighten the emperor as his palanquin went by. But it seems also to be true that Potemkin villages were not erected in order to beguile the emperor into supposing that his subjects were all gratefully enjoying the blessings of his reign.

Finally, an editorial in English, published in the *Japan Weekly Mail*, stated the purpose of the emperor's journeys in these terms:

> At the termination of the present tour, His Majesty will have seen more of the country than the great majority of his subjects. Schools, industrial establishments, objects of antiquarian or historical interest, will all receive attentive examination. The object of such progresses as this is not mere pleasure-seeking. Indeed, in many cases, a journey into the interior, even with all the luxuries of Majesty, must be quite the reverse of a pleasure. It is doubtless the desire of His Majesty and of his ministers that he should be acquainted, by personal observation, with the condition of the country over which he rules, and thereby fit himself more and more for the duties of the august station which he occupies.[15]

This is probably what the emperor himself and the members of the government believed at the time, although recent scholars have interpreted the progresses in terms of their effectiveness in building an imposing image of the emperor and causing the populace to think of him not simply as a benevolent ruler who wished to know the conditions under which his subjects lived but as an overseer whose unwavering gaze was fastened on their lives.[16]

The emperor set out as planned on June 16, 1880. He was accompanied by a retinue of 360 people, including Prince Sadanaru, the prime minister Sanjō Sanetomi, a councillor, a minister, high-ranking military officers, the minister of the imperial household, chamberlains, a court physician, mounted officers and men, foot soldiers, grooms, and so on. This was a large retinue by our standards, and it was augmented by local security agents wherever he went, but it was by no means large by Japanese standards of that time. Even on quite ordinary occasions, the emperor was accompanied by a large number of attendants,[17] and it is unlikely that people who saw the progress pass were stunned by its numbers or magnificence.

The first stop was at Hachiōji, where the emperor examined such local products as silk thread and material. He was offered fireflies from a nearby river that were forwarded to the empress dowager and the empress. The latter responded with a poem that suggested both her loneliness and the comfort the gift had brought.

The journey was far easier than the progress of 1878 to Niigata and the Hokuriku Provinces, but it was hardly a royal progress in European style. On June 18, for example, the emperor rose at four in the morning and was carried off in the rain over twisted mountain paths. He traveled all that day, sometimes in a sedan chair, sometimes in a horse-pulled carriage, reaching his destination at Sasago after five that afternoon. His quarters that night were no better than a ramshackle hut, for the village offered no more suitable accommodations.[18]

One new note was struck on this journey: whenever the emperor passed through beautiful scenery, he asked a photographer to take pictures. Later on, the emperor told the photographer not to wait for his command but to take pictures wherever the scenery was particularly beautiful. This was one way the emperor would have of recalling the sights he had passed.

The summer heat made the journey anything but a pleasure excursion. The emperor, as usual, inspected schools, factories, and (in Yamanashi Prefecture) a wine distillery. In Kōfu he visited a hospital founded in 1872 where he saw an exhibition of the more than twenty varieties of insects vomited by a girl suffering from some strange disease. He also examined the mummy of the priest Myōshin, who had died about fifty years earlier.[19]

In Kuwana the progress was greeted by particularly enthusiastic crowds, even though Kuwana had been one of the domains that held out longest against the imperial forces in the struggle between court and shogunate fourteen years earlier. The emperor observed a chemistry experiment conducted by two prize pupils at the teachers' training school in Tsu and later listened at the middle school to five pupils deliver lectures on the history of the world.

On July 8, although the weather was extremely hot, the emperor put on his dress uniform and, carrying the sword and jewel, went to worship at the Inner and Outer Shrines in Ise. The emperor, going first to the Outer Shrine, washed his hands, and then passed through the *tamagaki* (shrine fence) to the *hama-yuka*, a platform erected at the foot of the stairs of the sanctuary. He removed his hat and, in an attitude of deepest reverence, bowed in worship. Later he went to the Inner Shrine where an identical ceremony took place. The order of his visits to the two shrines was apparently based on the belief that Toyouke no ōkami, the goddess of agriculture, was fundamental to all existence. But experts in Shintō lore, learning of the proposed order of worship, insisted that he go first to the shrine of Amaterasu-ōmikami, the foundress of the imperial line. Their protest was rejected, and the emperor followed the precedent established in 1869 when, on his first visit to Ise, he worshiped first at the Outer Shrine.[20]

The weather was so hot when the progress reached Kameyama that the emperor rose at 3 A.M. to profit by the relative cool of early morning. He left his quarters at 5:30 A.M. to observe military maneuvers near Yokkaichi. The next day he rose at 2:30 A.M. and went on horseback to observe maneuvers between Kameyama and Seki. It has been justly said that Meiji liked nothing better than observing maneuvers.

The last stage of the journey, from Ōtsu to Kyōto, was by train. This was made possible by the new railway tunnel through the mountains east of Kyōto, the first such tunnel in Japan. No doubt the emperor was glad to be back in Kyōto, but disappointingly little is recorded concerning his activities. On July 15, the day after his arrival, he granted an audience to various high-ranking dignitaries, including Buddhist priests. He contributed 100 yen to the rebuilding of the Bukkō-ji, a temple burned during the fighting in 1864. On the sixteenth he visited the Sennyū-ji, the site of his father's tomb. On his way back, he stopped at the Myōhō-in and inspected its treasures. The attention the emperor gave to Buddhist temples was not surprising in Kyōto, a city full of temples; but it contrasted with the anti-Buddhist measures of the early years of his reign and indicated that the persecution had ended.

The moment that may have most affected the emperor during his stay in Kyōto was when, on the way to visit his aunt, Princess Sumiko, he stopped to look at the Sachi no i, the well dug in Nakayama Tadayasu's garden during the drought of 1853. Emperor Kōmei, pleased by the abundance of good water, had given the well the name Sachi, Meiji's childhood name.[21]

When the emperor arrived at the princess's residence, he gave her two cloisonné boxes, one containing confetti from Yamada in Ise, and the other rock candy from Ōsaka. The unpretentious nature of these gifts is endearing. The princess had arranged a program of five nō and four *kyōgen* to divert the emperor. The performance was attended also by members of the nobility still living in the old capital, a momentary revival of their former glory.

The rest of the emperor's journey passed without incident. From Kyōto he proceeded to Kōbe, from where he sailed to Yokohama, reaching Tōkyō on July 23. After a few weeks of recuperating from his journey, on August 16 he summoned the ministers and councillors to discuss the advisability of collecting peasants' land rents in rice rather than in cash. The various ministries had failed to reduce expenses, despite the government's injunctions, and the leaders were obliged to search for another way to redress the financial crisis. They concluded that the crisis had resulted from collecting rent on farm land in cash, and their solution was to revert to the old custom of collecting rent from the peasants in rice. The chief proponent of this policy was Councillor Ōki Takatō (1832–1899).

Proponents argued that the sudden general rise in prices could be attributed to the sharply higher price of rice, which had affected all other commodity prices. If the government received payments in rice, it would be able to control the price, for when the price was high, it would sell the rice it had stored, and when it was low, it would buy rice, thereby maintaining the price at an acceptable level. They noted without pleasure that the high prices paid for rice had brought such prosperity to the villages that farmers had begun to indulge in luxuries. Farmers were now buying costly imports, which hurt Japanese industry.

Kuroda Kiyotaka, one of the strongest proponents of a change in method of payment, pointed out that in the past, farmers were content with coarse grains, but now they ate rice as their staple food. The financial crisis had arisen because the sale of rice was left entirely to the farmers. Accordingly, they should be required to pay at least part of their rent in rice, which the government could use to keep the price stable.

The councillors were divided on the issue. On August 16 the prime minister and the minister of the left visited the palace to explain the proposal. They said that a decision by the emperor himself was the only way of breaking the impasse and suggested that representatives of both factions discuss the issue in his presence.[22]

On August 31 Iwakura proposed an eleven-point program for rescuing Japan from its financial crisis. The first point, which he considered to be the most important, provided that one-quarter of the rents be paid in rice. He deplored the tendency of even the humblest farmers, the beneficiaries of higher prices for rice, to shun other grains and eat rice themselves. This meant that there was not enough rice for the samurai, merchants, or artisans, necessitating its import. The farmers' newly acquired taste for luxury items had caused an increase in the demand for cotton cloth, sugar, coal, cooking oil, and the like. The farmers had also become lazy, a sign portending a decline in agriculture. They should return to their old ways and eat coarse grains, and when that happened, Japan, instead of importing rice, would become an exporter.[23]

The callousness of Iwakura and his supporters was not only surprising but shocking in their implicit rejection of the Confucian adage (to which all paid lip service) that agriculture is the foundation of a nation. Even if they now ate rice, the farmers were surely less extravagant than the Tōkyō officials,[24] but the latter deplored any improvement in the standard of living of the poorest class of society. The advice offered to the supposedly indolent farmers paraphrased Marie Antoinette: "Let them eat sorghum!"

Not all officials were won over by this promise of an easy solution to the financial crisis. Sasaki Takayuki, urging the importance of strict economy for all classes of society, blamed the upper classes for the taste for luxury now exhibited by the peasants: "They hear about the extravagant and frivolous ways of upper-class society, and they mistakenly suppose that this is what is meant by culture and freedom; in that way the whole country has come to imitate them [the upper classes]."[25]

Meiji's eventual decision to reject the councillors' recommendation that rents be collected in rice from the farmers was probably influenced by Sasaki and Motoda, both Confucianists.[26] He also benefited from the advice of Itō Hirobumi, with whom he discussed the matter of rice payments on September

15.[27] Itō seems to have realized that his only chance to overcome Iwakura's advocacy of the rice tax was by enlisting the emperor's support.

On September 18 the emperor summoned the ministers and gave them a rescript in which, though expressing appreciation for their efforts to resolve the financial crisis, he declared unambiguously his opposition to what he termed an "extremely alarming" plan. The only solution to the crisis was, as he had said many times, to practice strict economy, and he enjoined the councillors to consider ways of implementing his wishes.

Before issuing the rescript, the emperor had privately revealed to Sasaki and Motoda his opposition to the plan. He was sure that imposing a rice tax would cause extreme resentment by the farmers and that no region of the country would be immune to their rebellions. He noted in particular that it had been publicly announced in May 1880 that rents (in money) had been fixed until 1885. If they abrogated this declaration and returned to the old system of payment in rice, the public would lose confidence. This indeed was the chief reason not to revert to payments in rice.[28]

The third problem that faced Meiji at this time concerned the creation of a parliament and a constitution. In the first of the five oaths he swore at the beginning of his reign, he had promised that a legislative body would be created in which measures would be decided after open discussion. Regardless of the context in which the oaths were proclaimed in 1868, by this time they had acquired the character of an imperial promise that a parliament would be created and would operate within the framework of a constitution.

This was not the first time that the government had considered writing a constitution. As far back as May 1872 a member of the Sa'in, Miyajima Seiichirō (1838–1911), had urged that a constitution be drawn up defining the powers of the ruler. He believed this was necessary because, having learned of the polity of other countries, "ignorant people" were insisting on their rights in the name of individual freedom; some were even calling for a republic. Under present conditions, it was difficult to know how to deal with such people, but once the powers of the ruler were clearly defined by a constitution, anyone trespassing on them could be punished by law. Miyajima insisted that he did not favor a constitution that prescribed one-man government by the ruler; this would be oppressive to the people and would hamper modernization. The ideal solution would be joint rule by the sovereign and the people, but the level of education was still so low it was unlikely the people possessed the necessary intelligence to elect suitable representatives. So, Miyajima concluded, the sovereign should personally draw up a constitution but take into account the principle of joint rule. This proposal was forwarded to the Sei'in,[29] and preparations began for writing a constitution.

In June 1872 Gotō Shōjirō (1838–1897), the president of the Sa'in, and Ijichi Masaharu (1824–1886), the vice president, jointly proposed the creation of a lower house (*kagi-in*) as provided for in the Oath in Five Articles. Unless there were two houses—the upper house representing the nobles and samurai and the lower house, the common people—there could be no budget or even a foundation for the laws. The lower house, modeled on those in Europe and America, should serve as a forum where open discussions and public opinion could be heard. Although the Sa'in approved, it postponed acting on the proposal until the following year.

In 1873 the emperor commanded the Sa'in to draft a constitution that would serve as the foundation of the nation and provide the essentials of government. The Oath in Five Articles might, of course, be described as a constitution for all ages, but it also was necessary to have a constitution that would serve as the basic law of the land.

Little progress was made despite the general agreement that a constitution was desirable. In September 1876 the emperor sent a message to the Genrō-in commanding the members to prepare a rough draft that, though faithful to Japanese traditions, would benefit from the study of the constitutions of other countries.[30]

Soon afterward Prince Taruhito, the president of the Genrō-in, was appointed by the emperor to frame a first draft. He and the committee he appointed completed a draft in October. Despite the leisurely pace with which the draft had been compiled, it was evidently much discussed. General Grant, who arrived in Japan a year later, observed in his conversation with Meiji that "the theme now so popularly advocated by the press and some of the people of this country seems to be that of Elective Assembly." He offered these comments:

I do not know whether the proper time for it has come or not. But such assemblies are very good for all countries in due time. . . . An assembly will have to be established in this country sooner or later, and therefore the government ought to hold out to the people this idea, and educate them to the fact that in due time such an assembly shall be established for them. The people shall know that it is coming and they should be educating themselves for the responsibility. But you must always remember that privileges like this can never be recalled. When you give suffrage and representation you give them forever. Consequently in establishing such an assembly too great caution can not be taken. It is exceedingly dangerous to launch out too suddenly. You do not want to see anarchy as the result of any premature creation of an assembly.[31]

Coming from the former president of a country that was proud of its democratic traditions, these views struck a responsive chord among Japanese statesmen. Yamagata, a conservative military man and statesman, strongly favored a constitution and a legislative body, and in August 1880 Iwakura Tomomi, another conservative, proposed to the emperor the creation of an office for examining constitutions. It was rather late in the day for such a proposal, but

Iwakura evidently had decided that the time had come for implementing the provisions of the emperor's Oath in Five Articles:

> At the very outset of his reign, His Majesty intuitively grasped the world situation, and he swore in five articles that he would effect extraordinary reforms. In this manner he greatly enhanced the imperial rule and initiated the glorious achievements of the Restoration. All state affairs since then have been carried out in accordance with his oath.[32]

Iwakura went on to propose the compilation of a constitution, but first, he insisted, the constitutions of all European countries should be examined in detail, so that there would be no flaws in the Japanese constitution.

The caution with which Iwakura made his proposal suggested that his real object may have been to postpone action, but Itō Hirobumi, a more progressive man, was no less cautious. His superior knowledge of European history enabled him to give more positive reasons than Iwakura's why Japan should possess a constitution.

Itō pointed out that the influence of the French Revolution had by now been felt in every other country, sometimes resulting in a rejection of the past and a commitment to distinctly new ways and sometimes even leading to disorder. Some enlightened rulers anticipated changes without waiting for a revolution. But however the influence of the French Revolution made itself felt, no country has been able to escape the assumption that the ruler must share power with the people. European books, with their new theories of government, had flooded into Japan, reaching the remotest hamlet. Itō declared that there was no way to check the new concept of government.

He offered specific proposals concerning the future composition of a bicameral parliament, with the upper house to be composed of nobles and samurai and the lower house, of common people. He believed that it was extremely desirable for the sovereign and people to share the rule, but he insisted that changes not be made hastily. Itō was particularly desirous that the emperor take an active part in all deliberations.[33]

The draft constitution on which Prince Taruhito had begun to work in 1876 was not presented until December 1880, and the prince envisaged a further long period of study of other countries' constitutions.[34]

Prince Taruhito's draft constitution contained no note of urgency. Like Iwakura, Itō, and others, he seems to have considered that a gradual approach to democracy was better than prompt action. But many people felt otherwise. In April 1880, at a convention in Ōsaka, members of the Aikoku-sha (Society of Patriots) passed a resolution calling for the convening of an assembly and spread word of this decision throughout the country. In March, delegates from twenty-four prefectures met in Ōsaka and adopted as its name The League for Establishing a National Assembly.[35]

The league attempted to present a petition to the emperor asking for the convening of an assembly. Although frustrated by the government and the Genrō-in, the attempt was not without effect. Iwakura, who had insisted that changes must be gradual, suddenly began to urge speed in creating a constitution. His haste was occasioned by fears, aroused by the petition, of possible danger to the imperial household if no action was taken.[36] In December 1880 the league decided to form a political party, the Jiyū-tō (Freedom Party). The struggle of this and similar parties to create a national assembly lasted through the 1880s.

Chapter 34

The year 1881 was one of the most eventful years of Meiji's reign. It opened calmly with the emperor's ritual worship of the four directions, but changes were soon apparent even in the New Year ceremonies. He and the empress accepted congratulations both from the princes of the blood and high-ranking officers and from their wives. Later that day, the ministers of foreign countries, also accompanied for the first time by their wives, paid their respects.

No reason was given for the change, but presumably it reflected Japanese diplomats' knowledge of European court usages. The change immediately aroused problems. If Japanese women were to attend court on such an important occasion, what would be the appropriate attire? It was eventually decided that they should wear a trailing outer robe (*uchikake*) and trousers (*hakama*), but diplomats' wives who did not own these items of formal Japanese dress would be permitted to wear foreign clothes. Next, what should be the relative positions of husband and wife when advancing toward the throne? Should the wife trail behind the husband, as was customary when a Japanese wife accompanied her husband? It was decided that the couple should advance together, the husband on the right and the wife on the left, although left usually took precedence over right. These and similar decisions were not lightly reached. The officials in charge of protocol were creating traditions that would govern etiquette at the court for many years to come.

Sasaki Takayuki, one of the men closest to the emperor at this time, described the change in these terms:

This year for the first time husbands and wives offered New Year congratulations to the emperor. Most of the wives, however, stayed away. Foreigners think of participating in such ceremonies as a great honor, but people of our country have quite different reactions. Wives either actively dislike such experiences or avoid them because of unfamiliarity. Again, in foreign countries they do not allow women who were originally performers or prostitutes to mingle in upper-class society, not even if they are legal wives. Their practice, which I find admirable, is to look down on such women and not permit them ever to appear in public gatherings. In our country, too, this was the custom before the Restoration, but at the time of the Restoration many women of base birth became consorts of important men in the government, and this unfortunate practice has continued to this day. It is natural, then, that some people argue that it is inappropriate for such women to offer congratulations to the emperor. It is essential today that we revert to our former, admirable ways.[1]

The emperor presumably approved of this change in the ceremonies, but he refused to accept others. For example, when Foreign Minister Inoue Kaoru proposed that foreign diplomats, being guests, be permitted to pay their respects to the emperor ahead of Japanese, he did not approve. He replied that the central meaning of the reception of officials at the beginning of the year was to affirm the correct relationship between lord and vassals and that it was therefore proper for Japanese officials to pay their respects ahead of foreign visitors, even though normally, as guests, they would come first.[2]

On January 3 the emperor rode horseback. In the previous year he went riding 144 times, but this year he went only fifty-four times, an indication of the increasing demands on his time. In 1881 he attended sixty-six cabinet meetings, usually remaining from 10 A.M. to noon each time. On January 10, three days later than normal,[3] the emperor and empress heard their first lecture of the year, delivered by Motoda Nagazane on the mythical Chinese emperors Yao and Shun. Soejima Taneomi and Nishimura Shigeki also delivered lectures regularly during the remainder of the year, but whether because of the press of official duties or because the emperor had lost interest in Confucian wisdom, only seventeen were delivered in 1881.[4]

On January 5 foreign diplomats were invited for the first time to the traditional New Year banquet at the palace, another example of the court's willingness to accommodate itself to foreign usage. On this occasion the serving dishes, previously of pewter, were of silver, no doubt in honor of the foreign guests, although a policy of strict economy was still in effect.

Beginning this year, Meiji had regular luncheon meetings on Wednesdays and Saturdays with princes of the blood, ministers, councillors, and other high-ranking officials, evidence of his increased interest in running the government. Sometimes he chose these sessions to express personal opinions, although previously he had been hardly more than a mute witness. For example, on January 29, after the Saturday luncheon had ended, he called Sasaki Takayuki to his study and asked about the new penal law ending the death penalty. The new law was supposed to go into effect on July 1. In that case, asked the emperor, was it not true that quite a few criminals who had already been sentenced to death would (if not executed by that date) escape their sentences? He asked the opinion of Justice Minister Tanaka Fujimaro, who expressed the hope that the execution of criminals according to the old penal code would be delayed by special order until July when the death penalty was abolished—in other words, that there would be no further executions. The emperor felt that if the aim was to end executions, the people who framed the new law should have said so at the start. It would be highly irregular suddenly to issue special stays of execution. Either executions should be carried out in accordance with the present law, or when the verdict of death was passed on to a higher authority, the official in charge should delay acting on it until July and then administer the punishment prescribed by the new law. The emperor added that the trouble had arisen because of the haste with which the new penal code had been proclaimed. The haste was unavoidable in terms of the eagerness to revise the treaties with foreign powers—a lessening of the severity of punishments was likely to impress foreigners favorably—but the new penal code could not escape the charge of having been compiled carelessly.[5]

The particular issue that disturbed the emperor may not appear of major significance, but his active concern over a legal matter indicated a new maturity. It is noteworthy also that Sasaki did not hesitate later in the conversation to consult the emperor concerning the need to make changes in the Genrō-in, as divisions of opinion among the various factions had impeded its functions. The emperor answered with not only surprising frankness but also a confidence that indicated that although he had not spoken at cabinet meetings, he had formed opinions of the issues and politicians involved.

The emperor was not, however, so absorbed by politics that he forgot other diversions. In February 1881 he suddenly developed a passion for rabbit hunting. He always refused to escape the extremes of Tōkyō climate by going away during the winter or summer. When his advisers urged him to take a vacation, he would reply, "I will do what the majority of my people do," meaning that he did not feel free to escape cold or heat when he knew that most Japanese were busy at their places of work, regardless of the temperature.

Virtually the only exceptions he made to this refusal to travel for pleasure were the four times he went to the Tama area to shoot rabbits. At the time the region was scantily populated, and there were many more rabbits to shoot than at the Fukiage or the Akasaka Palace grounds, where hunts had earlier been conducted. The emperor liked to hunt until dark, and it was feared that he might have trouble finding his way back along the badly lit paths in Tama. People were ordered to put torches outside their houses to light his way. One night, after returning to his quarters in Fuchū, he mentioned he had noticed on the way a torch that proved to be a bamboo broom on fire. He asked people to find out who had put out the burning broom. It proved to be an old woman who lived alone and was so poor she had nothing but the broom to burn. The emperor summoned the woman and, praising her unselfish action, rewarded her.[6]

On February 23 the emperor had word from John Bingham, the American minister, that King Kalakaua of Hawaii would be arriving in Japan on a round-the-world journey. The king would be traveling incognito, but he had some state business to transact: he wished to encourage Japanese migration to Hawaii and to sign a treaty with the Japanese government. He was accordingly treated as a state visitor, and Prince Yoshiaki was appointed as the commissioner for the visit. Two other officials were charged with entertaining the king.

Kalakaua arrived in Yokohama on March 4. He was greeted with twenty-one-gun salutes by Japanese and foreign warships anchored in the bay. When the boat sent by the Japanese to take the Hawaiians from the *Oceanic* to their hotel touched shore, they heard the Hawaiian national anthem, played with explosive vigor by a Japanese military band. They were astonished that the Japanese musicians had learned the anthem of so remote and unimportant a country.[7] The king and the others of his retinue, touched, were all but in tears. Along the way to the palace where they were to stay, they noticed that the houses of Yokohama were decorated with crossed Japanese and Hawaiian flags. The king and his party were stunned by the welcome.

Kalakaua traveled to Tōkyō the next day aboard the imperial train and, after receiving an official reception at Shimbashi Station, proceeded directly to the Akasaka Palace. The emperor, following the etiquette of European courts that requires a monarch to receive a visiting monarch at the threshold of his palace, went to a room close to the entrance of the palace to meet his royal visitor. He was resplendent in a dress uniform studded with medals. The two monarchs shook hands. The Hawaiians, having been informed that the emperor normally did not shake hands, interpreted the gesture as a special honor. The two monarchs, after exchanging formal greetings, walked side by side into an interior room. W. N. Armstrong, the king's chamberlain and the chronicler of his journey around the world, had heard that because of his divine origin, the emperor had never before permitted anyone to walk by his side; even the empress followed him. "But, for the first time in his own reign, and in those of his predecessors, he walked by the side of his kingly guest."[8]

The empress was waiting for the royal visitor in the audience chamber. Meiji presented Kalakaua to the empress. "She did not rise, but returned the king's salutation with the least movement of her head and eyes." Sueko, the daughter of Inoue Kaoru, who had spent several years in England, served as her interpreter. (Armstrong wrote that she spoke perfect English.) Refreshments were served, but the Hawaiians, having been previously informed that they should not eat in the presence of the emperor, declined them.

The emperor was tall for a Japanese of that time, but Kalakaua was a giant of man. He was unusually dark for a Hawaiian, and this made the emperor, who was of a swarthy complexion, look much lighter. Earlier descriptions of Meiji's face by foreign visitors had always noted the prominent jaw, but it was now concealed by his beard. Armstrong mentioned instead the unusually high forehead and, above all, the eyes, which were black and penetrating; they seemed to say that he was not "one who would put himself entirely in the hands of his Ministers."[9]

The two monarchs chatted for some twenty minutes until the king, rather overwhelmed by the reception, decided it was time to leave. The emperor saw him off as far as the threshold. Kalakaua and his party left for the Enryōkan, the building at the Hama Detached Palace where foreign dignitaries were lodged. Later, the emperor, conforming to the rule of European etiquette that a monarch's visit must be returned within an hour, called on the Hawaiians, who had taken off their heavy uniforms and were relaxing in their underwear.

Kalakaua originally intended to spend only three days in Japan, but Foreign Minister Inoue Kaoru, believing that this first visit to Japan of a foreign monarch should be commemorated in some way, sent word that the emperor was planning various events, including "a grand ball in the palace, which, it was intimated, would be the most notable given since the new order of things was established; there would also be a grand review of the imperial troops, special theatrical exhibitions and other entertainments."[10] The king at once postponed his departure, expressing deep appreciation of the emperor's kindness. He also asked Armstrong, the legal expert in his suite, to inform Inoue that he would at once consent to abrogating the extraterritoriality clause in the treaty between Japan and Hawaii. Inoue, delighted, said that it "would give the emperor and the people of Japan unbounded pleasure."

Hawaii was only a small country, but even so, this crack in the wall of extraterritoriality was highly welcome to the Japanese. When informed of this action, the American minister approved of what had been done, but the instrument abrogating the old treaty was not executed, "owing to the strenuous remonstrances of the European governments." It required another seventeen years before the humiliating clause was removed from all the treaties.[11]

On March 11 the king, at his request, had a private interview with the emperor. After refreshments were served, all the Japanese officials with the exception of Inoue Kaoru, who served as the interpreter, withdrew. Kalakaua stated that he planned to have his coronation in the following year. He asked that the emperor send a delegation, and Meiji consented.

Kalakaua moved then to a matter that demanded secrecy: "The purpose of my travels this time has been to promote something that has been on my mind for many years, a league of the countries of Asia. The European countries make it their policy to think only of themselves. They never consider what harm they may cause other countries or what difficulties they may cause other people. Their countries tend to work together and cooperate when it comes to strategy in dealing with the countries of the East. The countries of the Orient, on the other hand, are mutually isolated and do not help one another. They have no strategy for dealing with the European countries. This is one reason why the rights and benefits of the countries of the East are today in the hands of the European countries. Consequently, it is imperative for the countries of the East to form a league to maintain the status quo in the East, in this way opposing the European countries. The time for action has come."

Meiji replied, "The general situation in Europe and Asia is indeed as you describe it. I share your opinion concerning a league of the countries of the East. But how can you be sure that the time for action is now?"

The king continued, "Up to the present the countries of the East have suffered under the oppression of every one of the European countries. I have come to realize that the time has arrived for us to act boldly. That is what I mean when I say now is the time to put this great plan into effect."

The emperor asked, "I would like to know more about your plan."

The king replied, "During my trip I intend to meet with the rulers of China, Siam, India, Persia, and other countries and to discuss with them the advantages and disadvantages of forming a league. However, my country is a tiny cluster of islands and its population is insignificant; it lacks the strength to carry out a great plan. Your country is exactly as I have heard—not only has your progress been truly astonishing, but the people are numerous and of a hardy disposition. That is why, if a league of the countries of Asia is to be initiated, Your Majesty must step forward and be its leader. I will serve Your Majesty as his vassal and devote my every energy to the cause. If Your Majesty becomes the head of the league and works to carry out its purpose, it will surely compel the European countries to abandon extraterritoriality. Just by chance, an exposition is to be held in New York in 1883. Your Majesty should take this opportunity to travel to America. You should also dispatch princes of the blood as secret envoys to the European countries and have them persuade the ruler of each country to meet in New York on the occasion of the exposition. If you directly address the rulers who attend the exposition on the urgent need to end extraterritoriality, this is certain to be effective. Then, after you return to your country, you should open an exposition to which the rulers of the countries of Asia and Europe are invited. In short, the end of extraterritoriality and the success or failure of the league of oriental countries depends on whether or not Your Majesty is willing to serve as head of the league."

The emperor said, "I understand your point of view. However, a country like China is big and arrogant in its ways. Even if invited, it is most unlikely to join."

The king replied, "It is too much to hope that the rulers of the countries of

Asia will, without exception, join. However, I am certain that the king of Siam, the king of Persia, and various kings of India will attend. This will be enough to get the league started. But a plan of this nature is not to be perfected in two or three meetings. I should mention that the invitations you extend to the rulers of European countries to the exposition in your country will be in order to avoid offending them. Of course, you will discuss matters close to your heart only with the rulers of the Asian countries. If Your Majesty has, to my good fortune, accepted my words, I would like to ask Your Majesty to bestow on me his ring."[12]

After some thought, the emperor responded, "I understand your views. However, the progress of my country is not what it may seem on the outside. There are many problems, especially with respect to China. The Chinese always consider that our country intends to commit aggression. It is difficult enough to maintain peaceful relations with China, and to do what you propose would be even more difficult. I will confer with my cabinet and after mature consideration give you my reply."

The king accepted this decision, and the conversation ended after an hour and twenty minutes. As he was leaving, the king offered the emperor a photograph of himself and a book describing the political situation in Hawaii. He also presented a photograph of his queen to the empress.[13]

During his conversation with Meiji, the king brought up two other matters. First was the need for a underwater cable linking Japan and Hawaii in order to expand communication between the two countries. Finally, he earnestly asked that his niece Kaiulani (then five years old) be accepted as the bride of Prince Sadamaro.[14] The king had been taken with Sadamaro, a sixteen-year-old student at the naval academy who had been in his escort, and decided he would make a good husband for his niece. Kalakaua, who had no children, had already decided that Kaiulani would be his successor. If his proposal had been accepted, the husband of the future queen of Hawaii would have been a Japanese. Kalakaua probably hoped this would protect Hawaii from annexation by the United States; conversely, the Japanese government may have feared that the marriage would antagonize not only America but the European powers. Answers to these two requests were not immediately forthcoming, but both were rejected in a letter sent to Kalakaua by Inoue Kaoru on February 10, 1882.[15]

Kalakaua was absolutely delighted with the reception he had received in Japan, far exceeding his expectations. Although he was a Christian, he was deeply impressed by the Buddhist temples, finding them much more to his taste than the austere New England–style churches built in Hawaii, and he told his chamberlain to look into the possibility of introducing Buddhism to Hawaii. He was disappointed only that the promised grand ball had to be canceled owing to the assassination of the czar of Russia, which required the Japanese imperial family to go into mourning.

According to Armstrong's account, in which he did not hesitate to mock his master, Kalakaua was not a wise or even thoughtful man, and his attention was easily diverted. This is what makes his plan of a league of the countries of Asia so surprising: it suggests that he had greater political insight than anyone in Hawaii suspected. But like almost everything else he proposed while in Japan, Kalakaua's plan was, in the end, rejected.[16] It was obvious to Meiji that even if a league of Asian countries were formed, the Chinese would never consent to its being headed by a Japanese. And although it was easy to speak of Siam, India, and Persia in terms of their sharing an Asian heritage, their languages and customs were not related, and it would be difficult to find anything uniting them except resentment over the aggression of the occidental countries.[17]

On March 14 when Kalakaua was about to leave Tōkyō, he called on the emperor, who personally pinned on the king the Grand Order of the Chrysanthemum, the highest Japanese decoration. He also bestowed the usual farewell presents—cloisonné flower vases, brocade, lacquer boxes, embroidery, and so on. The empress sent two lengths of white silk crepe to the queen of Hawaii.[18]

King Kalakaua's visit was certainly less important to Emperor Meiji than that of General Grant. Nothing ever came of Kalakaua's plans for a league of Asian nations, and the other proposals he made during his secret meeting with the emperor were soon forgotten. But in terms of Meiji's development as a statesman, the meeting was of considerable significance. During his conversation with Grant, his utterances had been confined to brief, noncommittal remarks, but when answering Kalakaua, he spoke with assurance and revealed that he was informed about the conditions prevailing in eastern Asia. Perhaps his self-confidence owed something to his feelings of superiority to the ruler of a few small islands whose army numbered seventy-five men, but he treated Kalakaua with faultless courtesy. In contrast to the inarticulate boy of ten years earlier, Meiji had become an imposing figure who deeply impressed his visitors.

Meiji had two more royal visitors later in 1881, Prince Albert Victor and Prince George, the sons of the future Edward VII of England, who arrived in Yokohama on October 21 aboard HMS *Bacchante*. They went by train to Tōkyō and then by carriage to the Enryōkan, where they were to stay. The account of their stay in Japan states that their first visit was to Asakusa, where they went by jinrikisha. No doubt the two young men had heard reports of this pleasure quarter and wished to examine it for themselves. That night at dinner they were visited by Sanjō Sanetomi and Iwakura Tomomi, and the emperor sent his "private band" to play for them during the meal. Prince George's reaction was: "The sounds that proceeded from the inner-room where these musicians were placed were so faint and plaintive that some of the party ignorantly mistook them for preparations of a band tuning up, and as it went on for some time inquired when they were going to begin to play."[19]

The two princes called on the emperor the next day. They wrote about him, "Although he is not thirty years old . . . he has a much aged look about the face. He is self-possessed and evidently strenuously anxious, though not nervous, to play his part well."[20] Judging from this description, the emperor was much less at ease than he had been with King Kalakaua. Even though the princes were still very young—the older eighteen and the younger sixteen—they came from the most powerful country in the world, and the emperor may have felt it necessary to produce an impression of age.

The princes were obviously more attracted to the empress. George (later George V) wrote, "She is very small and would be very pretty if she was not painted up so according to Japanese fashion." She attempted "in cheerful and genial manner" to begin a conversation. The older prince asked her to accept two wallabies that they had brought from Australia. "These were great pets with all aboard, as they went hopping and frisking and booming about at meal hours all over the decks, as wild as hawks." The empress seemed pleased with the gift, and the wallabies were sent off the next day to the palace. It is hard to imagine the wallabies hopping and frisking about the palace. It is equally hard to imagine George V, whose grave, bearded face became familiar to stamp collectors during the quarter century of his reign, asking a Japanese tattooer to decorate his arms: "He does a large dragon in blue and red writhing all down the arm in about three hours."[21]

On October 31 the princes invited the emperor to lunch aboard the *Bacchante*. Accompanied by three princes of the blood, Iwakura Tomomi, Inoue Kaoru, and various other dignitaries, the emperor went to the ship, greeted by salutes from the Kanagawa gun batteries and the vessels, both Japanese and foreign, in the harbor. He was treated aboard ship to an exhibition of torpedo firing.[22] The English princes sailed for Kōbe the next day and subsequently spent more than a week sightseeing in Kyōto, Nara, Ōsaka, and elsewhere in the Kansai region.

Earlier, on July 31, the emperor set out on another imperial tour, this time to Yamagata, Akita, and Hokkaidō. Some 420 men were to accompany him on his progress, but because of the inadequate lodgings en route, the number was reduced to 350.[23] The journey was comparatively uneventful, though the summer heat was broiling. The emperor often spent the night at elementary classes, in part because they were big enough to accommodate his large party, and also because this confirmed his abiding interest in education.[24] As usual, he visited classes wherever he went. He was surely pleased when in Tsuruoka a middle-school honor student gave a talk on the Chinese classic *Tso Chuan*, followed by an elementary-school pupil who discussed *Nihon shiryaku*.[25] Word seems to have spread that the emperor did not like to hear pupils delivering talks on ancient Rome.

Despite the extreme heat, there were splendid views to admire, displays of local products and antiques, and crowds lining the roads along which the emperor's carriage or palanquin passed. The *junkō* to the north was marked by one new feature, the marked improvement in communications. News reached the emperor not only from other parts of Japan but from the entire world. He was kept informed by telegraph, for example, of the illness and death of his aunt, Princess Sumiko, in Kyōto. He also learned almost immediately of the death of President James A. Garfield on September 19; two days later, he sent a telegram of condolence to Garfield's successor, Chester Alan Arthur.

The most important news the emperor received during the journey, however, related to a scandal that broke at this time. On August 21 Prince Yoshiaki, greatly upset over the public outcry aroused by revelations concerning the sale of properties belonging to the Hokkaidō Development Office, sent a letter to Prince Taruhito, who was then with the emperor in Saitama Prefecture, summarizing the situation. He stated that Kuroda Kiyotaka, the director of the Development Office, had been angered by the sudden announcement that Hokkaidō would become a prefecture. He told various high-ranking officials that the present development of Hokkaidō had been entirely due to his efforts and that the proper thing would have been to allow him to make decisions concerning the end of the office and the creation of a prefecture. He said that if this advice was accepted, he would at once announce support for ending the office. The officials consented. Thereupon Kuroda asked permission to sell properties of the Development Office to a samurai of the former Satsuma domain named Godai Tomoatsu (1834–1885), who while serving in the office, had founded a trading company in Ōsaka.[26]

The cabinet did not immediately approve Kuroda's request, arguing that in view of the emperor's forthcoming visit to Hokkaidō, a decision should be postponed until he had visited the site. The decision enraged Kuroda, who screamed imprecations at a certain high-ranking official, threw a candlestick at him, and completely lost control of himself.

On the day of his departure on the *junkō* to the north, the emperor had consented to the planned sale in accordance with the decision made in the previous year to sell factories, mines, and other governmental properties to private entrepreneurs. When, however, details of the plan—assets worth about 3 million yen were to be sold for 300,000 yen, payable in thirty years without interest—became known, there was a great outcry from the newspapers and advocates of people's rights. The fact that both Kuroda and Godai were from Satsuma made the proposed sale seem all the more suspicious.

Prince Yoshiaki, believing that he could no longer keep silent, decided to ask for an audience with the emperor while he was still on his *junkō*. He sent for Sasaki Takayuki and Hijikata Hisamoto (1833–1918), an official of the Interior Ministry, and asked them to accompany him. He said that he had never expressed political views to the emperor and was afraid that he would not be able to convince him. He was sure he would have a better chance of success if they, two men trusted by the emperor, accompanied him. But they thought it better that they not go. They believed that the emperor detested artifice and that the prince's best plan was to report the truth straightforwardly.[27] Yoshiaki, accepting this judgment, went to Saitama and informed the emperor.

But perhaps the emperor knew already. According to the newspapers, he had learned a month earlier (while in Hokkaidō) of the public's reaction to the proposed sale from a Household Ministry official who traveled all the way to Hakodate to inform him of the commotion that the sale had aroused. The emperor was also said to have read a newspaper article reporting that Satsuma politicians had joined forces to get rid of a certain councillor. He correctly guessed that the intended victim was Ōkuma.

Meiji returned to the Akasaka Temporary Palace on October 11. He sent for Motoda Nagazane, who urged him to dismiss Ōkuma immediately. He said that Ōkuma's recommendation that a parliament be immediately convened had aroused conflicting emotions and seemed likely to lead to disaster. The emperor hesitated to act. He asked if it was not true that the Satsuma councillors had banded together to get rid of Ōkuma. He also asked for proof that Ōkuma had conspired to do wrong. He was informed that although proof was difficult, evidence had been obtained from disciples of Fukuzawa Yukichi (1834–1901). It was alleged that Ōkuma, Fukuzawa, and Iwasaki Yatarō (1834–1885)[28] had joined in a conspiracy. Motoda insisted that not only the Satsuma councillors but all the rest were outraged by Ōkuma. He predicted that if the emperor ceased to trust the Satsuma councillors, the cabinet would be destroyed. The emperor yielded but commanded that Ōkuma should not be compelled to resign without being given an explanation.

Itō Hirobumi and Saigō Tsugumichi were delegated to go to Ōkuma and persuade him to resign. Ōkuma agreed without hesitation. In return, the emperor on October 12 directed Sanjō Sanetomi to withdraw permission for the sale of government properties. The government announced that Ōkuma had resigned because of a recurrent attack of rheumatism that made it impossible for him to carry out his political duties. Other politicians associated with Ōkuma also resigned.[29] The Satsuma and Chōshū cliques in the cabinet, which for some years had been on bad terms, had united in face of the threat from an outsider (Ōkuma was from Saga). But in order to mollify Ōkuma's supporters, it was officially announced that the promised parliament would convene in 1890, rather too soon for the advocates of gradualism.

Although Kuroda had been frustrated in his attempt to sell government properties, he was consoled by the dismissal of his enemy Ōkuma. He did not suffer any lasting disgrace despite his involvement in the scandal; indeed, in 1888 he became the prime minister. All the same, the incident, often referred to as the "political crisis of 1881," was not forgotten. It was a peculiarly unsavory example of power politics.

Meiji seems to have disliked most of the politicians involved. According to his chamberlain Ogi Masayoshi, who accompanied the *junkō* to the north, one night in the bath the emperor had expressed these opinions of the councillors: "Kuroda wants to become a minister and has the habit of pushing until he gets what he wants. He is utterly loathsome. Councillor Saigō [Tsugumichi] is always drunk, and when he speaks, he seldom makes sense. When Reed, a member of the British Parliament, came to Japan some years ago, Councillor Kawamura treated him in a way that was not at all what I intended.[30] It is Kuroda's practice not to attend court, alleging that he is ill, whenever his proposals are not carried out. And when he stays away, Saigō and Kawamura, for no reason, also stay away. It's extremely difficult to understand." Ogi added, "He is aware of Councillor Inoue [Kaoru]'s deviousness and dislikes him. As for the others, His Majesty commented that during the recent *junkō*, Ōki [Takatō] acted exactly like a wooden puppet. The only person he really trusts is Councillor Itō Hirobumi."[31]

From this time on, we can sometimes hear Meiji's voice in both the stereotyped phraseology of the rescripts and the distinctive tones of a man who, having heard much, has decided that the time has come for him to speak.

Chapter 35

The year 1881 was when demands for a constitution and a national assembly reached such intensity as to make it seem likely that the advocates would soon be successful. Little progress had been made toward drawing up a constitution during the years since the emperor had promised one in September 1876. Needless to say, nobody openly opposed a constitution, for that would have defied the emperor's stated wishes,[1] but a policy of "gradualism" was advocated by many who hoped that the implementation of a constitution could be put off indefinitely. However, advocates of a constitution and a legislative body had become tired of waiting, and many demanded prompt action.

There was pressure on the government, some of it from surprising quarters, to take concrete steps. In December 1879 Yamagata Aritomo had sent a long letter to the prime minister, Sanjō Sanetomi, stating his views on the advisability of constitutional government. After enumerating the various causes of discontent with the government—the loss of jobs, economic duress,[2] and the abandonment of traditional morality and customs—all of which had alienated the people and encouraged the rise of the Freedom and Popular Rights movement, Yamagata stated his belief that the most urgent need was a reform of the legislative, administrative, and judicial powers; otherwise, there were sure to be more armed disturbances like those that had already occurred in Saga, Kagoshima, and elsewhere. He had become convinced that the only way to restore people's confidence in the government was to promulgate a constitution. Such a constitution, given that it was likely to endure through many future generations, obviously could not be drawn up in a day and a night, but it was time to establish at least the basic principles. Once it became evident that the government as a whole and the various ministries in their different fields were conforming with these principles and that a future course had been determined, people would once again offer their allegiance.

Yamagata stressed that nothing in the new constitution should be construed as infringing on the authority of the imperial line. As far back as his Oath in Five Articles, the emperor himself had promised that there would be progress toward constitutional government. Already, at lower levels—in the prefectures, counties, and districts—assemblies had been created. The most gifted members of these assemblies should be selected for a national assembly, which would be the plebeian counterpart to the Genrō-in.

Sanjō approved of Yamagata's proposal, which was seconded by Iwakura Tomomi. They presented the proposal to the emperor, who was pleased to accept it. He also asked each councillor to submit a statement of his views on constitutional government.[3] Among the responses, Itō Hirobumi's was the most detailed. After describing the samurai's resentment of the changes that had occurred since the abolition of the domains, he contrasted the present situation with the days of the shoguns when the samurai were well educated, enjoyed stipends, and owned property. Despite the changes, the samurai class still considered that they should assume responsibility for affairs of state. When the samurai made political pronouncements, the common people were swayed: "If we may compare society to a human body, the samurai are like the muscles and bones; the common people are like the skin and flesh. When the muscles and bones move, the skin and flesh follow."[4]

Itō warned of the influence of the French Revolution, predicting that sooner or later every country would be affected. The notion of the government's sharing power with the people had entered Japan along with books and other imports from Europe. New ideas of government had gained currency among both samurai and commoners, and in the past few years the influence had spread irresistibly to the cities and villages. Some agitators were startling listeners with their wild words. Others moaned, although they were not ill, and bewildered people with their displays of demented behavior, oblivious of the plans the sovereign might have. But all this was as inevitable as plants springing up after rain had moistened the soil, and it was not worth marveling at.[5]

Itō seems to have accepted as inevitable the need to share with the common people the responsibility for government. He insisted, however, that plans for a parliament not be hastily drawn up, as some men advocated. This was to be an unprecedented change in Japanese polity, and it would take time to construct a firm foundation. Itō favored two houses of parliament, on the European model. The upper house (Genrō-in) would consist of 100 members chosen from among the nobility and samurai; its special function would be to support the imperial house and to preserve the Japanese heritage. Itō hoped that direct involvement in the government would mitigate the samurai's antipathy.

The lower house would consist of "inspectors" (*kensakan*) chosen from among members of local assemblies; its responsibilities would be limited to matters of finance. Obviously the upper house would be far more important than the lower house. Itō thought that this would make for stability and that the upper house would protect the lower house from radical tendencies.[6] He concluded by stating that he hoped the emperor himself would preside over the gradual establishment of a parliamentary government.

At first Councillor Ōkuma Shigenobu was reluctant to express his views, but the emperor asked Prince Taruhito to urge Ōkuma to disclose his thoughts concerning this crucial issue. Taruhito reported back that Ōkuma wished to present his views verbally, fearing that if he wrote them down, they might be leaked. The emperor, however, insisted on a written statement, and in March 1881 Ōkuma finally sent a memorial to the minister of the left, Prince Taruhito, asking that no one—not even the prime minister or the minister of the right— be permitted to see it before it was presented to the emperor. Taruhito agreed.

Ōkuma's memorial was in seven articles. The first called for a prompt public announcement of the date for the opening of the parliament, the selection of persons to draw up the constitution, and the commencement of construction of the parliament building.

The second article provided that the appointment of high-ranking officials would take into account their level of support from the people. The parliament that would operate under the future constitution had to reflect the wishes of the people. Decisions by the parliament also had to be in accordance with the wishes of a majority of its members. The head of the political party that enjoyed the most popular support should head the parliament.[7] The establishment of a constitutional monarchy would enable the emperor to find without difficulty the most suitable persons to assist him. By relying on elected officials, he would be spared the trouble of examining the credentials of potential advisers. However, Ōkuma pointed out, a political party elected by the voters might in time lose popularity because of its inept administration. In that case, it would hand over the government to the party with the greatest strength. The emperor would then choose a prime minister from this party and ask him to form a cabinet.[8]

Ōkuma's third article established a distinction between those officials who changed with the party in power and those who retained their positions permanently, regardless of which party was in power. The latter, who constituted the great bulk of officials (all but the top-ranking positions), were not permitted to become members of parliament but had to remain politically neutral.

As provided in the fourth article, the constitution would be promulgated by the emperor. It would be extremely simple, consisting entirely of general principles and combining a clarification of the responsibilities of administrative power and a similar clarification of the rights of the individual citizen. The fifth article proposed that a parliament be convened at the beginning of 1883, and in order to make this possible, a constitution should be promulgated in 1881 and the members of the parliament chosen by the end of 1882.

The sixth article asked that the various political parties establish platforms and that contests among the parties be among their different platforms (rather than among personalities). The seventh article called attention to the need for political parties to be faithful to the spirit of constitutional government. If they followed the letter but not the spirit, this would be unfortunate for the nation but a disaster for the administrators and would stigmatize their rule for generations to come.[9]

When Prince Taruhito read this document, he was astonished by the proximity of the date that Ōkuma suggested for opening the parliament. Disregarding his promise to Ōkuma, he secretly showed the memorial to Sanjō Sanetomi and Iwakura Tomomi and only then presented it to the emperor for his consideration. Hearing that a memorial from Ōkuma had been offered to the emperor, Itō Hirobumi asked Sanjō if he might see it. Sanjō obtained the document from the emperor and on June 27 showed it to Itō, who was enraged by the contents.[10] Not only was the date for the opening of the parliament a bare two years hence—far too soon in his opinion—but the proposal that even the advisers closest to the emperor be men chosen by popular election seemed a total denial of the sovereign's prerogatives. On July 1 Itō sent a letter to Iwakura stating his views and threatening to resign if Ōkuma's proposal was accepted. He wrote Iwakura again on the following day, saying that he could not attend meetings of the councillors if Ōkuma was present.[11]

After attempting without success to mollify Itō, Iwakura sent for Ōkuma and explained why he had showed the proposal to Itō and what Itō's reaction had been. Ōkuma defended his radical proposals, using the analogy of a crowd trying to get through a locked gate. If the gate were only half open, there would be indescribable confusion as people pushed and shoved to get in. It was therefore better to open the gate all the way and allow people inside. His plan for opening the parliament in 1883, a bold and even radical step, corresponded to opening the gate all the way. Ōkuma and Itō subsequently met at Iwakura's suggestion, and eventually their personal differences were reconciled and Itō again attended sessions of the cabinet, but they remained far apart on many political issues.

Itō, an advocate of gradualism, was intensely concerned about the emperor's future role. The emperor's personal decisions—against seeking a foreign loan and against making peasants pay taxes in rice—suggested that he might no longer be willing to play a passive or symbolic role but would insist on actively participating in major decisions. Itō feared that this tendency might lead to the emperor's being held responsible for political actions or might even lead to controversy over the institution of the emperor. He therefore preferred that the emperor play the role of an entirely symbolic leader at the head of a cabinet serving him. Itō was particularly wary of palace advisers who, without bearing personal responsibility, might exert influence through the emperor, as he was sure this could only lead to instability in the government.[12]

The one thing that drew Itō and Ōkuma together was a mutually shared dislike of Satsuma. When Kawamura Sumiyoshi, a Satsuma man, came up for appointment as navy minister, a position he had formerly occupied, Itō strongly opposed the appointment, although it was backed by the navy itself, and he was joined by Ōkuma. They deplored the tendency of Satsuma men to consider the navy as their private preserve and were sure that Kawamura was not capable of overseeing its future development. Kawamura was nevertheless appointed, mainly because of the desire of the other ministers to preserve peace in the cabinet by maintaining a balance between Chōshū and Satsuma men. They may have also hoped that if Kawamura were appointed, the other Satsuma councillors, who normally did not bother to attend cabinet meetings (in contrast to the diligent Chōshū councillors), would once again attend. The ministers had increasing cause to regret the loss of Kido and Ōkubo, who had maintained equilibrium between Chōshū and Satsuma in the cabinet.[13]

Despite this setback, Itō remained the strongest man in the government. He enjoyed the confidence of both the emperor and the *daijin* (the three top ministers). Sasaki Takayuki noted in his diary, however, that he expected the cabinet to collapse in the not too distant future. He was pleased at this prospect because it would afford the emperor an opportunity to assume the reins of government, as Sasaki had long hoped. He urged the emperor to prepare for this eventuality. The emperor replied that he had expected the minister of the left (Prince Taruhito), as a member of the imperial family, to be superior to the other two *daijin* in his objectives, but now that he had become a cabinet member, Taruhito seemed to have lost the confidence he displayed during his Genrō-in days. Sasaki defended Taruhito, pointing out his good qualities but admitting he showed insufficient energy. The emperor then made a most telling comment: "Even though the *daijin* and councillors performed meritorious service — acts of military valor — at the time of the Restoration, they had no real knowledge of government and had not since then employed people skilled in political affairs. That is what has made inevitable the present difficulties within the cabinet. One can only hope that in the course of time, real statesmen will join the cabinet. The present situation is a product of the times, and all we can do is wait until a sufficiently ripe opportunity permits us to do something about it."[14]

Here was the crux of a problem that beset the Meiji government. A display of bravery on the battlefield was no guarantee of competence in political office, but most of the cabinet members had been chosen because of distinguished war service, not because of political acumen. The failure of the Satsuma councillors to attend cabinet meetings probably was due to their boredom when having to listen to administrative reports. Meiji's dislike of the military men Kuroda Kiyotaka and Saigō Tsugumichi reflected his observation of their inability to apply themselves seriously to civil matters.

The problem of military participation in the government would last well beyond the Meiji period, but at this time it became imperative to keep military men from meddling in politics and, worst of all, disobeying their sovereign. As early as 1874 Katō Hiroyuki had written an essay in *Meiroku zasshi* that opened, "In enlightened and civilized countries, it is regarded as best and most important for military officials to earnestly obey their sovereigns' commands."[15] In the same year, three generals had resigned their commissions to express their disapproval of Ōkubo's foreign policy.[16] In reaction to these open displays of political views by the military and especially to the rebelliousness of the soldiers who had joined Saigō during the Satsuma Rebellion, in 1878 Yamagata had drawn up *Gunjin kunkai* (Admonitions to Military Men) for distribution to the troops. Among the principles he laid down was one forbidding military men to discuss the government or political events.[17]

Despite this command, members of the military became involved in the political manifestations that spread throughout the country at this time. In order to control demonstrations which (in its opinion) threatened public security, the government issued on April 5, 1880, sixteen regulations dealing with public gatherings. All manifestations—whether political addresses, attacks on the government's policy of gradualism, or support of a parliament—would henceforth require police permission. In addition, members of the army, the navy, the police, and the teaching profession were prohibited from taking part in mass meetings or joining political parties.[18] Military participation in the movement to obtain greater civil rights continued to be an issue: when the Imperial Rescript for Military Men was proclaimed in January 1882, the first article ordered soldiers and sailors not to be confused by public opinion and become involved in politics.[19]

Perhaps because of this pressure on the military to refrain from political action the movement to secure "freedom and popular rights" was led entirely by civilians, mainly men of middle- or lower-rank samurai status. The first political party dedicated to this aim, the Jiyū-tō, or Party of Liberty, was founded on December 15, 1880.[20] Well before this, however, political groups had been formed in many parts of the country, each with a distinctive and auspicious name but not necessarily any concrete objectives. Even those who called most vociferously for a constitution and the opening of a parliament gave little thought to what the constitution should contain or how the legislative body should be organized.[21]

The Risshi-sha (Self-Help Society) in Kōchi was the most prominent of these groups of samurai activists. It was founded in 1874 by Itagaki Taisuke and other men associated with the movement to secure "freedom and popular rights," but the name itself, derived from the title of Samuel Smiles's popular book *Self-Help* (*Saikoku risshi hen*), suggested that originally it was more concerned with education and self-improvement for samurai than with the creation of a parliament.[22] Perhaps that is why Itagaki founded in 1875 the Aikoku-sha (Society of Patriots), a specifically political group intended to create a link between the Risshi-sha and organizations working for freedom and popular rights.

It did not take long, however, before the Risshi-sha itself became involved in major national issues, although the Satsuma Rebellion caused a shift in its activities. Itagaki, who had been a firm supporter of Saigō, returned to Kōchi after the outbreak of the war in 1877. The defeat of Saigō's forces by the government army made it clear that it was useless to attempt to oppose the government by military means; therefore, the Risshi-sha's message would be spread by speeches and newspaper articles, not swords.

Although Itagaki was the founder and best-known member of the Risshi-sha, a more effective crusade for freedom and popular rights was carried out by the youthful Ueki Emori (1857–1892), only twenty at the time. Ueki came from a high-ranking Kōchi samurai family. In 1872 he went to Tōkyō to study.[23] He read widely, especially about law, political economy, and natural science, and he also became interested in Christianity, often attending church.

Ueki returned to Kōchi at the end of 1873. Five months later, an address by Itagaki at the Risshi-sha deeply impressed him, and he began to study theories of freedom and parliamentary structure. He returned to Tōkyō in 1875 to continue his studies, this time reading more traditional works, especially those of the Wang Yang-ming school of Confucianism.[24] In that year, he started contributing articles to the leading newspapers, his first positive steps as an activist in the cause of freedom and popular rights. In 1876 he was imprisoned for a piece he wrote entitled "Ape Men and the Government," in which he argued that what distinguished men from apes was their capacity for thought and imagination but that by imposing restrictions on speech, the government had reduced men to the status of apes.[25] As yet, however, Ueki had doubts about the country's holding elections before the populace was sufficiently educated to cast its votes intelligently.

In the same year, after the outbreak of the Satsuma Rebellion, Ueki returned to Kōchi. He lodged in Itagaki's house for a time and began to work actively for the Risshi-sha. He was the main author of a petition in favor of opening a parliament, and the Risshi-sha published various short-lived magazines to which Ueki contributed. Ueki also began to establish a reputation as a speaker. In 1877 alone, he gave thirty-four lectures, generally to crowds of 1,000 or 2,000. He recorded in his diary that on June 23 of that year he lectured at a theater that accommodated 2,000 people, but another 2,000 were turned away. The press was so great that the meeting had to be closed halfway through. Kōchi was the spearhead of the Freedom and Popular Rights movement, and intellectuals from all over the country were drawn there. By this time, Ueki had become absolutely convinced of the need for a parliament, and he blamed the Satsuma Rebellion for its absence.[26]

Ueki's advocacy of freedom extended to sex: he declared that the object of human beings was "to satisfy their desires, to exhaust their pleasures, and to attain the highest happiness."[27] His diary records the sexual fantasies of his dreams. In one he dreamed, "I slept in the same bed with the emperor, slept with the empress and had intercourse with her."[28] His strange identification with the emperor recurs again and again in the diary, where he often refers to himself as *tennō* (emperor) and uses the appropriate honorifics. From 1883 he even dated the beginning of each year by the years since Emperor Jimmu founded the nation, by the Christian calendar, and by the anniversary of the "birth of the Great Emperor of the Universe," meaning himself. On March 13, 1884, Ueki wrote in his diary, "The emperor this night made a progress to Yoshiwara. At the Kōzenrō he sent for the courtesan Nagao."[29]

Ueki nowhere explained why he kept referring to himself as the emperor. He certainly had an unusual interest in the person of the emperor. Entries in his diary, normally devoted exclusively to his own doings, from 1873 mention progresses of the emperor, the birth of royal children, and glimpses he had obtained of the "dragon countenance." It is conceivable that this obsession with the emperor was the reverse side of his antimonarchist sentiments. On August 2, 1879, Ueki had a dream that he recalled in these terms: "I was in Tōkyō, and somebody got angry with me because, he said, I had failed to show respect for the emperor in the course of an argument, or maybe it was that I said something close to advocating a republican form of government. Anyway, he sent two young men to stab me. I was slightly wounded, but did not die."[30]

Needless to say, such diary entries have no connection with Meiji himself, but Ueki's friend Yokoyama Matakichi wrote that in the final years of Ueki's short life, "One might say that he had gone crazy. He thought that he was the emperor."[31] If Ueki had been no more than a madman, his curious references to himself as the emperor would be of no interest; but at the time he wrote these words, he was actively engaged in giving lectures and writing articles in support of freedom and popular rights.

In January 1880 Ueki wrote an article in which he said that although some people feared a republican form of government, if truly understood, it would prove a blessing to the nation.[32] Generally speaking, however, Ueki seemed to take the existence of the monarchy in Japan as a "given." The constitution he drafted in 1881 provided for an emperor and mentioned some of his prerogatives. He did not openly advocate a republic.[33]

Ueki is also remembered for his article "Concerning Equal Rights for Men and Women," perhaps the earliest example of a Japanese call for equal rights. It was long claimed that Ueki wrote his famous editorial against prostitution (published in February 1882) in a brothel, but there is no evidence to support this. All the same, his advocacy of equal rights for women certainly began while he was still very actively indulging himself with prostitutes. Although he recognized the difficulty of abolishing prostitution in the near future, he urged that efforts be made to educate prostitutes in the principles of liberalism.

Ueki served the cause of freedom and popular rights through all the movement's convolutions. In 1880 the Aikoku-sha renamed itself the League for Establishing a National Assembly, and in 1881 it became the Jiyū-tō (Party of Freedom). Ueki prepared a draft of the party's principles and procedures.

It is not known what Meiji thought of these developments, but it is unlikely they pleased him. He was certainly aware of the Jiyū-tō members' anger over such events as the scandal of the Hokkaidō Development Office and thought it advisable to mollify them. On October 12, 1881, he announced that a parliament would be convened in 1890.[34]

The announcement took its urgency from the demands of the Jiyū-tō and other political groups to open a parliament, but many important matters of policy were still to be decided. Would the new government be modeled on the British or the Prussian system? Behind national differences was the basic question of whether the constitution would come from the people (British style) or be bestowed by the emperor (Prussian style).

An even more fundamental problem was the future legislators' almost total lack of training in parliamentary procedures. At the mass meeting of the Jiyū-tō in October 1881, Gotō Shojirō was chosen as the president and Baba Tatsui as the vice president, but (according to Baba's diary) Gotō almost never attended meetings. It was therefore left to Baba, who had studied at the Middle Temple in London and was well acquainted with the manner in which sessions of the British Parliament were conducted, to preside. Baba was dismayed by the party members' ignorance of even the basic rules of parliamentary discussion. When he rebuked them for their ignorance, they answered that regardless of how assemblies were conducted in Europe, they were Japanese and would behave in a "Japanese style." Baba persisted, and in the end the Jiyū-tō was officially formed.[35] Itagaki Taisuke was elected the chairman (*sōri*) of the new party.[36]

The Jiyū-tō's future objectives were by no means clear now that the emperor's proclamation had ensured the convening of a parliament. A rival party, the Rikken kai shintō (Constitutional Reform Party), formed by Ōkuma in April 1882, had a more definite objective, the creation of a British-style parliamentary democracy headed by a constitutional monarch. In his address at the founding of the Rikken kai shintō, Ōkuma emphasized the symbolic (rather than active) role of the monarch in the democratic government he favored: "There are some who, though they style themselves the party of 'respect for the emperor' and wear the trappings of that virtue, actually seek mainly to establish a few families as the bulwark of the Imperial Household or to protect the Imperial Household with troops. The extremists of this group would push the sovereign to the very forefront, and make him bear directly the administration. They would by their support of the Imperial Household place it in a position of danger."[37]

Ōkuma repeatedly emphasized his devotion to the imperial household. He stated in the same address, "I hope always to work with an ever firmer resolve for the achievement of the glorious work of the Restoration; for the laying of a foundation for our empire which will last through all eternity; and for the everlasting preservation of the dignity and prosperity of the Imperial Household and the happiness of the people."

On April 6, 1882, having just finished delivering an address in Gifu, Itagaki was attacked and wounded by a man wielding a dagger. Although the wounds were superficial and the assailant was immediately subdued, Itagaki, no doubt believing that he was dying, is reported to have cried, "Itagaki may die, but freedom will never die!"[38] The emperor was shocked by the news and immediately sent a chamberlain to find out what had happened.[39]

The incident created a great deal of sympathy for Itagaki, and the Jiyū-tō gained new members in all parts of the country. The government, however, imposed more and more stringent regulations on its activities. When members of the party protested the tyrannical actions of the governor of Fukushima in putting down a peasant revolt, they were imprisoned and eventually charged with treason.

The government had a more ingenious, even Machiavellian, plan for disposing of the Jiyū-tō's leadership. In March 1882 Itō Hirobumi, along with many advisers, went to Europe to investigate the constitutions of various countries. Itagaki visited him shortly before his departure, and Itō took the occasion to urge Itagaki, who had never been abroad, to go to Europe to study the politics and customs of the different countries. He declared that unless a man was personally acquainted with conditions in Europe, he was likely to be influenced by those who glorified everything foreign and to end up misleading the Japanese people. Itagaki was tempted and replied that he would go if the money for his travels could be arranged.[40]

Itō secretly conferred with Inoue Kaoru, and they agreed that the best way to deprive the Jiyū-tō of its strength was to get Itagaki and Gotō Shōjirō to spend considerable time abroad. Itō and Inoue set about raising funds for their travels, eventually obtaining a promise of $20,000 from the Mitsui Bank in return for extending for three years its contract with the army.

At the end of August 1882 Itagaki suddenly announced that he was going to Europe, and Gotō soon afterward did the same. The two men were completely unprepared to study conditions in Europe. According to Baba Tatsui, they could not even read roman letters, let alone a foreign language. There was no chance they could learn any significant information. Although an interpreter was supplied to assist them, the man's principal job (though they did not suspect this) was to spy on them and report their activities to Inoue.[41]

The two men were never given a satisfactory explanation concerning the source of the money for their travels, but this does not seem to have bothered them. They were so desperately eager to go abroad that they became quite irrational whenever members of the Jiyū-tō questioned the advisability of their making the journey.[42]

As might easily have been predicted, the stay in Europe did neither man any good. Gotō spent most of the time in Paris, occasionally (perhaps as a sop to his conscience) making trips to Prussia, Austria, or England. In Vienna, at Itō's suggestion, for some ten days he attended lectures given by the great Professor Lorenz von Stein. Itō had recommended study with Stein as an antidote to the excessive liberalism expounded by those under the influence of England, France, or the United States and as a way of strengthening the foundations of the imperial household. But Professor Stein's lectures that year were devoted to miscellaneous remarks about the coup d'état of Napoleon III, and Gotō derived nothing from them.

Itagaki was proud to have met Clemenceau and Victor Hugo, but his time in France was spent mainly in sightseeing, as the account of his travels published after his return to Japan demonstrated. He succeeded in meeting Herbert Spencer, the idol of Japanese intellectuals, but even as Itagaki was expounding one of his woolly arguments, Spencer cried out in exasperation, "No, no, no!" got up, and left the room.[43]

Itagaki and Gotō returned to Japan in June 1883. They discovered that in their absence, the two chief liberal parties, the Jiyū-tō and the Rikken kai shintō, had taken to furious exchanges of mudslinging. This, no doubt, was the result the conservative leaders of the government had hoped for when they bought off Itagaki and Gotō with a trip to Europe. Members of the Jiyū-tō who hoped that Itagaki would enlighten them about the republican form of government in France or the constitutional monarchy in England were disillusioned when they heard him deliver lectures in which he declared that although Japan lagged behind Europe in the standard of living, it was well advanced in government. He urged party members to devote greater efforts to raising the standard of living and warned of the peril to Japan if its navy were not strongly reinforced.[44] Nothing was left of the crusading liberal.

The Jiyū-tō was disbanded on October 29, 1884, and its bitter rival the Rikken kai shintō was effectively disbanded on December 17 of the same year when Ōkuma and Kōno Togama, its two chief officers, resigned. The liberal parties were dead and would have to be brought back to life during the coming years.

Chapter 36

After the turbulent incidents that marked the fourteenth year of Meiji's reign, 1882—or at least the first half of that year—seemed exceptionally peaceful. The year opened, as usual, with the emperor worshiping the four directions and performing other traditional New Year rituals.

The first noteworthy event of the year occurred on January 4. That day the emperor summoned Army Minister Ōyama Iwao and personally presented him with the Imperial Rescript for Military Men.[1] The rescript was subsequently distributed widely among the military and, by General Ōyama's command, printed at the head of the pocket notebooks distributed annually for the next sixty and more years to soldiers and sailors, to be read, memorized, and obeyed.

The rescript opens with an account of the service rendered by the military to the throne in the reign of Emperor Jimmu. In ancient Japan, the emperor himself had commanded the imperial forces, but in later times the court gradually lost its martial vigor as the result of the protracted period of peace. Military power fell into the hands of professional soldiers, the future samurai.

For some 700 years, the military ruled the country in disregard of the wishes of the imperial family, but by the 1830s and 1840s the shogunate was much weakened. It was just at this time that foreigners first posed a threat to Japanese security, causing Emperor Meiji's grandfather and father deep distress. He had been more fortunate. When he came to the throne, still young and inexperienced, he was assisted by loyal men who made it possible to return to the ancient system of government, rule by the emperor.

During the last fifteen years, great changes had taken place. The army and the navy were now personally commanded by the emperor. He declared to the military, "We are your commander in chief. We depend on you as Our trusted retainers; you look up to Us as your chief; our relations must be particularly intimate. Whether We can or cannot protect the nation, render thanks for the blessing of Heaven, and repay the debt We owe to Our ancestors depends on whether or not you carry out to the full your duties as military men."[2]

These statements are followed by a series of five commands indicating what the emperor expected of the military. The first was that as members of the military, they devote their entire loyalty to their country. He asked rhetorically, "Is there anyone born in our country who does not feel the desire to recompense his country?" It was not sufficient for a soldier to be skilled or learned. Unless he possessed the spirit of "recompensing his country," he would be no more than a puppet. A military man should consider his duty to maintain loyalty as weighty as the mountains but think of death as being as light as a feather.

The second injunction commanded lower ranks to show the same respect toward their seniors that they would toward the emperor himself. In return, the upper ranks were commanded not to behave with arrogance or contempt toward lower ranks but to treat them with kindness. Above and below should join in service to the emperor.

The third injunction was devoted mainly to the importance of courage. Soldiers were warned that real courage did not consist in recklessness; they were enjoined always to be governed by the sense of duty, by steady spiritual strength, and by their intelligence. The members of the military were commanded, moreover, to consider gentleness of the greatest importance in their dealings with civilians; they must try always to earn their affection and respect.

The fourth and fifth injunctions commanded the military to be true to its words and to practice simplicity.

The one feature that most clearly distinguishes these injunctions from those that any commander, regardless of country, might issue to his army was the emphasis on the direct connection between the emperor and the soldiers and sailors of his command. Emperor Meiji declared that he relied on his soldiers and sailors to serve as his "hands and feet" and commanded them to look up to him as their head, creating a relationship of mutual, personal dependence. If his men exerted themselves to the utmost, they would share his glory; if they did not, he too would fail.

A few days after the imperial rescript was issued, Chief of the General Staff Yamagata Aritomo prepared a memorandum on the state of the armed forces that he presented to Army Minister Ōyama Iwao. He complained of the insufficient number of soldiers—barely 40,000 men. Even nine years after conscription was instituted, established quotas of troops were not being filled. Garrisons in different parts of the country were short of infantry, artillery, and engineering personnel. Externally, too, the situation was by no means settled: Japan's relations with China and Korea were uncertain, and the status of the Ryūkyūs was a potential source of conflict. If the Japanese were to wait until a crisis arose before bringing their forces up to strength, it would then be too late. Yamagata was aware of the financial problems, but he was determined that the quotas prescribed in the conscription law be filled that year.[3] Yamagata's mention of China and Korea was noteworthy, as the latter part of 1882 was largely occupied with Japan's relations to these two countries.

The other important matter to occupy the court this year was the perpetual question of treaty revision. Again and again, the Japanese attempted to secure revision, offering various concessions to the foreign powers with which they had concluded unequal treaties. Although Japan had managed to secure the approval of most countries to revision, British opposition was unwavering.

Meiji himself at first was not directly involved in these problems. His name occurs most often in official records in connection with the gifts he made to people and institutions. On January 19, for example, he made a gift from his private purse of 1,000 yen to Kongōbu-ji on Mount Kōya to rebuild the great pagoda, destroyed by fire in 1843.[4] It is unlikely that Meiji was moved by Buddhist piety, though he no doubt had received instruction in Buddhism as a child.[5] Perhaps he felt, as did contemporary European monarchs, that it was incumbent on him as the father of his people to give money to religious and scholarly associations as well as charities.[6] Or the donation to rebuild a pagoda may have reflected his interest in reviving the past.

The emperor showed at this time an increasing concern for the preservation of Japanese traditions. He was pleased to learn that after a period of indiscriminate imitation of Western educational systems, Confucian virtues were being reinstituted as the foundation of education. He commented, "On examining the articles of the educational system now established by the Ministry of Education, I realized today that the recommendations I had made to the previous minister of education, Terashima Munenori, had at last been put into practice."[7] In a rescript he expressed the hope that in years to come, even if, for example, people urged the adoption of some feature of German education or of Russian education, the ministry would not be swayed by such demands but hold fast to the present system; ten years would surely demonstrate that it was a success.

Not long afterward, in response to questions from the emperor, Prime Minister Sanjō Sanetomi presented a written opinion concerning constitutional government. The time of the opening of a parliament had been set, and a draft constitution had been presented to the Genrō-in, but its provisions were copied from European constitutions and, not being suited to Japanese national feelings, could not be adopted without revision. Many opinions were expressed concerning how to put the constitution into effect and what its governing principles should be. One thing was definite: the constitution would be bestowed by the emperor and would not be the result of a struggle by the people. Debates continued, however, as to the locus of sovereignty. Some claimed that it resided with the people, others that it was shared by the sovereign and the people, still others that it resided entirely with the emperor; and they all quoted European theories and systems to prove their points.

Distressed by these divisions, the emperor asked Sanjō to submit a detailed report on the principles of the imperial constitution, the relationship between the parliament and imperial authority, and the state of preparations for opening the parliament. Sanjō's report, submitted on February 24, insisted on the sovereign's inviolability; his ministers bore full responsibility for acts committed on his behalf. Sanjō reiterated that the government's policy was gradualism. He was aware that many people favored rapid changes. He believed that this was because the Japanese for hundreds of years had lived securely in their own little world, despising everything outside. When suddenly they were brought into contact with foreign countries, they rushed to the opposite extreme, vying with one another in an attempt to be as advanced as possible. Recently, European extremist political thought had penetrated the cities and countryside, and the young people were inebriated with strange new ideas. The most urgent need was to guide these people and imbue them with objectivity and steadfastness.

Sanjō also emphasized the need to preserve the financial independence of the imperial household.[8] Indeed, he defined the main function of the nobility in the future upper house of the parliament to be its preservation. Next below the nobility came the samurai, but they had been impoverished by the changes in the government. Sanjō pleaded for measures to bring them relief. In a separate document, he listed steps that had been taken to prepare for the opening of the parliament.[9]

The emphasis on preserving Japanese traditions did not mean that the court had turned its back on guidance from abroad. In February, Terashima Munenori (1832–1893), the president of the Genrō-in, proposed that Itō Hirobumi be sent to Europe to study the various European constitutions in order to determine which features were suitable for adoption in the Japanese constitution; he himself would go to America as a minister plenipotentiary for the same purpose. The proposal was approved, and Itō resigned as president of the House of Councillors in order to make the journey. In March, before his departure, Itō received from the emperor a long list of matters to be investigated.

The question of treaty revision continued to bother the Japanese, and a preliminary conference on treaty revision met to consider the subject. Inoue Kaoru expressed the opinion that because the foreign countries had nothing to gain by revising the treaties and surrendering extraterritoriality, Japan would have to make major concessions. Two proposals for concessions were offered. The first, made by Councillor Yamada Akiyoshi, stated that if foreigners were willing to follow Japanese law in all matters, they would be permitted to live, work, and engage in trade anywhere in the country, exactly like Japanese.[10] The second, offered by Itō Hirobumi, promised less: foreigners would be permitted to engage in trade in the interior provided that they were subject to trial in

Japanese courts in cases of infractions of administrative rules or police regulations; the Japanese government would recover the right to decide all civil suits.

On March 5 Sanjō Sanetomi took the two proposals to the emperor and asked him to decide which he preferred. The emperor answered that first of all, he had hoped for unanimity of opinions on this major question, instead of bickering over minor differences. He also urged secrecy: if word of differences concerning treaty revision should leak out, there might be a repetition of the scandal that arose in the previous year when the sale of government properties in Hokkaidō was disclosed. Finally, he spoke out against Yamada's proposal, saying that the Japanese were still not the equal of the foreigners in knowledge and that they were very far from their equal in financial power. If foreigners were given the right to live and work in the interior and were permitted to engage in trade there, it might well lead to a lamentable result. He urged legislators to give earnest thought to possible future consequences.[11]

The emperor's advice failed to end the bickering. Inoue Kaoru, caught between the irresolution of the preliminary conference and the demands of the British minister for prompt action, finally tried to resign. The three *daijin* used every effort to calm him. In the end, K. F. H. Rösler, a German employee of the cabinet, rewrote the two proposals. The first proposal now included a clause permitting foreigners to own property but subjected them to Japanese law in all instances, both civil and criminal. The second proposal restricted to civil cases the trial of foreigners by Japanese courts but offered fewer privileges in return. The two proposals were once again submitted to the emperor. His decision was to open negotiations with foreigners on the basis of the first proposal. If that did not work, the second proposal should be tried. If neither proposal was acceptable, further discussions would have to be initiated and the results submitted to him.[12]

In April, at the seventh meeting of the preliminary conference, Inoue Kaoru read a memorandum stating that in order to realize its objectives in relations with foreign countries, Japan was prepared to make concessions to countries with which it had signed treaties. Before describing the concessions, he offered evidence of Japan's modernization and its qualifications for being accorded equality with the major powers. He claimed that Japan had always followed universally recognized principles of law and morality. It had ended the feudal system and enabled all men to enjoy equal rights. It had reformed the methods of government and separated the administrative and judicial systems. It had spread education and relaxed the ban on Christianity. It had established a postal system and joined the Universal Postal Union. It had built a telegraph system, a railway system, and lighthouses along the coasts. It had established a penal code and laws governing appeals. But the Japanese were not resting on these achievements; they were striving for greater progress and improvement and wished to establish ever closer connections with all countries in the belief that this would be mutually beneficial.

Unfortunately, there still were obstacles to friendship and trade with foreigners. According to the present treaties, foreigners were not allowed to live or trade outside the treaty ports. The government had long waited for the proper moment to remove these obstacles and believed that it had now arrived. On condition that foreigners obeyed Japanese laws, they would be free to travel throughout the country, live where they pleased, acquire movable and immovable property, engage in trade, and operate industries. On the day that this new system went into effect, foreign citizens would be subject to jurisdiction dissimilar to what they had experienced while in the treaty ports, but it would be fair. Inoue had not the slightest doubt that its fairness would be acknowledged. This would revolutionize the relations of Japanese and foreigners and build friendship between them. Trade would be free and foreign capital welcomed, in this way creating prosperity for industry and trade. He expected that a large-scale market for imported goods would be opened.[13]

On June 1 Inoue formally presented to the preliminary conference a bill (based on his April speech) for revision of the treaties. The bill provided that five years after the revised treaties were signed, the entire country would be opened to foreigners to travel, live, and work where they pleased, with all the rights the Japanese enjoyed in trade or employment. In order to allay foreigners' fears about Japanese laws, every effort would be made to secure their trust. The new laws would be based entirely on the legal principles prevalent in the West. All laws and regulations would be translated into at least one European language and would be distributed. Foreign judges would sit with Japanese judges. In the event that the jury system was adopted, in those cases involving foreigners, some jurors would be foreigners.

When the bill was read, the German minister at once expressed his admiration for the bill's plans for mutual benefit, praising particularly the generous guarantees to foreigners. He said he would report the content of the bill to his government and recommend revision of the treaties. He was followed by the ministers of Belgium, Portugal, Austria-Hungary, Holland, Spain, Italy, and Russia, all of whom agreed with the German envoy. The American envoy praised the reasonableness of the Japanese plan and said that he would be delighted to recommend that his government accept the plan. He added that the elimination of extraterritoriality would soften Japanese feelings of discontent and bitterness, preserve friendly relations with the Japanese people, and promote business and trade. Only Sir Harry Parkes, the British envoy, declined to join in the chorus of praise for the bill, saying that he would have to study it more carefully.[14]

On July 18 Parkes replied to the preliminary conference that the British government was adamantly opposed to Inoue's proposal and presented a memorandum explaining the reasons. He said that although Japan would commence having jurisdiction from the day after the approval of the revised treaties, it would not accord the promised privileges to foreigners for five years. During this time, the only advantage they would enjoy was the freedom to travel in the interior on business; they would not be able to live there, possess property, or use capital in their occupations. Moreover, the judicial system and judicial methods promised by the Japanese were extremely vague and by no means sufficient to guarantee foreigners' rights and benefits. Because the Japanese government had yet to formulate a civil or commercial code and the new penal code had been in operation for only one year, it would be exceedingly difficult for his government to judge whether or not the new laws would be effective. He expected that it would take considerable time before the proposal could be approved and so recommended that the governments of Japan and the other countries involved give it their most careful attention. Parkes believed that the present proposal could not enjoy the trust of Englishmen and that it would not be able to attract the flow of foreign capital into Japan necessary for Japan's future prosperity.[15] He quoted "an able Japanese publicist" who as late as the close of 1879 declared that "the laws did not duly protect the lives, liberties, and property of the Japanese themselves, and required very considerable reform before they could be generally approved by the Japanese people."[16]

Although England was the only country to speak out against the proposal, Parkes's voice was decisive. He suggested that the ministers of other countries discuss the proposal freely, but they decided instead to refer the matter back to their governments. Thus ended the sixteenth session of the preliminary conference on July 27.

In reading Parkes's objections to Inoue's proposal for eliminating extraterritoriality, it is difficult not to recognize the force of his arguments. Neither he nor his government saw any reason to hurry with treaty revision, and they were reluctant to give up rights they enjoyed without being absolutely sure the new system would work equally to their advantage. Parkes said in his memorandum that he sympathized with the desire of the Japanese to abolish completely consular jurisdiction, but his sympathy does not appear to have been deep. He seems not to have shared the awareness of the American minister (John Bingham) of the resentment the Japanese felt over the extraterritoriality imposed by foreign governments, an unmistakable indication of their belief that Japan was still uncivilized. Parkes's citation of the words of "an able Japanese publicist" did not allude to this resentment, which was probably more keenly felt by Japanese than any uncertainty over the new laws. In sum, Parkes was defending a system that had become odious to the Japanese as a negation of all they had achieved since the Restoration.

In the meantime, Japanese attention was diverted from the long-standing question of treaty revision to a more immediate problem, an uprising of Korean soldiers in Seoul on July 23. The ultimate cause was anger over reforms that the government had ordered in the armed forces. At the end of 1881, as part of their plan to modernize Korea, King Kojong and his consort, Queen Min,[17] had invited the military attaché of the Japanese legation, Lieutenant Horimoto Reizō, to serve as an adviser in creating a modern army. One hundred young men of the aristocracy were given Japanese-style military training, and it annoyed soldiers of the old army to see how much better equipped and treated these young men were than themselves. More than 1,000 soldiers, most of them old or disabled, had been discharged in the process of revamping the army, and the rest had not been given their pay in rice for thirteen months. In June, having been informed of the situation, the king ordered that a month's allowance of rice be given to the soldiers. He directed Min Kyom-ho, the overseer of government finances, to make the payment. Min handed the matter over to his steward, who sold the good rice he had been given and used the money to buy millet that he mixed with sand and bran. It was so rotten and foul smelling as to be inedible.[18]

The enraged soldiers headed for the residence of Min Kyom-ho, whom they suspected of having swindled them out of their rice. Min, getting word of the revolt, ordered the police to arrest some of the ringleaders and announced that they would be executed the next morning, assuming that this would serve as a warning to the others. When, however, the rioters learned what had happened, they broke into Min's house to take revenge. He was not there, so they dissipated their frustration by destroying his furniture and other possessions.

The rioters moved on to an armory, from which they stole weapons and ammunition. Better armed than ever before in their careers as soldiers, they headed for the prison and, overpowering the guards, released not only the men who had been arrested that day by Min Kyom-ho but many political prisoners. Min, who was in the royal palace, summoned the army to quell the rebellion, but it was too late: the original body of rioters had been swelled by the poor of the city and other malcontents, and the revolt had assumed major proportions.

One group of rioters went to Lieutenant Horimoto's quarters and took turns in stabbing the cowering military instructor, administering many small wounds until they slowly killed him.[19] Another group, some 3,000 strong, after arming themselves with weapons taken from a looted depot, headed for the Japanese legation. The royal palace had received word of the imminent danger, along with the admission that the king was powerless to subdue the rioters.[20] Inside the legation were the minister, Hanabusa Yoshimoto (1842–1917), seventeen members of his staff, and ten police officers. The mob surrounded the legation, shouting its intention of killing all the Japanese.

Hanabusa gave orders to burn the legation. His secretary at once doused important documents with oil and set them afire. The flames quickly spread, and under cover of flames and smoke, Hanabusa and the others escaped through a rear gate. The Japanese fled to the harbor, where they boarded a boat that took them down the Han River to In'chon. At first they took refuge with the In'chon commandant, but when word arrived of the events in Seoul, the attitude of their hosts changed, and the Japanese realized they were no longer safe. They escaped to the harbor in a driving rain, pursued by Korean soldiers. Six Japanese were killed, and another five were seriously wounded. The survivors, carrying the wounded, boarded a small boat and headed for the open sea. Three days later they were rescued by a British surveyor ship, the *Flying Fish*.[21]

On July 24, the day after the attack on the Japanese legation, the rioters forced their way into the royal palace. They found and killed Min Kyom-ho as well as a dozen other high-ranking officers. They searched for Queen Min, intending to kill her both because she belonged to the hated Min family and because they knew the corrupt government was completely under her control. The queen narrowly escaped, dressed as an ordinary court lady and carried on the back of a faithful guard who claimed she was his sister.[22]

The one member of the royal family on the side of the rioters was the *taewon'gun*,[23] the father of the king. He hated the Min family, which had deprived him of his power over the throne. The hapless king, now that Queen Min was not there to guide him, was again dependent on his father. He asked his father to return, and the *taewon'gun* joyfully resumed his former post after nine years of exile. Among his first acts were to order a state funeral for Queen Min, who was presumed to have died in the attack on the palace, and to abolish the modern, Japanese-trained army unit.

It may be imagined the indignation with which the news of these events was received after Hanabusa's return to Japan. Inoue Kaoru called a special session of the cabinet on August 30. The emperor commanded Inoue to go to Shimonoseki to take charge of the crisis. He also commanded Rear Admiral Nirei Kagenori to proceed with four warships, and Major General Takashima Tomonosuke to accompany him with a battalion of infantry, to Korea as an escort for Minister Resident Hanabusa when he returned to his post (and also to protect other Japanese who might be in Korea).

Inoue left Tōkyō on August 2. He met Hanabusa in Shimonoseki and gave him his instructions, which described the anger aroused by the outrages of the Korean ruffians and the affront to the reputation of the Japanese nation. The document blamed the Korean government for its laxness in suppressing these unruly elements. It had failed to attach sufficient importance to the relations that should prevail between neighboring countries. The Japanese nevertheless had judged, in view of Korean national feelings, that it was premature to send a punitive expedition. The minister would return to Seoul. He would be protected by army and navy units because there was no predicting what further violence might be unleashed by the rioters.

Hanabusa was commanded to meet with senior officials in Seoul and persuade them to set a date by which the rioters would be disposed of in a manner satisfactory to Japan. If the rioters were bold enough to make surprise attacks, Japan would feel compelled to use military force to subdue them, regardless of what measures the Korean government might take.

As yet there was no threat of war, but it was implicit. Hanabusa was instructed that if the Koreans showed any signs of hiding the culprits and not punishing them or if they refused to take part in the discussions demanded by the Japanese, this would constitute a clear breach of peace. In that case, the envoy would send a final letter to the Korean government indicting it for its crimes and then proceed without delay to Inch'on, along with army and navy forces that would occupy the port. On arrival in Inch'on, the envoy would at once send a detailed report to Tōkyō and await further orders. Hanabusa was advised that if China or any other nation offered to mediate, it should be refused. The instructions concluded on a surprisingly conciliatory note: the Japanese government did not consider that the Korean government had intentionally harmed peaceful relations. The envoy should therefore sincerely attempt to restore the traditional good relations between the two countries. The present incident might even provide a means of securing a lasting peace.[24]

Despite the optimism of these last remarks, the government authorized the call-up of reserves at the beginning of August. Inoue Kaoru notified ministers living in Tōkyō of the Japanese government's decision to send troops and ships to Korea to protect Japanese citizens. He emphasized that the government's intentions were entirely peaceful. An offer by the American government to mediate was, however, immediately declined.[25] The emperor, worried about the situation, sent Chamberlain Yamaguchi Masasada to Korea as a personal envoy. He remained in Korea until the Treaty of Chemulp'o[26] was signed.

While the Japanese and the Koreans were negotiating the terms of a treaty, there was much discussion in Japan concerning the urgent necessity to increase armaments. Proponents pointed out that the four warships sent to Korea constituted the entire Japanese navy, leaving not one ship to protect the country. Yamagata Aritomo presented a petition to the throne arguing in favor of armaments, recommending that the costs be met by increasing the taxes on cigarettes. On August 16 the emperor asked Iwakura for his recommendations. He replied that if China continued to consider Korea as a tributary state, war with China was inevitable. Iwakura said that it was essential that the armed forces be prepared for war and asked the emperor to issue secret instructions. On August 19 Yamagata sent Iwakura a letter expressing pleasure that Japan had been furnished with such a good opportunity to fight China.[27]

Hanabusa went on August 22 to the royal palace in Seoul, escorted by two companies of soldiers, to present the king of Korea with a list of Japanese demands. He gave the king three days to reply. The demands included the payment of 500,000 yen as an indemnity for the burning of the Japanese legation. The king ordered his government to reply within the allotted time, and the *taewon'gun* at once summoned a meeting of the cabinet. However, the cabinet members were so enraged by the unreasonable sum of money demanded by the Japanese (500,000 yen was about one-sixth of the Korean government's total revenues) that no answer was forthcoming. Judging that it was unlikely the Koreans would comply with the Japanese demands, Hanabusa decided to leave for Inch'on. War seemed inevitable. As prescribed in his orders, he wrote a final message to the king before leaving Seoul. The king at once wrote Hanabusa, begging him to return, but Hanabusa did not change his mind. He had been irritated by a discourteous letter he had received from a member of the government named Hong Sun-mok, who declared that the Japanese need not have sent a special envoy to Korea.[28] On August 25 Hanabusa reached Inch'on. The next day, a letter arrived from Hong stating his intention to resign his office and pleading for a further meeting. Hanabusa agreed to wait two days longer before sailing.

An unexpected complication in the situation was provided at this point by Queen Min, who, from her place of hiding, sent a letter to the king urging him to ask China, as the suzerain state, to send troops to Korea to put down the insurrection. The king, obedient as ever to Queen Min, sent men to Tientsin, where they met two high-ranking Korean officials stationed there. These officials traveled to Peking and transmitted to Li Hung-chang the king's request for Chinese troops. Li did not hesitate: this was a golden opportunity to revive Chinese sovereignty over Korea, which had been much attenuated over the years.

A Chinese fleet of three warships and six merchant ships was ordered to leave at once for Korea. The ships, carrying 4,000 troops, were to rendezvous off Inch'on. With such forces the Chinese could easily have seized Inch'on, but they were under instructions from Li Hung-chang not to create any unnecessary incident with the Japanese. When the Chinese saw the Japanese warship *Kongō* in Inch'on harbor (it had arrived ahead of the other Japanese ships), they at first withdrew, but on August 22 they returned, and on the following day landed some 200 of their troops.

The Chinese informed Hanabusa that they had come to put down a rebellion in their tributary state. Hanabusa, insisting that Korea was an independent country, said that the present tension between Japan and Korea was not China's concern. The Chinese proposed that they cooperate in suppressing the rebellion, but Hanabusa replied that he was waiting for a reply to his ultimatum to Korea and that no other country should intervene.

The Chinese, resigned to Japanese unwillingness to cooperate, embarked on quite a different course of action. Their three highest naval officers paid a courtesy call on the *taewon'gun*. As they were leaving, they asked him to attend an important meeting at their camp. The *taewon'gun* was obliged by rules of etiquette to return the call and went the next day (September 26) as requested. There were the usual exchanges of politenesses between the Chinese and the Koreans, but at a signal (the lifting of a wine glass in a toast to the long life of the *taewon'gun*), Chinese troops burst into the room, seized the *taewon'gun*, and bundled him into a palanquin. He was carried off to the warship *Wei-yüan* and, still in the palanquin, was taken to China. He was not released from the palanquin until the ship reached Tientsin. There he was interrogated by Li Hung-chang, who tried unsuccessfully to make him admit responsibility for the rebellion. Li ordered the *taewon'gun* put back in his palanquin, and he was carried off to a town about sixty miles southwest of Peking. For three years he was confined to one room and kept under strict surveillance.[29]

Now that the *taewon'gun*, the most impressive figure in the government, could offer no resistance, the Korean government had no choice but to negotiate with the Japanese. On August 30 the Treaty of Chemulp'o was signed, officially ending the tension between Japan and Korea. It provided that (1) within twenty days the Korean government would arrest and punish the rioters who had killed the Japanese; (2) the Korean government would give proper funerals for the Japanese victims; (3) the Korean government would pay an indemnity of 50,000 yen to the families of the dead and wounded; (4) the Korean government would pay an indemnity of 500,000 yen for the damage done by the rioters to the Japanese legation and the costs of the expedition, to be paid in five annual installments of 100,000 yen each; and (5) the Japanese legation would henceforth be protected by "a few" soldiers.

Patriotic fervor had been aroused among the Japanese by the incident, with some men volunteering for military service or offering money for war expenses. Hanabusa returned to Yokohama on September 28 and traveled by special train to Tōkyō, where he was welcomed by a platoon of cavalry. At the palace he was given an audience by the emperor, who awarded Hanabusa the Order of the Rising Sun.

Deploring the recent unhappy incidents, King Kojong sent three high-ranking officials to express his apologies and to offer gifts. The emperor received Pak Yong-hyo, the senior Korean envoy, who offered a letter from the king conveying his admiration for the emperor's glorious accomplishments and asking for peace and long friendship.[30]

On November 3 Lieutenant Horimoto and the other Japanese killed in Korea were enshrined in the Yasukuni Shrine. On November 17 the captain of the *Flying Fish*, which had rescued Hanabusa and other Japanese, was presented by the emperor with a pair of bronze vases and some books, including one on the ancient conquest of Korea. When Pak Song-hyo and his colleagues were about to leave Japan in December, the emperor received them in audience. Expressing regret over their departure, he asked them to convey his feelings of friendship to the king. He also gave them 500 guns for the king, no doubt a hint that he hoped they would be used to put down any future rebellions. Pak said that nothing was more needed than guns and he was sure that the king would be delighted to receive them.[31]

Pak also reported verbally to the emperor on current conditions in Korea and conveyed the king's hope that Japan would give financial aid to Korea to help preserve its independence. After his return to Korea, he and Kim Ok-kyun organized a new, progressive party that sought, with Japanese help, to free Korea from the shackles of Chinese domination and the accumulated burden of old evils. For these men, Japan was the model for the enlightenment they hoped to bring to Korea.[32]

The year ended on this rather optimistic note, although some members of the government warned against provoking China into a war that might last tens of years.[33] On December 23, 1882, Emperor Meiji issued a rescript that opened, "It is my earnest desire to preserve peace throughout the East. However, on this occasion there has been a request made by Korea, and we, with the friendship of a neighboring nation, plan to assist their ability to maintain their autonomy. We also intend to persuade other countries to recognize Korea as an independent country." One senses behind these words the causes that would lead twelve years later to the Sino-Japanese War.

Chapter 37

The familiar New Year ceremonies opened 1883. On January 4 the emperor attended the first meeting of the year of the Genrō-in, and on January 18, at the first poetry meeting in the palace, his New Year poem was composed on the topic "The Four Seas Are Pure."

This year the emperor's fondness for riding seems to have revived: he rode fifty-one times, generally ending his riding practice either with a visit to the Aoyama Palace, the residence of the empress dowager, or with a drinking party at the pavilion in the Shinjuku Royal Park.

The emperor occasionally took pleasure also in the performances of nō at the Aoyama Palace or at the nō theater opened in Shiba Park on April 16, 1881. The emperor and empress, along with members of the imperial family, councillors, officers of the Imperial Household Ministry, and so forth attended a particularly brilliant program of eight nō and six *kyōgen* on May 23, 1883, at the Aoyama Palace. Nō seemed to be on its way to being once again recognized as the official "music" of the regime, but despite regular gifts from the empress dowager, its most generous patron, there was not enough money to support the actors or to train successors. Not until the beginning of the twentieth century were the livelihoods of performers of nō made financially secure.[1]

The emperor probably took greater pleasure in the nō than in the lectures delivered before him this year. They were given by Motoda Nagazane on a section of the *Analects*, by Nishimura Shigeki on the Japanese translation of J. K. Bluntschli's *Allgemeines Staatsrecht*, by Takasaki Masakaze on the preface to the *Kokinshū*, and by Kawada Ōkō on *Jōkan seiyō*, a T'ang-period treatise on the art of government.

Although it began promisingly, 1883 would be marked by personal tragedies for the emperor. On January 26 his fourth daughter, Princess Fumiko, was born to the *gon no tenji* Chigusa Kotoko.[2] His third daughter, Princess Akiko, had been born to the same mother on August 3, 1880. As an infant, Akiko had been stricken with meningitis but had responded to treatment and seemed to have been completely cured. With the birth of Fumiko, the emperor had three children—Prince Yoshihito and the two princesses. But this joy did not last long. In August, Princess Akiko's illness recurred, induced (it was said) by the extreme summer heat, and this time the palace doctors' efforts to save her life were unsuccessful. She died on September 6. The infant Princess Fumiko, who had suffered from croup ever since her birth, showed symptoms of chronic meningitis on September 1. The emperor sent his personal physician, and when Fumiko's condition did not improve, he commanded the surgeon general, Hashimoto Tsunatsune (1845–1909), to treat her. Princess Fumiko died two days after her sister.[3]

Six of the emperor's seven children had died in infancy. The emperor's reactions to the deaths of his children were usually not recorded, but in face of this double blow, he was clearly grief stricken. In token of mourning, he canceled court business for a day and commanded that there be no singing or dancing for three days. He also ordered the army to fly flags at half-mast and to fire cannon in solemn tribute. On the day of the funeral, crowds gathered along the streets to watch in sorrow as the little coffins were carried off to the grave.

Asada Sōhaku,[4] the physician in attendance on the royal children, asked to be allowed to resign his position because of his failure to cure the two princesses. He blamed his failure on his having tried by turns Chinese and Western medicine. Despite the recent tragedy, however, the emperor continued to believe in using both to treat illnesses. He appointed the Western-trained Hashimoto as chief medical officer of the palace.[5] He, along with two other Western-trained physicians,[6] were expected to consult with doctors of traditional medicine in prescribing treatment. After the deaths of the princesses, the emperor was more deeply concerned than ever about his one remaining child, the crown prince, whose health had been a problem ever since he was born.[7]

The emperor's own health also suffered this year: in September he had an another attack of beriberi. The emperor's beriberi was, fortunately, not malignant, but, the doctors argued, it might well become so in Tōkyō, the most dangerous place for infection. They advised building a detached palace perhaps sixty or seventy miles from Tōkyō at a place with beautiful surroundings and pure air and urged the emperor to spend the dangerous time of year away from Tōkyō.[8] Needless to say, Meiji once again ignored their advice.

The doctors also expressed their grief over the deaths of the six princes and princesses, all of them victims of the same disease: meningitis. They believed that any royal infants who were born in the future should be brought up differently from the traditional palace customs. They recommended that a palace be built where the children might escape the summer heat. More important, they ascribed the deaths to some inborn infirmity and recommended all possible precautions be taken for their health from the time their mother's pregnancy was first recognized. The emperor gladly agreed to these suggestions. A palace was subsequently built at Hakone, and residences at Nikkō and elsewhere. The royal children born to the emperor's concubines were sent to these houses when it was thought they needed a change of air, but the emperor himself, who gave little thought to his health, never stayed at any of them. The emperor seems to have been happiest when he managed to get away from the court for a few days to observe maneuvers.[9]

During the first half of 1883, Itō Hirobumi was still in Europe studying various constitutions in the hopes of finding suitable models for the future Japanese constitution. He spent most of his time in Germany and Austria, believing that their constitutions best fitted Japan's needs. He was especially impressed by two scholars of constitutional law, Rudolf von Gneist[10] and Lorentz von Stein,[11] and invited Stein to accompany him when he returned to Japan to serve as an adviser in both preparing the constitution and establishing an educational policy for Japanese universities.

Stein declined the invitation, citing his advanced age, which made it impossible for him to travel abroad, and also his belief that a country's system of law must be based on the traditions of that country. He believed that if a people felt it advisable to borrow laws from another country, it must, first of all, trace back to their sources the reasons for the existence of these laws, to consider their history, and then to judge whether or not they were applicable to their own country.[12]

Itō was all the more impressed by Stein on reading this response, but it was clear he would not travel to Japan. Itō asked Bismarck if he could recommend someone else to take Stein's place. After highly praising Japan's progress, Bismarck mentioned three scholars. Itō at once cabled the cabinet for authorization to invite them. The foreign minister, Inoue Kaoru, sent Itō a cable giving him permission to make the appointments but warning that Japan must not be unduly influenced by Bismarck and German power. He recalled how French officers, invited to train the Japanese army, had insisted on following French procedures in all matters, resulting in dissension with the army minister. In any case, Inoue said, it was not the government's intention to adopt a purely German style of constitution and laws. German advisers should be chosen who, in the capacity of Japanese civil servants, would be capable of performing effectively under the terms of their contracts.

Despite this apparent lack of enthusiasm for his project, Itō did not abandon hope of receiving advice from German and Austrian legal experts. On October 10 the emperor agreed to appoint Stein as a member of the Japanese legation in Austria, to serve as an adviser on questions pertaining to the Japanese legal system.[13]

Itō returned from Europe early in August along with members of his mission. He had spent a year and a half visiting Germany, Austria, England, France, Russia, and Italy, studying their constitutions. He informed Iwakura that he had learned the general principles of state organization from Gneist and Stein and had obtained the essential knowledge to establish the foundations of the imperial house. He believed that the time had arrived to establish a constitutional monarchy, to perfect the imperial rule, and to establish legislative and judicial systems. He was aware that many in Japan had been seduced by the extreme liberalism of England and France, but he was convinced that such people could be kept under control by adopting his proposals.

Itō's thoughts were so much occupied with the future of Japan that he seemed not to notice that Japanese traditions were rapidly eroding despite efforts to revive festivals and other manifestations of traditional beliefs.[14] The death of Iwakura Tomomi on July 20 represented perhaps the sharpest break with the past. Iwakura had been appointed as a chamberlain to Emperor Kōmei in 1854, when Meiji was only two years old, and he probably figured in the emperor's earliest memories. Iwakura had played a vital part in almost every important event affecting the monarchy ever since that time. Although he came from the lower ranks of the nobility, he was a noble, a distinction that set him off from most members of the Meiji government. This distinction at times led to clashes with the samurai,[15] but it also enabled Iwakura to enjoy a special relationship with the emperor. He was a more active member of the Meiji government than other nobles, such as Prince Taruhito or Sanjō Sanetomi, although both were of higher status than himself.

Iwakura had gone to Kyōto in May to supervise plans for restoring the imperial palace. The emperor had become increasingly concerned over the dilapidation not only of the palace but of the entire city, and he readily agreed when Iwakura proposed that steps be taken to arrest further decay.[16] The emperor sent Iwakura and other officials to Kyōto to survey the situation.

Iwakura's plans included the establishment of a branch office of the Imperial Household Ministry to administer the palace, the imperial gardens, the detached palaces, and the tombs. An office would be created to deal with shrines and temples in the region. Festivals would be renewed and a shrine erected in the Gosho to the memory of Emperor Kammu, revered as the founder of the city of Kyōto. The area around the Gosho, where once the houses of the nobles stood, would be divided by roads; trees would be planted; and clean water would be sent flowing through the gutters. Unnecessary buildings would be removed. The Shugaku-in Detached Palace would be repaired, and Nijō Castle officially recognized as a palace. Western-style buildings would be erected in the area of the Kamo River as places where distinguished visitors from abroad might stay.[17]

These plans were eventually carried out, helping reverse the city's steady deterioration. Iwakura's enthusiasm for the project compelled him to remain at his task even after he began to feel chest pains and such acute stricture of the stomach that he was unable to eat or drink. When word reached the emperor of Iwakura's illness, he was greatly concerned and at once sent his personal physician, Itō Hōsei, to examine Iwakura.

Iwakura's condition improved sufficiently for him to return to Tōkyō, only to suffer a relapse after arriving. On July 5 the emperor, worried about Iwakura's health, expressed his intention of paying a visit to the sickroom. Overcome by awe and trepidation, Iwakura sent his son to decline the honor, but it was too late: the imperial carriage had already arrived. Iwakura, hastily changing clothes, left his sickbed and, supported by two sons, approached the emperor to convey his gratitude. At the sight of Iwakura's frail condition, the emperor was moved to tears.

A week later the empress, learning that Iwakura still showed no signs of recovery, wished to comfort him. "However," she said, "the minister of the right places great importance on showing the proper deference. If he hears I am coming he will unquestionably make every effort to welcome and send me off, regardless of the harm it may do him in his illness. This is not what I intend. I shall visit him today as Ichijō Tadaka's daughter, and we shall meet without his getting out of bed."[18]

The emperor visited Iwakura for the second time on July 19. As he was about to leave the palace, he told Tokudaiji Sanetsune, "I am going to take my last farewell of the minister of the right." He called for his palanquin and, not waiting for his full escort, left the palace. An equerry preceded the emperor. He informed Iwakura that the emperor would be coming. Iwakura sobbed and shed tears of gratitude. When the emperor arrived, Iwakura tried to raise himself and bow, but he was now so stricken that his body would not obey him. All he could do was join his hands to express his gratitude. Seeing Iwakura's condition, the emperor wept and could barely ask how he felt. Iwakura was unable to reply. For a few moments the emperor and his minister gazed at each other without words, and then the emperor departed. That day Iwakura's request to resign his office was granted. He died on July 20.

The emperor, deeply grieved, canceled all court business for three days and granted Iwakura a state funeral. In his eulogy, he bestowed on Iwakura the title of *dajō daijin*, the highest position a subject could attain. After praising the achievements that made Iwakura a "pillar of the state," he wrote movingly of his personal relationship: "I ascended the throne when I was still a child. I depended on him completely for guidance, and I imbibed the wisdom he unstintingly gave me. The kindness of my teacher was the same as a father's. Heaven did not spare him; how can I overcome these feelings of bitter grief?"[19]

Most of Meiji's official utterances consisted mainly of stereotyped phrases, but these words reveal his unmistakable grief over the loss of his mentor.[20]

The emperor bade farewell not long afterward to another person who for many years had figured importantly in his life: Sir Harry S. Parkes was being transferred to China. During the farewell luncheon, offered at the palace, the emperor delivered a rescript in which he expressed his regrets that Parkes was leaving Japan after eighteen years of service. The emperor graciously thanked Parkes not only for his efforts to cultivate relations between his country and Japan but also for having supported the Meiji Restoration and recommending many beneficial projects. In recognition of these services to Japan, the emperor had intended to give Parkes the Grand Order of the Rising Sun, but the British government would not permit this. Instead, he gave Parkes two of his own possessions, an incense burner and a flower vase. He said it would please him if Parkes cherished them as mementos of deep feelings.[21]

Here, too, the emperor's words have a ring of sincerity, for this was not the language he normally used when saying goodbye to foreign dignitaries. It is surprising, all the same, that the emperor spoke so warmly of Parkes, who was generally arrogant and irritable in his dealings with the Japanese and who at this time (according to Sir Ernest Satow) was "the bugbear of the Japanese public," as much hated and feared as Napoleon had been by the English.[22] Parkes's recent opposition to ending extraterritoriality surely did not endear him to the emperor, but he managed to surmount any feelings of annoyance to render a generous tribute. Satow, often critical of Parkes, also expressed admiration:

> Japan herself owes to his exertions a debt which she can never repay and has never fully acknowledged. If he had taken a different side in the revolution of 1868, if he had simply acted with the majority of his colleagues, almost insurmountable difficulties would have been placed in the Mikado's restoration, and the civil war could never have been brought to so speedy a termination.[23]

During the following year, 1884, the emperor figured surprising little in the major events. Most of his activities were repetitions of the previous year's. Perhaps the action that gave him the greatest pleasure was bestowing on the father of Emperor Kōkaku the posthumous title of Emperor Kyōkō.[24] Emperor Kōkaku had attempted for years, as an act of filial piety, to obtain for his father the title of *daijō tennō* (retired emperor), even though he had never reigned. The shogunate did not concur in Kōkaku's plan and finally (in 1792) ordered the emperor to postpone action. Among the nobles who supported Kōkaku, the most prominent was the former major counselor Nakayama Naruchika, the great-grandfather of Meiji's maternal grandfather, Nakayama Tadayasu. He was summoned to Edo for questioning and later placed under house arrest by the shogunate.[25] Meiji no doubt believed that in bestowing the title Emperor Kyōkō, he had rectified a long-standing injustice to his ancestors.

In April war broke out between China and France over the possession of

Annam. The Japanese government decided to cooperate with three other neutral nations (Germany, the United States, and England) in protecting the lives and property of their citizens in the areas affected by the war. This was the first time the Japanese had cooperated abroad in this fashion with other countries.[26]

Nothing is recorded of the emperor's reactions to this war, but probably he was pleased when the Chinese seemed to be holding their own against the French. As his conversation with the king of Hawaii revealed, he deplored the encroachments of the European powers in Asia. But at this time, Japan's relations with China were strained because of the Ryūkyū issue, and any pleasure in Chinese victories would have been muted.

In any case, it is unlikely that the emperor gave much thought to the Sino-French conflict. From the latter part of April, he frequently failed to attend cabinet meetings because of illness. The imperial household minister Itō Hirobumi, was greatly worried and asked the emperor to send for his physician, Ikeda Kensai. The emperor had always disliked doctors, and so when urged to have a doctor examine him, he refused, saying he was suffering from nothing worse than a cold. Only after Itō had repeatedly begged the emperor to see a doctor did he at last reluctantly consent.[27]

There is no indication what illness was troubling the emperor. It may be that he was suffering less from a physical ailment than from depression. The chamberlain Fujinami Kototada (1852–1926) late in life recalled how unapproachable the emperor had been at this time.[28] He mentioned how after sending word that he was indisposed, the emperor often failed to attend cabinet meetings. Even when Itō Hirobumi requested an audience with him in order to report on some court or national business, the emperor sometimes refused to see him. Palace rules prescribed that except in a great emergency, not even the prime minister might visit the emperor's sickroom, and Itō wondered whether the emperor was actually ill.

Itō was understandably upset. He was a minister and had matters of importance to report personally, but he was refused permission to appear before the emperor. Even supposing the emperor was indisposed, the illness seemed not to be so serious that he could not meet his ministers. Itō was convinced that urgent affairs of state must not be neglected even briefly. He wondered if the emperor found him personally offensive and for this reason was indisposed to discuss governmental business with him. Itō finally decided he could no longer bear the heavy responsibility of his office and, handing to an attendant his letter of resignation, left the palace.

Yoshii Tomozane (1828–1891) and others of Itō's staff, learning what had happened, were alarmed. Yoshii sent for the chamberlain, Fujinami Kototada. He told him, "His Majesty is indisposed and refuses to see the imperial household minister. He is hardly likely to see any of us. There is nothing we can do about this, so we are asking you to think of a way of enabling the minister to have an audience." He chose to make this request of Fujinami because he knew that he had served the emperor ever since he was a boy and that the emperor gave him free access to his private quarters.

Fujinami did not welcome the suggestion: "Reporting such matters is no part of a chamberlain's duties. If I did mention them, I would be forced to some extent to admonish the emperor. My job does not permit this."

Yoshii replied, "I understand your position. However, if speaking to the emperor makes him angry with you, we will do everything in our power to help you.[29] We are asking you to risk your life by speaking to him."

Faced with this appeal to his courage, Fujinami made up his mind to speak to the emperor. First he informed the empress of his resolution. Later, he also told the ladies-in-waiting. Watching for the right moment, he finally managed to have a private audience with the emperor. He said, "Recently the imperial household minister, Itō Hirobumi, has requested again and again an audience with Your Majesty to discuss state affairs, but you have refused to see him, saying you are confined by illness to your bed. Your Majesty is surely aware in your wisdom that affairs of state must not be neglected even for a day. I believe that it would also be highly improper for Your Majesty to learn from a third person what the minister wishes to report to you. I have read that the holy sovereigns of the past adjusted their dress and listened respectfully when their ministers made reports, but this is not possible under present conditions. I beg Your Majesty to grant Hirobumi an audience."

The emperor colored with anger and reprimanded Fujinami, "You are in no position to tell me anything of this kind. Bear in mind the nature of your duties."

Fujinami spoke again: "I am aware that addressing such matters to Your Majesty is in contravention of my duties, but for the sake of Your Majesty, for the sake of the nation, I cannot keep silent. That is what has possessed me to speak of such matters. I am ready to accept whatever punishment is due me, however severe. But I beg you with bended head to change your mind."

The emperor, in a rage, got up from his seat without a word and went directly into his bedroom. The empress indicated to Fujinami that he should go, and he left.

The next morning, after inquiring about the emperor's health, Fujinami set about performing his duties in his customary manner. When he went to another room, the emperor asked a page to see if Fujinami was still about. Fujinami told the page to inform the emperor that he had left. The emperor suddenly commanded: "Send for the imperial household minister!"

Itō went to the palace as soon as word reached him, and he was granted an audience with the emperor. Itō's face showed no sign of his irritation over the failure of his previous attempts to see the emperor, and the emperor did not allude to them. Itō described the state business that had piled up and left after requesting the emperor to give these matters his attention. Itō, realizing it was owing to Fujinami that he had been able to see the emperor, thanked him for his faithful service.

One day, about two months after this incident, the emperor called to Fujinami, who was on duty in the corridor. He said, "The other day you spoke very well on my behalf. I am extremely pleased with you. If in the future the same sort of thing should occur, do not hesitate to do the same. These are mere trifles, but I give them to you." He presented Fujinami with a gold watch and a bolt of silk. Fujinami wept profusely with gratitude.

This story fits in with the relative scarcity of mentions of the emperor's activities during the period from April into the summer of 1884. However, this period was by no means a total blank: not only did the emperor give audiences to foreign visitors and the like, but on June 25, when the railway line from Ueno to Takasaki was completed, he rode the train to Takasaki. All the same, compared with other years, the entries relating to the emperor are so skimpy as to suggest that the emperor may not have been giving full attention to state business. Fujinami's recollections of the incident were related long after the events, and he may have confused what happened at this time with Itō's attempt to resign as minister in July 1885 after the emperor had refused to see him when he had urgent business.[30] But surely Fujinami, even in old age, would not have invented the gift of the gold watch.

In any case, by the end of July the emperor had resumed his normal schedule. On July 28 he gave an audience to Medical Officer Second Class Mori Rintarō (later known as the celebrated author Mori Ōgai), who had been ordered to study in Germany. On the same day, he attended the graduation exercises of the Army Military Academy and presented gifts to graduates with the best marks.

A more important event of this month did not directly involve the emperor. The foreign minister, Inoue Kaoru, stressing the urgent need for treaty revision, proposed that the ban on Christianity be lifted. Although the ban had not been enforced since March 1873, when all persons who had been imprisoned for professing Christianity were released, it was technically still in effect, and this continued to rankle some foreign powers.[31]

Of equal concern was the rise of a reactionary group that called itself the Imperial Way (*kōdō*). Its members denounced Christianity and, terming its believers "religious bandits," called for their expulsion. They also expressed aversion for foreigners in general and demanded that European influence be purged from the country. Inoue believed that such people were acting contrary to the emperor's intentions as enunciated in his Oath and worried lest such people block national progress and impede negotiations for treaty revision.

Another religious problem was deciding on the extent of government control of Shintō and Buddhism. In 1872 the Ministry of Religious Instruction (*kyō-bushō*) and moral instructors (*kyōdōshoku*) of Shintō and Buddhism had been established, permitting the government to intervene directly in religious matters. Opposition to this system had developed, so the Ministry of Religious Instruction was abolished in 1877. Then the moral instructors were abolished in August 1884 and replaced with supervisors for each sect of both religions.[32] This liberalization of control over religion did not meet with unanimous acclaim. Shintō priests in Ōsaka, Kyōto, Kōbe, and elsewhere were dismayed to learn that the moral instructors had been abolished. They were sure this would lead to the spread of Christianity and bring about irreparable harm. The evil might well culminate in acts of irreverence toward the shrines of the founder of the empire (Emperor Jimmu); in destruction of shrines; in disrespect for the ruler and in dishonor for parents; in diminished regard for the state; in contempt for the laws; in a complete change in the concepts of loyalty, filial piety, and fidelity to principles; and, finally, in a complete collapse within the hearts of people. Eighty-one Shintō priests signed a document to this effect that was presented to Prime Minister Sanjō Sanetomi, with a request for prompt action to halt Inoue's proposal.

Late in October 1884 Emperor Meiji sent a message to King Kojong informing him that of the 500,000 yen that Japan had been awarded in indemnity by the Treaty of Chemulp'o, all but the 100,000 yen already paid by the Koreans would be returned. The emperor had previously advised cabinet members that with the objective of securing the peace throughout East Asia, it would be desirable to give Korea financial help. Kim Ok-kyun and Pak Yong-hyo, men dedicated to creating in Korea a strong and prosperous nation on the model of Japan, were now participating in the Korean government and making strenuous efforts to achieve national independence. However, the stringent financial situation made it impossible for the Koreans to progress. Accordingly, the emperor decided to send Takezoe Shin'ichirō (1842–1917) as minister resident[33] to communicate to the king of Korea the emperor's decision to return the indemnity. The king expressed profound gratitude.

In the meantime, leaders of the progressive faction in Korea, convinced that China's engagement in the war with France would prevent it from intervening in Korea, decided that the time had come to oust the corrupt government and replace it with one dedicated to the country's modernization.[34] The Japanese supported these men, saying it was essential to preserve Korea's independence from China.

At the time there were two "parties" in Korea. The government was controlled by the Sadaedang (Serving the Great Party). It was pro-Chinese (China was the great power Korea served), opposed to major changes, and closely associated with Queen Min and her family. The Kaehwadang (Progressive Party)[35] advocated Korean independence from China. It was led by men who had been impressed by the success of Japanese modernization. On November 4 leaders of the progressive faction met at the house of Pak Yong-hyo in Seoul. A member of the Japanese legation also attended. Various courses of action were considered, one of which was adopted: to stage a coup d'état on December 4, the day when the new post office was to open.

That evening Hong Yong-sik, recently appointed as postmaster general, gave a banquet at the post office. The dinner began at six, but about seven a fire alarm was sounded, interrupting the festivities. A house across the street was burning. A nephew of Queen Min went out to investigate the fire, only to be attacked with a sword by a man in Japanese clothes. The other guests, seeing what had happened, fled.[36]

Kim Ok-kyun and Pak Yong-hyo hurried to the Japanese legation to make sure that Japanese troops would help the progressives. The troops were in fact lined up and ready to attack. Kim Ok-kyun and the other progressives set out for the palace, which had been thrown into a state of confusion by explosions set off by their supporters in the palace compound. Kim and the others, entering the presence of the king, informed him that the Chinese were coming to capture him. The king did not believe this, but he was powerless to resist. Kim Ok-kyun asked the king to send for the Japanese minister requesting protection. He refused, but one of the rebels dashed off a note in the king's name. The minister and the Japanese soldiers arrived shortly afterward.

Early the next morning, Kim Ok-kyun, using the king's seal, sent a message to leaders of the Sadaedang commanding them to come to the palace. They were arrested and killed as they arrived. With Japanese help, the Kaehwadang had seized control of the government, and a new cabinet was formed consisting of its members. The coup seemed to have succeeded, and the king was preparing to proclaim a change in the government; but then Koreans who had learned what had happened went to Yüan Shih-kai, the commanding general of the Chinese forces in the city, and begged him to intervene. The Chinese forces, which outnumbered the Japanese troops by seven to one, attacked the palace and rescued the king, who at once declared his opposition to the rebels. Fighting ensued between the Japanese and the Chinese. The Chinese forces were augmented by Koreans who had seemed up until then to be pro-Japanese.

The Japanese lost more than 30 of their 150 men. They withdrew from the palace, taking the progressive leaders with them. Soon more than 300 people crammed into the Japanese legation, which did not have enough food to feed them for even one day. Takezoe decided that the Japanese must fight their way out of Seoul to the coast.[37] They did so, reaching Inch'on on December 8. On the following day a message from the king was delivered to Takezoe, sympathizing with his difficulties and asking him to return to Seoul to settle matters, apparently discounting the importance of the clash between the Japanese and the Chinese. The British and Americans also urged Takezoe to wait, but he and a shipful of Japanese and Korean refugees sailed for Nagasaki on December 11.

The incident was not yet over. On December 21 the emperor received Inoue Kaoru and told him that he was sending him to Korea as minister extraordinary and plenipotentiary. Inoue would be accompanied by high-ranking military officers. The emperor was prompted to take this step by the controversy that had been aroused by Takezoe's return with details of the failed coup. The Chinese minister to Japan had also reported that China had sent a large number of soldiers to Korea. Inoue would take a message to the Korean king stating that he was ready to confer with senior Korean officials in order to determine who was responsible for the recent incident, to see that the appropriate punishment was carried out, and that the Japanese received reimbursement for the damage to the legation. If in fact the king had requested protection from the Japanese minister (as the Japanese claimed), the king should send a letter of apology to the emperor so as to dispel all doubts, both at home and abroad, as to what had happened. The Chinese should be asked, in the interests of peace, to agree to join the Japanese in withdrawing their forces from Korea.

Inoue requested two battalions of troops to escort him to Korea, and this was agreed on. He would also be protected by three warships. By this time he had concluded that Japan had brought about the incident by its own actions. Having decided to promote Korean independence, Japan had intervened in Korea's internal politics to achieve this end; Japan had also tried to persuade other countries to accept Japan's position. Japan now had to decide between one of two courses. The first was to pursue its demands for Korean independence, even if this meant war with China. Of course, friendly relations with neighboring countries were important, but to temporize was to invite future trouble, and nothing should be tolerated that might harm Japanese prestige. Now that China was occupied with a war with France, if the Japanese presented their demands with a sufficient show of force, the Korean court was likely to accept. That was why Inoue had asked for the two battalions. If this course of action was found unacceptable, because maintaining peace was more important than any other consideration, the second alternative—abandoning plans for Korea's independence and recognizing China's suzerainty over Korea—should be adopted. Inoue asked for a prompt answer as to the course Japan would follow.[38]

He received the same day an answer from Sanjō urging that war with China be avoided at all costs. Sanjō reminded Inoue that he must obey his original orders to reach a peaceful solution acceptable to both Japan and China. He said that the two battalions were being sent not as a display of force but because it was feared Korea might be a dangerous place after the failed coup. He added that it was not possible at present to decide whether to support Korean independence, even at the risk of war with China.

Inoue arrived in Inch'on on December 30, still uncertain what course to follow. He was not the only one who was puzzled. For another decade, relations with China and Korea remained a riddle for Japanese diplomats to ponder.

Chapter 38

On November 28, 1883, the completion of the Rokumeikan, a two-story building in Western-style architecture, was celebrated in a ceremony presided over by the foreign minister, Inoue Kaoru, and his wife, Takeko. The old Enryōkan, where foreign dignitaries (beginning with the duke of Edinburgh) had previously been entertained, was a cheaply constructed building, originally erected by the shogunate as a training school for naval cadets. By now, despite the interior decorations added when the building was converted into a residence for foreign guests, the Enryōkan was badly showing its age.[1] A new building was needed.

The Rokumeikan was designed by the English architect Josiah Conder in "French Renaissance style" (so termed because of the mansard roof), but the arched portico of the facade had a vaguely Moorish look and the columns showed an Indian influence. Only the garden with its pines, pond, and stone lanterns indicated that this particular example of eclectic architecture was situated in Japan. The style of the building reflected Inoue's cosmopolitan tastes, and the presence of his wife at the opening ceremony, unthinkable on a state occasion fifteen years earlier, was a sign that women would participate prominently in the future activities of the new building.

The Rokumeikan was erected on the site of a former armory of the Satsuma domain at a total cost of 180,000 yen (compared with 40,000 yen for the Foreign Ministry building).[2] Surely nothing could be further from the spartan discipline characteristic of Satsuma samurai than the frivolity to which the new building was dedicated. The extent of the changes that had occurred in a bare fifteen years seemed to be symbolized by the fairy-tale appearance of the building, replacing the forbidding walls of an earlier era. The name Rokumeikan itself was derived from a "deer crying" (*rokumei*) song in the ancient Chinese book of poetry the *Shih Ching* that describes how a host had welcomed honored guests. The name was appropriate, for entertaining foreign guests would be a major function of the new building.[3] Foreigners, no longer denounced as excrescences who defiled the Land of the Gods, would be ceremoniously feted at the Rokumeikan.

An equally important function of the Rokumeikan was as a stage on which Japanese might display to foreigners that, having turned their backs on the antiquated ways of the past, they had become masters of European table manners and the decorum of the ballroom. The meals served at the Rokumeikan were elaborate, and the many courses were listed in French on the menus.[4] In the ballroom, Japanese gentlemen wearing evening clothes ordered from London and ladies in gowns designed in Paris danced the quadrille, waltz, polka, mazurka, or galop to the latest European tunes played by the army and navy bands. For those who had not yet learned how to dance, foreign residents of Tōkyō were available as tutors.[5]

Conservative commentators frowned on Japanese who participated in ballroom dancing, warning that men and women who embraced in public were likely to yield to immoral impulses. Here is how one dance was reported in the press:

A beautiful woman leans her head against a man's shoulder and turns her fair face toward the man's ears. Her bare arm circles the man's neck, and her undulant bosom touches the man's chest, rising and falling with her breathing. Her legs intertwine with the man's like vines on a pine tree. The man's strong right arm firmly encircles the small of the woman's back; with each move he presses her ever more tightly to his body. The light flowing in the beautiful woman's eyes is steadily directed at the man, but she is too dazzled to see anything. The music stirs her, but she does not hear the sounds. She hears instead the echoes of a distant waterfall and moves as in a dream, her body clinging to the man's. When a woman reaches such a state, where is the innate modesty of the virtuous maiden?[6]

Many Japanese shared these moral objections to ballroom dancing, but members of the upper classes had decided that it was a necessary social accomplishment. To improve their skill, they attended practice sessions that were held on Sunday nights from October 1884 at the Rokumeikan. A contemporary account reported:

Married ladies and young women of the gentry, from the wives of Councillor Inoue, Councillor Ōyama, and Minister of Education Mori on
down, gathered at the Rokumeikan at six in the afternoon on the twenty-
seventh of the month for a practice session of dancing. This was in preparation for the ball that will be held on the third of next month, on the
emperor's birthday. The steady improvement in the ladies' proficiency at
dancing means that gentlemen who are unfamiliar with this art will unfortunately be unable to enjoy the pleasure of being partners to the ladies
when the ball takes place. Officials of the Foreign Office, the Imperial
Household Ministry, and other agencies have consequently begun to take
lessons, and there is gossip concerning whether or not they are likely to
become proficient by the third of next month.[7]

Probably most of those who danced at the Rokumeikan had nothing more
profound in mind than displaying their expensive costumes and terpsichorean
skills, but Inoue hoped that by cultivating congenial relations with foreign dignitaries, he might persuade them that the Japanese had attained so high a degree
of European culture that they had to be treated as equals. His ultimate goal
was the abolition of extraterritoriality, the symbol of European distrust of Japanese justice and the most obvious instance of foreign feelings of superiority
toward the Japanese.

It is doubtful that the amenities of the Rokumeikan contributed significantly
to ending the unequal treaties. Contrary to the hopes of the Japanese, Europeans who attended balls were not impressed by Japanese efforts to prove that
they could successfully act like Europeans. In fact, they found the appearance
of Japanese men and women in expensive foreign clothes amusing and even
ludicrous. A cartoon by the French artist Georges Bigot shows a man and a
woman standing before a mirror. Her hair, starched to imposing heights, is
crowned with a feathered bonnet; her bustle and umbrella are the last word in
Parisian elegance. Her companion's moustache is waxed, and he carries a silk
hat, but the legs under his elegantly tailored jacket are matchsticks. The reflection in the mirror shows a pair of monkeys.[8]

Bigot's cruel jest is labeled "Monsieur et Madame vont dans le Monde."
This was how the Japanese guests at the Rokumeikan appeared to foreigners.
Pierre Loti, who arrived in Japan in July 1886 and was invited to the ball on the
emperor's birthday in November, described his experience in both his diary
and the story "Un bal à Yeddo,"[9] a visitor's impressions of a ball at the
Rokumeikan:

> The first European-style ball, held in the middle of Tōkyō, was quite
> simply a monkey show. Young ladies, dressed in white muslin and wearing
> gloves that reached above their elbows, sat on chairs, holding engagement

books white as ivory in their fingers and maintaining forced smiles on their faces. Presently, they could be seen dancing polkas and waltzes, more or less correctly, to tunes from operettas, though the sounds of our rhythms surely must fall most unpleasantly on their ears. . . .

This contemptible imitation is certainly interesting for the visiting foreigner to observe, but it reveals that this people has no taste and is absolutely lacking in national pride.[10]

Loti was more generous in his description of a few of the ladies. He was most impressed by Inoue Takeko, the wife of the foreign minister, who stood at the head of the stairs alongside her husband, greeting guests with a smile and words of welcome. Her ease and accomplished manner revealed that she had spent time abroad as one of the first Japanese women to accompany her husband to a diplomatic post. Loti repeated the rumor he had heard that she was formerly a geisha (a matter of speculation). He declared, in any case, that her costume could pass muster in Paris and that her manners were faultless. He concluded his description with an expression of admiration for the complete ease she displayed, even to holding out her hand for him to shake, like an American woman.[11]

Inoue's adopted daughter Sueko, twenty years old in 1885, had also accompanied him to Europe. She was not only beautiful but talented, able to entertain foreign visitors to the Rokumeikan with diverting conversation in both English and French.[12] Inoue had every reason to feel proud of his wife's and daughter's mastery of European etiquette, but contrary to his hopes, the parties at the Rokumeikan promoted the canard that the Japanese were a "race of imitators," who, lacking a culture of their own, merely borrowed and imitated the culture created in China or the West.

This was by no means the first time foreigners had seen Japanese in Western clothes. Japanese men had long ago realized that they would not be taken seriously if they persisted in wearing their quaint native garb. The women, too, particularly those of the upper classes, had enjoyed dressing in the European fashions of the day. But when Japanese, not content with wearing Western clothes as a sign of being modern, took to attiring themselves in the fancy dress typical of the Rokumeikan and practiced the etiquette appropriate to these clothes, the foreign guests laughed at these imitations of themselves.

A high point of the Rokumeikan culture was the costume ball staged two years later at the prime minister's residence by Itō Hirobumi. More than 400 members of the nobility and high government officials, as well as foreign diplomats and their wives, sported fancy dress. Itō and his wife, Umeko, were attired as members of the Venetian nobility, and their daughter as an Italian peasant girl.[13]

The adoption of Western culture—even a peculiar example of Western culture like the costume ball—into the mainstream of Japanese culture was nevertheless a central event of the time. The naïveté of Japanese enthusiasm for the West at this time is likely to excite smiles today, but writers of more recent times have experienced nostalgia for the brief flowering of the Rokumeikan, a time when some Japanese boldly stepped from the shadows of upper-class society of the past into a brightly lit ballroom evoking the Paris of Napoleon III.

Inoue Kaoru's ultimate objective of inducing foreigners to end extraterritoriality ended in failure, and in 1887 he resigned as foreign minister. Again and again, he had thought that treaty revision was near, only to be frustrated by the actions of some foreign power. As early as 1882, the Germans had expressed a readiness to give up extraterritoriality completely within eight to ten years if the Japanese would open up the entire country to foreign commerce and improve their legal system. The Americans had long since agreed to abolish extraterritoriality and control of customs, providing that other countries did the same. Both Germany and the United States were willing to make concessions over legal jurisdiction in return for commercial advantages.[14] Even the British, the most unyielding advocates of extraterritoriality, showed signs that they might make concessions.[15] A memorandum to Inoue in August 1884 from the British minister Francis Plunkett, Parkes's successor, declared that it was not England's intention to maintain extraterritoriality in perpetuity, that it would be abandoned just as soon as the Japanese government perfected its civil, commercial, and appeals laws and arranged to have them translated.[16] By 1886 the Board of Trade in England was expressing concern lest Britain's refusal to agree to Japan's demands on extraterritoriality harm its trade with Japan.[17]

But these promising signs failed to bring immediate results. Foreigners in Japan, convinced that once they were at the mercy of Japanese justice, they would be arrested without cause and subjected to oriental tortures, resisted change. The Japanese struggle to end extraterritoriality continued until this system was finally terminated on August 4, 1899. Tariff autonomy was not achieved until 1911, but as one scholar has pointed out,

> There is little doubt that the Japanese were anxious to recover tariff autonomy, but there is equally little doubt that the main thrust of the campaign against Bakumatsu-period treaties was the desire to end extraterritoriality and its slur on Japan's rights as a sovereign state. It was not fortuitous that the Japanese were prepared to postpone full tariff autonomy until 1911 in exchange for the abandonment of extraterritoriality in 1894–1898.[18]

The year 1885 marked the height of the prestige and glamour of the Rokumeikan. Quite apart from the brilliance of the parties held there, this was one of the memorable years of Japanese cultural history. Major works of literature and criticism that appeared this year included *The Essence of the Novel* (*Shōsetsu shinzui*) by Tsubouchi Shōyō, *Fortuitous Meetings with Beautiful Women*

(*Kajin no kigū*) by Tōkai Sanshi, and the remarkable translation of Bulwer-Lytton's novel *Kenelm Chillingly*.

As far as Meiji was concerned, however, 1885 (like 1884) was a depressing year during which he found it difficult to concentrate on his work. Although he would be known in later years for the long hours he spent each day at his desk, at this time he spent barely two hours a day—from ten in the morning until noon—in his office. Moreover, much of his time was spent in casual conversation about palace affairs with the head chamberlain and others of his staff, even while ministers and councillors were kept waiting fruitlessly for an audience at which they planned to discuss state business. Even Itō Hirobumi, who not only enjoyed the emperor's confidence but was responsible for palace affairs, could not have an audience with the emperor whenever he felt it was necessary. This so upset him that once again he expressed the intention of resigning his post as imperial household minister.

In a letter he wrote to Sanjō Sanetomi, Itō expressed fears that Meiji's reputation for intelligence and wisdom might in the end prove to have been hollow. At a time of unprecedented changes that called for the emperor to provide a model for all ages to come, his idle frittering away of his time was unworthy of his ancestors and future members of the imperial line. The emperor was leaving decisions on state business to ministers and lesser officers and seldom examined in detail reports of cabinet meetings submitted to him. Even on the rare occasion when he looked over the reports, he never asked a question about them. Itō asked if it was possible for the emperor, for all his inborn wisdom, to obtain a complete grasp of the extremely complicated state of affairs of the times. The emperor's chief confidants—Tokudaiji Sanetsune, the head chamberlain, and Motoda Nagazane, his Confucian tutor—were estimable men, but they were ignorant of the world situation and had no idea whether a particular policy was to Japan's advantage or disadvantage. Moreover, they were not elected officials and were therefore not responsible to anyone for their actions. Itō warned that at this critical time in world history, an error of judgment or policy might result in disaster to Japan's survival.[19]

It is not clear whether Itō actually sent this letter to Sanjō. It is not clear either why Meiji seemed so indifferent to state business. Perhaps the main cause was boredom. The matters that were of enormous importance to Itō probably did not excite the emperor. It might have done him good to attend a ball at the Rokumeikan, but that, of course, was beneath his dignity.[20]

Another cause of the emperor's depression might have been his health. During the previous year, as we have seen, he at times refused to meet his cabinet, alleging illness, and this year, too, he again and again suffered from colds and fever. In April he was to go to Fukuoka to observe a large-scale maneuver of troops from the Hiroshima and Kumamoto garrisons, and on his return from the maneuvers, he would make a *junkō* of Yamaguchi, Hiroshima, and Okayama Prefectures. But illness kept him from attending the maneuvers, and the *junkō* was postponed. Inability to attend maneuvers, one of the emperor's great pleasures, no doubt depressed him. He may have felt relieved not to have to make another *junkō*, but the people of the three prefectures expressed such disappointment that he promised to go later that month.

Another cause of depression may have been the unseasonable weather, particularly the heavy rains and wind that caused great damage to houses and crops. The emperor ordered that reports on damage to the crops—and on no other subject—be submitted to him. The news was dismal. The tea harvest was expected to be only half of normal, and of wheat, only 40 percent of normal. People recalled that it was just fifty years since the terrible famine that lasted from 1833 to 1836 and wondered uneasily whether they were to be afflicted with another one. In the spring and early summer, there were torrential rains, and the rivers overflowed their banks, causing flooding and much damage to houses.[21]

The emperor might have been cheered by his one surviving child, Prince Yoshihito, but the boy lived at the house of his great-grandfather, Nakayama Tadayasu, and Meiji probably saw little of him. Now that the prince had reached the age of seven years (by Japanese count), his education and health began to concern the emperor, and it was decided in March that he should henceforth live in the palace. Two years earlier the minister of education, Fukuoka Takachika, had proposed that a kindergarten be established in the palace where the prince might begin his education. This proposal was carefully considered, but (because it represented a departure from the education traditionally given an heir to the throne) steps to implement the proposal were taken cautiously. A pavilion for the kindergarten was erected in the Aoyama Palace, and boys of Yoshihito's age were selected as his classmates. He was of such delicate health, however, that the plan could not be carried out.[22] All the same, a start had to be made on his education, and the emperor asked his old tutor, Motoda Nagazane, to prepare a curriculum and a program of study.

Motoda's suggestions were surprisingly liberal. He recommended that the instructors not be bound by rules but give the prince informal guidance even while he was playing. The pace of instructing the prince should be set according to what was appropriate for gradual progress, rather than by a timetable. The prince would have two hours of instruction each morning in reading, writing, arithmetic, and morals and two hours of exercise each afternoon. In addition, every other day he would practice singing for half an hour.

The program was initiated in March 1885, but the prince's health remained uncertain. In June he was allowed to return to Nakayama Tadayasu's house for a visit. That night, back in the palace, he suddenly fell ill. He ran a high fever and suffered from convulsions. It took a month for him to recover.[23] Perhaps the illness was psychosomatic, induced by his reluctance to leave the nostalgic warmth of the Nakayama house for the solemnity of the palace.

The emperor decided in September that Prince Yoshihito would enter the

Gakushū-in in the following year, a break with the tradition of private instruction for children of the imperial family. Motoda and various others would be asked to prepare a curriculum for the prince's education, and between fifteen and twenty boys of the imperial family and high-ranking nobility would be chosen as his playmates. Later that year, the emperor commanded Nishimura Shigeki, a scholar of Western learning, to take charge of the prince's education, a reflection of his conviction that the old methods of education, based on the antiquated usages of the palace, were no longer viable. He wished Nishimura to give the future emperor an education suited to the modern age.[24]

On July 26 the emperor set out on his promised junkō of Yamaguchi, Hiroshima, and Okayama.[25] This was probably the most wearisome and least pleasurable of his travels, mainly because of the extreme heat.[26] People along the way wept with joy on beholding the imperial countenance, but the emperor himself was exhausted. Although he was normally ready to accept stoically the hardships of a journey, this time the blazing heat was too much even for him. When the imperial party reached Itsukushima, the emperor sent a chamberlain to worship at the shrine in his place, and when in the vicinity of Shizutani-kō, the Confucian academy founded in 1668 by Ikeda Mitsumasa—the kind of place Meiji normally most enjoyed visiting—he sent the chief chamberlain to make the inspection. Despite the heat, the emperor was obliged to meet local dignitaries and examine local products, however little appetite he may have had for such occasions.[27]

The emperor's ship returned to Yokohama on August 12, greeted by salutes from ships and shore. His junkō had lasted only eighteen days, but every day he rose at four or five in the morning and he did not get to bed until midnight. The journey itself, whether on land or sea, had been painful because of the incredible heat. His travels had brought joy to his subjects, but he had not been permitted even one day of rest.

Back in Tōkyō, the emperor's normal routine was resumed. King Kalakaua sent his portrait to the emperor, a mark of friendship and respect. Pope Leo XIII sent a letter expressing his thanks for the emperor's generous treatment of Christian missionaries and asking for relations between Japan and the Vatican similar to those formed with the rulers of the major countries of Europe and America. After consultation, the emperor granted the pope's envoy an audience at which he assured him that he intended Christian believers to enjoy the same protection as other Japanese.[28] King Umberto of Italy asked for some Japanese deer, and he received a pair from the emperor. The court went into mourning for twenty-one days on receiving word of the death of Alfonso XII of Spain.

Probably the most satisfactory aspect of 1885 for the emperor was in foreign relations. The year began promisingly when King Kojong of Korea sent in February a formal apology for the incident of December 1884 in which Japanese had been killed.[29]

In the same month, Lieutenant General Takashima Tomonosuke and Rear

Admiral Viscount Kabayama Sukenori, both of whom had seen service in Korea, submitted a document to the Court Council in which they contrasted the steady progress toward modernization Japan had achieved as the result of its adoption of the government, education, laws, and military systems of Europe and America with the obdurate clinging to the old ways of the Chinese. The two countries were headed in quite different directions, which had created in the Chinese feelings of envy and suspicion. Takashima and Kabayama recalled clashes between China and Japan in recent years, particularly the incidents of 1884 when the Chinese attacked Japanese units in Korea and inflicted casualties. They urged resolute action to clear away the sinister clouds and to eradicate the pestilential fumes; otherwise, there was no telling what disaster might occur between the two countries. They were sure that this was a unique opportunity to promote national power and to elevate the prestige of the imperial house.[30]

The Court Council's response was to dispatch Itō Hirobumi to China as ambassador plenipotentiary in order to deal with the increasing rift between China and Japan. It was hoped he would be able to sign a treaty that would keep the Chinese from further interfering in Korea. Enomoto Takeaki, the Japanese minister to China, was secretly instructed to ask the good offices of Sir Harry Parkes (long the bane of the Japanese but now a potential friend as the British minister in Peking) in sounding out Li Hung-chang's intentions. If Li refused to make arrangements with Japan concerning Korea, the Japanese government was prepared to seek satisfaction.

Itō was provided with credentials to be presented to the Chinese emperor and with instructions from the Japanese government describing its wishes for peace between the two countries but insisting that the Chinese meet two conditions: (1) the officer who commanded the troops involved in the December 6 incident should be punished; and (2) Chinese troops must be withdrawn from Seoul. If the Chinese accepted these terms, the Japanese were prepared to withdraw at the same time their troops guarding the Japanese legation in Seoul. If, however, the Chinese refused to sign such an agreement, the Japanese would be obliged to act in the interests of national self-defense. In that case, sooner or later there was bound to be a clash, and the responsibility would lie entirely with the Chinese.[31]

Itō and his party sailed for China on February 28. The emperor expressed full confidence in Itō's ability to reach a peaceful settlement, but popular feelings had been aroused against China and there were calls for conquest. The atmosphere was so reminiscent of the era when an invasion of Korea had been urged that Prime Minister Sanjō felt it advisable to send a memorandum to ministers and other high-ranking officials emphasizing the emperor's desire for peace.[32]

Itō arrived in Tientsin on March 14. The Chinese expected him to confer immediately with Li Hung-chang, who had been delegated with full powers, but Itō thought it advisable to proceed first to Peking for an audience with the emperor at which he might present his credentials. He hoped also to open discussions in Peking, but the Chinese ministers refused, pointing out that the emperor was still a child. They urged Itō to confer instead with Li in Tientsin. Itō and his party accordingly returned to Tientsin on April 2. The discussions between Itō and Li were difficult, but on April 15 they at last reached an agreement. They signed a treaty providing for the withdrawal of both countries' troops from Korea. The commander of the Chinese troops at the time of the December 6 incident would not be punished, but alleged crimes against Japanese would be investigated, and Chinese soldiers who were found guilty of committing them would be punished accordingly. Itō accepted this modification of his original demands because, he said, of the emperor's desire for peace in East Asia.[33]

When Itō returned to Tōkyō, he was warmly thanked by the emperor. The next day, the emperor sent word asking Sanjō whether Itō should be given the same reward (10,000 yen) that Ōkubo Toshimichi received after his successful negotiations in Peking concerning Taiwan or whether he should be promoted to first rank or perhaps given an annual stipend.[34] Some at the court thought Itō deserved to be made a marquis. Sanjō apparently recommended that Itō be given 10,000 yen plus a set of gold cups,[35] but during the following months, a horse, a gift from the emperor, was Itō's chief material reward.[36] He received an even more welcome sign of imperial approbation when on July 7 the emperor, together with more than twenty members of the nobility and high-ranking officials, visited Itō's residence.[37]

There could be little doubt of the emperor's high regard for Itō, although he did not share Itō's unbounded enthusiasm for Western culture. In September the emperor resumed his Friday lunches with princes, councillors, and other high-ranking members of the government and the military, perhaps a sign he had shaken off his apathy. In November, Itō, in his capacity of imperial household minister, proposed that in view of the increasingly heavy demands on the emperor's time, meals with Japanese and foreigners, evening parties, and balls be restricted to the period between chrysanthemum viewing and cherry-blossom viewing.

About this time, another politician began to figure prominently in the highest circles, Kuroda Kiyotaka. He had resigned in February 1883 his position as major general[38] and requested permission to make a tour of China, mainly in order to promote the sale in China of Hokkaidō products. Inoue Kaoru turned down the request, saying that in view of the tense relations between Japan and China, it was not an ideal time for a senior member of the government to be visiting China.[39] In February 1885 Kuroda again proposed going to China, this time in order to observe the war between China and France. He had an audience with the emperor, who agreed to send him because China, Japan's nearest neighbor, was a country of prime importance. The emperor asked Kuroda to submit reports on the Sino-French War.[40] Although this was to be an unofficial journey, the emperor gave Kuroda 4,000 yen for his expenses.

Kuroda traveled first to Hong Kong, arriving on the same day that Itō reached Tientsin, and from there he went to Singapore. He would have liked to travel farther south, but learning on April 16 of the treaty signed in Tientsin between China and Japan, he decided instead to go north to Peking, where he was soon drinking merrily with the Japanese minister, Enomoto Takeaki.[41] Kuroda returned to Japan on September 5.

At this stage Sanjō considered appointing Kuroda as minister of the right to fill the position left empty by Iwakura's death. He asked Itō's opinion. Itō replied that no one was better qualified than Kuroda and promised to do what he could to assist him. This inclined Kuroda to accept, but when Sanjō reported to the emperor, he received an unexpected reaction: the emperor said that the post of minister of the right entailed heavy responsibilities and that the occupant must therefore be a man of sterling reputation, which could hardly be said of Kuroda. He added astutely that if Kuroda were to take this office, he would soon discover that real power was in the hands of Itō and that he was likely to become resentful.[42]

Sanjō then proposed that Itō become minister of the right, but Itō, aware that if he accepted, he would be strengthening the *dajōkan*—the antiquated system of government—and would thereby lose the chance to abolish it, refused, insisting that Kuroda be appointed. Once again this was reported to the emperor, who asked if *all* the councillors had agreed on Kuroda. One councillor, Sasaki Takayuki, a man the emperor respected, had in fact not taken part in the decision. Sasaki privately expressed disapproval of Kuroda, citing his disorderly behavior, the adverse gossip about him, and especially his drunkenness.[43] Sanjō at length persuaded Sasaki not to voice his objections, probably by threatening to dismiss him from the post of minister of works.

Presumably it was because of his meritorious service in Hokkaidō that Kuroda was proposed as minister of the right, but it is baffling to a modern reader that a man seriously implicated in the Colonization Office scandal of 1881 should have been considered for the third-highest post in the government. His personal life was certainly not beyond reproach. He was known as the heaviest drinker in political circles of the Meiji era and was sometimes was too drunk to deal with difficult decisions. His drunkenness often induced him to display his fierce temper. Finally, his wife had died in 1878 under mysterious circumstances.[44]

When Sanjō informed Kuroda that he was unanimously supported by the councillors, he was once again surprised: Kuroda now refused the position, saying that he was unworthy to occupy a post that neither Saigō Takamori nor Ōkubo Toshimichi had attained. He also mentioned his reluctance to be Itō's superior. Whether or not these were his real feelings, it seems likely he had heard of the opposition to his appointment expressed by the emperor and Sasaki and was also aware of the motivation behind Sanjō's and Itō's support. Kuroda withdrew from public life for the time being. He was much gratified when despite persistent rumors that he had killed his wife, the emperor visited his house on November 11.[45]

When Sanjō Sanetomi proposed that the emperor appoint Kuroda Kiyotaka as minister of the right, it was in order to maintain a balance in the government between Chōshū (represented by Itō) and Satsuma (Kuroda's domain). He also wanted to shore up the *dajōkan*, suspecting that Itō was planning a reorganization of the government that would create a cabinet with himself as prime minister. Itō, realizing for the first time how reluctant Sanjō would be to give up his post, decided to humor him and go along with his recommendation of Kuroda.[46]

In the meantime, Itō's plans to change the form of government had gradually matured.[47] Abolishing the *dajōkan* in favor of a cabinet headed by a prime minister would not be simply an administrative change; it would mark the end of nominal rule by the nobility, replaced at the top by members of the samurai class.

Sanjō was understandably dismayed by the imminent loss of his position, but when the order came from the emperor to study how the government should be reorganized, he could not voice his opposition. On December 22 Sanjō had an audience with the emperor at which he advocated reform of the government and asked to be relieved of his post.[48] The emperor consented, and on the same day, the offices of prime minister, minister of the left, minister of the right, councillors, and the heads of the various ministries were abolished and replaced with a parliamentary cabinet consisting of a prime minister and ministers who headed each of the nine branches of the government.[49] Itō Hirobumi was appointed as prime minister, Inoue Kaoru as foreign minister, and Yamagata Aritomo as interior minister.

The selection of cabinet members was in accordance with Itō's recommendations. The emperor objected at first to the appointment of Mori Arinori as minister of education because he was a controversial figure with Christian leanings, but Itō did not yield. He guaranteed the emperor that while he was prime minister, nothing would occur that might disturb his tranquillity. The emperor, having already delegated the formation of the cabinet to Itō, decided to allow him to have his way for the time being and to watch what happened.[50] Itō had now attained the position of highest authority, second only to the emperor. The spirit of the Rokumeikan had triumphed.

Chapter 39

The nineteenth year of Meiji's reign, 1886, was unusual in that it did not begin with his performance of the traditional New Year observances. The official chronicle states, without further explanation, that he was prevented by illness from worshiping the four directions and that Nabeshima Naohiro performed various ceremonies in his place. However, the emperor participated as usual in other rites, suggesting that he was not totally incapacitated by illness. Again and again during the course of this year, the emperor's health was cited to explain why he had failed to attend a ceremony, but the nature of the illness was usually not disclosed.[1] We also know that he rode horseback twice as often in 1886 as the preceding year,[2] an indication that boredom with official ceremonies, rather than illness, was the cause of his repeated absences.

In February, Viscount Hijikata Hisamoto sent Sanjō Sanetomi a letter from Berlin describing the celebrations in honor of Wilhelm I's ninetieth birthday. He urged that Aoki Shūzō, a Foreign Office expert on Germany who was well acquainted with the particulars, make a report to the emperor. Hijikata hoped that this might stimulate him to travel abroad—to observe conditions and meet the rulers of Western countries.

Saionji Kinmochi, then minister extraordinary and plenipotentiary to Austria, had earlier made a similar suggestion in a letter to Itō Hirobumi, adding that this was a particularly good time for the emperor to travel to the West.[3] If the emperor had in fact attended the festivities in Berlin, the stimulation provided by unfamiliar sights would probably have shaken him from his apathy. It is not known, however, whether the matter was broached, and there is no indication he ever considered traveling abroad.

One result of the emperor's repeated illnesses and his failure to appear on important occasions was the increased prominence of the empress, who again and again took his place. Until this time her public role had been modest, but now she began to appear even at gatherings that were normally attended only by men of the nobility and high-ranking government officials. For example, when it was reported that the emperor was not well enough to attend the scheduled Friday dinner on March 26, the empress appeared in his place, and to keep her company, court ladies and wives of officials were also invited.

The emperor planned to visit the Yokosuka shipyard on March 30 for the launching of the warship *Musashi*, but he was indisposed that day and the empress went instead, traveling to Yokosuka aboard the warship *Fusō*. Even when the emperor managed to attend a ceremony, the empress often accompanied him. On April 13 they traveled to Akabane Village to observe the maneuvers of the Household Guards. The mock warfare staged between the "north" and "south" armies may have puzzled the empress, who had not been trained in the art of warfare, but, we are told, she observed the charge of the southern army from a horse carriage and then went to the south bank of the Arakawa to observe the blowing up of a bridge.[4]

On July 30 the empress wore Western dress for the first time in public when she visited the Peeresses' School (Kazoku jogakkō) to observe graduation exercises and the award of diplomas. On August 2, when she called on the empress dowager at the Aoyama Palace, she again wore Western attire, and from this time on not only the empress but most of the women of her entourage gradually adopted Western dress. On August 10, at a concert of Western music held in the palace by the emperor and empress, she received foreign guests for the first time in Western clothes. She probably dressed in this manner not in imitation of the West (in the manner of the Rokumeikan) but as a quiet assertion of her newfound role.

On January 17, 1887, the empress issued a memorandum on the subject of women's clothes. She contended that the clothes worn by contemporary Japanese women were a relic of the period following the warfare of the fourteenth century. Not only were they poorly adapted to modern conditions of life, but they were quite unlike the costumes worn by Japanese women of earlier periods. She believed that Western clothes were in fact closer to the dress of women in ancient Japan than the kimonos currently worn and urged that they be adopted as the standard clothes of the reign. In addition to the encouragement she gave Japanese women to dress in Western clothes, she hoped this would promote the sale of Japanese cloth.

The empress's advocacy of clothing reform was part of her new, active role in the government. On November 26, 1886, she and the emperor traveled to Nagaura to inspect the recently completed cruisers *Naniwa* and *Takachiho* and to observe naval maneuvers, including the firing of torpedoes. The empress composed several *tanka* on this occasion, including one entitled "Torpedo Fire":

koto shi araba	If a crisis should come
mi-kuni no tame ni	This is how, for our country's sake
adanami no	We shall destroy
yosekuru fune mo	Any ship that dares approach
kaku ya kudakan	Over the boisterous waves.

Needless to say, the subject matter of this poem was unconventional. It may be that the empress took to wearing Western clothes and composing poetry on such subjects as torpedoes because she too had become bored with life at court. Chamberlains who wrote memoirs of their years in the palace agreed that the emperor was always solicitous of the empress and never behaved like a despot. But she knew from early in the marriage that she could never have children, and because she was unable to fill the most important role of an emperor's consort—bearing his heirs—she was left with a mainly ornamental role at the court. This may have been frustrating to a woman of marked intelligence. It may also be true that even though she never expressed resentment of the various *gon no tenji* who served the emperor's bed, she envied them. At this time such feelings would have been exacerbated: the emperor (who had had children by four different women and divided his attentions among more) seems to have become devoted mainly to one *gon no tenji*, Sono Sachiko.[5] Those who have ventured to write about this aspect of the emperor's life are discreet, but it is a fact that Sono was the mother of his last eight children, born between 1886 and 1899. Four of them, all daughters, survived him.

Sachiko was the eldest daughter of Count Sono Motosachi,[6] who (although he lived until 1905) was most prominent during the 1860s. Sachiko's photographs do not reveal unusual beauty, and no anecdotes explain what quality of hers attracted the emperor, but, for whatever reason, she was his preferred bed companion during his later years.

Toward the end of 1885, when it became apparent that Sachiko was pregnant, there was a debate as to the kind of medical treatment she should receive.[7] The deaths in infancy of six of the emperor's previous seven children had made people wonder whether a physician of traditional medicine should again be relied on or whether it might not be better to choose a Western-trained physician. Nakayama Tadayasu's opinion was sought. Nakayama was committed to traditional ways, in medicine as in everything else, but after the deaths of the two baby princesses in September 1883 he began to waver in his stated conviction that children up until the age of ten should be treated by doctors of traditional medicine. He was now willing to admit that it was not necessarily superior to Western medicine. In addition, there seems not to have been a single traditional doctor of repute in Tōkyō, and Nakayama feared that the art might be dying out. He finally replied that he was incapable of choosing between the two kinds of medicine. Meiji, who still favored traditional medicine, commanded Nakayama and the chief chamberlain to search Tōkyō until they found a master of the art.[8]

The emperor's fifth daughter, Princess Shizuko, was born to Sono Sachiko on February 10, 1886. The emperor gave her her name, and that night there was a celebration in the palace attended by princes of the blood and other dignitaries, including Count Sono, the baby's grandfather.[9] The emperor had his first glimpse of the princess on March 12, when she was taken to the palace for his inspection. Like all the other children born to the concubines of the emperor, she would be officially considered to be a child of the empress, and her biological mother would have little part in raising her.

Princess Shizuko's life was brief. She died on April 4, 1887. On New Year's Day of that year, she suffered a sudden fever and regurgitated milk. Her illness was diagnosed as teething fever, but there were ominous signs of incipient meningitis, the cause of the deaths of the emperor's earlier children. The doctors—one trained by the Dutch, the other a practitioner of Chinese medicine—disagreed on the proper way of treating the illness, and finally the emperor's opinion was sought. He decided in favor of the Western-trained doctor and asked Ikeda Kensai, the most respected Western-style physician, to join in the consultations. At first the new treatment seemed to be effective, but during a cold spell in the latter part of March the princess's fever returned, and she died soon afterward.

The emperor's only surviving child, Prince Yoshihito, had been afflicted by repeated illnesses, and the emperor, in the light of painful experiences of losing one after another of his children, probably was anxious about Yoshihito's chances of surviving to maturity. This may be why he acceded to Prince Akihito's request that he adopt his son Sadamaro. The young man, now a naval officer studying in England, was formally adopted on May 1, 1886, and (as a prince of the blood) was given the name Yorihito.[10] As previously related, Sadamaro had so favorably impressed King Kalakaua that he hoped the Japanese prince would marry his niece. Perhaps Meiji also thought of Yorihito as a possible heir.

Regardless of the emperor's fears about Yoshihito's health, it was necessary to act as if there were no doubt that he would succeed to the throne. The prince's education had for years been a matter of great concern to the emperor. In December 1885 the emperor placed Nishimura Shigeki in charge of the prince's education. The choice of Nishimura, a specialist in Western learning, suggested that he felt the traditional palace education was unsuited to modern conditions.[11] The emperor personally informed Nishimura of his wishes concerning the subjects the prince should study during the coming year and the hours of his classes. A month later, in January 1886, the emperor decided that

Yoshihito should be permitted to visit the palace whenever he wished, although he had been allowed to see his parents only at prescribed times. This step was taken in the belief that it would be a good way of inculcating respect and affection for his parents.

In April 1886 Kadenokōji Sukenari and two other elderly nobles were asked to take turns in teaching the prince, but their notions of education were old fashioned and they had no success in tutoring a difficult boy. Itō Hirobumi, who was eager for the prince to obtain a systematic education, conferred with the minister of education, Mori Arinori. They recommended that the prince's education be in accord with modern principles, and Mori suggested as the prince's tutor Yumoto Takehiko (1857–1925), an official of the Ministry of Education. Yumoto was appointed on April 12.

Yumoto was asked to teach reading, writing, and arithmetic. Instruction was not to exceed thirty minutes at a time, but even so, Yumoto soon discovered that the prince was completely undisciplined, and his attention easily wandered. Yumoto recalled:

> My lessons were as I have already mentioned—the 50 kana symbols, 1, 2, 3 and that sort of thing—nothing difficult. But His Highness still had not the least conception of rules and had not made any progress in that direction. If he felt like it, he would study for 30 or 40 minutes, but when he did not feel like it, he would say, "Yumoto, that's enough." He would then get up and go out. His retainers and military escort, who had been waiting in the corridor, and his schoolmates, who were seated at their desks in the classroom, followed His Highness when he went out, leaving me dazed and alone in the classroom. When he was even more out of sorts, he would slam his desk down in front of him, and then go off somewhere. Once, when he was having a lesson in penmanship, he said, "Yumoto, that's enough." I answered, "No, you must study a bit longer," whereupon he lost his temper completely, picked up a big writing brush soaked with red ink and threw it right at me. The brush landed on the breast of my best, brand-new frock-coat and dripped all over it.[12]

Why did Yoshihito behave so outrageously? Perhaps it was because those around him, fearing that scolding might bring on convulsions, had permitted him to have his way in everything.[13] Yumoto sent in his resignation to Itō Hirobumi, the imperial household minister, but Itō persuaded him to remain at his post, saying that this constituted his duty as a loyal subject, that he would be offering up his life no less than a military man.

The emperor was informed of his son's capricious behavior in the classroom. Yumoto petitioned the emperor to have the prince call him "Yumoto *sensei*" and not leave his seat unless so directed by the teacher. The emperor commanded Yumoto to remain with the prince throughout the day, in the hopes of further influencing his conduct. He also sent chamberlains and women officials (and on occasion his own tutors) to Yumoto's classroom to observe the instruction. When the emperor asked Yumoto why he did not follow the textbooks that Motoda had chosen for instructing the young, he replied that they were too lofty to be used for this purpose. Yumoto prepared a new textbook and the prince began to make rapid progress, relieving the emperor's mind.[14] Later that year, Itō announced that the emperor had decided that Yoshihito would attend the Gakushū-in along with children of the nobility.

In September, the emperor, still worried about the prince's education, appointed a senior official, Hijikata Hisamoto, to take charge. He accepted, with the proviso that no one must be allowed to interfere with his decisions. The emperor agreed and sent the chief chamberlain to inform Nakayama Yoshiko that henceforth her guidance would not be needed. Yumoto was also instructed to consult with Hijikata on all educational matters. Yoshiko seems to have resisted being deprived of responsibility for her grandson's education. In October, Hijikata, obeying an imperial command, agreed to divide responsibility with Yoshiko; she would be in charge of matters concerned with the prince's upbringing in the palace, including his Japanese-style clothes and his meals. Finally, as had long been planned, Yoshihito entered the Gakushū-in on September 19, 1887. He traveled to school every day and studied in the company of other boys, his desk alongside theirs.[15] This was the first time an heir to the throne had received a public education.

Toward the end of 1886, Nishimura Shigeki delivered three lectures on Japanese morality at Imperial University.[16] Nishimura, formerly a member of the Meirokusha, had frequently delivered lectures on the West before the emperor and would continue to do so in the future, but these lectures on morality, later published as *Nihon dōtoku ron* (Essays on Japanese Morality) were anything but a summons to learn from the West.

In later years, Nishimura recalled how government officials at that time imitated the legal system, customs, and etiquette of the West, and the mindless aping of such Western diversions as dance parties, costume balls, and tableaux vivants that took place in the hopes of winning the respect of foreigners. He contrasted this subservience with the age-old Japanese morality based on such conceptions as loyalty and filial piety, righteousness, bravery, a sense of shame, and so on and asked how these virtues could be abandoned. He declared that grief over this situation had impelled him to deliver the lectures.[17]

The first lecture opened with a consideration of the differences between two systems of thought dealing with morality. The first he called "this-worldly teachings"; the second, "other-worldly teachings" (or religion). In the former category he placed Confucianism and Western philosophy; in the latter, Buddhism and Christianity. His sympathies were obviously with the former. In China, Confucianism was a native system of thought that had originated in remote antiquity. Buddhism, however, was no more than an imported religion and had never attained the influence of Confucianism. In Japan, however, both Confucianism and Buddhism had been imported. At first they were accepted by all classes of society; but in later times, although the lower classes continued to believe in Buddhism, extremely few of the middle and upper classes retained their faith. The Japanese therefore lacked a common morality shared by all classes; indeed, since the Restoration, all moral standards had disappeared.[18]

Asia was now menaced by the European countries, each of which had staked out an area for colonization. The threatened Asian countries were desperately attempting to modernize. Nishimura commented, "Civilization and enlightenment are to be hoped for, but unless a country exists, there can be no civilization or enlightenment. Once a country has been lost, civilization and enlightenment are obviously impossible." The crucial task for Japan was to preserve its independence and not permit any foreign country to trample on its dignity. But no matter how many warships or cannons a country possessed, if its people lacked morality, it would not be respected by other countries. History teaches us that the collapse of Rome was the result of the people's corruption and loss of morality. Or consider the most lamentable instance in recent history, the case of Poland. The people were not as corrupt as the Romans, but they were so divided into factions that they did not attempt to preserve the unity of their country; as everyone knows, the country was partitioned into three.[19] He went on to relate these generalizations to Japan:

> In Japan the three lower classes—the farmers, the artisans, and the merchants—have never been educated, and there is therefore no point in discussing either raising or lowering their morality; but the people of the samurai class and above have received from generations of their ancestors training in Confucianism. In addition, there is a special study in our country known as the Way of the Warrior (*budō*). These teachings can forge a man's character in such a way that he will devote his every energy to the task of defending his country. But Confucianism, which since the Restoration has acquired the status of a state religion, has greatly lost its influence, and today nobody still mentions the Way of the Warrior or anything similar.[20]

Nishimura expressed dismay over the loss of morality even among the samurai. They were eagerly turning to the West, forgetting that each of the countries of Europe and America followed a religion that preserved the morality of the people. He generalized:

> By nature most Japanese are basically quick and clever, but their thought is superficial, and they lack an awareness of the grand. They tend to echo other people's views and have only a feeble conception of what it means to stand on their own. In recent years, observing the exactness of Western

science and the strength and prosperity of those countries, they have been indiscriminately fascinated and do not know how to stand firm. . . . However, there are differences in human nature and in the cultural climate, and the learning of the West cannot be adopted without change in the East.[21]

Nishimura advocated a return to the morality of Confucianism. He did not specify the variety of Confucianism he preferred, but his insistence on putting into practice the morality one has learned suggests the teachings of Wang Yang-ming. Nishimura did not, however, gloss over the failings of both Confucianism and Western philosophy. He recognized also that both Buddhism and Christianity possessed merits that were worthy of adoption. The essential task was to create a morality for modern Japan, and once it had been established, elements could be borrowed from other systems of thought.[22]

The specific elements in Nishimura's morality are hardly startling. He favored education and giving alms to the deserving poor. He favored investment in enterprises that would benefit the nation. On the negative side, he rebuked men for retiring at the early age of forty-five instead of continuing to contribute to society and contrasted the Japanese institution of the "retired master" (inkyo) with the long productive lives of people in the West. He disapproved of early marriage because children produced before their parents are fully mature are susceptible to illness, leading to physical weakness of the people as a whole and, because early marriages tend to result in numerous offspring, to family impoverishment. Finally, Nishimura disapproved of extravagance, particularly lavish expenditures of money for marriages and funerals.[23]

It is hard to imagine anyone disagreeing with most of his recommendations, but the reaction to Nishimura's lectures was not merely favorable but overwhelming. Those who had been trained in Confucianism—mainly men of the samurai class over forty years old—responded to the call from the past. Mori Arinori, the minister of education, who had been Nishimura's associate in the Meirokusha and was known as an advocate of progress, was so impressed by Essays on Japanese Morality that he expressed the intention of adopting it as a text for middle schools and above.[24] But Itō Hirobumi was enraged by the book, considering it libelous to the regime and a block to political progress. He sent for Mori and rebuked him for praising the book. After learning of Itō's displeasure, Nishimura promised to make revisions, and he later deleted some criticisms of the government's pro-Western policy, but he had already challenged the government's utilitarianism. Nishimura's book was the first expression of opposition to Itō's policies, a forerunner of the ultranationalism that soon became prominent.

One more event of 1886 requires mention, the sinking of the British freighter Normanton. The ship set sail from Yokohama for Kōbe on October 23. The next day, off Wakayama Prefecture, it struck a reef and broke up. Although the members of the British crew were saved, they made no effort to rescue the twenty-five Japanese passengers or the twelve Indian crew members, all of whom drowned. As soon as word of this disaster became known, there was a great outcry over what seemed to be a conspicuous example of racial prejudice. On November 5 the captain of the *Normanton*, John William Drake, was questioned at the British consulate in Kōbe but was acquitted of any misdemeanor.

At first the Japanese leaders, at the time eagerly attempting to win the approbation of foreigners, did not protest, but so great was the clamor all over the country that it could not be ignored. The newspapers solicited funds for the families of the men lost on the *Normanton*, and speeches were delivered to crowds already angry over the flagrant display of white supremacy. Finally, the government formally asked the British to try the captain. (Because of extraterritoriality, Japan was unable to intervene.) A trial took place on December 8 at the British consulate in Yokohama. Captain Drake was found guilty of criminal negligence and sentenced to three months' imprisonment. The other members of the British crew were acquitted.[25] However, the *Normanton* incident continued to live in the memories in the Japanese, not least because of a song composed about the disaster.[26]

Although some Japanese who were versed in maritime law thought that the decision was just, the mild punishment meted out to Drake failed to satisfy most Japanese.[27] The *Normanton* incident, along with Nishimura's lectures on Japanese morality, represented a defection from Rokumeikan-style adulation of foreigners and set the stage for more serious attacks in the following year.

The New Year ceremonies at the beginning of 1887 followed tradition in all but one respect: the empress wore a formal Western gown when accepting congratulations from members of the court, and this became her normal costume for such occasions. The rumblings of discontent over the *Normanton* affair seem not to have reached the court, where the exchange of presents with foreign royalty continued unabated.[28] The construction of a new palace, long delayed, was finally under way, but financial problems had arisen, threatening completion.

On January 25 the emperor and empress set out for Kyōto in order to participate in observances on January 30 at the tomb of Emperor Kōmei, who had died twenty years earlier.[29] The most noteworthy aspect of this journey was the empress's presence. Otherwise, the trip to Kyōto and the visits to schools and famous places closely resembled the emperor's previous journeys. The royal couple remained in Kyōto until February 21.

They returned to Tōkyō on February 24 and resumed their usual activities. The empress visited schools, including an industrial college and the army officers school.[30] In April she joined her husband in observing maneuvers of the Household Guards regiment. Her role in official functions—even military maneuvers—had become indispensable.

In March 1887 the empress presented the Peeresses' School (Kazoku jo-gakkō) with two poems of an inspirational nature. The first opened:

> Even a diamond
> If you polish it
> Will shine all the brighter.
> People too
> Study so that later on
> Their true qualities will appear.[31]

The poems were later set to music and became the school song of the peeresses. The earnest moral tone suggests the Protestant hymns of the same period, but the pro-Western leaders of the government, unaffected by such calls for virtue, continued to frequent the Rokumeikan,[32] hoping that their affability and mastery of Western etiquette would gain for Japan the friendship and respect of the advanced countries of the West. They were convinced that the best way to overcome Japan's financial and military weakness and to preserve its independence was by proving that Japan was a modern nation that shared the same culture as the Europeans. To this end, they would dress and eat like Europeans and rid their society of its antiquated aspects. Some were willing to adopt not only the Western legal system but also Christianity and the use of English as the national language; others (in order to improve the Japanese physique) were ready to take European wives.[33]

The contrast between the outpouring of wealth for festivities at the Rokumeikan and the poverty in which the vast majority of the population lived aroused opposition. Motoda Nagazane, a staunch Confucianist, repeatedly attempted to see Itō in order to communicate his unhappiness over the extravagant construction of Western-style palaces and the lavish parties, but Itō was always too busy to see him. In May 1887 Katsu Kaishū issued a statement in twenty-one articles condemning the destruction of native Japanese virtues in the frantic effort to promote the adoption of European culture. In the late Tokugawa era, Kaishū had studied Dutch with the aim of acquiring a knowledge of navigation and naval gunnery, and he had served as the captain of the *Kanrin maru*, the first Japanese ship to cross the Pacific Ocean. He was certainly not a hidebound Confucianist, but he, no less than Motoda, was outraged by the effects of pro-Western policies on Japanese society, which were lowering moral standards by the conspicuous waste of wealth.

In the meantime, on April 22, 1887, in its twenty-sixth session, the Treaty Revision Conference decided to offer extreme concessions to the foreigners in order to obtain the abolition of extraterritoriality. They agreed that within two years after the exchange of documents of ratification of new treaties, all of Japan would be opened to foreigners. Rights and privileges enjoyed by Japanese citizens would be extended to resident foreigners. Within two years, the Japanese legal system would conform in every respect to practices in the West. All laws would be translated into English (the translations would be considered the original texts) and sent to foreign governments within sixteen months. Consular courts would continue to exist for another three years after opening the country to foreigners. Most judges passing on cases in which foreigners were involved would be of foreign nationality.[34] The Japanese seemed ready to yield to any foreign demand, provided that their country was symbolically recognized as an equal by ending the hated extraterritoriality.

Not all Japanese were willing to make such concessions. Tani Tateki (also known as Tani Kenjō, 1837–1899), the minister of agriculture and commerce, recently returned from Europe,[35] was appalled by what he considered to be the moral laxness of the times, and he spoke his mind. Itō had heard rumors that Tani had praised Rousseau and other French exponents of people's rights and attacked the government, and he interpreted this as meaning Tani had been infected by seditious radical ideas. The emperor, getting word of this, was profoundly disturbed that a cabinet minister should entertain such views. He had Sasaki Takayuki ask Tani face to face his political views.

Tani, a believer in *kokusui* (the genius of the nation), was anything but an advocate of people's rights, as he quickly convinced Sasaki. But in July, before resigning his post, he issued a stinging attack on the government's policies. He demanded that efforts to obtain treaty revision be discontinued and that action be taken to correct the worsening moral situation. Like Nishimura, Tani was shocked by the decadence and extravagance of those addicted to dancing at the Rokumeikan, and he deplored the hardships the people were suffering because their money was being wasted in the attempt to Europeanize the country. He informed Itō of his belief that efforts to secure treaty revision should be speedily discontinued. Tani presented the same view to the cabinet, where it led to a bitter argument with Inoue Kaoru. But despite the hostility, Tani persisted, denouncing policies that, he said, were advocated without consideration of their lasting harm. Inoue and the others claimed that revising the treaties was necessary in order to end extraterritoriality, but, Tani asked, would it not be worse to allow foreigners to meddle in the country's internal affairs? He accused the Foreign Ministry of acting in secret without consulting anyone else and asked that the opinions of all the other ministers be sought lest some grave error be committed.[36]

Itō and Inoue were infuriated and quickly retorted that at a time when Japan was taking the advanced countries of the West as its model in all things, it was unavoidable that its laws be revised to accord with those of the West. Tani, realizing that his recommendations would not be accepted by the cabinet, decided to take a bold step. On July 20 he obtained an audience with the emperor at which he related in detail his reasons for opposing treaty revision and for believing that the corruption of the times must be corrected. He requested the emperor to ask the opinions of his advisers as to whether treaty revision was desirable, suggesting in particular that Kuroda Kiyotaka, who had recently returned from Europe, be consulted. The emperor listened attentively but made no comment. Tani withdrew and immediately afterward submitted his resignation.

Tani's request reveals that he was familiar with the views critical of the administration earlier expressed in discussions of men close to the emperor— including Sasaki Takayuki, Hijikata Hisamoto, and Motoda Nagazane. When Tani returned from abroad and they discovered that he shared their doubts about treaty revision, they decided to work with him and to search for others of like mind. Many influential men in the government (including Kuroda Kiyotaka) openly expressed opposition to the agreement for treaty revision.

When the emperor asked Motoda's opinion, he replied that he believed Tani had spoken out of loyalty and that nobody in the whole country could disagree with his denunciation of the evils of the time. Motoda was sure that unless the concessions made to foreign countries in order to obtain treaty revision were at once discontinued, incalculable disaster would result.[37]

About this time Gustave Boissonade, a Frenchman who served as a legal expert to the cabinet, expressed his opposition to the agreement for treaty revision. He attempted unsuccessfully to present his objections to Inoue Kaoru, and when he stated his position to Yamada Akiyoshi, the minister of justice, Yamada said he was unable to consider the matter because it was outside his competence. At this point Inoue Kowashi, the cabinet librarian, who had grave doubts about the advisability of treaty revision, secretly visited Boissonade and listened to his arguments against the agreement. Boissonade was convinced it would cause the nation great harm. Inoue Kowashi, persuaded, decided to use his every effort to end treaty revision.

Boissonade tirelessly presented position papers to members of the cabinet explaining why revision must be stopped. He contended that it would inevitably harm Japanese prestige, weaken security, and lower Japan's position. He attacked every provision of the agreement, including the use of foreign judges: they would have to be paid a salary that satisfied them, which would be a considerable drain on national resources. He warned that the Japanese people, indignant at the harm to Japanese interests and the damage to national prestige, might revolt once new treaties were approved that might lead to foreign intervention.[38]

Inoue Kowashi wrote Inoue Kaoru on July 12 stating his reasons for opposing the agreement, declaring that it would reduce Japan to the level of a semi-independent state. He predicted also that the country would be divided into two camps, for and against the revisions, which might lead to open conflict and immense losses. In the end, Inoue Kaoru was forced to recognize the turmoil that his plans had created. He saw that if he plunged ahead without modifying his original agreement with the foreign powers on the operation of Japanese courts, it would cause a national crisis. At the conference meeting on July 18 he informed the delegates that the Japanese government had decided it was necessary to make certain changes in the treaty with respect to the courts.

On September 17 Itō resigned as imperial household minister, though retaining his post as prime minister. At first the emperor was unwilling to accept Itō's resignation, and he rejected Itō's suggestion that Kuroda Kiyotaka succeed him. The Imperial House Act had yet to be framed and the property of the imperial household had not been systematically defined. Itō was the only one capable of dealing effectively with these matters. As for Kuroda, his character was such that the emperor would not wish him to remain long in the palace. The emperor asked Motoda Nagazane his opinion. Motoda replied that although in principle it was best in a constitutional monarchy for palace and state to be united, this depended on the particular man. In China there had been Chu-ko Liang, and in Prussia there had been Bismarck, men of great sincerity and ability. Itō had enormous ability, but his moral qualities were not yet sufficient. His continued presence in the palace might prove harmful. Motoda urged the emperor to accept Itō's resignation as imperial household minister.[39]

The emperor was loath to lose Itō, but in the end he accepted his resignation and appointed Hijikata Hisamoto to succeed him. Kuroda was named minister of agriculture and commerce. Motoda's recommendation that Inoue be dismissed as foreign minister was effected on September 16. For the time being, Itō would serve as foreign minister as well as prime minister.[40]

Although these political changes greatly disturbed the emperor, his year was not entirely gloomy. On August 22 his fourth son, Prince Michihito, was born to Sono Sachiko. On August 31 Prince Yoshihito, whose ninth birthday was that day, was confirmed both as heir to the throne and as the "true child" (*jisshi*) of the empress. That evening, with the emperor, the empress, the dowager empress, and Yoshihito in attendance, a birthday party was held. Thirty-nine members of the imperial family and palace officials were invited. The emperor, happy and relaxed, called one after another of the guests to his side. With his own hands, he poured saké for the empress dowager, the empress, and Yoshihito. Soon the dining room was filled with happy shouts induced by the liquor. The emperor commanded various people to sing and dance. The chronology of his reign comments that probably so joyful an occasion, shared alike by ruler and ruled, had never before been witnessed.[41] There were indeed few such moments in the emperor's life.

Chapter 40

During much of 1888, Emperor Meiji was prevented by illness from performing his ritual duties or attending field maneuvers and graduation ceremonies. The most severe illness, which lasted from February 7 until May 5, was diagnosed as catarrhal pneumonia.[1] After the emperor had passed out of danger, his doctors recommended that he recuperate at a salubrious site along the coast, but he refused to leave the palace, obsessed as always with a sense of monarchical duty.[2] Later that year, he suffered from disabling colds, but his dislike of doctors was so intense that he paid no attention to their advice. On various occasions, especially when he was ill, the empress took his place, receiving envoys from Siam, launching a warship, or inspecting the medical and scientific facilities of Tōkyō Imperial University.

The record of the court physicians was dismal, but the emperor, still clinging to traditional "Chinese" medicine, was reluctant to replace them.[3] One more of the emperor's children, Michihito, died of meningitis on November 12, despite the efforts of the court physicians (and despite also the ministrations of army and navy surgeons called in at the last moment). Another daughter (the emperor's sixth) was born to Sono Sachiko in September. As usual, there was a banquet to celebrate the birth, but surely most of those present, remembering how many of the royal children had died, must have wondered whether their toasts to the health of the infant Princess Masako would have much effect.

Early in the new year, the emperor listened as usual to lectures: by Fukuba Bisei on the section of the *Records of Japan* describing the reign of the emperor

Keikō, by Motoda Nagazane on a passage in the *Doctrine of the Mean*, and by Nishimura Shigeki on "the meaning of autonomy" from Henry Wheaton's *Elements of International Law*.[4] The choice of subjects for these lectures reflects the continuing efforts made to achieve a balance in the emperor's education among Japanese historical traditions, Chinese moral teachings, and Western practical learning.

Among the few intimate glimpses we get of the emperor at this time, one is of particular interest. Believing that a portrait of the emperor more recent than the photographs taken by Uchida Kuichi in 1872 was needed for presentation to foreign monarchs and other dignitaries, Imperial Household Minister Hijikata Hisamoto asked the Italian artist Eduardo Chiossone, an employee of the Printing Bureau, to prepare a suitable likeness. The simplest way would have been to take a photograph, but the emperor's dislike of being photographed made this impossible. Not long before, Itō Hirobumi had repeatedly begged the emperor to allow a new photograph to be taken, but the emperor refused each time. Realizing how unlikely it was that the emperor would change his mind, Hijikata asked Chiossone to sketch his features secretly, promising to take responsibility if anything went amiss.

After securing the consent of the chamberlains and other officials, Hijikata waited for a suitable occasion. The day chosen was January 14, when the emperor dined out. Chiossone, hidden behind a sliding partition, carefully sketched in crayon the dragon countenance, the emperor's posture, and the changes of expression as he chatted.[5] Hijikata was delighted with the finished Chiossone portrait and decided to show it to the emperor, first apologizing for not having secured his permission in advance. When the emperor saw the portrait, he said not one word, of either approbation or displeasure. Hijikata wondered what the emperor's silence signified, but he could not very well ask for an explanation. Just at this time, a request was received from Europe for the emperor's picture. Hijikata asked him to sign for presentation a photograph of Chiossone's portrait. The emperor did so, to the great relief of Hijikata, who interpreted this as meaning that he was pleased with the portrait.[6] From this time on, photographs of Chiossone's picture (based on his original sketches) were widely distributed to foreign royalty and schools around the country, and generations of children bowed in reverence before the imperial portrait (*goshin'ei*). The picture was so realistic that most people assumed it was a photograph.[7]

On February 1, 1888, the emperor appointed Ōkuma Shigenobu as foreign minister. As we have seen, Ōkuma's predecessor, Inoue Kaoru, had had to resign as the result of opposition to his plans for treaty revision, but he hoped that Ōkuma might succeed in his place.[8] The main problem in making the appointment lay in persuading Kuroda Kiyotaka, an adviser to the cabinet, to accept a man with whom relations had been strained ever since the scandal over the sale of Hokkaidō Development Office properties.

Itō Hirobumi, the prime minister, agreed to help persuade Kuroda. He had his own reservations about Ōkuma: although Ōkuma's party, the Kaishin-tō (Constitutional Reform Party), was less radical than the Jiyū-tō, it advocated changes of which Itō disapproved.[9] Nonetheless, surmounting his political antipathy, Itō urged Kuroda to support Ōkuma. His persuasion was effective, for one day Kuroda suddenly appeared at Ōkuma's residence, apologized for what had happened in the past, and promised to cooperate with him in the future.[10]

Ōkuma was moved by Kuroda's gesture, but he was reluctant to enter the cabinet because of the possible adverse effects on the Kaishin-tō. He stipulated conditions for accepting the post: the establishment, within seven or eight years of the convening of the Diet, of a cabinet composed of members of parliament; agreement that the qualifications for voters in the election of the new parliament should not be set higher than those for voters in local elections; and assurance that orderly and steady progress would be made.[11] Ōkuma also asked that if his conditions were met, they would be publicly announced. For some months Itō was so reluctant to accept these conditions that he continued to serve as foreign minister, but eventually a compromise was reached and Ōkuma took office.

Ōkuma was no less determined than Inoue Kaoru to end extraterritoriality. His modified version of Inoue's proposals included the controversial permission to foreigners to travel, reside, and own property in the interior of Japan. However, under his plan the role of foreign judges would be limited, and the authoritative version of the new civil codes would be the Japanese, not the English, text.[12] These concessions did not placate opponents of treaty revision within the government, and criticism was levied at Ōkuma's proposals through 1888 and much of 1889.

In the meantime, on April 28, 1888, the emperor created the Privy Council (Sūmitsu-in). His edict stated, "Whereas We deem it expedient to consult personages who have rendered signal service to the State, and to avail Ourselves of their valuable advice on matters of state, We hereby establish Our Privy Council which shall henceforth be an institution of Our Supreme counsel."[13]

The main function of this body was to discuss matters relating to the enactment of a constitution.[14] Members of the Privy Council would be senior persons (over forty years old) who had performed conspicuous service to the state. The council would consist of some fifteen members, including the president and vice president. When the constitution came into force, the Privy Council would serve as both an intermediary between the government and the Diet and an advisory body to the emperor.

Itō was the chief proponent of the Privy Council. He firmly believed that the constitution must be considered to be a gift bestowed by the emperor, whose authority was inviolable and whose decisions were final. The Privy Council would guide him, especially when a conflict occurred between the government and the Diet—for example, on whether to replace a minister or to dissolve the Diet.

To emphasize the importance of the newly formed body, Itō resigned as prime minister to become the president of the Privy Council. At Itō's suggestion, Kuroda Kiyotaka was appointed as his successor. Although reluctant to lose Itō as prime minister, the emperor granted him permission to move to the Privy Council, probably because Itō was the only person who could control the discussions.[15] Meetings of the Privy Council would be enhanced by the presence of the emperor, who attended every session except when he was ill. He listened carefully to the proceedings without ever once saying a word, although afterward he occasionally sent for speakers to ask questions.[16] During the summer months, the room where the discussions took place sometimes became unbearably hot, but Meiji, apparently unaffected by the heat, listened tirelessly.

Why did the emperor willingly spend so many hours listening to debates that must often have been inept and repetitious? Perhaps, in contrast to the boredom of the annual court rituals and the countless meetings with foreign visitors, he had at last found something that engaged his attention. The discussions may have helped him understand his role in the future of Japan.

In April 1888 Itō presented to the Privy Council a draft of a constitution. As far back as 1884 he had been asked by the court to study the framing of a constitution, and he had met with Inoue Kowashi, Itō Miyoji, and Kaneko Kentarō, as well as with K. F. H. Rösler, the German adviser to the *dajōkan* (later, professor of law at Tōkyō Imperial University); but other duties had kept him from making progress. In 1886 he began to work seriously on drawing up a constitution. Itō divided the different aspects of the task among his three associates, delegating to Inoue chief responsibility for the actual writing.

Itō had studied constitutional law in Vienna, and his views probably reflected what he had learned there about the importance of an "axis" (*kijiku*) to constitutional governments. In his speech delivered to the Privy Council on June 18, 1888, Itō mentioned that in Europe, where the seeds of constitutional government had germinated in antiquity and had steadily grown over the centuries, people were at home with this form of government. Moreover, religion, the axis of the European nations, deeply penetrated their peoples and unified them. Buddhism and Shintō, the religions of Japan, were too weak to affect people's hearts and so could not serve as axes; the only axis the Japanese possessed was the imperial family. Itō declared that a realization of this truth was always in the minds of the men framing the constitution. Out of respect for the sovereign's prerogatives, they had striven to avoid restricting his actions in any way. The prerogatives of the sovereign thus formed the axis of the draft constitution that Itō and his colleagues had prepared.[17]

Discussions of the constitution continued at a leisurely pace through the rest of the year. Other issues, such as efforts to end extraterritoriality, were not forgotten, but little progress was made until November, when a treaty was signed with Mexico that gave Mexicans the right to live in the interior and buy property, but not extraterritoriality. This was the first treaty signed by the Japanese on the basis of equality between the two contracting powers, but no other country followed Mexico's example. Although vigorously protested by the British and French, who claimed that the most-favored-nation clause in their treaties signed with Japan automatically extended to them any privileges enjoyed by Mexico, the treaty had no immediate effect, as at the time there was only one Mexican in Japan.[18]

The new palace was completed toward the end of the year, and the imperial family was scheduled to move there on January 11, 1889. Since 1873, Meiji and his court had lived in a crowded "temporary palace." The emperor's dislike for extravagance had made him reluctant even to consider the construction of a new palace, but he at last yielded to the argument that Japan's prestige demanded a more suitable residence for its monarch.

The palace, built at great cost, was intended to convey the grandeur of the Japanese crown, and visiting foreigners for the most part were impressed.[19] The east wing of the palace was reserved for the emperor's appearances as a public figure, when he sat on a gilded throne receiving foreign guests. The west wing, his private quarters, was in Japanese style. At the back were Shintō shrines where he performed ritual observances. The buildings, connected by Japanese-style passageways, had gardens around them.

Meiji seems to have been totally indifferent to the appearance of the new palace. Viscount Hinonishi recalled, for example, that artificial flowers decorating the corridors would hang there for three or four years at a time until they had lost their original color. The emperor seems not to have noticed them. By the time of his death, the blossoms had become so dirty they had to be burned.[20] The palace was wired for electricity, which was used in state rooms, but the emperor refused to allow electric lights in his private quarters, fearing that a short circuit might cause a conflagration. But the use of candles blackened the ceilings, contributing to the palace's rather forlorn appearance, especially in the emperor's later years.

The move to the new palace took the form of a procession from the temporary palace. The emperor and empress, accompanied by princes of the blood and members of the cabinet and other dignitaries, set out at ten in the morning, arriving an hour later. Schoolchildren along the course of the procession sang the national anthem, *Kimi ga yo*, and music was otherwise provided by military bands. When the procession reached the Double Bridge over the moat surrounding the palace grounds, there were daytime fireworks, and enormous crowds of people shouted, "Banzai!"

The emperor's health was better in 1889 than in the previous year, although illness sometimes kept him from attending to state business. This was one of the most hectic years of his reign because his decisions were constantly being sought. A particularly difficult decision concerned Lieutenant General Tani Tateki. Although Tani was undoubtedly an able man, he was contentious and had quarreled with both Itō Hirobumi and Inoue Kaoru, leading (as we have seen) to his resignation as minister of agriculture and commerce. He had now been out of office for a year and a half. The government, suspicious of what he might be secretly planning, sent detectives to spy on him.

The emperor feared that Tani might join with other dissidents and, following in the footsteps of Etō Shimpei and Saigō Takamori, might even start a rebellion. He believed that the best plan would be to neutralize Tani by including him in the Privy Council. In December 1888 he directed Motoda Nagazane to visit Tani and find out whether he was willing to serve in the Privy Council. Tani refused any appointment and would not be budged.

In the attempt to persuade him to change his mind, Soga Sukenori, who was Prince Yoshihito's tutor[21] and an old friend of Tani's, visited him repeatedly in the company of Motoda. But even though Tani wept with emotion on learning that the emperor ardently wished him to accept an appointment, he said that he could not break his promise to his comrades. Tani had assured them that he planned to expound antigovernmental views from a seat in the upper house,[22] and so if he joined the government at this stage, his friends would no longer trust him. He insisted that his opposition to the government was not a sign of disrespect toward the imperial household, that members of the Japanese opposition (unlike German socialists or Russian anarchists) were loyal to the throne. He asked that the government call off its detectives.[23]

Deliberations continued in the Privy Council. Itō proposed in January 1889 that the draft constitution be translated into a European language so that council members might benefit from the opinions of foreign legal experts. He realized that no matter how carefully the new constitution was framed, a certain amount of criticism was unavoidable, but he was determined to avoid leaving future generations an obviously flawed document. Even at this stage, he still had modifications to offer; for example, at his last-minute suggestion, the constitution specified that succession to the throne be restricted to male heirs.[24]

On February 5 the Privy Council adopted the Imperial House Act, the Imperial Constitution, the Diet Act, the Rules for Election of Members of the House of Representatives, and the House of Peers Act. Copies of each were made, two for presentation to the emperor.[25] Six days later, on February 11, the anniversary of Emperor Jimmu's accession, the emperor promulgated the Imperial House Act and the Imperial Constitution at a ceremony held in the Hall for State Ceremonies. In the formal statement addressed to his ancestors read on this occasion, he attributed to their guidance the momentous events of this day. He vowed to abide by the provisions of the constitution. Immediately afterward, he worshiped at the Imperial Ancestors' Shrine and again read his address.

The constitution was publicly pronounced at a ceremony held later that morning. Members of the imperial family, the cabinet, high-ranking nobles, governors of prefectures, judges, and high-ranking representatives of other organs of the state, as well as the ministers of foreign countries, assembled to hear the emperor's rescript. He paid tribute not only to his ancestors but also to his subjects, the descendants of loyal subjects of his ancestors. Together, he promised, they would promote the glory of the empire, both at home and abroad, and strengthen for all time to come the work of his ancestors.[26]

After reading these words, the emperor presented the Constitution of the Empire of Great Japan to the prime minister, Kuroda Kiyotaka, in a symbolic gesture indicating that he was bestowing the constitution on the nation. The description of the ceremony by Dr. Erwin Baelz, the German physician who served the imperial family, evokes the scene:

> In front of the Emperor, somewhat to the left, were ranged the ministers of State and the highest officials. Behind were the chief nobles, among whom I noticed Kamenosuke Tokugawa, who, but for the Restoration, would now be Shogun; also Prince Shimadzu of Satsuma, the only one who (though wearing a western uniform) had his hair dressed in the old Japanese style. He cut a strange figure! Immediately to the left of the Emperor were the diplomatic corps. The gallery surrounding the hall had been opened to the other high officials and to a number of foreigners. The Empress followed with the princesses and the court ladies. The Empress wore a European dress, pink, with a train. On either side of the throne a high dignitary now stepped forward, one of them Duke Sanjo, formerly imperial chancellor, each of them with a roll of parchment. The one Sanjo held was the constitution. The Emperor took the other document, opened it, and read it in a loud voice. It contained the decision to give the people voluntarily the promised constitution. Then the Emperor handed the charter itself to the prime minister, Kuroda, who received it with a deep reverence. Thereupon the Emperor nodded and left the hall, followed by the Empress and suite. The whole business lasted about ten minutes. Meanwhile salutes were being fired, and bells were being rung everywhere. The ceremony was dignified and brilliant. The only trouble was that the throne-room, a very fine apartment, is colored red, and was therefore too dark.[27]

The 1889 constitution was the most advanced possessed by any Asian country and was more liberal than those of many European countries; but the insistence on the "sacred and inviolable" person of the emperor and the rights of sovereignty invested in him indicates how far the constitution was from granting sovereign power to the people.[28] The granting of the constitution nevertheless marked the beginning of representative government in Japan. An imperial edict, issued on the same day, stated that a parliament would be convened in 1890 and that the constitution would go into effect the same day.

As part of the celebrations, the newly created Grand Cordon of the Rising Sun and the Paulownia Flower was bestowed on Itō Hirobumi. It was recommended that (to balance this award to a Chōshū man), the prime minister, Kuroda Kiyotaka (from Satsuma) should be similarly decorated, but Meiji refused, even though Motoda spoke in support of the award to Kuroda.[29] In an effort to heal old wounds on this felicitous occasion, some men who had been put to death as rebels were not only pardoned but decorated: Saigō Takamori was promoted to the senior third rank, and Yoshida Shōin to the senior fourth rank.

That same day, when the minister of education, Mori Arinori, was about to set out for the palace to attend the ceremonies, a man requested an audience. Mori asked someone to attend to the visitor and was leaving the house when the visitor leaped on him and severely wounded him with a knife. The assailant, Nishino Buntarō, was killed immediately. It was discovered that Nishino had been informed that Mori, on a visit to the Great Shrine of Ise, not only had failed to remove his shoes on entering the sacred building but had lifted with his cane the curtain hiding the sacred mirror and peeped in. Nishino was so enraged by Mori's actions, considering them a profanation of the divine presence and an insult to the imperial family, that he decided to kill Mori.

In the statement of vindication found on his body, Nishino wrote that he had traveled to Ise to verify that Mori had actually committed the offense and was satisfied that the rumor was not false. (However, after Mori's death an investigation conducted by the vice minister of education concluded that there was no truth to the rumor.) Mori died the next day. The emperor sent a message expressing grief and appreciation of Mori's achievements and promoted him posthumously to the senior second rank.[30]

Once the excitement of the constitution's proclamation had died down, members of the government returned to unfinished business, especially treaty reform. Ōkuma believed that it was essential to destroy the unity with which the European and American governments tended to act vis-à-vis Asia. He decided therefore to conduct separate negotiations with each of the different countries. A new treaty had been concluded with Germany in November 1888, and in December, Ōkuma gave the American minister a draft of a revised treaty with the request that it be expeditiously approved by the American government. He promised that regardless of what other countries might decide, American citizens would enjoy the benefits of the new treaty. If other countries claimed the same benefits under the most-favored-nation clause, they would be informed that unless they also accepted the end of extraterritoriality, they would not receive the benefits.

Ōkuma was aware that unless Japan was able to persuade European nations to accept the revised treaties, the treaty with America would not mean much.

But he believed that if he could tell other countries that a new treaty was about to be signed between Japan and the United States, this would encourage their ministers in Japan to work for a similar settlement.[31]

The treaty of friendship, commerce, and navigation signed by Ōkuma and the American minister, Richard B. Hubbard, marked a major step toward the end of extraterritoriality. The treaty would take effect on February 11, the same day as the proclamation of the constitution. The Japanese rushed the signing because they feared that the new Republican administration might not approve of actions taken by Hubbard, a Democratic appointee.[32]

As might have been foreseen, Britain opposed the treaty revision, even though the Japanese had devoted their greatest efforts to persuading the British to agree. On December 29, 1888, Ōkuma reminded the British minister that Britain was the country from which Japan imported most and that trade between the two countries amounted to one-third of Japan's total foreign trade. About half the foreign nationals residing in Japan were British, and their interests far exceeded those of any other country. According to Ōkuma, the Japanese had not forgotten how much they owed Sir Harry Parkes for his help at the time of the Restoration, but gratitude might turn to hatred if Britain kept blocking treaty reform. If Britain accepted revision, the other countries would follow, and the Japanese would truly be grateful for British support. This newly emerged nation, with a population of 40 million, an army of 180,000 troops, and a fleet of dozens of warships, would become Britain's ally.

Despite Ōkuma's pleading, Britain was not ready to accede to the Japanese request. The reply noted that Japanese laws did not conform to Western standards and gave specific instances of inadequacies in the revised treaty. If the Japanese really wanted foreigners to comply with Japanese justice, they should open the interior of the country at once. Then, after five years had passed, if the structure of the courts was established, the compilation of the codes of laws was completed, and the Japanese were able to offer guarantees concerning the satisfactory administration of the courts, the consular courts would be abolished and extraterritoriality ended. Similar conditions were laid down for revision of the tariffs.[33]

Doubts about the revised treaties from the Japanese side were first expressed by Mutsu Munemitsu, the minister plenipotentiary to America. He noted that for at least twelve years after the treaties were signed, foreign judges would be appointed to the supreme court. Mutsu believed this provision violated articles 24 and 58 of the constitution.[34] Ōkuma replied that there was in fact no conflict, but the dispute over foreign judges continued.

On June 11 1889, Japan and Germany signed the revised treaty. At the last moment further concessions were asked of the Japanese, but the Japanese minister to Germany, Saionji Kinmochi, appealed to the German foreign minister, Herbert von Bismarck, who yielded to the Japanese. The Japanese government, delighted with this success, asked the resident ministers to send copies of the revised treaty to their home countries.[35]

The successful negotiations with the United States and Germany did not end the internal opposition to the revised treaties. The *Yūbin hōchi shimbun*, an organ of the Kaishin-tō, printed a series of fourteen articles devoted to questions and answers about the new treaties. The role of the editor, Yano Fumio (1850–1913), was to reassure those who were concerned about the possible effects of the treaties. Some people feared, for example, that the employment of foreign judges might lead to meddling by other countries in Japanese internal affairs, but Yano answered that the appointment and dismissal of these judges would be entirely in the hands of the Japanese. If, moreover, the judges were naturalized as Japanese, what danger could there be of foreign meddling? Again, in response to those who feared that opening the interior of the country to foreigners or permitting them to buy land was a threat to Japanese sovereignty, Yano insisted that there must be equality in international relations. Japanese already could travel freely in other countries and could buy land, and it was therefore unfair not to allow foreigners the same privileges. As for the fear that foreigners would buy up Japanese land, there were many more profitable investments; there was no danger of foreigners flocking to Japan to purchase land.[36]

Yano's arguments were persuasively presented, but Japanese opposition to the revised treaties became increasingly vocal. The emperor sent Motoda Nagazane to ask Ōkuma whether there was anything to the charge that provisions of the revised treaties violated the new constitution. Ōkuma denied that there was, but Motoda urged the emperor to consult with Itō. The emperor, following Motoda's suggestion, sent for Itō on July 24 to ask how naturalization laws might affect the employment of foreign judges. Itō initially had been favorably impressed by Ōkuma's plans for treaty revision and had recommended that the emperor approve them, but as the cries of opposition became increasingly vociferous, Itō began to waver. On the twenty-ninth, when the emperor sent for him again, Itō (who said he was too ill to visit the palace) was pessimistic. He predicted future difficulties and confessed he had no solutions to offer.[37]

Many questions remained to be answered. First, if a major country refused to accept the revised treaty, should the present treaty with that country be revoked? Britain, the most important "major country," showed no sign of willingness to consider revising the treaties. As foreseen, when the Japanese granted the Americans the right to trade in the interior, the British demanded the same rights under the most-favored-nation clause. Ōkuma refused, saying that it was still premature to consider the issue. The negotiations dragged on. In the meantime, Japan signed a revised treaty with Russia in August.

On August 14 a group of high-ranking officials, headed by Soejima Taneomi, visited the foreign minister's residence to discuss treaty revision. General Torio

Koyata (1847–1905) brought up the matter of foreign judges. He believed that hiring these judges was unconstitutional and asked why the Japanese were so quick to protect foreign interests and so indifferent to Japanese interests. Ōkuma admitted that there was something to this criticism but said that the harm done to Japan by extraterritoriality far exceeded that of the proposed concessions and that if the Japanese wished to get rid of the major harm, concessions were unavoidable. Torio asked if Ōkuma really intended to go through with treaty revision. Ōkuma replied that he was determined to do so but that if the emperor failed to ratify the new treaties, that would end the matter. Torio retorted that Ōkuma's only possible course was to resign and put an end to his plan.[38]

Opposition to the revised treaties was by no means confined to politicians. Throngs of people from the provinces arrived in Tōkyō to demand the cancellation of treaty revision. On August 18 representatives of various organizations, including antigovernmental newspapers, convened a meeting of a nationwide Anti-Treaty-Revision League. More than 180 people attended, and for three days, beginning on the twenty-fifth, there were large-scale lecture meetings. On the twenty-second, the Nippon Club was founded as an organ of resistance to treaty revision (and to Westernization in general). A mounting campaign against treaty reform was launched in the press, and attempts were made to appeal to the emperor through his trusted advisers, especially Motoda and Sasaki Takayuki. Before long, there were calls for Ōkuma's resignation and even his impeachment.[39]

The tone of the protests became openly xenophobic. The proposed use of foreigners as judges in Japanese courts was attacked with particular vehemence. Rhetorical questions were voiced: How is it possible that men who were so brave in face of the shogunate armies are so afraid of foreign countries? What will become of national independence if the revised treaties are put into effect?[40]

Inoue Kowashi sent a letter to the prime minister urging him to cease negotiations for treaty revision. At first Inoue had favored using naturalized foreign judges, but he was now convinced that the country faced irremediable disaster unless attempts to revise the treaties were abandoned altogether. He decided he must resign and pleaded unsuccessfully with Prime Minister Kuroda to resign as well. He sent a letter to Minister of Justice Yamada Akiyoshi recalling that when Iwakura Tomomi was on his deathbed in 1883, he had commanded him never to forget that the fate of the nation hung on not allowing foreigners to dwell in the interior as long as they demanded legal privileges. Inoue feared that if Japan went ahead with treaty revision, advocates of national rights would become increasingly emotional, and in the end patriots would join with crass politicians to rid the country of foreigners. In that case, Japan would surely suffer the fate of Egypt.[41]

The emperor, who had earlier seemed to favor treaty revision as advocated by his chief ministers, was now worried. He sent for Ōkuma and asked about the state of negotiations with Britain and about relations with Russia since the treaty was signed. Ōkuma assured the emperor that despite the difficulties, he was confident that a treaty with Britain would soon be signed. The emperor was not convinced. He had the impression that Kuroda left everything to Ōkuma, who was trying to run the country single-handedly, and he wondered whether it was safe to leave matters in one man's hands. When Itō first brought up the question of treaty revision, he did not suggest that there might be a conflict with the constitution, and for this reason the emperor had assented. The question was what to do now. Should attempts to revise the treaties be abandoned? Or should the revised treaties be revised still further? He asked Itō to submit a plan.[42]

Itō had no plan to offer, but the antirevisionists grew more and more strident in their demands that Ōkuma be compelled to resign. At this stage, prophets of disaster raised their voices. Nishimura Shigeki gave as his reason for opposing revision of the treaties the fierce and unruly dispositions of Europeans and Americans that compelled them to commit incessant acts of aggression. If the Japanese, impressed by foreigners' learning and dazzled by their wealth, believed their fair words and were led astray by their religion, in the end they would fall into the foreigners' trap, and Japan would suffer the same fate as India, Turkey, Egypt, and other countries. Considering the relative strength of Japan to the West—the comparative levels of information and wealth—if foreigners were allowed to live among Japanese in the interior and to buy property there, it was likely to benefit them only and to bring the Japanese only losses. After a hundred years, all the landowners would be foreigners, and the present landowners would be tenant farmers. Land that had been in the possession of the imperial household for thousands of years, ever since the foundation of the country, would belong to foreigners. Business and industry would also be in the hands of the foreigners. Japanese would be treated by them exactly like slaves. The present treaties were not without faults, but compared with the revised treaties, the harm they did to Japan was minor. The present treaties had the effect of keeping the foreigners at a distance, but the revised treaties would bring them close, and that would be a disaster.[43]

Although Nishimura had been chosen as a lecturer to the emperor because of his special knowledge of Western institutions, he was harsh in his appraisal of foreigners. Extraterritoriality had been considered for years as the most hateful manifestation of Western feelings of superiority to Japan, but Nishimura felt it was of only minor significance compared with the sacrifices Japan would be obliged to make in exchange for ending extraterritoriality. Ironically, the British, far from considering that the Japanese were victims, were astonished that the Germans were willing to yield so much to Japan in return for so little![44]

On October 3, increasingly concerned over the situation, the emperor sent an official to ask Kuroda to meet with Itō and decide whether to push ahead with treaty revision. Kuroda was determined to carry out the revision, regardless of how many obstacles there might be, but Itō, who had previously supported it, had lost the courage to carry it through. Alleging illness, he refused to see anyone.[45] Sasaki Takayuki, long one of the emperor's trusted advisers, reported that opposition to treaty revision was growing every day. He foresaw great turbulence if the emperor did not deliver a decision, but the emperor preferred to wait until the negotiations with Britain had been concluded. He was also waiting for a decision to emerge from the deliberations of Itō, Kuroda, and Ōkuma.

A meeting of delegates from all parties was held in the presence of the emperor, but it ended in a stalemate, with neither side willing to change its viewpoint. The participants, despairing of reaching a solution, repeatedly appealed to the emperor to pass judgment, but he seemed reluctant to act without a concrete proposal from Itō. Both sides attempted to win Yamagata's support, but he only counseled delay.

On October 18 Ōkuma was seriously wounded by a "patriot." That day, as he was leaving court to return to his house, a man leaped out and threw a bomb at his carriage. Ōkuma was badly wounded. Dr. Baelz, who was summoned to treat him, concluded that there was no choice but to amputate Ōkuma's leg above the knee. Baelz added, "Ōkuma, who with much labour and skill had at length achieved what the Japanese had almost universally and for so long had been desiring, was now decried as an enemy of his country, as one who would hand it over to foreigners. Much nonsensical talk of this kind has culminated in the abominable attempt to assassinate him. A few days ago Count Ito, president of the Council of State, resigned. He is an artful dodger!"[46]

Ōkuma eventually recovered from the wound and the loss of his leg, but treaty revision was doomed, at least for the time being. Baelz wrote in anger, "To listen to the Japanese talking about it or to read Japanese newspapers, one would suppose that it is the foreigners who have been trying to effect revision, and have wanted to force it upon the Japanese! . . . A year hence they will see things more clearly, and will probably want revision once more."[47]

Kuroda said he was willing to accept full responsibility for the failure of the treaty revision and tendered his resignation to the emperor. He favored Yamagata as his successor, but Sanjō Sanetomi, a safe but hardly dynamic figure, was appointed instead as a kind of interim prime minister until Yamagata was ready to take the position. Ōkuma resigned as foreign minister. The struggle to revise the unequal treaties was over, at least for the time being.

Chapter 41

On New Year's Day of 1890, the emperor, now in his thirty-ninth year, once again failed to worship the four directions. It was given out that he was ill, but we may suspect that having spent many hours listening to debates about the constitution and other matters of vital concern, the emperor was not so much ill as bored with his formal duties. But even though he sometimes neglected rituals, he devoted himself to his work this year with greater enthusiasm than ever before, hardly taking a day of rest. On July 17 Tokudaiji Sanetsune, the chief chamberlain, noted in his diary that regardless of the weather—even when it was broiling hot—the emperor went every day to his office to make decisions on state affairs and, not showing the least sign of ennui, devoted himself to studying plans for the government.[1]

The observance of protocol had come to be fairly time-consuming. Not only was there a steady stream of foreign visitors who had to be received with repetitions of set expressions of greeting or farewell, but as the result of the court's eagerness to associate itself with foreign royalty, the emperor had to send messages of congratulations whenever a child was born to the royal families of Europe. A much more tedious obligation was the necessity of going into mourning whenever word was received of the death of a foreign monarch or other member of royalty. In Europe this obligation was intelligible in terms of the blood and marital relations that joined most of the royal houses, but the death on January 8 of Empress Augusta, the consort of Wilhelm I, although it could not have meant much to Emperor Meiji, plunged the Japanese court into mourning for twenty-one days. On January 20 the death of the duke of Aosta necessitated another six days of mourning. Deaths among the emperor's "cousins" were so frequent that regulations governing the appropriate periods of mourning had to be drawn up. The various foreign countries were divided into major (Russia, England, Germany, China, and Italy) and minor (Holland, Spain, Belgium, Hawaii, Sweden, Portugal, and so on) The deaths of the sovereigns, consorts, and crown princes of major nations required twenty-one days of mourning, but the deaths of the royalty of minor countries might require no more than three days of mourning.[2]

Closer at hand, the emperor's worries about the crown prince's health continued. Although Sono Sachiko gave birth in February to the emperor's seventh daughter, the health of Yoshihito, his son and heir, was a source of unending concern.

Another concern of the emperor was the plight of the former high-ranking nobles, many of whom had been reduced to penury. One solution was to appoint them as Shintō priests, but this often proved unsatisfactory. The most eloquent member of the imperial family, Prince Asahiko, tried the patience of the emperor with repeated pleas for special treatment for his class. When the emperor visited Kyōto in April, he felt so sorry for the impoverished nobles that he presented them with 10,000 yen.[3]

These matters directly affected the emperor and were important to him, but his main interest had shifted to politics, especially to the forthcoming general election, scheduled for July 1. This would be an event without precedent in Asia. Revision of the foreign treaties, a matter of such bitter dispute in the preceding year, had certainly not been forgotten, but time went by with little progress being made. On January 29 the new foreign minister, Aoki Shūzō (1844–1914), who had been appointed on December 24 of the previous year, presented for the emperor's approval a memorandum on treaty revision to be sent to the foreign countries with which Japan had concluded treaties. The minister of the imperial household, Hijikata Hisamoto, expressed his conviction that unless the emperor himself was roused into action in support of this new plan, it would be impossible to bring the negotiations to a successful conclusion. Action by the emperor would also be essential in order to win the heartfelt support of the people.

Deeply concerned, the emperor consulted with Itō Hirobumi and Sasaki Takayuki. Sasaki, a long-time adviser, insisted that the cabinet was the appropriate agency for dealing with the matter. This might not be true of other countries, he said, but the national polity (kokutai) and the respect offered by the Japanese people to the gods distinguished Japan from the nations of Europe and America. The emperor, by way of criticizing those officials who claimed to speak for the entire Japanese people, commented that there was a great gap between what persons in the cabinet or in the upper classes thought and what ordinary people thought. His skepticism impressed even the highly conservative Sasaki, who wept with emotion.[4]

The emperor continued to consult with Itō about the Diet's future work. His questions show a new acuity: "What would happen if the Diet failed to pass a bill, even though it was absolutely essential to the administration?" Itō replied that nothing could be done without parliamentary consent and that in such a case, members of the cabinet would have to exert every effort to obtain this consent. The emperor asked next what would be done if the House of Peers and the House of Representatives disagreed or if differences in the views of the Diet and the cabinet could not be resolved. Itō replied that in such instances the Privy Council would have to play a major role.[5]

The emperor's questions, though not profound, revealed that he had become seriously interested in politics. This was true also of the cabinet members. Previously, attendance at cabinet meetings had been casual, as the emperor had complained, but now the ministers had to attend all meetings without fail; those who were physically unable to attend had to notify the others in advance. When bills proposed by a particular minister were being discussed, he would be expected to have copies of his explanations of the contents and to point out salient features to the ministers present. These changes, it was hoped, would contribute to the efficiency of the cabinet meetings.[6] For the first time, gatherings of the high-ranking officers of the state seemed to be professional, rather than occasions for cronies or rivals to exchange banter and divide up political spoils. Itō's studies of parliamentary procedures had begun to bear fruit.

On February 8 Aoki sent a memorandum to the countries with which Japan had concluded treaties, stating that equality would be the necessary condition of any future treaties. With the convening of the Diet and the implementation of the constitution, it seemed evident that the concessions that had been proposed by earlier ministers of foreign affairs in the hopes of securing revisions to the treaties were no longer appropriate. Now that it possessed a legislative body and a constitution, Japan should no longer be considered to lag behind the advanced nations of the West. Aoki specified four changes to the concessions that had been proposed by Inoue Kaoru and Ōkuma Shigenobu: (1) the promise to appoint judges of foreign extraction to the high court was rescinded; (2) the agreement concerning the organization and publication of a survey of the Japanese laws was canceled; (3) the agreement giving foreigners the right to own property was retracted; and (4) some restrictions relating to the agreement granting foreigners the same rights as Japanese would be applied.[7] Aoki added that although he recognized that certain rights accorded to foreign countries thirty years earlier could not be swept away in a day, the new Japan would not tolerate anything harmful to the interests of its people or its dignity as a sovereign state.

It was hardly likely that the European nations (especially Great Britain) would accept these unilaterally decreed changes, but the outcry against proposed treaty revisions during the previous year had made it imperative to produce a new basis for negotiations. The matter of treaty revision could not simply be ignored. The emperor had conveyed to Motoda Nagazane his unhappiness over the failure of the previous year's negotiations, and Motoda had brought this to the attention of the Privy Council. But little, if any, progress could be made through diplomatic channels; instead, the Japanese set about reforming their legal system in order to deny the European nations grounds for apprehension over what their nationals might suffer under primitive or unwritten laws.

On March 18 it was decided that the courts should be reorganized, the first of many changes this year. On the twenty-seventh of the month, the civil code was promulgated, the fruit of long preparation. As far back as 1876, a committee had been appointed to draft a code, which was completed in 1878. The government, still not satisfied, had sent men abroad to examine legislative and political theory in the hopes of producing a better code of law. In 1880 Gustave Boissonade was hired by the Ministry of Justice to prepare a code, which was elaborated and eventually translated in 1886. Other modifications were made, but despite efforts to hasten its completion, the code was not approved by the Genrō-in and the Privy Council until this time.[8] Codes of civil suits and mercantile law were also promulgated. These developments should have reassured foreigners that Japanese justice would not be arbitrary or corrupt, but they showed no signs of willingness to satisfy the Japanese desire for equality.[9]

The emperor's reactions to these changes in the legal system were not recorded. Perhaps his mind was already preoccupied with thoughts of the Grand Maneuvers he was to observe in Aichi Prefecture. He left by train for Nagoya on March 28 and, after numerous rest stops along the way, arrived at five that afternoon. The city greeted the emperor with boundless enthusiasm and joy. The sincerity of the welcome was emphasized by fireworks that rose into the sky, red lanterns that glowed along the streets, and evergreen arches erected over the course he followed. The emperor's journey to Nagoya does not figure among his *junkō*, presumably because its purpose was to observe maneuvers and not to acquaint the emperor with the lives of his people; but it contributed no less than a *junkō* to enhancing the emperor's popularity.

The maneuvers took the form of a mock war between the East Army (Japan) and the West Army (the invaders). The West Army was able, thanks to its powerful fleet, to control the sea, and it successfully landed troops on various islands and coastal districts. The East Army's mission was to defend Tōkyō Bay from attack by West Army units approaching from various directions. The maneuvers were hampered by driving rain that began to fall on March 30 and continued to fall steadily through the whole of the thirty-first. The emperor braved the wind and rain, seeming not to notice the extreme muddiness of the roads.

The "fighting" at first seemed to favor the East Army, but the invading West Army, under such capable officers as Nogi Maresuke, held its own, perhaps disappointing the emperor, who probably hoped that the invaders would be repulsed. After five days of combat on land and sea, the maneuvers were halted, but not before anecdotes had accumulated describing how, for example, the emperor ate lunch at an elementary school, drinking tea from a cup made for the pupils' use, and using a classroom desk for his table.[10]

The empress joined the emperor in Nagoya, and they traveled together to Kyōto. The railway line between Tōkyō and Kyōto had been completed in October 1889, making travel far more convenient than ever before. When they arrived that evening at the Gosho, they discovered that the cherry blossoms were in full bloom, stirring nostalgic thoughts in the emperor, who still considered Kyōto to be his "old home." He composed this poem:

furusato no	When I came and saw
hana no sakari wo	The cherry-trees in full bloom
kite mireba	In my old village.
naku uguisu no	How nostalgic I was made
koe mo natsukashi.	By the voice of the song-thrush.[11]

Hardly had they arrived than they went to pay their respects at the tomb of Emperor Kōmei. Later, the empress visited a school for the blind and deaf, and the emperor, a middle school where he observed calisthenics and military drill. On April 9, at the earnest request of the governors of Kyōto and Shiga Prefectures, the emperor and empress visited the recently completed aqueduct, bringing water from Lake Biwa to Kyōto.[12]

On April 15 Arthur, duke of Connaught, the third son of Queen Victoria, and his wife, Louise Marguérite, arrived in Tōkyō for a visit. Luckily for them, the emperor and empress were in Kyōto and thus spared the necessity of entertaining these important visitors. They did not hurry their return to the capital. The emperor, who feared he had been neglecting the navy, left Kyōto on the eighteenth to observe a naval review at Kure. He later visited the chief naval stations, at Kure and Sasebo. The empress traveled instead to Nara, visiting the principal Shintō shrines in the city and the surrounding countryside. They did not return to Tōkyō until May 6.

In the meantime, the duke and duchess had been amusing themselves with riding in jinrikishas, buying curios, and admiring the cherry blossoms. Mary Fraser, the wife of the British minister, wrote,

The Duchess, indeed, is an ardent sightseer, and seems to have only one dread; namely, that she should miss some interesting experience which the ordinary traveler would ferret out for himself. Before the party arrived, word was sent that they wishes to travel quite unofficially so as to have all possible freedom for sight-seeing.[13]

The emperor did not return to Tōkyō until two days before the duke and duchess sailed for Vancouver on May 8. On the morning of their departure, Prince Komatsu arrived at the British legation, where the royal couple were residing, bringing gifts from the emperor and empress. Japanese often startled foreigners by arriving for a visit with excessive punctuality, a tradition that has lingered. Mrs. Fraser recalled, "Prince Komatsu came, without warning, at a quarter to nine, and neither the Duke nor the Duchess was quite prepared for such an early pleasure."[14]

The visit of the duke and duchess of Connaught passed without incident and without unnecessary fuss, suggesting new maturity in dealing with distinguished foreign visitors. Soon after their departure, Yamagata Aritomo, the new prime minister, made significant changes in his cabinet that indicated a new era in Japanese politics had arrived. The changes had begun some months earlier with Yamagata's decision to place at the head of the Metropolitan Police Force someone who was not from Satsuma. For years the police had been dominated by Satsuma, and many abuses of power had resulted from this unvarying control. Yamagata, determined to change the situation before the convening of the first Diet, appointed Tanaka Mitsuaki from Tosa as the superintendent general in December 1889.

The appointment broke precedents but not too much: Tosa (the present Kōchi), after all, was one of the four western domains that shared a monopoly of cabinet posts.[15] Yamagata's next move was more dramatic. He included in his cabinet two men who were not from the four domains — Yoshikawa Akimasa (from Awa, the present Tokushima) as minister of education, and Mutsu Munemitsu (from Kii, the present Wakayama) as minister of agriculture and commerce.[16] These appointments aroused opposition among politicians from the four domains, and even the emperor expressed reservations. He had long disliked Mutsu and doubted that his character had improved since "what happened ten years ago."[17] Yoshikawa, the emperor added, was conspicuously lacking in popularity. He urged Yamagata to give due thought before choosing these men.

Yamagata answered that Mutsu's crime had been expiated by the years he spent in prison. If he was not given a post worthy of his abilities, he might join some political party that would create problems for the government. Yamagata guaranteed that there would be no repetition of Mutsu's earlier errors that he would personally assume responsibility. As for Yoshikawa, an old friend, he might not yet be ready for interior minister, but he was quite capable of handling the work of the Ministry of Education. Yamagata promised to give guidance to Yoshikawa. He declared he was fully aware of the importance of education, which was why he had tried for so long to persuade Enomoto Takeaki, the minister of education, to set future goals, but Enomoto had vacillated and nothing had been achieved. If Yoshikawa was appointed as minister of education, he would see to it that principles of education would be laid down that would not require alteration even after another man became minister of education. The emperor at length gave his consent.[18] The appointments were good, and the emperor, impressed by Yamagata's capability, promoted him in June to general.

Many problems remained before an elected, constitutional government could commence its activities. On June 28, immediately before the election, the administrative code was approved, and two days later the spheres of activity of the Privy Council and the Cabinet were defined in last-minute efforts to have the government in working order for the newly elected Diet.

The election took place on July 1. It was carried out under the provisions of the Law of Election of Members of the House of Representatives, which had been enacted by the emperor on February 11, 1889, at the same time that he sanctioned the constitution.[19] A total of 300 seats were contested, covering the entire country with the exception of Hokkaidō, Okinawa, and the Ogasawara Islands. The franchise was severely limited. Women could not vote, and for men there were qualifications of age, residence, and property. A voter had to be twenty-five years of age, to have lived as a permanent resident in a prefecture for one year, and to have paid at least 15 yen in national taxes. This meant that only 450,365 men were entitled to vote, about 1.14 percent of a population of nearly 40 million. About 95 percent of those who were eligible to cast ballots did so, although there was no penalty for failing to vote, a mark of the great interest aroused by the election.[20]

The elections were carried out without violence and with surprising smoothness, considering the civil strife that had torn the country not long before. On the whole there seem to have been few violations of the electoral laws, although petty deceptions may have been carried out when illiterates cast ballots.[21] But as R. H. P. Mason commented, "in complete contrast to what went on at the time of the second general election two years later, the Government refrained from abusing its executive or judicial powers to secure the defeat of its opponents. The law was neutral, and so was its enforcement by the police and the higher political or judicial authorities."[22]

The emperor did not express his reactions to the election. It is hard to imagine that he was indifferent to the results, even if they did not affect him directly. His continued efforts to persuade Itō Hirobumi either to accept the post of president of the House of Peers or to resume his post as head of the Privy Council suggest his deep concern about the future of the government. Itō, although he repeatedly refused both appointments, eventually accepted the presidency of the House of Peers, provided he could resign after the first session of the Diet.[23]

The adoption of parliamentary government led to greater freedom of assembly and formation of political organizations than had been hitherto permitted. On July 25 a law was promulgated simplifying procedures for obtaining permission to hold political meetings or forming parties. At the same time, however, new regulations were imposed prohibiting women and children from attending political meetings or joining political parties. During sessions of the imperial Diet, outdoor gatherings or large-scale movements of people were prohibited within seven miles of the Diet buildings.[24]

One other feature of the history of the imperial household at this time was the steady increase of crown lands in different parts of the country, properties newly incorporated into the palace holdings.[25] This addition in the lands and revenues naturally bolstered imperial authority. Even though the emperor himself almost never took advantage of the various hunting preserves, hot springs, and scenic spots that were constantly added to the imperial domains, they probably served to reassure the people around him that there was no danger he would ever have to endure the poverty experienced by some emperors in the past.

The Diet did not convene until November 29. During the intervening months, various last-minute changes were proposed. On September 24 a group of high-ranking political figures headed by Sasaki Takayuki submitted a proposal to the prime minister asking for the establishment of a government agency that would be responsible for Shintō worship. This agency would be in charge of national religious observances, ceremonies, and the oaths taken by civilian and military officials. The chief officer would be of the highest rank in order to enhance the post's importance. He would advise the emperor and bear responsibility for the religious life of the nation. Sasaki was convinced that the preservation of order in the state required the maintenance of the eternal, unchanging national polity. Worship of the gods was indispensable to this polity, and the unity of the people was strengthened by the expansion of the imperial way of fidelity to the sovereign and love of country. He declared that the greatest deficiency in Meiji's holy reign was the lack of a high governmental agency for the worship of the imperial ancestors and the gods of heaven and earth.[26]

Yamagata referred the proposal to the cabinet. At first it seemed as though there would be no difficulty in obtaining agreement to form a Shintō agency within the Ministry of the Imperial Household, but the minister, Yamada Akiyoshi, though agreeing in principle with Sasaki's insistence on the importance of worshiping the gods, saw practical difficulties. According to Sasaki's plan, all Shintō shrines would be placed under the agency's jurisdiction, but there were more than 30,000 shrines scattered over the country, and if one added unofficial shrines, the number would exceed 80,000. Yamada asked how it would be possible to supervise all of them. Faced with this problem, the cabinet chose the safest course, to submit the proposal to the emperor for his consideration.

The emperor in turn sent word to Itō Hirobumi, asking whether he favored or opposed the proposal. Itō replied that it went without saying that it was appropriate to worship the gods but that because establishing a governmental organization was a major undertaking; it should be thoroughly examined by members of the cabinet before being submitted to the emperor for his decision.

When Yoshii Tomozane, the vice minister of the imperial household, asked Sanjō Sanetomi his opinion, Sanjō opposed Sasaki's proposal, citing the cost of establishing an agency, and warned against unnecessarily increasing the number of Shintō priests. Other cabinet ministers also raised objections. They argued that if the proposal were adopted, it might make people in foreign countries wonder whether this were not a political maneuver whose objective was the expulsion of foreign religions; at home, it might make Buddhists suppose that it was intended to establish Shintō as the state religion and to discriminate against themselves. It was not advisable, they said, to mix religion and politics at a time when parliamentary government was first being instituted.

Sasaki replied that ancestor worship was the polity of the imperial land and that creating a Shintō agency was a means of placing the Japanese gods above religion, making clear the special nature of the imperial land, and ensuring the freedom of religion.[27] In the end, no decision was reached, but the special relations between Shintō and the state would be of major importance in the years to come.

In October there was another development that, though minor in itself, had long-lasting repercussions. Photographs of the emperor and empress, at first distributed only to schools established by the central government, were later distributed also to prefectural schools and to locally established elementary schools and kindergartens. The photographs were to be worshiped by teachers and pupils on the three major holidays as a means of inculcating loyalty and patriotism.[28] Probably most teachers and students, initially at least, accepted this obligation as an act of patriotism. But the fact that the object of worship was a photograph, rather than a flag or some other symbol, in time caused some to refuse to bow for religious or other reasons. The seeds of emperor worship and even of the elevation of the emperor to godhead were planted in those who bowed their heads in reverence before the imperial photographs.

On October 30 the emperor, having just returned from observing exhausting maneuvers in Ibaraki Prefecture, issued his rescript on education. The emperor had long displayed unusual interest in education and had encouraged Motoda Nagazane, his Confucian adviser, to write books that would inculcate in the young loyalty and filial piety as the basis of education. Motoda conceded that it had been necessary to adopt and imitate Western material things and institutions in order for Japan to maintain its independence and dignity in a threatening world, but he deplored the accompanying tendency to ignore the essence of national polity and the wellsprings of education. At a conference of provincial leaders held that February, delegates had urged the minister of education to end the disproportionate emphasis on the West and to encourage the indigenous morality of Japan. They asked that a new educational policy be established as soon as possible.[29]

The emperor, sharing these concerns about education, had commanded Enomoto Takeaki, the minister of education, to compile a set of educational precepts to be read and memorized by students. Enomoto spent some months attempting to compose a suitable set but in the end was unsuccessful. When Yoshikawa Akimasa succeeded him, the emperor once again commanded the compilation, and Yoshikawa subsequently drew up the first draft of an imperial edict incorporating the emperor's wishes. In brief, it stated that loyalty, filial piety, benevolence, and righteousness were the Way of Japan. These virtues were both easy to learn and easy to practice. They were truly the essence of national polity and the fountainhead of education; an educational policy for Japan was not to be sought elsewhere.[30]

The most apparent flaw in this presentation of educational policy was that it was so markedly Confucian—at least what people of the day supposed to be Confucian—that it seemed to contain nothing new and nothing specifically Japanese. Indeed, it would be hard to imagine any people who denied the value of loyalty and filial piety, virtues said to be the essence of Japanese national polity. Perhaps the only way to make educational policy seem uniquely Japanese was to stress the importance of the imperial household. This course would in fact be adopted when the rescript on education was prepared.

Inoue Kowashi (1844–1895), who was recognized as an expert in intellectual matters (he was said to be Itō Hirobumi's "brain"), was asked his opinion of Yoshikawa's draft rescript. He objected to it on various grounds. First of all, he said that a rescript on education should not be the same as one devoted to politics or the same as a set of commands appropriate to military education. He insisted that it was not advisable to risk arousing religious disputes by mentioning in the rescript respect for heaven or worship of the gods. He also advised that the rescript not be abstrusely philosophical or colored by a political tinge. It should be clear and easy to understand, and the tone should not be such that it pleased one faction and angered another. Inoue admitted that to avoid these dangers would be more difficult than erecting a twelve-story building.[31]

As is apparent from this synopsis of his views, Inoue's criticism was largely negative, but he later compiled a draft rescript of his own. He showed it to Motoda and, in the light of his criticisms, drew up a second draft. Yamagata and Minister of Education Yoshikawa approved this version, and after a few stylistic problems had been corrected, they submitted a temporary draft to the emperor. He read it with great care. Some points did not satisfy him; he mentioned in particular the inadequate treatment of the four Confucian virtues. Motoda returned the manuscript to Inoue on August 26, conveying the emperor's opinions. Inoue and Motoda conferred many times over the text, adding a character here and deleting a character there. At last the final text was ready, and on October 21 it was again presented to the emperor for his inspection. The emperor read and pondered every word, not giving his approval until October 24.

The rescript itself it short and uncomplicated, but the use of rare and obscure

characters makes it harder to understand in the original than in English translation. The official translation opens:

> Know ye, Our subjects:
> Our Imperial Ancestors have founded Our Empire on a basis broad
> and everlasting, and have deeply and firmly implanted virtue; Our sub-
> jects ever united in loyalty and filial piety have from generation to gen-
> eration illustrated the beauty thereof. This is the glory of the fundamental
> character [*kokutai*] of Our Empire, and herein also lies the source of Our
> education. Ye, Our subjects, be filial to your parents, affectionate to your
> brothers and sisters; as husbands and wives be harmonious, as friends
> true; bear yourselves in modesty and moderation; extend your benevo-
> lence to all; pursue learning and cultivate arts, and thereby develop in-
> tellectual faculties and perfect moral powers; always respect the Consti-
> tution and observe the laws; should emergency arise, offer yourselves
> courageously to the State; and thus guard and maintain the prosperity of
> Our Imperial throne coeval with heaven and earth. So shall ye not only
> be Our good and faithful subjects, but render illustrious the best traditions
> of your forefathers.[32]

There can be no question of the Japaneseness of a document that opens with
reference to the Imperial Ancestors. Although the virtues of loyalty and filial piety are mentioned as if they had been passed down from remote antiquity, they
are not prominent, say, in the *Kojiki*, and they are not necessarily true to the
teachings of Chu Hsi, the founder of the orthodox school of Neo-Confucianism.
Chu Hsi certainly preached the importance of filial piety, but in place of loyalty
to the state, he insisted on the virtue of respect for elders, typified by a younger
brother's respect for his older brother. But the importance that Chu Hsi gave to
the study of the principles of nature is missing from the rescript, whose emphasis
is not on scholarly excellence but on the many generations of Japanese, going
back to the foundation of the empire, who have loyally and faithfully served the
imperial family. The rescript states at the conclusion:

> The Way here set forth is indeed the teaching bequeathed by Our Im-
> perial Ancestors, to be observed alike by Their Descendants and their
> subjects, infallible for all ages and true in all places. It is Our wish to lay
> it to heart in all reverence, in common with you, Our subjects, that we
> may all attain to the same virtue.[33]

Apart from a reference to the desirability of the emperor's subjects pursuing
learning and cultivating arts, the rescript has little to say about the content of
education present or future. The emperor's subjects, in their capacity as good

citizens, were enjoined to respect the constitution and observe the laws. They were also commanded to offer themselves courageously to the state if an emergency arose. But other, germane, questions were not touched on. Was education to be compulsory for all? If so, up to what level? Should girls receive the same kind and degree of education as boys? Should Western learning (science, law, medicine, and the like) be considered as important as moral training? Were traditional Japanese artistic skills to be considered an integral part of education? Was physical education important? The rescript was less progressive in outlook than the charter oath sworn by the boy emperor.

The rescript (though not the charter oath) was nevertheless not only acclaimed but worshiped. In January 1891, only a few months after its issuance, Uchimura Kanzō (1861–1930), a teacher in a high middle school, was asked (along with the other teachers and students) to bow before the imperial signature affixed to the Rescript on Education "in the manner we used to bow before our ancestral relics as prescribed in Buddhist and Shintō ceremonies." Uchimura recalled in a letter he wrote to an American friend two months after the event,

> I was not at all prepared to meet such a strange ceremony, for the thing was the new invention of the president of the school. As I was the third in turn to go up and bow, I had scarcely time to think upon the matter. So, hesitating in doubt, I took a safer course for my Christian conscience, in the august presence of sixty professors (all non-Christians, the two other Xian prof.'s beside myself having absented themselves) and over one thousand students, I took my stand and did *not* bow! It was an awful moment for me, for I instantly apprehended the result of my conduct.[34]

When urged by his friends at the school to bow, he replied that "the good emperor must have given the precepts to his subjects *not* to be bowed unto but to be obeyed in our daily walks in life." In the end, however, having been assured by the principal of the school, who did not wish to fire him, that bowing did not mean worship, Uchimura decided to bow "for the sake of the school, the principal, and my students."[35] No doubt other men, like Uchimura, "believed the ceremony to be a rather foolish one," but it took courage to refuse to bow when all one's colleagues were bowing. Whatever resistance such men may have felt in their hearts, most ended by bowing and joining in the chorus of praise for the "great foundation of education."[36]

The effects of the Rescript on Education were not immediately apparent. Early in November the minister of education issued a statement on higher education. Without referring to the rescript's ideals, he noted and deplored the tendency for universities to be concentrated in Tōkyō. Indeed, there were said to be 5,000 university students in Tōkyō, quite a disproportionate part of the national number. Some private universities had established connections with political parties. Others were so wedded to England, France, or Germany that they gave no thought to Japanese traditions. Young men of no educational attainments were aimlessly studying a bit of the law or of political science and then abandoning themselves to empty speculations or getting bogged down in theories instead of devoting themselves to the welfare of the nation.[37]

On November 29 the ceremonies of the long-awaited opening of the Diet took place. That morning the emperor left the palace at 10:30 and proceeded toward the House of Peers. He was accompanied by Prince Taruhito, Interior Minister Sanjō Sanetomi, Prime Minister Yamagata Aritomo, President of the Privy Council Ōki Takatō, and various high officials. On reaching the Diet building, the emperor was met by other dignitaries. The members of both Houses were already assembled for the ceremony, as were the ministers and other officers of the different foreign legations, officials personally appointed by the emperor, men decorated with first-class orders, and specially invited guests. The emperor appeared in the Hall of Ceremonies, ushered in by the grand master of ceremonies. Chamberlains bearing the sacred sword and jewel formed a line that was joined by princes of the blood and personal attendants of the emperor. The emperor seated himself on the throne, whereupon all present bowed deeply. The prime minister came forward to offer the text of the rescript, and the emperor read it aloud.

The rescript expressed the emperor's satisfaction with the progress toward establishing institutions of government during the twenty or so years since he ascended the throne. He hoped that this progress would result in making known abroad the glory of the country and the loyalty and bravery of its people. He was pleased that friendly relations had been secured with foreign countries and hoped that trade would be broadened and would raise the nation's level of prosperity. He also hoped that relations with countries with which Japan had concluded treaties would be ever more cordial.[38]

The tone was certainly more international than the Rescript on Education, but it, too, attributed to the Imperial Ancestors the progress of the Japanese people. Itō Hirobumi, the president of the House of Peers, came forward to accept the document from the emperor. Once again, all present made a deep bow, acknowledged by the emperor with a nod. Then he withdrew. The ceremony was over.

The convening of the first Diet was the realization of the dreams of many men, notably Ōkuma Shigenobu. Even the authors of popular fiction had been caught up in the excitement of the impending opening of the Diet. A new kind of fiction—the political novels of the 1880s—had been written with the hopes of appealing to a large body of readers who anticipated with joy the day when Japan, like the advanced countries of the West, would be ruled by a parliament that guaranteed the liberty of all Japanese and promised them a better life. Many who entertained such high hopes would soon be disillusioned by the squabbles that marked the actual proceedings of the Diet, but it can hardly be doubted that Japan had taken an immense step toward achieving democracy, even though the path ahead was in shadows.

Chapter 42

On New Year's Day 1891, the emperor performed the traditional rites, only to be stricken two days later with a serious illness. An influenza epidemic had swept the country, and not even the imperial family was spared. First to fall ill were some court ladies, then the empress, and finally the emperor, who was confined to his bed for forty days. He did not resume his duties until February 16, although court officials kept him abreast of matters that demanded his attention.

The epidemic claimed victims who were close to the emperor. On January 22 Motoda Nagazane died after a week's illness. As soon as the emperor heard that Motoda was unwell, he sent Dr. Erwin Baelz to examine him and repeatedly inquired about his condition. Word came on the twenty-first that Motoda was sinking. The emperor, in recognition of Motoda's twenty years' service as his tutor and Confucian adviser, made him a baron and promoted him to the junior second rank. The emperor sent Privy Council Adviser Inoue Kowashi to Motoda's bedside to inform him. Motoda, joining his hands and bowing his head, wept. He died soon afterward.

Motoda had transmitted to the emperor his Confucian belief in the importance of education and the necessity of faithfully performing his Heaven-appointed duties. Even after attaining his majority, the emperor continued to consult Motoda on state policy, respecting his opinions as those of a teacher. Although Motoda (unlike the Confucian scholars of earlier times) knew a fair amount about the West, he was basically conservative and reluctant to recognize the value of the new learning. In this respect he does not seem to have influenced Meiji, but the emperor's extraordinary devotion to duty, his dislike of extravagance, and his determination to share the hardships of his people surely owed much to this teacher. When Itō Hirobumi learned of Motoda's death, he said that he hoped the emperor would not replace him. "What Nagazane did was done well only because he was Nagazane. No man, no matter how studious and erudite, could replace him."[1]

The epidemic persisted well into February. Sanjō Sanetomi died on February 18. On the preceding day the emperor, learning that Sanjō's illness had taken a turn for the worse, decided he must see him before he died. Refusing to wait until a suitable escort could be assembled, he and three chamberlains, protected by only two guards and three cavalry orderlies, set out for Sanjō's house. The emperor had earlier sent the imperial household minister with a rescript praising Sanjō's achievements and bestowing on him the rank of senior first grade. He feared that if he himself presented this decoration, Sanjō might try to leave bed to receive it, worsening his condition. On being ushered into the sickroom, he asked Sanjō how he felt. The latter, not mentioning his illness, expressed gratitude for the great benevolence the emperor had always shown him and his shame over receiving the emperor while lying in a sickbed. He begged the emperor's forgiveness.

The emperor left after a brief visit, but soon afterward issued a rescript proclaiming his indebtedness to Sanjō, whom he described as a teacher and father. The language recalls his words of grief after the death of Iwakura Tomomi, but surely there was a difference in his feelings. Before the Restoration, Sanjō had been a hot-headed noble of the sonnō jōi faction. In 1863 he had physically forced Emperor Kōmei, much against his will, to make a pilgrimage to Iwashimizu to pray for jōi. In the following year, he had joined six other noble extremists in a flight to Chōshū in opposition to the court's policy of kōbu gattai. Meiji may have been too young at the time to be fully aware of these instances of disobedience to the emperor, but whatever he later learned could not have inspired affection for Sanjō.

After the Restoration, Sanjō became a totally different man. Famous mainly for his vacillation, he seemed incapable of ever reaching a firm decision. Meiji certainly depended far less on Sanjō than on Iwakura, Kido, or Itō; Sanjō's importance to the government stemmed mainly from his being a high-ranking noble. So few nobles contributed to the formation of the new government that the emperor, who never forgot the importance of birth, may have credited Sanjō with greater wisdom than he actually had. Sanjō was given a state funeral and was buried at the Gokoku-ji in Tōkyō. Although he had done nothing to ingratiate himself with the common people, it is said that crowds flocked along the roads and wept as they watched the funeral procession pass.[2]

Because of the emperor's and empress's illness, the first poetry gathering, usually held soon after the New Year, did not take place until February 28. The emperor's poem on the topic "Praying for the World Before a Shrine" (*shatō kisei*) was

tokoshie ni	I pray to You that
tami yasukare to	The people will be at peace
inoru naru	For all time to come
wa ga yo wo mamore	Preserve and protect my reign,
Ise no ōkami	O Great Goddess of Ise.[3]

This *tanka* was entitled "Poem of Grievance" (*jukkai*), suggesting that it was the emperor's way of conveying his apprehensions about a year that had begun with an epidemic and the loss of two men who were close to him. But worse was to come.

On January 9, while the emperor was suffering from influenza, he received word of the planned visit to Japan of Czarevitch Nicholas, the Russian crown prince. No doubt the news greatly pleased him. Although Japan had clashed with Russia over the possession of various islands to the north, Russia was a neighbor, and good relations between the two countries was essential. Again, although Meiji had received other royal visitors, Nicholas would be the most important to pay a state visit.[4] As the eldest son of Czar Alexander III, he would one day be the czar of all the Russias, the ruler of the biggest country in the world.

Nicholas would be traveling with his cousin, Prince George of Greece. Count Sergei Witte, probably the most able man in the Russian government at the time, recalled in his memoirs the background for the two princes' journey:

> When he [the czarevitch] reached his majority . . . it was decided to send him abroad, to round out his political development. At this point Emperor Alexander III had the idea of sending the Tsesarevich to the Far East. The Tsesarevich was accompanied on the trip by his brother George, who had to return home before the trip was over because he began to show signs of having consumption, brought on either by a cold or through some kind of carelessness. Also accompanying the Tsesarevich was Prince George of Greece, whose behavior could not serve as a model for grand dukes or princes.[5]

In anticipation for the visit, the Japanese made elaborate preparations. In Tōkyō the royal guests would stay at the Western-style residence of Prince Arisugawa Taruhito in Kasumigaseki, and the large sum of 20,000 yen was set aside for repairing and refurnishing the house.[6] Mary Fraser, the wife of the British minister, described the excitement in Tōkyō over the forthcoming visit:

Very great preparations are being made for this royal visit. The apartments in the palace by the sea[7] have all been furnished and decorated anew; there are to be triumphal arches and illuminations and Court balls; and the Emperor intends to lavish honours—and fun—on his guest.[8]

Nicholas and his suite arrived in Nagasaki on April 27. They had left St. Petersburg in November of the previous year and had boarded the warship *Pamiat Azova* in Trieste, the major port of the Austro-Hungarian Empire. The ship had called at Egypt, Bombay, Ceylon, Singapore, Java, Saigon, Bangkok, Hong Kong, Canton, and Shanghai before reaching Japan. Nicholas was scheduled to visit different regions of Japan and then go on to Vladivostok, where he would inaugurate the construction of the Ussuri Railroad from Vladivostok to Khabarovsk.[9] The decision to send the youthful (he was twenty-three) Nicholas to the East undoubtedly reflected the growing interest of Russia in East Asia.

In Nagasaki, Nicholas received a state reception. Prince Takehito (the younger brother of Prince Taruhito) headed the welcoming party and would accompany the Russian prince throughout his stay in Japan. The reception given Nicholas was on a grand scale and planned to the last detail, down to which kind of tea or cakes would be offered at each stop during the princes' tour of the city.[10]

It seems likely that young Nicholas was hoping for other things than tea and cakes. The night before landing in Nagasaki, Nicholas read Pierre Loti's *Madame Chrysanthème*, a book that seems to have inspired a desire to acquire a temporary Japanese "wife." The evening of his arrival in Nagasaki, he met eight junior officers of the Russian navy stationed in the Inasa district and learned that each had married a Japanese wife. He commented, "I would like to follow their example." He added, "But how shameful to think of such things, just as Holy Week, when Christ suffered, is about to begin."[11]

May 3 was Easter Sunday, and Nicholas was expected to spend the preceding week in prayers. The Japanese, learning of this, did not schedule any official ceremonies until May 4, but Nicholas was so impatient to see the city that instead of devoting himself to prayers aboard ship, he secretly went sightseeing in a jinrikisha.[12] He was delighted with the cleanliness of the streets and houses and with the friendliness of the people. Wherever he went, he was trailed by Japanese plainclothes police responsible for his safety. Their secret reports on his movements reported precisely when Nicholas went where and what he bought at souvenir shops.[13] In imitation of Loti, Nicholas had a dragon tattooed on his right arm; it took seven hours, from nine in the evening until four the next morning.[14]

On May 4 Nicholas, free of religious impediments to his activities, enjoyed a rousing welcome from the citizens of Nagasaki. The long association—more than thirty years—of the Russian Pacific Fleet with the city had fostered a friendly attitude toward Russians. In his diary Nicholas expressed surprise at the number of people who could speak Russian. That day he was entertained at an elaborate Japanese banquet offered by the governor of Nagasaki. After the meal, he and the Greek prince were shown a display of Arita ceramics and other Japanese artistic wares and then were taken to see the Suwa *jinja*, the principal Shintō shrine in the city. They returned to the ship afterward, but that evening Nicholas and George slipped ashore and went to Inasa, where they met the resident Russian officers and their Japanese wives. Geishas danced for them. Nicholas mentioned in his diary that everyone had a little to drink.[15]

The secret police report on that evening's amusements supplied details not recorded in Nicholas's diary. They mentioned that the Russians were entertained by five geishas from Maruyama. Then followed a drinking party at which the geishas danced and the two princes sang Russian songs. Late that night, they went to a Western-style restaurant run by one Morooka Matsu. They did not return to the ship until four in the morning. Another source states that Matsu arranged private entertainment for the two princes on the second floor of her establishment; the names of the ladies involved are a matter of dispute.[16] Nicholas much regretted leaving Nagasaki, which he praised especially for its cleanliness.

The next port of call was Kagoshima, a curious choice considering the xenophobia for which Satsuma was renowned. Shimazu Tadayoshi was particularly conservative, as was apparent from his refusal to cut his hair or to wear European clothes, and he was not fond of foreigners; but when he learned that the Russian prince was to visit Japan, he decided to invite him to Kagoshima. The Russians arrived on May 6.

The entertainment offered by Shimazu Tadayoshi was of an earlier day. When Nicholas reached Tadayoshi's residence, the latter, along with 170 elderly samurai all dressed in traditional armor, came out to welcome him. The samurai performed warlike dances led by Tadayoshi's six-year-old son, Tadashige, and Tadayoshi himself led the display of mounted archery.[17] Nicholas was delighted with his reception in Kagoshima. He was particularly pleased that he saw no other Europeans in the city, proof that the place was still "unspoiled." He enjoyed the elaborate Japanese meal, but above all he was pleased with the conservatism of Shimazu Tadayoshi, which accorded with his own taste.

Not all the Russians were so impressed: Prince E. E. Ukhotomskii, who accompanied the czarevitch, complained that Kagoshima, the birthplace of "samurai-ism" and xenophobia, was a hotbed of Shintō and feudal tradition. He found the music for the samurai dances gloomy, and the battle cries raised by the samurai, cacophonous.[18] But a bond had been formed between Nicholas and the Shimazu family that would be maintained in years to come. The Russian ships left the same day at dusk.

May 7 and 8 were spent at sea. The *Pamiat Azova* passed through the Shimonoseki Straits and proceeded through the Inland Sea to Kōbe, arriving a little after midday on the ninth. After about two hours visiting the sights of the city, the Russians boarded a train for Kyōto, arriving that evening. Nicholas was delighted with Kyōto. He referred to it as the Moscow of Japan, alluding to the fact that both cities had once been capitals. He stayed at the Tokiwa, a modern hotel, but declined the Western-style room prepared for him, preferring a traditional Japanese room. That night Nicholas suddenly said that he would like to see some "Kyōto prostitutes" dance. He was taken to the Nakamura-rō in Gion, where he remained until two in the morning.

The next day was spent in sightseeing and shopping. He visited (among other places) the Gosho, Nijō Castle, and both East and West Honganji, the two biggest Buddhist temples. He saw *kemari* played by members of the Asukai family and observed long-distance firing of arrows. He seemed delighted by whatever he saw, and needless to say, wherever he went, he was acclaimed by crowds. He spent more than 10,000 yen on art objects and at the Nishi Honganji donated 200 yen for relief of the poor. The Japanese were impressed by his thoughtfulness in asking before he entered any building if he should remove his shoes.

The next morning Nicholas, George, and members of their suite left the hotel in Kyōto for Ōtsu in order to enjoy the sights of Lake Biwa and the surrounding mountains. Nicholas, dressed in a striped woolen suit and wearing a gray bowler hat, rode in a jinrikisha. At the border between Kyōto and Shiga Prefectures had been erected an arch of evergreens surmounted with crossed Japanese, Russian, and Greek flags. Once the party had passed through the arch, they were welcomed by the Ōtsu regimental commander, the chief of the Shiga police, city officials, teachers, schoolchildren, and so on, all lined up along the road.[19]

As the long procession of jinrikishas, stretching back more than 300 feet, entered Ōtsu, the crowds, like those in the other Japanese cities Nicholas had visited, cheered and waved flags. The procession headed first to the Miidera, where the royal guests were shown treasures of the temple and told of its long history. They enjoyed the views of Lake Biwa from the temple and presently were escorted to the shore of the lake, where they boarded the *Hoan maru*. The ship, gaily decorated with green leaves and flowers, sailed to Karasaki, where, as the foreign princes approached, daytime fireworks (invisible but audible) greeted them. After inspecting the display of armor in the shrine, they returned to the *Hoan maru*, which took them back to Ōtsu.[20]

The czarevitch had lunch at the prefectural office, and at half-past one he and his party set out on the return journey to Kyōto. The procession of jinrikishas was headed by four in which police and civil officials of Shiga and Kyōto rode. Nicholas was in the fifth jinrikisha, George in the sixth, and Prince Takehito in the seventh.[21] There had been rumors that something untoward might happen to the Russian prince this day, and police were stationed along the way. The procession had traveled some six or seven *chō* from the prefectural office, barely making its way through the crowds on both sides of the narrow street, when suddenly a policeman leaped out and, aiming at the czarevitch's head, attacked with his saber. The first blow lopped off the brim of the prince's hat and dealt him a wound on the forehead. Nicholas recorded in his diary:

> I was returning along the same street in a jinrikisha. Crowds were lined up on both sides of the street. We turned left on the narrow street. Just then I felt a sharp sensation on my right temple. I turned back and a policeman, so ugly as to turn my stomach, was swinging a saber in both hands and coming at me for a second attack. The next instant I jumped from the jinrikisha onto the paved road, shouting all the while, "What do you think you're doing?" The reprobate came pursuing me. No one tried to stop the man. Pressing my hand against the bleeding wound, I ran as fast as I could. I wanted to hide in the crowd, but I couldn't because the Japanese had panicked and were scattering in all directions.
>
> As I ran I looked back once again, and I noticed George running after the policeman who was pursuing me. After I had run about sixty feet I stopped at the corner of a narrow lane and turned back. To my great relief, the attack was over. George, to whom I owe my life, had knocked the reprobate down with a blow from his bamboo whip. When I went up to the place, I saw our jinrikisha coolies and several police officers were dragging the reprobate by the legs, and one of them was cutting at the reprobate's neck with a saber.
>
> Everyone was standing there in a daze. I could not understand why George and I and the madman had been left alone on the street, why not one person had run up to help me and to stop the policeman. I could, however, understand why nobody in our escort had been able to help me. Prince Arisugawa, third in the line, couldn't have seen anything. In order to reassure them, I deliberately remained on my feet as long as I could.[22]

Nicholas's account should have been definitive, but the testimony of numerous other witnesses makes it clear that he erred in several particulars. He was incorrect in stating that George had knocked down the policeman and that nobody had helped him and George when they were threatened. At the trial, witnesses testified that George was indeed first to resist the attacker. He used the bamboo whip purchased that day as a souvenir. However, the whip did not cause the assailant to fall down; it only made him flinch, but that was long enough for Nicholas's ricksha coolie to tackle him. The saber dropped from the policeman's hand as he fell, and one of George's coolies, picking it up, slashed the man's neck and back. The vital role of the two rickshaw coolies in saving the Russian prince was soon recognized not only by the Japanese but also by the Russians.[23]

The mistakes in Nicholas's account can be attributed to extreme agitation and to the effects of the wounds, but the reward he bestowed on the rickshaw coolies prove that he later came to recognize their courage. All the same, every year on May 11, the anniversary of the Ōtsu incident, in his prayers he thanked George (not the coolies) for saving his life.[24]

We may conjecture, however, that the sensation of being abandoned by a crowd that was more concerned with its own safety than with saving two unarmed men from a maniac may have embittered Nicholas toward the Japanese. There is no overt indication of this feeling in his diary; on the contrary, it mentions how moved he was to see Japanese kneeling along the streets, their hands clasped in prayer, apologizing for the disaster that had befallen him.[25] Moreover, he assured Prince Takehito immediately after the attack that his trifling wounds would certainly not make him think ill of Japan.[26]

But in his memoirs, Count Witte interpreted the prince's reactions quite differently:

> It seems to me that the attack left the Tsesarevich with an attitude of hostility toward and contempt for Japan and the Japanese, as can be seen from official reports in which he refers to the Japanese as *"macaques"* [baboons].
>
> If not for his belief that the Japanese are an unpleasant, contemptible, and powerless people who could be destroyed at one blow from the Russian giant, we would not have adopted a policy in the Far East that led us into the unfortunate war with Japan.[27]

Witte's own "hostility and contempt" for Nicholas II may have colored his account, but he knew his sovereign well and it is unlikely that he invented the prejudices he attributed to him. The incident at Ōtsu, trivial as it may seem at this distance, may have marked a significant step toward the Russo-Japanese War thirteen years later.

The reports to reach Tōkyō of the attempted assassination were at first highly exaggerated. According to Mary Fraser, the very first message stated: "Two deep wounds on the head; recovery impossible." Later, as additional telegrams came in, she was able to report, "He was very much hurt, poor young fellow; but not dangerously so, as in the terror of the moment somebody wired that he was."[28] But even when it had become clear that Nicholas would recover from his slight wounds, the shock to the Japanese was profound.

The primary emotion was probably fear. Many Japanese were convinced that the attack on the czarevitch would lead to war with Russia, a war in which Japan would be no match for the immense empire that stretched across Europe and Asia. There was also an awareness that a great blow had been dealt to Japanese prestige as a civilized, modern nation. Mary Fraser wrote about the attack:

Had it happened in Europe, it would have been looked upon as a great misfortune, but no more. No deductions would have been drawn from it; no enemies could have brandished its record in the stricken face of the nation to show that no civilised people should have friendship with her, that treaties were an absurdity, equality a dream. All that happened to poor Japan, smarting under the wound, to her the most bitter of all — a wound to her honour. The Emperor's welcome guest had been betrayed.[29]

The first word of the incident at Ōtsu to reach Meiji was a telegram sent by Prince Takehito twenty minutes after the attack. It said that the Russian prince had suffered severe wounds and asked that the army surgeon General Hashimoto Tsunatsune be sent to the scene at once. An hour later Takehito sent a personal message to the emperor asking him to come to Kyōto. The emperor, alarmed by the shocking event, conferred with the prime minister and other cabinet members. He sent Prince Yoshihisa at once to Kyōto. He also ordered Dr. Hashimoto and several other doctors, including his personal physician, to go immediately to the wounded man's side. He then informed Prince Takehito that he would go to Kyōto himself early the next morning to see the czarevitch. Meiji also sent a telegram to Nicholas expressing grief and outrage over the attack on his "dear friend" and prayers for his speedy recovery. The czarevitch in reply regretted that he had caused the emperor to worry and stated that he felt surprisingly well. Meiji also sent a personal message to Alexander III informing him that his son had been wounded. The empress sent a similar message to the czarina.[30]

The emperor set out for Kyōto as planned, leaving from Shimbashi Station at 6:30 A.M. That night, soon after his arrival, he went to the hotel where the Russian prince was recovering from the attack and asked to see him. The Russian minister refused, explaining that a visit late at night would not be good for the patient. This must have been one of the rare occasions in Meiji's life when a request of his was refused, but he did not insist, saying he would return the next morning. In the meantime, the doctors sent by the emperor had asked to examine the prince's wounds, but they were refused by the Russian doctors, who said that there was nothing unusual about the wounds and that they did not wish to have the bandages removed. They said that the prince was unwilling to be examined by other doctors. On the following day when the Japanese doctors returned, they were again refused, and because the prince was moved that day to the *Pamiat Azova*, they were never allowed to examine him.[31]

The next morning the emperor left the Gosho, where he had spent the night, and went to visit Nicholas at his hotel. He was met by Prince George, who led him to the wounded prince's room. The emperor expressed his deep regrets over the incident and his sympathy for Nicholas's parents, who, far from their son, were surely greatly worried. He assured the prince that the criminal would be promptly punished and expressed the hope that the prince, as soon as he recovered from his wounds, would visit Tōkyō and see scenic spots elsewhere in Japan. Nicholas replied that the slight wounds he had received would not cause any change in his gratitude for the many kindnesses shown him by the emperor and the Japanese people. As for a visit to Tōkyō, he would have to await orders from home.[32]

That day Nicholas was moved from Kyōto to Kōbe; by command of his mother, he was to recuperate aboard the *Pamiat Azova*. When the emperor learned that the prince was returning to his ship, he was shocked, realizing this meant the prince would not visit Tōkyō. He sent Itō Hirobumi to ask the Russian minister to persuade the prince to remain in Japan. The minister explained the Russian people's great fears for the prince's safety and, in particular, the czarina's deep concern. Although the prince personally wished to go to Tōkyō, he had no choice but to obey his parents. Finally, the minister, in tears, begged Itō to ask the emperor to think of the prince as his own son and travel with him to Kōbe in order to ensure his safety.[33] Itō agreed to transmit the minister's request and predicted that the emperor, in his supreme benevolence, would grant it.

Despite his disappointment, the emperor agreed to the minister's request. His carriage called at the prince's hotel, and they rode to the railway station. They boarded the imperial train (*omeshi ressha*) together, accompanied by Prince George and Prince Takehito. The train was heavily guarded, and the route that the party would take between the railway station and the harbor where the *Pamiat Azova* was anchored was lined with soldiers. In Kōbe the emperor accompanied the czarevitch as far as the pier, where they shook hands.

This was not the last time the two men met. On May 16 Nicholas sent Meiji a letter informing him that he was obliged to leave Japan on the nineteenth by command of his father.[34] The emperor invited Nicholas to lunch in Kōbe on the nineteenth, but he replied that his doctors had advised against his leaving the ship. Nicholas in turn invited the emperor to lunch aboard the *Pamiat Azova*, and the emperor accepted. When word of the invitation reached members of the cabinet, they were appalled. They remembered how the *taewon'gun* of Korea had been abducted by the Chinese, carried off on a ship, and kept a prisoner in China for three years. They were sure that the Russians (who had more ships in Kōbe harbor than the Japanese) would carry off their emperor. The emperor calmly replied to their protests that he would go nevertheless: the Russians were not barbarians, how could they do anything of the kind the ministers feared?

On May 18 the emperor, accompanied by Princes Taruhito and Yoshihisa, boarded the Russian ship. The meal went well. The Russian minister later reported that he had never heard the emperor laugh so loudly. The emperor apologized for the incident at Ōtsu, to which the czarevitch responded that there were lunatics in every country and that in any case his wounds were slight, nothing to cause the emperor worry. They both observed the Russian custom of smoking during the meal, each offering the other a cigarette.[35] The emperor left the ship at two that afternoon, and the ship sailed for Vladivostok a few hours later. By command of the emperor, Prince Yoshihisa, aboard the *Yaeyama*, saw off the Russian ship as far as Shimonoseki.[36]

The visit to the ship had passed without incident. Probably it did much to bring the two men together and erase painful memories from Nicholas's mind. It had required considerable courage on the emperor's part, showing once again his determination to do what he thought necessary, regardless of his ministers' opinions.

In the meantime, national agitation over the incident had mounted. Perhaps the most deeply affected person was the empress. Mrs. Fraser wrote:

> Meanwhile there was one person who could do nothing to help the poor young Prince or to punish his assailant; the valiant gentle Empress forgot all the repressions of her up-bringing, all the superb calm which as a part of her rank she had shown in every circumstance of her life, and for the whole of that wretched night walked up and down, up and down, weeping her heart out in a flood-tide of grief . . . her only thought was for the boy—and his mother.[37]

The whole of Japan seems to have grieved. Lafcadio Hearn began "Yuko: A Remembrance" with this passage:

> Strange stillness in the city, a solemnity as of public mourning. Even itinerant venders utter their street cries in a lower tone than is their wont. The theaters, usually thronged from early morning until late into the night, are all closed. Closed also every pleasure-resort, every show—even the flower-displays. Closed likewise all the banquet-halls. Not even the tinkle of a samisen can be heard in the silent quarters of the geisha. There are no revellers in the great inns; the guests talk in subdued voices. Even the faces one sees upon the street have ceased to wear the habitual smile; and placards announce the indefinite postponement of banquets and entertainments.[38]

Hearn went on to describe the "universal spontaneous desire to repair the wrong." Rich and poor stripped themselves of their most valued heirlooms, their most precious household treasures, in order to send them to the *Pamiat Azova*.

Hearn was moved most of all by "a serving-maid named Yuko, a samurai name of other days, signifying 'valiant.'" He wrote,

Forty millions are sorrowing, but she more than all the rest. How and why no Western mind could fully know. Her being is ruled by emotions and by impulses of which we can guess the nature only in the vaguest possible way.[39]

On May 20 Yuko stabbed herself to death in front of the prefectural office in Kyōto. She was twenty-seven. On her body, people found letters, one (in Hearn's words) "praying that the Tenshi-Sama may be petitioned to cease from sorrowing, seeing that a young life, even though unworthy, has been given in expiation of the wrong."[40] A monument was later erected to her memory.[41]

People from all over the country sent gifts to the *Pamiat Azova*, so many that "it seemed likely to sink with gifts."[42] There were tens of thousands of messages sent to the prince conveying the shame and regret of the Japanese people over the incident.[43]

In contrast to the overpowering sympathy expressed for the Russian prince, the Japanese had nothing but hatred for Tsuda Sanzō, the would-be assassin. The village of Kanayama in Yamagata Prefecture even passed an ordinance prohibiting anyone living in the village from bearing the surname Tsuda or the personal name Sanzō.[44] Tsuda, although only a policeman, was of a samurai family that had served the daimyos of Iga in the hereditary capacity of physicians. Sanzō was born in the twelfth month of 1854 (or late January 1855 by the solar calendar).[45] He had attended the domain school where as a samurai boy he studied the Chinese classics and the military arts. In 1872 he entered the army and subsequently served with distinction in the Satsuma Rebellion, winning a seventh-class decoration and a promotion to sergeant.[46] In 1882 he was demobilized and became a policeman, at first in Mie and later in Shiga Prefecture. People remembered him as an unsociable man of few words.[47]

The question immediately arouse as to Tsuda's motivation. Dr. Baelz offered the simplest explanation:

Probably the offender was only a sort of Herostratus, craving for notoriety.[48] There can be no doubt, however, that the Japanese hatred of the Russians, which has gradually been increasing for several years, must have played a contributory part. Russia is continually expanding, and swallows up her smaller neighbours. This makes the Japanese anxious.[49]

Other sources mention Tsuda's indignation over the ceding of Sakhalin to the Russians; his conviction that the Russian prince had come to Japan as a spy, in preparation for invading the country; and his anger that Nicholas had gone to Nagasaki and Kagoshima to amuse himself instead of proceeding first to Tōkyō for an audience with the emperor.[50] The most intriguing explanation of Tsuda's motivation originated in the rumor that Saigō Takamori, who had not really died, had returned to Japan with the Russians. Tsuda, who had fought in the Satsuma Rebellion, did not welcome Saigō's return. He even feared that he might be deprived of the honors he had won during the war.[51]

At his trial, Tsuda revealed that he had first decided to kill the Russian prince while on duty earlier that day at the Miidera. In order to get a better view of the scenery, Nicholas and George had climbed in their jinrikishas a hill known as Miyukiyama, or Imperial Visit Mountain, commemorating Meiji's visit to the site in 1878. A monument stood there, erected to the memory of soldiers from Ōtsu who had died in the Satsuma Rebellion. Tsuda, seeing the inscription, contrasted his time of glory during the war with his present humble status as a policeman, and this aroused irritation with the foreign visitors. He thought of killing the Russian prince in order to dissipate his feelings of frustration. Just at this time two foreigners appeared. They showed not the slightest respect for the monument to the dead but asked the jinrikisha coolies about the scenery. Tsuda interpreted their questions as proof that they were engaged in spying, and his anger grew the more intense. He was not sure, however, which of the two foreigners was the Russian prince, so he decided to put off action, remembering the words of the police chief who had stressed to his men the importance to the emperor of the prince's visit.[52] Later, at Karasaki, he was close enough to assault Nicholas but delayed. But when Nicholas and his party were about to leave Ōtsu, Tsuda realized that this was his last chance, and if he allowed Nicholas to leave unscathed, he would one day return as an invader. This was why he struck.[53]

It was clear that Tsuda's attack on the czarevitch had been premeditated. Almost everyone assumed that he would be speedily executed; the only question was under which provision of the criminal code this would be. The Genrō and the cabinet ministers argued that unless Tsuda was executed, Russia would not be satisfied and that there was no telling what might happen. They were sure that Tsuda should be executed in order to satisfy the czar and the Russian people. Article 116 of the criminal code provided that anyone who attempted to kill the emperor, the empress, or the crown prince should be punished by death. The only question was whether this provision applied to foreign royalty.

On May 12 Prime Minister Matsukata and Minister of Agriculture and Commerce Mutsu Munemitsu summoned Kojima Korekata, the chief justice of the supreme court, and warned him of the danger of harming Russian feelings. Kojima replied that there was no reason to assume article 116 applied to a foreign prince, and he insisted on the authority of the law. But Matsukata said that only when a nation existed could there be laws, that it was folly to insist on the importance of the law and to forget the survival of the state. Mutsu pointed out that article 116 said only *tennō* (emperor), not the *tennō* of Japan, and therefore it applied to any monarch, regardless of country; but Kojima replied that when the Genrō-in revised the penal code in 1880, they had deliberately not specified "emperor of Japan" because *tennō* referred only to the Japanese sovereign. Kojima refused to budge.

On the following day Kojima met with the other judges of the supreme court. All agreed that *tennō* referred exclusively to the emperor of Japan. The minister of justice threatened to impose martial law, which would take precedence over the penal code. On the same day the judge of the court in Ōtsu that was to try Tsuda reported that his crime should be dealt with in accordance with articles 292 and 112 of the penal code—the attempted murder of an ordinary person. The most severe penalty was life imprisonment.

This did not end the matter, and Kojima had to fight valiantly for the integrity of Japanese justice, answering every threat. He pointed out that under Russian law, an attempt on the life of the sovereign of another country was dealt with far more leniently than with an attempt on the czar and that under the German penal code, the penalty was merely one to ten years in prison. Committing Tsuda to prison for life would actually be a more severe punishment than in other countries.[54] He insisted that if the law was bent to suit particular occasions, it would destroy the constitution. In response to warnings about what terrible vengeance the Russians would exact if Tsuda were not executed, he replied that Russia was not a barbarian country and that there was not the slightest indication that any act of vengeance was contemplated. Foreigners were constantly complaining about the inadequacies of the Japanese law and judges; now was the time to demonstrate Japanese respect for the law.

On May 20 Kojima and other judges of the supreme court visited the Gosho and received a rescript from the emperor: "The present incident relating to the Russian crown prince is of great importance to the nation. Using care, dispose of the matter promptly." The interpretations of this oracular pronouncement differed conspicuously: some took "using care" as a warning not to provoke the Russians, whereas others thought the emperor meant that they must not tamper with the new constitution.[55] Kojima interpreted the emperor's command as meaning that he must oppose the cabinet's efforts to bend article 116 to include foreign royalty.

Immense pressure was exerted on the seven judges who were to pass on the constitutionality of applying article 116 to Tsuda Sanzō. Members of the cabinet approached judges from the same domain as themselves and seemed to have success in persuading them to vote to use article 116, but in the end the judges' judicial conscience won out. Five of the seven judges were against using article 116. On May 24, the day before Tsuda's trial was to begin, Kojima informed Yamada Akiyoshi, the minister of justice, that there was no possibility of applying article 116.

Yamada was greatly surprised, but Minister of the Interior Saigō Tsugumichi was enraged. He demanded a detailed explanation from Kojima of the reasons for this decision. Kojima replied that the judges had simply respected the command from the emperor. Applying article 116 would break a statute of the penal code, violate the constitution, and leave a stain on the history of Japan that not a thousand years could expunge, a profanation of the imperial virtues. It would also leave the judges with a reputation for iniquity and insincerity.

Saigō said, "I don't know anything about legal arguments, but if we adopt the measures you propose, it will not only violate the emperor's words but the Russian fleet will be swarming off Shinagawa, and with one shot, our empire will be blasted to smithereens. In such a case the law would be not a means of preserving the peace of the nation but a means of destroying the nation." He added that the emperor was much grieved by this development, which was why he and the others had come, by command of the emperor. He asked Kojima if judges intended to refuse to obey even an imperial order. But Kojima still did not yield.[56]

When Yamada, Saigō, and the others realized that there was no changing Kojima's mind, they approached the other judges, but all managed to evade them. On May 25, as scheduled, the trial of Tsuda Sanzō began. There was no difficulty in reaching a decision: Tsuda Sanzō was sentenced to life imprisonment. When news of the verdict reached Russia, the authorities did not send a Russian fleet to bombard Shinagawa; in fact, the Russian minister informed the minister of foreign affairs that if the sentence had been death, the czar would have asked the emperor to exercise mercy.[57] Tsuda was incarcerated in a Hokkaidō prison where he died of pneumonia on September 30, 1891.[58]

The Ōtsu incident did not lead to war, as many in the government had feared. It is possible that as the result of the attempted assassination, Nicholas formed anti-Japanese prejudices that contributed to the Russo-Japanese War thirteen years later, but this has been disputed. The most important result of the incident was undoubtedly the strengthening of the Japanese judiciary, thanks to the courage of Kojima Korekata. He himself did not suffer because of his opposition to the politicians: in 1894 he was made a member of the House of Peers. His diary describing the Ōtsu incident, was banned in his day and was not published until 1931.[59] Kojima is surely one of the heroes of modern Japanese history.

Even if foreigners living in Japan at the time showed sympathy for the wounded prince, they were still highly suspicious of the Russians. Dr. Baelz wrote that the Japanese were foolish to have ceded Sakhalin to Russia in 1875 and, as a sign of likely Russian aggression in the future, cited the building of an enormous Orthodox church at Surugadai, adding, "What makes this seem particularly absurd is that, apart from the legation staff, there are no Russians in Tōkyō."[60]

Perhaps the most sympathetic appraisal of the attempted assassination came from Lafcadio Hearn in a letter dated August 26, 1893, to his friend Nishida Sentarō:

By the way, I think Tsuda Sanzo will be more kindly judged by a future generation. His crime was only "loyalty run mad." He was insane for the moment with an insanity which would have been of the highest value in a good cause and time. He saw before him the living representative of the awful Power which makes even England tremble;—the power against which Western Europe has mustered an army of more than 1,500,000 of men. He saw, or thought he saw—(perhaps he really *did* see: time alone can show)—the Enemy of Japan. Then he struck—out of his heart, without consulting his head.[61]

Chapter 43

The remainder of 1891, once the excitement of the Ōtsu incident had died down, was relatively tranquil. The most important political change occurred while the czarevitch Nicholas was still in Kyūshū: Yamagata Aritomo announced his intention of resigning his post as prime minister. He had caught influenza during the epidemic in March, and although he had since recovered, he still did not feel himself. He recommended as his successor the president of the House of Peers, Itō Hirobumi. The emperor, having ascertained that it would not be possible to induce Yamagata to remain as prime minister, joined in the effort to persuade Itō to accept the post. Itō, who had submitted his resignation as president of the House of Peers, was traveling in the Kansai region when emissaries caught up with him and asked him to return to Tōkyō.

On April 27 Itō had an audience with the emperor during which the emperor stated his intention of appointing him as prime minister. Itō refused the appointment. He recalled that when Ōkuma Shigenobu had proposed convening a parliament in 1881, he had opposed Ōkuma, believing that preparations were incomplete and the Japanese people were not yet sufficiently mature. He had proposed delaying the opening of a parliament until he had investigated the constitutions and political institutions of various foreign countries and was later authorized to make such a journey. After his return, the constitution was promulgated, followed by the convening of the first Diet; but the intellectual level of the people remained low, and it was truly difficult to carry out constitutional government. Itō was sure that no matter who might become prime minister, he would not long remain in office. If he himself was obliged to serve in that position, he might well be assassinated. He would have no special regrets about losing his unimportant life, but if he were killed, who would assist the imperial household and preserve the government?[1]

Itō suggested that either Interior Minister Saigō Tsugumichi or Finance Minister Matsukata Masayoshi (1835–1924) would be suitable. On being informed of Saigō's unwillingness to accept the post, the emperor then chose Matsukata, who at first declined. The emperor refused to listen to his disclaimers, and Matsukata was sworn in as prime minister on May 6. The six months or so that he served in this capacity were marked by constant bickering in the Diet, leading in December to its dissolution and an election in the following year.

In July, Commodore Ting Ju-ch'ang, in command of the Chinese Northern Seas Fleet, had an audience with the emperor. The audience was marked by the customary exchange of "oriental" courtesies, but the six warships of the Chinese fleet (more powerful than any in the Japanese navy) inspired fear among some Japanese.

The visit of the Chinese fleet served as an occasion for those Japanese who had received a traditional education to demonstrate how much they knew about Chinese culture. Some referred deferentially to the Chinese as their "elder brothers."[2] Commodore Ting and the other high-ranking Chinese officers were feted wherever they went, and they fitted into the Japanese scene in a way impossible for Europeans. The pleasure that Japanese literary men and scholars experienced in exchanging poems in Chinese with these visiting dignitaries was possible because the writing of characters transcended national boundaries and the ideal of the "gentleman scholar" was shared by China and Japan. Probably none of those who participated in the various manifestations of friendship dreamed that in little more than two years' time Japan and China would be fighting a bitter war.

Perhaps the most welcome news for the emperor in the summer of 1891 was the birth on August 7 of his eighth daughter, Nobuko, to Sono Sachiko. He now had three children—the crown prince, Princess Masako, and Princess Nobuko. After having lost so many children in infancy, he could anticipate with pleasure the growth to maturity of his children.

Nothing much else happened that year, but in October the emperor sent the Russian crown prince a set of armor, a broadsword, a dirk, bows and arrows, and a photograph of himself, together with a personal letter.[3] Probably the gifts were by way of further apology for the Ōtsu incident.

The first important event of 1892 was the election held on February 15. The emperor was worried about the future of the Diet. He told Matsukata he feared that if the same members kept getting reelected, this would lead again and again to the Diet's dissolution. He suggested that leading regional officials encourage good people in their districts to run for office.

The cabinet minister who took these words most to heart was Interior Minister Shinagawa Yajirō (1843–1900). He sent directives to regional officials explaining governmental policy and urging the election of distinguished men who were fair, impartial, and not affiliated with parties; men deeply involved with political parties should be dismissed.[4] Shinagawa directed the police to deal severely with acts of intimidation or bribery, implying that was the work of the political parties. But despite the high-flown sentiments of his directives, the election of 1892 was probably the most corrupt in Japanese history, and the worst offender was none other than Shinagawa himself.

Unlike the peaceable elections of the previous year, the election of 1892 was marked by violence and arson. Clashes between officials and ordinary citizens resulted in deaths and injuries in many parts of the country.[5] Ruffians stole ballot boxes in Kōchi Prefecture, and made voting impossible in parts of Saga Prefecture. It was generally believed that these irregularities had been planned by Shinagawa, who had decided that political parties opposed to the government were disloyal and must be suppressed. Yet for all the scheming and brutality, the populist parties maintained their majority in the House of Representatives—163 seats against 137 for the progovernment forces.[6]

Soon after the election, the emperor, disturbed by reports of intimidation and violence, sent chamberlains to the four prefectures where violations had been most conspicuous: Ishikawa, Fukuoka, Saga, and Kōchi.[7] The new House of Representatives was convened on May 6. On May 11 the House of Peers passed a resolution condemning the manner in which the election had been conducted:

> It needs hardly be said that officials should not have used their authority to interfere in the election of members of the House of Representatives. There was consequently no reason for the government to issue orders or warnings concerning interference. Nevertheless, at the time when the elections of members were held in February of this year, officials interfered in the contests, and this precipitated reactions on the part of the people, leading finally to terrible scenes of bloodshed. These events have been the focus of public attention and the subject of universal protest. In every region, there is now indignation over the interference of officials in the elections and the officials are looked on as enemies. The government must now speedily deal with this situation and demonstrate to the public its fairness. If this is not done immediately, it will truly harm the security of the nation, and will in the end invite great and irremediable misfortune. This House consequently hopes that the government will reflect deeply on the matter, and by taking appropriate action at present, end future abuse.[8]

There were conflicting views in the cabinet concerning the election. Matsukata decided to visit Itō and ask his advice; but Itō, getting wind of his intention, sent a letter to Mutsu complaining that whenever a problem arose in the cabinet, Matsukata always asked him to settle it. He refused to become involved at this stage, suggesting that Matsukata and the members of his cabinet first reach an accord on future policies before asking his advice. Their conclusion when they conferred was that the only way to surmount the crisis was for Itō himself to form a cabinet. They begged him to accept, but he refused.[9]

The problem was complicated by Itō's repeated attempts to resign as president of the House of Peers. As was usual in such cases, he alleged illness, but the emperor refused his request, fearing the consequences if he were deprived of the services of the man he trusted most in the government. On March 11 the emperor sent Tokudaiji Sanetsune, the senior chamberlain, to Itō's house with this message: "I am aware of the extremely earnest nature of your request. However, I hope I shall always have you by my side and be able to depend on your frank advice. Reassure me by getting plenty of nourishment and rest. I am unable to release you from your post as my adviser."[10] Itō, moved to tears of gratitude, hastened to the palace to accept the emperor's command.

Shinagawa Yajirō was not at all satisfied with the cabinet's reactions to what he considered to be his loyal behavior during the election. Sure that he had acted appropriately and angry that his intentions had been misunderstood, he decided to resign.[11] Matsukata, embarrassed by the need to make a cabinet change at the very outset of the new administration, asked Yamagata to dissuade him, but Shinagawa presented Yamagata instead with two *tanka* that obliquely conveyed his feelings. The second was

oroka naru	What a shameful thing
mi wo mo wasurete	To have offered promises
ametsuchi ni	To Heaven and earth
chikaishi koto no	Forgetting even how great
hazukashiki kana	Was my own incompetence.[12]

Shinagawa's request to resign for reasons of health was granted by the emperor the same day. Various men (naturally including Itō) were suggested as possible successors in the post of interior minister. The most likely candidate was Soejima Taneomi, but the emperor objected to Soejima, saying that he was too old for such a demanding position, and he feared that Soejima might resign midway. The emperor recommended instead Kōno Togama, but Matsukata, pointing out that Soejima's reputation was far higher than Kōno's and that Kōno enjoyed little popularity with provincial officials, decided to appoint Soejima despite the emperor's disapproval.[13]

This episode demonstrates that Meiji (although he seldom expressed political views openly) kept a close watch on the officers of his government and formed his own judgments of their capabilities. It also shows that even when he intervened concerning an appointment, he did not necessarily have his own way.

The emperor's opinions of the principal figures of the government are most clearly recorded in the diaries kept by his long-time adviser Sasaki Takayuki. For example, during their conversation on March 19 the emperor said, "Shinagawa is honest, but he is narrow-minded and has no patience. Even at cabinet meetings he sometimes flies into a rage, weeps and behaves in a completely unreasonable way. The other day Itō questioned him about irregularities in the election and criticized his interference, whereupon Shinagawa became greatly excited and said he had heard Itō intended to resign and organize a political party. Then he said, 'Your political party is no concern of mine, but if you persist in your abusive language, I will deal with you by putting emergency measures into effect immediately.' Itō became angry, and his face colored as he answered, 'Do you think you can dispose of Itō as you please, even if you use your authority as Interior Minister?'"[14]

Meiji had obviously listened with the utmost attention as Shinagawa and Itō exchanged threats, and his comments on the characters of the two men, as well as on Soejima, Gotō Shōjirō, and Mutsu Minemitsu, were frank and illuminating. Sasaki was one of the few people to whom the emperor could express his views freely, and Sasaki in turn spoke his mind to the emperor, although he naturally was always deferential.

As the emperor predicted, Soejima did not last long in office. He resigned in June and was appointed as an adviser to the Privy Council, the standard assignment for ministers who resigned or were dismissed. The political situation was marked by so many quarrels between individuals and parties that Inoue Kowashi concluded that the emperor was the only hope for a stable government. He appealed to the emperor to give a "great command" and take the lead in giving the country a course to follow. He specifically asked the emperor, who was known for his love of simplicity, to eliminate wasteful expenditure on ceremonies, suggesting that a reduction of 10 percent in court expenditures might be used for augmenting the navy.[15]

The emperor no doubt agreed in principle to Inoue's call for economy, but even though he preferred to have his uniform patched rather than buy a new one, he was surrounded by the luxury of others and had to respond appropriately. When he visited the house of a minister or other dignitary, he expected to be suitably entertained, regardless of the cost. On July 4, for example, the emperor visited the residence of Gotō Shōjirō in Takanawa. He was obliged by precedent to give Gotō the customary gifts—a set of silver cups with the imperial crest, a pair of cloisonné vases, and 1,000 yen, along with a bolt of silk for Mrs. Gotō and presents for their children. Gotō offered in return a valuable sword, a Korean tea jar, and a porcelain badger. That afternoon there were performances of nō by outstanding actors of the day—Kanze Tetsunojō, Hōshō Kurō, and Umewaka Minoru. After dinner the imperial party was entertained with recitations by Momokawa Joen and performances of Satsuma biwa by Nishi Kōkichi, both recognized masters of their art. Apart from these special entertainments, musicians of the Household Ministry played Japanese and Western music all day long. At night, thousands of lanterns were lit and bonfires burned under the trees. Tens of thousands of fireflies were released over the pond, making a sight more beautiful than any picture. The emperor did not leave until after midnight. The next day, similar entertainment was offered to the empress.[16] Despite his predilection for simplicity, the emperor enjoyed the extravagant entertainment that Gotō had provided that evening.

Less than a week later, on July 9, he visited the residence of Nabeshima Naohiro. The entertainment was not quite on the scale that Gotō had offered, but there was the usual exchange of gifts, followed by demonstrations of martial sports, a banquet, conjuring, recitations, and so on, but not any nō plays.[17] Such visits by the emperor, though profoundly appreciated by his hosts, did nothing to foster his policy of thrift.

Again, although the emperor informed the Interior Ministry that he desired economies to be practiced in the imperial household in order to raise money for building warships, he specified that in two areas there must be no skimping of funds—the expenses of observances for his ancestors and for maintenance of their tombs, and the household expenses of the empress dowager. When the empress dowager learned of the economies being practiced in the palace, she indicated that she too wished to cut the expenses of her household by one-tenth, but the emperor indignantly refused to allow any reduction, saying that she should not worry about such matters.[18]

In any case, much of the money from the royal purse was used by the emperor and empress not on themselves but to relieve suffering or rebuild schools in towns and villages where there had been fires and other disasters. There was also a royal obligation to protect and encourage the arts. For example, on July 12 the empress presented the Japanese Women's Association for the World's Columbian Exposition in Chicago with 10,000 yen to improve the quality of the Japanese exhibition.[19] Buddhist temples that had long been neglected were given funds to repair their buildings and works of art. There were also gifts to members of the imperial family, even relatively distant members, on the occasion of their marriages or when they built new residences. Even if the emperor and empress had desired nothing more than to live in perfect simplicity, they still needed funds to meet these public obligations.

The most important political development of 1892 was Itō's emergence from his retirement in Odawara, where he had worked behind the scenes as a manipulator of the government. Again and again, he had refused reappointment as prime minister. When approached after Matsukata's resignation at the end of July, he at once left Tōkyō and returned to Odawara, alleging sudden illness. It seemed as if he was trying (as before) to escape appointment, but when the emperor sent the imperial household minister to ask Itō to return to Tōkyō, he apparently judged the time was ripe for assuming the post of prime minister. He insisted, however, that he must have assurances that all the *genrō* would join the cabinet and assist him. This wish was granted. Itō's cabinet included Yamagata Aritomo (minister of justice), Kuroda Kiyotaka (minister of communications), Inoue Kaoru (minister of the interior), Ōyama Iwao (minister of the army), Gotō Shōjirō (minister of agriculture and commerce), Mutsu Munemitsu (foreign minister), Kōno Togama (minister of education), Nirei Kagenori (minister of the navy), and Watanabe Kunitake (finance minister). It would be hard to imagine a more impressive array of able men.[20]

When Itō went before the emperor to accept his appointment as prime minister, he promised that he would leave all major decisions to the emperor but would take responsibility for everything else. The emperor responded by promising not to interfere in any decisions; all he asked was that when making reports, Itō would give him the benefit of his opinions.

The cabinet was more effective than its predecessors and remained in office longer, but in November the jinrikisha in which Itō was riding was overturned by a passing horse carriage. Itō suffered head and face injuries that kept him from attending court until February 1893.[21]

That year opened in what was now the standard fashion: the emperor did not perform the ritual worship of the four directions, and most of the other New Year observances were performed by the chief protocol officer, Nabeshima Naohiro. Lectures were offered to the emperor on British history, a section from the Confucian classic the *Book of Rites*, and poetry from the *Man'yōshū*. The emperor paid his customary New Year visit to the empress dowager at the Aoyama Palace. The subject of the poetry meeting this year was "Turtles on the Rocks."

Everything seemed quite normal, but the festive New Year mood was rudely broken on January 12 when the House of Representatives voted to cut appropriations for officials' salaries and warship construction. Although the government had constantly called for economy, these were areas where it would not tolerate any cuts. The reductions amounted to about 11 percent of the budget submitted by the government. Members of the House of Representatives argued that the cuts in wages for officials were reasonable and would not result in any loss of efficiency. They also argued that it was premature to increase the size of the navy without having first established a policy of national defense. Watanabe Kunitake, the finance minister, replied that the proposed cuts in the appropriation for civil officials would impede the functions of administrative organs. Neither side would yield, and the House was adjourned for five days. This was the first head-on collision between the government and the Diet, and it brought up the fundamental question of whether the government was entitled to have its way in matters it deemed to be of vital importance, even if this violated the Diet's constitutional privileges.[22]

Deciding that their only recourse was the emperor, members of the House of Representatives submitted a petition with 146 signatures. The emperor's response was to suspend sessions until February 6.²³ On February 7 Hoshi Tōru (1850–1901), president of the House, submitted a petition to the emperor justifying the decision to cut the budget and appealing for his intercession in preserving the rights of the Diet as stipulated in the constitution. Also on February 7 the House voted to submit to the emperor a petition condemning the cabinet and begging for the emperor's intercession.²⁴ Itō responded with a plea to the House of Representatives to reconsider its decision and not trouble the emperor, but the House affirmed its decision by a vote of 281 to 103.

The only person who could end this confrontation was the emperor himself. He is often portrayed by historians as a mere figurehead, but this was one of many occasions when the pleas, couched in ritual formulas, for the emperor to vouchsafe his wisdom were not empty formalities. His was the only decision that everyone would have respected.

In a memorial submitted on February 9, Itō recommended that the emperor choose one of two courses: (1) to command the House of Representatives and the government to open negotiations with the purpose of securing a rapprochement (if the House of Representatives failed to obey this command or if negotiations failed to achieve the desired results, the House should be dissolved) or (2) to dissolve the House immediately. On the following day the emperor issued his decision. He reiterated his belief that it was necessary to increase Japanese military preparedness at a time when other nations were steadily growing more threatening. He had decided therefore to reduce palace expenditures and, for six years, to make an annual grant of 300,000 yen from palace funds for armaments. At the same time, the salaries of all civil and military officials would be reduced by 10 percent for the costs of building warships.²⁵

The House of Representatives responded deferentially, accepting the emperor's command and promising to reach a compromise with the government. Members of the House of Peers also agreed on February 14 to donate one-tenth of their salaries to the costs of building warships. The emperor's decision represented a compromise: civil and military officials would have their salaries reduced—as the House of Representatives had proposed—but the money saved would be used for warships—not what the House had voted. The imperial family as a whole voluntarily reduced its expenditures by 5 to 15 percent, but the empress insisted on reducing her palace expenditures by 20 percent during the coming six years.²⁶

The other major undertaking of the House of Representatives in 1893 was its action on treaty revision. The unequal treaties, most of them signed during the waning days of the shogunate, had been a source of discontent for the Japanese for many years. Everyone desired the end of extraterritoriality and the recovery of tariff autonomy, but the price for the Japanese to achieve these goals had again and again proved to be a stumbling block. Some people had asserted that it was easier to bear the humility of extraterritoriality than the danger of allowing foreigners to exploit the chance to control the lands and livelihoods of the Japanese.

The House of Representatives prepared in May 1892 a bill for submission to the emperor calling for the end of extraterritoriality and foreign control of customs. The ultimate objective was to secure equality, and to achieve that objective, it would allow foreigners to live in the interior, although it would deny them permission to own land or to own or operate mines, railways, canals, and shipbuilding facilities. It also called for most-favored-nation treatment from all countries with which it concluded treaties.[27] But the bill went nowhere because the Diet was dissolved. It was introduced again in December when the new Diet was convened and was discussed in secret sessions (by request of the government) in February 1893.

Even though there was little progress, the issue was by no means forgotten. In July the House passed a bill calling for the end of extraterritoriality. The foreign minister, Mutsu Munemitsu, believed that the history of attempts to modify the treaties had been a history of failures and that the causes of failure were always internal, based on the Japanese inability to act together. He himself drew up a new treaty of commerce and navigation and presented it to the cabinet for its consideration. In preparing the treaty, he consulted the British-Italian treaty concluded in 1883 and the Japanese-Mexican treaty, both of which were based on equality. He proposed that the treaty take effect five years after being signed, giving adequate time for the transition between the old and new systems.[28]

Mutsu believed that the best course was to open separate negotiations with the various nations, and he chose to begin negotiations with England, the long-time opponent of equal treaties. He selected as his negotiator Aoki Shūzō, the minister plenipotentiary to Germany. The emperor approved the plan. Aoki met Hugh Fraser, the British minister to Japan (then on leave in London), in September and started preliminary preparations for discussions with the British government.

Treaty reform would be by no means easy. Foreigners living in Japan repeatedly protested the prohibition on their residing in the interior, contrasting this with the freedom that Japanese enjoyed to travel and live anywhere within the principal Western countries. Some Japanese, fearful of the disasters that would occur if foreigners were permitted to live among them, had committed acts of violence against the foreigners. They hoped that this show of violence would make foreigners understand that they were not welcome, but their actions made it difficult for the Japanese government to reassure foreigners who feared that if extraterritoriality was ended, the Japanese courts would not punish such acts of violence. But treaty reform was of immense psychological importance to most Japanese, as it would signify that Japan had been recognized as a modern nation.

The opposition between those who favored treaty revision and those who preferred to extend the existing treaties (rather than allow foreigners to live in the interior), continued throughout 1893. At the heart of the matter was the xenophobia common to most Japanese. In December, when Mutsu examined the various proposals concerning treaty revision before the House of Representatives, he was dismayed by their content. He commented,

> These bills look on foreigners as if they belonged to a different species, rather the way the Russian government still treats the Jews. This runs counter to the imperial policy of opening the country to the world. The government must at this time make it absolutely clear that its policy ever since the Restoration has been one based on this policy; and it must adopt means of eradicating and suppressing contrary movements that oppose this policy. If it fails to do so and merely watches on in silence, these tendencies will spread increasingly throughout the country. There is a danger that eventually this will create great confusion in internal and external negotiations and will be a major obstacle to the negotiations now under way for treaty reform. The government must not hesitate another day.[29]

Mutsu made a similar statement at a cabinet meeting on December 11. When the cabinet appeared reluctant to take positive action, he announced his intention of resigning. Itō reminded Mutsu, however, that a display of impatience was not the way to settle the important matter before them. He urged Mutsu not to be rash. Mutsu, mollified, withdrew his resignation.

Opposition to treaty revision continued in the House of Representatives. A resolution was put forward on December 19 calling on the government to clarify Japan's rights and duties as prescribed in the treaties. To this resolution were appended descriptions of the rampant disorders of foreigners that would accompany any relaxation of national control over the interior.

The debate became so heated that an edict suddenly arrived from the emperor adjourning the Diet for ten days. During the debate, the emperor had been greatly upset by the acrimonious arguments. He sent chamberlains to listen to the proceedings and keep him informed. When disputes arose over major matters, these men reported the situation to him moment by moment by telephone.[30]

On December 29 debates were resumed in the House of Representatives. Mutsu delivered a speech against renewing the existing treaties, once again insisting that the government's basic policy ever since the Restoration was one of an open country and progress. The renewal of existing treaties would be contrary to national policy. These treaties did not suit the modern society that had evolved since the time they were first signed. Now was the time to reject the shogunate's policy of "close the country and expel the foreigners" and to recoup the rights that had been lost. In return, it was appropriate to reward the foreigners with privileges not provided in the existing treaties. Moreover, the Japanese should not forget that if foreigners were free to travel inland, the money they would spend would enrich the people living there. And if Japan wished to modify the treaties, the only way would be to make the foreigners aware how greatly Japan has progressed, which could be done only by following a policy of "open country." In conclusion, Mutsu asked the House to withdraw the proposal to preserve the existing treaties. He failed to get support for this motion. An edict was issued ordering a suspension of the Diet for another fourteen days.[31]

On December 30 Prime Minister Itō and President of the Privy Council Yamagata Aritomo had an audience with the emperor, after which the House was dissolved. Itō had requested permission to suspend debates in order to keep the House from passing its resolution in favor of extending the existing treaties. This had been the reason for the two-week suspension issued the previous day, but the House showed no signs of reconsidering. Itō decided that there was no other way to deal with the situation than to dissolve the House. The emperor ordered this the same day.

The emperor had reached the same conclusion as Itō—no matter how many times debates might be suspended, there was unlikely to be any change of attitude. Not long afterward he confided to Sasaki Takayuki that he felt such collisions between the government and the House of Representatives were caused by the excessive haste with which the Diet had been established.[32] From this point on, the emperor's political views seem to have become more conservative. He had begun to think that the granting of the constitution and establishment of the Diet, in which he had taken pride, had been premature.

Chapter 44

On New Year's Day 1894, worship of the four directions and other prescribed ceremonies were again performed not by the emperor but by a surrogate. The emperor's failure to perform these ceremonies probably did not surprise anyone. In recent years he had often declined to appear, sometimes alleging indisposition, sometimes without explanation. People seem to have forgotten that for centuries the performance of such rites was an emperor's chief duty.

The most memorable feature of the day for those in the palace was probably the visit of the crown prince to congratulate the emperor on the arrival of the new year. Visits by the prince to the emperor became more frequent this year—several times each month—suggesting that their relations, previously governed by court decorum rather than by ties of affection, had become closer. Of course, the emperor had worried each time the crown prince was stricken with illness, but his chief concern was probably for the succession to the throne rather than for the life of this particular son. All his other male offspring had died in infancy, and it seemed increasingly likely that Yoshihito, despite his delicate health, would be his successor. The emperor probably had many occasions to regret that his son was not as healthy and energetic as he had been at the same age.

All the same, it was necessary to prepare the prince for his future position. The emperor was determined that his son receive a proper education. As we have seen, he early decided that the prince would attend Gakushū-in along with other boys instead of receiving the private tuition that had been normal for members of the imperial family. The prince was an indifferent student, but his lack of scholarly aptitude did not result in the termination of his studies. It was essential to Meiji that the next emperor of Japan be acquainted not only with Japanese and Chinese history and culture but with the West. The prince would also have to write an acceptable hand and compose poetry in the traditional manner.[1] But although much consideration was given to planning the prince's education, his health always took precedence, and his studies were frequently interrupted by illness or by the decision of physicians that Tōkyō was too hot or too cold for the prince to remain in school.

The prince seems to have been intimidated by a father who never showed him parental tenderness. Meiji's coldness was not unusual: he treated his son in the manner customary in orthodox Confucian fathers. Perhaps he modeled his behavior on remembrances of Emperor Kōmei's severity toward himself; but he did not follow Kōmei in giving his son daily guidance in composing *tanka*. The emperor seems to have contributed little to the education of his heir.

The increased frequency of Yoshihito's visits to the palace in 1894 suggests that the natural affection of father and son had at last taken hold. Toward the end of the year there was proof. On November 17, 1894, Yoshihito arrived in Hiroshima intending to visit his father (who had moved there during the Sino-Japanese War). The prince appeared at headquarters at ten-thirty the next morning and, after chatting briefly with his father, went with him to inspect a Manchurian horse. They later climbed together to the castle tower, from where they enjoyed a splendid view of the entire city of Hiroshima. A palace attendant, serving as their guide, explained the sights with the aid of a telescope and maps. The emperor and his son ate lunch together. Members of the emperor's staff, who had long wondered whether the emperor had any affection for his son, were so delighted to see his kindness this day that they decided to inform the empress. But this rare intimacy did not keep the emperor from his duties; he was able to find time for lunch with Yoshihito only twice more before the prince left for Tōkyō on November 24.[2]

Although the crown prince actually spent little time in his father's presence, from 1887 he was frequently portrayed along with the emperor and empress in *nishikie*, the cheaply produced, often gaudy, prints popular at the time. Sometimes the prints depict the prince standing between his parents, as if to emphasize the domestic harmony within the imperial family.[3] Another glimpse of their family life was provided in 1894 by the public celebrations of the twenty-fifth wedding anniversary of the emperor and empress. The wedding anniversaries of Japanese sovereigns had never before been a matter for public rejoicing, but when the emperor was informed that it was customary in foreign countries for royalty to celebrate "silver weddings," he gladly gave his consent to the proposed celebrations. To make sure they maintained the proper tone, a committee was formed to investigate foreign examples. It was announced that the celebration would take place on March 9.

In honor of the occasion, gold and silver medals were struck, suitably engraved with auspicious designs such as the imperial chrysanthemum and paired cranes.[4] Permission was granted to those who purchased the medals to wear them for the rest of their lives and then pass them on to their descendants. On March 9, 15 million postage stamps were issued in honor of the occasion, the first Japanese commemorative stamps.

The day of the celebration opened with observances in the palace sanctuary. Neither the emperor nor the empress took part in these ceremonies, but the crown prince, princes of the blood, and members of the cabinet joined in worship. Royal salutes were fired by the Household Guards artillery regiment and by ships at sea. At eleven that morning the emperor and empress appeared in the Phoenix Room, where they were joined by more than 200 members of the nobility, the cabinet, and their wives. The emperor wore his formal uniform and all his decorations. The empress wore a white gown, decorations, and a crown. The train of her gown was decorated with designs of flowers and birds worked in silver thread. Later, messages from their governments were delivered by the ministers of France, England, Germany, Russia, the United States, Belgium, Korea, and Austria, to each of which the emperor responded graciously.

At two that afternoon the emperor and empress, riding in the same carriage, traveled to the Aoyama parade grounds to review the troops. Outside the main palace gate, students from Tōkyō Imperial University formed ranks along with members of other organizations to acclaim the royal couple as they emerged from the palace. The streets were lined with crowds of people eager to catch a glimpse of their Majesties. About 2:45 they reached their destination, where they were welcomed by Prince Akihito and high-ranking officers. The different units presented arms, and a military band played the national anthem. After receiving the guests, who included both Japanese and foreign dignitaries, the emperor and empress again boarded their carriage and, with the hood removed, rode around the grounds, receiving the acclamation of the crowd. After this they reviewed the troops.

The celebration continued all day, concluding with performances of *bugaku* and a banquet. Although the words "silver wedding" were not officially used,[5] the presents given to the guests or offered to the imperial couple were mainly of silver. Persons who were not lucky enough to be invited to the festivities were permitted to offer gifts. These, however, tended not to be of silver but included poems, saké, shōyu, dried cuttlefish, swords, paintings, ceramics, lacquerware, bonsai, and so on. Twenty-five men and twenty-five women (the number chosen because of the twenty-fifth anniversary), including members of the nobility, cabinet ministers, and participants in the regular palace poetry gatherings, offered poems on the theme "Song-thrush in the Blossoms Promise Ten Thousand Springs!" The exhausted emperor and empress did not get to bed until 1:45 in the morning.[6]

The festive mood of the silver wedding ceremonies had hardly dissipated when word was received that on March 28, the Korean politician Kim Ok-kyun

(1851–1894) had been murdered at a Japanese inn in Shanghai. The murderer, who had accompanied Kim from Japan, had acted under orders from the conservative leaders of Korea who hated Kim because he belonged to the progressive faction.

Kim had lived in Japan before the failed coup of 1884. Soon after his first visit in 1881, he became friendly with Fukuzawa Yukichi, who strongly favored the "enlightenment" faction in Korea and believed that Japan must take the lead in enabling both Koreans and Chinese to modernize their countries.[7] But in 1885, after it had become clear that the "enlightenment" faction was unable to keep control of the Korean government, Fukuzawa published his famous article "Datsua ron" (On Escaping from Asia) in which he asserted that Japan could not wait for neighboring countries in Asia to achieve enlightenment, that it was imperative that Japan share the future of the advanced countries of the West.

Kim fled to Japan in December 1884 along with eight other Koreans who believed that their country should follow the Japanese example of modernization. These Koreans took Japanese names and wore Western dress in the attempt to ingratiate themselves with the Japanese leaders.[8] They probably expected to be well treated by the Japanese government, but they received only minimal protection. In February 1885 the Korean government sent a mission to Japan requesting the Japanese to turn over Kim to them. When the Japanese refused, assassins were sent to Japan, provided with orders signed by King Kojong to kill Kim and his associate, Pak Yong-hyo.[9] Kim, learning of the plot, informed the prime minister, Itō Hirobumi, and the foreign minister, Inoue Kaoru. Inoue sent a message to the Korean government asking that the assassins be recalled, promising in return to expel Kim from Japan.

Kim was staying at the time at the Grand Hotel in Yokohama. Inoue ordered the governor of Kanagawa Prefecture to remove Kim forcibly from the hotel, then under consular jurisdiction, and detained him under arrest in a villa belonging to the Mitsui family. In June 1886 the minister of the interior, Yamagata Arinori, ordered the governor to expel Kim from the country within fifteen days on the grounds that he was a menace to Japanese security and an obstacle to peace with foreign countries.[10] The Japanese officials regarded Kim as a nuisance, despite his pro-Japanese views, and feared that his presence might provoke a war before Japan was ready for one.[11] In the end, Kim was sent not to a foreign country but to a remote island, Chichijima in the Bonin Islands, where for two years he led the lonely life of an exile. The climate was deleterious to his health, and he was therefore sent under escort from the hot climate of the Bonins to the northerly cold of Hokkaidō, where he remained until permitted to return to Tōkyō in 1890.[12] He survived his years of exile with the help of gifts of money from numerous Japanese sympathizers.

In March 1894, having given up hope of assistance from the Japanese government in bringing enlightenment to Korea, Kim left for Shanghai. His purpose was to meet Li Hung-chang. Kim had become friendly with Li Ching-fang (the son of Li Hung-chang), who was then the Chinese minister to Japan, and continued to correspond with him after Ching-fang's return to China. Kim hoped that Ching-fang would enable him to meet his father, the most powerful man in China. He hoped especially to put before this senior statesman his plan for cooperation among the three nations of East Asia to prevent further aggression by the Western powers.[13] Kim was warned of the danger in making this journey,[14] but he was sure it would be worth taking the risk if there was a chance of having even five minutes with Li Hung-chang.[15]

Funds for the journey (and for paying the debts Kim had incurred while in Japan) were provided by Yi Il-sik, a Korean resident of Ōsaka. Yi also gave Kim a bill of exchange to cover his expenses while in China but informed him that in order to cash the bill, he would have to be accompanied by Hong Chong-u, a Korean who had until recently been studying in France.[16] The party included Kim's Japanese friend Wada Enjirō.

Kim arrived in Shanghai on March 27. On the following day while Wada was out on an errand, Kim was reading a book in bed when Hong broke into his room and shot him twice. Kim crawled from his bed to the corridor, only to be shot from behind, this time fatally. The brilliant, erratic, charming victim was forty-three years old.[17]

Wada bought a coffin for Kim and arranged with the captain of the *Saikyō maru*, the ship on which Kim and the others had come to Shanghai, to take the coffin back to Japan. However, the night before the ship was to sail, a man from the Japanese consulate ordered Wada to wait. When Wada refused to delay, the consulate informed the settlement authorities, who took the coffin and turned it over to the Chinese.[18] Li Hung-chang, informed of the murder, ordered the coffin and the murderer to be sent to Korea aboard the warship *Wei-yüan*. Both the Chinese and Japanese governments seemed to be eager to be rid of a troublesome idealist.

When the coffin reached Korea, the government had Kim's body removed. His head, hands, and feet were severed and hung from poles with an inscription proclaiming him a traitor; the torso was left lying on the ground nearby.[19] The vengeance of the Korean government did not stop with this atrocity: members of Kim's family were also executed.[20] Hong Chong-u was given a hero's welcome.

The Japanese were outraged by Kim Ok-kyun's murder. Their feelings of hatred were directed toward the Chinese in particular for their role in the incident. Hayashi Tadasu, the deputy foreign minister, wrote in his memoirs that he was sure the outbreak of war with China a few months later was precipitated by the murder of Kim Ok-kyun and the Chinese involvement in the crime.[21]

Fukuzawa Yukichi wrote sympathetically of the murdered man, expressing anger that the Chinese had turned the corpse over to the Koreans, and horror over the shameful mutilation of the corpse by the Koreans. He accused the Chinese of having violated the Treaty of Tientsin, which provided for China and Japan to cooperate in maintaining order in Korea, attributing misguided Chinese policies to the "rottenness at the core" resulting from the obstinate refusal of the Manchu rulers to permit progress. He predicted that a clash would be unavoidable if the Chinese continued to consider Korea as a vassal state. and expressed doubt that China would be able to maintain its independence if it showed no signs of progress.[22]

There was still, however, no immediate reason for opening hostilities with China. This would be provided by the rebellion staged by a Korean religious group called the Tonghak. In April and May 1894 this group rose in rebellion throughout the provinces of Cholla and Ch'ungch'ong.[23] The founder of the Tonghak movement, Ch'oe Che-u (1824–1864), had urged his followers to drive out Western influences and restore the native Korean beliefs, which he called Eastern learning (the meaning of *tonghak*). Although in principle he opposed Confucianism because its doctrines had originated in China, a foreign country, his religion was in fact a mixture of Confucianism, Buddhism, and Taoism; its chief enemy was Christianity.[24] The government prohibited the Tonghak movement not so much because of its teachings as because of its popularity among the peasants, whom the authorities feared might be incited to rise in rebellion.

Ch'oe Che-u was eventually captured and beheaded by order of the government—as a Catholic. Some Tonghak religious practices superficially resembled those of Roman Catholicism, then being persecuted in Korea, which prompted the police to give an anti-Christian zealot a martyr's death. Having lost its founder, the Tonghak religion went underground but maintained its hold over the peasantry, for whom its appeal was not its mysterious spells and incantations but its promise of equality and this-worldly benefits.[25]

The religion grew in numbers despite the prohibition, and by 1893 the southern half of the Korean peninsula was under the control of the Tonghaks. In January of that year, the new leader, Ch'oe Si-hyong, called a meeting of believers at which he demanded the exoneration of Ch'oe Che-u and the end of the prohibition of the Tonghak religion. In March a delegation of believers went to Seoul to beg for an admission of Choe's innocence. They remained prostrated on the ground before the main gate of the palace for three days and three nights, imploring the king to exculpate the founder of their religion.[26] Although their petition was not granted, they had succeeded in demonstrating the strength of their convictions. From this time, the Tonghaks' antiforeign slogans proliferated; originally directed against Europeans, they came now to include the Japanese. The peasants had only a vague notion of Europeans, but they all had personal experience of unscrupulous Japanese merchants who bought their rice crops and lent them money at usurious rates.

The Tonghak believers, emboldened by the fears their movement aroused in the Korean government, plastered the walls of foreign legations and consulates with antiforeign slogans and shouted abuse at the foreign diplomats inside.[27] Even the Chinese legation was not spared the abuse. Yüan Shih-k'ai, the representative of the Chinese government, realizing that these actions might easily escalate into much larger disturbances, sent an urgent message to Li Hung-chang asking for two warships. Li immediately sent the *Ching-yüan* and the *Lai-yüan* to Inch'on. Members of the Japanese legation, fearing attack, armed themselves with swords and readied themselves for action.

Mutsu Munemitsu's account of the circumstances leading up to the outbreak of the Sino-Japanese War is of particular importance because he not only was an alert observer of the events he describes but, as foreign minister, was actively involved in decision making. His record of the war, *Kenkenroku*,[28] opens with a consideration of the Tonghak revolt:

> Some have regarded the Tonghak as a type of religious group, imbued with a mixture of Confucianism and Taoism. Others have considered them to be an association of political reformers. Others have seen them merely as a lawless gang spoiling for a fight. Here, we are less concerned with their character and motivation than with the simple fact that in April and May of 1894, a group of insurgents calling themselves Tonghak rose in rebellion throughout the provinces of Cholla and Ch'ung-ch'ong. After they had pillaged homes and expelled the local officials in these provinces, they continued their rampage toward Kyonggi Province and occupied Chonju (the capital city of Cholla) for a time.[29]

The reactions in Japan to the Tonghaks' early successes were mixed. Some favored sending Japanese troops into Korea in order to help the feeble Korean government suppress the revolt. Others believed that the Tonghaks were reformers whose aim was to rescue the suffering Korean people from a corrupt government. In recent years, some scholars have discounted the importance of the Tonghak religion to the rebellion, insisting that (despite its garments of religion) it was essentially a peasant movement.[30]

At first, observers believed that the Tonghaks were not strong enough to overthrow the existing regime, but when the Tonghaks approached Seoul, the Korean government panicked and appealed to Yüan Shih-k'ai for help in putting down the revolt. On June 2 Mutsu had word of the Korean request from Sugimura Fukashi, the chargé d'affaires at the Japanese legation in Seoul, and at once informed the cabinet of his intention to send "a substantial number" of Japanese troops to the peninsula in order to maintain the balance of power between the Japanese and the Chinese. The cabinet concurred unanimously, and the prime minister went to the palace to obtain the emperor's approval. The emperor gave his consent in a brief rescript stating that during this period of revolts and disorders in Korea, troops would be sent to protect the lives of resident Japanese.[31]

The Japanese minister to Korea, Ōtori Keisuke (1832–1911), who happened to be on a leave of absence in Japan, was sent back to Korea on June 5 with instructions to devote his full energies to achieving the Japanese objectives of national honor and a balance of power with China. Insofar as possible, a peaceful solution should be sought. Mutsu wrote, "In the event a Sino-Japanese conflict occurred, we were determined to have the Chinese be the aggressors, while we ourselves assumed the position of the aggrieved party."[32]

Through the minister plenipotentiary to Japan, Wang Feng-tsao, the Chinese government informed the Japanese government that at the request of the king of Korea, it was sending "a small number" of troops to Korea in order to suppress the Tonghak faction. According to Mutsu, Wang "had foolishly concluded that Japan was too debilitated internally to engage in conflict with another power."

The Chinese had obtained this impression from the endless, acrimonious debates in the Diet, a political phenomenon unknown in their own country. Exasperated by the constant attacks on himself and his cabinet, Itō Hirobumi said that even though five years had passed since the constitution was put into effect, members of the Diet were still wandering like "lost sheep." Each political party tried to outdo the others in opposing the government, even if this was harmful to the future of the country. Itō's solution was for the emperor to summon the leaders of all parties and command them to hearken to the imperial will.[33] It is not clear whether Itō actually submitted this request; in any case, Meiji did not react.

Noticing the sharp divergence of views expressed in the Diet, the Chinese could not easily appreciate (and the exasperated Itō sometimes forgot) the intense patriotism of the Japanese, which would sweep away divergences if ever their country was threatened by another. The assumption of the Chinese that their army and their navy were superior to Japan's was shared by many Japanese. Hayashi Tadasu wrote, "Before the Sino-Japanese War, Japanese would laugh at the backwardness of the Chinese and speak of them with contempt, but they were in fact extremely afraid of them."[34]

On June 7 Mutsu wired instructions to Komura Jutarō (1855–1911), the Japanese chargé d'affaires in Peking, directing him to notify the Chinese that the Japanese government, in keeping with the Treaty of Tientsin, intended to send troops to Korea. The Chinese replied that they were acting in compliance with a Korean request for assistance in subduing a rebellion. This, they said, was in keeping with their traditional practice of protecting tributary states. The last words could not be passed over without comment by the Japanese. Mutsu in his reply stated that "the Japanese government did not and never had recognized Korea as a tributary state of China."[35] Throughout the ensuing war, the Japanese never ceased to insist on this point, but the fact remained that the Koreans had asked the Chinese—and not the Japanese—to protect them.

Ōtori arrived in Inch'on on June 9 and proceeded to Seoul, accompanied by 300 Japanese marines. He was followed by a battalion of army troops. In the meantime, the Tonghaks had become discouraged and had virtually ceased their advance on Seoul, the direct cause of the Chinese presence. Discovering that Seoul was surprisingly calm, Ōtori recommended that no large body of Japanese troops be sent to Korea, but this did not alter Mutsu's belief that "the issue would be settled by whichever side enjoyed superior troop strength."[36] On June 11 a mixed brigade under the command of General Ōshima Yoshimasa left Ujina for Inch'on. By the fifteenth of the month, the Tonghak rebellion seemed to have ended, but the Chinese and Japanese armies showed no signs of leaving the peninsula.[37]

At this juncture Itō proposed that the Chinese and Japanese cooperate to terminate the rebellion and, when this had been accomplished, send commissioners to improve Korea's internal administration, especially finances and military preparation. If the Chinese refused to join the Japanese, the Japanese would assume sole responsibility. The plan was sent to the emperor for his approval, but he seemed uneasy about the provision (which Mutsu had added to Itō's original plan) that Japan would act unilaterally if necessary. He sent the chief chamberlain to question this provision. Mutsu came to the palace to explain in detail, and the emperor finally gave his consent.[38]

As Mutsu had expected, the Chinese were unwilling to accept the plan. On June 21 the Chinese minister reported that his government had rejected the Japanese plan, for three reasons:

First, as the disturbance in Korea had already been quelled, it was no longer essential for Chinese forces to act on behalf of the Korean government in finishing off the rebels. It followed that there was equally no need for China and Japan to act jointly in suppressing the disturbance. Second, while the Japanese government's ideas about Korea's future might well be excellent ones, it was for the Koreans themselves to reform their country.... Finally, the terms of the Treaty of Tientsin obliged both Japan and China to withdraw their troops as soon as the disturbance occasioning their dispatch had been quelled. A mutual withdrawal of Japanese and Chinese troops at this point was thus completely justified and required no further discussion.[39]

The arguments of the Chinese were irrefutable, but Mutsu declared that "from the outset, however, our government had insisted that we would not feel secure until the evils lying at the root of the rebellion in Korea had been eradicated." He informed the Chinese that the Japanese government found it impossible to order the withdrawal of Japanese troops from Korea. Japan could not stand by while Korea was in such a wretched condition, as this would be contrary to the friendship that should prevail between neighboring nations. It also ran counter to Japanese security needs. Yamagata Aritomo observed on June 23 that war between China and Japan was inevitable.

On June 26 Ōtori Keisuke had an audience with King Kojong at which he insisted on the importance of internal reform. On the twenty-eighth he demanded that the Korean authorities disclose whether Korea was an independent country or only a vassal of China. The Korean court was thrown into a state of panic by the question, and the discussions did not reach any conclusion. At this stage, Ōtori received from the Japanese government instructions that reform in Korea could not be expected until Chinese influence had been destroyed. No doubt this made Ōtori intensify his demands for an answer. On June 30 the Korean court at last affirmed that it was an independent country.[40]

On July 3 Ōtori, with the assurance that Korea was an independent country, had an audience with the king of Korea during which he proposed reforms in Korea's administration, finances, laws, military, and education. The court was still dominated by the reactionary Sadaedang, which stood in awe of China and detested reforms, but Ōtori's proposal was backed by the might of the Japanese armed forces, and they could not refuse. The king issued a rescript blaming himself for the crisis, expressing shame over the years of bad government and grief over the repeated internal revolts. He attributed all that had gone wrong to his own lack of virtue and the incompetence of his officials. He set up a committee for reform and ordered it to consult with the Japanese minister.[41]

One after another of the principal Japanese figures came out in favor of war. Count Matsukata Masayoshi, learning that at its meeting the previous day the cabinet had not reached a decision to open hostilities against the Chinese, visited Itō Hirobumi on July 12 to express his concern over the government's hesitation. He declared that the arrogance of the Chinese grew worse each day and accused them of committing outrages of every sort in Korea. He deplored the government's failure to take advantage of the opportunity it had been given to carry out its mandate. Itō thought that there was still insufficient reason for declaring war, but Matsukata declared that the public, even enemies of the government, was united in support of war. He predicted that if action were not taken in the next couple of days, it would be impossible to control public unrest and that there would be no guaranteeing that some foreign power might not intervene. Withdrawing Japanese troops from Korea would lower Japan's national prestige in the eyes of foreigners, and its national unity would be once again imperiled. Matsukata ended by threatening never again to see Itō if he disregarded his advice.

Itō agreed to consider Matsukata's views, but unlike Matsukata, who was not in the government, he could not forget his responsibilities as prime minister. Moreover, he was close to the emperor and knew that he was extremely reluctant to open hostilities, fearing that war between Japan and China might give some third country an opportunity to intervene.[42]

Li Hung-chang asked the Russians to mediate, and they gladly agreed. Russia's interest in Korea, particularly in obtaining an ice-free port there, would be an important factor in developments in the region for years to come. The Japanese thanked the Russians for the offer of mediation but said they would withdraw from the peninsula just as soon as conditions permitted.[43]

The British also expressed their desire for peace in East Asia. In April 1894 the British government agreed on a revised treaty. Although the British refusal to give up extraterritoriality had long been a sore point with the Japanese, England was about to become the first major country to grant Japan equality.[44] Prime Minister William Gladstone, who had newly formed a cabinet, declared that he not only considered the continuation of consular courts in Japan to be inappropriate but also believed that the abolition of these courts was of urgent importance in strengthening the ties of friendship between the two nations. But when the British offered on July 17 to mediate, the Japanese, who by this time had decided on war and were uninterested in the British proposal, deliberately proposed conditions that they knew the Chinese could not accept. The Japanese declared that any reinforcement of Chinese troops in Korea would be considered a provocation. The British protested, saying that this stipulation was in contravention of the Treaty of Tientsin, but the Japanese replied that the matter was not one on which they were subject to questioning by the British. The latter gave up their efforts to mediate.[45]

On July 23 Japanese troops of the mixed brigade entered Seoul at dawn. As they approached the royal palace, Korean soldiers suddenly opened fire. The Japanese answered this fire and entered the palace precincts, driving out the Korean troops and taking their place in guarding the palace. The king called on his father, the *taewon'gun*, to assume charge of the government. Although the *taewon'gun* had been bitterly anti-Japanese, his experiences as a prisoner of the Chinese had changed his outlook, and he now welcomed Ōtori to the palace. He informed him that the king had delegated to himself full powers to reform the government. He promised that he would always consult with Ōtori before taking any steps. On July 25 the *taewon'gun* announced the abrogation of the Korean treaty with China.[46]

The first battle of the war (which had not yet been declared) took place on July 25 when elements of the Japanese fleet encountered two Chinese warships, a cruiser and a gunboat, heading toward Asan. Not only did the Chinese ships fail to salute the Japanese flag, but their battle stations were manned. When the two fleets had closed to about 10,000 feet, the cruiser *Chi-yüan* opened fire, and the three Japanese ships returned it. After a battle lasting for more than an hour, the *Chi-yüan*, badly damaged, fled, and the gunboat was beached and abandoned. Two other ships approached, the warship *Ts'ao-chiang* and the British merchant ship *Kao-hsing*, carrying a thousand Chinese troops to Asan. During the ensuing action, the *Ts'ao-chiang* raised the white flag of surrender. The *Naniwa*, commanded by Captain Tōgō Heihachirō, ordered the *Kao-hsing* to weigh anchor and follow behind. When this order was disregarded, he sank the ship. The captain and two other British officers were rescued, but the Chinese crew and the thousand soldiers were left to drown. The sinking at first aroused anger in England, but British experts defended the Japanese action as appropriate in wartime, and the matter was allowed to drop, since that was to the advantage of the British government.[47]

The first land engagement took place on July 29 when the mixed brigade commanded by General Ōshima encountered the Chinese at Song-hwan. As usual, Japanese accounts of the battle state that the Chinese opened fire first and that the Japanese did no more than answer their fire. The Japanese, in any case, were victorious, putting the Chinese to rout and capturing their base at Asan.

On August 1 the Japanese declared war on China. The emperor issued a rescript to the military, urging them to fight on land and on the sea until the nation's objectives were attained. They were urged to use all means at their disposal to achieve victory, providing that they did not violate international law.[48]

There can be no doubting the intense enthusiasm engendered by the war among the Japanese. This was the first time since Hideyoshi's abortive attempt in the sixteenth century to conquer Korea that Japanese troops were fighting foreigners abroad, and it seemed a confirmation of Japan's new status among the nations of the world. China, by contrast, appeared to the Japanese like the embodiment of all that Japan had rejected—an "unenlightened" country that prided itself on past glories rather than on present achievements.

Fukuzawa Yukichi, the prime exponent of enlightenment, published an article in which he declared that a war with China was necessary in order that the Chinese might benefit by the enlightenment that had been denied them by their obstinate Manchu rulers. He considered China's interference in Korea to be an intolerable attempt to prevent the spread of enlightenment, and the war itself not merely a struggle between two countries but a "battle for the sake of world culture."[49]

Uchimura Kanzō, who was later known for his pacifism, published in August 1894 an article in English entitled "Justification of the Corean War." He was certain that the "Corean War now opened between Japan and China" was a righteous war.[50] He wrote,

> The Corean War is to decide whether Progress shall be the law in the East, as it has long been in the West, or whether Retrogression, fostered once by the Persian Empire; then by Carthage, and again by Spain, and now at last (last in the world's history, we hope) by the Manchurian Empire of China, shall possess the Orient forever. Japan's victory shall mean free government, free religion, free education, and free commerce for 600,000,000 souls that live on this side of the globe.[51]

Uchimura concluded by declaring, "Japan is the champion of Progress in the East, and who, except her deadly foe, China—the incorrigible hater of Progress—wishes not victory for Japan!"

The initial victories of the Japanese military in Korea brought on a wave of patriotic fervor that was heightened by the *nishikie* drawn and published as fast as news reached Japan. The battle of Song-hwan produced two heroes whose deeds were commemorated pictorially by various artists and in poetry composed by both Japanese and foreigners. The first hero at Song-hwan was Captain Matsuzaki Naoomi. Struck by a bullet in the leg, he went on fighting until another bullet struck his head. *Yarareta* (I'm done for!) was his last utterance. Matsuzaki's fame, however, was soon eclipsed by that of an ordinary private, Shirakami Genjirō,[52] who fell in action on the same day, July 29, 1894. Reports told how Shirakami, though struck by a bullet, continued to blow his bugle to his last breath. When his corpse was found, the bugle was still pressed to his lips. Before long, a flood of poetry and *nishikie* had been inspired by the heroic bugler. For example, Toyama Masakazu composed the lengthy poem "I Am a Bugler," which opens in this manner:

> *Okayama kenjin Shirakami Genjirō.*
> *Kare wa mata ikko no rappashu narishi nari.*
> *Hito wa ieri. Kare was tadatada rappafuki nari to.*
> *Kare wa ieri. Ware was tadatada rappafuki nari to.*[53]

> Shirakami Genjirō, Okayama man,
> He too was a bugler.
> People said, "He is just a bugle-blower."
> He said, "I am just a bugle-blower."

The unspoken point of these lines is that Shirakami did not belong to the samurai class but was a mere conscript who merely blew a bugle. Indeed, most of the heroes of the Sino-Japanese War were men of humble social origins. The fact that these soldiers performed acts of bravery of a kind that had hitherto been associated exclusively with the samurai class proved that the entire Japanese people possessed the virtues of bravery and loyalty.

On August 11 the emperor's ancestors were officially informed of the proclamation of war. Ceremonies were held in the palace sanctuary, and high-ranking nobles were dispatched to the Ise Shrine and to the tomb of Emperor Kōmei to report the news. Some days earlier, shortly after the emperor's declaration of war had been issued, Imperial Household Minister Hijikata Hisamoto visited the emperor to ask which envoys he wished sent to Ise and the tomb of Emperor Kōmei. The emperor answered, "Don't send anybody. I have not been in favor of this war from the start. It was only because cabinet ministers informed me that war was inevitable that I permitted it. It is very painful for me to report what has happened to the Ise Shrine and the tomb of the previous emperor." Hijikata, astonished by these remarks, admonished the emperor, "But Your Majesty has already issued a declaration of war. I wonder if Your Majesty might not be mistaken in giving me such a command." The emperor flew into a rage and said, "Not another word out of you. I don't wish to see you again." Hijikata withdrew in fear and trepidation.[54]

After he returned to his home, Hijikata gave earnest thought to the situation. The proclamation of war had already been disseminated at home and abroad, and units of the army and navy were on their way to the front. He could not bear to think of the effect the emperor's words might have on the future of the war, yet there was no doubting he meant his words. Hijikata considered consulting with Itō but feared that would only make things more complicated. He could not sleep that night for worry and anguish. The next morning, however, the chief chamberlain came with a message from the emperor commanding Hijikata to waste no time in choosing envoys to be sent to Ise and to Kyōto. Hijikata hurried to the palace, where he found the emperor in good humor, quite changed from the previous night, Hijikata gave him the names of two men, then burst into tears of emotion.

Evidently, on thinking over the matter, the emperor had decided that it was impossible to call off the war at this late stage. But what had made him so loath to approve the declaration of war? Perhaps, as he had earlier said, he feared that war might permit some other country to intervene, to Japan's detriment. Or it might be that the thought of a war in which many Japanese soldiers would surely be killed was so distasteful that he wanted no part of it. Or conceivably, he may have feared that Japan might not be a match for China. The foreign press was unanimous in predicting a Chinese victory once Japan's initial advantages of discipline and preparedness had dissipated.[55] Finally, it may be that the emperor, whose education had been so heavily based on the Confucian classics, did not wish to fight against the country that had given birth to the Sage.

We shall probably never know why Meiji was reluctant to report to the gods or to his father's tomb the declaration of war; but by the next morning he had changed his mind, and from then on until the end of the war he did not waver in his devotion to the Japanese fighting on the Asian mainland and on the sea.

Chapter 45

The war with China went so well for the Japanese that soon there were discussions of what policy should be adopted toward Korea after the victory. Mutsu Munemitsu presented four plans to the cabinet meeting on August 17, 1894:

1. Having declared the independence of Korea and the need for reforms in its internal administration, the Japanese government should let the Koreans work out for themselves the future of their country.
2. Although nominally treating Korea as an independent country, the Japanese government should support its independence both directly and indirectly on a permanent or long-term basis and strive to keep Korea from being humiliated by other countries.
3. If the Japanese government believes that Korea lacks the strength to be independent and that it would be unwise for Japan to protect it single-handedly, Japan and China should jointly assume responsibility for the integrity of Korean territory.
4. If the third plan is thought not to be advisable, the neutrality of Korea should be guaranteed by the major powers, in the manner of Belgium and Switzerland in Europe.

The cabinet decided that it was still premature to adopt a fixed policy, but for the time being the second plan would be the general strategy.[1]

In keeping with this policy of friendly support to Korea, on August 20 the emperor commanded the adviser to the Privy Council, Saionji Kinmochi, to go to Korea with presents and a message for King Kojong. The letter expressed Meiji's great concern over recent events in Korea and his confidence that the king in his wisdom and resolution would strengthen the foundations of national prosperity. In token of unchanging friendship, the emperor sent gifts—a sword and a pair of vases. The king, replying in kind, expressed joy that Meiji had strengthened the ties of friendship between Japan and Korea and thanked him for sending Japanese troops to preserve Korean independence.[2]

The Japanese were anxious about the impression produced on foreign countries by their actions in Korea. Foreign Minister Mutsu Munemitsu sent identical messages to the minister plenipotentiary Ōtori Keisuke and the Japanese army and navy commanders in Korea, reminding them that they must avoid any act that violated Korean independence, even if this resulted in military inconvenience or was uneconomical. He realized that at times there might be no choice but to make demands of the Korean government, but these demands should never exceed what the government of Korea, as an independent country, could accept without losing face. Finally, he reminded them that Korea was not an enemy but an ally of Japan and that goods needed for military or other purposes must be paid for, the sum being sufficient to satisfy the sellers. Under no circumstances should an impression be given of plundering the country.

On August 26 Japan and Korea signed an alliance providing that the two countries would cooperate to drive Chinese troops from Korean soil, strengthen Korean independence, and promote the interests of both Japan and Korea.

The emperor, though (as we have seen) at first reluctant for Japan to become engaged in a war with China, quickly threw himself into his role as supreme commander of the armed forces. Because he alone combined political and military authority, his decisions were needed frequently. During the Sino-Japanese War, about ninety meetings were held in his presence, attended not only by the chief military officers but also, at the emperor's request, by Itō Hirobumi.[3] Itō's attention as a civil official was divided between the successful prosecution of the war and the possibility that other countries might seek to intervene in the war, especially if it was prolonged.[4] Fortunately, negotiations with the British for treaty revision had at last been successful, and the end of the hated extraterritoriality was in sight.[5]

On September 1 the emperor received Prince Taruhito, the chief of the general staff, who asked that the imperial headquarters be moved to Hiroshima in order to improve communications with the forces fighting in Korea. The proposal of moving headquarters had originated with Itō, who suggested that Shimonoseki (in his native Chōshū) would be suitable because it was the closest port to Korea; but the military favored Hiroshima, the headquarters of the Fifth Division. Hiroshima was the western terminus of the railway from Tōkyō, and

Ujina, the port of Hiroshima, was the embarkation point for troops on their way to Korea. Moving the headquarters to Hiroshima would improve communications with the front, but it would also hamper negotiations with foreign diplomats, all of whom remained in Tōkyō.[6]

The order to move headquarters to Hiroshima was issued on September 8. As commander in chief, the emperor also moved, and he was accompanied by chamberlains, personal physicians, secretaries, and so on. Prime Minister Itō Hirobumi was asked to go with the emperor to Hiroshima.[7]

The emperor left Tōkyō by train on September 13. Many dignitaries saw him off at Shimbashi Station. Along the route to the station, soldiers, students, and ordinary civilians lined the streets, crying "Banzai" as his carriage went by. At every village the emperor's railway carriage passed, the entire population, on both sides of the railway tracks, respectfully greeted the emperor. The emperor spent the night in Nagoya, leaving the next morning for Kōbe. Land and sea security measures were extremely strict in Kōbe because of the large Chinese population, but the emperor, indifferent to the possible danger, that night admired the autumn moon, chatting and laughing with his entourage until very late. Those who waited on him were impressed by his ability to rise above petty concerns.[8]

The emperor arrived in Hiroshima on the evening of September 15 and went at once to imperial headquarters, located in a simple, two-story wooden structure.[9] Meiji's quarters—an office, bath, toilet, and dressing room—were on the second floor. The rest of that floor and the whole of the floor below were occupied by the quarters of his staff and war council rooms. The only unusual feature of the emperor's office was a gold screen behind his seat and two tables, on one of which were placed the sacred sword and jewel and on the other the imperial seal. The same room was used for his official business, his meals, and his sleeping. In the morning, while he was washing, his bed was removed and replaced by a desk and a chair. Except for the desk, the chair, and a few other items brought from Tōkyō, the room contained no furniture, and the only decoration on the wall was a cheap clock.[10] Later, the room acquired some decorations, including artificial flowers made by the noncommissioned officers and sailors of the Kure garrison as well as trophies from the front.

The emperor was unwilling to have his quarters made more comfortable. A chamberlain suggested that he use an easy chair or (as it grew colder) a stove, but he refused, asking if such things were to be found at the front. When someone else proposed that an addition be made to the building to give the emperor more space, he again refused, saying that he did not wish the building to be extended for his comfort. He said of his quarters, "When I think of the hardships our officers and men are experiencing at the front, how can this be called discomfort?"[11]

On the same day that the emperor moved to his quarters in Hiroshima, Japanese forces in northern Korea attacked the Chinese entrenched in Pyongyang. The Chinese and Japanese troops involved in the fighting were about equal in numbers, some 12,000 men, but it was an accepted principle that a successful siege required three times more attacking soldiers than defenders. The Chinese, moreover, were armed with more modern weapons than the Japanese.[12] On top of these material disadvantages, the Japanese troops were exhausted by the long march to Pyongyang. They nevertheless opened an all-out attack.

Chinese resistance was stubborn, and although the Japanese captured some positions, the main fortifications proved too strong to assault. At a critical moment in the fighting, a Japanese soldier scaled the wall and opened the northern Gembu Gate, and the Japanese troops flooded into the city. Most of the Chinese inside, including the supreme commander, Yeh Chih-chao, seeing that the battle was going against them, abandoned the city, fleeing toward the Yalu River, the border between Korea and China. One Chinese officer is remembered for his somewhat quixotic bravery: Tso Pao-kuei, considering that surrender was dishonorable, put on the dress uniform that the emperor of China had given him, and led his men in a charge. He was struck by a Japanese shell and died on the field.[13] The Japanese suffered 180 men killed and more than 500 wounded, but more than 2,000 Chinese soldiers died and 600 were taken prisoner. Pyongyang was the last Chinese base in Korea; from this point on, the fighting was on Chinese soil.

A hero emerged from the victory at Pyongyang, a first-class private named Harada Jūkichi, the man who opened the Gembu Gate. For his achievement (which made possible the Japanese victory), he was promoted on the spot to superior private, a modest acknowledgment of extraordinary courage. He was also awarded the Order of the Golden Kite. More lasting tributes to his bravery are found in the many *nishikie* showing him in the act of the climbing the wall in order to open the gate from the other side; battling Chinese soldiers inside the wall; or standing on top of the wall, a Chinese he has just killed at his feet, in solitary contemplation of the burning city.[14] Harada was also celebrated in song, including one that opens

> Diving under bullets thicker than rain,
> He scrambles up the castle wall,
> Just like a monkey,
> And lightly jumps inside; this man
> Is none other than Mr. Harada Jūkichi.[15]

Harada's story was made into a play called *Repeated Victories on Land and Sea, the Glorious Rising-Sun Flag* presented at the Kabuki Theater with Onoe Kikugorō in the role of Harada (called Sawada Jūshichi in the play). But the role of a hero was apparently too demanding for Harada. After the war he sold his Order of the Golden Kite and drank the proceeds. For a time he appeared on the stage, reenacting his epic deed. One reason for his dissipation may have been the discovery that he was *not* the first man over the wall. A suicide squad had already scaled the wall, and a member of this squad named Matsumura Akitarō, at first supposed dead, survived and returned to Japan. The authorities, fearing that if known, his story would lessen Harada's glory, forbade him to disclose it.[16]

After learning of the capture of Pyongyang, the emperor issued a rescript of congratulations praising the soldiers' loyalty and bravery. This was relayed by telegram to Nozu Michizane, the commanding general of the Fifth Division, whose reply stated that all the officers, noncommissioned officers, and soldiers had wept tears of emotion on learning of the emperor's praise and had pledged to repay the imperial graciousness by continuing to advance at the risk of their lives.[17]

Japan's success on land was followed by a major victory at sea. On September 17, the day after the fall of Pyongyang, a battle was fought in the Yellow Sea between the Japanese Combined Fleet and the Chinese Northern Sea Fleet, the first naval battle fought between ships using steam power. The Japanese fleet, consisting of eleven warships, was under the command of Vice Admiral Itō Sukeyuki aboard the flagship *Matsushima*. The Chinese fleet of twelve ships had somewhat smaller tonnage and was slower than the Japanese, but two of the ships (the flagship, *Ting-yüan*, and the *Chen-yüan*) were ironclads and said to be the most powerful ships in the East.[18] German, British, and American officers were aboard some of the Chinese ships.

On the morning of the battle, a column of smoke was detected on the horizon, and soon many similar columns made it clear that the Chinese fleet had been encountered. At about one in the afternoon the *Ting-yüan* opened fire at a distance about 10,000 feet. The Japanese fleet responded with intense fire. The Japanese ships suffered severe damage, including a hit on the *Matsushima*, but not a single Chinese ship escaped damage, and three were sunk. Although the two ironclads managed to retreat to Port Arthur, control of the seas around not only Korea but also north China had passed into the hands of the Japanese.[19]

This naval battle also produced a hero, a sailor aboard the *Matsushima* who had been badly wounded by a shell from a Chinese ironclad. With his dying breath he asked the officer who comforted him, "Hasn't the *Ting-yüan* sunk yet?" Sasaki Nobutsuna composed a poem using these words which, set to music, became the most haunting of the many songs that came out of the war. It concludes:

> "Hasn't the *Ting-yüan* sunk yet?"
> These words, though brief,
> Will long be engraved in the hearts
> Of loyal subjects who strive for Our Country.

"Hasn't the *Ting-yüan* sunk yet?"
These words from a sincere heart
Will be recorded in the burning breasts
Of loyal subjects who love Our Country.[20]

The sailor, like the bugler and the wall climber, was a humble member of the Japanese armed forces. Their elevation to immortality made the victory over China seem that of the entire Japanese people rather than (as in earlier Japanese warfare) a victory won by samurai swords.

Although the emperor was the supreme commander, he did not intervene in the conduct of the war. His reason for being in Hiroshima was to reassure the fighting men that he was with them in spirit and to inspire them to perform deeds of valor and patriotism.[21] This was why he insisted on enduring discomfort, not permitting himself any luxury denied to men at the front. He refused to have the empress or court ladies serve him because there were no women helping the men at the front, and he depended instead on chamberlains who performed household duties awkwardly.[22]

When not reading dispatches from the front, the emperor occasionally amused himself by playing *kemari* (kickball) or archery. In an attempt to relieve the tedium, members of his staff showed him swords and objects of art from different parts of the Hiroshima region. Sometimes the emperor had members of his staff with a reputation for skill at drawing paint pictures on subjects he assigned. Once in a while he himself drew pictures. Hinonishi Sukehiro, a chamberlain, recalled, "His pictures were not very good, but I thought if I were given one it would be a treasure for my house. But he would tear up a picture at once and I never received one."[23]

It is surprising that the emperor did not compose more poetry during his stay in Hiroshima.[24] He did, however, compose the war song "The Battle of Song-hwan," which contains such lines as

Our dauntless warriors
Stepping over the corpses of friend and foe,
Advance, their spirits high.[25]

The poem, set to music, on October 26 was sung to the accompaniment of a military band while the emperor had his dinner. The music, however, did not please the emperor, and two days later it was sung to the music of "The Sound of Bugles" by Katō Yoshikiyo, a piece the emperor liked so much that he had it played after dinner almost every evening.[26] The emperor also composed a nō play called *The Battle of Song-hwan*. He asked an official of the Interior Ministry to add musical notation, and the resulting work was sung in his presence.[27]

The emperor's life in Hiroshima was enlivened by the special session of the imperial Diet that met in Hiroshima from October 18 to October 22. Minister of Communications Kuroda Kiyotaka and Interior Minister Inoue Kaoru had proposed to Itō Hirobumi that the Diet meet in Hiroshima, arguing that it would have a more powerful effect on the Diet members if the emperor himself read his rescript on opening the session, rather than if somebody else read it in Tōkyō, and it was so arranged. The emperor's message expressed regret that China, having forgotten its duty to maintain peace in the Orient, had brought about the present situation. Now that hostilities had broken out, Japan would not stop until its goals had been attained. He hoped that subjects of the empire, joining their efforts behind him, would achieve complete victory, speedily restoring peace in the Orient and enhancing the national glory.[28]

The Diet session was given over largely to discussions of how to finance the war. It was agreed to issue 100 million yen in bonds to meet the deficit. The points of view of the Diet members differed somewhat, but all were determined to see the war to a successful conclusion, and all expressed gratitude to the emperor for personally commanding the armed forces.

Even as the Diet was debating in Hiroshima, Japanese First Army troops had advanced to the banks of the Yalu River and on October 24 crossed the river. Chinese resistance was stiff, but the Japanese continued to be victorious in every clash between the two armies. On November 2 the emperor attended a banquet at the temporary Diet building to celebrate the victories. The walls were decorated with pictures depicting the boastful Yüan Shih-k'ai, the weeping Li Hung-chang, the death in battle of Tso Pao-kuei, and similar subjects. Later that day, there were performances of nō and kyōgen.[29] On the following day, the emperor's birthday, there was a party at which the emperor himself sang Yuya.[30]

On November 8 the American minister to Japan, Edwin Dun, sent the foreign minister, Mutsu Munemitsu, this message from his government:

> The deplorable war between Japan and China endangers no policy of the United States of America in Asia. Our attitude toward the belligerents is that of an impartial and friendly neutral, desiring the welfare of both. If the struggle continues without check to Japan's military operations on land and sea, it is not improbable that other powers having interests in that quarter may demand a settlement not favorable to Japan's future security and well-being. Cherishing the most friendly sentiments of regard for Japan, the president directs that you ascertain whether a tender of his good offices in the interests of a peace alike honorable to both nations would be acceptable to the government of Japan.[31]

Behind these words we can sense the usual American mistrust of England and the desire to have the Japanese recognize America as a friend with no territorial or other ambitions in East Asia. But Mutsu, though expressing appreciation for the American offer to mediate, replied (with the consent of the government and the emperor): "The universal success which has thus far during the conflict attended the arms of Japan would seem to relieve the imperial government of the necessity of invoking the cooperation of friendly powers to bring about a cessation of hostility." Mutsu believed that "unless the Chinese were subjected to further military attacks, they would not feel truly repentant or sincerely desirous of peace. Also, considering that war fever in Japan continued to be rampant, we concluded that any commencement of peace talks would be premature."[32]

Mutsu assured Dun that Japan had no wish to "press its victories beyond the limits that will guarantee to Japan the just and reasonable fruits of the war," but other Japanese had more ambitious plans. Yamagata submitted to the emperor a memorandum on the future of Korea in which he expressed the conviction that it would be extremely difficult to guarantee the independence of Korea and to keep China from interfering. He mentioned the existence of a secret agreement to build a railway between Pusan and Seoul but said that this would be insufficient, that Japan would surely regret it later if the railway did not go all the way to Uiju, north of Pyongyang. This was a strategic area, and Japanese should be encouraged to settle there in order to minimize Chinese influence. The way between Pusan and Uiju was a highway that extended to India, and if Japan were to gain hegemony in Asia, it would have to start building the railway immediately.[33]

Yamagata's recommendation was not acted on, but ever since the Second Army had taken Chin-chou-ch'eng on November 6, Yamagata had urgently pressed for Japanese expansion on the continent. The Chinese, unable to prevent incursions by Japanese forces deep into their territory, were desperately eager to end the war as quickly as possible. It was reported that Li Hung-chang had decided to make peace with Japan, regardless of the reparations that might be demanded. He asked various countries, including Germany and Russia, to ascertain Japanese conditions for peace. The German foreign minister refused to mediate, recommending instead that negotiations be undertaken directly with the Japanese government. The Russian foreign minister made a similar response.

The next major battle was at Port Arthur, the strongly defended home port of the Chinese North Sea Fleet. The Chinese had been building up the fortifications at great expense for more than ten years, and it was reputed to be one of the three strongest fortresses in the world. More than 10,000 troops[34] manned the many gun emplacements. The Japanese commenced their assault at 1:30 A.M. on November 22. The first line of defense was difficult to penetrate, but once these positions were taken, Chinese resistance crumbled, almost all the defenders running from the scene. Port Arthur, despite its vaunted fortifications, had fallen to the Japanese.[35]

On November 22, the same day that Japan and the United States concluded a new treaty of commerce and navigation, Charles Denby, the American minister in Peking, sent a cable to Edwin Dun in Tōkyō stating that the Chinese government had authorized and requested him to make "direct overtures for peace talks." The terms offered by the Chinese were recognition of Korea's independence and the payment of a reasonable indemnity for military expenditures.[36] The Japanese interpreted the offer (which they termed "minimal") as meaning that the Chinese were not seriously desirous of peace. They replied that if the Chinese really wished for peace, they should appoint plenipotentiary envoys who would be informed of the Japanese conditions for ending the war.

Everything seemed to be going favorably for the Japanese when reports sent by foreign newspaper men who had witnessed the occupation of Port Arthur not only horrified readers abroad but for a time threatened Japan's reputation as a modern, civilized country.

The first report on the Japanese troops' actions after conquering Port Arthur was made by Thomas Cowen, a foreign correspondent of the *Times* of London. After leaving Port Arthur, he reached Hiroshima on November 29 and had an interview the following day with Foreign Minister Mutsu. Cowen astonished Mutsu with his detailed descriptions of the ghastly scenes he had witnessed. That night Mutsu sent a telegram to Hayashi Tadasu:

Today I met with a *Times* correspondent who has returned from Port Arthur. He says that after the victory the Japanese soldiers behaved in a outrageous manner. It seems to be true that they murdered prisoners who had already been tied up, and they killed civilians, even women. He said that this situation was witnessed not only by newspaper men of Europe and America, but also by officers of the fleets of different countries, notably a British rear admiral.[37]

Cowen asked Mutsu what Japan proposed to do to remedy the situation. Mutsu replied that if the report was true, it was most deplorable but that he could not answer until he had heard from General Ōyama, the commander of the Second Army. He found it difficult to believe that Japanese soldiers, who always maintained discipline, could have committed such acts, but if in fact they had occurred, there must have been some cause, and if the cause were known, it might diminish the offense somewhat. Mutsu asked Hayashi to inform him of any information that reached him.

Cowen's first dispatch on the fighting appeared in the *Times* of December 3. It opened by giving the official Japanese view of what had occurred: Chinese soldiers, discarding their uniforms, had put on civilian clothes and carried hidden weapons, including bombs. Civilian snipers had also participated in the fighting, firing from inside the houses. The Japanese military had therefore judged that it was necessary to exterminate them. The Japanese army was further aroused by the sight of the bodies of Japanese prisoners who had been burned alive or had had their hands and feet cut off.

Cowen then described his own experiences. He had been in the city during the four days following the victorious attack by Japanese forces. He stated as a fact that although there had been no resistance in the city, almost every male inhabitant had been slaughtered, and some women and children had also been killed accidentally. Japanese soldiers had looted the whole city. He had reported to Viscount Mutsu that he had seen many Chinese prisoners, both hands tied behind their backs and stripped of their clothes, who had been hacked and slashed with swords. The intestines of some men had been torn out and their hands and feet cut off. Many corpses were partly burned.[38]

The immediate reaction of the Japanese government to this and similar dispatches that appeared in the foreign press was to send out reports favorable to the Japanese.[39] Bribes were given to Reuters to circulate pro-Japanese articles. Some newspapers like the *Washington Post* were directly paid to print articles favorable to Japan.[40] Various foreign journalists were by this time in the Japanese pay.[41]

Military censorship of the Japanese press was initiated at this time. A set of four regulations was drawn up, headed by the following instructions: "Reports should record insofar as possible true facts concerning acts of loyalty, courage, righteousness, and nobility and should encourage feelings of hostility toward the enemy." Those who violated these regulations would be suitably punished.[42]

Worldwide attention was drawn to the events that had occurred at Port Arthur by a brief cable dispatch from James Creelman, a foreign correspondent of the New York newspaper the *World*:[43]

> The Japanese troops entered Port Arthur on Nov. 21 and massacred prac-tically the entire population in cold blood.
>
> The defenseless and unarmed inhabitants were butchered in their houses and their bodies were unspeakably mutilated. There was an un-restrained reign of murder which continued for three days. The whole town was plundered with appalling atrocities.
>
> It was the first stain upon Japanese civilization. The Japanese in this instance relapsed into barbarism.
>
> All pretenses that circumstances justified the atrocities are false. The civilized world will be horrified by the details.
>
> The foreign correspondents, horrified by the spectacle, left the army in a body.[44]

The response of the Japanese press was to justify Japanese actions in terms of the unspeakable trickery of the Chinese soldiers who, even after shedding their uniforms and putting on civilian clothes, continued to resist. They were as dangerous as mad dogs let loose among the population, and the Japanese army had no choice but to kill them before they could bite.[45] The atrocities perpetrated against the bodies of captured Japanese were repeatedly cited as the cause of the hatred of the Japanese troops for the Chinese.[46]

As for the "massacre," it was claimed that the British in India had committed worse. Maoris had been massacred in New Zealand. The recent massacre of Armenians by a Bulgarian army unit in the service of the Turkish government was termed far worse than anything that had occurred in East Asia. The lynching of a black man in Texas, whose only crime was to aspire to a good education, was cited not (as one might expect) as a deplorable instance of racial prejudice but to show that civilized people (like the American lynchers or the Japanese) found it hard to sympathize with barbarians (like the black man or the Chinese).[47]

The full accounts of the massacre at Port Arthur, as seen by three foreign correspondents (Cowen, Creelman, and Frederic Villiers of the *North American Review*), are horrifying. They all bear witness to the fact that the Japanese troops killed everyone in sight, even though there was no resistance. Old people, kneeling and begging for mercy, were stabbed with bayonets and their heads cut off. Women and children who fled to the hills were pursued and shot. The shooting was indiscriminate: anything that moved, even a dog, a cat, or a stray donkey, was shot. Cowen declared that as far as he could see, not one shot was fired from inside the houses at the Japanese, but this did not keep the Japanese from reckless shooting. The streets were filled with corpses, as the photographs show, and a river of blood flowed. According to the foreign correspondents, none of the corpses looked like soldiers or carried weapons.[48]

No prisoners were taken, although it was officially announced that 355 were being well treated in captivity and would soon arrive in Tōkyō.[49] The *Yorozu chōhō* for December 4 asked why there were so few prisoners, and then answered its own question by saying that if the Japanese army and navy had wished to take prisoners, they could have taken as many as they pleased. But a large number of prisoners would have been a nuisance, so the Second Army killed every man who either was armed or looked as if he might resist the Japanese soldiers. That was why there were so few prisoners.[50]

A few Chinese were in fact not killed, probably because their help was needed in burying the dead. They were given white tags bearing such inscriptions as "This man is obedient. Do not kill him" and "Do not kill this man. By order of the XX unit."[51]

Although prohibited by international law from bearing arms, coolies with the Japanese army eagerly took part in the slaughter. In time, when it became impossible for the army to deny that a massacre had occurred, drunken coolies were blamed for what happened. The looting by the Japanese army, which stripped the houses of Port Arthur of every article of value, was formally denied by General Ōyama.[52]

On November 23 the Harvest Festival was celebrated with a party in the Port Arthur shipyard. At the height of the party Ōyama Iwao and other high-ranking officers were treated to being tossed in the air in celebration of the victory. That night Ariga Nagao, the legal officer of the Second Army, visited the foreign correspondents. Ariga had been a brilliant student at Tōkyō University, reputedly the only student who fully understood Ernest Fenollosa's lectures on art,[53] but at this time he was an apologist for the Japanese military. He urged Villiers to say without hesitation whether he considered what had happened during the past days to constitute a massacre. Villiers avoided a direct answer, but in his article he characterized the events with another term, "cold-blooded butchery."[54]

If there had been no foreign correspondents, these unspeakable events might never have been recorded.[55] The massacre at Port Arthur remains a painful issue: How did it happen that men who were not monsters could have performed these terrible acts? In the heat of battle, and provoked by the sight (or report) of the dismembered bodies of their comrades, normal discipline may have been forgotten and individual convictions, including inborn decency as human beings, melted into an undifferentiated mass emotion characterized only by the instinct to kill.[56]

If people in the West had read reports of the massacre of the "natives" of some distant part of the world by the troops of a European or American country, they might have shrugged them off, saying that savages had to be taught to behave like civilized men. But when they read of the atrocities committed by Japanese troops, it confirmed the suspicions of some of them that Japan, for all its beautiful scenery and picturesque art, was a barbarian country that could not be dealt with as an equal.[57]

Ratification of the Japan–United States treaty by the Senate was immediately affected. On December 14 Minister Kurino Shin'ichirō cabled Mutsu: "The secretary of state[58] says that if the rumors concerning the murders of Chinese in Port Arthur are true, they will surely cause very great difficulties in the Senate." Mutsu immediately wired back to Kurino that "while reports regarding the Port Arthur incident are greatly exaggerated, some unnecessary bloodshed and killing did occur. I believe, however, that there must have been provocation on that occasion, since the conduct of our soldiers everywhere else has been exemplary." The Senate, after much delay, finally took up the treaty. Some senators opposed abandoning extraterritoriality in the light of Japanese behavior in China. Then an amendment was proposed that, according to Mutsu, "would have had the effect of virtually nullifying the entire treaty."[59] Not until February 1895 did the Senate approve the treaty.

Cowen was sure that the generals and other high-ranking officers were aware that the massacre had continued day after day.[60] But it seems unlikely that the emperor in Hiroshima knew what had happened. The men close to him would hardly have disturbed him with reports that cast shame on the behavior of the imperial forces. The emperor scarcely looked at the newspapers, but even if he had read them carefully, he would have found only denials of the articles by foreign correspondents, and he had no reason to trust foreigners more than his own countrymen.

Perhaps the emperor's most intimate knowledge of the fighting came from the wartime booty presented for his admiration. Although the booty included works of art, it consisted mainly of Chinese items of clothing, flags, and similar items. Most memorable was the pair of camels first offered to General Yamaji by the Japanese soldier who found them. Yamaji in turn offered them, together with a crane, to the emperor.[61] The camels arrived in Ujina on November 29. The emperor, in a good mood, jovially suggested that they be given to Horikawa.[62] The puzzled nobleman somehow contrived to avoid the unwelcome gift,[63] so in February the camels were presented to the Ueno Zoo as a gift from the crown prince.[64]

The emperor composed two *tanka* on the subject of the fighting at Port Arthur:

kazu shirazu	The sounds of gunfire
ada no kizukishi	As our soldiers boldly charge
toride wo mo	Against the countless
isamite semuru	Fortified positions
tsutsu yumi no oto	Constructed by the enemy
yo ni takaku	How loudly they sound
hibikikeru kana	Echoing through the heavens
Shōjuzan	The shouts of triumph—
semeotoshitsuru	Our men have taken by storm
kachidoki no koe	The fort at Pine Tree Mountain.[65]

These were his most overt expressions of his feelings on learning of the capture of Port Arthur.

Chapter 46

After the disastrous defeat at Port Arthur, the Chinese tried once again to end the war. At Li Hung-chang's suggestion, a German commissioner of customs at Tientsin named Gustav Detring was sent to Japan with a letter from Li to Prime Minister Itō. The letter related that the emperor of China had commanded Li to send Detring to Japan because he had "held office in our empire for many years and proved himself faithful, true and worthy of our highest trust." Detring's mission was to effect a settlement, and he was instructed by Li to "learn the conditions upon which peace may be regained and amicable intercourse be reestablished as of old."[1] Li also enclosed a private letter to Itō reminding him of their friendly meeting some years earlier in Tientsin and expressing the conviction that Itō and he had a common purpose.

Detring arrived in Kōbe on November 26, 1894. He requested an interview with Itō through the governor of Hyōgo Prefecture, but Itō categorically refused to meet him, citing Detring's lack of proper qualifications as an emissary from a country at war with Japan.[2] His rejection of an emissary on technical grounds suggests that Japan was basically uninterested at this stage in ending a war that was developing so strongly in its favor.

In the meantime, the First Army, under the command of General Yamagata Aritomo, had advanced beyond the Yalu River into China. His supply lines were extremely extended, and he was faced with a difficult decision—whether to continue the advance or to go into winter quarters. Imperial headquarters favored the latter, believing it was advisable at this point to shift from the attack

498 EMPEROR OF JAPAN

to defense, but hoping to rival the victory of the Second Army at Port Arthur and fearful that a protracted period of waiting might seriously impair morale, the senior officers of the First Army were eager to penetrate deeper into Chinese territory. Yamagata had already (on November 3) submitted three possible plans of future action to the imperial headquarters and expressed his readiness to carry out whichever one they chose. The plans were (1) landing in the vicinity of Shanhaikuan and securing a base for an attack on Peking, (2) massing his forces in the Port Arthur peninsula and establishing a supply base at an ice-free port on the coast, or (3) marching to the north and attacking Feng-t'ien (the present Hsien-yang).[3]

Imperial headquarters rejected all three plans, but Yamagata, dissatisfied with this response, on November 25 issued an order to the Third Division to attack Hai-ch'eng, a strategic communications junction. Itō Hirobumi, enraged by Yamagata's disregard of imperial headquarters, persuaded the emperor to issue a rescript on November 29 recalling him to Japan. The official line was that Yamagata was suffering from a stomach ailment and that the emperor was concerned about his health, but the central message was the command that Yamagata return to Japan at once, ostensibly so that the emperor might hear from him personally about the situation at the front.[4]

By this time, however, the First Army had already reached the area of Hai-ch'eng, where it encountered the stiffest Chinese resistance to date. Japanese troops occupied Hai-ch'eng on December 13, but the Chinese, in sharp contrast to their actions after earlier battles of the war, did not resign themselves to losing the city. They tried five times to take back Hai-ch'eng,[5] and it was with the utmost difficulty that the Japanese repelled these attacks. For a time it even seemed that the Chinese might reverse the tide of the war.[6] The most serious threat came toward the end of February when the Chinese commanding general, Liu K'un-i, drew up a plan to mobilize 100,000 men and use this force to encircle and destroy the Japanese army at Hai-ch'eng. The plan was opposed by the Chinese imperial headquarters, and permission from the emperor was not obtained. The failure of the Chinese high command to implement Liu's plan may have saved the Japanese from a disastrous battle.

The Japanese troops at the front suffered more from the cold than from enemy action. Hundreds of soldiers were stricken with frostbite. On December 19 troops of the Third Division left Hai-ch'eng at dawn to attack Chinese forces heading toward Niu-chang. There was more than a foot of snow on the roads, which severely hampered their movements. The Japanese fought well, taking several fortified places, but Chinese resistance was strong, and by the end of the day the Japanese were exhausted by the fighting and the cold. As it grew dark, the commanding officer, Katsura Tarō, ordered the troops to return to Hai-ch'eng at once, but they were so worn out that it was not until the next morning that they straggled back to Hai-ch'eng.

Among the innumerable *nishikie* executed during the Sino-Japanese War, the most affecting are those that show soldiers in the intense Manchurian cold and snow, sometimes gathered around a fire, sometimes lying in the snow as they aim their rifles, sometimes mounted on horses that are suffering as much as the men from the cold.[7] At first the Japanese troops, despite the intense cold, were dressed in summer uniforms because winter uniforms had not caught up with them, and the feet of horses that carried men over the icy surfaces were not protected by horseshoes. But the advance continued.

After Detring's failure to meet with Itō, the Chinese sent messages through the American minister to China, Charles Denby, and the American minister to Japan, Edwin Dun, asking for a summary of Japanese peace terms and saying that they could not appoint an envoy without this knowledge. The Japanese reply stated that they would not state their terms until after they had met with a plenipotentiary delegate equipped with the proper credentials.[8] Once again using American ministers as their intermediaries, the Chinese informed the Japanese that they would follow the Japanese suggestion and appoint plenipotentiaries, and they requested a meeting with Japanese delegates in Shanghai. The Japanese replied that the meeting must take place in Japan. The Chinese proposed Nagasaki as the site because of its proximity to China, but the Japanese insisted on Hiroshima. They promised that a meeting would take place within forty-eight hours after the arrival of the Chinese.[9]

Despite the urgency of Chinese appeals to end the war, their representatives did not reach Hiroshima until January 31. The Japanese government appointed Itō Hirobumi and Mutsu Munemitsu to meet with their opposite numbers, but from the outset there were complaints that the Chinese delegates were of comparatively minor office and rank, giving rise to doubts as to whether the Chinese were sincerely interested in negotiating. It was further discovered that they did not bear certificates of investiture with full powers but only what they called an official paper and an order from the Chinese emperor appointing the two men to the mission. The powers of these men to negotiate were not plainly stated. The Chinese emperor clearly expected them to report by telegram each development and to await his commands before proceeding. The Japanese asked the Chinese to reply in writing whether they in fact possessed plenipotentiary powers in conducting negotiations for peace. In the note they submitted on February 2, they admitted that they lacked the authority to make decisions on their own. Itō thereupon declared that further negotiations were not possible.[10]

Even while these meetings were taking place, Japanese troops, which had landed January 20 at Ying-ch'eng Bay on the northern coast of the Shantung Peninsula, were advancing on Weihaiwei, the last stronghold of the Chinese fleet. On February 2 the Second Army occupied the city of Weihaiwei without resistance, and the Japanese Combined Fleet succeeded in bottling up the remainder of the Chinese North Sea Fleet in the bay.[11] There was still severe shelling from Chinese batteries on Liu-kung Island, hampering action against the Chinese fleet. Japanese torpedo boats managed to sneak past the island on the night of February 5 and, approaching to 150 or 300 feet of their targets, were able to sink or heavily damage three of the principal Chinese warships.[12] Another attack, carried out on the night of the sixth, damaged two more warships. On the seventh, Japanese warships bombarded two islands in the bay, Liukung-tao and Jih-tao. The ammunition depot on Jih-tao was hit and exploded. This disaster seems to have destroyed the Chinese will to resist.[13]

About noon on February 9, a Japanese shell hit the magazine of the warship *Ching-yüan*, causing it to explode. When the captain of the *Ting-yüan* saw this happen, he ordered his ship (which had been damaged) to be scuttled and then turned his pistol on himself. On the following day the captains of the surviving Chinese warships urged Admiral Ting Ju-chang to surrender. Ting sent word commanding them to fight to the finish, but not one officer concurred. Admiral Ting, having no choice, sent word to Admiral Itō Sukeyuki (1843–1914) asking to surrender. Earlier, Admiral Itō had proposed surrender to Admiral Ting. His letter, written in English in order to permit Admiral Ting's foreign advisers to participate in the discussions for surrender, read in part:

> Honored Sir: The unfortunate turn of events has made us enemies; but as the warfare of today does not imply animosity between each and all individuals, we hope that our former friendship is still warm enough to assure Your Excellency that these lines, which we address to you with your kind permission, are dictated by a motive higher than that of a mere challenge to surrender.[14]

When Admiral Itō received the message from Admiral Ting indicating that he wished to surrender, he sent back wine, champagne, and dried persimmons in a gesture of consolation and *politesse*. On the morning of February 12, the Chinese gunboat *Chen-pei*, raising a white flag, approached the *Matsushima*, flagship of the Combined Fleet, with a message from Admiral Ting to Admiral Itō formally asking to surrender. He sought a guarantee of safety for the Chinese troops and foreign advisers in exchange for the surrender of ships and arms in the Weihaiwei area. On the sixteenth, Admiral Ting composed a poem in which he took responsibility for the loss of the Chinese navy and then drank poison.

Admiral Ting's final gesture earned him the respect of the Japanese. His last moments before drinking the poison were depicted sympathetically by artists of the *nishikie*. In Mizuno Toshikata's print, Admiral Ting, holding the glass of poison in his hand, looks out on the ships burning in the harbor; Migita Toshihide's print of the same moment shows a much heavier man, slumped in his chair, a vial of poison on a nearby table, as he reads over his final testament.

On learning of Admiral Ting's death, Admiral Itō ordered the ships of his fleet to display flags of mourning and to refrain from playing music except for ceremonies. He asked a Chinese officer who was arranging details of the surrender which of the Chinese ships could carry the most men. The officer replied that because all but the *Kuang Chi* were warships, they were not intended to carry troops; however, the *Kuang Chi* was originally a transport and could probably carry 2,000 men. Itō then revealed that he had been discussing with other Japanese officers what should be done with Admiral Ting's coffin. They suggested that it be loaded aboard a Chinese junk with other coffins and taken out to sea, but Admiral Itō replied, "He was the supreme commander of the Northern Sea Fleet. . . . Even though he has been defeated, a son of Japan could not bear to allow the coffin of a commodore to be loaded aboard a mere junk. As a mark of my esteem for his soul, I will exempt the *Kuang Chi* from impounding and will allow you to dispose of it as you see fit. After the commodore's coffin is loaded aboard, if there is room for others, I will not prevent you from taking aboard other military personnel."[15]

A foreign observer reported, "The Japanese fleet paid a touching tribute to the memory of a brave opponent. As the ship steamed out of the harbor, all the vessels had their flags at half-mast, and from Count Itō's flagship minute guns were fired for some time after the vessel sailed. The European warships at Weihaiwei also lowered their flags, as a testimony to the bravery exhibited by the late admiral."[16]

Admiral Itō was extraordinarily generous to his fallen foe. He not only authorized the Chinese to evacuate as many soldiers as could be accommodated aboard the *Kuang Chi* but permitted civilians to leave Weihaiwei if that was their choice. The battle for Weihaiwei had ended not only in a Japanese victory but also with a vindication of the Japanese code of the samurai after the horrors of Port Arthur.

As commander in chief, the emperor undoubtedly learned of the victory soon afterward, but his days seem otherwise to have been passed monotonously. He attended many policy sessions, but (as was true of his presence at meetings at which the constitution was hammered out), he apparently never said a word. On New Year's Day 1895, none of the usual palace ceremonies was performed, but the emperor watched others play *kemari*[17] and had an officer read to him passages from the *Tale of the Heike*. This was probably the first time the traditional lecture delivered before the emperor at the beginning of the year consisted of a work of his own choice.

In December, Prince Taruhito was stricken with typhoid fever. Again and again he seemed to be recovering, only for the illness to return. He left Hiroshima to recuperate at his villa on the coast at Maiko, but the change of air did him no good. The emperor bestowed decorations on the dying man, including the Order of the Golden Kite; Taruhito was the first recipient of this award. Despite the medical attentions showered on him, Taruhito died on January 15. His illness had been kept a secret, for fear it might have an adverse effect on the troops, but on the twenty-third, it was officially announced that he was in critical condition. His body was sent back to Tōkyō, but not even the emperor was informed that Taruhito was dead. On the twenty-third an officer he sent to inquire after Taruhito's health first learned of his death. A state funeral was held on January 29. The emperor sent a pair of *sakaki* branches to the funeral, the first time this gift was made to a person who was not an imperial prince or princess.[18]

The emperor's emotions on learning of Taruhito's death are not known, but surely it was a blow to lose another of the figures who had been by his side at the time of the Restoration. Taruhito's successor as chief of the general staff was Prince Akihito.[19]

On March 19 the empress arrived in Hiroshima. Those serving the emperor at imperial headquarters knew how inadequately he was cared for by his chamberlains[20] and had long hoped that the empress would pay a visit, and the emperor had at last consented. The empress traveled with a retinue of palace ladies, including Chigusa Kotoko and Sono Sachiko,[21] the emperor's favorites among his concubines. *Gon no tenji* almost never left their quarters in the palace; it was unprecedented for them to travel so far.

It is hard to think of a European woman making so magnanimous a gesture. The empress, solicitous of her husband's needs, brought him women who, she knew, would take her place in his bed. Nothing in the official accounts suggests that the emperor had female companionship in Hiroshima before this time, and there is no indication of his reactions on seeing the two concubines. Viscount Hinonishi Sukehiro recalled that during the empress's stay in Hiroshima she lived in a building behind imperial headquarters but that for nearly a month after her arrival, the emperor did not visit her, continuing to live as before in his solitary room. One night he had occasion to visit her house, and from then on he went there every evening, not returning until morning to imperial headquarters.

The day after she arrived in Hiroshima, the empress expressed the wish to visit the hospitals where wounded men were recuperating. Her doctors advised her to rest after the fatigue of the long journey, but beginning on March 22 she went every other day to a hospital to comfort the wounded soldiers. *Nishikie* depict the empress solicitously visiting a ward where bandaged patients crouch on their beds in attitudes of profound awe. The empress remained in Hiroshima for more than a month.

On the same day that the empress arrived in Hiroshima, a Chinese delegation headed by Li Hung-chang arrived in Shimonoseki to open negotiations with the Japanese for the conclusion of the war. This time there could be no question of the qualifications of the delegate: Li was the chief minister of the Chinese government. Shimonoseki had been chosen by the Japanese partly because the name was familiar in the West ever since allied warships bombarded the city in 1864.[22]

The negotiations began the day after the Chinese delegation's arrival. The Japanese side was represented by Itō Hirobumi, Mutsu Munemitsu, and others. Credentials were exchanged, this time without incident. On the same day Li formally requested an armistice along the lines proposed some months earlier by the American minister to Peking.

On March 20 Itō laid down his conditions: Japan was to occupy Taku, Tientsin, Shanhaikwan, and the fortifications surrounding these three cities. Chinese units at these places were to surrender to the Japanese all their military equipment and supplies. Japanese military officials were to have jurisdiction over the railway between Tientsin and Shanhaikwan. During the period of the armistice, the Chinese would be responsible for the expenses of the Japanese army. If the Chinese took exception to any of these provisions, they would have to submit their own armistice conditions; the Japanese would not revise theirs. Li Hung-chang was stunned by the severity of the provisions but asked for three days to consider the Japanese proposal.

On March 24 Li, Itō, and their staffs met in Shimonoseki. Li withdrew his proposal of a cease-fire, replacing it with a request to enter immediately into negotiations for a treaty of peace. Itō promised to submit a plan for a treaty the next day. After the meeting Li was on his way back to his hotel when a deranged man named Koyama Toyotarō fired a pistol at Li, wounding him in the face.[23]

When word of the attempted assassination reached imperial headquarters in Hiroshima, the emperor was at once informed. He was greatly upset by the news and sent two high-ranking army physicians to Shimonoseki to minister to Li. The next morning, the empress sent a nurse to Shimonoseki along with bandages that she herself had made. On the following day the emperor issued a rescript expressing his profound grief and regret—even though Japan was at war with China—that such an attack had occurred. He declared that the assailant (who had been captured) would be punished according to the law and enjoined all his subjects to strive to the utmost to keep from further besmirching the honor of Japan.[24]

Until the attempt on his life, Li Hung-chang had been depicted in *nishikie* as a doddering old man, a fit representative of the weak yet deceitful Chinese people, and there were songs mocking him. But the attack created immense sympathy, and a steady stream of presents and messages of condolence flooded into Shimonoseki. Mutsu Munemitsu recalled, "Many of the same people who had used the most abusive language conceivable in personal attacks on Li Hung-chang suddenly spoke in laudatory terms approaching sheer adulation as they expressed their sorrow over the assault on him. Some even went so far as to recapitulate all of his past achievements and to assert that peace in the Far East hinged on whether he could recover from his wound."[25]

Reaction to the attempted assassination was not the same as that to the attack on the Russian crown prince in Ōtsu, as the Chinese were unlikely to take vengeance. But there was the danger that Japan's reputation abroad, established by victories during the war, might be tarnished and that Li might use the incident to gain the West's sympathy. This would provide the perfect opportunity for intervention in the war by a third power.[26]

Mutsu felt that some grand gesture was required in order to convince China and the rest of the world that Japan sincerely regretted the attack. He urged that Li's original request for an armistice for a period of several weeks be granted unconditionally. Itō Hirobumi, agreeing with Mutsu, persuaded cabinet members and imperial headquarters to accept a cease-fire, even though some believed that this would work to the disadvantage of Japan. The emperor's consent was obtained, and on March 28 Mutsu brought to Li's bedside a draft of the cease-fire convention. The preamble began: "His Majesty the emperor of Japan, in consideration of the fact that the progress of the peace negotiations has been interrupted by an untoward incident, issues instructions to the empire's peace plenipotentiaries to agree to a temporary armistice."[27]

Mutsu commented, "The convention thus declared that the cease-fire was entirely the product of His Majesty's gracious will." It is clear, however, that the emperor's role was minimal; he merely accepted the plan, originally conceived by Mutsu, that Itō had offered him. The intent of the preamble may have been to augment the authority of the emperor in the eyes of the Chinese.[28] In any case, Li accepted the armistice with evident pleasure and said that although he was physically unable to be present at the conference table, he would gladly open talks in his bedroom. The armistice, signed on March 30, provided that all naval and army units would cease fire for three weeks from that day.

On April 1 the Japanese forwarded to Li Hung-chang a draft of their treaty proposals. The terms were severe. Apart from the recognition of Korea as an independent country, already accepted by the Chinese months earlier, the treaty required China to cede to Japan the southern part of Feng-t'ien Province, Taiwan, and the Pescadores Islands. China would also pay Japan an indemnity of 300 million taels. Commercial privileges for Japanese subjects in China were also specified.

Li tried every line of approach to reduce the Japanese demands. Earlier, he had unsuccessfully tried to persuade the Japanese that the Chinese and Japanese peoples must "formulate a common approach to preventing our inundation and preparing for the union of the yellow races against the white man."[29] Now he warned that if Chinese territory were ceded to Japan, it would arouse indignation and hostility among the Chinese people, leading to a desire for revenge, and would prevent any future amelioration of relations between the two countries.

Li next questioned the huge sum the Japanese were demanding in indemnities, reminding them that the Japanese had started the war and invaded Chinese territory. He was nevertheless willing (as he had previously informed the American minister) to pay an indemnity, but the sum had to be reasonable. Setting so high a price for peace was dangerous: if the Chinese were unable to pay the sum demanded, it might lead to a fresh outbreak of hostilities with Japan. He closed his memorandum with an appeal for mercy:

I have served my country for half a century, and it may be that I am nearing the end of my days. This mission of peace is probably the last important service I will be permitted to render my sovereign and his subjects. . . . Our efforts here will determine whether our two great East Asian nations can henceforth live together in enduring friendship, mutual security, and prosperity. I pray, therefore, that Your Excellencies will take the greatest care to exercise mature judgment in your policies.[30]

The Japanese were unmoved by these arguments and reminded Li that the Japanese were the victors and the Chinese the losers. If the talks should fail, sixty or seventy Japanese ships were loaded with troops awaiting the command to head toward the battle area, and the fate of Peking itself was in doubt. Itō demanded an answer of yes or no to the Japanese demands.

The Chinese made a counterproposal that reduced the amount of territory to be ceded to Japan and cut the indemnity to 100 million taels. Li also proposed that if in the future disputes should arise between Japan and China, a third nation would be requested to arbitrate. If a nation could not be agreed on, the president of the United States would be suitable.[31]

The Japanese delivered their final proposal on April 10. Once again, they required a yes or no answer. They reduced their territorial demands to the Liaotung Peninsula, Taiwan, and the Pescadores Islands and cut the indemnity to 200 million taels. Other provisions were left intact. After one more, futile, attempt to secure greater concessions, Li accepted the Japanese conditions. The treaty of peace was signed on April 17. Mutsu commented, "Thanks to the might and virtue of His Majesty, our nation's prestige has been enhanced, our people's happiness has been augmented, and East Asia was once again blessed with peace."[32]

On April 21 the emperor issued a rescript on the resumption of friendly relations between Japan and China. He opened by stating his conviction that the fortunes of a country could be enhanced only in times of peace; and it was his belief, passed down from his ancestors, that it was his mission to preserve peace. This had been his aim ever since he succeeded to the throne, but hostilities had unfortunately broken out between the two countries and he had been unable to terminate the warfare that had lasted more than ten months. He expressed his gratitude to all who had made victory possible, especially the troops, who had endured innumerable hardships: "Although this result may be attributed to the spirits of my ancestors, how could it have been attained without the extraordinary devotion, bravery, and sincerity of my officials and subjects?"[33]

The rescript concluded with the warning that the Japanese must not let victory make them arrogant, despising others without reason and losing the trust of friendly countries. He expressed the hope that once the peace treaty with

China was signed, friendly relations between the two countries would be resumed, and neighborly feelings would become stronger than ever.[34]

This statement, regardless of whether the emperor himself composed it, probably accorded with his real feelings. He was saying, in effect, that it was not (as official statements had declared) thanks solely to his might and virtue that the war had been won and Japanese prestige abroad enhanced; rather, victory could not have been attained without the efforts and sacrifices of his people. He did not express pleasure in having triumphed over a hateful enemy (in the manner of twentieth-century Western rulers) or in having removed the Chinese threat to Korean independence. Instead, he prayed that the two countries would resume the traditional ties of friendship that had been interrupted by an unavoidable war. This expression of hope that neighborly relations between Japan and China would become stronger than ever may explain his anger when he first heard of the decision to go to war with China.

After the peace treaty was signed in Shimonoseki, the emperor expressed his intention of proceeding to Kyōto. He had always been fond of the old capital, and he may have looked forward to a stay at the Gosho after his cramped life in Hiroshima. The departure for Kyōto would be on April 27.

On April 23 the ministers of Russia, Germany, and France called on Hayashi Tadasu, the vice minister of foreign affairs, and informed him that their three governments were opposed to the cession to Japan of the Liaotung Peninsula. The message from the czar of Russia stated that Japan's possession of this territory would destroy Korean independence and that the threat to Peking posed by the occupation of Liaotung would be a perpetual obstacle to peace in the Far East. The czar urged, in his capacity as a sincere friend of the emperor, that Japan give up the Liaotung Peninsula.[35] Needless to say, the Japanese did not take this profession of friendship at face value.

All three European powers had territorial ambitions in China and were suspicious of Japanese expansion on the continent. Russia was the leader of the coalition. On April 11 at a special meeting to determine Russian policy toward Japan, Count Sergei Witte, the finance minister, said that as the victor, Japan was entitled to a considerable indemnity and that Russia was prepared to allow the cession of Taiwan to Japan, as provided in the peace treaty. However, at all costs (with military force, if necessary), Japanese troops must be driven from the Liaotung Peninsula.[36] He advised taking direct action if the Japanese failed to agree. Since the end of March, reports had reached Japan of a massing of Russian naval strength in Vladivostok and of troop convoys being readied in Odessa.[37]

The Russian government invited France and Germany to join the alliance. The decision of the French to join was, on the surface at least, puzzling, as French interest in China had hitherto been almost entirely confined to the south. When the French learned that the British had refused to join the coalition, for a time they debated whether to withdraw; but in the end they decided they could not oppose their ally, Russia. The British, normally the leaders in developments in the East, did not join the coalition because they believed that as it stood, the peace treaty was not harmful to their interests. The Germans joined, hoping that closer relations with Russia might weaken the Franco-Russian alliance. They also hoped that a pro-Chinese action might earn them a military base from the grateful Chinese.

The general reaction of the Japanese, needless to say, was utter dismay. The euphoria of the victory and the peace treaty had been chilled by threats from three of the strongest countries in Europe. On April 24 Itō listed the following options for the Japanese:

1. The advice of the three powers should be firmly rejected, even if this had the unhappy result of creating new enemies.
2. A conference of the major powers should be called to settle the question of the Liaotung Peninsula.
3. The proposal of the intervening three powers should be accepted and the Liaotung Peninsula returned to China as a benevolent gesture.[38]

Members of the cabinet who considered the three options unanimously rejected the first. The main strength of the navy and army was now in China, and the Japanese islands were almost defenseless. The troops were, moreover, exhausted by ten months of war, and supplies were low. Japan was in no position to oppose Russia, let alone three foreign countries. The third option would certainly show that the Japanese were generous of spirit, but it might be interpreted as a sign they feared the Europeans and, for this reason, had to be rejected. It was privately agreed to follow the second option, but no conference was ever arranged.[39] The third option was eventually followed, distasteful though it was.

Both Britain and America insisted on remaining neutral, although the Japanese judged that America was basically in sympathy with them. Italy, to Japan's surprise, announced unqualified support, but it was not in a position to assist Japan.

There were differences among the three nations. Although insistent on their demands, the Russians and French expressed them politely, but the German minister delivered an angry tirade to the effect that Japan, ignoring Germany's well-intentioned advice, had signed a treaty demanding excessive concessions, and it was only to be expected that his country should protest. When Hayashi Tadasu asked if Germany was threatening war if Japan did not comply, the minister backed down, saying that his heated remarks should be expunged from the record. But the threat remained.[40]

On April 27 the emperor left Hiroshima for Kyōto, where the imperial head-quarters would henceforth be located. He expressed no reactions to the Three

Power Intervention, apparently resigned to the loss of the Liaotung Peninsula.[41] The public was still unaware of the three foreign powers' demands, and in celebration of the victory, every house between Hiroshima to Kyōto flew the flag. People greeted the emperor's train with heartfelt shouts of "Banzai," and at every station great crowds acclaimed the emperor.

The empress, who had arrived in Kyōto the day before, welcomed him by the steps of Hall of Audiences. This was the emperor's first visit to the Gosho in years, and he happily toured the buildings and gardens. He related to the chamberlains accompanying him the histories of the different sites, pointing out where he had played as a child. Climbing to a little hill in a garden originally planned by his father, Emperor Kōmei, he picked up a stone, brushed off the dirt, and gave it to his military attaché, urging him to preserve it. The man wept at the display of filial piety.[42]

Meiji obviously loved being back in Kyōto, and when it was announced that the imperial headquarters would move back to Tōkyō on May 29, he resisted leaving, saying that some major figures in the victory over China had not yet had their triumphal return. But when the last of the heroes of the war had returned in triumph, there was no longer any excuse for remaining in Kyōto, and the emperor left for Tōkyō on May 29.

The war, however, was not quite over. According to the terms of the peace treaty, Japan was to receive the island of Taiwan as part of the settlement, but as yet no Japanese troops had landed there. Naval General Staff Admiral Kabayama Sukenori (1837–1922) was designated to accept control of the island from the Chinese administrators. It was essential that Japanese ownership of the island be asserted as soon as possible. The Chinese, hoping that there would be a repetition of the Three Power Intervention, asked that Kabayama's departure for Taiwan be delayed, but the Japanese government, guessing their reasons, refused, saying that the case of Taiwan was quite different from that of Liaotung, Kabayama left Kyōto on May 17 to take up his post.[43]

The inhabitants of Taiwan were by no means eager for their island to become a Japanese possession. Once the provisions of the peace treaty were learned, there were numerous outbreaks of violence. The Japanese expected some resistance, but they had no idea how many men would be needed to quell it. The government decided to send the Household Guards division, which had reached China too late to see action. It would leave China on May 22 and 23 for Taiwan, where it would serve as a garrison. Just at this time the Japanese received a report that the Chinese government was recalling on May 20 its civil and military officials from Taiwan, so there would be nobody with whom to negotiate.[44]

When the Taiwanese realized there would be no Three Power Intervention on their behalf, one group decided to establish a republic with a military man, T'ang Ching-sung, as its president. A flag (a yellow tiger on a blue background) was devised, and the independence of the new republic was declared to both the island and the countries of the West. At the time, there were about 50,000 Chinese soldiers on the island, plus nearly that number of irregulars—farmers who took up arms in emergencies.

The landing of the Household Guards under Prince Yoshihisa began on May 29 near Keelung, and the town was occupied on June 3. There was resistance from the "bandits," as the Japanese termed the irregulars, estimated to number between 2,000 and 3,000 men. The Japanese killed at least 200 in this first engagement. When the leader of the rebels heard the news of the defeat, he and some 1,000 Chinese soldiers fled the island on June 6 to Amoy. The chief city, Taipei, fell to the Japanese on June 7. The north of the island was pacified by June 25, but in the south, resistance against the Japanese continued. Admiral Kabayama, deploring the hardships that the fighting was causing the people of the island, sent a letter to the rebel leader suggesting that he surrender, but he refused.[45]

The Japanese seem not to have anticipated that the warfare on Taiwan would last so long. Casualties mounted steadily, and on July 9 the empress presented 3,000 bandages she had made for wounded soldiers. Not until August 3 were irregulars cleared from the area between Taipei and Hsin-chu. Another 20,000 rebels were estimated to be in southern Taiwan. On October 21 advance units of the Japanese forces entered Tainan, the last remaining rebel stronghold. The entire island had been pacified.[46]

The cost had been heavy. Only 396 men were killed in action, but 10,236 men had died of tropical diseases.[47] Among those who died of malaria was Prince Yoshihisa.[48] His death was kept a secret until November 4. In the meantime, he was praised by the emperor for bravery on the battlefield as if he were still alive, awarded the Order of the Chrysanthemum and the Order of the Golden Kite, and promoted to general. After the official announcement of his death, the emperor ordered a state funeral for the erstwhile renegade and issued a eulogy praising a life devoted to the military.[49]

As the result of the fighting, Japan had acquired a major possession, the island of Taiwan. The loss of the Liaotung Peninsula had enraged patriots, and the bitterness lingered, but Japan was now more of an "empire" than ever before in its history. The emperor was acclaimed in every proclamation as the source of the victory, and undoubtedly most Japanese accepted this as true. Abroad, too, he was praised as never before. An editorial in the *New York Sun* published in December 1894 opened,

> At the beginning of this year little still was known about the Emperor, but now, at the end of the year, he has come to occupy the highest place among the rulers of the world. No one acquainted with the facts will doubt that he is an extraordinarily enlightened ruler. He completed the great achievement of the Restoration and ended the feudal system. Next, he promulgated a constitution, and inaugurated a parliament. He adopted

European civilization while maintaining the traditional customs of his country. He put his Navy and Army in order, and made Japan the strongest country in the East. He encouraged industry.

The conclusion was that the world in all its history had never seen such a monarch.[50]

Another American newspaper reported in April 1895,

Ever since the Chicago Exposition [of 1892–93] foreigners have gradually acquired some knowledge of Japanese culture, but it was limited to the fact that Japan produces beautiful pottery, tea and silk. Since the outbreak of the Sino-Japanese War last year, however, an attitude of respect for Japan may be felt everywhere, and there is talk of nothing but Japan this and Japan that. . . . Most amusing is the craze for Japanese women's clothes. Many American women wear them to parties, although they are most unbecoming, and the praise they lavish on the Japanese victories sounds exactly as if they were boasting about their own country.[51]

Okakura Kakuzō wryly commented that as long as Japan indulged in the gentle arts of peace, it had been regarded as barbarous, but victory in war had induced the foreigners to call Japan civilized.[52]

Chapter 47

The war with China had ostensibly been fought to preserve Korean independence. The emperor stated in his rescript of May 10, 1895, immediately after the signing of the peace treaty with China, "We have always longed for peace, and our objective, which ultimately led to conflict with China, was in fact none other than the establishment of a firm and everlasting peace in the East." King Kojong on May 30 sent a message to Emperor Meiji thanking him for his recognition of Korean independence.[1]

If the Japanese supposed that victory in a war fought to obtain recognition of Korea's independence would induce the grateful Koreans to strengthen their ties with Japan, they were soon disabused of this notion. The strong pro-Russian faction at the court included the minister of the interior, Pak Yong-hyo, who had lived as an exile in Japan for ten years following the failure of the 1884 uprising. Pak had been permitted to return to Korea as the result of the intercession of Inoue Kaoru, who, on assuming his post as minister to Korea on October 20, 1894, immediately secured from Kojong a pardon for Pak.[2] No doubt Inoue hoped this would make Pak a firm ally, but he (like Kim Ok-kyun) had not been well treated while in Japan, and this probably militated against gratitude.[3]

Inoue returned temporarily to Japan and on June 21 had an audience with the emperor. He hoped to persuade the government to change its policies toward Korea; otherwise, he feared, the country would fall under Russian domination. At the beginning of July, Inoue presented his recommendations concerning a loan, Korean railways and telegraph, the defense of Seoul, and restrictions on Japanese permitted to stay in Korea. He pointed out that the recent warfare had exhausted the Koreans, physically and financially, and he proposed giving Korea 5 million to 6 million yen from the reparations that China was to pay. Three million of this amount would be repaid; half the remainder would be presented to the royal house; and the other half would be used for starting government-sponsored industries.[4] Inoue proposed that a railway be laid between Seoul and Inch'on and that the telegraphic lines installed by the Japanese army be turned over to the Koreans but maintained by the Japanese. He favored stationing about two battalions of Japanese to defend the palace, but only if specifically requested by the king. Finally, he warned against Japanese who had recently been going to Korea. He described them as being of extremely shady background and declared that their activities were creating anti-Japanese feelings among the Koreans. The greatest care would have to be exercised to keep such people under control.[5]

Inoue Kaoru seems to have had the interests of the Koreans at heart. Even contemporary Korean scholars, usually quick to condemn any action by a Japanese in Korea, have praised Inoue's efforts.[6] Inoue's wife, Takeko, the belle of the Rokumeikan, was on friendly terms even with Queen Min, the avowed enemy of Japan.[7] Indeed, if Inoue had continued to serve as the Japanese minister to Korea, the tragic events of that year might not have occurred.

Inoue had planned to reform the Korean government along the enlightened lines of the Japanese government. In the opinion of Miura Gorō, his successor, Inoue failed because the Koreans could not understand the urgency of reform in financial and other matters. When, for example, a Japanese tax expert insisted that it was necessary to establish a budget and keep spending within its limits, this irritated Kojong, who, despite his lack of financial resources, was accustomed to spend money whenever he pleased. Even if he nodded in agreement while listening to a sermon on the importance of financial solvency, it did not take long for him to revert to his normal extravagance.[8]

The success of the three powers in forcing Japan to give up the Liaotung Peninsula had made the Koreans sharply aware that Japan was not as strong as the Japanese pretended. At this time Queen Min became friendly with the Russian minister, Carl Waeber, and his wife. Waeber was pleased by her affability and sought, by exploiting it, to eliminate Japanese influence at the court. He sent word to the queen reminding her that the Japanese and the Min, her family, had a history of bad relations. Although people spoke of Korea and Japan as neighbors, the two countries were in fact separated by an expanse of ocean. They were by no means as close as Korea and Russia, whose lands were contiguous. Even from a geographic point of view, it was clear that it was desirable for Korea and Russia to be friends. Moreover, Russia was the most powerful country in the world, as the enforced return of Liaotung had proved. Russia would not violate Korea's independence, nor would it interfere in internal matters. The safest course for Korea was to depend on Russian protection. Russia, an absolute monarchy, would unquestionably protect the rights of Korea's ruler.[9]

The king, whose actions generally were dictated by the queen, on July 6 suddenly accused Pak Yong-hyo of insubordination, stripped him of his rank, and ordered his arrest.[10] Pak managed to escape, but now there was no one to restrain the queen. Inoue returned to Korea at this juncture. He sensed that the atmosphere had changed and that his main task now was not to encourage reform but to please the king and queen. At an audience with the king, he reported that the Japanese government was about to present him with 3 million yen. He also attempted to ingratiate himself by cultivating the queen's relatives, and he kept a distance from the Reform Party, his former allies.[11] Despite his efforts, however, Inoue soon realized that the court was not to be swayed even by generous gifts; the atmosphere remained strongly anti-Japanese and pro-Russian. He asked to be relieved of his post.

On July 19 Miura Gorō was appointed as minister plenipotentiary extraordinary.[12] According to his recollections, he was extremely reluctant to accept the post. He protested that he was an amateur in diplomacy and had no competence in such matters. In the past, he had refused when he was considered for the post of minister to France, and he refused the present appointment several times; but pressure was brought to bear on him, and in the end he had no choice but to accept. Even after he accepted, he still had no idea what was expected of him. He said he needed to know the government's intentions. Was Korea to be made independent? Or was it to be annexed by Japan? Or did the government intend to share control with Russia? He asked to be plainly informed which policy the government favored.[13] But, Miura claimed, all he had ever received by way of instructions was a directive from Yamagata Aritomo to take up his post in Korea as soon as possible. In the absence of guidance, he would have no choice but to act as seemed best to him.

Miura presented his credentials to Kojong on September 3. Despite his professed ignorance of what the Japanese government expected of him, the choice of a military man indicated that the leaders hoped he would take action— perhaps very strong action—against the enemies of Japan now that Inoue's policy of friendly assistance had been discredited. Inoue himself had recommended Miura as his successor, and although the ailing Mutsu Munemitsu had opposed the appointment, it was pushed through by the Chōshū clique.

When Miura left for Korea, he was accompanied by various advisers, including Okamoto Ryūnosuke, an extremist, who was deeply involved in the plot to kill Queen Min but who had been a friend of the progressive Kim Ok-kyun. When he learned that Kim had been assassinated in Shanghai, Okamoto rushed there from Japan, intending to retrieve Kim's remains and prevent them from being dishonored by his enemies, whether Korean, Japanese, or Chinese.[14] Although Okamoto arrived too late to accomplish his mission, he was loyal to his Korean friend. His involvement in the plot on Queen Min's life was inspired by a belief in Japanese imperialism as well as the need for progress in Korea.

When Miura was presented to the Korean court soon after his arrival, he created a favorable impression by describing himself as an ordinary soldier who was unfamiliar with the fancy language of diplomacy. He said that unless he was summoned by the king, he would remain in the legation, copying sutras[15] and enjoying the beauties of nature in Korea. He hoped to present to the queen a copy of the Avalokitesvara sutra in his hand.[16]

True to his word, Miura rarely left the legation. He spent so much of his time reading the sutras that he was known as "the sutra-reading minister,"[17] but he was privately planning to kill the queen of Korea. It is not clear what Miura had learned about Queen Min before leaving Japan, but once he reached Seoul, he was undoubtedly informed by members of the legation and leaders of the Japanese community that the queen was vehemently anti-Japanese and an unyielding opponent of progress. In his uncomplicated, soldierly manner (and in the absence of contrary instructions from Japan), he apparently decided that the only remedy for the situation was to get rid of the queen, the major obstacle to good relations with Japan.

Originally, Miura planned to carry out the assassination in November 1895, but the date was moved up when word was received that the king (probably following the queen's recommendation) intended to disband the Training Unit (Hullyon Togam), a battalion of some 800 well-equipped soldiers who had been trained by the Japanese.[18] Because this pro-Japanese unit was necessary to Miura's plan, the assassination had to be carried out before it was disbanded.[19]

Miura devised a plan that would shift responsibility for the queen's murder away from the Japanese: it would be announced that her death had occurred during a coup d'état staged by the *taewon'gun*. Japanese military (stationed near the royal palace in accordance with the peace treaty with China) would be available to back up the coup, but the murder of the queen would be left to unruly Japanese elements in Seoul, known as *sōshi*. Korean participation would be limited to the Training Unit. The plan was kept secret from all but a handful of Japanese.[20]

It was necessary to obtain the *taewon'gun*'s consent to lead the coup, but not even he was informed of the plan to kill the queen. On October 5 Okamoto Ryūnosuke (at Miura's request) called on the *taewon'gun*, saying that he wanted to pay his respects before returning to Japan. He mentioned his belief that an uprising was imminent and asked if the *taewon'gun* would approve a set of four "promises" drawn up at the Japanese legation. The first was a promise to confine his future activity to palace matters and not to meddle in politics. The second and third promises related to future appointments, and the fourth was to send his grandson to study in Japan for three years.[21]

The *taewon'gun*'s response to these promises is not known. At the trial in

Hiroshima of persons involved in the murder of Queen Min, one man testified that the *taewon'gun* happily agreed to all four promises without changing a word;[22] but Okamoto recalled that on the contrary, the *taewon'gun* at first said he was an old man and lacked the energy to become involved in anything new, and he asked to be left to die as he was. It took considerable persuasion to get him to consent.[23] Okamoto left the next day for Inch'on; the queen, learning of his departure, was reassured.[24]

Civilians were recruited mainly by Adachi Kenzō, the editor of the Japanese-language newspaper *Kanjō shimpō*. Miura is reported to have said to Adachi soon after his arrival in Korea, "We'll have to go on a fox hunt one of these days. How many young people do you have at your place?" Adachi, guessing that by "fox" was meant the queen, replied that he had some, but they were all mild-mannered newspapermen he had brought with him from Japan. If Miura needed vigorous young men, he would send a telegram in code to Kumamoto and would have no trouble in collecting as many as were needed.[25] Miura said this would not be necessary and warned Adachi to keep the conversation an absolute secret. Adachi started to gather volunteers locally without telling them the purpose. On the afternoon of October 7 Miura sent for Adachi and told him that the changing situation had necessitated making the attack that night. When Adachi informed the others of the plan to kill the queen, they agreed without hesitation to take part.

In the early morning hours of October 8, a party of Japanese civilians and policemen, some dressed in Korean uniforms,[26] barged into the residence of the *taewon'gun*. Okamoto Ryūnosuke, who had secretly made his way back from Inch'on, was among them. Some accounts say that the *taewon'gun* joyfully welcomed the Japanese and expressed eagerness to leave for the royal palace,[27] but in fact the *taewon'gun* was fast asleep when the Japanese arrived, not foreseeing that the Japanese would visit him that night. Even after being awakened, he seemed still to be in a daze and dawdled over preparations to leave. Finally some *sōshi*, fearing that the delay might make it impossible to kill Queen Min before it grew light, dragged him outside and deposited him in a palanquin. On the way to the royal palace the *taewon'gun* stopped his palanquin in order to extract from Okamoto a promise that neither the king nor the crown prince would be harmed.[28] It is not known if the *taewon'gun* realized that those around him intended to kill the queen.

By the time the *taewon'gun*'s palanquin reached the palace, it was growing light. There it was joined by sixty or so *sōshi* and Japanese military, some in mufti. Men scaled the palace walls and opened the gates. Inside, they were met with scattered fire from soldiers of the Self-Defense Unit but soon put them to flight. The "Official Report on Matters Connected with the Events of October 8th, 1895, and the Death of the Queen" issued by Korean authorities reported what ensued when the *sōshi* broke into the quarters of the king and queen:

These Japanese *sōshi*, numbering thirty or more, under the leadership of a head Japanese, rushed with drawn swords into the building, searching the private rooms, seizing all the palace women they could catch, dragging them round by the hair and beating them and demanding where the queen was. This was seen by many, including Mr. Sabatin, a foreigner connected with His Majesty's guard, who was in the court-yard for a short time. He saw the Japanese officers in command of the Japanese troops, saw the outrages committed on the Korean court ladies and was himself asked often by the Japanese where the queen was and was threatened and put in danger of his life because he would not tell. . . .

After searching the various rooms, the *sōshi* found the queen in one of the side rooms where she was attempting to hide, and catching hold of her cut her down with their swords.

It is not certain whether, though so grievously wounded, she was then actually dead; but she was laid upon a plank, wrapped up with a silk comfort (used as bed-clothing) and taken out into the court-yard. Very soon afterward, under the direction of the Japanese *sōshi*, the body was taken from the court-yard to a grove of trees not far distant, in the deer park, and there kerosene oil was poured over the body and faggots of wood piled around and all set on fire. . . .

It was thus that our beloved and venerated queen of Korea and mother of His Royal Highness, the crown prince, was cruelly assassinated and her body burned to destroy evidence of the crime.[29]

This official Korean report did not exaggerate the circumstances of the murder. Witnesses at the trials in Japan and Korea reported that brute force had been used by the Japanese against the king and the crown prince. The intruders who broke into the king's apartment demanded that the king and crown prince reveal where the queen was hiding. When they failed to answer, they were manhandled and threatened with swords and pistols. Court ladies were also threatened by *sōshi* who demanded they reveal the queen's whereabouts, but not understanding Japanese, they could only scream in fright.[30]

Brushing off the king's attempt to bar the way, the Japanese intruders stormed into the next room, where they killed the minister of the royal household, Yi Kyong-jik, who was attempting to defend the queen's apartment. In the queen's apartment, they killed three court ladies, all of them beautiful, but they could not be sure which one was the queen, since none of the men had ever seen her. Other court ladies and the crown prince were dragged into the room to make the identification.[31]

It is not clear who actually killed Queen Min. Okamoto Ryūnosuke was accused of the murder, but other men proudly took credit. A medicine peddler named Terasaki Yasukichi recalled how he and two other Japanese had broken into the queen's apartment:

We went on inside. When we got into XX's room there were some 20 or
30 court ladies there. We flung them off one at a time. Then, when we
looked under the bedding, there was someone dressed exactly the same
as the other court ladies, but quite self-possessed, not making a fuss, looking like somebody important, and this told us it was XX. Grabbing her
by the hair, we dragged her from her hiding place. Just what you'd expect,
she wasn't in the least bit ruffled. . . . I swung my sword down on her
head. Nakamura was holding her by the hair, so his hand got slightly cut.
I let her have it from the head, so one blow was enough to finish her.
The others criticized me saying I was too reckless, killing her before we
had identified that it was XX, but later on it turned out it really was XX.

Terasaki boasted of his achievement, as did other Japanese, including some
who had not so much as entered the room where the queen was murdered.[32]

Once Queen Min was dead, other *sōshi* stole her possessions. The Japanese
consul Uchida Sadatsuchi reported: "Sassa Masayuki stole a perfume sachet
and other valuable articles that were on the queen's body, and other intruders
stole various things from the queen's room."[33]

It was reported that after the queen had been wounded in two or three places,
"they stripped her naked and examined her private parts." Her body was carried
out to the garden and burned there. She was in her forty-fifth year, but she
looked no more than twenty-five or twenty-six.

Queen Min was an arrogant and corrupt woman.[34] She was certainly not
"beloved and venerated" by Korean people who were acquainted with her activities, even if they admired her resolutely anti-Japanese stand. But the manner
in which she was killed was unspeakably barbaric, and contrary to Japanese
hopes, her death did not solve their problems in Korea. In the words of a Korean
diplomat,

> Despite the attempt of the Japanese officials to minimize their responsi-
> bility for the incident, it did more harm to Japan in the eyes of the Western
> world than anything else at that time. Japan, at one blow, lost all the
> influence in Korea which her success in the war with China had won for
> her. Indeed, it was not regained until she had fought another and a greater
> war against Russia.[35]

News of the murder was slow in reaching the rest of the world and might
have been kept secret indefinitely had not two foreigners—General William
M. Dye, the American who had trained the Self-Defense Unit, and the Russian
electrical engineer Alexander Sabatin—witnessed the events.[36] They told others
what had happened, and rumors spread throughout the foreign community in
Seoul.

The American and Russian ministers called on Miura to ask for an explanation. He was calmness itself and noted with wry pleasure that their knees were shaking. He told them, "You haven't got any of your people living here, but I have a whole Japanese community to look after. With respect to what happened, I bear a heavy responsibility toward my home government, but there is no reason why I should be questioned by you about my responsibility. It may well be, as you say, that Japanese were involved in this incident, but we won't know until an investigation has been completed whether they were all Japanese. Koreans sometimes deliberately pose as Japanese, aware that otherwise they will be looked down on. That's why they sometimes use Japanese swords. And that's why we must investigate, to discover how many were real Japanese and how many were fakes. To say that because they acted like Japanese and carried Japanese swords proves they were Japanese is jumping to conclusions. But that is my responsibility. And there is no reason why I must be subjected to questions by you."[37] He refused to submit to any further questioning.

Quite by accident, Colonel John Albert Cockerill, the celebrated correspondent of the *New York Herald*, happened to be in Seoul. Learning from Dye of the assassination, he attempted to cable a dispatch to his newspaper, but Miura applied pressure on the telegraph office to prevent the message from getting out. On October 14 word finally reached Washington. The Japanese legation, when asked to confirm the report, stated that it

> merely received advices to the effect that a portion of the Corean army, excited by the report that the queen proposed to disarm and disband them, marched upon the castle, headed by Tai Won Kun. The dispatch failed to say whether or not the queen had been killed, but the attachés infer from its content that she has met such a fate.[38]

Miura intended that the world believe that what had happened was a purely Korean affair—the *taewon'gun* had staged a coup d'état with the help of Korean troops who were unhappy about the queen's decision to disband them.[39] This fabrication would probably have been believed if not for the two foreign witnesses who knew that Miura was lying. His first report to Tōkyō (which arrived on October 9) was so vaguely phrased that the Japanese government suspected that something was being concealed. The emperor was much disturbed by the extreme lack of clarity in the message sent to him from the Foreign Ministry.[40] He is said to have remarked with a frown to the military attaché Kawashima Reijirō, who informed him of what had happened, "Once Gorō makes up his mind about something, he doesn't hesitate to carry it out."[41] The emperor evidently surmised that Miura had been behind whatever had occurred.

On the evening of October 9 the emperor sent Kawashima to the General Staff Office to inquire about the incident in Seoul and to ask the army to investigate. Kawashima was received by the second in command, who promised to send someone at once to Seoul to investigate. On the thirteenth an order was issued prohibiting unauthorized Japanese from traveling to Korea, as it was feared that "lawless elements" might create fresh diplomatic problems.[42] On October 17 Miura Gorō was recalled to Japan. He would be replaced as minister by Komura Jutarō, a career diplomat.

On October 19 an ambassador arrived in Tōkyō from Korea with gifts for the emperor and empress from the king. There was also a letter in which the king expressed his joy over the signing of the peace treaty between China and Japan and declared that the independence of Korea and the governmental reforms were thanks entirely to the depth of the emperor's neighborly feelings. The ambassador, in turn, was given presents from the emperor and empress to take back to the king.[43] The ritual exchange of presents at a most inappropriate time masked whatever real feelings were involved.

On October 21 Itō Hirobumi decided to send Inoue Kaoru to Korea as special ambassador. He said that the recent incident involving Queen Min not only was a violation of the policies that hitherto had been followed by the Japanese government but had given rise to extraordinary international reactions. For this reason, he was giving Inoue precise instructions concerning his powers and duties lest misunderstandings arise in the future. Inoue's mission was to convey to the king the imperial household's sympathy over the death of Queen Min and its regret that Japanese subjects had participated in the incident.[44]

As for future Japanese policy toward Korea, Itō believed that it served no useful purpose to aid internal reforms in Korea, much less attempt to force them on the Koreans. A policy of disengagement—leaving Korean affairs to the Koreans—would gradually be put into effect. He believed that Japanese policy toward Korea should be passive. If the necessity ever arose to take more positive measures, the resident minister should await instructions from the Japanese government before acting.

On October 24 when the Korean minister to Japan was about to return to his country, having completed his tour of duty, the emperor received him in audience and expressed regret over the death of Queen Min.[45] On the same day Miura Gorō was officially relieved of his post because of his failure to obey government orders. On November 5 his privileges as a member of the nobility were suspended.

The assassination of Queen Min had brought disaster to almost everyone concerned. The king of Korea not only had lost his beautiful wife but had been forced to sign a royal edict in which he blamed Queen Min for having "made dull our senses, exposed the people to extortion, put Our Government in disorder, selling offices and titles." He had accordingly deposed her from the rank of queen and reduced her to the level of the lowest class.[46] Miura, the chief architect of the assassination, was in disgrace. Itō Hirobumi's overarching plan for Japan to gain recognition as equal among the eminent countries of the world had been frustrated by an unseemly action. Inoue Kaoru's hopes for reforming the Korean government would be annulled by the new policy of keeping hands off Korea's internal policies. Furthermore, with the death of Queen Min, the Russians had lost influence at court.[47]

The only person likely to have felt satisfaction over these developments was the *taewon'gun*. No sooner had "his" coup succeeded than he demanded that Kojong replace members of the cabinet with pro-Japanese men of his choice.[48] The Self-Defense Unit, the king's personal guard, was amalgamated into the Training Unit, which kept the king a virtual prisoner. The king helplessly agreed to everything demanded of him, but he became convinced that people were trying to poison him and refused to eat food unless it had been prepared in the kitchen of one of the foreign legations.[49]

Pressure was mounting, however, to punish the Japanese who had been involved in the murder, and Miura could no longer pretend that no Japanese had participated. He decided to conduct an investigation that would result in severe punishment for "several people" and the banishment from Korea of some twenty more. Because Japan enjoyed extraterritoriality in Korea, the investigation would be conducted not by Koreans but by the Japanese police headed by a commissioner who himself was deeply involved in the incident.[50]

Shiba Shirō, another of Miura's advisers,[51] obtained 6,000 yen, supposedly from the *taewon'gun*, for distribution among his "benefactors." This money probably came not from the *taewon'gun* but from Miura as a means of shoring up his claim that the *taewon'gun* had instigated the incident.[52] It would also buy the silence of those banished from Korea. The Japanese government refused, however, to go along with this plan, giving instructions that no disposition of those involved in the incident be made until the new minister, Komura Jutarō, arrived. Everyone suspected of involvement would be sent to Japan for trial, a demonstration by the government of its resolve to abide by international law.

Three groups of suspects were sent back to Japan—the *sōshi*, Minister Miura and his staff, and remaining elements. They left Seoul in three stages, on October 19, 20, and 21. The ships sailed directly to Ujina in Hiroshima Prefecture. On arriving at the army quarantine station, they were directed to take a bath, and on emerging from the bath, they were served with warrants of arrest and put in handcuffs, accused of premeditated murder and conspiracy.[53]

Miura was given the same treatment as the others when he arrived in Ujina. He naturally was enraged and refused to talk to anyone below the status of cabinet minister. He was escorted to a rather comfortable prison cell where he remained for some ninety days.[54]

On January 14, 1896, a court-martial was held for the Japanese army officers accused of participating in the murder of Queen Min. On January 20 the preliminary inquiry held at Hiroshima District Court to consider the charges against Okamoto Ryūnosuke, Miura Gorō, and Sugimura Fukashi found that "there is no sufficient evidence to prove that any of the accused actually committed the crime originally meditated by them." The defendants were released.

The court's findings were detailed and accurate insofar as they went. The decision made it clear that Japanese and not Koreans had planned and carried out the attack on the palace and the murder of Queen Min. For example, it stated that

Miura Gorō further issued instructions to Major Umayabara Muhon, Commander of the Japanese Battalion in Seoul, ordering him to facilitate the Tai Won-kun's entry into the palace by directing the disposition of the *Kunrentai* troops, and by calling out the Imperial force for their support. Miura also summoned the accused Adachi Kenzō and Kunitomo Shigeakira, and requested them to collect their friends, meeting Okamoto at Yong-san, and act as the Tai Won-kun's bodyguard on the occasion of His Highness's entry into the palace. Miura told them that on the success of the enterprise depended the eradication of the evils that had done so much mischief to the kingdom for the past twenty years, and instigated them to dispatch the queen when they entered the palace.[55]

The report even mentions that after assembling "the whole party" outside the gates of the *taewon'gun*'s house, Okamoto declared that "on entering the palace the 'fox' should be dealt with as exigency might require, the obvious purport of this declaration being to instigate his followers to murder Her Majesty the queen." The report follows Okamoto and the others into the palace through the Kwang-hwa Gate and then to the inner chambers but stops abruptly at this point. Having presented irrefutable evidence of the involvement of Miura and the others in the crime, the court could not seem to take the final step of finding them guilty. The Japanese jurists seemed to have tried to the utmost to preserve their integrity as men of the law but in the end submitted to the government's order that they acquit the accused.

The failure of Miura's policy in Korea was dramatically demonstrated on February 11, 1896, when Kojong escaped from the palace where he had been kept in confinement and took refuge in the Russian legation. The escape had been carefully planned. According to the "Official Report,"

His Majesty confided his intention to no official in the Palace nor to any one connected with the Cabinet, and though closely watched managed, early in the morning to go out through the East Gate of the Palace in a closed chair such as is used by the palace women. The Crown Prince accompanied him in a similar chair. It had been customary for ladies of the Court and the women connected with the Palace to pass in and out of this gate in such chairs and the guards, supposing that they contained women, permitted them to pass without question.

His Majesty and the Crown Prince had no escort, and the people in the Palace, supposing that they were asleep, did not discover for some time that they had left. They proceeded at once to the Russian Legation, where they arrived about twenty minutes past seven, and at once summoned a number of Koreans whom His Majesty knew to be faithful to himself, and issued edicts dismissing most of the members of the old Cabinet, appointing others in their place, and denouncing six persons. . . . The prime minister of the old Cabinet, Kim Hong Chip, and the Minister for Agriculture, Chung Pyung Ha, though not denounced in any proclamation, were arrested by the police and in the tumult and excitement were killed and their bodies exposed upon the street, where they were stoned and otherwise maltreated by the infuriated populace.[56]

The king's reasons for taking refuge in the Russian legation were not revealed, but he apparently had heard the report that the *taewon'gun* intended to depose the king and put his own grandson on the throne. The king had not forgiven the Japanese for the murder of Queen Min, and his first statement emanating from the Russian legation was a call for extreme punishment to be meted out to the murderers.

Kojong's dismissal of the pro-Japanese cabinet was the boldest action of his life. Japanese influence in Korea, which had seemed so strong a few months earlier, now dropped to its nadir, and the Russian legation became the core of the Korean government. At an audience with the king, Komura, the Japanese minister, urged him to return to his palace, but the king ignored this recommendation. The military units trained by the Japanese were disbanded, and most of the Japanese advisers to the government were dismissed.

These events naturally caused great consternation in Japan, where the king's flight to the Russian legation was officially interpreted not merely as a serious blow to Japanese ambitions but as a threat to Korean independence, a matter of grave concern for the future of the Orient. General Miura, far from being punished for the fiasco, went on to have a distinguished political career. King Kojong left the Russian legation and returned to his palace in February 1897. In August he changed the reign-name to Kwang mu (Martial Brilliance) and in October proclaimed the establishment of the Great Han Empire.[57] It is ironic that a king so little endowed with martial brilliance should have chosen such a time to proclaim himself an emperor.

Chapter 48

On January 1, 1896, Meiji once again did not perform the customary New Year ceremonies. Now in his forty-fifth year, he had apparently lost interest in the performance of traditional rituals. His mind was preoccupied not by the past but by the future role of Japan in a world of conflicting powers. Japan had won the war with China, its longtime mentor, but victory had not ended the tensions in East Asia. The situation in Korea remained confused and potentially dangerous, and although Taiwan had officially been pacified, there were still sporadic outbreaks of resistance to Japanese rule. A rare agreeable development, the reestablishment of friendly relations with China, may have inspired the cheerfulness of the poem the emperor composed at the first poetry gathering of the year:

ame no shita	How delightful is
nigiwau yo koso	The prosperity that reigns
tanoshikere	Beneath the heavens:
yama no oku made	Roads have been opened up
michi no hirakete	To the depths of the mountains.[1]

On January 25 Princesses Masako and Fusako paid a visit to the palace.[2] They were accompanied by Sadako, the wife of Sasaki Takayuki, their guardian. After the audience with the emperor had ended, the empress called Sadako to her and remarked that although all the emperor's other children, including the crown prince, had been prone to illness, the two princesses looked the picture of health. This, she said, had greatly comforted the emperor, and he always praised the efforts of Sasaki and his wife. Despite his professed interest in his two daughters, however, the emperor could not find time to see them again that year until December 29, when, at an audience before their father, they displayed their skill at reading, conversation, and drawing.[3]

Granted that the emperor had many state duties to perform, it is surprising that he should have permitted almost a year to elapse without once seeing his daughters. Most of his children had died young, and the crown prince's frequent illnesses were a constant problem. One would suppose that the emperor would be eager to see two such healthy children. Early in September, Sasaki, confessing that he had great trouble looking after the princesses, asked when they would be permitted to return to the palace. He recalled that until 1891 it had been extremely easy for the princesses to have an audience with the emperor, but such occasions had gradually become fewer, and this year he had granted them an audience only once. Sasaki tried without success to communicate his disappointment to the emperor. Later that month, Sasaki took the princesses to the palace, hoping that the emperor would be pleased to see how they had grown, but he again declined to give them an audience.[4] Perhaps the emperor felt that a display of special interest in his children would be unbecoming. As a result, he seemed a cold and unaffectionate father.[5]

The education of the two princesses remained a matter of concern throughout 1896. Sasaki Takayuki was informed in January that Masako would, after the summer vacation, be brought up at the Akasaka Palace under the guidance of Kagawa Keizō. Sasaki would continue to be responsible for Fusako's education and for that of the next child, expected in May. Sasaki protested: first of all, he and his wife were no longer young and would probably be unequal to the task of raising a newly born infant. He also expressed the belief that Fusako was now old enough to leave his care. In any case, he did not think it was a good idea to separate the two princesses. The emperor yielded to the extent of allowing both princesses to be educated by Kagawa Keizō, but he was quite determined that Sasaki be in charge of raising his next child. Perhaps the emperor attributed the survival of the two princesses, after so many early deaths among his children, to Sasaki's ministrations.[6]

The survival of these children was, of course, a matter of rejoicing, but they were girls, and succession to the throne had been limited to males. In April 1896 the chief chamberlain, Tokudaiji Sanetsune, begged the emperor to summon more court ladies to his side. He explained that the people were secretly worried by the fewness of the emperor's male heirs. More children would promote the glory of the imperial household and contribute to the prosperity of the nation. Yamagata Aritomo, Matsukata Masayoshi, and many other patriotic subjects had again and again discussed the matter with Tokudaiji, asking him to implore the emperor to summon additional court ladies to serve him as soon as possible; he needed sons who in the future would serve in the army and navy and command the armed forces.

Tokudaiji waited until the imperial headquarters had been disbanded and peace restored before broaching this matter to the emperor. He explained that increasing the number of concubines was desirable not for the emperor's pleasure but as an act of piety toward his ancestors. The emperor, however, chose not to take this advice.

All of the emperor's last eight children were born to the same *gon no tenji*, Sono Sachiko. Six were girls, four of whom survived; neither of the two boys lived to be two years old. The curse of meningitis persisted to the emperor's last offspring, Princess Takiko, his tenth daughter, who died of this disease on January 11, 1899, when she was less than a year and a half old. Tokudaiji and the other members of the government may have been correct in their belief that if the emperor divided his affections among more women he would produce more heirs, but (contrary to gossip that persists to this day) the emperor, although he regarded succession to the throne as a matter of the highest importance, had no desire to acquire a harem. The strict manner in which his heir, the future emperor Taishō, was raised suggests that Meiji had come to disapprove of the profligacy that had been a traditional privilege of the sovereign.

On May 11, 1896, the emperor's ninth daughter, Toshiko, was born to Sono Sachiko. Undoubtedly there was disappointment that the baby was not a boy, and it now seemed inevitable that the crown prince would succeed to the throne. The day after the celebration of Princess Toshiko's birth, it was announced that the crown prince would henceforth visit the palace every Saturday.

The education of sons of the nobility was also reconsidered at this time. It had previously been assumed that graduates of the Gakushū-in would become officers in the military or members of the House of Peers, but Konoe Atsumaro (1863–1904), who had been appointed as principal of the school in 1895, believed that the Gakushū-in should also train future diplomats for service in the different countries of Europe. To this end, he proposed modifying the curriculum, and in June 1896 he received permission. Courses to be added included sociology, the history of Western and European diplomacy, public and private law, and foreign languages; but Eastern and Western philosophy, Japanese and Chinese literature, aesthetics, and other "useless" subjects were to be dropped from the curriculum.[7] The decision had been made that even young aristocrats must receive a modern education.

Meiji's busyness, the cause of his inability to find time to see his daughters, was probably due to both external and internal causes. Among the external causes none was more time-consuming than the situation in Korea. King Kojong continued to live through 1896 in the Russian legation in Seoul, showing no signs of returning to his palace, even though he had clearly outstayed his welcome. Russian influence in Korea kept growing, and in order to maintain whatever influence they still possessed, the Japanese had no choice but to join with the Russians in guaranteeing Korea's independence and promising mutual supervision of its internal affairs. Komura Jutarō, the Japanese resident minister, and Carl Waeber, the acting Russian minister, signed a memorandum to this effect on May 14. They agreed that the king should soon return to his palace, at which time they would urge him to appoint tolerant and moderate ministers and to govern humanely.[8] They also agreed to limit both Russian and Japanese military strength in Korea and to withdraw all troops once the country was entirely peaceful.

The coronation of Nicholas II in May was the occasion for further Russo-Japanese discussions on the future of Korea. The emperor sent Yamagata Aritomo as his personal representative to the coronation. On May 22 Yamagata had an audience with the czar at which he presented a letter from Emperor Meiji. In accepting the letter, the czar said that he was well aware of Yamagata's special qualifications for such a mission. He probably did not know, however, that in April 1895 Yamagata had strongly recommended an alliance with Russia to Foreign Minister Mutsu Munemitsu. He believed that Japan could not single-handedly maintain supremacy in the East, and he was sure that the Russian crown prince's visit to Japan in 1891 had been inspired by friendly feelings. The incident at Ōtsu was unfortunate, but far from making this a pretext for hostile measures, the Russians had demonstrated that they desired friendly relations promoting the interests of both countries. Yamagata urged that Japan change its foreign policy and ally itself not with England but with Russia.[9]

Nothing seems to have come of Yamagata's suggestion, but it probably was not forgotten. At the same time he was informed that he would be sent to the coronation as a special ambassador, he was directed to take the opportunity to engage in basic discussions with the Russians on the defense of Korean independence. On May 24, the day after his audience with the czar, Yamagata met the Russian foreign minister, Aleksei Lobanov-Rostovskii, and gave him a draft proposal for the two countries' future cooperation in Korea. He was unaware that a few days earlier Lobanov-Rostovskii had secretly concluded with Li Hung-chang (who also had come for the coronation) a treaty of alliance between China and Russia. The main purpose of the treaty was to secure Chinese consent to the Russians' building a railway from Siberia through Mongolia and northern Manchuria to Vladivostok. The Chinese were offered in return a promise by the Russians to defend Chinese territory from any aggressive action by Japan.[10] Lobanov-Rostovskii, naturally not mentioning the treaty, reached an agreement with Yamagata on matters connected with the Korean financial crisis.

The agreement between Japan and Russia had two secret provisions. The first provided that in the event of disturbances or threatened disturbances to peace and order in Korea, the two countries, by mutual agreement, might send additional troops into the country. In such a case, so as to prevent a clash between units of the two countries, there should be a buffer zone occupied by neither. The second provided that until a force of Korean soldiers had been trained to defend their country, Japan and Russia might station the same number of troops in Korea to protect their citizens.[11] The Russians, however, did not abide by their promise to cooperate with the Japanese; instead, they took exclusive control of training Korean troops and of managing Korean finances and replaced with Russians the British advisers to the government.

Domestic problems were even more perplexing to the emperor. Foreign Minister Mutsu resigned because of ill health.[12] Prime Minister Itō decided that since he had to replace his foreign minister, he should take advantage of the opportunity to change other members of the cabinet. He appointed Matsukata Masayoshi as finance minister and Ōkuma Shigenobu as foreign minister. When Home Minister Itagaki Taisuke learned of these appointments, he declared that if Ōkuma entered the cabinet, he would resign. Itō considered appointing only Matsukata, but Matsukata said that unless Ōkuma was appointed at the same time, he would not accept his post. Itō was faced with a difficult choice. If, despite Itagaki's opposition, he appointed both Ōkuma and Matsukata, this would cause a break with the Jiyū-tō. But if he decided not to appoint Ōkuma, he would cut himself off from the Shimpo-tō, the other important party. Unable to reach a decision, he tendered his resignation on August 20, alleging ill health.

Now it was left to the emperor to decide which course to follow. In the end, he appointed both Matsukata and Ōkuma but accepted Itō's resignation, even though Itō was the politician he most trusted. He replaced him with the president of the Privy Council, Kuroda Kiyotaka, to serve as provisional prime minister, in addition to his Privy Council post, until a new prime minister was selected. The appointments of Ōkuma and Matsukata aroused consternation in some quarters; it was alleged that the intent was to exclude the Chōshū faction from the new cabinet.[13] Yamagata, the senior Chōshū leader, was asked to confer with other members of the new cabinet on a successor to Itō. The emperor in fact intended to appoint Yamagata as the prime minister, but when Yamagata learned this, he declined, saying he was ill and unequal to the demands of the position.

Nobody seemed to want to succeed Itō as prime minister. The emperor, unwilling to become further involved in the matter, left it to the Genrō to choose the successor. At this point Baron Sonoda Yasukata (1850–1924), the superintendent general of the Metropolitan Police, deploring a situation in which no one was willing to assume the duties of the office, sent a letter to the emperor stating his belief that this was not a time for reticence. He urged the emperor to step forward and reveal plainly to the world what was meant by personal rule. The German kaiser had announced, "I am the prime minister of my cabinet."[14] Sonoda hoped that the emperor would exercise personal control over the cabinet and not leave the appointment of ministers to the Genrō.

He declared that although cabinet ministers were supposedly appointed by the emperor, this was not in fact the case; men were able to take their places in the cabinet, regardless of whether they had the emperor's trust. Sonoda said the cabinet was the scene of endless conflicts that disturbed the peace of the nation. If the emperor were to assume personal control, who would object? He urged the emperor to take this step and appoint trusted people to help him. He termed this the emperor's most urgent task.[15]

Personal government by the emperor had been an ideal of the Restoration, but with the promulgation of the constitution and the establishment of the Diet, this ideal had been forgotten and replaced by a conception of the emperor as a distant, ultimate authority, not as an active participant in political affairs. The emperor's powers were, in principle, absolute, but he rarely chose to exercise them. The "reticence" of which Sonoda complained had become his chosen stance. There is no record of the emperor's reactions to the letter; probably there were none. Fortunately, he in no way resembled the tyrannical kaiser.[16]

The crisis over finding a new prime minister was resolved when Matsukata Masayoshi was appointed simultaneously as prime minister and finance minister. Matsukata was extremely reluctant to accept the post of prime minister because he could think of no solutions to the problems facing the government. At first, after much soul-searching, he refused the command with the usual display of awe and trepidation. But the emperor, not taking no for an answer, directed Matsukata to discuss the matter with Kuroda. Matsukata finally yielded. The new cabinet, sworn in on September 20, consisted almost entirely of familiar faces. The emperor was particularly concerned about the choice of a minister of the army, reminding Matsukata that armaments were being expanded and troops were still being shipped to Taiwan. It was essential that the new minister get along with the general staff and be able to deal efficiently with army administration. Matsukata appointed as army minister Takashima Tomonosuke, who had served in the same capacity in the first Matsukata cabinet.[17]

The most controversial figure in the cabinet was Ōkuma Shigenobu. He favored greater freedom of speech, assembly, and the press and believed that expansion of the army should be limited to twelve divisions, out of which three brigades would be stationed in Taiwan. He also proposed that finances be regulated, declaring that if these views were not acceptable to other members of the cabinet, he would refuse appointment. His views were opposed by the army minister, who objected to limiting future expansion, but in the end Ōkuma's conditions were met.

The first major test of the new freedom of the press came when a magazine in Ōsaka published in October a stinging attack on Hijikata Hisamoto, the imperial household minister, listing his misdeeds. The article was reprinted the following month in the newspaper *Nihon*, giving it wide circulation. Hijikata tendered his resignation, at the same time denouncing the story as a fabrication and claiming that it sullied the dignity of the imperial house. He appealed to

Matsukata and members of the cabinet to mete out severe punishment to the offenders, by which he probably meant not merely suppression or (at the very least) suspension of the magazine and newspaper but charges of lèse-majesté and libel of a government official.

Matsukata asked the cabinet if an administrative disposition was an appropriate way of deciding whether to ban the periodicals. Ōkuma opposed any such action as contravening the principle of freedom of the press, which the government had adopted. Other members of the cabinet expressed the view that banning the periodicals was unavoidable. The minister of justice, Kiyoura Keigo, who had studied the legal aspects of the matter, opposed sending the dispute to the courts. The article had slandered the imperial household minister but had not directly criticized the imperial house; therefore it did not constitute lèse-majesté. Moreover, if the writer were prosecuted for having libeled an official, this would magnify the incident and give the defendant and his counsel the opportunity to attack the Imperial Household Ministry in court, leading to a real profanation of the dignity of the imperial house.

Matsukata informed Hijikata that the cabinet had decided not to deal with the matter either administratively or legally. Hijikata naturally was upset. However, the chief chamberlain and Kuroda Kiyotaka joined to persuade Matsukata that administrative action was unavoidable, and in the end, the offending magazine was banned and the newspaper suspended publication. Hijikata was not mollified; he thought that the punishment was still too light. The general public was disappointed that despite its stated policy of freedom of speech, the cabinet had acted otherwise.[18]

The last echoes of the Sino-Japanese War were heard at a party the emperor attended in December at the house of Prince Sadanaru. It was a gala occasion. The two outstanding nō actors of the time, Hōshō Kurō and Umewaka Minoru, performed *Kosode Soga* and other plays. At the emperor's request Umewaka Minoru sang "Seikan no eki" (The Battle of Song-hwan), the war song written by the emperor, and Hōshō Kurō sang the empress's nō play *Heijō* (Pyongyang).[19] The music for both, newly revised by Umewaka Minoru, exalted the bravery of the Japanese troops. On December 21 the ban on travel to Korea was lifted because the country was now completely calm.

In sum, 1896 had been a rather dull year for the emperor after the excitement of the two years during the war with China. The emperor once more seemed to withdraw into himself. He did not participate in any of the traditional rituals on New Year's Day 1897, and the empress took his place in receiving greetings from foreign dignitaries.

Soon after the new year began, the empress dowager, who had not been well, caught a severe cold. On January 8 she felt a sudden chill. Her coughing increased and she complained of acute pains in her chest. She was examined by Surgeon General Hashimoto Tsunatsune, who pronounced that she was suffering from catarrhal pneumonia. On the tenth Dr. Erwin Baelz, who often treated members of the imperial family, examined the dowager and confirmed Dr. Hashimoto's diagnosis. Baelz warned that the illness was extremely serious, and if it was followed by a heart attack or pulmonary edema, the dowager's life would be endangered.[20]

On January 11 the emperor and empress asked a court physician about the condition of the empress dowager. They had earlier been informed that she had a cold and were taken aback to learn now that she was gravely ill. They decided to pay a visit to her sickroom at the Aoyama Palace but were dissuaded by the doctors and others because they themselves were suffering from bad colds and in no condition to pay a visit. The emperor insisted nevertheless that he and the empress go as planned at 9:30 in the morning. Word reached the palace early that morning that the dowager was in critical condition. The emperor and empress immediately set out at 8:50 without waiting for a proper escort.

As soon as the emperor entered the dowager's sickroom, he fell on his knees and in this position crawled closer to her bed. Seeing how emaciated she was by illness, he could not restrain his intense grief and wept aloud. The dowager turned toward him. The emperor, looking at her, could only weep and bow. The dowager, also weeping, asked an attendant to convey her thanks to the emperor and empress for their visit, explaining that she was incapable of leaving her bed to bow before them. An attendant of the emperor, fearing that a longer stay might worsen both the empress dowager's illness and their own, urged the emperor and empress to leave, and they departed shortly thereafter.

The empress dowager died that evening. She was in her sixty-fourth year and had been a widow for exactly thirty years, ever since the death of Emperor Kōmei in January 1867. Although the emperor was well aware that his natural mother was Nakayama Yoshiko (now known as Nii-dono), the empress dowager was officially considered to be his mother, and he always showed her filial reverence. The emperor's grief on this occasion was genuine: quite apart from ties of personal affection, the empress dowager was a precious contact with the world of his boyhood, one of the last. Although Meiji was often surrounded by men weeping tears of awe and gratitude, he himself rarely wept. His tears at this time were surely not occasioned by regret that he had not been a good son. It can hardly be doubted that he had done everything possible to ensure that the empress dowager's years after the death of her husband were most agreeably spent traveling, watching nō plays, attending exhibitions of art, and similar pleasures.

For five days after the empress dowager's death, court business was halted, and a period of mourning of a year was decreed, beginning on the day she died. Mourning clothes would be worn at court, and other Japanese were to desist for thirty days from song, dance, and music. Flags would be flown with black streamers. For the next fifteen days and on the days of the departure of the coffin and of the burial, criminals were not to be executed.[21]

Some people believed that the funeral, reflecting the present glory of the imperial house, should be on a grand scale. Members of the Commission of Imperial Mourning expressed the view that Emperor Kōmei's tomb was too small and that the empress dowager should have a bigger one. The emperor gave his opinion: "Of course, the empress's funeral should be impressive, but there is a limit to everything. We must not exaggerate and surpass the scale of the funeral of my late father."[22]

The imperial Diet at first budgeted 800,000 yen for the funeral, but Prince Takehito, calling attention to the emperor's wishes, asked that the sum be reduced, and so it was set at 700,000 yen. The emperor and empress were unable to attend the funeral in Kyōto because they both were ill, and it was feared that the exposure to winter weather might aggravate their illness. Prince Takehito and his wife represented them.

The emperor commanded that henceforth the empress dowager would be known as Dowager Empress Eishō. This was a most unusual distinction, no doubt reflecting his devotion. There were scarcely any previous instances of an empress dowager or empress being given a posthumous name.[23] Eishō was not a Buddhist title but was derived from the poem "Purple Wisteria over a Deep Pool" by the T'ang-dynasty statesman Li Tê-yu.[24] This name was chosen for the empress dowager because she was from the Fujiwara (Wisteria Field) family.

On February 2 Eishō's coffin left the Aoyama Palace for the Ōmiya Gosho in Kyōto. A ceremony before the departure was attended by members of the imperial family, cabinet members, the president of the Privy Council, ministers of foreign countries, and their wives. Despite their persisting illness, the emperor and empress wished to go to the Aoyama Palace for a last farewell, but the palace doctors strictly forbade them to brave the weather.

The funeral in Kyōto took place on February 7. The procession from the Ōmiya Gosho to the Tsukinowayama Funeral Hall was long and impressive. The hearse was drawn by four oxen, and nobles and great men of state, all dressed in formal robes, walked behind it. Shintō priests carrying *sakaki* branches, brocade pennants, and halberds, or flaming torches walked to the left and right of the procession. A guard of honor from the Household Guards and Fourth Division, along with naval personnel, accompanied the hearse. Field artillery of the Fourth Division fired salutes of minute guns, and a military band played "Kanashimi no kiwami" (Extremity of Grief), the dirge played at the funerals of senior members of the imperial family.[25]

When the funeral procession reached the Yume no Ukihashi (Floating Bridge of Dreams), just before reaching the Sennyū-ji, the road became so narrow that the coffin was transferred to a handcart. At ten that night the procession arrived at Tsukinowayama, and at eleven a service was performed. The coffin was placed at the center of the funeral hall, and the mourners formed lines flanking the temporary altar. Then, one by one, the mourners came forward from left and right to bow before the bier and offer a sprig of *sakaki*. It must have been a sight of extraordinary solemnity and beauty, despite being performed in honor of a woman who in life was unknown to more than a handful of those who bowed in worship. The funeral of Queen Victoria could not have been more impressive.

Perhaps the funeral's most surprising feature was the absence of Buddhist elements—no priests, no chanting of sutras, no incense.[26] In the past, Shintō priests had been unwilling to conduct funerals for fear of being infected by the pollution of death, but ever since the Restoration, when Buddhism had fallen from favor, Shintō funeral rites had been performed.

The ceremony ended at twelve minutes after midnight on the eighth of February, but the casket was not placed in the grave until 5:30 A.M., and the burial was not completed until 11:55. The only foreign worshiper at the funeral was probably the ambassador extraordinary and plenipotentiary Yi Ha-yong, sent by the king of Korea with a pair of vases of artificial flowers to be placed before the coffin. This gesture was much appreciated by the Japanese. Yi Ha-yong was decorated with the Order of the Rising Sun, and the emperor at an audience for the ambassador expressed his gratitude. On November 22, 1897, when a funeral service was held for Queen Min, the Japanese reciprocated by sending their minister with condolences and a pair of silver incense burners.[27]

The emperor and empress were not able to go to Kyōto for the funeral, but on April 19 they paid their respects together before the tomb of Dowager Empress Eishō. They remained in Kyōto for more than four months. They were scheduled to return to Tōkyō in the middle of May when word was received of an epidemic of measles, and the court doctors warned them that returning might be dangerous. The emperor was enjoying his stay in the old capital, and even when the measles epidemic had abated, he showed no inclination to return to Tōkyō. Not until August 22 did he tear himself away from Kyōto, having at last conceded that the measles epidemic seemed to be over.[28]

On the morning of his departure from Kyōto, the imperial train was to leave at 8:55, but the emperor suddenly announced that he would like the train to leave twenty minutes later. He gave no reason; perhaps he merely wished to enjoy Kyōto a bit longer. The Transport Section of the Ministry of Communications indicated that changing the timetable would be difficult, but the emperor retorted, "Why should it be impossible to rearrange the schedule, considering that this is a special train for my use?" He was extremely displeased. In the end, the train's departure was postponed. This was a rare instance of self-indulgence on the emperor's part, and (as in the other cases) he probably regretted it the next day.

Another internal matter that disturbed the emperor in 1897 and would have future ramifications was the copper poisoning caused by the mines at Ashio. On March 24 a cabinet committee was established to investigate the situation. The extent of the harm to the environment and the suffering of the inhabitants of the region could hardly be exaggerated. Fish had disappeared from the Watarase River and its tributaries. Innumerable dry and wet fields had been ravaged. In recent years there had been frequent flooding, and the damage increased each year. At every session of the Diet, Tanaka Shōzō (1841–1913), a member of the House of Representatives, described the terrible damage, appealing for preventive measures and relief. However, neither the government nor the mine owners did anything to help the people of the region, and it was feared they might stage a march on Tōkyō to appeal directly to the government.[29]

Shortly before the investigating committee was established, the minister of agriculture and commerce, Enomoto Takeaki, traveled to Ashio in mufti to observe the effects of mineral poisoning. He was so shocked by what he saw that he resigned his post, taking blame for the disaster.[30] The emperor was much upset when he was informed of conditions in Ashio, and on April 7, at his request, Tokudaiji Sanetsune sent letters to the governors of Gumma, Tochigi, Saitama, and Ibaraki Prefectures asking if they thought that the sudden spate of public criticism was occasioned by the damage caused by the flooding of 1896 or if it went back to 1892 and 1893 when the frightening effects of pollution were first discovered.

At the time some observers blamed the disasters on the indiscriminate felling of trees, resulting in landslides that filled the riverbeds. The rivers, unable to flow freely in their normal courses, had broken through the embankments and spread the poison in their water over the land. The governors were requested to reply without concealing anything and appending relevant documents.[31]

As a result of the reports received from the cabinet committee, on May 27 Furukawa Ichibei, the operator of the mines, was issued a set of thirty-seven orders requiring him to provide settling ponds, filter beds, and similar facilities to prevent the mine water from overflowing and to eliminate smoke pollution. He was told that these improvements must be completed within 150 days and that mining operations would be halted until the settling ponds and filter beds were ready. In the event that Furukawa disobeyed these orders, he would be forbidden to engage in further mining.[32]

On November 27 the cabinet, satisfied that the work of the committee investigating the mineral poisoning at Ashio was more or less completed, relieved the committee of its functions, and assigned to the appropriate ministries the supervision of preventive measures and restoration of affected land.[33] Judging from the persistence into the late Meiji era of the issue of copper poisoning, it is obvious that the pollution controls ordered by the government at this time were not strictly enforced. The desire to build a modern, rich country was so strong that the Japanese tended to tolerate environmental pollution, even when it was as extreme as at the Ashio copper mines.

Eleven years earlier, in 1886, Suehiro Tetchō had published *Setchūbai* (Plum Blossoms in the Snow), a work often praised as the finest of the Meiji-period political novels. It is set in 2040, the 173rd year of the reign of Emperor Meiji, and opens with the sounds of cannons and bugles blowing to celebrate the 150th anniversary of the proclamation of the constitution. The accompanying illustrations depict the Tōkyō of the future. It is a city of grim rows of brick buildings from which innumerable tall chimneys emit black smoke. Tetchō wrote enthusiastically, "Telegraph wires spread like spiders' webs, and trains run to and fro to every point of the compass. The electric lamps are so bright that even at night the streets look no different than in broad daylight."[34]

A reader today may shudder at the thought of a city so devoid of amenities and so tainted by industrial pollution, but Tetchō undoubtedly believed that his readers would be delighted by a future rich with the progress represented by chimneys belching smoke; he seems to have thought that the more Tōkyō resembled London, the greatest of the Western cities, the happier the Japanese would be.

The chamberlain Hinonishi Sukehiro recalled:

> Whenever His Majesty made a journey in the Kansai region, a little before the train passed Ōsaka he would say, "We're getting close to the smoke capital. . . . Now we're in the smoke capital." Whenever we approached Ōsaka, he would look out of the window at the landscape. When he saw a great deal of smoke rising, he would be extremely satisfied.[35]

For Emperor Meiji, no less than for Suehiro Tetchō, the "smoke capital" was a term of praise; but the copper mines at Ashio served as a grim reminder of the cost to the environment and to human lives of such progress.

Chapter 49

Another cabinet crisis occurred at the end of 1897. The prime minister, Matsukata Masayoshi, who never paid much attention to the political parties' wishes, tried to push legislation through the Diet without first obtaining the parties' consent. In response to the president of the Privy Council, Kuroda Kiyotaka, who questioned Matsukata's tactics, he replied that he was following instructions from the emperor to devote his every effort to matters of state, without worrying about allies or enemies in the political parties or the reactions of the Diet. A motion of no confidence in the cabinet was proposed in the House of Representatives, and Matsukata's enemies decided to petition for a dissolution of the Diet.[1] He was defeated, faced with opposition even from members of his own cabinet.

On December 25, 1897, Matsukata dissolved the Diet and, taking responsibility for the cabinet's disunity, informed the emperor of his wish to resign. The members of his cabinet made the same request. The emperor asked Matsukata to await further orders, at the same time ordering other ministers not to leave Tōkyō. Undoubtedly he remembered how often it had happened that ministers were off in the remote countryside just when he needed their advice. Absence from Tōkyō was second only to ill health as an excuse for not responding to the emperor's commands.

The emperor realized that dissolution or at least adjournment of the Diet was unavoidable. He also knew that there was no way to alter Matsukata's resolve to resign. On the same day, December 25, he sent Tokudaiji Sanetsune to

Kuroda Kiyotaka's house to explain what had happened and to inform him that he wished to discuss the situation. Kuroda replied that he was ill and asked for three or four days' leave before going to the palace. The emperor seems to have doubted that Kuroda was really ill. Three hours later, Tokudaiji was back at Kuroda's house with another message, this one asking him to report to the palace immediately: the Diet was about to be dissolved and the prime minister had asked to resign. Kuroda, unperturbed, said he would go to the palace on December 28. Tokudaiji returned on the twenty-sixth to inform Kuroda that the emperor was greatly upset by his failure to appear. Kuroda yielded, but only to the extent of going to the palace on December 27. For all the reiterated declarations of absolute loyalty to the throne, the emperor's ministers disregarded his wishes when they found them inconvenient.

While disclaiming any desire to intervene in the choosing of a successor, Matsukata suggested that either Itō Hirobumi or Yamagata Aritomo would be suitable. This crisis, like most of the other changes in prime ministers and cabinet ministers at this time, is no longer in itself of great interest, but the unspoken assumptions are significant. Matsukata, a Satsuma man, having failed as prime minister, suggested that either Itō or Yamagata, both Chōshū men, would make appropriate successors. Although the political parties had a role in the Diet, the party favored by his successor was not an important factor in Matsukata's recommendation. Regardless of Itō's or Yamagata's political allegiance, his qualifications to become prime minister were recognized ability (though not specifically for the tasks immediately confronting the government) and birth in one of the two domains that alternately supplied the chief officers of the state. Although the prospective prime minister's political affiliations were not yet a factor, this situation would soon change.

That night, by command of the emperor, Hijikata Hisamoto, the imperial household minister, sent Itō a telegram asking him to come to the palace the following day. Itō, then in his villa at Ōiso, sent back a message saying that he had not kept up with the situation either at home or abroad since he had resigned from office in the preceding year and feared that if the emperor asked his opinions, he might only mislead the holy wisdom. Besides, he had been suffering of late from an eye complaint. He requested a delay in reporting to the palace.[2]

On December 28 the emperor sent a chamberlain to Kuroda to inform him of his intention of appointing Itō as prime minister. Kuroda was asked to transmit this decision to Itō and, by describing the difficult situation that prevailed in the cabinet, to persuade him to accept the appointment. Kuroda went that day to Ōiso and urged Itō to leave for Tōkyō at once and to comfort the emperor by acceding to his wishes. Itō, moved by these words, agreed.[3]

Itō arrived in Tōkyō on December 29 and went to the palace. The emperor informed Itō why he had been summoned, and Itō replied that he was well aware of the gravity of the situation. He was willing to form a new cabinet.

The year 1898 opened as usual with New Year rituals being performed not by the emperor but by a surrogate. Learning that Itō was suffering from a cold, the emperor sent a chamberlain to inquire after his health and to express the hope that he would render ever greater services to the nation. He sent Itō what was now his standard gift, a dozen bottles of wine together with ten ducks.

Yamagata called on Itō and urged him to display his mettle by forming a cabinet. In his reply, sent the next day, Itō confessed to Yamagata that by nature he was given to going from one extreme to another. He mentioned also that Inoue Kaoru was highly emotional and had a tendency to break down in tears. He feared that these deficiencies might wreck any cabinet he might form. In contrast, when Yamagata served as prime minister, he had displayed his unique ability to balance lenience with stringency. He asked Yamagata's assistance.[4]

On January 8 Itō requested a meeting in the presence of the emperor to discuss the formation of a cabinet. He would, of course, count on Yamagata and Saigō Tsugumichi to continue serving as ministers of the army and navy. He had planned to invite Ōkuma Shigenobu, the leader of the Shimpo-tō, to join the cabinet in order that relations with the political parties be cemented. But at the end of 1897, when he discussed with Ōkuma the possibility of his joining the cabinet, Ōkuma had not readily consented. His price was the post of interior minister, and he asked that three other members of the Shimpo-tō be appointed to major cabinet posts. Itō was unable to accept these demands.[5]

Itō tried next to establish relations with the Jiyū-tō. He approached Itagaki Taisuke, only for him also to demand the post of interior minister in return for his cooperation. Itō rejected this condition, believing that if the head of a political party became interior minister, this would skew the coming election. He accordingly reported to the emperor on January 8 his failure to shore up the new cabinet with party support. Despite this failure, the tense situation in East Asia and many other problems, both domestic and foreign, permitted no delay in forming a government. Itō therefore urged the emperor to summon the *genrō* and have them discuss the situation. Itō would present his views at this meeting.

The meeting took place on January 10. Itō presented a gloomy appraisal of the situation in East Asia. Russia was exerting pressure on China from Siberia and had occupied Liaotung, Dairen, and Port Arthur. France had occupied the Yunnan region in the south of China. Britain controlled the mouth of the Yangtse. Germany had taken possession of Kiang-chou Bay and the Shantung area. British warships were threatening Inch'on. If a quarrel should arise between Britain and Russia, with which country should Japan side? In his opinion, in view of Japan's military unpreparedness and the uncertain state of its finances, the best course would be to remain neutral and preserve its safety.

Yamagata and the other *genrō* supported this conclusion, and the emperor agreed. In the past, the emperor had generally remained silent during discussions conducted in his presence, but he was now outspoken in expressing his views. The *genrō* unanimously recommended that Itō, the only person capable of handling the present crisis, form a new cabinet. They favored retaining from the previous cabinet only the navy and foreign ministers and proposed Inoue Kaoru as finance minister, Katsura Tarō as army minister, Saionji Kinmochi as education minister, and Yoshikawa Akimasa as interior minister. Itō had at last formed a cabinet, and Matsukata resigned on January 12.

In preparation for the general election of the House of Representatives on March 15, the home minister invited prefectural governors to the Interior Ministry to explain to them the importance of the elections. He cited abuses in election procedures and the need to control them in order to enable voters to elect the candidates of their choice. It was all too apparent that previous elections had not been conducted fairly. Votes had been purchased with money, gifts in kind, promissory notes, or property. Voters had been subjected to violence or threats, and there had been disturbances at polling places and at election meetings. All these activities were strictly prohibited, but the abuses had grown increasingly flagrant. Elections were coming up in a month, and the government must see to it that they were properly conducted. Candidates should not have to spend money in order to be elected, nor should voters be subjected to violence or threats.[6] Emergency orders were issued on February 8 prohibiting persons engaged in election activities from carrying guns, spears, or clubs.

The elections resulted in the Jiyū-tō winning 98 seats; the Shimpo-tō, 91 seats; and the Yamashita Club, 48 seats.[7] Sixty-three seats were won by minor parties and independents. The cooperation between the government and the Jiyū-tō, initiated by the appointment of Itagaki as interior minister in the second Itō cabinet, had not yet ended, even though Itō refused to include Itagaki in his new cabinet. After the election the Jiyū-tō demanded Itagaki's inclusion in the cabinet, threatening otherwise to create difficulties in the Diet. But the cabinet threatened to resign if any of its members were dismissed in order to make room for Itagaki. On April 15 Itō sent a letter to the Jiyū-tō refusing to appoint Itagaki and indicating that there would be no further cooperation with his party.[8]

The Diet was convened on May 19. On the twenty-sixth, the government offered a bill to increase taxes on land, income, and saké. Faced with a serious shortage in the balance of payments with foreign countries, the Matsukata cabinet had earlier introduced a bill increasing the taxes on land and saké, but the Diet had been dissolved without the bill's being put to a vote. When the bill was again submitted, this time by the Itō cabinet, it was rejected on June 20 by a crushing margin of 247 to 27, followed by Itō's dissolution of the Diet.[9]

The stalemate between the cabinet and the Diet led to an unexpected development. A new political party, the Kensei-tō (Constitutional Government Party), was formed by a union of the erstwhile enemies, the Jiyū-tō and the Shimpo-tō. At a gathering on June 16 Ōkuma and Itagaki delivered speeches on the urgent reasons for joining the two parties, and on the twenty-first, both parties were dissolved in preparation for the formation of the new party on the following day. The official announcement stated,

> It will soon be ten years since the promulgation of the constitution and the opening of the Diet. During this period the Diet has been dissolved no fewer than five times, and constitutional government has yet to bear fruit. The political parties likewise have made no progress, and as a consequence, the lingering evils of the domain cliques are still frozen solidly. This has shattered the harmony between the government and the people and delayed matters of state, something that all men who love their country deeply deplore. We, in consideration of the situation at home and abroad, have dissolved the Jiyū and Shimpo parties in order to organize one large political party, rallying men of like mind. We hope that renewal and renovation will create a fully constitutional government.[10]

Of the nine points of the new party's program, the most important was the second: in the future, cabinets would be formed by a prime minister chosen from the strongest political party, in place of the prevailing practice of the emperor's choosing as prime minister someone who was from either Satsuma or Chōshū, normally a man who had rendered service at the time of the Restoration.

Itō's first reaction to this program was to initiate plans for a political party of his own, which would consist of businessmen and public-spirited patriots. He quickly received the support of members of his cabinet. They pointed out, however, that in order to appeal to voters in the coming election, Itō would have to deliver speeches all over the country and explain the government's policies. He was also reminded how little time was left for campaigning before the election. Kuroda Kiyotaka promised that if Itō founded a political party, he would accompany him wherever he gave speeches, although he was now so old he would have to hobble around, leaning on a cane.

When Inoue Kaoru visited Yamagata to ask his support, he answered, "It is not improper for people of the same mind to form a political party, but to allow a political party to form a cabinet would be to destroy the history of the Meiji government and to violate the imperial constitution. If this is done, we shall undoubtedly share the fate of countries like Spain and Greece."[11] Yamagata rejected Itō's plan in such strong terms that Kuroda changed his mind about supporting a new party, and Itō himself finally abandoned the project.

After the Kensei-tō had been formed, the army minister, Katsura Tarō, who was resolved to maintain the existing political system, met with Yamagata, Inoue, and Saigō. After expressing regret that Itō intended to resign if his desire to form a political party was rejected, he suggested that if Itō could not deal with the political situation, the *genrō* must step into the breach. If the Diet continued to oppose the government, it could be dissolved, and if necessary, the constitution could also be suspended.[12]

The emperor, deeply disturbed by the situation, summoned a meeting on June 24 with Itō, Kuroda, Yamagata, Saigō, Inoue, and Ōyama Iwao. At the meeting Itō said that the new political party of Ōkuma and Itagaki had a majority in the Diet and that there was no way to avoid asking the two men to form a cabinet. Yamagata and Kuroda strongly opposed Itō, sure that if forming a cabinet were left to Ōyama and Itagaki and their cabinet was based on the program of a political party, this would be a contradiction of the national polity and a gross violation of the spirit of the imperial constitution.

The debate in the emperor's presence continued without reaching a resolution. The emperor grew increasingly apprehensive and summoned Itō after the meeting had ended in order to reveal his own opinions. He thought that while remaining as prime minister, Itō should ask the Jiyū-tō to cooperate with him, as it had in the past. Itō replied that this was no longer possible because of the two parties' merger. He suggested that the best plan was to let Ōkuma and Itagaki take responsibility for dealing with the difficult situation. Itō asked not only to resign but also to return his rank and title.[13]

On June 25 the emperor summoned Yamagata, Kuroda, Ōyama, Saigō, and Inoue. He announced that Itō could not be dissuaded from resigning. According to Itō, the consensus of opinion was that there was no choice but to recommend Ōkuma and Itagaki as his successors. Seven cabinet ministers immediately asked to resign. That night, Itō met Ōkuma and Itagaki privately, briefing them on the extremely critical situation, both internal and external. He said that he had recommended them to the emperor because they controlled a majority in the House of Representatives, which would enable them to pass necessary legislation for dealing with the crisis. He urged them to accept if the emperor asked them to serve. On the following day they informed him that they would not decline the responsibility, heavy though it was. On June 27 the emperor commanded Ōkuma and Itagaki to form a cabinet. The two men vowed to exert themselves to the utmost to repay their debt to the emperor.[14]

On June 28 Ōkuma and Itagaki, at an audience with the emperor, reported that they had completed their selection of cabinet ministers. Looking over the list, the emperor asked questions about the personalities of the men they had chosen. Most were Diet members, and there was no need to ask about their official career, court rank, or decorations, but the emperor wished to know what they were like as human beings. Ōkuma and Itagaki by turns described the different men. When the emperor reached the name of Ozaki Yukio, he expressed surprise, asking how it happened they had recommended as a cabinet member a man who some years earlier had been condemned to disciplinary punishment and who had not yet been pardoned.[15] The next day when Ōkuma and Itagaki visited the palace, the emperor reiterated that the office of cabinet member was of such importance that anyone appointed to this position must perform his duties with the utmost devotion and make no mistakes in dealing with matters of state, perhaps an indirect criticism of Ozaki.

Itō had become convinced that there was no way to prevent the majority party in the Diet from appointing the cabinet. He knew that this would mean the end of the domination of Satsuma and Chōshū and of rule by old friends with whom he had been closely associated since the days of the Restoration. The emperor also was distressed by the new state of affairs. Matsukata later told friends that he had never seen the emperor look so sad.[16]

No sooner did it become apparent that a cabinet controlled by a political party would become a reality than it was predicted that it would not last. This proved to be true of this particular party cabinet: the cabinet was destined to fall apart, not because the members belonged to political parties, but because the beliefs of Ōkuma and Itagaki were irreconcilable. On June 30 the new cabinet was invested by the emperor. Among those sworn in, Ōkuma became both prime minister and foreign minister; Itagaki, home minister; and Ozaki Yukio, education minister.

Shortly after taking office, Ōkuma called a meeting of prefectural governors at which he explained the special features of a party cabinet and promised fair elections and a reform of prefectural administration. He particularly stressed the elections as the bone marrow of constitutional government and said that in order to ensure fair elections, strict controls would be maintained over elections in order to forestall the violence, bribery, intimidation, and the rest that had marred previous elections.[17]

On July 14 Sasaki Takayuki visited the palace with the two princesses who had been left in his care. After the audience granted by the emperor, Sasaki, one of the few people with whom the emperor spoke freely, said that he could imagine how upset the emperor had been by the change in the cabinet. The emperor replied, "The present major change in the cabinet, like a tidal wave that sweeps in a moment over the shore, was of irresistible force. It had been brought about by the times, and that was why I listened to Itō's recommendation and commanded Ōkuma and Itagaki to form a cabinet. I believed at first that because Ōkuma was the head of the Shimpo-tō and Itagaki the president of the Jiyū-tō, the two of them would lead and guide the Kensei-tō and select cabinet appointees. This was definitely not the case. Their strength within their party is nil, and their wishes are paid not the slightest attention. The selection of members of the cabinet was made at party headquarters. Moreover, the Jiyū and the Shimpo factions have yet to resolve their differences. If the Jiyū faction recommends something, the Shimpo faction disapproves, and if the Shimpo faction advocates something, the Jiyū faction is against it. Ōkuma and Itagaki can do nothing about it. They are constantly being manipulated by party members and harassed by their demands. As long as the two of them are at cabinet sessions, everything is peaceful, but once they return to their residences, dozens of party members, relying on their numbers, are there to ask for various favors, and their demands never stop. At first I thought that if I entrusted the situation to Ōkuma and Itagaki, they would suitably reorganize general affairs and would be able to carry out the administration, but I was completely mistaken."[18]

Sasaki asked if, considering the present lamentable state of affairs, the coalition would in the future be able to manage state business. The emperor replied that it was difficult to predict the future, but there were likely to be problems. The worst of all would probably be the Ministry of Education: "People say that Toyama Masakazu, who served as minister and earlier as assistant minister, is a scholar and that Kikuchi Dairoku is a skillful administrator. Hamao Arata apparently had no special ability. They say that the new minister, Ozaki Yukio, is a good match for Hamao, although he may have some ability. The general opinion is that there is not much chance that his coping with problems at the ministry will lead to any advancement in education."[19] The emperor's sarcasm directed at Ozaki Yukio seems to reflect a deep personal dislike.

On July 8 the grand duke Kiril Vladimirovitch, a cousin of Nicholas II, paid a state visit. He was suitably received by the emperor and empress, although such visits had become so common that they no longer aroused much interest at the court. On August 5 Itagaki asked Ōkuma to relinquish his post as foreign minister, claiming that he had been allowed to occupy the post in order to facilitate receiving and entertaining the Russian grand duke. Now that the grand duke's visit had ended, it was time for Ōkuma to give up this second post and reestablish parity between the two parties. Itagaki favored Hoshi Tōru or Ebara Soroku as the new foreign minister. Ōkuma's reluctance to step down caused the first clash within the coalition. The emperor was consulted as the final court of appeal. He thought that Ōkuma should remain as foreign minister. The emperor's decision was, of course, obeyed but deepened the rift between the two factions.

The next clash between the two factions of the Kensei-tō came when the Shimpo faction proposed that the Metropolitan Police Office be abolished. Itagaki composed a statement for the emperor stating the reasons why it should not be abolished. No action was taken. In this and later clashes of opinions, the Jiyū faction, despite its traditions of liberalism, showed itself to be fundamentally more conservative than the Shimpo faction.

On August 11 the Ministry of Education abolished all the various ministerial ordinances, official notices, unofficial notices, directives, private instructions, and so forth that it had issued since 1881 to control freedom of assembly, speech, association, and the like. Explaining this sweeping action, Ozaki Yukio said that many of these ministerial orders had been rendered unnecessary by the enactment of related laws. Other orders, intended to remedy some specific abuse of their day, had become obsolete because of the changes brought about with the passage of time. A few, it is true, still were relevant, but he considered that educational problems were best resolved by school principals, teachers, and other persons engaged in education. Ozaki believed that the ordinances were a burdensome legacy of the past and, by abolishing them, hoped to reform education.[20]

On August 22 Ozaki delivered an address at the concluding ceremonies of the Imperial Educational Society Summer Institute. One remark gained undue prominence: he said that although it was unlikely Japan would ever became a republic, if it did, the candidates for president would likely be from Mitsui and Mitsubishi. This probably was his way of implying that the worship of money had become so prevalent that one day wealth (symbolized by the two giant companies) might rule the nation. These lightly delivered words gave Ozaki's political enemies a golden opportunity for questioning his patriotism. They demanded how the minister of education dared mention the possibility of a republican government in Japan. If this was not intended to destroy the national polity, what was it? The *Tōkyō nichinichi shimbun* harshly attacked Ozaki in the language of righteous indignation. Ozaki, upset that the newspaper account had falsified his words, published the stenographic record of his address in order to correct the newspaper article, but his opponents claimed that he had tampered with the record. The accusations grew ever more hysterical, and Ozaki's speech became a major question both inside and outside the government.[21]

On August 25 Tokudaiji Sanetsune sent word to Ozaki asking for the manuscript of his address. Not having a copy of his extemporaneous remarks, Ozaki submitted instead a clean copy of the stenographic report.[22] The chief chamberlain's request suggests that the emperor, having heard rumors about Ozaki's offensive remarks, wished to examine the words. The emperor also sent Iwakura Tomosada to Ōkuma privately with the message: "Ozaki has delivered a speech about a republic and suchlike matters, arousing public opinion. There is no telling what kind of trouble he may stir up in the future. One cannot trust such a minister. You should get him to resign at once."

Overcome with awe and trepidation, Ōkuma wished to go to the palace and personally explain the situation to the emperor, but Iwakura said, "His Majesty has already made up his mind. There is no point in your speaking to him. If you have anything to say to His Majesty, tell me. I will transmit it for you." Ōkuma asked Iwakura, "Is there no confidence in me either?" Iwakura answered, "It's not for me to say." Iwakura returned to the palace where he reported to the emperor his conversation with Ōkuma. The emperor said, "The matter I mentioned concerns only the minister of education. It has nothing to do with any other minister. Report this, and inform them all of the situation. And see to it that they get Ozaki to submit his resignation afterward."[23]

The emperor's reactions to one unfortunate phrase in Ozaki's speech is likely to strike modern readers as excessive. Granted that a mention of even the possibility that some day a republic might exist in Japan was repugnant to Meiji as a threat to the unbroken line of emperors, surely it should have been apparent that Ozaki's ironic comment was directed not against the monarchy but against business interests whose sole consideration was money. Meiji seems to have disliked Ozaki ever since his participation in the 1887 incident. We know of the emperor's reactions on this occasion because they are preserved in Sasaki Takayuki's diary. Years earlier, this diary had recorded the emperor's criticism of various men around him, but he had never before expressed his dislike so openly.

The emperor's command created problems for a parliamentary government. If he had been the ruler of an absolute monarchy, he could have ordered Ozaki's head chopped off or banished him without trial to some distant island; but Japan had a constitution and a cabinet that consisted not of sycophants but of members of a political party with a program. Iwakura feared that Ōkuma might cite this as a reason for not obeying the emperor's command to get rid of Ozaki but discovered to his relief that Ōkuma was quite ready to obey the emperor.

The emperor secretly sent Iwakura and Tokudaiji to inform Katsura Tarō, the army minister, of his command to Ōkuma. Katsura passed the word on to the navy minister, and they debated the next step. If the emperor were to dismiss a minister without waiting for the prime minister's request, the newspapers would be sure to feature it, and people would wonder what lay behind the dismissal.

Soon there were rumors that Ozaki had been denounced by the chamberlains and others close to the emperor. Sasaki Takayuki bluntly asked Tokudaiji if this was true. The latter replied that although he had been greatly upset by Ozaki's address, he had discreetly refrained from mentioning it to the emperor. However, the interior minister, Itagaki Taisuke, had been so shocked by the impropriety of Ozaki's words that he had demanded Ōkuma take action against him.

An editorial appeared in the reformist newspaper *Yorozu chōhō* denouncing fake royalists and fake loyal ministers, in this way referring to the "patriots" who had attacked Ozaki. Takada Sanae, an officer of the Ministry of Education, also delivered a speech along the lines of the *Yorozu chōhō*'s editorial. People guessed that Ozaki was behind the speech, and Itagaki ordered the Metropolitan Police Office to investigate. Although the police were unlikely to find positive proof of collusion, Itagaki was convinced that the *Yorozu chōhō*'s editorial and Takada's speech stemmed ultimately from Ozaki, and he pressed Ōkuma to punish him.

Itagaki, not obtaining satisfaction from Ōkuma, denounced Ozaki to the emperor, which led to the emperor's command that Ōkuma get rid of Ozaki. When Sasaki asked Tanaka Mitsuaki, the imperial household minister, if it was true that Ozaki was dismissed because he had been denounced to the emperor by a chamberlain, he answered that the direct cause was Itagaki's denunciation, and behind Itagaki were Katsura Tarō, the minister of the army, and Kawakami Sōroku, the chief of the general staff. Tanaka added that he had frequently been approached by Katsura and Kawakami to do something about Ozaki, but he always refused, saying that he did not think this was proper for someone in his position.

Everyone whom Sasaki questioned agreed that it was Itagaki who had denounced Ozaki to the emperor.[24] He had been incited by the military, whose aim was not simply the dismissal of Ozaki but the replacement of the Ōkuma cabinet by one headed by Yamagata. Katsura, the army minister, intimidated cabinet members by declaring (without presenting any evidence) that Ozaki's "republic speech" had caused a disquieting atmosphere to spread among the armed forces throughout the country. Itagaki, the interior minister, sent out false reports of popular unrest.[25]

Katsura recalled in his memoirs that he had urged Ōkuma to persuade Ozaki to make an abject apology to the emperor as soon as possible. He was sure that the emperor, in his magnanimity, would not hold a grudge against Ozaki. He also warned that any delay in apologizing might implicate the prime minister in the responsibility. Ōkuma told this to Ozaki, who went at once to the palace and apologized profusely for his crime. He made the mistake, however, of attempting to explain what had led him to speak as he had, sounding as if he were trying to justify his comments. This did not please the emperor. Ozaki finally resigned. Katsura wrote that he regretted not having been able to apologize for Ozaki. But this is unlikely, considering that it was Katsura who had deliberately inflated the scandal so as to get Ozaki dismissed.[26]

Once Ozaki was out of the way, the next step was to appoint a successor as education minister. The two factions of the Kensei-tō could not agree. Itagaki proposed the educator Ebara Soroku, with the proviso that if Ōkuma did not favor Ebara, he could appoint anyone else he liked as education minister but, in return, would resign as foreign minister and give the position to Hoshi Tōru. Ōkuma brushed aside these suggestions. He went to the palace to report his choice of education minister, Inukai Tsuyoshi. The emperor approved, and Inukai was inducted on October 27. Ōkuma showed no sign of resigning as foreign minister.

Itagaki, predictably, was furious. At an audience with the emperor, he denounced Ōkuma's bad faith. He declared that in view of Inukai's appointment as education minister, he and two other members of the cabinet had no choice but to resign. On October 29 at a mass meeting of the former Jiyū-tō, members voted to dissolve the existing Kensei-tō and to form a new party with the same name, from which members of the Shimpo-tō would be excluded.[27] A memorial was submitted to the emperor detailing Itagaki's grievances.

The emperor was distressed by this development. Reluctant to lose Itagaki from the cabinet, he sent Chamberlain Iwakura Tomosada to ask Itagaki to remain. Unfortunately, the emperor's usual adviser, Itō Hirobumi, was in China. Yamagata and Inoue also were out of Tōkyō. For want of better advice, he turned to Kuroda and Matsukata for help in dealing with the split in the

Kensei-tō. He feared that if the three Jiyū-tō cabinet members who had resigned were replaced with Shimpo-tō men, the Jiyū-tō would create trouble. The question was, should a new cabinet be formed with both parties represented? Or would it be better to accept resignations from the entire cabinet and organize an new one?

Ōkuma, unwilling to resign, wanted the cabinet to continue in power with replacements from the Shimpo-tō for the three Jiyū-tō men who had resigned. On October 29 he asked for an audience with the emperor to explain his views. The emperor did not approve of Ōkuma's plan, favoring instead Katsura Tarō's suggestion that Itagaki be persuaded to remain. Kuroda, however, wanted to end the party cabinet, and was delighted that Ozaki's speech had afforded an opportunity. When Itagaki announced his resignation, Kuroda opposed allowing Ōkuma to remain as prime minister. He enlisted the help of the ministers of the army and the navy and finally succeeded in making Ōkuma resign on the thirty-first, citing (as usual) illness. His resignation was followed by that of all cabinet members belonging to the Shimpo-tō. Only the nonparty army and navy ministers were left. The emperor, accepting the resignations, asked the assistance of Kuroda, Matsukata, and Ōyama Iwao in planning future policy.[28] The first party cabinet had failed.

On November 1 Yamagata returned to Tōkyō and, on the following day, was summoned to the palace along with Kuroda, Saigō, Matsukata, and Ōyama to consider forming a new cabinet. The emperor posed several questions: Should a nonparty cabinet be formed and attempt, as in the past, to get the Diet to pass its legislation without depending on party assistance? Would passing legislation be easier if a new cabinet were formed of a combination of men from the strongest political party and elder statesmen? Not directly responding to the questions, Yamagata replied that he thought that everything depended on the emperor's choice of a man to form a cabinet.

When faced with difficult decisions, the emperor had often turned for advice to Itō, and this time was no exception. An urgent telegram was sent to Itō in China asking him to return immediately. Kuroda, afraid that when Itō got back, he might again advise appointing Ōkuma as the prime minister, persuaded Yamagata to join in recommending—without waiting for Itō's return—that Ōkuma be dismissed immediately and a new prime minister appointed. The emperor finally agreed, with the understanding that Yamagata and Kuroda would inform Itō what had transpired.

Yamagata was asked to form a cabinet on November 5, even though Ōkuma had not yet formally resigned. Still hoping for Itō's support, Ōkuma sent urgent telegrams to China. Kuroda and Yamagata, on the other hand, recommended all possible haste in appointing a new cabinet in order that it would be functioning when the next session of the Diet began; they emphasized the need to have a cabinet that was above party lines. Believing that the old Jiyū-tō consisted

essentially of uncomplicated, well-meaning men who could easily be manipulated, they hoped that members, now Ōkuma's enemies, would support the
new cabinet.[29] On November 8 Yamagata informed the emperor of his choice
of cabinet members. They included Aoki Shūzō as foreign minister, Matsukata
Masayoshi as finance minister, and Saigō Tsugumichi as interior minister.
Ōkuma, along with his cabinet (except Katsura Tarō), resigned the same day.

As far as the emperor was concerned, 1898 was not a good year. Apart from
the complicated political developments, in which he was more deeply involved
than ever, the year was marked by his continuing concern about the crown
prince's health and education. The prince was twenty-one by Japanese count
this year, meaning that he had attained his majority; but his education had
been seriously delayed by repeated bouts of illness. Itō recognized that improving the prince's health was a priority, but he insisted that the prince's mental
development not be neglected either. He therefore urged that the prince attend
sessions of the Diet as a way of learning about political and military concerns.[30]
The prince showed signs of taking his new responsibilities seriously, and in June
he gave his first reception to foreign diplomats, shaking hands and graciously
conversing.

On occasion, however, the emperor had cause to admonish his son. He was
disturbed to learn that the crown prince had been telling people he intended
to fire members of his staff because they were incompetent. The emperor reprimanded the prince, saying that this was not the proper way to treat his staff,
that if he was dissatisfied with their service, he should report this privately to
the imperial household minister and await orders from the emperor.[31]

The crown prince was promoted to the ranks of major in the army and
lieutenant commander in the navy. The emperor had refused to permit this
promotion the previous year, saying that the prince had not been in grade long
enough to warrant it, but this year he yielded.[32] Needless to say, the prince did
not perform the duties associated with these military ranks, although his health
improved noticeably late in the year.[33]

Probably the emperor's most enjoyable experience this year was observing
the Grand Maneuvers held in the Ōsaka area. He rose every morning at five
and, regardless of the weather, traveled to the "front" to observe the mock
warfare staged between the South Army (foreign invaders seeking to capture
Ōsaka) and the North Army defending the city. After the maneuvers had ended,
he expressed his satisfaction but, warning that rapidly changing world conditions did not permit a relaxation of preparedness, he exhorted the officers to
make an even greater effort.[34]

Unfortunately, we do not have a more personal expression of the emperor's
feelings. The poems he composed this year, though skillfully expressed, are
conventional in sentiment, but perhaps the following *tanka* was meant to convey private emotions:

samidare no	A day that is spent
oto nomi kikite	Listening only to the sound
kurasu hi wa	Of the summer rain—
miya no uchi dani	How depressing it has been,
ibusekarikeri	Even within the palace.[35]

Chapter 50

The long struggle to end extraterritoriality at last bore fruit in 1899, bringing Japan equality among the nations of the world. As far as Emperor Meiji was concerned, however, the most important events of his forty-eighth year were personal and not related to treaty revision.

The year began inauspiciously with the death in January of the last-born of his children, Princess Takiko. She died on the same day, exactly two years later, as Dowager Empress Eishō. Flags were flown at half-mast; teaching at public and private schools was canceled; and the usual order was issued prohibiting singing and dancing in Tōkyō and environs. However, the emperor's New Year poem, on the subject "Smoke from a Country Chimney," revealed no trace of grief.

This year, for the first time, the crown prince participated in the first poetry meeting, an indication that having attained his majority, he was expected to compose poetry. The prince's education would be much discussed during the year in terms of how to increase the content of his studies without impairing his health. His relations with his father remained formal and distant. Even when he and his sisters visited the palace, the emperor rarely granted them an audience. In February, when the two princesses were about to leave for Kamakura to escape the Tōkyō winter, they were taken to the palace to say goodbye to their father. He refused to allow them into his presence because of a cold, but the empress, although she was also ill, insisted on seeing them.[1]

The court ladies found it impossible to understand why the emperor, whose love for his daughters was demonstrated even in such trivial matters as his care over the patterns of the kimonos he gave them, persisted in refusing to see them. They often pleaded with him to see his daughters from time to time, but he never took their advice.

Sasaki Takayuki explained the emperor's apparent coldness in terms of his Confucian education. He had revered the Chinese classics ever since childhood and had taken to heart their accounts of why certain countries prospered and others perished. His refusal to take the advice of court ladies may have been the result of reading the examples of disasters that had occurred when an emperor gave heed to his women. Sasaki admitted that the emperor may have been excessively cautious and at times seemed to reject good advice even from those closest to him, but Sasaki believed this was preferable to allowing the court to be swayed by opinions emanating from the women's quarters of the palace. The emperor might even be said to be rectifying a long-standing evil. Perhaps Sasaki was correct, but Meiji seems to have taken the lessons of history too literally.

In February 1899 the emperor's personal physicians recommended that he spend time in Kyōto for his health. They asked Tokudaiji Sanetsune, the chief chamberlain, to persuade the emperor, but he was unsuccessful. Next, they asked the imperial household minister, Tanaka Mitsuaki (1843–1939), who, when received into the emperor's presence, bluntly reported that the physicians believed the emperor was becoming obese. They warned that if he did not overcome his corpulence by exercise, the overweight was likely to affect his heart. Tanaka spoke with old-fashioned eloquence: "Your Majesty is the lord of the nation, the bulwark of the myriads of your people. Your body is Your Majesty's own, but at the same time, it is not yours alone; it is not solely for Your Majesty's sake that you must take good care of your body but for the sake of the people of the whole nation. However, in recent years you have allowed yourself to become exhausted under the pressure of state business. As long as Your Majesty remains in Tōkyō, there is little chance of your enjoying a moment's respite. I have heard that in the twenty-eighth year of your reign, when negotiations to end the war with China had been concluded, you traveled from Hiroshima to Kyōto and rested there for a month. During that time you exercised morning and evening, and your health was extremely good. No doubt it is because Your Majesty was born in Kyōto and its mountains, rivers and landscapes are all familiar to Your Majesty that the site is particularly conducive to your health. It is true that thirty years have passed since you first took up residence in the castle of Tōkyō, but the castle formerly belonged to the shogunate, and even though the surroundings are not lacking in spacious gardens and charm, this is not Your Majesty's old abode. It is, moreover, so strictly guarded as to make it difficult for you to enjoy a leisurely stroll. Last year, when you supervised the special army maneuvers on the Settsu-Izumi plain, Grand Headquarters were in Ōsaka, a mere twenty or twenty-five miles from Kyōto, yet you did not go there. People at the time wondered why Your Majesty went to Ōsaka but not to Kyōto. They asked, 'Doesn't His Majesty love Kyōto?' But your long stay in 1895 demonstrated this was not the case. I humbly implore Your Majesty to take the advice of your physicians, and go to Kyōto for a vacation. You will surely regain your health."

Tanaka knew that his words were unwelcome. The emperor, his face coloring with anger, said, "I did not reject the chief physician's advice without good reason. Kyōto is my old home, a place I have always loved, as you know. But just because I love the place, is it right for me to take a vacation there? It may be good for my health, but what will happen if state business falls hopelessly behind because I am not here? Last year, when I went to Ōsaka to supervise the Grand Maneuvers, I deliberately did not go to Kyōto. I was afraid I might get carried away by my love for Kyōto and, once settled there, might not wish to return to Tōkyō. Couldn't you and your colleagues understand that? What you ask of me, of course, is not unreasonable, but if I should neglect state business for even one day, the repercussions would affect every official. This is why I cannot neglect state business on my own account, not even for a single day. The one thing incumbent on me is to carry out diligently the Way of the emperor, fulfilling my Heaven-appointed mission. If this should bring about my death, I ask nothing more. I shall be content."

His expression gradually softened as he spoke. He went on, "You must stop worrying about me. From now on I will exercise and do what I can to restore my health. Don't worry so much about me any more." Afterward, he occasionally took a stroll in his private garden or performed exercises, but before long he abandoned these efforts.[2]

The emperor was sensitive about his weight. According to Chamberlain Viscount Hinonishi Sukehiro, the emperor stopped reading newspapers because an article in the *Chūō shimbun* had stated that the emperor weighed more than 170 pounds. Angered by the article, he said, "It wouldn't bother me if what they printed was the truth, but I can't abide lies. I'll never look at a newspaper again."[3]

All the same, a poem composed in 1905 indicates that the emperor continued to read newspapers, at least occasionally, although their mistakes continued to irritate him:

minahito no	How good it would be
miru niibumi ni	If in the newspapers that
yo no naka no	Everybody reads
atonashigoto wa	They didn't write such falsehoods
kakazu mo aranan	About doings in this world.[4]

The emperor's weight was clearly related to his loss of interest in riding, which in the past had been his favorite diversion. The only thing that seemed to interest him now was his work. It is not clear how many hours he actually spent each day in his office, but it does not seem that, like his contemporary Emperor Franz Josef of Austria, he was at his desk from morning to late at night perusing official documents. He continued to drink heavily, although by this time he had switched from saké to wine. His appetite remained good, judging from the menus of the dinners he offered visiting dignitaries.[5]

The personal matter that most occupied the emperor's attention at this time was finding a bride for the crown prince, who in 1899 became twenty years old. The emperor hoped that a girl could be found in the imperial family, but if there was not one who would make a suitable bride in that class, girls of the high aristocracy might also be considered. If even this enlargement of the search failed to uncover a likely bride, one might be sought among girls whose fathers were *kōshaku*.[6] As far back as 1891, the emperor had asked Tokudaiji Sanetsune to send to the Takanawa Palace as playmates for Princesses Masako and Fusako some girls of the upper classes who were of the right age to marry the crown prince. He further directed Sasaki Takayuki to examine the appearance and personality of each. One candidate stood out, Princess Sachiko, the daughter of Prince Sadanaru, the commanding general of the Tenth Division. Shimoda Utako, the head mistress of the Peeresses' School, recommended her strongly, as did the imperial household minister, who described her in a report to the emperor. It seemed certain that she would be chosen as the crown prince's bride.

In December 1896 the emperor and empress visited Prince Sadanaru's house for a look at the princess, but the first official meeting devoted to the subject of her suitability as a bride for the crown prince did not take place until February 1899.[7] During the discussion, it was discovered that Princess Sachiko had suffered appendicitis two years earlier, and although she had recovered completely, the medical report of the palace doctors mentioned hearing a vesicular murmur in her right chest. This caused some fear about her health, but most of the physicians believed that she was likely to outgrow the problem in two or three years.[8] The emperor, however, was distressed by the news, fearing that this defect in the princess's health might threaten the continuation of the imperial line. On March 22, 1899, he sent the imperial household minister to Prince Sadanaru to announce that the engagement had been broken.

The crown prince does not seem to have been disappointed by this development; indeed, he may not even have been aware a search had been conducted. In any case, he had not completely recovered from his serious illness of 1895, and he was doing poorly in his studies. The prince was capricious and difficult to please, as his servants complained. The emperor was also annoyed by the prince's infatuation with the West. Even though his command of traditional learning was by no means assured, he loved to sprinkle French words in his conversations.[9] His fondness for the West may have been inspired by the decorations he began to receive at this time, including the Order of the Golden

Fleece from Spain, the Légion d'Honneur from France, and the Order of the Elephant from Denmark.[10]

The most striking feature of the crown prince's activities at this time was the frequency of his visits to his villas in Hayama and Numazu. His avoidance of Tōkyō, which became almost a mania in later years, was perhaps occasioned by dislike for the court solemnity that was so carefully cultivated by the emperor and his advisers.

On August 28, 1899, the emperor was the host of a banquet to celebrate the revision of the treaties, which had become effective on August 4. Toasts were offered to the health of the rulers of all countries represented at the gathering, and the emperor and empress shook hands with the guests. Extraterritoriality ended not with a bang but with the popping of champagne corks. This should have been the occasion for nationwide celebration, but the day passed with only a subdued awareness of the occasion's importance.

Although many foreign residents had feared the worst when the protection afforded them by consular courts had ended, there were no mass arrests, no raids by Japanese policemen armed with books of minute regulations, no reports of foreigners being tortured. As time passed, the old fears proved to have been groundless, and the foreigners began to wonder why they had ever supposed that without the shield of extraterritoriality, they would be cruelly treated. But even after the new era had begun, it was not easy for foreigners to discard their feelings of superiority, and many Japanese had become embittered by the efforts they had been required to make in order to prove to foreigners that they were qualified to run their own country. As one British scholar commented, "Attitudes had become fixed and too much had been said which could not be forgotten."[11] That may be why the end of extraterritoriality did not bring many overt expressions of joy.

On August 21 it was decided that the crown prince would marry Sadako, the fourth daughter of *kōshaku* Kujō Michitaka, but that the uncertain condition of the prince's health would necessitate a delay of the marriage until the spring of the following year. The crown prince was not informed of this decision until February 1900, when the emperor sent Iwakura Tomosada to Hayama with a terse message informing the prince of the name of the bride chosen for him.[12]

Erwin Baelz, one of the physicians serving the imperial family, wrote on March 23, 1900:

> Important conference today about the crown prince, that is to say about his state of health, and whether this will allow of his marriage in May. Together with Hashimoto and Oka, I agreed that it would, though there are some small counter-indications. He has not by a long way regained the weight of last year. No reference is, however, to be made to this fact in the report to the Emperor, who would have liked to defer the marriage till the body weight has been fully recovered. Marquis Ito and Prince

Arisugawa, and the members of the crown prince's entourage in general, are of opinion that the marriage must not be any longer delayed—the determination being (oriental customs notwithstanding) that he is not to touch any other woman before his marriage. In view of all the circumstances, both general and particular, I therefore agreed that a prompt marriage is likely to have a good effect.[13]

In October 1889 the crown prince traveled by warship from Numazu to Kōbe, Hiroshima, Shōdojima, Etajima, and other places in the Inland Sea region. He would embark on an even more ambitious tour of Kyūshū a year later. These travels acquainted the prince with the country he would one day rule and strengthened ties with his future subjects, but they were by no means as arduous or important as the *junkō* of the early part of Meiji's reign. By this time, travel had become much easier and industrialization had advanced. The sights the prince visited were typified by the steelworks in Yawata and the Mitsubishi shipyard in Nagasaki.

The marriage of Crown Prince Yoshihito and Kujō Sadako took place on May 10, 1900. On May 8 the emperor sent the crown prince a set of ceremonial robes and a sword of state. Even as the prince was receiving these gifts, Yanagihara Naruko, the prince's biological mother, happened to pay a visit. The prince asked her to thank the emperor. It is reported that when the prince first learned that he was Naruko's son, he expressed surprise and dismay, having always assumed he was the child of the empress.[14] This story circulated among the court ladies and even reached Naruko's ears. She had been the prettiest and most intelligent of Meiji's concubines, but she was blamed (and blamed herself) for the crown prince's physical infirmity. Her name hardly appears in the pages of the chronology of Meiji's reign.[15]

On May 9, the day before the marriage, the empress awarded Sadako the Order of the Sacred Crown, First Class, the highest decoration for which a woman was eligible. In celebration of the occasion, the emperor and empress presented the city of Tōkyō with 80,000 yen and Kyōto with 20,000 yen, to be used for education.[16] The emperor also presented Fukuzawa Yukichi, the central figure of the Japanese enlightenment, with 50,000 yen and a rescript expressing appreciation of his contribution to education.

The following day at dawn, the marriage was reported to the palace sanctuary. At 8:40 the prince and his bride worshiped in the sanctuary. The prince offered a declaration to the gods, and the couple drank ritual saké before the altar. The master of ceremonies reported to the emperor and empress the completion of the marriage rites, and army and navy guns fired salutes. At 10:40 the emperor, in ceremonial attire, appeared with the empress inside the Hall of Audiences. The prince and princess were ushered by the master of ceremonies into the imperial presence. The emperor and empress offered cups of saké to the prince and his bride.

The ceremonies were now concluded, and at 11:20 the prince and princess boarded a carriage for the crown prince's palace. The crowd outside the main palace gate was so dense that for twenty minutes their carriage could make no headway, and it was with difficulty that a path wide enough for the carriage to pass was cleared. The emperor sent the chief chamberlain to the crown prince's palace with the Supreme Order of the Chrysanthemum. After the prince and princess had partaken of a ritual offering, they returned to the palace, where they ate a meal with the emperor and empress. At 4:30 the imperial family appeared in the Phoenix Hall to receive congratulations from members of the nobility, high-ranking officers, and the diplomatic corps.[17]

Excitement over the royal marriage had hardly died down when Yamagata Aritomo, who had often expressed the desire to resign as prime minister, on May 24 again asked the emperor's permission. He pointed out that he had served for a year and a half, during which time the revised treaties had been put into effect. He believed that future prime ministers should be men who were well acquainted with conditions abroad. He himself, though lacking this qualification, had accepted the post of prime minister because of the disturbed situation prevailing in the government after the fall of the Ōkuma cabinet; but now that the political world was peaceful and no crisis loomed, he asked to be relieved of his post.

The emperor repeatedly tried to persuade Yamagata to change his mind, but he absolutely refused to remain in office. The emperor, at last resigned to losing Yamagata, sent word to Itō Hirobumi that he wished him to accept the post. Itō refused, saying he was unable to accept the command, even though it came from the emperor. In his opinion, a cabinet could be formed constitutionally only with the Diet's approval, and the government was obliged to act in cooperation with the political parties. Unlike Yamagata, he could not issue orders like a general in the field, and any misstep on his part might well involve the throne.

The emperor next commanded Matsukata Masayoshi to assume the post of prime minister temporarily, in addition to his post as finance minister. Matsukata refused, proposing instead Katsura Tarō, the army minister; but the emperor could not agree to this suggestion because it would certainly exacerbate the existing rivalry between the army and the navy.

Just at this time, the court learned of disturbances in China. The emperor, deeply concerned, sent a message on May 31 to Yamagata saying that he was well aware how strongly Yamagata desired to resign his post but believed that it would be highly inadvisable to change prime ministers at such a time. He asked Yamagata to postpone his resignation. Yamagata replied that the disturbances in North China were nothing more than the temporary uprisings of ignorant peasants and were not to be taken seriously. They certainly were not important enough to change his mind about resigning. He agreed, however, to remain in office for another month or two if no successor had been found.[18]

Yamagata vastly underestimated the importance of the unrest in North China, known in the West as the Boxer Rebellion.[19] The emperor, who seems to have had a better grasp than Yamagata of the seriousness of the situation in China, fell back on Yamagata's offer to remain in office for the time being.

It took some 45,000 troops[20] (about half of them Japanese) from eight countries to suppress what Yamagata had belittled as a minor uprising. Tens of thousands of Chinese died in the fighting. The rebellion—more properly termed a war[21]—was a major conflict between China and eight foreign powers. Even more important, it was a direct cause of the Anglo-Japanese Alliance of 1902 and the Russo-Japanese War of 1904/1905.

The Chinese name for the rebels, *i-ho-t'uan* (Righteous and Harmonious League), indicates that unlike uprisings in the past whose aim had mainly been to set a new ruler on the throne of China, its members believed that they were fighting a crusade for higher ideals. They were sure that the only way to achieve their goal was to rid China of both foreigners and Chinese infected with Christianity.[22] Not all the rebels (referred to as "bandits" in the documents of the time) were fanatics, but most believed that they were protected by the Chinese gods. They killed without mercy, convinced of the justice of their cause. In the course of the rebellion, they killed some 250 European missionaries, many foreign military, and perhaps 23,000 Chinese Christians.[23]

The rebellion was the most recent of a series that had broken out during the nineteenth century as discontent mounted with both the corrupt Manchu regime and the repeated acts of humiliation imposed by the foreign powers. The biggest disturbance, known as the T'ai P'ing Rebellion, lasted from 1851 to 1864 and cost an estimated 20 million people their lives. The T'ai P'ing Rebellion had for its ideology a quasi Christianity that might be described as primitive communism. All property was to be owned in common by believers. Men and women enjoyed equal rights. Prostitution and slavery were prohibited, as were foot binding, gambling, opium, liquor, and tobacco. Such ideals (many adopted by the Boxers) suggest the discontent aroused by prevailing conditions in Chinese society. The T'ai P'ing Rebellion was put down only with great difficulty, and it might have succeeded had the foreign powers not intervened.

Another revolt, this one by members of a Buddhist sect called the White Lotus,[24] raged from 1861 to 1863 in Shantung Province, a part of China that had not been involved in the T'ai P'ing Rebellion. The Boxer Rebellion also originated in Shantung, from where it spread to other parts of North China. It was based on religious beliefs, a combination of devotion to traditional gods and a hatred of Christianity which, the members believed, had destroyed village peace and harmony. The Boxers were fervently supported by the impoverished peasantry, but relatively few of the literati of the region, even if they shared the peasants' hatred of foreign religion, became involved, perhaps because they could not renounce the pacific ideals of Confucius, a native of Shantung.

The Boxers' hatred of Christian converts seems to have stemmed from the ruthlessness with which the latter, carried away by their religion, had smashed "idols" and erected churches, sometimes on the sites of shrines worshiped by the majority of the villagers.[25] The division between Christians and non-Christians had altered the structure of village life, and resentment of the changes had led to the violence directed against the "foreign devils" and Chinese converts to Christianity.[26]

The violence in Shantung Province began in 1897 with the murder of two German missionaries. The German government profited by this incident to force the Chinese in 1898 to grant them a ninety-nine-year lease on Tsingtao and an area around Kiaochow Bay. In 1898 the British, benefiting by the concession to Germany, took over Weihaiwei on the northern coast of Shantung from the Japanese, who had been holding it since the end of the Sino-Japanese War as security against payment of the indemnity agreed on at Shimonoseki. These developments provoked all the greater antiforeign activity, which spread from Shantung to neighboring Hopei.

In the villages, people formed bands intended to protect the local shrines from attacks by Christians. It was expected that the gods would in return protect the villagers, and altars were erected where the worshipers might receive mysterious powers from the gods. Those who were thus endowed were supremely confident of victory, sure that the foreigners' weapons would be powerless to harm them.[27] As preparation for the forthcoming struggle, they threw themselves into boxing and other martial sports but scorned using foreign guns.

The Boxer leaders resembled members of the Shinpūren and similar groups in Japan who had been committed to destroying foreign influence. Some recent historians have expressed admiration for the Boxers' courage in resisting foreigners who threatened the traditional Chinese way of life. Xenophobia, however, is not a virtue, and it should not be forgotten that most of the Boxers' victims were Chinese peasants.

On May 30, 1900, the foreign minister, Aoki Shūzō, presented to the emperor a report on the activities of the "bandits" in North China. Aoki had been informed earlier that month by the American secretary of state of the murder of the German missionaries by the Boxers.[28] Aoki's report (not mentioned in his memoirs) described how once China's weakness had been exposed by defeat in the Sino-Japanese War, the European powers, demanding concessions, had leased territories that soon developed into strategic bases. Although there had formerly been a strong progressive faction in the Chinese government, aggressive actions by the foreigners had enabled the conservative faction, which demanded expulsion of the foreigners, to seize control of the government under the reactionary empress dowager, Tz'u-hsi; the powerless emperor was confined to his palace.

Manifestations of hatred, whether on the level of insults to foreigners encountered in the street or actual violence, became frequent. The government was reportedly planning to close the ports and drive out the barbarians. It may have seemed to the Japanese like a reenactment of their own past of forty years earlier; and just as the loyalists had joined in the cry *sonnō jōi*, the Boxers cried "Save the Ch'ing and destroy the foreigners." This apparent profession of devotion to the Manchu monarchy pleased the government,[29] but when the Boxers cried "Save the Ch'ing," they were urging the rescue not of the Manchu dynasty but of China itself from the hated foreigners.[30]

On June 6 Aoki received from Tei Nagayasu, the Japanese consul in Tientsin,[31] a description of the rebellion's mounting intensity. The Chinese government, doing nothing to calm the situation, gradually began to express its support of the rebels. Reports reached Japan of Russian troops heading to China from Siberia and of German troops about to arrive from Tsingtao. A member of the Japanese legation was killed by the rebels, and the Japanese felt that they could not merely stand by. The cabinet, meeting on June 15, decided to send infantry, artillery, cavalry, and engineering troops to protect the lives of Japanese citizens in China. The emperor at once approved.[32]

Ships of the "allies"[33] had by this time assembled off Taku, the port of Tientsin. On June 17 the allied fleet opened fire on the Chinese batteries. The ostensible purpose of this (and subsequent military actions) was to save the lives of nationals trapped in Peking, but the Chinese were infuriated, and the government decided to use the Boxers to drive out the foreigners and Chinese Christians.

On June 19 Japanese ships under the command of Vice Admiral Tōgō Heihachirō, in cooperation with the other allies, occupied the batteries at Taku. The Chinese Foreign Ministry at once sent messages to the ministers of all countries represented in Peking, ordering them to leave the city in twenty-four hours; they would be escorted to Tientsin by Chinese troops. On the following day the German minister was assaulted and killed by Chinese soldiers while on his way to the Foreign Ministry. This made the foreigners (who had earlier agreed to leave for Tientsin) doubt the protection promised by the Chinese government. They decided to withdraw to their legations and defend themselves until reinforcements arrived.[34]

On June 21 the emperor of China issued a rescript opening hostilities with the allies. The emperor declared that although China had always treated the foreigners well, the foreigners had responded by occupying Chinese territory and menacing and robbing Chinese citizens. Their wanton actions had caused patriots to burn churches and kill Christians. The government had done its utmost to protect the foreigners despite their outrageous behavior, but not showing the slightest gratitude, they had used force to compel the Chinese to abandon the forts at Taku. The emperor declared he had vowed, swallowing his tears, that rather than live and endure such humiliation, he would use all the strength available to him in fighting a war with the foreigners. He hoped that patriots would join in the war or at least provide the expenses.[35]

On June 29 the emperor issued a completely contradictory rescript calling for suppression of the rebels and the resumption of friendly relations with foreign countries. It was said that the earlier rescript had been dictated by Prince Tuan and that the emperor's real sentiments were in the later rescript.[36] But the second rescript seems to have been ignored: the fighting continued, and the siege of the legations lasted for about two months until Peking was relieved by the allies.[37]

In the meantime, Boxer forces, admitted to Peking by command of the empress dowager, went on a rampage, burning churches and foreigners' houses and searching for Christian converts and others who had associated with foreigners, slaughtering all they found. The legations were under constant attack, and some of the buildings were burned, but the foreigners did not capitulate.

On July 3 the emperor of China sent a telegram to Emperor Meiji asking him to intercede in order to restore order. The opening salutation revealed that he appealed to Meiji as his equal, and he cited the mutual dependence "as close as lips and teeth" that joined China and Japan. He expressed profound grief that a member of the Japanese legation had been killed, but he added that even while the Chinese authorities were in the process of apprehending and punishing the guilty persons, the foreign powers had attacked and seized the Taku forts. He warned of a confrontation between East and West and asked if the emperor thought that the covetous, "tiger-like" glares of the Western countries were directed only at China. If by some chance China proved unable to withstand the foreigners' aggression, it would be difficult for Japan to stand alone. He urged that Japan and China halt the fighting and, putting aside their petty differences, join in maintaining stability. He assured the Japanese emperor that Chinese troops would be unremitting in disposing of the bandits.[38]

Meiji did not respond to the Chinese emperor's proposal. Instead, he declared that if the Chinese government succeeded in suppressing the revolt—in this way making it clear that it did not desire war with foreign countries—Japan would be glad to resume its traditional friendship. He insisted that the Chinese government lift the siege of Peking and that if it failed to do so, Japan would have no choice but to send troops to pacify the rebels and rescue its citizens.[39]

Just at this time the chief chamberlain, Tokudaiji Sanetsune, submitted a request to the emperor that he be permitted to resign his post. The emperor, enraged, replied, "Any member of the nobility who serves at the court must be resolved to perform his duties faithfully, regardless of the sacrifices this may involve. Anyone who seeks to resign his office without good reason, merely in order to enjoy a life of ease, is truly hateful. No matter how many times you may try to resign your post, I will unconditionally refuse. Most present-day officials who come from the samurai class are self-indulgent and undisciplined. They tend to use resignation as a means of evading some temporary crisis and ensuring their personal safety. I always find this reprehensible. But for someone from the nobility to imitate them and cause me distress—that is the worst possible example of disloyalty."[40]

Meiji himself, earlier in his reign, had been rebuked by Itō Hirobumi and others for neglecting his work, but now he seems to have been entirely absorbed in state business. He had come to think of being the emperor as a responsibility and not a privilege, and it was also incumbent on a noble like Tokudaiji to show a greater sense of responsibility than a member of the samurai class. The concept of duty had come to dominate his thought, and he regarded each instance of resignation "for reasons of health" as a betrayal.

A major battle was fought on July 9 in the vicinity of the Tientsin racetrack between the allied army and the Chinese. Japanese troops, which formed the vanguard, did most of the fighting that day, dislodging the Chinese defenders, who consisted of 2,000 elite troops and some 500 Boxers. The Chinese general was killed, and after suffering heavy losses, his troops were put to flight. Allied casualties consisted of thirty or so Japanese and eight British soldiers. The bravery and skill displayed by the Japanese infantry earned the admiration and praise of the other countries.

The allied attack on Tientsin itself began on July 13. Japanese, British, American, and French troops attacked from the south; Russian and German troops, from the northeast. The Chinese forces consisted of about 14,000 regulars and about 10,000 Boxers; the allies, about 8,000 men. The city was surrounded by steep walls about twenty-six feet high. The fighting on the thirteenth was inconclusive, but at three in the morning of July 14, Engineer Lieutenant Inoue Kenkichi, who had been ordered to blow up the southern gate of the walls, crept up with six men. They laid explosives by the gate, but the electrically operated fuse was cut by enemy gunfire. Inoue and his men, compelled to ignite the explosives manually, were very nearly killed, but the gate was pulverized. The allied forces, led by Japanese troops shouting war cries, rushed through, only to be confronted by an inner wall with enemy soldiers on top. Not fazed by this difficult situation, First Class Private Masuda Sentarō climbed over the wall and opened the gate from the inside. Japanese troops poured into the city, followed by French, British, and American soldiers. The Chinese left 400 dead. More than 860 allied troops were killed or wounded, 400 of them Japanese.[41]

On August 8 Kaiser Wilhelm II sent a cable to Emperor Meiji requesting that General Alfred Waldersee be appointed as commander of the allied forces. Although Germans constituted a much smaller part of the allied forces than the Japanese, the emperor immediately consented, perhaps because of the murder of the German minister. The emperor was probably not aware that late in July, when the German Expeditionary Force was about to set sail for China, the kaiser had delivered an address to the officers and men commanding them to show no mercy and take no prisoners, in this way ensuring that the Chinese would never again dare to look down on Germans.[42]

The kaiser's address was much criticized by the allies when it became known abroad. Hearing that a German had been appointed to head the allied force,

Makino Nobuaki, the minister to Austria, objected on the grounds that the kaiser's speech had aroused strong opposition.[43] But Meiji had already sent a telegram agreeing to the kaiser's request. Without realizing it, the emperor was cooperating with a monarch obsessed with a hatred of the "Yellow Peril."

As it happened, however, the allied advance on Peking was so rapid that the German general did not have time to assume the post of commanding officer. Instead, in keeping with a Japanese proposal supported by other allies, a Russian general was chosen as the commander. On August 14 Peking fell to the allies; the siege of Peking was lifted; and the foreign nationals were rescued. The Chinese emperor and empress dowager fled to the northwest. Japanese and American troops secured the imperial palace, but elsewhere in the city, the allies engaged in unbridled looting.[44]

The China crisis was at an end.

Chapter 51

Once the Boxer Rebellion had been suppressed, Yamagata Aritomo again asked the emperor's permission to resign the post of prime minister.[1] Meiji, no longer able to insist that Yamagata was urgently needed to deal with an emergency, resigned himself to losing Yamagata's services. The obvious successor was Itō Hirobumi, but he had earlier refused, and he was also occupied with the formation of a new political party. Itō believed that political parties were necessary to a constitutional monarchy and that a cabinet lacking a party base was likely to have its legislation blocked by factions in the Diet. There were in fact several established parties, but they were moribund and incapable of exercising leadership. Itō believed that an entirely new party, to be headed by himself, was needed to correct long-standing abuses in the government. He informed Yamagata of his intention and asked the imperial household minister to report it to the emperor.

The emperor not only granted Itō permission to form a new party but on September 14 sent Iwakura Tomosada to Itō's residence with a gift of 10,000 yen and a roll each of red and white silk crepe. He also sent a message conveying his trust in Itō's devotion and his abiding eagerness to benefit by Itō's frank advice.[2]

On September 15, 1900, the formation of a new party was announced. It was called the Rikken seiyūkai,[3] and Itō was its president. At this point the members of the Kensei-tō declared their party's dissolution and their intention of joining the new party and forming its nucleus. Some cynics remarked that in view of Itō's having obtained palace authorization before organizing the Seiyūkai, he really should have called it the Imperially Sanctioned Party.[4]

On September 24 the emperor sent for Matsukata Masayoshi and Inoue Kaoru and asked them to persuade Itō to succeed Yamagata. The two men visited Itō separately, but both received a firm refusal. Yamagata somehow learned that Inoue had gone to see Itō, which may have precipitated his submission on September 26 of a memorial to the emperor, asking to resign. He alleged that his health made it impossible for him to continue performing the exhausting duties of his office. The decision of the Kensei-tō, no longer willing to cooperate with Yamagata, to join forces with Itō's party may also have spurred Yamagata's decision, for his cabinet was now completely lacking in party support.

Matsukata also attempted to persuade Itō to become prime minister, only for Itō to urge Matsukata to take the post himself. Finally, the emperor, realizing that intermediaries would not succeed, summoned Itō to court and commanded him to accept the post. Itō still would not yield. He had his hands full organizing the Seiyūkai, and he was suffering from a debilitating cold. The imperial command could not have come at a worse moment. Matsukata made one last attempt on October 6. This time Itō agreed, having by then reached the conclusion that neither the domestic nor the foreign situation permitted further delay. On the following day in the presence of the emperor, Itō formally accepted the command to form a cabinet.

Itō was invested as prime minister in a ceremony at the palace on October 19. From the outset, there were clashes among the members of the new cabinet. On October 20 Army Minister Katsura Tarō (a holdover from the previous cabinet) asked to resign for reasons of health. The emperor refused, saying that at a time of great tension, the office of army minister must not be vacant for even a single day.[5]

On November 15 the emperor, resuming his practice of earlier days, traveled to Ibaraki Prefecture to observe maneuvers, spending the night in an elementary school. The weather the next day was terrible—unremitting rain and wind with occasional snow flurries—and it was bitingly cold. The roads over which the emperor's carriage passed were supposed to have been repaired, but days of rain and the heavy traffic of soldiers and horses had turned them into deep mud. At a place called Nagakata the emperor left his carriage and walked to a height from which he could observe the mock battle between the two armies. He remained there for more than an hour, buffeted by rain and wind that grew steadily more intense, until the maneuvers had ended. He probably considered that as emperor, he was obliged to set an example of fortitude for the troops.

The emperor did not suffer ill effects from his prolonged exposure to the elements, but toward the end of the year he contracted an illness that confined him to his bed until January 13, 1901. As a result, he did not participate in any of the traditional observances at New Year. The emperor was now fifty years old by Japanese count.

On January 23 Japan received word of Queen Victoria's death. England, at the zenith of its power, had long been the greatest obstacle to recognition of Japan as an equal to the major powers of Europe, but the Japanese court, showing not the slightest sign of resentment, went into three weeks of mourning. Hayashi Tadasu, the minister to Great Britain, was designated as special ambassador to the funeral. He would figure prominently in the negotiations later in this year for an alliance between Japan and England, the extraordinary resolution of the often tense relationship between the two countries.

Having formed a political party, as he had long hoped, Itō organized a cabinet that consisted entirely of Seiyūkai members. The House of Peers was vociferous in its denunciation of party government, but Itō ignored the complaints, exacerbating the mutual feelings of hostility. The problems facing Itō were manifold. The government was faced with the urgent need to pay the expenses incurred in quelling the Boxer Rebellion. The House of Representatives attempted to raise funds by imposing taxes on saké and sugar and increasing customs duties. Greater revenues were also expected from the tobacco monopoly. However, the House of Peers opposed any raise in taxes and seemed certain to vote against the bill. On February 27 the emperor (at Itō's request) suspended the Diet for ten days.

Itō hoped that during these ten days he would be able to induce the House of Peers to compromise, but it remained adamant in its demand for full debate over the revenue bill. Itō expected Yamagata, who had influence in the House of Peers, to mediate, but he was in Kyōto, and when he and Matsukata met, they decided against mediation. Itō, in exasperation, asked the emperor to summon the two men back to Tōkyō. A chamberlain sent telegrams to Yamagata and Matsukata, who left for Tōkyō the following day.

At an audience on March 5 Itō explained to the emperor the gravity of the situation caused by the refusal of the House of Peers to cooperate in raising money needed to pay national debts. He feared severe repercussions in the world of finance and suggested that the emperor ask advice from four genrō — Yamagata Aritomo, Saigō Tsugumichi, Matsukata Masayoshi, and Inoue Kaoru. The emperor received Yamagata and Matsukata shortly afterward, and messages were sent to Saigō and Inoue asking them to join in finding a solution to the crisis.[6]

Yamagata and Matsukata reported the failure of their efforts to mediate. The suspension of the Diet would soon end, and Itō could not restrain his impatience. He drew up a plan that he passed on to the imperial household minister, requesting that the emperor issue a rescript to the House of Peers reproving its obstruction. The emperor, complying with this request, on March 12 summoned Konoe Atsumaro, the president of the House of Peers, and told him, "I was recently informed that the House of Peers has expressed unwillingness to pass the tax increase and has clashed with the government on the matter. I find this most deplorable. I ordered Yamagata and others to mediate, but their efforts were unfortunately not successful. The government has further informed me that it cannot accede to the proposals of the House of Peers. I am deeply disturbed, as you will see from the enclosed note. I ask you to show it to all members of the House, and to discuss ways of restoring harmony as soon as possible."

The emperor's note left no doubt as to his position:

"I am deeply distressed by the difficult situation both at home and abroad. It is essential at this time for the nation to pay the necessary war expenses and to establish plans for putting its finances on a sound basis.

"As I indicated when not long ago I opened the Diet, these are my wishes. Moreover, the various measures to increase taxes, which I commanded the government to submit, have already been passed by the House of Representatives.

"I believe that the members of the House of Peers, being loyal to the throne, surely must share my unremitting concern. I hope that they will speedily approve these plans made by the court and not give the nation cause for regret in the future."[7]

Konoe had foreseen the possibility that matters might develop in this way, but he was greatly upset by the emperor's reprimand. He called on Iwakura Tomosada, supposing that Iwakura, who deplored Itō's habit of asking the emperor to issue a rescript whenever he was in a tight situation, would know what had occasioned this one. Iwakura, however, had heard nothing. When Konoe showed him the rescript, Iwakura was astonished to see that it neither had the emperor's signature or seal nor had been countersigned by a minister. This was highly irregular. That night, Iwakura sent a copy of the rescript to Itō and asked if members of the cabinet were already familiar with its contents.

The following day, Itō called on Konoe at the House of Peers and related in detail his own efforts ever since the suspension of the Diet to open negotiations with the House of Peers and how the emperor had commanded Yamagata to mediate. It seemed as if the emperor, disappointed at the failure of mediation efforts and extremely worried about the situation, had taken things into his own hands. Itō added that no one in the cabinet had known in advance of the rescript, but regardless of whether anyone knew, as the head of the cabinet he bore the heavy duty of advising the emperor, and it was natural that this responsibility should extend to advising the emperor with respect to politics.[8]

Itō's words implied that although no one in the cabinet had prior knowledge of the rescript, his own advice may have influenced the emperor to write in these terms. The absence of a signature or countersignature suggested that the emperor may have acted on his own, perhaps on the spur of the moment.

Konoe presented the rescript to the House of Peers on March 24. The emperor's admonition caused an immediate change in the members' attitudes, and the revenue bill was passed without modification.[9]

Later that month, the emperor displayed his authority in quite a different area. On March 27 the minister of justice, Kaneko Kentarō, asked the emperor's authorization to dismiss sixteen judges and public prosecutors who had asked permission to resign their offices. The cause of their action was the decision by the House of Representatives not to grant salary increases to members of the judiciary, even though there were good reasons to do so. The annual budget was consequently passed without a provision for a salary increase. The disappointed judges and prosecutors started a campaign against the bill. Some provincial magistrates left their posts to participate in strike actions in the capital.

Kaneko issued frequent warnings to the strikers, reminding them they must not violate official discipline, but his warnings had no effect. The ringleaders called for a general resignation, and soon letters of resignation were streaming into Tōkyō by mail and telegraph. Kaneko, determined to maintain the dignity of the judiciary, decided that rather than yield to the strikers' demands for higher pay, he would accept their resignations. He forwarded to Itō the letters of resignation, with the request that they be submitted to the emperor.

Itō informed the emperor of the circumstances and requested his decision. The emperor asked if the minister of justice would be able to replace men who might resign. Itō in turn asked Kaneko who, by way of reply, showed him a list of more than 800 persons qualified to serve as judges and prosecutors. He said that there would be no difficulty in replacing the strikers. Itō showed the list to the emperor, who at once accepted the resignations, saying, "If from now on anybody submits a resignation, an answer should be sent immediately, even if it's in the middle of the night. I will give permission immediately." The emperor's decision had the effect of breaking the strike; people who had already submitted resignations, assuming that they would not be accepted, asked to withdraw them.[10]

The emperor's decision did not take into account the hardships that judges and prosecutors might be suffering because of inadequate salaries. His only concern was whether the strikers could be replaced. As a Confucian ruler, he should have displayed greater compassion, but Meiji probably thought of the strikers primarily as violators of the law, and in his dislike of disorder, he was like the Tokugawa shoguns, who were also good Confucians.

On May 2 Itō asked the emperor's permission to resign as prime minister. He declared that although he had recovered sufficiently to be able to attend court functions, his health still did not permit him to cope with the arduous tasks ahead, notably the budget. Itō's poor health was more than a mere excuse, as the emperor tacitly recognized. On the day he received Itō's letter, he appointed Saionji Kinmochi as acting prime minister, to serve during Itō's illness.[11]

Itō was not exaggerating the difficulties facing the government. The budget for the coming year and a bill to increase taxes had at last passed the Diet, but the financial crisis was still not solved. Ever since the ending of the Sino-Japanese War in 1895, the government had made building up the military its chief priority, and a large part of the national wealth had been funneled into military projects and plans, resulting in serious deficits. Tax increases followed on earlier tax increases, and loans were floated on earlier loans; the process seemed unending. Financial stringency threatened to precipitate a panic.

The finance minister, Watanabe Kunitake (1846–1919), submitted a bill of financial retrenchment involving the suspension of government enterprises, but he was opposed by five members of the cabinet, mainly because of their personal annoyance with him. Itō was called in to mediate, but the solution he proposed only intensified the conflict. Finally, the entire cabinet except for Watanabe submitted their resignations.

On May 3 Watanabe presented to the emperor his views on the financial situation. Afterward, the emperor sent for Saionji and asked him what he thought of Watanabe's opinions. Saionji replied that allowing Watanabe to have his way would set a bad example. He proposed asking Watanabe to resign. If he refused, Saionji would inform him that the emperor desired his resignation.

Saionji went to see Watanabe and, after considerable exhortation, persuaded him to resign. That day, Watanabe went to the chief chamberlain, Tokudaiji Sanetsune, with two different letters of resignation and asked him which one he should submit. In the first, he gave failing health as his reason for resigning; in the second, he said he was resigning because everybody else in the cabinet was resigning. Tokudaiji said it was customary in such circumstances to attribute one's resignation to one's health. Watanabe followed his advice.[12]

In the meantime, the emperor's first grandchild, a boy, was born to the crown prince's consort on April 29. Officials crowded the crown prince's palace to voice congratulations, but the crown prince did not return from Hayama for a look at his son until May 3.[13] The baby was healthy, and joy over his birth was not tinged with the apprehension that had accompanied the births of the emperor's children. On May 5 the emperor gave the infant a name and title. From among three names submitted, he chose Hirohito, and from two titles, Michinomiya.[14] The emperor inscribed the names on separate sheets of parchment and gave them to Tokudaiji for delivery to the crown prince, who returned to Odawara the next day.[15]

Itō's petition to resign was finally accepted by the emperor on May 10. Inoue Kaoru was asked to form a cabinet but failed. On May 26 the emperor commanded General Katsura Tarō, who had been strongly recommended by the *genrō*, to form a cabinet. Katsura delayed responding, saying that he hoped to persuade Itō to change his mind. He asked the emperor to join his voice in urging Itō to reassume the post of prime minister. The emperor had Tokudaiji telegraph Itō, requesting him to come at once to Tōkyō for an audience.[16]

Itō firmly declined to reassume his post. Katsura, whose hesitation to accept the premiership seems to have been prompted by deference to Itō and not by doubts of his own ability, asked Tokudaiji to inform the emperor on June 1 that preparations for the new cabinet had been completed. He requested that the inauguration ceremony take place on the following day.

The cabinet consisted entirely of new men except for the army and navy ministers who, at the emperor's request, remained in office. It was unusual in that it contained not one *genrō*. The military coloring of the cabinet was not confined to Katsura: all members were associated with Yamagata. This facilitated relations with the House of Peers, although it posed a problem regarding relations with the House of Representatives, now controlled by the Seiyūkai.

On June 21 Hoshi Tōru (1850–1901), a member of the House of Representatives and a leading figure in the Seiyūkai, was assassinated. Hoshi is one of the most enigmatic figures of the entire Meiji era. Encyclopedia articles describe him as an arrogant and corrupt politician and sometimes compare him with similar Japanese politicians of recent times. Hoshi's meritorious acts are usually passed over quickly by writers who prefer to dwell on his faults, but he may strike a modern reader as the first specifically modern politician in the good as well as the bad sense.

Hoshi was the first major political figure to come not merely from the class of commoners but from the lowest depths of society. His father, an alcoholic plasterer, deserted his wife and their three children, leaving them penniless. Hoshi's eldest sister was sold to a brothel, and his second sister was indentured as a servant. His mother was so exhausted by the strain of feeding herself and her baby that she planned to throw Hoshi into a pond, only to decide at the last moment to let him live because he was a male.[17] Later she married a kindly man—a quack doctor and fortune-teller by profession—and the family of five was able to live together in an Edo slum.

When Hoshi was old enough to go to school, his stepfather sent him to study under the doctor who had been his own teacher, planning to have the boy follow in his profession. Hoshi was not unusually bright, but with dogged perseverance he learned not only the rudiments of medicine but also the Confucian classics. More important to his future career, he also began to study English. In 1866, when Hoshi was sixteen, he was adopted by a childless samurai who sent him to the Kaiseisho, a school for children of shogunate retainers, where he studied English with Maejima Hisoka, the founder of the Japanese postal service. Maejima was so favorably impressed that he enabled Hoshi to remain at the school even after his samurai ties had been broken.[18]

Hoshi was introduced by Maejima to Ga Noriyuki (1840–1923),[19] a professor of English at the Kaiseisho, who recognized the boy's ability and obtained for him his first job as a teacher of English at a naval school. The school was disbanded after the shogunate was overthrown, and Hoshi wrote to Ga asking for another job. Ga introduced him to Mutsu Munemitsu, the governor of

Hyōgo, who hired Hoshi to teach at a school he had founded in Kōbe. Mutsu's patronage was crucial to Hoshi's success.

Hoshi's career was characterized by absolute determination to rise in the world despite his lowly birth and physical weakness. His resentment over his lot in life revealed itself in his hatred of the samurai class and his urge to triumph over those who ran the government. The more elevated his opponent was, the more his fighting spirit would be aroused.[20] He overcame the handicap of birth by intelligence and unremitting study and his physical weakness by the constant practice of martial sports. The photographs of Hoshi taken in late years show him as a portly, ugly man who exudes self-confidence.

Mutsu was appointed as governor of Kanagawa Prefecture in 1871; two years later, Hoshi obtained a position in the Finance Ministry on Mutsu's recommendation. His main occupation was translating the tax laws of various foreign countries. He lost this job and was placed under house arrest after assaulting a rickshaw coolie and refusing to obey the restraining policemen. He used the time at home to translate a book on heroic men of foreign countries. When Hoshi was released from house arrest, Mutsu urged him to behave himself in the future and (a sign of how highly he regarded Hoshi's ability) invited him to live in his residence. Hoshi and two students took advantage of this offer and were soon translating Blackwood's *British Laws*.

In 1873 Mutsu obtained for Hoshi a position in the Yokohama customs. He rose rapidly, in January 1874 becoming the tax adviser and superintendent of customs. Everything seemed to be going well when Hoshi's nemesis struck. In an exchange of documents with the British consulate, he translated the words "Her Majesty" not as *jotei* (empress) but as *joō heika* (Her Majesty, the queen). He was accused by the British of lèse-majesté. Hoshi, defending himself, pointed out that Victoria referred to herself as queen and not as empress, but Sir Harry Parkes personally went to the Foreign Ministry to protest and demand that Hoshi be fired and made to apologize. Sanjō Sanetomi, the prime minister, and Terashima Munenori, the foreign minister, urged Hoshi to apologize, but he refused, saying that he was not mistaken. The government, afraid of antagonizing the British, removed Hoshi from his post in order to mollify Parkes.[21]

Hoshi retained his post of tax adviser, however, and it was in this capacity that he was sent to study in England in September 1874. In January 1875 he enrolled at the Middle Temple, and two years later he became the first Japanese to obtain the degree of barrister-at-law. Hoshi spent almost all his time in London in his room, studying books of law and philosophy.[22]

After his return to Japan, Hoshi was appointed as *daigennin* (barrister) attached to the Justice Ministry. His main occupation at this time was as a lawyer, but he became increasingly involved with the movement for Freedom and Popular Rights and the Jiyū-tō, attracting the attention of the authorities. In 1882 members of the Jiyū-tō in Fukushima were arrested for having protested against the actions of a tyrannical governor.[23] They were accused of attempting to overthrow the government. Hoshi, defending Kōno Hironaka, the central figure among the accused, demonstrated with irrefutable logic that the charge of insurrection did not apply, but the defendants were found guilty all the same.[24]

In the meantime, Hoshi had joined the Jiyū-tō, whose program corresponded closely to his own beliefs about society. He felt, however, that the official party newspaper was couched in such high-flown language that the mass of Japanese were unable to understand it. In May 1884 he founded a popular newspaper, written in easy-to-understand language and containing pictures, in order to appeal to the class from which he himself had originated. This attempt to educate the masses was unprecedented at a time when the vote was confined to a fraction of the population.

In July 1884 Hoshi delivered in Niigata a speech entitled "The Limitations of Government" in which he attacked the despotic, militaristic governments of Russia and Germany for their interference in the private lives of their citizens. Although he carefully refrained from mentioning Japan, the implications were obvious, and the police, acting under a regulation promulgated in 1880, halted the lecture and dispersed the meeting.

Hoshi was ordered to report to the Niigata Police Station, but he ignored the summons, saying that the police had no authority to summon him. They finally arrested him anyway and charged him with having slandered public officials. Hoshi had not criticized any official, but he was nevertheless found guilty of having slandered Prime Minister Sanjō and the ministers of the interior, army, navy, education, agriculture and commerce, public works, and imperial household. He was condemned to six months in prison and ordered to pay a fine of forty yen. He was also stripped of his credentials as barrister.[25]

Hoshi was not chastened by his time in prison. He continued publishing his illustrated newspaper and waited for the chance to reestablish the Jiyū-tō, which had been dissolved while he was incarcerated. However, in 1888 he was again arrested, this time on the charge of having published secret documents dealing with the negotiations over treaty revision. He was sentenced to a year and a half in prison and had no choice but to sell his newspaper.[26]

Hoshi spent his time in prison studying. It was by no means a good place to read books, but from the crack of dawn until nightfall, he read books written in Japanese, English, German, French, and Italian. He was pardoned and released in the amnesty celebrating the proclamation of the constitution in February 1889.

After leaving prison Hoshi traveled to America and Europe to study their political institutions. What this meant in practice was that wherever he went he visited bookshops, buying books that seemed useful and then shutting himself up in a cheap hotel room to read them. He scorned to imitate politicians like Itō Hirobumi, who boasted of having sat at the feet of Rudolf von Gneist,

Lorenz von Stein, and other eminences. Hoshi said that these men were not as famous in Europe as in Japan and that it was ludicrous to give oneself airs just because one had heard them lecture.

Hoshi visited almost every country of Europe and North America. The journey seems to have changed him. He disappointed his former associates in the Freedom and Popular Rights movement by delivering a speech after his return to Japan in which he urged strengthening armaments,[27] acquiring colonies, encouraging Japanese emigration, and starting an active Japanese propaganda campaign abroad.[28] His experience abroad, or perhaps the books he read, seems to have opened his eyes to the realities of the world situation, and he talked in terms of power politics.

Once back in Japan, Hoshi threw himself into refounding the Jiyū-tō as the Rikken jiyū-tō. At the party convention in March 1891, Hoshi's faction won control. In the second general election in February 1892, Hoshi was elected to the House of Representatives and (with Mutsu Munemitsu's help) was chosen as president. Everyone expected that Hoshi would take advantage of his position to advance bills favored by the Jiyū-tō, but in fact he was scrupulously fair and did not favor members of his own party.[29]

Hoshi was soon at loggerheads with Matsukata, the prime minister, whose authority was derived from backers in the Satsuma and Chōshū domains. Hoshi's arrogance also alienated many members of the House of Representatives. The politics of the time are confusing and need not be treated at length here; suffice it to say that Hoshi was accused of improprieties. He was able to prove his innocence of all charges, but this did not erase the impression that he was guilty; an aura of corruption has clung to him ever since.[30] Hoshi was removed from his position as president of the House.

In 1896 Hoshi was appointed as minister to the United States, mainly (it has been conjectured) because Itagaki and others of the Jiyū-tō found him an embarrassment and wanted him out of the way.[31] His two years as minister were successfully spent in dealing with two crucial issues, the threatened rise in import duties on Japanese products and the effects on Japanese in Hawaii of the impending American annexation.

Hoshi was able to dissuade senators who favored the higher tariffs sponsored by the Republican administration.[32] With respect to Hawaii, Hoshi was determined to secure from the Americans the concessions granted earlier to the Japanese by the Hawaiian monarchy. At one point he moved to an extreme position of advocating the annexation of Hawaii by Japan, even if this risked war with the United States.[33] Ōkuma Shigenobu, the foreign minister, rejected the proposal as being provocative, but Hoshi succeeded in obtaining a guarantee that Japanese residents of Hawaii would enjoy the same rights as citizens of European countries.[34]

When Hoshi learned of the formation of a new political party (the Kensei-tō), he decided to return at once to Japan, hoping for the post of foreign minister in the next cabinet. He telegraphed the ministry that he was returning, only to be ordered by the ministry to remain at his post. Although Hoshi paid no attention to this directive, he failed in the end to obtain the coveted post of foreign minister, mainly because of Ōkuma's opposition.

Hoshi later helped organize the Seiyūkai and, as the strongest figure within that party, was rewarded in 1900 with the post of minister of communications in the fourth Itō cabinet. This was not a major cabinet post, but never before had a man of Hoshi's birth, without domain connections, been appointed to such an exalted position. In addition to being a member of the cabinet, Hoshi was elected in 1899 to the Tōkyō Municipal Assembly and served as its presiding officer. It was widely believed that he ran the city government mainly for the profit of himself and his faction.[35] This rumor was not substantiated, but he had clearly built up a political machine, and some of his underlings did not hesitate to use strong-arm methods. Hoshi himself did not profit by his alleged crimes. Despite accusations by the newspapers that he made a fortune out of government contracts, he left only debts when he died.

Hoshi was forced to resign in October 1900 as a member of the Tōkyō Municipal Assembly and in December as minister of communications, although he insisted to the end that he had committed no wrongdoing. All the same, public indignation against him continued to mount, and in June a fencing teacher named Iba Sōtarō, a devout believer in Confucian morality, was so enraged by the corruption he sensed in the government that he waylaid Hoshi and stabbed him to death.[36]

Many people unquestioningly believed the rumors of corruption, but there were also many who still admired Hoshi, and thousands of them followed the funeral cortege as it advanced to the solemn strains of music provided by a company of the emperor's guards. Hara Takashi and Matsuda Masahisa, two major politicians of the next generation, headed the funeral committee, and Itagaki Taisuke gave the eulogy.[37] Despite the accusations (and the bad reputation that has lasted to this day), Hoshi, more than any other man, had shaped the future of modern, Japanese-style party politics. The emperor promoted Hoshi to the junior third rank and posthumously bestowed on him the Order of the Sacred Treasure.[38]

The emperor was kept abreast of the controversy surrounding Hoshi Tōru, and on occasion his decision was sought. Even after the House of Representatives had passed a vote of no confidence in November 1893, Hoshi continued to occupy the president's chair. On December 2 the vice president, Kusumoto Masataka, visited the palace with a petition reporting to the emperor the vote of no confidence and apologizing for having recommended Hoshi to the emperor. After reading the petition, Meiji summoned Kusumoto and said it was not clear what was being asked of him. Was he being requested to replace the president? Or were the members of the House apologizing for having made a mistake?

The emperor wished to avoid being put in the position of commanding Hoshi to vacate the president's chair. His response had the effect of making Kusumoto abandon the hope that the emperor would personally expel Hoshi. It is not known what the emperor thought of Hoshi, but his decision to decorate him posthumously suggests that he recognized Hoshi's contributions to the state.

On July 6 the emperor and empress visited the crown prince's palace, where they inspected the wedding gifts the crown prince and princess had received the previous year. They also visited their grandson, Hirohito. On the following day the infant was taken to the residence of Admiral Kawamura Sumiyoshi in Mamiana. The emperor and empress gave 100 yen to the admiral, asking him to watch over the infant prince during his childhood. It was announced that the crown prince requested this arrangement, but in fact it was the emperor's wish.[39] This survival of an old practice perplexed Erwin Baelz, the emperor's personal physician, who wrote,

> At five to call on Count Kawamura. The crown prince's son has been put under the care of this elderly admiral, who must be nearly seventy. What a strange idea! I hoped that the unnatural and cruel custom of taking little princes away from their parents and handing them over to strangers had fallen into desuetude. It is not so, however. The poor crown princess was compelled to hand over her baby, which cost her many tears. Now the parents can see their child only for a brief period once or twice a month. . . . Why can they not in this matter follow the example of the German or the English royal family as they do in so many others? Little Prince Michinomiya is a lively and good-looking youngster.[40]

On August 1 Baron Hayashi Tadasu (1850–1913), the minister plenipotentiary to the Court of St. James, sent a telegram to Sone Arasuke, the foreign minister, reporting that after conferring about China with Lord Henry Lansdowne, the British foreign minister, he had learned that the British government wished to conclude an alliance with Japan. He asked, "Is the Japanese government prepared to sign a treaty with them? If they are willing to accept our conditions, are we ready to enter an alliance with them? Please send the government's reply as soon as possible."[41]

The proposal to create an alliance between England and Japan had its origins in Russian policy in the Far East. As noted earlier, after the conclusion of the Sino-Japanese War, the Japanese had been forced by three European powers to return the Liaotung Peninsula to China. However, Russia not long afterward leased this territory, signed a secret treaty with China, and began constructing a railway. The Russians now administered Port Arthur and Dairen and were steadily expanding their hold over northwestern China. Russian towns had been founded along the railway line. Other countries with interests in East Asia were concerned about Russia's moves in Korea, and many believed that a clash between Russia and Japan was inevitable. However, the Japanese were by no means adequately prepared for such a conflict, and it was obvious that it would be extremely difficult for the country, unaided, to dislodge the Russians.

Japan had two possible courses of action. One (favored by Itō Hirobumi) was to reach an understanding with Russia whereby Manchuria would be yielded to the Russians. In return, Japanese predominance in Korea would be recognized.[42] The other (favored by most other Japanese officials) was for Japan to act in concert with major European powers in order to contain Russia. It was unlikely that France would join an anti-Russian coalition, as France and Russia had recently concluded an alliance. Japan's most likely partners were Germany and England, both of which were convinced that the Russians were infringing on their rights in East Asia. In April 1901, in conversation with Lansdowne, Hayashi had voiced the opinion that in order for there to be permanent peace in East Asia, a firm relationship between Japan and England was essential. Lansdowne agreed, but this was only the private opinion of the two men.[43]

Even before this time, men in Japan and England had advocated such an alliance. In 1895 Fukuzawa Yukichi had written an editorial proposing an alliance;[44] and in England Joseph Chamberlain, the minister for the colonies, had informally discussed the subject with the Japanese minister.[45] In 1898 the Japanese government, about to end the occupation of Weihaiwei, consented to the British proposal to lease the city from the Chinese, adding that it hoped that the British would in return be sympathetic and offer help if Japan needed to take action to ensure its security or promote its interests.[46] A pro-Japanese mood swept England in 1900 after the Japanese army rescued British subjects in Peking besieged by the Boxers. Hayashi Tadasu, who became minister to Great Britain that year, concluded that England was the only country with which Japan could form an alliance against Russia.[47]

The discussions between Hayashi and Lord Lansdowne reached agreement on six points:

1. An open door must be maintained in China.
2. Apart from concessions already made by treaty, no further acquisition of Chinese territory was to be permitted.
3. Japan's freedom to act in Korea was recognized because Japan had greater interests there than any other country.
4. If one member of the alliance engaged in hostilities with another country, the other member would preserve neutrality, but if a third power helped the enemy, the other member would enter the war.
5. The Anglo-German agreement on China would remain in force.
6. The alliance would be restricted to the Far East.[48]

After much discussion and some apparent setbacks to the alliance, the British prepared a draft of the proposed treaty and asked for a prompt Japanese reply.[49] Japanese revisions to the text, telegraphed to London on November 30, mainly concerned language. The telegram mentioned that when shown the proposed treaty, the emperor had asked it be shown to the *genrō* and to Itō for their opinions.[50]

After a heated debate the *genrō* approved of the treaty as revised and recommended that it be made effective as soon as possible. Only Inoue Kaoru, who had favored an alliance with Russia rather than England, expressed dissatisfaction on the grounds that Itō's opinion had still not been heard. The awaited telegram from Itō, received on December 8, raised objections to the treaty. He declared that the wording left many points obscure and noted that it was not known what Germany would think of an Anglo-Japanese alliance. It was possible also that negotiations with Russia would result in a treaty. He urged extremely careful consideration and requested that his opinions be conveyed to the emperor.[51]

Prime Minister Katsura took Itō's telegram to the emperor the next day. The emperor always placed great value on Itō's opinions, but he said now that in view of the treaty's approval by both the cabinet and the *genrō*, he thought that Japanese consent could not be delayed. He asked Katsura to ascertain the reactions of the *genrō* to Itō's message. Katsura went to the *genrō* but, before asking their views, pointed out that there was no guarantee that a treaty would be concluded with Russia and that any delay might cause the British to withdraw its offer of an alliance. On December 10 he reported to the emperor that the majority supported the treaty with England. With the authorization of the emperor, a telegram was sent to Hayashi on the twelfth stating that Japan had accepted the revised treaty.[52] On January 30, 1902, Hayashi and Lansdowne signed the treaty in London., and it was announced to the public on February 12.

It is difficult to appraise the benefits to Japan brought by the treaty. Hayashi believed that the alliance enabled Japan's victory in the Russo-Japanese War.[53] It accounted for Japan's participation in World War I and its acquisition of an overseas empire when it captured former German colonies in the South Pacific. More important than material benefits was the joy felt by the Japanese, from the emperor on down, that Japan had been recognized as an equal partner of the strongest nation in the world, a nation that in the past had humiliated Japan again and again.[54]

Chapter 52

The year 1902 opened with a minimum of ceremonial. The one-day postponement of the New Year banquet, normally held on January 5, typified the steady
erosion of New Year rituals: that day was a Sunday, and it was judged to be
more important to observe the Christian day of rest than Japanese tradition. A
few days later, the emperor heard the usual three New Year lectures, one each
on Japanese, Chinese, and Western history. The lecture on the West this year
was devoted to parliamentary reform in England, possibly because of the Anglo-
Japanese Alliance.

On January 10 the court lady Muromachi Kiyoko died in her sixty-third year.
Soon after entering palace service in 1856, she had been appointed as governess
to the future emperor, then a child of four. On his accession to the throne in
1867, she had been given the position of *tenji* (lady-in-waiting) and had served
the emperor in this capacity for forty-six years. If ever she disapproved of anything the emperor said or did, she did not hesitate to scold him. He would
invariably reject her advice, calling her *otafuku*, a Kyōto word for an ugly
woman; but there was affection in his tone. To this rebuke she would respond,
"I was born an *otafuku*. There's nothing I can do about it, no matter what Your
Majesty may command. But I beg you to take the advice I offer." The emperor
would not reply but in the end did what she suggested. In recognition of Kiyoko's long service, the emperor and empress donated 2,000 yen for her funeral,
an unprecedented amount for someone of her position.[1]

So few of Meiji's "human" contacts with the people who served him have been recorded that this trifling anecdote is endearing. The use of the word *otafuku* suggests also that the emperor in private used Kyōto language, even though other anecdotes always transmit his words in standard Japanese.

The one traditional ceremony observed that spring was the first poetry meeting. The emperor did not like the two topics ("Cockcrows Herald the Dawn" and "Prayers to the Gods") proposed by the head of the Imperial Poetry Office, Takasaki Masakaze, who then had to supply a more conventional topic. The emperor composed this *tanka* on the theme "New Year Plum Blossoms":

tachikaeru	Blossoms of the plum
toshi no asahi ni	Returning with the new year
ume no hana	In morning sunlight
kaorisometari	Have begun to be fragrant
yukima nagara ni	In between breaks in the snow.[2]

The poem is felicitous but hardly memorable. All the same, the emperor was about to enter his most fruitful period as a poet, as most of his best-known poems were composed from this time until the end of his reign.

The festive New Year mood was harshly interrupted when on January 28 a report was received that a battalion of the Fifth Infantry Regiment had been buried in a blizzard. The emperor had retired for the night when the news arrived, but a chamberlain immediately went to inform him.

Telegrams sent back and forth between Tōkyō and Aomori gradually revealed the terrible story. The battalion of more than 200 men, out on a winter maneuver, had been caught on January 23 in a sudden fierce snowstorm near Mount Hakkōda. Maneuvers at more clement times of the year had familiarized the soldiers with the terrain of the region, but they were not equipped for such weather and lost their way in the blinding snow and lacerating wind. Rescue parties, sent out when the battalion failed to return to its base, were hampered in their search by the unrelenting storm. On the twenty-seventh, a survivor was found, all but dead from exposure. He described to the rescuers what had happened, and they battled their way through the snow to reach the site of the disaster. They found a handful of survivors and the bodies of about three-quarters of the victims. It was not until the snow melted in May that the last bodies were found.[3]

The emperor, deeply distressed to learn of the tragic event, at once sent his military attaché, Miyamoto Teruaki, to the scene. Word came from Miyamoto on February 7 that ninety-four rifles had been recovered, but only much later was the full extent of the disaster known: 199 officers and men had perished, and only eleven had survived.[4]

The first reaction when the tragedy became generally known was an outcry against the military for its recklessness in subjecting troops to maneuvers in a raging storm without proper winter uniforms, but when the full details of the tragedy were released, the prevailing sentiment shifted from anger to sympathy. The families of the victims were even said to have rejoiced, convinced that the deaths of their sons or grandsons were not in vain but would contribute to future victories of the imperial forces.[5]

On April 8 Foreign Minister Komura Jutarō reported to the Diet that Russia and China had signed an agreement providing for the restitution of Manchuria to China. This development was highly welcome to the Japanese, especially because they themselves had been forced by the Three Power Intervention, headed by Russia, to return the Liaotung Peninsula to China.

Negotiations on Manchuria between Russia and China went back to 1896, when Li Hung-chang traveled to Moscow to attend the coronation of Nicholas II.[6] A secret treaty signed between Russia and China provided for (1) mutual assistance in the event of aggression by a foreign power, (2) the use of Chinese ports by Russian warships in emergencies, and (3) the construction of a railway, administered by Russian personnel with extraterritorial rights, through northern Manchuria to Vladivostok, to be used by Russia to transport troops and supplies. The treaty was to remain in force for fifteen years.[7]

Although the framers of the treaty had assumed that aggression against China would be Japanese, the German seizure of Kiaochow Bay in 1897 was clearly aggression and therefore (under the treaty) involved the Russians as well as the Chinese. Ian Nish described the situation:

> China reacted to Germany's action in the only way she knew, by calling on Russia to neutralize and discourage the Germans. When news reached Peking that the Germans had landed at Kiaochow, Li Hung-chang issued under the Russo-Chinese alliance of 1896 a direct invitation to Russia to occupy temporarily a Chinese port as a countermeasure to German action.[8]

This was exactly what the Russians had hoped for, and they soon forgot their own claim to Kiaochow. The Russians secured from China the right to lease Port Arthur and Dairen and to build a railway through southern Manchuria. They now possessed the long-desired ice-free harbor on the Pacific. By the end of the year, the Chinese realized that their tactic of setting one barbarian off against another had failed.[9]

On April 25, 1898, Japan and Russia signed a protocol confirming the independence of Korea and agreeing to abstain from interference in that country's internal affairs. In the event that Korea requested counsel and assistance on military or financial matters from either Japan or Russia, that country should not take any measures without consulting the other. Russia agreed not to obstruct commercial and industrial relations between Japan and Korea. The agreement was the first to recognize the particular role of Japan in the economic development of Korea.[10]

Two years later, in 1900, destruction of the tracks of the Trans-Siberian Railway in Manchuria by Boxer insurgents gave the Russians an excuse to send an army to occupy three eastern provinces of Manchuria. They insisted that they had no intention of annexing Manchuria and that once order had been restored, they would immediately withdraw their troops.[11] The Russian occupation naturally upset the Japanese. In February 1901 they warned China not to yield to further Russian demands, but Li Hung-chang seemed willing to sacrifice Chinese rights in Manchuria in exchange for the Russian alliance. In the autumn of 1901, other countries that had participated in the suppression of the Boxer Rebellion withdrew their troops from Peking, but the Russians continued to occupy Manchuria.

The Japanese and British repeatedly protested. At first the Japanese protests were muted because Itō Hirobumi and Foreign Minister Nishi Tokujirō (who had studied at the University of St. Petersburg) believed in the importance of an understanding with Russia. They continued to hope that if Russia's ambitions in Manchuria were satisfied, it would recognize Japanese preeminence in Korea.

Itō visited Russia in November 1901 and was received cordially by the Russians. He was presented with the Gold Cordon of St. Alexander Nevsky, and the czar urged him to return to Japan by the Trans-Siberian Railway. Count Sergei Witte assured Itō that Russia sought nothing in Korea and was glad to permit Japan to operate freely there. In fact, the Russians were willing to make only nominal concessions in Korea and wanted in return a free hand in Manchuria. Itō was much disappointed. He still hoped to obtain concessions from Russia, but the Japanese government decided instead to proceed with the Anglo-Japanese Alliance and no longer sought an alliance with Russia.[12] All the same, both Japan and Russia still wanted to preserve the peace.

During 1902 the Japanese continued to strengthen their position in Korea, building up a nucleus of pro-Japanese Korean politicians. A large number of Japanese decided to settle in southeastern Korea, and Japan gradually took control of mines, the post, and telegraph. At this time Japan acquired a new ally, the United States, which had traditionally refused to become entangled in foreign affairs. Early in 1902, Theodore Roosevelt, who had become president a few months earlier, sent a message to Emperor Meiji expressing his friendship. He joined with Japan and Britain in warning China that special rights granted to Russia would be in contravention of the Open Door policy.[13] The chief reason for American participation was the fear that the Russification of not only Manchuria but also North China would seriously hamper American trade with China.

In January 1901 the Kokuryūkai (Amur River Society)[14]was founded with the professed aims of pan-Asianism and the removal of the Russians from Manchuria to the Amur River, the frontier between Manchuria and Siberia. In September the Kokumin dōmeikai (Peoples' Alliance), formed by Prince Konoe

Atsumaro, recommended measures to prevent the Russians from occupying Manchuria permanently and advocated Japanese construction of railways in Korea and Manchuria.[15] These and similar groups founded at this time were fully aware that if their policies were adopted, this might lead to war with Russia.

The construction of railways was important to the Japanese for trade and eventual control of Korea, but to the Russians, the Trans-Siberian Railway represented an almost mystical conception. A guide to the railway published in 1900 stated,

> The civilizing policy of Russia in the East, which may be regarded as an exception to that of other countries, was guided by other principles and was directed to the mutual welfare of nations by the maintenance of peace throughout the immense extent of her dominions. The honour of having planted the flag of Christianity and civilisation in Asia is due to Russia.[16]

Among the sponsors of the railway none was more active than Count Witte, the minister of finance. He pushed forward the project relentlessly, without regard to cost, and the railway was rapidly extended. It was almost unbelievable that a country that had always lagged behind the advanced nations of Europe should have embarked on such an immense project, but it was sustained by an "imperialist drive." A railway battle between Russia and Japan seemed inevitable.

In August 1902 at the request of the czar, Count Witte traveled to the Far East where he visited Vladivostok, Port Arthur, and Dairen. He was dismayed by what he saw and on his return to Russia went to the Crimea to convey to the czar his impressions of the enormity of the problems Russia faced in colonizing Siberia. He later submitted a report in which he wrote that normality could return to East Asia only if the Russians withdrew their troops from Manchuria. He also emphasized the need for an agreement with Japan, predicting that without it, things would go very badly.[17]

In April 1902 Russia had signed an agreement with China to withdraw its troops gradually from Manchuria, providing that no disturbances arose. The Russians also agreed to restore to the owners a railway line that they had occupied since 1900. Japan and England greeted this announcement with enthusiasm as a triumph for the Open Door policy, but the proviso that there must be no disturbances left a large loophole for the Russians, as disturbances were frequent in that part of the world. Count Witte later admitted that there had never been any serious intention of carrying out the evacuation treaty.[18]

Apart from the tensions with Russia, 1902 was uneventful for Emperor Meiji. The health and progress of the crown prince continued to worry him, although the prince was surprisingly diligent in his studies this year. Dr. Erwin Baelz, finding the relationship between the emperor and his son disagreeably cold and distant, wrote in his diary,

When he [the crown prince] visits his father, it is always in an extremely ceremonial fashion, and numerous officials are present. Should he fall ill, the Emperor makes frequent enquiries after the health of his son, but does not visit him unless the illness is so severe as to endanger life.[19]

In May the crown prince set out on a tour of prefectures in central and northern Honshū. Before he left, the emperor gave orders that since the object of the *junkō* was for the prince to observe customs and geography, local officials should not be kept from their work by welcoming, seeing off, or waiting on him.[20] The journey was in fact carried out with the simplicity the emperor had prescribed and could not have been very exciting to the crown prince. He visited schools, the Zenkō-ji in Nagano, local legislative bodies, factories, and other noteworthy places. The *junkō* was cut short when word came of an epidemic of measles in Fukushima.

A slight indisposition contracted during the journey gave the crown prince an excuse to recuperate for a month in his beloved Hayama. The birth of his second son was celebrated at the end of June by members of the imperial family and other dignitaries, but the crown prince (though informed) remained in Hayama. The emperor gave the newly born prince the name Yasuhito, with the title of Atsunomiya.[21]

In the meantime, a palace was being erected for the crown prince. The initial budget of 2.5 million yen had been approved by the emperor, but at the beginning of August the officer in charge of construction reported that costs had risen because of inflation. The new estimate for the palace, scheduled to be completed in 1907, was 5 million yen, a huge sum for the time. The emperor, who had insisted on simplicity and economy when his own palace was built in 1889, was appalled by the estimated cost of the prince's palace and later that year directed the architects to avoid fancy decorations and to concentrate on sturdy construction. The emperor gave strict orders that no further requests might be submitted for additional funds.[22]

The willingness of the Japanese government to spend so much money on a palace for the crown prince indicates that it did not anticipate the outbreak of war. Relations between the Japanese and Russian courts continued to be friendly. On August 27, for example, the emperor sent the czar a telegram thanking him for the cordial reception given to Prince Akihito while he was in Russia. But some men predicted war and urged suitable preparation. In a memorial to the throne on national defense, Yamamoto Gonnohyōe (1852–1933), the navy minister, described how the emperor's contribution of personal funds for building warships had brought about victory in the war with China. He declared,

It would seem that in the lands of the Orient, ominous clouds and baleful mists have now been happily cleared away, but I fear that in all probability the situation in China and Korea contains seeds of disaster imminently threatening the peace. At present the Imperial Navy may be said to reign supreme in the Orient, but military preparations of the powers are advancing rapidly. This is true especially of the neighboring power that has recently expanded its navy and plans before long to have a fleet in the Orient many times stronger than the empire's. If an emergency should arise, will the sea-girded empire of Japan be able to sleep in peace?[23]

Yamamoto asked for a total of 115 million yen with which to build and equip three first-class battleships, three first-class cruisers, and two second-class cruisers. Needless to say, the power against which Japan had to defend itself was Russia, whose eastward advance was deplored by the *genrō* when they approved this request for naval expansion.

In November 1902 Meiji set out for Kumamoto Prefecture to observe special grand maneuvers. An outbreak of cholera had occurred some months earlier, and the disease had been rampant. Whether or not to call off the imperial visit was debated, but fortunately, with the return of cool weather in October, the epidemic had subsided. On November 7 the emperor boarded a train at Shimbashi Station, seen off by the empress and the crown princess. The crown prince, still in Hayama, sent a chamberlain to Ōfuna Station to watch as the imperial train sped by.[24]

The emperor's journey to Kumamoto was made in leisurely stages with stops along the way. He composed *tanka* at various places, the most memorable as the train passed Tabaruzaka, the site of the fierce battle in 1877 between the government armies and Saigō Takamori:

mononofu no	At Tabaruzaka
semetatakaishi	Where warriors once attacked
Tabaruzaka	And fought in battle,
matsu mo oiki ni	Now even the sapling pines
narinikeru kana	Have turned into aged trees.[25]

He presented this poem to Lieutenant General Nogi Maresuke, a member of his escort, no doubt because Nogi had fought in the battle at Tabaruzaka. Nogi's poem was more vivid:

no ni yama ni	In fields and mountains
uchijini nashishi	Where my friends fought and found
tomobito no	Death in battle
chi no iro misuru	The autumn leaves on the trees
kigi no momijiba	Show the color of their blood.

The emperor's renewed interest in poetic composition was probably the most positive aspect of the journey. He usually enjoyed going on maneuvers, but this time he was strangely uninterested, and he even had a fit of temper on November 14 when a banquet was held in the castle for members of the imperial family and many high-ranking persons, both Japanese and foreign. The banquet was to begin at 2:30 that afternoon, but when Chief Chamberlain Tokudaiji informed the emperor that it was time to leave for the banqueting hall, he refused to go. The guests in the banquet hall were worried when the emperor failed to appear, wondering what had happened. General Yamagata stopped an attendant and demanded why the emperor was so late when the guests were eagerly waiting for him. When he failed to get a satisfactory answer, Yamagata himself went to the emperor and urged him to attend the banquet. The emperor refused, saying that he had his reasons.

Yamagata, astonished by this response, told the emperor that officers and men had been deeply moved and encouraged to see how the emperor, following the traditions of Emperor Jimmu, had day after day exposed himself to the elements. He imagined how disappointed they would be if he failed to appear at the banquet and reminded the emperor that his every action served as a model for his worshipful subjects. If now, without reason, he refused to appear, this would dampen the ardor of the entire army and disappoint the officials and people of the region. The emperor might be indifferent to the possibility that people might doubt his wisdom, but he, Yamagata, could not endure this. His voice rose with excitement as he concluded, begging the emperor to change his mind and go to the banquet hall.

The emperor, interrupting him, said, "When the plan for me to go to the west first came up, the officials asked to cancel it because of a cholera epidemic, but the military were against this and said that as long as strict control was exerted over what I ate and drank, there was no danger of infection. They claimed it would make a tremendous difference to the morale of the troops whether or not I went and begged me to make the trip. I decided they were right and made the journey. Ever since I arrived, the officials have been all fear and trembling about my health and have taken every precaution with the kitchen. I have also been extremely careful, as you are well aware. Now the maneuvers have ended. A banquet like the one today has only one purpose— to reward people who took part. I am still being careful about what I eat and drink, and I don't feel like attending. That's why I am not going. But you come here and keep insisting that I go. You urged me to travel to the west on condition that I was careful in what I ate and drank, but now you are forcing me attend a party where there will be food and drink. Are you and the rest trying to have fun at my expense?"

The emperor's expression was extremely severe. Although filled with fear and trepidation, Yamagata persisted, and finally the emperor yielded and sent for his carriage. It was now 3:20. As soon as the carriage reached the banquet hall, the emperor went to his seat and, after nodding to those present, left immediately, without touching the liquor or food.[26]

It is difficult to understand why the emperor was so determined not to attend the banquet. Perhaps it was simply that he had been tired by maneuvers and was not feeling well; but he may have resented being manipulated by men who, although they pretended to worship him, gave no consideration to his wishes. Nobody asked if he *wished* to travel to Kumamoto; Yamagata and the other leaders of the government decided he would go, even though there was danger of cholera infection. Now Yamagata was insisting that he attend the banquet, regardless of his wishes. The commands that the emperor do this or that were phrased in reverential language, but they were commands all the same, and the emperor was greatly annoyed.

The emperor did not enjoy the Kumamoto maneuvers, but on the return journey he directed his military attaché (*jijū bukan*) to compose a war song commemorating the occasion:

> *Meiji sanjū / yū go nen*
> *koro wa shimotsuki / nakabagoro*
> *daigensui no / mihata wo ba*
> *Hi no Kumamoto ni / susumerare* ...

> In the five and thirtieth year of Meiji
> Along about the middle of November
> Our commander in chief advanced his flag
> To Kumamoto in the land of Hi ...

The rest of the poem describes both the maneuvers and the return journey, referring also (by mentioning a captured Chinese warship) to the Japanese victory in the Sino-Japanese War:

> *ryūgan itomo / uruwashiku*
> *Tsukushi no kisha ni / mesaretsutsu*
> *kangyo no roji mo / Chōshū naru*
> *oki ni wa Saien / teihaku shi* ...[27]

> His dragon countenance extremely pleased
> He boarded a train in Tsukushi
> And on the way back, off the Chōshū coast,
> The *Chi-yüan* was anchored ...

At the end of December 1902, the House of Representatives was again dissolved, this time because of the failure of the government's proposal to raise property taxes in order to pay for a bigger navy. The opposition parties, headed by Itō Hirobumi's Seiyūkai, were against the plan. The impasse was not resolved by repeated suspensions of the Diet by the emperor, and on the twenty-eighth the House of Representatives voted in favor of dissolution and a new election on March 1, 1903.

The only novelty in the New Year rituals for 1903 was the choice of subject for the lecture on Western history delivered before the emperor on January 6. This year it was devoted to the section of William H. Prescott's *History of the Reign of Ferdinand and Isabella the Catholic* describing Columbus's appeal for funds for his exploration. As usual, there is no indication if Meiji was interested in this lecture, but now, when his country was about to acquire colonies and join the imperialistic powers, he may have wished that a Japanese endowed with the vision of Columbus would appear before him and promise an empire.

But whatever dreams Meiji may have had concerning the future expansion of Japan, with respect to matters closer at hand he remained conservative. On January 9 Sasaki Takayuki, who was charged with the education of Princesses Masako and Fusako, sent word to the chief chamberlain that he was thinking of moving the girls to a place on the coast where they could escape the cold of the Tōkyō winter. When the emperor was consulted, he refused to allow the princesses to leave the city. He reasoned that they were approaching marriageable age and that when a woman married, she had to accommodate herself to the ways of the family she joined. The family into which a woman married might not be sufficiently rich to travel in order to avoid the cold and heat. If the princesses grew accustomed to spending every summer and winter outside the city, this would become a habit, and it might not be easy for them to discard it. It might even be bad for their health. It would be better for them to learn to endure cold and heat. The princesses would spend this winter in Tōkyō. If outdoor exercise was necessary for their health, they might from time to time visit one of the detached palaces or imperial properties.[28]

Although he himself never went anywhere to escape the heat or cold, the emperor did not insist that the crown prince remain in Tōkyō. Probably he feared that heat or cold might seriously affect the prince's health. He may also have feared that forcing the prince to do what he disliked might bring on convulsions or some other nervous disorder, as it had in the past. The crown prince was the one member of the imperial family who lived as he pleased.

On February 2 the crown prince's tutor, Prince Takehito, expressed to the emperor his belief that the office of tutor should be abolished. He said that the crown prince of late not only had made great progress in his studies but was even inclined to study on his own, and his illness had gradually subsided. He believed that the time had come for the prince to be more independent. Now that he was twenty-five years old, people thought it was strange that he should still need a tutor, and this reflected on the imperial household. The emperor responded that if having a tutor was considered inappropriate for the crown prince now that he was a grown man, the title should be changed. In other words, the emperor believed that the prince still needed a tutor, regardless of the title. When consulted by Takehito at the end of the previous month, Itō Hirobumi had also expressed the opinion that the prince still required a tutor, but he recognized that Takehito was exhausted by the physical and mental strain to which he had been subjected for some years, that it would be inhumane to ask him to continue. On February 6 Takehito's title was changed to the crown prince's adviser, but his duties remained the same.[29]

A month later, Takehito again reported to the emperor on the need to foster a spirit of independence in the crown prince, but the emperor had become increasingly cautious about his son's behavior and does not seem to have favored giving him greater independence. He issued the order that if henceforth anyone wished to ask the crown prince's opinion, it should be in writing, and the crown prince's answer should also be in writing.[30]

On January 28 the statue of another problem member of the imperial family, the late Prince Yoshihisa, was erected in front of the barracks of the First and Second Infantry Regiments of the Household Guards.[31] Yoshihisa's wartime service and death in Taiwan no doubt occasioned the erection of the statue, but his earlier career—whether as Rinnōjinomiya or as an extravagant and capricious student in Germany—hardly justified this honor. In contrast, not one statue of Meiji was ever erected, although other sovereigns (such as his near contemporary, Queen Victoria) had no objection to being immortalized in stone or bronze.

On April 7 Meiji left for Kyōto and Ōsaka to observe a Grand Naval Review and the Fifth National Industrial Exhibition. He traveled by train, making several stops along the way and arriving on the following afternoon at Maiko, where he stayed at Prince Takehito's villa. When his train passed Kōbe, the warships outside the harbor, all fully dressed, fired salutes, and at Maiko, the warships anchored offshore were decked with pennants by day and illuminated at night. For two hours before and after dinner, the navy band played. At the emperor's request they played the war song composed in November on his return from army maneuvers in Kumamoto.[32]

The emperor's preference for the army over the navy was no secret. He disliked being aboard warships, in part because he found the smell of oil unpleasant. On April 10, the day of the Grand Naval Review, he chose to wear an army uniform,[33] the one he wore in both winter and summer, regardless of the occasion or season. Although he commanded his military attaché to compose a war song about the occasion and presented it to the navy, the naval personnel were disappointed that the emperor had failed to wear his uniform as commander in chief of the navy.

Several years after the review of 1903, when the Imperial Navy was about to stage another review, a naval uniform was made for the emperor with the request that he wear it at the ceremony. He did not reply, and the navy minister,

Yamamoto Gonnohyōe, fearing that this signified a refusal, requested an audience with the emperor, hoping to change his mind. Before he could say a word, the emperor, guessing what was on Yamamoto's mind, asked, "You've come about the uniform, haven't you?" He promised to wear his new naval uniform. The sight of the emperor in naval attire is said to have greatly raised morale among men of the fleet.[34]

The emperor left Maiko for Kyōto on April 13. On the train he composed a poem in the manner of a war song. He had Chamberlain Sawa Nobumoto write it down and commanded him to say it was his own composition when he showed it to other people:

> *Maiko hamabe no / kashiwayama*
> *kari no miyai wo / gubu nashite*
> *hashiru ressha ni / makasetsutsu*
> *haya Ōsaka ni / tatsu keburi*
> *hikage mo ōte / sora kuraku*
> *kore shōgyo no / hanjō wo*
> *hajimete satoru / gubu no tomo*
> *fuku harukaze mo / samukarazu*
> *yagate Kyōto ni / tsukinikeri*[35]

> Having served His Majesty
> At the temporary Palace of Kashiwayama
> On the shore at Maiko,
> We, his attendants, boarding a speedy train,
> In no time at all reach Ōsaka
> Where smoke rises, obscuring the sunlight,
> And we realize for the first time
> That this shows the prosperity of commerce.
> The blowing spring wind is not cold,
> And soon we arrive at Kyōto.

Sawa suggested that this composition by the emperor, extolling Ōsaka's prosperity, would give great pleasure to people of the city if they knew about it, but the chief chamberlain refrained from asking the emperor's permission to publish it, fearing that this might incur his wrath.

On April 20 the emperor attended the opening ceremonies of the Fifth National Industrial Exhibition in Ōsaka. No doubt it greatly pleased him to see the progress that Japan had achieved in industry as well as in agriculture, commerce, and education.[36] He and the members of his escort wore full-dress regalia for the ceremonies, where they were joined by the ministers of thirteen foreign countries and many Japanese dignitaries. It was an occasion for satisfaction in the "smoke capital" of Japan.

In the meantime, however, disquieting reports were being received from China on the slow progress of the withdrawal of Russian troops from Manchuria. The Russians had promised to withdraw in three stages. One stage had been completed, and the railway between Shan-hai-kwan and Ying-k'ou (Newchang) had been returned, but all this meant was that the Russians had moved their troops from Liao-hsi, a region where they had few interests, to their major base at Liaotung. The Russians were far more reluctant to carry out the second-stage withdrawal, which included Port Arthur and Dairen. The deadline of April 8 passed without any Russian withdrawal; instead, the Russians presented the Chinese government with seven demands that it would have to fulfill if it wanted its territory returned. The demands amounted to complete control over the administration and economy of Manchuria, which would mean that commercial relations with all other countries would be blocked.[37]

The Japanese were dismayed to learn of the new demands but could not agree on how to react. On March 15 at a meeting of the genrō, Itō Hirobumi had stated that England and Germany would not use force against Russian actions in Manchuria. If Japan, not backed by any other power, opposed Russia, this might lead to a conflict of views that in the end could be resolved only by war. He favored modeling Japan's responses on those of England and Germany. With respect to Korea, the goal should be to preserve the status quo; Japan should try to reach an understanding with Russia that there would be no conflict between the two countries.

Itō's opinions were not easily disregarded, but when the foreign minister, Komura Jutarō, learned of Russia's new demands on China, he at once sent a severe warning to China not to yield. At the same time he believed that the time had come to open direct negotiations with Russia. He persuaded Itō to go with him to Yamagata Aritomo's residence in Kyōto to discuss basic policy.

Just at this time a telegram arrived from the minister to China reporting that the Russian army had begun moving. One battalion was preparing to occupy the forest on the bank of the Yalu River. A similar communication was received from the Japanese minister to Korea.

Those meeting at Yamagata's villa on April 21 came to the conclusion that Russia's activity in Manchuria and northern Korea threatened Korea's existence and was incompatible with Japanese policy. The four men[38] decided that although they were willing to make concessions on Manchuria, they would insist on their rights in Korea, even at the risk of war.[39]

There is no indication that the emperor had been apprised of the potentially dangerous situation. He was staying in Kyōto but traveled to Ōsaka repeatedly to visit the exposition. The empress usually went on the following day to the same places the emperor had visited. On May 2 the emperor listened to a phonograph that had been lent to the exhibition by Matsumoto Takeichirō of Ōsaka. The emperor, greatly pleased with this new invention, purchased it for seventy-five yen. Later, Matsumoto presented the emperor with five wax cylinders. The first was a recording of "Kimigayo," the national anthem. The second was a performance by Tachibana Chijō, the master of the Chikuzen biwa, playing "Lord Kusunoki at the Battle of Sakurai." The remaining cylinders were devoted to war songs.[40] Matsumoto evidently knew the emperor's tastes.

On the following day after the emperor had visited the tombs of Emperor Kōmei and Empress Eishō at Tsukinowa behind the Sennyū-ji, he wrote one of his most moving poems:

tsuki no wa no	When I visited
misasagi mōde	The tombs at Tsukinowa
suru sode ni	On my sleeves
matsu no furuba mo	Old needles from the pines
chirikakaritsutsu	Kept falling.[41]

When the emperor left Kyōto to return to Tōkyō on May 10, he was seen off by all the nobles and other great dignitaries. The visit had been a happy interlude, but two days later, back in Tōkyō, the emperor learned from Ōyama Iwao, the chief of the general staff, of the critical situation developing in Korea. According to reports received from the army attaché in Korea, Russia had occupied Korean territory on the left bank of the Yalu River estuary and had begun to construct military facilities intended to block any Japanese advance. It was clear that the Russians had no intention of withdrawing from Manchuria; Ōyama believed that their aim was permanent possession of the three eastern provinces.

Ōyama compared the relative military strength of Russia and Japan. Although the completion of the Trans-Siberia Railway had made it possible to transport Russian troops to East Asia more quickly than before, the railway was still not functioning adequately. All the same, troops would be steadily reinforced. At present, Russian naval strength was only about three-quarters that of the Japanese, but it was likely to surpass Japanese strength in a few years if current plans for expansion were completed.

In view of this situation, Ōyama concluded, Japan must act now in order to control the boundless greed of the Russians, to preserve the independence of China and Korea, and to maintain the rights of the Japanese. The longer Japan waited, the harder it would become to realize its objectives. If Japan yielded Manchuria to the Russians and allowed them to extend their long arms into Korean territory on the other side of the Yalu River, it would mean that Korean independence was no more and China was in danger. If these two countries perished, how could Japan alone hope to remain safe?

Ōyama revealed that he had warned Korea of the Russians' moves, but the Korean government was powerless to act, and the Japanese government therefore had no choice but to convey to the Russians its determined opposition.[42]

The emperor's reactions to this report are not known, but surely he must have been startled by the likelihood that war with the most powerful country in the world was imminent. After the idyllic visit to Kyōto where he had relived the past, he was suddenly faced with the shock of the present.

Chapter 53

On June 1, 1903, seven doctors of law sent Prime Minister Katsura Tarō a memorial concerning Japan's future policy with respect to Russia.[1] The tone was hard-line, interpreting the current tension between Japan and Russia as the latest in a series of crises and all but calling for war if Russia failed to meet Japanese demands. Their arguments were typical of those expressed by many Japanese leaders during the following eight months of negotiations with Russia.

The first crisis, said the doctors of law, was occasioned by Japan's inability after the Sino-Japanese War to retain the Liaotung Peninsula in the face of the demands of the three powers (Russia, Germany, and France); this was the ultimate cause of the present crisis in Manchuria. Next, Japan had lacked the sea power necessary to repulse the Germans when they were casting covetous eyes on Kiaochow Bay. If Japan had been able to prevent the Germans from seizing Chinese territory, the Russians would not have found it so easy to demand leases of Port Arthur and Dairen. Finally, the failure to establish a detailed schedule for the withdrawal of troops from Manchuria after the Boxer Rebellion had given the Russians the chance to procrastinate over their withdrawal.

The new crisis arose from the Russians' failure to carry out the promised second phase of withdrawal. If Japan let this pass unquestioned, it would be tantamount to missing a golden opportunity for action. The seven doctors of law believed that Japan had already missed three such opportunities, and they were anxious not to let this happen again. They pointed out that Russia had steadily encroached on Manchuria, strengthening its position on land by building railways, ramparts, and batteries and, on the sea, by devoting immense efforts to its fleet. Recent reports made it clear that the purpose of these armaments was to intimidate Japan. Every day of delay increased the danger. Japan could maintain its military superiority for less than a year at the longest.

At present, they said, Russia could not match Japan militarily, but once the Russians felt confident in their forces, it could hardly be doubted that, not content with Manchuria, they would turn their attention to Korea. Once Korea was in their hands, it is obvious where they would look next. Unless the question of Manchuria was resolved, Korea was doomed, and if Korea was doomed, Japan could not hope to defend itself.

But there was hope for Japan; in fact, there was a Heaven-sent chance. The Russians still did not have a firm base of operations in the Far East. Japan had the geographic advantage. Forty million and more Japanese were as one in their secret hatred of Russian actions. If the Japanese failed to take advantage of these factors, the heritage from their ancestors would be endangered, and the happiness of their descendants would be destroyed.

The seven doctors, urging prompt action, rebutted those who said Japan must act cautiously in foreign relations, first studying the attitudes of England and America and the intentions of Germany and France. But the attitudes of these countries were clear. Although Germany and France would not support Japan, they also would not support Russia, because in accordance with Japan's alliance with England, making an enemy of Japan meant making an enemy of Britain. And Britain would not be willing to face this danger for the sake of Manchuria. The Americans' objective was the Open Door, and as long as the door was kept open, they did not care whether the sovereignty was Chinese or Russian; all that interested them was commercial profits. To wait for the Americans to make up their minds—to assume that they were Japan's steadfast comrades in a foreign policy aimed at ensuring peace in the Far East and the security of China—would be to deprive Japan of its freedom to act.

People say that under no circumstances should Japan lose Korea. This is correct, but to protect Korea, Japan must not let Manchuria fall into the Russians' hands. Therefore it is essential in diplomatic disputes that Japan not allow the Russians to limit the discussion to Korea, as if Manchuria were already acknowledged to be under Russian influence.

In legal terms, the seven doctors of law continued, Russia must withdraw its troops from Manchuria, which does not mean moving troops from place A to place B in Manchuria. The railway guards must also be withdrawn. Japan has the right to demand that Russia fulfill its part of the agreement. Above all, Japan must be wary of Russian politicians who with honeyed tongues propose an exchange of Manchuria for Korea or any similar temporizing measure. Japan must take definitive measures to solve fundamentally the problem of the return of Manchurian territory and to maintain peace in the Far East.

Although the seven doctors did not say so plainly, they obviously believed that Japan should present Russia with an ultimatum, and if the Russians refused to comply with Japanese wishes on Manchuria, Japan should declare war while it held the upper hand militarily.

The seven doctors had sympathizers, but war did not seem imminent. Soon after the presentation of this memorial, the Russian minister of war, General Alexis Nikolaevich Kuropatkin, and nine other high-ranking officers who had made a tour of inspection of Vladivostok and Port Arthur, visited Japan. They were treated as state guests and on June 13 had audiences with the emperor and empress. The luncheon given by the emperor for the Russian visitors and legation personnel was attended by Yamagata Aritomo, Ōyama Iwao, and members of the cabinet. On the same day Kuropatkin was decorated with the Order of the Rising Sun, First Class, and members of his suite received lesser decorations. Kuropatkin's visit, made by command of the czar, was for the purpose of observing the situation in Japan and learning Japanese intentions, but the Japanese felt honored.

The Japanese naturally avoided discussing military matters with the visiting Russians, but in casual conversations they expressed regret that the two countries were constantly opposed on questions relating to the Far East. Kuropatkin expressed the hope that war could be avoided and the situation dealt with peacefully. Before he left Tōkyō to return to Russia, he conveyed the czar's verbal message to the emperor: "Your country, unlike other countries, is a neighbor, and for this reason I hope that the relations between our two countries will be particularly close. I hope also, now that the Siberian Railway has been completed, that our future relations will be increasingly intimate."[2]

Despite these friendly words, the war parties in both countries became ever more vociferous. On June 22 Ōyama Iwao, the chief of the general staff, expressed his conviction to the emperor that the question of Korea urgently required settlement, by military force if necessary. He submitted to the cabinet on the same day a written opinion declaring that if Japan let things take their natural course, the Korean peninsula would become Russian territory in three or four years. This would leave Japan with nothing more than narrow strip of water separating it from a country that was as ferocious as a tiger or a wolf. Ōyama favored efforts to achieve a peaceful settlement with Russia through negotiations, but if, unfortunately, war broke out, the Japanese army was a fair match for the Russian army. Now was the best time to settle the Korean question in such a way as to guarantee national security for a hundred years.[3]

On June 23 at the request of Katsura and Komura, the emperor summoned nine of the country's outstanding men to discuss in his presence Japan's future policy toward Russia.[4] Komura read a statement that, like the memorial by the seven doctors of law, declared that Russia's failure to live up to its promise of withdrawing troops from Manchuria presented the Japanese with an opportunity for settling the Korean question, which had hung fire for several years. First of all, Komura insisted, Korea must not yield territory to Russia, regardless of the reasons. But some concessions might be made to Russia with respect to Manchuria, where it had the preponderance. He suggested that a conference be held in Tōkyō.[5] Katsura was equally determined not to allow Russia to take any part of Korea, but he believed that if Korea were openly made a Japanese possession, this would invite a clash.

The Japanese minister in St. Petersburg was instructed to ask if the Russians were willing to attend a conference with the Japanese. However, the show of unity during the discussion before the emperor was deceptive. Itō's party, the Seiyūkai, though conciliatory on this occasion, continued its attacks on Katsura, especially concerning the property tax. On the following day Katsura invited Itō, Yamagata, and Navy Minister Yamamoto to his residence. He informed them that because he felt incapable of dealing with the crisis, he wished to resign his office. He believed that only a *genrō* was capable of assuming leadership and asked either Itō or Yamagata to form a cabinet. He himself, although he would withdraw to the sidelines, would cooperate in every way. Itō and the others protested, but Katsura nevertheless submitted his resignation, alleging illness.[6]

No solution being found to this impasse, the matter (as so often) was left for the emperor to decide. He summoned Katsura and informed him that at a critical time, when negotiations were about to begin with the Russians on Korea and Manchuria, he could not permit the resignation. He urged Katsura to remain in office while recuperating from his illness.

On July 13 the emperor appointed Itō Hirobumi as president of the Privy Council. There can be little doubt that the emperor valued Itō's opinions more highly than those of anyone else in the government. On July 6 he had sent for Itō to discuss relations with Russia. The emperor said that Japan might be on the brink of war with Russia over Manchuria and Korea. The prospects were by no means reassuring, and he wanted Itō to serve in the Privy Council so that he might advise him on major national issues. Itō asked for a few days to think it over. On the eighth, the emperor sent Itō a message in writing explaining that it was because he needed Itō's frank opinions that he was imposing on him by asking him to take an additional position: "I have depended on and trusted your service over the years, and I hope that with your sound advice and faithful assistance we shall successfully accomplish the task ahead."[7]

This was probably the most unambiguous statement of esteem that the emperor ever gave to any of his subjects. Itō replied that he would accept His Majesty's gracious command, but in his heart he was by no means pleased, suspecting that Yamagata had suggested this tactic to the emperor. Yamagata himself met Itō and used all his eloquence to persuade Itō to accept the appointment. In the end Itō agreed, provided that both Yamagata and Matsukata also become members of the Privy Council. Finally, the emperor summoned Katsura, supposedly from his sickbed, and informed him that Itō would accept his new post only if Katsura remained in office. Itō confirmed this later that day when Katsura visited him, and Katsura, after long deliberation, withdrew his resignation.

The Japanese government was now unified. On July 28 Foreign Minister Komura asked Kurino Shin'ichirō, the minister to Russia, to deliver to the Russian foreign minister, Count Vladimir Nikolaevich Lamsdorf, a verbal message indicating that the Japanese hoped to open negotiations concerning Manchuria and Korea. If the Russians were in general agreement, the Japanese government would send proposals concerning the nature and scope of the negotiations. Kurino was also asked to relate that in the interests of friendship and amity, the Japanese hoped that such negotiations could be opened without delay.[8]

On August 12 Kurino delivered to Lamsdorf the text of the Japanese proposals. They were in six articles:

1. The two countries promise to respect the independence and territorial integrity of China and Korea and to maintain a policy of equal commercial and industrial opportunities for all countries.
2. Russia and Japan mutually recognize the special interests of Japan in Korea and of Russia in the railway administration in Manchuria.
3. Japan and Russia mutually promise not to interfere with the development of each other's commercial and industrial enterprises—Japan in Korea and Russia in Manchuria.
4. In the event that disturbances in Korea or Manchuria require the expedition of troops, they should not exceed the number actually needed, and once they have completed their mission, they should be at once withdrawn.
5. Russia recognizes that Japan has the exclusive right to aid and assist (including militarily) Korea in the interests of good government.
6. This treaty is to take the place of all previous agreements reached by Japan and Russia with respect to Korea.[9]

The Japanese government submitted this plan with confidence that it could serve as the basis for an agreement between Japan and Russia, and it was hoped that the Russian government's modifications or contrary views would be made in a friendly spirit. Although these proposals were telegraphed to Kurino on August 3, he was unable to meet Count Lamsdorf until August 12. The excuse was that he was busy. The real cause was a major change in the administration of Russian territories in the Far East. On August 12, the day that Kurino was at last able to deliver Komura's proposal, the czar signed a ukase establishing the viceroyalty of the Far East, which unified all military, economic, and diplomatic affairs of the Russian possessions in the provinces and territories east of Lake Baikal under Viceroy Evgenii Ivanovich Alekseev.[10]

The change came as a great and painful surprise to Count Sergei Witte, the minister of finance and the most able man in the Russian government. On

August 28[11] when he delivered his regular monthly report, the czar suddenly informed him that he had been transferred from the position of minister of finance to the eminent but meaningless position of chairman of the committee of ministers. Witte believed that he was being removed from an active role in the government because he opposed policies that, he was sure, would lead to war with Japan.[12] When Witte learned that Alekseev, a man he despised as an "egregious careerist" with "the mentality of a sly Armenian rug dealer,"[13] had been appointed as viceroy, he interpreted this as meaning that the czar had accepted the views of hard-line extremists that the Russians could obtain whatever they wanted in the East because the Japanese would not dare to fight. He added that the czar "in his heart thirsted for the glory that would come from a victorious war. I am convinced that had there been no war with Japan there would have been a war with India [over Afghanistan] or, more likely, war with Turkey, over the Bosphorus, and such a war would, of course, have turned into a larger war."[14] The czar, for his part, wrote laconically in his diary on the day of Witte's dismissal, "Now I rule."[15] Witte recalled the Japanese proposal in these terms:

> Not long after my return to Russia, Kurino, the Japanese minister to Russia, came to see me. In July 1903, while I was still minister of finance, he had presented a proposal to me and Count Lambsdorff that would have made a peaceful settlement of our differences possible. I favored acceptance, but to no avail, because it was sent to Viceroy Alekseev and became the subject of endless and fruitless discussion.
>
> This intelligent man [Kurino] told me how my country was dragging out negotiations while his was acting with dispatch. Japan would make a proposal, Lambsdorff would say that matters were in Alekseev's hands, while Alekseev and [Roman] Rosen [the Russian minister to Japan] would say that their hands were tied because the Emperor [czar] was away. To Japan this sort of tactic meant that we wanted war, and he felt it a matter of honor to do what he could to prevent conflict. Time was short, he argued. Japanese public opinion was becoming increasingly aroused and was therefore difficult to keep under control. After all, he declared, Japan was a sovereign state, and it was humiliating for her to have to negotiate with some sort of "viceroy of the Far East," as if the Far East belonged to Russia and Japan was but a protectorate.[16]

Kurino's comments were perceptive. He was aware, of course, that Komura's proposals could not be accepted unchanged by the Russians. The second item was perhaps the least acceptable to them. All that was given to Russia in return for recognizing the preponderance of Japanese interests in Korea was the administration of railways in Manchuria. This was clearly an unequal bargain, but when Komura advanced this proposal, he no doubt expected to make further concessions. The Russians' failure to respond promptly to Komura's proposals was interpreted by the Japanese as a deliberate insult, and this, on top of their failure to fulfill their promise of a second-stage withdrawal from Manchuria, had inflamed Japanese public opinion. Patriots, headed by the seven doctors of law, now openly called for war.[17]

The Japanese had to wait fifty-two days for a counterproposal from Russia. Count Lamsdorf gave as reasons the absence of the czar and the need to discuss some points with Alekseev. He suggested that negotiations take place in Tōkyō.[18] This was originally proposed by the Japanese but now was unwelcome because of the establishment of the viceroyalty: in Tōkyō the Japanese would have to negotiate not with the highest echelon of Russian command but with the Russian minister Baron Rosen, an underling of Alekseev, and this would represent a loss of face for them.[19] In the end, the Japanese yielded, and on October 3 the first Russian counterproposals were delivered to the Japanese government.

The counterproposals amounted to an almost complete rejection of the original Japanese proposals. The first article in the counterproposals guaranteed the independence and territorial integrity of Korea but not of China, and there was hardly a mention of Manchuria in any of the articles, implying that Russian control was not to be discussed. The eighth article, the only one that did mention Manchuria, demanded that Japan recognize that Manchuria and its littoral were completely outside its sphere of influence. A new element was a proposed neutral zone to be established in Korea north of the thirty-ninth parallel into which neither country should introduce troops, thus limiting Japanese powers in that country.[20] The differences between the two countries' proposals were so great as to make compromise seem impossible.

Komura met with Baron Rosen in an attempt to reconcile the Japanese and Russian proposals and find a basis for a settlement, but Rosen said he was not empowered to make any alterations. On October 30 Komura handed to Rosen the second set of Japanese proposals, in eleven articles. The first article, as before, was a mutual affirmation of the independence and territorial integrity of China and Korea. Articles 2 to 4 called for Russia's recognition of Japan's preponderance in Korea. Article 5 was a promise by Japan not to erect fortifications that might interfere with free passage through the Korea Strait. Article 6 provided for a neutral zone of thirty miles on both sides of the border between Korea and Manchuria. Articles 7 and 8 stipulated that Manchuria was outside the Japanese sphere of influence and that Russia had the right to take necessary measures to protect its interests there. The remaining articles dealt with trade and railways.[21]

The Japanese waited for more than forty days for the Russian reply, which finally arrived on December 11. The Russians attributed the delay to the illness of the czarina, who had been stricken while traveling with the czar. At such a time his ministers did not dare to approach the czar with such "trifles" as the situation in the Far East which, the czar supposed, had already calmed down.

The new Russian proposals were even more one-sided than the old ones: those concerning Korea were reiterated, but every mention of Manchuria had been deleted. The Japanese, believing that they had made many concessions in the spirit of compromise, were dismayed by what they interpreted as a display of Russian arrogance.[22]

Not every Russian was so intransigent. On December 10 General Kuropatkin transmitted to the czar a long memorandum on Russian aims in the Far East that recommended:

> To give Kwantung back to China with Port Arthur and Dalny [Dairen]; to hand over the southern branch of the Chinese Eastern Railway to China, but in return to receive all the rights in northern Manchuria, in addition to 250,000,000 rubles in compensation for the Russian expenses incurred in the building of the railroad and Port Arthur.[23]

Witte was in general sympathy with Kuropatkin's plan, but he wrote in his memoirs:

> Manchuria could not be ours. We should have been content with the Kwantung Peninsula that we had taken so perfidiously and with the Chinese Eastern Railroad. Not America, not England, not Japan, nor any of their open or secret allies, nor China would have ever have agreed to let us have Manchuria.[24]

Even the czar, for all his yearning for military victory, telegraphed Alekseev in October: "I do not want a war between Russia and Japan and will not allow it. Take all measures so that war will not occur." At the special conference called by the czar on December 28, 1903, he observed, "War is unquestionably undesirable. Time is Russia's best ally. Every year strengthens us."[25]

By this time, however, Japanese patience was exhausted, and they felt humiliated by the Russian lack of diplomatic courtesy. On December 16 at a meeting of the prime minister, the *genrō*, and members of the cabinet, two decisions were reached: (1) that a solution by diplomatic means should be sought first to last with respect to Manchuria, and the use of "ultimate means" should be avoided; and (2) that with respect to Korea, Japan would maintain the principles enunciated in the revised proposal of October 30, but if the Russians refused to accept these principles, they themselves would resort to arms to achieve their objectives.[26]

The meeting decided to make one more, final, attempt to reach a diplomatic solution. Katsura felt uncomfortable at the idea of a "final step," but on December 18 he called a meeting of cabinet ministers and informed them of the decision. Afterward, he and Komura went together to the palace to report to the emperor and ascertain his views. From this point on, although Komura continued to devote every effort to the negotiations, Katsura repeatedly met with the ministers of the army, the navy and the treasury, and these men prepared for war.

On December 21 instructions were sent to Kurino to present orally the third Japanese proposal.[27] The most noteworthy change was the elimination of article 6, which had provided for the establishment of a neutral zone. The Japanese were willing to create such a zone, even though it would encompass about one-third of Korea, provided that the Russians would create a similar buffer zone on the Manchurian side of the frontier; but the Russians had not deigned to respond to this suggestion.

The new Japanese proposals were pessimistically received in Russia. On December 23 Admiral Alekseev addressed the czar: "The new Japanese proposals, transmitted to me by telegram from Baron Rosen on December 22, are tantamount to a demand for formal recognition by the Russian government of a protectorate of Japan over Korea."[28]

Naturally, the Russians were unwilling to grant this, although the possibility of referring to Manchuria in their next proposal was seriously considered. In Tōkyō, however, more and more members of the government thought that war could not be avoided. On December 28 a special cabinet council was called to discuss the final preparations for war.[29]

During these months of increasing tension, the emperor's thoughts were preoccupied by the possibility of war. He probably had little time to think of his family, although the crown prince's behavior may have worried him. The prince was promoted in October (after two years in grade) to colonel in the army and captain in the navy. His military duties were minimal, but he traveled that month to Wakayama, Kagawa, Ehime, and Okayama Prefectures. In addition to the obligatory visits to schools and displays of local products, the crown prince enjoyed seeing Yashima, the site of the great battle between the Heike and the Minamoto, the hot springs at Dōgo, and various temples. Before returning to Tōkyō, he recuperated at his villa in Numazu.[30]

The education of his daughters continued to concern the emperor. Sasaki Takayuki, who was entrusted with the upbringing of Princesses Masako and Fusako, proposed at this time that science and classical Chinese be added to their studies. The emperor did not object to classical Chinese but thought that science was too elevated and might interfere with more necessary studies.[31] He also maintained that they needed most to study the geography of the world and European languages. Perhaps the emperor had in mind the possibility that one or more of his daughters might marry foreign princes, in the manner of European royalty.

The only novel feature of New Year's Day 1904 was that because the crown prince and princess happened to be in Tōkyō, they paid their respects to the emperor. They also held a court of their own for the first time.[32] On the following day Konoe Atsumaro, the most promising member of the high nobility, died in his forty-second year. This must have been a particular blow to Meiji, who worried about the future role of the nobility in governing Japan.

On January 6 Rosen delivered to Komura the Russian response to the third set of Japanese proposals.[33] The Russians still demanded the establishment of a neutral zone within Korea (but not within Manchuria) and insisted that the Japanese not use Korea for strategic purposes. If both these conditions were met, within Manchuria, Russia would not "impede Japan, nor other powers in the enjoyment of the rights and privileges acquired by them under existing treaties with China, exclusive of the establishment of settlements."[34] This was a concession, but the Japanese considered that the Russians had not responded to key issues and saw little reason to continue the negotiations.

On January 12 a conference attended by sixteen men, including genrō, cabinet members, and high-ranking army and navy officers, was held in the presence of the emperor. Although Katsura and Komura had concluded that there was no room for further negotiations and that the issue would have to be decided by military means, naval preparations for a war were not yet complete. The transports needed to carry men to the continent could not be assembled at Sasebo before the twentieth of the month. It would therefore be disadvantageous to Japan if war broke out earlier. Katsura had Komura prepare one last revised proposal; even if it failed to win Russian concessions, it would at least give the Japanese needed time before commencing hostilities.[35]

The final proposals opened with the request to suppress the clause in article 5 stating Japan was "not to use any part of Korean territory for strategic purposes" and to suppress all of article 6 concerning the establishment of a neutral zone. The Russian proposals concerning Manchuria would be modified to include an agreement by Russia to respect the territorial integrity of China in Manchuria.[36]

The Japanese could have had little hope that Russia would agree to these changes. The Russians found the language so provocative as to constitute an ultimatum that did not allow for further discussion. Their reply, as usual, was slow in coming. In the meantime, preparations were initiated by the Japanese for the war that would follow if negotiations broke down. On January 16 orders were given to the army to ready four battalions of infantry for transport to Inch'on, the port of Seoul. Japan planned to occupy Seoul and make it the center of operations during the war.[37]

On January 18 the annual lecture on European history delivered before the emperor was devoted to reading an extract from David Hume's *History of England* describing the defeat of the Spanish Armada by the British, a curiously prophetic choice.[38] The emperor's *tanka*, composed on the theme of "Pines on the Rocks" at the first poetry meeting of the year, was ambiguous enough to be interpreted as a prayer of safety for Japan in the war that threatened.[39]

By this time, both Japan and Russia seem to have resigned themselves to war, but in France efforts continued to avert a conflict. The French were in a difficult position, being tied to Russia by an alliance but having recently become close also to England, an enemy of Russia and an ally of Japan. The French had enormous investments in Russia that they were determined to preserve. On January 23 Maurice Paléologue, the deputy director of political affairs at the Ministry for Foreign Affairs in Paris, wrote in his diary:

> [Foreign Minister Théophile] Delcassé is skilfully continuing his efforts to bring St. Petersburg and Tōkyō near together. He has hit upon certain ingenious formulae which would simultaneously solve both the Manchu and Korean problems. He has been equally skilful in exploiting the support he has managed to get from London. Lansdowne, Komura and Lamsdorf have been showering thanks upon him.
> "I think I'm going to bring it off," he said to me this morning.
> His face was radiant and his eyes positively sparkled.
> I told the Minister of the latest revelations which make me feel certain that Russia wants war, or at any rate is putting herself in a position to send Japan a threatening ultimatum which will almost inevitably result in war.
> Delcassé's face clouded over at once:
> "You don't expect me to believe *that*, do you? I'm corresponding daily with the Tsar. Only yesterday he thanked me for comprehending his views so well and working so hard in the cause of peace. And, according to you, he means war all the time! What next!"[40]

Delcassé was sure, on the basis of personal contacts, that Czar Nicholas II was extremely anxious to settle the quarrel between Japan and Russia by diplomatic means. But (as Paléologue elsewhere pointed out) he dreamed of extending his frontiers still farther and annexing not only Manchuria and Korea but also Tibet, Persia, and perhaps Turkey. Paléologue described the character of Nicholas II in these terms: "He is not very intelligent, but timid, credulous, slack, vacillating, very susceptible to occult influences. . . . And he lets himself be led by a gang of visionaries, speculators and filibusters who are absolutely set on war."[41]

Paléologue related how Nicholas II (whom he termed "shifty and a dissembler—like all weak creatures") had got around ministers who opposed the collision course with Japan by creating the viceroyalty of the Far East without even consulting them. If the viceroy had been truly outstanding, the situation might have been remedied, but as Witte wrote of Admiral Alekseev, who during the ensuing war became commander in chief of the Russian armed forces, "he knew nothing about the army and little about the navy." He had risen to eminence because when Grand Duke Alexis was interrogated by the police after behaving in a disorderly fashion at a Marseilles brothel, Alekseev had taken the blame, saying there had been a confusion between Alexis and Alekseev. The grateful grand duke, for this reason, recommended Alekseev as chief of the Kwantung region.[42]

It is astonishing that the czar chose such a man for a position of extraordinary importance. Witte attributed such unpredictable actions to Nicholas's "feminine character," quoting a remark that it was only by a whim of fate that Nicholas was born with the traits that distinguish male from female. Everyone who knew Nicholas said that he had fundamentally a good character and that he was passionately devoted to his wife and children, but his vacillation made him a difficult master to serve. His conviction that he derived his authority from God, to whom alone he was responsible, might account for his sense of the coming war with Japan as a holy mission. He was certain that Russia would win, even though it might require some effort.[43]

Nicholas was also under the influence of Wilhelm II of Germany. It is hard to imagine a worse influence. As early as April 1895, the kaiser wrote to his "cousin,"[44] "I shall certainly do all in my power to keep Europe quiet and also guard the rear of Russia so that nobody shall hamper your action toward the Far East! For that is clearly the great task of the future for Russia to cultivate the Asian Continent and to defend Europe from the inroads of the Great Yellow race. In this you will always find me at your side ready to help you as best I can."[45] Again and again in his letters to the czar, the kaiser vented his hatred of the Yellow Peril and his conviction that it was Russia's mission to defend "the old Christian European culture against the inroads of the Mongols and Buddhism."[46] (In one letter, the kaiser sketched a drawing of the powers of Europe, represented by their respective genii called together by the Archangel Michael "to unite in resisting the inroad of Buddhism, heathenism and barbarism for the Defense of the Cross.")[47]

"Willy," as the kaiser signed his letters, had a vision of himself as admiral of the Atlantic and Nicholas as admiral of the Pacific. He encouraged Nicholas's ambitions at every stage. On January 3, 1904, for example, he wrote, "It is evident to every unbiassed mind that Korea must be and will be Russian. When or how that is nobody's affair and concerns only you and your country."[48]

It is terrifying to realize that these two emperors were absolute masters of the lives of millions of their subjects. The third emperor to be involved in the approaching war, Meiji, was the only one deserving of his title.

As late as January 30, at an extraordinary council held in St. Petersburg, Foreign Minister Lamsdorf "vigorously and persistently emphasized that the present dispute in no way involves the vital interests of Russia and does not therefore justify the enormous risks of a war which, in any event, the Russian people would not understand. His conclusion was that the Tsar's government should leave no stone unturned to find some peaceful solution of the crisis."[49]

Lamsdorf was backed by all members of the council except Admiral Alexander Ageevich Abaza, described by Witte as a "knave and a scoundrel"[50]—and a tool of the viceroy. Nicholas had allied himself with a band of political adventurers, and each day brought the opening of hostilities closer.

The Russian response to the Japanese "final" proposal was not approved by the czar until February 2. In the meantime, Komura repeatedly instructed Kurino to urge the Russians to reply promptly. Kurino reported that the Russians were stalling to gain time to strengthen military preparations.[51] On January 30 at a meeting in the prime minister's residence, Itō drafted a memorandum stating that the time had come for Japan to reach a resolute decision. He was supported by all the *genrō* and cabinet ministers present. Two days later, the chief of the army general staff, Ōyama Iwao, advised the emperor that Japan should strike first.

The emperor's most trusted advisers expressed no confidence about the outcome of a war but dwelled on only Japan's desperate military and financial position. The army calculated that Japan had a fifty–fifty chance of winning a war; the navy expected that half its forces would be lost but hoped that the remaining half could destroy the enemy forces.[52] Despite the pessimistic appraisal of Japanese chances, all the decision makers favored a war. They were convinced that it was futile to negotiate any further with the Russians, and they believed that the Russians were a serious threat to both Korea and Japan.

It is conceivable that if the Russian response to the Japanese fourth proposal had arrived earlier, the elimination of the clause "exclusive of the establishment of settlements" in the article concerning rights and privileges acquired by existing treaties from China might have induced the Japanese to reconsider the decision to open hostilities. But the message sent to Admiral Alekseev on February 3, which should have been received in Tōkyō by February 4 or 5 at the latest, did not reach Baron Rosen until February 7.[53]

In the meantime, on February 3, at an audience with the emperor, Prime Minister Katsura and Foreign Minister Komura reported in detail why war with Russia was now inevitable. They asked him to summon a meeting of the *genrō* and cabinet ministers the next day and announce his decision. No Russian reply had been received, even after two weeks of waiting and numerous requests for prompt action. Katsura attributed this discourtesy to Russian contempt for the seeming Japanese lack of the will to fight. He advised that no more time be wasted.[54] The Japanese minister in Paris was instructed to make no further attempt to obtain a reply from the Russian government.

On the following day a break between the two countries was approved at the imperial council.[55] On February 5 the Japanese imperial government, through its minister in St. Petersburg, informed the Russian foreign minister that the Japanese government had decided to terminate negotiations and take such action as it deemed necessary to preserve the freedom and territorial integrity of

Korea. On the same day the emperor issued a rescript to the army and navy informing them that Japan's relations with Russia had been broken, despite all the Japanese efforts to maintain peace.

A poem written by the emperor at this time seems to suggest (though very indirectly) his anxiety:

omou koto	This year, too, when
ōki kotoshi mo	There are so many problems
uguisu no	It is not surprising
koe wa sasuga ni	The voice of the song-thrush
matarenuru kana	Is so longingly awaited.[56]

Chapter 54

The Russo-Japanese War opened without a prior declaration of war by either side. The Japanese navy, determined to wait until the cruisers *Kasuga* and *Nisshin* (recently purchased from Italy) were available for action against the Russian fleet,[1] repeatedly vetoed plans to open hostilities, much to the army's annoyance. Only when the cruisers had safely reached Singapore, the bastion of Japan's ally, did the naval authorities agree to fire the first shots. They realized that it was essential to strike before a powerful Russian fleet, then on its way, arrived in Far Eastern waters.

Before making the decision to fight the Russians, the Japanese had waited in vain for a Russian reply to their proposals. Indeed, the immediate cause of the outbreak of war seems to have been the wounds to Japanese pride. During the past year, the Japanese had again and again been kept waiting by the Russians, who seemed indifferent to the effect that their dilatory behavior might have on Japan. This attitude was an intolerable affront to members of the Japanese government, even those well aware of Russia's military strength. The Japanese might have acted even more quickly if they had known with what pejorative language they and their country were scorned by the czar and his cronies.

Regardless of what the two governments might do, people at the time seemed convinced that war between Japan and Russia was inevitable. The poet Ishikawa Takuboku wrote in his diary on January 13:

The storm winds of East Asia have grown tempestuous. Preparations are under way for the military to move out, and there is a report that a declaration of war is being drafted. Of late people have been in high spirits. There is no avoiding a war now. Since it can't be avoided, I think it the sooner it starts the better, and I look forward to the valiant deeds of a great people.[2]

At our distance from the events, this war may not seem quite so inevitable. It is hard to take seriously, in view of subsequent developments, the ostensible cause of the war: Japan's determination to preserve Korean independence. The Japanese themselves destroyed Korean independence in the year the Russo-Japanese War ended, forcing the Korean emperor to sign a treaty that made Korea a protectorate of Japan. Five years later, Japan annexed Korea. Korean independence was clearly no more than a pretext. Ian Nish wrote,

> In its origins the Russo-Japanese War stands in interesting contrast to other wars. It was not the result of economic pressures, for example the scarcity of resources for the number of people. Certainly Japan was the initiator: she also suffered from a shortage of raw materials and a rapidly growing population. But Korea was not sought for her raw materials or as a place to locate surplus population. Nor was Manchuria at this stage a place for great overseas settlement by Japanese or indeed of great commercial activity. . . . Nor can one say that Japan was in a state of social disintegration and was seeking war as a way of diverting attention from domestic problems. There was not in 1904 an appeal to xenophobia or nationalism or war-lust on the part of the Japanese people in order to deflect them from thoughts of poverty, revolution or political discontent. The decision for war in both countries was taken on a narrow basis and probably owed most to strategic considerations.[3]

The chief strategic consideration was, of course, which country would dominate in Korea and Manchuria. The Japanese were determined not to yield; perhaps their victory in the Sino-Japanese War had given them confidence that they were a match for any country, no matter how big or militarily strong. They informed the Russians on February 6, 1904, that they were terminating negotiations and that they intended henceforth to take such independent action as they deemed appropriate. They may have supposed that this statement was tantamount to a declaration of war,[4] but the sudden commencement of hostilities against Russian ships at Port Arthur and Inch'on was denounced by the Russians as a shameful violation of international law.[5]

The Japanese naturally defended their action, and they were not without support from other countries. Maurice Paléologue of the French Foreign Ministry wrote, "In thus commencing hostilities without a declaration of war, the Japanese are repeating against their enemy the mean tactics which the Russians themselves employed against the Turks on November 30th, 1853, when they surprised and destroyed the Ottoman Black Sea squadron, at anchor off Sinope."[6]

E. J. Dillon, known as "the greatest foreign authority on things Russian,"[7] wrote in 1918,

> The Japanese were accused of hitting below the belt when they fell foul of the Russian squadron unexpectedly, and the charge is still believed by many. I feel bound to state that having followed the ups and downs of the crisis as closely as my sources of information would permit, I formed the conviction that from beginning to end in war, as in peace, the Mikado's government displayed chivalrous loyalty and moderation. The notion that the Russians would have behaved differently from their enemies in dealing the first blow so unexpectedly is, I fear, erroneous. There is extant a telegram [dated February 8] from the Tsar to his viceroy containing this significant injunction: "If on the west of Korea the (Japanese) fleet should sail northward past the 38th parallel, it is open to you to attack them without waiting for the first shot from their side. I rely on you. May God aid you."[8]

The telegram indicated that the Russians would not have hesitated to attack, even without a declaration of war, but the Japanese beat them to the punch. On February 6 the Japanese cabled their minister to Russia to return to Japan, and on the same day the Russian minister to Japan, Baron Roman Rosen, was summoned to the residence of Foreign Minister Komura Jutarō and informed that Japan was severing diplomatic relations with Russia. On returning to the Russian legation, Rosen learned from the Russian naval attaché

> that at 6 A.M. that morning the Japanese fleet had weighed anchor for an unknown destination, divided in two squadrons, one of which was convoying transports having on board two divisions of troops, evidently destined to be landed on the Korean coast, probably at some point on the west coast of the peninsula. The other squadron was no less evidently destined to attack our fleet, which was at anchor in the outer roadstead of Port Arthur, a fact which was known to the Japanese.[9]

Rosen's information was correct, but he was powerless to warn the Russian government, as the Japanese government had suspended the sending of telegrams to foreign countries in order to preserve secrecy. While Rosen and his family were waiting for a ship to take them from Japan, a touching incident took place. My wife was alone in her drawing-room when the arrival of the Grand Mistress of the Empress's household was announced. She said that she had been commissioned by the Empress to express Her Majesty's profound sorrow at seeing us depart under such painful circumstances, and that she begged my wife to accept from her a small souvenir in remembrance of our sojourn in Japan. This souvenir consisted of two small flower vases in silver, adorned with the Imperial Arms.

Baroness Rosen, though somewhat embarrassed to receive a gift from the empress now that their two countries were at war, accepted it in the spirit with which it was offered and asked to have her thanks conveyed.[10] Old-fashioned courtesy lingered on, in a manner hard to imagine today.

On February 8 an expeditionary force, escorted by ships under the command of Rear Admiral Uryū Sotokichi, landed at Inch'on. With little opposition, the troops took Seoul and moved northward toward the Yalu River. At the time two Russian warships and a merchantman were in the harbor. Admiral Uryū ordered the Russian ships to leave the harbor by noon on the following day. If they failed to comply, he would sink them inside the harbor. At ten minutes after twelve the next day, the two warships steamed out of the harbor. Baron Rosen heard that

the *Variag*, followed by the gunboat *Koreetz*, having accepted the Japanese admiral's challenge, slowly steamed, colours flying, officers and men on parade, past the foreign men-of-war anchored in the roads, saluted by our national anthem, heroically going to meet certain destruction at the hands of an enemy who had spread the numerous and powerful vessels of his squadron in a wide semicircle, rendering escape a matter of utter impossibility.[11]

Japanese accounts relate more prosaically that when the *Variag* emerged from the harbor, the *Asama* opened fire. After about an hour of gunfire exchanges, a fire broke out on the *Variag*, which fled back into the harbor. The ship later blew up and sank. That night, the *Koreetz*, engulfed in flames, also sank, and the merchant ship was scuttled by the crew. The Japanese fleet suffered no damage in this first victory.[12]

The main body of the Japanese Combined Fleet sailed from Sasebo on February 6. Two days later, destroyer units at Port Arthur staged night attacks against Russian ships, damaging two battleships and a cruiser. Admiral Tōgō Heihachirō, the commanding officer of the Combined Fleet, ordered the fifteen ships in his command to advance into the harbor at Port Arthur. At 11:30 the next morning, he raised signal flags with the famous message: "Victory or defeat will be determined by this battle. All hands, do your utmost."

At the outbreak of war the naval strength of Russia in the Far East consisted of six first-class battleships and one second-class battleship, nine first-class and two second-class cruisers, as well as smaller craft. All the battleships and second-class cruisers and four of the first-class cruisers were at Port Arthur, while four of the latter were at Vladivostok and one at Inch'on.[13] During the next few weeks, most of this Russian fleet was severely damaged, and the Japanese gained control of the sea, enabling them to blockade Port Arthur and to land forces in Manchuria. The psychological importance to the Japanese of these early victories was, of course, enormous. On reading the somewhat exaggerated newspaper account of the success of the attack on Port Arthur and the battle off the Korean coast, Takuboku exclaimed, "Overcome by joy, I went about three to school, a newspaper under my arm, and discussed the war with the people there."[14]

The Russian declaration of war in the name of the czar was promulgated on February 9. The Japanese declaration was issued on the following day, in the names of the emperor and members of the cabinet.[15] By this time Japanese excitement over the forthcoming war had reached fever pitch, as we can gather from this entry for February 7 in Takuboku's diary:

> Today's newspaper reports that the situation between Japan and Russia has suddenly become critical. I hear that reserves in the village are being called up. The gauntlet has been thrown. A Heaven-sent chance has come. A marvelous thing.[16]

The ensuing Japanese victories at sea and on land are too well known to be recounted in detail again here. They attracted worldwide attention. Naturally, the Japanese were overjoyed, at least until reports came of the heavy casualties. The Koreans, whose land was once again the site of warfare, were less enthusiastic, but they had little choice but to acquiesce in the Japanese occupation. Japan proposed that China remain neutral, explaining that (however welcome China's natural resources and limitless manpower would be) no additional strain should be placed on the exhausted Chinese finances. They also feared that Chinese involvement in the war might cause a recrudescence of the antiforeign violence of the Boxer Rebellion. The Japanese promised to respect China's neutrality, provided the Russians did the same.[17]

England, as the ally of Japan, was bound by the treaty of alliance to fight by Japan's side if a third country joined Russia. Because no other country joined Russia, England did not participate militarily in the war, but great enthusiasm was manifested for the Japanese cause. The most extreme example is found in *A Russo-Japanese War Poem* by Jane H. Oakley, a poem about 250 pages long in 84 cantos. This little-known example of doggerel is in rhymed iambic pentameter. Almost any section is equally ludicrous; the following, from an early canto, describes why the Japanese were successful and the Russians defeated at the naval engagement off Inch'on:

> The Russian sailors were for prowess famed,
> And hardihood, in sailing ships of yore;
> Mechanic skill they seemed inapt to grasp;
> The Japanese excel in science more.
> Japan's Mikado, "Mutsu Hito" named,
> Belongs to oldest dynasty of Kings
> Throughout the world; the Founder's reign
> To times of "Bel" the Babylonian, brings.[18]

The British not only were allies of Japan but from long before had been anti-Russian. The revelation of Russian indifference to the loss of human life during an incident that took place on the night of October 21, 1904, intensified this dislike into such hatred that many favored an immediate declaration of war against Russia. On that night the Second Squadron of the Russian Pacific Fleet, comprising thirty-five ships, was crossing the North Sea when it encountered a fleet of English trawlers on the Dogger Bank. They took these harmless vessels for Japanese destroyers, not considering how unlikely it was that Japanese ships would be operating in the North Sea, and opened fire. One trawler sank, and several others were damaged. Maurice Paléologue commented, "That a fleet of warships, traversing at night a fishing bank well known to all sailors, should mistake a fleet of trawlers for an ambush of enemy destroyers, particularly as these trawlers were carrying the regulation lights—has positively dumbfounded the British public." The last straw was the decision of the Russian admiral, after realizing his mistake, to continue on his way without stopping to pick up the unfortunate fishermen.[19]

English public opinion was unanimous in demanding reparation from the Russian government. The French foreign minister told Paléologue, "It would not surprise me if war broke out at any moment." But he thought that public opinion in Russia probably had been equally aroused because Russia regarded England as the traditional enemy, an enemy hated far more than the Japanese. The incident was finally settled with help from the French, and the Russian squadron continued on its way toward its fatal rendezvous with the Japanese fleet off Tsushima.

Baron Rosen was disappointed by public opinion in other countries. He said it "was everywhere arraigned against us, even in America, where we would least have expected it. To some extent this was probably due to the apparently glaring disproportion of the combatants, which naturally, as a purely sporting proposition, enlisted the sympathies of neutral onlookers on what had seemed to be the weaker side."[20]

Rosen's surprise that the United States favored Japan was probably based on his assumption that the problem of Japanese immigration to California would predispose the Americans in favor of Russia. But President Theodore Roosevelt detested the Russians, as he revealed in a letter of August 1905: "No human beings, black, yellow, or white could be quite as untruthful, as insincere, as arrogant—in short, as untrustworthy in every way—as the Russians under the present system." Occasionally he also criticized Japan (in much milder terms), but on the whole he remained pro-Japanese both because he hated the Russian government and its "preposterous little Czar"[21] and because, as an ardent advocate of physical fitness, he was impressed by the samurai tradition as described in *Bushidō* by Nitobe Inazō, one of his favorite books.[22]

Americans who wrote about the war were usually pro-Japanese. Dr. Sidney Gulick, a Christian minister, wrote *The White Peril in the Far East* in answer to Kaiser Wilhelm's denunciation of the Yellow Peril. Gulick was able to justify all of Japan's actions, even the prohibition on Christianity during the Tokugawa period and the xenophobia of the late Tokugawa era. He blamed *sakoku* (the closure of the country) on the Japanese discovery of the White Peril and concluded: "No nation has on the whole left a more honourable record in regard to its attitude toward foreigners than has Japan."[23]

The generous treatment of Russian prisoners of war by the Japanese illustrated Gulick's contention that the Japanese had fully absorbed the occidental code of behavior. Wounded Russian sailors from the *Variag* who were brought to Matsuyama were treated as "guests." They were supplied with ample quarters, a special surgeon, an interpreter, a pharmacist, and eleven nurses. Beds of foreign style were supplied, as well as blankets, sheets, pillows, and pillowcases. Foreign foods were also prepared for them. Fresh-cut flowers were provided for their rooms every few days. As the "guests" recovered, they were given much freedom. Gulick speculated, "I doubt if these men had ever had such a delightful time in their lives before."[24]

In contrast, he noted, "Profound resentment and anger have been roused in Japan by Russian treatment of her interests and rights in the Far East, by the methods of her diplomacy and by her cruelty to Japanese women, scouts and wounded soldiers." After enumerating all the wrongs Japan had suffered on account of Russia, he added, "The white peril as embodied in Russia assumes its worst form for it adds hypocrisy to aggressive greed and cloaks its crimes with the very religion which condemns them." His conclusion was: "The white race must abandon its cherished conviction of essential racial superiority and of its inherent right to dominate the earth, and to subordinate all coloured races to its own economic interests. So long as this conviction is held as an ideal, so long is the white race to continue a peril to the peace and welfare of the earth."[25]

James Price, a former member of the British cabinet who met Kaneko Kentarō in Washington in October 1904, told him, "Since coming to America I have traveled to every part of the country and met with people of every walk of life, and have been astonished by the great sympathy felt for your country. They support your country with an enthusiasm that one does not easily see even in my country, England, which is an ally of yours, and the antipathy they have for Russia was truly quite unexpected." Among the reasons he cited for the pro-Japanese and anti-Russian sentiments were the warm relations created by Japanese who, ever since the Restoration, had studied in the United States.[26]

The Japanese government was eager to maintain goodwill abroad. It sent Suematsu Kenchō, a Cambridge graduate, to England and Kaneko Kentarō, a Harvard graduate, to the United States.[27] Kaneko not only was remarkably effective in his dealings with President Roosevelt but became his trusted friend. His first meeting with the president at the White House took place on March 26, 1904. Although thirty or more persons were waiting, as soon as the president saw Kaneko's card, he came out and, after shaking his hand, ushered him into his office. He told Kaneko that he had been eagerly awaiting his visit and had wondered why Kaneko had not appeared earlier.[28]

On March 20, 1905, shortly after the Japanese army won a great victory at the battle for Mukden, Roosevelt sent Kaneko a telegram inviting him to have lunch at the White House. Kaneko was met by the president, whose face shone with joy over the unprecedented victory. Roosevelt was about to leave for Colorado to hunt bears and would be away for six weeks. Normally the president would not divulge where he planned to travel, but he told Kaneko that if for some reason he wished to discuss the war situation, he would return to Washington immediately.[29]

Recalling that the bear was a symbol for Russia, Kaneko said to the president, "The Russian fleet is about to enter the Pacific, and there is certain to be a great naval battle with our fleet in the near future. If you should kill a bear, this will be an augury of victory for the Japanese fleet. I pray that you will have great success." To this Roosevelt said merely, "I fully intend to." After the conclusion of the peace treaty, when Kaneko was about to return to Japan, the president gave him the skin of a bear he had shot, together with a note in his own hand, and asked him to present it personally to the emperor.

Although official relations between Japan and the United States were extremely friendly, the novelist Arishima Takeo detected anti-Japanese feelings in Europe. He wrote, "With the outbreak of the Russo-Japanese War the fact that it was a conflict between a Christian and a non-Christian nation suddenly became a matter of importance. Granted that it was inevitable that Russia, having become the enemy of Japan, should have felt animosity toward Japan, it is obviously also true that the peoples of the countries of Europe as a whole felt jealous of Japanese successes because the Japanese belonged to a different race and religion."[30]

The French, the allies of the Russians, were in the most difficult position. Few in the government wanted to get involved in the war. When French officials learned of the plan to send the Baltic Fleet to Japan, they urged the Russians to have the fleet make the voyage by way of Cape Horn, at the southern tip of

South America. This route, though the longest, had the advantage of avoiding British possessions, whose inhabitants would no doubt inform the Japanese of Russian fleet movements they observed. An even more important consideration to the French was that this route also avoided French possessions, sparing the French the obligation to assist the Russian fleet.

The French believed that Russia was likely to be defeated in the war. A French general who had served as an observer with the Russian army in Manchuria, concluded that the Japanese would win and urged Russia to make peace as soon as possible, on any terms it could secure, because the Russian position could grow only worse. The French ambassador to Russia, who arrived in Paris from St. Petersburg at the beginning of November, reported, "The war in the Far East . . . is getting more and more unpopular with the masses in Russia; they regard it as an enterprise promoted by private interests, a vast filibustering expedition engineered by the Court. In many villages the departure of reservists has been accompanied by riots. One of the most common phrases to which public discontent has given currency is: Our masters have declared an unjust war. Is it surprising that God does not bless our arms?"[31]

In St. Petersburg and Moscow, students were reportedly organizing seditious meetings at which the "Marseillaise" was sung. High-ranking Russians in Paris assured Paléologue that "Russia must fight on, cost what it may, until dirty little Japan begs for mercy, even if the war lasts two more years." But other Russians stated that not a week passed without a mutiny in the barracks or riots along the line when reservists leave for the front.[32]

The Russian admiral chose for his fleet a route along the west coast of Africa and around the Cape of Good Hope, expecting to obtain help from the French whenever the fleet passed their colonies. The French, not wishing their cooperation to be known to the Japanese, urged the Russian admiral to put in at deserted places, but he insisted on anchoring at the chief ports. After rounding the Cape of Good Hope, the Russian fleet asked permission to remain for an extended period in Madagascar. Delcassé refused for fear of Japanese retaliation, but this did not prevent the Russians from sojourning there.

On January 2, 1905, Port Arthur, the "Gibraltar of the Far East, the great fortress which, symbolizing Russian determination in the China Seas, crowns the extremity of the Liao-tung Peninsula" surrendered to the Japanese. A Russian destroyer that had succeeded in escaping from Port Arthur brought the following telegram from General Anatolii Mikhailovich Stoessel to Czar Nicholas:

> The Japanese are in possession of all our lines. We cannot hold out much longer; we shall have to surrender. Great Sovereign, forgive us; we have done everything possible. Be merciful in your judgment upon us. The constant struggle for eleven months has worn down our strength. Three-quarters of the garrison are in the hospitals or the cemeteries. The last

quarter is holding no less than 27 versts and cannot take turns even to snatch a short rest. The men are shadows.

Although he was harshly criticized by many Russians for surrendering while the fortress still had ample supplies, General Stoessel received a most courteous message from General Yamagata Aritomo: "His Majesty the Mikado is graciously pleased to advise me that, in view of your gallant conduct, He desires that you shall be granted military honours. His Majesty has therefore commanded that your officers should retain their swords."[33]

The fall of Port Arthur had immediate repercussions in Russia. On January 19 an attempt was made on the life of the czar, and on January 21 no fewer than 140,000 workers paraded the streets of St. Petersburg in a general strike. Discontent with the war rose as each Japanese military success in Manchuria was reported. Paléologue heard that "the government and people of Russia are still pinning their last hopes to the *Invincible Armada*, which is still at Madagascar." However, for all the fleet's repute, the French naval attaché in St. Petersburg declared, "The naval and military value of the 2nd Squadron is less than mediocre. It is not a homogeneous, cohesive organism but a motley collection, a hodge-podge of ships of all ages and types. . . . The efficiency of the crews is no higher than that of the fleet. There are few experienced officers; the engineering staff is of poor quality; there are no petty officers and most of the sailors have had no military training nor ever been to sea."[34]

The Russian squadron spent more than a month in Madagascar, training the crews for action against the Japanese. In the meantime, internal opposition against the war increased in Russia. On February 17 Grand Duke Sergei, governor general of Moscow, was blown to pieces by a bomb thrown by a terrorist. On February 27 the women of Moscow sent a petition to the czarina, expressing their fervent hope of peace: "We are horrified to see in the recent troubles the beginning of calamities which promise to overwhelm the whole of Russia, unless the Tsar unites with the people to take steps to prevent them."[35]

The French foreign minister, hoping to shake the czar's resolve to fight the war to the bitter end, sent him a letter saying, "Every day the war continues makes it more difficult for Your Majesty's Government to secure a peace which it can regard as acceptable."[36]

On March 17 the Russian squadron finally left Madagascar, heading northeast for the western extremity of Sumatra. This was the worst possible route because the fleet would be in full view of the British in Malaya, and the Japanese would therefore be able to follow the approach of the Russian squadron hour by hour. But the Russians still maintained their unbelievable confidence in the Baltic Fleet. No one doubted that with a great naval victory, Russia could still deprive Japan of control of the sea, after which the Russian armies would take a brilliant revenge.[37]

On April 14 the Russian squadron anchored off the coast of Annam in French Indochina, 200 miles north of Saigon. The French wanted nothing more than for the Russians to leave, but there was little they could do to persuade them, and the squadron's prolonged stay raised a storm of anti-French demonstrations in Japan. At this point the Germans, who had played a mischievous part in the war, now encouraging the Russians to save Christianity, now inciting the Japanese, suddenly informed the French that they would not hesitate to go to war if they saw no other means of safeguarding German rights and interests in Morocco. The French chief of staff exclaimed, "A sudden attack by Germany! We couldn't resist it! It would be worse than 1870! Our defeat would be even more rapid and complete! Just think a minute—in the first place, not a vestige of help from Russia! What should we have with which to meet the 1,500,000 men of the German Army? 900,000 at the outside—of which 100,000, possibly 200,000, would refuse to take the field."[38] France was in no position to help its Russian ally.

The Russian squadron entered Japanese waters on May 26, 1905. The Japanese fleet, commanded by Admiral Tōgō, blocked its path, and in one of the decisive naval engagements of history, Tōgō's fleet annihilated the Russians. On May 29 the French learned that "the 2nd Squadron of the Pacific Ocean" had ceased to exist. Paléologue predicted that the naval battle off the island of Tsushima would mark the end of Russian domination in Asia.

On June 16 Paléologue reported, "Something new and unexpected has happened—something which seems to presage important developments in world politics. For the first time in history, the United States of America is intervening in European affairs. Hitherto it has regarded a studied aloofness from the problems of the old continent, 'European entanglements,' as a national dogma."[39] Now, at the request of the German kaiser, President Roosevelt was considering how to compose the grave difference that had arisen between France and Germany over the Moroccan question.

On June 20 Paléologue wrote, "President Roosevelt, who decidedly appears to be setting up as universal arbiter, has just offered Russia and Japan his good offices to put an end to hostilities."[40] Meanwhile in Russia, a revolutionary storm was raging from the Baltic provinces to the plains of the Volga. "Repression is frequently impossible," Paléologue noted, "as the troops refuse to intervene."

Count Sergei Witte stated in his memoirs that after the crushing defeat of the Russian navy at Tsushima, everyone, even the czar, recognized that peace must be negotiated. The Japanese, too, although they had won memorable victories on land at Port Arthur and Mukden and on the sea at Tsushima, were exhausted by the human and financial cost of the war. When they heard that President Roosevelt had offered to mediate peace talks between Russia and Japan, Count Lamsdorf, the foreign minister, reacted favorably. He recommended that the czar appoint Witte as the chief plenipotentiary in the peace negotiations, but the czar did not respond, no doubt because of his reluctance to recognize that everything Witte had predicted about the consequences of following the war party had come true.[41]

Meiji's name, unlike the czar's, hardly appears in accounts of the war or the peace negotiations. During the war years, he of course performed his usual duties—receiving reports from his ministers, granting audiences to important foreign visitors, and so on. But unlike during the Sino-Japanese War, when he moved to Hiroshima in order to be closer to the troops and spent dreary months waiting for victory, during this war he gave little overt sign of involvement. However, the chamberlain Hinonishi Sukehiro recalled that the emperor did not allow any heating in his rooms, and apart from the time he spent eating and sleeping, he was at his desk the entire day. Hinonishi said that the event that worried the emperor most was the siege of Port Arthur. According to the emperor, "I am sure that Port Arthur will fall, sooner or later, but it's terrible killing soldiers that way. Nogi's a good general, but the way he kills soldiers is really upsetting."[42]

Little has been recorded concerning the emperor's private life at this time, but a letter of the British minister to Japan, Sir Claude MacDonald, gives us a welcome, though momentary, glimpse:

I sat opposite to the Emperor at the lunch given to Admiral Noël and the officers of our Fleet. Besides plying a very healthy knife and fork, His Majesty chatted most amicably with everybody all around. The Imperial Princes, Arisugawa and Kanin who sat on either side, treated him with marked deference, but Marquis Ito and Count Inoue (the latter sat next to me) seemed to speak on absolute terms of equality and cracked jokes which made this direct descendant of the Sun roar with laughter. It was a great revelation to me and one which pleased me very much for, though a Mikado, he seems very human.[43]

If the emperor, like the Russian czar, had insisted on appointing his commanding generals and admirals himself or, because of some personal quarrel, had refused to appoint the most suitable man to represent Japan at the peace negotiations, he could probably have had his way, however much this harmed Japan. Fortunately, this did not occur. Perhaps that is one reason that Baron Rosen said of the emperor in his memoirs that his "name will go down in history as that of one of the greatest sovereigns the world has ever known."[44]

Chapter 55

The destruction of the Russian fleet off Tsushima on May 27–28, 1905, caused "a shadow of gloom and consternation" to spread over all Russia. The kaiser, who not so long before had incited the czar to fight Japan, now congratulated the Japanese minister to Germany on Japan's great success and declared that the naval battle was the most important since the victory of the British fleet over the French and Spanish fleets at Trafalgar in 1805, exactly 100 years earlier. Kaneko Kentarō, who was in New York when the news arrived, sent a note to President Roosevelt declaring that the battle was "the greatest naval victory of the world's history."[1] Roosevelt agreed. He replied to Kaneko, "This is the greatest phenomenon the world has ever seen. Even the battle of Trafalgar could not match this. I could not believe it myself, when the first report reached me. As the second and third reports came, however, I grew so excited that I myself became almost like a Japanese, and I could not attend to official duties."[2]

The defeat forced the czar to reconsider his determination to continue the war. The "war party," which had long dominated high-level discussions, was losing ground, and even before the czar indicated a willingness to open peace negotiations, those Russian leaders who hoped for peace began to think of President Roosevelt as the best mediator.

The Japanese had also decided to ask Roosevelt to initiate peace talks. On January 7 and 8 (immediately after the Japanese captured Port Arthur) Kaneko visited Roosevelt in the White House to discuss the possibility of a peace conference and Japanese plans once the war had ended. Roosevelt expressed his conviction that Japan was entitled to take possession of Port Arthur and to incorporate Korea within its sphere of influence, but he believed that Manchuria should be returned to China and neutralized under guarantees from the Western powers. Although Roosevelt was firm in the view "that we cannot permit Japan to be robbed a second time of the fruits of victory,"[3] he emphasized that Japan must agree to maintain the Open Door in Manchuria, a matter of great concern to America because it directly related to trade. On being informed by Takahira Kogorō, the Japanese minister to the United States, that Roosevelt expected and desired a Japanese victory in the war, Komura Jutarō, the foreign minister, decided to reveal openly to Roosevelt Japan's intentions and hopes concerning Manchuria, Korea, and Port Arthur, and they proved to be more or less the same as Roosevelt's.[4]

During the next months, various attempts were made, especially by the French, to bring Japan and Russia together at a peace conference. The Japanese were suspicious of France, the ally of Russia, and they were also reluctant to promise before a conference that they would not seek an indemnity or Russian territory. They obviously preferred that Roosevelt, rather than the French, call the peace conference. Komura was at pains to assure him that Japan fully adhered to the position of maintaining the Open Door in Manchuria and of restoring that province to China.[5]

The battle for Mukden in Manchuria was the largest that had taken place in modern history. It ended on March 10 with a Japanese victory, but by the time the Russians fled to the north, the Japanese were too exhausted to pursue them effectively. The Japanese had won a major battle, but the Russians were by no means on their knees. Even at the peace conference, the Russians contended that they had lost some battles but not the war. Indeed, the need for peace was probably felt more keenly by the Japanese than the Russians. On March 8 while the battle still raged at Mukden, the army minister, Terauchi Masatake, informally approached the American minister, Lloyd Griscom, and asked him to inform President Roosevelt that the time had come for the war to cease.[6]

In the end, nothing came of Terauchi's initiative because Komura insisted that the czar take the first step toward peace. But Komura's attitude also changed before long. On April 25 Minister Griscom wrote to Washington that the Foreign Ministry "was anxious to effect the peace through Roosevelt, and that it was really anxious for peace."

Sentiment in America was overwhelmingly pro-Japanese. Meiji seems to have been aware of this. On January 24 he sent for Griscom to express his thanks for the warm reception Prince Sadanaru had received during his recent visit to the United States. Of course, it was normal for thanks to be expressed for hospitality given to members of the imperial family when they traveled abroad, and sometimes decorations were bestowed, but on this occasion the emperor's language seems to convey genuine feeling: "When I think of the profound goodwill that your country has always displayed toward our country, I am over-come with joy. I congratulate His Excellency, the president, on his good health, and pray for the prosperity of his country. At the same time, I hope that in the future the friendship between our two countries will grow ever closer."[7]

During the Russo-Japanese War, the emperor never felt impelled to offer advice on the conduct of the war, and he rarely revealed his emotions, even when told of Japanese victories. As soon as he learned of the fall of Port Arthur, the vice chief of the general staff, Nagaoka Gaishi, rushed to the palace to inform the emperor. The emperor was just leaving his study to perform morning worship, but when he was informed that Nagaoka had requested an audience, he returned to the study. Nagaoka, too overcome by joy even to wait for the emperor to be seated, declared that serving as the messenger of glorious news was the greatest blessing of his life. Having blurted out these words, he started to make his report. He looked up at the emperor's face. It was calm and self-possessed, exactly as it always was, not revealing a trace of emotion. During the fifteen or sixteen minutes while Nagaoka described the victory, the emperor nodded almost imperceptibly a few times. When Nagaoka completed his report, the emperor proceeded to the altar, as he had planned before the interruption.

Nagaoka was deeply disappointed. He was aware that the emperor's temper-ament only rarely permitted him to reveal any emotion—whether joy or an-ger—in his expression, but the event he reported was so extraordinary that he expected the emperor to look pleased or at least seem relieved. The siege of Port Arthur had cost the lives of many Japanese soldiers, and there had been scenes of appalling carnage during three all-out attacks against the Russian defenders. The whole nation had impatiently waited for months for the news received this day. The victory not only was of key importance to the future conduct of the war but would exert an enormous influence over national policy. Yet the emperor had not shown the slightest change of expression. Nagaoka, embarrassed by his unrestrained excitement, felt the sweat down his back as he left the emperor's presence.[8]

The emperor may have seemed unmoved because he had already received word of the victory at Port Arthur. That same day, Yamagata Aritomo had tele-phoned the chief chamberlain describing the victory. But when the chamber-lain conveyed the news to the emperor, his first reaction was not an exclamation of joy but of admiration for General Stoessel's unwavering loyalty to his country. He ordered Yamagata to make sure that Stoessel was allowed to maintain his dignity as a soldier. Yamagata transmitted the order to General Nogi Maresuke who communicated it to all members of his command. Perhaps the emperor, aware of the display of Japanese brutality at the time of the capture of Port Arthur from the Chinese ten years earlier, feared a recurrence.

Even though the emperor's joy over the victory was not disclosed to those around him, it was found in this *tanka*:

atarashiki	How happy I was
toshi no tayori ni	To hear at the beginning
ada no shiro	Of the year the news
hirakinikeri to	That the enemy's fortress
kiku zo ureshiki.	Had fallen to our soldiers.[9]

The emperor had composed war songs in the past, but his poems during the Russo-Japanese War were seldom warlike. Before the first poetry gathering of the year on January 19, 1905, the chief of the poetry bureau, Takasaki Masakaze, had proposed two topics: "The Whole People Rejoice" and "Rejoicing on the Way." The emperor rejected both, presumably because they related too closely to the war. The topic he finally chose was the innocuous "Mountains at New Year." Meiji's poem was

Fuji no ne ni	The sky at the start
niou asahi mo	Of the new year is so calm
kasumu made	That the morning sun
toshi tatsu sora no	Glowing over Mount Fuji
nodoka naru kana	Seems hazy.[10]

The emperor's lack of excitement, even after Japan had won a great victory at Port Arthur, may have reflected his caution: Was it fitting to celebrate while a powerful enemy still retained its military capability? Was it fitting to celebrate when so many Japanese soldiers had lost their lives in the effort to take Port Arthur?

If reluctant to show unseemly joy, the emperor did not hesitate to voice concern over the hardships endured by Japanese troops in the bitter cold of North China:

himugashi no	Even the sky over
miyako no sora mo	The Eastern Capital
haru samushi	Is chilly this spring
saekaeruran	How bitterly cold must be
hoku Shina no yama	The mountains of North China.[11]

When the emperor learned of the Japanese army's great victory at Mukden, he issued this rescript to the Manchurian army:

Mukden was the place where the enemy, having constructed strong defense fortifications and manned them with imposing numbers of soldiers ever since last autumn, intended to test which side was the stronger, in the expectation of certain victory. Our Manchurian army, taking the initiative, plunged ahead and, for more than ten days and nights battled valiantly amid numbing cold, snow, and ice, until it at last crushed the stubborn resolve of the enemy to defend the city to the death. The army has taken more than 10,000 prisoners, dealt great destruction, and driven the enemy in the direction of T'ieh-ling. By its unprecedented great victory, it has displayed at home and abroad the authority and might of the empire. We have rejoiced to learn of the untiring patience and tremendous efforts you officers and men have offered, and we urge you to perform even greater deeds.[12]

This message expressed the emperor's appreciation of the army's heroic struggle to take Mukden, but if we imagine the bombast that would have accompanied a proclamation by the German kaiser or Russian czar after a similar victory, we cannot fail to be struck by Meiji's restraint. We wonder, too, how the emperor would have expressed disappointment if the Japanese army had been defeated.

We know how the czar reacted to the Russian defeat. At a meeting with Minister Takahira, President Roosevelt said that although many Russians had recognized the magnitude of the defeat at Mukden and a majority of the czar's advisers leaned toward seeking peace, the czar insisted on continuing the war. Despite the series of defeats Russia had suffered during the past year, it seems not to have occurred to the czar to end the war in order to spare the lives of his soldiers. Roosevelt confessed that he could not understand what the czar might be thinking but judged it unlikely he would make the first move for peace. Roosevelt thought it might be a good idea for Japan to find some way to convey to the powers its desire for peace negotiations and, if possible, to state its conditions.[13] After the great victory at Mukden, no one would suppose that the Japanese were acting out of weakness.

Not long afterward, Kaneko Kentarō in Washington sent a telegram to Tōkyō stating that he had been invited to the White House by President Roosevelt. The president said his sympathies were entirely with Japan because Japan was fighting for civilization. His greatest worry was how he might best help Japan by persuading Russia to enter peace negotiations.[14]

The extraordinary victory of the Japanese fleet in the great naval battle fought on May 27–28 prompted Meiji for the first time to issue a rescript that openly revealed his pleasure:

The joint fleet met the enemy fleet in the straits of Korea and, after several days of fierce fighting, completely annihilated it to achieve an unprecedented success. We rejoice that, thanks to your unswerving loyalty, We are able to report this to the divine spirits of Our ancestors. The road ahead is still long. May you devote ever greater efforts to the war and in this way bring to completion your military achievements.[15]

Mention of the imperial ancestors may recall the mentions of God that figured so prominently in the czar's utterances, but Meiji did not assert that it was because the gods of Shintō were on his side that the Japanese had been victorious. President Roosevelt was more direct in his expression of joy: he opened a letter to Kaneko on May 30 with BANZAI, followed by three exclamation points.[16]

With the destruction of the Russian fleet, it was generally agreed that the time was ripe for peace talks. On May 29, the day after the victory, Roosevelt discussed with Minister Takahira the possibility of peace negotiations with the Russians. On May 31 Foreign Minister Komura telegraphed Takahira, instructing him to request Roosevelt's aid in arranging such negotiations. Komura's message, formally presented to Roosevelt on the following day, asked him "directly and entirely of his own motion and initiative to invite the two belligerents to come together for the purpose of direct negotiations."[17]

Roosevelt was entirely willing to undertake this responsibility, but he warned Takahira that the Russians were unlikely to respond to peace overtures if the Japanese demanded an indemnity. He reminded him also that even though the Japanese army and navy had been everywhere successful, they had not penetrated Russian territory. He told Takahira that if the Japanese hoped for an indemnity of the kind Germany had received after the Franco-Prussian War, it would not happen until Japanese troops surrounded Moscow.

Roosevelt was even blunter with the Russians. He summoned the Russian ambassador, Count Arturo Cassini, and declared that the war was absolutely hopeless for the Russians.[18] Cassini expressed concern over the merciless demands the Japanese were likely to make but promised to transmit to St. Petersburg the president's message advising peace. At this juncture, to Roosevelt's surprise, the kaiser supported his efforts. We know the kaiser's mood from a letter he sent his cousin, the czar, on June 3:

> From the purely military strategic point of view the defeat in the straits of Corea ends the chances for a decided turn of the scales in your favour: the Japanese are now free to pour any amount of reserves, recruits, ammunition, etc. into Manchuria for the siege of Vladivostok, which will hardly be able to resist very long without a fleet to support it. . . . Formally it is of course possible, even under these adverse circumstances, to continue the war for any amount of time. But then on the other hand the *human* part must not be overlooked. Your country has sent thousands of its sons to the front, where they died, or were taken ill and were left crippled for the rest of their lives. . . . Is it compatible with the responsibility of a ruler to continue to force a whole nation against its declared will to send its sons to be killed by hecatombs only for his sake?[19]

The kaiser offered to do what he could to bring about peace but added toward the close of his letter:

> I may perhaps turn your attention to the fact that no doubt the Japanese have the highest regard for America before all other nations. Because this mighty rising Power with its tremendous fleet is next to them. If anybody in the world is able to influence the Japanese and to induce them to be reasonable in their proposals, it is President Roosevelt.[20]

The reason for the kaiser's change of attitude was suggested by remarks he made to the American ambassador, who reported to Washington: "He looks upon continuation of the war, from the Russian side, as hopeless. The people are strongly opposed to it, they will not sustain it longer, and unless peace is made, they will kill the Tsar."[21] Roosevelt was pleased by this unexpected communication from the kaiser, who had not previously been known as a peacemaker. For all his bluster, the kaiser no doubt feared that an uprising by the Russian people against the czar would represent a danger to all monarchs.[22]

The kaiser's letter may have had an effect on the czar. Although the czar's message to Roosevelt, delivered by Ambassador Cassini on June 6, said that Russia did not seek peace or mediation, on the same day, during the discussions with high-ranking nobles and military officers, the czar finally agreed to negotiate for peace. The next day, he told the American ambassador that he would consent to the president's suggestion that Russia and Japan have a meeting without intermediaries "in order to see if we can make peace."[23]

On June 8 President Roosevelt sent identical letters to the American ambassadors in Tōkyō and St. Petersburg. asking them to convey to the two governments his willingness "to do what he properly can if the two Powers concerned feel that his services will be of aid in arranging the preliminaries as to the time and place of meeting" of negotiations to end the war. The Japanese Ministry for Foreign Affairs on June 10 sent a reply stating its readiness to "appoint plenipotentiaries of Japan to meet plenipotentiaries of Russia at such time and place as may be found to be mutually agreeable and convenient for the purpose of negotiating and concluding terms of peace directly and exclusively between the two belligerent Powers."[24]

The Russian reply, conveyed to the American ambassador, stated, "With regard to the eventual meeting of Russian and Japanese plenipotentiaries, 'In order to see if it is not possible for the two Powers to agree to terms of peace,' the Imperial Government has no objection in principle to this endeavour if the Japanese Government expresses a like desire."[25] However, the word "like" was not in either the original French text or the Russian translation. Without this word, the Russian reply meant that they were willing to participate if the Japanese first expressed the desire for a meeting. In order not to upset the Japanese by the arrogance of the Russian note, the Americans had deliberately softened the expression.[26]

The haughtiness of Foreign Minister Lamsdorf (although he was a supporter of Count Witte and favored peace) would continue to try the patience of President Roosevelt, whose irritation with the Russians mounted until on June 16 he wrote to Senator Henry Cabot Lodge, "Russia is so corrupt, so treacherous and shifty, and so incompetent, that I'm utterly unable to say whether or not it will make peace, or break off the negotiations at any moment."[27] Roosevelt many times voiced similar sentiments. Even though these were not publicly expressed, his hostility to the Russian government was surely sensed. It is difficult to understand why the Russians were willing to attend a peace conference called by a president who was so obviously anti-Russian.[28]

The site of the conference was the first problem. Roosevelt at first proposed The Hague in Holland. Japan, rejecting this site, proposed Chefoo, a port on the northern coast of the Shantung Peninsula, across the Gulf of Chihli from Port Arthur. Washington was Japan's second choice. The Russians' first choice was Paris, but Washington was also their second choice. Roosevelt therefore settled on Washington. Just as he was informing the Russian ambassador of his decision, a cable came from Lamsdorf saying that he preferred The Hague because Washington was so distant and so hot in summer. However, Komura not only had rejected The Hague but had declared that the Japanese would not go to any site in Europe.[29] Roosevelt refused to reopen the question. Lamsdorf sent a memorandum to the czar asking his opinion. Fortunately, the czar wrote in response, "I decisively do not see any objections to Washington as a place for the meeting for the preliminary discussions between our and the Japanese plenipotentiaries."[30] This ended the discussion, but the words "preliminary discussions" suggested the czar did not expect decisions of importance to emerge from the peace conference.

The time of the conference was the next problem. It would take the Japanese delegation at least a month to reach the east coast of the United States. This meant that the conference would have to take place in the summer. In order not to subject the delegates to the unbearable heat of a Washington summer, Roosevelt considered alternative, cooler sites, finally choosing the Portsmouth Navy Yard in New Hampshire. Both Japan and Russia accepted Portsmouth as the site of the conference.

Roosevelt proposed beginning deliberations during the first ten days of August in order to allow the Japanese sufficient time to reach Portsmouth. The czar, though at first reluctant to consent to peace negotiations, was now eager to have negotiations start as soon as possible, as he feared that the Japanese might take advantage of a delay to seize Sakhalin.[31] There was reason for this fear, for according to Kaneko, Roosevelt had recommended that Japan immediately invade Sakhalin to improve its prospects at the conference table.[32]

The choice of plenipotentiaries was not easy for either side. Itō Hirobumi was the obvious choice to head the Japanese delegation, but he had been known before the outbreak of war as an advocate of accommodation with Russia. His friends warned him that his sympathy for Russia would be blamed if the Japanese delegation failed to win the peace terms demanded by the public. Itō was fortunately spared the headache of choosing whether to serve when the emperor informed Prime Minister Katsura Tarō that he needed Itō in Tōkyō for consultation during the peace negotiations.[33]

The choice of Russian plenipotentiaries was complicated by the czar's interference. Although Lamsdorf argued convincingly that a specialist on financial and economic matters was essential, Nicholas remained opposed to Witte, clearly the best-qualified man. The situation in Russia at this time took a sudden turn for the worse when there was a clash between striking workers and government troops in Odessa on June 25, followed by a mutiny aboard the battleship *Potemkin* two days later. The *Potemkin* mutiny was symptomatic of the unrest in Russia. This unrest was fostered by Japanese agents who gave money to opponents of the czar's government (including Lenin) and were especially active in Finland and Poland, parts of the Russian Empire that yearned for independence.[34]

The Japanese and Russian delegates began their deliberations on August 10. On the following day the Japanese presented a formal list of twelve demands, including Russia's recognition of Japan's paramount political, military, and economic interests in Korea; evacuation of Manchuria by the Russian army; transference of the Port Arthur leasehold from Russia to Japan; cession of Sakhalin to Japan; payment to Japan of the expenses of the war; and restriction of Russia's use of the railway connecting Manchuria to Vladivostok to commercial and industrial purposes.[35]

The Russian reaction to the Japanese demands was one of dismay. Witte told a colleague, "The Japanese conditions were more heavy than anything it was possible to expect." In fact, however, only two of the demands caused trouble in the ensuing negotiations: the cession of Sakhalin and the payment of an indemnity. The czar asserted again and again that Russia would never pay one ruble in indemnity nor yield one square inch of Russian soil. His refusal in both instances was based on considerations of honor rather than practical policy. He wrote on an initial draft of the instructions to the Russians going to the conference, "Russia has never paid an indemnity; I shall never consent to this." The word "never" was underlined three times.[36]

The czar was equally opposed to yielding Sakhalin. Russia had owned Sakhalin only since 1875 when a treaty with the Japanese gave them possession of the island in exchange for the Kuriles. Its desolation had been known to the

Russians ever since the report published by Anton Chekhov, who visited the prison colony in 1890. Yet the czar, the ruler of an immense country that stretched over Europe and Asia, was ready to prolong a disastrous war in order not to give up a square inch of wasteland.

Komura Jutarō also seems to have been driven by a concept of honor. In April when a cabinet conference decided on concrete terms for peace (to which the emperor gave his assent), there were only three "absolutely indispensable" items: (1) to have Russia acknowledge Japan's complete freedom of action in Korea, (2) mutual military evacuation of Manchuria within a period to be specified, and (3) transference to Japan of Russia's Port Arthur leasehold and the branch railway running from Port Arthur to Harbin.[37] There were also four "items not absolutely indispensable but to be secured insofar as possible," including an indemnity and the cession of Sakhalin. If Komura had been satisfied with obtaining the three "absolutely indispensable" items, the negotiations would have gone smoothly, but his insistence on an indemnity and his failure to inform the Japanese government of the czar's willingness to compromise on Sakhalin (he was willing to divide the island between Japan and Russia) very nearly resulted in a collapse of the negotiations and a resumption of the war.[38] On August 26 Komura sent a telegram to Tōkyō announcing his intention of breaking off the negotiations.[39]

On August 28 the prime minister held a meeting of cabinet members and three genrō—Itō Hirobumi, Yamagata, and Inoue Kaoru. Although they regretted that Russia had failed to respond to Japanese efforts to reach a compromise, they agreed that the only alternative to continuing negotiations was war. They recognized that it might not be difficult to capture Harbin before the year was out but that this would require additional military forces, and Japan lacked the financial reserves to equip and send them into the field. Moreover, even supposing that Harbin and, eventually, Vladivostok were captured, this would still not deal Russia the coup de grâce. They concluded, after hours of debate, that it was essential to make peace, even if it meant Japan would have to abandon an indemnity and the acquisition of Sakhalin.[40]

That afternoon a meeting of the three genrō and cabinet ministers was held in the presence of the emperor. They decided to cable Komura that although the cabinet was aware of both the Russian refusal to compromise and the great difficulty of continuing negotiations, military and economic conditions compelled Japan to negotiate for peace, regardless of the loss of an indemnity and Sakhalin. In any case, Japan's basic objective in fighting the war—the settlement of important problems relating to Korea and Manchuria—had been achieved. Komura was directed to yield first on the indemnity, asking in return that the Japanese occupation of Sakhalin be accepted as a fait accompli. If the Russians refused to budge on Sakhalin, Komura should ask President Roosevelt to recommend to the Japanese that they withdraw their claim for territory for the sake of peace and humanity.[41] This last was obviously intended as a face-saving device to spare the Japanese the embarrassment of unilaterally withdrawing their claim.

Members of the Japanese delegation were so shaken by these instructions, which seemed to be a confession of defeat at the conference table, that they began to weep and sob. On August 28 Witte also received a discouraging telegram. Lamsdorf relayed the czar's words: "Send Witte my order to end discussion in any case. I prefer to continue the war than to await gracious concessions on the part of Japan."[42] The two Russian delegates, Witte and Rosen, disagreed about whether to obey this imperial command. Witte decided to ignore it and to repeat his offer to make peace by giving up the southern half of Sakhalin.

At a secret meeting held on August 29, Witte agreed to the cession, and Komura, following instructions from Tōkyō, accepted the arrangement. They also agreed on the withdrawal of troops from Manchuria and the disposition of the Manchurian railways.[43] All problems had been settled. When Witte emerged from the conference room, he announced that peace had been achieved, that the Japanese had agreed to everything.[44]

Later that morning at the formal session, Komura, following instructions, asked for the whole of Sakhalin. Witte refused, whereupon Komura stated that Japan, for the sake of peace and humanity, would accept the Russian offer to divide the island at the fiftieth parallel. This was just so much playacting for the benefit of spectators, but the session ended with Witte's recommendation that immediate steps be taken to conclude an armistice, lest soldiers be unnecessarily killed. The peace treaty was not signed by Komura and Witte until September 5. In the meantime, word that a settlement had been reached quickly spread. The czar was stunned to learn of the agreement. He wrote in his diary, "At night there came a telegram from Witte with the news that the negotiations about peace have been brought to an end. All day after that I went around as in a trance."[45]

The Russians' first reactions were almost all unfavorable, none more so than those of the English wife of a Russian prisoner: "Peace of the new diplomacy! Peace of the Twentieth Century! Peace as she is made in America! Peace as she is hammered out at the American Cronstadt! All the traditions are broken with. Japan and Russia have not made peace—nor wanted it. Oh, no! That terrible American President, *Il Strenuoso*, he has made it. He wanted it, he would have it. And I believe him capable of locking the conferees in a room and starving them into obedience."[46]

Most Russians who had not actually witnessed the fighting thought it was absurd that peace should be made when the Russian armies in Manchuria were in better condition to fight the Japanese than ever before. The American ambassador to Russia, George Meyer, wrote in his diary that although Roosevelt had earned the gratitude of the world for his role in the peace negotiations, he should not expect gratitude from the Russians, who believed that without his interference they would have won the war.[47] But a Russian officer who had held a high position on the general staff throughout the war said that the two armies were so strong and so dug in that an attack by either would almost certainly end in disaster and terrible losses.

The Russian delegates did not doubt that they had performed a miracle. They had managed to avoid paying an indemnity, and the only territory they had yielded was half of a bleak island that the Japanese had already occupied. It is small wonder that they drank champagne toasts at the celebration after the signing.

The Japanese did not attend the celebration. Komura and his colleagues had signed a treaty quite against their own wishes because they had been so ordered, and they could easily imagine the stormy reception they would receive after their return to Japan.

The happiest person was probably President Roosevelt. Praise came from France, Germany, and even England, although some Britons at first expressed astonishment that their ally Japan had yielded so much. Just at this time, the Anglo-Japanese Alliance was renewed for five years, and one publication stated that the reassurance the Japanese received by the renewal caused them to moderate their peace terms. Whatever criticism was made of Roosevelt, it quickly subsided, and he received telegrams of thanks from both Meiji and Nicholas. Just before the peace treaty was signed, he wrote the American minister in Peking, "I was pro-Japanese before, but after my experience with the peace commissioners I am far stronger pro-Japanese than ever."[48] He was awarded the Nobel Peace Prize in 1906 for his efforts to end the war.

When the provisions of the peace treaty were published in the Japanese press, there was a great outcry. A "people's mass meeting" was planned for September 5 at Hibiya Park to discuss the rejection of the treaty and the impeachment of the cabinet ministers, but the police would not permit demonstrators to enter the park. The protesters, some 30,000 in number, broke through the barricades erected around entrances to the park, and the outnumbered police could not control them. Troops were called out to protect the palace, ministries, and foreign legations.

The noise of the clashes in the park could be heard in the palace, and the emperor, unable to sit tranquilly in his chair, paced back and forth listening to the tumult. Suddenly there was a sound of rifle fire; the military police were firing pistols to intimidate the protesters. The emperor, normally so impassive, was extremely agitated by the noise outside.[49] Soon afterward, Prime Minister Katsura rushed to the palace to report on the situation, and that night the emperor repeatedly sent chamberlains to discover the latest developments.

The demonstrations continued for two more days. On the second day, the protesters set fires, burned ten or more streetcars, and stormed from place to place burning police boxes. Martial law, declared for Tōkyō and vicinity, was not lifted until November 29. There were smaller-scale meetings of protest in other Japanese cities. Heavy rains on the third day of riots discouraged the demonstrators, and the situation returned to normal.

The demonstrations against the treaty were widely reported abroad, sometimes as manifestations of xenophobia or anti-Christian sentiment, although this was quickly denied by competent foreign observers in Tōkyō. President Roosevelt thought that the Japanese government was to blame for having allowed the public to expect Russia would pay a large indemnity.[50] Sure that peace was desirable and proud to have had a part in obtaining it, he wrote to Minister Takahira, "You have crowned a great war by a great peace."[51]

Chapter 56

The first alliance between Japan and England, signed in 1902, was for a period of five years, but in 1905, while the treaty was still in effect, it was modified and extended. During the Russo-Japanese War, the British aided the Japanese in various ways, the most important of which was selling munitions, without which the Japanese could not have fought the war.[1] The British kept the Japanese informed when they sighted Russian warships, and they also had been instrumental in preventing ships of the Russian Black Sea Fleet (which might have reinforced the naval forces sent against Japan) from passing through the Dardanelles.[2] But Britain's announced policy during the war was one of strict neutrality and officially did not favor Japan.[3]

Japan was nevertheless well aware of the importance of the alliance. In December 1904 Sir Claude M. MacDonald, the British minister in Tōkyō, reported that in talks with Prime Minister Katsura Tarō and Foreign Minister Komura Jutarō, both had said that "if Japan was successful in war, she would seek for a closer alliance with England."[4] Britain was also eager for a renewal of the alliance, as may be inferred from various suggestions made to the prime minister: that in the interests of strengthening ties between the two countries, Britain present the Order of the Garter, its highest honor, to the emperor; that the post of minister to Japan be raised to the ambassadorial level; and that Britain offer to renew the alliance for another five years.

On February 12, 1905, at a dinner given by the Japanese foreign minister to celebrate the third anniversary of the alliance, Komura not only proposed a toast to the health of King Edward VII in the customary manner but also expressed the hope that the alliance would grow in strength and solidity. The British were uncertain just how seriously Komura's speech should be taken, but Claude Lowther, a Conservative member of Parliament, urged the government on March 29 to renew the alliance on a firmer basis because he believed it was "the only possible means by which we could secure retrenchment and efficiency with safety to the Empire."

Lowther was worried by the threat that Russia posed to India. Now that the Russians had built, at great expense, railways that enabled them to move quickly to the Indian frontier an army of more than 500,000 men, the most economical means of defending India was with Japanese troops. He advised that the treaty not be merely renewed but be given a new character: in the event that either country's Asian possessions were attacked, they should mutually help each other—Great Britain with its fleet and Japan with its army. This arrangement would relieve Great Britain of the upkeep of an Indian army, which had threatened to become an intolerable burden on British taxpayers. It would also save Japan the expense of building a fleet.[5]

It is difficult to imagine the Japanese government consenting to send a Japanese army to the north of India in order to protect the British Empire from a Russian attack, but nonetheless, Japan was extremely eager to continue the alliance. Its main advantage to the Japanese was that it seemed the best way to discourage Russia from staging a war of revenge; it would also "neutralize the schemes which were being devised by the Russians and French at present to form a European union to oppose Japan under the banner of the Yellow Peril."[6]

Some members of the British government, believing they could overcome Japanese reluctance to defend India, proposed that in the event that Russia threatened the northern Indian frontier, Japan be asked to supply 150,000 troops. They clung to the belief that Japanese help in India would be no more than a fair exchange for British naval support and acquiescence in whatever moves Japan might make in Korea.

The Japanese naval victory in the battle of the Tsushima Strait greatly strengthened the Japanese negotiators' bargaining position. The final agreement, signed on August 12, 1905, in London, bound the two powers for ten more years and imposed a measure of cooperation in disputes arising in East Asia, India, and countries east of India. There were no secret clauses, and Japan did not promise to send soldiers to India, but it recognized Britain's special interests in all that concerned the security of the Indian frontier.[7] The treaty, though signed while peace negotiations were in progress at Portsmouth, had little influence on the conference.

Soon after the new treaty had been negotiated, Prime Minister A. J. Balfour announced the resignation of his ministry. Before leaving office, however, the Conservatives honored Japan by raising the British legation in Tōkyō to an embassy. France, Germany, Italy, and the United States followed this example, symbolic recognition that Japan had emerged as a first-class power. As a second mark of respect for Japan, the government recommended that the Order of the Garter be conferred on the emperor. Edward VII had earlier resisted a similar proposal on the grounds that the Garter could not be given to a non-Christian sovereign, but in 1903, for political reasons, the order had been conferred on the shah of Persia despite the king's opposition. Taking advantage of this precedent, the government insisted on making the offer to the emperor, and the king had no choice but to acquiesce. He appointed Prince Arthur of Connaught to head the mission that would confer the decoration, on February 20, 1906.[8]

Among the members of the distinguished delegation was Lord Redesdale (A. B. Mitford), who had served as an interpreter at the British legation in Tōkyō from 1866 to 1870. His joy at returning to Japan was conveyed in the opening pages of his book-length report *The Garter Mission to Japan*:

> Never did the winter sun rise in greater glory than it did on the 19th of February 1906, when H.M.S. *Diadem*, Captain Savory, carrying Prince Arthur of Connaught and the Garter Mission to Japan, steamed at daybreak into the harbour of Yokohama. Never did it shine upon a fairer scene. The King's standard was flying at the main; the buildings on shore and the vessels in the bay, blue as that of Naples, were all dressed; eleven great warships thundered out a Royal welcome, their bands playing "God Save the King"; in the distance was the pine-clad Hakoné range, beautiful as my recollection of it; but, best of all, Fuji, the Peerless Mountain, covered with snow and glittering in the morning rays, was lifting its mystic cone to heaven, without a cloud to mar the grace of its outline; for the goddess of the mountain, "the princess that causes the trees to blossom," had risen in her beauty to give us a foretaste of the greeting which the spirit of old Japan was making ready for the messengers of her friend and ally, King Edward the Seventh.[9]

Redesdale was absolutely delighted by the welcoming crowd along the streets of Yokohama:

> The streets were very crowded; every soul in the place must have turned out to line them—the grown-up people behind, the children in front according to their stature, the best place belonging by prescriptive right to the tiniest. Every child was armed with two flags, one Japanese and one English, which were waved most conscientiously, and then there arose such a shouting of "Banzai" from shrill treble and deep bass![10]

The members of the mission boarded a train that took them to Shimbashi, where a ceremony took place which must have stirred to their profoundest depths the hearts of all the Japanese who witnessed it. Never before, since the first creation of Japan, was such a compliment paid as that which awaited Prince Arthur. Surrounded by the Crown Prince and all the other Princes of the Blood, the Emperor had come in person to greet his guest. This august Sovereign, whom his subjects revere as something, if not actually divine, at any rate far removed above the rest of mankind, had come, for the first time in all the history of the country, publicly to acclaim a foreign prince. . . . When the Emperor so warmly shook hands with the Prince it was a message to his people which said in unmistakable terms, "This is MY friend."[11]

Like every other king, prince, or president who ever met Emperor Meiji, Prince Arthur was convinced that the emperor had never displayed such friendship and respect toward any predecessor. Redesdale also congratulated himself: "I was the only European present who could remember the old days of mystery and seclusion in which the Emperors of Japan had lived for upward of eight centuries."[12] He was obviously deeply impressed by the emperor, seen again after forty years: "From all that we can gather, the strength which is written in his face is his great characteristic. His whole time, so the Japanese statesmen tell us, is given to public work. His few leisure moments he solaces with writing poetry."

The ceremony of the conferring of the Order of the Garter was imposing.[13] This order of knighthood, founded in the fourteenth century by King Edward III, had its origins (at least according to legend) in a court lady's garter that fell to the palace floor. The king, retrieving the garter, offered it to the lady. Some of those present laughed, but the king rebuked them in French, "*Honni soit qui mal y pense*" (Shame on anyone who thinks ill of it!), a phrase inscribed on the decoration.

The order, as Prince Arthur informed the emperor, is restricted to the king, the Prince of Wales, and twenty-five knights and is recognized as the most noble British order of knighthood. In addition to the British knights, it has been the custom to confer the dignity on those emperors, kings, and princes who are in special and peculiar amity or alliance with the king of England.

Meiji was not overawed. He seemed pleased at first when he was informed that he would receive the decoration and accepted, but later he summoned the imperial household minister, Tanaka Mitsuaki, and told him, "I can't stand receiving British envoys. Tell them not to come."

The stunned Tanaka said, "But Your Majesty has accepted. You can't decline it now. Prince Connaught will already have left his country. Such an act would violate the trust that must prevail among allies in matters affecting them both. It is absolutely impossible. All Your Majesty can do now is to await the prince and receive him."

The emperor was by no means pleased by these words, but he fell silent and issued no further commands. His reluctance to meet Prince Arthur probably had nothing to do with the prince himself or his country; rather, the emperor had come to dislike receiving foreign guests. He was always in a bad mood before an audience, and he often rebuked members of his staff for arranging it. But once the guest arrived, the emperor never revealed the slightest displeasure; on the contrary, those whom he received were invariably impressed by his sincere affability.[14]

Even after he reluctantly agreed to receive Prince Arthur and accept the Garter, the honor seems not to have meant much to the emperor. When Saionji Kinmochi, who had replaced Katsura Tarō as prime minister in 1906, asked the emperor to go to Yokohama to meet the prince's ship, he refused, saying there was no precedent. He agreed to go only as far as Shimbashi Station. This gesture, though much less than what Saionji had requested, had struck Redesdale as being "an act of kingly hospitality most graciously conceived, most graciously carried out."

The emperor's resistance continued to the end. His protocol officer informed him that the recipient of the Garter must not wear any other decorations at the ceremony, but the emperor insisted on wearing several Japanese decorations. He finally removed the Order of the Chrysanthemum, but kept the eighth-grade Paulownia Leaf pinned to his chest, as if to assert the importance of Japanese decorations.

Redesdale did not mention this violation of the etiquette of the Garter, nor did he mention the awkward incident that occurred during the conferment. As the prince was buckling the Garter below the emperor's knee, the pin pricked his finger, and the decoration was stained with his blood. The prince, who was only twenty-three, was obviously nervous, but the emperor seemed quite unperturbed by the sight of blood. The chamberlain Hinonishi Sukehiro related how, once the ceremony had ended, the emperor, still wearing the hat and other insignia received during the ceremony, left the Hall of Ceremonies and retired to his private quarters. He removed the hat, and as he passed it to a palace lady, he gave a great laugh, as much as to say "*Nanda, konna mono wo*" (What am I supposed to do with such a thing?)[15] At lunch that day with Suematsu Kenchō (an adviser to the Privy Council) and others, the emperor related what had happened and expressed admiration for Prince Arthur's composure. Later, he showed Suematsu and a few others the bloodstains.[16]

That evening, the emperor paid the obligatory return visit to Prince Arthur. According to Lord Redesdale, he expressed great admiration of the ceremony and of the smoothness with which it had been conducted, diplomatically avoiding mention of the mishap. Then, producing a lacquer box, he took from it the ribbon and star of the Order of the Chrysanthemum and with his own hands put the ribbon over the prince's shoulder and pinned the star to his breast. Once again, Lord Redesdale was overcome: "Never before, not even in the case of the Crown Prince, has His Majesty deigned to invest a recipient. As a rule he has handed the box containing the Insignia unopened. Sometimes he has gone so far as to open it. But no man save Prince Arthur alone can boast that the Emperor put on the ribbon or fixed the star for him."[17]

That evening the emperor gave a state dinner in honor of Prince Arthur and the Garter mission. Prince Arthur led the way to the banquet hall with Princess Arisugawa; next came the emperor wearing the star and collar of the Garter and leading Princess Higashi Fushimi; and after them, the rest of the princes and princesses. The dinner, according to Lord Redesdale, was excellent and not too long:

> As soon as the sweet course was reached, the Emperor rose and gave the toast of the King of England, which was drunk in all solemnity, the band playing "God Save the King." Shortly afterward Prince Arthur got up and wished "health, long life, and prosperity to His Majesty, the Emperor of Japan," and now burst forth the stately National Anthem of Japan. This, it may be noted, is the first occasion upon which an Emperor of Japan has ever proposed a toast.[18]

Redesdale concluded his description of the day in these exhilarated tones:

> So ended a memorable day, a day which has broken all records and established many precedents, a day of happy augury, marking a new epoch in the relations between the two countries. Some forty years ago I was looking with a Japanese gentleman at a map of the world on Mercator's projection; pointing to England in the west and Japan in the east, he said, "Look at those two island kingdoms! are they not like the two eyes in a face? If they could only see together!" That pious wish of a man who has been dead for many years has now been realised — realised, it may be hoped, as a security for peace, at any rate in the Far East.[19]

On February 24 a program of entertainment was given in honor of Prince Arthur of Connaught at the Kabuki Theater. It opened with a kabuki play specially written for the occasion by Masuda Tarō, which concludes with the Englishman Miura Anjin[20] marrying a Japanese girl named Otsū. The ceremony ends with a geisha dance and a song of welcome to the young prince. The final words, according to Redesdale, were

> Now the two countries unite in love for ever, and ever, and ever.
> *Chorus—Wakamiya* Welcome
> *Yoi, Yoi, Yoiya, Sa.*[21]

The festivities officially ended with the emperor visiting the Kasumigaseki Detached Palace on February 26 to say goodbye to Prince Arthur, but the prince remained in Japan until March 16 in order to sightsee in Kyōto, Nara, Kyūshū, and Nikkō.

The renewal of the alliance with Britain changed Japan's relations with Korea. The Japanese had been worried that the powers might object if wartime measures in Korea were developed into a policy of permanent occupation, but Britain had made it plain that it would not cause any difficulties. The power most sympathetic to Korea, the United States, also indicated that it was willing for Japanese influence to prevail in Korea.[22] On November 2 the emperor sent for Itō Hirobumi and commanded him to travel to Korea as a special ambassador. Itō was to take this letter from Emperor Meiji to Emperor Kojong:

> The emperor of Great Japan respectfully addresses his dear friend His Majesty, the emperor of Korea.
>
> In order to complete the defenses of the empire and to maintain peace throughout East Asia, I was recently obliged to open hostilities with a neighboring country and, after twenty months of warfare, was finally able to achieve peace. During this time Your Majesty always shared my joys and sorrows, and the peoples of both countries experienced together the dangers and comforts. I am accordingly sending as special ambassador a man I trust, Marquis Itō Hirobumi, of the senior second rank of Grand Merit, the president of the Privy Council, to report to Your Majesty the achievement of an honorable peace. It will give me the greatest pleasure if he is granted a personal audience with Your Majesty at which he can convey without concealment the sincerity of my earnest wishes for the future peaceful relations between our two countries. I believe that we have reached a point where we must expect that relations between our two countries will become closer than ever. The defenses of Your country unfortunately are not yet sufficient, and the foundations of self-defense are still not solid. This has meant that they have been inadequate to secure peace throughout East Asia, a situation that Your Majesty and I have both had the occasion to deplore. For this reason, a treaty was concluded last year between our two countries that delegated responsibility for the defense of your country to mine. Even though, happily, peace has been restored, it is extremely important to make the union between our two empires firmer than ever, in order to maintain peace permanently and to prevent future troubles in East Asia. I have instructed my government to establish and execute the appropriate measures. I promise Your Majesty that the security and dignity of Your imperial house will not suffer in the slightest but will be safely preserved. Hoping that Your Majesty, giving profound consideration to tendencies in the world and considering

the welfare of Your country and people, will vouchsafe to listen to my most sincere advice, I pray for Your Majesty's happiness and the tranquillity of Your imperial house.[23]

Itō's mission was to inform the Koreans that in the treaty of peace signed at Portsmouth, Russia had recognized Japanese political, military, and economic rights in Korea and had promised not to interfere with any measures Japan might take to guide and protect Korea. He was empowered to sign a new treaty with Korea that would guarantee its territorial integrity and future peace in East Asia.

On November 15 Itō had an audience with Emperor Kojong, but before he could say a word concerning his mission, the emperor poured out his complaints about Japanese actions in Korea. He began with an expression of regret that Inoue Kaoru, the most enlightened Japanese minister to Korea, a man whose advice he had gladly followed, had been recalled, leading to an indescribable event (the murder of Queen Min). If only Inoue had remained longer, this calamity would never have occurred. It is true that the ringleaders of the plot were Koreans, but it cannot be doubted that they depended on Japanese might.

However, the emperor continued, there was no point in dwelling on long-ago events; he would discuss what had taken place since Itō first visited Korea in March of the preceding year. The Japanese had established a banking system that was supposed to be exclusively in Korean hands, but in fact a Japanese bank, the Daiichi Bank, controlled the transactions, causing the Korean people great financial distress. The Japanese had meddled in even the private property of the imperial house. When the emperor complained to General Hasegawa, the resident commander in chief, he declared that this was necessary, and the imperial family had said no more.

Financial matters were not the only problem. Postal and telegraphic communications—the lifeblood of any society—were entirely in the hands of the Japanese as the result of "improvements" proposed by the Japanese and accepted by the unsuspecting Koreans. Meiji's letter had mentioned the inadequate state of Korean defenses, but this was the result of Japanese intervention. The Korean armed forces had been so severely reduced by order of the Japanese that they were powerless to suppress even banditry, let alone foreign attack. The Japanese military had issued orders protecting railways and telegraphic communications, but badly educated Koreans could not be expected to understand a notice tacked up somewhere, and those who violated the Japanese orders were sentenced by military law to be shot by a firing squad.

At first, the emperor continued, the Japanese were welcomed, but people eventually came to cry out in angry voices. Of late, there had been rumors that foreign affairs would henceforth be in the hands of the Japanese, and this had created even more apprehension. These developments had made Koreans, high and low alike, suspect the sincerity of Japanese intentions. The emperor urged Itō to put himself in the place of Koreans faced with the present crisis.

Itō probably had not been expecting these charges but replied that he was well aware of the discontent described by the emperor. He had one question to ask, however: On whom had Korea depended for its very survival to this day? And thanks to whom was Korea independent? Did the emperor, knowing these things, still complain?

The emperor interrupted him, saying, "I am perfectly well aware of these matters. Yes, our independence was made clear in the Treaty of Tientsin of 1885 and the Treaty of Shimonoseki of 1895. This was entirely due to Japan's strength and to your truly great skills as a negotiator."

The emperor then proceeded at length to justify his decision in 1896 to take refuge in the Russian legation. Itō, who had yet to describe his mission, could not conceal his displeasure, and even while the emperor's remarks were being interpreted into Japanese, he forcibly interrupted. He said, "I have come before Your Majesty with an imperial command from His Majesty, and I was about to deliver it when I was obliged to listen to Your Majesty's tales of long ago. Those are secondary matters. I do not object to hearing them, and some other day, when I have time, I will be glad to listen in detail. But now I intend to inform you of the substance of my mission."[24]

Despite his impatience with references to the past, Itō began his oration with his meeting in 1885 in Tientsin with Li Hung-chang. On that occasion he had insisted on preserving the independence of Korea and had prevented Li from carrying out plans that would have threatened it. Again, in 1894 China had sought to take advantage of the Tonghak rebellion to impose its rule on Korea, but Japan had defeated China in the ensuing war. The greatest menace to Korean independence then became Russia, which encircled Korea by land and sea and seemed ready to annex Korea. But Japan willingly sacrificed the lives of its citizens and its national wealth to rescue East Asia from this menace. As the result of the war, Korean territorial integrity had been preserved, as the world recognized. Itō was aware that some suffering in Korea had been caused by measures taken by Japan, but this was unavoidable, and he was sure that it was not asking too much of the Koreans to put up with these difficulties. As the result of Japanese policy, Korean territory had been preserved and peace in East Asia won.

Itō moved at last to current issues: the emperor of Japan, desiring to maintain peace permanently and to prevent future threats to East Asia, had sent him to Korea to meet His Majesty and to inform him of his desire that the union between Korea and Japan be made even firmer. Korean relations with foreign countries would be managed by the Japanese government, but internal affairs would continue to be left to the Korean emperor to decide. This change would end disturbances in East Asia, ensure the peace and dignity of the Korean imperial household, and promote the happiness of the Korean people.[25]

The emperor replied that he was grateful for Meiji's solicitude, and he was not unwilling to have Japan run Korean foreign affairs. But he asked that the form, if not the reality, be left in his hands, meaning that he hoped negotiations with foreign powers would continue to be carried out in his name, even though Japan in fact decided them. Itō denied this request, saying that in foreign affairs, form and substance could not be divorced. If the Koreans insisted on running foreign affairs, it would certainly lead to trouble in East Asia, and Japan could not tolerate this. That was why Japan wanted to act for Korea in foreign affairs. The Japanese had evolved this policy after considering every possible alternative and in the light of past experience; it was not to be altered. Itō had brought a copy of the treaty and asked the emperor to examine it.

After reading through the treaty, the emperor expressed his appreciation for Itō's efforts, saying he relied more on Itō than on his own ministers. However, if he were not to be allowed even the semblance of being in command of foreign affairs, would not Korea be in the same position as Hungary with respect to Austria or the countries of Africa to their European conquerors?

Itō insisted that the treaty was indeed intended to benefit both the Korean monarchy and Korea itself. He denied that the Japanese had any intention of deceiving the emperor or of reaping profits for themselves. The analogy with Hungary did not apply: Hungary had no monarch of its own, but Japan and Korea each has its own monarch, and both preserve their independence. As for Africa, hardly a single country had ever in its history been an independent state. Comparing the relations between Japan and Korea with such examples was misleading. All Japan was asking in the interests of eradicating a possible source of calamity was to manage external affairs; everything else would be left untouched.

The emperor pleaded again and again to be allowed at least a modicum of authority, but Itō replied each time that there was absolutely no room for flexibility. All he needed to know was the emperor's decision. He was free to accept or reject the treaty, but he should be aware that the Japanese government had decided what it would do if he rejected it.

Emperor Kojong pleaded that this was an extremely serious matter and he could not make a decision on the spot. It was customary in such cases to consult his ministers and to determine the will of the people. He begged for time. Itō agreed to allow the emperor to consult his cabinet, but he was suspicious of any plan to ascertain public opinion. He commented, "Your country does not have a constitutional government. Is it not true that it is an absolute monarchy where everything is decided by Your Majesty?" Itō feared that the real purpose of ascertaining public opinion was to stir up the people against Japan. The Korean people were easily swayed because they were ignorant of foreign affairs, and that was why Japan felt compelled to act in Korea's place. The emperor protested that he did not mean a poll of public opinion but a consultation with the Chungch'uwon (Privy Council). Itō was willing to allow the emperor to consult the Chungch'uwon but warned that Japan would not tolerate delay.

The emperor asked that the treaty be sent through diplomatic channels, but Itō refused. He demanded that the emperor summon his cabinet that very night and get them to consider the treaty. The emperor promised to do as Itō commanded. He had one final request: that his plea for token recognition in foreign affairs be communicated to the emperor and the Japanese government. Itō advised him to abandon any such hope.

The discussion between Emperor Kojong and Itō Hirobumi lasted for four hours.[26] The emperor must have felt humiliated, but he had no choice but to yield: Itō had made it clear that if he refused, the Japanese would intervene militarily and overthrow his dynasty. In descriptions of Itō in other situations, he is usually portrayed as an urbane, highly civilized man, but he now demonstrated he had an iron fist inside his velvet glove. His refusal to allow the emperor even the barest modicum of self-respect—by pretending that orders actually issued by the Japanese had originated with the emperor—was couched in suitably polite language, but Kojong recognized the seriousness of the threat. Kojong himself, hitherto described in most sources as a nonentity, especially in contrast with his consort, Queen Min, showed dignity and strength in this great crisis of his reign.

On November 16 Itō invited members of the Korean cabinet and senior statesmen to his hotel for a friendly chat which turned into a fierce argument that lasted until midnight.[27] According to one Korean account: "The ministers, before coming to the hotel, had sworn to one another that they would not yield to the Japanese demands under any circumstances. The Japanese used every kind of reasoning, offered them immense bribes, cajoled them, and finally threatened to kill them if they refused to yield."[28]

On the following day a meeting between the Japanese (Itō, Minister Hayashi Gonsuke, and General Hasegawa Yoshimichi) and the Korean cabinet took place at the Japanese legation. Members of the cabinet continued to voice their opposition to the treaty, and no decision could be reached. The emperor appealed to Itō for a delay, lest forcing the issue lead to disorder, but Itō refused. Instead, the Japanese army and military police were called out. The same Korean account states, "Machine guns were everywhere in the streets, and even field guns were brought out to command the strategic points of the city. They made feint attacks, occupied gates, put their guns into position, and did everything short of actual violence to prove to the Koreans that they were prepared to enforce their demands."[29]

That night another conference took place, this time in the palace. Itō demanded an audience with the emperor, but he refused on the grounds that he had a painfully sore throat. Itō, paying no attention to the emperor's wishes, forced his way into Kojong's presence. The emperor, refusing to discuss the treaty with Itō, asked him to consult members of his cabinet. Returning to the conference room, Itō announced, "Your emperor has commanded you to confer with me and settle the matter."[30] He ordered the acting prime minister, Han Kyu-sol, to ask each member to state whether he approved of the treaty; he wanted to know the reasons of those who opposed it. In the end, all but three — one ambiguously — were persuaded or intimidated into voting in favor of the treaty.[31]

Itō declared that only two members of the cabinet were irrevocably opposed to the treaty and that the will of the majority should be respected. He called on the prime minister to follow the established procedures for signing the treaty. He realized that the acting prime minister (one of the two unyielding opponents) was loath to approve of the treaty but said that in his capacity as a representative of the emperor, he would not remain silent if he thought anyone was taking him lightly.[32]

The acting prime minister assured Itō that he was by no means anti-Japanese. He well knew that Korean independence could not have been preserved without Japanese help. But he was unable to change his mind concerning the treaty. This was perhaps a case of the proverb "Even a lowly man will not abandon his principles." His inadequate intelligence was no doubt responsible for his inability to accommodate himself to the times, and as a result he had defied the wishes of his sovereign and held views at variance with those of the rest of the cabinet. He could only await his punishment. "Try to imagine what is in my heart!" he cried, bursting into uncontrollable weeping and sobs. Itō urged him to wipe away the tears and show greater courage.[33]

Emperor Kojong was willing to approve the treaty, but he wanted a statement inserted that the present treaty would cease to be valid when Korea became rich and strong enough to maintain its independence by itself. To please the emperor (and perhaps privately sure that such a day would never arrive), Itō with his own brush wrote in the clause the emperor had requested.[34]

On November 18, 1905, the treaty of protection was signed.[35] It was in five articles:

1. Japan would henceforth conduct foreign relations for Korea and, through its diplomatic and consular personnel abroad, protect Korean subjects and their interests.
2. Japan would carry out the provisions of treaties already concluded by Korea with foreign countries, but Korea would promise henceforth not to conclude international treaties without the prior consent of the Japanese government.
3. Japan would station in Korea as its representative a resident general who would be concerned exclusively with foreign affairs. He would have the privilege of audiences with the emperor. The Japanese government would

station "residents" at opened ports and such other places in Korea as it
deemed essential.

4. All existing agreements between Japan and Korea would remain in force,
providing they did not conflict with the provisions of the present treaty.

5. Japan guaranteed it would preserve the safety and dignity of the Korean
imperial household.[36]

There was naturally bitter resentment in Korea over the treaty imposed by
Japan. Word of how the ministers had voted soon leaked out to the press, and
newspapers courageously published editorials denouncing the treaty and those
ministers who had betrayed their country by yielding to the Japanese demands.
The following days were marked by "howls of grief" and mass demonstrations
in the square in front of the palace. Shops and schools closed in protest, and
Christian churches were filled with the sounds of lamentation.[37]

Itō Hirobumi was appointed as the first resident general on December 21,
1905.[38] His activities in Korea, despite his assurances to Emperor Kojong, were
by no means restricted to foreign affairs. He determined, for example, to rid
the palace of corruption in order to end its protection of banditry and uprisings
elsewhere in the country. With the permission of the Korean emperor, Itō took
personal command of the palace guards.[39]

On the surface Emperor Kojong welcomed the new relationship with Japan,
but in a letter to President Roosevelt, smuggled out of the country, he declared
that he had never sanctioned the new treaty, that it had been forced on the
Koreans by bayonets, and that it was without validity.[40] The letter did not stir
Roosevelt into action, perhaps because he had already written off Korea as an
area of Japanese domination.

Emperor Kojong had no choice but to continue playing the role of a loyal
ally of Japan. When a celebration and review of the troops was held in April
1906 to celebrate the Japanese victory over Russia,[41] Kojong sent Lieutenant
General Prince Ui to attend the review. The prince carried a message of congratulations from the emperor and his prayer for eternal friendship between the
two countries. Kojong mentioned in particular his joy over Itō Hirobumi's appointment as resident general. This praise contradicted the extreme dislike he
always displayed toward Itō, especially after being informed of his appointment
as the first governor general,[42] but Meiji, probably unaware of the Korean emperor's real feelings, expressed pleasure that Kojong was satisfied with Itō's
administration.

Messages were exchanged from time to time between the emperors of Japan
and Korea, always expressing joy over the ever-deepening friendship between
the two countries.[43] When Meiji was informed that the Korean crown prince
was to be married, he sent the imperial household minister to the wedding with
presents for everybody. Perhaps Meiji actually believed in the pledges of friendship he exchanged with Kojong, but Itō's report to the emperor in April 1907

painted a gloomy picture of unrest. He mentioned assassination plots directed against cabinet ministers who had voted for the treaty and hinted that the Korean emperor might be deeply involved. People suspected of implication had been arrested and questioned, and many had confessed, but the investigation continued.[44]

Kojong last attempted to resist the Japanese by sending a three-man delegation to the Second International Peace Conference held in The Hague in June 1907. The delegates were Yi Sang-sol, the former vice prime minister; Yi Chun; and Yi Wi-jong, all men who had resigned in protest against the Convention of 1905. They secretly made their way from Seoul to Vladivostok, where they met the missionary Homer Hulbert. They traveled together on the Trans-Siberian Railway to St. Petersburg and from there to The Hague. The Koreans' attempts to get a hearing at the conference were largely rebuffed, although Yi Wi-jong was invited to present his case before a meeting of journalists that took place at the same time. He claimed that (1) the Convention of November 15, 1905, had never been agreed to by the Korean emperor and was therefore invalid; (2) Japan consequently had no authority to control Korea's foreign relations; and (3) Korea therefore had the right to send delegates to international conferences.

Yi Sang-sol was allowed on July 5 to present the Korean petition to the conference. His address so moved the delegates that they decided to send a telegram to Seoul to verify that the delegation actually represented the views of the Korean government, but the service was controlled by the Japanese and the telegram fell into the hands of Itō Hirobumi. He went to the palace and confronted the emperor with the telegram. Itō demanded how Kojong could have violated the treaty so flagrantly. Rather than reject Japan's protection, he might better have declared war. The chagrined emperor replied in a low voice that he knew nothing about it. This avowal was all Itō needed: he sent a reply to the effect that the Korean government had not authorized the delegation. On the motion of the British delegate (loyal to the Anglo-Japanese Alliance), the Korean appeal was rejected.[45]

The Japanese government could not allow the emperor's action to pass unpunished. Itō, accompanied by Hayashi Gonsuke, the Japanese foreign minister, called on Emperor Kojong on July 18 and demanded that he abdicate. He refused but, bowing to intense pressure, agreed late that night that the crown prince might serve as his regent. Kojong's refusal to abdicate was ignored by the Japanese, who announced that the feeble-minded Sunjong had succeeded to the throne.[46] On July 21 Emperor Meiji sent his congratulations, but despite his promise to maintain the security and dignity of the Korean monarchy, the dynasty was in its death throes.

Chapter 57

The Japanese victory in the Russo-Japanese War gave rise to powerful repercussions in many parts of the world. As the first military victory of an Asian country over a European power in modern times, it captured the imagination of people living in Asian and African countries that were under the yoke of a European conqueror.[1] Within Japan itself, however, the wartime exhilaration and sense of triumph stemming from the defeat of a powerful enemy rapidly faded. Even during the war, some intellectuals had expressed doubts about the necessity of fighting Russia. In August 1904 Arishima Takeo wrote in his diary, even as Japanese troops were pressing in on Port Arthur, "They spend an average of 500,000 dollars a day on war expenses. Is this not to be wondered at? They could build a splendid university with the money saved from two days of war. I don't know whether or not the present war is necessary. But war is unnecessary."[2]

Ishikawa Takuboku, who at the outset of hostilities with Russia had burned with enthusiasm for the war, wrote in his diary in December 1906, "When I teach my pupils that Russia, which lost the war is a finer country than Japan which won it, I wonder what kind of human beings I am trying to create."[3] Takuboku did not explain why he had taught his pupils that Russia was superior to Japan; perhaps he was indirectly expressing the disillusion that he and other Japanese intellectuals felt when they realized that the acclaimed wartime victories had been hollow. The Japanese had paid a very heavy price for the meager territorial acquisitions, and the threat from Russia was by no means ended. The satisfaction of having gained recognition as a power, thanks to the victory, did not compensate for the terrible loss of Japanese lives during the battles at Port Arthur and Mukden.

Emperor Meiji composed poems during the war, most of them lacking in the kind of fervor typical of European wartime poems. One of his best-known *tanka*, said to have been admired by President Theodore Roosevelt,[4] even expressed puzzlement (real or feigned) over why there should be such things as wars:

yomo no umi	In this world of ours
mina harakara to	Where all within the four seas
omou yo ni	Should be as brothers,
nado namikaze no	Why is it that waves and wind
tachisawaguran	Should rise and cause such tumult?[5]

Another poem described the effects of the war on those at home:

kora wa mina	All his sons have
ikusa no niwa ni	Quit their home, on their way to
idehatete	The theater of war;
okina ya hitori	Only the old man is left
yamada moruran	To guard the hillside paddies.[6]

Meiji's poems by no means expressed jubilation even after the naval victory in the Tsushima Strait or the army victory at Mukden. Foreign monarchs acclaimed these successes as being unparalleled in world history, but he soberly commented:

mukashi yori	In battles like these,
tameshi mare naru	Whose likes have rarely been seen,
tatakai ni	Throughout the ages,
ōku no hito wo	How many of our soldiers
ushinaishi kana	Have we lost in the fighting![7]

Years later, when General Nogi committed suicide in 1912 following Emperor Meiji's death, the overwhelming majority of Japanese believed that he had been moved by remorse over the tens of thousands of the men who had died in the repeated all-out attacks he had ordered during the battle for Port Arthur.[8] At the time of the victory celebration in Tōkyō in January 1906, Nogi wrote a *kanshi* expressing shame, not exultation, over Japan's success:

> *ōshi hyakuman kyōryo wo sei su*
> *kōjō yasen shikabane yama wo nasu*

hazu ware nan no kambase atte furō ni kan sen
gaika konnichi ikunin ka kaeru[9]

Imperial troops, a million strong, conquered the
arrogant enemy;
But siege and field warfare left a mountain of corpses.
Ashamed, what face can I show to old parents?
How many men have returned this day of triumphal song?

The celebrated poem by Yosano Akiko, "Kimi shinitamau koto nakare" (Do Not Die, My Brother), is often praised as an expression of antiwar sentiment, although in its day it was attacked for this very reason. In fact, Akiko, who was not a pacifist and insisted on her family's tradition of loyalty to the throne, intended to convey in the poem not pacifist convictions but fears for the safety of a brother about to leave for the front in China. Even if the poem actually had no political overtones, one can hardly imagine a similar poem being published during the Sino-Japanese War (a relatively easy campaign with few casualties), let alone during the Pacific War (when the press operated under totalitarian controls that allowed no deviation from state policy).

The naturalist movement in literature, a literature of disillusion, developed immediately after the Russo-Japanese War. A typical example of naturalist fiction, Tayama Katai's story "Ippeisotsu" (One Soldier), based in part on his experiences as a war correspondent in China, was considered to be so antimilitaristic that for years it could be printed only with passages excised.

The generation that grew to maturity during the years after the Russo-Japanese War seemed to be alienated. This alienation often began with shock at the wartime casualties and disappointment over the results of the war but later took such forms as socialism in politics. This in turn caused the older generation to express gloom over the loss by the young of their traditions. Yamazaki Masakazu characterized the times as "the morose era."

Oka Yoshitake wrote of the same period, "Some youths were swallowed up by scepticism and despair in the course of their search for meaning in life. In fact, that tendency had showed signs of emerging even before the Russo-Japanese war, but it became much more apparent following the cessation of hostilities."[10]

One might suppose that victory in the war and the admiration voiced abroad would have made the Japanese self-confident, if not proud, but critics of the time worried about the "anxious pessimism" that had become fashionable among young men and women.[11] This pessimism, ironically, may have contributed to the extraordinary flourishing of literature during the ten years after the conclusion of the Russo-Japanese War.

On the whole, 1906 was an uneventful year for the emperor, now in his fifty-fifth year. In January he commanded Saionji Kinmochi to form a cabinet after Katsura Tarō resigned. It probably pleased the emperor to have a member of the nobility as prime minister, for in recent years the nobles had played a minor role in the government.

At the end of January a delegation of members of the Chinese imperial family visited Tōkyō. At their audience with the emperor, the chief of the delegation, Prince Tsai Tse, informed him that they had been sent by the Chinese emperor to study the Japanese political system. He declared that the emperor's martial glory and civic virtues shone throughout the five continents and that he and his colleagues had been deeply impressed by the manner in which politics and education in Japan were daily being perfected. Prince Tsai Tse hoped that the emperor would recognize their sincerity and, displaying his compassion, enable them to study the excellent technology and other praiseworthy features of Japan. They intended to make Japanese civilization a model for China, hoping in this way to ensure the future security of East Asia and to promote the happiness of the people.[12]

Of course, these compliments can be discounted as mere flattery, but it is nonetheless true that a Chinese prince had addressed the Japanese emperor in terms that would have been inconceivable at any previous time during the long relationship between the two countries. Meiji seems to have been pleased: he offered the prince a chair, something he rarely did to visitors.[13] He also invited the Chinese delegation to lunch and later sent the chief chamberlain to the Shiba Detached Palace (where the Chinese were staying) with decorations for the visitors and other gifts.[14] The delegation, a small-scale Chinese replica of the Iwakura mission, after inspecting facilities in Japan and studying the Japanese constitution, left for America (and Europe) on February 13. The Chinese government genuinely seemed eager to modernize, and although other countries were also studied, Japan offered the examples most easily adopted by the Chinese.

Later that month, a delegation arrived from Korea, headed by a high-ranking officer, Yi Chae-wan. He brought with him a letter from Emperor Kojong thanking Emperor Meiji for having sent Itō Hirobumi to Korea. There were lavish gifts for the emperor, empress, crown prince, and crown princess. The next day, the emperor sent decorations to all members of the delegation, the level determined by the station of each.[15]

In February a British delegation arrived for the presentation of the Order of the Garter, as described in an earlier chapter. These attentions from foreign governments undoubtedly pleased the emperor, in contrast to developments at home. In March, for example, the foreign minister, Katō Takaaki (1860–1926), resigned over differences with other members of the cabinet concerning a bill recommending government ownership of the railways. Katō opposed the bill as an invasion of private rights, and when the bill passed despite his opposition, he submitted his resignation to Prime Minister Saionji. Members of the government who resigned invariably gave failing health as the reason, but Katō stated his real reasons.

The emperor, always a stickler for precedents, asked Saionji why Katō had disregarded custom. Saionji explained that when a man who asks to resign gives poor health as the reason, he may or may not be telling the truth. He implied that Katō was a rare example of an honest man; in any case, he asked the emperor to forgive Katō's action and accept his resignation. The emperor was persuaded, and as a consequence Saionji, in addition to being prime minister and minister of education, temporarily became foreign minister.[16]

That year, natural disasters occurred in various parts of the world. There was a major earthquake in Taiwan on March 27 in which more than 1,100 people died. On April 11 Mount Vesuvius erupted in Italy with considerable loss of life. And on April 21 there was the celebrated San Francisco earthquake. The imperial family, as they always did in the case of major disasters, contributed money for the relief of the victims—10,000 yen for the victims in Taiwan and 200,000 yen for those in San Francisco.[17] Possibly the size of the latter gift was meant to reflect Japanese gratitude for American support in the negotiations after the Russo-Japanese War.

In July the emperor was faced with a decision of somewhat less than earth-shaking importance. It was vigorously debated at the time whether the boundary stone between Japanese and Russian territory in Sakhalin should be decorated with a rising sun or a chrysanthemum. On July 5 the emperor offered his decision: it should be a chrysanthemum.[18]

Nothing much happened for the rest of the year until December 11, when a Korean delegation was granted an audience with the emperor. They brought a letter from the Korean emperor and verbal messages of eternal friendship between the two countries. The Korean emperor also expressed the deepest trust in Itō Hirobumi and deplored rumors that Itō would be replaced as governor general. A change of governor general would not only be untimely but cause the government and the people to lose heart for the future. He begged the emperor not to replace Itō.[19] At this distance from the events, we can only marvel that the Korean emperor, who detested Itō, was capable of such politic lies.

On December 28 the emperor officially opened the Diet. An American visitor to the Diet that day, Professor George Ladd of Yale University, recorded his impressions:

The occasion was the opening of the Diet by the emperor in person. . . . None might enter the House later than ten o'clock, although His Majesty did not leave the palace until half-past this hour.
    As soon as His Majesty arrived, all those who had been waiting were conducted to their proper chambers in the gallery of the Peer's House, . . .

Not more than five minutes later His Majesty entered, and ascending to the throne, sat down for a moment; but almost immediately rose and received from the hand of Marquis Saionji, the Prime Minister, the address from the throne inscribed on a parchment scroll. This he then read, or rather intoned, in a remarkably clear but soft and musical voice. The entire address occupied not more than three minutes in the reading. After it was finished, Prince Tokugawa, President of the Peers, went up from the floor of the House to the platform, and then to a place before the throne; here he received the scroll from the Emperor's hand. After which he backed down to the floor again, went directly in front of His Majesty and made a final bow. The Emperor himself immediately descended from the throne and made his exit from the platform by the door at which he had entered, followed by all the courtiers.[20]

Ladd characterized himself:

I am only a teacher; and I have had no ambition for any higher title than that of "teacher," no desire for any more imposing kind of service. But His Majesty's painstaking to recognise, and to signalise with his favour before the nation, his appreciation for any service rendered to the "moral education" of his people, has been as unmistakably sincere as it has been distinctive. And there is abundant reason to believe that this painstaking regard for the moral and other welfare of his people, irrespective of considerations of diplomatic policy, or rank, or expectation of similar favours in return, characterises throughout the Imperial rule of the present Emperor of Japan. One would have to search hard among the world's present day rulers to find another so affectionate, so solicitous, so self-sacrificing, where the interests of his people are concerned, as Mutsuhito.[21]

The fortieth year of Meiji's reign, 1907, opened without special celebrations of the anniversary. As had been true for many years, the emperor did not perform the prescribed worship of the four directions, and he had a deputy perform other traditional acts of reverence.

On January 8 the emperor went to the Aoyama parade grounds to review the troops. He had always performed the review on horseback, but this time an order was issued to open the hood of his carriage, and he reviewed the troops without leaving the carriage. It had also been customary for him to grant audiences to elder statesmen, ministers, and foreign diplomats who had come to witness the review, but this year the practice was discontinued, and the reception of visitors was left to the Ministry of War. It has been suggested that the change was made because so few foreign visitors attended the review this year,[22] but perhaps the emperor, whose state of health was unknown because of his dislike of being examined by doctors, was feeling the fatigue of age or of incipient illness.

Another sign of a deterioration of the emperor's health may be found in his decision, because of bad weather, not to attend, as planned, the graduation ceremonies at the military academy.[23] In the past, the emperor had always been indifferent to even the worst storms.

A curious, and similar, incident occurred just before the emperor's visit to the Special Festival of the Yasukuni Shrine on May 3 of the same year. The weather was fine that day, and the emperor was dressed in full regalia for the occasion. Tanaka Mitsuaki, the imperial household minister, hoped that the emperor would allow the families of men killed during the war (and other spectators) to see his "dragon countenance" as his carriage passed along the streets to and from the Yasukuni Shrine. With this in mind and without asking permission before-hand, Tanaka ordered the master of the horse to open the hood of the carriage. The day was hot and humid, but the emperor had not asked to have the windows of the carriage, much less the hood, opened. On two or three occasions in recent years when he was to pass through the foreign settlements or was on his way to an exposition, he had granted the pleas of officials that the hood be removed so that people could see him; but this time, when he was about to leave the palace, he noticed that the hood was open. He called to Chief Chamberlain Tokudaiji and ordered him to shut the hood, standing by the carriage until this was done.[24]

The officials, needless to say, were petrified at the thought they had acted in contravention of his wishes. Probably the emperor was simply annoyed that the hood had been opened without his permission. But the fact that despite the heat, he had not wanted the carriage windows opened suggests that it was not solely annoyance that made him insist that the hood be closed; he may have had an old man's fear of the cold.

At the beginning of February 1907, in response to an inquiry from the em-peror, the chiefs of the army and navy general staffs prepared a memorandum on national defense. The first and most important point was that Japan must be ready to attack any country that infringed on its rights. They claimed that apart from the Tokugawa period, when a retrogressive policy was followed, a forward-looking policy—meaning a readiness to attack—had always been typi-cal of Japan and exemplified the Japanese character.

In drawing up defense plans, the chiefs considered probable enemies. Ever since its defeat in the Russo-Japanese War, Russia had been steadily building up its military in the Far East. It also had plans to rebuild its navy and seemed to be watching for an opportunity to take revenge. Russia therefore ranked as the prime hypothetical enemy.

Next came the United States. Although America seemed to wish to maintain friendly relations with Japan, Japan could not be sure that at some time in the future there would not be a violent clash caused by geographic, economic, racial, and religious factors. Again, the alliance with England was a basic part of national defense, but in accordance with the renewed treaty, Japan was still obligated to send military assistance in the event of Russian aggression against India.

The conclusion was that the Japanese army must be able to attack its hypothetical enemy, Russia, and the Japanese navy its hypothetical enemy, the United States. To this end plans must be put into effect, beginning in the following year, to build army strength to nineteen divisions and navy strength to eight 20,000-ton battleships and nine 18,000-ton armored cruisers.[25] The emperor's reactions were not stated, but he may well have pondered the great cost of these ambitious plans at a time when Japan had yet to recover economically from the Russo-Japanese War.

A week after receiving this report, the emperor had word that miners at the copper mine in Ashio in Tochigi Prefecture had rioted, demanding better conditions and higher wages. The revolt was suppressed at the request of the governor of Tochigi by soldiers of the Fifteenth Infantry Regiment. This was not the first time the emperor had heard of the Ashio mine. In March 1897 a cabinet committee had been established to study copper poisoning of the soil resulting from the Ashio mine's operation.[26] At that time improvements in the mine's conditions were ordered, and the owner was warned that if the orders were disobeyed, he would henceforth be forbidden to engage in mining. Enforcement of the orders, however, was lax. The pollution continued, and the miners were increasingly dissatisfied with the conditions under which they worked.

The emperor was also reminded of the deplorable situation at the mine when in December 1901, Tanaka Shōzō, who had resigned from the House of Representatives to protest its indifference to his pleas to end copper poisoning, in desperation attempted to push a petition into the emperor's carriage as it was returning from the Diet to the palace. Tanaka was stopped by members of the police escort and arrested, but this did not end protests over pollution.

The protests were amply justified, but they came too early to be effective: the period was marked by desperate attempts to make Japan a major industrial power, and the harm suffered by the miners and farmers of the Ashio region probably seemed of only minor national significance to the emperor and others in the government. In the course of suppressing the violence in 1907, eighty-two miners, convicted of inciting a riot and damaging mine property, were sent to prison. In June of the same year, violence by miners at a copper mine in Ehime Prefecture over a reduction in wages was also suppressed by the militia. In July a gas explosion at a coal mine in Fukuoka Prefecture caused the deaths of more than 420 men. The emperor and empress gave 1,200 yen to the prefecture for the relief of those who suffered in the disaster, and the emperor sent a chamberlain to examine the circumstances.[27] Each of these incidents contributed to the general somber mood of the times.

Relations with foreign countries, however, were generally good. A trade treaty was signed with Russia in March, the first step toward reconciliation between the two countries. In August, on a visit to the Privy Council, the emperor delivered a rescript looking forward to removing the causes of conflict with Russia and returning to peaceful relations. A new treaty was signed with Russia that included a secret protocol in which each nation promised to respect the rights of the other north or south of a line in Manchuria.[28] This was followed by a directive proclaiming renewed friendship with Russia.

In August, Itō Hirobumi, temporarily back in Japan from Korea, received a rescript from the emperor praising his achievements in Korea. The emperor said that Itō had, by virtue of his diligence and hard work, succeeded in perfectly realizing his own desire to maintain peace in East Asia and assist Korea. In September Itō was promoted to *kōshaku*.[29]

On August 27 Sunjong, the new emperor of Korea, was officially crowned. His younger brother, the extremely handsome but dissolute Prince Yi Kan (known in Japan as Gi Shinnō), should have became crown prince, but his behavior was so outrageous that he was replaced on August 7 by Yi Eun (Ei Shinnō), his younger brother. Once Yi Eun had been installed as crown prince, Itō Hirobumi proposed that the ten-year-old boy be sent to Japan for his studies. Although he was never so described, the prince served as a hostage, as the Korean emperor realized.[30] Itō also requested that the Japanese crown prince travel to Korea in the interests of promoting friendly relations between the two countries. Although Emperor Meiji was enthusiastic about Yi Eun studying in Japan, he at first opposed sending Yoshihito abroad because of security risks, but Itō swore on his life he would safely escort the prince. The emperor finally consented, provided that Prince Takehito accompanied the crown prince.

Itō hurried back to Seoul, where he had an audience with Emperor Sunjong at which he disclosed the crown prince's forthcoming visit and presented specific plans for the Korean crown prince's study in Japan. Prince Yoshihito arrived in Seoul on October 16, accompanied by both Prince Takehito and former Prime Minister Katsura Tarō, Admiral Tōgō Heihachirō, and other high dignities. The effect of this visit, interpreted as a great gesture of friendship toward Korea, was to make it impossible for the Korean emperor to refuse to allow Yi Eun to study in Japan.[31] Later that year, at the request of Emperor Sunjong and with the approval of Emperor Meiji, Itō became the grand preceptor of the Korean crown prince, and it was he who escorted Yi Eun to Japan in December 1907.[32]

Probably the event of 1907 that most directly and strongly affected Meiji was the death in October of his mother, Nakayama Yoshiko. This was not her first illness. Dr. Erwin Baelz mentioned in his diary for November 28, 1893, that he had examined the emperor's mother, who was then suffering from a stomach ailment. On January 20, 1900, he wrote about a more serious illness:

Had good luck with the emperor's mother. When the old lady was at her worst, with high fever and pneumonia, and the court chamberlain asked me whether she had any chance, I said that there was hope she would pull through if she could last two days more. My words were evidently misreported to the emperor. When, two days later, Dr. Oka appeared to give his report, he found the emperor watch in hand. The emperor nodded to him saying: "I know, it's all right, she is saved." Dr. Oka, speechless with astonishment, said he did not quite understand, but he was delighted to be able to inform His Majesty that there really was a shade of improvement. The emperor rejoined: "Baelz said she would recover if only she could live forty-eight hours longer. He knew!" Oka begged permission to say that perhaps my words had been a little misrepresented. But the emperor stuck to his opinion.

Actually, the mother is better.[33]

This anecdote, though Dr. Baelz tells it with humor, is touching because the emperor so rarely revealed his emotions. He was obviously extremely concerned about his mother's illness, and when Baelz said that there was hope she might recover if she lasted two days more, the emperor's anxiety made him interpret this as meaning that if his mother lasted two days more, her recovery was certain. Dr. Oka's description of Meiji waiting, watch in hand, for the forty-eighth hour to pass, is particularly appealing, for at that moment he seemed to have forgotten he was an emperor and behaved merely like a son.

On October 4, 1907, the emperor received word from Dr. Oka that he was treating Nakayama Yoshiko for pneumonia and that her condition was serious. The empress immediately decided to pay a visit, but first she sent the *tenji* Yanagihara Naruko to wait on the stricken woman. Her reasons for choosing Naruko were not stated, but perhaps it was because Naruko, like Yoshiko, would one day be the mother of an emperor.

The empress herself was so impatient to leave for Yoshiko's residence that she did not wait for a proper escort to be composed. The emperor, too, as soon as he heard of Yoshiko's illness, commanded the surgeon general, Viscount Hashimoto Tsunatsune, to devote himself entirely to treating his mother, regardless of what this might involve. However, Yoshiko was over seventy and her illness was severe, and although Dr. Hashimoto exhausted every remedy at his disposal, her condition grew worse each day. There was no hope for her recovery. Finally, the doctor reported to the emperor that he had no way to cure her illness. The emperor looked extremely upset, and those around him could only gaze at him with apprehension.

The morning he received word of how serious his mother's condition was, the emperor was seated at the breakfast table. Pointing at the milk that he was served every morning at breakfast, he said to the empress, "They say Ichii [Nakayama Yoshiko's title] can't get down food or drink. But maybe she could swallow this." He took one of the three bottles on the table, each containing about half a pint, and gave it to the empress. As soon as the empress reached the mother's sickroom, she took out the milk and offered it to Yoshiko, also repeating the emperor's words. Yoshiko, overcome with emotion, drank the milk to the last drop.

The anecdote rings true even in the crucial detail, not explicitly mentioned, that the emperor was not free to visit his mother on her deathbed. He had gone to the side of his official mother, the empress dowager, and revealed then the depth of his affection, but he could not visit his real mother because her status was insufficiently elevated. Obviously, no one could have prevented him from visiting his mother if he so chose. It is unlikely there would even have been words of remonstrance. But Meiji could not violate what he believed to be the proper behavior for an emperor; he was in effect the prisoner of his conscience. Years earlier, Dr. Baelz had written in his diary that although the emperor ceremoniously visited his official mother several times a year, he was not free to visit his real mother because she was only a subject. "Strange flowers of etiquette!" had been his comment.[34] The emperor could not violate the code of etiquette, however much he may have yearned to see his mother once again before she died.

Early on the morning of October 5 Nakayama Yoshiko died in her seventy-third year. On the twelfth the emperor and empress gave 30,000 yen for funeral expenses and supplemented this with a gift of 15,000 yen in recognition of her services. The crown prince and princess gave 10,000 yen, and the four imperial princesses gave another 5,000 yen.

The funeral took place on October 14. The emperor sent Chamberlain Hōjō Ujiyasu to mourn in his place at Nakayama Yoshiko's bier. Later that day, Ujiyasu went to the Gokoku-ji, a Shingon temple associated with the imperial family, to offer prayers. The emperor also offered the Gokoku-ji *tamagushi* (wands of *sakaki*, the sacred tree of Shintō), to be placed before the Buddhist altar. On the previous day he had sent a set of seven ritual implements (*shinsen*) for offering food and drink to the Shintō gods. The combination of Shintō offerings and a Buddhist altar suggests that the separation of Buddhism and Shintō, promulgated early in the emperor's reign, had broken down. Perhaps the mixture of the two religions was unavoidable because Shintō funerals were unpopular.[35]

The ties between the imperial family and Buddhism had become tenuous, but they could not be completely broken, as the imperial tombs (including Emperor Kōmei's) were at Sennyū-ji in Kyōto. Two *gon no tenji* who had died giving birth to offspring of Emperor Meiji had been buried at Gokoku-ji, and all the other concubines of the emperor would eventually be buried within the precincts of a Buddhist temple. There was also a secular element present at Nakayama Yoshiko's funeral: by command of the emperor, a battalion of infantry served as an honor guard in the funeral procession.

Nakayama Yoshiko's surviving letters suggest that although she came from a distinguished noble family, she was not an educated woman. She probably did not attempt to understand the extraordinary changes that had occurred in Japan since her son had become emperor. But by all accounts she showed no hesitation about speaking her mind to the emperor if ever she disapproved of anything he did. He followed her advice, seeming to fear her stern rebukes, but his attitude was not solely one of respect: the affection he formed for Yoshiko as a child continued throughout his life. In her old age, she frequently visited the palace for the pleasure of seeing her son, and although he rarely enjoyed meeting anyone, he was always glad to see her.[36]

In November 1907, after a considerable hiatus, the emperor resumed one of his favorite activities, observing army maneuvers. They were held this year in Tochigi Prefecture. The emperor traveled to the site by train, at each stop on the way granting an audience (through the windows of his train compartment) to local officials who had come to welcome him. It was a festive occasion for all who rejoiced over the changes that had occurred in their lives in the forty years of the emperor's reign. In every village there were strings of paper lanterns, flags, red and white bunting, white sand spread for the emperor to tread on, and arches of green leaves.

The maneuvers, concluded at a command from the emperor, were followed by a banquet attended by 4,800 nobles, ministers, and military. The emperor, in a good mood, offered saké to some sixty of them.[37]

On December 7 Prince Yi Eun arrived in Shimonoseki, escorted by Itō Hirobumi. The prince was met by Chamberlain Iwakura Tomosada, who accompanied him to Tōkyō, which they reached on December 15 after a stop in Kyōto. Prince Takehito rode in the same carriage with the young Korean prince to the Shiba Detached Palace, where he was to stay. That afternoon, Yi Eun visited the imperial palace. The emperor went as far as the entrance to the Phoenix Hall to welcome him. In conversation with the emperor and empress, the prince said that he had come, by command of the Korean emperor and empress, to study in Japan. He asked for guidance in all matters.

After lunch the Korean prince offered the emperor, empress, and crown prince presents from his country including a jade flute, a tiger skin, and a porcelain vase with a design of cranes and clouds. On December 20 the emperor, returning the visit, called on Yi Eun at the Shiba Detached Palace. He told the prince that he regretted his stay in Japan would be so short[38] but said he hoped the prince would make the most of his time. So saying, he personally gave the prince a gold watch with the imperial crest, saying that he should use it to mark the time of his studies. The prince looked delighted.

On December 19 an envoy arrived from the emperor of Korea to thank the emperor for having sent General Hasegawa Yoshimichi as his deputy at the time of his coronation. The envoy, the uncle of the Korean emperor, brought a letter from him expressing in arcane phraseology his admiration for Emperor Meiji and his desire for a continuing friendship between the two countries. The Korean emperor clearly did not realize that within a few years, he would lose his crown to the monarch he had praised in such fulsome language.

Chapter 58

Although 1908 opened with traditional rituals, the emperor's participation was minimal. On January 6 three lectures were delivered in his presence; the first was devoted to the Code of Hammurabi (Western learning), the second to Chu Hsi's commentary on the *Doctrine of the Mean* (Chinese learning), and the third to a passage from the *Kojiki* (Japanese religion.) The emperor probably listened attentively, whether or not the lectures were engrossing, but he probably found the following day more to his taste.

It began with a visit from Yi Eun, the Korean crown prince, who had come to the palace (along with various Korean and Japanese dignitaries) to offer New Year greetings. The emperor gave Yi Eun a toy horse, a silver anchor, and various ornaments, and the empress gave him a gilt French figurine holding a clock.[1] These gifts, unlike the fresh fish or saké more commonly offered by their majesties to devoted subjects, regardless of their age or preferences, were obviously intended to please a boy of eleven. The emperor may have treated this foreign prince with greater consideration than his own children because he believed it was required by international courtesy; but perhaps his kindness indirectly expressed his regret that his own son was not more like Yi Eun.

On January 20 his son, Yoshihito, the crown prince, left Tōkyō for the mild coast of Hayama, where he would take refuge from the Tōkyō cold. The empress, also in delicate health, went for the same reason to Numazu, staying there from January 12 to April 14. The emperor was pleased that Yi Eun remained in Tōkyō, diligently attending to his studies regardless of the cold. When Yi Eun visited the palace on January 29, the emperor told him,

> I have been greatly pleased to learn that Your Highness has enjoyed per-fect health ever since taking up residence in Tōkyō, despite the differ-ences in climate and surroundings. Your studies of the Japanese language advance day by day, and I am sure that you have noted many things here that are unlike those in your own country. I hope you will show ever greater diligence in your studies and achieve even better results.[2]

At this time the emperor also sent a message to Emperor Sunjong, informing him that he was doing everything possible to ensure that the Korean prince did well in his studies.[3] On February 9 Yi Eun moved from the Shiba Detached Palace to his own house in Toriizaka Street. This was the occasion for more gifts from the emperor, the empress, and the crown prince. In May the emperor sent Yi Eun a cricket bat and a bookcase.[4]

The Japanese and the Korean courts exchanged messages on Yi Eun's prog-ress in his studies, and occasionally a Korean official visited Japan to confirm that the prince's education was proceeding satisfactorily. The Japanese made every effort to convince the Koreans that Yi Eun was happy and benefiting from his stay in Japan, part of their long-range plan to bring Japan and Korea even closer.

The emperor, however, does not seem to have been entirely convinced by the glowing reports he kept receiving of the successful collaboration between the two countries. When Itō Hirobumi returned to Korea at the end of March, the emperor sent with him an official who was asked to find answers to such ques-tions of the emperor as

1. While Itō was back in Japan, was there a decline in efficiency in the ad-ministration under Vice Resident General Sone Arasuke?
2. To what degree do the Korean emperor and retired emperor trust Sone?
3. How strong is the pro-Japanese faction in the Korean cabinet?
4. The only Koreans in the cabinet are the ministers themselves, and all the assistant ministers and bureau chiefs are Japanese. Does this mean the minister is merely a figurehead? Do the vice ministers act in a high-handed manner? Do the ministers and vice ministers work together harmoniously?
5. To what degree has Sone won the confidence of the Koreans in general?
6. What are the reactions at different levels of Korean society to the pro-longed stay of the crown prince, Yi Eun, in Japan?

The official spent about a month investigating such matters in Korea, returning early in May to report to the emperor.[5]

It was, of course, highly unlikely that the emperor would be informed that relations between the Koreans and the Japanese were deteriorating or that Sone was not trusted by the Koreans, but the fact that he had such questions suggests he was unwilling to accept at face value the optimistic reports submitted by his advisers.

The emperor was right to question the assurances he had received. There were continual outbreaks of violence in Korea against Japanese domination of the country, and the Japanese army was hard-pressed to subdue them. In May, Itō Hirobumi cabled Army Minister Terauchi Masatake asking for more Japanese troops in Korea. The matter was brought to the attention of the emperor, who told Itō that he was granting permission for sending additional troops to Korea and hoped Itō would use them to put a speedy end to the disturbances.[6]

On October 13 the emperor issued a rescript expressing concern over the gradual deterioration since the Russo-Japanese War in the spirit of the people, revealed especially in their tendency toward frivolity. He opened his message with an affirmation of his belief that the cultures of East and West were steadily drawing closer together, to the advantage of both. He mentioned his own efforts to establish friendly relations with other countries and the likelihood that benefits would result from these new relations. However, he noted, even during the short time since the war ended, the people had become lax. He urged the Japanese to bestir themselves and work together diligently in a spirit of trueheartedness.[7]

The morose mood of the Japanese after the Russo-Japanese War, already mentioned, seems to have come to the emperor's attention, although he interpreted it not as a sign of depression or disillusion with the current situation but as a flabbiness of spirit revealed in an attraction to superficial pleasures. He seemed to be asking why the Japanese did not show (by working harder) their gratitude for the blessings they now shared with the peoples of other countries.

In November the emperor left for Nara and Hyōgo Prefectures, where there were to be army and navy maneuvers. In Nara, the Grand Headquarters were in the Nara Club, a far cry from the primitive conditions under which earlier maneuvers had been carried out. The land maneuvers, attended by military attachés from eighteen countries, lasted for four days. A special character was given to these maneuvers by the site, the Three Mountains of Yamato, celebrated in poetry ever since the *Man'yōshū*. The emperor supervised the maneuvers from an observation post on Mount Miminashi. He did not overtly express pleasure to be in these historic surroundings, but his attendants, reasoning that Mount Miminashi was not far from the tomb of Emperor Jimmu northwest of Mount Unebi, another of the Three Mountains, wondered whether the emperor might not wish to pay his respects at the tomb. They accordingly made preparations, but when the emperor's expected command to arrange for a visit to the tomb did not materialize, an attendant plainly asked the emperor his intentions. He responded that it would be disrespectful to worship at an imperial tomb simply because it happened to be in the vicinity: "I came here in order to supervise the Grand Maneuvers. I will come at another time to pay my respects." It is said that the attendant was dismayed to think he had so badly misunderstood the emperor's wishes.[8]

The emperor, probably for similar reasons (although it may have also reflected his indifference to Buddhism), showed no desire to sightsee at the Hōryū-ji or any of the other famous temples in the region, but he sent a chamberlain to the Danzan Shrine and another to the tomb of the famous loyalist Kitabatake Chikafusa. From Nara he traveled to Kōbe, where he observed a naval review. Although the review was undoubtedly more interesting and more aesthetically pleasing than the maneuvers he had just witnessed, the emperor's partiality for the army was no secret, and he probably was relieved when the review was over.[9]

Although 1908 was not a particularly exciting year, there was no lack of personal events. The emperor's eldest daughter, Masako, was married to Prince Tsunehisa on April 30. Several distinguished foreigners were received at the court, including the great German scientist Robert Koch and the Swedish explorer Sven Hedin. The painter Hashimoto Gahō, the jurist Kojima Korekata, and the founder of the Ezo Republic, Enomoto Takeaki, died that year. Word was also received of the deaths of foreign monarchs—King Carlos of Portugal (the victim of an assassination), King Oscar II of Sweden (after a long and peaceful reign), and Emperor Kuang-hsü and Empress Dowager Tz'u-hsi of China (after a particularly disastrous reign). Prime Minister Saionji resigned in July and was replaced once again (in Cox and Box fashion) by Katsura Tarō, whose statement of political views, presented to the emperor, included a warning that socialism was spreading.[10] As far as the emperor was concerned, however, the most memorable feature of the year may have been the presence of Yi Eun, his surrogate son.

The next year, 1909, opened with the customary rituals, given a novel touch this year because Prince Yi Eun took part in the New Year ceremony of congratulations in the Phoenix Hall along with members of the Japanese imperial family. This may have been a further sign of the Japanese government's intention of uniting Japan and Korea, but perhaps it was no more than a sign of the emperor's high regard for the Korean crown prince.

On February 22 the Korean minister of the imperial household, Min Pyongsok, arrived in Tōkyō and stayed at the Metropole Hotel. On the twenty-fifth he and four other Korean officials visited the palace and, accompanied by Itō Hirobumi, had an audience with the emperor in the Phoenix Hall. Min brought a letter from the Korean emperor expressing his thanks for the message of encouragement he had received when he set out on a hunting tour of the Korean hinterland. This chief purpose of this excursion, in imitation of the *junkō* carried out by Meiji early in his reign, was acquainting the emperor with conditions among his people. Meiji ordered ships of the Japanese fleet to sail to Pusan so that when the Korean emperor's travels took him to southern Korea, he would be able to inspect the ships.[11] The Korean emperor's letter expressed gratitude for a gesture that had deeply moved him. He sent the letter to Emperor Meiji in the hope that the friendship between the two sovereigns would be perpetual and increasingly cordial.

The Korean emperor's letter included many kind words for Itō Hirobumi who, he said, was completely informed about the situation in Korea. Ever since taking up his post as governor general, Itō had made improvements in the Korean government and had helped the emperor in innumerable ways. For example, although Itō was an old man, he had not avoided the fatigue and cold of the emperor's journey to remote parts of the country but had accompanied the emperor on his *junkō* and done everything possible to be of service. He had patiently counseled the officials and people of both countries and had in this way cleared up the misunderstandings of uneducated Koreans, which would surely be of great value in the country's future development. The Korean emperor directed Min to voice his unbounded thanks for the emperor's great concern for Korea exemplified by his stationing Itō permanently in Korea.[12]

Emperor Sunjong sent lavish presents to the emperor, empress, crown prince, and crown princess. It is hard to imagine, however, despite his praise and his gifts, that he was really grateful for Itō's directives on not only foreign policy but also internal affairs. Nor could he have forgotten the brutality Itō displayed in forcing Emperor Kojong to abdicate. Some of Itō's reforms were in fact probably beneficial, but Sunjong tactfully did not refer to the constant incidents of violence in every part of the country in protest against Japanese rule.

By contrast, relations between the emperor and the Korean crown prince were extremely friendly. On April 30, for example, Yi Eun visited the palace and was granted an audience with Emperor Meiji. On this occasion the emperor presented the prince with a silver vase and a telescope. The silver vase was a conventional gift, but the telescope was intended to please a twelve-year-old boy. Yi Eun had a favor to ask of the emperor. Eight high-ranking Korean dignitaries had come to Japan for sight-seeing, and the prince asked the emperor to receive them. This was not the kind of request to which the emperor readily granted, but he at once consented. He told the group, "We have granted you an audience today because the crown prince of your country has wished it. We hear that you have come here for sight-seeing. We hope that you will have sufficient opportunity to carry out your observations."[13] The emperor's words were hardly genial; instead of mentioning, in the conventional manner, his pleasure in seeing these visitors, he stated his reason for granting the audience: the Korean crown prince had wished it.

Itō must have found it an increasing strain to have to administer a country where he not only was hated but was in constant danger of violence. In his memorial to the throne on May 25, he mentioned with pride his achievements in Korea but said he was tired after three and a half years in his post and asked to resign. The emperor at first refused, but on June 14 he accepted the resignation, appointing in Itō's place Sone Arasuke (1849–1910), previously the vice governor general. Itō resumed his position as president of the Privy Council. The emperor bestowed a rescript on Itō, praising him for his loyalty and his great success in the post of governor general. The rescript was accompanied by a gift of 100,000 yen, a fortune in those days. The empress sent Itō two silver bowls.[14]

On July 6 Katsura Tarō was received in audience by the emperor. The emperor approved of Katsura's policy with respect to the matter at hand, the annexation of Korea. During the past months, there had been a gradual increase in the number of intellectuals in both Japan and Korea who believed that a union of the two countries was inevitable. In March the foreign minister, Komura Jutarō, in assessing the gains that had been achieved since Japan took Korea under its protection, declared that in order for Japanese strength to be firmly established on the Korea peninsula and for the national policy on Korea to be successful, it would be necessary at some appropriate time to incorporate Korea into Japanese territory. He proposed that the government bear in mind the annexation of Korea as its eventual goal and that until that time projects relating to Korea should always accord with this goal. Katsura, accepting the suggestion, asked Itō his opinion. Itō was reputed to oppose annexation, but when he replied that he had no objection, Katsura decided to secure the approval of the entire cabinet. Now he also had the emperor's consent.[15]

Itō paid a short visit to Korea in July for the official transfer of his position to Sone Arasuke. He returned to Japan on July 20. The emperor sent a carriage to Shimbashi Station to welcome Itō back. Itō's reception ranked second only to that accorded to a victorious general of the army. He was escorted to the palace by a guard of honor consisting of a regiment of Imperial Guards infantry and a platoon of Imperial Guards cavalry.

On July 26 Itō was appointed as director of education of the Korean crown prince, an indication of his importance to Japan. On the same day Sone Arasuke handed the Korean prime minister, Yi Wan-yong, a memorandum relating to the Central Bank of Korea. It was an agreement for the establishment of a central monetary agency, known as the Bank of Korea, all of whose activities were to be in the hands of the Japanese government.[16]

The dedication of the new shrine building at the Ise Shrine, a ceremony that occurs once every twenty years, took place on the night of October 2. The emperor sent officials to represent him but remained in Tōkyō, where he performed "distant worshiping" from the palace. On this occasion the emperor, unusually of late, wore traditional robes, and all the chamberlains and civil and military officials were attired in appropriate vestments.[17] Although for years the emperor had declined to participate in most of the traditional rites, at the time of this important Shintō ceremony, he felt impelled to manifest his firm belief in the gods.

On October 9 Itō, about to leave for Manchuria, had an audience with the emperor. He sailed from Moji on the sixteenth for Dairen, where he visited the sites of the battle for Port Arthur. He left Port Arthur for Harbin by train. On arriving in Dairen, Itō stated that his journey was essentially a pleasure tour to a country that he had not previously visited.[18] More likely, however, the real purpose of the journey was to discuss with Finance Minister V. N. Kokovtsev the forthcoming Japanese annexation of Korea.

Itō's train arrived in Harbin on October 26 at nine in the morning. Kokovtsev boarded the train to welcome Itō. Russian guards were lined up along the railway platform, but judging from the photograph taken at the time, no special security precautions were in effect.[19] Itō was asked by Kokovtsev, the honorary commander of the railway guards, to review them, and he consented. He, Kokovtsev, and other officials stepped down from the train onto the platform. A photograph taken at this moment shows Itō, recognizable by his white moustache and beard, lifting his hat in salutation to the director of the Eastern Chinese Railway.[20]

When the review ended, Itō turned back to greet a delegation of Japanese residents of Harbin who had come to welcome him. He had taken a few steps in their direction when suddenly a young man in Western clothes leaped forward from behind the troops and, aiming his pistol at Itō,[21] fired six shots, the first three mortally wounding him.[22] Members of Itō's party carried him back inside the train, and doctors administered emergency treatment, but he died half an hour later. He was informed shortly before he breathed his last that the assailant had been a Korean. His last words are said to have been, "Damned fool!" (*baka na yatsu ja*).[23]

The assassin, An Chung-gun, was quickly seized by Russian guards, but before he was carried off, he managed to emit three cries of "Korea hurrah!"[24] This was the first anyone realized that he was a Korean. It is hard to blame the Russians for having failed to distinguish his nationality at first sight. He was about the same height as the average Japanese (five feet, three inches), and his features were such that he could easily pass for a Japanese. He had also taken the precaution of dressing in the best Western clothes he could afford[25] in order to look like a prosperous Japanese resident of Harbin welcoming Itō to the city.

An Chung-gun was born in 1879 to a *yangban* (noble) Korean family that could trace its ancestors back twenty-six generations.[26] Seven moles on his chest and abdomen led to the nickname he often used, An Un-chil.[27] It was expected that he would become a scholar, following his family's traditions. His grandfather had six sons, all known for their literary skill, and among them Chung-gun's father was the most brilliant. At the age of eight or nine, he was able to read the Four Books and the Three Classics of Confucianism and was acclaimed as a genius. Chung-gun, however, did not become a man of letters (although he was an accomplished calligrapher) but a man of action. Even as a boy he was known as a skillful marksman, and he preferred hunting to books. When he was first interrogated after being arrested, he gave as his profession "hunter."[28]

In the account of his life he wrote in a prison cell while awaiting the death sentence, An related what had led to his conversion to Catholicism. His father, incensed over the violently anti-intellectual Tonghak rebellion, had formed a "righteous army" of some seventy soldiers who assumed responsibility for protecting their village from the rebels.[29] An Chung-gun joined them, but they were no match in numbers for the Tonghak. He wrote that fighting them was like throwing eggs against a rock. But the "righteous soldiers" persevered and eventually won some victories against the superior Tonghak forces, only to be attacked by the new pro-Russian government.[30]

Fleeing the fighting, An Chung-gun took refuge with a priest named Wilhelm, known by his Korean name, Hong Sok-ku. He remained in hiding for several months in Wilhelm's church. The priest encouraged An to use his enforced leisure to study Christianity, and he complied, spending much of his time reading the Bible and discussing Christianity with Wilhelm. The priest finally convinced An of the truth of Christianity, and An was baptized in January 1897. His baptismal name was Thomas.[31] For several years afterward, he and his father actively propagated the faith, and he remained a convinced Catholic to death. In his last letter, addressed to his wife, he asked that their elder son become a priest.[32]

An recalled in the narrative of his life that he had studied French for about three months with Father Wilhelm;[33] it was the only foreign language he ever learned. When a friend asked why he had stopped studying French, An responded, "Anyone who studies Japanese becomes the slave of Japan. Anyone who studies English becomes the slave of England. If I were to learn French, I could not avoid becoming the slave of France. That is why I gave it up. Once the reputation of Korea rises in the world, people all over the world will come to use Korean."[34] It is apparent from An's remarks that he had had some sort of disagreement with Wilhelm. Even though An's faith in Christianity was not shaken, he no longer trusted foreign people.[35]

An was intensely nationalistic, but he also envisaged a union of the three great countries of East Asia—China, Korea, and Japan. Perhaps this conception was first suggested to him, paradoxically, by the doctrine of the Yellow Peril, the evil brainchild of the kaiser. An warned of the White Peril, exemplified by the predatory European nations that were pouncing on helpless Asia. The best way for the East Asian nations to end the threat of aggression from the Western powers was to unite. China and Korea especially, because they were even at that moment victims of European aggression, must cooperate to resist the European powers; if they did, the Europeans would withdraw and peace would return to East Asia.[36]

An was not anti-Japanese. The man he most admired was undoubtedly Emperor Meiji, and one of his most vehement accusations against Itō Hirobumi was that he had intentionally deceived the emperor, who desired not the subjugation of Korea but peace in East Asia and Korean independence.[37]An's knowledge of the emperor's wishes was derived from the statement of Japanese objectives in starting a war with Russia in 1904.[38]An was delighted to read about Japanese victories over the Russians and claimed that his compatriots shared his joy over the defeats suffered by one of the agents of the White Peril.[39] He regretted only that Japan had broken off the war before Russia was reduced to total submission.

An was sure that many Japanese shared his hatred of Itō Hirobumi's policies. He described conversations with various Japanese prisoners of war. One, a member of the garrison stationed in Korea, wept as he told An how much he missed the family he had left behind in Japan. An said that if peace were restored to East Asia, there would be no need for a Japanese garrison in Korea. The soldier agreed, commenting that it was because wicked ministers had disturbed the peace that he had been compelled to come to this distant place, much against his wishes. He added that although he could not do it all alone, he would like somehow to kill Itō.

An had similar conversations with a Japanese farmer, a merchant, and a Christian minister, all prisoners. They deplored the present situation in Japan, and the merchant, like the soldier before him, wished he could kill Itō. An received from these men a strong impression of hatred for Itō, and he supposed that they typified the entire Japanese populace.[40] He reasoned that if even Japanese wished to kill Itō, it was easy to imagine why Koreans, whose family and friends had been murdered on Itō's orders, detested him. An claimed to have assassinated Itō in his capacity as a "lieutenant general of the righteous army" because Itō, by disturbing the peace of East Asia, had estranged Japan and Korea.[41]

An still hoped that relations between the two countries would become closer, providing a model for the whole world to imitate. An urged a sympathetic Japanese prosecutor not to worry about whether or not he would be condemned to death; all he asked was that the emperor of Japan be told why he had committed the crime.[42] He was sure that if the emperor realized how mistaken Itō's policies had been, he would understand An's action and rejoice. An expected that if in the future, following the wishes of the emperor of Japan, administrative policy with respect to Korea was improved, peace between Japan and Korea could be maintained for 10,000 ages.

By blaming on Itō every crime committed against Korea by the Japanese, An absolved from guilt not only the emperor, in whose name many of these crimes had been committed, but the entire Japanese people. Once Japan was free of the cancer that had corrupted relations between the two countries, which were meant to be friends because of the many traditions they shared, there was no reason that they could not enjoy peace for all ages to come. In such writings, An seems to have been obsessed with his image of the archfiend Itō, a modern equivalent of the Satan he read about in the Bible.

An accused Itō of fifteen specific crimes, including the murder of Queen Min. An's most surprising accusation was that forty-two years earlier, Itō had killed Emperor Kōmei. He asserted that all Koreans knew this, but even if this rumor were true, it is hard to know why An thought killing Kōmei was a crime against the Korean people.[43] An's other accusations describe the unspeakable consequences suffered by the Koreans from the unequal treaties the Japanese had imposed on them. The last of the fifteen crimes of which Itō stood accused was that he had deceived the emperor of Japan and the rulers of other countries by pretending that Korea was at peace and thriving.[44]

It was undoubtedly with exhilaration that An fired his gun at the great enemy of the Korean people. No sooner had An fired six shots than he was overcome by Russian guards and carried off to prison. The *Tōkyō nichinichi shimbun* for November 3 quoted An as saying in his prison cell, "I have ventured to commit a serious crime, offering my life for my country. This is the behavior expected of a noble-minded patriot. But giving me such inedible food is not the treatment a patriot should receive. I absolutely refuse to eat it."[45]According to the same article, he refused to eat anything for two days.

His treatment improved markedly after the Russians turned him over to the Japanese. Mizobuchi Takao, the public prosecutor, offered him gold-tipped cigarettes after finishing his interrogations and, in their chats afterward, showed his sympathy. An recorded in his autobiography that when he had revealed Itō Hirobumi's fifteen crimes, Mizobuchi had exclaimed, "From what you have just told me, it is clear that you are a righteous man of East Asia. I can't believe a sentence of death will be imposed on a righteous man. There's nothing to worry about."[46]

The other Japanese officials at the prison also were deeply impressed by An, whose attitudes and actions, much in the mold of a Japanese hero, seems to have struck a responsive chord in them. At New Year, An and the two Koreans who had been arrested as his accomplices were treated to traditional Japanese New Year's delicacies. His bold calligraphy was so much in demand by his captors that he wrote more than fifty scrolls for them, all signed "An Chung-gun, a Korean in the Port Arthur Prison."

An began to write his autobiography on December 13 and continued writing it during his trial, which began on February 7, 1910. At the trial, in accordance with the agreement signed between Japan and Korea providing that Japan would henceforth protect Korean citizens abroad, An was not permitted to have a Korean defense attorney. Everyone involved in the conduct of the trial—the judge, the prosecutors, the defense council, and the interpreter—was Japanese.

This created a particular hardship because An did not understand Japanese. The interpreter did his job with the utmost care,[47] and An's attorneys sincerely attempted to secure an acquittal,[48] but he felt almost unbearably isolated.

Despite Mizobuchi's reassurances, the verdict was predictable. On February 14 An was sentenced to death.[49] The decision was made not by persons in the courtroom but by the Foreign Ministry. On December 2 Foreign Minister Komura Jutarō sent a cable saying, "As far as the government is concerned, An Chung-gun's crime is extremely grave, and it considers that it is appropriate in his case, as a means of discouraging crime, for the extreme penalty to be applied."[50]

Although An had expected this verdict, he was greatly incensed when it was pronounced. He had hoped that he might be recognized not as an assassin but as a prisoner of war, a righteous soldier who had killed an enemy of his country. This plea was ignored. Judge Hiraishi had earlier promised An that even if he were found guilty, a stay of execution of at least a few months would surely be granted, but the order from Tōkyō called for prompt action. The date for the execution was set for March 26. An did not appeal the verdict, considering that it would be useless. All he asked was a postponement of two weeks in the execution so that he might complete his study "On Peace in East Asia." He asked the help of the prison warden, Kurihara Sadakichi, but Kurihara, though deeply sympathetic, was powerless to change the date. As a last favor, An asked for white silk Korean clothes in which to die, and Kurihara obliged.[51] Not long afterward, depressed over his failure to save An, Kurihara resigned as warden and returned to Japan.

On March 9 and 10 Father Wilhelm heard An's confession, said mass, and administered the sacraments.[52] During the last weeks of his life, An continued writing. On the morning of his execution, he put on white clothes. A photograph taken at that time shows him looking calmly into the distance. All that is visible inside the whiteness of the clothes is his head with its intensely black hair, eyes, and mustache and his hands folded together over his knees. An was hanged later that morning, on March 26. A Japanese doctor pronounced him dead at ten that morning. An's body was carried to a common burial grounds about two miles away.

Emperor Meiji's reactions to An Chung-gun's death are not known, but probably he felt it was appropriate that the man who had killed his most valued adviser, Itō Hirobumi, should be punished by death. Despite An's earnest request, it is unlikely the emperor was informed of his reasons for assassinating Itō. In any case, Itō's death came as a terrible blow to the emperor. He did not reveal this openly; his activities were much the same as before Itō's death. But Hinonishi Sukehiro, who served the emperor as chamberlain for many years, recalled that his shock on learning of the death of Itō was so great that he seemed to have suddenly become an old man. Itō's funeral in Tōkyō attracted a crowd of 400,000 mourners.

An Chung-gun has been treated as a patriot and hero, especially in the theater. In China, among the plays was one written by Chou En-lai and his wife, Teng Yin-chao. In Korea, An is celebrated as a national hero, and Harbin has acquired for Koreans the character of a sacred place because it is the site of the revival of their national spirit.[53]

There was a speedy reaction in Japan to news of Itō's assassination. Ishikawa Takuboku published in the *Iwate nippo* the following day an article that opened

October 26. Cloudy. Shortly after three this afternoon a dispatch arrived from afar that caused unimagined consternation in a corner of Tōkyō. Cries of disbelief, words of shock and grief spread moment by moment; then, when day was at last coming to an end after a light rain, shouts of "Extra!" in voices filled with sinister overtones, filled the whole city, throwing people's hearts into sudden commotion, as if a hundred tides had gushed forth at one time. Everyone, old or young, high born or low alike, was equally stupefied by this shocking news that has affected our entire people. Indeed, the news was so bad it truly astonished the people of Japan, and at the same time it was a major event of worldwide importance. And this news spread today from one corner of our empire to the other. It was a day when in every part of the country voices were raised in an overflow of grief. Ah, Lord Itō is dead![54]

Takuboku went on to recall Itō's recent visit to the Tōhoku region:

I can visualize the expression on the faces of the people of Morioka when they learn this tragic news. It is less than a hundred days since they welcomed and said goodbye to his lordship when he traveled in the north. Yes, no sooner had he returned to his country after resigning his post of governor general, before he had even time to warm his seat, he toured the Tōhoku and Hokkaidō with the Korean crown prince. He returned to Japan, only to hurry off on a journey to northern Manchuria.

Takuboku concluded the essay: "He was reproached by some critics. But who can deny that today's Meiji Japan owes most to the low-keyed progressivism that characterized his entire life?"

Chapter 59

The annexation of Korea by Japan, formally proclaimed in the treaty signed by both parties on August 22, 1910, was precipitated by the assassination of Itō Hirobumi ten months earlier. Undoubtedly the murder by a Korean of the most respected Japanese statesman intensified feelings in Japan that the Koreans were lawless and could not govern themselves. It is also likely that if Itō had not been assassinated, he would have served as a restraining influence on the advocates of annexation, even though the decision to unite the two countries had been made a year earlier and the Japanese government was waiting only for a suitable occasion to carry out this plan.

Japan had fought two wars with the ostensible purpose of preserving Korean independence. But more important than the independence of Korea, a matter of limited interest to most Japanese, was Japan's determination to prevent China and Russia from interfering with its own plans to exploit Korean resources. Some Koreans (like An Chung-gun) accepted the Japanese war aims stated by the emperor in his declarations of war on China and Russia as expressions of genuine determination to maintain Korean independence. A few Koreans, even more impressed by the Japanese than An Chung-gun, began openly to advocate a union of the two countries.

In 1904 Song Pyong-jun, an interpreter for the Japanese during the Russo-Japanese War, formed the Ilchin-hoe, a party committed to cooperating with Japan. The new party took in such figures as Yi Yong-gu, earlier associated with the Tonghaks, and came to collaborate with Japanese right-wing nationalists, notably Tōyama Mitsuru, Sugiyama Shigemaru, and Uchida Ryōhei, the founder of the notorious Amur River Society.[1] Uchida, a part-time employee of the Residency General, became an adviser of the Ilchin-hoe in October 1906 and from then on served as an intermediary between Itō Hirobumi and pro-Japanese Koreans. Itō decided late in 1906 to make use of the Ilchin-hoe and, from the following January, the Residency General provided the party with monthly grants of about 2,000 yen.[2]

The first Korean cabinet to be formed after the creation of the Residency General was headed by Pak Che-sun. Although Pak, a well-educated man, favored the reforms proposed by Itō and got along well with him, he became depressed over reports that he was the prime target of anti-Japanese activity. There were also increasing outbreaks of "righteous army" resistance. Despite Itō's request that he remain in office, Pak insisted on resigning. Itō had to organize a new cabinet in May 1907 and chose Yi Wan-yong[3] as prime minister and Song Pyong-jun as minister of agriculture and industry.

Itō delivered to the new cabinet a "pep talk" that included these words:

> Whether Korea is to progress as at present or to be destroyed depends on no other country but Korea itself. . . . I am doing all that lies within my power to help you and to enable Korea to stand on its own feet. How is it possible for Koreans not to have awakened to this fact? . . . The most appropriate and urgently needed policy for the continued existence of Korea is the resolution to cultivate sincere friendship with Japan, and to share its future with Japan.[4]

These words confirmed Itō's conviction that cooperation with Japan was essential to Korea's future prosperity, but he stopped short of proposing an immediate union of the two countries. He was, however, implicitly warning that if the Koreans failed to appreciate all that Itō was doing on their behalf, harsher policies might be adopted.

Anti-Japanese activity by "righteous army" soldiers in every part of the peninsula should have made it clear that the Korean people as a whole bitterly resented Japanese rule in their country, even though *some* Koreans were impressed by the reforms initiated by Itō, and others hoped that collaboration with the Japanese might bring material benefits to the country.

The members of Yi Wan-yong's cabinet were solidly pro-Japanese, but otherwise there were divisions among them. For example, Yi himself was hostile toward the Ilchin-hoe, in part because he was an aristocrat and it was led by a man of humble origins. Itō's chief concern, however, seems not to have been squabbles among the Koreans or anti-Japanese activity but the possibility of Russian intervention. In 1906, when a new Russian consul general was appointed to Seoul, the Russian government sent his credentials to the Japanese Foreign Office, in keeping with the convention of 1905 that provided for Japanese control of Korean foreign relations. However, the credentials were addressed to the emperor of Korea, an indication that Russia still considered Korea to be an independent nation.[5] Itō feared this meant that Russia had not renounced its ambitions of intervening in Korea. Indeed, it was probably in the hopes of improving relations with Russia that he made his fatal journey to Harbin.

Song Pyong-jun openly advocated Japan's annexation of Korea, insisting that it would make possible a more successful administrative policy in Korea than the halfway status of a protectorate.[6] He was disappointed to learn in November 1906 that Itō, cautiously waiting to see how the present situation developed, was reluctant to take immediate action to force the Korean emperor to abdicate.[7] In 1908 Uchida Ryōhei, deciding that Itō had no intention of annexing Korea, joined the Ilchin-hoe's appeal to the Japanese government to get rid of Itō. Song resigned his cabinet post in 1909 and went to Japan, where he urged Prime Minister Katsura Tarō to waste no time in annexing Korea.[8] Itō, fearing that Song's resignation might lead to the cabinet's collapse, promoted him to minister of the interior.

In any case, Itō himself had decided to resign, disappointed that during the three and a half years of the protectorate he had not won the allegiance of the Korean people. His gradualist policy had obviously failed. The intensification of activity by the "righteous army" as well as attacks from Japanese politicians, who claimed that Itō's conciliatory policy had weakened Japanese prestige, made him feel there was no point in wasting more time in a thankless post. But even after his resignation as resident general in June 1909, Itō still wielded influence within the Japanese government, and his death meant that an important obstacle had been removed from the path of annexation.

The Ilchin-hoe (now headed by Yi Yong-gu) stepped up its advocacy of annexation after Itō's death. On December 5, 1909, the Japanese press reported that on the previous day the Ilchin-hoe had issued a manifesto calling for annexation. Memorials to this effect were submitted to the Residency General and Prime Minister Yi with the request that they be transmitted to the emperors of Japan and Korea.[9] This was not mere opportunism: Yi Yong-gu was convinced that Korea was moribund, at death's door, and that the only hope for its recovery was a union with Japan that would bring benefits to be shared alike by the Korean and Japanese peoples. His memorial to the emperor of Korea seems to reflect genuine convictions:

I, Yi Yong-ku, the president of the Ilchin-hoe, representing a million members and 20 million other subjects, in profound awe and trepidation, bow my head in respect and offer a hundred reverences in addressing these words to Your Majesty. . . . Our country, Korea, is now like a sick man whose pulse has for long been on the verge of failing. For us, Your subjects, to cry out our griefs to our country has been exactly like holding a corpse in our arms and vainly howling our sorrow. . . . Fortunately, we come originally from the same race as the Japanese, and there never has been between us any greater difference than between the *karatachi* and the *tachibana*.[10] If now, before quarrels intensify, we boldly obliterate the national boundaries and remove the high walls separating the two neighbors, and the two peoples, enabled to live freely under one regime, receive equally the blessings of living together under the same government, who will say that this one is the elder brother or that that one is the younger brother? Indeed, it is certain that His Majesty, the emperor of Japan, in his great humanity will nurture and educate our 20 million compatriots and raise them to the same level [as the Japanese]. . . . Let us shake off the name and reality of being the inferior people of a protectorate and, in one leap, rise up, a great new union of peoples, into the ranks of the finest nations of the world. This indeed will be like the first blooming of an *udombara*, and the lucky stars and the phoenix will see each other.[11]

The memorial, signed by Yi Yong-gu and "1 million people," was submitted on December 4, arousing public outcry against the Ilchin-hoe, whose members were branded as traitors.[12] It was rejected by the Korean government, and Sone Aramaki, the resident general, told a Japanese reporter that he still was not in a position to say anything definite about the union of Japan and Korea. He stressed that the Japanese government was in no way involved in the Ilchon-hoe's declaration. The Japanese government considered unification a very serious matter and would not act until the appropriate time, and then only after proper preparation. It was to be regretted that the Ilchon-hoe had not waited and had made no preparations.[13]

Yi Yong-ku's assertion that the Koreans and Japanese were fundamentally the same people with the same traditions would be repeated many times in years to come, mainly by the Japanese in justifying their conquest of Korea.[14] The destruction of the formal line dividing the two countries even caused some Japanese to refer to Koreans as "people of the peninsula" (*hantōjin*), a term the Koreans found highly offensive because it denied the existence of Korea except as a mere projection of land. Perhaps Yi meant no more than that both the Koreans and the Japanese were recipients of Chinese civilization. That is, a Korean gentleman raised on the Four Classics of Confucianism had no trouble in "conversing with the brush" with a Japanese gentleman of similar education, and the elaborate courtesies observed by both courts were ultimately derived from the same Chinese models. But it is astonishing that a former advocate of Tonghak xenophobia should have contemplated with equanimity being ruled by a foreign people who not only spoke a different language but had a government that, unlike the Korean one, was thoroughly Westernized.

The Japanese seem to have had no doubts about the propriety of occupying a country whose traditions were as old as their own. Korea was now militarily weak and had fallen far behind in the race of East Asian countries to modernize. The Japanese authorities were actually puzzled by Korean resistance to their gift of modern civilization and could attribute it only to ignorance. Yamagata Aritomo, the least sympathetic to Korea of the Japanese leaders, declared, "Korea has neither the basic knowledge nor sufficient capacity to absorb the new civilization. The Korean people, high and low alike, are indecisive and rather indolent."[15]

Annexation was undoubtedly the goal of the Residency General, but its officers were determined to suppress "righteous army" resistance before the union took place. Accordingly, a harsh campaign to wipe out this resistance was initiated in the south of Korea in September 1909. The brutal "churning method," employed with devastating success, was followed by similar campaigns elsewhere in the country. It seems likely that the hatred of Japan felt even today by many Koreans dates from this time.[16]

In May 1910 the ailing Sone was replaced as resident general by Terauchi Masatake (1852–1919), who continued to serve also as army minister. In July, shortly before Terauchi was to sail for Korea, Prime Minister Katsura Tarō and Foreign Minister Komura Jutarō reported to the emperor on the situation in Korea. After hearing their report, the emperor asked that Terauchi take with him a personal letter and various gifts to the emperor of Korea.[17] It is surprising that the emperor, so shortly before his government deprived the Korean emperor of his crown, should have followed the old oriental practice of exchanging gifts with other sovereigns. Perhaps he had not yet been informed of how drastically annexation would affect the Korean monarchy.

One of Terauchi's first actions on assuming office, even before he arrived in Korea, was to unify under Japanese command all police functions in the country. On being asked why the number of Japanese military police had been so greatly increased, he is said to have commented, "It is easier to use military than ordinary police to control a primitive people."[18]

From the time of his appointment to the post of resident general, Terauchi waited patiently for the right moment to set in motion the mechanism of unifying the two countries. The moment seemed to have arrived in August. Terauchi received an increasing number of reports that Koreans, irrespective of their social status, were becoming resigned to annexation by Japan. But one major concern remained to be cleared up. People expressed fears concerning the treatment of the Korean imperial house and the future position of the prime minister and other high-ranking statesmen. Terauchi secretly sent word to members of the Korean cabinet explaining that the emperor of Japan was generous and his government fair, that they would never allow the Koreans, whether they were members of the imperial household or humble peasants, to fall into adversity. If the members of the cabinet chose to resign in a body, the Japanese government would not try to stop them, but it would try to make them see that shirking their responsibility could only harm themselves and the nation.[19] This stirred the prime minister, Yi Wan-yong, into resolving to face the crisis rather than flee it. Terauchi, guessing that Yi's attitude had changed, sent for him on August 16.

As soon as Yi arrived in the Residency General, Terauchi handed him a memorandum concerning the treaty of annexation. It opened with what were now familiar generalizations—that Japan and Korea were neighboring countries; that their cultures were the same; that from ancient times they had shared weal and woe, profit and loss; and that their relations were so close they should no longer remain separate. That was why Japan had twice fought wars, sacrificing tens of thousands of soldiers and vast sums of money. Ever since then, the Japanese government had zealously devoted its energies to helping Korea, but under the present complicated structure of the protectorate, it found itself unable to ensure in perpetuity the security of the Korean imperial house or to protect to the full the welfare of the Japanese and Korean peoples as a whole. For this reason, the two countries should be brought together and made one.

Needless to say, the memorandum continued, this union of two countries must not be thought of as being the result of a war or hostility. Rather, the agreement is to be carried out in a spirit filled with the friendliest of feelings. In view of the current situation, the emperor of Korea will voluntarily cede his sovereign powers to the emperor of Japan. He will abdicate his throne and in the future occupy a position of perfect security. It was in order to protect the tranquillity of the emperor, the retired emperor, the crown prince, and other members of the imperial family, as well as to ensure the prosperity of the Korean people, high and low alike, that Japan felt it necessary to conclude the treaty of annexation.[20]

As finally presented to the Korean government, the treaty was in eight articles, which mainly reassured the emperor of Korea and the nobility that they would be well treated after unification.[21] This promise, on the whole, was honored by the Japanese. Members of the Korean imperial family and other high nobles received Japanese titles and sufficient stipends to carry on their lives in the manner to which they were accustomed.[22] After abdicating, Emperor Sunjong and Retired Emperor Kojong continued to live in the Toksu Palace in Seoul. In 1920, after receiving an excellent education in Japan, Yi Eun, the crown prince, married Masako, the eldest daughter of Prince Nashinomoto. During his distinguished career as a Japanese army officer, Yi Eun eventually rose to the post of commandant of the First Air Force.

The memorandum that Terauchi showed to Yi Wan-yong contained a somewhat earlier version of the treaty articles. It proposed, for example, that the Korean emperor be known henceforth as *taikō denka* (His Highness, the archduke) and the crown prince as *kōdenka* (His Highness, the prince). These titles would be hereditary. The memorandum recognized that some people might object that this represented a demotion from their present status, but these titles would be Japanese, not merely Korean. Besides, if one examined the matter historically, one would find that it had been only since Japan gave Korea its protection and proclaimed Korean independence that the king of Korea had assumed the title of emperor. It was nonsense to claim that his title went back centuries; indeed, it was not necessarily true, regarding his status of thirteen or fourteen years earlier, to say that he would suffer a demotion. In any case, there would be not the slightest reduction in court appropriations. Most important, as the recipient of the privileges of a member of the Japanese imperial family, he would enjoy a position that was permanent and stable and would never suffer any alterations in his status.[23]

The memorandum promised that members of the Korean aristocracy would be given equivalent titles in the Japanese aristocracy and that their annual allowances would actually be increased, thanks to the generosity of the Japanese emperor. Members of the present Korean cabinet would remain in office until their terms expired and then would be given pensions that would enable them to live comfortably for the rest of their lives. Ordinary citizens would be given grants to enable them to carry on with their livelihoods.[24]

After listening to a lengthy exposition of Japan's future policy that promised benefits for all, Yi Wan-yong had only two requests to make of Terauchi. The first was that even after unification, the country would still be known as Han-guk, and the second was that the Korean emperor be allowed to retain the title of king. Although Yi welcomed annexation, he evidently feared that unless the name of the country and the title of king were preserved, Korean identity would be lost. Terauchi replied that keeping the name of the country and the title of king would contradict the reality of a postunification Korea, that if the two countries became one, a name that suggested a wholly independent state would be inappropriate, and a king had no functions when the emperor of Japan ruled over joined countries. Yi asked to consult with his adviser Cho Chung-ung, the minister of agriculture and industry, and Terauchi agreed.

Cho (who spoke fluent Japanese) called that night on Terauchi and told him that he and Yi agreed that unless the name Han-guk and the title of king were retained, no compromise could be reached. They were apparently under the impression that annexation would be a union of two countries, each retaining sovereign status, rather in the manner of Austria-Hungary or Sweden-Norway. Terauchi was surprised by this lack of understanding of Japanese aims, but he finally agreed to allow the country to be known by the old name of Chōsen. In response to the request that the title of king be retained, Terauchi compromised to the extent of allowing the emperor to be known as *riō denka* (His Highness the Yi king). The title *ō* was not the same as *kokuō* (king); in Japan, *ō* meant no more than a prince, but this concession seemed to satisfy the Koreans' wounded pride.[25] Retired Emperor Kojong would be known as *taiō denka* (His Highness, the great king), and Crown Prince Yi Eun, as *ōseishi denka* (His Highness, the heir to the king). Cho agreed to these changes and informed Yi, who told Terauchi that he was confident he would be able to persuade the cabinet at the meeting on the next day to accept Terauchi's compromise.

On August 18 Katsura Tarō reported to the emperor on Terauchi's negotiations with the Korean cabinet. Mentioning the two concessions he had made, Terauchi asked the government's approval, promising that once it had been obtained, the treaty could go into effect within a few days.[26] The emperor gave his consent, and Katsura wired this to Terauchi, who at once informed Yi Wan-yong. He advised Yi to take steps to ratify the treaty. Yi summoned the cabinet the same day and asked them to support unification. A cabinet meeting in the presence of the Korean emperor was arranged for August 22.

The meeting was attended by the emperor, the prime minister, representatives of the imperial family, and other high-ranking personnel. The emperor announced that he was ceding to the emperor of Japan sovereignty over Korea and that he had personally signed and affixed the imperial seal to the commission of full power. He gave the document to Yi Wan-yong, who in turn submitted the treaty of annexation for the emperor's inspection and explained its provisions. The emperor was pleased to approve them.

As soon as the meeting had ended, Yi Wan-yong went to the Residency General to inform Terauchi what had happened at the meeting and to show him the commission of full power. He asked Terauchi to sign the treaty. Terauchi, after inspecting the document, pronounced it to be complete and accurate. He remarked that it was a blessing for both Japan and Korea that such a restrained and amicable solution to the political situation had been found, that it was an occasion for congratulations. He and Yi put their signatures to both Japanese and Korean texts of the treaty.[27]

On August 29 the text of the treaty was published in Japan along with an imperial rescript:

> We, bearing in mind the necessity of maintaining peace permanently in East Asia and ensuring the future safety of Our empire and, taking cognizance of the fact that Korea has always been a hotbed of disorder, in the past asked Our government to reach an agreement with the Korean government to place Korea under the protection of the empire, in the hopes of extirpating disorders at their source and ensuring peace.
>
> During the more than four years that have elapsed since then, Our government has assiduously striven to improve Korean facilities, and its achievements have been considerable; but they have still not been sufficient to make complete the maintenance of order under the present system in Korea. Feelings of fear abound within the country, and the people do not live in peace. It has become clear that in order to maintain peace within the community and to advance the well-being of the people, reform of the existing system is inevitable.

We, together with His Majesty the emperor of Korea, reached the conclusion, in view of this situation, that there was no alternative to uniting Korea with the Japanese Empire, in this way responding to the demands of the times; We have therefore decided to unite Korea permanently with the empire.

His Majesty the emperor of Korea and members of the imperial family will, after unification, receive appropriate and generous treatment, and the people, direct recipients of Our compassion, will know greater security and happiness. Industry and commerce will see marked development under good government and peace. We are absolutely certain that peace in East Asia will as a result have stronger foundations than ever before.

We shall appoint a governor general of Korea, and expect him, in keeping with Our orders, to command the army and navy and to exercise general control over all governmental business. We expect that government officials and public servants, in obedience to Our wishes and in accordance with the situation, will choose whether it is preferable to be fast or slow in the development of facilities and, in this way, inspire confidence in the people in the blessings of order and peace.[28]

As usual in the case of rescripts issued in the emperor's name, it is not clear what part (if any) he had in the expression, but probably the text accorded with his opinions concerning Korea's immediate fate. At this distance from the events, we can see that everyone involved in the decision to join Korea to Japan was seriously mistaken. Koreans who believed that the union would result in mutual prosperity should have foreseen, in the light of their experiences with foreign countries, that profit for the foreign country would always take precedence over any desire to bring prosperity to the Koreans. They should have realized, too, that even if figureheads like their king were permitted to enjoy a comfortable retirement, the mass of Koreans were likely to be exploited. The Japanese, who were ahead of the Koreans in every aspect of modern civilization, would surely not hesitate to take advantage of this superiority.

Those Japanese who sincerely believed in the professed aims of their country should have realized that there was nothing to indicate that the military men who ruled in Korea as governor generals would display any real interest in Korea except as a possible springboard for further Japanese expansion on the continent. And although it should have been easy to predict, no one seems to have feared the worst aspect of the annexation: that the Japanese in Korea would conduct themselves with the arrogance of a master race, and the Koreans, in order to survive under Japanese rule, would have to learn how to please the Japanese, humiliating although this sometimes proved.

Even if it had foreseen how Japanese rule would affect its people, at this stage the Korean government was incapable of resisting. The emphasis in the treaty of annexation on the good treatment that would be accorded to the king and the nobility probably reflected the belief of the Japanese that as long as the upper classes were satisfied, it did not much matter if there was discontent among the ignorant masses.

The Korean emperor, soon to be only a king, could not be a rallying point for Korean independence, as he made clear in a rescript issued on August 29 in which he spoke of his futile efforts to reform the government ordinances. Furthermore, he was handicapped by a long-standing debility, originating twelve years earlier when he drank poisoned coffee. His exhaustion had reached its limits, and there was no hope that he would recover his strength. Day and night he had attempted to think of some solution to the problems facing the country, but in the end he had found nothing, and it seemed best to turn over the responsibility to someone else. He had decided to surrender Korea's sovereign power to His Majesty, the emperor of Great Japan, the neighboring country, a man he had long trusted, believing that he would ensure peace in East Asia and preserve the livelihoods of the people of the entire country. He urged the people not to worry about the state of the nation or the times but to go about their work tranquilly, obeying the civilized new regime of the Japanese Empire and enjoying the blessings. He declared that his abdication did not mean that he had forgotten his people; rather, he had acted entirely out of a deeply felt desire to save them.

It is unlikely that Emperor Sunjong personally wrote this rescript, but the intensity of the conveyed emotions suggest that whoever wrote it was familiar with the emperor's deepest feelings, and these *may* have been his words. Sunjong was frail, prematurely old, and toothless, but he wanted the Korean people to know that he had not given in to the Japanese without first exhausting his limited strength in a vain attempt to find some other solution to the crisis facing the country.[29]

On the same day, August 29, a series of imperial ordinances were issued, proclaiming that Han-guk was henceforth to be called Chōsen, that the government general of Chōsen had been established, that an amnesty was to be put into effect in Chōsen, and that there would be an extraordinary imperial bounty in Chōsen. Other ordinances dealt with duties on Korean merchandise imported into Japan, patents, designs, copyrights, and similar commercial matters.[30] After long years of laxness under their own rulers, the Koreans were getting an early taste of Japanese efficiency.

Emperor Meiji expressed his gratitude to Katsura for his skillful handling of the treaty of annexation. On September 1 rites commemorating the annexation of Korea were celebrated with religious observances in the palace, with Iwakura Tomotsuna standing in for the emperor. On the same day the emperor sent Kujō Michizane to the Ise Shrine to report the annexation. On the third he sent Kujō to inform the tomb of Emperor Jimmu and on the fourth, the tomb of Emperor Kōmei.[31] Judging from the number of sacred places where the good news was reported, the annexation was judged to be of even greater importance than the victories in the wars with China and Russia.

On a much humbler level, on August 29, the *Yorozu chōhō* printed a song including, "Have you seen the likes? Don Saigō is having a drinking party with King Enma."[32] Some thirty years earlier, Saigō had espoused the conquest of Korea, but Korea had now become a Japanese possession without having to fight a war. Saigō was celebrating with Enma, the king of hell.

The changed relations with Korea did not affect the emperor's affection for Yi Eun, and from time to time he sent the prince a box of cakes or fruit. Now that the prince no longer had the title of crown prince, it was decided that he would be known as the Ch'angdok young prince.[33]

In October, Terauchi sent an official report describing events from the time he took office as resident general up to the annexation of Korea. He had reorganized the administrative organs and simplified procedures. He had drastically reduced expenses with a view to promoting regional administration. As the consequence of these measures, high and low, nobles and plebes in Korea all basked in the blessings of the emperor's influence and were profoundly moved by the generous treatment and special favors they had received.[34]

Terauchi did not mention it in his report, but he had prohibited the use of the Korean *nengō*; all official documents would henceforth bear a date according to the year of Meiji's reign. The name of the capital, Hansong, although it had been used for more than 500 years, ever since the Yi family built their capital on the site, was forbidden and replaced by Keijō.[35] Even at this early stage of the union, Terauchi seems to have been determined to destroy the Koreans' national consciousness.

It is likely that some Koreans, particularly those of the upper classes, felt grateful for the greater efficiency of the government and the greater security for themselves under Japanese rule, but the vast majority were acutely unhappy under the rule of strangers, who treated them as inferiors in their own country and who eventually sought to rob them of their language and even their names. Most Japanese were pleased and proud to think that their emperor now ruled over not only the Japanese islands but Taiwan, Sakhalin, and now Korea. In the Far East, the Japanese had done better than the British, who had only Hong Kong and a couple of Chinese ports; the French, who had not gone beyond Indochina; or the Americans, whose rule in the Philippines was plagued by unrest. Few Japanese of the time seemed to be aware that colonialism was a poison that attacked not only the victims of colonialism but also the colonizers.

Chapter 60

The year 1911 began quietly. The emperor was now in his sixtieth year, and there were further signs that his health was failing. He was scheduled to go to the Aoyama parade grounds on January 7 for the first military review of the year, but on the recommendation of the chief surgeon, he canceled the review for reasons of health.

On January 10 he and the empress went to the Phoenix Hall to hear the annual first lectures of the year. As usual, there was one lecture each devoted to Western, Chinese, and Japanese learning.[1] On the eighteenth the first poetry gathering took place in the customary manner. The emperor's poem on the topic "A Cold Moon Shines on the Plum Blossoms" was

teru tsuki no	The light of the moon
hikari wa imada	Shining in the sky is still
samukeredo	Cold, but already,
haru ni kawaranu	No different from in spring,
ume ga ka zo suru	The plum blossoms are fragrant.[2]

The poem is graceful, although the fragrance of plum blossoms in the early spring had been noted by earlier poets.

On the same day that this elegant gathering took place, the supreme court passed death sentences on twenty-four persons who had been found guilty of planning to assassinate the emperor. Two other defendants were sentenced to life imprisonment at hard labor. In the afternoon, Prime Minister Katsura Tarō went to the palace with a transcript of the verdict and reported to the emperor on the circumstances of the case. The emperor listened to Katsura with evident distress and directed him to consider an amnesty and a reduction of the sentences.[3]

It is almost unbelievable that the emperor should have learned now, for the first time, of the trial of Kōtoku Shūsui and the other defendants, the subject of immense interest throughout the country ever since the trial began on December 10. The only explanation is that people at the court, aware that he did not read the newspapers, had deliberately not informed the emperor.[4] If, indeed, he had no knowledge of the planned attempt on his life, the fact that any Japanese would have desired to kill him must have come as a shock. From time to time, Meiji had received word of assassinations of foreign heads of state. Czar Alexander II of Russia, King Umberto I of Italy, and King Carlos I of Portugal had all been killed in recent years.[5] President Sadi Carnot of France and Presidents James Garfield and William McKinley had been assassinated. Queen Min of Korea had been killed by Japanese ruffians. In addition, there had been unsuccessful attempts on the lives of Alfonso XIII of Spain and even of Queen Victoria.[6] Closer at hand, a Japanese policeman had attempted to kill Crown Prince Nicholas of Russia at Ōtsu in 1891.

The emperor regularly sent telegrams of grief when he learned of assassinations and telegrams of joy when he heard that the intended targets of assassination attempts had escaped, but probably it never occurred to him that he himself might one day be a target.

The plot against his life, characterized as "high treason" (taigyaku), was planned by anarchists whose spiritual mentor was Kōtoku Shūsui (1871–1911), a journalist and translator.[7] Kōtoku grew up in Tosa Nakamura, a small town in Shikoku, where he early demonstrated unusual scholarly ability, A poem in Chinese he wrote when he was seven years old has been preserved.[8]

In his autobiographical "Why I Became a Socialist," Kōtoku suggested various reasons that he was attracted to socialism while still a boy. He recalled one misfortune with resentment: his family had suffered such severe financial reverses during the period after the Restoration that he was unable to continue his studies.[9] He did not mention two other misfortunes—the death of his father when Kōtoku was a year old, depriving him of parental protection, and the discrimination he suffered at school because he did not belong to the samurai class.

As a boy, Kōtoku felt restive in the closed world of Tosa Nakamura. Recognizing his unusual ability, his family made sacrifices in order that he might attend a school in Kōchi, but he hated the regimen and felt like a "prisoner."[10] His restlessness (and the poor food) is said to have induced pleurisy, the first of many illnesses that dogged him. When he recovered, he returned to middle school, but his long absence had a deleterious effect on his studies, and he decided to quit school and go to Tōkyō. He raised money for the journey by selling his books. He had just turned sixteen when he arrived in Tōkyō in September 1887.

Kōtoku found work as a houseboy, attending an English-language school in his free time. Three months later, he, along with others members of the Tosa Freedom Party, an association of Kōchi men with advanced political views, was ordered by a public security ordinance to leave Tōkyō. Their principal crime was having protested against the weakness of the government's handling of treaty revision. This "crime," shared by persons of many varieties of political belief, probably would have escaped punishment had it not occurred just as the draft of the new constitution was being completed. The government (especially Itō Hirobumi) feared that such protests might threaten the successful completion of the constitution and therefore issued the decree in the name of preserving public order. Kōtoku was one of 570 men ordered to stay away from Tōkyō for a period of three years.[11]

Kōtoku walked all the way back to Tosa Nakamura, and his suffering on the road from cold and hunger created in him a hatred of Itō that he never lost. No sooner did he get back home than he was subjected to complaints that he was not doing anything to relieve the family's financial problems. Once again he decided to run away, this time to China, but his money took him only as far as Ōsaka. This city turned out to be of critical importance to Kōtoku, as it was in Ōsaka that he met Nakae Chōmin (1847–1901), a materialist philosopher and popular-rights advocate who, by his own testimony, was his only teacher. Kōtoku, now in his eighteenth year, served for two and a half years as Nakae's houseboy and disciple.

Nakae (who was also from Kōchi Prefecture) was living in Ōsaka because he, too, had been ordered to leave Tōkyō. Ōsaka was an exciting place: most of the liberal or radical thinkers who had been expelled from Tōkyō had settled there, giving rise to discussions, meetings, and publications devoted to political issues.

Kōtoku began at this time to keep a diary of his impressions. On February 11, 1889, the day the constitution was proclaimed, Mori Arinori, the minister of education, was stabbed and killed by a young man named Nishino Buntarō. Kōtoku wrote nothing in his diary about the constitution, but he composed a funeral oration in classical Chinese expressing sympathy and admiration for Nishino, identifying himself with an assassin who had chosen the dangerous course of implementing his convictions with direct action.[12] Kōtoku's admiration hinted at his future politics, although at the time he was not even a socialist, much less an anarchist.

Although the constitution was joyfully welcomed by most Japanese, Kōtoku's silence probably reflected the influence of Nakae, who questioned the value of this "gift" from the emperor and mocked the foolishness of Japanese who acclaimed the word "constitution" without any conception of its probable effects.[13]

To earn a living, Kōtoku for a time wrote plays for a popular actor, including one on the assassination of Mori Arinori, contrasting the arrogance of the cabinet minister with the powerlessness of ordinary Japanese. Kōtoku also began to write articles for political magazines. Once the celebrations of the proclamation of the constitution had passed without incident, the ban on radicals in Tōkyō was lifted, and the center of political activity reverted to the capital. Nakae moved back, taking Kōtoku with him.

In 1890, when he was nineteen, Kōtoku failed a physical fitness test for army service, the one fortunate result of his lingering illness. He studied at a government English-language school, graduating in 1893. In the meanwhile, he had become addicted to the pleasures of the Yoshiwara district. Nakae predicted that Kōtoku would become a writer rather than a political figure, but Kōtoku insisted that he intended to become a cabinet minister.[14]

In September 1893 Kōtoku took a job with the *Jiyū shimbun*, a newspaper that had stood for liberalism in the traditions of Itagaki Taisuke but had been bought and turned into a government organ. Kōtoku's work was mainly translating articles that had appeared in English-language publications. Although he had learned at the language school to read Macauley, Dickens, and Carlyle, translating political dispatches was quite a different matter. In later years, he vividly recalled how hard this work had been.

As Kōtoku gradually became more adept at reading political works in English, he fell under influence of the writers. He mentioned in a personal memoir having read early in his career the works of Albert Schäffle and Henry George, but he was still far from being a convinced socialist. Kōtoku first attracted attention with an article he wrote in 1897 on the funeral of the empress dowager. Its reverent loyalty to the throne made the editor suppose that Kōtoku was a model young Japanese, and he was promoted to writing editorials.[15]

Kōtoku first came in contact with socialist organizations in the following year. He joined a study group that met monthly to hear and discuss lectures on issues related to socialism. Kōtoku was at first an inconspicuous member of the group, probably because his knowledge of socialism was limited, but on June 25, 1899, he delivered a lecture entitled "Present-Day Political Society and Socialism" that brought attention, particularly because he dealt with socialism in Japan, unlike the other lecturers, who delivered papers on foreign socialists like Charles Fourier, Louis Blanc, Karl Marx, and Henry George.[16]

In 1898 Kōtoku moved (as an editorial writer) to the *Yorozu chōhō*, the most progressive of the major Tōkyō newspapers, and wrote editorials for five years. His first (published in February 1898) bore the provocative title "Grief over Empire Day." It opens:

It was just ten years ago today that our people, excited by the mere report of the proclamation of a constitution, had instant visions of an age of gold and danced for joy, all but crazed with happiness. Quite a few months

and years have passed since then, but the absolutist, oppressive administration has not changed. The constitution has frequently been dishonored
by the Satsuma clique, and the legislature has been trampled on by the
Chōshū clique. The political parties are anesthetized, and society advances day by day in the direction of corruption and degeneration.[17]

Kōtoku's criticism of the government, particularly its monopoly by the
Satsuma–Chōshū cliques, was severe, but he had not abandoned hope for the
political parties. In November he wrote an editorial welcoming the new Yamagata cabinet, not because he admired its policies, but because the failure of
the Ōkuma–Itagaki cabinet had demonstrated that the existing political parties
were not worthy of the name. He felt it was preferable to have as the prime
minister someone who did not even pretend to lead a party. Kōtoku continued
to call for such reforms as an equalization of income between rich and poor,
the spread of education, fair elections, an end to the aristocracy, the establishment of an inheritance tax, the establishment of laws to relieve poverty and to
supervise the workplace, and the nationalization of monopolies and land.[18] He
still seemed to hope that the existing political system could be reformed and
made beneficial to the mass of the Japanese people.

Kōtoku considered going into politics and seeking office. He joined a movement that advocated the creation of a system that would enable anyone who so
desired to run for election. His goal at this time was a democracy based on the
constitution, but as a result of his participation in the study group, his writings
began to treat socialism more overtly. In an editorial written in September 1899,
he recognized that the Japanese were not yet ready for socialism but urged
readers before rejecting or persecuting socialism to study it seriously.

The central figure of the study group was Katayama Sen (1859–1933), a major
figure in the history of Japanese socialism. Katayama had received a good education but had become dissatisfied with its traditional content. He declared that
the study of Chinese texts was stupid, and that writing Chinese poetry and prose
was of no use in earning a living.[19] In 1884, at the age of twenty-five he went to
America and remained there for eleven years, earning a living as best he could
while studying at various institutions.[20] In 1886, while in California, he "discovered God" and became a member of the First Congregational Church of
Alameda. Although in later years he sometimes mocked his conversion in terms
of having prayed to Jesus, the god who dwelled in America, only because the
Japanese gods were so far away, his Christian faith was of prime importance in
his development. Katayama left the United States with a master of arts and a
bachelor of divinity. But even more valuable than these degrees were his contacts with the social thought of advanced Protestant leaders, confirming his
concern for workers and other exploited members of society.[21] Katayama wrote
that socialism was the "new gospel" that would save twentieth-century society.

After his return to Japan in 1895, Katayama became the director of the first

Japanese settlement house. His firsthand knowledge of the suffering poor undoubtedly contributed to his socialist convictions. The period following the
conclusion of the Sino-Japanese War was marked by rapid industrialization, an
increase in salaried workers, rising prices, and great social change. But no matter
how hard-pressed, workers had no means to protest against exploitation. In 1897
Katayama was active in the formation of labor unions and served as the editor
of the first union periodical. The success of the railway strike of 1898 brought
him celebrity and proved that the strike was an effective weapon with which
workers could enforce their rights. But Katayama was convinced that efforts to
improve the workers' situation should always be in accordance with the law; he
had no sympathy for anarchists.

In 1900 the Yamagata cabinet pushed through the "Security Police Law,"
which included provisions directly affecting union activities. It did not prohibit
strikes but punished both those who incited them and those who used violence
to end them. This might seem evenhanded, but in fact the intent of this and
similar clauses in the new law was to control the unions and prevent them from
striking. Kōtoku wrote an editorial on the new law for the *Yorozu chōhō* in which
he said that although "violence, defamation, coercion, enticement, and agitation" were all undesirable, they should be available to the labor movement
because workers "lack education, money, writing, or speech-making ability, and
haven't the vote." He argued that in their struggles with capitalists, they had no
choice but to resort to what otherwise would be considered misdemeanors.

Kōtoku, who emerged as Katayama's chief rival as leader of the left wing,
published in 1901 his study *Imperialism, the Monster of the Twentieth Century*.
Although he disclaimed any originality, saying that he had done no more than
repeat what European and American scholars had already written, this was a
pioneer work.[22] His discussion of imperialism was effective, if not unique; his
comments on the emperor were distinctive:

> The emperor of Japan, unlike the young kaiser of Germany, is not fond
> of war; he places high value on peace. He does not delight in the bar-
> barous vanity of victory for one country and desires that culture thrive for
> the benefit of the entire world. . . . He is definitely not one of the so-
> called patriots or imperialists.[23]

Kōtoku was convinced that Emperor Meiji used troops only for the sake of
peace, humanity, and justice. He was sure that the emperor would prefer that
soldiers fight not for him or out of loyalty but for these same three ideals. At
this stage of his career Kōtoku revered the emperor. In response to articles by
Yamakawa Hitoshi condemning the crown prince's arranged marriage, Kōtoku
expressed extreme regret that even two or three people were capable of "such
insane impiety." He hoped for a union of the people and the imperial house.[24]

At this time the suppression of the Boxer Rebellion in Peking attracted the attention of Kōtoku and other progressive writers, who considered the intervention of the European powers (and Japan) to be a crass instance of imperialism. Kōtoku was moved to write a series of forty editorials denouncing imperialism and advocating pacifism, two concerns that occupied a prominent place in his later writings.

In May 1901 Kōtoku, Katayama, and others who had acquired reputations as socialists decided to form a socialist party, to be called Shakai minshū-tō (Social-Democratic Party). The collapse of the Jiyū-tō (Freedom Party) in the previous year and the renunciation of its ideals by former members who joined Itō Hirobumi's newly formed Seiyūkai had created the need for a party that stood for the rights of the underprivileged. At Nakae Chōmin's request, Kōtoku wrote an editorial mourning the loss of the Jiyū-tō. It was brilliantly composed in the elaborate language then in favor and earned Kōtoku the reputation of an exceptional stylist.

Abe Isoo (1865–1949), a member of the former socialist study group, drew up a manifesto for the new party. Before long, most of its demands would be realized, but at the time they seemed dangerously revolutionary to the authorities. The demands included public ownership of the railways, free and compulsory elementary-school education, a prohibition on night work for children and women, and an end to the death penalty.[25] No sooner was the manifesto issued than the government decided to ban the formation of the party and confiscated the manifestos.

According to Abe's notes, the police leaked to him the information that the government would not prohibit the formation of the party provided that three of its demands were excised: the call for a reduction or an abolition of armaments, the advocacy of a popular referendum on every major decision, and the demand that the House of Peers be abolished. But Abe, an idealist, stubbornly refused to change a word.

The decree banning the party was issued by the minister of the interior, Suematsu Kenchō (1855–1920).[26] Sakai Toshihiko (1870–1933), a close associate of Kōtoku's on the *Yorozu chōhō* and an acquaintance of Suematsu, went to ask why the party had been banned. Suematsu's answer was simple: "Other countries all have their hands full with the socialist party and are doing their best to suppress it. We in Japan must likewise devote all our efforts to suppressing it." Kōtoku, learning of Suematsu's attitude, wrote a withering reply saying that if Suematsu really wanted to prohibit socialism, he would have to drive all the socialists out of the country, burn all the relevant documents, and forbid the importation of foreign books. If he had the courage, the willpower, and the ability to do this, he might succeed in holding up socialism for one generation at most.[27]

Shortly afterward (on May 30, 1901), Kōtoku wrote "Japanese Democracy." In the epigraph he quoted two *tanka* by Emperor Meiji: "Whenever I look at the writings of long ago, I wonder what will happen to the country I rule" and

"When I put on layers of figured silks and brocade, I think of those who have not even sleeves to keep off the cold."[28] Kōtoku stated that the message conveyed by these two poems was democracy itself. Anyone who did not seek to carry out the emperor's aims "committed a crime against His Majesty." The emperor, the incarnation of democracy, deeply desired the happiness of his people, but some people in the government sought only their own profits and blocked the happiness of the people. Kōtoku called for new principles and new ideals to suit the new age.

In September 1901 Kōtoku met Tanaka Shōzō, a valiant battler against the pollution stemming from the copper mine at Ashio. In February 1900 some 3,000 farmers from Gumma and Tochigi Prefectures had traveled to Tōkyō to stage a peaceful demonstration, but the government ordered armed police to break up the demonstration and arrest the leaders. Tanaka, concluding that it was hopeless trying to appeal to the government, decided to throw himself on the mercy of the emperor by making a direct plea. He felt incapable of writing the fancy language needed for such a document and asked Kōtoku, now known as a stylist, to compose the appeal. On December 10, 1901, Tanaka attempted to push the document into the emperor's carriage, but it never reached his eyes. Tanaka was arrested, as was Kōtoku as his accomplice. The government, not knowing what to do with the two men, finally released them as madmen.[29]

Three days after this incident, Nakae Chōmin died of cancer. When doctors informed him that he had only a year to live, he decided to devote his remaining days to writing his memoirs. His book, A Year and a Half, sold 10,000 copies in three days and went through twenty-two printings, evidence that liberal thought, despite governmental suppression, was of great interest to the public. Kōtoku, who thought of Chōmin as his only teacher, wrote a moving tribute that was published the next year.

In 1903 Kōtoku published The Essence of Socialism, an exposition of the principles of socialism. He acknowledged in the introduction his indebtedness to Marx, Engels, and others. His conclusion was that once socialism was put into effect, liberty, brotherly love, progress, and happiness would be solidly established. He earnestly hoped men of goodwill would come forward to help achieve socialism.[30] The work had seven printings.

In October 1903 Kōtoku resigned from the Yorozu chōhō. Its editorial policy had changed from that of a free forum, allowing even sharply contrasting opinions in its pages, to a mouthpiece of the government in its bellicose policy toward Russia.[31] Kōtoku and Sakai decided that they would publish a periodical in which they could print their opinions without having to defer to anyone else. The first issue of the weekly Heimin shimbun (Common People's Newspaper) appeared in November 1903, published by the Heiminsha, the newspaper's parent organization.[32] An announcement appeared at the top of the front page, stating the weekly's future policy: the Heimin shimbun would promote liberty, equality, and fraternity. It advocated democracy, socialism, and pacifism. It hoped, to the degree the law permitted it, to obtain the active cooperation of many people. And while absolutely renouncing the use of force, it vowed to promote the socialist movement.

Even after war with Russia began to seem inevitable, the *Heimin shimbun* continued to print editorials denouncing warmongering. Kōtoku asked in one article who had the power to declare war. According to the constitution, it was the emperor's prerogative, but before this prerogative could be exercised, someone else made the decision—not public opinion, the elected members of the Diet, or the administrative officials, but the "the usurers called bankers."[33]

Even though Kōtoku's writings could not prevent war with Russia, he continued his untiring efforts to douse the mindless war frenzy. In March 1904 he published his "Memorandum to the Russian Socialist Party," calling its members his "comrades" and blaming the imperialistic greed of both countries for the war. He told his "brothers and sisters" of the Russian Socialist Party that both peoples had the same common enemies—so-called patriotism and militarism. His article, given also in translation in the English-language section of the *Heimin shimbun*, had a great impact on other countries where it was soon reproduced or translated. *Iskra*, the organ of the Russian Socialist Party, praised Kōtoku's message as a document of the highest historical significance and joined in the cry of "Down with Militarism!"[34]

Despite the encouragement from the Russians, Kōtoku and the other members of the Heiminsha were no match for the war fever that gripped all Japan. In March, Kōtoku published the leading article "Alas, a Tax Raise!" in which he criticized the rise in taxes to pay for the war. The government, deciding that the article was harmful to national interests and disruptive to social order, sentenced Sakai, the publisher and editor of the *Heimin shimbun*, to two months of minor imprisonment, the first instance of a prison sentence being imposed because of socialist activity.[35]

The November 13, 1904, issue of *Heimin shimbun* was intended to celebrate the first anniversary of the publication. It was decided to devote the issue to a translation of the *Communist Manifesto*. But before the periodical appeared, Kōtoku, Nishikawa Mitsujirō, and Ishikawa Sanshirō, all members of the Heiminsha, were charged with disruptive activity against the state. Kōtoku was sentenced to five months' imprisonment and a fine of fifty yen. The issue of *Heimin shimbun* carrying the translation by Kōtoku and Sakai of the *Communist Manifesto* was confiscated, and Kōtoku and Sakai had to pay an additional eighty yen in fines.

Kōtoku went to prison in July 1905. He spent the five months studying works of political doctrine and Joseph-Ernest Renan's *Life of Jesus*. The period of uninterrupted time for study was a blessing in disguise, but he had never enjoyed robust health, and his stay in prison further weakened him. When he emerged, he was in no condition to attempt to revive the Heiminsha, as his old colleagues hoped. In a letter he wrote to the American anarchist Albert Johnson on August 10—the day the peace treaty between Japan and Russia was concluded—he revealed that although he went into prison as a socialist of the Marxist variety, he had returned to the outside world as a "radical anarchist."[36] He also listed the reasons that he thought he should go abroad. First, he wanted to master the foreign languages needed to understand international Communism and the anarchist movement. He wished also to visit revolutionary leaders in foreign countries and learn directly from their activities. Finally, he wished to go where the emperor's poisonous hand did not reach and where he could discuss freely the emperor's position as well as the political and economic system.[37]

Kōtoku did not explain the startling change in his attitude toward the emperor. His friend Kinoshita Naoe, like Kōtoku a socialist and pacifist, had in the past criticized the inconsistency exemplified by Kōtoku's insistence on employing only legal means and his deferential attitude toward the emperor. But he now believed that as the result of his five months in prison, Kōtoku had become thoroughly and rigorously consistent in his views.[38]

While Kōtoku was in prison, the Heiminsha was forced by developments in the war to change its stand on pacifism. Attacks on the war were of little interest to Japanese who, after the victories at Port Arthur and Mukden, were sure that the triumphant end of the war was in sight. There still was enthusiasm for socialism, as shown by the huge turnout for the first May Day celebration in Japan, but the Heiminsha's financial backers began to withdraw, and there was dissension in the ranks, especially between Christian and materialist socialists. Even Sakai decided to leave the Heiminsha and earn his living by editing a family magazine. On August 27 Kōtoku published a letter to his comrades stating that he planned to go to America. On September 26 after a party to celebrate Nishikawa Mitsujirō's release from prison, all its members decided to disband the Heiminsha.

Kōtoku left for the United States in November 1905. Funds for the journey and his living expenses while in America were provided by friends and family. At the time of departure Kōtoku wrote in his diary,

> Ah, why have I left Japan? I could not stop myself. Ever since governmental oppression caused the collapse of the Heiminsha, my sickness and poverty have made it impossible to do anything. On the night of the eighth, at the farewell party given by my comrades, Kinoshita said that seeing me off was like seeing off a wounded warrior. I am not a warrior, but it is true that I am going off like a fugitive from a defeated army, hiding from the world and seeking a refuge.[39]

Kōtoku discovered when he arrived in America that his reputation had preceded him. He was given a rousing welcome in Seattle and San Francisco by Japanese residents who had read his writings, notably the memorandum to the

Russian Socialist Party. He was in great demand for lectures, and he mentioned having a steady stream of visitors. In San Francisco he was introduced to a Russian woman, a passionate anarchist, in whose house he rented a room. As he wrote to Johnson, while in prison he had become an anarchist, but it was only on coming in contact with his landlady[40] that he was made aware of the general uselessness of elections and the need to assassinate rulers.[41] He had come to believe that violence was necessary in order to topple oppressive governments and allow the birth of a society without government, in which everyone worked harmoniously for the good of the whole society.

During his six months in America, Kōtoku did not follow the program of studies he originally sent to Johnson, but he met many people and took an active part in founding the Social Revolutionary Party in America. It did not take him long, however, to discover that even in the United States there were limits to freedom of speech, and he had harsh comments about the racial prejudice that condemned Japanese immigrants to being either schoolboys or houseworkers.[42] He was in San Francisco when the famous earthquake struck. Kōtoku rejoiced in the flames: "In their path, there are no gods, no wealth, no authority of any kind. Of all the many imposing churches and towering municipal buildings, the many banks, the many fortunes, every last one fell in a rain of sparks."[43]

On the ship going back to Japan, Oka Shigeki, a member of the San Francisco branch of the Heiminsha, told Kōtoku that the first step in starting a revolution in Japan must be the overthrow of the emperor. He suggested that Kōtoku volunteer as a guard in the House of Peers as a way of gaining access to the emperor.

While Kōtoku was in America, there had been many changes in Japan. Of particular importance to the socialists was the resignation of the reactionary Katsura cabinet in December 1905 and the formation of the Saionji cabinet the following month. The new cabinet let it be known that it recognized socialism as a major current in the world and that it would not use police power indiscriminately to suppress it. This led some socialists in January 1906 to request permission to found the Nihon heimin-tō (Japan People's Party). The government gave its permission. Another group (headed by Sakai Toshihiko) asked to found the Nihon shakai-tō (Japan Social Party), and this too was permitted. Socialist parties were now legally established in Japan.

Kōtoku, however, was no longer interested in parliamentary socialism, which he contrasted with what he called "pure socialism," by which he meant anarchosocialism. He was intoxicated with the anarchism of flames, like those he had seen in San Francisco. His first lecture after returning to Japan shocked and confused fellow socialists. He urged direct action—a general strike—rather than legal and peaceful parliamentary strategies. This uncompromising attitude led inevitably to disputes, especially with those socialists who had aspired to legal recognition.

In January 1907 a daily newspaper, called like its predecessor *Heimin shimbun*, published 13,000 copies, priced at one sen. It insisted on freedom of speech and declared that it would not tolerate any interference, restraint, or restriction in what it published. It soon became apparent, however, that it was dominated by a direct-action "hard-line" faction, although Kōtoku declared that he would not attempt to force anyone to accept his beliefs. He insisted that revolution was a natural tendency, and as if in confirmation of his thesis, there was a series of spontaneous strikes at this time, including a major strike at the Ashio copper mines. The mine strike was put down by troops sent at the request of Hara Takashi, the interior minister.

On February 17, 1907, the Second Japan Socialist Party Congress was opened in Tōkyō. A serious division soon became apparent between the socialists, who revered Marx, and the anarchists (including Kōtoku), who turned to Bakunin. The Social Revolutionary Party, an organization of Japanese living in America, led the anarchists' attacks. Its magazine published in late December 1906 a fierce attack on the rulers of the different countries, including a demand that the "mikado," who represented the capitalist class, be speedily overthrown. In November 1907 a similar publication featured "An Open Letter to Mutsuhito, Emperor of Japan, from Anarchists-Terrorists."[44] This development could be traced back to Kōtoku, who had organized the Social Revolutionary Party while he was in the United States and wrote every month for its magazine.

Pressure against the socialists increased. In April 1907, after three months of publication, the daily *Heimin shimbun* was forced to close down, largely because of an article by Yamaguchi Koken urging readers to "kick their fathers and mothers"—an appeal to overthrow the establishment. Apart from the government pressure on socialists, the rivalry between Kōtoku and Katayama became increasingly bitter. Kōtoku's faction was known as the "hard-line" and Katayama's as the "soft-line," the difference being Kōtoku's refusal to compromise in their anarchist demands. Kōtoku defended anarchism, insisting that it was not an organization of assassins and declaring that its mission was "to demolish the foundations of tyrannical oppression and to ignite the divine fire of insurrection in the hearts of the timid."[45]

In June 1908, while Kōtoku was recuperating from illness in Tosa Nakamura, members of the "hard-line faction" staged a demonstration in Tōkyō during which red flags inscribed with the words "anarchism" and "anarchocommunism" were paraded through the streets.[46] The incident was relatively minor, but most of the anarchist leaders were arrested and their punishment was severe. It was symptomatic of the intensified stridency of the anarchists and the harshness of the police. Yamagata, the most vigorous opponent of socialism, decided that Saionji was too soft on the radicals and schemed to get the emperor to replace him with Katsura. He was successful: in July 1908 Katsura was asked to form a cabinet, which soon adopted extremely repressive measures to control the socialists.

Meanwhile, in many parts of Japan, anarchist opposition to the government was springing up. The daily *Heimin shimbun* had converted many of them to anarchism, but most, far from being intellectual theorists, were farmers, factory workers, or unemployed. Despite the police surveillance of suspected radicals, they managed to form small groups known as the "Kishū Band," the "Hakone Band," the "Shinshū Band," and so on. In Hakone, for example, the Buddhist priest Uchiyama Gudō privately published a pamphlet called *A Memento of Prison: Anarcho-Communism*, which included such passages as

The present boss of the government, the one they call "the son of Heaven," is not the child of the gods or anything of the kind, regardless of what you have been told by your elementary school teachers. . . . You tenant farmers have to struggle even to get enough to eat each day. You can't be in the least grateful that Japan is the Land of the Gods or whatever it's called. . . . And because you've been taught to spend your whole life working for and being used by a descendant of robbers who wears the mask of a god, you will never be able to free yourselves from poverty.[47]

The "enemy" in anarchist writings, whether in Japan or California, now stood revealed as the emperor rather than any corrupt politicians or greedy capitalists. The proposed weapon to be used in effecting change also had shifted from general strikes to bombs. Kōtoku argued that a successful assassination would not require many participants. He favored a suicide squad of fifty people.

At first there was little liaison among the different groups, each of which had arrived at its own program of action. Uchiyama Gudō had dynamite that could be used but thought it would be easier to kill the crown prince than the emperor. Miyashita Taikichi of the Shinshū Band had the most concrete plan: he proposed making bombs himself and using them on the emperor. But when Miyashita called on Kōtoku in February 1909, Kōtoku expressed doubts about his plan's feasibility, although he admired Miyashita's courage. Kōtoku was in poor health, and he wanted to complete other projects before he died, including the translation of Peter Kropotkin's *Conquest of Bread* and a massive attack on Christianity. Perhaps, too, despite his reiteration of anarchist principles, his long reverence for the emperor made it difficult for him to join bomb throwers.[48]

Probably the most extreme anarchist was a woman, Kanno Suga. After being forced by her family into a loveless marriage, she ran away and lived for a time with the writer Arahata Kanson, who converted her to his leftist views. They both were arrested in the Red Flag incident, but she was released for lack of evidence. While Arahata was still in prison, Suga shifted from him to Kōtoku and eventually became his mistress. Kōtoku thought that he at last had found the wife of his dreams who shared his revolutionary ideals, but Suga was so fanatically determined to carry out the assassination that Kōtoku's ardor was cooled and they separated.

Even after Kōtoku had made it clear that he would not take part in the assassination attempt, Miyashita was still determined to carry out his plan. He recruited three others—Kanno Suga, Niimura Tadao, and Furukawa Rikisaku. On November 3, 1909,[49] he successfully exploded one of his bombs. On May 17, 1910, the four drew lots to decide each person's role when the emperor's carriage approached on its return from the military review on November 3, the emperor's birthday. Suga drew the lucky number: she would throw the first bomb.

On May 20 the police, who had been suspicious of Miyashita for some time,[50] raided his rooms and discovered two tin canisters. Next they searched the lumber mill where he worked and found chemicals and additional canisters. On the twenty-fifth a bill of indictment was issued, and five members of the Shinshū Band were arrested. Other arrests followed, including that of Kōtoku, on June 1. The arrests led from one group to another, with the last made on October 18.

The trial began on December 10 and ended on December 29. The twenty-six defendants were accused of having violated article 73 of the criminal code, which prohibited harming or intending to harm the emperor or the imperial family. During the trial, Kanno Suga insisted that only four persons were involved in the plot, and quite apart from her testimony, it was evident that Kōtoku had not been involved. Nevertheless, he was accused of having inspired the others with his anarchist teachings.[51] The police were determined not to let him escape.

The verdicts were read on January 18, 1911. Twenty-four of the twenty-six defendants were sentenced to death, and the remaining two, to imprisonment. On January 19 in accordance with the emperor's wishes, concerned judges and officials met to consider an amnesty. They recommended that the sentences of twelve defendants be reduced one degree to life imprisonment. This was accepted, but the remaining twelve (including Kōtoku) were executed by hanging on January 24 and 25.[52]

The harsh sentences passed even on persons who were only tangentially related to the grand treason plot shocked some in the Japanese literary world, and there were protests from abroad, but probably most people at the time believed that the anarchists' plot was a loathsome act of rebellion for which the death penalty was fully justified.[53] The trial and conviction of the twenty-six defendants satisfied the authorities who were eager to stamp out socialism. It would take another decade for the socialists to emerge from the winter of their discontent.

At this distance from the events, one tends to sympathize with the executed men and woman, who were motivated by ideals, not by a lust for power. The failure of the planned murder of the emperor makes it easy to forgive the would-be killers and deplore their execution. Unfortunately, this was not the last assassination plot planned or carried out in Japan, although the assassins of the next thirty years were not anarchists but fanatics of the extreme right.

Chapter 61

Once the excitement of the grand treason had died down, the forty-fourth year of Emperor Meiji's reign was marked by few dramatic incidents. The noteworthy events included the signing of new treaties of commerce with America, France, Spain, and other countries, ending most of the economic and legal discrimination against Japan that had characterized earlier treaties. However, the question of Japanese immigration marred the generally friendly relations with the United States and remained a source of bitter feelings for years.

The Anglo-Japanese Alliance was renewed for a third time in July 1911, though weakened by modifications of the original provisions. The Americans, dismayed over the buildup in the Japanese navy and Japanese expansion in Korea and Manchuria, blamed the alliance for these unwelcome developments and were doubtless hoping that the alliance would be terminated.[1] The British could not completely ignore American objections, if only because they were about to sign a treaty with the United States providing for compulsory arbitration in the event of differences between the two countries. Compulsory arbitration, however, contradicted the terms of the Anglo-Japanese Alliance. If Japan and the United States went to war, Britain would be obligated by the alliance to join Japan in fighting the United States; but if Britain were bound to submit to arbitration, the arbitrators might rule against participation in a war. For their part, the Japanese refused to submit to arbitration their differences with other countries. Experience had taught them that whenever a conflict arose between a country of the white race and a country of the yellow race and it was submitted to arbitration, the country of the white race always won.[2]

In the end, however, the Japanese saved the alliance by agreeing that in the event the Japanese went to war with a country with which Britain had concluded a treaty of arbitration (for example, the United States), Britain would not be obligated to support the Japanese.[3] The Japanese made this concession because they still believed that the alliance helped preserve peace in the Far East, but the alliance had in fact lost much of its original importance to the Japanese, both as a symbol of equality with a European power and as a bulwark against Russian aggression.

There were signs also that the intensely pro-Japanese feelings that had swept through Britain when the alliance was first proclaimed had cooled, especially since the Russo-Japanese War. Antipathy toward the Japanese, possibly originating in latent racial and religious prejudices, took the form of fears over the development of Japanese commerce and industry, concern that Japan was using the alliance to its own advantage, and a growing conviction that Japan had violated China's territorial integrity and (despite its professed adherence to the Open Door policy) was monopolizing vital interests in Manchuria.[4] Some in Britain called for an end to the alliance, but Sir Edward Grey, the foreign secretary, favored renewal because he felt the Japanese navy was needed to counter the growing German navy.

About this time, in July 1911, Yamagata Aritomo presented a memorial to the throne deploring the laxness that had crept over the Japanese since the Russo-Japanese War. He urged rearmament, pointing out that Russia had recovered from the war, that the Chinese army was far more effectual than in the past, and that (although it was hard to imagine) war was sure to occur sooner or later between Japan and the United States because the latter's Pacific Ocean policy so frequently clashed with Japanese interests.[5]

Despite such dire prospects, the prevailing atmosphere in Japan was peaceful. There was even leeway for thinking about the hitherto neglected parts of the population. For the first time, the emperor demonstrated his awareness of the plight of those who had been left behind in the rapid development of the Japanese economy. On February 11 he issued a rescript to Katsura Tarō (once again the prime minister) containing these words:

> One matter causes me constant concern—the possibility that there may be needy people, with no one they can turn to, who are unable to live out their natural span of life because they lack medical care. I intend therefore to broaden the channels for saving lives by providing free medicine and medical care. I shall give funds for this purpose from my private purse, to be used as capital. I call on you to implement my wishes and take the proper steps so that our entire people will always have something they can depend on.[6]

That day, the emperor informed the minister of the treasury that he intended to give 1.5 million yen for medical care for the poor. This was not the emperor's first gift to poor people in need of medical attention. In 1878, distressed by the prevalence of trachoma in Niigata, he had given money for treatment.[7] Whenever there was a fire, a flood, or an earthquake anywhere in Japan (and sometimes abroad), he had made donations to the victims. But the scale this time was so much larger than before that it seemed an entirely new kind of concern. Perhaps as the emperor himself began to feel the weight of old age and illness, his thoughts had turned to others who bore the same burdens.

This year the emperor began to cancel appearances if they seemed likely to prove harmful to his health. On April 20, for example, he and the empress were scheduled to attend a cherry-blossom viewing at the Hama Detached Palace, but a strong wind was raising dust, and he decided not to go.[8] He had never enjoyed garden parties, where he had to be cordial to whoever attended, and he may have felt as if he had shaken hands a sufficient number of times with foreign diplomats, but he had always submitted to these irksome duties. Now, however, not even his Confucian training enabled him to overcome physical weariness.

Meiji put himself to what would be a final test of endurance later that year when he attended the Special Grand Army Maneuvers in Fukuoka Prefecture. He left Tōkyō by train on November 7 and, after stops on the way at Shizuoka and Himeji, arrived on the ninth at Mitajiri in Chōshū, where he was the guest of Mōri Motoaki. They were joined by a number of distinguished Chōshū men, including Yamagata Aritomo, Katsura Tarō, and Hara Takashi. That night, Mōri offered entertainment calculated to please the emperor—musical ballads played on Satsuma and Chikuzen biwas commemorating heroic deeds of the past, followed by motion pictures, probably the first he had seen. The films showed whaling off the Aomori coast, a skit about a badger turning into a man, and travel down the rapids in deepest Africa. A member of the emperor's party provided explanations.[9]

The emperor left the next day for Shimonoseki, where he boarded a naval vessel for Moji and from there went by train to Kurume, the site of Grand Headquarters. On November 11 the emperor left Kurume and traveled by train and carriage to the site of the maneuvers. He was able to climb to an observation post on the top of a hill, thanks to a flight of sixty wooden steps up the hill that had been built for his convenience. A bamboo railing on which he could lean as he climbed was provided along the stairs. It was evident to everyone that the climbing exhausted him, but he reached the top and observed maneuvers for about two hours.

A photograph of the emperor bending over a map was taken at this time by an army photographer.[10] This profile photograph was published after his death along with a facsimile of his signature, but the posture was rotated ninety degrees to make him stand straight. It probably was the first photograph taken of the emperor in thirty-nine years, since he posed for Uchida Kuichi in 1873.[11]

On the return journey the emperor again received hospitality from Mōri Motoaki at Mitajiri and was entertained by music and a mixture of informative and humorous films. The emperor learned after his return to Tōkyō that a man who had been responsible for temporarily derailing the emperor's train on November 10, causing a delay of one hour, had atoned for his mistake by throwing himself under the wheels of another train. The emperor sent 300 yen to his family.[12]

In February 1912, plans for the annual autumn Grand Maneuvers were presented to the emperor for his approval. They specified that he would spend only the second night of maneuvers in Kawagoe and that on the remaining three nights he would return to Tōkyō. This provision was obviously made out of concern for the emperor's failing health.

The emperor was unusually slow to approve the plans. When the general staff could wait no longer, the chief of the General Affairs Department visited the palace and asked (through the senior chamberlain) the emperor's wishes. He replied, "When I looked at the plans for the maneuvers, I saw I was to spend only one night in Kawagoe. The troops are to sleep in the open, regardless of whether it is windy or raining, and then carry out actual warfare. How could I be the only one to sleep happily in the palace? I can't approve such plans." The plans were accordingly revised to provide that the emperor would spend the full period of the maneuvers in Kawagoe. When the new plans were submitted, he approved them on the same day.[13] The emperor insisted (as he had during the Sino-Japanese War) on sharing the hardships of the soldiers and was unwilling to admit that observing maneuvers might prove a strain on his health.

Soon after the emperor's return to Tōkyō from Fukuoka, he received word of major disturbances in China. The Japanese government was inclined to watch developments for a time rather than act precipitously, but of late the haplessness of the Chinese court had been all too apparent, and hopes that it might restore order without foreign intervention had more or less disappeared. Reports stated that revolutionary forces seeking to overthrow the Manchu regime had established bases in various places, but they lacked unity. Internal dissension among the rebel leaders and the lack of training of their hastily mustered troops vitiated their strength, and it was doubtful they could maintain order in the areas they occupied. If the disturbances continued over a long period of time, they would interfere with trade and might also revive Boxer-style xenophobia. In view of this tense situation, the Japanese government concluded that countries with major concerns in China could not merely watch with folded arms.

The Japanese ambassador in London was asked to determine what steps Britain intended to take in the face of the crisis. He was also directed to explain that Japan could not accept the arguments of those who sought to establish a republic in China. Japan favored a government that, though nominally in the hands of the Manchus, was actually run by Chinese.[14]

Concern over the situation in China continued to grow in Japan. General Yüan Shih-k'ai, named as premier by the Manchu court in a desperate gesture to maintain its existence, was well known to the Japanese. He had played a prominent role in Korea before the Sino-Japanese War and after the war had established a reputation by rebuilding the Chinese army. Now he seemed to be the monarchists' last hope, but in fact he saw a chance to become the first president of China. British support of the Manchus wavered, and even within the Manchu government, some high-placed men were disposed to accept a republic.

Although the Japanese did not change their opinion that a constitutional monarchy was the best form of government for China, they realized that Japan could not be the only country to insist that China remain a monarchy, nor could Japan continue indefinitely to worry about China's future. On November 27 the emperor opened the twentieth session of the Diet. In his rescript, he referred to the unrest in China: "I am deeply concerned over the disturbances in China. I hope that order will be promptly restored and peace prevail."[15] His constant references to his desire for peace in East Asia (as opposed, say, to Kaiser Wilhelm's insistence on German glory) surely reflected his real feelings. That was why such men as An Chung-gun and Kōtoku Shūsui, despite their hatred of the Japanese government, had respected him.

On December 28, 1911, the Manchu government issued a statement appealing for an end to hostilities and calling for a fair election to determine whether the people desired a constitutional monarchy or a republic. The following day, without reference to this appeal, an election was held in Nanking for the president of the provisional republican government. Sun Yat-sen was elected and took office on January 1, 1912.

In the meantime, the Japanese minister plenipotentiary to China, Ijūin Hikokichi (1864–1923), and the Confucian scholar K'ang Yu-wei, who led the movement for creating a constitutional monarchy on the lines of the Meiji government, called on Yüan Shih-k'ai. They said they had been informed that no progress had been made in the negotiations between governmental and revolutionary forces. There were also rumors that the emperor would abdicate. They asked what was really happening. Yüan answered that negotiations with the revolutionary army had indeed reached a stalemate. The two sides could not agree even on where to open a parliament. The government proposed Peking, but the revolutionaries strongly objected. In any event, the government army's financial situation was growing more desperate by the day, and there was no way to replenish the funds available for military expenses. Civil organizations and local officials in Shanghai and Hong Kong were demanding the speedy abdication of the emperor and the establishment of a republican form of government.

Faced with this opposition at home and abroad, the cabinet abandoned hope for a constitutional monarchy. Opinion among the nobles was divided, and the situation was chaotic. Yüan concluded by asking Ijūin to offer his advice.[16]

Ijūin replied that Japan had no easy solution to offer, but he conveyed the Japanese hope for a constitutional monarchy, even if this reduced the emperor to being a mere figurehead. He added that the Japanese government was unlikely to recognize any government unless it demonstrated it was capable of suppressing disturbances. Until such time, Japan would have no choice but to treat China as a country without a government. This response upset Yüan greatly.[17]

The end of the Manchu dynasty, after 300 years of rule, came a few weeks later. On February 12, 1912, the six-year-old Emperor Hsüan T'ung announced his abdication. Yüan Shih-k'ai formed a provisional republican government and was granted full powers to negotiate with the people's army on unification. On the thirteenth Sun Yat-sen, recognizing Yüan's military capability, offered his resignation as president to the Assembly in Nanking and proposed that Yüan Shih-k'ai be the new president. The Assembly agreed, and on March 10, in a ceremony held in Peking, Yüan took the oath of office as the first president of China.

Emperor Meiji's reactions to the abdication of the Chinese emperor are not recorded, but he was undoubtedly more affected than, say, when he heard that the king of Portugal had been driven from his throne. Not only was China far closer than any European country, but his respect for China lingered despite the decisive defeat Japan had administered in the Sino-Japanese War. China may have lost its preeminence among the nations of East Asia, but when letters were exchanged between the emperor of China and the emperor of Japan, they both wrote in Chinese, and Meiji's rescripts were dotted with Chinese words and phrases borrowed from Confucian texts.

Nationalists did not hesitate to say that the Japanese, rather than contemporary Chinese, were the true heirs to the ancient glories of Chinese civilization. The fall of the Chinese monarchy, breaking traditions of more than 2,000 years since the first emperor, could not be dismissed as most Japanese had dismissed the fall of the Ryūkyūan or the Korean monarchy as the unavoidable fate of a weak country in the modern world. During the next forty years or so, China was subjected by the Japanese military to humiliation and the ravages of war, but it continued to exercise a powerful attraction on Japanese intellectuals who felt that the Chinese past was in large part their own.

Although the emperor's physical condition had plainly deteriorated, he maintained an active interest in the affairs of state. In October 1911, when the chief of the general staff, Oku Yasukata, who had been suffering from deafness, was about to retire, Yamagata Aritomo suggested to the emperor that Oku be succeeded by Nogi Maresuke. The emperor sent word the next day to Yamagata that he feared it might prove difficult to find a successor for Nogi as president of the Gakushū-in. This in fact may have been the emperor's true opinion; he may have hoped that while at the Gakushū-in, his three grandsons would have the benefit of Nogi's guidance.[18] But the emperor was surely aware that Nogi would have been far happier to be appointed as chief of the general staff, the highest post to which a military man could aspire, than to remain as principal of the Gakushū-in. To deny Nogi this promotion was an unkindness. Perhaps the emperor still had not forgiven Nogi for the enormous loss of life at Port Arthur. Although Nogi was idolized by the Japanese public as the hero of the Russo-Japanese War and foreign governments had decorated him, he had been shunted aside to an educational post for which he had no qualifications apart from the excellence of his character.[19] The emperor's refusal to appoint Nogi as chief of the general staff was, of course, final, and Yamagata, withdrawing his recommendation, asked that General Oku be permitted to remain in his post.[20]

The new year, 1912, was the forty-fifth of the emperor's reign. This year Meiji would celebrate his sixtieth birthday.[21] In view of his ailments, however, there was not much likelihood of festivities.

The traditional New Year's events were observed. The lectures of the year opened with one on Aristotle's *Politics*. Arrangements for the first poetry gathering were complicated by the emperor's dislike of the two topics suggested by Takasaki Masakaze: "Cranes by the Sea" and "Cryptomeria Before the Shrine." Takasaki submitted two more topics, but the emperor did not like these either. He chose to compose a *tanka* on a topic of his own, "Crane in the Pines."[22]

The most unusual feature of this particular gathering was the participation of the *gon no tenji* Sono Sachiko. The *gon no tenji*, the least prominent members of the court, normally did not take part in court functions, but perhaps the emperor wished to show special favor to Sono, who had given birth to his four surviving daughters. Perhaps also he sensed that this might be his last poetry gathering and wished it to be memorable. Three days later, his personal physician, Oka Genkei, recommended that, for the time being, the emperor not eat meat or fowl, shellfish, mushrooms, eels, or Western food, and orders to this effect were passed on to the imperial kitchen.[23]

The emperor continued to observe his daily routine of granting audiences to members of the cabinet and foreign visitors, though in his weakened physical condition, this had become taxing. He also bestowed money on deserving and suffering people and attended such public functions as the graduation exercises at military schools. In April he (and 2,040 other people) attended the cherry-blossom viewing at the Hama Detached Palace.

In May the emperor attended graduation exercises at several navy and army colleges and on July 10 went to the exercises at Tōkyō Imperial University. The effort to climb stairs seemed to exhaust him, and he used his sword to support him.[24] On the morning of the fourteenth when his physician paid his usual call, the emperor mentioned that he had felt some pain early that morning and was heavy in the stomach. He also complained of fatigue in his limbs and dozed off from time to time. All the same, he did not forget to send a palace officer to Prince Yi Eun with a message praising his diligence in his studies and urging him to keep up the good work while on summer vacation.

On July 15 a secret treaty between Japan and Russia was signed in St. Petersburg, setting boundaries on the spheres of influence of the two countries in Manchuria and Inner Mongolia. Before the meeting of the Privy Council at which the treaty was to be discussed, the emperor summoned Yamagata Aritomo and gave him a rescript expressing pleasure that the causes for conflict between Japan and Russia were to be removed, thereby ensuring peace in East Asia. Despite his indisposition, he attended the session of the Privy Council. Normally, the emperor's bearing was solemn and serene, and once he had taken his seat, he hardly stirred for long periods, but today his posture was slovenly, and at times he dozed off, to the consternation of ministers and advisers. After the emperor returned to the palace, he told people that he had made the effort to attend the meeting because the subject of discussion was of particular urgency, but he was so fatigued that without realizing it, he had fallen asleep two or three times.[25]

From this day on, the emperor's pulse was irregular and skipped beats, but even though he was not feeling well, he continued to go as usual to his office. His periods of drowsiness, however, became more pronounced. When he was offered refreshments in the afternoon or his favorites tunes were played on the phonograph, he did not take his usual pleasure in either. He looked absolutely exhausted.[26]

On July 17 he was examined by Dr. Oka, who noted skipped beats in his pulse, hardening of the liver, and pain in the legs beneath the knees. The emperor walked extremely slowly but went as usual to his office.

From July 18 the emperor suffered a loss of appetite. He did not attempt to go to his office, spending the entire day in a daze. In the evening he asked that the phonograph be played and seemed to enjoy it, but kept dozing off. At night, however, he did not sleep soundly.

The emperor's suffering was intensified by the exceptionally hot summer. For days, the temperature did not drop below 90 degrees, and on the nineteenth it reached 94 degrees. At the dinner table after drinking two glasses of wine, he complained of pain in his eyes. He left his chair, only to stagger and fall. Everyone was alarmed, and a temporary bed was quickly made where he fell. He was running a high fever and in a coma. At two in the morning, the empress and three officials were sent for.

The next morning, the empress suggested that two physicians (both professors at Tōkyō University) who had not previously examined the emperor be summoned. They diagnosed his illness as uremia. The two physicians, along with the chief of the Court Medical Bureau, informed the assembled genrō, ministers, members of the Privy Council, generals, and admirals of the emperor's condition. That afternoon, they issued a statement disclosing to the nation for the first time that the emperor was seriously ill. The report mentioned that he had suffered since 1904 from diabetes, to which in 1906 chronic hepatitis had been added. These two ailments had continued to afflict him, sometimes acutely. Since July 14 he had been suffering from gastroenteritis and since the fifteenth from a tendency toward lethargy, which had grown more pronounced. There had been a loss of appetite, and from the nineteenth, brain fever had left him in a state of daze. His temperature, urination, and breathing were described in detail.

From that day, his four daughters and the crown princess took turns watching by his bedside. The crown prince could not be present because he was suffering from chicken pox. The empress sent the court ritualist Miyaji Iwao to the Ise Shrine to pray for the emperor's recovery, but his condition continued to deteriorate. There was a steady stream of visitors, but he was incapable of speaking to them. Everyone blamed the emperor's physicians for not having prescribed treatment after his illness of 1904. The physicians defended themselves, claiming that although they went every morning to the palace intending to examine him, he always refused, saying he did not need an examination. They had not dared to oppose his commands.[27]

Even when the emperor, realizing that he was definitely suffering from some ailment, had consented to let a doctor examine him, he was always an unwilling patient. Chamberlain Hinonishi Sukehiro recalled that he had been taken ill while in Hiroshima during the Sino-Japanese War. "We thought it was just a cold, but later on we discovered it was pneumonia." Hinonishi continued, "He had had trouble with his eyes and teeth from some time back, but he never complained to anyone. He had difficulty seeing things at a distance. . . . When he ate he was always very careful about what he put in his mouth and absolutely refused anything hard. But he never had any dental care. He put up with the pain. . . . He avoided doctors as much as possible."[28]

Those serving him had begged him to listen to the doctors' advice. At the time of the Grand Maneuvers in Kurume, his extreme fatigue was apparent to everyone. On the way back, going from Mitajiri to Nagoya, the rocking of the train had bothered him. He blamed the clumsy engineer for making the train go too fast. "Tell him to go slower," he commanded. Chamberlain Bōjō Toshinaga, who was in attendance, said that the train was traveling at normal speed, to which the emperor responded sharply, "You're taking the side of the railways." The train slowed down, and it arrived an hour late in Nagoya.[29]

Such outbursts by the emperor were extremely rare. Whatever physical pain he might be experiencing, he had endured, trying not to let others see. His stoical acceptance of suffering, like his indifference to summer heat or winter cold, was an integral part of his conception of what it meant to be an emperor. Moreover, he felt that he must not only accept hardship but also deny himself pleasure. He once told Saionji Kinmochi, "I love Kyōto. That's why I don't go there."[30] But inevitably there were moments of weariness. In the privacy of his private quarters he was heard to say after his return from Kyūshū, "What will become of the world when I am gone? I wish I were already dead."[31]

Meiji's interpretation of how a Confucian ruler should behave explains his sometimes puzzling behavior. His determination to observe the maneuvers in Kurume at a time when he was suffering from a heaviness in his limbs that made walking, let alone climbing, difficult, is otherwise hard to understand, but he willingly accepted physical pain as a part of his duties. He did not feel sorry for himself, and when he refused to accept the proposed easy schedule for the maneuvers in Kawagoe, he was not being masochistic. Rather, he was convinced that it was his duty to share the hardships of his soldiers. The long journey to Kyūshū made little sense in terms of what he actually did while observing maneuvers. Although he was the supreme commander, he did not utter a word of command or try in any way to display his knowledge of warfare. He went because he believed that his position demanded it and because he knew the effect that his presence would have on the maneuvers. The soldiers, aware that he was watching, would do their best, determined not to disgrace themselves in his presence. He knew that he could inspire them without resorting to oratory or insisting on his own importance. Duty was his primary concern: he had no desire for glory and did not worry about how history would judge him.

The emperor's end occurred shortly after midnight on the morning of July 30, 1912. The immediate cause was heart failure. The news was announced jointly by the minister of the imperial household and the prime minister. At one in the morning, the home minister went to the Hall for State Ceremonies bearing the sacred sword and jewel, the imperial seal, and the seal of state. The ceremony of transmission of the sword and jewel was performed, and the new emperor in an imperial rescript announced that his reign-name would be Taishō.[32]

The next morning, Bōjō Toshinaga helped Emperor Taishō put on his clothes for the accession ceremony. He had been wearing a lieutenant general's uniform but changed now to that of the supreme commander. After the ceremony the new emperor went to an inner room where he prayed before his father's remains. Empress Shōken, who was now the dowager, wished to yield the place of honor in the room to her son, considering that he ranked higher than herself. He insisted that she keep her place, but she said in gentle but firm tones, "You have acceded to the position of the sovereign of the entire realm, and you must sit in the place of honor." Although Taishō wished to manifest to the full his respect for his mother, he quietly bowed and took his seat in the place of honor, from which he delivered a few words on ascending the throne.[33]

Soon after Meiji's death, men who had known him best were asked to relate their recollections.[34] All commented on his insistence on simplicity, his exceptional powers of memory, his concern for other people, but their comments somehow failed to create a portrait of the man. The reason is probably to be found in the statement made at the time by the politician and diplomat Makino Nobuaki:

> The emperor had almost no private side to him. He also had no prefer-
> ences. There was nothing to choose between his living quarters and those
> of the aristocracy. If anything, his were simpler. They merely served his
> needs. When he made a journey, it was never for pleasure but always for
> the sake of the country. He initiated public works but never because of
> his own tastes; everything was done because it was necessary for the na-
> tion. He did not give permission for public buildings to be erected unless
> they were needed to receive foreign visitors or for state business. He did
> not buy things because he wanted them but in order to encourage in-
> dustry or protect art. He led almost no life apart from his work.[35]

Chapter 62

There were no religious or other ceremonies on the day of Emperor Meiji's death, but Viscount Fujinami Kototada obtained permission from the empress dowager to measure the late emperor's height. The emperor had always refused to be measured even when new clothes were made for him. The tailor would cut a suit that was more or less the right size, and the emperor would try it on, saying that one place was too tight or another too loose, and alterations were made without actually taking measurements.[1] The emperor's height, as measured by Fujinami, proved to be 5 *shaku* 5 *sun* 4 *bun*, or about 5 feet, 4 inches.[2]

It is not clear why Fujinami asked to measure the emperor. Asukai Masamichi, who believed that Fujinami may have been Meiji's only friend, wrote that it was thanks to Fujinami that the exact height of the emperor, not found in any other document, is known.[3] Descriptions of the emperor generally mentioned that he was tall,[4] but his tallness was relative; Itō Hirobumi, Nogi Maresuke, Tōgō Heihachirō, and other prominent figures of the period would probably seem very short by contemporary Japanese standards. The emperor's weight was not taken at this time, but we know from various accounts that he had been overweight for years and was sensitive on the subject.

On July 31 the new emperor, empress, and empress dowager went to the room in the palace where Emperor Meiji was lying in state on a platform covered with pure white *habutae* silk. His body was also enshrouded in a burial garment made of the same kind of silk. Members of the imperial family, including the three young sons of Emperor Taishō, bade farewell to the late emperor, and they were followed by 171 other mourners, members of the nobility, and high-ranking officials who had personally served the late emperor. At eight that evening the ceremony of placing Meiji's body in the coffin was performed. A decree was issued suspending court activities for five days, during which period criminals would be spared penal servitude, the death penalty and whipping of criminals halted, and singing, dancing, and playing music forbidden.

On August 1 the late emperor's coffin was sealed. Even after the five-day ban on music and dancing had been lifted, the inhabitants of the city continued to refrain from making music or indulging in other entertainments. The streets were silent and passersby few.

On August 6 it was announced that the funeral services would take place from September 13 to 15. Breaking the long tradition of Buddhist rites after the death of an emperor, the observances would be purely Shintō in character, although the lack of precedents would require the invention of suitably "ancient" rituals.[5]

It was further announced that the place of interment would be Kojō-san (Old Castle Mountain), south of the city of Kyōto. The selection of this site for the emperor's tomb was said to have been in keeping with his wishes. Meiji apparently made this decision in April 1903 when he was in Kyōto for the naval Grand Maneuvers and the opening of the Fifth National Industrial Exhibition. One night, while having dinner with the empress, during a conversation about the former capital, he suddenly said that he had decided that after he had lived out his "hundred years," his tomb should be at Momoyama. The *gon no tenji* Chigusa Kotoko, who was then waiting on the emperor, was so struck by these words that she wrote them down in her diary. When the emperor's condition took a serious turn for the worse, the empress, apparently recalling his wish, commanded that the tomb be situated on Momoyama.[6]

Momoyama had been the site of Toyotomi Hideyoshi's Fushimi Castle. It was a place of exceptional scenic beauty, but during the Tokugawa period, the deserted castle had fallen into ruins and become overgrown. All that was left to show that a castle had once stood on the spot was the name, Old Castle Mountain. Later, the peach trees planted on the site had given the mountain a new name, Momoyama. This name, though euphonic, was judged to be rather mundane for the site of the emperor's tomb, so it was capped with Fushimi, the name of a nearby village often mentioned in poetry, and the mountain came to be known as Fushimi Momoyama.

As soon as they learned of the gravity of the emperor's illness, many people in Tōkyō petitioned the authorities to choose some spot of special purity near their city for his tomb, but their prayers went unanswered. The wish of the late emperor to be buried in Kyōto had the force of an imperial command.[7] The creation of the Meiji Shrine in Tōkyō was probably intended to soothe the wounded feelings of the inhabitants.[8]

The late emperor's coffin was moved on August 13 to an *arakinomiya* (temporary burial hall) where it remained, worshiped daily by the emperor, empress, and empress dowager, as well as many officials, until September 13, when it was placed aboard the imperial hearse. On August 27 the late emperor was officially given his posthumous name, Meiji. This was the first time in either Japan or China that the posthumous name of an emperor had been taken from the *nengō*. Indeed, the *nengō* Meiji was so closely linked to the extraordinary events of his reign that no other name seemed suitable.[9]

In the meantime, newspapers all over the world carried tributes to the late emperor. Two large volumes of Japanese translations of tributes that had appeared in the foreign press were published a year after the emperor's death. Needless to say, the comments were uniformly laudatory, regardless of the country where they were published. Some newspapers devoted their accounts mainly to a description of the amazing changes that had occurred in Japan during Meiji's reign, but the emperor's personal contribution to this progress was also praised. The British editorials were the most perspicacious, as the following (from the *Times*) may suggest:

An opinion prevailed among outsiders that the *fainéant* tradition of old times was still observed, and that the Emperor did not take any active part in the management of State affairs. It was a notion based on ignorance. Those who were in a position to know bore unanimous witness to his Majesty's zeal in the discharge of administrative duties. He possessed a remarkable faculty of judging character, and where his confidence had once been given, occasion to recall it never occurred. He possessed also a rarer trait, absolute willingness that others should wear the laurels of success, for he asked of the nation nothing except that it should honour and trust the Throne's servants, reserving to the Throne only the reverence born of prestige. Thus his own efforts were never obtrusive. But they were none the less earnest.[10]

The *Globe* echoed these sentiments:

How far the wonderful progress of Japan was due to the personal ability of the late Mikado, and how far to the wisdom and foresight of the statesmen by whom he was surrounded in his early years, it is impossible for Westerners, with their still imperfect knowledge, to estimate with exactitude. But it would probably be accurate to say that but for the personality of the Monarch the statesmen would have been able to accomplish very much less, and to do it much more slowly. Among the qualities attributed to him are the power of judging character—probably the most valuable that a Sovereign can possess; great assiduity in business, as was shown by his invariable attendance at the Conferences preceding the grant of a

Constitution; a wonderful memory for detail; great courage, both physical and moral; and complete disregard of his own personal comfort.[11]

It is not clear how the journalists who wrote these eulogies gained their knowledge of the emperor's character. Probably, word was "leaked" to the foreign press by Japanese who were close to the emperor.

The French editorials for the most part devoted greater attention to the events of Meiji's reign than to the emperor himself, but the newspaper *Le Correspondant* not only presented its own views but quoted comments by Japanese statesmen. The first was by Itō Hirobumi:

Quelles que puissent être les causes qui ont aidé le Japon dans ses progrès et quelque importante qu'ait pu être la part que nous avons eue dans les succès des années, tout cela devient insignifiant quand on le compare avec ce que le pays doit à Sa Majesté l'empereur. La volonté impériale a toujours été l'étoile qui a guidé la nation. Quelle qu'ait pu être l'oeuvre accomplie par ceux qui, comme moi-même, ont essayé de l'aider dans son gouvernement éclairé, il eut été impossible d'obtenir d'aussi remarquables résultats, n'eût été la grande, sage et progressive influence toujours derrière chaque nouvelle mesure de réforme.[12]

A second quotation was from Suematsu Kenchō:

Sa Majesté apporte l'attention la plus soutenue à chaque branche des affaires de l'État. Chaque jour, depuis le matin de bonne heure jusqu'à une heure avancée il s'occupe dans son cabinet des affaires publiques. Il est au courant de ce qui intéresse chaque département, surtout de ce qui touche à l'armée et à la marine. . . . Parfois il étonne par sa connaisance d'événements qui se produisent parmi son peuple. Il prend le plus vif intérêt à tout ce qui se passe dans les grands pays du monde, son unique désire étant de prendre des leçons des autres nations.[13]

The comment of the French editorialist was astute:

L'empereur a pu, à certains moments, influencer la politique de ses ministres, car son activité, son intelligence ne sont pas douteuses. Mais son oeuvre principale, et il l'accomplit avec une remarquable sagesse, fut d'être le chef de l'État, le vivant symbole de la vie nationale, du sentiment du pays. . . . Les grands rois ne sont pas ceux qui, comme Philippe II, veulent diriger eux-mêmes les affaires de l'État, mais ceux qui, ayant mis leur confiance en de grands ministres, les soutiennent de tout le prestige de la royauté.[14]

A Belgian newspaper praised Emperor Meiji for having awakened the Japanese people from long slumbers, as if with a magic wand, and compared him with the heroes of ancient Greece.[15] A Russian newspaper, after pointing out resemblances between Emperor Meiji and Peter the Great, decided that the two men were fundamentally different. Peter had fought as a soldier, knew navigation, and had even worked as a carpenter, but the mikado had never fought on the battlefield, never built a ship, and never climbed a mast. Peter needed such talents in order to create single-handedly a new Russia, whereas the mikado could do without them. Japan had so many able men that the mikado had only to choose the most capable to assist him.[16]

The Chinese newspapers expressed much sorrow over the death of Emperor Meiji. One Chinese newspaper mourned him in these terms:

Ah, the summit of Fuji is hidden in clouds, darkening the spirits of the ruler; and the waves lapping the shores of Lake Biwa seem to be weeping, mourning the death of a father or a mother. This hero of a generation, the Emperor of Japan, brought a country consisting of [merely] three islands onto the stage of the major Powers of the world, and left behind a land like the dragonfly, a national destiny like the dragon or tiger, and fifty millions of the Yamato people.[17]

The writer, unable to contain the grief that swelled in his breast, spoke words of mourning in place of the Chinese people. Looking for a parallel between Meiji's achievements and those of other illustrious men of world history, he decided that although he could not be compared with the great Chinese of the past, Meiji was superior to Attila, Ogodei (the founder of the Yüan dynasty), and Mohammed because they, being essentially nomadic chieftains, were barbarians and lacked the qualifications of an emperor. It was thanks to the emperor that Japan had defeated Russia in war and secured an alliance with England. The writer mourned the emperor especially because he had brought light to the "yellow men," no doubt referring to Japan's leadership among the nations of East Asia in achieving a modern state.[18]

This may have been the first time that the Chinese thought of themselves as belonging to the same race as the Japanese. In the past, the Chinese were accustomed to thinking of their country as unique because of its long history and culture. The similarity of the facial features of its people to those of the Japanese had not been thought worthy of comment. The success of Japan under Emperor Meiji in gaining equality with the chief countries of the West, notably by defeating Russia in war, seems to have induced the Chinese to feel a bond with the Japanese as fellow members of the yellow race. But even at this time one Chinese journalist wrote, "The Japanese are brave and gifted at imitation. The country has no indigenous culture."[19] Some writers praised the achievements of Emperor Meiji by criticizing indirectly the self-satisfaction of Chinese who were so sure of the superiority of their own culture to all other cultures that they refused to adopt the new Western learning: "There are more than ten countries, big and small, in the eastern and western regions of the Asian continent. Japan is the only one of them which has maintained its own culture, absorbed the new civilization of the West, and achieved what it can proudly call a constitutional state."[20]

These comments from foreign newspapers, made soon after the death of the emperor, were followed by descriptions of the funeral. The article by the reporter for *La Revue* (G. de Banzemont) opened by describing the sorrow of the Japanese people on learning of the emperor's death:

> Mutsu-hito ne fut pas seulement un des plus illustres Empereurs du Japon, mais encore un des plus grands monarques du monde moderne. On se souvient de l'angoisse qui étreignit la nation japonaise lors des premières nouvelles relatives à l'indisposition du souverain. Plusieurs jours durant, la foule éplorée défila sans souci d'une chaleur véritablement torride, sous les fenêtres du palais imperial; à genoux, le front dans la poussière, d'une commune voix, elle implora les dieux. Et dès qu'une lanterne sourde, éclairant la chambre du moribond, annonça que le monarque entrait en agonie, ce fut la plus violente explosion de douleur qu'on puisse imaginer.[21]

Many Japanese left accounts of their stunned reactions on learning of the emperor's death. Even Tokutomi Roka, a novelist who had frequently been critical of the government and had protested the execution of those involved in the grand treason incident, was shocked to think that the reign in which he had been born and lived all his life had come to an end. He recalled,

> When an emperor dies the *nengō* also changes. I was certainly not unaware of this, but I felt as if the *nengō* Meiji would last forever. I was born in the tenth month of the first year of Meiji, in the year when the emperor Meiji had his coronation and in the month when he traveled to Tōkyō from Kyōto, in a village some 300 *ri* from Tōkyō called Ashikita no Minamata in Higo, close to the Satsuma border. I had become accustomed to thinking of the age of Meiji as my own age, and being the same age as Meiji was at once my pride and my shame.
>
> The death of His Majesty closed the volume of Meiji history. When Meiji became Taishō, I felt as if my own life had been cut off. I felt as if Emperor Meiji had gone off taking with him half my life.
>
> A gloomy day. The long drawn-out note of the flute a candy-man was blowing on the other side of the rice paddy seemed to penetrate my vitals.[22]

Natsume Sōseki related in his diary for July 20 his annoyance that the *ka-wabiraki*, the traditional annual festival "opening" of the Sumida River at Ry-ōgoku, had been called off:

The emperor hasn't died yet. There was no need to prohibit the *kawa-biraki*. There must be many poor people who will suffer because of this. The authorities' lack of common sense is incredible. It seems there's a great debate raging over whether or not to close the theaters and other entertainments. The emperor's illness deserves the sympathy of the entire people. But the livelihood of the people, providing it is not directly harm-ful to the emperor's health, should be allowed to continue as usual. . . . If people are forced to suspend their normal business, no matter how reverent and sympathetic they may seem on the surface toward the im-perial household, they will certainly feel bitterness, and this dissatisfaction will build up in their hearts.[23]

But even Sōseki, once he learned that the emperor had died, wrote a pan-egyric.[24] He, like virtually everyone else in the entire country, mourned the emperor who had provided unwavering support for the enormous changes that had occurred during his reign. Although Sōseki deplored many of these changes, he realized also that there had been no alternative and that the ugly aspects of modernization had to be endured, if only to maintain the indepen-dence and authority of Japan in a world that had become increasingly obtrusive and intolerant of East Asian traditions.

The funeral service, held on September 13 at the Aoyama parade grounds, was on a lavish scale. The coffin left the *arakinomiya* and was placed aboard the hearse at seven in the evening. The hearse, roofed in Chinese style like the one used at the funeral of Dowager Empress Eishō, was lacquered black all over and decorated with more than 3,000 metal ornaments, the whole weighing more than three tons. The hearse was drawn by five specially chosen oxen. At eight, when it was already quite dark, the solemn procession began to move slowly from the court entrance, illuminated by lanterns. The procession was headed by the former chief chamberlain, Tokudaiji Sanetsune, Chamberlain Hōjō Ujiyasu, and Master of the Horse Fujinami Kototada, dressed in formal robes of mourning and wearing swords; they and other nobles pulled the ropes of the funeral carriage. Two nobles who had personally served the late emperor walked on either side of the carriage, holding aloft torches to illuminate the way. The emperor, the empress, and the empress dowager, who had earlier proceeded to the Double Bridge, were waiting for the funeral cortege. As it passed over the bridge, they bade a last farewell to Emperor Meiji. At that moment the army began to fire salutes of minute guns, and from the distance, the navy responded with minute salutes from warships off Shinagawa. The bells of temples inside and outside the city tolled in unison.[25]

At 8:20 the funeral carriage passed through the main gate of the palace where twelve horsemen joined the vanguard of the procession, clearing the way. The Guards Cavalry Regiment followed behind the twelve horsemen and was in turn followed by the Guards Military Band playing "Kanashimi no kiwami" (Extremity of Grief). Ubukata Toshirō, a newspaper reporter who had been assigned to cover the funeral, declared that nothing in the world could compare in sadness with the thin, prolonged, choked sounds of this music: "The tens of thousands of people present swallowed their voices and corrected their posture. Then they surrendered themselves completely to the waves of sound suffused with grief."[26]

The funeral cortege was led by two officers bearing torches. They were followed by some 300 men carrying torches, drums, bells, white flags, yellow flags, quivers, bows, shields, halberds, imperial pennants decorated with the sun and moon, and chests containing articles of war and of Shintō worship. These men, in rows of two or three, served as the advance guard for the hearse. Other officials followed, and the hearse itself was preceded by fifty *Yase no dōji* in two ranks.[27] Officials, including chamberlains, who had personally served the late emperor walked close to the hearse and directly behind them came other chamberlains. Next came twenty-eight generals, admirals, field officers, captains, and commanders, guarding the flanks, and behind them members of the nobility, headed by Prince Kotohito, representing the emperor, Prince Sadanaru, the commissioner in chief of the imperial funeral, other princes of the blood and lesser princes, and Yi Kang, the elder son of the former emperor of Korea. They in turn were followed by members of the nobility, the prime minister, members of the cabinet, the governor general of Korea, high-ranking army and navy officers, and other civil and military officials, all in full dress.

The Tōkyō municipal authorities had hastily repaired the streets to be taken by the hearse and sprinkled them with white sand. Along the route were branches of *sakaki*, brocade pennants, gas beacons, and arc lanterns and in between, white and black cloths twisted into ropes. Before each building the procession passed, a white lantern was hung as a mark of grief and as a farewell to the late emperor. The area of the funeral services, although it was extremely crowded with mourners, was pervaded by a reverential silence.

The hearse arrived at 10:56 P.M. at the Aoyama funeral hall. Officers representing the emperor, empress, and empress dowager went out to meet the hearse which, after passing through the first and second torii, was taken into a curtained enclosure in front of the funeral hall. Here the oxen were released from the shafts of the hearse, and the coffin was carried into the funeral hall. Presently the curtains opened, and the emperor and empress entered the temporary shrine, followed by an officer representing the empress dowager, Prince Arthur of Connaught (representing the king of England), ambassadors, and special delegates. All took their seats, and the ceremony began.

A Shintō prayer (*norito*) was read. After this the new emperor left his seat, approached the coffin, bowed, and read the funeral eulogy prepared by Katsura Tarō. The emperor's voice was low and filled with sorrow. Those present sobbed with grief as they listened. A roar of cannons echoed through the capital, a signal for the city to observe a moment of silent prayer. Sixty million people bowed in distant worship. The services ended at 12:45 on the morning of September 14.[28]

That night as the imperial hearse was leaving the palace, General Nogi Maresuke and his wife, Shizuko, committed *junshi* (suicide following one's lord) at their residence. Nogi had set a small desk beside a window facing in the direction of the palace, covered it with white cloth, and placed above it a portrait of the late emperor and an offering of *sakaki*. Both Nogi and his wife left poems of mourning for the emperor. He also left this farewell poem (*jisei*):

utsushiyo wo	In longing for
kamisarimashishi	The great god who, as a god,
ōkami no	Has departed from,
mi ato shitaite	This transient world of ours,
ware wa yuku nari	I shall follow his traces.[29]

Nogi slit his abdomen with his military sword and then stabbed his throat, falling over forward. His wife stabbed her heart with a dagger.

Nogi's farewell note explained that feelings of shame about the loss of a regimental flag during the Satsuma Rebellion had make him court danger at the time, hoping to make amends for losing the flag by his death but that death had eluded him.[30] During the Sino-Japanese and Russo-Japanese Wars, he had again hoped to be killed but had been denied an opportunity. During the Russo-Japanese War, tens of thousands of men, including his own two sons, had died in the attacks he ordered on Port Arthur. He felt deeply ashamed about the loss of His Majesty's "children," but the emperor, not blaming him, had appointed him after the war to head the Gakushū-in.

Nogi felt more than ever the depth of the emperor's solicitude, and he regretted that in his old age he had so little time left to repay this kindness. During the emperor's last illness he had gone every day to the palace to offer his respects and to pray for the emperor's recovery, but to no avail. The death of the emperor had caused him such profound grief that he had decided to offer his life as an expression of loyalty to the holy spirit of the emperor.

Years earlier, on the day of his triumphal return to Tōkyō after the Russo-Japanese War, Nogi had expressed to the emperor his desire to commit *seppuku* by way of making amends for the loss of the many officers and men who died in the attacks he ordered at Port Arthur. The emperor at first said nothing, but as Nogi was leaving, the emperor called to him and said, "I understand very well the feelings that make you want to apologize by committing *seppuku*, but this is not the time for you to die. If you insist on killing yourself, let it be after I have departed this world."[31]

It is reported that when word of Nogi's suicide reached the Aoyama funeral hall, everyone was stunned by his display of nobility and unswerving loyalty.[32] Mori Ōgai, who at first doubted that Nogi had really committed suicide, when he learned that the rumors were true wrote during the next four days "Okitsu Yagoemon no isho" (The Last Testament of Okitsu Yagoemon). The central theme of this short work is the *junshi* of a samurai who follows his master in death. The story suggests that Ōgai felt unqualified admiration for Yagoemon's decision to prove by his suicide the depth of his grief; but in his next story, "Abe no ichizoku" (The Abe Clan), Ōgai seemed less certain about the desirability of *junshi*. In this story, he told how many men who had only indirect connections with the late daimyo, or even none at all, killed themselves, acting as if they were doing merely what was expected of them.

The resolve of a samurai to display in an unanswerable manner the depth of his loyalty to his late master was usually praised. But if all the most capable and trusted retainers of a deceased daimyo were to commit suicide, the daimyo's heir would be deprived of their guidance. Suicide, even if nobly motivated, might be irresponsible. A vogue for *junshi* in the seventeenth century had in fact inspired a decree stating that anyone who killed himself without authorization would be considered to have died like a dog. The prohibition had been incorporated in the Laws for the Military Houses, as revised in 1782.[33]

Nogi's suicide was in contravention of this law, but this was not why it was criticized. Katō Hiroyuki, the last surviving member of the Meirokusha, a group of intellectuals who had promoted "enlightenment" during the early years of the Meiji era, commented that although people in the past might have admired the general's action, it was now an anachronism. He asked why this fanatically loyal man had not considered offering his loyalty to the new emperor. The military clique, perhaps fearing that other officers might emulate Nogi's *junshi*, attempted to conceal his motivation, attributing his suicide to mental derangement.[34] The most frequent criticism of Nogi's suicide was that it had deprived Meiji's heir of his guidance. Although no one said so plainly, Taishō's education had been hampered not only by his physical ailments but also by his teachers' inability to give sufficient guidance to a difficult child. The emperor hoped that Taishō's sons would benefit by the inspiration provided by a man of absolute rectitude. This was why he had chosen Nogi as the president of Gakushū-in, but now that he was dead, the three princes could not benefit from his influence.

The reasons Nogi gave for his suicide were probably sincere, but they seemed to belong to another era. Other officers had lost regimental flags without feeling obliged to expiate their guilt by suicide, and gratitude to the late emperor for his kindness need not have been expressed by self-immolation. All the same, Nogi's death reminded most Japanese of the old samurai virtues. Others remained skeptical or even hostile. This was particularly true of the writers of the Shirakaba school, men who had studied at Gakushū-in. Mushakōji Saneatsu published an article denouncing Nogi's suicide as "an act that could be praised only by the warped intelligence of men who have been nurtured on thought shaped by a warped age through a misuse of nature."[35] He contrasted Nogi's suicide, which he said was totally lacking in human qualities, with Van Gogh's, which revealed the nature of humanity.

Shiga Naoya's first reaction to Nogi's suicide, as recorded in his diary entry for September 14, was, "What an idiot!" the same kind of feeling aroused in him when he heard a maid had done something stupid. On the next day he described Nogi's suicide as "a surrender to temptation."[36]

Criticism of Nogi's act was by no means restricted to former Gakushū-in students. The *kanshi* poet Nagai Ussai's sarcastic poem "Loyalty" contains these lines:

> General Nogi was a model of loyalty,
> Emperor Meiji the embodiment of saintly majesty.
> If the general knew proper behavior, who did not?
> Unfortunately, the court is unaware of tradition . . .
>
> Warriors in the middle ages gladly performed the act,
> But *junshi* was never a custom of the court
> Who would have guessed a mighty general
> Would behave like a eunuch or a priest's concubine?[37]

Even the newspapers were at first by no means unanimous in praising Nogi's suicide. Some criticized him for failing to fulfill his duty of receiving guests of state like Prince Arthur of Connaught; others, for not serving the new emperor. But two days later the tone changed. On September 16 the journalist Kuroiwa Ruikō (1862–1920) wrote of General Nogi, "Should the people worship him as a god? Yes, if he is not worshiped, who should be worshiped? . . . Truly General Nogi was a god." On September 19 the *Tōkyō nichinichi shimbun*, expressing regrets over Nogi's death, asked whom future people would take as the model of the ideal Japanese and answered, comparing him with Kusonoki Masashige, that it would be Nogi Maresuke. From this time on, Nogi became the incarnation of loyalty to the emperor, a legendary hero whom it was impossible to criticize.[38] Nogi was worshiped as the perfect exemplar of a soldier's loyalty and devotion to the imperial house.

At 1:40 on the morning of September 14, a few hours after Nogi committed suicide, the coffin containing the emperor's body was placed aboard a special train that would take it to Kyōto. The train consisted of seven cars. The middle one carried the coffin, and the mourners, headed by Prince Kotohito and Prince Sadanaru, rode in the remaining cars. The train stopped for a few minutes at each of the principal stations between Tōkyō and Kyōto. At the stations and even along the tracks between stations, crowds bowed in reverence. The train reached Momoyama at 5:10 that afternoon. Guns of the Twenty-second Field Artillery Regiment fired minute salutes as the coffin neared its destination, and the army and navy bands, lined up along the way, played "Kanashimi no kiwami."

One hundred five *yase no dōji* in two ranks were the pallbearers, and alongside them walked high-ranking army and navy officers who had personally served the late emperor and his chamberlains. At 7:35 that evening, the procession arrived at the funeral pavilion. The rain, which had been falling for some time, cleared, and there was faint moonlight. The coffin was moved from the palanquin in which it had traveled and taken to the graveside, where it was placed inside a stone sarcophagus. After personal possessions of the late emperor had been placed inside the sarcophagus, the lid was closed. *Haniwa* depicting the generals of the four directions were placed at the corners of the grave, and a stone marker with the words "Fushimi Momoyama Ryō" in the hand of Prince Sadanaru was erected. Prince Sadanaru, stepping forward to the grave, bowed three times and placed clean earth on the sarcophagus. Last, he covered the top of the sarcophagus with pure sand.

The burial was completed at 7 A.M. on the morning of September 15. By 9:55, the entire service had ended.[39]

Chapter 63

Emperor Meiji, unlike most of the Japanese emperors who had reigned during the previous 500 years, was not forgotten after his death. Because his name was derived from the *nengō*, it inevitably appeared in the titles of the many studies of the Meiji Restoration and later Meiji history; and references to "Meiji culture," "Meiji thought," and the like abound, even in books that do not mention the emperor.

The events of the Meiji period have been studied from every conceivable angle by scholars fascinated by the extraordinary changes that occurred in Japan during the half century following the opening of the country in the 1860s. The emperor himself has been made the object of research much less frequently. During his lifetime, he was idolized by the mass of the people, less as a man with distinct attributes than as the motivating force behind the transformation of Japan from an obscure oriental monarchy into a modern nation ranking as one of the great powers. After his death he was elevated to the ranks of the gods and duly worshiped, especially at the great shrine in Tōkyō named after him. His birthday, November 3, proclaimed a national holiday, came to be considered among the most important celebrations of the entire year.[1]

With the steady dwindling number of Japanese who lived and worked during his reign, Meiji tended to become mainly a name, and his achievements were often confused with those of the military and civil officials who served him. He is still popularly remembered, for example, in terms of his heroic role in leading the country to victory in the wars with China and Russia, even though in fact his role in both wars was minor. Although he has not been forgotten, most Japanese would have trouble naming a single deed that indubitably should be credited to the emperor.

Not only have memories of the man faded, but many of the buildings that stood as tangible reminders of his reign have disappeared. Some were destroyed during the great earthquake of 1923 or the bombings of 1945, but even more were the victims of later generations of Japanese less interested in preserving the past than in accruing commercial profits. The Rokumeikan, the emblematic building of the Meiji era, was razed in 1941. The rows of red brick buildings in front of Tōkyō Station that seemed to represent the hopes entertained by Japanese of the late Meiji era that Tōkyō might one day achieve the commercial success of London, survived the war, only to be condemned afterward as inefficient and to be torn down. Other relics of the era have been moved to Meiji Village, where examples of city architecture are tastefully grouped in bosky surroundings.

Each New Year, the Meiji Shrine attracts the greatest number of worshipers of any shrine or temple in Japan, but probably no more than a handful of those who fight their way to the altar, hoping that theirs will be a record-breaking crowd, recall the enshrined emperor as they bow, asking his blessings in the year to come. Meiji's tomb in Kyōto is generally deserted. Meiji and his era grow more and more remote, as this often-quoted haiku by the poet Nakamura Kusatao suggests:

furu yuki ya	The falling snow—
Meiji wa tōku	Meiji has receded
narinikeri	Into the distance.

It is the task of the biographer to make his subject come alive again. Leon Edel, the celebrated biographer of Henry James, once said that a biographer must "fall in love" with his subject. It is hard to fall in love with Meiji, who even in his most informal moments never forgot himself or his ancestors and rarely revealed his feelings. Many accounts relate how the emperor at a party kept drinking as long as there was any liquor on the table and then staggered off. Such anecdotes provide a "human" touch to the portrait of the emperor, but in the end they prove only the uninteresting fact that like millions of other Japanese, he enjoyed drinking saké. They do not make us feel any closer to him. The gossip about his affairs with anonymous women, including those allegedly provided by hosts during his travels, is equally unilluminating.

Meiji seems almost to repel attempts by a biographer to come closer. Perhaps we would feel differently if those who knew him best had not been so reluctant to write down their memories. Obviously, Empress Shōken would never have revealed details of her married life (for example, how she felt about the various *gon ni tenji*), nor could we expect that the future Emperor Taishō would explain the causes of his strained relations with his father, but we would know Meiji much better if Fujinami Kototada had related what it was like to be the emperor's friend or if Sono Sachiko, the mother of his last eight children, had indicated if this seemingly cold and distant man had a warmer side.

It may be that there was no other side to Meiji than the one that could be observed in public. He was a stoic who rarely expressed preferences and almost never complained of heat, cold, fatigue, hunger, or the other afflictions of ordinary men. He was almost ostentatiously impassive. A chamberlain recorded that during maneuvers when cannons were fired, he refused to stuff cotton into his ears, even though every member of his staff took this precaution.[2]

Meiji's indifference to comfort has been ascribed to his Confucian training, but this training was essentially the same as that received by his father and by other members of the court, yet none of them resembled Meiji in his stoicism. Unlike his father, he seldom gave way to anger or acted in a manner that might be termed arbitrary or irresponsible. He seems to have possessed some inner force that enabled him to follow with rare deviations a code of behavior that was his own creation. He followed this code to the very end, when he painfully dragged himself to the Tōkyō University graduation exercises and to a session of the Privy Council. He was unwilling to admit, even to himself, that he was in pain.

Chamberlain Hinonishi Sukehiro recalled that the emperor seldom revealed his emotions by his expression: "I served him a long time, but I never saw him either extremely happy or extremely sad." Hinonishi was unable for two or three days to summon up the courage to break the news to the emperor that Itō Hirobumi had been assassinated, but all the emperor said when informed that his most trusted minister had been killed was *un*. At a session of the constitutional convention, when the emperor learned of the death of Prince Akihito, he said *muu muu* and nodded. The meeting went on.[3]

In the early years of his reign, he did not complain about the grueling progresses to different parts of the country, even though the accommodations at his destinations were likely to be primitive. In keeping with his personal code of behavior, he endured the torture of riding all day in a sweltering hot palanquin, sitting erect for long hours. He could not enjoy even the relief of being alone even after he arrived. As soon as he reached a destination, he would be surrounded by local officials, probably verbose in expressing their joy over his visit, and he had to listen to them all attentively, as if grateful for their words, never revealing boredom. He was obliged by his sense of duty also to examine carefully local products and relics, even when he was exhausted.

What did he think about while being tossed for hours in a palanquin? Much of the time, especially when the going was most arduous, he may have reminded himself, "This is *my* land." He never forgot that he was the descendant of a long line of emperors who had ruled over the country through which he was passing, and he was obligated to see every part, following the ancient practice of *kunimi*. He never relaxed in his resolve to follow precedents established by his ancestors, and he was determined to do nothing that might disgrace himself in their eyes.

In the same way, the emperor also recognized the people he encountered on his travels as *his* people. He probably never saw farmers or fishermen at work until his first journey to Edo, but he knew when he saw them that they were his people. He did not think of them, in the manner of a Heian-period aristocrat, as menials who were scarcely human. He never disdained to share with the common people their pleasures at the circus, the horse races, or displays of fireworks, and sometimes, on his travels, he shared their simple food.

Although the emperor felt a special closeness to Iwakura Tomomi, a nobleman who for many years had been his mentor and whom he associated with the world of his childhood at the Gosho, the men closest to him in later life, like Itō Hirobumi, were of humble stock, and he did not look down on them because of their birth. As the case of Itō proves, talented men could rise within the ranks of the new aristocracy, regardless of their forbears.

In his dealings with foreigners, Meiji was invariably courteous and even cordial, ready to smile and shake hands with anyone who was presented to him. His meeting with former President Grant was especially memorable; probably no advice that he received is his lifetime created a deeper impression than Grant's. He was friendly toward the king of Hawaii, although he expressed doubts concerning the feasibility of the king's plan for a league of Asian nations to be headed by himself. His solicitude for Crown Prince Nicolas after he had been wounded at Ōtsu was dictated not merely by fear of a Russian attack but by compassion for a prince who had been attacked while in a distant country. Each member of foreign royalty who was presented to the emperor was persuaded by his gracious reception that never before had the emperor shown such friendship to a visitor.

Meiji's meetings with foreigners were not confined to heads of state. Hardly a day passed without his receiving some foreign technician or teacher about to return to his country. Innumerable foreign dignitaries—chiefly military men and politicians but also such figures as the general of the Salvation Army— called on him to convey their compliments during their sojourns in Japan, and the emperor met most of them. Many foreigners received high-ranking decorations from the court; few countries have ever been so generous with their decorations as Japan during the reign of Emperor Meiji.

It is difficult to say how the emperor responded to the changes in Japan during his reign. Although like many who followed Confucian doctrines, he generally looked to the past for guidance, he seemed increasingly unwilling to perform such traditional duties of the emperor as the worship of the four directions at the New Year. He undoubtedly believed in Shintō, but he seldom visited shrines. When he returned to Kyōto, he worshiped at the tomb of his father, rather than at a shrine; his religion was less Shintō than ancestor worship.[4] It did not bother him that many of his ancestors had been devout Buddhists, even though he himself was indifferent or even hostile to Buddhism.

Well-meaning missionaries sometimes presented the emperor with copies of the Bible, but nothing suggests that he ever read them. Even if he had diligently perused the Japanese translation, it is unlikely that the Bible would have shaken his conviction that he was descended from the gods, the scion of an unbroken line of emperors. Christianity was too alien for him to consider its teachings, but many young intellectuals of his time became converts.

Even though he was not interested in Christianity, Emperor Meiji seems to have felt no antagonism toward the European things that flooded into Japan during his reign. In his daily life, he usually wore a military uniform or a frock coat and was rarely seen in public wearing Japanese clothes. He did not object, for that matter, to the empress's preference for wearing European clothes. He seems to have enjoyed Japanese food best, but at formal dinners Western food was always served, and he ate it without complaint and even with relish. During the day, he sat on a chair in front of a desk in his study, and all the public rooms of his palace were in Western style. He disliked electric lights not because they were foreign but because he feared that faulty wiring might cause a conflagration.

After a fire destroyed his old palace, he put off as long as possible the construction of a new one, reluctant to allow money to be spent for this purpose. He eventually realized that in order to impress foreign visitors, the prestige of the country demanded that he have a palace of some magnificence; but those parts of the palace to which visitors were not admitted were shabbily maintained. He always seemed reluctant to spend money on himself, as the tales of his patched uniform attest.

Meiji's pleasures included listening to the phonograph and singing along with it, especially martial tunes.[5] Late in life, a new pleasure came his way, the films. His enjoyment of nonnative diversions did not imply any rejection of traditional Japanese arts but merely demonstrated his acceptance of the latest inventions. But the sports he played—*kemari* and archery—were traditional, and he often expressed a preference for Japanese works of art.

The emperor had his foibles. Erwin Baelz recalled that

> he could not endure that the empress' throne should be as lofty as his. He wanted a higher one, but Inouye protested. When Inouye, paying a casual visit to the palace, found that a thick silken mat had been smuggled beneath the emperor's throne, he dragged it out and flung it into the corner of the room, which naturally led to a great "row."[6]

He seems also to have had a streak of sadism, as when he deliberately dropped asparagus on the dusty dining-room floor, to be retrieved and eaten by a chamberlain. Perhaps this kind of sadism was inevitable in someone who (in theory at least) had absolute power; he may have wanted to see to what extremes of obedience he could obtain from a comically devoted retainer.

The emperor's sadism (if that is the proper word) was closely related to his sense of humor. Everyone who knew and wrote about him mentioned the humor of this imposing, even awesome man. His humor, if the examples given are typical, was of masculine heartiness rather than witty. Chamberlain Hinonishi recorded this anecdote:

> One day when I appeared in his presence, I found him laughing. He said something interesting had occurred the previous night. When I asked what it was, he said, "Last night Yamaguchi and Ayanokōji were sleeping in the next room. Yamaguchi was snoring loudly and Ayanokōji was grinding his teeth. Between them they made a most unusual concert." Yamaguchi, who was standing nearby, said, "No, I believe that Your Majesty snored even louder." At this His Majesty laughed a great deal.[7]

The emperor was also reputed to have an extraordinary memory, but the examples given of his powers of memory are by no means dazzling. Chamberlain Hinonishi wrote,

> Everyone agrees that Emperor Meiji had an extraordinary memory, but I can't remember any specific examples. However, when I accompanied him to Kyōto, he told me in detail how a certain room was used in the past. Or he recalled that when he was still a small boy, there was a ditch that ran along the wall of the crown prince's pavilion, and he often used to catch *medaka* [killifish] there.[8]

The emperor's intellectual interests were limited. Hinonishi wrote,

> I almost never saw him read anything. Apart from when he was listening to lectures at the beginning of the year, I never saw him look at a book. Probably when he was still at the Akasaka Temporary Palace, he had more leisure and read books, but this must have ended when the pressure of state business became more intense and there were many other things to occupy him. In all the time that I served him, I never saw any indication that he had been reading.[9]

Even if Meiji did not read books or newspapers, he managed to acquire considerable information about the world from the officials he daily consulted. No doubt he was briefed before he met foreign visitors about conditions in their countries, and his knowledge impressed them. The lectures he heard early each year may have stimulated his interest in history or philosophy, but he was never inspired to make a deeper study of the subjects described. He seems not to have read contemporary works of literature or contemporary *tanka* poetry, let alone scholarly monographs.

The emperor's formal studies, mainly in the Confucian tradition as interpreted by Motoda Nagazane, lasted until he was in his thirties and undoubtedly contributed to his abiding sense of duty. On rare occasions he refused to do what was expected of him, as when he obstinately insisted on not attending the banquet ending the maneuvers in Kumamoto. He seems to have disliked particularly the feeling that his ministers (or others) were forcing him to accommodate himself to their plans. This was revealed most clearly when he refused to take advantage of being in Nara to worship at the tomb of Emperor Jimmu. It was not that he was averse to worshiping at the tomb but that he did not like other people to decide what he should do. Generally, however, he yielded in the end to persuasion, and when he did not, he apologized afterward. There were periods in his reign when he seemed loath to perform even his ordinary daily business as the ruler, perhaps out of boredom with paperwork or with his advisers. On the whole, however, he was highly responsible and seldom went against the advice of his ministers.

Meiji's reliance on his ministers makes it difficult to be sure whether decisions made in his name were in fact his or actually made by his ministers. At the very least the wording of his rescripts was surely the work of men better trained than he in classical Chinese; but we have no way of knowing the degree to which his personal opinions were reflected in his rescripts. Probably it is safe to say that nothing in the rescripts was contrary to his wishes.

One theme recurs in his rescripts so often that it is tempting to view it as an expression of the emperor's deepest conviction—his repeated hopes for peace. This may seem no more than a convention, or even the excuse for crushing enemies as "obstacles to peace," but the emperor's behavior during the wars of his reign suggests that despite his fondness for uniforms and for observing maneuvers of his army, he genuinely disliked war.

During the Satsuma Rebellion, he was so given to apathy that he refused to perform his duties as head of the state or even to pursue his studies. He opposed the declaration of war on China in 1894. When informed of the victory at Port Arthur during the Russo-Japanese War, his first reaction was not a cry of elation but the command that the enemy general be given proper treatment. The emperor's insistence on his desire for peace impressed even An Chung-gun, the man who assassinated Itō Hirobumi, the emperor's most trusted adviser.

Perhaps the emperor's greatest achievement was reigning so long. In this respect he resembled his near contemporary Queen Victoria, who for years was attacked by the press for indulging in her griefs to the neglect of her duties; but in the end, thanks to the length of her reign, she acquired the reputation of a great monarch.[10] If Meiji, like his father, had died at the age of thirty-six, he would hardly be remembered today except as a young man who happened to be on the throne at a time of great changes in Japan. But the length of his reign, and the impression he increasingly created of unwavering steadfastness, gave him an awesome, almost sacred authority. Immediately after his death, a special issue of the magazine *Taiyō* was published with the title *Meiji seitenshi* (Meiji, the Holy Emperor). The day after his death, an article on the front page of the *Ōsaka mainichi shimbun* referred to the late emperor as *taitei* (the Great), in the manner of Peter the Great, and this term was frequently used of him until the end of the Pacific War in 1945. Asukai Masamichi explained why he used it as the title of his *Meiji taitei*: "It was because in modern history—no, in the whole of Japanese history—there was no other 'great emperor' except this one. Emperor Meiji definitely left behind the footprints of a great monarch."[11]

NOTES

Preface

1. I shall refer to him as Meiji, even though this was a posthumous designation. During his lifetime he was referred to by Japanese simply as *tennō*, or emperor; his personal name, Mutsuhito, was used mainly when communicating with foreigners or signing rescripts.

2. It is often said that Meiji's boyhood name, Sachinomiya, was taken from the name of the well, but the well was not drilled until the drought in Kyoto in the eighth month of 1854, when Meiji was about a year old. The name Sachinomiya (or Prince Sachi) was chosen by Emperor Kōmei from among seven names suggested by the imperial councillor (*sangi*) Gojō Tamesada. Emperor Kōkaku (1771–1840), Meiji's great-grandfather, had had the same childhood name. The well took its name from the prince, rather than the other way round; Emperor Kōmei himself, pleased with the quality of the well water, named it Sachi no i (*Meiji tennō ki*, 1, p. 59).

   Although it is commonly believed that Meiji was first bathed with water from the Sachi well (see, for example, Kurihara Kōta, *Ningen Meiji tennō*, p 1), the official record plainly states that the water used was drawn from the Kamo River north of the Demachi Bridge (*Meiji tennō ki*, 1, pp. 20, 23).

3. The building itself cost 100 *ryō*, and Tadayasu asked for a loan of 200 *ryō*. The request went through various officials and finally reached the chancellor (*kampaku*), who refused, stating there was no precedent for lending more than 100 *ryō*. Tadayasu therefore borrowed the money, promising to pay back the loan in installments over the next fifteen years. Fortunately, Tadayasu's great-aunt, Naka-

yama Isako, was serving as senior lady-in-waiting, and he was able to borrow an additional 50 *ryō* in her name, to be repaid in ten years (*Meiji tennō ki*, 1, pp. 8–9). Tadayasu no doubt expected that if a child was safely delivered, his daughter would receive presents that would enable him to repay these debts.

4. His many poems were written on scraps of paper, copied by expert lady calligraphers, and then destroyed.

5. The Seitoku kinen kaigakan (Memorial Picture Gallery) at the Meiji jingū contains eighty large paintings depicting highlights of Meiji's life from his birth to his funeral. They were painted between 1926 and 1936 by outstanding artists of the period, but probably none of the artists had actually seen Meiji. The Italian painter Edoardo Chiossone (1832–1898) was one of the few to depict Meiji from life; his drawing, supposed by most people to be a photograph, was worshiped in schools throughout Japan.

6. Kimura Teinosuke recalls (when he was seven and Meiji was eight), "If ever anything occurred that displeased him in some way, he usually clenched his little fists and struck whoever was to blame. I can't tell you how many times I was the recipient of blows from his gracious fists. At any rate, because I was a year younger than he, I tended not to show sufficient awe. I was always venturing to do something that went contrary to his wishes, and each time he would deign to drub me" ("Meiji tennō no go-yōji" p. 17).

7. Bōjō Toshinaga, *Kyūchū gojūnen*, p. 15.

8. For an account of why he stopped reading newspapers, see Hinonishi Sukehiro, *Meiji tennō no nichijō*, p. 53.

9. Ibid., pp. 44, 175.

10. See ibid., p. 59, where Hinonishi mentions that sometimes Meiji spent tens of thousands of yen on diamond rings. About the perfume, see p. 146, where it says he used up a bottle of French perfume every two or three days.

11. Giles St. Aubyn comments, "Almost all nineteenth-century constitutional text books implied that the Queen was a cipher . . . . Nothing, in fact, could be further from the truth, and Gladstone must have smiled ruefully at such nonsense" (*Queen Victoria*, p. 218).

Chapter 1

1. The lack of individuality in official portraits of emperors may have been due to their having been painted after the emperor's death by an artist who might never have seen his subject. We know the circumstances of one portrait: on November 4, 1846, Toyooka Harusuke, who had painted Emperor Kōkaku's portrait, was commanded to paint a portrait of Emperor Ninkō, eight months after the latter's death. Toyooka was paid ten pieces of silver and two *tan* of silk for the portrait (*Kōmei tennō ki*, 1, pp. 270–71; Fujita Satoshi, *Bakumatsu no tennō*, p. 141).

2. For details on the children of these three emperors, together with Ōya Sōichi's views on why mortality was so high, see *Ōya Sōichi zenshū*, 23, pp. 24–26.

3. The mortality rate for infants in Japan in 1899 was 153.8 per thousand. Even if it was somewhat higher forty years earlier, this was still a far cry from the mortality rate in the imperial family (Katō Hitoshi, "Meiji tennō o-tsubone go-rakuin den," p. 62).

4. The ceremonies were, of course, of the utmost importance to the court, and it had therefore happened twice during the Tokugawa period that because the male heir to the throne was still too small even to make a pretense of performing these ceremonies, a princess was chosen to rule as empress until the heir was more mature. Herschel Webb wrote, "Cycles of ceremonies, attestations of appointment, and calendrical affairs were the whole 'national' business of the emperor and his court" (*The Japanese Imperial Institution in the Tokugawa Period*, pp. 119–20).

5. Higashikuze Michitomi, *Ishin zengo*, p. 41.

6. It was actually a week before his birthday. At the time, Kōmei was eight years old by Western count. Although I have elsewhere converted dates from the lunar to the solar calendar and the ages of people from Japanese to Western count, when making direct translations I have followed the original.

7. Higashikuze, *Ishin*, p. 32. For an official account of this ceremony, compiled from various sources, see *Kōmei tennō ki*, 1, pp. 43–45.

8. See the account by Sanjō Sanetsumu of the devious activities of the *dōjō kuge*, nobles of the highest rank who were permitted to appear in the emperor's presence (quoted in Fukuchi Shigetaka, *Kōmei tennō*, p. 21). He mentions, for example, how they sold medicine, which they claimed had been passed down in their families for centuries, pretending that it was highly efficacious. Or when encountering a military person or rich merchant on the street, they would allege some trivial offense and demanded money by way of apology. Sanjō, himself a high-ranking noble, said that the get-rich-quick schemes of the *dōjō kuge* were as numerous as bamboo shoots, popping up in all directions.

9. *Koji ruien*, 12, p. 747.

10. Confucian texts. The Four Books were the *Analects*, the *Doctrine of the Mean*, the *Great Learning*, and *Mencius*. The Five Classics were the *Book of Changes*, the *Book of Odes*, the *Book of Documents*, *Spring and Autumn Annals*, and the *Book of Rites*.

11. Higashikuze, *Ishin*, p. 33. *Gagaku* is the ancient ritual music still performed in the imperial palace and at some shrines. It is often accompanied by *bugaku* dances.

12. Higashikuze, *Ishin*, p. 33. The seven shrines were Ise, Iwashimizu, the two Kamo shrines, Matsuo, Inari (Fushimi), and Kasuga; the seven temples were Ninna-ji, Tōdai-ji, Kōfuku-ji, Enryaku-ji, Enjō-ji, Tōji, and Kōryū-ji. It is noteworthy that all the Buddhist temples were affiliated with the old Nara sects or the Tendai and Shingon sects, not with the sects that arose to prominence in the Kamakura period or later.

13. Higashikuze, *Ishin*, p. 34.

14. Ibid., p. 35.

15. Ibid., p. 35.

16. The shogun's chief representative in Kyōto.

17. She did not actually become his wife until January 10, 1848 (*Kōmei tennō ki*, 1, p. 764). Asako was born in 1834, but because this was an unlucky year, her birth was officially put back to 1833 (Fukuchi, *Kōmei tennō*, p. 35). Even after she was recognized as Kōmei's consort, her title remained *junkō*, or "next after the empress." There are several variants of this title, of which the most common was

jusangū, meaning "next after the three princesses"—the grand empress dowager, the empress dowager, and the empress. She was Meiji's official mother, and after he ascended the throne, her title was changed to empress dowager (*kōtaikō*).

18. *Kōmei tennō ki*, 1, p. 255. Further descriptions of the emperor's message, from the *Buke densō kiroku* and other sources, are given on pp. 255–58.

19. *Kōmei tennō ki*, 1, p. 370.

20. Ibid., 1, p. 371. Of course, Kōmei had in mind the *kamikaze* that had destroyed the fleet of the Mongol invaders in the thirteenth century.

21. Fukuchi, *Kōmei tennō*, p. 44. On November 30 even ordinary people were admitted to the Gosho. According to Yamashina Tokinaru, whose diary *Tokinaru-kyō ki* is a major source of information on this period, the crowds of miscellaneous visitors who came to see the decorations for the coronation were "as dense as clouds, as dense as mist," and the congestion was so great there was not a empty space (*Kōmei tennō ki*, 1, p. 432).

22. *Kōmei tennō ki*, 1, p. 512. This *tanka* was composed on the twenty-fifth day of the second month of 1848 at an anniversary service for Sugawara no Michizane. The plum tree (*ume*) was the first to blossom, which may be why it is mentioned; but there was also a traditional connection between Michizane and plum trees.

23. *Kōmei tennō ki*, p. 950. For an interesting account of the prohibition of *narimono* (noisemakers) after the death of a member of the imperial or shogunal family, see Fujita, *Bakumatsu*, pp. 30–32.

24. *Kōmei tennō ki*, 2, p. 39.

25. Ibid., 2, p. 81.

Chapter 2

1. Court officials, five or six in number at this time, who waited on the emperor and transmitted his words to members of the nobility.

2. Imperial court officers, two in number at this time, who maintained liaison with the shogunate. They carried ceremonial messages and received shogunal officers at the court.

3. *Meiji tennō ki*, 1, p. 2.

4. Ibid., 1, p. 3. A knife, called a *tekōnagatana*, normally used in the *gembuku* ceremony to cut the hair of a boy who has come of age, substituted in the ceremony for the umbilical cord. The authors of the *Meiji tennō ki* commented that this was probably a remnant of some "old custom."

5. The sardines were of the kind called *gomame*, and they were considered to be felicitous because their name includes the word *mame*, meaning "healthy."

6. A very simple doll, rather like a modern *kokeshi* except for the arms, which stick out at right angles from the body, forming a kind of cross. Such dolls were placed beside the bed of an infant to absorb evil influences and thereby protect the child. They were kept by the bed until the child had reached its third year. The doll was about a foot and a half tall.

7. "Hardhead" is a free translation of *kanagashira*, otherwise known as the "gurnard." The choice of this particular fish was dictated by word magic: "hardhead," the literal translation of the fish's name, suggested that the baby would be unusually strong. The blue stones had the same significance.

8. *Meiji tennō ki*, 1, p. 27. Obviously, the baby's declared wishes were supplied by "interpreters" of his infant howling.
9. *Meiji tennō ki*, 1, p. 46.
10. Hori Tatsunosuke (1823–1892) was a member of a line of official interpreters and translators of Dutch. He later learned English and was the translator of the letter that James Biddle brought to Uraga in 1846. He later founded a school for teaching English and published an important manual for learning English.
11. This was not a pretext. Tokugawa Ieyoshi (1793–1853) died on July 27. News of his death was kept secret by the shogunate for another month (*Meiji tennō ki*, 1, p. 55).
12. *Meiji tennō ki*, 1, p. 53.

Chapter 3

1. Putiatin's fleet arrived on August 21, 1853, but it took the shogunate about a month to get around to reporting the event to the court in Kyōto (*Meiji tennō ki*, 1, p. 57). For a good account of the background of Putiatin's mission, see Wada Haruki, *Kaikoku*.
2. For the background of the Russian government's decision, which Putiatin learned of while in the Bonin Islands, see Wada, *Kaikoku*, pp. 89–91. The Russian appraisal of Japanese feelings was correct: the Japanese who dealt with the Russians favorably contrasted their peaceable ways with American brashness (p. 101).
3. For an account of Putiatin's movements at this time, see Wada, *Kaikoku*, pp. 109–11. He was anxious for word from Russia because it seemed likely that war would soon break out between Russia and Turkey and possibly also with Turkey's allies, England and France. While in Shanghai, Putiatin wrote to Commodore Perry, then in Hong Kong, proposing that they join forces and asking to be lent 40 tons of American coal in Shanghai. Perry politely refused an alliance but agreed to lend the coal. Once the coal was loaded, Putiatin sailed back to Nagasaki, having learned by this time that war had broken out in Crimea.
4. *Meiji tennō ki*, 1, p. 57. See also Wada, *Kaikoku*, pp. 99–100.
5. *Meiji tennō ki*, 1, p. 58.
6. Ibid., 1, p. 60.
7. Ibid., 1, p. 62.
8. Fujita Satoru, *Bakumatsu no tennō*, pp. 11–12.
9. Wada, *Kaikoku*, pp. 157–58. See also *Kōmei tennō ki*, 2, pp. 155–56, and *Meiji tennō ki*, 1, p. 64.
10. At the time, Shimoda was a village of some 1,000 houses with a population of 4,000 to 5,000. It was difficult to reach except by sea and was situated in an area often struck by typhoons.
11. *Meiji tennō ki*, 1, p. 78. The date corresponds to May 11, 1854.
12. If Putiatin's fleet of three ships had gone as before to Nagasaki, there would have been trouble: a fleet of four British ships was anchored there, and since this was the time of the Crimean War, they probably would have attacked the Russian ships. Putiatin headed instead for Hakodate, a port that had been opened to the Americans. It was there he learned of the British fleet in Japanese waters from a grateful Japanese whom he had returned the previous year to Japan. Putiatin

informed the Japanese that he was proceeding to Ōsaka, but his letter was not delivered until after his ships had appeared (Wada, *Kaikoku*, pp. 133–35).

13. See Kawaji Toshiakira's comments in my *Travelers of a Hundred Ages*, pp. 393–94.
14. For an account of the complicated negotiations, interrupted by the loss of the *Diana* during another storm, see Wada, *Kaikoku*, pp. 146–60.
15. The seven names considered by the scholars, together with the source for Ansei in *Hsün Tzu*, are given in *Meiji tennō ki*, 1, p. 88. Burton Watson translated the sentence: "And once the common people feel safe, then the gentleman may occupy his post in safety" (*Hsün Tzu*, p. 37).
16. *Meiji tennō ki*, 1, pp. 89–90.
17. The relevant excerpts from Kawaji Toshiakira's diary are quoted in Wada, *Kaikoku*, pp. 153–54. An example of the more favorable treatment accorded the Russians was the opening of three ports (Nagasaki, Shimoda, and Hakodate), as opposed to the two opened to the Americans.
18. *Meiji tennō ki*, 1, pp. 98–99. The ship was built at Heda on the western coast of the Izu Peninsula and was accordingly named the *Heda*. After the wreck of the *Diana*, the Russians salvaged diagrams showing how a warship was constructed at Kronstadt; these were used as models by the Japanese when building their first ship to European specifications. The Russians who took passage on the German ship were taken prisoner by the British, who intercepted the ship off Sakhalin.
19. *Meiji tennō ki*, 1, p. 91.

Chapter 4

1. *Meiji tennō ki*, 1, p. 113.
2. Ibid., 1, p. 117.
3. Ibid., 1, p. 118. "Child of the sun" (*hi no miko*) was a poetic name for the emperor or a prince, and because "sun" is mentioned, the poem opens with the related word "rising" (*noboru*). The term *ama no iwahashi*, literally "stone bridge of heaven," refers to the actual bridge the prince crossed but suggests such terms as *ama no ukihashi*, "the floating bridge of heaven" (connecting heaven and earth), and *ama no iwato*, "the stone chamber of heaven," the cave where the goddess Amaterasu hid herself.
4. *Meiji tennō ki*, 1, p. 120. This account is derived from Japanese sources, including *Higashibōjō Tokinaga nikki* and *Dai Nihon komonjo*. It does not accord with Harris's own version of the events, as found in his diary. He wrote on August 22, 1856, the day after his arrival in Shimoda, that he went ashore and visited the village of Kakizaki, opposite Shimoda. "The temple of this place—Yokushen [Gyokusen] of the Shinto sect—is set apart for the accommodation of Americans. The rooms are spacious and very neat and clean, and a person might stay here for a few weeks in tolerable comfort . . . . The Temple Rioshen [Ryōsen] at Shimoda is also set apart for the use of Americans—perhaps I may have to reside in it until a house can be prepared for me" (Mario Emilio Cosenza, ed., *The Complete Journals of Townsend Harris*, pp. 203–4). Harris mentions on August 27 the officials' efforts to persuade him to "go away and return in about a year," but he resisted all such attempts. On August 28 he was informed by the "vice governor" "that he was ready to receive me with all the honors due to my high place, and

to assign me the only place that was habitable for my residence—the Temple of Jocksend [Gyokusen-ji] at Kakizaki" (pp. 209–10). It is possible that the government in Edo was deliberately misinformed about the local resistance put up to Harris's landing and residence in Shimoda.

5. *Meiji tennō ki*, 1, p. 121.

6. Ibid., 1, p. 121.

7. Erwin Baelz, *Awakening Japan*, trans. Eden Paul and Cedar Paul, p. 124.

8. *Meiji tennō ki*, 1, p. 124.

9. This was a small building situated north of the Tsune goten, or ordinary palace of the emperor. From 1840 it was more often called Tōgū goten, or Crown Prince's Palace, but in this instance the older name was used, perhaps because Sachino-miya had not yet been designated as crown prince.

10. Baelz, *Awakening Japan*, p. 101.

11. Diary entry, September 16, 1901, in ibid., p. 144.

12. *Meiji tennō ki*, 1, p. 126.

13. While still living in the Nakayama household, Meiji was vaccinated by command of his grandfather, Nakayama Tadayasu (*Meiji tennō ki*, 1, p. 454). For the spread of vaccination elsewhere in the country, see my *Travelers of a Hundred Ages*, p. 382, where the diarist Iseki Takako (1785–1845) gives her favorable opinion of vaccination, introduced by Dutch doctors in Nagasaki.

14. *Meiji tennō ki*, 1, p. 129.

15. Ibid., 1, pp. 127–28. This is a translation from the Japanese translation of the original letter written in Dutch.

16. For an account of the demonstrations around the Gosho, see Fujita Satoru, *Bakumatsu no tennō*, pp. 55–70.

17. Gosakuramachi is reported to have distributed 30,000 apples, one to a person, on the afternoon of a single day (Fujita, *Bakumatsu*, p. 60).

18. *Meiji tennō ki*, 1, p. 130. For more detailed reports, see also *Komei tennō ki*, 2, pp. 644–45.

19. The text is in Cosenza, ed., *Complete Journals*, pp. 573–74. See also *Meiji tennō ki*, 1, p. 131.

20. At the time, there was probably no one who could interpret directly from English to Japanese or vice versa; instead, Harris's words were translated into Dutch by Heusken and then from Dutch into Japanese by a Japanese who had been trained in Dutch, the only European language in which Japanese were fluent. For an account of Heusken (especially concerning his death), see Reinier Hesselink, "The Assassination of Henry Heusken."

21. Cosenza, ed., *Complete Journals*, p. 412. See also *Meiji tennō ki*, 1, p. 136.

22. For a description of the audience in Harris's words, see Cosenza, ed., *Complete Journals*, pp. 468–80.

23. Ibid., p. 475. The Japanese text of the shogun's remarks is reproduced photographically on p. xxx.

24. *Meiji tennō ki*, 1, pp. 137–38. Harris's version of the meeting with Hotta, although it follows the same lines, is much less specific; there is no mention made, for example, of possible British and French territorial ambitions. See also *The Cambridge History of Japan*, vol. 5, p. 278.

25. *Kōmei tennō ki*, 2, p. 708; *Meiji tennō ki*, 1, p. 140. Harris's version is contained in Cosenza, ed., *Complete Journals*, pp. 496–500.
26. This translation follows *Meiji tennō ki* 1, p. 142. The original letter is much more extensive (*Kōmei tennō ki*, 2, pp. 725–26).
27. *Meiji tennō ki*, 1, p. 139. The poem was discovered after her death among Naka-yama Yoshiko's effects with a note in her handwriting giving the time of compo-sition. For the poem, see chapter 5.

Chapter 5

1. *Meiji tennō ki*, 1, p. 143.
2. Ibid., 1, p. 142. The original letter is in *Kōmei tennō ki*, 2, p. 730.
3. The letter is translated in full in W. G. Beasley, ed. and trans., *Select Documents on Japanese Foreign Policy*, pp. 180–81.
4. This title has been variously translated as "regent," "chancellor," "president of the councillors," and the like. The meaning of the term changed with time, but the position was essentially that of the senior "elder," the most powerful adviser of the shogun.
5. *Meiji tennō ki*, 1, p. 148. The text of letter is in *Kōmei tennō ki*, 2, p. 856.
6. The text is in *Kōmei tennō ki*, 1, p. 892. See also *Meiji tennō ki*, 1, p. 150. This was only one of several similar *semmyō* composed by Kōmei on this occasion.
7. The English text is in Mario Emilio Cosenza, ed., *The Complete Journals of Townsend Harris*, pp. 578–84.
8. He mentions in the letter *san shinnō* (three princes of the blood) but gives only two names, Fushimi and Arisugawa. Fushimi referred to Fushiminomiya Sada-nori; Arisugawa, to Arisugawanomiya Takahito and his son Taruhito. All three men had been adopted by the emperor Ninkō and had subsequently been given the title of *shinnō*, apparently in order to ensure continuance of the imperial line, even though their connections with the blood line of the imperial family were distant (Asukai Masamichi, *Meiji taitei*, pp. 77, 207).
9. *Kōmei tennō ki*, 2, pp. 923–24.
10. Tōyama Shigeki, ed., *Ishin no gunzō*, pp. 56–57.
11. A treaty with France was signed in the ninth month.
12. *Meiji tennō ki*, 1, p. 153.
13. He wrote in a letter dated November 1 to the minister of the left (Konoe Tadahiro) that he was too exhausted to meet Manabe (*Kōmei tennō ki*, 3, p. 102).
14. *Kōmei tennō ki*, 3, pp. 155, 156.
15. *Meiji tennō ki*, 1, p. 170.
16. The text is in *Kōmei tennō ki*, 3, p. 227. A summary is in *Meiji tennō ki*, 1, p. 171.

Chapter 6

1. The 100,000 *tanka* he composed were written on scraps of paper and then tran-scribed onto more suitable paper by a court lady. Afterward, the original manu-script was destroyed (Hanabusa Yoshimoto, "Sentei Heika ni kansuru tsuioku," p. 322). The only comment made on Meiji's handwriting by members of the court

was that it was extremely difficult to decipher (Hinonishi Sukehiro, *Meiji tennō no go-nichijō*, pp. 54–55, 181, 187).

2. For the poem (and translation), see chapter 5.

3. *Meiji tennō ki*, 1, p. 167. The bream (*tai*) is still a gift of good augury because its name is a homophone of part of the word *medetai*, "felicitous."

4. Watanabe Ikujirō, *Meiji tennō*, 1, p. 85. Watanabe is quoting *Tadayasu nikki*. The characters *naka* and *yama* made up the surname of his mother's family, which may be why he chose them, but he also would have learned these two simple characters at the start of his study of calligraphy.

5. *Meiji tennō ki*, 1, p. 212. He began the *sodoku* reading of *The Great Learning* on September 14, 1860, and completed reading this text on December 23. He began studying the *Doctrine of the Mean* on December 28 (p. 231), and he began the *sodoku* reading of the *Analects* on July 23, 1861 (p. 257).

6. Kimura Ki, *Meiji tennō*, p. 91. Kimura apparently acquired this information during a conversation with Uramatsu Tarumitsu.

7. Watanabe Ikujirō, *Meiji tennō*, 1, p. 86. See also *Meiji tennō ki*, 1, p. 245, where it mentions how Sachinomiya tricked his mother into believing he had completed his assignment.

8. Both poems are in *Meiji tennō gyoshū*, 2, p. 714. The first is quoted in Watanabe Ikujirō, *Meiji tennō*, 1, p. 86. The "bamboo horse" (*takeuma*) of the second verse probably meant "stilts."

9. Watanabe Ikujirō, *Meiji tennō*, 1, p. 84.

10. Kimura Teinosuke, "Meiji tennō no go-yōji," pp. 22–23.

11. Watanabe Shigeo, *Meiji tennō*, pp. 4–5.

12. Ibid., pp. 5–6.

13. According to the account by Prince Takahito, by the end of 1857, when Meiji was five years old, he had begun to compose *tanka* (Watanabe Ikujirō, *Meiji tennō*, 1, p. 86).

14. Kimura Ki, *Meiji tennō*, p. 92. Meiji read such works as *Genpei seisuiki*, *Taiheiki*, and *Taikōki*.

15. *Meiji tennō ki*, 1, pp. 199–202.

16. Ibid., 1, p. 221.

17. Ibid., 1, p. 223.

18. Ibid., 1, p. 228.

19. Ibid., 1, pp. 206–7. For a paraphrase of Kōmei's response, see also *Kōmei tennō ki*, 3, pp. 379–80. Kōmei mentioned that because Kazunomiya was born of a different mother, she did not have to obey his commands.

20. *Meiji tennō ki*, 1, p. 218. See also Takebe Toshio, *Kazunomiya*, pp. 39–41.

21. Brief summary in *Meiji tennō ki*, 1, p. 218; for the full text, see *Kōmei tennō ki*, 3, p. 410.

22. *Meiji tennō ki*, 1, p. 218. See also Takebe, *Kazunomiya*, pp. 44–45.

23. Takebe claims that the promise to get rid of the foreigners was not the shogunate's real intent but was forced on it by Kōmei's insistence on specific plans for *jōi* (*Kazunomiya*, p. 46).

24. Ishii Takashi, *Bakumatsu hiun no hitobito*, p. 60. Ishii believed that the opposition of Kazunomiya's mother, Kangyō-in, and her uncle, Hashimoto Saneakira, had strengthened her resistance to the marriage.

25. Takebe, *Kazunomiya*, p. 48.
26. According to Ishii, a henchman of Konoe Hisatada (the chancellor) named Shimada Sakon hinted to Kazunomiya that if she persisted in her refusal, her mother and uncle would be severely punished (*Bakumatsu*, p. 61). He also induced her nurse to persuade Kazunomiya to accept. Takebe says that two retainers of the chancellor had plotted to get a relative of Kazunomiya's nurse to inform the nurse that the court had decided to punish mother and uncle and, in this way, shake Kazunomiya's resolve (*Kazunomiya*, pp. 51–52). In any case, it seems likely that underhanded methods were employed in the hopes of persuading Kazunomiya to agree to marry the shogun.
27. Takebe, *Kazunomiya*, p. 53.
28. Ibid., p. 54.
29. Ishii, *Bakumatsu*, p. 62.
30. *Ōya Sōichi zenshū*, 23, p. 259; Takebe, *Kazunomiya*, p. 55.

Chapter 7

1. *Meiji tennō ki*, 1, p. 144.
2. Ibid., 1, p. 244.
3. For a description of the activities of the Russians on Tsushima, see George Alexander Lensen, *The Russian Push Toward Japan*, pp. 448–51. Lensen's account is based mainly on Russian sources.
4. *Meiji tennō ki*, 1, p. 243.
5. Ibid., 1, pp. 242–43. Konishi Shirō emphasized the importance of the resistance to the Russians by the inhabitants of Tsushima (*Kaikoku to jōi*, p. 226). If they had not battled to save their land from the Russian invaders, the affair would not have ended so easily with the British action.
6. *Kōmei tennō ki*, 4, pp. 243–47. See also *Meiji tennō ki*, 1, p. 243. The Tsushima daimyo was Sō Yoshiaki (1847–1902).
7. A large-scale mission was dispatched to Europe in 1862. For a study of this mission, see Haga Tōru, *Taikun no shisetsu*, and my *Modern Japanese Diaries*.
8. *Kōmei tennō ki*, 3, pp. 611–16. See also *Meiji tennō ki*, 1, pp. 255–56.
9. *Meiji tennō ki*, 1, pp. 256, 257.
10. There was confusion and even alarm in the shogunate when it was discovered that the treaty was not solely with Prussia but with other states of what would shortly be the North German Confederation. The Japanese thought they had been tricked into signing a treaty with several countries (*Meiji tennō ki*, 1, pp. 234–35; *Kōmei tennō ki*, 3, pp. 488–89).
11. For Kazunomiya's letter, see *Kōmei tennō ki*, 3, pp. 489–90. See also Takebe Toshio, *Kazunomiya*, p. 66.
12. The name Chikako was given to her by Kōmei after she had been proclaimed an imperial princess (*naishinnō*) in May 1861 (*Kōmei tennō ki*, 3, p. 559).
13. A letter sent by Kazunomiya to Kōmei at this time has been preserved. It includes the words "For the sake of peace in the country I have no choice but to accept, though it is truly hateful" (Takebe, *Kazunomiya*, p. 60).
14. *Meiji tennō ki*, 1, p. 267. Nakayama also fell out of favor, but Imadegawa Saneaya (1832–1864) rapidly recovered from the disgrace and was appointed in 1863 as the

imperial messenger to the tomb of Emperor Jimmu, where he prayed for the expulsion of the barbarians.

15. The number of men in the procession has been variously estimated. A frequently cited source stated that there were 7,896 men, 280 horses, 7,440 futon, 1,380 pillows, 8,060 rice bowls, 5,210 soup bowls, 1,040 trays, and 2,110 plates (Takebe, *Kazunomiya*, p. 83; Konishi, *Kaikoku to jōi*, p. 214). Additional guards were supplied at various places en route. Ōya Sōichi estimated the escort as 20,000 men (*Ōya Sōichi zenshū*, 23, p. 278).

16. Ōya, 23, p. 278. The *enkiri enoki* was in Itabashi, just north of Edo.

17. A section of the text of their manifesto is in *Kōmei tennō ki*, 3, pp. 764–65.

18. The letter was an outright forgery (*Ōya*, 23, p. 276).

19. According to the rumor, Townsend Harris had decided to get rid of Kōmei as an obstruction to opening the country and had suborned Andō to commit the deed. The two scholars (Hanawa Jirō and Maeda Kensuke) whom he allegedly had employed were both assassinated in January 1863 (*Ōya*, 23, p. 276).

20. Fujita Satoru, *Bakumatsu no tennō*, p. 190.

21. *Meiji tennō ki*, 1, p. 273. The poem contains two wordplays: *tachi* is both "sword" (a reference to the gift Kōmei has received) and "nature" (of the patriotic donor); *saya* is both "scabbard" and "brightly."

22. *Meiji tennō ki*, 1, pp. 282–83.

23. Ibid., 1, p. 300.

24. The four "villains" (*kan*) were Koga Takemichi, Iwakura Tomomi, Chigusa Aribumi, and Tominokōji Hironao. The two "ladies" (*hin*) were Imaki Shigeko and Horikawa Motoko. All six were in some way connected with Kazunomiya's betrothal to the shogun.

25. *Meiji tennō ki*, 1, p. 312.

Chapter 8

1. The text of the message (in Chinese) is in *Kōmei tennō ki*, 4, p. 195. A rather free translation into Japanese is in *Meiji tennō ki*, 1, p. 312.

2. The hall of audiences (*ōhiroma*) was in three tiers. The bottom level (*gedan*) was the level of an ordinary tatami; the middle level (*chūdan*) was the height of two layers of tatami; and the upper level (*jōdan*) was three tatami high.

3. *Meiji tennō ki*, 1, p. 312.

4. Ibid., 1, pp. 320–21. See also *Kōmei tennō ki*, 4, pp. 353–54.

5. Nakagawanomiya (1824–1891) was born the son of Fushiminomiya Kuniie. He had several childhood names and acquired more when he was sent as an acolyte in 1831 to the Honnō-ji. In 1836 he was transferred to the Ichijō-in, an abbacy of the Kōfuku-ji in Nara, to study (with still another name) under his uncle, the superior of the temple. That year, at the age of twelve, he was adopted by Emperor Ninkō and succeeded his uncle as the superior, although he was not formally inducted as a priest until 1838. He moved by imperial command in 1852 to the Shōren-in, a major Tendai temple in Kyōto, and was accordingly known as Shōren-no-miya Son'yu, the name most commonly found in documents of the late Tokugawa period. (He was also known as Awatanomiya or Awataguchinomiya from the location of the temple). Among those who gathered around him were

Umeda Unpin, Ikeuchi Daigaku, Maki Izumi, Hashimoto Sanai, and Sakuma Shōzan, and various others who were either murdered or purged in the Ansei incident. These men were attracted not only by the prince's advocacy of *jōi* but also by his noble character, attested to by his followers' writings. His popularity with the *shishi* did not escape the notice of the shogunate, and at the time of the Ansei purge, he was condemned to perpetual confinement at the Shōkoku-ji, where he spent more than two years in a tiny, dilapidated hut (Ōnishi Gen'ichi, "Ishin kaiten no kōbo to Kuni-no-miya Asahiko Shinnō," p. 79). This treatment of the prince enraged the *shishi*, and obtaining his release became their first objective (p. 86). Some even spoke of making the prince the *seii taishōgun* of an army that would overthrow the shogunate, although the prince remained to the end a believer in *kōbu gattai* (p. 82). Sanguinary plans for disposing not only of shogunate officials but of all foreigners were pushed forward with the expectation that the prince would lead the attacks (p. 87). The prince was released from confinement and allowed to return to the laity in 1862 as part of the amnesty declared in honor of the marriage of the shogun and Kazunomiya (p. 98). Only then did he become known as Nakagawanomiya. After the Restoration his enemies still did not relent, and he was exiled to Hiroshima on what seems to have been a trumped-up accusation. His last years were spent as the lord custodian of the Great Shrine at Ise.

While at the Kōfuku-ji, the prince studied both the literary and the martial arts, especially spearmanship. In Nara he made an important acquaintance, Kawaji Toshiakira, an official of the shogunate who prominently figured in efforts to open the country, even though the prince remained throughout an advocate of *jōi*.

6. Fujita Satoru referred to the prince as "the right arm of Emperor Kōmei" (*Bakumatsu no tennō*, p. 219).
7. Kurihara Ryūichi, *Zankanjō*, p. 107.
8. For a text of the accusation directed against the Ashikaga shoguns, see ibid., p. 115. For an excellent account in English of this event, see Anne Walthall, "Off with Their Heads! The Hirata Disciples and the Ashikaga Shoguns."
9. Walthall, "Off with Their Heads," pp. 162–68. The official responsible for apprehending these men was Matsudaira Katamori (1835–1893), who had been appointed as the Kyōto *shugo* in 1862. This action brought the young, little-known daimyo of Aizu to the attention of the court. His determination to catch the culprits was inspired by the symbolic importance of the act: in beheading the statues of long-ago shoguns they were threatening the present shogun.
10. *Kōmei tennō ki*, 4, p. 455. See also *Meiji tennō ki*, 1, p. 325.
11. *Meiji tennō ki*, 1, p. 325. It is said that Iemitsu was accompanied by 307,000 men. It is hard to take this literally, but probably this was the impression conveyed by the throng of escorts he brought with him in the hopes of thoroughly impressing the court.
12. As mentioned previously, he had in fact been forced by the conflagration that destroyed the palace in 1854 to leave the Gosho and take refuge elsewhere.
13. His decision to make this pilgrimage seems to have been the result of repeated petitions offered to the throne by Mōri Sadahiro (1839–1896), the heir of Mōri Takachika, the daimyo of Hagi. Sadahiro said that it was not fitting at a time of

crisis for the emperor to remain shut up in his palace and urged him to worship not only at the two Kamo Shrines but also at the Sennyū-ji and the Iwashimizu Hachiman Shrine (*Meiji tennō ki*, 1, p. 327).

14. *Meiji tennō ki*, 1, pp. 326–27.

15. Yoshimura Toratarō (1837–1863), a *shishi* from Tosa, wrote a letter to his parents describing the scene: "When the imperial palanquin came close, I naturally was overcome with tears. I prostrated myself, but more than that I cannot say. I later heard from others that more than four hundred thousand people—men and women, old and young—had gathered this day along the roads, hoping to catch a glimpse of his countenance inside the beaded curtains, and all of them were weeping" (quoted in Nishijima Ryōsaburō, *Nakayama Tadamitsu ansatsu shimatsu*, p. 39).

16. *Meiji tennō ki*, 1, p. 330. Nakayama Tadamitsu in his capacity as chamberlain served his nephew Mutsuhito.

17. *Kōmei tennō ki*, 4, pp. 592–93. See also Ishii Takashi, *Bakumatsu hiun no hitobito*, pp. 68–69.

18. *Meiji tennō ki*, 1, pp. 330–31.

19. Nishijima, *Nakayama*, pp. 22–24, 34.

20. By "advocate of justice," he probably meant someone devoted to the *sonjō* cause (Nishijima, *Nakayama*, p. 34).

21. Nishijima, *Nakayama*, p. 35.

22. Ibid., p. 49.

23. There are at least eight different theories as to the day in the eleventh moon when the assassination occurred (Nishijima, *Nakayama*, p. 197). Nishijima gives the names of men sent by the Zokurontō, the anti-*jōi* faction then dominant within the domain, to kill Tadamitsu (p. 201).

Chapter 9

1. *Meiji tennō ki*, 1, p. 331.

2. *Kōmei tennō ki*, 4, pp. 707–10. See also *Meiji tennō ki*, 1, p. 335.

3. Yoda Yoshiie, "Kindai tennōsei seiritsu no zentei," p. 10. He quotes a passage to this effect from the letter sent by Kōmei to Konoe Tadahiro dated April 7, 1859. For the full text of the letter, see *Kōmei tennō ki*, 2, pp. 787–89.

4. *Meiji tennō ki*, 1, pp. 338–39. In the end, Shimazu Mochihisa accepted the British demands and paid more than 6 million *ryō* in gold by way of indemnity.

5. *Meiji tennō ki*, 1, pp. 340–41. For a much fuller account of Ikeda Yoshinori's views, see *Kōmei tennō ki*, 4, p. 741.

6. *Meiji tennō ki*, 1, p. 341.

7. Ibid., 1, p. 344.

8. Ibid., 1, p. 345. Far richer documentation and fuller quotation from Kōmei's message are found in *Kōmei tennō ki*, 4, pp. 791–820. For example, Prince Nakagawa recalled to an interviewer that Kōmei had said he could not take command of any army that attacked the shogunate, because Princess Chikako (the former Kazunomiya) was now a Tokugawa, and if he attacked the Tokugawa family, he would have to kill her. This would be unforgivable to the late emperor, the father of Chikako, and to her relations. If a time came when such an attack was necessary,

he would attack, but the time would have to be right. From all he had heard, it was too early to open an attack, if only because adequate weapons were still not available. He had therefore decided to defer temporarily assuming personal command (*Kōmei tennō ki*, 4, p. 791). It is not clear when Nakagawa made this statement. Probably it was years after the events, and slips of memory and inventions may have colored his recollection.

9. *Meiji tennō ki*, 1, p. 345. The seven nobles left behind a brief message stating that just when the great enterprise of restoring imperial power was moving toward a successful conclusion, traitors had disturbed the imperial mind with their machinations. Unable to tolerate this, the seven signers had decided to go to the west where they would raise an army. They appealed to all patriots to join them (Kurihara Ryūichi, *Zankanjō*, p. 178).

10. They included *Ehon Asakusa Reigenki*, *Ehon Sangokuki Yōfuden*, *Ehon Taikōki*, *Ehon Hikoyama Reigenki*, *Genpei seisuiki zue*, and *Ashikabi sōshi*.

11. *Meiji tennō ki*, 1, p. 353.

12. The *nengō* was changed from the fourth year of Bunkyū to the first year of Genji on the twentieth of the second month because this was a "revolutionary" year. A full list of the twenty-four *nengō* recommended at the time is in *Kōmei tennō ki*, 5, pp. 84–88. One of the recommended *nengō* was Meiji.

13. The text is in *Kōmei tennō ki*, 5, p. 20; the translation, in W. G. Beasley, ed. and trans., *Select Documents on Japanese Foreign Policy*, pp. 263–64.

14. The text is in *Kōmei tennō ki*, 5, p. 20; the translation, in Beasley, ed. and trans., *Select Documents*, p. 264.

15. *Meiji tennō ki*, 1, p. 376. For details, see *Kōmei tennō ki*, 5, pp. 226–30, esp. p. 230. Kido Takayoshi, who was in another part of the building, barely managed to escape.

16. These plans were learned by the Shinsengumi from Furutaka Shuntarō (1829–1864), a loyalist-activist (*kinnō shishi*) whom they captured and tortured. They also learned the names of the people involved (Fukuchi Shigetaka, *Kōmei tennō*, pp. 182–83; Tōyama Shigeki, ed., *Ishin no gunzō*, p. 55).

17. *Meiji tennō ki*, 1, p. 337. Hikone was the seat of the Ii family, powerful *fudai* daimyos, which was probably why it seemed like a suitable and easily defensible place for the emperor to reside.

18. *Meiji tennō ki*, 1, p. 377. The statement left at the Gion Shrine by the assassins, explaining why they killed Shōzan, mentioned his study of Western learning, his advocacy of foreign trade and opening the ports, and his collaboration with the "villainous" Aizu and Hikone Domains. He was accused also of plotting with Prince Nakagawa to move the capital to Hikone (Kurihara, *Zankanjō*, pp. 247–48). There seem to have been grounds for the belief that a removal of the capital was being planned.

19. Ishii Takashi, *Bakumatsu hiun no hitobito*, p. 84. This description is from Nakayama Tadayasu's diary, quoted in *Kōmei tennō ki*, 5, p. 302.

20. *Meiji tennō ki*, 1, p. 378.

21. This description is from Higashibōjō Tadanaga's diary, quoted in *Kōmei tennō ki*, 5, p. 305. See also Ishii, *Bakumatsu*, p. 85.

22. *Meiji tennō ki*, 1, p. 379.

23. Ibid., 1, p. 380. See also *Kōmei tennō ki*, 5, p. 303.

24. Ninagawa Shin, *Meiji tennō*, p. 21. Ōya Sōichi was perhaps the first to state that the prince had been so frightened by the sound of gunfire that he fainted (*Ōya Sōichi zenshū*, 23, pp. 30–32). But as Asukai Masamichi pointed out, this statement originated in a misreading of the text of *Nakayama Tadayasu nikki* (*Meiji taitei*, p. 97).

25. This is the theory of Asukai, *Meiji taitei*, p. 98.

Chapter 10

1. The French text of this treaty is in W. G. Beasley, ed. and trans., *Select Documents on Japanese Foreign Policy*, pp. 273–74. It provided that the Japanese government had to deliver to the French minister in Edo, within three months of the return of the Japanese embassy, 140,000 "piastres mexicains, dont 100,000 piastres seront payées par le Gouvernement lui-même, et 40,000 piastres par l'Autorité de la Province de Nagato."

2. A translation of Ikeda's long letter to the shogunate explaining his actions is in Beasley, ed. and trans., *Select Documents*, pp. 274–82.

3. *Meiji tennō ki*, 1, p. 387.

4. Ibid., 1, p. 388.

5. Ibid., 1, p. 395. This entry is dated February 16. His name appeared again on March 8, when he urged precisely the opposite course of action: to allow the nobles to return to the capital and to restore them to their positions. He seems to have changed his mind as the result of an order from the daimyo of Satsuma, Shimazu Mochihisa.

6. *Meiji tennō ki*, 1, p. 407.

7. The foreigners always referred to the emperor as the mikado, a title that they believed was that of a religious, rather than a secular, authority.

8. *Kōmei tennō ki*, 5, p. 653. The original French text of the memorandum, signed on October 30, 1865, in Yokohama by the ministers in Japan of Great Britain, France, the United States, and Holland, is in Beasley, ed. and trans., *Select Documents*, pp. 293–96. The contents differ in many small ways from the Japanese version given in summary here.

9. *Meiji tennō ki*, 1, p. 416.

10. The information on the dealings with the foreigners at Hyōgo, found in *Kōmei tennō ki*, 5, pp. 654–55, is derived from *Zoku saimu kiji*, the records kept between 1862 and 1867 by Matsudaira Yoshinaga (1828–90), the daimyo of Echizen.

11. *Kōmei tennō ki*, 5, p. 654.

12. Mario Emilio Cosenza, ed., *The Complete Journals of Townsend Harris*, pp. 371, 518.

13. Beasley, ed. and trans., *Select Documents*, p. 300. The letter is dated November 21, 1865.

14. It is true that the foreigners on occasion (and as far back as Townsend Harris) had threatened to take a disputed matter to the mikado in Kyōto, but this was the first time they—or anyone else—had been informed that the emperor ranked higher than the shogun. For mention of foreigners who had earlier shown awareness of the importance of the emperor, see F. V. Dickins and S. Lane-Poole, *The Life of Sir Harry Parkes*, 2, p. 43. But William Elliot Griffis wrote, "English scholarship

first discovered the true source of power, exposed the counterfeit government in Yedo, read the riddle of ages, and rent the veil that so long hid the truth. It was the English minister, Sir Harry Parkes, who first risked his life to find the truth; stripped the shogun of his fictitious title of 'majesty;' asked for at home, obtained, and presented credentials to the mikado, the sovereign of Japan" (*The Mikado's Empire*, p. 577)

15. I have followed here the account given by Matsudaira Yoshinaga, as quoted in *Kōmei tennō ki*, 5, p. 655. It differs in details from the account in *Meiji tennō ki*, 1, p. 418, which states, for example, that it was Parkes who, seeing Inoue about to cut his finger, said he took his word.

16. *Meiji tennō ki*, 1, p. 419.

17. Quoted in Ishii Takashi, *Bakumatsu hiun no hitobito*, p. 91.

18. *Meiji tennō ki*, 1, p. 420. For a translation of the message from the court to the shogunate, see Beasley, ed. and trans., *Select Documents*, p. 304.

19. *Meiji tennō ki*, 1, p. 421.

20. Quoted in Tōyama Shigeki, ed., *Ishin no gunzō*, p. 56. His translation is very free and omits a good deal, but by so doing he makes better sense than the original. Ishii quotes phrases from the same letter, dated August 29, 1865 (*Bakumatsu*, p. 89). The letter does not appear in *Kōmei tennō ki* but is in *Asahiko Shinnō nikki*, 1, pp. 336–37.

21. *Asahiko Shinnō nikki*, 1, pp. 336–37. Tōyama says this statement is to be found in *Zoku sōri meichū* (*Ishin*, p. 57), but it is not there. He also quotes the diary of Nakayama Tadayasu to the effect that "the palace is exactly like the licensed quarter; every day is spent in pleasure."

22. Ishii, *Bakumatsu*, p. 88.

23. Tōyama, *Ishin*, p. 51; Ishii, *Bakumatsu*, p. 77. Because of this position, the prince was referred to as *in no miya*.

24. The relevant part of the letter sent by Kōmei to Nakagawanomiya on January 11, 1864, is in *Kōmei tennō ki*, 4, p. 940. Ishii quotes the section in which the emperor, denouncing the rumor as the work of villains seeking to overturn the changes achieved on September 30, said he was sure the *in no miya* could see into his heart, just as he could see into the *in no miya*'s heart (*Bakumatsu*, p. 77). Kōmei concluded with the assertion that he entertained absolutely no suspicions of the prince.

25. Tōyama, *Ishin*, p. 52.

26. According to Ninagawa Shin, "The emperor Meiji ascended the throne on the ninth day of the first month of the third year of Keiō. On the twenty-fifth day of the twelfth month of the previous year his father, Kōmei tennō, was assassinated by Iwakura and others, and on the twentieth day of the ninth month of that year the fourteenth shogun, Iemochi, was killed by an unknown assailant while in Ōsaka Castle" (*Meiji tennō*, p. 11).

27. The Chōshū men included such outstanding figures as Kido Takayoshi, Takasugi Shinsaku, Inoue Kaoru, and Itō Hirobumi (*Meiji tennō ki*, 1, p. 429).

28. For the negotiations at this time, see Marius B. Jansen, *Sakamoto Ryōma and the Meiji Restoration*, pp. 217–22.

29. For the six articles of the agreement, see ibid., pp. 220–21.

30. Iemochi's illness had begun in May of that year and, after various ups and downs, had become serious at the end of the July while he was in Ōsaka. For a detailed account of his illness, see Conrad Totman, *The Collapse of the Tokugawa Bakufu*, p. 516.

31. The diary of a court lady mentions Princess Chikako's fears that Kamenosuke was too young to cope with the difficult times (quoted in *Kōmei tennō ki*, 5, p. 799).

32. *Kōmei tennō ki*, 5, p. 798. The memorial to the throne is dated simply "seventh month" but elsewhere is identified as having been sent on the twenty-ninth day of the seventh month. However, Iemochi died on the twentieth day of the seventh month. It is not clear, therefore, whether Iemochi wrote the memorial at some previous time or whether it was written by someone else.

33. The text of the proposal is in *Kōmei tennō ki*, 5, pp. 804–6.

34. This is the view of Ishii, *Bakumatsu*, p. 95. I have tried without success to imagine Kaiser Wilhelm II listening patiently as a stinging attack was made on his policies.

35. *Meiji tennō ki*, 1, p. 442.

36. The announcement said merely that hostilities were being discontinued "for a while" (*shibaraku*) (*Kōmei tennō ki*, 5, p. 832).

Chapter 11

1. Ōkubo Toshiaki, *Iwakura Tomomi*, p. 138.

2. Ishii Takashi, *Bakumatsu hiun no hitobito*, pp. 97–98.

3. *Meiji tennō ki*, 1, p. 445.

4. Ibid., 1, p. 445.

5. Ibid., 1, p. 445.

6. Ibid., 1, p. 454; documentation is in *Kōmei tennō ki*, 5, p. 916.

7. Higashikuze Michitomi, *Ishin zengo*, pp. 41–42. For a citation from Nakayama Tadayasu's diary in which he mentioned that the emperor was so robust that he never even caught a cold, see also *Kōmei tennō ki*, 5, p. 927.

8. Haraguchi Kiyoshi, "Kōmei tennō wa dokusatsu sareta no ka," p. 48. See also *Kōmei tennō ki*, 5, p. 918.

9. *Nakayama Tadayasu nikki*, 3, p. 652.

10. Tankai's diary stated that the emperor was well on the way to recovery (Nezu Masashi, "Kōmei tennō wa byōshi ka dokusatsu ka," p. 33).

11. Haraguchi, "Kōmei," p. 49. Kōmei's death was officially said to have occurred on the twenty-ninth of the twelfth month, although he actually died on the twenty-fifth. It had been the practice ever since the seventeenth century for the "official" day of an emperor's death to be later than the day on which he actually died, perhaps to allow more time for preparing the funeral. It was decided in October 1867 to change the day of mourning for Emperor Kōmei to the day on which he had actually died (*Meiji tennō ki*, 1, p. 816).

12. Haraguchi, "Kōmei," p. 57.

13. Haraguchi discusses the article by Yoshida Tsunekichi, first published in 1949, insisting that smallpox was the cause of Kōmei's death, in ibid., pp. 49–50.

14. Nezu Masashi, who emerged as the leading exponent of the poison theory, somewhat melodramatically stated that "anyone who, prior to the defeat, expressed the slightest doubt concerning this official fact [that Emperor Kōmei died a natural

death] was branded as impious or else pursued by the law and thrown into prison. No scholar even considered investigating it. Not one document written in Japanese openly stated that Emperor Kōmei had been poisoned, but Satow's *A Diplomat in Japan* reported it as a rumor. This passage was cut from the Japanese translation of Satow's book" ("Kōmei," p. 28). But Nezu himself mentions that in July 1940, at a meeting of the Nihon ishi gakkai Kansai shibu (Kansai Division of the Society for the History of Japanese Medicine), Dr. Saeki Riichirō, after examining the diary of a court physician in the possession of Irago Motoyoshi, concluded that the course of the smallpox was normal up until January 22 or 23, when Iwakura Tomomi took advantage of the emperor's illness to have his niece, a court lady, administer poison. Dr. Saeki said he had heard the facts directly from the woman in question, who subsequently became a nun at the Reikan-ji convent at Shishigatani, to the east of Kyōto (pp. 34–35). Among the problems is the fact that the court lady in question was a sister, not a niece, of Iwakura's. Ishii, who supported the poison theory, felt compelled to state that the sister, Horikawa Motoko, could not have committed the crime, if only because she was not on duty in the palace at that time (*Bakumatsu*, p. 114).

I also recall hearing from my teacher, Dr. Tsunoda Ryūsaku, that about 1910 a neighbor at a bar in Honolulu told him that he had taken part in the assassination of Kōmei and for this reason could not remain in Japan. This would be pertinent information if I could be sure that (1) my memory of Professor Tsunoda's conversation was accurate forty years after hearing it; (2) Professor Tsunoda's memory of the alleged conversation in Honolulu was accurate forty years later; and (3) the man at the bar was not drunk.

15. Sir Ernest Satow, *A Diplomat in Japan*, pp. 185–86. *Baku-fu* is used for the shogunate, and Shitotsubashi (Hitotsubashi) for Tokugawa Yoshinobu.

16. Nezu, "Kōmei," p. 35.

17. This theory is mentioned by Ōya Sōichi in *Ōya Sōichi zenshū*, 23, p. 294.

18. Ishii gives the names of two court ladies (Takano Fusako and Nakamikado Yoshiko) who seem to him to be not above suspicion (*Bakumatsu*, p. 113). He also says, without further elucidation, that the culprit probably was a court lady, although a mastermind man was doubtless working behind the scenes. However, Sasaki Suguru suggested that the poisoner may have been Ōkubo Toshimichi, working in cahoots with Iwakura, who was hampered in his movements by his exile to Iwakura Village (*Boshin sensō*, p. 9). In any case, Sasaki felt sure that somebody working behind the scenes had planned the assassination. However, when his book was reprinted thirteen years later (in 1990), he wrote that he had been persuaded by Haraguchi's articles that Kōmei died of smallpox.

19. Maruya Saiichi amusingly imagined the performance of kabuki that Emperor Meiji witnessed on April 26, 1887 (*Aoi Amagasa*, pp. 273–74). An addition to the program consisting of the play within the play from *Hamlet*, would be performed in the presence of not only the emperor but also Iwakura Tomomi, whose crime — poisoning the emperor like Claudius — would be enacted as Meiji stared at the guilty man. But as Maruya was fully aware, Iwakura died in 1883.

20. Ōkubo, *Iwakura*, pp. 181–82. A description by Iwakura of his overpowering grief on learning of the illness and death of Kōmei is in *Iwakura-kō jikki*, 1, pp. 1135–36.

21. Haraguchi Kiyoshi, "Kōmei tennō to Iwakura Tomomi."

22. Haraguchi Kiyoshi, "Kōmei tennō no shiin ni tsuite," pp. 2–3.

23. The art of vaccination had been transmitted to Japan in the 1830s by physicians at the Dutch trading station in Nagasaki. By this time it was being practiced fairly widely among the upper classes.

24. *Meiji tennō ki*, 1, pp. 459–60.

25. Ibid., 1, p. 470.

Chapter 12

1. This is an excerpt from a letter dated February 21, 1867. It is in *Iwakura Tomomi kankei monjo*, 3, p. 277. See also Fujita Satoru, *Bakumatsu no tennō*, pp. 239–40.

2. *Asahiko Shinnō nikki*, 2, p. 268. Shōki (Chung Kuei) was a mythic being of fierce countenance (distinguished by his full beard and big eyes) who was believed to have the power to drive away the god of plague and other demons with the sword he brandishes. He appeared in the dream of the T'ang emperor Hsüan-tsung, who had the painter Wu Tao-tzu draw his portrait.

3. *Asahiko Shinnō nikki*, 2, p. 272.

4. Tōyama Shigeki, ed., *Ishin no gunzō*, p. 57.

5. *Meiji tennō ki*, 1, pp. 463, 479. See also Watanabe Ikujirō, *Meiji tennō*, 1, p. 88.

6. *Meiji tennō ki*, 1, p. 466.

7. Ibid., 1, p. 467.

8. The ancient practice of bestowing on a deceased emperor a posthumous name derived from the Chinese classics and referring to him as *tennō* , which had fallen into desuetude for 955 years, was revived in 1840 for Emperor Kōkaku in honor of his long reign (Fujita Satoru, *Bakumatsu no tennō*, pp. 129–33). Before this return to ancient usage, emperors were normally known posthumously by a place-name followed by the word *in*, meaning that the emperor had entered priestly orders before his death. Ichijō-in and Momozono-in are examples. Kōmei *tennō* is an example of the new (but also ancient) usage.

9. *Meiji tennō ki*, 1, pp. 826–27.

10. Ibid., 1, pp. 469–70.

11. Ibid., 1, p. 477. For the complete text of the shogun's letter, see Tada Kōmon, ed., *Iwakura-kō jikki*, 2, pp. 42–43, and W. G. Beasley, ed. and trans., *Select Documents on Japanese Foreign Policy*, pp. 308–10.

12. The text is in Tada, ed., *Iwakura*, 2, p. 44; the translation, in Beasley, ed. and trans., *Select Documents*, p. 310.

13. *Meiji tennō ki*, 1, p. 480. The text is in Tada, ed., *Iwakura*, 2, pp. 44, 45; the translation, in Beasley, ed. and trans., *Select Documents*, pp. 310–11.

14. The text is in Tada, ed., *Iwakura*, 2, p. 47; the translation, in Beasley, ed. and trans., *Select Documents*, p. 319.

15. *Meiji tennō ki*, 1, p. 481. Nakayama Tadayasu continued to give the young emperor lectures on the Japanese classics, and other men lectured on Chinese works (pp. 500, 507).

16. *Meiji tennō ki*, 1, p. 497. Meiji also had instruction from Takatsuji Osanaga and Nagatani Nobuatsu in the Chinese classics (pp. 500, 508). The one Chinese classic mentioned by name was the *Shu Ching* (Book of History).

17. *Meiji tennō ki*, 1, p. 474.

18. Ibid., 1, p. 481.
19. Ibid., 1, p. 484.
20. On December 17 the American minister resident, R. B. Van Valkenburgh, sent a message conveying the thanks of President Andrew Johnson for the Japanese efforts (*Meiji tennō ki*, 1, p. 549).
21. At this time her name was Masako, but it was changed to Haruko, the name by which she was known abroad. For the sake of uniformity, I shall call her Haruko throughout.
22. Horaguchi Michihisa, *Shōken kōtaikō*, p. 9.
23. *Meiji tennō ki*, 1, pp. 502–3.
24. Ibid., 1, p. 504.
25. Ibid., 1, pp. 504–5. A *nyōgo* was ranked immediately below empress.
26. According to the Japanese calendar, it was on the twenty-eighth day of the twelfth month of the previous year. A full description of the marriage ceremonies is in *Meiji tennō ki*, 1, pp. 941–44.
27. *Meiji tennō ki*, 1, pp. 940–41.
28. She was known as *jungō*, meaning literally, "next after the empress."
29. *Meiji tennō ki*, 1, p. 943.

Chapter 13

1. *Meiji tennō ki*, 1, p. 495.
2. Ibid., 1, pp. 497, 500. The text states that in extreme cases husbands and wives separated and relatives broke off relations, estranged by the change in circumstances.
3. *Meiji tennō ki*, 1, p. 511.
4. Ibid., 1, p. 656.
5. Ibid., 1, p. 681.
6. Ibid., 1, p. 682. Sir Ernest Satow describes Sir Harry Parkes's meeting with Gotō Shōjirō and Date Munenari (Muneki) on May 22, 1868: "With the latter we had a discussion about the recently published edict against Christianity; it revived the ancient prohibition, but in less stringent terms. Daté admitted that the wording was objectionable, and said that he had caused it not to be exhibited on the public notice-boards at Ozaka and Hiōgo. He had tried to get the expression (translated 'evil' or 'pernicious' sect) altered, but said it would be impossible to suppress the proscription of Christianity altogether . . . . Afterwards I had a long talk with Nakai [Hiroshi] on this subject, and suggested that instead of specifically mentioning Christianity the decree should merely forbid 'pernicious sects' in general. It was clear that the Japanese Government would not be induced to revoke the law completely, for that would be to give a free hand to the Roman Catholic missionaries at Nagasaki, who had already made themselves obnoxious by the active manner in which they had carried on their proselytism" (*A Diplomat in Japan*, p. 368).
7. *Meiji tennō ki*, 3, p. 42.
8. Ishii Takashi, *Boshin sensō ron*, p. 1.
9. For Oguri's advocacy of *Tokugawa zettai shugi*, see Ishii Takashi, *Bakumatsu hiun no hitobito*, pp. 188–221.

10. Ishii, *Boshin*, p. 21.

11. Terajima Munenori (also known as Matsuki Kōan, 1832–1883) was an exception to this generalization. During the brief "war" between Satsuma and the British, he deliberately became a prisoner in order to travel abroad. His knowledge of the rest of the world, especially of India and China, convinced him that the only way Japan could resist colonization at the hands of foreign powers was by unifying the country under one ruler, the emperor (Ishii, *Boshin*, p. 22). After the outbreak of the war between the shogunate and Chōshū in the summer of 1866, Fukuzawa Yukichi presented a memorandum expressing his hope that after Chōshū was crushed (with the aid of foreign troops if necessary), the feudal system would be changed; he hoped the shogun would establish an absolutist regime (p. 29).

12. *Yonaoshi* often took the form of people dancing in the streets and crying, "Ii ja nai ka." Here is Satow's description of one such manifestation: "Some difficulty was experienced in making our way through the crowds of people in flaming red garments dancing and shouting the refrain *ii ja nai ka*. They were so much taken up with their dancing and lantern-carrying that we passed along almost unnoticed" (*A Diplomat*, p. 289).

13. Ishii, *Boshin*, p. 38.

14. Ōhashi Akio, *Gotō Shōjirō to kindai Nihon*, p. 76. For the meeting of the two men, see Marius B. Jansen, *Sakamoto Ryōma and the Meiji Restoration*, pp. 265–66.

15. For Sakamoto's proposals, see Jansen, *Sakamoto*, pp. 295–96, and Ōhashi, *Gotō*, p. 91.

16. Ishii, *Boshun*, p. 61. See also *Meiji tennō ki*, 1, pp. 501–2. Ōhashi gives a somewhat different paraphrase (*Gotō*, pp. 95–96). See also Jansen, *Sakamoto*, pp. 300–301.

17. *Meiji tennō ki*, 1, p. 516.

18. Ibid., 1, p. 518.

19. The name is also read Yamanouchi; Yōdō was the *gō* by which he was commonly known, but his personal name was Toyonobu.

20. Ōhashi, *Gotō*, pp. 99–101.

21. The text is in *Meiji tennō ki*, 1, p. 520.

22. Satow was shown a copy of this proposal by Gotō Shōjirō and Nakai Hiroshi (called Kōzō by Satow): "They produced a copy of the Tosa memorial of last month, advising the Tycoon to take the step he had since adopted, and proposing various reforms. Of these the most important were the establishment of an assembly composed of two houses, the erection of schools of science and literature in the principal cities, and the negotiation of new treaties with foreign powers" (*A Diplomat*, p. 284).

23. The text is in *Meiji tennō ki*, 1, pp. 521–22. See also Jansen, *Sakamoto*, pp. 312–17.

24. *Meiji tennō ki*, 1, pp. 519–20.

25. The text is in ibid., 1, p. 525. It is reproduced photographically in Ishii, *Boshin*, p. 67.

26. Yoshinobu is called Minamoto rather than Tokugawa because the Tokugawa family claimed to be descended from the Minamoto, the shoguns during the Kamakura period.

27. The court was still in mourning for Kōmei.

28. I have followed the interpretation of the text given in Ishii, *Boshin*, pp. 66–67. Not everything is clear, but this is the general sense.

29. They were Nakayama Tadayasu, Ōgimachisanjō Sanenaru, and Nakamikado Tsuneyuki.
30. Ishii, *Boshin*, p. 70. For Iwakura's relations with Tamamatsu, see Tada Kōmon, ed., *Iwakura-kō jikki*, 2, pp. 59–62.
31. Tada, ed., *Iwakura*, 2, p. 70.
32. Ishii, *Boshin*, p. 71.
33. Although the second edict was dated the day after the first, they both were sent on the same day (*Meiji tennō ki*, 1, p. 526). Katamori was the Kyōto *shugo* and Sadanori, the Kyōto *shoshidai*.
34. Tada, ed., *Iwakura*, 2, pp. 84–85. According to Iwakura, the emperor directed the three nobles who had signed the edicts to wait and see what happened now that Yoshinobu had announced his intention of yielding political power to the throne. Despite Iwakura's words, the young emperor was unlikely to have made this decision by himself.
35. Conrad Totman wrote, "Mindful of our evidence that Edo had been making substantial progress in restoring Tokugawa power and prestige, Yoshinobu's decision of 10/12 commands attention and prompts a query: Why did he make it?" (*The Collapse of the Tokugawa Bakufu*, pp. 381–82). After offering various possible answers in terms of immediate and long-range causes, Totman concluded, "In sum, then, given the very worrisome context, Yoshinobu's ambiguity of purpose, his ambivalence about governing, the relatively concessive orientation of those about him, the absence of forceful countervailing pressure, the limited objectives of the Tosa proposal, and the very real likelihood that it would peter out in any case as its predecessors had done—given all these considerations, Yoshinobu's decision was not so surprising after all" (p. 386).
36. *Meiji tennō ki*, 1, p. 527.
37. Elizabeth Longford, *Queen Victoria*, p. 61.
38. Ashikaga Takauji assumed the office of shogun in 1338, and the last Ashikaga shogun, Yoshiaki, resigned in 1588. This means that there were fifteen years without a shogun between 1588 and 1603, but during most of this period Toyotomi Hideyoshi was shogun in all but name.
39. *Meiji tennō ki*, 1, p. 560. For a fuller account, see Tada, ed., *Iwakura*, 2, p. 60.
40. Satow, *A Diplomat*, p. 324. The original text (in *kambun*) is in *Meiji tennō ki*, 1, p. 595. The message was delivered to the ministers of six countries by Higashikuze Michitomi. The use of the plural in the translation is, of course, the royal "we." For an analysis of a similar, but far from identical, imperial proclamation announcing that the emperor had abolished the office of shogun and that he would decide both internal and external matters once they have passed meetings of *dōmei reppan*, see also Sasaki Suguru, *Boshin sensō*, pp. 17–18.

Chapter 14

1. *Meiji tennō ki*, 1, p. 541.
2. Income was calculated in terms of rice; a *koku* was about 5.1 bushels.
3. Ōhashi Akio, *Gotō Shōjirō to kindai Nihon*, p. 118.
4. *Meiji tennō ki*, 1, p. 532. They seem to have had some success: Asahiko was de-

prived of his title *shinnō* in September 1868 for having attempted to help the Tokugawa family restore its control over the government (p. 793).

5. *Meiji tennō ki*, 1, pp. 531–32. Iwakura was accompanied on this occasion by Nakaoka Shintarō.

6. For details, see Marius B. Jansen, *Sakamoto Ryōma and the Meiji Restoration*, pp. 343–44, and *Meiji tennō ki*, 1, pp. 545–46. It is not clear who sent the assassins, although it has been suggested it was probably a "hit squad" of the shogunate.

7. Construction had started on October 19 (*Meiji tennō ki*, 1, p. 516). The shogunate had raised the needed money by levying a tax of 3 percent on each 100 *koku* of village income throughout the country (p. 528).

8. Paper currency, valid for two years, was issued by the shogunate on December 14 (*Meiji tennō ki*, 1, p. 548). These questions were four of eight specific points raised at this time (pp. 532–33).

9. Tokugawa Yoshinobu's recollections of the inexperienced court are related in Ōkubo Toshiaki, *Sekimukai hikki*, p. 271.

10. *Meiji tennō ki*, 1, pp. 532–33. The text of the edict is on p. 534.

11. Sir Ernest Satow, *A Diplomat in Japan*, p. 285. Satow dates this impression December 7, 1867.

12. Ishii Takashi, *Boshin sensō ron*, p. 74.

13. This description of the contents of Nishi's *Gidai sōan* is derived from ibid., pp. 75–76.

14. Quoted in ibid., p. 77.

15. The term in Japanese is *taikun no monaruki* (Ishii, *Boshin*, p. 78).

16. In *Boshin*, Ishii favored the former view. Sasaki Suguru expressed the later interpretation in *Boshin sensō*, pp. 11–12. A similar view was expressed in Haraguchi Kiyoshi, *Boshin sensō*, p. 45.

17. The text of the proclamation and other details are given in *Meiji tennō ki*, 1, pp. 557–60. See also Ishii, *Boshin*, p. 86. The three titles, all created at this time, were short-lived. The office of *sōsai*, established in January 1869 and abolished in May, was a supervisory post filled by a prince. It was one of the three highest posts (*sanshoku*).The office of *gijō*, created at the same time, was an administrative office filled by a prince, a *kōshaku*, or a daimyo. At first it was one of the *sanshoku*, but after the *sanshoku* were abolished, four *gijō* were appointed to supervisory posts. The office of *san'yo* (counselors), created in January 1868 as the third of the *sanshoku*, was filled by nobles, daimyos, and retainers with supervisory duties over all branches of the government. It was abolished in August 1869.

18. This summary of Yōdō's statement is a conflation of materials in Shibusawa Eiichi, *Tokugawa Yoshinobu-kō den*, 4, p. 127, and *Meiji tennō ki*, 1, p. 561. The most detailed account of the meeting is found in Tada Kōmon, ed., *Iwakura-kō jikki*, 2, pp. 157–61. Ishii, not citing sources, wrote that Yōdō "roared" (*dogō*) his anger over the underhanded way in which *ōsei fukkō* had been brought about. Ishii attributed Yōdō's overbearing manner to chronic alcoholism (*Boshin*, pp. 86–87).

19. Tada, ed., *Iwakura*, 2, p. 159.

20. Ibid., 2, p. 159. See also Shibusawa, *Tokugawa*, 4, p. 127.

21. This probably meant that he would suffer a reduction of one degree in his court rank, not that he would totally deprived of rank. Yoshinobu's court rank was junior

second rank. The return of land was expected to bring the government 2 million *koku* of Yoshinobu's income of 4 million *koku*, but Yoshinobu later told envoys of the court that the shogunate's income was not, as supposed, 4 million *koku* but only 2 million *koku* (Shibusawa, *Tokugawa*, 4, p. 132; Ōkubo Toshiaki, *Iwakura Tomomi*, p. 207).

22. Tada, ed., *Iwakura*, 2, pp. 159–60; Shibusawa, *Tokugawa*, 4, pp. 127–28. Iwakura began his impassioned address by conceding that Tokugawa Ieyasu's benefits to the country had not been insignificant, but he deplored the many offenses of Ieyasu's successors and especially the shogunate's actions since the arrival of the foreigners in 1853.

23. Tada, ed., *Iwakura*, 2, p. 160; *Meiji tennō ki*, 1, p. 562; Sasaki, *Boshin sensō*, p. 14. Ōkubo's speech, as summarized in Shibusawa, *Tokugawa*, 4, p. 128, does not call for subjugating Yoshinobu if he failed to obey the court.

24. Tada, ed., *Iwakura*, 2, p. 160.

25. Ōkubo, *Iwakura*, p. 208. Similar accounts are in Mōri Toshihiko, *Iwakura Tomomi*, p. 83; Inoue Kiyoshi, *Saigō Takamori*, 2, p. 52; and Ikai Takaaki, *Saigō Takamori*, p. 22. Neither *Meiji tennō ki* nor *Iwakura-kō jikki* mentions Saigō's remark.

26. This is the view of Ishii, who wonders whether Gotō did not see the post of *san'yo* flickering before his eyes (*Boshin*, p. 88). Gotō was in fact appointed as a *san'yo* on the twelfth day of the twelfth month, along with fourteen other men from five domains—Satsuma, Owari, Aki, Echizen, and Tosa (*Meiji tennō ki*, 1, p. 565).

27. Shibusawa, *Tokugawa*, 4, p. 132. See also *Meiji tennō ki*, 1, pp. 562–63, and Tada, ed., *Iwakura*, 2, p. 162.

28. *Meiji tennō ki*, 1, p. 569. Satow wrote, "He [Yoshinobu] began by explaining his policy, vindicating his retirement from Kiōto, and expressing his determination to abide by the decisions of a general council. His reply to the particular question asked by the ministers was that foreigners should not trouble themselves about the internal affairs of Japan, and that until the form of government was settled he regarded the conduct of Foreign Affairs as his own function" (*A Diplomat*, p. 304).

29. Apparently a reference to Iwakura, Sanjō, and others who were exiled during the reign of Emperor Kōmei.

30. The summary and translation represent a conflation of *Meiji tennō ki*, 1, pp. 571–72, and Tada, ed., *Iwakura*, 2, pp. 187–88. The latter purportedly presents Yoshinobu's text as composed, but it is too prolix to be quoted here.

31. *Boshin* was the cyclical designation for the year 1868.

32. For details, see Shibusawa, *Tokugawa*, 4, pp. 167–68. In a more recent account, Ikai Takaaki attributes the incidents to Sagara Sōzō, acting under orders from Saigō (*Saigō Takamori*, p. 25). See also *Meiji tennō ki*, 1, p. 581, where Saigō and Ōkubo Toshimichi are jointly given responsibility. Not all the incidents were the work of *rōnin*; some were committed by bandits who only pretended to be *rōnin* (*Meiji tennō ki*, 1, p. 574).

33. Rumors circulated at this time that the *rōnin*, taking advantage of this and other fires they had set, had abducted the widows of two previous shoguns (Iemochi and Iesada), and carried them off to Satsuma (Inoue, *Saigō*, 2, p. 61). Because Tenshō-in, the widow of Iesada, had originally been from Satsuma, it was also rumored that she was in contact with Satsuma samurai and had helped them burn

the castle (Shibusawa, *Tokugawa*, 4, pp. 168–69). Satow heard the same rumor: "The Satsuma people had contrived to set a part of the castle on fire, and carried off Tenshō-In Sama, a princess of theirs who had married the last Tycoon but one. Thereupon the government people attacked all the Satsuma *yashikis* in Yedo and burnt them, and the occupants getting on board their steamer put to sea" (*A Diplomat*, p. 309). Note that in this citation Satow refers to the supporters of the shogun as "the government."

34. *Meiji tennō ki*, 1, p. 575. The English seem not to have been impressed by the uniforms. Satow described a similar drill: "Their uniform was in imitation of European style, black trousers with red stripes down the side, and black coats; happy the soldier who could muster a pair of boots, the rest had only straw sandals. On their heads they had hats of papier-maché, either conical or of dish-cover shape, with two horizontal red bands. They used the English infantry drill, with the quaint addition of a shout to indicate the discharge of their firearms" (*A Diplomat*, p. 263).

35. Inoue, *Saigō*, 2, p. 59.

36. Ibid., 2, p. 65.

37. The memorandum consisted of eight points, mainly dealing with where the emperor should be moved, who should accompany him, who should remain in Kyōto, and so on. For the text, see Tada, ed., *Iwakura*, 2, pp. 231–32.

38. Inoue, *Saigō*, 2, p. 65. See also *Meiji tennō ki*, 1, p. 583. Asukai Masamichi provides an additional twist: the imperial palanquin would be sent off toward Hiei-zan, to make the shogun's forces suppose the emperor had escaped in that direction (*Meiji taitei*, p. 117).

39. For example, in 1159 Emperor Nijō, disguised as a woman, left his palace to seek safety with Taira no Kiyomori at Rokuhara. The incident is described in *Heiji monogatari*.

40. Sasaki, *Boshin*, p. 23.

41. Ishii, *Boshin*, p. 66.

42. A sword bestowed by the emperor on the commander of an army when he sets out to do battle.

43. *Meiji tennō ki*, 1, p. 585. The shogun was known as *seii taishōgun* (great general, conqueror of barbarians)," but in this instance the commanding general was charged with conquering the east, the stronghold of the Tokugawa shoguns.

44. Sasaki, *Boshin*, p. 26.

45. Satow gives a brief but unflattering description of Yoshiaki: "Just after leaving the prince's residence we were stopped in the road to let Ninnaji no Miya pass. He was on horseback, a stoutish, swarthy, thick-lipped young man, with his hair just beginning to sprout; for until recently he had been in the Buddhist priesthood" (*A Diplomat*, p. 357).

46. In a letter dated April 7, 1867, to Tsuchimochi Masateru, Saigō characterized himself as *ikusa zuki*—someone who loves war (Ikai, *Saigō*, p. 28).

47. Sasaki, *Boshin*, p. 27.

48. It has been claimed that Yoshinobu mistakenly boarded the American ship, unable to distinguish it in the dark from the *Kaiyō maru*, but it is generally agreed that he knew it was the *Iroquois* (Ishii, *Boshin*, pp. 106–7).

49. Shibusawa, *Tokugawa*, 4, p. 190; Sasaki, *Boshin*, p. 30.

Chapter 15

1. *Meiji tennō ki*, 1, pp. 595–96.
2. Sir Ernest Satow, *A Diplomat in Japan*, p. 324.
3. The text is in *Meiji tennō ki*, 1, p. 596. See also Ishii Takashi, *Boshin sensō ron*, p. 114. Satow stated that "a notification, signed by Iwashita, Itō and Terashima, as officers of the Foreign Department, was placarded about the town, informing the people that the Mikado would observe the treaties, and enjoining on them proper behaviour towards foreigners" (*A Diplomat*, p. 326). He may have been referring to a separate document, sent on February 16 to the ministers of the different countries.
4. *Meiji tennō ki*, 1, pp. 600–601. The intended recipient of the letter, Hashimoto Saneyana (1834–1885), had already left for the east. Princess Chikako's messenger found him at Kuwana. Hashimoto, extremely moved by the letter, gave it to the messenger to take back to Kyōto and show it to the *san'yo* Madenokōji Hirofusa for consideration by the Court Council.
5. Ishii, *Boshin*, pp. 120–1.
6. Ibid., p. 123.
7. Ibid., p. 124.
8. *Meiji tennō ki*, 1, p. 618. Kōgen was the Buddhist name of the ninth son of Fushiminomiya Kuniie. He was more commonly known at this time as Prince Yoshihisa or Rinnōjinomiya.
9. *Meiji tennō ki*, 1, p. 603. Mention of a monarch mingling with the common people probably refers to Queen Victoria, though it was also true of King Louis Philippe.
10. *Meiji tennō ki*, 1, pp. 602–3.
11. Ibid., 1, p. 611. The only previous time he had left the Gosho was when a fire consumed most of the palace.
12. *Meiji tennō ki*, 1, p. 627.
13. Ibid., 1, p. 628.
14. Satow, *A Diplomat*, p. 337.
15. Ibid., pp. 347, 353; *Meiji tennō ki*, 1, p. 630.
16. Satow, *A Diplomat*, p. 347. Satow's colleague A. B. Mitford (later Lord Redesdale) was of a different opinion. He heard from the French officers who were present "to witness the horror" that "when the first condemned man came out he plunged the dirk into his stomach with such force that his entrails protruded; he held them up in his hand and began singing verses of hatred and revenge against the detested foreigners who were polluting the sacred soil of the Land of the Gods till death stopped his ghastly song" (Redesdale, *Memories of Lord Redesdale*, p. 446). According to what Mitford heard, after eleven men had died in this way, "the French could hold out no longer, and Captain du Petit Thouars prayed the nine remaining men might be spared."
17. The term is better known in the West as *harakiri*. Purists in Japanese prefer *kappuku*. But regardless of name, the act consisted of drawing a dagger deeply across the abdomen to reveal that the intestines were free of impurity.
18. Satow described the incident in Kōbe during which members of the Bizen Domain under Taki Zenzaburō's command fired on foreigners, killing an American

sailor (A *Diplomat*, pp. 319–20, 344). Taki subsequently was ordered to commit *seppuku*.

19. Satow, *A Diplomat*, pp. 346–47.

20. Roches was the senior diplomatic officer in terms of service in Japan. Van Pols-broek, although of lesser rank, may have been granted an audience ahead of Parkes because of the long-standing relationship between Japan and Holland.

21. Also known as Yamashinanomiya (1816–1898). The eldest son of Fushiminomiya, he entered Buddhist orders at the age of eight (in 1824) but returned to the laity and worked actively for the Restoration. Mitford, who met him shortly before he was presented to the emperor, left this description: "The Prince was robed in the old court dress of a purple colour with the curious cap (*yéboshi*) of wrinkled black paper. His teeth were blackened, but as that process has to be renewed every two, or at most three, days, and as they were at that moment in a transition stage, they did not look their best. When we saw him again a few days later they had been newly polished up, and shone like patent leather" (Redesdale, *Memories*, p. 447).

22. *Meiji tennō ki*, 1, p. 635.

23. Satow, *A Diplomat*, p. 359. Another account of the attack on the British party is given by Mitford. One passage is particularly memorable: "I heard pistol shots and the clatter of swords and cries of, 'We are attacked!' 'Kill him!' 'Shoot him!' and the like. I jumped out of my palanquin more quickly than I ever in my life have jumped out of anything, and rushed forward. There were pools of blood in the street, and I saw the murderer coming at me, by this time himself wounded, but not seriously, and full of fight. His sword was dripping and his face bleeding, I knew enough of Japanese swordsmanship to be aware that it was no use to try and avoid his blow, so I rushed in underneath his guard and wrenched the bleed-ing sword out of his grip. I handed him over to the men of the 9th [regiment], but he managed to wriggle away from them and bolted down a passage into a courtyard, I ran to see whether Parkes was safe. To my great relief he was sitting on a horse, quite unmoved, with Satow, whose pony was bleeding, also mercifully unhurt. As I came up with them I stumbled over something; it was a man's head" (Redesdale, *Memories*, p. 450).

On the first day of the ninth month, the queen of England bestowed swords on Gotō and Nakai for having saved the life of the British minister (*Meiji tennō ki*, 1, p. 639).

24. Satow, *A Diplomat*, p. 360. A photograph was taken of this priest, whose name was Saegusa Shigeru, two hours before he was executed. He glares at the camera with no visible trace of penitence. Mitford, who conversed with his would-be murderer after he was captured, also mentioned the prisoner's reiterated wish to have his head cut off as soon as possible (Redesdale, *Memories*, pp. 452–53). A photograph of the severed head of the other assailant, Hayashida Sadakata, is on the facing page of *Yomigaeru bakumatsu*, pp. 164–65. On April 15 the heads of Saegusa and Hayashida were exposed, and three men who were accused of being accomplices were exiled to Oki. Three days later, a proclamation was issued warn-ing people against attacking foreigners and stating that this was not only in defi-ance of the wishes of the court but was harmful to the prestige of the emperor and likely to lead to international conflicts (Redesdale, *Memories*, pp. 455–56; *Meiji tennō ki*, 1, p. 639).

25. *Meiji tennō ki*, 1, p. 636.
26. Satow, *A Diplomat*, p. 361.
27. Redesdale, *Memories*, pp. 451–52.
28. Satow could not accompany them to the palace because, as Mitford explained, "not having at that time been presented at our own Court, could not, according to etiquette, be presented to a foreign sovereign" (Redesdale, *Memories*, p. 458).
29. Redesdale, *Memories*, pp. 456, 457.
30. The "blue blood" of the aristocrat.
31. Redesdale, *Memories*, pp. 459–60.
32. *Meiji tennō ki*, 1, p. 638.
33. Redesdale, *Memories*, p. 461. Itō Shunsuke is, of course, Itō Hirobumi. He had gone to England in 1863 to study and had acquired a good command of English.
34. The Shinsengumi, a group of handpicked *rōnin* soldiers, was founded in 1863 by the shogunate mainly to suppress *jōi* activity in Kyōto. Members of the Shinsengumi crushed the plotters at the Ikeda-ya in 1864. Even after the defeat at Toba and Fushimi, the members continued to fight fiercely for the former shogun. Although unsuccessful in most of its encounters with the imperial forces, it acquired a special aura and has been much written about, no doubt because of the extreme loyalty its members displayed for a lost cause. For a contemporary account of the battle, see Shin jimbutsu ōrai sha, ed., *Shinsengumi shiryō shū*, pp. 205–14.
35. Ishii, *Boshin*, pp. 126–27.
36. *Meiji tennō ki*, 1, p. 589. This text gives *miya-san*, rather than *miya-sama*, as sung in the Gilbert and Sullivan operetta. The meaning is something like "Your Excellency, your Excellency, what is it that fluttering before your horse?" *tokoton'yare ton'yare na*. "That's the brocade pennant given me with the command, 'Conquer the *chōteki*!' Don't you recognize it?"

Chapter 16

1. In ancient times, the word *matsurigoto* designated both worship of the gods and the government of the country. The edict was printed in *Daijōkan nisshi* (The Daily Record of the Ministry of State), first published on February 12, 1868. Copies were sent to the administrative office of each domain and each region of direct shogunal control (*Meiji tennō ki*, 1, p. 632; Asukai Masamichi, *Meiji taitei*, p. 128).

    The revival of Shinto led to many instances of burning and destruction of Buddhist texts, works of art, and sacred implements that had been preserved at Shinto shrines, leading the government to forbid Shinto priests to indulge in such wanton behavior (*Meiji tennō ki*, 1, pp. 665–66).

2. *Meiji tennō ki*, 1, p. 646. Those who did not wish to yield their Buddhist positions were ordered to make a separate application. On April 21 a decree was issued prohibiting the mixture of Shinto and Buddhism. Buddhist images, known as the "original substances" (*honji*) of Shinto gods, were to be removed immediately from Shinto shrines along with Buddhist ritual implements, temple bells, gongs, and so on. There were even voices raised calling for the prohibition of Buddhism (*Meiji tennō ki*, 1, p. 663).

3. The earliest example of *honji suijaku* thought seems to date from 937, when two gods were declared to be avatars of bodhisattvas. In time it was claimed that every

god was an avatar of one or another buddha or bodhisattva. Most of the "original substances" of the different gods proved to be the thirteen buddhas of Shingon Buddhism. Shinto worship came to include the incantations, ritual fire ceremonies, charms, signs, and methods of instruction of Shingon Buddhism. The most important form of union between Buddhism and Shinto was called *ryōbu shintō*, a term derived from the equation made between the two mandalas of Shingon Buddhism and the Inner and Outer Shrines at Ise.

4. The term *haibutsu kishaku* (abolish Buddhism and destroy Shakyamuni) was frequently used during this period, though the official policy was one of separating the two religions, not of destroying Buddhism. For a study in English of the persecution of Buddhism during the Meiji period, see James Edward Ketelaar, *Of Heretics and Martyrs in Meiji Japan.*

5. The traditional position of the emperor according to the Chinese cosmogony was in the north, facing his ministers and vassals to the south.

6. The text of this Shinto prayer of dedication is in *Meiji tennō ki*, 1, p. 648. It describes the circumstances of the occasion leading up to the vow that the emperor is about to pronounce.

7. The first draft by Yuri Kimimasa, the revisions made by Fukuoka Takachika, and the suggestions of Kido Takayoshi are given in detail in *Meiji tennō ki*, 1, pp. 652–55.

8. Tōyama Shigeki, *Meiji ishin*, pp. 192–93. Tōyama believed that the Charter Oath and similar, seemingly liberal measures promulgated at the beginning of Emperor Meiji's reign were "no more than anesthetics to relieve the birth-pangs of sending into the world emperor-system absolutism, and was typical of an era antedating that of enlightened despotism." He also gave more concrete criticism of the oath: for example, he stated that Yuri Kimimasa's mention in the third article of the common people being allowed to pursue their own calling meant only that for financial reasons, rich merchants and rich farmers would be allowed a measure of voice in the government. Tanaka Akira dismissed the first article of the oath as being no more than a slogan that was gradually consigned to oblivion (*Mikan no Meiji ishin*, pp. 24–28). He believed also that its liberal tone was inspired by the need to convince foreign countries, in the wake of various acts of violence against foreigners in Japan, that the new government was enlightened. Tanaka also quoted a document written by Kume Kunitake stating that in 1872 Kido seemed to have almost completely forgotten the oath that he had had a hand in writing, an indication that he did not consider it to be of much importance.

9. When on June 19 reforms were made in the administration, it was stated that their objectives were in consonance with the Charter Oath (*Meiji tennō ki*, 1, p. 708). In addition, Tanaka states that the leaders of the Freedom and Popular Rights Party admired the democratic character of the Charter Oath (*Mikan*, p. 28).

10. *Meiji tennō ki*, 1, p. 649.

11. Ibid., 1, pp. 649–52.

12. Tanaka, *Mikan*, p. 28.

13. Sir Ernest Satow, *A Diplomat in Japan*, pp. 365–66.

14. *Meiji tennō ki*, 1, p. 671.

15. Ibid., 1, p. 661.

16. This opinion was not necessarily shared by people of the time. For example, Kido Takayoshi wrote in his diary, "If the current situation prevails for another year that the Realm will be reduced to poverty goes without saying, and in the end Imperial rule cannot be established" (Sidney DeVere Brown and Akiko Hirota, trans., *The Diary of Kido Takayoshi*, 1, p. 32). This is only one of several gloomy predictions Kido made concerning the outcome of the fighting.

17. More commonly known as Akira Shinnō (1816–1898), the eldest of Fushiminomiya's many sons. He entered the priesthood at the age of eight but returned to the laity in 1864 to found the house of Yamashinanomiya. In 1866 he, along with Iwakura Tomomi and others, was sentenced to house arrest for his political actions. After the Restoration, he became a *gijō* and at this time was *gaikoku jimu sōtoku*.

18. Satow, *A Diplomat*, pp. 370–71. The account of the audience given in Japanese sources contains one detail not mentioned by Satow: when Sir Harry Parkes presented the letter from Queen Victoria to the emperor, he seemed so overcome with reverence and awe that Prince Akira had to support him (*Meiji tennō ki*, 1, p. 686). This certainly does not sound like the Sir Harry we know from other descriptions.

19. Ōkubo Toshimichi nikki, 1, p. 452. See also Asukai, *Meiji taitei*, p. 125.

20. Brown and Hirota, trans., *Diary*, 1, p. 12.

21. Asukai, *Meiji taitei*, p. 125. The text of Yokoi's remarks is given somewhat differently in *Meiji tennō ki*, 1, pp. 705–6.

22. *Meiji tennō ki*, 1, p. 670.

23. See the excerpt of a letter from Ōkubo to Kido, dated May 23, quoted in Asukai, *Meiji taitei*, p. 126. See also Ōkubo's memorandum proposing the moving of the capital to Ōsaka in Tōyama Shigeki, *Tennō to kazoku*, pp. 6–8.

Chapter 17

1. The text is in Tōyama Shigeki, *Tennō to kazoku*, p. 9. The proclamation was issued on June 13, 1868 (*Meiji tennō ki*, 1, p. 705).

2. The *kōkyū*, often called simply *oku*, the emperor's private quarters, presided over by female officials; what might be called the seraglio in other parts of the world.

3. "At eight" (*tatsu no koku*) is supplied from another text (Tōyama, *Tennō*, p. 9).

4. Men in the highest posts of the bureaucracy at the time; Iwakura Tomomi and Sanjō Sanetomi were concomitantly *gijō* and *hoshō*.

5. *Hakkei no ma*, the office of the *hoshō*, so called because of the paintings of Eight Views, perhaps the Eight Views of Ōmi. *Meiji tennō ki* amplifies the text by adding a phrase to suggest that the emperor would go to the *hoshō*'s office in order to observe him busily engaged in state affairs.

6. This seems a clear indication, not provided elsewhere, that by this time Meiji smoked.

7. Personal attendants of the emperor, a new office, established at this time. The regulations provided (1) that they never divulge any matter revealed in the imperial presence, (2) that they not permit direct appeals on state matters that had not passed through the proper channels, (3) that they absolutely refrain from vulgar or impolite speech or action in the imperial presence, and (4) that (it goes without

saying) they never while on duty, day or night, presume in the slightest on the imperial benevolence and thereby profane the imperial dignity or flaunt their authority inside or outside the palace. The remaining six regulations dealt with the performance of their duties (*Meiji tennō ki*, 1, pp. 706–7). Other provisos enumerated the qualifications the *kinjū* were expected to possess. It was difficult to find members of the nobility who fulfilled all the demands, but ten were eventually chosen. For the names, see p. 707.

8. The paraphrase is in *Meiji tennō ki*, 1, pp. 705–6.

9. Sir Ernest Satow wrote that he had seen several "constitutions," the most recent of which was dated June of that year. He commented, "It showed marked traces of American political theories, and I have little doubt that Okuma and his fellow-clansman Soyéjima, pupils of Dr Verbeck, had had a considerable part in framing it. 'The power and authority of the *Daijōkan* (i.e., government), threefold, legislative, executive and judicial,' was the wording of one article. By another it as provided that 'All officers shall be changed after four years' service. They shall be appointed by a majority of votes given by ballot. When the first period for changing the officers of government arrives, half of the present staff shall be retained for an additional space of two years, in order that there be no interruption of the public business.' In this we seemed to hear an echo of the 'spoils system.' Okuma explained that the 'executive' represented the executive department in the United States Constitution, 'consisting of the president and his advisers,' but that in fact it was the head of the Shinto religion, finance, war and foreign departments" (*A Diplomat in Japan*, p. 377).

10. *Meiji tennō ki*, 1, p. 708. Among the second-rank officials who were given rank at this time were Gotō Shōjirō, Kido Takayoshi, Ōkubo Toshimichi, Soejima Taneomi, and Yokoi Shōnan—a dazzling cluster of brilliant men.

11. In order to provide continuity, however, some of those elected in the first election would serve an additional two years.

12. Iwakura Tomomi asked on September 11 to be sent to the front at the head of 2,000 soldiers from the Saga Domain. In his petition to the throne, he admitted that having been born into a noble family, he had no knowledge of warfare, but he desired all the same to test his wormlike skill in battle with the traitors in the north. He was subsequently dissuaded, but not because of inadequate military training (*Meiji tennō ki*, 1, p. 774).

13. This is the name by which he is called in most documents describing his activities in 1868, but I shall refer to him as Rinnōjinomiya, the name by which he was best known during the entire period.

14. *Meiji tennō ki*, 1, p. 618. See also Arima Yorichika, "Kitashirakawa no miya shōgai," pp. 239–40.

15. Arima, "Kitashirakawa," p. 239.

16. Ibid., p. 240.

17. Arima estimated that someone of Rinnōjinomiya's status would have been escorted by several hundred men ("Kitashirakawa," p. 244).

18. Arima, "Kitashirakawa," p. 241.

19. Mori Ōgai, "Yoshihisa shinnō jiseki," in *Ōgai zenshū*, p. 516.

20. Arima, "Kitashirakawa," p. 242. Virtually the identical account is in Mori Ōgai, "Yoshihisa," p. 516.

21. Mori Ōgai, "Yoshihisa," p. 517.

22. Arima expressed the belief that Iwakura Tomomi was afraid that Rinnōjinomiya might influence the emperor and interfere with his plans for taking Edo Castle. Arima was convinced that Iwakura was determined not to let Edo Castle be attacked, even though the expeditionary army had been sent to the east, because he thought Katsu Kaishū, the chief negotiator in the castle, was too valuable a man to be sacrificed ("Kitashirakawa," p. 247).

23. Takigawa Masajirō, "Shirarezaru tennō," p. 125.

24. Arima, "Kitashirakawa," p. 249.

25. Ibid., p. 250. See also Shibusawa Eiichi, *Tokugawa Yoshinobu-kō den*, 4, pp. 247, 248.

26. Arima, "Kitashirakawa," p. 250.

27. Mori Ōgai, "Yoshihisa," p. 532.

28. Ibid., p. 533.

29. Ibid., p. 535. For a description of the prince's disguise (as a physician on his way to a sick man's residence), see p. 536.

30. *Meiji tennō ki*, 1, p. 736.

31. Takigawa, "Shirarezaru," p. 126. Takigawa wrote that he had heard this directly from the late Dr. Osatake Takeshi. He himself had not seen the document, but he had the highest respect for Osatake as a source of information.

32. The prince's title as "emperor" was *tōbu*, or "Eastern Warrior."

33. *Meiji tennō ki*, 1, p. 736. Satow must have heard rumors to this effect. He wrote, "Rinōji no Miya, the imperial prince who had always resided there in the character of abbot, and whom the recalcitrant Tokugawa men talked of raising to the throne as Mikado, was carried off by the survivors at the end of the day" (*A Diplomat*, p. 375).

34. The oath was called *shiroishi meiyaku sho* (for details, see Sasaki Suguru, *Boshin sensō*, pp. 115–23). See also Ishii Takashi, *Ishin no nairan*, pp. 122–27.

35. Sasaki, *Boshin*, p. 131.

36. An artist of historical portraits. His *Senken kojitsu*, portraying more than 500 illustrious people (including emperors, loyal retainers, and heroic women) with commentary, covers the 2,000 years from Emperor Jimmu to Emperor Gomurakami. It was published between 1836 and 1868.

37. Sasaki, *Boshin*, p. 132. The name *tōbu*—Eastern Warrior (the homonym of *tōbu*, eastern region)—indicates that he was emperor of only the eastern part of the country, leaving the west to Meiji. According to Kikuchi, however, he was known as *kōtei*, the term used for foreign kings or emperors, rather than as *tennō*.

38. Mori Ōgai, "Yoshihisa," p. 546.

39. Ibid., p. 553.

40. Ibid., p. 557. On February 14, 1872, he was promoted to *sanbon*, a high rank in the *kōzoku*. On the same day, his brother Prince Asahiko, an equally ambiguous figure, was also named *sanbon*. Tokugawa Yoshinobu was appointed the junior fourth rank, and Date Yoshikuni, who had been "acting great general quelling barbarians" during the short-lived reign of Emperor Tōbu, was appointed to the junior fifth rank. The government's leniency was all but incredible.

41. *Meiji tennō ki*, 1, pp. 792–93. For a more detailed account of Asahiko's plot, see Shibusawa, *Tokugawa*, 4, pp. 268–69.

42. *Meiji tennō ki*, 2, p. 623.
43. Ibid., 1, p. 927.
44. For an account of the creation, international relations, and fall of Enomoto's government, see Ishii, *Ishin*, pp. 204–49.
45. William Elliot Griffis, *The Mikado*, p. 182. I have not identified the protagonists of this attempt.
46. *Meiji tennō ki*, 2, pp. 422–24.
47. Griffis, *Mikado*, p. 184.
48. *Meiji tennō ki*, 2, pp. 603–4.
49. Ishii, *Boshin*, p. 149.
50. Ishii says that if the peasant revolts in the northeast had been directed against the government, the result of the war between the government and the rebels of the Nagaoka Domain would have been hard to predict, but they were directed against the *shōya* instead (*Ishin*, p. 149).
51. For example, on August 12, 1868, he personally presented Prince Yoshiaki, who was about to leave for Aizu, as commanding general of the punitive expeditionary force, with the brocade pennant that symbolized imperial authorization (*Meiji tennō ki*, 1, p. 754). Again, on August 22 he sent an envoy to the north with a personal message meant to comfort the troops and ordinary people suffering because of the fighting. Saké and food were also sent to the military as a gift of the emperor (p. 757). Similar gifts intended to "comfort" the troops continued as long as the fighting lasted.

Chapter 18

1. *Meiji tennō ki*, 1, p. 794.
2. The globe in fact figured prominently in the coronation ceremonies (*Meiji tennō ki*, 1, p. 805).
3. *Meiji tennō ki*, 1, p. 796. The prayers were not answered, for it rained heavily during the ceremonies.
4. The imperial regalia consisted of a sword, a mirror, and a *magatama* jewel. The mirror was normally enshrined at Ise, but the other two treasures were in the emperor's possession.
5. A wooden stick to which were attached strips of paper or cloth. A priest waved the stick before a person in order to drive off baleful influences.
6. Literally, a reader of the *senmyō*. A *senmyō* was an imperial command, written in words of purely Japanese origins. The *senmyō-shi* on this occasion was Reizei Tametada.
7. *Meiji tennō ki*, 1, p. 812. This poem of felicitation is number 344 in the *Kokinshū*.
8. *Meiji tennō ki*, 1, p. 812.
9. Ibid., 1, p. 804. The term *tenchō* was part of the formula *tenchō chikyū*, wishing the emperor life as long as the heavens and as lasting as the earth. After the adoption of the solar calendar in 1873, Tenchō-setsu came to be celebrated on November 3, converting the day of Meiji's birth in 1852 from the lunar to the solar calendar. However, in 1868 the birthday according to the solar calendar was November 6. Sir Ernest Satow wrote, "November 6th was celebrated with much

pomp and ceremony as being the Mikado's birthday" (A Diplomat in Japan, p. 386).

10. The reasons for this decision were not stated. Probably, as Japanese became familiar with the Western system of designating years, the Japanese system of frequently changed nengō came to seem inefficient.

11. Meiji tennō ki, 1, p. 787.

12. Ibid., 1, p. 814.

13. Satow wrote in his diary, "On the 23rd [of August 1868] I dined with Komatsu [Tatewaki] and Nakai [Hiroshi] to meet Okubo, the Satsuma statesman who had suggested the removal of the Capital from Kiōto to Ozaka earlier in the year. I have no doubt that the final decision to make Yedo the centre of government, and to change its name to Tōkiō or Eastern Capital was largely his work" (A Diplomat, p. 380). In February 1868, Ōkubo stated his reasons for advocating a move of the capital to Ōsaka. He later came to prefer Tōkyō (Tōyama Shigeki, Tennō to kazoku, pp. 6–8).

14. Satow, A Diplomat, p. 366.

15. Meiji tennō ki, 1, p. 838.

16. Ibid., 1, p. 839.

17. Ibid., 1, p. 847. Tada Kōmon gives another anecdote strikingly similar in content (Iwakura-kō jikki, 2, p. 570). On November 6, when the emperor's palanquin reached Ishibe, a station on the Tōkaidō, Date Munenari, going to a rice field by the side of the road, picked five stalks and offered them to the emperor with the following poem: kimi mimase / itsuki no ame no / furisugite / kariho no ine no / torimi sukunaki. Both anecdotes and poems have the same meaning: they were intended to inform the emperor, who had never before seen peasants toiling in the fields, of the hardships they suffered because of the poor harvest.

18. Tada, ed., Iwakura, 2, p. 572.

19. Meiji tennō ki, 1, p. 852. The point of the poem is the pun on Arai, the name of a nearby town, and arai, meaning "rough." Although the name suggests a rough crossing, it was actually smooth.

20. Meiji tennō ki, 1, p. 865.

21. Ibid., 1, pp. 865–66.

22. This was the opinion of Iwakura Tomomi (Meiji tennō ki, 1, p. 906).

23. Kinoshita Hyō, Meiji shiwa, p. 3.

24. Meiji tennō ki, 1, p. 906.

25. Ibid., 1, pp. 905, 913. On February 20, 1869, the dispatch of Akitake to the north was called off, on the grounds that rebel forces had suffered such severe setbacks that their submission was imminent; but plans for his going to Hokkaidō had advanced so far that Akitake petitioned to be allowed to leave as planned. He in fact left early the next month (Meiji tennō ki, 2, p. 11).

26. Kinoshita, Meiji shiwa, p. 12.

27. Satow, A Diplomat, p. 404.

28. Meiji tennō ki, 1, p. 915.

29. Ibid., 1, pp. 917–19.

30. Taki Kōji's Tennō no shōzō, an extremely interesting account of how the image of the emperor was presented to the people, describes the variety of colored prints (nishikie) produced in conjunction with the emperor's journey to the east. These

prints sold quite well, especially those showing the emperor entering Tōkyō, and provided the common people with a kind of political experience (pp. 9–11).

Chapter 19

1. It would be more accurate to say "the second year of Meiji" rather than 1869. The discrepancy between the lunar and the solar calendar is particularly noticeable at New Year, for the first day of the lunar calendar was February 11 by the solar calendar.
2. *Meiji tennō ki*, 2, p. 4.
3. At this time most imperial pronouncements were written by Tamamatsu Misao (1810–1872) (*Meiji tennō ki*, 2, p. 19).
4. *Meiji tennō ki*, 2, p. 7. The text of their charges against Yokoi is in Morikawa Tetsurō, *Meiji ansatsu shi*, p. 29. One of the assassins, Ueda Tatsuo, was particularly incensed because Yokoi had been seen wandering around the Tsukiji foreign quarter wearing Western clothes and a foreign-style hat.
5. For the development of practical learning in China and Japan, see Wm. Theodore de Bary and Irene Bloom, *Principle and Practicality*, pp. 189–511.
6. H. D. Harootunian, *Toward Restoration*, p. 335.
7. George B. Sansom, *The Western World and Japan*, p. 283.
8. Translated by Paul Varley as *A Chronicle of Gods and Sovereigns*.
9. Diary entry, October 9, 1868, in Sidney DeVere Brown and Akiko Hirota, trans., *The Diary of Kido Takayoshi*, p. 105.
10. The *gijō* Nakamikado Tsuneyuki sent a message to this effect to Iwakura Tomomi on May 10, 1869. He stated that the emperor was now riding every other day and urged that he confine his riding to the prescribed six days a month (*Meiji tennō ki*, 2, p. 109).
11. *Meiji tennō ki*, 2, p. 30.
12. German (rather than English or French) was chosen presumably because of the close influence of German law on the evolving new Japanese law. Katō Hiroyuki, one of the emperor's mentors, had studied German and become fluent in that language ("Yo ga jidoku ni measarishi koro," p. 38 [*Taiyō* 18, p. 13]).
13. *Meiji tennō ki*, 2, p. 27.
14. Ibid., 2, p. 44.
15. For details, see Katō Hitoshi, "Meiji tennō o-tsubone go-rakuin den."
16. In "Meiji," Katō discussed the claims made by various persons who believe that they are Meiji's illegitimate descendants, but he was reluctant to admit the validity of these claims.
17. Diary entry, May 19, 1874, in Brown and Hirota, trans., *Diary*, 3, p. 32.
18. Diary entry, August 20, 1875, in ibid., p. 199.
19. Diary entry, October 13, 1876, in ibid., p. 375.
20. Takashima Tomonosuke, "Jinmu irai no eishu," p. 33, quoted in Asukai Masamichi, *Meiji taitei*, p. 148.
21. Quoted in Katō, "Meiji," p. 60.
22. Hinonishi Sukehiro, *Meiji tennō no go-nichijō*, p. 81. Hinonishi also described how after the emperor had been drinking at Count Hijikata's house, he had trouble walking and had to lean on Hinonishi. Unfortunately, Hinonishi was not very

tall, and he found it extremely difficult to keep the heavy emperor under control. They had almost reached their destination when both men fell down (p. 83).

23. Charles Lanman, *Leading Men of Japan*, p. 18.

24. Bōjō Toshinaga, *Kyūchū gojūnen*, pp. 14, 16.

25. Takatsuji Osanaga, "Go-yōji no shinkō," p. 30.

26. Katō, "Yo ga jidoku no measareshi koro," p. 38.

27. Ibid.

28. Ariji Shinanonojō, "Yūsō, kattatsu, saishin, kiken no wataraseraru," p. 52.

Chapter 20

1. *Meiji tennō ki*, 2, p. 10.

2. Tada Kōmon, ed., *Iwakura-kō jikki*, 2, pp. 688–89; *Meiji tennō ki*, 2, p. 31.

3. *Meiji tennō ki*, 2, p. 53.

4. Ibid., 2, p. 55.

5. John R. Black, *Young Japan*, 2, pp. 254–55.

6. It may have been a coincidence, but years later (about 1875) when his tutor, Motoda Nagazane, asked Meiji who of the emperors of most ancient time he most admired, he replied, "Jimmu and Keikō." Both emperors were associated with the foundation and unification of Japan (Yasuba Sueki, "Junchū shisei no taiju Motoda Nagazane sensei," p. 9).

7. *Meiji tennō ki*, 2, pp. 77–78.

8. Ibid., 2, p. 79.

9. As late as May it was reported that the rebels' "craftiness" had prevented the government forces from making headway; but on May 28 they launched a successful land and sea attack.

10. *True Records of Three Reigns*, the last of the six imperially sponsored histories of Japan, compiled in 901.

11. *Meiji tennō ki*, 2, p. 95.

12. Ibid., 2, pp. 97, 109–10. It was reported on July 14 that outside the three main cities (Kyōto, Tōkyō, and Ōsaka) the people still did not trust paper money, and in these cities there was sharp inflation, causing hardship (p. 135).

13. *Meiji tennō ki*, 2, pp. 100–101.

14. Ibid., 2, p. 112.

15. Ibid., 2, p. 108.

16. For his studies, see ibid., 2, pp. 119, 124, 131–32, etc.

17. Ibid., 2, p. 140.

18. Black, *Young Japan*, 2, p. 267.

19. Ibid., 2, pp. 266, 267.

20. F. V. Dickins and S. Lane-Poole, *The Life of Sir Harry Parkes*, 2, pp. 121, 142. The same wording is in Black, *Young Japan*, 2, pp. 267–68. Black seems to have had access to Parkes's letter to the earl of Clarendon, dated August 23, 1869, in which this statement appears. Iwakura's detailed account of the formalities that were to be observed during the duke's visit is in Tada, ed., *Iwakura*, 2, pp. 768–73.

21. Black, *Young Japan*, 2, pp. 268–69.

22. Parkes explained this ceremony: "Kan-jin, literally the God of China. This is the revival of an extremely ancient ceremonial which dates from a time when there was no intercourse with abroad, excepting with China through Korea. Kan-jin is, therefore, the patron saint of foreigners, who are all united under his protection with the generic name of Tōjin, or 'men of the Tang Dynasty of China'" (Dickins and Lane-Poole, *Life of Parkes*, 2, p. 143). A. B. Mitford, who presumably was Parkes's source, uses the identical wording (Redesdale, *Memories of Lord Redesdale*, 2, p. 496). Japanese sources say little about this ceremony and do not explain the term, but *Meiji tennō ki*, 2, p. 159, mentions the *kanjin-sai* performed on the twenty-third of the seventh month; on this occasion, Nakayama Tadayasu read a *norito*. Tada stated that the *kanjin-sai* would be performed several days before the duke arrived (*Iwakura*, 2, p. 768).

23. Redesdale, *Memories*, 2, p. 496. In addition, *A Guide to the Works* states that "by order of the Japanese government, the same mark of respect was paid to His Royal Highness that is observed when an Imperial Progress takes place. The windows of the upper stories of the houses were all sealed with paper, that none might look down upon the Queen's Son" (p. 45).

24. Dickins and Lane-Poole, *Life of Parkes*, 2, p. 143.

25. Redesdale, *Memories*, 2, p. 497.

26. Fukuzawa Yukichi explained the title (and text) in terms of Portman's desire to attract the attention of the president, who was "not in the habit of personally reading the reports of the ministers in foreign lands unless they contained very pertinent or unusual matters" (Kiyooka Eiichi, trans., *The Autobiography of Yukichi Fukuzawa*, pp. 205–6).

27. Watanabe Ikujirō, *Meiji tennō*, 1, p. 104. According to William Elliot Griffis, "At a convenient distance from the hall of audience, rites with wands of *gohéi* and other Shinto appliances were performed by the white robed and black capped priests, in order to exorcise any evil spirits or influences which might have accompanied representatives from such outlandish countries as England and Scotland, which orthodox Shinto commentators taught had been made from the sea foam and mud left over after the creation of the Heavenly Country, Japan, by the ancestors of the Mikado" (*The Mikado*, p. 159).

28. Redesdale, *Memories*, 2, p. 499.

29. Dickins and Lane-Poole, *Life of Parkes*, 2, p. 147.

30. Sir Henry Keppel, *A Sailor's Life Under Four Sovereigns*, 3, pp. 289, 292. Keppel wrote, "Tomorrow we are to have a procession and the Prince's visit to the Mikado, which we look forward to as rather a bore" (p. 289).

31. The gifts included "lacquerware, wakizashi, netsuke, bronzes, pottery, enamels" (*Guide to the Works*, p. 45).

32. *Meiji tennō ki*, 2, p. 168.

33. The entertainment included a Japanese meal (probably more authentic than the food served to visiting dignitaries at present!), sumo, displays of swordsmanship, acrobatics, juggling, and (in a more somber mood) a program of nō and *kyōgen* (*Meiji tennō ki*, 2, p. 165). This was said to be the first time nō had been witnessed by foreigners (Redesdale, *Memories*, 2, p. 498). The program consisted of four nō (*Yumi Yawata*, *Hagoromo*, *Kokaji*, and *Tsunemasa*) and two *kyōgen* (*Suminuri* and *Tachiubai*) (Nakayama Yasumasa, *Meiji hennenshi*, 1, p. 303). Mitford prepared

outlines of the plays to help the duke and his entourage understand them, but it is hard to believe that they sat through these plays in entirety; this would have taken close to ten hours. Perhaps only excerpts were performed. The great actor Hōshō Kurō appeared in *Hagoromo*.

34. Dickins and Lane-Poole, *Life of Parkes*, 2, p. 151. Black commented about the piano, "Whether it has done anything towards reconciling the Imperial ear to foreign music is very doubtful. I have heard it reported more than once that the Empress was taking lessons on the piano—but I gave no credence to the statements" (*Young Japan*, 2, p. 273).

35. Black, *Young Japan*, 2, p. 274. However, the two letters sent by Meiji to the Austrian emperor do not contain any word for "brother" (*Meiji tennō ki*, 2, pp. 190–93). Although it was customary among European monarchs to address one another as "brother" or "cousin," this was not the practice in Japan. Meiji referred to Franz Josef as *kōtei heika*, "His Majesty, the emperor," the same title that would have been applied to the emperor of China.

Chapter 21

1. *Meiji tennō ki*, 2, p. 224.
2. Ibid., 2, p. 221.
3. A highly important ritual, performed by an emperor once in his lifetime, generally in the early winter following his coronation.
4. *Meiji tennō ki*, 2, pp. 277–78, 445.
5. Asukai Masamichi, *Meiji taitei*, p. 137.
6. *Meiji tennō ki*, 2, p. 109. He suggested that Meiji ride only on the third, thirteenth, twenty-third, eighth, eighteenth, and twenty-eighth of each month.
7. The most detailed description of his studies is given for the sixth month of the second year of Meiji, when he had lessons every day except for the first, sixth, eleventh, sixteenth, twenty-first, and twenty-sixth. In addition to reading texts, he had lectures on Japanese history from Fukuba Bisei, and he took part in the reading by turns (*rindoku*) of *Jōgan seiyō*, an eighth-century Chinese study of politics that had long formed a part of the education of Japanese emperors (*Meiji tennō ki*, 2, pp. 131–32; also pp. 299–300). His teachers included Nakanuma Ryōzō, Matsudaira Yoshinaga, and Akizuki Tanetatsu.
8. Motoda Takehiko and Kaigo Motoomi, eds., *Motoda Nagazane monjo*, p. 45. In this section of *Kanreki no ki*, his autobiography, Motoda related how his father, anxious for Nagazane's future career, suggested that he temporarily give up his study of *jitsugaku* and no longer attend lectures on the subject by Nagaoka Korekata, a former *karō* who had fallen out of favor with the Kumamoto daimyo. The preceding passage was Nagazane's response to his father's suggestion. See also Kose Susumu and Nakamura Hiroshi, *Motoda Tōya, Soejima Sōkai*, p. 27.
9. Yagi Kiyoharu, "Keikenteki jitsugaku no tenkai," p. 176. Yagi quotes in his essay several works by Minamoto Ryōen, an outstanding authority on the subject. The *jitsugaku* of Yokoi Shōnan, Motoda's teacher, was mentioned in chapter 19.
10. Shortly after his disagreement with his father, Motoda began to suffer from an eye ailment, and his doctor forbade him to engage in research. This accident had the

effect of causing Motoda to discontinue his studies of *jitsugaku* under Nagaoka Korekata (Kose and Nakamura, *Motoda*, pp. 28, 33).

11. Kose and Nakamura, *Motoda*, p. 45.

12. Yasuba Seika, "Junchū shisei no taiju Motoda Nagazane sensei," p. 6. The author of this article was the adopted son of Yasuba Yasukazu (1835–1899), a close friend of Motoda's and, like him, a disciple of Yokoi Shōnan.

13. Motoda and Kaigo, eds., *Motoda*, pp. 118–19. See also Kose and Nakamura, *Motoda*, p. 46.

14. *Meiji tennō ki*, 2, p. 475. The texts of lectures delivered by Motoda in the presence of the emperor beginning on the seventh day of the first month of the fifth year of Meiji are in Motoda and Kaigo, eds., *Motoda*. They are composed in easily understood classical Japanese.

15. "Unofficial History of Japan," a celebrated work by Rai San'yō (1780–1832) that described Japanese martial traditions over the centuries.

16. Motoda and Kaigo, eds., *Motoda*, p. 126; Kose and Nakamura, *Motoda*, p. 47.

17. Yasuba, "Junchū," p. 7. See also Motoda and Kaigo, eds., *Motoda*, p. 127, and Kose and Nakamura, *Motoda*, p. 48.

18. The Mima (or, more commonly, Omima) were three small rooms to the southwest of the Tsunegoten where the emperor granted informal audiences.

19. Motoda and Kaigo, eds., *Motoda*, p. 127; Kose and Nakamura, *Motoda*, p. 49.

20. For example, he was unpopular with the chamberlains because they thought he was teaching the emperor to behave in an old-fashioned manner (Hinonishi Sukehiro, *Meiji tennō no go-nichijō*, p. 120).

21. Yasuba, "Junchū," p. 4.

22. The Four Books: *Ta Hsüeh* (The Great Learning), *Chung Yung* (The Mean), *Lun Yü* (The Analects), and *Meng Tzu* (Mencius) plus *Shih Ching* (The Book of Songs) and *Shu Ching* (The Book of History).

23. Kose and Nakamura, *Motoda*, pp. 53, 225. This text is dated 1871.

24. Ibid., pp. 72–74.

25. *Meiji tennō ki*, 2, p. 295. On this occasion, battalions of infantry, artillery, and cavalry from three domains were for the first time organized as a single regiment. Because the troops of each of the three domains were trained differently (in accordance with English, French, or Dutch practice) and attired in different uniforms, they presented a somewhat heterogeneous appearance.

26. Baron Alexander de Hubner, *Promenade autour du monde*, 2, p. 10. For a brief account of Hubner's audience with Emperor Meiji, see *Meiji tennō ki*, 2, p. 516.

27. Among the entries in *Meiji tennō ki*, 2, mentioning Meiji's eating of Western food during the first years of his reign: on the twelfth day of the eighth month of the third year of Meiji, he ate Western food at the Enryōkan; on the twenty-first day of the eleventh month of the fourth year of Meiji, he ate a Western lunch; on the fourth day of the twelfth month of the fourth year of Meiji, both the emperor and the empress, at the recommendation of a court physician, drank milk for the first time, and on the seventeenth day of the twelfth month of the fourth year of Meiji, the long-standing ban on the eating of animal flesh was lifted, and the emperor began to eat beef and mutton.

28. William Elliot Griffis, *The Mikado*, p. 194. Griffis wrote disparagingly of the troops of Satsuma's Shimazu Saburō who appeared in the capital in May 1872: "When

he and his band of two hundred Samurai arrived they seemed most sadly medieval
and obsolete. All wore high clogs, long red scabbarded swords, had the front and
sides of their noddles shaved, went bareheaded and often bare armed, and in
general looked like a pack of antiquated ruffians. They found themselves so stared
at, and indeed so looked upon as men behind the times that they actually begged
their lord to allow them to take off their killing tools" (p. 238).

29. For a description of the photograph, see *Meiji tennō ki*, 2, p. 599. The photograph
is reproduced in the front matter of *Taiyō*, September 1912. It has recently been
rediscovered (*Asahi Shimbun*, May 25, 2001, p. 20).

    A few foreigners, on the other hand, took to wearing Japanese clothes. Sir
Harry Parkes wrote of Peshine Smith, "an American lawyer of some eminence"
who was serving as an adviser to the Japanese Foreign Affairs Ministry, that he
"did his best to bring his employers into ridicule by going about in a Japanese
split jacket and loose trousers with a couple of swords stuck in his girdle, and
declaring in public 'that not one foreigner in ten in Japan was murdered who
ought to have been murdered'" (quoted in F. V. Dickins and S. Lane-Poole, *The
Life of Sir Harry Parkes*, 2, p. 193).

30. *Meiji tennō ki*, 2, p. 527.

31. Ibid., 2, p. 324.

32. Ibid., 2, p. 522.

33. Eiichi Kiyooka, trans., *The Autobiography of Yukichi Fukuzawa*, pp. 225, 226. See
also Nagao Kazuo, *Ansatsusha*, p. 12.

34. A brief but useful chronology of Ōmura's life is in Ezaki Masanori, "Ōmura
Masujirō," p. 74.

35. The fighting is described in gory detail in Nagao, *Ansatsusha*, pp. 16–20.

36. Morikawa Tetsurō, *Meiji ansatsu shi*, p. 35.

37. Hirosawa was sleeping with his mistress when he was killed, and some thought
that jealousy, rather than politics, had led to the murder. Sasaki Takayuki, an
adviser of the emperor, wrote in his diary that he suspected someone close to Kido
Takayoshi of the crime but gave no reason (Kurihara Ryūichi, *Zankanjō*, p. 363).
Hirosawa, like Kido, was from Chōshū.

38. Kurihara, *Zankanjō*, p. 362. Meiji raised Hirosawa's rank posthumously and gave
3,000 *ryō* to his family (*Meiji tennō ki*, 2, p. 392). When the emperor stated that
Hirosawa was the "third minister" to be assassinated, he was presumably referring
indirectly to Yokoi Shōnan and Ōmura Masujirō.

Chapter 22

1. During the period since *hanseki hōkan* had been adopted, various domains (*han*)
had memorialized the throne, asking that they be abolished and replaced by prefectures (*ken*) (*Meiji tennō ki*, 2, pp. 499–501). The four daimyos summoned on
this occasion were men who had offered detailed reasons why they wished their
domain to be abolished. The Tokushima daimyo Hachisuka Mochiaki deplored
the lack of unity within the country caused by the existence of the domains and
thought it advisable that all domain soldiers be placed under the command of the
Ministry of War. Similar petitions were made by the daimyos of the Nagoya,
Kumamoto, and Tottori Domains (pp. 404–5). On May 17, 1881, the Marugame
daimyo Kyōgoku Akiyuki asked permission to abolish the domain and replace it

with a prefecture; this was granted on May 28 (p. 446). The Mito Domain governor Kuki Takayoshi went even further: he not only asked that domain officials be dismissed and their powers transferred to the court, but advocated gradually turning the samurai of the domain into farmers and merchants. He also favored abolishing the distinctions of *kazoku* (nobles) and *shizoku* (samurai) (pp. 470–71, 500). The daimyos of Ōmizo and Tsuwano successfully petitioned to be incorporated within larger domains (pp. 478, 483). These developments, though not typical of the country as a whole, indicate that the atmosphere was conducive to *haihan chiken*.

2. *Meiji tennō ki*, 2, p. 498.
3. William Elliot Griffis, *The Mikado*, p. 181.
4. Ibid., pp. 190–91.
5. Kinoshita Hyō, *Meiji shiwa*, pp. 50–51. See also my *Dawn to the West*, 1, p. 41. The poem is forty lines long.
6. Shiba Ryōtarō, *Meiji to iu kokka*, p. 111. He states that until the 1920s the bureaucracy and academia were occupied by members of the samurai class because they quickly realized that they could escape from their economic predicament only by education. He further states that it was not until the end of the Taishō era that the samurai class began to influence the merchant and agricultural classes.
7. In 1868, when it was arranged for the ministers of foreign countries to visit the Shishinden, the ladies of the *ōoku*, led by Meiji's mother, Nakayama Yoshiko, protested violently, weeping and screaming, enraged by the prospect of the emperor's meeting foreigners. Higashikuze Michitomi sent for the principal female officials and persuaded them to cease their opposition. But Nakayama Yoshiko got her father, Nakayama Tadayasu, to ask for a delay on the grounds that a doctor had said the emperor had a fever. Iwakura asked another doctor to examine the emperor, who was pronounced well. The meeting took place as scheduled (Asukai Masamichi, *Meiji taitei*, p. 123).
8. *Meiji tennō ki*, 2, pp. 504–5.
9. Ibid., 2, pp. 505–6.
10. For an account of the officers of the court who were dismissed and their successors, see ibid., 2, p. 506. Murata was appointed as *kunai daijō*.
11. *Meiji tennō ki*, 2, p. 507. Three were appointed as *gon no tenji*, the title given to the emperor's concubines.
12. *Meiji tennō ki*, 2, p. 509. See also Asukai, *Meiji taitei*, p. 142.
13. *Meiji tennō ki*, 2, p. 175. A *kuni* was a large area corresponding to a prefecture, and a *gun* was a subprefecture.
14. *Meiji tennō ki*, 2, p. 267.
15. Ibid., 2, p. 463.
16. Ibid., 2, pp. 463–64.
17. Ibid., 3, p. 30. They met in Tōkyō rather than in the north. Soejima proposed buying Sakhalin for 200,000 yen, but Biutsov countered by offering to give the Japanese the Kurile Islands in return for obtaining sole possession of Sakhalin. Neither budged in his stand. Perhaps to break the deadlock, Soejima said that Japan would yield all of Sakhalin to the Russians provided they would sign an agreement permitting Japanese troops free passage across their territories in the event that Japan engaged in military action on the Asian continent. Biutsov replied

that he was not authorized to discuss such matters, and there the matter was dropped.

18. *Meiji tennō ki*, 3, p. 31. The text of Kuroda's memorandum is in "Soejima Haku keireki gūdan" (part 3), pp. 23–24.

19. *Meiji tennō ki*, 3, pp. 444–45.

20. Ibid., 2, pp. 327, 333. Itagaki Taisuke was originally selected to head the four-man team of observers but declined because of domain duties. The senior member was Ōyama Iwao, a cousin of Saigō Takamori, who later became minister of war and commanding general of the Second Army during the Sino-Japanese War. Another member, Shinagawa Yajirō, who remained in Europe for five years, later rose to be minister of the interior.

21. Takashima Tomonosuke, "Jimmu irai no eishu," p. 34. Watanabe Ikujirō wrote, however, that the German minister (not a ship's captain) showed and explained the photographs (*Meiji tennō*, 1, p. 129).

22. Watanabe Ikujirō, *Meiji tennō*, 1, p. 129.

23. *Meiji tennō ki*, 2, p. 666.

24. Ibid., 2, p. 582. For a fuller description of the departure, see Kume Kunitake, *Beiō kairan jikki*, 1, pp. 42, and Tanaka Akira, *Iwakura shisetsudan*, pp. 8–10.

25. This would be in October 1872, but it was generally believed that reconsideration would be possible on July 1, 1872 (Tanaka, *Iwakura*, p. 41). Similar treaties had been signed with Holland, Russia, England, France, Portugal, Prussia, Switzerland, Belgium, Italy, and Denmark. When trade treaties were later signed with Sweden-Norway, Spain, Germany, and Austria-Hungary, they followed the American model, and the Japanese were unable to eliminate the objectionable features (*Meiji tennō ki*, 2, p. 547).

26. *Meiji tennō ki*, 2, pp. 548–50.

27. Ōkubo Toshiaki, *Iwakura shisetsu no kenkyū*, pp. 257–58. Ōkubo reproduces sections from William Elliot Griffis, *Verbeck of Japan*. Although he considered himself to be an American (technically, he was a stateless person), Verbeck was born and educated in Holland. In 1859 he was sent by the Dutch Reformed Church to Nagasaki, where in addition to proselytizing, he taught English, law, politics, economics, and Western technology. (His original university degree was in engineering.) His pupils included Itō Hirobumi, Ōkubo Toshimichi, Ōkuma Shigenobu, and Soejima Taneomi.

28. It is not clear what Iwakura meant by "your chief officers."

29. Ōkubo, *Iwakura*, p. 254. The authenticity of Verbeck's claim was bolstered by the discovery in the Gardner A. Sage Library of the Reformed Church in New Brunswick, New Jersey, of a copy in Verbeck's hand of his original proposal, sent to Ōkuma on June 11, 1869 (Tanaka, *Iwakura*, p. 28).

30. Ōkubo, *Iwakura*, p. 257.

31. Mōri Toshihiko, *Meiji rokunen seihen*, p. 23. Mōri mentions that Mori Arinori, then in Washington, D.C., overestimated the friendliness of the Americans and believed that it was an opportune time for treaty revision. His sentiments were shared by Itō Hirobumi (*Meiji tennō ki*, 2, p. 659). Mori was detested by members of the mission because he openly criticized Japan in front of the Americans. Kido Takayoshi's diary contains such passages as "In recent days Mori's behavior has

been appalling. By contrast, Americans understand our feelings very well, and know our customs. But, our students who are now studying in the United States lack a deep understanding of our country's traditional ways. They admire American customs without knowing the tradition on which they themselves stand. They advocate liberty and republicanism so thoughtlessly that I can hardly bear to listen to their light-hearted frivolous ideas. It is talked about that Mori, who is the Minister of our country here, scorns the customs of his own land indiscriminately in the presence of foreigners" (diary entry, April 15, 1872, in Sidney DeVere Brown and Akiko Hirota, trans., *The Diary of Kido Takayoshi*, 2, pp. 149–50).

32. Ōkubo and Itō seemed to believe they had obtained the credentials to negotiate treaty revision with America, but in fact all they were empowered to do was to open negotiations. They were not to modify the treaty with America alone but were directed to meet in Europe with representatives of all countries with which treaties had been signed and negotiate there. Iwakura was sent telegraphic instructions to ask if the Americans would send an envoy extraordinary to the site of negotiations. The emperor on June 19, 1872, sent a message to his "good friends," the kings and presidents of the various countries, describing the chief members of the embassy who would visit their capitals and who were empowered to conduct negotiations with the aim of achieving ever more peaceful and friendly relations with their countries. He reminded them that it would soon be the time set for treaty revisions and hoped that these revisions would be carried out for the benefit of all (*Meiji tennō ki*, 2, pp. 677–79; Mōri, *Meiji*, p. 26).

33. Miyake Setsurei, *Dōjidai shi*, 1, pp. 339–43, quoted in Mōri, *Meiji*, pp. 32–33.

34. However, Griffis recorded his pleasure over the new promptness of the Japanese in dealing with would-be assassins: "On January 13, 1871, two Englishmen in Tokyo were attacked by three two sworded men and wounded very severely. With Verbeck, I had the pleasure of helping to nurse them back to health. With the utmost promptness, the three assailants were caught and their confessions extorted from them before their punishment was decreed. What surprised and pleased the British Minister was the production of a new criminal code, two out of five volumes being then ready. According to its provisions two of the guilty ruffians were strangled and one sentenced to ten years of hard labor, all three being degraded from the rank of Samurai . . . . The innovation of putting gentlemanly scoundrels and murderers to death on the common execution ground, where vulgar felons were beheaded, soon made assassination unpopular" (*Mikado*, pp. 183–84).

Chapter 23

1. Chūgoku referred to the northern shore of the Inland Sea (Hiroshima, Okayama, etc.); Saigoku at this time was another name for Kyūshū.

2. In order to take advantage of the high tide, the emperor and his party left the palace at three in the morning, traveled to Hama Rikyū, where they boarded the warship *Ryūjō*, and sailed to Uraga, reached that evening. The *Ryūjō* spent the night anchored in Uraga Bay and then sailed back to Hama Rikyū the following morning.

3. *Meiji tennō ki*, 2, p. 674.

4. Taki Kōji, *Tennō no shōzō*, p. 6.

5. Baron Alexander de Hubner wrote after an audience with Emperor Meiji, "Conformément à l'étiquette, l'empereur, en me parlant, ne faisait que murmurer entre ses dents des sons inarticulés et à peine saisissables" (*Promenade autour du monde*, 2, p. 16). A. B. Mitford, who was present when "the Mikado" first gave an audience to Sir Harry Parkes, the English minister, wrote, "As might be expected from his extreme youth and the novelty of the situation to one who had only recently left the women's apartments, the Mikado showed some symptoms of shyness. He hardly spoke above a whisper, so the words were repeated aloud by the Prince of the Blood on his right side and translated by Ito Shunske" (quoted in Hugh Cortazzi, *Mitford's Japan*, p. 121). Frank Brinkley recalled that he and the other Englishmen "offered him our most profound salutations, but His Majesty sat erect, not so much as blinking his eyes. He did not vouchsafe a word . . . . Some wondered if he might not be a doll, he was so god-like in his attitude" ("Sentei heika," p. 46).

6. For example, Hugh Cortazzi quotes an article dated August 15, 1872, from *The Far East* in which it mentions "a slight stiffness in his gait, as if unused to boots" (*Victorians in Japan*, p. 81). Lady Brassey, who saw the emperor in November 1873, wrote, "He is a young, not very good-looking man, with rather a sullen expression, and legs that look as though they did not belong to him—I suppose from using them so little, and sitting so much on his heels; for until the last few years the Mikado has always been considered far too sacred a being to be allowed to set foot on the earth" (quoted in ibid., p. 333).

7. Taki, *Tennō*, p. 9.

8. Ibid., p. 10.

9. Peter Burke, *The Fabrication of Louis XIV*, p. 11.

10. Ibid., p. 44.

11. Baron de Hubner wrote of his audience with Meiji, "Excepté en nous addressant la parole, Sa Majesté se tint immobile comme une statue" (*Promenade*, p. 15).

12. Burke, *Fabrication*, p. 180.

13. Ibid., p. 61.

14. Norbert Elias, *The Court Society*, p. 126.

15. *Meiji tennō ki*, 2, pp. 675, 683. Needless to say, no one had previously sat on chairs in the Gosho.

16. The costume is more fully described in *Meiji tennō ki*, 2, p. 691: the basic material is black wool embroidered on the chest with gold thread in the shape of chrysanthemum blossoms and leaves. On the back at the waist there is an embroidered phoenix. The trousers are of the same black wool with a stripe about an inch wide of gold braid. The cocked hat, of black velvet, is embroidered on both sides with phoenixes of gold thread and is bordered by a stripe of gold braid. The "hooks" (*hokku*) seem to refer to the fastenings of the upper garment.

   The emperor was measured for Western clothes on May 13 by a European tailor from Yokohama. This may have been the only time that he was ever measured (*Meiji tennō ki*, 2, p. 666).

17. *Meiji tennō ki*, 2, p. 711.

18. Ibid., 2, p. 691.

19. At this point, *Meiji tennō ki*, 2, p. 695, sounds a cautionary note: "It is said that the crying of *banzai* in the modern period began in 1889 at the time of the

proclamation of the constitution. The statement given here that the citizens of Ōsaka cried *banzai* is based on records of the time, but did the people in fact cry *banzai*? Or was it merely that the records used the expression 'cry *banzai*,' often found in classical texts of both Japan and China, to indicate a state of joyfulness? This is still not clear. There is also a text stating that in the ninth month of 1870, at the ceremony performed by the navy in honor of the emperor's birthday, everyone lined up on deck in order of ranks at eleven in the morning and shouted *banzai*."

20. *Meiji tennō ki*, 2, p. 696.

21. Princess Sumiko, the third daughter of Emperor Ninkō, was a member of the Katsuranomiya family; this high-ranking princely family came to an end with her death in 1881.

22. *Meiji tennō ki*, 2, p. 700.

23. Ibid., 2, p. 711.

24. Asukai Masamichi, *Meiji taitei*, p. 150.

25. *Meiji tennō ki*, 2, p. 719.

26. I am thinking of Philemon and Baucis, but also of such Japanese examples as the receptions given in humble cottages to Saimyōji *nyūdō* Tokiyori, who had a habit of visiting people in disguise.

27. So reported in *Meiji tennō ki*, 2, p. 726, which further says that similar reports were transmitted from the other places visited by the emperor as exemplifying the people's worship of the imperial house.

28. *Meiji tennō ki*, 2, pp. 727–28. In recognition of Saigō Takamori's unique qualities of leadership, the emperor appointed him as a marshal soon after his return to Tōkyō (p. 733).

29. *Meiji tennō ki*, 2, pp. 735–37.

30. Ibid., 2, pp. 744–47. The Japanese would profit by this gratitude during their negotiations with the Chinese in February 1873.

31. Mōri Toshihiko, *Meiji rokunen seihen*, p. 40.

32. William Elliot Griffis, *The Mikado*, p. 226.

33. For an account of Dickins as a scholar of Japanese literature, see Kawamura Hatsue, *F. V. Dickins*. In 1866 Dickins published a translation of the collection of poetry *Hyakunin isshu*.

34. Mōri, *Meiji rokunen*, pp. 52–54.

35. The text is in ibid., pp. 54–55. See also *Meiji tennō ki*, 2, pp. 767–68.

36. For a brief description of the Wakan and the reasons for its existence, see Kamigaitō Ken'ichi, *Amenomori hōshū*, pp. 90–93. A somewhat more detailed description is in Kang Bom-sok, *Seikanron seihen*, pp. 16–19. Kan makes interesting comparisons between the Wakan and the Dutch "factory" on Deshima.

37. The Korean government was informed in January 1869 by Higuchi Tetsushirō, a senior officer of the Tsushima clan sent as its envoy by the Japanese government, of the restoration of imperial rule and the termination of the shogunate (*Meiji tennō ki*, 2, p. 944; see also Kang, *Seikanron*, p. 11).

38. Asukai Masamichi, "Saigō Takamori wa heiwa shugisha datta ka," p. 109. He states that from the Korean standpoint, the Meiji government had overthrown by force the government of the Tokugawa shoguns and was therefore a usurper. The Koreans also considered that the use of such words as *kō* (emperor) and *choku* (re-

script) by the new government was an unsanctioned use of words that were properly used only of the Chinese emperor. Kido Takayoshi wrote in his diary that he favored sending an envoy to Korea to question officials about their discourtesy. "If they do not acknowledge their fault, let us proclaim it publicly and launch an attack on their territory to extend the influence of our Divine Land across the seas to cover their territory" (diary entry, January 26, 1869, in Sidney DeVere Brown and Akiko Hirota, trans., *The Diary of Kido Takayoshi*, 1, p. 167). See also Kang, *Seikanron*, p. 11.

39. *Meiji tennō ki*, 2, p. 741.

40. Ibid., 2, p. 742. There were seven articles in all; others dealt with such matters as the return to Japan of Japanese officials who were not essential to the station, the discontinuance of the annual ship from Tsushima, and the return of castaways to Korea.

41. Kido, who was in London at the time, had read in the New York newspapers that Korea had detained one Japanese envoy and expelled another. He wrote in his diary, "The stupidity and obstinacy of that country is detestable." He added, "Moreover, when our trade with the West is beginning to flourish, Asian countries which lie near us must make a successful advance toward civilization or else we cannot fully achieve our future purposes." He implied that if the Koreans were unwilling to modernize their ways, this would be detrimental to Japanese interests and that war might be the only course open to the Japanese (diary entry, September 1, 1872, in Brown and Hirota, trans., *Diary*, 2, p. 206).

42. *Meiji tennō ki*, 2, p. 755.

43. The text of the *mikotonori* is in ibid., 2, p. 756. It opens with a declaration of the emperor's authority as the heir to the 10,000 ages of unbroken imperial authority and the vast area he ruled. The edict goes on to state why the Ryūkyū king was being honored. His country shared the same customs and language with Japan and was long tributary to Satsuma. The king himself had demonstrated his loyalty. Finally, it commanded the *han-ō* to give due weight to the responsibilities of his domain and to assist the imperial house.

44. *Meiji tennō ki*, 2, p. 781. For the text of the rescript, see Tōyama Shigeki, *Tennō to kōzoku*, pp. 31–32. At the same time, the twenty-four hours of a day were made uniform in length; previously the hours of light and dark were of different lengths.

Chapter 24

1. *Meiji tennō ki*, 2, p. 9. Only two ladies were presented, the wives of the American and Russian ministers, but this established a precedent.

2. *Meiji tennō ki*, 3, p. 6. This was essentially the schedule established after the major changes in the palace on September 15, 1871 (Ikujirō, *Meiji tennō*, 1, pp. 113–14). The lectures on *Kokushi sanron*, a collection of historical essays on emperors from Jimmu to Goyōzei published by Yamagata Taika in 1839, would be delivered by Fukuba Bisei and Motoda Nagazane; those on *Saikoku risshi hen*, by Fukuba Bisei, Katō Hiroyuki, and Motoda Nagazane; and those on poetry, by Sanjōnishi Suetomo and Fukuba Bisei.

3. *Meiji tennō ki*, 3, p. 28.

4. A photograph of the text of the *jōyu* (imperial order) is in Wayne C. McWilliams, "East Meets East," p. 241. For a *yomikudashi* version, see *Meiji tennō ki*, 3, p. 38.

5. These details of Soejima's orders were given by the emperor to Sanjō Sanetomi, the prime minister, for transmission to Soejima (*Meiji tennō ki*, 3, pp. 38–39).

6. Acting on LeGendre's suggestion, Soejima proposed occupying the southern part of Taiwan. He believed this could be obtained by negotiations with China and that possession of the southern part of the island would make it possible to obtain the rest of the island by diplomatic means in four or five years (McWilliams, "East Meets East," p. 243).

7. The interpreters, Tei Nagayasu and Hirai Yoshimasa, spoke both Chinese and English. Both served in the Foreign Ministry. Tei was of Chinese origin.

8. According to Soejima, the plan worked: when the two warships arrived in Shanghai, he was referred to by Chinese officials as the "great Japanese general Soejima" ("Soejima Haku keireki gūdan," p. 24).

9. *Meiji tennō ki*, 3, p. 39. The *Kanrin maru*, which traveled to San Francisco in 1860, was not, strictly speaking, a warship.

10. "Soejima Haku," p. 24. The content of their talk is not known.

11. McWilliams quotes letters from the American consul in Tientsin to Frederick Low, the American minister in Peking ("East Meets East," p. 248).

12. McWilliams quotes a letter from LeGendre to General O. E. Babcock dated July 2, 1873 ("East Meets East," p. 248).

13. McWilliams quotes part of a letter sent on May 7, 1873, from the American consul in Tientsin to Low, the American minister in Peking: "The fact that the Japanese had seemingly identified themselves with the foreigners . . . was so entirely at variance with the viceroy's own ideas of Oriental superiority that he could not resist giving his cousins from the 'Rising Sun' a left-handed slap for submitting to or seeking after the guidance of western barbarians" ("East Meets East," pp. 248–49).

14. This account is derived from "Soejima Haku," p. 25.

15. Ibid., p. 17.

16. Ibid., pp. 17–18.

17. "Shinkoku to no shūkō jōki tsūshō shōtei teiketsu ni kansuru ken," pp. 147–48, quoted in McWilliams, "East Meets East," p. 256. This diary, referred to as "Shi shin nikki" by McWilliams, is found in *Nihon gaikō monjo*, 6.

18. From "Shinkoku," p. 152, quoted in McWilliams, "East Meets East," p. 258.

19. From "Shinkoku," p. 166, quoted in McWilliams, "East Meets East," p. 259.

20. "Soejima Haku," p. 29; McWilliams, "East Meets East," p. 265.

21. He was the first foreign envoy to be granted an audience with the emperor since 1793, some eighty years earlier, when Lord Macartney was received.

22. Kose Susumu and Nakamura Hiroshi, *Motoda Tōya, Soejima Sōkai*, p. 158.

23. "Soejima Haku," p. 32. However, he was given only a nineteen-gun salute, according to "Shinkoku," p. 198.

24. The text of the letter is in "Soejima Haku," p. 33. See also McWilliams, "East Meets East," p. 273.

25. Kose and Nakamura, *Motoda*, p. 159.

26. *Taewon'gun* was the title given to the father of a reigning king who had not himself reigned, but it is often used to refer to one particular man, Yi Ha-ung, the father

of King Kojong. The *taewon'gun* had placed his second son on the throne but governed behind the scenes, rather in the manner of the *insei* in late Heian Japan.

27. The document is referred to by the Japanese as the *Tōraifu denreisho*. Tōraifu (or Tong-nai-pu in Korean) was the district where the Wakan was situated.

28. The full text is in *Meiji tennō ki*, 3, p. 115. See also Tada Kōmon, ed., *Iwakura-kō jikki*, 3, pp. 45–46. This volume (pp. 1–90) contains other documents relative to relations between Japan and Korea.

29. Kang Bom-sok, *Seikanron seihen*, pp. 44–46. The merchants in question were sent by the Mitsui Gofukuten. The names of three employees of Mitsui who were planning to go to the Wakan to engage in trade are given in a letter sent by the *gaimu daijō*, Hanabusa Yoshikata, to Murayama Shigeru, dated January 21, 1873 (p. 45).

30. *Meiji tennō ki*, 3, p. 116.

31. Ibid., 3, p. 116.

32. Ibid., 3, pp. 117–18.

33. Soejima had not yet returned from China at the time of the debate. Kido and Ōkubo had returned from Europe, but Kido was (really) ill and could not attend the Court Council. Ōkubo, not being a *sangi*, was not qualified to attend. Iwakura was still abroad. Among those supporting the proposal were the three *sangi* Itagaki Taisuke, Gotō Shōjirō, and Etō Shimpei.

34. *Meiji tennō ki*, 3, p. 118. Saigō would repeat this prediction in the letter he sent on August 17 to Itagaki Taisuke, in which he wrote, "I need hardly say that it [his proposal to send an envoy to Korea] is at the same time a far-reaching scheme which will divert abroad the attention of those who desire civil strife, and thereby benefit the country" (Ryūsaku Tsunoda, Wm. Theodore de Bary, and Donald Keene, trans., *Sources of Japanese Tradition*, p. 657; original in Ōkawa Nobuyoshi, *Dai Saigō zenshū*, 2, p. 756).

35. *Meiji tennō ki*, 3, pp. 118–19. Soejima (who returned to Japan on July 23) expected to be sent to Korea, only to encounter Saigō's determination to become the envoy.

36. *Meiji tennō ki*, 3, pp. 111–12, 114. The royal party traveled by train from Shimbashi to Kanagawa and from there by horse-drawn carriage. The journey took two days.

37. Kang, *Seikanron*, pp. 54–55. The Koreans had previously (in 1868) repulsed attacks by French and American warships (Tsunoda Fusako, *Mimpi ansatsu*, pp. 58–59, 66, 80–81).

38. Tsunoda et al., trans., *Sources of Japanese Tradition*, pp. 655–56; original in Ōkawa, *Dai Saigō*, 2, pp. 736–38.

39. Tsunoda et al., trans., *Sources of Japanese Tradition*, p. 656; original in Ōkawa, *Dai Saigō*, 2, pp. 751–52. See also Kang, *Seikanron*, pp. 131–32.

40. Kang, *Seikanron*, p. 129. The doctors thought that Saigō's corpulence was the cause of his high blood pressure and prescribed strong laxatives, five or six times a day, in order to reduce his weight. It can easily be imagined how this must have weakened him.

41. Kang, *Seikanron*, pp. 135–36, 150. In later years, Ōkuma Shigenobu, describing the reasons that different men advocated *seikan*, said that Saigō was looking for a place to die (Kose and Nakamura, *Motoda*, p. 168).

42. Mōri Toshihiko, *Meiji rokunen seihen*, pp. 117–18, 127–31.

43. Saigō's exalted reputation is difficult for non-Japanese to understand. His personality and appearance and the legends that have grown up around him seem to have induced Japanese to condone both his attitude at this time and his later rebellion against the government, but it is doubtful if many Koreans share this admiration.

44. Diary entry, September 3, 1873, in Sidney DeVere Brown and Akiko Hirota, trans., *The Diary of Kido Takayoshi*, 2, pp. 370–71. See also Kang, *Seikanron*, pp. 167–73.

45. He asked that Itō Hirobumi also be made a *sangi*, but Itō was an officer of the second rank, and an appointment to *sangi* would have involved jumping over the first rank, which was deemed impossible. Ōkubo also asked, as a condition of becoming a *sangi*, that Sanjō and Iwakura swear that once they made up their minds on *seikan* they would not waver! (Mōri, *Meiji rokunen*, p. 166).

46. *Meiji tennō ki*, 3, pp. 139–41; Kose and Nakamura, *Motoda*, pp. 164–65. Although Kido was a *sangi*, his absence from the sessions prevented him from voting.

47. *Meiji tennō ki*, 3, pp. 143–44, 147–49.

48. Ibid., 3, p. 150.

49. Kose and Nakamura state that the four men, concerned about how their resignations would be interpreted abroad, decided they were "somehow or other" ill (*Motoda*, p. 167).

50. It has been suggested that even those most opposed to intervention in Korea were essentially in favor of it but had special reasons for their opposition at this point. Kido is said to have favored *seikan* but thought it would be too expensive under the stringent financial conditions in Japan at the time (Mōri, *Meiji rokunen*, p. 144). Ōkubo is said not to have been unduly worried about sending Saigō as an ambassador (Kang, *Seikanron*, p. 192); he is even said to have told Soejima that he would have agreed to *seikan* if he had first been given fifty days in which to create the Ministry of the Interior (Kose and Nakamura, *Motoda*, p. 167). But it is difficult to reconcile the claim that Ōkubo was essentially sympathetic to *seikan* with his detailed statement on why he opposed the Korean expedition (Tsunoda et al., trans. *Sources of Japanese Tradition*, pp. 658–62; original in Kiyozawa Kiyoshi, *Ōkubo Toshimichi*, pp. 28–31).

Chapter 25

1. *Meiji tennō ki*, 3, p. 130.

2. Ibid., 3, pp. 65–66. Meiji limited the expenditures to not more than 50,000 yen.

3. *Meiji tennō ki*, 3, p. 70.

4. Ibid., 3, pp. 57–58.

5. For the photograph and an account of the circumstances, see Taki Kōji, *Tennō no shōzō*, pp. 116–18. *Meiji tennō ki*, 2, p. 739, states that "previously" Uchida had taken photographs of the emperor and empress which were presented to the empress dowager on September 9, 1872. The empress dowager, in turn, had her photograph taken by Uchida on October 9. On October 17 Uchida presented to the emperor the total of seventy-two photographs he had taken of him, the empress, and the empress dowager. Some show the emperor in *sokutai*, others in *nōshi*. There was also a photograph taken (at some time before February 1873) showing the emperor on horseback. These photographs, with two or three excep-

tions, have never been published and are known to me only by the descriptions in *Meiji tennō ki*.

6. However, the emperor himself seems not to have disliked the photographs. He presented one to Soejima Taneomi on March 9, 1873, when the latter was about to leave for China (*Meiji tennō ki*, 3, p. 39). He also gave a copy to his aunt, Princess Chikako, on March 20 (p. 42). The same photograph (or another taken at the same time) was sent to Japanese legations abroad for display (Taki, *Tennō*, pp. 118–19).

7. The emperor's uniform was determined on June 3 after a study of the uniforms worn by other monarchs. For details, see *Meiji tennō ki*, pp. 77–78.

8. Ibid., 3, p. 47. On the morning of the day on which the emperor's hair was to be cut, he had a court lady arrange his hair and powder his face lightly as usual. He went to his study where, by his command, the chamberlain Ariji Shinanojō put scissors to his locks. The chief chamberlain Yoneda Torao and the chamberlain Kataoka Toshikazu took turns in cutting the emperor's hair. When he reappeared in the *ōoku*, the palace ladies were surprised and dismayed by his changed appearance.

9. The photograph is reproduced in Taki, *Tennō*, p. 121. His description of the photograph is on p. 118. Two portraits were taken on this occasion, one full-length and the other half-length (*Meiji tennō ki*, 3, p. 134). The duke of Genoa, who was then in Japan, was presented with a large-sized example of the full-length photograph. A copy of the same photograph was subsequently sent to each prefecture. The half-length photograph has not been published.

10. It was known as the *rusuban seifu* because so many of the top leaders were abroad with the Iwakura mission.

11. *Meiji tennō ki*, 3, p. 42.

12. For a description of this uprising, see ibid., 3, pp. 73–74.

13. Ibid., 3, p. 87. Another armed revolt occurred later in June in Meitō Prefecture (Nagoya). This was similar in character to the one in Hōjō Prefecture, arising from a misunderstanding of the term *ketsuzei*. The leaders of this revolt were punished with extreme severity, and more than 16,890 suffered some form of punishment (pp. 93–94).

14. *Meiji tennō ki*, 3, p. 181.

15. For a detailed account of the incident, see Tada Kōmon, ed., *Iwakura-kō jikki*, 3, pp. 94–96, and *Meiji tennō ki*, 3, p. 189. John Russell Young, a member of General Grant's party, who met Iwakura in 1879, noted that "Iwakura has a striking face, with lines showing firmness and decision, and you saw the scar which marked the attempt of an assassin to cut him down and slay him" (*Around the World with General Grant*, 2, p. 527).

16. For the text of the sentence passed on eight of the nine assailants, see Kurihara Ryūichi, *Zankanjō*, pp. 366–67.

17. For the program advocated by the Yūkoku-tō, see Sonoda Hiyoshi, *Etō Shimpei to Saga no ran*, p. 144. Another of the points was a rejection of Christianity as a pollution of the religions of Japan. Immediately after the attempted assassination of Iwakura, the Yūkoku-tō drew up a new statement of purpose but did not express opposition to *seikan* (p. 145).

18. A third party, the Chūritsu (or Neutral) Party, eventually sided with the government forces.
19. Mōri Toshihiko, Etō Shimpei, p. 202.
20. Soejima was also asked to return to Saga, but he yielded to Itagaki's strong pressure to remain in Tokyo (Mōri, Etō, p. 205). Etō, disregarding Itagaki's (and Ōkuma's) advice, went.
21. Nakano Yoshio shared my bewilderment over the reasons for Etō's decision ("Saga no ran to Etō Shimpei," p. 213).
22. Nakano, "Saga no ran," p. 215. Etō did not elaborate on what a "second ishin" would involve, but it may have included seikan.
23. Mōri, Etō, p. 206.
24. Sonoda, Etō, pp. 154–55. A shorter form of what is essentially the same statement is in Meiji tennō ki, 3, p. 212. The Chōshū war is discussed in chapter 21.
25. Sonoda, Etō, p. 156. Etō had received assurances from men not only from these two prefectures but also from Aichi and Kumamoto. See also Nakano, "Saga no ran," p. 216.
26. Evidence suggests that Nakayama Ichirō, whom Etō sent to see Saigō Takamori in Kagoshima, reported back that if Saga rose in rebellion, Saigō's party would follow its lead, but it seems hardly possible that Saigō would have committed himself in this way (Nakano, "Saga no ran," p. 216).
27. Sonoda gives a paraphrase of Etō's statement on this occasion (Etō, pp. 194–95). He said that unless the army were disbanded, every man of the rank of corporal and above would be killed by the government army. He asked that they put aside their military garb, scatter through the region, and await the time (which would certainly come) for a second uprising.
28. Meiji tennō ki, 3, pp. 221–24. For a detailed account of the fighting, see Sonoda, Etō, pp. 163–90.
29. The details are given in Sonoda, Etō, p. 200. Etō's opens: "Age 41. Tall and rather heavy. Long face with high cheek bones. Eyebrows thick and long."
30. Kido remarked ironically that "what we are advocating now, Etō was advocating last year." He seems to have been equating Etō's eagerness to conquer Korea with the Japanese war of conquest in Taiwan that was then being waged (quoted in Sonoda, Etō, p. 205).
31. Sonoda, Etō, pp. 190–91.
32. Ibid., p. 207.
33. Ibid., p. 208.
34. This is what he told his servant, urging him to return home lest he become implicated in the crime of rebellion (Sonoda, Etō, p. 209).
35. The text of the letter is in Sonoda, Etō, p. 210. Although the envelope was addressed to Iwakura only, the letter itself also bears the names of Kido, Ōkubo, Ōkuma, and Ōki as addressees. The sender's name on the envelope was part of the alias that Etō used in his guise as a secret agent, but his real name was given in the letter.
36. Sonoda, Etō, p. 211.
37. He was captured on March 7 (Meiji tennō ki, 3, p. 239).
38. Sonoda, Etō, p. 219. The wording of Etō's outburst varies somewhat according to the source.

39. Sagi Ryūzō, *Shihōkyō Etō Shimpei*, p. 408. Nakano states that the *Tōkyō nichinichi shimbun* denounced the sale in Kyūshū of photographs of the severed heads of Etō and Shima ("Saga no ran," p. 218). He said that he was reluctant to believe that Ōkubo was behind this but that there were rumors to this effect.

40. In his diary for April 2, 1874, Kido Takayoshi wrote, "Today was the day for members to affix their seals to the resolution on Taiwan; therefore, I told the two Ministers of State, Sanjō and Iwakura, that I am refusing to sign. The reason is, as I observed in my statement in response to the Imperial inquiry last year, that in surveying the present condition of the country I am conscious of the poverty of the people. We should devote ourselves exclusively to domestic administration, and to advancing the people's living standards, and afterwards, it will not be too late to undertake an overseas expedition."

41. *Meiji tennō ki*, 3, pp. 234–35.

42. Ibid., 3, pp. 243–44.

43. Ibid., 3, p. 245.

44. The American ship the *Shaftsbury* was renamed the *Sharyō maru*, and the British ship the *Delta* was renamed *Takasago maru*. Both names refer to Taiwan: Sharyō was the port the Japanese would use for their expedition, and Takasago was the name the Japanese gave to the natives of the island (*Meiji tennō ki*, 3, p. 259).

45. *Meiji tennō ki*, 3, p. 280.

46. Ibid., 3, p. 282.

47. Ibid., 3, p. 325.

48. Ibid., 3, pp. 368–73.

Chapter 26

1. *Meiji tennō ki*, 3, p. 377.

2. He was at the time an officer of the Ministry of Education (*Meiji tennō ki*, 3, p. 378).

3. *Meiji tennō ki*, 3, p. 383.

4. The daughter of the nobleman Yanagihara Mitsunaru (*Meiji tennō ki*, 2, p. 292). She was appointed as *gon no tenji* on February 20, 1873. She bore Meiji four children; three of them died, but the remaining one was the future Emperor Taishō.

5. Earlier in the same month a series of regulations had been formulated concerning the ceremonies to be observed after the birth of a prince or princess. They prescribed that in keeping with the practice in the imperial family ever since the time of Emperor Seiwa, male children should have names ending in -hito and female children names ending in -ko (*Meiji tennō ki*, 3, pp. 384–85).

6. It had long been the custom to bestow on courtesans names derived from the female characters in *The Tale of Genji*. Originally, this may have been to give merchants who bought the favors of prostitutes the impression that they, like Genji in ancient times, had slept with Murasaki no Ue or Rokujō no Miyasudokoro. Meiji bestowed on his ladies the names of plants and trees. These names were used by both the emperor and the court ladies themselves when calling one another. In addition to their Genji names, the ladies had nicknames, also bestowed by the emperor.

7. Saitō Keishū, *Jokan monogatari*, pp. 91, 93.

8. Katō Hitoshi, "Meiji tennō o-tsubone go-rakuin den," p. 60.

9. Yamakawa Michiko, "Kindan no jokan seikatsu kaisōki," p. 196.

10. Yamakawa Michiko, *Jokan*, p. 16.

11. Katō, "Meiji," p. 60. The senior court lady (*jokanchō*) during much of Meiji's lifetime, Takakura Kazuko, seems to have been a redoubtable figure. She would inform the *gon no tenji* she had chosen as the emperor's companion for the night, "*Kyō wa, anata*" (It's your turn today).

12. When Yamakawa Michiko entered the emperor's service in 1909, Ogura Fumiko and Sono Sachiko were the only two women who shared the emperor's bed.

13. Yamakawa, "Kindan no jokan," p. 196. She quotes an unnamed aged woman who served Yanagihara Naruko for many years. The woman recalled that Naruko's hysteria was such that not only the other palace ladies but even the nurses ran from her.

14. Yanagihara Naruko was one of seven *gon no tenji* portrayed by the ukiyoe artist Tsukioka Yoshitoshi in a series of prints published in 1878. All the women are beautiful in much the same way, but Naruko's picture offended the Ministry of the Imperial Household because her pose recalled those of the courtesans Yoshitoshi so often depicted. (The print is reproduced in *Impressions*, no. 21, 1999.) It is said that consequently, ukiyoe artists were henceforth forbidden to depict the emperor in their prints, but if such an order was actually issued, it was frequently disobeyed in later years.

15. For details, see *Meiji tennō ki*, 3, p. 623.

16. Ibid., 3, p. 405.

17. Ibid., 3, p. 406. The expression was derived from the Chinese historical work *Tso Chuan*. If China fell, Japan would feel the Siberian cold from Russia.

18. *Meiji tennō ki*, 3, p. 407.

19. Ōkubo Toshiaki, *Iwakura Tomomi*, pp. 218–19.

20. The emperor gave Sanjō a memorandum urging Saigō to return and, as a loyal subject, to take part in reviving the spirits of the people and planning for a prosperous and militarily strong country (*Meiji tennō ki*, 3, pp. 427–28).

21. Genrō-in was a translation of "Senate." It was expected to perform legislative and advisory functions. The Taishin-in was the highest judicial court.

22. *Meiji tennō ki*, 3, pp. 425–26.

23. Ibid., 3, p. 436.

24. Ibid., 3, pp. 444–45. The treaty was signed on May 7 by Enomoto Takeaki, representing Japan, and Duke Alexander Gorchakov.

25. The decision was issued by the czar on May 29 (*Meiji tennō ki*, 3, p. 453). Despite this welcome development, many Japanese continued to believe that Russian expansion in East Asia was the chief menace to Japanese security.

26. *Meiji tennō ki*, 3, p. 473.

27. Iwakura, exasperated by Shimazu Hisamitsu's obsessive insistence on what Iwakura considered to be trifles, decided not to meet him again (*Meiji tennō ki*, 3, p. 498). Hisamitsu nursed a secret plan for correcting the woes of the time: it was to adopt the policy of Emperor Hsüan Tsung of the T'ang dynasty who, after putting down a rebellion, had strictly forbidden luxury and had commanded that

all elegant things be burned (p. 500). When Iwakura heard of this "secret plan," he merely laughed.

28. For Korean interpretations of the incident and its place in the chain of events leading to the treaty between Japan and Korea, see Kan Je-on, *Chōsen no jōi to kaika*, pp. 140–42, 163–71.

29. *Meiji tennō ki*, 3, pp. 496–97. Other sources give somewhat different dates. The place where the boat from the *Un'yō* attempted to land was directly in front of the main gun emplacements on the island, an obvious challenge to the Korean defenders (Kan, *Chōsen*, p. 164).

30. For press coverage in Japan of the incident (which undoubtedly affected public opinion), see Kinebuchi Nobuo, *Nikkan kōshō shi*, pp. 30–48.

31. *Meiji tennō ki*, 3, pp. 520–22.

32. Ibid., 3, pp. 541–42.

33. Woonsang Choi, *The Fall of the Hermit Kingdom*, p. 6. *Meiji tennō ki*, 3, p. 568, gives two platoons, not three companies, of marines. The two warships were the *Nisshin* and *Mōshun*.

34. Choi, *Fall of the Hermit Kingdom*, pp. 6–7.

35. *Meiji tennō ki*, 3, p. 569.

36. A translation of the treaty is in Choi, *Fall of the Hermit Kingdom*, pp. 124–27. It was in twelve articles. The fourth article provided that trade should be continued at the Wakan at Pusan without restricting it to the Tsushima Domain. Two other ports would be opened "for commercial intercourse with Japanese subjects."

37. Joseph H. Longford, *The Evolution of New Japan*, p. 105.

38. *Meiji tennō ki*, 3, p. 578.

39. Ibid., 3, pp. 584–85.

40. The site of the villa, near the present Komagome Station, is marked by a stone pillar with an inscription commemorating Meiji's visit.

41. *Meiji tennō ki*, 3, p. 590.

42. Kido Takayoshi noted in his diary, "I am the first *shizoku* whose villa His Majesty has chosen to visit. Nine years ago I was summoned into the Imperial Presence, the first man without court rank to be honored with an Imperial audience" (diary entry, April 11, 1876, in Sidney DeVere Brown and Akiko Hirota, trans., *The Diary of Kido Takayoshi*, 3, p. 281).

43. *Meiji tennō ki*, 3, p. 606.

44. Diary entry, May 19, 1876, in Brown and Hirota, trans., *Diary*, 3, p. 297.

45. *Meiji tennō ki*, 3, p. 599.

46. The journey is described in great detail in a series of accounts given in Yoshino Sakuzō, *Meiji bunka zenshū*, 1, pp. 341–572. See also *Meiji tennō ki*, 3, pp. 614–81.

47. Kishida Ginkō, "Tōhoku go-junkō ki," p. 342; *Meiji tennō ki*, 3, p. 616.

48. *Meiji tennō ki*, 3, p. 646. The portrait of Hasekura is no doubt the one now displayed in the Sendai Museum.

49. On July 11, however, much to Kido's relief, the emperor walked some 100 yards down a steep hill (*Meiji tennō ki*, 3, p. 664).

Chapter 27

1. Shinpū is the *on* reading of characters usually pronounced *kamikaze*. The members took this name for their organization by way of signifying that they, like the

"divine wind" that had foiled the Mongol invasion, would protect Japan from harm.

2. *Meiji tennō ki*, 3, p. 709. The ideal of the Jitsugaku-tō, derived from its mentor, Yokoi Shōnan, was the creation of an American-style democracy.

 Despite the prominent activity of its samurai nationalists, Kumamoto was also known for its Christian thought. In 1876, the same year as the Shinpūren rebellion, the "Kumamoto Band," a group of thirty-five young men who had been converted to Christianity by L. L. Janes, an American teacher, swore an oath to save their country through Christianity. For more about Janes, see F. G. Notehelfer, *American Samurai*.

3. *Meiji tennō ki*, 3, p. 710. For the text of the manifesto composed (and read aloud to Shinpūren members) by Kaya Harukata, see Araki Seishi, *Shinpūren jikki*, p. 138. Among other charges, the government was attacked for seeking to ingratiate itself with the foreigners by forbidding the wearing of swords, secretly promoting the dissemination of Christianity, and intending to sell land to foreigners.

4. Ōtaguro had become the chief priest of the Shinkai daijingū in 1875 as the result of the policy of Yasuoka Ryōsuke, the governor of Kumamoto Prefecture, of appointing members of the Shinpūren as priests of the principal Shinto shrines. The rite of divination (as performed by Ōtaguro) was known as *ukei*. In order to obtain an oracle from the gods, three alternative courses of action were inscribed on slips of paper which were then inserted in a hollow tube. The tube was shaken, and whichever slip dropped from the tube was taken to be the will of the gods. All of the Shinpūren's important decisions were made in this manner, and the answer vouchsafed by the gods was absolutely followed, even if it disappointed the inquirer by denying support for some action. Ōtaguro had several times been forbidden by the gods to attack the government forces before he at last receiving a command sanctioning action (Shiba Ryōtarō, *Tobu ga gotoku*, 6, pp. 227–28).

 For the importance of *ukei* in the spiritual thought of the Shinpūren, see Araki, *Shinpūren jikki*, pp. 35–36. The mentor of the Shinpūren, Hayashi Ōen (1798–1870), wrote a study of the practice of *ukei*, tracing its origins back to the dispute between Amaterasu Ōmikami and Susano-o no mikoto, described in the *Kojiki*, over his failure to obey her command.

5. Members of the Shinpūren detested Buddhist priests and regarded them as unclean because their religion had originated outside Japan and was therefore alien.

6. These and other equally amusing examples of Shinpūren fanaticism are given in Kobayakawa Hideo, *Kesshi Kumamoto keishintō*, pp. 22–23. The author, although generally sympathetic to the Shinpūren, described such actions as "sick" (*byōteki*).

7. Mishima Yukio gives a highly dramatic account of the Shinpūren, from the time Ōtaguro first sought permission from the gods to stage his uprising until the final defeat (*Homba*, pp. 458–504). Mishima's account cannot be accepted as historical evidence, but he had evidently read widely in the surviving materials.

8. Shiba, *Tobu*, 7, p. 42.

9. Their name, meaning "shield and castle unit," indicated their determination to protect their lord (presumably the emperor) from all enemies.

10. They evidently did not know that the rebellion in Kumamoto had failed.

11. *Meiji tennō ki*, 3, p. 712. *Hōkoku* means literally "repaying [one's] country."

12. *Meiji tennō ki*, 3, p. 713.

13. Ibid., 3, p. 715. *Junkoku* means "to die for one's country."

14. *Meiji tennō ki*, 3, pp. 742–44.

15. Diary entry, January 4, 1877, in Sidney DeVere Brown and Akiko Hirota, trans., *The Diary of Kido Takayoshi*, 3, p. 419. For the text of the emperor's brief announcement, see *Meiji tennō ki*, 4, p. 4.

16. *Meiji tennō ki*, 4, p. 6.

17. The announcement of the forthcoming journey was made on November 22, 1876 (*Meiji tennō ki*, 3, p. 729).

18. *Meiji tennō ki*, 4, p. 30.

19. The text and prefatory material are from *Shinshū Meiji tennō gyōshū*, 1, p. 45. The poems are in reverse order in *Meiji tennō ki*, 4, p. 19.

20. *Meiji tennō ki*, 4, p. 21.

21. *Shinshū Meiji tennō gyōshū*, 1, p. 46. Both the prefatory note and the poem mention "rowing" into the harbor at Toba, probably a poetic term for the maneuvering of the steamship.

22. *Shinshū Meiji tennō gyōshū*, 1, p. 46.

23. Meiji was so upset when he saw how run-down the buildings had become during the bare eight or nine years since he had taken up residence in Tokyo that he arranged for 4,000 yen to be paid every year for their maintenance and commanded the Kyōto prefectural administration to consider how best to preserve them (*Meiji tennō ki*, 4, p. 48).

24. The insistence that the schools were "private schools" (*shigakkō*) was in order to make it clear that they were not under the control of the government-sponsored educational system.

25. Paraphrase in *Meiji tennō ki*, 4, p. 26. In surviving examples of Saigō's calligraphy, the maxim is given as *keiten aijin* (Revere heaven and love mankind), but in the private schools, *sonnō*, the term familiar from *sonnō jōi* days, was used.

26. The traditions were largely Confucian in origin, but instruction in the "private schools" did not deal with such "mainstream" Confucian works as the Four Books because it was believed they were intended for prospective officials rather than for samurai.

27. They included ten policemen (*junsa*) and several students, all natives of Kagoshima. These men were samurai but, being from the hinterland, were scorned by samurai stationed at Kagoshima Castle. Feeling was bitter on both sides, which no doubt was why Nakahara and the others cooperated with the central government.

28. The main points of the confession are in Saitō Nobuaki, *Saigō to Meiji ishin kakumei*, pp. 361–62. Nakahara had told a trusted old friend (who immediately passed on the information to his superiors) that the chief objective of his mission was to alienate samurai from the private schools. This would be easy in outlying parts of Kagoshima Prefecture but difficult within the city. The best way to destroy the private schools in the city would be to kill Saigō and his two lieutenants, Kirino Toshiaki and Shinohara Kunimoto. In his formal confession, Nakahara stated that as soon as Saigō was assassinated, a telegram would be sent to Tokyo, followed by armed intervention by the army and navy. Saitō, who believed in the veracity of the confession, admitted that it was obtained by means of torture but insisted that the use of torture was legal at the time.

29. *Meiji tennō ki*, 4, pp. 35–36. Ueda Shigeru stressed how unlikely it was that Na-kahara and those with him were acting under orders to assassinate Saigō, who was recognized to be a moderating influence (*Saigō Takamori no higeki*, pp. 157–59). Saigō's death was likely to stir up a hornet's nest, as those in the government were well aware. Ueda suggested that the government had deliberately circulated the rumor of a planned assassination in order provoke a reaction.

30. On this occasion, he saw *Okina, Miwa, Hagoromo, Ataka, Shōson*, and *Sesshōseki* (*Meiji tennō ki*, 4, p. 34). If these plays were presented in entirety, they would have taken a full day to perform.

31. Diary entry, February 5, 1876, in Brown and Hirota, trans., *Diary*, 3, p. 435. After describing the seizure of army and navy ammunition by Kagoshima samurai on January 30 and 31, Kido commented, "This is a very different situation from the one described by Hayashi Tomoyuki on the basis of his observations early in January. Today the powerful reputation of Satsuma reverberates to all corners of the land; malcontented *shizoku* in more than ten prefectures are observing the movements of Satsuma."

32. *Meiji tennō ki*, 4, p. 46. The prefectures mentioned were Kumamoto, Saga, Fu-kuoka, Kōchi, Okayama, Tottori, Hikone, Kuwana, Aizu, and Shōnai, some of which were subsequently abolished.

33. *Meiji tennō ki*, 4, p. 47.

34. Ibid., 4, p. 47.

Chapter 28

1. Diary entry, February 5, 1876, in Sidney DeVere Brown and Akiko Hirota, trans., *The Diary of Kido Takayoshi*, 3, p. 434.

2. This *tanka* is complicated. *Yaso uji* means "many clans," but the *kakekotoba* leads into Uji River, where soldiers of many clans once fought. The moon is clear in the water, but there is probably a pun on *sumu*, meaning "to dwell"—the moon dwells in the river. In the light of the moon Asahiyama, whose name means "morning sun," can be seen, a contrast between moon and sun.

3. The Komparu school was especially strong in Nara.

4. *Meiji tennō ki*, 4, p. 54.

5. This day was known as Kigen-setsu. It was proclaimed as a day of celebration in 1873, the year that the solar calendar was adopted.

6. Diary entry, February 10, 1877, in Brown and Hirota, trans., *Diary*, 3, p. 441.

7. *Meiji tennō ki*, 4, p. 61. See also Roger F. Hackett, *Yamagata Aritomo in the Rise of Modern Japan*, pp. 77–78.

8. The text is in *Meiji tennō ki*, 4, p. 77. See also Yamashita Ikuo, *Kenkyū seinan no eki*, p. 132.

9. The text is in Yamashita, *Kenkyū*, p. 133.

10. This is the figure given in *Meiji tennō ki*, 4, pp. 77–78. A breakdown of the component members of the total of some 30,000 men who fought during the war under Saigō is in Yamashita, *Kenkyū*, p. 137. The main body of troops consisted of the 13,000 "students" of the private schools.

11. Yamashita, *Kenkyū*, p. 152. This information is derived from various contemporary documents such as *Teichū Dan'u nikki* by Kawahigashi Sukegorō, and *Kesshi seinan eki* by Takeno Masayuki.

12. The text of the entire song is in Yamashita, *Kenkyū*, pp. 127–29. The author is unknown. Mention of *"shide no tabi"* (a journey to the other world) in the last line indicates that it was composed about the time of the move into Kumamoto. Each line of the poem begins with a different syllable, following the order of the *i-ro-ha* poem.

13. *Meiji tennō ki*, 4, p. 100.

14. *Kido Takayoshi monjo*, 7, p. 334, quoted in *Meiji tennō ki*, 4, p. 108. This statement is recorded in the letter Kido sent Itō Hirobumi, probably on March 4, 1877.

15. Ikai Takaaki, *Saigō Takamori*, p. 224.

16. *Meiji tennō ki*, 4, p. 121.

17. Ibid., 4, p. 120. See also Kido's letter to Shishido Tamaki, March 4, 1877, in *Kido Takayoshi monjo*, 7, p. 331.

18. *Meiji tennō ki*, 4, p. 119.

19. Ibid. By an extraordinary coincidence, both the siege of Metz and that of Kumamoto lasted fifty-four days.

20. *Meiji tennō ki*, 4, p. 125. See also diary entry, March 14, 1877, in Brown and Hirota, trans., *Diary*, 3, p. 463. The *battōtai* (Drawn Sword Unit) was subsequently immortalized in poetry and song.

21. *Meiji tennō ki*, 4, pp. 130–31.

22. Ibid., 4, p. 134. Kido made this observation on March 22 (Brown and Hirota, trans., *Diary*, 3, p. 468).

23. *Meiji tennō ki*, 4, p. 146.

24. For an account of Saigō's victory at Mitai-mura on August 19, see ibid., 4, pp. 237.

25. Ibid., 4, p. 181.

26. Ibid., 4, p. 223.

27. See also ibid., 4, pp. 247–49. Takasaki became Meiji's tutor of poetry at the end of August.

28. This was a building within the compound of the Aoyama Gosho, the empress dowager's residence.

Chapter 29

1. *Meiji tennō ki*, 4, p. 269.

2. Ibid., 4, p. 313. The emperor's gesture was not intended to cure the wounds, in the manner of the sovereign's touch in Europe.

3. *Meiji tennō ki*, 4, p. 276. He did not attend meetings on days of rest or religious holidays. He had still not entirely recovered from the beriberi he contracted in Kyoto, and the doctors urged him to devote himself above all to recuperating his health.

4. *Meiji tennō ki*, 4, p. 279. Yen Hui (Gankai in Japanese) was the favorite disciple of Confucius. A gourd was commonly used as a container for saké.

5. *Meiji tennō ki*, 4, p. 291. They read *Tsugan Ran'yō* (T'ung-chien Lan-yao), a historical work compiled by Yao P'ei-ch'ien and Chang Ching-hsing during the Ch'ing period, on Chinese history from ancient times to the Ming dynasty.

6. *Meiji tennō ki*, 4, p. 292. The empress's poem was "Unless one mends one's ways and lets fall the flowers in one's hair, even the light of the morning sun will not

be bright." The meaning seems to be that a life of indolence (flowers in the hair) destroys true happiness.

7. *Meiji tennō ki*, 4, p. 329. Fukuba Bisei, Nishimura Shigeki, and Nishi Amane were among the lecturers this day. Beginning on January 7, 1878, an even more demanding series of lectures was given in the presence of the emperor and empress, including one by Motoda on the *Analects*, another by Nishimura Shigeki on a textbook of morals written by an American, and a lecture by Kondō Yoshiki on the *Kojiki*. These and other lectures were delivered, except when the emperor was indisposed, until he left on his tour of the Hokuriku and Tōkai regions. For more detailed information on the contents of the lectures, see pp. 350–51.

8. *Meiji tennō ki*, 4, p. 316.

9. The *jiho* were officers appointed by the emperor to serve him by advising ("remonstrating") and supplementing his decisions. The position was established in 1877 and abolished in 1879.

10. *Meiji tennō ki*, 4, pp. 355–56.

11. Ibid., 4, p. 330. The letter, sent on December 17, 1877, accepted the invitation extended to Japan to participate in the exposition that would be held in Paris the next year.

12. *Meiji tennō ki*, 4, p. 338. The letter was delivered on December 28 by the new Chinese minister.

13. *Meiji tennō ki*, 4, pp. 331–32. The emperor commanded that all documents relating to the war, including the oral testimonies of members of the defeated army, be delivered to a historiographical institute (*shūshikan*). He also commanded the compilation of a history of the war.

14. His first attack was while in Kyōto in 1877. Ever since then, he had been prone to attacks at the change from summer to autumn. The attack in 1882 was particularly severe, requiring several months for recovery. Beriberi was common at the time, particularly among the military. It was estimated that more than a third of naval personnel suffered from the disease, seriously reducing the efficiency of ships at sea. A report prepared by the surgeon admiral in response to the emperor's request attributed beriberi to the poorness of the food served to the men. The food was improved; the number of patients dropped dramatically, and in three years it had virtually disappeared (*Meiji tennō ki*, 6, pp. 140–41). It is unlikely that the emperor's beriberi was caused by poor food. Japanese doctors probably did not know about the importance of vitamins, although the Royal Navy had long given lime juice to British sailors to avoid beriberi.

15. *Meiji tennō ki*, 4, pp. 368–69.

16. Somewhat abbreviated from Takashima Tomonosuke, "Jimmu irai no eishu," p. 33.

17. Hinonishi Sukehiro, *Meiji tennō no go-nichijō*, p. 80.

18. *Meiji tennō ki*, 4, pp. 372–73.

19. Ibid., 4, pp. 386–87.

20. Ibid., 4, pp. 399–400.

21. Ibid., 4, p. 253.

22. Tōya Hiroki, *Toshimichi ansatsu*, p. 27.

23. Ibid., p. 33. Tōya, to whose brilliant study of the assassination I am indebted, suggested that while in Kagoshima, Chō had come to embrace the ideal of a military dictatorship by the samurai.

24. The name was derived from the Buddhist temple in Kanazawa where the group met.

25. Tōya, *Toshimichi*, p. 80. Tōya's commentary on the manifesto (*zankanjō*) is on pp. 81–92.

26. For an exhaustive account of Kuga Yoshinao's activities before this time, see Kokuryūkai hombu, ed., *Seinan kiden*, 3, 1, pp. 407–18, and 3, 2, pp. 1014–17. Kuga spent time in Kagoshima, where he frequently met with Saigō's lieutenant, Kirino Toshiaki. It was Kuga who introduced Chō Tsurahide to Kirino and arranged for Chō to be "educated" by him (3, 2, p. 411).

27. Tōya, *Toshimichi*, p. 66.

28. Kokuryūkai, ed., *Seinan*, 3, 2, p. 1004. See also Tōya, *Toshimichi*, p. 65.

29. The full text of the *zankanjō* (in two parts) is in Kokuryūkai, ed., *Seinan*, 3, 1, pp. 436–57.

30. Kokuryūkai, ed., *Seinan*, 3, 1, p. 43; Tōya, *Toshimichi*, p. 82. For the full explanation of these crimes in the *zankanjō*, see Kokuryūkai, ed., *Seinan*, 3, 1, pp. 440–57.

31. Kokuryūkai, ed., *Seinan*, 3, 1, p. 438. See also Tōya, *Toshimichi*, p. 83.

32. Tōya, *Toshimichi*, pp. 70, 83.

33. Kokuryūkai, ed., *Seinan*, 3, 1, p. 439; Tōya, *Toshimichi*, p. 84.

34. Tōya, *Toshimichi*, p. 94.

35. Ibid., p. 100. Shimada also said that they would not have the time to tell people their reasons after committing the crime.

36. Excerpts from these letters are in Tōya, *Toshimichi*, pp. 102–4.

37. Ibid., pp. 101–2. This *chōka*, in alternating lines of seven and five syllables, goes on to list further crimes of Ōkubo and his associates and describes the heroic struggle in Satsuma.

38. Tōya, *Toshimichi*, pp. 127–28.

39. Ibid., p. 138.

40. An article from the *Times* (London) is quoted in translation in ibid., pp. 154–55.

41. *Meiji tennō ki*, 4, pp. 410–11.

42. Ibid., 4, pp. 413–14.

Chapter 30

1. *Meiji tennō ki*, 4, p. 414.

2. Taki Kōji, *Tennō no shōzō*, pp. 81–82.

3. Imperial Household Minister Tokudaiji Sanetsune was of the opinion that there was no objection to the free sale of the photographs. He requested the government's authorization, but in March 1874 it ruled that permission could not be granted and directed Tōkyō Prefecture to keep under surveillance persons who sold the photographs. In May, Foreign Minister Terashima Munenori appealed this decision. He said that foreigners were disappointed not to be able to obtain photographs of the emperor, even though in the West photographs of monarchs were freely sold. Now that the Japanese had become enlightened, there surely was no danger that selling the emperor's photograph would encourage disrespect; in fact, photographs would induce feelings of respectful affection. In December an official in Kanagawa Prefecture stated that in the absence of a prohibition, the

local police were allowing the sale of photographs of the emperor, empress, and dowager empress. He asked for a ruling. The following March the government prohibited the sale of the photographs (*Meiji tennō ki*, 4, pp. 435–36).

4. He was accompanied by more than 300 ranking officials, chamberlains, physicians, cavalry troops, foot soldiers, grooms, and so on, plus about 400 police (*Meiji tennō ki*, 4, p. 466). This entourage was still much smaller than the customary size of a daimyo's procession.

5. *Meiji tennō ki*, 4, p. 468.

6. Ibid., 4, p. 490.

7. Ibid., 4, p. 503.

8. Ibid., 4, p. 528.

9. Ibid., 4, p. 512.

10. George H. Kerr, *Okinawa*, p. 374.

11. Ōta Masahide, *Kindai Okinawa no seiji kōzō*, p. 92.

12. *Meiji tennō ki*, 4, p. 585. See also Kerr, *Okinawa*, p. 377.

13. *Meiji tennō ki*, 4, pp. 603–4.

14. For Meiji's edict, see ibid., 4, p. 628.

15. Ibid., 4, p. 642.

16. Ibid., 4, p. 659.

17. Ibid., 4, pp. 663–64.

18. Ibid., 4, pp. 665–66.

19. Hugh Borton, *Japan's Modern Century*, pp. 160–61. Borton gives in Chinese the phrase identifying the murdered fishermen as Japanese (p. 169).

20. The figure is according to *Meiji tennō ki*, 4, p. 690. According to Ōta, there were ninety-six retainers (*Kindai*, p. 104).

21. Liliuokalani, the queen of Hawaii, was not nearly as well treated by the Americans, who deposed her in 1893.

22. One party, known as the Kaika-tō, favored modernization of the country; the other, the Ganko-tō, opposed all change as destructive to tradition. The former tended to favor Japan; the latter, China. For a fuller description of the two parties, see Nakahara Zenchū, *Ryūkyū no rekishi*, pp. 131–32.

23. Nakayama Morishige, *Ryūkyū shi jiten*, p. 419.

24. Sasamori Gisuke, *Nantō taiken*, 1, p. 131.

25. Ibid., 2, p. 123.

26. Ibid., 2, p. 204. Ōta describes instances of violent opposition to the Japanese occupation of the islands (*Kindai*, pp. 106–7).

Chapter 31

1. William S. McFeely, *Grant*, p. 450.

2. Ibid., p. 457.

3. Ibid., pp. 453, 463, 472.

4. Li Hung Chang referred to his suppression of the T'ai P'ing Rebellion in the same years that Grant had conquered the rebellion of the southern states (McFeely, *Grant*, p. 474).

5. John Russell Young, *Around the World with General Grant*, 2, p. 411.

6. Ibid., 2, pp. 443, 447–48.

7. Ibid., 2, p. 451.

8. Ibid., 2, p. 533.

9. This took place at the Hibiya army parade grounds on the morning of July 7 (Young, *Around the World*, 2, p. 532). For a detailed description, see *Meiji tennō ki*, 4, pp. 702–3.

10. Young, *Around the World*, 2, p. 477.

11. Ibid., 2, p. 481.

12. Ibid., 2, p. 529. It is not clear whether this was true. It is possible that Meiji shook hands with earlier visitors such as Prince Alfred.

13. Young, *Around the World*, 2, p. 567.

14. Ibid., 2, pp. 533, 530.

15. Ibid., 2, pp. 542, 526, 538, 548.

16. Ibid., 2, pp. 527–28. An abbreviated version of this account is in *Meiji tennō ki*, 4, pp. 698–700.

17. The formal message of welcome from the emperor to Grant and Grant's reply are in *Meiji tennō ki*, 4, pp. 699–700. Meiji expressed his pleasure at meeting a man whose fame had long preceded him, his gratitude for the friendship Grant had shown Japanese visitors (especially at the time of the Iwakura mission) during his presidency, and his joy that Grant had visited Japan during his round-the-world voyage.

18. Young, *Around the World*, 2, p. 534.

19. *Meiji tennō ki*, 4, p. 703.

20. Ibid., 4, p. 703.

21. Ibid., 4, p. 704.

22. Ibid., 4, p. 705.

23. *Shimbun shūsei Meiji hennen shi*, 4, p. 75.

24. *Meiji tennō ki*, 4, p. 712. Saigō Tsugumichi and Mori Arinori were also sent to Nikkō.

25. Young, *Around the World*, 2, pp. 558–59.

26. *Meiji tennō ki*, 4, pp. 708–10. A detailed account of the conflicting views of Japan and China on the Ryūkyū question was published by John Russell Young in the August 15 and September 1 issues of the *New York Herald*. A translation into Japanese, published from October 14 to October 27 in the *Hōchi shimbun*, may be found in *Guranto shōgun to no gotaiwa hikki*, pp. 69–95.

27. *Meiji tennō ki*, 4, p. 720.

28. A page from the original English transcript is reproduced in *Guranto shōgun*, p. xiii. It is in normal, rather distinguished script, not in shorthand. Some words have been corrected, perhaps because the scribe in his haste made mistakes or because Grant himself, speaking impromptu, had made mistakes of grammar. The corrections seem to be in Grant's hand. The comments made by the emperor are very much shorter than Grant's words of advice. Sometimes comments are in the third person ("Expressed his hope for the most peaceful and harmonious relations with China"), suggesting that the interpreter had passed on to Grant only a summary of the emperor's words. Both the English text and the Japanese translation by Shimada Tanemori were at first preserved in the house of Yoshida Kiyonari, but later given to the Kyōto University Library (*Guranto shōgun*, p. 99).

29. *Guranto shōgun*, pp. 21–22. The English expression is unnatural, but the meaning is clear enough. The fault may lie with the typesetters of the English text I have used, rather than with Grant or the interpreter.

30. *Guranto shōgun*, pp. 22–23.

31. Young, *Around the World*, 2, p. 605.

32. *Guranto shōgun*, pp. 15, 18–19.

33. Ibid., p. 22.

34. Young wrote, "One of the odd phases of the English policy in the East is, that while England allows her own colonies to do as they please in tariffs, to have free-trade or protection, she insists that Japan and China should arrange their imports and tariffs solely with the view of helping English trade" (*Around the World*, p. 582).

35. On January 5, 1879, Sir Harry Parkes wrote a letter from "Yedo" in which he said, "The Americans have made a Treaty with Japan—such a Treaty! but they have protected themselves from its consequences by stipulating that it is not to take effect until other nations agree to a similar Treaty, which we, for one, are certainly not likely to do" (quoted in F. V. Dickins and S. Lane-Poole, *The Life of Sir Harry Parkes*, 2, p. 268). For provisions of the American treaty (which was never put into effect), see *Shimbun shūsei Meiji hennen shi*, 4, pp. 72–73. The treaty, signed in Washington by Yoshida Kiyonari and Secretary of State William M. Evarts, was dated August 7, 1878. It was approved by Meiji on February 7, 1879.

36. *Guranto shōgun*, p. 26.

37. Ibid., p. 17.

38. Asukai Masamichi, *Meiji taitei*, p. 183.

39. Asukai wrote that because Grant's advocacy of gradualism came from a leader of an advanced country, it probably greatly strengthened the hand of the emperor, who had already demonstrated his preference for a gradual approach to the creation of a parliament (*Meiji taitei*, p. 183). At this time, by contrast, Ōkuma Shigenobu favored setting a timetable for calling a parliament within two years.

40. *Meiji tennō ki*, 4, pp. 729–32. Grant urged the Japanese to withdraw the harsh words they had used about the Chinese, and the Chinese, to withdraw the equally harsh language they had used about the Japanese. A useful summary in English of the negotiations between Japan and China is in George H. Kerr, *Okinawa*, pp. 389–92.

41. Kerr, *Okinawa*, p. 389.

42. *Shimbun shūsei Meiji hennen shi*, 4, p. 75.

43. For a full account of the festivities, see *Meiji tennō ki*, 4, pp. 735–40.

44. Young, *Around the World*, 2, p. 573.

45. The curtain was crimson with the word *shōhei*, or "peace," embroidered in white. To one side were the words "Guranto yori" (from Grant) woven in gold thread.

46. For an account of the play, see *Engeki hyakka daijiten*, 2, p. 477. Although the cast included the greatest stars of kabuki—the ninth Ichikawa Danjūrō, the first Ichikawa Sadanji, the third Nakamura Nakazō, etc.—it was not a success.

47. McFeely, *Grant*, p. 468.

48. Yanagizawa Hideki, *Hōshō Kurō den*, p. 34.

49. *Meiji tennō ki*, 4, p. 741. A similar, but not identical, speech is in *Shimbun shūsei Meiji hennen shi*, 4, p. 97. I have quoted elements of both.

50. Young, *Around the World*, 2, p. 602.

Chapter 32

1. Harunomiya was a name denoting the crown prince, but the infant had not yet been so designated.

2. *Meiji tennō ki*, 4, pp. 755–56. Probably Naruko was still suffering from the hysterics she had at the time of the birth.

3. *Meiji tennō ki*, 4, pp. 821, 827. These works of art reached Japan in June. The government was of the opinion that they should be accepted by the Imperial Household Ministry, but it was not until December that these works were acknowledged. Ugolini was sent money and various expensive gifts. His portrait of the emperor is included in *Meiji tennō no Go-Shōzō*.

4. *Meiji tennō ki*, 4, pp. 746, 820. Meiji soon afterward sent a telegram to Alfonso XII congratulating him on his narrow escape from an assassin (*Meiji tennō ki*, 5, p. 2).

5. *Meiji tennō ki*, 4, pp. 773–74.

6. Ibid., 4, pp. 777–78.

7. Ibid., 4, p. 245. The *jiho*, a name proposed by Itō Hirobumi, was an office within the Imperial Household Ministry whose members were to serve and advise the emperor, compensating for possible deficiencies in the administration.

8. Asukai Masamichi, *Meiji taitei*, pp. 175–76.

9. This and the previous poem are quoted from Watanabe Ikujirō, *Meiji tennō*, 1, p. 159. Watanabe did not indicate that the former dated from 1907 and the latter from 1909 (*Shinshū Meiji tennō gyoshū*, pp. 911, 1023). Watanabe seems to have believed that both these two poems, written from quite different points of view, were characteristic of Emperor Meiji.

10. Kishida Ginkō, "Tōhoku go-junkō ki," p. 396.

11. Asukai, *Meiji taitei*, p. 173.

12. *Meiji tennō ki*, 4, pp. 364–65.

13. Watanabe Ikujirō, *Meiji tennō*, 1, p. 220.

14. For a brief account of the directive (as issued by the Ministry of Education on September 5, 1871), see Kokuritsu kyōiku kenkyūjo, ed., *Nihon kindai kyōiku hyakunen shi*, pp. 477–89. The plan called for 8 university districts, further subdivided into 32 middle-school districts, with each middle-school district divided into 210 elementary-school districts. This would be a total of 53,760 elementary schools, or 1 school for each 600 pupils. The organization of the school system was an indication of French influence, and several of the men responsible had written or translated studies of French education (Katsube Mitake and Shibukawa Hisako, *Dōtoku kyōiku no rekishi*, p. 11). The curriculum actually followed in the schools tended to be modeled on American examples, under the influence of Guido Verbeck and other Americans. But France was the only major country with *instruction morale et religieuse* as an integral part of the curriculum, and this appealed to the Japanese (Katsube and Shibukawa, *Dōtoku*, p. 211).

15. Asukai, *Meiji taitei*, p. 176.

16. Katsube and Shibukawa, *Dōtoku*, p. 13. The term *shūshin* was defined as *gyōgi no satoshi* (instruction in deportment). *Shūshin* remained a part of the curriculum until the end of 1945.

17. *Meiji tennō ki*, 4, p. 758.

18. Ibid., 4, pp. 758–59.
19. Ibid., 4, p. 759.
20. Ibid., 4, pp. 760–63. A translation of Itō's memorial to the throne is in Herbert Passin, *Society and Education in Japan*, pp. 230–33.
21. Asukai, *Meiji taitei*, p. 178.
22. *Meiji tennō ki*, 4, pp. 760–64.
23. Kōno's explanation of why it was necessary to change the educational system, presented to the emperor on December 9, is in *Meiji tennō ki*, 5, pp. 248–50. He denied that there had been excessive "meddling" by government officials in running the schools. See also Kokuritsu kyōiku kenkyūjo, ed., *Nihon kindai kyōiku hyakyunen shi*, p. 930.
24. *Meiji tennō ki*, 5, p. 250.
25. Asukai, *Meiji taitei*, p. 178.

Chapter 33

1. On February 17 Meiji sent a telegram of congratulations to Czar Alexander II on his having escaped a bomb that destroyed part of his palace (*Meiji tennō ki*, 5, p. 21).
2. Sakamoto Kazuto, *Itō Hirobumi to Meiji kokka keisei*, p. 24. The emperor had previously (from April 4, 1879) attended cabinet meetings on Monday, Wednesday, and Friday mornings, but after the change made on March 17, 1880, in the regulations governing cabinet meetings, the emperor attended all meetings except those held on Sundays or holidays. For the regulations, see *Meiji tennō ki* 5, pp. 35–36. Note that the word *naikaku* (cabinet) did not have the modern meaning of "cabinet"; rather, it was the body of *sangi* (councillors), who were officially (*hohitsu*) "advisers" to the *daijin* (ministers) (Sakamoto, *Itō*, p. 20).
3. Sakamoto discusses Itō's reasons for desiring the emperor's participation in cabinet meetings (*Itō*, pp. 12, 15, 19). It was essentially as a symbolic leader whose presence lent authority rather than as a sponsor of new ideas or as the spokesman of the conservative views typical of the *jiho*.
4. This presupposed exchanging paper for specie at a rate of 1 yen 15 sen for 1 yen in specie (*Meiji tennō ki*, 5, p. 71).
5. Sakamoto, *Itō*, p. 29.
6. *Meiji tennō ki*, 5, pp. 74–75.
7. He actually visited other prefectures in the course of the journey (including Kanagawa, Nagano, and Shiga), but the journey was officially to these three prefectures.
8. Tōyama Shigeki, *Tennō to kazoku*, p. 81.
9. An account of the journey by a reporter named Noda Chiaki was published in the *Chōya shimbun*. Excerpts are in Tōyama, *Tennō*, pp. 82–86. The first excerpt is the account of an old man who attempted to present a petition directly to the emperor but was prevented by the police. They contended that the man was deranged and drove him away, but the subject of the petition was probably quite rational, the convening of a parliament. The second excerpt concludes with a brief account of action taken by the police against a reporter for the *Iroha shimbun* who had mentioned in an article that a policeman had discovered a noble in the

emperor's escort sleeping with a geisha he brought with him from Tokyo. The police, warning the reporter that printing groundless rumors could cause immeasurable harm, required him in the future to submit articles in advance to a police officer, a beginning of censorship of the press.

10. *Ōsaka shimpō*, May 29, 1880, in Tōyama, *Tennō*, p. 94.

11. Tōyama, *Tennō*, pp. 94–95. The article by Takizawa Shigeru, describing the Niigata segment of the *junkō*, confirms that the expenses were met by local rich people ("Hokuriku junkō to minshū tōchi," p. 36). Because they were enjoined not to be extravagant in their reception of the emperor, many falsified their expense reports. In the most extreme case, real expenses of 45,000 yen were reported as a mere 90.30 yen.

12. Tōyama, *Tennō*, p. 88.

13. Historians speak of the Six Great Imperial Tours (*roku daijunkō*). Not all travels by the emperor were known as *daijunkō*. Of his three later lengthy journeys, the one in 1881 (to northern Honshū and Hokkaidō) and the one in 1885 (to Yamaguchi, Itsukushima, Hiroshima, and Okayama) are counted among the *daijunkō*, but the emperor's voyage in 1890 to Kure, Etajima, and Sasebo is not so termed, perhaps because it was made by sea rather than land.

   Meiji also made numerous day excursions to the race track in Yokohama, to maneuvers in Chiba, and to the launching of ships at Yokosuka, and so on, and he spent much of 1894 and 1895 in Hiroshima during the Sino-Japanese War. These travels were of course quite dissimilar in character to the *junkō*.

14. Tōyama, *Tennō*, p. 90.

15. Ibid., p. 101.

16. See especially T. Fujitani, *Splendid Monarchy*: "Through these pageants and various written and nonwritten representations of them the people could begin to imagine that the emperor was at the apex of a panoptic regime and that he was the Overseer who disciplined the realm and the people within his gaze" (pp. 55–56). For a somewhat different interpretation of the facts, see Takizawa Shigeru, "Hokuriku junkō to minshū tōchi," pp. 24–25.

17. For example, on April 11, 1881, when the emperor went to the horse races at the Fukiage Garden, he was accompanied by more than 160 persons (*Meiji tennō ki*, 5, p. 328).

18. *Meiji tennō ki*, 5, p. 87.

19. Ibid., 5, p. 93.

20. Ibid., 5, p. 128. See also *Meiji tennō ki*, 2, pp. 76–77.

21. *Meiji tennō ki* 5, p. 144. Meiji was known as Sachinomiya until he received the name Mutsuhito.

22. *Meiji tennō ki*, 5, p. 164.

23. Ibid., 5, pp. 171–73.

24. Perhaps the worst example of extravagance was the Naval Ministry, which eagerly bought whatever new weapons were invented in Europe and America, sometimes getting quite different items from what they thought they had ordered (*Meiji tennō ki*, 5, p. 182).

25. *Meiji tennō ki*, 5, p. 179.

26. Watanabe Akio detected an "extremely dense coloring" of the views of Motoda and Sasaki in Meiji's pronouncements on the need for economy ("Tennōsei kokka

keisei tojō ni okeru 'tennō shinsei' no shisō to undō," p. 2). This was also true of his other proclamations at this time.

27. *Meiji tennō ki*, 5, p. 176. See also Sakamoto, *Itō*, p. 37.

28. *Meiji tennō ki*, 5, p. 181.

29. The highest political organ of the state, established in 1871 and abolished in 1877. It consisted of the *dajō daijin*, the *sadaijin*, the *udaijin*, and the *sangi*.

30. *Meiji tennō ki*, 3, p. 696. Meiji's command to Prince Taruhito, directing him to frame a constitution, was issued on September 7, 1876 (*Meiji tennō ki*, 5, p. 245).

31. *Guranto shōgun to no go-taiwa hikki*, p. 17. See also *Meiji tennō ki*, 4, p. 722.

32. *Meiji tennō ki*, 5, p. 168.

33. Ibid., 5, p. 234. See also Sakamoto, *Itō*, p. 43.

34. He advocated borrowing the content from England, the United States, and France but borrowing the form from Germany, Austria, Holland, Belgium, Italy, Spain, and Portugal (*Meiji tennō ki*, 5, p. 246).

35. *Meiji tennō ki*, 5, p. 49.

36. Kasahara Hidehiko, *Tennō shinsei*, p. 174.

Chapter 34

1. Sasaki Takayuki, *Hogo Hiroi*, 10, pp. 1–2.

2. *Meiji tennō ki*, 5, p. 254.

3. On January 7, when it was customary for him to hear his first lectures of the year, the emperor went to Yokohama to inspect the Italian warship aboard which the duke of Genoa was about to leave Japan (*Meiji tennō ki*, 5, p. 257).

4. *Meiji tennō ki*, 5, p. 259. This was even fewer than the twenty-three delivered in 1880, itself an extremely low figure. Soejima lectured on the Confucian classic the *Doctrine of the Mean*. Nishimura may have lectured on moral philosophy, a subject that preoccupied him at the time. Motoda attended all lectures, even when he did not speak.

5. *Meiji tennō ki*, 5, pp. 265–66. See also Sasaki, *Hogo Hiroi*, 10, pp. 66–68. Sasaki's own account gives many more details of the conversation.

6. Mori Senzō, *Meiji jimbutsu yawa*, pp. 19–20. See also *Meiji tennō ki*, 5, pp. 281–82.

7. The music of the anthem had been borrowed from a foreign woman who had served as a missionary in Hawaii by American Consul General Robert Walker Irwin (a descendant of Benjamin Franklin), who had in turn passed it on to the Japanese military band (Aramata Hiroshi, *Karakaua-ō no Nippon gyōten ryokōki*, p. 70).

8. William N. Armstrong, *Around the World with a King*, p. 37.

9. Ibid., p. 39.

10. Ibid., pp. 47–48.

11. Ibid., p. 50.

12. The exchange of rings was probably intended to signify the emperor would not break his unwritten promise. Apparently, Meiji did not give Kalakaua his ring.

13. This account of the secret meeting between Meiji and King Kalakaua is taken from *Meiji tennō ki*, 5, pp. 294–98. It is not found in Armstrong's *Around the World with a King*, evidence that Kalakaua did not reveal to members of his suite

what he had proposed. Armstrong expressed annoyance with the king for his mysterious departure from their quarters: "It was a neglect of his own suite which was entirely contrary to etiquette. Its secrecy puzzled us, as he usually placed the fullest confidence in us" (p. 62). *Meiji tennō ki* gives no fewer than thirteen sources for its account, but the letters of Inoue Kaoru and the report of Nagasaki Seigo (the interpreter) probably provided the bulk of the information about the secret meeting.

14. *Meiji tennō ki*, 5, p. 296. Yamashinanomiya Sadamaro (1865–1921) was the son of Prince Fushiminomiya Akira. His letter to Kalakaua, dated January 14, 1882, in which he explains why he cannot marry Princess Kaiulani, is in the Bishop Museum in Honolulu. The prince revealed that he had been engaged as a small child and that he was therefore not at liberty to consider marriage to the princess. Although the prince did not say so, there was undoubtedly opposition to a member of the imperial family's marrying a foreigner. According to Armstrong, "The emperor received his suggestion with excellent humour and politeness, but declared that it required much reflection and would be a startling departure from Japanese traditions" (*Around the World*, p. 63). (Prince Yoshihisa, who had married a member of the German nobility while residing in Europe, had been forced to divorce her.) Armstrong, who dismissed the planned marriage as something conceived by the king in "the curious recesses of his Polynesian brain," was sure that "had the scheme been accepted by the emperor, it would have tended to make Hawaii a Japanese colony; a movement distasteful to all of the Great Powers."

15. Aramata, *Karakaua-ō*, pp. 298–300. There were two problems connected with the cable. The first was the lack of Japanese funds for such a project; the second was the prior request by an American, Cyrus Field (who had successfully laid the Atlantic cable linking the United States and Great Britain), which would have to be given preference (*Meiji tennō ki*, 5, p. 674).

16. There was one exception. Inoue Kaoru enthusiastically accepted the king's request that Japanese be encouraged to emigrate to Hawaii (*Meiji tennō ki*, 5, p. 674; Aramata, *Karakaua-ō*, p. 151).

17. On January 24, 1882, Meiji sent Kalakaua a letter in which he expressed his appreciation of Kalakaua's proposal that he head the league of Asian monarchs, and his wholehearted support of the project; but he reiterated his belief that it would be exceedingly difficult to create a league because of the diversity of the countries involved. He also declined, in deferential language, to head the league. The letter is preserved in the Bishop Museum in Honolulu (Kapiolani-Kalanianaole Collection) (Aramata, *Karakaua-ō*, pp. 299–300).

18. Aramata, *Karakaua-ō*, p. 139; *Meiji tennō ki*, 5, p. 298.

19. Hugh Cortazzi, "Royal Visits to Japan in the Meiji Period," p. 84. The source of this information is *The Cruise of Her Majesty's Ship 'Bacchante' 1879–1882*, compiled from the two princes' journals, letters, and notebooks.

20. Quoted in Cortazzi, "Royal Visits," p. 85.

21. Quoted in ibid., pp. 85, 87.

22. *Meiji tennō ki*, 5, p. 567.

23. Ibid., 5, p. 417.

24. He also stayed at the houses of rich men, Buddhist temples, a museum (in Yamagata), county offices, a medical school (in Fukushima), and the like.

25. *Meiji tennō ki*, 5, p. 506. At Yonezawa he heard a middle-school honor student lecture on *Nihon gaishi* and an elementary-school honor student lecture on *Nihon ryakushi* (p. 521).
26. *Meiji tennō ki*, 5, p. 535.
27. Ibid., 5, p. 536.
28. The founder of the Mitsubishi enterprises; he was said to have been annoyed not to have had the opportunity to purchase government assets that were being sold.
29. *Meiji tennō ki*, 5, p. 548.
30. I do not know in what way Kawamura irritated the emperor. Edward James Reed and his son visited Japan in January 1879. He had supervised the building of three Japanese warships in England—the *Fusō*, the *Kongō*, and the *Hiei*. When he visited Japan, he was given an audience by Meiji, who praised Reed's part in the launching of ships that were to become the backbone of the Japanese navy (*Meiji tennō ki*, 4, pp. 596–97.
31. Sasaki Takayuki, *Hogo Hiroi*, 14, p. 495. The account in *Meiji tennō ki*, 5, p. 558, is based on Sasaki, but differs in wording and minor details. I have incorporated elements from both versions in my translation.

Chapter 35

1. There had been opposition earlier to the idea of a popularly elected assembly. See, for example, Katō Hiroyuki, "An Abridged Translation of Bluntschli's '*All-gemeines Staatsrecht*' on the Inappropriateness of Establishing a Popular Assembly," in William R. Braisted, trans., *Meiroku zasshi*, pp. 47–49. Katō followed the translation with these remarks: "I beg the readers to believe that this translation is in no sense an effort to deny the validity of public discussion and public opinion. I only desire to explain the error of recklessly trying to expand public discussion without reference to the times and the condition of the people." See also Gotō Yasushi, *Jiyū minken*, p. 39.
2. The price of rice doubled between 1877 and 1880, and other commodity prices also soared (Gotō, *Jiyū minken*, p. 135).
3. *Meiji tennō ki*, 4, pp. 832–36.
4. *Meiji tennō ki*, 5, p. 228.
5. Ibid., 5, p. 229.
6. Ibid., 5, p. 231. See also Sakamoto Kazuto, *Itō Hirobumi to Meiji kokka keisei*, pp. 42–43.
7. *Meiji tennō ki*, 5, p. 309. Ōkuma was obviously much influenced by the British parliamentary system, which was a lingering source of antagonism between him and statesmen who preferred the Prussian model.
8. *Meiji tennō ki*, 5, p. 310. There was, of course, nothing new in Ōkuma's proposals; he was merely describing how the British Parliament functioned. However, the concept of a government run in response to the wishes of the people (or, at any rate, the electorate) was still quite unfamiliar to the Japanese. I have omitted some of Ōkuma's explanatory details.
9. *Meiji tennō ki*, 5, p. 313.
10. Gotō, *Jiyū minken*, p. 162.

11. *Meiji tennō ki*, 5, p. 314. For Iwakura's version of the events and the text of Itō's letter, see Tada Kōmon, ed., *Iwakura-kō jikki*, 3, pp. 698–700. Iwakura says that he asked Ōkuma if his views on the matter were the same as Itō's, as expressed in Itō's memorial presented on December 14, 1880. Ōkuma replied that the differences were minor. A few days later, Iwakura met Sanjō and suggested that Ōkuma's proposals be shown to Itō in order to verify whether or not his views were more or less the same as Ōkuma's. Sanjō agreed and obtained the document from the emperor. When Itō read it, he was dismayed and asked to resign his post as councillor. I have followed the account in *Meiji tennō ki*, based on many contemporary sources.

12. Sakamoto, *Itō Hirobumi*, p. 44.

13. *Meiji tennō ki*, 5, pp. 318–19.

14. Sasaki Takayuki, *Hogo Hiroi*, 10, pp. 152–53. See also *Meiji tennō ki*, 5, p. 319; the wording is somewhat dissimilar, but the meaning is essentially the same as in Sasaki's account.

15. Braisted, trans., *Meiroku zasshi*, p. 90.

16. Gotō, *Jiyū minken*, p. 45. The generals were Yamada Akiyoshi, Torio Koyata, and Miura Gorō.

17. *Meiji tennō ki*, 4, p. 464.

18. Gotō, *Jiyū minken*, pp. 144–45. *Meiji tennō ki*, 5, p. 47, briefly mentions the proclamation of the sixteen regulations but does not enter into details. It mentions, however, that Sasaki Takayuki (with the support of Iwakura Tomomi and Ōki Takato) had earlier opposed adoption of the regulations because of the public anger they were likely to arouse, but their advice was not taken.

19. *Meiji tennō ki*, 5, p. 602.

20. Various dates are given for the formation of the Jiyū-tō. Some sources state that it was on December 15, 1880, when delegates of the Kokkai kisei dōmei met in Tokyo. At this gathering, Ueki Emori delivered an address in which he proposed changing the name of the organization to Jiyū-tō. He met with considerable opposition but, in the end, succeeded getting a vote in favor of a promise to form the Jiyū-tō. On this occasion, a program for the party in four articles was drawn up. It was agreed to meet again the following October (*Meiji tennō ki*, 5, p. 235; Yonehara Ken, *Ueki Emori*, p. 96).

   A more frequently given date is October 29, 1881, when the Kokkai kisei dōmei and the Jiyū-tō merged to form (the augmented) Jiyū-tō. This marked a more formal establishment of the party than the agreement reached in December 1880. Its announced program remained the same (*Meiji tennō ki*, 5, p. 566; Gotō, *Jiyū minken*, pp. 173–74).

21. Gotō, *Jiyū minken*, p. 171.

22. Yonehara, *Ueki Emori*, p. 24.

23. He was sent to a military academy in Tokyo after the domain school in Kōchi was abolished. The instruction at the academy was largely in French. Ueki dropped out of the school, possibly because he could not learn French. For details of his early life, see Yonehara, *Ueki Emori*, pp. 17–26.

24. This school of Confucianism prescribed a combination of knowledge and action.

25. Yonehara, *Ueki Emori*, p. 32.

26. Ibid., pp. 44, 52.

27. Ibid., p. 56.
28. Diary entry, February 2, 1881, in *Ueki Emori shū*, 7, p. 258.
29. Diary entry, March 13, 1884, in ibid., 7, p. 338.
30. Diary entry, August 2, 1879, in ibid., 7, p. 205.
31. Yonehara, *Ueki Emori*, p. 14. See also Ienaga Saburō, *Ueki Emori kenkyū*, p. 300.
32. Sonezaki Mitsuhiro, *Ueki Emori to onnatachi*, p. 53.
33. Yonehara, *Ueki Emori*, p. 112. The entry in his diary concerning his writing of the constitution is simplicity itself: *"Nihon koku kempō wo sō su"* (I drafted a constitution for Japan) (diary entry, August 28, 1881, in *Ueki Emori shū*, 7, p. 273).
34. The date chosen followed the recommendation of Sanjō Sanetomi and the councillors from Satsuma. Iwakura had proposed a delay of seven years before opening a parliament, and Ōki Takatō had recommended a delay of thirty years. For the text of the emperor's message, see *Meiji tennō ki*, 5, p. 547. He stated that he had long desired to establish a constitutional form of government and mentioned the gradual steps that he had caused to be taken in this direction, such as the establishment of the Genrō-in in 1875 and the opening of assemblies at the prefectural level in 1878. He said that the opening of a parliament in 1890 would represent the realization of long-standing wishes.
35. See the excerpts from Baba's diary in Hagihara Nobutoshi, *Baba Tatsui*, pp. 145–46. Hagihara points out that the diary was written in 1885, after Baba had broken with Itagaki Taisuke, so his account of the formation (and especially of his relations with Itagaki) should be read with caution. See also Yonehara, *Ueki Emori*, pp. 117–18.
36. According to Ōhashi Akio, Itagaki (who was off on a speaking tour of the Tōhoku region when the vote was taken) wished Gotō to become the *sōri*, and the meeting actually chose him, but Gotō declined the post (*Gotō Shōjirō to kindai Nihon*, p. 217).
37. Watanabe Ikujirō, *Ōkuma Shigenobu*, p. 93. Translation from Ryūsaku Tsunoda, Wm. Theodore de Bary, and Donald Keene, *Sources of Japanese Tradition*, p. 693. When he wrote about those who claimed their party stood for "respect for the emperor," Ōkuma may have been thinking of the Rikken teiseitō (Constitutional Imperial Rule Party). This right-wing political party favored a constitution bestowed by the emperor rather than one originating with the people. It was founded in March 1882 by Fukuchi Gen'ichirō (Ōchi). For a concise statement of Fukuchi's views as of 1880, see "Kokuyaku kempō kaigi wo hiraku no gi," in *Fukuchi Ōchi shū*, pp. 364–66. The party, supported largely by the Shinto and Buddhist clergy, was disbanded in September 1883 but, like other political parties, died only to be revived again and again, breathing its last in 1940.
38. Ōhashi comments that (despite the fame of this outcry), it is not known whether it was actually pronounced (*Gotō*, pp. 221–22). The assailant was an elementary-school teacher who had been influenced by the harsh criticism of Itagaki published in the *Tōkyō nichinichi shimbun* (edited by Fukuchi Ōchi). It was reported that because the local doctors knew that the governor of Gifu was anti-Jiyū-tō, they declined to treat Itagaki's wounds, fearing this might stigmatize them as pro-Jiyū-tō. He was treated instead by Gotō Shimpei, a physician who later became a prominent political figure.

39. *Meiji tennō ki*, 5, p. 687. At first it was suggested that he send the chief chamberlain, Tokudaiji Sanetsune, as *chokushi*, but the emperor disagreed, saying that an ordinary chamberlain would be more appropriate. This suggests a certain coldness toward Itagaki, but the governor of Gifu (notoriously anti-Jiyū-tō) was far colder. He acted as if he knew nothing of the incident and refrained even from asking about Itagaki's condition. This enraged supporters of the Jiyū-tō, who claimed that the attempted assassination had been instigated by the government. Some of Itagaki's followers believed that he should not have accepted the 300 yen that the emperor gave to Itagaki to comfort him, but he, reproving them, declared that it was out of the question for a mere subject to decline a gift bestowed by the emperor. It was only after the governor heard of the emperor's gift that he sent someone to ask about Itagaki's condition.

40. Ōhashi, *Gotō*, p. 223.

41. The interpreter, Imamura Kazuo, had studied in France and was a competent interpreter of French. Shortly before, he had been appointed by Inoue to a position in the government (Ōhashi, *Gotō*, p. 229).

42. Ōhashi, *Gotō*, pp. 227–28.

43. Ibid., p. 236. The account of Spencer's reaction to Itagaki's theories is found in a letter sent by Mori Arinori, then Japanese minister in London, to Itō.

44. Ōhashi, *Gotō*, pp. 237–38.

Chapter 36

1. *Meiji tennō ki*, 5, p. 600. The word *gunjin* naturally also included the navy as well as the army.

2. *Meiji tennō ki*, 5, pp. 601–2.

3. Ibid., 5, p. 608.

4. Ibid., 5, pp. 617–18.

5. A tiny figurine of the bodhisattva Monju (Manjushiri), said to have been Meiji's personal talisman (*nenjibutsu*), is preserved at Sennyū-ji, the Shingon temple in Kyōto closely associated with the imperial family. (For a photograph, see *Kōzoku no mitera*, p. 36.) The connection with Shingon Buddhism may have disposed him favorably toward rebuilding a pagoda on Mount Kōya. He gave only 50 yen toward rebuilding the Saikyō-ji, an important Tendai temple (*Meiji tennō ki*, 5, p. 651). Meiji was not the only member of the imperial family to make donations to temples: the empress dowager and the empress gave 500 yen toward rebuilding a building at the Tōfuku-ji, a Rinzai Zen temple in Kyōto (p. 690).

6. In *Royal Bounty*, Frank Prochaska describes the gift giving of British royalty (mainly in the nineteenth century) to schools, hospitals, orphanages, and miscellaneous charities. On occasion, Meiji gave money to schools and hospitals. On August 5, 1881, at the time of an epidemic, he donated the very large sum of 70,000 yen from his private purse to Tōkyō Prefecture for hygiene and disease prevention (*Meiji tennō ki*, 4, pp. 736–37). On July 27, 1882, during a cholera epidemic, he gave another 1,000 yen for epidemic relief (*Meiji tennō ki*, 5, p. 747). He even more frequently bestowed largesse on religious or scientific organizations. On February 3, 1882, for example, the emperor agreed to give the Kōten kōkyū-sho—a newly formed school for the study of the Japanese classics, Shinto, rites

and music, martial arts, etc. — an annual grant of 2,400 yen for ten years (*Meiji tennō ki*, 5, pp. 624–25).

7. *Meiji tennō ki*, 5, p. 633.

8. The emperor's personal property was a matter often considered. In theory, the entire land of Japan was the emperor's land, but there were no documents to prove this. With the end of the prohibition on selling land in 1872, even commoners came to hold title over land. In 1876 Kido Takayoshi had realized the importance of the imperial household's having a suitable amount of wealth. If the princes and members of the imperial family could not afford to live in a style proper to their station, how could they preserve their dignity? Kido declared that in no other country of the world did the royal family possess so little wealth (*Meiji tennō ki*, 5, p. 644).

9. *Meiji tennō ki*, 5, pp. 640–41.

10. Reference is being made to the restrictions on foreigners traveling in the interior of the country. They might be issued passports on application for "health, botanical research, or scientific investigation." Isabella L. Bird, who traveled in 1878 from Tōkyō to Hokkaidō with a passport obtained by the intercession of Sir Harry Parkes, recited the conditions for travel stipulated in English on the cover of the passport: its bearer must not light fires in woods; attend fires on horseback; trespass on fields, enclosures, or game preserves; scribble on temples, shrines, or walls; drive fast on a narrow road; or disregard notices of "No thoroughfare." He must "conduct himself in an orderly and conciliating manner towards the Japanese authorities and people"; he "must produce his passport to any officials who may demand it," under pain of arrest, and, while in the interior, "is forbidden to shoot, trade, to conclude mercantile contracts with Japanese, or to rent houses or rooms for a longer period than his journey requires" (*Unbeaten Tracks in Japan*, pp. 33–34).

11. *Meiji tennō ki*, 5, p. 657.

12. Ibid., 5, p. 658.

13. Ibid., 5, pp. 683–84.

14. Ibid., 5, pp. 712–13.

15. Ibid., 5, p. 743. See also Hugh Cortazzi, "Sir Harry Parkes," p. 15.

16. Cortazzi, "Sir Harry Parkes," p. 15. His source, quoted here, is F. V. Dickins and S. Lane-Poole, *The Life of Sir Harry Parkes*, 2, pp. 319–22.

17. Min is invariably used as if it were her personal name, but it was the name of her family, rather as if Marie Antoinette were known as Queen Hapsburg.

18. Woonsang Choi, *The Fall of the Hermit Kingdom*, p. 17; *Meiji tennō ki*, 5, p. 746; Katano Tsugio, *Richō metsubō*, p. 56.

19. Katano, *Richō*, p. 57.

20. Tsunoda Fusako, *Minbi ansatsu*, p. 115. Although this work is in the form of a novel, it obviously is the product of serious research.

21. For a somewhat different description of these events, see Hilary Conroy, *The Japanese Seizure of Korea*, p. 102.

22. Tsunoda, *Minbi*, p. 121. See also Choi, *Fall of the Hermit Kingdom*, p. 18, and Ki-baik Lee, *A New History of Korea*, trans. Edward W. Wagner, p. 273.

23. He is known by this title, which was reserved for a monarch's father who had not occupied the throne. His personal name was Yi Ha-ung.

24. *Meiji tennō ki*, 5, p. 750.

25. Ibid., 5, p. 752.

26. Chemulpo was the old name for Inch'on, the port of Seoul.

27. *Meiji tennō ki*, 5, pp. 759–62, 766–67.

28. Ibid., 5, p. 771. The immediate cause of Hanabusa's leaving Seoul is given variously. According to Choi, it was because, when Hanabusa demanded redress for damage suffered by the Japanese, the *taewon'gun* had "retorted that if the Japanese insisted on an indemnity the Korean government would feel obliged to levy a tax on all Japanese merchants doing business in Korea" (*Fall of the Hermit Kingdom*, p. 18). Katano states that when the allotted three days had passed, Hanabusa was informed that an answer would not be forthcoming because of the funeral of Queen Min (*Richō*, p. 68). In a rage that this internal matter had taken precedence over his mission, he screamed that he had abandoned hope for peacefully solving the crisis. According to Choi Suk-wan, the Korean court was shocked by Hanabusa's demands, especially the limit of three days in which to reply (*Nisshin sensō e no dōtei*, p. 33). Hong Sun-mok, who had been delegated by the king to respond to Hanabusa, had tried to secure a delay because of pressing state business, but Hanabusa, interpreting this as a sign of unwillingness to negotiate seriously, left for Inch'on after sending the king a final message on August 22.

29. Katano, *Richō*, pp. 61–63.

30. *Meiji tennō ki*, 5, p. 800.

31. Ibid., 5, p. 818, 838.

32. Ibid., 5, p. 840; Lee, *New History*, p. 276.

33. This was the view of Iwakura Tomomi (*Meiji tennō ki*, 5, p. 841).

Chapter 37

1. The *gagaku* musicians were better treated by the government, no doubt because their music was directly related to court ceremonies. They were guaranteed lifetime employment at salaries sufficient to pay for their living expenses (*Meiji tennō ki*, 6, p. 299).

2. Kotoko was the third daughter of the nobleman Chigusa Aritō.

3. *Meiji tennō ki*, 6, pp. 105–6.

4. Asada Sōhaku (1815–1894), a doctor of Chinese medicine (*kampōyaku*), had served as palace physician (*ōoku no jii*) at the end of the Tokugawa period.

5. Hashimoto Tsutatsune (1845–1909) had studied Western medicine with Matsumoto Ryōjun and later with the Dutch physician A. Bauduin in Nagasaki. In 1870 he became the medical officer of the Army Ministry (*hyōbushō*), which sent him to Germany for study. In 1885 he became surgeon general of the Japanese army.

6. They were Itō Hōsei (1832–1898) and Iwasa Jun (1836–1912), both trained in Dutch medicine. Itō Hōsei studied Dutch medicine at first with the celebrated Itō Gemboku and later with Pompe van Meerdevoort in Nagasaki. He also studied at the University of Utrecht, returning to Japan shortly after the Restoration (*Meiji tennō ki*, 6, p. 68). Iwasa studied with both Pompe and Bauduin in Japan and in 1884 traveled to Europe to study.

7. In December 1884 Prince Yoshihito suffered from what may have been influenza.

The emperor was extremely worried, and when he heard that Nakayama Tadayasu (the boy's great-grandfather) and Nakayama Yoshiko (his grandmother) were both praying to the gods and buddhas for his recovery, he sent word urging them to continue their prayers. It took Yoshihito about a month to recover completely (*Meiji tennō ki*, 6, p. 316).

8. The emperor's beriberi may have been caused by a vitamin deficiency, probably not yet recognized in Japan as a cause of the disease.

9. For example, from April 16 to 20 the emperor observed the spring maneuvers of units of the Imperial Guards at Hannō in Saitama Prefecture and vicinity (*Meiji tennō ki*, 6, pp. 37–42).

10. Rudolf von Gneist (1816–1895) was more liberal in his political ideas than Itō stated when recommending him. Gneist was indebted to British democracy in forming his philosophy of government.

11. Stein (1815–1890) was a professor at the University of Vienna. He was conservative in his political views, opposing universal suffrage and party government. His influence was particularly strong on the framers of the Japanese constitution.

12. *Meiji tennō ki*, 6, pp. 14–15.

13. Ibid., 6, p. 121. He received the substantial salary of 2,000 yen.

14. For example, the ancient rituals of the Kamo and Otokoyama festivals were revived after falling into desuetude at the time of the Restoration. Iwakura Tomomi was the moving spirit behind the revival; it was part of his plan to preserve Kyōto (*Meiji tennō ki*, 6, pp. 56, 111). The first revival of the festival in accordance with the old rites took place on May 15, 1884 (p. 206).

15. One matter of contention was whether members of the samurai class who had performed distinguished service should be considered to be members of the aristocracy (*kazoku*). Itō Hirobumi strongly advocated including such men in the upper house of the projected parliament along with the hereditary *kazoku*, but Iwakura was adamantly opposed (see, for example, Ōkubo Toshiaki, *Iwakura Tomomi*, p. 236). The issue was settled in July 1884, after Iwakura's death, with the Peerage Act, which provided for five ranks of nobility, replacing the old aristocratic titles, awarded on the basis of both the family rank (*kakaku*) and meritorious deeds (*kunkō*) (*Meiji tennō ki*, 6, pp. 220–25).

16. The emperor had been dismayed to see the dilapidation of the city when he stopped there during his Hokuriku *junkō*. It had occurred to him then that just as in Russia, major rites (royal burials and coronations) were performed in the old capital, Moscow, similar Japanese rites might be held in Kyōto. This was officially proclaimed in April 1883. Iwakura had earlier (in January of that year) submitted a detailed proposal for the city's preservation. He advocated not merely preserving the old palace but maintaining the city on the scale of the old Heian-kyō, and he wished to make plans for its future prosperity. Iwakura described the city's beautiful natural surroundings and glorious history and declared that preserving it was of crucial importance (*Meiji tennō ki*, 6, pp. 46–48) The acts of preservation Iwakura proposed in January were for the most part carried out when he went to Kyōto in May.

17. *Meiji tennō ki*, 6, p. 56.

18. Ibid., 6, p. 81. Before her marriage, the empress was indeed known as Ichijō Tadaka's daughter. By visiting Iwakura in that capacity (much humbler than that of empress), she spared him the obligation to leave his sickbed to welcome her.

19. *Meiji tennō ki*, 6, pp. 89–90.

20. A more formal eulogy of Iwakura, to be engraved on his monument, was composed by command of the emperor, listing Iwakura's achievements. The text was by Shigeno Yasutsugu (*Meiji tennō ki*, 6, p. 96).

21. *Meiji tennō ki*, 6, p. 99.

22. Hugh Cortazzi, "Sir Harry Parkes," p. 16. Satow's comment was made in 1881 in a letter to Parkes's future biographer, F. V. Dickins. Satow, who was Parkes's interpreter for many years, frequently mentioned Parkes's outbursts of temper— for example: "A great discussion took place on the Christian question, in which the Japanese spoke very reasonably, and Sir Harry likewise, until he unfortunately lost his temper over the arguments used by Kido, and made use of very violent language such as I do not care to repeat" (*A Diplomat in Japan*, p. 398).

23. Satow, *A Diplomat*, p. 141.

24. The proclamation was made on March 19, 1884. Earlier (on December 28, 1883) the emperor informed his maternal grandfather, Nakayama Tadayasu, that it had been unofficially decided to give Prince Kan'innomiya Sukehito a *songō*. The name is also pronounced Keikō.

25. Fujita Satoru, *Bakumatsu no tennō*, pp. 102–12.

26. *Meiji tennō ki*, 6, p. 200. On September 9 Japanese neutrality in the war was officially announced (p. 285).

27. *Meiji tennō ki*, 6, p. 210. This entry is dated June 1, indicating that by this time the illness had lasted more than a month.

28. *Meiji tennō ki*, 5, pp. 339–42.

29. Yoshii said he would personally take all responsibility if the emperor became angry with Fujinami.

30. *Meiji tennō ki*, 6, pp. 349–42.

31. Japanese seemed to have ceased to worry about the ban on Christianity, and the number of converts steadily grew. By 1882 there were 93 Protestant churches and more than 4,300 believers. However, the ban on Christianity was not completely lifted until the promulgation of the constitution on February 11, 1889. Article 28 stated that subjects had freedom of religion except insofar as this might obstruct peace and order or be in contravention of their duties as subjects.

32. *Meiji tennō ki*, 6, pp. 275–76.

33. Takezoe Shin'ichirō (1842–1917) wrote the extraordinary travel diary *San'un kyōu nikki*, describing his travels in China. See my *Modern Japanese Diaries*.

34. One curious consequence of the outbreak of the war was the French proposal of an alliance between France and Japan, citing the two countries' common interests. If the Japanese lacked sufficient funds for a war with China, the French promised to assist the Japanese by raising funds in Paris under the most advantageous conditions. However, the Japanese failed to respond, and the matter lapsed (*Meiji tennō ki*, 6, pp. 328–29).

35. It was sometimes called the Toknipdang (Independence Party). For a description of the Progressive Party, see Ki-baik Lee, *A New History of Korea*, trans. Edward W. Wagner, pp. 275–76.

36. For a contemporary description, see Hilary Conroy, *The Japanese Seizure of Korea*, p. 154.
37. *Meiji tennō ki*, 6, pp. 318–21. I have also derived material from Woonsang Choi, *The Fall of the Hermit Kingdom*, pp. 21–23. Choi's account, in turn, is based mainly on accounts by Europeans who were in Seoul at that time.
38. *Meiji tennō ki*, 6, p. 337.

Chapter 38

1. Tomita Hitoshi, *Rokumeikan*, p. 58.
2. Isoda Kōichi, *Rokumeikan no keifu*, p. 23. See also Tomita, *Rokumeikan*, p. 116; he states that the cost of erecting the building was shared by the Foreign Ministry, Army Ministry, and other ministries together with Tōkyō Prefecture.
3. Tomita, *Rokumeikan*, p. 7. The name Rokumeikan originated with Nakai Hiroshi, the previous husband of Mrs. Inoue. Nakai was not only well acquainted with Chinese poetry but a connoisseur of Paris; he founded the Miyako-odori dances in Kyoto as equivalents of revues (p. 51). Although the Rokumeikan was used mainly for balls, dinners, bazaars, and similar social functions, some particularly distinguished foreign visitors stayed there while in Tokyo.
    The poem that inspired the name, no. 161 in the *Shih Ching*, opens:

    > Yu, yu cry the deer
    > Nibbling the black southernwood in the fields.
    > I have a lucky guest. (Arthur Waley, *The Book of Songs*, p. 192)

4. A typical menu is in Tomita, *Rokumeikan*, pp. 189–90.
5. One particularly successful tutor was a German, Johannes Ludwig Janson, who was otherwise a teacher at the Tokyo Komaba Agricultural School (Tomita, *Rokumeikan*, pp. 165–67).
6. *Jogaku zasshi*, July 9, 1887, quoted in Tomita, *Rokumeikan*, p. 174.
7. Tomita, *Rokumeikan*, p. 164.
8. There is a photograph of the cartoon in ibid., p. 215.
9. Foreigners, proud to know the old name Edo (Yedo, Yeddo, etc.), were reluctant even as late as 1885 to use the new name, Tōkyō. This essay is part of Pierre Loti's *Japoneries d'automne*.
10. Quoted in Isoda, *Rokumeikan*, p. 23.
11. Quoted in Kondō Tomie, *Rokumeikan kifujin kō*, p. 154.
12. Ibid., p. 146. Sueko had served as the interpreter for the empress four years earlier, during King Kalakaua's visit (chapter 34).
13. For a list of some prominent participants and the guises in which they appeared, see Kondō, *Rokumeikan*, pp. 187–89. Photographs of two members of the government attired as the gods of good fortune Ebisu and Daikoku, and of two ladies dressed as Matsukaze and Murasame in the nō play *Matsukaze*, are in Tomita, *Rokumeikan*, p. 177. See also *Meiji tennō ki*, 6, pp. 732–33.
14. James E. Hoare, "Extraterritoriality in Japan," p. 95.
15. Tomita, *Rokumeikan*, p. 70. The foreign minister sent a memorandum to this effect to Mori Arinori, the Japanese minister to Great Britain, on December 11, 1883.

16. Tomita, *Rokumeikan*, p. 71. See also *Meiji tennō ki*, 6, p. 272. Plunkett's friendliness, a marked contrast to Parkes's intransigence, earned him the approbation of Emperor Meiji who (in July 1886) granted him an audience during which he conveyed his gratitude. The text of the emperor's statement on this occasion (which included praise for the similar attitude of the German minister) is in *Meiji tennō ki*, 6, pp. 615–16.

17. Hoare, "Extraterritoriality," p. 95.

18. Ibid., p. 72. See also Tomita, *Rokumeikan*, p. 31.

19. *Meiji tennō ki*, 6, pp. 447–48.

20. The empress and the empress dowager went to the Rokumeikan on November 19, but not for dancing or feasting. There was a charity bazaar at which they bought a few things (*Meiji tennō ki*, 6, p. 497). The emperor's dislike of excessive fondness for Western things, combined with a Confucian conception of the proper behavior for a ruler, kept him from attending a ball at the Rokumeikan. It was rumored, however, that on his visit to the house of Prince Akihito in June 1885, he asked what *dansu* meant. The prince responded by dancing with his wife, and the emperor expressed approval. For the rumor, see Kondō, *Rokumeikan*, p. 186; for the visit, see *Meiji tennō ki*, 6, p. 421.

21. In August, while on his *junkō*, he sent Prince Yoshihisa to inspect areas in Ōsaka, Kyōto, and Shiga that had been particularly hard hit by flooding. Rivers broke dikes at more than 2,000 places in Shiga, and nearly 40,000 people, threatened with starvation, were given assistance. Of this number, it was estimated that 23,000 would have great difficulty in surviving on their own resources (Kanai Yukiyasu, "Seijun nichijō," p. 628; *Meiji tennō ki*, 6, pp. 462–63, 468–69).

22. *Meiji tennō ki*, 6, pp. 377, 382, 385.

23. Ibid., 6, pp. 426, 443.

24. Ibid., 6, pp. 504, 510.

25. For an account of the *junkō*, see Kanai, "Seijun nichijō," pp. 604–31.

26. After exhausting all their adjectives to describe the steadily increasing heat, on August 10 the sober compilers of *Meiji tennō ki* declared that the heat stabbed through people like arrows!

27. *Meiji tennō ki*, 6, p. 453.

28. Ibid., 6, p. 475.

29. The text of the apology is in ibid., 6, p. 365. Meiji's brief reply is on p. 366. The Korean king referred to Meiji as *daikōtei* (great emperor) and to himself as *daikunshu* (great monarch). Meiji called the Korean king *daiō* (great king).

30. *Meiji tennō ki*, 6, p. 367.

31. Ibid., 6, pp. 369–70.

32. For the text of Sanjō's message, see ibid., 6, p. 373.

33. Ibid., 6, pp. 397–98. Many Japanese were incensed over the lack of firmness in their country's foreign policy. A number of men hatched a plot intended to secure the independence of Korea from Chinese influence by killing the Korean prime minister and others in the Sadaedang and replacing them with Pak, Kim, and other progressives, in this way eradicating Chinese influence. They believed that this would also help create a parliamentary system in Japan. Twenty or more Japanese crossed over to Korea, intent on destroying the Sadaedang. They drew up a manifesto and distributed it throughout the country. However, the lack of

funds and internal conflicts within the conspiracy led to arrests. Altogether some 130 men were involved, of whom 58 were tried in Japan in April 1887 (pp. 500–502).

34. *Meiji tennō ki*, 6, pp. 405–6.

35. Ibid., 6, p. 406. This information is found in the diary of Tokudaiji Sanetsune rather than in more official records. Itō was not the only person who was to be rewarded on this occasion: Inoue Kaoru received 10,000 yen for his efforts in settling the situation in Seoul, and Saigō Tsugumichi and Enomoto Takeaki 6,000 yen each. Inoue received his gift from the emperor on May 9, but no date was set for the other men to be rewarded.

36. *Meiji tennō ki*, 6, p. 433.

37. Ibid., 6, p. 436. Lavish preparations were made for the imperial visit, and the emperor gave Itō a set of silver cups with the imperial crest, a pair of bronze vases also with the imperial crest, and 1,000 yen. These gifts seem to have been made in honor of the visit rather than as a reward for service in China.

38. The strange circumstances that led to Kuroda's appointment in 1873 as a major general are given by Iguro Yatarō in *Kuroda Kiyotaka*, pp. 91–92. Yamagata originally opposed the appointment, and Prince Taruhito said that it would only invite disaster.

39. *Meiji tennō ki*, 6, pp. 15–16.

40. Ibid., 6, p. 371. At the end of May, when Kuroda was in Shanghai, on his way from southern China to Peking, he sent Sanjō a report describing recent acts of European imperialism in East Asia. He mentioned also what he had heard about defenses along the Kwangtung and Fuchow coasts.

41. Iguro, *Kuroda*, pp. 195–96.

42. Ibid., p. 200.

43. Ibid., p. 201. No doubt Sasaki's views, communicated to the emperor, had influenced him.

44. Iguro, *Kuroda*, p. 118. It was rumored that Kuroda, in a drunken state, had killed his wife, by either stabbing or beating her.

45. *Meiji tennō ki*, 6, p. 503. Normally, when the emperor visited the house of some dignitary, he was entertained with nō, but Kuroda provided instead sumo matches in a ring specially built in his mansion.

46. Iguro, *Kuroda*, pp. 198–99.

47. Itō's success in steadily pushing forward his program of government reform is described by Sakamoto Kazuto in *Itō Hirobumi to Meiji kokka keisei*. For an account of Itō's activities between 1883 (when he returned from Europe where he had studied the Prussian constitution) and 1885 (when his plans for a cabinet government were approved by the emperor), see pp. 105–36.

48. *Meiji tennō ki*, 6, p. 514. His message to the throne, explaining his reasons, is on pp. 514–16.

49. It is difficult to convey in English the change in the government. The previous government (*dajōkan*) had consisted of three *daijin*: *dajōdaijin* (prime minister), *sadaijin* (minister of the left), and *udaijin* (minister of the right). In addition there were *kyō* (ministers) heading each of eight ministries. Under the cabinet (*naikaku*) system, there was a *sōri* (prime minister) and *daijin* (ministers) heading each of nine ministries. Itō was working toward a parliamentary democracy like that in

England, with a cabinet consisting of members of the same party who were members of parliament and responsible to those who elected them. The English word "minister" translates not only *kyō* and *daijin* but *kōshi*, a minister to a foreign country.

50. *Meiji tennō ki*, 6, pp. 516–17. The emperor's proclamation on December 23 announcing the reorganization of the government is on pp. 518–19.

Chapter 39

1. A rare instance of mention of the nature of the emperor's illness is in *Meiji tennō ki*, 6, p. 595, where it says he was suffering from a gastric ailment.
2. *Meiji tennō ki*, 6, p. 530.
3. Ibid., 6, pp. 542–43.
4. Ibid., 6, p. 572. Shortly afterward, a stray bullet some twenty or thirty feet from the emperor's carriage hit a groom, passing through his leg. The commander of the Household Guards felt this was so grave an offense that he asked to resign his post. However, the emperor decided about a month later that the offense did not require a resignation.

    The empress seems to have taken an increased interest in military matters from this time. On March 28, 1887, she visited the Rikugun shikan gakkō and observed the various activities there (p. 721).
5. According to Yamakawa Michiko, toward the end of his life Meiji favored just two *gon no tenji*, Sono and Ogura Fumiko ("Kindan no jokan seikatsu kaisō ki," p. 194). Ogura was barren and for this reason does not figure in the gallery of portraits of the emperor's ladies.
6. Sono Motosachi was the third son of Sono Motoshige. Naruko, the wife of Nakayama Tadayasu, was the adopted daughter of Motoshige. This means that Motoshige was both the great-grandfather of Meiji and the grandfather of Sono Sachiko.
7. *Meiji tennō ki*, 6, p. 509.
8. Ibid., 6, p. 509.
9. Ibid., 6, p. 544. It is not clear from this account which variety of medicine was employed for the birth of the princess.
10. *Meiji tennō ki*, 6, p. 579.
11. Ibid., 6, pp. 504, 510.
12. Iizawa Tadashi, *Isetsu Meiji tennō den*, p. 53.
13. According to *Meiji tennō ki*, 6, p. 630, everything to do with the prince had been left in the hands of Nakayama Yoshiko (the emperor's biological mother). Although she was strict with Mutsuhito, Yoshihito's delicate health may have induced her to be excessively lenient with him.
14. *Meiji tennō ki*, 6, pp. 570–71.
15. Ibid., 6, p. 808.
16. The name of Tōkyō University was changed to Teikoku daigaku on March 1, 1886. The change was at the instigation of the minister of education, Mori Arinori, and reflected his belief that the principal function of education was to train persons who would be of service to the state. For a description of the changes in the structure of Imperial University at this time, see *Meiji tennō ki*, 6, pp. 551–52.

17. Quoted by Yoshida Kumaji in "Kaisetsu" to Nishimura Shigeki, *Nihon dōtoku ron*, p. 117. The lectures were given on December 11, 17, and 26 in the university's lecture hall and were open to students as well as the community at large.

18. Nishimura, *Nihon dōtoku ron*, pp. 10–11.

19. Ibid., pp. 12, 14.

20. Ibid., p. 14.

21. Ibid., p. 15.

22. For five failings of Confucianism (such as the lack of dignity for people of humble status and the inequality sanctioned between men and women), see ibid., pp. 28–29, and for four failings of philosophy, pp. 31–33.

23. Nishimura, *Nihon dōtoku ron*, pp. 60–64.

24. *Meiji tennō ki*, 6, p. 670.

25. This account is derived mainly from Kawai Hikomitsu, "Norumanton gō jiken," pp. 4–5. See also *Meiji tennō ki*, 6, pp. 644, 666–67.

26. The opening of the song ("Normanton-gō chimbotsu no uta"), a translation, and the music are in William P. Malm, "Modern Music of Meiji Japan," p. 287. The song opens: *Kishi utsu nami no / oto takaku / yowa no arashi ni / yume samete / ao unabara wo / nagametsutsu / waga harakara wa / izuko zo to / yobedo sakebedo / koe wa naku.*

27. Dissatisfaction was not confined to the Japanese. The French artist Georges Bigot published a cartoon showing members of the British crew safely ensconced in a rowboat while Japanese, only their heads visible, float in the water. The captain is demanding money from any Japanese who wants to be saved. The cartoon is reproduced in Irokawa Daikichi, *Kindai kokka no shuppatsu*, p. 438.

28. It is probable, however, that the warm feelings the Japanese court entertained toward foreign royalty were not fully reciprocated. In June 1887 Prince Akihito represented the Japanese court at the celebration in London of the fiftieth anniversary of Queen Victoria's reign. The prince was disgruntled to see that his name was missing from the list of foreign dignitaries participating in the ceremonies. And his hotel accommodations were inferior to those of European members of royalty. When he was about to go to Westminster Abbey, he was not provided with a state vehicle but had to hire a cab, and when he arrived, he discovered he was seated with Siamese and Hawaiian royalty rather than with members of the European royal houses. This (and other affronts) persuaded him that the British still thought of Japan as being no more than a small island in the Orient (*Meiji tennō ki*, 6, pp. 764–65).

29. They would be joined in Kyōto by the empress dowager, who had arrived there on January 14.

30. *Meiji tennō ki*, 6, p. 721.

31. Ibid., 6, pp. 712–13.

32. The Tōkyō Club was founded in 1881 as a place where gentlemen of both Japan and the West might form friendly relations.

33. *Meiji tennō ki*, 6, p. 732. See also Donald H. Shively, "The Japanization of the Middle Meiji," p. 94. He quotes a passage from the book *Jinshu kairyō ron* by Takahashi Yoshio, published in 1884, in which the author claimed that the Japanese, "with their weak minds and bodies," could not hope to compete with white men and would only be exhausted in the attempt. The only remedy was to

strengthen the race with intermarriages with the white race. When asked his opinion in 1892, Herbert Spencer advised against it.

34. *Meiji tennō ki*, 6, pp. 735–36. See also Inoue Kiyoshi, *Jōyaku kaisei*, pp. 108–9.
35. He returned to Japan on June 23 after more than a year in Europe, where he had observed agricultural, commercial, and industrial conditions. He had seen how armaments had increased, which had made him aware of the dangerous world situation. Perhaps that is why he also studied international law with Lorenz von Stein in Vienna (*Meiji tennō ki*, 6, pp. 765–66, 777).
36. *Meiji tennō ki*, 6, pp. 778–79.
37. Ibid., 6, p. 782.
38. Ibid., 6, pp. 788–89. See also Inoue, *Jōyaku kaisei*, pp. 112–13.
39. *Meiji tennō ki*, 6, p. 804.
40. Ibid., 6, pp. 803–6.
41. Ibid., 6, p. 799.

Chapter 40

1. *Meiji tennō ki*, 7, p. 20.
2. In the summer of 1888, the tutors of Prince Yoshihito (who had been afflicted with whooping cough in April) suggested that he be taken to Hakone to escape the heat. Meiji's permission was requested, but he was obviously displeased and gave his consent reluctantly, stipulating that it should be for only a week and that the prince must be accompanied by Motoda Nagazane (*Meiji tennō ki*, 7, p. 116). Probably he felt uneasy at the thought the prince would be so far away, but he may also have felt that it was incumbent on the prince, as on himself, to suffer through the summer heat along with millions of other Japanese. However, the stay in Hakone was evidently beneficial to the prince's health, and it became customary for him to leave Tokyo in both the summer and the winter for places with more equable climates.
3. Palace doctors of Chinese medicine were replaced in December 1888 with Western-trained doctors (*Meiji tennō ki*, 7, p. 167). In February 1889 the emperor asked army and navy surgeons to conduct an investigation as to why so many of his children had died (p. 203).
4. *Meiji tennō ki*, 7, p. 4.
5. A photograph would, of course, have been an even more exact likeness, but Chiossone (at a time when taking a photograph indoors required considerable time and illumination) could not have photographed the emperor indoors without his being aware.
6. *Meiji tennō ki*, 7, p. 7.
7. Baroness Albert d'Anethan, wife of the Belgian minister to Japan, recorded in her diary, "We went to tea with Signor Chiossoné, an Italian, who has lived here very many years, and we saw his wonderful collection of bronzes, lacquer, Japanese prints, and ancient embroideries. He also showed us his drawings of the Emperor and the Empress, which are the originals of the only existing portraits of their Majesties. Signor Chiossoné developed these excellent likenesses from sketches from memory, it being against the ideas of the Japanese etiquette or loyalty to the throne that the Emperor or Empress should permit themselves to

pose for either a painting or photograph" (*Fourteen Years of Diplomatic Life in Japan*, pp. 53–54).

Meiji's dislike of photographs was not shared by the empress. On June 24, 1889, she sent for the photographer Suzuki Shin'ichi and had him take her picture. On the following day, she sent for another photographer, Maruki Toshiaki, and he also took her picture (*Meiji tennō ki*, 7, p. 287). For the distribution of photographs to elementary schools, see p. 424.

8. *Meiji tennō ki*, 7, p. 16. Inoue's immediate successor had been Itō, who temporarily served as both prime minister and foreign minister.

9. For an account of the objectives of Ōkuma's party, see Joyce C. Lebra, *Ōkuma Shigenobu*, pp. 69–76.

10. For a brief account of Kuroda's meeting with Ōkuma, see Watanabe Katsuo, *Meiji nijūninen no jōyaku kaisei hantai undō*, p. 4.

11. *Meiji tennō ki* 7, p. 17. See also Lebra, *Ōkuma*, pp. 84, 164. Ōkuma's conditions changed in the course of negotiation; for details, see Watanabe Katsuo, *Meiji*, pp. 6–18.

12. Lebra, *Ōkuma*, p. 86.

13. *Meiji tennō ki*, 7, p. 50; this rather free translation is in Hugh Borton, *Japan's Modern Century*, p. 141.

14. The five functions of the Sūmitsu-in are listed in *Meiji tennō ki*, 7, p. 51. All relate to the contents of the proposed constitution and the procedures for modifying its provisions.

15. *Meiji tennō ki*, 7, p. 52.

16. Ibid., 7, pp. 74–75, 92, 94. See also Hijikata Hisamoto, "Eimei kurabenaki dai-kōtei": "Sometimes fiercely intent debates lasted for several hours, but His Majesty listened assiduously to each speech, and even after he had retired for the night he would comment that in today's debate so-and-so's point of view was correct; he would pass judgment on the good or bad of the different opinions. I was impressed by the accuracy and clarity of his evaluations" (p. 58).

17. *Meiji tennō ki*, 7, p. 93.

18. Ibid., 7, pp. 164–65, 324–25. See also Mary Crawford Fraser, A *Diplomat's Wife in Japan*, p. 27.

19. According to Dallas Finn, "But most foreigners, as diverse as Dr. Baelz, the Belgian Baroness d'Anethan, Britain's Lord Redesdale, and New York financier Jacob Schiff, found the palace magnificent" (*Meiji Revisited*, p. 94). Baroness d'Anethan, for example, wrote of the Throne Room that it was "a magnificent and vast apartment, laid with parquet floors" (*Fourteen Years*, p. 48).

20. Hinonishi Sukehiro, *Meiji tennō no go-nichijō*, p. 71.

21. At the time Yoshihito was spending the winter months at Atami, where Tani was also residing. This made it convenient for Soga to approach Tani repeatedly.

22. *Meiji tennō ki*, 7, pp. 192–93. Tani specified that he would serve in the upper house (House of Peers) because he had been created a viscount in recognition of his military service.

23. When the emperor learned that Tani was unwilling to serve in the Privy Council, he refused to take no for an answer. He directed the senior chamberlain to send an official of the Imperial Household Ministry to persuade Tani to change his mind. Tani was moved to hear of the emperor's disappointment, but he asked for time to reconsider (*Meiji tennō ki*, 7, pp. 201–2). Tani was later offered a choice

of a position in the Sūmitsu-in or the cabinet. He was not adverse to the latter but did not wish to fill a cabinet vacancy at the same time as Gotō Shōjirō. In the end, Prime Minister Kuroda appointed Gotō but not Tani (p. 246). The post of minister of education was filled by Enomoto Takeaki, and Gotō succeeded to Enomoto's former post of minister of communications.

24. *Meiji tennō ki*, 7, p. 197.

25. Ibid., 7, p. 200.

26. Ibid., 7, pp. 206–7.

27. Erwin Baelz, *Awakening Japan*, trans. Eden Paul and Cedar Paul, pp. 81–82. "Kamenosuke Tokugawa" was the boyhood name of Tokugawa Iesato (1863–1940). He figured importantly in the creation of the constitution. "Duke Sanjo" was, of course, Sanjō Sanetomi. Baelz described him as having been the "imperial chancellor," the German equivalent of prime minister.

28. Borton gives the provisions of the 1946 alongside the corresponding sections of the 1889 constitution (*Japan's Modern Century*, pp. 490–507).

29. Knowing of the emperor's aversion to Kuroda, Motoda cited an episode from Chinese history as textual evidence for rewarding a man with egregious faults: Han Kao Tzu killed one of his favorite ministers and enfeoffed a minister he detested in order to induce the common people to submit willingly to his rule (*Meiji tennō ki*, 7, pp. 213–14). The emperor, not persuaded by Motoda's argument, decorated only Itō.

30. According to Baelz, the newspapers made a hero of the murderer, and "there is a regular pilgrimage to Nishino's tomb in Ueno. The pilgrims are of all sorts, including students, actors, and geishas" (*Awakening Japan*, pp. 85–86).

31. *Meiji tennō ki*, 7, pp. 226–27.

32. Ibid., p. 227. Benjamin Harrison, a Republican, was sworn in as president on March 4, 1889.

33. *Meiji tennō ki*, 7, p. 237.

34. Article 24 stated, "No Japanese subject shall be deprived of his right of being tried by judges determined by law." Article 58 states in part, "The judges shall be appointed from among those who possess proper qualifications according to law. No judge shall be deprived of his position unless by way of criminal sentence or disciplinary punishment."

35. *Meiji tennō ki*, 7, pp. 284–87.

36. Ibid., pp. 297–98.

37. Ibid., p. 315.

38. Ibid., p. 333.

39. Ibid., pp. 339–40.

40. Ibid., p. 342. These were the questions of Katsu Awa (Kaishū).

41. *Meiji tennō ki*, 7, p. 349.

42. Ibid., p. 352.

43. Ibid., pp. 364–65. The source is Nishimura's Kengen-kō (Draft Memorial), written in September 1889. For a lurid picture of what would happen to the Japanese if they permitted foreigners to live outside the settlements and serve as judges of the High Court, see Nihon kōdōkai, ed., *Hakuō sōsho*, 1, pp. 395–411, esp. pp. 399–402, 409. For a study of Nishimura in English, see also Donald H. Shively, "Nishimura Shigeki." It should be noted that before this time many Japanese were

enthusiastic about the prospect of foreigners dwelling among them (*naichi zakkyo*) (Inō Tentarō, *Jōyaku kaiseiron no rekishiteki tenkai*, pp. 266–68).

44. *Meiji tennō ki*, 7, p. 325. According to Baelz, "What the Japanese want is to have the treaties revised in this sense, that they are to get everything and to give nothing in return" (*Awakening Japan*, p. 90).

45. *Meiji tennō ki*, 7, p. 371.

46. Baelz, *Awakening Japan*, pp. 91–92.

47. Ibid., p. 93.

Chapter 41

1. *Meiji tennō ki*, 7, p. 600.

2. Ibid., 7, p. 463. See also p. 568, where mention is made of the court's going into mourning for nine days after the death of the consort of the king of Korea.

3. *Meiji tennō ki*, 7, pp. 684–87, 691–93. On July 3 imperial property at Ikaho in Gumma Prefecture was set aside for the rest and recreation of the *kōzoku* (p. 586).

4. *Meiji tennō ki*, 7, p. 467.

5. Ibid., 7, p. 471.

6. Ibid., 7, p. 472.

7. Ibid., 7, p. 475.

8. Ibid., 7, pp. 507–10.

9. On July 15, 1890, the long-awaited British response to Aoki's modified proposals was received. After noting how greatly these proposals differed from those made in the previous year, Lord Salisbury predicted that it would take at least five years before the British would surrender their special privileges.

10. *Meiji tennō ki*, 7, p. 521. The emperor on occasion ate the simple food of inferiors, presumably as a gesture of solidarity with them. When, for example, he visited the warship *Yaeyama*, he ate the food served in the petty officers' mess (p. 484).

11. *Meiji tennō ki*, 7, p. 524.

12. Ibid., 7, pp. 526–27.

13. Mary Crawford Fraser, *A Diplomat's Wife in Japan*, p. 159.

14. Ibid., p. 166.

15. In addition to men from Satsuma, Chōshū, Tosa, and Hizen, two men who came from none of these domains (Katsu Awa and Enomoto Takeaki) had also received appointment to cabinet posts, probably because of long service to the shogunate.

16. Roger F. Hackett, *Yamagata Aritomo in the Rise of Modern Japan*, p. 135.

17. Mutsu was sentenced in 1878 to five years' imprisonment because of his involvement in the Tosa risshisha plot to overthrow the government. He was incarcerated for four years and four months. The emperor, who had pardoned others implicated in the plot, refused to pardon Mutsu. For a brief account of these events, see Hagihara Nobutoshi, *Mutsu Munemitsu*, pp. 47–48.

18. *Meiji tennō ki*, 7, p. 554.

19. Ibid., 7, p. 211. Three laws promulgated at this time were Giin-hō, Shūgiin giin senkyo-hō, and Kizokuin-rei (R. H. P. Mason, *Japan's First General Election*, pp. 27ff).

20. The House of Peers, although convened at the same time as the House of Representatives, was not elected in the same manner. The 251 members belonged to

such categories as members by right for life (imperial princes, princes, and marquises), members by election, and imperial nominees for life. For a good discussion of the House of Peers, see Andrew Fraser, "The House of Peers (1890–1905)," in Andrew Fraser, R. H. P. Mason, and Philip Mitchell, *Japan's Early Parliaments*.

21. Suematsu Kenchō, who declared, "If an illiterate asked for a proxy, Gombei was written as Hachibei or Gosuke as Rokusuke, as a result of collusion between the headman and the clerks. I was often a witness to the most baneful, for the electors, practice" ("Nijūsannen no sōsenkyo," in *Meiji bunka zenshū*, 3, p. 217), is quoted in Fraser et al., *Japan's Early Parliaments*, p. 43.

22. Fraser et al., *Japan's Early Parliaments*, p. 52.

23. Hackett, *Yamagata*, p. 137. Itō was formally appointed as president of the House of Peers on October 24 (*Meiji tennō ki*, 7, p. 658).

24. *Meiji tennō ki*, 7, p. 603.

25. See, for example, *Meiji tennō ki*, 7, pp. 532, 564, 565, 583, 586, 595, 596, 602, 607, 614, 621, 622, etc. A list of imperial properties, drawn up in November 1890, is on pp. 698–700. It is not complete, possibly because it listed only properties that were transmitted hereditarily. The holdings as of December 31, a total of more than 1,016,045 *chō* of *daisshu seden goryō* and more than 2,633,756 *chō* of *dainishu goryōchi*, are listed on p. 701.

26. *Meiji tennō ki*, 7, pp. 636–37. For the full text of Sasaki's proposal, see Tsuda Shigemaro, *Meiji seijō to Shin Takayuki*, pp. 698–703. The Kyōbushō (Ministry of Religious Instruction) was abolished in 1877, and nothing had taken its place.

27. *Meiji tennō ki*, 7, p. 638.

28. Ibid., 7, p. 645. The three holidays were New Year (Worship of the Four Directions), Kigen-setsu (the anniversary of Emperor Jimmu's accession), and Tenchō-setsu (the emperor's birthday).

29. *Meiji tennō ki*, 7, pp. 671–72.

30. Ibid., 7, p. 672.

31. Ibid., 7, p. 673.

32. Quoted from Ryūsaku Tsunoda, Wm. Theodore de Bary, and Donald Keene, trans., *Sources of Japanese Tradition*, p. 646.

33. Ibid., p. 647.

34. *Uchimura Kanzō zenshū*, 20, pp. 206–7, in ibid., pp. 852–53.

35. Tsunoda et al., *Sources of Japanese Tradition*, pp. 853–54.

36. *Meiji tennō ki*, 7, p. 676.

37. Ibid., 7, pp. 681–82.

38. Ibid., 7, p. 704.

Chapter 42

1. *Meiji tennō ki*, 7, p. 737.

2. Ibid., 7, pp. 754–56.

3. Ibid., 7, p. 759.

4. Earlier royal guests had been mainly second or third sons of monarchs (or grandsons in the case of the two English princes).

5. Count Sergei Iulevich Witte, *The Memoirs of Count Witte*, trans. Sidney Harcave, pp. 126–27. Nicholas's brother George returned to Russia after the ship reached India (*Meiji tennō ki*, 7, p. 795).

6. *Meiji tennō ki*, 7, p. 751. By contrast, the emperor gave only 200 yen for repairing the Kōryū-ji, the oldest temple in Kyoto, known for its magnificent sculpture (p. 780).

7. No doubt she is referring to the Hama rikyū.

8. Mary Crawford Fraser, *A Diplomat's Wife in Japan*, p. 275.

9. Yasuda Kōichi, *Nikorai nisei no nikki*, p. 9; Witte, *Memoirs*, p. 125. Nicholas took part in the ceremony on May 18, 1891.

10. For an extremely detailed account of the visit of the Russian prince to Nagasaki, see Nomura Yoshifumi, *Ōtsu jiken*, pp. 9–88.

11. Yasuda, *Nikorai*, pp. 22, 21.

12. Yasuda reproduces a photograph of Nicholas in a Nagasaki jinrikisha in ibid., p. 25.

13. All the purchased items, together with their prices and the shops where they were purchased, are listed in Nomura, *Ōtsu jiken*, pp. 80–85.

14. Yasuda, *Nikorai*, p. 24. Nicholas's cousin, the future George V of England, also was tattooed while in Japan.

15. Yasuda, *Nikorai*, p. 31.

16. Ibid., pp. 32–33. According to one local historian, Nicholas was entertained by the geisha Kikuyakko and George by O-ei, but Nomura believed that O-ei was the recipient of Nicholas's favors (*Ōtsu Jiken*, p. 86).

17. Yasuda, *Nikorai*, p. 36. On p. 39 a photograph of the *samurai-odori* performed on this occasion is reproduced.

18. Ibid., p. 39.

19. Nomura, *Ōtsu jiken*, p. 111. At lunch the same day, Nicholas made a point of complimenting the regimental commander on the splendid impression he had received of Japanese soldiers, the first he had seen since his arrival in Japan (Andō Tamotsu, *Ōtsu jiken ni tsuite*, 1, p. 144).

20. Detailed reports of the excursion (from contemporary sources) are given in Andō, *Ōtsu jiken ni tsuite*, 1, pp. 141–44.

21. For a diagram of the positions of the different jinrikishas at the time of the attack, see ibid., 1, p. 177.

22. Yasuda, *Nikorai*, pp. 11–12.

23. *Meiji tennō ki*, 7, p. 828. The czarevich summoned the two coolies to his ship and personally presented them with 2,500 yen each. He also decorated them with the Order of St. Anna and offered them a lifetime pension of 1,000 yen, although he expressed concern lest these ignorant men use the money in a way detrimental to themselves. Meiji was also worried about this and directed the foreign minister, Aoki Shūzō, to urge the two men not to use the money in an unworthy manner. Aoki not only warned them but directed the governors of Kyōto and Ishikawa Prefectures (where the two men originated) to keep watch on the newly rich coolies. For a account of one of the coolies, Mukōhata Jisaburō, see Osatake Takeshi, *Ōtsu jiken*, pp. 252–57.

24. Yasuda, *Nikorai*, pp. 16–17. The last such entry in his diary was written in 1916, the year before his death.

25. Yasuda, *Nikorai*, p. 12.

26. Osatake, *Ōtsu jiken*, pp. 51–53.

27. Witte, *Memoirs*, pp. 126–27.

28. Fraser, *Diplomat's Wife*, pp. 281, 284.

29. Ibid., p. 283.

30. *Meiji tennō ki*, 7, pp. 812, 813–14.

31. Ibid., 7, pp. 817–18. One of the doctors sent by the emperor was actually not a Japanese. Dr. Scriba was a foreign professor at the medical university. Erwin Baelz wrote, "Scriba and the leading Japanese surgeons, whom the emperor sent to Kyoto, were not admitted to the tsarevich's presence. They say that the Russians' attitude was most unfriendly" (*Awakening Japan*, trans. Eden Paul and Cedar Paul, p. 96).

32. *Meiji tennō ki*, 7, pp. 819–20.

33. Osatake, *Ōtsu jiken*, pp. 100–101. See also *Meiji tennō ki*, 7, p. 821. There is some confusion in the latter account; it says on the same page that Nicholas, fearing for his own safety, begged the emperor to accompany him, but this does not accord with other statements made by Nicholas at this time.

34. The letter is given (in Japanese translation) in *Meiji tennō ki*, 7, p. 825.

35. The emperor normally did not carry cigarettes, but he was specially prepared on this occasion, no doubt informed by someone of the custom.

36. *Meiji tennō ki*, 7, pp. 829–31.

37. Fraser, *Diplomat's Wife*, pp. 286–87.

38. Lafcadio Hearn, *Out of the East*, p. 254.

39. Ibid., p. 256.

40. Ibid., p. 260. A more sober account of Hatakeyama Yūko is given in Osatake, *Ōtsu jiken*, pp. 257–63. It does not contain Hearn's quotation.

41. *Meiji tennō ki*, 7, p. 826.

42. Fraser, *Diplomat's Wife*, p. 289. A drawing reproduced by Yasuda shows the deck crowded with screens, chests, and other bulky items (*Nikorai*, p. 55). Mary Fraser wrote that even very poor people brought presents—rice, shōyu, or eggs. It was estimated that the gifts would have filled sixteen chests (*nagamochi*) (*Meiji tennō ki*, 7, p. 823).

43. A list of organizations that sent messages to the wounded prince is in Andō, *Ōtsu jiken ni tsuite*, 1, pp. 489–93.

44. Osatake, *Ōtsu jiken*, pp. 79–80.

45. Mary Fraser described him as "an old sergeant-major in the army," but he was only thirty-six at the time of the Ōtsu incident.

46. Details of Tsuda's service during the war are in Andō, *Ōtsu jiken ni tsuite*, 1, p. 251. See also Kojima Koretada, *Ōtsu jiken nisshi*, pp. 193–94.

47. Kojima, *Ōtsu jiken*, p. 193. For fuller biographical information, see Osatake, *Ōtsu jiken*, pp. 248–52.

48. The reference is to the man who burned the temple of Diana of the Ephesians in order to achieve a place in history.

49. Baelz, *Awakening Japan*, p. 95.

50. His anger over these three points is found in the testimony he gave at his trial (Osatake, *Ōtsu jiken*, pp. 133–34; *Meiji tennō ki*, 7, pp. 834–35).

51. Andō, *Ōtsu jiken ni tsuite*, 1, pp. 248–54. His brother-in-law testified that Tsuda had said he believed the rumor and worried about the consequences of Saigō's return.

52. Kojima, *Ōtsu jiken*, p. 192; Osatake, *Ōtsu jiken*, p. 135.

53. Osatake, *Ōtsu jiken*, pp. 135–36.

54. *Meiji tennō ki*, 7, p. 840.

55. See the admirably clear presentation of the situation in Barbara Teters, "The Otsu Affair," p. 55.

56. *Meiji tennō ki*, 7, pp. 848–49.

57. Teters, "Otsu Affair," p. 59.

58. Kojima, *Ōtsu jiken*, p. 194. There is no indication that the pneumonia was induced by conspicuously bad treatment.

59. The diary and related materials are now easily available, edited by Ienaga Saburō, in the Tōyō bunko series. In June 1892 rumors circulated to the effect that Kojima was addicted to gambling, especially *hana-awase*, with his colleagues (*Meiji tennō ki*, 8, p. 86). The case against Kojima was dropped for want of evidence the following month (p. 97). However, on August 23 Kojima resigned his post, alleging illness. Apparently the gossip about his gambling, even if untrue, had made him feel disqualified to serve as a judge (p. 120).

60. Baelz, *Awakening Japan*, p. 95.

61. The letter is in the library of the University of Virginia.

Chapter 43

1. *Meiji tennō ki*, 7, p. 804.

2. Donald Keene, "The Sino-Japanese War of 1894–95 and Japanese Culture," pp. 261–62.

3. It is not clear which photograph was sent; possibly it was not a photograph but a reproduction of Chiossone's etching. On November 25 of the same year, tacit permission was given to sell portraits of the emperor, empress, and dowager empress (*Meiji tennō ki* 7, p. 934).

4. *Meiji tennō ki*, 8, p. 5. Shinagawa's first fame was as a composer.

5. There were 25 deaths and nearly 400 injuries.

6. *Meiji tennō ki*, 8, p. 19. In *Yamagata Aritomo in the Rise of Modern Japan*, Roger Hackett gives the figure of 183 for the popular parties.

7. *Meiji tennō ki*, 8, pp. 25–26.

8. Ibid., 8, p. 67. The Shūgi-in passed a similar resolution, affirming that officials had interfered with the election and demanding that the cabinet ministers accept responsibility (p. 68).

9. *Meiji tennō ki*, 8, p. 22.

10. Ibid., 8, p. 32.

11. Shinagawa was unrepentant about the methods he employed during the election. He explained, "If the obstructionists were re-elected it would endanger the nation's safety; therefore, various means were used to influence the election so that they would be defeated and loyal representatives would be elected. If similar conditions should prevail in the future, I would do the same again and exterminate

the obstructionists" (Okutani Matsuji, *Shinagawa Yajirō den*, pp. 286–87, as quoted in Hackett, *Yamagata*, p. 152).

12. *Meiji tennō ki*, 8, p. 32.

13. Ibid., 8, p. 33.

14. Ibid., 8, p. 39. Other evaluations by the emperor of the men around him are quoted from Sasaki's diary, pp. 107, 126–27.

15. *Meiji tennō ki*, 8, p. 94.

16. Ibid., 8, pp. 100–101.

17. Ibid., 8, pp. 103–4.

18. Ibid., 8, p. 227.

19. Ibid., 8, p. 104. The empress subsequently (on November 25, 1892) made a supplemental gift of 5,000 yen to the Sekai hakurankai Nihon fujinkai.

20. *Meiji tennō ki*, 8, p. 117.

21. Ibid., 8, p. 161.

22. Ibid., 8, pp. 187–88. As we have seen (in chapter 41), Meiji anticipated this possibility. Itō had told him that in such cases the government would have to try to persuade the Diet to change its mind.

23. *Meiji tennō ki*, 8, p. 189.

24. The text is in ibid., 8, pp. 195–97.

25. Ibid., 8, p. 206.

26. Ibid., 8, pp. 209, 239.

27. Ibid., 8, pp. 211–12.

28. Ibid., 8, pp. 273–74.

29. Ibid., 8, p. 340. He made a similar statement at a cabinet meeting on December 11.

30. *Meiji tennō ki*, 8, p. 348.

31. Ibid., 8, p. 359.

32. Ibid., 8, p. 372.

Chapter 44

1. The prince (the future Emperor Taishō) became an excellent calligrapher, and the *kanshi* he composed are surprisingly skillful. It has been stated that he spoke English, French, and German fluently (see, for example, Julia Meech-Pekarik, *The World of the Meiji Print*, p. 128), but this seems improbable.

2. *Meiji tennō ki*, 8, pp. 584, 586, 595.

3. The print by Hashimoto Chikanobu entitled *Fusō kōki kagami*, published on August 8, 1887, shows the crown prince standing between the emperor, seated to the right, and the empress, seated to the left. His face is turned in the direction of the empress, but he is gesturing toward the emperor. Three books lie on the table behind the prince, perhaps intended to suggest that he was a diligent student (reproduced in color in Meech-Pekarik, *World of the Meiji Print*, plate 23). A somewhat later (August 23, 1887) print by Chikanobu entitled *Kanjo Yōfuko saihō no zu* shows the crown prince, the empress, and a little girl in a room where one court lady operates a sewing machine and another measures fabric (reproduced in color, plate 24).

4. The gold medals were intended for members of the imperial family (*kōzoku*) (*Meiji tennō ki*, 8, pp. 382–83).

5. However, the best known of the *nishikie* depicting the celebration, showing various Japanese and foreign dignitaries presenting their messages of congratulations to the emperor, is Nansai Toshitada's *Dai Nihon teikoku ginkon goshiki*, evidence that the term "silver wedding" (*ginkon*) was used at least informally. The scene depicted in this print was imagined, as it was published before the actual ceremony. For a reproduction, see Konishi Shirō, *Nisshin sensō*, pp. 16–17. Other prints published at the same time by Toyoharu Kuniteru and Shunsai Toshimasa included the word *ginkonshiki* in their titles (pp. 18–19).

6. *Meiji tennō ki*, 8, pp. 384–90. For the menu of the dinner served in the palace, see *Tennōke no kyōen*, p. 41.

7. For a discussion of Fukuzawa's relations with Kim Ok-kyun and other Korean intellectuals, see Kan Je-on, *Chosen no jōi to kaika*, pp. 193–203. Kinebuchi Nobuo's *Fukuzawa Yukichi to Chōsen* is a full-length study of Fukuzawa's opinions on Korea.

8. Kim took the name Iwata Shūsaku shortly after arriving in Japan in 1884, but when he went to China in 1894 he changed his name to Iwata Sanwa, *sanwa* (three peace) being a reference to his plan for the three nations of East Asia to cooperate in keeping out foreigner aggressors (Kan, *Chōsen*, pp. 174, 184).

9. On May 17, 1894, thirty-five members of the Jiyū-tō presented a question to the government concerning the assassination of Kim Ok-kyun and the attempted assassination of Pak Yong-hyo. They claimed that Korean assassins had crossed into Japan three times with this mission, each time claiming it was by order of the king (*Meiji tennō ki*, 8, p. 412).

10. Kan, *Chōsen*, p. 185. See also *Meiji tennō ki*, 6, pp. 624–25.

11. Kan, *Chōsen*, p. 183.

12. Ibid., p. 185; Kinebuchi Nobuo, *Nikkan kōshō shi*, p. 107.

13. Tsunoda Fusako, *Minbi ansatsu*, p. 186.

14. For example, Hayashi Tadasu, at the time the deputy foreign minister, recalled in his memoirs that he had advised Kim to give up his plan of going to Shanghai, asking, "Isn't that, as far as you are concerned, enemy territory?" Kim answered that Shanghai was neutral ground (referring presumably to the international concessions) and therefore not dangerous, but he promised to consult Fukuzawa Yukichi on the advisability of travel to Shanghai as soon as Fukuzawa returned from a tour of Kyūshū (Hayashi Tadasu, *Ato wa mukashi no ki*, pp. 73, 253).

15. He made this statement to Miyazaki Tōten (Kan, *Chōsen*, pp. 174–75).

16. Kan says that the bill of exchange (*kawase tegata*) was fake (*Chōsen*, p. 176). Hong was the first Korean to study in France. After leaving Paris in 1893 he did not return to Seoul but went instead to Tokyo. He contacted Koreans in Japan, hoping for their assistance in getting a job in the Korean government. Yi Il-sik apparently promised his assistance if Hong killed Kim (Tsunoda, *Minbi*, p. 188). Hayashi Tadasu (who knew Hong personally) thought he had killed Kim in order to win favor with the queen of Korea (*Ato wa mukashi*, p. 73).

17. For Kim's personality and achievements, see Kan, *Chōsen*, pp. 187–93. See also the brief account in *Meiji tennō ki*, 8, p. 396.

18. This account is derived from Wada's recollections, as given in Kan, *Chōsen*, pp. 179–80. The chief authority in the International Settlement was the British consul general. He turned Kim's body over to the Chinese without following the proper procedures, laying the British open to the charge of having condoned the crime (Kinebuchi, *Fukuzawa*, p. 160). A different account was given in the Shūgi-in on May 18: Moriya Koresuke of the Rikken kaishintō asked the government why, after having been loaded aboard the ship and all formalities completed, Kim's coffin should have been seized by the Chinese and loaded aboard a Chinese ship. He considered the Chinese action to be an insult to Japan. On May 31 the government replied with its own version of what had happened. It said that Wada had received the coffin but, instead of loading it aboard ship, left it lying by the road and went away. The chief of police of the International Settlement, following regulations, moved the coffin to the police station. Wada returned to Japan without making any arrangement for receiving the coffin. The Chinese government had indeed disposed of the body, but there was no "snatching away" of the coffin as alleged, and there was no occasion for the Japanese government to intervene. Regardless of whether or not this official account is correct, it shows how reluctant the Japanese government was to become involved (*Meiji tennō ki*, 8, p. 413).

19. For a drawing of this grisly sight, as depicted in the *Jiji shimpō* of April 24, 1894, see Kinebuchi, *Nikkan*, p. 118. Kinebuchi gives extracts from the Japanese press reporting the crime. There is also a blurred photograph of the exposed head and the inscription in Fujimura Michio, *Nisshin sensō*, p. 48.

20. Fujimura, *Nisshin*, p. 49.

21. Hayashi wrote, "There is no doubt that the dispatch of troops to Asan was the fuse leading to the Sino-Japanese War, but I believe that it was in fact precipitated by the assassination of Kim and the actions of the China at this time" (*Ato wa mukashi*, p. 74). According to Fujimura, Hayashi "testified" that Foreign Minister Mutsu decided on a war with China because of the assassination of Kim and the Chinese actions (*Nisshin*, p. 49).

22. Kinebuchi, *Fukuzawa*, pp. 156–60.

23. Mutsu Munemitsu, *Kenkenroku*, trans. Gordon Mark Berger, p. 5.

24. See the brief account in Ki-baik Lee, *A New History of Korea*, trans. Edward W. Wagner, pp. 258–59; see also *Meiji tennō ki*, 8, p. 428.

25. Katano Tsugio, *Richō metsubō*, p. 103.

26. Ibid., p. 104.

27. Ibid.

28. Gordon Mark Berger, who translated the work, preferred to leave the title in romaji, but he gave as a literal translation "A Record of Arduous and Selfless Service to the Throne" (Mutsu, *Kenkenroku*, p. 257).

29. Mutsu, *Kenkenroku*, p. 5.

30. See, for example, Ōe Shinobu, *Higashi Ajia shi toshite no nisshin sensō*, p. 282. He compared the Tonghak rebellion (a term he avoided) with the Wat Tyler revolt in England, the peasant war in Bohemia associated with Jan Hus, and the T'ai P'ing revolt in China.

31. *Meiji tennō ki*, 8, p. 428.

32. Mutsu, *Kenkenroku*, p. 8.

33. *Meiji tennō ki*, 8, p. 427.

34. Hayashi, *Ato wa mukashi*, p. 69.
35. Mutsu, *Kenkenroku*, p. 15. See also *Meiji tennō ki*, 8, pp. 433–34.
36. Mutsu, *Kenkenroku*, p. 20.
37. *Meiji tennō ki*, 8, p. 437.
38. Ibid., 8, p. 437.
39. Mutsu, *Kenkenroku*, p. 24. See also *Meiji tennō ki*, 8, pp. 441–42.
40. *Meiji tennō ki*, 8, p. 446.
41. Ibid., 8, p. 452.
42. Ibid., 8, p. 456.
43. Ibid., 8, p. 449.
44. For an account of the final negotiations to end extraterritoriality and the text of the draft treaty prepared by Mutsu Munemitsu, see Louis G. Perez, *Japan Comes of Age*.
45. *Meiji tennō ki*, 8, p. 464.
46. Ibid., 8, p. 466.
47. Ibid., 8, p. 467. For the opinion of Dr. T. E. Holland, a leading English authority on international law, who concluded that the Japanese had behaved properly and that "no apology is due to our government" see Mutsu, *Kenkenroku*, pp. 89–90.
48. *Meiji tennō ki*, 8, p. 473.
49. *Fukuzawa Yukichi zenshū*, 14, p. 500. See also Donald Keene, "The Sino-Japanese War of 1894–95 and Japanese Culture," p. 263.
50. *Uchimura Kanzō zenshū*, 16, p. 27.
51. Ibid., p. 35. See also Keene, "The Sino-Japanese War," pp. 263–64.
52. It was later discovered that this identification had been mistaken and that the bugler was not Shirakami but Kiguchi Kohei. Kiguchi's name soon replaced Shirakami's and acquired a legendary character; he became the symbol of the virtue of loyalty. "Kiguchi Kohei died with the bugle pressed to his lips" was featured in elementary-school textbooks as the perfect example of loyalty (Keene, "Sino-Japanese War," pp. 278–79).
53. *Chuzan sonkō*, 2, p. 309. See also Keene, "Sino-Japanese War," p. 278.
54. *Meiji tennō ki*, 8, p. 481.
55. Keene, "Sino-Japanese War," p. 266.

Chapter 45

1. *Meiji tennō ki*, 8, p. 486. Mutsu Munemitsu dismissed these different proposals as being "nothing more than private thoughts whispered among a few individuals" (*Kenkenroku*, trans. Gordon Mark Berger, p. 29). He added, "In my view, the reforms in Korea should focus primarily on Japan's national interests; and there should thus be no cause for hardship or sacrifice for the sake of reform." See also Fujimura Michio, *Nisshin sensō*, p. 106.
2. *Meiji tennō ki*, 8, pp. 487, 488.
3. Shirai Hisaya, *Meiji kokka to Nisshin sensō*, pp. 81–82.
4. *Meiji tennō ki*, 8, p. 497. Itō participated in military as well as political decisions. He stressed particularly the need to win a quick victory before the great powers could intervene, and the emperor frequently consulted with him on wartime policy (Shirai, *Meiji kokka*, p. 82).

5. On August 25 Mutsu reported to the emperor that the negotiations in London by Aoki Shūzō, initiated in December of the previous year, had been successful despite many obstacles. He felt confident that similar treaties would gradually be concluded with other allied countries. He now had the "joyful duty" of informing the emperor that the revised treaty had been signed by Queen Victoria. The new treaty of commerce and navigation was publicly announced on August 27 (*Meiji tennō ki*, 8, p. 493).

6. Fujimura Michio suggested that Itō's real reason for advocating the move of Daihon'ei was to demonstrate to the people that the war was being fought under the leadership of the emperor and to unite them in support of the war (*Nisshin sensō*, p. 112).

7. *Meiji tennō ki*, 8, p. 505.

8. Ibid., 8, p. 510.

9. It stood on the site of Hiroshima Castle, erected in 1589 by Mōri Terumoto, one of Toyotomi Hideyoshi's generals. At the time when Meiji resided in Hiroshima, all that was left of the castle was the five-story keep.

10. *Meiji tennō ki*, 8, p. 511. Viscount Hijikata Hisamoto recalled that the emperor's private quarters consisted of two rooms, one of eight mats and the other of ten mats. He used one for sleeping and the other for state business. It was extremely cramped: "In such crude surroundings His Majesty lived, read telegrams that arrived from the front in a steady stream, and gave endless audiences to officers about to go overseas. He was extremely busy, but showed no sign of weariness" ("Eimei kurabenaki daikōtei," p. 70).

11. *Meiji tennō ki*, 8, p. 512.

12. Shirai, *Meiji kokka*, p. 83.

13. Ibid., p. 516.

14. Some prints depicting Harada in action are reproduced in Shumpei Okamoto, *Impressions of the Front*, p. 24. See also Henry D. Smith, *Kiyochika*, p. 86.

15. Donald Keene, *Nihonjin no biishiki*, pp. 149–50.

16. Donald Keene, "The Sino-Japanese War of 1894–95 and Japanese Culture," p. 280; Muneta Hiroshi, *Heitai hyakunen*, pp. 109–14.

17. *Meiji tennō ki*, 8, p. 517.

18. Although the tonnage of the Japanese and Chinese ships was small by modern standards, for their time these ships were by no means inconsequential, as one can gather from the account in *L'Illustration* for August 11, 1894, which anticipated: "Une lutte dans laquelle tous les engins les plus puissants et les plus perfectionnés de la science moderne seront, pour la première fois, mis aux mains de deux nations, non pas certes barbares, mais d'une civilisation complètement différente de la nôtre" ("Iryusutorashion" *Nihon kankei kiji shū*, 2, p. 166).

19. *Meiji tennō ki*, 8, pp. 518–20. Ten *nishikie* depicting the battle of the Yellow Sea (also known as the battle off Takushan and as the battle of Hai-yang-tao) are given in Okamoto, *Impressions*, pp. 25–30.

20. Keene, "Sino-Japanese War," p. 280. A *nishikie* by Kobayashi Kiyochika depicting the dying sailor is reproduced in Okamoto, *Impressions*, p. 28.

21. The noted journalist Tokutomi Sohō stated that the Sino-Japanese War had caused not only the military but the entire people to draw closer to the imperial household (Shirai, *Meiji kokka*, pp. 89–91).

22. Hinonishi Sukehiro, *Meiji tennō no go-nichijō*, p. 44. Hinonishi described himself as *futsutsuka*, an incompetent.

23. Hinonishi Sukehiro, *Meiji tennō no go-nichijō*, p. 27.

24. The collection *Shinshū Meiji tennō gyōshū* (1, p. 252) contains only two *tanka* that allude to the war. However, *Meiji tennō ki*, 8, pp. 528–29, includes a war song (*gunka*) not in the collection and mentions two others (on the victories on the Yellow Sea and at Pyongyang).

25. *Meiji tennō ki*, 8, p. 529.

26. Horiuchi Keizō related how Katō, on hearing the story of Shirakami Genjirō's bravery, was immediately inspired to write a poem and set it to music (*Ongaku gojūnen shi*, pp. 155–56). He first tried blowing the tune on a clarinet, but his breath gave out. Next he tried a baritone trumpet, but again his breath failed. Finally, he scribbled the words on a blackboard. Still in this white-hot fury of creativity, but with the help of another musician, he completed music and words in half an hour.

27. I have unfortunately been unable to examine this work. See *Meiji tennō ki*, 8, p. 529, where mention is also made of the *gunka* (war song) on the victory at Pyongyang composed by the empress (at the emperor's request) when she visited him in Hiroshima. Sakurai also supplied the music for the empress's poem.

28. *Meiji tennō ki*, 8, pp. 524–25, 549.

29. Ibid., 8, p. 568. The nō plays performed were suitably martial in tone—*Ōeyama* and *Eboshiori*. The *kyōgen* was *Utsubosaru* (p. 569).

30. *Meiji tennō ki*, 8, p. 571.

31. Mutsu, *Kenkenroku*, p. 138. See also *Meiji tennō ki*, 8, p. 576.

32. Mutsu, *Kenkenroku*, p. 139.

33. *Meiji tennō ki*, 8, pp. 577.

34. *Meiji tennō ki* gives "more than 10,000" (8, p. 589), but Shirai gives a figure of 15,000 (*Meiji kokka*, p. 141).

35. Shirai, *Meiji kokka*, p. 143. For an eyewitness account of the battle, see Kamei Koreaki, *Nisshin sensō jūgun shashinchō*, pp. 172–77. Kamei, the first Japanese war photographer, kept an extremely detailed war diary that included information from other sources. He quotes the report of the battle by an observer, a foreign officer who accompanied the Second Army on pp. 172–73.

36. Mutsu, *Kenkenroku*, p. 140. See also *Meiji tennō ki*, 8, p. 594.

37. Inoue Haruki, *Ryojun gyakusatsu jiken*, pp. 25–26. I owe much of the following to Inoue's brilliant, scholarly book. The British "rear admiral" was probably Vice Admiral Sir Edmond Robert Fremantle, the commander in chief of the China station. He went ashore in Port Arthur on November 25, soon after the Japanese victory (p. 127).

38. Inoue, *Ryojun*, pp. 26–27. On November 24 Kamei Koreaki photographed coolies digging a hole in which to bury the Chinese corpses shown in the foreground of the picture. His description of the piles of corpses littering the streets is even more horrible than Cowen's, but he clung to the explanation that every male in Port Arthur over fifteen had been ordered to resist the Japanese army and that it was impossible to distinguish civilians from soldiers (Kamei, *Nisshin sensō*, pp. 197–99).

39. Inoue described how Central News, a Japanese-owned news agency, fed "information" to newspapers abroad (*Ryojun*, p. 29). For example, in response to Cowen's first article, it stated that not one Chinese had been killed except for those lawfully killed in warfare.

40. Inoue, *Ryojun*, p. 72. The Japanese were not always successful in their attempts to bribe the foreign press. On December 6 during the course of an interview with Cowen, Itō Miyoji, the president of the progovernment newspaper *Tōkyō nichinichi shimbun*, stated that the Japanese government would pay his expenses and would not charge the *Times* for telegrams, regardless of the length (p. 98). Cowen refused.

41. Notably Francis Brinkley, the owner of the *Japan Mail* in Yokohama, which published various English-language newspapers. Brinkley not only received a monthly grant from the Japanese government during the Sino-Japanese War but was decorated for his services and given 5,000 yen (Inoue, *Ryojun*, pp. 31–32).

42. Inoue, *Ryojun*, p. 40.

43. The *World*, a newspaper owned by Joseph Pulitzer, was at this time known mainly as a scandal sheet, but this did not prevent Creelman's articles from being believed.

44. English text is in Inoue, *Ryojun*, p. 55.

45. Ibid., p. 58.

46. James Allan, a British writer, described seeing "the bodies of the Japanese soldiers, killed in encounters with the enemy as they closed on the place, were often found minus the head or right hand, sometimes both, besides being ferociously gashed and slashed. Corpses were still hanging on the trees when the fortress fell, and it is not surprising that their former comrades should have been maddened by the sight, though of course the officers are greatly to blame for permitting the fearful retaliation which ensued to be carried to such lengths" (*Under the Dragon Flag*, p. 67).

   Inoue states that the heads of three Japanese soldiers who had been taken alive in the fighting near Tu-ch'eng-tzu three days before the battle for Port Arthur were suspended from a willow beside the road. The noses had been cut off, and their ears were missing. A little farther on, two more heads were suspended on wires from the eaves of a house. The Chinese had also decapitated the corpses of Japanese of the Second Army who had fallen at Tu-ch'eng-tzu. The bellies were slit open and filled with stones; the right arms and the testicles were also cut off. The Chinese government had offered rewards for the heads of Japanese soldiers, and one foreign journalist told Creelman that he had seen the money being paid (*Ryojun*, pp. 146–47).

47. Inoue, *Ryojun*, pp. 82, 85. It was reported in the December 20 issue of the *Ōsaka mainichi shimbun* that 6,000 to 10,000 Armenians had been killed.

48. Inoue, *Ryojun*, pp. 153, 157, 176.

49. Ibid., p. 64. Prisoners did reach Japan, but they were not necessarily captured at Port Arthur.

50. Inoue, *Ryojun*, p. 186. The decision not to take prisoners was also justified in terms of the amount of food that would be needed to feed them.

51. Inoue, *Ryojun*, pp. 202–4. Mutsu quotes Dr. T. E. Holland, described as "a leading English authority on international law and a man who had hitherto been

unstinting in his praise of Japan's wartime conduct," as having said in an article, "At last but thirty-six Chinamen were left alive in the city. They had been spared only to be employed in burying their dead countrymen, and each was protected by a slip of paper fastened in his cap, with the inscription: 'This man is not to be killed'" (*Kenkenroku*, p. 75).

52. Inoue, *Ryojun*, pp. 48, 189, 192.

53. Donald Keene, *Dawn to the West*, 1, p. 100.

54. Inoue, *Ryojun*, p. 195.

55. Ibid., p. 86.

56. A Japanese soldier gives a brief account in a letter written to a friend describing how, after some initial distaste, he quickly acquired the knack of cutting off Chinese heads (Inoue, *Ryojun*, p. 187).

57. For example, an English-language newspaper in Bombay printed an editorial saying of the Japanese that "their enlightenment was only skin-deep, and with time they have shown their true natures as barbarians" (Inoue, *Ryojun*, p. 102).

58. Walter Q. Gresham, the secretary of state, expressed his gratitude to the *World* for having printed Creelman's articles. At first, he had supposed that Creelman must have exaggerated, for it seemed improbable that no representative of the American government would have informed him of so major an event. However, he interpreted Mutsu's telegram as a confirmation of Creelman's articles, and he now realized that the atrocities after the fall of Port Arthur were even worse than at first reported (Inoue, *Ryojun*, p. 70).

59. Mutsu, *Kenkenroku*, pp. 75, 76.

60. Inoue, *Ryojun*, p. 222.

61. The *tanchōzuru* was captured at Chin-chou. For mention of the emperor examining war booty, see *Meiji tennō ki*, 8, p. 606. The same work mentions that the emperor examined booty from Ryojun and elsewhere that was placed on display in the garden (p. 610). He also looked at photographs of the battle of the Yellow Sea and at Chinese *nishikie*.

62. Viscount Horikawa Yasutaka, who about this time was in charge of cataloguing the imperial treasures in the Shōsōin.

63. For the anecdote about Horikawa and the camels, see Hinonishi, *Meiji tennō*, p. 27. See also *Meiji tennō ki*, 8, p. 607. Hinonishi mentioned that Chinese prisoners were shown to the emperor but said merely that "he looked on them from above." This suggests he was curious to see what Chinese looked like but did not wish to get too close.

64. Inoue, *Ryojun*, pp. 191–92.

65. *Shinshū Meiji tennō gyoshū*, 1, p. 252. The second *tanka* originally ended *semi-otoshitaru / totsugeki no koe*. The poems were composed in 1895, probably some months after the fall of Port Arthur.

Chapter 46

1. Mutsu Munemitsu, *Kenkenroku*, trans. Gordon Mark Berger, p. 128.

2. Ibid., pp. 128–29. See also *Meiji tennō ki*, 8, pp. 600–601.

3. Shirai Hisaya, *Meiji kokka to Nisshin sensō*, p. 145.

4. The text of the rescript is in *Meiji tennō ki*, 8, p. 601. See also Shirai, *Meiji kokka*, p. 146. Yamagata received the rescript on December 8 and on that day sent a telegram to Prince Taruhito stating that he had been recalled, would turn over command of the First Army to Major General Nozu, and would leave for Japan on December 9 (*Meiji tennō ki*, 8, p. 602).

5. The counterattacks took place on January 17, January 22, February 16, February 21, and February 27 (*Meiji tennō ki*, 8, pp. 642–43, 645–46, 679, 687, 695).

6. Shirai, *Meiji kokka*, pp. 146–47.

7. Reproductions of some of the prints that evoke the cold and snow are in Tamba Tsuneo, *Nishikie ni miru Meiji tennō to Meiji jidai*, pp. 160–65.

8. *Meiji tennō ki*, 8, p. 604.

9. Ibid., 8, p. 617.

10. Mutsu, *Kenkenroku*, pp. 152–57. See also *Meiji tennō ki*, 8, p. 658.

11. Weihaiwei was a much larger military harbor than Port Arthur and was heavily fortified. At the time of the Japanese attack, eight warships and smaller vessels were at anchor (*Meiji tennō ki*, 8, p. 637).

12. For details of the attack, see *Meiji tennō ki*, 8, pp. 665–66. Shirai says that a torpedo boat attack had been attempted on January 30, but the temperature was 30 degrees below zero (Celsius) (*Meiji kokka*, pp. 161–62). Waves breaking over the decks of the boats froze, and icicles formed over the mouths of the torpedo-launching tubes making an attack impossible.

13. Shirai, *Meiji kokka*, p. 162.

14. The text is in Miyake Setsurei, *Dōjidaishi*, 3, p. 44; the translation, in Shumpei Okamoto, *Impressions of the Front*, p. 44.

15. *Meiji tennō ki*, 8, p. 684.

16. Trumbull White, *The War in the East*, p. 641, quoted in Okamoto, *Impressions*, p. 44.

17. On December 12, while the emperor was playing *kemari*, he was struck by a ball kicked by a chamberlain, who was appalled by what he had done. However, the emperor said with a smile, "The navy has fired a torpedo." He did not blame the poor chamberlain (*Meiji tennō ki*, 8, p. 609).

18. *Meiji tennō ki*, 8, p. 653.

19. Ibid., 8, p. 648.

20. For example, it was reported that the emperor was obliged by the lack of suitable female attendants to cut his own fingernails and toenails.

21. *Meiji tennō ki*, 8, p. 721.

22. Ibid., 8, p. 717.

23. Li was in a sedan chair (*kago*) when the assailant fired. The bullet grazed his right cheek under the eye, injuring him only slightly. For details from the Japanese press, see Ishida Bunshirō, *Meiji daijihen kiroku shūsei*, pp. 225–28.

24. *Meiji tennō ki*, 8, pp. 730–32. The complete text of the rescript is in Mutsu, *Kenkenroku*, p. 174.

25. Mutsu, *Kenkenroku*, p. 175. See also *Meiji tennō ki*, 8, pp. 738–39.

26. Mutsu, *Kenkenroku*, p. 176.

27. Ibid., p. 178.

28. The armistice did not include Taiwan or the Pescadore Islands. The latter islands were occupied by Japanese forces between March 24 and 26 (*Meiji tennō ki*, 8, p. 733).

29. Mutsu, *Kenkenroku*, p. 168.
30. Ibid., pp. 186–87. See also *Meiji tennō ki*, 8, pp. 751–53.
31. *Meiji tennō ki*, 8, p. 756.
32. Mutsu, *Kenkenroku*, p. 199.
33. *Meiji tennō ki*, 8, p. 773.
34. Ibid., 8, p. 774.
35. Mutsu, *Kenkenroku*, p. 203. The German and French governments sent roughly the same notes. See also *Meiji tennō ki*, 8, p. 776, and Shirai, *Meiji kokka*, p. 183.
36. *Meiji tennō ki*, 8, p. 778. See also Shirai, *Meiji kokka*, p. 182.
37. Mutsu, *Kenkenroku*, p. 211; Shirai, *Meiji kokka*, p. 183.
38. *Meiji tennō ki*, 8, pp. 780–81. See also Mutsu, *Kenkenroku*, p. 207.
39. *Meiji tennō ki*, 8, p. 781. See also Mutsu, *Kenkenroku*, p. 207.
40. *Meiji tennō ki*, 8, p. 780.
41. Mutsu, *Kenkenroku*, p. 210.
42. *Meiji tennō ki*, p. 806.
43. Ibid., 8, p. 817.
44. Ibid., 8, p. 822.
45. Ibid., 8, p. 849.
46. Ibid., 8, p. 920.
47. For a table of casualties during the Sino-Japanese War, see Fujimura Michio, *Nisshin sensō*, p. 183. During the campaign on the Asian mainland, the Japanese lost a total of 2,647 men; during the Taiwan campaign, there were 10,841 casualties.
48. He was known at various times of his career as Michinomiya, Kōgen, Rinnōji-nomiya, and Kitashirakawanomiya (chapter 17). He died on October 28 in Tainan (*Meiji tennō ki*, 8, pp. 923–24).
49. The text of the eulogy is in *Meiji tennō ki*, 8, p. 932.
50. Ibid., 8, pp. 622–23. Later, the same article compares Emperor Meiji with the rulers of Germany, Austria-Hungary, Italy, England, France, and the United States, each time deciding that the emperor is superior. The article also compared him with such historical figures as Augustus in Rome, King Alfred of England, Napoleon, and Wilhelm I, all of whom fell far short.
51. Donald Keene, "The Sino-Japanese War of 1894–95 and Japanese Culture," p. 294.
52. Okakura Kakuzō, *The Book of Tea*, p. 7.

Chapter 47

1. *Meiji tennō ki*, 8, pp. 807, 829.
2. Woonsang Choi, *The Fall of the Hermit Kingdom*, pp. 26–27.
3. *Meiji tennō ki*. 8, p. 846.
4. Ibid. He also offered an alternative plan that, although less welcome to the royal house and the government, would probably lessen the burden on the common people.
5. *Meiji tennō ki*, 8, p. 851. Joseph H. Longford wrote, "The worst rogues and bullies of Japan—and Japan produces an abundance of both types—poured into the unfortunate country, and robbed and browbeat the terrified natives in a way that

filled European witnesses with indignation and horror, and increased tenfold the traditional hatred of the natives of the very name of Japan" (*The Evolution of New Japan*, p. 118).

6. For example, Choi contrasted Inoue with his successor, Miura Gorō, in these terms: "Unlike Count Inoue, who was a man of great ability and had done much for the reform of Korea, Miura proved to be lacking in every quality of constructive and administrative statesmanship" (*Fall of the Hermit Kingdom*, p. 27).

7. Queen Min in principle never appeared before foreign men, but she met foreign women. Takeko, who was a year older than the queen, was the only Japanese woman to meet her. The famous traveler Isabella L. Bird also met the queen and left this description: "Her Majesty, who was then past forty, was a very nice-looking slender woman, with glossy raven-black hair and a very pale skin, the pallor enhanced by the use of pearl powder. The eyes were cold and keen, and the general expression one of brilliant intelligence" (*Korea and Her Neighbours*, 2, p. 39). See also Tsunoda Fusako, *Minbi ansatsu*, pp. 278–79.

   According to Kuzuo Yoshihisa, when Inoue had audiences with the king, the queen's voice could be heard from behind a curtain giving the king directions (*Tōa senkaku shishi kiden*, 2, p. 521). Gradually she showed half her face and finally, opening the curtains completely, joined in conversation with the king and Inoue. This account, as far as I know, is not confirmed by other writers.

8. Miura Gorō, *Kanju shōgun kaiko roku*, p. 269.

9. *Meiji tennō ki*, 8, p. 866. Waeber is said to have sent this message to the Korean court with the American Charles W. LeGendre, who had formerly been employed by the Japanese Foreign Ministry. He was hired by the Korean government in 1890 (*Meiji tennō ki*, 3, p. 586; Tsunoda, *Minbi ansatsu*, p. 180).

10. *Meiji tennō ki*, 8, p. 866. This action is puzzling, considering Pak's pro-Russian views; however, he was a longtime advocate of reforming the country, and this made people suppose he was actually pro-Japanese. After escaping from Seoul, Pak found refuge once again in Japan (p. 891).

11. *Meiji tennō ki*, 8, p. 867. The Kaehwadang was also known as the Progressive Party.

12. Miura, who was from Chōshū, was recommended by three members of the Chōshū clique—Itō Hirobumi, Yamagata Aritomo, and Inoue Kaoru. With such backing, he could hardly fail to be appointed.

13. Miura, *Kanju shōgun*, pp. 266–67.

14. Okamoto Ryūnosuke, *Fūun kaiko roko*, pp. 222–23.

15. Miura was in fact a devout Buddhist. Not long before, he had been called on to mediate a dispute between two factions of the Sōtō sect of Zen Buddhism (Miura, *Kanju shōgun*, pp. 245–65).

16. Tsunoda, *Minbi ansatsu*, p. 283; Kojima Noboru, *Ōyama Iwao*, 4, p. 237.

17. Tsunoda, *Minbi ansatsu*, p. 284; Kojima, *Ōyama Iwao*, 4, p, 238. Kuzuo says Miura was called *nembutsu kōshi*, but as a believer in Zen Buddhism, Miura probably did not say the *nembutsu* (*Tōa*, 1, p. 517).

18. Pak Jong-keun, *Nisshin sensō to Chōsen*, p. 241.

19. Another unit of some 500 men, called the Self-Defense Unit, had been formed in June 1895. It was trained by an American officer, William M. Dye, to defend

the royal palace, but most members were unarmed. It was anti-Japanese (Pak, *Nisshin sensō*, p. 241).

20. Even the commanding officer of the second battalion of the Training Unit, a Korean, was not informed of the plan. On October 7 he hurried to the Japanese legation to inform Miura that the king had privately ordered the dissolution. He arrived just as Miura and two others were drawing up final plans for the attack. This would have been a natural moment to inform him of plans for the following day, but he was led to another room and was told nothing. Apparently, even a pro-Japanese Korean was not trusted to keep the secret (Pak, *Nisshin sensō*, p. 235).

21. *Meiji tennō ki*, 8, p. 909. See also Kobayakawa Hideo, *Binkō ansatsu*, p. 318. Another Japanese visitor to the *taewon'gun*, the consul Horiguchi Kumaichi, went in the guise of a Japanese tourist and carried on a conversation with the *taewon'gun* in classical Chinese with writing brushes (*Gaikō to bungei*, pp. 118–31). The *taewon'gun* entertained Horiguchi with champagne and Havana cigars, but most appreciated of all was his promise that if Miura helped him, he would resume his old position in the government (p. 130).

22. Kobayakawa Hideo wrote this in *Binkō ansatsu*, p. 318. Kuzuo was of the same opinion (*Tōa*, 1, p. 523).

23. Pak, *Nisshin sensō*, p. 233. Pak believed it was impossible that the *taewon'gun* accepted all four promises without changing a word. His actions immediately after the murder showed he was by no means willing to yield his political authority.

The photographs of the *taewon'gun* suggest that he was indeed a very old man, but Horiguchi, who saw him shortly before Queen Min's murder, wrote that his complexion was that of a young man and his eyes were piercing. He seemed overflowing with energy. Horiguchi thought the *taewon'gun* was in his early fifties but looked much younger; in fact, he was over seventy (*Gaikō*, p. 119).

24. Tsunoda, *Minbi ansatsu*, p. 300.

25. Adachi Kenzō, *Adachi Kenzō jijoden*, p. 57. Adachi was an important political figure in Kumamoto, his native place; Kumamoto was known for its toughs. Miura used the word *sōshi*, but Adachi's account changed it to *wakai mono* (young people). Adachi did not date this conversation, but it was probably at the beginning of October.

26. The uniforms and hats were taken from Korean guards at the *taewon'gun*'s palace (Pak, *Nisshin sensō*, p. 237). Some *sōshi* were dressed in Japanese clothes; others, in Western clothes. Some carried a broadsword on their shoulders, some a Japanese sword at their waist; others, pistols (Kobayakawa, *Binkō ansatsu*, p. 330).

27. Pak, *Nisshin sensō*, p. 237. Kobayakawa, who was present when the *taewon'gun* was roused from sleep, stated that he happily accepted the proposal that he accompany the Japanese to the royal palace (*Binkō ansatsu*, p. 333).

28. Kobayakawa, *Binkō ansatsu*, p. 337.

29. "Official Report on Matters Connected with the Events of October 8th, 1895, and the Death of the Queen," p. 126.

30. Kobayakawa, *Binkō ansatsu*, p. 352.

31. Tsunoda, *Minbi ansatsu*, p. 321. Choi gives a somewhat different account: "Okamoto, after cutting down the Queen, had three other palace ladies identify the

dying Queen, then murdered them all to leave no evidence and to make sure of his work" (*Fall of the Hermit Kingdom*, p. 34).

32. Pak, *Nisshin sensō*, p. 246. XX is, of course, Queen Min. Some believe that although the murderer was a Japanese army officer, the authorities blamed the *sōshi*.

33. Pak, *Nisshin sensō*, p. 247.

34. However, a highly favorable account of Queen Min is presented by Isabella Bird, who visited Korea four times between 1894 and 1897. She was granted several audiences with the king and queen. She described the king as rather ordinary but sensed that the queen exerted great influence over the king. Miss Bird was also impressed by the queen's enemy, the *taewon'gun*, though she mentioned with disapproval the murder by his orders of 2,000 Korean Catholics in 1866 (*Korea and Her Neighbours*, 2, pp. 39–49).

35. Choi, *Fall of the Hermit Kingdom*, p. 30.

36. Katano Tsugio, *Richō metsubō*, p. 159. There is a story to the effect that when a Japanese officer noticed General Dye, he told Horiguchi Kumaichi, a consul, to order the foreigner to leave. Horiguchi passed on the message to Dye in French, but the general did not understand French. Another man repeated the message in English, but the general replied, "I am an American. I don't take orders from a Japanese" (Tsunoda, *Minbi ansatsu*, p. 320). Adachi Kenzō, though, wrote that the normally arrogant Dye was so frightened by the Japanese that he removed his hat and bowed, an ingratiating look on his face. Adachi found this change "extremely ludicrous" (*Adachi Kenzō*, p. 61).

The discovery of the diary kept by Alexander Sabatin was reported in 1995. Although Sabatin did not actually see Queen Min killed, he saw Japanese in plainclothes drag court ladies by the hair from the building where they and the queen slept and was within a few feet of the actual murder. The discovery was made by Professor Kim Rekho of the Russian Academy of Sciences (*Asahi shimbun*, June 20, 1995, p. 29).

37. Miura, *Kanju shōgun*, pp. 282–83.

38. The article is reproduced photographically in the front matter of Tsunoda, *Minbi ansatsu*.

39. Kojima, *Ōyama Iwao*, 4, p. 261. Kojima's account of the murder of Queen Min is most detailed, but unfortunately he does not give his sources (pp. 250–83).

40. *Meiji tennō ki*, 8, p. 911. The message, as given by Kojima, was simply, "Last night there was an incident in the royal palace. The whereabouts of the queen are unknown" (*Ōyama Iwao*, 4, p. 263).

41. Kojima, *Ōyama Iwao*, 4, p. 263.

42. *Meiji tennō ki*, 8, p. 914.

43. Ibid., 8, p. 917.

44. Inoue had an audience with the king on November 5 at which he expressed the emperor's deep concern over the incident. He also offered the gifts from the empress and emperor (*Meiji tennō ki*, 8, p. 930). Inoue (and Komura) had another audience with the king on November 15, before Inoue's return to Japan. The king expressed regret that Inoue could not remain longer, and when they parted, the king shook Inoue's hand (p. 935).

45. *Meiji tennō ki*, 8, p. 921.

46. "Official Report," p. 133. The text of the king's condemnation of the queen is given in full along with the names of the officials who signed the document, in Bird, *Korea and Her Neighbours*, 2, pp. 69–70. See also *Meiji tennō ki*, 8, p. 943. The king signed this edict on October 10. At the time he was still unaware that the queen had been killed. (Mourning for Queen Min was not decreed until December 5.) When first confronted with the edict and told he must sign it, the king said he would rather have his hands cut off than sign (Bird, *Korea and Her Neighbours*, 2, p. 69; Shirai, *Meiji kokka*, p. 215). He finally yielded to pressure from Miura, who promised in exchange to remove Japanese troops from the palace area (Pak, *Nisshin sensō*, p. 250). The message was sent to the various legations. Miura, in response, expressed profound shock and distress that the queen, whose actions had been inspired by regard for the royal line and the well-being of the people, should be so treated. Dr. Allen, the representative of the United States, replied in a single sentence, "I cannot recognise this decree as coming from His Majesty" ("Official Report," p. 135).

    On the following day, a compromise was reached: it was announced that out of consideration for Queen Min's status as the mother of the crown prince, she would be raised from the ranks of commoners to *pin*, or concubine (Tsunoda, *Minbi ansatsu*, p. 333). On November 22, 1897, she was given an elaborate state funeral and a posthumous title. She was remembered now chiefly as an unfortunate victim (Kojima, *Ōyama Iwao*, 4, p. 266).

47. *Meiji tennō ki*, 8, p. 943.

48. Pak, *Nisshin sensō*, p. 249.

49. Tsunoda, *Mimbi ansatsu*, p. 334. See also Bird, *Korea and Her Neighbours*, 2, p. 73. The king's fears were not groundless; on September 12, 1898, the king and crown prince were poisoned at dinner (*Meiji tennō ki*, 9, p. 497).

50. Pak, *Nisshin sensō*, p. 260.

51. He was better known, however, as the author of *Kajin no kigū* (Chance Meetings with Beautiful Women), a novel that enjoyed great popularity in the 1890s (Donald Keene, *Dawn to the West*, 1, pp. 82–86).

52. Pak, *Nisshin sensō*, pp. 260–61. Pak quotes Adachi Kenzō as saying that he was given the money (200 yen for each man) by Sugimura, a secretary of the Japanese legation, strongly suggesting that the money came from Miura, not from the *taewon'gun*.

53. Kojima, *Ōyama Iwao*, 4, pp. 271–74. Kojima gives a vivid account of a wild drinking party held in Seoul on October 17. When Yamada Ressei, one of the *sōshi*, suggested that they might be accused of premeditated murder or of conspiracy, he was greeted with raucous laughter. Another *sōshi* answered him: "We acted under the direction of Minister Miura, the representative of our empire. We responded to the trust of the *taewon'gun*. We fought for our country. We had nothing to do with premeditated murder or conspiracy."

54. Miura, *Kanju shōgun*, p. 286.

55. "Official Report," p. 123.

56. Ibid., p. 141. *Meiji tennō ki*, 9, pp. 20–21, differs from this report in important details. It states, for example, that the prime minister of the pro-Japanese cabinet (Kim Hong-jip) and the minister for agriculture (Chong Pyong-ha) were arrested and executed with swords. Kojima states that the two men were traveling to the

palace in sedan chairs when they were surrounded by a mob that killed them and left their bodies on the street. Kojima also states that about fifty Russian soldiers, who had slipped into the palace late at night, escorted the king and crown prince to the Russian legation (Ōyama Iwao, 4, p. 279). According to Choi, Yi Pom-jin and Yi Wan-yong, the leaders of the pro-Russian party, arranged with Carl Waeber, the Russian minister, to land 100 marines from a Russian warship at Inch'on under the pretext of guarding the Russian legation (Fall of the Hermit Kingdom, p. 37). Yi Pom-jin then went to see the king and urged him to seek asylum at the Russian legation. Choi added that "the palace ladies also brought hot food to the guards. Such acts of kindness naturally lulled their vigilance towards the ladies' chairs" (p. 50).

57. Ki-baik Lee, A New History of Korea, trans. Edward W. Wagner, p. 301.

Chapter 48

1. Meiji tennō ki, 9, p 11.
2. Nobuko, the eighth daughter of the emperor, does not appear in these and other mentions of her sisters, probably because she was reared separately from her sisters by Viscount Hayashi Tomoyuki (Meiji tennō ki, 7, p. 899).
3. Meiji tennō ki, 7, p. 172.
4. Ibid., 7, p. 120. The emperor deigned, however, to accept the presents the two princesses had brought—pictures of the detached palace and some sweet potatoes—and it brought Sasaki some consolation to hear that these gifts had pleased the emperor.
5. He was certainly not an indulgent father. His daughter Kitashirakawa Fusako, who later became the presiding dignitary at the festival of the Ise Shrine, recalled that the first time she ever heard Meiji laugh aloud was when she took her infant son to the palace and the child misbehaved ("Meiji tennō to sono kyūtei," p. 44).
6. At the end of 1897, Princess Fusako was taken ill. Sasaki wished to report the progress of her illness to the emperor, but he was told that the emperor had so many other worries on his mind that unless the illness was extremely serious, he should not be informed until the princess had recovered. However, the empress was given a detailed report on the illness (Meiji tennō ki, 9, pp. 365–66).
7. Meiji tennō ki, 9, pp. 94–95.
8. Ibid., 9, pp. 71–72. The king did not leave the Russian legation until February 20, 1897 (Katano Tsugio, Richō metsubō, p. 165).
9. Meiji tennō ki, 8, pp. 746–47.
10. For the negotiations that led to the treaty, see Count Sergei Iulevich Witte, The Memoirs of Count Witte, trans. Sidney Harcave, pp. 227–38.
11. Meiji tennō ki, 9, p. 88.
12. He resigned on May 30, 1896, and died on August 24, 1897 (Meiji tennō ki, 9, pp. 80, 292).
13. Meiji tennō ki, 9, p. 112. Matsukata was from Satsuma; Ōkuma, from Hizen.
14. I have not found this quotation, but Kaiser Wilhelm II made many similar remarks. He told the Prince of Wales, "I am the sole master of German policy and my country must follow me wherever I go" (quoted in John C. G. Röhl, The Kaiser and His Court, p. 12).

15. *Meiji tennō ki*, 9, pp. 119–20.

16. Röhl makes it clear how much more of a despot the kaiser was than Meiji: "It must be remembered that not a single appointment to an official position, and no political measure, could be undertaken without the express consent of the Kaiser. Each statesman and official, each army and naval officer, each political grouping within the ruling elite, each member of the court society, all were condemned to try to enlist the favour of the 'All-Highest Person'" (*Kaiser and His Court*, p. 117).

17. *Meiji tennō ki*, 9, p. 123.

18. Ibid., 9, pp. 152–53.

19. Ibid., 9, p. 160.

20. Ibid., 9, p. 177.

21. Ibid., 9, p. 180.

22. Ibid., 9, p. 183.

23. If a grand dowager empress, dowager empress, or empress had entered Buddhist orders, she would usually be known by a title ending -mon'in or -in, like Kenreimon'in. However, this empress dowager had not entered Buddhist orders, and such a title would have been inappropriate. There were only three cases of a posthumous title (*shigō* or *okurina*) being given to a grand dowager empress, dowager empress, or empress, all from the Nara period, more than a thousand years earlier. The official in charge opposed giving the present empress dowager a posthumous title, preferring her to be known simply by her surname, followed by a posthumous name (*imina*). Later, he was willing to allow a *shigō*, provided it was the name of the place where she lived; he proposed Aoyama Kōtaigō (*Meiji tennō ki*, 9, pp. 194–95).

24. The concluding line of the poem is "Luxuriant clusters of *blossom reflect* in the dark waters of the pool." The name Eishō means literally "blossoms reflect." Li Tê-yu was better known as a statesman than as a poet.

25. *Meiji tennō ki*, 9, p. 199.

26. The non-Buddhist nature of the empress dowager's funeral established a precedent for the imperial family. When Prince Akira, an adopted son of Emperor Kōmei, died in February 1898, his family wished him to have a Buddhist funeral in accordance with his wishes, expressed in his testament, but this request was rejected. The vice president of the Privy Council, Count Higashikuze Michitomi, ruled that funerals of members of the imperial family must be carried out in accordance with ancient examples—meaning Shinto. The emperor supported this ruling (*Meiji tennō ki*, 9, pp. 397–98).

27. *Meiji tennō ki*, 9, pp. 200–201, 207, 343. Queen Min was elevated to the rank of empress as the result of the proclamation by the king of Korea on October 12 that he was henceforth to be the emperor of Korea. The name of the country was changed from Choson to Taehan (Great Han), and the reign-name to Kwangmu (p. 319).

28. *Meiji tennō ki*, 9, pp. 256, 291. Hinonishi Sukehiro, who served as a chamberlain from 1886 until the emperor's death in 1912, recalled that when Meiji was in Kyōto in April 1897, the chamberlains were worried about the emperor's delay in returning to Tōkyō. Just at this time, a great storm caused train service to be suspended. The emperor, with a pleased expression, said, "Low pressure system, is

it? Yes, a low pressure system is just fine." Train service was presently restored, but in the meantime an epidemic of measles had broken out in Tōkyō. This led to a second postponement of the emperor's departure. Not long afterward, word was received that the epidemic had died down, but the emperor said, "I'm sure there must still be some cases. Investigate." The chamberlains investigated and found there were two cases of measles in Tokyo. When this was reported to the emperor, he said, "You see! Didn't I tell you that there would still be cases?" It was no easy matter persuading him to return to Tōkyō (Hinonishi Sukehiro, *Meiji tennō no go-nichijō*, pp. 173–74).

29. *Meiji tennō ki*, 9, p. 218.
30. Ibid., 9, p. 225.
31. Ibid., 9, p. 233.
32. Ibid., 9, p. 260.
33. Ibid., 9, p. 345.
34. Donald Keene, *Dawn to the West*, 1, p. 90.
35. Hinonishi, *Meiji tennō*, p. 98. I am reminded of the story of the emperor Ōjin, related in the *Kojiki*. When he stood on a hill and, looking out over a village, noticed that no smoke was coming from the chimneys, he realized that the people did not have enough money to cook food. He accordingly remitted taxes. When next he stood on the hill and surveyed the village, he was happy to see smoke rising from the chimneys, a sign that it was now prosperous.

Chapter 49

1. *Meiji tennō ki*, 9, pp. 360–61.
2. Ibid., 9, p. 363.
3. Ibid., 9, p. 364.
4. Ibid., 9, p. 370.
5. Ibid., 9, pp. 371–72.
6. Ibid., 9, pp. 384–85.
7. The Yamashita Club was a faction that favored industrial interests. It did not have a strong party organization and was dissolved at the time of the sixth general election.
8. *Meiji tennō ki*, 9, p. 425.
9. Ibid., 9, p. 445.
10. Ibid., 9, p. 451.
11. Presumably he cited Spain and Greece as examples of countries torn by internal warfare.
12. *Meiji tennō ki*, 9, p. 454.
13. Ibid., 9, p. 455.
14. Ibid., 9, pp. 457–58.
15. This probably refers to an incident in December 1887. Various secret matters were leaked to the press and stirred up agitation among *sōshi* who demanded a reduction of taxes, freedom of speech and assembly, and a recovery from the errors of foreign policy. Their anger had been aroused in particular by Inoue Kaoru's plan to allow foreign judges to sit in Japanese courts and to allow foreigners to live in the interior. Yamagata, the interior minister in the first Itō cabinet, issued security

regulations in seven articles prohibiting secret associations, outdoor assemblies, disturbance of the peace, and so on. Ozaki Yukio was one of more than 570 persons who were banished from Tokyo because of their participation in the agitation (*Meiji tennō ki*, 6, pp. 856–58).

16. *Meiji tennō ki*, 9, p. 460. The emperor is said to have been heartened at this time by a long attack on democracy if democracy meant that a nation's sole raison d'être was private interests and private benefits. The attack was made by Nomura Yasushi, a member of several cabinets, who believed that party politics were incompatible with the monarchy.

17. *Meiji tennō ki*, 9, p. 467.

18. Ibid., 9, p. 474.

19. Ibid., 9, p. 475. Although harshly appraised in these words, Hamao Arata was in fact a distinguished educator who twice served as president of Tokyo University.

20. *Meiji tennō ki*, 9, p. 489.

21. Ibid., 9, p. 491.

22. Ibid., 9, p. 492.

23. Ibid., 9, p. 514.

24. Shimba Eiji, *Itagaki Taisuke*, p. 296. Shimba wrote that Itagaki's philosophy of freedom and people's rights had completely "faded."

25. Shimba, *Itagaki*, p. 297. Shimba believed that the plot against Ozaki was ultimately the work of Hoshi Tōru. Hoshi, who had been dismissed in 1892 from his post as chairman of the Shūgiin, was at this time minister to the United States but, hearing of the formation of a coalition cabinet under Ōkuma and Itahaki, had rushed back to Japan without permission, eager to be close to the action.

26. *Meiji tennō ki*, 9, p. 517.

27. Ibid., 9, p. 527.

28. Ibid., 9, p. 531.

29. Ibid., 9, p. 540.

30. Ibid., 9, p. 441. For mentions of worry over the crown prince's health, see pp. 393, 412, 414, 418, 544.

31. Ibid., 9, p. 405.

32. Ibid., 9, p. 537.

33. He was given a physical examination on November 11. The doctor reported that there was no change in the moist rale in his left chest, that his gastroenteritis was improving, and that his appetite was better (*Meiji tennō ki*, 9, p. 544).

34. *Meiji tennō ki*, 9, p. 548.

35. *Shinshū Meiji tennō gyoshū*, 1, p. 318.

Chapter 50

1. *Meiji tennō ki*, 11, p 586.

2. *Meiji tennō ki*, 9, pp. 595–96. The source seems to be a recorded conversation with Tanaka Mitsuaki.

3. Hinonishi Sukehiro, *Meiji tennō no go-nichijō*, p. 53. This anecdote appears in various forms in the different accounts based on Hinonishi's conversations. The version quoted is from the 1976 (Shingakusha kyōyūkan) edition. Another version appears in the 1953 (Sokokusha) edition, pp. 54–55. Morita Seigo suggested, giving

amusing examples, that newspapers were much freer at this time to carry gossip about the emperor than in later years (*Meijijin monogatari*, pp. 37–54).

4. *Shinshū Meiji tennō gyoshū*, 2, p. 719. The word *niibumi* is a "pure" Yamato pronunciation of *shimbun*.

5. They included the dinner offered on July 26, 1905, to William Howard Taft, the heaviest man ever to become president of the United States (*Tennō-ke no kyōen*, pp. 84–85).

6. *Meiji tennō ki*, 9, pp. 613–14. A *kōshaku*, sometimes translated as "duke" or "prince," ranked above a marquis. Many of the *kōshaku* were former daimyos.

7. It was attended by Tokudaiji Sanetsune, Hijikata Hisamoto, Tanaka Mitsuaki, Kagawa Keizō, and Kawaguchi Takesada.

8. One physician, Oka Genkei, was sure that Sachiko was suffering from tuberculosis and intemperately attacked the proposed marriage. Years later, when the crown prince, married to another woman, had his second son, Oka went to congratulate the emperor. He commented that if the crown prince had married his original fiancée, there wouldn't have been such a celebration. The emperor interrupted him angrily, saying that Sachiko's failure to have a child even after a year of marriage was not necessarily her fault (*Meiji tennō ki*, 9, p. 615).

9. *Meiji tennō ki*, 9, p. 751. When Sasaki Takayuki at this time (January 1900) asked the emperor's permission to have the princesses taught French, the emperor refused, saying it was too early. Perhaps his refusal was occasioned by irritation with the crown prince's fondness for that language.

10. These and other European decorations were awarded to the crown prince between December 1897 and March 1900, presumably in connection with his coming of age. In October 1900 he also received a royal decoration from Siam. The Japanese frequently bestowed decorations on foreigners, even those with minimal connections with Japan. For example, Europeans who had been kind to members of Japanese royalty when they traveled abroad often received first-class decorations. Decorations were also bestowed on foreign monarchs; for example, the dowager empress of China was awarded the *kun ittō hōkanshō* (*Meiji tennō ki*, 9, p. 652). Again, after the crown prince received the Order of the Elephant, one of the most distinguished in Europe, the emperor responded by giving the Prince Waldemar of Denmark, who had brought the decoration to Japan, the *daikun'i kikka daijushō*.

11. James E. Hoare, "Extraterritoriality in Japan," p. 97.

12. *Meiji tennō ki*, 9, pp. 694, 761.

13. Erwin Baelz, *Awakening Japan*, trans. Eden Paul and Cedar Paul, pp. 119–20. See also *Meiji tennō ki*, 9, p. 758.

14. Katō Hitoshi, "Meiji tennō o-tsubone go-rakuin den," p. 67.

15. Taishō referred to his mother as *nii*, her rank after he became emperor. When there were leftovers from the palace table, he would often say, "*Nii ni yare*" (give them to Nii) (Katō, "Meiji," p. 66).

16. *Meiji tennō ki*, 9, p. 811.

17. Ibid., 9, pp. 813–14.

18. Ibid., 9, p. 823.

19. So called because many of the insurgents practiced boxing and other martial sports before participating in the fighting.

20. In addition to the foreign troops who suppressed the Boxers, about 170,000 Russian troops invaded Manchuria at this time.

21. On June 19 the Chinese government declared war on the allies, who, however, continued to insist that they were not fighting a war but were engaged solely in a mission to rescue their nationals.

22. The Boxers had roots going back to the eighteenth century when the Eight Diagram Sect was formed as a secret religious and martial organization. The purpose of this secret society (and similar ones) was the overthrow of the Ch'ing (Manchu) dynasty and the restoration of the Ming. For a description of the study of the origins of the Boxer sect by Lao Nai-hsüan, see Chester C. Tan, *The Boxer Catastrophe*, pp. 43–44.

23. Kobayashi Kazumi, *Giwadan sensō to Meiji kokka* , p. 55. He gives these figures for those killed: 188 Protestant missionaries, 5,000 Chinese Protestants, 5 Catholic bishops, 48 Catholic priests, and 18,000 Chinese Catholics. He claims, however, that many were killed not by the Boxers but by Chinese troops after the Manchu government joined with the Boxers in the summer of 1900. In addition, several German and Japanese diplomats were killed in the early stages of the rebellion.

24. This sect gained notoriety for the sexual promiscuity it encouraged, but scholars who are favorably inclined toward the nineteenth-century rebellions in China have interpreted even such sexual excesses as having prepared the ground for the liberation of women from the feudal restraints of Confucianism (Kobayashi, *Giwadan*, pp. 7–8).

25. The first such instance in Shantung seems to have occurred in 1886 when a French priest, with the aid of Chinese Christian converts, destroyed a Taoist shrine (Kobayashi, *Giwadan*, p. 66).

26. For the disruption of village life, see Kobayashi, *Giwadan*, pp. 36–38, 43–44. Kobayashi mentions in particular the loss of tradition—the locally worshiped gods, heroes, public-spirited men, legendary men of super ability—and the loss of the beliefs, rites, and votive theatricals that accompanied these traditions (p. 43).

27. Kobayashi, *Giwadan*, pp. 50, 58. Ōyama Azusa describes the red turbans and red sashes worn into battle by believers; the sashes carried such inscriptions as "The Justice and Peace Sacred Band will raise the Ch'ing and destroy the foreigners" (*Pekin rōjō, Pekin rōjō nikki*, p. v).

28. Sakane Yoshihisa, ed., *Aoki Shūzō jiden*, p. 325.

29. Prince Tuan Chün, the father of the crown prince, had secret connections with the Boxers and was even known as their "chief patron" (Tan, *Boxer Catastrophe*, p. 137; Ōyama, "Kaisetsu," in *Pekin rōjō*, p. iv).

30. Kobayashi, *Giwadan*, p. 90.

31. Ōyama, "Kaisetsu," in *Pekin rōjō*, pp. iii–iv. For Tei's service as an interpreter at the time of the Soejima mission to China, see chapter 24.

32. *Meiji tennō ki*, 9, pp. 836–37.

33. The "allies" consisted of Japan, England, France, Germany, Russia, Italy, Austria, and the United States. The degree of participation in the war varied greatly.

34. Ōyama, ed., *Pekin rōjō*, pp. 244, 16.

35. *Meiji tennō ki*, 9, p. 843.

36. Ibid., 9, p. 844.

37. Absorbing accounts of the siege are in Ōyama, ed., *Pekin rōjō*. It consists mainly of lectures delivered on his experiences by Colonel Shiba Gorō (a younger brother of Shiba Shirō, who had been active in Korea), and the diary kept by Professor Hattori Unokichi, a student in Peking when hostilities broke out.

38. *Meiji tennō ki*, 9, p. 851. Mention of a confrontation between East and West brings to mind the "Yellow Peril" doctrine of the German kaiser.

39. *Meiji tennō ki*, 9, pp. 852–53.

40. Ibid., 9, p. 854. The source of this incident is the diary of Tokudaiji Sanetsune.

41. *Meiji tennō ki*, 9, pp. 862–63.

42. His actual words were "You will be fighting against a well-armed power, but at the same time you must avenge the death not only of the envoy but of many other Germans and Europeans. When you come before the enemy, you must defeat him, pardon will not be given, prisoners will not be taken. Whoever falls into your hands will fall to your sword. Just as a thousand years ago the Huns under King Attila made a name for themselves for ferocity which tradition still recalls; so may the name of Germany become known in China in such a way that no Chinaman will ever again dare to look a German in the eye even with a squint" (quoted in John C. G. Röhl, *The Kaiser and His Court*, pp. 13–14). See also the drawing made by the kaiser showing the nations of Europe as goddesses being led into battle by the Archangel Michael against the "Yellow Peril" (represented by an image of Buddha) (p. 203).

43. *Meiji tennō ki*, 9, pp. 872–73.

44. Ibid., 9, p. 878. Looting by Japanese soldiers was at first dismissed as minor, but it was later revealed that high-ranking officers had stolen quantities of silver bullion. The officers were subsequently dismissed (*Meiji tennō ki*, 10, pp. 228–29, 239).

Chapter 51

1. *Meiji tennō ki*, 9, p. 895.

2. Ibid., 9, pp. 890–91.

3. A literal translation would be Constitutional Party of Friends of Government. It was normally referred to in Japanese simply as Seiyūkai, and it will be so called here.

4. *Meiji tennō ki*, 9, p. 891.

5. Ibid., 9, p. 913. Katsura again requested permission to resign on November 14, and the emperor finally consented on December 23 (pp. 923–25).

6. *Meiji tennō ki*, 10, p. 26.

7. Ibid., 10, pp. 29–30.

8. Ibid., 10, p. 30.

9. For the text of Konoe's note agreeing to follow the wishes of the emperor, see ibid., 10, p. 31.

10. Ibid., 10, pp. 40–42.

11. Ibid., 10, p. 54.

12. Ibid., 10, pp. 54–57.

13. Ibid., 10, pp. 53, 57.

14. The characters were chosen because they appeared in auspicious passages in Chinese classics. The tradition of using words found in the Chinese classics for the names of members of the imperial family (and *nengō*) has not been abandoned, even today.

15. *Meiji tennō ki*, 10, pp. 58–59.

16. Ibid., 10, p. 68.

17. Biographical details are drawn from Ariizumi Sadao, *Hoshi Tōru*, pp. 3–15. The terrible experiences of his sister in the brothel may have inspired his resolve never (in the manner of most Meiji men) to seek pleasure with prostitutes. He was faithful to his wife (p. 9).

18. As part of the contract of adoption, Hoshi's family was required to pay a "dowry" of 50 *ryō*. The family proved unable to provide the money, and the adoption into the Koizumi family was annulled after one year (Ariizumi, *Hoshi*, p. 13).

19. Ga was the descendant of a refugee from Ming China. Well known for his ability in English and his knowledge of the West, he was a member of the Iwakura mission. He was later appointed by the emperor to the House of Peers. Maejima and Mutsu Munemitsu were pupils of Ga.

20. Suzuki Takeshi, *Hoshi Tōru*, p. 22.

21. Ibid., p. 33.

22. He is said to have read again and again Jeremy Bentham's *An Introduction to the Principles of Morals and Legislation* (Ariizumi, *Hoshi*, p. 49).

23. This was the Fukushima incident. The governor, Mishima Michitsune, decided to build a road, the costs to be borne by the people of the prefecture. He ignored the resolution against the road passed by the Prefectural Assembly and went ahead with the construction. Farmers who could not give either money or labor for the road were told that their property would be put up for public auction. Several Jiyū-tō members were arrested for protesting, whereupon a thousand people attacked the Kitakata police station where the arrested men were held. This, in turn, led to the arrest and trial of some fifty Jiyū-tō members.

24. Nakamura Kikuo, *Hoshi Tōru*, pp. 50–54.

25. Suzuki, *Hoshi*, pp. 59–61.

26. Ibid., pp. 79–80.

27. He believed Japan should possess a fleet that was at least as strong as the British East Asian Fleet (Nakamura, *Hoshi*, p. 86).

28. Suzuki, *Hoshi*, p. 91; Nakamura, *Hoshi*, pp. 85–89. In the same speech, Hoshi urged that a new policy be adopted toward China to protect it from British or Russian aggression. He also stated that in view of the unlikelihood of obtaining both the end of extraterritoriality and the end of foreign control of tariffs, the latter was of greater urgency.

29. Nakamura, *Hoshi*, p. 104. Nakamura quotes part of Hoshi's greeting on taking office as House president. He declared that he would act not as a member of the Jiyū-tō but impartially, as befitted someone entrusted with a public duty. He urged members to correct him if they thought he was mistaken and promised to change if they were right.

30. For an account of the charges leveled against Hoshi in the Diet, see Nakamura, *Hoshi*, pp. 116–17. See also *Meiji tennō ki*, 8, pp. 328–29.

31. Nakamura, *Hoshi*, p. 156.

32. Hoshi testified before a Senate subcommittee on the probable adverse effects of a tariff increase on silk. He spoke to such good effect that the tariff was actually lowered (Nakamura, *Hoshi*, pp. 163–64). Ōkuma was so impressed that he bestowed on Hoshi the Order of the Rising Sun, Third Class.

33. The text of his proposal is in Nakamura, *Hoshi*, pp. 175–77.

34. Ibid., p. 182.

35. Suzuki, *Hoshi*, pp. 150–51.

36. For an account of the assassination of Hoshi, see Nagao Kazuo, *Ansatsusha*, pp. 135–59. The verdict handed down after Iba was tried for the murder recognized that he had acted out of a sense of moral justice and sentenced him to life imprisonment rather than execution (p. 159).

37. For further details of the funeral, see Nagao, *Ansatsusha*, p. 158. There is a photograph of the funeral procession in Suzuki, *Hoshi*, p. 191.

38. *Meiji tennō ki*, 10, pp. 80–81. This account mentions the scandal that was created by the exposure in the previous year of Hoshi's taking bribes but does not explain why (if this report was true) such a man was favored by the emperor.

39. *Meiji tennō ki*, 10, p. 89.

40. Erwin Baelz, *Awakening Japan*, trans. Eden Paul and Cedar Paul, p. 144.

41. *Meiji tennō ki*, 10, p. 98.

42. In August 1901 Inoue Kaoru urged Itō, who was about to leave for America and Europe, to visit Russia. Inoue had become convinced that an entente with Russia was the best way of solving the question of Korea. Katsura Tarō, the prime minister, believed that an alliance with either Britain or Russia would achieve this goal. Itō had come to feel that an alliance with England would serve no useful purpose and would antagonize Russia and France. When Hayashi Tadasu met Itō in Paris in November, Itō (who was unaware of the progress of negotiations with England) expressed the opinion that an agreement with Russia was essential to end tension over Manchuria and Korea (Hayashi Tadasu, *Ato wa mukashi no ki*, pp. 343–45).

43. Hayashi, *Ato wa mukashi*, pp. 328–29.

44. Ibid., pp. 306–7.

45. For what the author terms "the first voices" in favor of an Anglo-Japanese alliance, see Kurobane Shigeru, *Nichiei dōmei no kiseki*, 1, p. 21. The conversation between Chamberlain and the Japanese minister, Katō Takaaki, took place on March 17, 1898.

46. Kurobane, *Nichibei*, p. 23.

47. Hayashi, *Ato wa mukashi*, pp. 321, 327.

48. Ibid., pp. 330–31.

49. The agreement, signed on October 16, 1900, proclaimed the Open Door policy in China and the integrity of Chinese territory. The special relations between England and Germany at this time are discussed in Kurobane, *Nichiei*, pp. 24–34. The German minister to England, Hermann Freiherr von Eckardstein, proposed to Hayashi Tadasu, on March 18, 1901, a three-way alliance including Germany, but he acted without authorization from the German Foreign Ministry (pp. 29–30).

50. For details of the Japanese revisions, see Hayashi, *Ato wa mukashi*, pp. 349–50.

51. Ibid., p. 159.

52. Ibid., p. 160.
53. Ibid., p. 306.
54. Baelz described Japanese reactions to the signing of the Anglo-Japanese alliance in these terms: "February 14, 1902. The Japanese can hardly contain their delight at the new alliance. It is unquestionably a triumph for them that the one power which on principle has abstained from alliances should now enter into an alliance, on terms of perfect equality, with the Japanese, who are of an utterly different race. The students of the Keiogijuku School had a torchlight procession and gave three cheers in front of the British legation" (*Awakening Japan*, p. 154).

Chapter 52

1. *Meiji tennō ki*, 10, pp. 176–77.
2. Ibid., 10, p. 181.
3. Ibid., 10, pp. 184–87.
4. Ibid., 10, p. 187. As of February 7 there were 17 survivors, 108 dead, and 85 unaccounted for. Some of the survivors died in the hospital (p. 198).
5. *Meiji tennō ki*, 10, p. 187.
6. See chapter 48.
7. Ian H. Nish, *The Origins of the Russo-Japanese War*, p. 31. The provisions of the treaty were not fully divulged until 1922.
8. Nish, *Origins*, p. 39.
9. Ibid., p. 41. According to Andrew Malozemoff, at a meeting of the Russian czar and the German kaiser in August 1897, the czar had assented to a temporary visit by the German squadron to Kiaochow Bay in time of need (*Russian Far Eastern Policy*, pp. 96–101). The Germans, taking advantage of this agreement, entered the bay in November 1897. The Russians, who were not seriously concerned, decided in December to send a squadron to occupy Port Arthur temporarily, following the Chinese proposal. Malozemoff writes, "William II was delighted. On December 17 he conveyed his approval of the action through the Foreign Office. On the nineteenth he himself telegraphed to the Tsar: 'Please accept my congratulations on the arrival of your squadron at Port Arthur.' On the same day, he charged Baron Osten-Sacken [the Russian chargé in Berlin] to convey to Nicholas II the message: 'Your enemies, whether they be called Japanese or English, now become my enemies; and every troublemaker, whoever he may be, who wishes to hinder your intentions by force, will meet the German squadron side by side with your warships.'"
10. For the Nishi-Rosen Convention, see Malozemoff, *Russian*, p. 110. Baron Roman R. Rosen, the Russian minister to Japan, later termed this agreement a "rather lame and pointless convention."
11. Malozemoff, *Russian*, p. 146. See also *Meiji tennō ki*, 10, pp. 224–25.
12. Malozemoff, *Russian*, pp. 172–73. Count Sergei Witte recalled Itō's visit in these terms: "Unfortunately, he was received coldly . . . . In the end we countered his proposal with our own, which did not accept the basic wishes of Japan. We sent our draft proposal to Ito, who was by this time in Berlin: he did not respond to it, nor could he have, for seeing how his friendly proposals had been received in Petersburg, he no longer opposed having an agreement with England, by which

she would pledge herself to support Japan in a quarrel with Russia, an agreement that would lead to a war that was disastrous for us" (*The Memoirs of Count Witte,* trans. Sidney Harcave, p. 303).

13. According to Nish, "It is broadly accepted that Open Door ideas developed in the brains of Alfred Hippisley, one of the senior officials of the Chinese Maritime Customs, and William H. Rockhill, a junior of John Hay at the State Department in Washington" (*Origins,* p. 55).

14. The literal translation of *kokuryū* as "Black Dragon" may account for this society's sinister reputation.

15. Nish, *Origins,* p. 95.

16. Quoted in ibid., p. 17.

17. Witte, *Memoirs,* p. 307.

18. Nish, *Origins,* p. 142.

19. Erwin Baelz, *Awakening Japan,* trans. Eden Paul and Cedar Paul, p. 249.

20. *Meiji tennō ki,* 10, p. 243.

21. Ibid., 10, p. 261. The prince would later be known as Chichibunomiya.

22. *Meiji tennō ki,* 10, pp. 275, 346. Akasaka Detached Palace, as it came to be known, was completed in 1908, but during the Meiji period it was not used by the crown prince or anyone else. When the emperor examined an album of photographs of the completed palace, his only comment was "Such extravagance!" a blow to the architect Katayama Tōkuma, who had made several journeys to Europe and America to study buildings erected for royalty and the very rich. The palace is mainly in neobaroque but contains elements of many other styles. The materials used were equally varied. As Dallas Finn, the author of a study of surviving Meiji-period buildings, wrote, "Wherever he could, Katayama used Japanese materials: *hinoki* wood for rafters, native copper for roofing, Ibaraki granite for sheathing, Kyoto silk, and thirteen million local bricks. For the interior, however, he had to import, as he put it, the best from everywhere: marble from France, Morocco, Spain, and Italy; plate glass and carpets from England; heating, plumbing, and electrical equipment from the United States, and mantels, mirrors, mosaics, and chandeliers from France. France also provided furniture and a pervasive ambience" (*Meiji Revisited,* p. 236).

23. *Meiji tennō ki,* 10, p. 300.

24. Ibid., 10, p. 306.

25. Ibid., 10, p. 308.

26. Ibid., 10, pp. 318–19.

27. Ibid., 10, pp. 325–27.

28. Ibid., 10, p. 355.

29. Ibid., 10, pp. 366, 368.

30. Ibid., 10, p. 381.

31. Ibid., 10, p. 364.

32. Ibid., 10, p. 392.

33. Ibid., 10, p. 395.

34. *Mori Senzō chosaku shū zokuhen,* 5, p. 12.

35. *Meiji tennō ki,* 10, pp. 399–400.

36. For details, see ibid., 10, p. 406.

37. Ibid., 10, p. 405. For an English rendition of the seven demands, see Nish, *Origins*, p. 146.
38. They were Yamagata Aritomo, Itō Hirobumi, Katsura Tarō, and Komura Jutarō (Ōyama Azusa, *Nichiro sensō no gunsei shiroku*, p. 27).
39. Ōyama, *Nichiro sensō*, p. 28. See also *Meiji tennō ki*, 10, pp. 409–10.
40. *Meiji tennō ki*, 10, p. 416.
41. Ibid., 10, p. 417.
42. Ibid., 10, pp. 423–26.

Chapter 53

1. The text is in *Meiji tennō ki*, 10, pp. 444–49. Copies of the memorial were also sent to Field Marshal Yamagata Aritomo, Count Matsukata Masayoshi, Navy Minister Yamamoto Gonnohyōe, Foreign Minister Komura Jutarō, and Army Minister Terauchi Masatake.
2. *Meiji tennō ki*, 10, p. 452.
3. Ibid., 10, p. 458.
4. The nine were Itō Hirobumi, Yamagata Aritomo, Ōyama Iwao, Matsukata Masayoshi, Inoue Kaoru, Katsura Tarō, Yamamoto Gonnohyōe, Komura Jutarō, and Terauchi Masatake. These men have been referred to as the "oligarchs" who ran Japan at the time. For an extended treatment of this subject, see Shumpei Okamoto, *The Japanese Oligarchy and the Russo-Japanese War*.
5. *Meiji tennō ki*, 10, p. 460.
6. Ibid., 10, p. 464.
7. Ibid., 10, p. 469.
8. Ibid., 10, p. 475.
9. Ibid., 10, p. 479. For a translation of the six points, see Ian H. Nish, *The Origins of the Russo-Japanese War*, pp. 184–85.
10. Andrew Malozemoff, *Russian Far Eastern Policy*, p. 224.
11. Witte's memoirs gives August 13 according to the Julian calendar, then used in Russia. Other accounts give August 28, the date in the Gregorian calendar, used elsewhere in Europe and in Japan.
12. Count Sergei Iulevich Witte, *The Memoirs of Count Witte*, trans. Sidney Harcave, pp. 315–16.
13. Ibid., p. 365.
14. Ibid., p. 366.
15. Malozemoff, *Russian*, p. 226.
16. Witte, *Memoirs*, p. 368.
17. *Meiji tennō ki*, 10, p. 477. See also Okamoto, *Japanese Oligarchy*, pp. 94–95. He quotes the diary of Dr. Erwin Baelz, who recalled, "On the train I met a fashionably dressed Japanese man. He told me, 'the people's indignation toward Russia is no longer under control. The government should declare war immediately. Otherwise, there will be, I fear, a civil rebellion. In fact, even the throne is threatened.'" Baelz commented, "Life is easy for such irresponsible men as this man" (diary entry, September 25, 1903). Okamoto quoted from the Japanese translation made by Baelz's son, Toku Baelz. The English translation does not contain this entry.

18. Malozemoff, *Russian*, p. 238.

19. *Meiji tennō ki*, 10, p. 484. See also John Albert White, *The Diplomacy of the Russo-Japanese War*, pp. 102–3.

20. Text of the first exchange of Japanese and Russian proposals is in White, *Diplomacy*, pp. 351–52.

21. The text is in *Meiji tennō ki*, 10, pp. 516–17; the translation of the second exchange of proposals, in White, *Diplomacy*, pp. 352–54.

22. *Meiji tennō ki*, 10, p. 542. The new Russian proposals were probably the work of Alekseev and Rosen (Malozemoff, *Russian*, p. 243).

23. Malozemoff, *Russian*, p. 243.

24. Witte, *Memoirs*, p. 366.

25. Alexis Kuropatkin, diary entry, December 28, 1903, quoted in Malozemoff, *Russian*, pp. 243, 245.

26. *Meiji tennō ki* 10, pp. 545–46.

27. The text is in ibid., pp. 549–50; the translation of the Japanese proposal and the Russian counterproposal of January 6, in White, *Diplomacy*, pp. 354–55.

28. White, *Diplomacy*, pp. 112–13.

29. Okamoto, *Japanese Oligarchy*, pp. 99–100; *Meiji tennō ki*, 10, pp. 555–62.

30. *Meiji tennō ki*, 10, pp. 503–4.

31. Ibid., 10, p. 508.

32. Erwin Baelz, *Awakening Japan*, trans. Eden Paul and Cedar Paul, p. 240.

33. The text is in *Meiji tennō ki*, 10, pp. 568–69; the translation in White, *Diplomacy*, pp. 356–57.

34. *Meiji tennō ki*, 10, p. 569; White, *Diplomacy*, p. 355.

35. The reasons that the Japanese submitted the fourth set of proposals, although they were convinced it would do no good, differ. In addition to the need for more time to assemble the transport fleet in Sasebo (*Meiji tennō ki*, 10, p. 575), White suggested three possible reasons: (1) the natural reluctance to become embroiled with a formidable adversary, (2) the natural reluctance to be considered an aggressor, and (3) the Japanese desire to prove itself a worthy and acceptable member of the society of nations (*Diplomacy*, p. 120).

36. The text of the fourth Japanese proposal is in *Meiji tennō ki*, 10, pp. 577–79; the translation, in White, *Diplomacy*, pp. 356–58.

37. *Meiji tennō ki*, 10, p. 582.

38. Ibid., 10, p. 583.

39. Sasaki Nobutsuna, *Meiji tennō gyoshū kinkai*, p. 202; *Meiji tennō ki*, 10, p. 584.

40. Maurice Paléologue, *Three Critical Years*, pp. 4–5. White wrote that the hope of using France's good offices to moderate the rigid demands of the two antagonists went back to Lamsdorf's visit to Paris in October 1903 (*Diplomacy*, pp. 124–25). Delcassé accepted this responsibility at the request of both England and Japan, and Russia had also approved. But the Japanese were convinced that further delay would serve Russia's interests, and Russia showed no signs of relenting in what for Japan were totally unacceptable demands.

41. Paléologue, *Three Critical Years*, p. 6.

42. Witte, *Memoirs*, p. 382.

43. Ibid., p. 369.

44. Wilhelm was Queen Victoria's grandson; Alexandra, the wife of the czar, was her granddaughter.
45. Isaac Don Levine, *Letters from the Kaiser to the Czar*, p. 10. The kaiser's letters to Nicholas were written in English. Nicholas's replies have not been published.
46. Levine, *Letters*, p. 13. When the kaiser spoke of "Mongols," he meant all members of the yellow race, but especially the Japanese. Itō Hirobumi, in a conversation with Dr. Erwin Baelz, said, "There can be no shadow of doubt that the Mongols he had in mind were chiefly the Japanese; for, if any Mongol power should threaten Europe, it could not be impotent China, but only Japan, the rising power of the Far East" (quoted in Baelz, *Awakening Japan*, p. 222).
47. Levine, *Letters*, p. 17. See also chapter 50.
48. Levine, *Letters*, pp. 96, 100.
49. Paléologue, *Three Critical Years*, p. 8.
50. Witte, *Memoirs*, pp. 365, 368.
51. Okamoto, *Japanese Oligarchy*, p. 100.
52. Ibid., p. 101.
53. White, *Diplomacy*, p. 129. He mentions a rumor that the message was purposely delayed by the Japanese telegraph.
54. *Meiji tennō ki*, 10, p. 593.
55. The text is in ibid., pp. 595–96.
56. Sasaki, *Meiji*, p. 158.

Chapter 54

1. The two cruisers did not reach Yokosuka until February 16, 1904 (*Meiji tennō ki*, 10, p. 639).
2. *Ishikawa Takuboku zenshū*, 5, p. 37.
3. Ian H. Nish, *The Origins of the Russo-Japanese War*, pp. 255–56.
4. The Japanese government, replying to accusations by the Russian government, stated that it had informed the Russian government of its intention to act independently: "An independent action implies all, including, as a matter of course, the opening of hostile acts. Even if Russia were unable to understand it, Japan has no reason to hold herself responsible for the misunderstandings of Russia. The students of international law all agree that a declaration of war is not a necessary condition for beginning hostilities, and it has been customary in modern warfare for the declaration to follow the opening of the war. The action of Japan had, therefore, no ground for censure in international law" (quoted in K. Asakawa, *The Russo-Japanese Conflict*, p. 354). Asakawa, a Japanese scholar living in the United States, wrote that this was translated from a statement published in the Japanese press on March 3, 1904.
5. The *Times* (London) of February 24, 1904, carried this statement by the Russian government: "Although the breaking-off of diplomatic relations by no means implies the opening of hostilities, the Japanese Government, as early as the night of the 8th, and in the course of the 9th and the 10th, committed a whole series of revolting attacks on Russian warships and merchantmen, attended by a violation of international law. The decree of the emperor of Japan on the subject of the

declaration of war against Russia was not issued until the 11th instant" (quoted in Asakawa, *Russo-Japanese Conflict*, p. 351).

6. Maurice Paléologue, *Three Critical Years*, p. 16.

7. Baron Roman Rosen, *Forty Years of Diplomacy*, 1, p. 107.

8. E. J. Dillon, *The Eclipse of Russia*, p. 288.

9. Rosen, *Forty Years*, 1, pp. 231–32.

10. Ibid., 1, pp. 232–33. By the time Rosen got back to Russia, rumors had spread that his wife had "received from the Mikado a complete dinner service in gold of great value" (p. 246). The czar had heard the rumor, but he assured Rosen that his wife had done exactly right in accepting the empress's gift. For a Japanese account of the same incident that discloses that Rosen had forgotten some of the gifts received from the empress, see *Meiji tennō ki*, 10, pp. 623–24.

11. Rosen, *Forty Years*, 1, p. 235.

12. *Meiji tennō ki*, 10, p. 613.

13. John Albert White, *The Diplomacy of the Russo-Japanese War*, p. 146.

14. *Ishikawa Takuboku zenshū*, 5, p. 43.

15. For the texts of both declarations, see *Meiji tennō ki*, 10, pp. 618–22.

16. *Ishikawa Takuboku zenshū*, 5, p. 42.

17. *Meiji tennō ki*, 10, p. 616.

18. Jane H. Oakley, *A Russo-Japanese War Poem*, p. 9. Bel was the chief deity of Babylon, the lord of heaven and earth, who, King Hammurabi stated, had given him "the black-headed people" and enlarged his kingdom. The name was used in the poem to suggest the great antiquity of the Japanese dynasty.

19. Paléologue, *Three Critical Years*, p. 100.

20. Rosen, *Forty Years*, 1, p. 235. Arishima Takeo, who was studying in America at this time, recalled in later years how extremely displeased he was when his classmates praised Japan every time news came in of a Japanese victory. He detected behind the praise their secret pleasure in the victory of a little dog over a big dog (preface to *Ribinguston den* [1919], 4th ed., in Ishimaru Akiko, ed., *Arishima Takeo*, pp. 49–50).

21. Tyler Dennett, *Roosevelt and the Russo-Japanese War*, pp. 119, 120.

22. Roosevelt read the book at the suggestion of Kaneko Kentarō and was so impressed that he ordered thirty copies for distribution among interested friends, including members of Congress. He felt that the book had given him a new insight into the Japanese character (Kaneko Kentarō, *Nichiro sen'eki hiroku*, pp. 119–21; see also White, *Diplomacy*, p. 158).

23. Sidney Lewis Gulick, *The White Peril in the Far East*, pp. 17–18.

24. Ibid., pp. 95–96. Gulick's description of the treatment given to Russian prisoners of war was confirmed by Eliza Ruhamah Scidmore, the wife of a Russian prisoner in Japan. She wrote that "the government furnishes here as much privacy and more foreign comforts than any tourist can command in a tea house; while the rank and file are in a heaven of plenty, cleanliness, comfort, and idleness they never dreamed of before" (*As The Hague Ordains*, p. 293).

25. Gulick, *White Peril*, pp. 118, 153, 173–74.

26. *Meiji tennō ki*, 10, p. 899.

27. According to Kaneko's own account, he was extremely reluctant to go to America because he was convinced that the Americans were pro-Russian. He gave various

reasons for this belief, including Russian support for the United States during the War of 1812 and the frequent marriages between American heiresses and impoverished members of the Russian aristocracy. He said it would be beyond his powers to induce the Americans to feel sympathy for the Japanese cause, but Itō Hirobumi persuaded him to accept the assignment (*Nichiro*, pp. 11–20).

28. Kaneko, *Nichiro*, pp. 57–59. Roosevelt had been informed in advance by Minister Griscom of Kaneko's forthcoming visit.
29. Kaneko Kentarō, "Meiji tennō to Ruzuberuto daitōryō," p. 123.
30. Ishimaru, ed., *Arishima Takeo*, p. 49.
31. Paléologue, *Three Critical Years*, p. 112.
32. Ibid., pp. 126, 133. For an excellent account of Russian opposition to the war, see Adrian Jones, "East and West Befuddled."
33. Paléologue, *Three Critical Years*, p. 153.
34. Ibid., pp. 163, 90.
35. Ibid., p. 175.
36. Ibid., p. 181.
37. Ibid., p. 200.
38. Ibid., p. 207.
39. Ibid., pp. 221, 255. The Moroccan crisis of 1905 was caused by German apprehension about the increasing French influence in Morocco.
40. Paléologue, *Three Critical Years*, p. 258.
41. Count Sergei Iulevich Witte, *The Memoirs of Count Witte*, trans. Sidney Harcave, pp. 420, 422.
42. Hinonishi Sukehiro, *Meiji tennō no go-nichijō* p. 49.
43. Sir Claude MacDonald to Lord Lansdowne, October 24, 1905, quoted in Nish, *Origins*, p. 9.
44. Rosen, *Forty Years*, 1, p. 29.

Chapter 55

1. Report by the British ambassador to Russia, quoted in Raymond A. Esthus, *Double Eagle and Rising Sun*, p. 38.
2. Gaimushō, *Gaikō bunsho: Nichiro sensō*, no. 5, pp. 231–32, quoted in Shumpei Okamoto, *The Japanese Oligarchy and the Russo-Japanese War*, p. 119.
3. Tyler Dennett, *Roosevelt and the Russo-Japanese War*, p. 173. Roosevelt was referring to the Three Power Intervention after the Sino-Japanese War that deprived Japan of the Liaotung Peninsula.
4. Dennett, *Roosevelt*, pp. 23–27.
5. Ibid., p. 180. This message was in a telegram sent by Komura to Takahira on April 25.
6. Esthus, *Double Eagle*, p. 25.
7. *Meiji tennō ki*, 11, p. 33.
8. Ibid., 11, pp. 3–4.
9. Sasaki Nobutsuna, ed., *Meiji tennō gyoshū kinkai*, p. 244. A different version of the last line—*tsutae kinikeri*—is in *Meiji tennō ki*, 11, pp. 4–5.
10. *Meiji tennō ki*, 11, p. 30.
11. Sasaki, *Meiji*, p. 254. *Himugashi no miyako* was a poetic way of referring to Tōkyō.

12. *Meiji tennō ki*, 11, pp. 83–84. A similar (but shorter) message was sent to the Yalu River Army.

13. *Meiji tennō ki*, 11, p. 93.

14. Ibid., 11, p. 101.

15. Ibid., 11, p. 156.

16. Kaneko Kentarō, *Nichiro sen'eki*, p. 217.

17. Esthus, *Double Eagle*, p. 39. The original document is in *Nihon gaikō bunsho: Nichiro sensō*, 5, pp. 233–34, 252–54.

18. Esthus, *Double Eagle*, p. 40.

19. Isaac Don Levine, *Letters from the Kaiser to the Czar*, p. 172.

20. Ibid., p. 175.

21. Dennett, *Roosevelt*, p. 219. The American ambassador to Germany, Charlemagne Tower, reported this to the president in a letter dated June 9.

22. Dennett, *Roosevelt*, p. 220. In a letter dated June 4, the kaiser wrote Ambassador Tower, "Considering the grave dangers to all of us, which might arise in case something serious happened to His Imperial Majesty, I have written him a letter counselling him to open negotiations for Peace." He told Tower, "Unless peace is made, they will kill the Tsar." See also Esthus, *Double Eagle*, p. 41.

23. Esthus, *Double Eagle*, pp. 43, 45.

24. Dennett, *Roosevelt*, pp. 224–25, 225–26. The Japanese text is in *Meiji tennō ki*, 11, p. 173.

25. Dennett, *Roosevelt*, p. 226.

26. Esthus, *Double Eagle*, p. 48.

27. Quoted in ibid., p. 47.

28. Roosevelt was aware of the danger of causing the czar and the Russian government to suspect he was pro-Japanese (*Meiji tennō ki*, 11, p. 103).

29. *Meiji tennō ki*, 11, pp. 176, 177.

30. Quoted in Esthus, *Double Eagle*, p. 51.

31. When the American ambassador George von Lengerke Meyer went to see the czar to persuade him to consent to direct negotiations, the czar finally yielded and then suddenly confessed, "You have come at a psychological moment; as yet no foot has been placed on Russian soil; but I realize that at almost any moment they can make an attack on Sakhalin. Therefore it is important that the meeting should take place before that occurs" (quoted in Dennett, *Roosevelt*, p. 194). On March 31 an order was issued for the Japanese Thirteenth Infantry Division to assemble, for the purpose of occupying Sakhalin (*Meiji tennō ki*, 11, p. 106).

32. Kaneko, *Nichiro sen'eki*, p. 225. Kaneko wrote that on June 8 Roosevelt urged him to send a message to the Japanese government, advising it to seize Sakhalin before negotiations began and even specifying the number of troops and gunboats that would be needed. Roosevelt believed that unless the Japanese occupied Russian territory, they would be in a weak position at the conference table. Exactly a month after Roosevelt gave this advice, Japan sent two gunboats and a mixed brigade to Sakhalin. Kaneko said he was not sure if this action was inspired by Roosevelt's advice. See also Esthus, *Double Eagle*, p. 46.

33. The emperor's reliance on Itō during the war began earlier. When Itō decided to send Kaneko to America, he admitted that it would be better if he himself went,

but the emperor had made it clear he needed his counsel and would not let him go abroad (Kaneko, *Nichiro sen'eki*, p. 16).

34. Matsumura Masayoshi, *Nichiro sensō to Kaneko Kentarō*, pp. 234–41; Akabane Shigeru, *Nichiro sensō shiron*, pp. 287–311. Colonel Akashi Motojirō, who was based at the Japanese legation in Stockholm, operated a network of spies that provided him with information on conditions in Russia. He was enabled by Konni Zilliacus, a Finnish patriot, to meet various Russian revolutionaries, including Lenin, and generously backed them. Zilliacus said of Akashi's activities, "Half the people to whom Japanese money is distributed don't know where it comes from — and the other half don't care" (quoted in Noel F. Busch, *The Emperor's Sword*, p. 122).

Soon after the end of the Russo-Japanese War, a booklet called *Rakka ryūsui* describing Akashi's secret activities was published by the Russian state police. His cooperation with Russian revolutionary elements may have helped the success of antigovernmental movements in 1905 and 1917. An English translation of parts of *Rakka ryūsui* was published in Helsinki in 1988. Japanese intelligence activities during the war are described in John Albert White, *Diplomacy of the Russo-Japanese War*, pp. 138–42. E. J. Dillon wrote, "The strikes, the demonstrations, the subterranean agitation, the spread of revolutionary leaflets, and the brisk, illegal traffic between Finland and Russia, were in varying degrees evidences of Japanese propaganda" (*The Eclipse of Russia*, p. 184).

Kaneko Kentarō recalled in later years that the celebrated historian and author Henry Adams, whom he described as the "brain" (*chiebukuro*) of John Hay, the secretary of state, had advised him that Japan should send secret agents to Finland and Sweden to stir up the people there and create unrest. Kaneko and Adams met in Washington on January 15, 1905 (Kaneko, *Nichiro sen'eki*, pp. 70–76; Busch, *Emperor's Sword*, p. 122; Elizabeth Stevenson, *Henry Adams*, pp. 315–16).

35. Esthus, *Double Eagle*, pp. 82–83. The original instructions given to the Japanese emissaries on June 4 are listed in *Meiji tennō ki*, 11, p. 198. They differ somewhat from the demands made at Portsmouth. For example, at the suggestion of President Roosevelt, the demand that Vladivostok be demilitarized was removed from the list.

36. Esthus, *Double Eagle*, pp. 84, 61.

37. Okamoto, *Japanese Oligarchy*. p. 117.

38. Esthus writes, "From the records that are available, it is impossible to determine conclusively whether Komura was deliberately misleading his government on the Sakhalin question" (*Double Eagle*, p. 151). Komura did not inform the Japanese government of the Russian proposal to divide Sakhalin until the czar's decision had already been reported in the press. President Roosevelt wrote the kaiser proposing binding arbitration on the money question, but Komura could not be reached for confirmation. Esthus thought that Komura's failure to respond may have been deliberate (p. 153).

39. *Meiji tennō ki*, 11, pp. 281–84.

40. Ibid., 11, pp. 286–87.

41. The full English text sent by Katsura to Komura is in Morinosuke Kajima, *The Diplomacy of Japan*, 2, pp. 349–50.

42. Esthus, *Double Eagle*, p. 158.

43. Kajima, *Diplomacy of Japan*, 2, p. 351.
44. Esthus, *Double Eagle*, p. 159.
45. Ibid., p. 164.
46. Eliza Ruhamah Scidmore, *As The Hague Ordains*, p. 346. The reference to Kronstadt may simply equate this Russian naval port with the similar Portsmouth. *Il Strenuoso* is an ironic reference to Theodore Roosevelt's love of the strenuous life.
47. Esthus, *Double Eagle*, p. 165.
48. Ibid., pp. 171, 173.
49. *Meiji tennō ki*, 11, pp. 314–15.
50. Esthus, *Double Eagle*, p. 188. He quotes a letter written by Roosevelt on September 6.
51. Theodore Roosevelt to Takahira Kogōro, September 8, 1905, quoted in ibid.

Chapter 56

1. Iguchi Kazuki, *Nichiro senō no jidai*, pp. 127–28. Iguchi declared that without Britain's support, Japan lacked the fighting strength to pursue the war with Russia. The Japanese, as yet incapable of casting the main and secondary guns for their battleships and armored cruisers, depended on the British not only for the guns but also for charging the missiles fired. The British also supplied the Japanese navy with 20,000 tons of coal each month.
2. Ian H. Nish, *The Anglo-Japanese Alliance*, p. 289. Britain decided that it could not "permit any ship now in the Black Sea to take part in warlike operations," and at Britain's request, Turkey refused to allow vessels of the Russian Black Sea Fleet through the Straits.
3. Nish wrote that "Britain may have given the impression of being more a neutral and less an ally" (*Anglo-Japanese Alliance*, p. 292).
4. Sir Claude MacDonald to Charles Hardinge, British ambassador to Russia, December 23, 1904, quoted in Nish, *Anglo-Japanese Alliance*, p. 299.
5. Nish, *Anglo-Japanese Alliance*, p. 303.
6. Telegram, Hayashi Tadasu, Japanese minister to England, to his government, quoted in ibid., p. 309.
7. The English text of the agreement is in Nish, *Anglo-Japanese Alliance*, pp. 331–33.
8. Ibid., p. 346. Prince Arthur's father, also called Prince Arthur of Connaught, had made an unofficial visit to Japan in 1890, spent mainly in sightseeing and acquiring "curios." It is surprising that the son, rather than the father, should have been assigned so important a task as the conferment of the Garter, but the father was occupied in India.
9. Lord Redesdale, *The Garter Mission to Japan*, pp. 1–2.
10. Ibid., pp. 5–6.
11. Ibid., pp. 7–8.
12. Ibid., p. 8.
13. It is described in detail in ibid., pp. 16–20.
14. *Meiji tennō ki*, 11, p. 492.
15. Hinonishi Sukehiro, *Meiji tennō no go-nichijō*, p. 184.
16. *Meiji tennō ki*, 11, p. 493.
17. Redesdale, *Garter Mission*, pp. 22, 23.

18. Ibid., p. 25.

19. Ibid., p. 29.

20. The name by which William Adams (1564–1620) became known after he decided to live permanently in Japan.

21. Redesdale, *Garter Mission*, pp. 76–81. *Yoi, yoi, yoiya, sa*, the burden of the song, has a vaguely felicitous meaning.

22. Nish, *The Anglo-Japanese Alliance*, pp. 350–51.

23. *Meiji tennō ki*, 11, pp. 374–75.

24. Ibid., 11, pp. 376–79.

25. Ibid., 11, pp. 380–81. See also Kim Un Yon, *Nikkan heigō*, pp. 187–88.

26. *Meiji tennō ki*, 11, pp. 381–84. Kim gives a shortened but very similar account (*Nikkan heigō*, pp. 183–91). According to Woonsang Choi, the last utterance of Emperor Kojong was "Assent to your proposal would mean the ruin of my country, and I will therefore sooner die than agree to it" (*The Fall of the Hermit Kingdom*, p. 46).

27. For an account of the opinions expressed, see Katano Tsugio, *Richō metsubō*, pp. 217–18. The Koreans called attention to the paradox that Japan, the ostensible defender of Korean independence, proposed to rob the country of its independence.

28. Choi, *Fall of the Hermit Kingdom*, p. 47.

29. Ibid., p. 47.

30. Ibid., p. 48.

31. Katano gives a vivid description of Itō's asking each cabinet member by turn whether he was for or against the treaty (*Richō metsubō*, pp. 221–22). Vague responses were tallied as "not opposed" and marked O, and only the determinedly opposed were marked X. Katano does not give his source. See also Peter Duus, *The Abacus and the Sword*, pp. 190–92.

32. Kim, *Nikkan heigō*, p. 195. Choi gives an account of how Japanese officers dragged the defiant acting prime minister into a side room where, the other cabinet ministers feared, he was likely to be killed (*Fall of the Hermit Kingdom*, pp. 48–49). This action by the Japanese induced several of the cabinet ministers to consent to the treaty. Choi says of the different accounts of the conference, "All authors vary little in describing the substance of the conference scene, namely its coercive nature" (p. 54). However, Duus states that the acting prime minister left the room in so highly agitated state that he accidentally wandered into the women's quarters (*Abacus*, p. 191, citing Japanese authorities). Petrified by his mistake (and the shrieking of the women), he had fainted dead away. The discussion continued without him. The marked discrepancy between the two accounts suggests that neither may be completely reliable.

33. Kim, *Nikkan heigō*, p. 195.

34. Ibid., p. 196.

35. Historians do not agree on whether or not the emperor signed the treaty. For the controversy, see Duus, *Abacus*, pp. 193–94.

36. *Meiji tennō ki*, 11, p. 408.

37. Katano, *Richō metsubō*, pp. 225–26. The five ministers who had voted in favor of the treaty were branded by the public as *ulsa ojok*, the five bandits of 1905.

38. *Meiji tennō ki*, 11, p. 435. He was succeeded as president of the Privy Council by Yamagata Aritomo. He took leave of Emperor Meiji on February 2 and, after arriving in Korea, was formally installed as the first resident general on March 3.

39. *Meiji tennō ki*, 11, pp. 596–98. Itō was particularly concerned about rebellions that seemed to be backed by influential persons in the palace. Most rebellions were directed against the treaty, but there were also some without ideological content.

40. *Meiji tennō ki*, 11, p. 228. The letter was sent by secret messenger to Chefoo in China, and from there by cable to Washington where Homer Hulbert, an American missionary who enjoyed the confidence of the Korean emperor, delivered it to Elihu Root, the secretary of state, who in turn passed it on to Roosevelt. It had no effect, perhaps because the American minister to Korea had warned the secretary of state that Hulbert's judgments were often "colored by prejudice" in favor of the Koreans (Duus, *Abacus*, p. 206).

41. *Meiji tennō ki*, 11, pp. 536–37. The review took place on April 30 at the Aoyama parade grounds. It was notable otherwise because Meiji wore for the first time the khaki uniform that had become standard in the Japanese army.

42. According to Katano, the emperor did not utter a word when Itō presented his credentials on March 9 (*Richō metsubō*, p. 238).

43. See, for example, *Meiji tennō ki*, 11, pp. 642–44.

44. *Meiji tennō ki*, 11, pp. 661, 724.

45. Choi, *Fall of the Hermit Kingdom*, pp. 61–63. See also Katano, *Richō metsubō*, pp. 242–45, and *Meiji tennō ki*, 11, pp. 765–66.

46. Sunjong, earlier known as I Chok, was Kojong's son by Queen Min. He was poisoned in 1898, and although doctors saved his life, the poison affected his mind (Kitano, *Richō metsubō*, pp. 254–55).

Chapter 57

1. When I visited Madagascar in 1963, I learned that Japan enjoyed the reputation of being "the land of liberty." At the time, although the country was officially independent, the French still controlled the radio. They seemed eager to broadcast my lecture until they learned it was to be on Japan, a dangerous subject!

2. *Arishima Takeo zenshū*, 10, p. 475.

3. *Ishikawa Takuboku zenshū*, 5, p. 118.

4. The poem was shown to the president in the translation by Arthur Lloyd, a professor at Waseda University (Chiba Taneaki, *Meiji tennō gyosei kinwa*, p. 203).

5. *Shinshū Meiji tennō gyoshū*, 1, p. 638.

6. Ibid., 1, p. 613. The poem is discussed in *Meiji tennō ki*, 11, pp. 456–57.

7. *Shinshū Meiji tennō gyoshū*, 2, p. 732.

8. Asukai Masamichi, *Meiji taitei*, p. 278.

9. Matsushita Yoshio, *Nogi Maresuke*, p. 188.

10. Oka Yoshitake, "Generational Conflict After the Russo-Japanese War," trans. J. Victor Koschmann, p. 199.

11. Ibid., p. 207.

12. *Meiji tennō ki*, 11, p. 468.

13. According to Chamberlain Bōjō Toshinaga, the emperor offered chairs to only three Japanese: Prince Taruhito, Itō Hirobumi, and Yamagata Aritomo(*Kyūchū gojūnen*, p. 17).

14. *Meiji tennō ki*, 11, p. 469. Tsai Tse received the Order of the Paulownia Leaf, First Class; the other Chinese received lesser decorations.

15. *Meiji tennō ki*, 11, pp. 472–74.

16. Ibid., 11, pp. 501–2. The emperor appointed Makino Nobuaki as minister of education on March 27, replacing Saionji. Hayashi Tadasu succeeded Saionji as foreign minister on May 19.

17. *Meiji tennō ki*, 11, p. 535.

18. Ibid., 11, p. 586.

19. Ibid., 11, p. 643.

20. George Trumbull Ladd, *Rare Days in Japan*, pp. 18–22.

21. Ibid., pp. 339–40. For an estimation of Ladd's contribution to Japanese education, see *Meiji tennō ki*, 11, p. 796.

22. *Meiji tennō ki*, 11, p. 661.

23. Ibid., 11, p. 754.

24. Ibid., 11, p. 726.

25. Ibid., 11, pp. 671–78.

26. See chapter 48.

27. *Meiji tennō ki*, 11, pp. 749, 778.

28. Ibid., 11, pp. 773–76.

29. Ibid., 11, pp. 777–78, 790. *Kōshaku* was the highest rank of the peerage, sometimes translated as "duke."

30. Katano Tsugio, *Richō metsubō*, pp. 255–56.

31. On November 19 the emperor of Korea issued an edict to his people explaining why the crown prince was going to study in Japan. He cited the European practice of sending crown princes from an early age to study abroad and mentioned that sometimes they even had these princes join the armed forces of another country. He said that he was entrusting the education of Yi Eun to Emperor Meiji (*Ei shinnō rigin den*, p. 70; Katano, *Richō*, pp. 256–57).

32. A photograph showing Itō in what looks like a naval uniform with Yi Eun in a Japanese *haori* and *hakama* is reproduced in *Ei shinnō rigin den*, p. 7. On the same page there is a picture of Yi Eun in the uniform of a Korean army officer but wearing a Japanese decoration.

33. Erwin Baelz, *Awakening Japan*, trans. Eden Paul and Cedar Paul, p. 117.

34. See chapter 4.

35. For Shinto funerals, see Helen Hardacre, *Shinto and the State*, pp. 34, 47. She wrote, "For Shinto clergy, funerals were problematic because of the concept of death pollution, but revenues from funerals and ancestral rites were a considerable incentive to overcome such taboos" (p. 47).

36. *Meiji tennō ki*, 11, pp. 803–5.

37. Ibid., 11, p. 835.

38. It may originally have been intended that Yi Eun remain for a relatively short period of time, but in fact he married a Japanese princess and it was not until 1963 that he returned permanently to Korea, where he died in 1970.

Chapter 58

1. *Meiji tennō ki*, 12, p. 3.
2. Ibid., 12, p. 13. A photograph of an essay written in Japanese on November 7, 1908, by Prince Yi Eun indicates that he had made remarkable progress with the Japanese language (*Ei shinnō rigin den*, p. 8).
3. *Meiji tennō ki*, 12, pp. 13–14.
4. Ibid., 12, p. 57. On September 4, when Yi Eun returned to Tokyo from a visit to the Kansai region, the emperor presented him with a motion-picture machine (*katsudō shashin kikai*) and another set of cricket gear (p. 102). It is not known if the Korean prince ever played cricket.
5. *Meiji tennō ki*, 12, p. 36.
6. Ibid., 12, pp. 54–55.
7. Ibid., 12, p. 121.
8. Ibid., 12, p. 138. See also Hinonishi Sukehiro, *Meiji tennō no gonichi*, p. 153.
9. *Meiji tennō ki*, 12, p. 149, does not state what uniform the emperor wore on this occasion. He normally wore his unique army uniform, but he was sometimes persuaded to wear a naval uniform instead. On May 15, for example, when he attended the graduation ceremonies at the naval academy, he wore a naval dress uniform (p. 229).
10. *Meiji tennō ki*, 12, p. 85.
11. Ibid., 12, p. 173.
12. Ibid., 12, p. 189.
13. Ibid., 12, pp. 221–22.
14. Ibid., 12, pp. 231–33, 242.
15. Ibid., 12, p. 255. See also Saitō Michinori, *Itō Hirobumi wo utta otoko*, pp. 62–63, and Kinebuchi Nobuo, *Nikkan kōshō shi*, p. 267.
16. *Meiji tennō ki*, 12, p. 263.
17. Ibid., 12, pp. 283–84.
18. For excerpts from his speech, as reported in the *Tōkyō Asahi shimbun* on October 22, see Kinebuchi, *Nikkan*, p. 268.
19. The photograph is reproduced in Saitō, *Itō Hirobumi*, p. 9. It shows in the foreground Russian officers chatting, some with their backs to the train, and the main body of guards some distance down the platform. The laxness of the Russian guards was mentioned by the correspondent of the *New York Herald*, who expressed surprise that soldiers from a country famed for its assassinations should not have been more alert (p. 10).
20. The photograph is reproduced in Saitō, *Itō Hirobumi*, p. 8.
21. An Chung-gun was not sure which of the Japanese was Itō, never having seen even Itō's photograph. He chose as his target a man "with a yellow face and white whiskers" who seemed to lead the others (Nakano Yasuo, *An Jūkon*, pp. 45, 192). He fired at Itō from a distance of two and a half *ken* (about fifteen feet, or five meters). After killing Itō, he fired at two other Japanese, thinking that one or the other might be Itō, but his shots went astray, possibly because a Russian guard interfered with his aim (Saitō, *Itō Hirobumi*, p. 35).
22. An Chung-gun fired a Browning automatic pistol that held seven shells. After firing three shots at Itō, he fired three more at two other Japanese. At his trial he

was asked if he had saved the last bullet for himself, but he denied that he had any thought of suicide (Nakano, *An Jūkon*, pp. 45–46).

23. Saitō, *Itō Hirobumi*, p. 184. Doubt has been cast on the truth of this utterance. If Itō actually said these words, he may have meant that An was a fool to think that killing him would prevent the annexation of Korea. According to another source, however, Itō's last words were to ask who had shot him and if anyone else had been shot.

24. Nakano, *An Jūkon*, p. 4. So reported by witnesses, but An stated in courtroom testimony that he had cried out not in English or Russian but in Korean, *Taihan mansei* (Long Live Great Han), Han being a name for Korea (Saitō, *Itō Hirobumi*, p. 10).

25. Nakano, *An Jūkon*, p. 191; Saitō, *Itō Hirobumi*, p. 23. It was reported in the November 3 issue of *Tōkyō nichinichi shimbun* that An's overcoat and suit had been made in France (Saitō, *Itō Hirobumi*, p. 46). An also wore a cloth cap as part of his costume as a Japanese.

26. Nakano, *An Jūkon*, p. 103. For an extended account of the An family, see Norbert Weber, *Im Lande der Morgenstille*, pp. 331–49.

27. An explained in court that he had used the name "An of the Seven Moles" ever since, three years earlier, he had become a *uibyong* (righteous soldier) (Nakano, *An Jūkon*, p. 39). In ancient China, seven moles on a person's body were interpreted as a sign of greatness, probably because they were associated with the seven stars of the Big Dipper.

28. Saitō, *Itō Hirobumi*, p. 34.

29. For more on the *uibyong* (righteous army), see Peter Duus, *The Abacus and the Sword*, pp. 117, 224–27.

30. For a description of the fighting at this time, see Nakano, *An Jūkon*, pp. 108–10.

31. Ibid., pp. 118–19; Saitō, *Itō Hirobumi*, p. 63. Nakano states without explanation that both An Chung-gun and his father, An Tae-hun, were baptized at this time after passing a test in the catechism (*An Jūkon*, p. 118), but he earlier says that Tae-hun had been baptized at some previous date and given the baptismal name of Petrus (p. 108). The name Thomas was rendered in Chinese characters that indicate the intended pronunciation was *to-ma* (as in French).

32. The son died in 1916 at the age of twelve in Vladivostok, where the family had fled after the assassination (Nakano, *An Jūkon*, pp. 225–56; Saitō, *Itō Hirobumi*, p. 121).

33. Nakano, *An Jūkun*, p. 39. Although Father Wilhelm's name suggests that he was German rather than French, he may have taught French to An because French missionaries played the most important role in propagating Catholicism in Korea.

34. Nakano, *An Jūkon*, p. 127.

35. It may have been not Wilhelm but his superior, the bishop of Seoul, who annoyed An. When An presented to the bishop his plan for a university in Korea, the bishop disapproved, saying that education would be harmful to the Koreans' faith (Nakano, *An Jūkon*, p. 127). An was probably disappointed when Wilhelm, whom he supposed was on his side, agreed with his superior. For another theory as to why An and Wilhelm became estranged, see pp. 144–45. An was so annoyed that he considered appealing directly to the pope. However, he was delighted when Wil-

helm visited him shortly before his death. A photograph shows the two men conversing over a table (Saitō, *Itō Hirobumi*, p. 110).

36. Saitō, *Itō Hirobumi*, p. 114. These remarks are found in An's essay "On Peace in East Asia," left unfinished at his death.

37. See, for example, Saitō, *Itō Hirobumi*, p. 84.

38. Saitō pointed out, however, that An must have been thinking of the emperor's proclamation at the opening of the Sino-Japanese War (*Itō Hirobumi*, p. 90). The proclamation for the Russo-Japanese War was significantly different, calling for not for peace in East Asia but "peace and order," and not the independence of Korea but its "integrity."

39. Saitō, *Itō Hirobumi*, p. 178. See also Nakano, *An Jūkon*, pp. 209–10. An condemned as a "crime against Heaven" the actions of Prime Minister Yi Wan-yong, who had helped Russia and fought against Japan during the Russo-Japanese War, although he added that if Yi were to raise a "righteous army" and fight against Japan, this would be in consonance with the will of Heaven; Itō's outrageous behavior had made the difference (Nakano, *An Jūkon*, p. 160).

40. An released all the prisoners unharmed and even gave them back their rifles (Nakano, *An Jūkon*, p. 171).

41. An did not explain how he had come to be a lieutenant general or if there was a general who ranked above him. *Uibyong* (*gihei* in Japanese), translated here as "righteous army" or "righteous soldiers," has no exact equivalent in English. It means soldiers who are moved by righteous principles, as opposed to ordinary soldiers whose only thought is to obey orders.

42. Nakano, *An Jūkon*, p. 14.

43. In 1867 Itō was not of sufficiently high rank to appear before the emperor. At the time of Kōmei's death, moreover, Itō was seriously ill in Chōshū and not in Kyōto.

44. For the fifteen charges with a brief commentary on each, see Saitō, *Itō Hirobumi*, pp. 172–75.

45. Quoted in ibid., p. 46.

46. Nakano, *An Jūkon*, pp. 17, 13.

47. Saitō, *Itō Hirobumi*, p. 100.

48. They gave examples of men who, because political ideals had inspired their assassinations, were given relatively light sentences. They did not mention, however, the nearest parallel: in 1907, an American named Durham W. Stevens, who had been in the employ of the Japanese in Korea, announced at a press conference given on arriving in San Francisco on his way to Washington that Itō Hirobumi had done much to benefit the Korean people. He was assassinated the next day by two angry Koreans. One of them, Chang In-hwan, served fifteen years in prison for the crime. The Japanese newspaper article reporting Stevens's murder is in Kinebuchi, *Nikkan*, pp. 266–67. See also *Meiji tennō ki*, 12, p. 41, and Woonsung Choi, *The Fall of the Hermit Kingdom*, p. 78.

49. Saitō, *Itō Hirobumi*, p. 103.

50. Nakano, *An Jūkun*, pp. 29–30. Saitō mentions the discussion between Judge Hiraishi and Kurachi Tetsukichi of the Foreign Ministry, who had come to Port Arthur under orders from Komura (*Itō Hirobumi*, p. 101). Kurachi conveyed the opinion of the government that the death penalty was advisable.

51. Saitō, *Itō Hirobumi*, p. 124.

52. Katano Tsugio, *Richō metsubō*, p. 284.
53. Saitō, *Itō Hirobumi*, pp. 31, 32.
54. "Hyakkai tsūshin," in *Ishikawa Takuboku zenshū*, 4, p. 192. A Korean scholar has suggested that Takuboku's poem "A Spoonful of Cocoa," usually considered to refer to the execution of Kōtoku Shūsui, might actually have expressed his feelings about An (Saitō, *Itō Hirobumi*, pp. 150–51). However, the tone of Takuboku's remarks in "Hyakkai tsūshin" is one of shock, not of sympathy with the terrorist.

Chapter 59

1. Kinebuchi Nobuo, *Nikkan kōshō shi*, p. 274. See also Moriyama Shigenori, *Nikkan heigō*, pp. 128–29.
2. Moriyama, *Nikkan*, p. 129.
3. Yi Wan-yong had an unusually checkered career. In 1896 he was one of the leaders of the pro-Russian party that urged King Kojong to take refuge in the Russian legation. Later that year, he was elected vice president of the Independence Club, which was anti-Russian and opposed foreign intervention in Korean affairs. In 1905, as minister of education, he was the first of the five "traitors" to sign the convention providing for Japanese control of Korea's foreign relations. In 1906, exasperated by Kojong's refusal to cooperate more positively with the new government, he proposed to the Japanese that the emperor be deposed (Moriyama, *Nikkan*, p. 125). This earned Yi Wan-yong the confidence of the Japanese, and when Itō formed a new cabinet in May 1907, he chose Yi Wan-yong as prime minister.
4. Moriyama, *Nikkan*, p. 130.
5. Ibid., p. 131.
6. Woonsang Choi, *The Fall of the Hermit Kingdom*, p. 70.
7. Moriyama, *Nikkan*, p. 129.
8. Kinebuchi, *Nikkan*, p. 274.
9. Ibid.
10. The *karatachi* (*Citrus trifoliata*) and the *tachibana* (*Citrus tachibana*) are similar members of the same family that also includes the tangerine. The *karatachi* was also known as *karatachibana* or simply as *tachibana*, evidence of how easily the two plants were confused.
11. Quoted from the Japanese version of the text, originally printed in the *Tōkyō Asahi* on December 8, 1909, in Kinebuchi, *Nikkan*, p. 276. According to legend, the *udombara* blossomed only once in 3,000 years. Both the lucky stars and the phoenix were auguries of future good fortune.
12. Peter Duus, *The Abacus and the Sword*, pp. 239–40.
13. Kinebuchi, *Nikkan*, p. 277.
14. For an excellent analysis of how the "common culture" and "common ancestry" of the Japanese and Koreans was discussed by Japanese at the time, see Duus, *Abacus*, pp. 413–23.
15. Ibid., p. 197. His source was Ōyama Azusa, *Yamagata Aritomo ikensho*, p. 284. In contrast, Itō was far more optimistic about the possibility of the Koreans accepting modern civilization. He believed that the reason that the Koreans had fallen behind the Japanese was not because they were inherently indolent but because of the upper classes' corruption and resistance to change (Duus, *Abacus*, p. 199).

16. Moriyama, *Nikkan*, p. 178.

17. *Meiji tennō ki*, 12, p. 430.

18. Choi, *Fall of the Hermit Kingdom*, p. 74. Choi's source was Fukuda Tōsaku, *Kankoku heigō kinen shi*, p. 597.

19. *Meiji tennō ki*, 12, pp. 455–56.

20. Ibid., 12, pp. 451–52.

21. The text is in ibid., 12, pp. 461–62; the translation, in Choi, *Fall of the Hermit Kingdom*, pp. 136–38. There were only five articles in the version presented to Yi Wan-yong by General Terauchi. The preamble, the first two articles (stating the willingness of the Korean emperor to cede his rights of sovereignty and the Japanese emperor's willingness to accept the annexation of Korea), and the eighth article (the promulgation of the treaty) are missing, but the remaining articles are more or less the same.

22. In October 1910 seventy-six Korean nobles were given Japanese titles: six marquises, three counts, twenty-two viscounts, and forty-five barons (*Meiji tennō ki*, 12, p. 488). In December of that year the former Korean emperor was made a general of the Japanese army. The crown prince became a first lieutenant of infantry, and his dissolute elder brother, Yi Kan, and other nobles became lieutenant generals. Probably the crown prince was the only one of these officers to take his military duties seriously. For the others, the superior treatment and attendants that went with their ranks were all that mattered (p. 535).

23. *Meiji tennō ki*, 12, pp. 452–53.

24. Ibid., 12, pp. 453–54.

25. Katano Tsugio, *Richō metsubō*, p. 293.

26. *Meiji tennō ki*, 12, p. 457.

27. Ibid., 12, p. 460.

28. Ibid., 12, pp. 464–65.

29. When Yi Wan-yong informed Sunjong in August of Japan's decision to annex Korea, he listened at first to Yi's explanation without showing any reaction. He seemed incapable of judging the situation correctly, but when Yi had finished, Sunjong opened his toothless mouth and gave a look of disgust, his mute reaction (Katano, *Richō metsubō*, p. 289).

30. *Meiji tennō ki*, 12, pp. 467–68.

31. Ibid., 12, pp. 469–70.

32. Kinebuchi, *Nikkan*, p. 289. Enma was the king of hell. "Don Saigō" was an imitation of the usage in Kagoshima, with *don* both a shortened form of *dono* and an equivalent of the Spanish *don*.

33. *Meiji tennō ki*, 12, p. 503. Ch'angdok was the name of the palace in Seoul where the former emperor Sunjong was living.

34. *Meiji tennō ki*, 12, p. 500.

35. Katano, *Richō*, p. 294.

Chapter 60

1. The first was on evidence in classical texts of ancestor worship in Greece and Rome; the second, on a passage in the *I Ching*; and the third, on the *kunibiki* episode in the *Izumo fudoki*.

2. *Meiji tennō ki*, 12, p. 544.

3. Ibid., 12, pp. 545–46.

4. Hinonishi Sukehiro, who served the emperor as a chamberlain from 1886 to 1912, stated that "seven or eight years" after 1895 "he stopped reading the newspapers altogether" (*Meiji tennō no go-nichijō*, p. 53).

5. Alexander was killed on March 13, 1881; Umberto, on July 29, 1900; and Carlos, on February 1, 1908. Although the assassins in each case said they were anarchists, they were killers hired by political enemies of the kings (*Meiji tennō ki*, 12, p. 15).

6. A bomb was thrown at Alfonso XIII on the way from the church where he had just been married, on May 30, 1906. He was unhurt (*Meiji tennō ki*, 11, p. 565).

   There were at least seven attempts on the life of Queen Victoria. The first was on June 10, 1840, when she and her consort, Prince Albert, were out on a drive in an open carriage: "Suddenly she heard an explosion and at the same time felt Albert's arms flung round her. . . . She smiled at his excitement but next moment saw 'a little man on the footpath with his arms folded over his breast, a pistol in each hand. . . .' As he aimed at her and fired again she ducked" (Elizabeth Longford, *Queen Victoria*, p. 151). The would-be assassin was tried for high treason, a crime punishable by death, but he was eventually sent to an asylum. On July 27, 1850, Queen Victoria was struck violently on the head by a retired lieutenant and knocked unconscious. The assailant was sent abroad as a convict for seven years. The sixth attempt, on February 28, 1872, had the most modern overtones: the assassin intended not to kill the queen but to frighten her into signing a document ordering the release of certain political prisoners (pp. 390–91). The last attempt on the queen's life was on March 2, 1882. The would-be assassin, who aimed a fully loaded revolver, was sent to a lunatic asylum (p. 446). The motives of all the would-be assassins were vague and confused, which was the reason that they were sent to asylums.

7. His major translation was of *La Conquête du pain* by Prince Peter Kropotkin, completed not long before he was executed. The Japanese translation was made from an English translation.

8. Nishio Yōtarō, *Kōtoku Shūsui*, p. 9. Kōtoku's original text is reproduced photographically in the front matter. If this was really his composition and calligraphy at the age of seven, he was unusually precocious. Kōtoku wrote *kanshi* (poems in Chinese) to the end of his life. For an account in English of Kōtoku's early life, see F. G. Notehelfer, *Kōtoku Shūsui*, pp. 8–20.

9. Sakamoto Taketo, *Kōtoku Shūsui*, p. 78. See also Nishio, *Kōtoku Shūsui*, p. 8.

10. Nishio, *Kōtoku Shūsui*, p. 20.

11. The decree was particularly severe on men from Tosa (Kōchi) because they led the opposition to the Satsuma–Chōshū government.

12. Sakamoto, *Kōtoku Shūsui*, pp. 50–51; Nishio, *Kōtoku Shūsui*, pp. 27–28.

13. Nishio, *Kōtoku Shūsui*, p. 28.

14. Sakamoto, *Kōtoku Shūsui*, p. 55. After graduation, Kōtoku left employment with Nakae, who gave Kōtoku the *gagō* of Shūsui, a name with poetic rather than political overtones.

15. Sakamoto, *Kōtoku Shūsui*, p. 60. See also Nishio, *Kōtoku Shūsui*, p. 46. By this time, Kōtoku had left the *Jiyū shimbun* because of discontent over working for a

mouthpiece of the government and was at the *Chūō shimbun*, where he worked chiefly as a translator.

16. Sakamoto, *Kōtoku Shūsui*, pp. 102–4. On p. 102, he gives a list of all the lectures delivered to the society.

17. Ibid., p. 99.

18. This is the opinion of Sakamoto, but Nishio believed that Kōtoku made his start as a socialist in 1897 (*Kōtoku Shūsui*, p. 48).

19. Ōhara Satoshi, *Katayama Sen no shisō to taigyaku jiken*, p. 15.

20. He attended Hopkins Academy in Oakland, Maryville College, Grinnell College, Andover Theological Seminary, and Yale Divinity School.

21. Ōhara, *Katayama sen*, p. 16. For works such as R. Ely's *Social Aspects of Christianity* that strongly influenced Katayama, see pp. 18–19.

22. Sakamoto pointed out that Kōtoku's book was published a year before John Hobson's study of imperialism and fifteen years before Lenin's (*Kōtoku Shūsui*, p. 125).

23. Sakamoto, *Kōtoku Shūsui*, p. 127. See also Notehelfer, *Kōtoku Shūsui*, pp. 85–87.

24. Nishio, *Kōtoku Shūsui*, p. 69. Yamakawa's articles brought him a sentence of four years in prison for lèse-majesté.

25. For the twenty-eight demands framed by Abe Isoo, see Sakamoto, *Kōtoku Shūsui*, pp. 74–75.

26. Suematsu had studied in England, where he published a partial translation of *Genji monogatari*.

27. Sakamoto, *Kōtoku Shūsui*, pp. 134, 135.

28. Ibid. The first poem, *Inishie no / fumi miru tabi ni / omou kana / ono ga osamuru / kuni wa ika ni to* (*Shinshū Meiji tennō gyoshū*, 1, p. 50), was composed before 1878. The second poem, *Aya nishiki / torikasanete mo / omou kana / samusa ōwan / sode mo naki mi wo*, does not appear in this collection.

29. Sakamoto, *Kōtoku Shūsui*, p. 140; Nishio, *Kōtoku Shūsui*, p. 82.

30. For a summary of the contents of the book, see Nishio, *Kōtoku Shūsui*, p. 86.

31. Sakamoto, *Kōtoku Shūsui*, pp. 152–53. Until this time, three gifted writers had regularly published antiwar editorials—Kōtoku, Uchimura Kanzō, and Sakai Toshihiko. Other newspapers had for some time been prowar, but the *Yorozu chōhō* held out until it became clear that Russia would not fulfill its promise of withdrawing troops from Manchuria. The founder and editor of the *Yorozu chōhō*, Kuroiwa Ruikō, decided that in the interests of national unity, he would support the government's prowar policy. This decision prompted Kōtoku, Sakai, and Uchimura to resign from the newspaper.

32. All together, sixty-four issues were published, the last on January 29, 1905. The first issue sold 8,000 copies, but the average sale of later issues was about 4,000 copies (Nishio, *Kōtoku Shūsui*, pp. 96–97).

33. Sakamoto, *Kōtoku Shūsui*, p. 160.

34. Ibid., p. 163.

35. Ibid., p. 164.

36. Nishio, *Kōtoku Shūsui*, p. 135.

37. Sakamoto, *Kōtoku Shūsui*, pp. 168–69.

38. Nishio, *Kōtoku Shūsui*, p. 136.

39. For details, see Sakamoto, *Kōtoku Shūsui*, pp. 170, 171.

40. Her name was Mrs. Fritz. For the little that is known about her, see Notehelfer, *Kōtoku Shūsui*, pp. 124–27.
41. Sakamoto, *Kōtoku Shūsui*, p. 173.
42. Nishio, *Kōtoku Shūsui*, p. 153.
43. Donald Keene, *Modern Japanese Diaries*, p. 444. The source is Shioda Shōhei, *Kōtoku Shūsui no nikki to shokan*, p. 235.
44. Nishio, *Kōtoku Shūsui*, p. 177.
45. Ibid., pp. 189–94, 202–3, 204.
46. For a vivid account of the Red Flag incident, see Sakamoto, *Kōtoku Shūsui*, pp. 202–6.
47. Nishio, *Kōtoku Shūsui*, p. 220.
48. Sakamoto, *Kōtoku Shūsui*, p. 215.
49. Miyashita chose this day, the emperor's birthday, to try out his homemade bomb, hoping that the sound of the explosion would not be noticed amid the fireworks set off in celebration (Nishio, *Kōtoku Shūsui*, p. 245).
50. There were rumors to the effect that Miyashita had been betrayed to the police by the disgruntled husband of a woman with whom he had had relations or by a police spy in the movement.
51. For the charges against Kōtoku, see Nishio, *Kōtoku Shūsui*, pp. 276–77.
52. The prison authorities, with a curious show of delicacy, executed Kanno Suga, the one woman involved, on January 25, a day after the men.
53. Yoshida Seiichi quotes Masamune Hakuchō: "If someone should ask me whether, in view of the gravity of the incident, I personally did not feel secret indignation deep down in my heart, feel loathing for the government and the judges, curse life itself, lose all interest in food and all capacity to sleep soundly at night, I would have to reply that I experienced nothing even remotely resembling such emotions" (*Kindai bungei hyōron shi: Taishō hen*, pp. 48–49).

Nagai Kafū, though, wrote some years later, "Of all the worldly incidents I have ever seen or heard about, none has ever inspired such unspeakable disgust as this one. As a writer, I should not have kept silent about this question of ideology . . . . But I, like the other writers of the day, did not say one word. I felt extremely ashamed to be a writer. I was assailed by unbearable pangs of conscience" (*Nagai Kafū shū*, 1, p. 319).

Katayama Sen declared that "the decision passed on Kōtoku and the others was fair, and there are no points to criticize. It is unfortunate, however, that the trial was not open to the public. Socialist party members in various countries have criticized the case in their party organs, and in extreme instances they have even argued that the Japanese government's refusal to open the trial shows that contrary to tendencies elsewhere in the world, it intends to eradicate the Socialist Party. This shows their complete ignorance of our country's laws and the true facts of the case" (quoted in Ōhara, *Katayama Sen*, p. 68). Also, "The Japanese government is definitely not persecuting socialism; the persons who died on the gallows were all active anarchists" (p. 69).

Chapter 61

1. Ian H. Nish, *The Anglo-Japanese Alliance*, p. 377.
2. Kurobane Shigeru, *Nichiei dōmei no kiseki*, 1, p. 207.

3. For the terms of the treaty, see *Meiji tennō ki*, 12, pp. 628–30. The concession made by the Japanese is in article 4.

4. *Meiji tennō ki*, 12, p. 584.

5. Ibid., 12, pp. 637–38.

6. Ibid., 12, p. 555. Prime Minister Katsura on May 30 announced the establishment of a foundation to be called the Onshi zaidan saseikai. In addition to the money given by the emperor, funds had been obtained from volunteers throughout the country. When the emperor was informed of the name of the organization, he objected that funds had come not only from himself but from many other people. At his suggestion, the first four characters of the name (Imperial Gift Foundation) were always to be given in small print (p. 612).

7. See chapter 30.

8. *Meiji tennō ki*, 12, p. 593.

9. Ibid., 12, p. 689.

10. The photograph taken at this time, and three similar photographs taken at maneuvers in Nara, Tochigi, and Okayama Prefectures, are reproduced in *Meiji tennō no go-shōzō*, pp. 20–21.

11. Two or three other snapshots of the emperor are preserved from this period, but they were taken at so great a distance that they do not clearly show his features.

12. *Meiji tennō ki*, 12, pp. 702–3.

13. Ibid., 12, pp. 744–45.

14. Ibid., 12, pp. 705–6.

15. Ibid., 12, pp. 718, 719.

16. Ibid., 12, p. 730.

17. Ibid., 12, p. 731.

18. Minamoto Ryōen, "Nogi taishō no jisatsu to sono seishinshiteki haikei," p. 17. The three grandsons were the future Emperor Shōwa and Princes Chichibu and Takamatsu.

19. Early biographers of Nogi lavished praise on his work at the Gakushū-in, calling him "Pestalozzi with a sword" (quoted in Minamoto, "Nogi," p. 17). But see the different opinion of a more recent biographer, Matsushita Yoshio, *Nogi Maresuke*, pp. 193, 197. Matsushita also called attention to an incident that occurred during the Grand Maneuvers of 1908 (p. 195). On the final day, Nogi was suddenly replaced by another general as commander of the "Southern Army." He had ignored an order from the supervisor of the maneuvers (General Oku) to withdraw, saying that the Southern Army was not losing and there was no reason to withdraw. This independence of spirit was not prized.

20. *Meiji tennō ki*, 12, p. 673. Nogi was subsequently given a lesser post as supervisor of maneuvers carried out between the Fourth and Sixteenth Divisions (p. 683).

21. Sixty by Japanese count; fifty-nine by Western count. In Japan and China the completion of sixty years was considered very important because it meant that the person had lived through one whole cycle.

22. *Meiji tennō ki*, 12, p. 733. Takasaki Masakaze died not long afterward, on February 28, 1912.

23. *Meiji tennō ki*, 12, pp. 734–35.

24. Bōjō Toshinaga, *Kyūchū gojūnen*, p. 23.

25. *Meiji tennō ki*, 12, pp. 803–4.

26. Ibid., 12, p. 805.
27. Ibid., 12, p. 813. See also Bōjō, *Kyūchū*, p. 23.
28. Hinonishi Sukehiro, *Meiji tennō no go-nichijō*, pp. 71–72.
29. Ibid., p. 160.
30. Quoted in Suematsu Kenchō, "Go-jiseiryoku no o-tsuyokarishi sentei heika," p. 325.
31. Quoted in Hinonishi, *Meiji tennō*, p. 75.
32. *Meiji tennō ki*, 12, p. 819. Both the accession of the new emperor and the announcement of the new reign-name (*gengō*) were unprecedentedly prompt. Meiji waited for more than a year and a half before changing the reign-name Keiō to Meiji. Kume Kunitake (among others) criticized the unseemly haste with which the *nengō* was changed ("Sentei hōgyo ni saishite yo no kansō," p. 317).
33. Bōjō, *Kyūchū*, pp. 49–50.
34. A special issue of the magazine *Taiyō*, published in September 1912, was devoted entirely to reminiscences of the late emperor.
35. Makino Nobuaki, "Go-Shinsei shoki no tsuioku," p. 48.

Chapter 62

1. Hinonishi Sukehiro wrote that although the emperor's clothes never fitted him, this never bothered him (*Meiji tennō no go-nichijō*, p. 89). This statement was questioned by the compilers of *Meiji tennō ki*, who recorded that a European tailor came from Yokohama to take the emperor's measurements in the spring of 1872 (2, p. 666). The measurements taken at this time, even if accurate, would not have been of much use after the emperor grew stouter, and the tailors probably had to guess what changes had occurred.
2. *Meiji tennō ki*, 12, p. 828.
3. Asukai Masamichi, *Meiji taitei*, p. 29. Fujinami does not figure prominently in *Meiji tennō ki* or other accounts of Meiji's life, perhaps because his relations with the emperor were informal and private.
4. Erwin Baelz wrote that "in aspect Emperor Mutsuhito was, for a Japanese, tall and stately" (*Awakening Japan*, trans. Eden Paul and Cedar Paul, p. 395).
5. Asukai, *Meiji taitei*, p. 33.
6. *Meiji tennō ki*, 12, pp. 830–31. See also Asukai, *Meiji taitei*, pp. 48–49; he noted that Chigusa Kotoko seems not to have left a diary, and it was therefore uncertain whether or not this was actually the emperor's wish.
7. Asukai pointed out that although the capital of Japan had never officially been moved from Kyōto to Tōkyō, when the emperor traveled to Kyōto, it was stated that he had "gone" there, not that he had "returned" (*Meiji taitei*, pp. 46–47). According to the Kōshitsu tempan, promulgated in 1889 at the same time as the constitution, coronation ceremonies and the *daijōsai* were to be carried out in Kyōto. In fact, however, the *daijōsai*, a ceremony the emperor performed only once in his lifetime, took place in 1871 in Tōkyō. The emperor, although fond of Kyōto, accepted the reality of Tōkyō as the capital; but he may have felt that when his worldly duties had come to an end, he was entitled to be buried in the place he chose.
8. *Meiji tennō ki*, 12, p. 831.
9. Ibid., 12, p. 833.

10. Mochizuki Kotarō, ed., *Sekai ni okeru Meiji tennō*, 2, p. 11; *Times* (London), July 30, 1912.

11. Mochizuki, ed., *Sekai ni okeru Meiji tennō*, 2, p. 37.

12. Ibid., 2, pp. 118–19; original Japanese text, in ibid., 1, pp. 228–89. It is not clear when Itō made this statement.

13. Mochizuki, ed., *Sekai ni okeru Meiji tennō*, 2, p. 119; original Japanese text, in ibid., 1, p. 229.

14. Ibid., 2, p. 119.

15. Ibid., 1, p. 687.

16. Ibid., 1, pp. 599–600.

17. Ibid., 2, p. 1205; *Kuo Kuang Hsin-wen* (Peking), August 2, 1912.

18. Mochizuki, ed., *Sekai ni okeru Meiji tennō*, 2, p. 1206.

19. Ibid., 2, p. 1233. The translator (from Chinese into Japanese) added a note to the effect that the reporter was still imbued with the superiority complex of the Chinese.

20. Mochizuki, ed., *Sekai ni okeru Meiji tennō*, 2, p. 1211.

21. Ibid., 2, p. 175.

22. Quoted in Asukai, *Meiji taitei*, pp. 31–32. See also Carol Gluck, *Japan's Modern Myths*, p. 220. The Japanese text is in Tokutomi Roka, "Meiji tennō no hōgyo no zengo," in *Mimizu no tawagoto*, in *Meiji bungaku zenshū*, 42, p. 338. Gluck gives an excellent account of the atmosphere surrounding the emperor's funeral. See also the description by Ubukata Toshirō, a newspaper reporter who covered the events of the funeral, in his *Meiji taishō kenbun shi*, pp. 189–211.

23. *Sōseki zenshū*, 20, p. 398. Natsume Sōseki's diary entry was inspired by a newspaper extra that for the first time revealed the seriousness of the emperor's illness.

24. "Meiji tennō hōtō no ji," in *Sōseki zenshū*, 26, p. 312. Sōseki praised especially the emperor's devotion to education. The emperor's death and Nogi's *junshi* figure importantly in Sōseki's novel *Kokoro*.

25. An emergency session of the Diet appropriated 1,545,389 yen for funeral expenses (*Meiji tennō ki*, 12, p. 832). A detailed account of the funeral is found on pp. 838–43.

26. Ubukata, *Meiji Taishō kenbun shi*, p. 207.

27. Men from Yase, a section of Kyōto near Mount Hiei, were called from ancient times *Yase no dōji*. They were known as *dōji*, or "boys," because they did not shave their front locks. They traditionally served as palanquin bearers for the chief abbot of the Enryaku-ji, the Tendai monastery on Mount Hiei, and for the imperial family.

28. This description summarizes the account of the funeral in *Meiji tennō ki*, 12, pp. 838–43. Sōseki composed a haiku on the funeral procession: *ogosoka ni / taimatsu furiyuku ya / hoshizukiyo* (*Sōseki zenshū*, 24, p. 84).

29. *Meiji tennō ki*, 12, p. 844.

30. In the diary he kept during the Satsuma Rebellion, Nogi made no mention of having lost the regimental flag. Perhaps at the time it did not seem so important to him (Asukai, *Meiji taitei*, pp. 254). For the text of a part of Nogi's farewell note, see p. 248.

31. Yamaji Aizan, *Nogi taishō*, pp. 305–6, quoted in Minamoto Ryōen, "Nogi taishō no jisatsu to sono seishinshiteki haikei," p. 15. This moment was witnessed by only

a few people, including Chief Chamberlain Tokudaiji and the *jijū bukan*, General Okami. They kept it secret, but after Nogi's death, Okami revealed what the emperor had said. Minamoto's article is an excellent study of the background of Nogi's suicide (*Kokoro*, December 1963).

32. *Meiji tennō ki*, 12, p. 845. However, some who heard the first report of Nogi's suicide did not believe it. Ubukata at first supposed that the report was nothing more than a bad joke (*Meiji Taishō kenbun shi*, pp. 214–15). Mori Ōgai "half believed" the news (Asukai, *Meiji taitei*, p. 247).

33. Matsushita Yoshio, *Nogi Maresuke*, p. 213.

34. Quoted in Minamoto, "Nogi Taishō," pp. 16, 17.

35. *Mushakōji Saneatsu zenshū*, 1, p. 495. In his miscellaneous writings of the period, Mushakōji returned again and again to the subject of Nogi's suicide, always viewing it unfavorably.

36. *Shiga Naoya zenshū*, 10, p. 636. See also Asukai, *Meiji taitei*, p. 277. Shiga noted three days later in his diary that the poet Yoshii Isamu had called Nogi's suicide "one of the most disagreeable events of recent days."

37. Harada Norio, *Nihon kanshi sen*, pp. 246–47. After studying *kanshi* with Soejima Taneomi, Nagai Ussai had lived for a long time in China, where he was better known than in Japan.

38. Quoted in Asukai, *Meiji taitei*, p. 279.

39. *Meiji tennō ki*, 12, pp. 846–47.

Chapter 63

1. His birthday was officially proclaimed as a national holiday in 1927, but in 1948 (during the American Occupation) the holiday was renamed Culture Day.

2. Hinonishi Sukehiro, *Meiji tennō no go-nichijō*, p. 109.

3. Ibid., pp. 125, 151.

4. For his ancestor worship, see, for example, Bōjō Toshinaga, *Kyūchū gojūnen*, pp. 34–35.

5. Chamberlain Hinonishi recorded that during the Russo-Japanese War, the emperor had lost all interest in amusements and devoted himself entirely to state business. His only recreation was listening to the phonograph (Hinonishi, *Meiji tennō*, p. 124). According to Chamberlain Bōjō, the emperor's phonograph was a very old-fashioned model with a horn that played wax cylinders (*Kyūchū gojūnen*, p. 40). The recordings were "healthy pieces," presumably meaning that they were not popular songs but stirring ballads.

6. Erwin Baelz, *Awakening Japan*, trans. Eden Paul and Cedar Paul, p. 97. The "Inouye" mentioned was Inoue Kaoru, an advocate of modern ways.

7. Hinonishi, *Meiji tennō*, p. 46.

8. Ibid., p. 52. The *medaka* is a killifish.

9. Hinonishi, *Meiji tennō*, p. 53.

10. After the death of her beloved consort, Prince Albert, Queen Victoria so gave herself to grief that for five years she refused to open Parliament. The *Times* published an editorial urging her "to think of her subjects' claims and the duties of her high station, and not to postpone them longer to the indulgence of an unavailing grief" (quoted in Giles St. Aubin, *Queen Victoria*, p. 344).

11. Asukai Masamichi, *Meiji taitei*, p. 2.

GLOSSARY

bakufu	Shogunate, the government headed by the shogun in Edo
biwa	Musical instrument resembling a mandolin
bugaku	Dances of continental origin performed mainly at shrines and at the court
buke densō	Liaison officers of the court who transmitted orders from the bakufu
chō	Distance of about 100 yards
chokushi	Envoy of the emperor
chōteki	Enemy of the court
daijin	Government minister
daijō-e	Highly important ritual, usually performed by the emperor in the winter following his coronation
daimyo	Landholding military lord
dajō daijin	Prime minister of state, the highest-ranking official in the government
dajōkan	Great Council of State, the supreme organ of government responsible to the emperor but abolished during the Meiji era
fukasogi	Ceremony for both boys and girls, performed when they were between the ages of three and five, during which their hair was trimmed

gagaku — Oldest surviving court music, orchestral and often performed with bugaku

gembuku — Coming-of-age ceremony for boys, performed when they were between the ages of twelve and fifteen

genrō — Elder statesman, usually someone who had served with distinction in the Restoration

gijō — Administrative office, filled by daimyos

gisō — Court spokesmen, usually three or four, who conveyed the commands of the emperor

gon no tenji — Concubine of the emperor

Gosho — Imperial palace in Kyoto, usually including the extensive area around the palace proper; used also for other palaces, such as the Aoyama Gosho

gyokuza — Emperor's seat, usually higher by one tatami than the tatami-covered floor

haihan chiken — Abolition of the domains and establishment of the prefectures

hōkoku — "Repayment" due to one's country as a loyal citizen

hoshō — Men in the highest posts of the bureaucracy

jiho — Officers appointed by the emperor to advise him and supplement his decisions, a position established in 1877 and abolished in 1879

jijū — Chamberlain

jitsugaku — "Practical learning" that can be applied to government service, as opposed to purely philosophical learning

jōi — Expulsion of foreigners, advocated by those who opposed opening the country

junkō — "Progresses" made by the emperor to different regions of the country

kampaku — Chancellor, the highest-ranking official in the government under the old system

karō — Senior retainer of a daimyo

kemari — "Kickball," an elegant sport popular particularly with the nobility

kinjū — Personal attendant of the emperor

kōbu gattai — Union of the aristocracy and the military, the political creed of Emperor Kōmei

koku — Measure of rice, about five bushels; also used to calculate a samurai's income

kokutai — National polity, often used to refer to the "emperor system"

nengō — Era name, which always changed twice at fixed times in the cycle of sixty years but could be changed at any time in response to momentous events

nishikie	Woodblock prints, especially those of the nineteenth century depicting contemporary scenes, known as "brocade pictures" because of their many colors
nusa	Flapper waved by Shinto priests to drive away evil influences
nyōgo	Court lady who ranked immediately below the empress
onyōji	Yin-yang diviners
ōoku	Private areas of the palace to which the emperor retired each day after completing his duties, as opposed to public areas, where he met people and studied documents
ōsei fukkō	Restoration of royal rule
rōnin	Masterless samurai, who no longer served a daimyo or another high-ranking person
ryō	Unit of weight, used in the past for gold and silver currency
sa'in	Legislative branch of the government, established in 1871
sakoku	Closure of the country, the system that prevailed from the early seventeenth century to the end of the Tokugawa period
sangi	Councillor, a position in the early Meiji government
san'yo	Counselor, an office established and abolished in 1869
sei'in (shōin)	Highest political organ, established in 1871 and abolished in 1877
seii taishōgun	"Great general and subduer of barbarians," a title bestowed on the shogun by the emperor
sensei	Teacher, a title of respect used even of people who are not teachers
settō	Sword bestowed by the emperor on a commander when he set out to do battle
shinnō	Prince of the blood
shizoku	Samurai class
shō	Traditional musical instrument resembling a panpipe
shōin	Executive branch of the government, established in 1871 and headed by the emperor
shoshidai	Representative of the bakufu in Kyōto who oversaw all the activities in the palace, the city, and the surrounding area, a position established in 1600 and abolished in 1867
shugo	Constable, a high-ranking position, especially during the Muromachi period
songō	Honorific title, usually *dajō tennō*, given to the father of an emperor who had not reigned as emperor
sonjō	Shortened form of the compound term *sonnō jōi*
sonnō	Respect for the emperor, a loyalist slogan
sōsai	High-ranking supervisory post filled only by a member of the imperial family, a position established in January 1869 and abolished in May 1869

sōshi	Nationalist ruffian
taewon'gun	In Korea, the father of an emperor who had not reigned as emperor
tairō	Senior statesman who assisted the shogun
taisei hōkan	Return of political power by the shogun to the emperor
tanka	Classical verse form in thirty-one syllables
tenchū	Punishment of heaven, the word used to justify the assassination of men suspected of disloyalty
tenji	Court lady of relatively high rank, often promoted from *gon no tenji*
Tenshi-sama	Old-fashioned appellation for the emperor
Tōkaidō	Highway between Kyōto and Edo
u-in	Judicial branch of the government, established in 1871
yatoi	Foreign employee of the government during the Meiji period

BIBLIOGRAPHY

Adachi Kenzō. *Adachi Kenzō jijoden*. Tōkyō: Shinchōsha, 1968.
Akashi Motojirō. *Rakka Ryūsui: Colonel Akashi's Report on His Secret Cooperation with the Russian Revolutionary Parties During the Russo-Japanese War*. Helsinki: SHS, 1988.
Allan, James. *Under the Dragon Flag*. New York: Stokes, 1898.
Andō Tamotsu. *Ōtsu jiken ni tsuite*. 2 vols. Shisō kenkyū shiryō series. Kyōto: Tōyō bunkasha, 1974.
Arai Tsutomu. *Ōtsu jiken no saikōsei*. Tōkyō: Ochanomizu shobō, 1994.
Araki Seishi. *Shinpūren jikki*. Tōkyō: Shin jimbutsu ōrai sha, 1971.
Aramata Hiroshi. *Karakaua-ō no Nippon gyōten ryokōki*. Tōkyō: Shōgakukan, 1995.
Ariizumi Sadao. *Hoshi Tōru*. Tōkyō: Asahi shimbun sha, 1983.
Ariji Shinanonojō. "Yūsō, kattatsu, saishin, kiken no wataraseraru." *Taiyō*, September 1912. [*Meiji seitenshi* special issue]
Arima Yorichika. "Kitashirakawa no miya shōgai." *Bungei shunjū bessatsu*, September 1968.
Arishima Takeo zenshū. 12 vols. Tōkyō: Chikuma shobō, 1981–82.
Armstrong, William N. *Around the World with a King*. Honolulu: Mutual, 1995.
Asahiko Shinnō keigyō roku. Uji Yamada: Kuninomiya Asahiko gojūnensai kinen kai, 1942.
Asahiko Shinnō nikki. 2 vols. Tōkyō: Tōkyō daigaku shuppankai, 1969.
Asakawa, K(an'ichi). *The Russo-Japanese Conflict*. Boston: Houghton Mifflin, 1904.
Asukai Masamichi. *Meiji taitei*. Tōkyō: Chikuma shobō, 1989.
Asukai Masamichi. "Saigō Takamori wa heiwa shugisha datta ka." In Fujiwara Akira et al., *Nihon kindaishi no kyozō to jitsuzō*. Tōkyō: Ōtsuki shoten, 1990.

Baelz, Erwin. *Awakening Japan*. Trans. Eden Paul and Cedar Paul. New York: Viking Press, 1932.

Beasley, W. G., ed. and trans. *Select Documents on Japanese Foreign Policy, 1853– 1868*. Oxford: Oxford University Press, 1955.

Bird, Isabella L. *Korea and Her Neighbours*. 2 vols. Tōkyō: Tuttle, 1986.

Bird, Isabella L. *Unbeaten Tracks in Japan*. Tōkyō: Tuttle, 1973.

Black, John R. *Young Japan*. 2 vols. Yokohama: Kelly, 1880, 1881.

Bōjō Toshinaga. *Kyūchū gojūnen*. Tōkyō: Meitoku shuppansha, 1960.

Borton, Hugh. *Japan's Modern Century*. New York: Ronald Press, 1955.

Braisted, William R., trans. *Meiroku zasshi*. Cambridge, Mass.: Harvard University Press, 1976.

Breen, John. "The Imperial Oath of April 1868: Ritual, Politics, and Power in the Restoration." *Monumenta Nipponica* 51, no. 4 (1996).

Brinkley, Francis. "Sentei heika." *Kanri kōri* 5, September 1912.

Brown, Sidney DeVere, and Akiko Hirota, trans. *The Diary of Kido Takayoshi*. 3 vols. Tōkyō: Tōkyō University Press, 1983–86.

Burke, Peter. *The Fabrication of Louis XIV*. New Haven, Conn.: Yale University Press, 1992.

Busch, Noel F. *The Emperor's Sword*. New York: Funk & Wagnalls, 1969.

The Cambridge History of Japan. Vol. 5, ed. Kozo Yamamura. Cambridge: Cambridge University Press, 1989.

Che Sok-wan. *Nisshin sensō e no dōtei*. Tōkyō: Yoshikawa kōbunkan, 1997.

Chiba Taneaki. *Meiji tennō gyosei kinwa*. Tōkyō: Dainippon yūbenkai kōdansha, 1938.

Choi, Woonsang. *The Fall of the Hermit Kingdom*. Dobbs Ferry, N.Y.: Oceana, 1967.

Cohen, Paul A. *History in Three Keys*. New York: Columbia University Press, 1997.

Conroy, Hilary. *The Japanese Seizure of Korea, 1868–1910*. Philadelphia: University of Pennsylvania Press, 1960.

Cortazzi, Hugh. *Mitford's Japan*. London: Athlone Press, 1985.

Cortazzi, Hugh. "Royal Visits to Japan in the Meiji Period." In Ian H. Nish, ed., *Britain & Japan: Biographical Portraits*. Vol. 2. Folkestone: Japan Library, 1997.

Cortazzi, Hugh. "Sir Harry Parkes, 1828–1885." In Ian H. Nish, ed., *Britain & Japan: Biographical Portraits*. Vol. 2. Folkestone: Japan Library, 1997.

Cortazzi, Hugh. *Victorians in Japan*. London: Athlone Press, 1987.

Cosenza, Mario Emilio, ed. *The Complete Journals of Townsend Harris*. Rutland, Vt.: Tuttle, 1959.

d'Anethan, Baroness Albert. *Fourteen Years of Diplomatic Life in Japan*. London: Stanley Paul, 1912.

de Bary, Wm. Theodore, and Irene Bloom. *Principle and Practicality*. New York: Columbia University Press, 1979.

Dennett, Tyler. *Roosevelt and the Russo-Japanese War*. New York: Doubleday, 1925.

Dickins, F. V., and S. Lane-Poole. *The Life of Sir Harry Parkes*. 2 vols. 1894. Reprint. Wilmington, Del.: Scholarly Resources, 1973.

Dillon, E. J. *The Eclipse of Russia*. New York: Doran, 1918.

Dōmon Fuyuji. *Meiji tennō no shōgai*. Tōkyō: Mikasa shobō, 1991.

Duus, Peter. *The Abacus and the Sword*. Berkeley and Los Angeles: University of California Press, 1998.

Ei shinnō rigin den. Tōkyō: Kyōen shobō, 1978.

Elias, Norbert. *The Court Society*. New York: Pantheon, 1983.

Esthus, Raymond H. *Double Eagle and Rising Sun*. Durham, N.C.: Duke University Press, 1988.

Ezaki Masanori. "Ōmura Masajirō." In Tōyama Shigeki, ed., *Ishin no gunzō*. Jimbutsu Nihon no rekishi series, no. 20. Tōkyō: Yomiuri shimbun sha, 1973.

Falt, Olavi K. "Collaboration Between Japanese Intelligence and the Finnish Underground During the Russo-Japanese War." *Asian Profile* 4, no. 6 (June 1976).

Finn, Dallas. *Meiji Revisited*. New York: Weatherhill, 1995.

Fraser, Andrew, R. H. P. Mason, and Philip Mitchell. *Japan's Early Parliaments, 1890–1925*. London: Routledge, 1995.

Fraser, Mary Crawford. *A Diplomat's Wife in Japan*. Ed. Hugh Cortazzi. New York: Weatherhill, 1982.

Fujimura Michio. *Nisshin sensō*. Iwanami shinsho series. Tōkyō: Iwanami shoten, 1973.

Fujita Satoru. *Bakumatsu no tennō*. Kōdansha sensho mechie series. Tōkyō: Kōdansha, 1994.

Fujitani, T. *Splendid Monarchy*. Berkeley and Los Angeles: University of California Press, 1996.

Fujiwara Akira, Imai Seiichi, Uno Shun'ichi, and Awaya Kentarō, eds. *Nihon kindai shi no kyozō to jitsuzō*. Tōkyō: Ōtsuki shoten, 1990.

Fukuchi Ōchi shū. Meiji bungaku zenshū series. Tōkyō: Chikuma shobō, 1966.

Fukuchi Shigetaka. *Kōmei tennō*. Tōkyō: Akita shoten, 1974.

Fukuda Tōsaku. *Kankoku heigō kinen shi*. Tōkyō: Dai Nippon jitsugyō kai, 1911.

Fukuzawa Yukichi zenshū. 19 vols. Tōkyō: Iwanami shoten, 1964.

Gaimushō, ed. *Dai Nihon gaikō monjo*. 45 vols. Tōkyō: Nihon kokusai rengō kyōkai, 1947–63.

Gluck, Carol. *Japan's Modern Myths*. Princeton, N.J.: Princeton University Press, 1985.

Gotō Yasushi. *Jiyū minken*. Tōkyō: Chūō kōron sha, 1972.

Griffis, William Elliot. *The Mikado: Institution and Person*. Princeton, N.J.: Princeton University Press, 1915.

Griffis, William Elliot. *The Mikado's Empire*. New York: Harper, 1906.

A Guide to the Works of Art and Science Collected by Captain His Royal Highness the Duke of Edinburgh, K.F., during his Five-Years' Cruise Round the World in H.M.S. 'Galatea,' 1867–1871 and lent for Exhibition in the South Kensington Museum February, 1872. London: Strangeways, 1872.

Gulick, Sidney Lewis. *The White Peril in the Far East*. New York: Revell, 1905.

Guranto shōgun to no go-taiwa hikki. Kokumin seishin bunka bunken series, no. 14. Tōkyō: Kokumin seishin bunka kenkyūjo, 1937.

Hackett, Roger F. *Yamagata Aritomo in the Rise of Modern Japan*. Cambridge, Mass.: Harvard University Press, 1971.

Haga Tōru. *Taikun no shisetsu*. Tōkyō: Chūō kōron sha, 1968.

Hagihara Nobutoshi. *Baba Tatsui*. Tōkyō: Chūō kōron sha, 1967.

Hagihara Nobutoshi. *Mutsu Munemitsu*. Tōkyō: Asahi shimbusha, 1997.

Hanabusa Yoshimoto. "Sentei heika ni kansuru tsuioku." *Taiyō*, September 1912. [*Meiji seitenshi* special issue]

Harada Ken'yū. *Nihon kanshi sen*. Kyōto: Jimbun shoin, 1974.

Haraguchi Kiyoshi. *Boshin sensō*. Tōkyō: Hanawa shobō, 1963.

Haraguchi Kiyoshi. "Kōmei tennō no shiin ni tsuite." *Meiji ishin shigaku kaihō*, no. 15 (October 1989).

Haraguchi Kiyoshi. "Kōmei tennō to Iwakura Tomomi." *Meijō shōgaku* 39 (1990).

Haraguchi Kiyoshi. "Kōmei tennō wa dokusatsu sareta no ka." In Fujiwara Akira, Imai Seiichi, Uno Shun'ichi, and Awaya Kentarō, eds., *Nihon kindaishi no kyozō to ji-tsuzō*. Tōkyō: Ōtsuki shoten, 1990.

Hardacre, Helen. *Shintō and the State, 1868–1988*. Princeton, N.J.: Princeton University Press, 1989.

Harootunian, H. D. *Toward Restoration*. Berkeley and Los Angeles: University of California Press, 1970.

Hasegawa Takurō, ed. *Meiji taitei*. Tōkyō: Dai Nippon yūbenkai kōdansha, 1927.

Hashikawa Bunsō. *Seiji to bungaku no henkyō*. Tōkyō: Tōjusha, 1970.

Hayashi Tadasu. *Ato wa mukashi no ki*. Ed. Yui Masaomi. Tōyō bunko series. Tōkyō: Heibonsha, 1970.

Hearn, Lafcadio. *Out of the East*. Boston: Houghton, 1895.

Hesselink, Reinier. "The Assassination of Henry Heusken." *Monumenta Nipponica* 49, no. 3 (Autumn 1994).

Higashikuze Michitomi. *Ishin zengo*. Bakumatsu ishin shiryō sōsho. Tōkyō: Jimbutsu ōrai sha, 1969.

Hijikata Hisamoto. "Eimei kurabenaki daikōtei." *Taiyō*, September 1912. [*Meiji seiten-shi* special issue]

Hinonishi Sukehiro. *Meiji tennō no go-nichijō*. Tōkyō: Sokokusha, 1953.

Hirai Banson, ed. *Fūun kaiko roku*. Chūkō bunko series. Tōkyō: Chūō kōron sha, 1990.

Hoare, James E. "Extraterritoriality in Japan, 1858–1899." *Transactions of the Asiatic Society of Japan*, 3d ser., vol. 18 (July 1983).

Hoare, James E. *Japan's Treaty Ports and Foreign Settlements*. Folkestone: Curzon Press, 1994.

Hobsbawm, Eric, and Terence Ranger. *The Invention of Tradition*. Cambridge: Cambridge University Press, 1983.

Horaguchi Michihisa. *Shōken kōtaigō*. Tōkyō: Shōtokukai, 1914.

Horiguchi Kumaichi. *Gaikō to bungei*. Tōkyō: Daiichi shobō, 1934.

Horiuchi Keizō. *Ongaku gojūnen shi*. Tōkyō: Kōdansha, 1977.

Hoshi Ryōichi. *Matsudaira Katamori to sono jidai*. Tōkyō: Rekishi shunjū sha, 1984.

Hough, Richard. *The Potemkin Mutiny*. Annapolis, Md.: Naval Institute Press, 1996.

Hubner, Baron Alexander de. *Promenade autour du monde*. Paris: Hachette, 1873.

Ienaga Saburō. *Ueki Emori kenkyū*. Tōkyō: Iwanami shoten, 1960.

Iguchi Kazuki. *Nichiro sensō no jidai*. Tōkyō: Yoshikawa kōbunkan, 1998.

Iguro Yatarō. *Kuroda Kiyotaka*. Tōkyō: Yoshikawa kōbunkan, 1977.

Iizawa Tadasu. *Ishi Meiji tennō den*. Tōkyō: Shinchōsha, 1988.

Ikai Takaaki. *Saigō Takamori*. Iwanami shinsho series. Tōkyō: Iwanami shoten, 1992.

Imatani Akira. *Buke to tennō*. Tōkyō: Iwanami shoten, 1993.

Inō Tentarō. *Jōyaku kaiseiron no rekishiteki tenkai*. Tōkyō: Komine shobō, 1976.

Inoue Haruki. *Ryojun gyakusatsu jiken*. Tōkyō: Chikuma shobō, 1995.

Inoue Kiyoshi. *Jōyaku kaisei*. Iwanami shinsho series. Tōkyō: Iwanami shoten, 1955.

Inoue Kiyoshi. *Saigō Takamori*. 2 vols. Chūkō shinsho series. Tōkyō: Chūō kōron sha, 1970.

Inoue Kiyoshi, Ezaki Masanori, et al. *Shinsei no enshutsu*. Jimbutsu Nihon no rekishi series. Tōkyō: Shōgakukan, 1976.

Irokawa Daikichi. *The Culture of the Meiji Period*. Trans. Marius B. Jansen. Princeton, N.J.: Princeton University Press, 1985. [Translation of *Meiji no bunka*]

Irokawa Daikichi. *Kindai kokka no shuppatsu*. Nihon no rekishi series. Tōkyō: Chūō kōron sha, 1960.

Irokawa Daikichi. *Meiji no bunka*. Tōkyō: Iwanami shoten, 1970.

Iryusutoreshon Nihon kankei kiji shū. 3 vols. Yokohama: Yokohama kaikō shiryōkan, 1990.

Ishida Bunshirō. *Meiji daijihen kiroku shūsei*. Tōkyō: San'yō shoin, 1932.

Ishii Takashi. *Bakumatsu hiun no hitobito*. Yūrin shinsho series. Yokohama: Yūrindō, 1979.

Ishii Takashi. *Boshin sensō rōn*. Tōkyō: Yoshikawa kōbunsha, 1984.

Ishii Takashi. *Ishin no nairan*. Tōkyō: Shibundō, 1974.

Ishikawa Takuboku zenshū. Vol. 5. Tōkyō: Chikuma shobō, 1978.

Ishimaru Akiko, ed. *Arishima Takeo*. Sakka no jiden series. Tōkyō: Nihon tosho sentaa, 1998.

Isoda Kōichi. *Rokumeikan no keifu*. Tōkyō: Bungei shunjū, 1983.

Iwai Tadakuma. *Meiji tennō*. Tōkyō: Sanseidō, 1997.

Iwakura Tomomi kankei monjo. Tōkyō: Tōkyō daigaku shuppankai, 1969.

Iwata, Masakazu. *Ōkubo Toshimichi, the Bismarck of Japan*. Berkeley and Los Angeles: University of California Press, 1964.

Jansen, Marius B. *Sakamoto Ryōma and the Meiji Restoration*. Princeton, N.J.: Princeton University Press, 1961.

Jones, Adrian. "East and West Befuddled: Russian Intelligentsia Responses to the Russo-Japanese War." In David Wells and Sandra Wilson, eds., *The Russo-Japanese War in Cultural Perspective*. Basingstoke: Macmillan, 1999.

Kajima, Morinosuke. *The Diplomacy of Japan, 1894–1922*. 3 vols. Tōkyō: Kajima Institute of International Peace. 1976.

Kamei Koreaki. *Nisshin sensō jūgun shashinchō*. Tōkyō: Kashiwa shobō, 1992.

Kamigaitō Ken'ichi. *Amenomori Hōshū*. Chūkō shinsho series. Tōkyō: Chūō kōron sha, 1989.

Kan Je-on. *Chōsen no jōi to kaika*. Tōkyō: Heibonsha, 1977.

Kanagaki Robun. "Guranto's Life, Yamato Bunsho." *Century Magazine* 50, no. 28 (July 1895).

Kanai Yukiyasu. "Seijun nichijō." In Yoshino Sakuzō, ed., *Meiji bunka zenshū*. Vol. 1. Tōkyō: Nihon hyōron sha, 1928.

Kaneko Kentarō. "Meiji tennō to Rūzuveruto daitōryō." *Chūgai shinron*, May 1919.

Kaneko Kentarō. *Nichiro sen'eki hiroku*. Tōkyō: Hakubunkan, 1929.

Kang Bom-sok. *Seikanron seihen*. Tōkyō: Saimaru shuppan sha, 1990.

Kanzaki Kiyoshi. *Taigyaku jiken*. 4 vols. Tōkyō: Ayumi shuppan, 1977.

Kasahara Hidehiko. *Tennō shinsei*. Chūkō shinsho series. Tōkyō: Chūō kōron sha, 1995.

Katano Tsugio. *Richō metsubō*. Tōkyō: Shinchōsha, 1994.

Katō Hiroyuki. "Yo ga jidoku ni mesareshi koro." *Taiyō*, September 1912. [*Meiji seitenshi* special issue]

Katō Hitoshi. "Meiji tennō o-tsubone go-rakuin den." *Shinchō* 45 (September 1988).

Katsube Mitake and Shibukawa Hisako. *Dōtoku kyōiku no rekishi*. Tōkyō: Tamagawa daigaku shuppanbu, 1984.

Kawai Hikomitsu. "Norumanto gō jiken." *Nihon kosho tsūshin*, February 15, 1958.

Kawamura Hatsue. *F. V. Dickins*. Tōkyō: Shichigatsudō, 1997.

Kawamura Hatsue. "Frederick Victor Dickins to Nihon bungaku." *Ryūtsū keizai daigaku ronshū* 28, no. 2 (1993).

Keene, Donald. *Dawn to the West*. 2 vols. New York: Holt, Rinehart & Winston, 1984.

Keene, Donald. *Landscapes and Portraits*. Tōkyō: Kodansha International, 1971.

Keene, Donald. *Modern Japanese Diaries*. New York: Holt, 1995.

Keene, Donald. "The Sino-Japanese War of 1894–95 and Japanese Culture." In Keene, *Landscapes and Portraits*. Tōkyō: Kodansha International.

Keene, Donald. *Travelers of a Hundred Ages*. New York: Holt, 1989.

Keene, Donald. *Nihonjin no biishiki*. Tōkyō: Chūō kōron sha, 1990.

Keppel, Sir Henry. *A Sailor's Life Under Four Sovereigns*. London: Macmillan, 1899.

Kerr, George H. *Okinawa: The History of an Island People*. Rutland, Vt.: Tuttle, 1958.

Ketelaar, James Edward. *Of Heretics and Martyrs in Meiji Japan: Buddhism and Its Persecution*. Princeton, N.J.: Princeton University Press, 1990.

Kido Takayoshi monjo. 8 vols. Tōkyō: Tōkyō daigaku shuppankai, 1971.

Kido Takayoshi nikki. 3 vols. Tōkyō: Tōkyō daigaku shuppankai, 1967.

Kim Un-yon. *Nikkan heigō*. Tōkyō: Gōdō shuppan, 1996.

Kimura Ki. *Meiji tennō*. Tōkyō: Bungei shunjū, 1967.

Kimura Teinosuke. "Meiji tennō no go-yōji." *Taiyō*, September 1912. [*Meiji seitenshi* special issue]

Kinebuchi Nobuo. *Fukuzawa Yukichi to Chōsen*. Tōkyō: Sairyūsha, 1997.

Kinebuchi Nobuo. *Nikkan kōshō shi*. Tōkyō: Sairyūsha, 1992.

Kinoshita Hyō. *Meiji shiwa*. Tōkyō: Bunchūdō, 1943.

Kishida Ginkō. "Tōhoku go-junkō ki." In Yoshino Sakuzō, ed., *Meiji bunka zenshū*. Vol. 1. Tōkyō: Nihon hyōron sha, 1928.

Kitashirakawa Fusako. "Meiji tennō to sono kyūtei." *Readers' Digest*, October 1968.

Kiyooka Eiichi, trans. *The Autobiography of Yukichi Fukuzawa*. New York: Columbia University Press, 1966.

Kiyozawa Kiyoshi. *Gaiseika toshite no Ōkubo Toshimichi*. Chūkō bunko series. Tōkyō: Chūō kōron sha, 1993.

Kobayakawa Hideo. *Binkō ansatsu*. Tōkyō: Chikuma shobō, 1962.

Kobayakawa Hideo. *Kesshi Kumamoto keishintō*. Tōkyō: Ryūbunkan, 1910.

Kobayashi Kazumi. *Giwadan sensō to Meiji kokka*. Tōkyō: Kyūko shoin, 1986.

Koishikawa Zenji. *Ōtsu jiken to Meiji tennō*. Tōkyō: Hihyōsha, 1998.

Kojima Korekata. *Ōtsu jiken nisshi*. Tōyō bunko series. Heibonsha, 1971.

Kojima Noboru. *Nichiro sensō*. 8 vols. Bunshun bunko series. Tōkyō: Bungei shunjū sha, 1994.

Kojima Noboru. *Ōyama Iwao*. Vol. 4. Bunshun bunko series. Tōkyō: Bungei shunjū sha, 1985.

Kokuritsu kyōiku kenkyūjo, ed. *Nihon kindai kyōiku hyakunen shi*. Vol. 3. Tōkyō: Kyōiku kenkyū shinkōkai, 1974.

Kokuryūkai hombu, ed. *Seinan kiden.* 4 vols. Tōkyō: Kokuryūkai hombu, 1911.

Kōmei tennō ki. 5 vols. Tōkyō: Yoshikawa kōbunkan, 1967–69.

Komiya Toyotaka. *Japanese Music and Drama in the Meiji Era.* Trans. Donald Keene and Edward Seidensticker. Tōkyō: Ōbunsha, 1956.

Komori Michiyo. "Kinjirareta onna." *Kaizō,* October 1953.

Kondō Tomie. *Rokumeikan kifujin kō.* Tōkyō: Kōdansha, 1980.

Konishi Shirō. *Kaikoku to jōi.* Nihon no rekishi series. Tōkyō: Chūō kōron sha, 1966.

Konishi Shirō. *Nisshin sensō.* Nishiki-e bakumatsu Meiji no rekishi series. Tōkyō: Kōdansha, 1977.

Kose Susumu and Nakamura Hiroshi. *Motoda Tōya, Soejima Sōkai.* Tōkyō: Meitoku shuppan sha, 1979.

Kōshitsu no mitera: Sennyū-ji. Kyōto: Sōhonzan mitera sennyūji, 1991.

Kublin, Hyman. *Asian Revolutionary: The Life of Sen Katayama.* Princeton, N.J.: Princeton University Press, 1964.

Kume Kunitake. *Beiō kairan jikki.* 5 vols. Iwanami bunko series. Tōkyō: Iwanami shoten, 1977–82.

Kume Kunitake. "Sentei hōgyo ni saishite yo no kansō." *Taiyō,* September 1912. [*Meiji seitenshi* special issue]

Kurihara Kōta. *Ningen Meiji tennō.* Tōkyō: Surugadai shobō, 1953.

Kurihara Ryūichi. *Zankanjō.* Tōkyō: Gakugei shorin, 1975.

Kurobane Shigeru. *Nichiei dōmei no kiseki.* Vol. 1. Tōkyō: Hakubunsha, 1988.

Kurobane Shigeru. *Nichiro sensō shiron.* Tōkyō: Sugiyama shoten, 1982.

Kurobane Shigeru. *Nichiro sensō wa ika ni shite tatakawaretaka.* Tōkyō: Bunka shobō hakubunsha, 1988.

Kurushima Takehiko. *O-tsubone seikatsu.* Tōkyō: Bunrokudō shoten, 1907.

Kusunoki Seiichirō. *Kojima Korekata.* Chūkō shinsho series. Tōkyō: Chūō kōron sha, 1997.

Kuzuo Yoshihisa. *Tōa senkaku shishi kiden.* Tōkyō: Kokuryūkai shuppan, 1933.

Ladd, George Trumbull. *Rare Days in Japan.* New York: Dodd, Mead, 1910.

Lanman, Charles. *Leading Men of Japan.* Boston: Lothrop, 1883.

Lebra, Joyce C. *Ōkuma Shigenobu.* Canberra: Australian National University Press, 1973.

Lee, Ki-baik. *A New History of Korea.* Trans. Edward W. Wagner. Cambridge, Mass.: Harvard University Press, 1984.

Lensen, George Alexander. *The Russian Push Toward Japan.* Princeton, N.J.: Princeton University Press, 1959.

Levine, Isaac Don. *Letters from the Kaiser to the Czar.* New York: Stokes, 1920.

Longford, Elizabeth. *Queen Victoria.* New York: Harper & Row, 1964.

Longford, Joseph H. *The Evolution of New Japan.* New York: Putnam, 1913.

Loti, Pierre. *Japoneries d'automne.* Paris: Calmann Lévy, 1889.

Makino Nobuaki. "Go-Shinsei shoki no tsuioku." *Taiyō,* September 1912. [*Meiji seitenshi* special issue]

Malm, William. "Modern Music of Meiji Japan." In Donald H. Shively, ed., *Tradition and Modernization in Japanese Culture.* Princeton, N.J.: Princeton University Press, 1971.

Malozemoff, Andrew. *Russian Far Eastern Policy, 1881–1904.* New York: Octagon, 1977.

Makino Nobuaki. "Go-Shinsei shoki no tsuioku." *Taiyō*, September 1912. [*Meiji seitenshi* special issue]

Maruya Saiichi. *Aoi Amagasa*. Tōkyō: Bungei shunjū, 1995.

Mason, R. H. P. *Japan's First General Election, 1890*. Cambridge: Cambridge University Press, 1969.

Matsumoto Sannosuke. *Meiji seishin no kōzō*. Dōjidai raiburarii. Tōkyō: Iwanami shoten, 1993.

Matsumura Masayoshi. *Nichiro sensō to Kaneko Kentarō*. Tōkyō: Shin'yūdō, 1980.

Matsushita Yoshio. *Nogi Maresuke*. Jimbutsu sōsho series. Tōkyō: Yoshikawa kōbunkan, 1960.

McFeely, William S. *Grant: A Biography*. New York, Norton, 1982.

McWilliams, Wayne C. "'East Meets East': The Soejima Mission to China, 1873." *Monumenta Nipponica* 30, no. 3 (1975).

Meech-Pekarik, Julia. *The World of the Meiji Print*. New York: Weatherhill, 1986.

Meiji no hyōka to Meijijin no kanshoku. Tōkyō: Dōkōsha, 1967.

Meiji tennō ki. 13 vols. Tōkyō: Yoshikawa kōbunkan, 1968–75.

Meiji tennō no go-shōzō. Tōkyō: Meiji jingū, 1998.

Minamoto Ryōen. "Nogi taishō no jisatsu to sono seishinshiteki haikei." *Kokoro*, December 1963.

Mishima, Yukio. *Runaway Horses*. Trans. Michael Gallagher. New York: Knopf, 1973.

Miura Gorō. *Kanju shōgun kaiko-roku*. Chūkō bunko series. Tōkyō: Chūō kōron sha, 1988.

Miyake Setsurei. *Dōjidaishi*. 6 vols. Tōkyō: Iwanami shoten, 1950.

Mochizuki Kotarō. *Sekai ni okeru Meiji tennō*. 2 vols. Tōkyō: Hara shobō, 1973.

Mori Senzō chosakushū zokuhen. Vol. 5. Tōkyō: Chūō kōron sha, 1993.

Mori Senzō. *Meiji jimbutsu yawa*. Tōkyō: Tōkyō bijutsu, 1969.

Mōri Toshihiko. *Etō Shimpei*. Chūkō shinsho series. Tōkyō: Chūō kōron sha, 1987.

Mōri Toshihiko. *Iwakura Tomomi*. Tōkyō: PHP, 1989.

Mōri Toshihiko. *Meiji ishin no saihakken*. Tōkyō: Yoshikawa kōbunkan, 1993.

Mōri Toshihiko. *Meiji rokunen seihen*. Tōkyō: Chūō kōron sha, 1979.

Morikawa Tetsurō. *Meiji ansatsu shi*. Tōkyō: San'ichi shobō, 1969.

Morita Seigo. *Meijijin monogatari*. Iwanami shinsho series. Tōkyō: Iwanami shoten, 1998.

Moriyama Shigenori. *Nikkan heigō*. Tōkyō: Yoshikawa kōbunkan, 1992.

Motoda Takehiko and Kaigo Muneomi, eds. *Motoda Nagazane monjo*. Vol. 1. Tōkyō: Motoda monjo kenkyūkai, 1969.

Muneta Hiroshi. *Heitai hyakunen*. Tōkyō: Shin jimbutsu ōrai, 1968.

Mushakōji Saneatsu zenshū. Vol. 1. Tōkyō: Shōgakukan, 1987.

Mutsu Munemitsu. *Kenkenroku*. Trans. Gordon Mark Berger. Princeton, N.J.: Princeton University Press, 1982.

Nagai Kafū shū. Vol. 1. Gendai Nihon bungaku taikei series. Tōkyō: Chikuma shobō, 1969.

Nagao Kazuo. *Ansatsusha*. Tōkyō: Keizai ōrai sha, 1972.

Nagao Kazuo. *Tennō no gendaishi*. Tōkyō: Shin jimbutsu ōrai sha, 1974.

Nakahara Zenchū. *Ryūkyū no rekishi*. Naha: Bunkyō tosho, 1978.

Nakamura Fumio. *Taigyaku jiken to chishikijin*. Tōkyō: San'ichi shobō, 1981.

Nakamura Kikuo. *Hoshi Tōru*. Tōkyō: Yoshikawa kōbunkan, 1963.

Nakano Yasuo. *An Jūkon: Nikkan kankei no genzō*. Tōkyō: Aki shobō, 1991.

Nakano Yasuo. *An Jūkon to Itō Hirobumi*. Tōkyō: Kōbunsha, 1996.

Nakano Yoshio. "Saga no ran to Etō Shimpei." *Shinchō*, April 1965.

Nakayama Morishige. *Ryūkyū shi jiten*. Naha: Bunkyō tosho, 1969.

Nakayama Tadayasu nikki. Tōkyō: Tōkyō daigaku shuppankai, 1973.

Nakayama Yasumasa. *Meiji hennen shi*. Tōkyō: Rinsensha, 1934.

Nakayama Yasumasa. *Shimbun shūsei Meiji hennen shi*. Vol. 4. Tōkyō: Zaisei keizai gakkai, 1935.

Nezu Masashi. "Kōmei tennō wa byōshi ka dokusatsu ka." *Rekishigaku kenkyū* 173 (July 1954).

Nihon kōdōkai, ed. *Hakuō sōsho*. Tōkyō: Hakubunkan, 1909.

Ninagawa Shin. *Meiji tennō*. Kyōto: San'ichi shobō, 1956.

Nish, Ian H. *The Anglo-Japanese Alliance*. London: Athlone Press, 1966.

Nish, Ian H. *The Origins of the Russo-Japanese War*. London: Longman, 1985.

Nish, Ian H., ed. *Britain & Japan: Biographical Portraits*. 2 vols. Folkestone: Japan Library, 1994, 1997.

Nishijima Ryōsaburō. *Nakayama Tadamitsu ansatsu shimatsu*. Tōkyō: Shin jimbutsu ōrai sha, 1983.

Nishimura Shigeki. *Nihon dōtoku ron*. Iwanami bunko series. Tōkyō: Iwanami shoten, 1935.

Nishio Yōtarō. *Kōtoku Shūsui*. Tōkyō: Yoshikawa kōbunkan, 1959.

Nomura Yoshifumi. *Ōtsu jiken*. Fukuoka: Ashi shobō, 1992.

Notehelfer, F. G. *Kōtoku Shūsui: Portrait of a Japanese Radical*. Cambridge: Cambridge University Press, 1971.

Oakley, Jane H. *A Russo-Japanese War Poem*. Brighton: Standard Press, 1905.

Ōe Shinobu. *Baruchikku kantai*. Chūkō shinsho series. Tōkyō: Chūō kōron shinsha, 1999.

Ōe Shinobu. *Higashi Ajia shi toshite no Nisshin sensō*. Tōkyō: Rippū shobō, 1998.

"Official Report on Matters Connected with the Events of October 8th, 1895, and the Death of the Queen." *The Korean Repository*, vol. 3, 1896.

Ōgai zenshū. Vol. 3. Tōkyō: Iwanami shoten, 1962.

Ōhara Satoshi. *Katayama Sen no shisō to taigyaku jiken*. Tōkyō: Ronsōsha, 1995.

Ōhashi Akio. *Gotō Shōjirō to kindai Nihon*. Tōkyō: Yoshikawa kōbunkan, 1993.

Oka Yoshitake. "Generational Conflict After the Russo-Japanese War." Trans. J. Victor Koschmann. In Tetsuo Najita and J. Victor Koschmann, eds., *Conflict in Modern History*. Princeton, N.J.: Princeton University Press, 1982.

Okada Yoshirō. *Meiji kaireki*. Tōkyō: Taishūkan, 1994.

Okakura, Kakuzo. *The Book of Tea*. Tōkyō: Kodansha International, 1989.

Okamoto Ryūnosuke. *Fūun kaiko roku*. Chūkō bunko series. Tōkyō: Chūō kōron sha, 1990.

Okamoto, Shumpei. *Impressions of the Front*. Philadelphia: Philadelphia Museum of Art, 1983.

Okamoto, Shumpei. *The Japanese Oligarchy and the Russo-Japanese War*. New York: Columbia University Press, 1970.

Okazaki Hisahiko. *Komura Jutarō to sono jidai*. Tōkyō: PHP, 1998.

Ōkawa Nobuyoshi, ed. *Ōnishi Kyō zenshū*. Vol. 2. Tōkyō: Ōnishi Kyō zenshū kankōkai, 1926–27.

Ōkubo Toshiaki. *Iwakura shisetsu no kenkyū*. Tōkyō: Munetaka shobō, 1981.

Ōkubo Toshiaki. *Iwakura Tomomi*. Chūkō shinsho series. Tōkyō: Chūō kōron sha, 1990.

Ōkubo Toshiaki. *Sekimukai hikki*. Tōyō bunko series. Tōkyō: Heibonsha, 1966.

Ōkubo Toshimichi nikki. 2 vols. Tōkyō: Nihon shiseki kyōkai, 1927.

Okutani Matsuji. *Shinagawa Yajirō den*. Tōkyō: Kōyō shoten, 1940.

Ōnishi Gen'ichi. "Ishin kaiten no kōbo to Kuninomiya Asahiko shinnō." In *Asahiko Shinnō keigyō roku*. Uji Yamada: Kuninomiya Asahiko gojūnensai kinen kai, 1942.

Osaragi Jirō. *Tennō no seiki*. 17 vols. Tōkyō: Asahi shimbun sha, 1977.

Osatake Takeshi. *Ōtsu jiken*. Iwanami bunko series. Tōkyō: Iwanami shoten, 1991.

Ōta Masahide. *Kindai Okinawa no seiji kōzō*. Tōkyō: Keisō shobō, 1972.

Otabe Yūji. *Nashimoto-no-miya Itsuko no nikki*. Tōkyō: Shōgakukan, 1991.

Ōtani Tadashi and Harada Keiichi, eds. *Nisshin sensō no shakaishi*. Ōsaka: Fōramu A, 1994.

Ōya Sōichi zenshū. 24 vols. Tōkyō: Sōyōsha, 1981.

Ōyama Azusa. *Nichiro sensō no gunsei shiroku*. Tōkyō: Fuyō shobō, 1973.

Ōyama Azusa. *Yamagata Aritomo ikensho*. Tōkyō: Hara shobō, 1966.

Ōyama Azusa, ed. *Pekin rōjō, Pekin rōjō nikki*. Tōyō bunko series. Tōkyō: Heibonsha, 1965.

Pak Chong-gun. *Nisshin sensō to Chōsen*. Tōkyō: Aoki shoten, 1982.

Paléologue, Maurice. *Three Critical Years, 1904–05–06*. New York: Speller, 1957.

Passin, Herbert. *Society and Education in Japan*. New York: Teachers College, Columbia University Press, 1965.

Perez, Louis G. *Japan Comes of Age*. Cranbury, N.J.: Associated University Presses, 1999.

Pinguet, Maurice. *La Mort volontaire au Japon*. Paris: Gallimard, 1984.

Prochaska, Frank. *Royal Bounty: The Making of a Welfare Monarchy*. New Haven, Conn.: Yale University Press, 1995.

Redesdale, Lord [A. B. Mitford]. *The Garter Mission to Japan*. London: Macmillan, 1906.

Redesdale, Lord [A. B. Mitford]. *Memories*. 2 vols. London: Hutchison, 1915.

Röhl, John C. G. *The Kaiser and His Court*. Cambridge: Cambridge University Press, 1994.

Rosen, Baron Roman. *Forty Years of Diplomacy*. 2 vols. New York: Knopf, 1922.

Rowe, John Carlos. *New Essays on the Education of Henry Adams*. Cambridge: Cambridge University Press, 1996.

Rubin, Jay. *Injurious to Public Morals*. Seattle: University of Washington Press, 1984.

St. Albyn, Giles. *Queen Victoria*. New York: Atheneum, 1992.

Sagi Ryūzō. *Shihōkyō Etō Shimpei*. Tōkyō: Bungei shunjū, 1998.

Saitō Keishū. *Jokan monogatari*. Tōkyō: Nittōdō shoten, 1912.

Saitō Michinori. *Itō Hirobumi wo utta otoko*. Tōkyō: Jiji tsūshin sha, 1994.

Saitō Nobuaki. *Saigō to Meiji ishin kakumei*. Tōkyō: Sairyūsha, 1987.

Sakamoto Kazuto. *Itō Hirobumi to Meiji kokka keisei*. Tōkyō: Yoshikawa kōbunkan, 1991.

Sakamoto Moriaki. *Fukuzawa Yukichi to Ōkubo Toshimichi no tairitsu*. Tōkyō: Hyōgensha, 1971.

Sakamoto Taketo. *Kōtoku Shūsui: Meiji shakai shugi no ittōsei.* Tōkyō: Shimizu shoin, 1984.

Sakane Yoshihisa, ed. *Aoki Shūzō jiden.* Tōyō bunko series. Tōkyō: Heibonsha, 1970.

Sansom, George B. *The Western World and Japan.* London: Cresset Press, 1950.

Sasaki Nobutsuna. *Meiji tennō gyoshū kinkai.* Ōsaka: Asahi shimbun sha, 1924.

Sasaki Suguru. *Boshin sensō.* Chūko shinsho series. Tōkyō: Chūō kōron sha, 1977.

Sasaki Takayuki. *Hogo Hiroi.* 12 vols. Tōkyō: Tōkyō daigaku shuppankai, 1978–79.

Sasamori Gisuke. *Nantō taiken.* Tōyō bunko series. Tōkyō: Heibonsha, 1982–83.

Satō Shigerō. *Bakumatsu ishin no minshū sekai.* Tōkyō: Iwanami shoten, 1994.

Satomi Kishio. *Meiji tennō.* Tōkyō: Kinseisha, 1968.

Satow, Sir Ernest. *A Diplomat in Japan.* Tōkyō: Tuttle, 1983.

Scidmore, Eliza Ruhamah. *As The Hague Ordains.* New York: Holt, 1908.

Shiba Ryōtarō. *Meiji to iu kokka.* Tōkyō: Nihon hōsō kyōkai, 1997.

Shiba Ryōtarō. *Tobu ga gotoku.* Bunshun bunko series. Tōkyō: Bungei shunjū, 1980.

Shibusawa Eiichi. *Tokugawa Yoshinobukō den.* 4 vols. Tōyō bunko series. Tōkyō: Heibonsha, 1968.

Shiga Naoya zenshū. Vol. 10. Tōkyō: Iwanami shoten, 1973.

Shimba Eiji. *Inukai Taisuke.* Tōkyō: Shinchōsha, 1988.

Shimbun shūsei Meiji hennen shi. 15 vols. Tōkyō: Honpō shoseki, 1982.

Shimomura Fujio. *Kindai no sensō: Nichiro sensō.* Tōkyō: Jimbutsu ōrai sha, 1966.

Shin jimbutsu ōrai sha, ed. *Shinsengumi shiryō shū.* Shin jimbutsu ōrai sha, 1995.

Shinshū Meiji tennō gyōshū. 2 vols. Tōkyō: Meiji shoin, 1964.

Shioda Shōhei. *Kōtoku Shūsui no nikki to shokan.* Tōkyō: Miraisha, 1954.

Shirai Hisaya. *Meiji kokka to Nisshin sensō.* Tōkyō: Shakai hyōron sha, 1997.

Shively, Donald H. "The Japanization of the Middle Meiji." In Donald H. Shively, ed., *Tradition and Modernization in Japanese Culture.* Princeton, N.J.: Princeton University Press, 1971.

Shively, Donald H. "Motoda Eifu: Confucian Lecturer to the Meiji Emperor." In David S. Nivison and Arthur F. Wright, eds., *Confucianism in Action.* Stanford, Calif.: Stanford University Press, 1959.

Shively, Donald H. "Nishimura Shigeki: A Confucian View of Modernization." In Marius B. Jansen, ed., *Changing Japanese Attitudes Toward Modernization.* Princeton, N.J.: Princeton University Press, 1965.

Smith, Henry D. *Kiyochika: Artist of Meiji Japan.* Santa Barbara, Calif.: Santa Barbara Museum of Art, 1988.

"Soejima Haku keireki gūdan." *Tōhō kyōkai kaihō* 44 (1898).

Sonezaki Mitsuhiro. *Ueki Emori to onnatachi.* Tōkyō: Domesu shuppan, 1976.

Sonoda Hiyoshi. *Etō Shimpei to Saga no ran.* Tōkyō: Shin jimbutsu ōrai sha, 1974.

Sōseki zenshū. 29 vols. Tōkyō: Iwanami shoten, 1996–97.

Stevenson, Elizabeth. *Henry Adams.* New Brunswick, N.J.: Transaction Books, 1997.

Suematsu Kenchō. "Go-Jiseiryoku no o-tsuyokarishi sentei heika." *Taiyō*, September 1912. [*Meiji seitenshi* special issue]

Suzuki Kōichi, ed. *Meiji Nippon hakkutsu.* Tōkyō: Kawade shobō shinsha, 1994.

Suzuki Masayuki. *Kindai no tennō.* Tōkyō: Yoshikawa kōbunkan, 1993.

Suzuki Masayuki. *Kōshitsu seido.* Tōkyō: Iwanami shoten, 1993.

Suzuki Takeshi. *Hoshi Tōru*. Chūkō shinsho series. Tōkyō: Chūō kōron sha, 1988.

Taiyō, September 1912. [*Meiji seitenshi* special issue]

Tada Kōmon, ed. *Iwakura-kō jikki*. 3 vols. Tōkyō: Hara shobō, 1968.

Takashima Tomonosuke. "Jimmu irai no eishu." *Taiyō*, September 1912. [*Meiji seitenshi* special issue]

Takatsuji Osanaga, "Go-yōgi no shinkō." *Taiyō*, September 1912. [*Meiji seitenshi* special issue]

Takebe Toshio. *Kazunomiya*. Jimbutsu sōsho series. Tōkyō: Yoshikawa kōbunkan, 1965.

Taki Kōji. *Tennō no shōzō*. Tōkyō: Iwanami shoten, 1988.

Takigawa Masajirō. "Shirarezaru tennō." *Shinchō*, October 1950.

Takizawa Shigeru. "Hokuriku junkō to minshū tōchi." *Niigata shigaku* 24 and 26 (1990–91).

Tamabayashi Haruo. "Kōgen hōshinnō." *Denki*, September 1935.

Tamba Tsuneo. *Nishikie ni miru Meiji tennō to Meiji jidai*. Tōkyō: Asahi shimbunsha, 1962.

Tan, Chester C. *The Boxer Catastrophe*. New York: Octagon Books, 1967.

Tanaka Akira. *Iwakura shisetsudan*. Kōdansha gendai shinsho series. Tōkyō: Kōdansha, 1977.

Tanaka Akira. *Meiji ishin no haisha to shōsha*. Tōkyō: Nihon hōsō shuppan kyōkai, 1980.

Tanaka Akira. *Meiji ishin to tennōsei*. Tōkyō: Yoshikawa kōbunkan, 1992.

Tanaka Akira. *Mikan no Meiji ishin*. 2d ed. Tōkyō: Sanseidō, 1993.

Tanaka Akira. "Ōkubo seiken ron." In Tōyama Shigeki, ed., *Kindai tennōsei no seiritsu*. Tōkyō: Iwanami shoten, 1987.

Tennō-ke no kyōen. Tōkyō: Nihon kenkō kurabu, 1983.

Teters, Barbara. "The Otsu Affair: The Formation of Japan's Judicial Conscience." In David Wurfel, ed., *Meiji Japan's Centennial*. Lawrence: University Press of Kansas, 1971.

Tokushige Atsukichi. *Kōmei tennō go-jiseki ki*. Tōkyō: Tōkōsha, 1936.

Tokutomi Iichirō. *Kinsei Nihon kokumin shi*. Vol. 61. Tōkyō: Kinsei Nihon kokumin shi kankōkai, 1963.

Tomita Hitoshi. *Rokumeikan*. Tōkyō: Hakusuisha, 1984.

Totman, Conrad. *The Collapse of the Tokugawa Bakufu, 1862–1868*. Honolulu: University of Hawaii Press, 1980.

Tōya Hiroki. *Toshimichi ansatsu*. Tōkyō: Kōjinsha, 1986.

Tōyama Shigeki. *Meiji ishin*. Iwanami zensho series. Tōkyō: Iwanami shoten, 1951.

Tōyama Shigeki. *Meiji ishin to tennō*. Iwanami seminaa bukkusu series. Tōkyō: Iwanami shoten, 1991.

Tōyama Shigeki. *Tennō to kazoku*. Nihon kindai shisō taikei series. Tōkyō: Iwanami shoten, 1988.

Tōyama Shigeki, ed. *Ishin no gunzō*. Jimbutsu Nihon no rekishi series. Tōkyō: Yomiuri shimbun sha, 1973.

Tsuda Shigemaro. *Meiji seijō to Shin Takayuki*. Tōkyō: Jishōkai, 1928.

Tsunoda Fusako. *Minbi ansatsu*. Tōkyō: Shinchōsha, 1988.

Tsunoda, Ryūsaku, Wm. Theodore de Bary, and Donald Keene. *Sources of Japanese Tradition*. New York: Columbia University Press, 1958.

Ubukata Toshirō. *Meiji Taishō kenbun shi*. Chūkō bunko series. Tōkyō: Chūō kōron sha, 1978.

Uchimura Kanzō zenshū. Vols. 16 and 20. Tōkyō: Iwanami shoten, 1933.

Ueda Shigeru. *Saigō Takamori no higeki*. Tōkyō: Chūō kōron sha, 1983.

Ueki Emori shū. Vols. 7 and 8. Tōkyō: Iwanami shoten, 1990.

Wada Haruki. *Kaikoku: Nichiro kokkyō kōshō*. NHK Books series. Tōkyō: Nihon hōsō shuppan kyōkai, 1992.

Waley, Arthur. *The Book of Songs*. Boston: Houghton Mifflin, 1937.

Walthall, Anne. "Off with Their Heads! The Hirata Disciples and the Ashikaga Shoguns." *Monumenta Nipponica* 58, no. 2 (Summer 1995).

Watanabe Akio. "Tennōsei kokka keisei tojō ni okeru 'tennō shinsei' no shisō to undō." *Rekishigaku kenkyū* 254 (June 1961).

Watanabe Ikujirō. *Meiji tennō*. 2 vols. Tōkyō: Munetaka shobō, 1958.

Watanabe Ikujirō. *Meiji tennō to hohitsu*. Tōkyō: Chikuma shobō, 1938.

Watanabe Ikujirō. *Ōkuma Shigenobu*. Tōkyō: Jiji tsūshin, 1958.

Watanabe Katsuo. *Meiji nijūninen no jōyaku kaisei hantai undō*. Tōkyō: Kōbundō, 1981.

Watanabe Shigeo. *Meiji tennō*. Tōkyō: Jiji tsūshin sha, 1966.

Watson, Burton, trans. *Hsün Tzu*. New York: Columbia University Press, 1963.

Webb, Herschel. *The Japanese Imperial Institution in the Tokugawa Period*. New York: Columbia University Press, 1968.

Weber, Norbert. *Im Lande der Morgenstille*. St. Ottelien, Oberbayern: Missionsverlag, 1923.

Wells, David, and Sandra Wilson, eds. *The Russo-Japanese War in Cultural Perspective*. Basingstoke: Macmillan, 1999.

White, John Albert. *The Diplomacy of the Russo-Japanese War*. Princeton, N.J.: Princeton University Press, 1964.

White, Trumbull. *The War in the East: Japan, China, and Corea*. Philadelphia: Ziegler, 1895.

Witte, Count Sergei Iulevich. *The Memoirs of Count Witte*. Trans. Sidney Harcave. Armonk, N.Y.: Sharpe, 1990.

Yagi Kiyoharu. "Keikenteki jitsugaku no tenkai." In Rai Kiichi, ed., *Jugaku, kokugaku, yōgaku*. Nihon no kinsei series, no. 13. Tōkyō: Chuō kōron sha, 1993.

Yamakawa Michiko. *Jokan*. Tōkyō: Jitsugyō no Nihon, 1960.

Yamakawa Michiko. "Kindan no jokan seikatsu kaisō ki." *Jimbutsu ōrai*, April 10, 1959.

Yamashita Ikuo. *Kenkyū seinan no eki*. Tōkyō: San'ichi shobō, 1977.

Yanagizawa Hideki. *Hōshō Kurō den*. Tōkyō: Wan'ya shoten, 1944.

Yasuba Seika. "Junchū shisei no taiju Motoda Nagazane sensei." *Kingu*, May 1927.

Yasuda Kōichi. *Nikorai nisei no nikki*. Tōkyō: Asahi shimbun sha, 1990.

Yasumaru Yoshio. *Kindai tennōzō no keisei*. Tōkyō: Iwanami shoten, 1992.

Yoda Yoshiie. "Kindai tennōsei seiritsu no zentei." *Shakai kagaku Tōkyū* 29, no. 1 (October 1983).

Yomigaeru bakumatsu. Tōkyō: Asahi shimbun sha, 1986.

Yonehara Ken. *Ueki Emori*. Tōkyō: Chūō kōron sha, 1992.

Yoshida Seiichi. *Kindai bungei hyōron shi: Taishō hen*. Tōkyō: Shibundō, 1980.

Yoshino Sakuzō, ed. *Meiji bunka zenshū*. Vol. 1. Tōkyō: Nihon hyōron sha, 1928.

Young, John Russell. *Around the World with General Grant*. New York: American News Company, 1879.

INDEX

Meiji *(continued)*

POLITICAL/GOVERNMENTAL AC-
TIONS: political views of, 73; approval of edict against Yoshinobu by,
116; and government reform, 121–23;
on Korea, 231, 234, 476, 478, 657–58,
675–76; on Taiwan, 245; on crisis in
Kumamoto, 278; interest in, 296,
344–45; and abolition of Ryūkyū domain, 303; decisions of, not consensus based, 322–23; regularity of, 331;
on financial matters, 339, 466; on
draft constitution, 340; on changes in
Genrō-in, 345; on Ōkuma, 353; on
convening of parliament, 363; appointment of Stein as adviser to,
381–82; lack of attention to, 396; on
China, 400–401, 481, 504; on political appointments, 401, 417–18,
462–63, 555, 563; on Privy Council,
418–19; and promulgation of Imperial House Act and Imperial Constitution, 421; on treaty revision,
426–28, 468–69; rescript of, on education, 437–41; rescript of, on punishment of Czarevitch Nicholas's attacker, 456; as supreme commander
of armed forces, 485–86; and recall of Yamagata, 498; on political
crisis of 1898, 540–41; reaction of, to
Ozaki's speech, 543–44; on formation of new cabinet, 545–46; on Itō's
forming new political party, 562; rescript of, against House of Peers,
564–66; on judges' strike, 566; on
Russia, 593–94, 604

READING: ceremony of first reading, 3,
48; *Classic of Filial Piety* (Confucian
text), 47; Confucian classics, 47; literary preferences of, 51; books on warfare and prodigies, 77; *Analects*, 88;
Mencius, 88; newspapers, 263

TRAVELS AND MISSIONS *(junkō)*: to
Nijō Castle, 131; to Ōsaka, 143–46; to
Tōkyō, 159–65, 178–81; to Kyōto
from Tōkyō, 166–67; to Chūgoku
and Saigoku, 211–12, 213–16; to

northeast, 260–62; to Yamato Province, 274–75; function of, 275; to
Hokuriku and Tōkai, 297–302; pains
of, 300; distance covered by, 301–2;
to Yamanashi, Mie, and Kyōto Prefectures, 333–37; expense of preparing for, 334; to Yamagata, Akita, and
Hokkaidō, 351; to Yamaguchi, Hiroshima, and Okayama, 398; suggestion
for trip to West, 403–4; to Kyōto,
with empress, 411; to Nagoya to observe military maneuvers, 432–33; to
Kyōto and Ōsaka, 586; to ancestral
tombs, 659; day excursions, 790n.13;
Six Great Imperial Tours *(roku daijunkō)*, 790n.13

Meiji literature, 163
Meiji Restoration. *See* imperial rule
Meiji Shrine (Meiji jingū, Tōkyō), x,
705, 717
Meiji tennō ki (Record of the Emperor
Meiji), x–xi, xii, 10–14, 84
Meirokusha (intellectual group), 713
Meitō Prefecture, 774n.13
*Memento of Prison: Anarcho-Commu-
nism, A* (Gudō), 691
"Memorandum to the Russian Socialist
Party" (Kōtoku), 687
memorials, 191–192, 251, 259–60, 694
mercantile law, 432
Mexico, 309–10, 420
Meyer, George von Lengerke (American
minister to Russia), 627, 844n.31
Michihito, Prince, 415, 416
Michinomiya. *See* Hirohito; Yoshihisa,
Prince
Mie Prefecture, 267, 301
Miho no Matsubara (Pine Grove at
Miho), 166
Mikado. *See* emperors
Mikado, The (Gilbert and Sullivan), 136
military, 18, 360, 367–68, 545, 567. *See
also* army; conscription; Household
Guards; military drills and maneu-
vers; navy
*Military Account of the Later Three-Year
War in Ōshū, A* (Mokuami), 318

Motoda Nagazane *(continued)*
VIEWS: on sovereign's relation with
subjects, 289; on foreign loan, 332;
on dismissal of Ōkuma, 353; on
Western-style palaces, 412; on union
of palace and state, 415
mourning, 101, 380, 429–30, 530, 531, 564
Mukden, Manchuria, 618, 620–21
Murata Shimpachi, 278
Muromachi Kiyoko (court lady), 576
Mushakōji Saneatsu (writer), 714
Mutsu Munemitsu (minister to United
States, *later* agriculture and commerce minister, *later* foreign minister): on treaty revision, 424, 467; as
agriculture and commerce minister,
434; Meiji's dislike of, 434; on Article
116 of criminal code, 455; on xenophobia, 468; on Tonghak revolt, 476;
on Sino-Japanese War, 477, 490–91,
504, 505; and Korea, 478, 484, 485;
report of, on Port Arthur massacre,
492; on attack on Li Hung-chang,
503; resignation of, as foreign minister, 527; and Hoshi, 568–69; imprisonment of, 809n.17
Mutsuhito. *See* Meiji

Nabeshima Naohiro (chief protocol offi-
cer), 465
Nagai Kafū (writer), 857n.53
Nagai Kaoyuki (shogunate official), 120
Nagai Ussai, 714
Nagai Uta, 57–58, 59
Nagano, Meiji's visit to, 299
Nagaoka, Meiji's visit to, 300–301
Nagaoka Gaishi (vice chief of general
staff), 619
Nagasaki, 20, 35, 109–12, 446–47
Nagasaki Express (newspaper), 215
Naha (port city), 14
Nakae Chōmin (materialist philoso-
pher), 681, 686
Nakagawa, Prince (Son'yu, Kayanomiya,
Prince Asahiko): as confidant of Kō-
mei, 67; and *kōbu gattai* faction,
76–77; as target of planned Chōshū

attack, 79; on foreigners, 87; rumors
about, 88–89; Kōmei's belief in, 89;
on nobles' meeting with Kōmei, 93;
resignation of, 93; and Meiji,
99–100, 289, 430; exile of, 155; and
Kawaji, 736n.5; multiple names of,
67, 735n.5
Nakagawanomiya. *See* Nakagawa,
Prince
Nakahara Hisao, 271, 780n.28
Nakai Hiroshi, 134, 801n.3
Nakajima Saburōsuke (Uraga magis-
trate), 15
Nakamikado Tsuneyuki (nobleman), 91,
93, 119, 189
Nakamura Kusatao, 717
Nakaoka Shintarō, 89, 113, 119
Nakatsugawa village, 299
Nakayama Isako (Meiji's great-great-
aunt), 100
Nakayama Naruchika, 384
Nakayama Tadamitsu (Meiji's uncle),
70–73, 171
Nakayama Tadanaru (Meiji's uncle), 12
Nakayama Tadayasu (Meiji's maternal
grandfather, *later* adviser to the
throne), 119; false accusations against,
67–68; action of, on son's plotting
against Iwakura Tomomi, 72–73;
memories of, 77; on palace women's
quarters, 100; as chair of meeting on
new government, 121; on site of capital, 131; at Charter Oath ceremonies,
138–39; as head of Ministry of
Shintō, 183; antiforeign sentiments
of, 254; on traditional medicine, 405
Nakayama Tadayasu, and Meiji: and
Meiji's birth, x, 10, 12, 13; first New
Year presents to Meiji from, 14; on
Meiji's visits to palace, 29; anger of,
at Meiji's behavior, 48; concern of,
over Meiji's dreams, 84; as grandfather of Meiji, 98; at Meiji's wedding
ceremonies, 107; at Meiji's audience
with foreign ministers, 133–34; travel
with Meiji to Tōkyō, 161; on Meiji's
second visit to east, 179–80; on

Meiji's "mission" to distant parts of Japan, 213; Meiji's visits to, 214; as godfather of Meiji's son, 320
Nakayama Takamaro (Meiji's cousin), 48
Nakayama Tsunako (Meiji's great-grandmother), 23, 27, 29, 31
Nakayama Yoshiko (Meiji's mother, Nii no tsubone, Nii-dono, Ichii): and Meiji's birth, ix–x, 10; journey with baby Meiji to Kōmei, 13; at ritual meal for Meiji's first colored clothing, 26; relinquishing of maternal rights by, 31; as supervisor of Meiji's calligraphy, 52, 103; at court after Kōmei's death, 100–101; and Yoshihito, 321, 408; final illness and death of, 652–54; funeral of, 654; relationship with Meiji, 654–55
names: inauspicious, 61; god names, 85; of emperors, posthumous, 101, 743n.8; of empresses, posthumous, 531, 829n.23; for empress dowager, 727n.17; Genji, for concubines, 776n.6; Chinese classics as source of imperial, 835n.14. See also nengō
Naniwa (cruiser), 404–5
Nansai Toshitada (artist), 815n.5
Narashinohara (Maneuver Fields), 236
national defense, 17, 27, 34, 57, 375, 650–51. See also army; navy; warships
national holidays, 159, 716
national polity, 436, 437, 438
national religion, 328–29. See also Buddhism; Shintō
Natsume Sōseki, 709
natural disasters, 27, 648, 802n.21
natural resources, 318
Naval Ministry, 790n.24
navy: Meiji's interest in, 165; Meiji's personal command of, 367; reviews of maneuvers held by, 433, 659; battles fought by, 488; and Russo-Japanese War, 603, 605, 608, 609; sailors' suffering from beriberi, 783n.14
navy band, 213–14, 586
nengō (reign-name), 154, 709; Meiji, xiii,

159, 705; Ansei (Peaceful Government), 26; Mannen, change to Bunkyū, 57; Genji, change to Keiō, 84; Kōka, change to Kōmei, 101; in China, 303; in Korea, 522, 678
Nesselrode, Karl Robert (foreign minister, Russia), 21
New Year, 14, 43, 222, 344. See also lectures
newspapers, 215, 263, 334, 551, 686–87, 690
Nezu Masashi, 96, 741–42n.14
Nicholas (czarevitch of Russia): visit of, to Japan, 445–53; assassination attempt on, 448–53; Japanese doctors prohibited from seeing, 451; Meiji's visit to, 451–52; Meiji's luncheon with, 452–53
Nicholas II (czar of Russia): coronation of, 526; message of friendship to Meiji from, 593; expansionist views of, 596, 601; on war with Japan, 598; character of, 601–2; attempt on life of, 614; reaction of, to defeat at Mukden, 621; and peace negotiations with Japan, 623, 625, 627
Nihon dōtoku ron (Essays on Japanese Morality; Nishimura), 408–10
Nihon heimin-tō (Japan People's Party), 689
Nihon shakai-tō (Japan Social Party), 689
Nii no tsubone. See Nakayama Yoshiko
Niigata, Meiji's visit to, 300
Niimura Tadao (anarchist), 692
Nijō Akizane (chancellor), 3
Nijō Castle, 68
Nijō Nariyuki (regent, chancellor), 87, 93, 103, 105
Nikkō, Meiji's visit to, 261
Ninkai (priest of Iwashimizu Hachimangū shrine), 89
Ninkō (Meiji's paternal grandfather), 1–2, 7
Nippon Club, 426
Nirei Kagenori (rear admiral), 374, 465
Nish, Ian, 578, 606

Rosen, Roman (Russian minister to Japan), 596; and negotiations with Japan, 597, 600, 627; knowledge of Japanese troop movements, 607–8; on world opinion against Russia, 610–11; on Meiji, 616

Rösler, K. F. H., 370, 419

Russia: trade with, 17, 20–23, 25–26, 651–52; fleet of, 26, 27, 612–13, 614–15, 617; treaties with, 26–27, 41, 425, 700; encampment on Tsushima Islands, 56–57; Meiji on, 203–4, 651; and China, 251–52, 506–8, 526, 578, 595–604; and Sino-Japanese War, 479–80, 506–8; and Korea, 522, 525–26, 527, 595–604, 669–70; agreement with Japan, secret provisions of, 526–27; Far East policy of, and Anglo-Japanese Alliance, 573–74; military strength of, 589, 609; administration of territories in Far East, 595–96; attack of, on British trawlers, 610; unpopularity of Russo-Japanese War in, 613, 614; Japanese agents in, 625; as prime hypothetical enemy, 650. See also Putiatin, E. V.; Russo-Japanese War; Sakhalin

Russian Socialist Party, 687

Russification, 579

Russo-Japanese War, 605–29; Ōtsu incident as precursor to, 450; causes of, 556, 605, 606; actions and negotiations before outbreak of, 591–604; Japan's preparations for, 600; declarations of, 609; treatment of Russian prisoners of war during, 611; defeat of Russian fleet in, 615; Meiji's involvement in, 616; and Meiji's rescript on naval victory, 621; peace negotiations during, 622–28; Japan's objectives for, 626; protests against peace treaty, in Japan, 628–29; and Britain, 630; repercussions of Japan's victory in, 644–46; war fever during, 687

Russo-Japanese War Poem, A (Oakley), 609–10

Ryōjo (chief abbot of Kakushō-in), 23

Ryūkyū Islands, 14, 314

Ryūkyū kingdom (later domain), 220–21, 233, 253, 302–7

Sabatin, Alexander, 516, 517

Sachi no i (Sachi's Well, Well of Good Fortune), ix, 22, 337, 725n.2

Sachiko, Princess, 552

Sachinomiya. See Meiji

Sadaedang (Serving the Great Party), 388, 389, 479, 802–3n.33

Sadamaro, Prince (Yorihito), 349, 406, 792n.14

Sadanaru, Prince, 335, 711, 715

Saegusa Shigeru, 751n.24

Saeki Riichirō, 742n.14

Saga Castle, 241

Saga rebellion, 239–45

Sagara Nagaoki (major), 305

Saigō Takamori (army minister, later interior minister): and Sanjō's exile, 84; and Chōshū domain, 89; and shogunate, 113, 115, 125; at meeting on government reform, 122; as commander of imperial forces, 127; and Katsu, 142–43; at surrender of Edo Castle, 143; advocacy of haihan chiken by, 199; and Ministry of the Imperial Household, 201; on Meiji's Westernized dress, 213; and Household Guards, 216; on Korea, 232–33; and Etō, 242; on actions against native Taiwanese, 245–46; and China, 246, 803n.35; opposition of, to government, 252; private schools founded by, 271; and Satsuma Rebellion, 280; and Meiji, 281, 360, 769n.28; last stand of, 284; mission of, to Ōkuma, 353; posthumous promotion of, 423; and new cabinet, 546; as interior minister, 547; and revenue bill, 564; treatment of, for corpulence, 772n.40; exalted reputation of, 772n.43; students as troops under, 781n.10. See also Kagoshima: army of